Macromedia® Flash™ MX 2004 Bible

Macromedia® Flash™ MX 2004 Bible

Robert Reinhardt and Snow Dowd

Wiley Publishing, Inc.

Macromedia® Flash™ MX 2004 Bible

Published by
Wiley Publishing, Inc.
111 River St.
Hoboken, NJ 07030
www.wiley.com

Copyright © 2004 by Wiley Publishing, Inc., Indianapolis, Indiana

Library of Congress Control Number: 2003116419

ISBN: 0-7645-4303-2

Manufactured in the United States of America

10 9 8 7 6 5 4 3 2

1B/TR/QR/QU/IN

Published by Wiley Publishing, Inc., Indianapolis, Indiana
Published simultaneously in Canada

WILEY

About the Authors

After discovering Macromedia Flash while working on an art project combining film, photography, animation and audio, Robert soon realized there was a need for more comprehensive documentation of its capabilities. In 1998, not many people had even heard of Flash and publishers were wary of the limited market, but IDG Books Worldwide, Inc. (now Wiley Publishing, Inc.) committed to doing the *Flash 4 Bible*. The rest, as they say, is history. After studying and working together for five years in Toronto, Robert Reinhardt and Snow Dowd established a multimedia consulting and design company in Los Angeles in 1999, called [*the* MAKERS] (www.theMakers.com). In addition to work for entertainment companies, [*the* MAKERS] has done work for independent artists and nonprofit organizations.

Robert Reinhardt — With a degree in photographic arts, Robert takes a holistic approach to computer applications for the creation of compelling multimedia. Since January 2000, in addition to design and content creation through [*the* MAKERS], Robert has worked with the Content Project (www.contentproject.com) in Santa Monica, California. As a Director of Multimedia Applications, Robert has led various assignments including multimedia data analysis applications for Nielsen's Media and Entertainment division and creating interactive advertising for Warner Bros. films *Dreamcatcher*, *Kangaroo Jack*, *The Matrix: Reloaded*, and *Terminator 3: Rise of the Machines*.

Robert continues to teach and write about Flash. In addition to this book, he is the coauthor of the *Flash MX 2004 ActionScript Bible* (Wiley), as well as *Macromedia MX: Building Rich Internet Applications* (Macromedia Press). He has developed and taught Flash workshops for education centers in California, including Lynda.com and Art Center College of Design, as well as doing on-site training and seminars for clients in the United States and Canada. Robert has been a regular featured speaker at the FlashForward, FlashintheCan, and SIGGRAPH conferences.

Snow Dowd — Snow initially collaborated with Robert Reinhardt on multimedia, film, and photography-based installation projects while earning a BFA in Image Arts at Ryerson University. During this time, she was also the production manager for Design Archive, one of Canada's preeminent architectural photography studios (www.designarchive.com). Working with renowned photographers and an exacting international client base of architects and designers helped her gain a deeper appreciation for architecture and industrial design. She also learned to love color printing, but the novelty of darkroom chemicals quickly faded. Fortunately, multimedia design offered a rewarding alternative to the health hazards of traditional photography.

Now fully immersed in digital production, Snow is able to synthesize her background in visual arts and communication theory with an ever-expanding software toolkit. Focusing on content architecture and interface design, Snow strives to make print and Web projects that are beautiful, functional and memorable. A recent challenge was designing a Flash interface for a project to deliver legal information to remote Navajo and Hopi communities. The content is available in three languages, online as well as through touch-screen kiosks hosted in the offices of DNA People's Legal Services, a nonprofit legal services organization.

About the Technical Editors

Damian Burns — Damian is a user interface design expert with more than six years of international experience. His most recent American stint was a two-year tenure with Macromedia in San Francisco where he worked on the Flash Communication Server with the Flash MX Products Development Team. Damian has won several international awards for his work in advertising and Web site design, including a Gold Pencil Award from The One Show Interactive and a Gold Icon Award (*Adweek*) for the Intel WebOutfitter Service. He specializes in user interface design, Web design, motion graphics, and Rich Internet Applications. Currently, Damian resides in Vancouver, British Columbia where he is working on Web to wireless solutions with Mobile Operandi Communications.

Graham Pearson — Graham is a Certified Webmaster and Macromedia Coldfusion Developer with twenty years experience in the computer industry. He currently lives and works in Mishawaka, Indiana where he has been the local Macromedia User Group Manager and continues to help others solve their computer-related problems — from general technical issues to Rich Internet Application development issues.

As an instructor, Graham has taught Macromedia Coldfusion Server and presented Macromedia Flash Communication Server classes to local educational facilities in an effort to show how these powerful server applications can make everyday classroom instruction more interactive and enjoyable for students.

Credits

Senior Acquisitions Editor
Michael Roney

Project Editor
Timothy Borek

Development and Copy Editors
Dana Lesh
Elizabeth Kuball
Nancy Rapoport

Technical Editors
Damian Burns and Graham Pearson

Editorial Manager
Robyn Siesky

Vice President and Executive Group Publisher
Richard Swadley

Vice President and Publisher
Barry Pruett

Project Coordinator
Regina Snyder

Graphics and Production Specialists
Amanda Carter
Carrie Foster
Lauren Goddard
Joyce Haughey
Jennifer Heleine
Lynsey Osborn
Heather Ryan

Quality Control Technicians
John Greenough
Andy Hollandbeck
Carl William Pierce

Senior Permissions Editor
Carmen Krikorian

Media Development Specialist
Marisa Pearman

Proofreading and Indexing
TECHBOOKS Production Services

This version of the *Flash Bible* is based, in part, on ideas and content originally developed by Jon Warren Lentz, jwl@flash-guru.com.

To all of my friends in the Flash community, for their generous spirit even in trying times.

RJR

To California . . . for daily reminders that life is bizarre and beautiful.

SD

Foreword

Macromedia Flash has become an essential part of the interactive designer's toolkit. Whether you are a design professional who develops large commercial Web sites, or a beginner who just wants to make an interesting presentation for the boss, Flash is for you. It's a highly capable yet straightforward authoring platform for making interactive, visually interesting, and quick-downloading applications. The new MX 2004 version takes Flash to an even higher level, and the *Macromedia Flash MX 2004 Bible* is your guide to all the features for beginners, professionals, and everyone in between.

As an interactive developer and core faculty member in Art Center College of Design's graduate Media Design Program, I see an amazing array of creative Flash applications. Illustrators and animators with little digital experience use Flash to deliver their animations and portfolios on the Web. Web designers create highly interactive sites, combining Flash, audio, video, text and HTML. Product designers use it to prototype interfaces for futuristic mobile devices. And our graduate designers create groundbreaking media systems. For example, in a recent term they built a life-sized interface powered by Director and Flash with proximity sensors and a micro-controller. Users walked up to an 8-foot screen and simply reached out to make a selection from the Flash interface.

But Flash is not only about media presentation. Developers are now using Flash to create integrated Web applications that access corporate databases. These applications deliver up-to-date content and information, and break the obsolete stereotype that Flash is just eye-candy that's hard to update.

One of the most exciting aspects of Flash is how it bridges design, business, and technology. The old model was that designers made the visuals, programmers made it work, and business people sold the application. But design today is much more than visual styling. It's is evolving into a comprehensive practice that combines research, entrepreneurialism, content development, interaction design, media of all types, and software. From building prototypes for use in research and funding pitches, to creating and integrating media in applications, to building the software that supports the interaction approaches, Flash helps designers participate in every stage of the development process.

Flash MX 2004 adds new features that make this development process even better. The new Behaviors capability allows designers to make interactive applications with just a click or two, and helps them develop scripting skills by example. The new Spell Checking, Search/Replace, and Alias text features help deliver cleaner content. The Slides feature in Flash MX Professional 2004 allows novices and pros alike to create presentations with all the power of Flash, without using a timeline authoring metaphor. CSS (cascading style sheets) support and the new Project panel helps with the use of Flash in larger Web productions. The History panel and Command features allow the automation of repetitive tasks by recording steps in Flash as reusable macros. Of course, as a designer with a background in programming and database development, I can't leave out the new data connectivity features that enable designers to easily establish links to Web services and databases.

The *Macromedia Flash MX 2004 Bible* is a comprehensive introduction to all aspects of Flash development. Whether developing Web applications, CD-ROMs, kiosks, cell phone and PDA applications, installations, broadcast graphics, or corporate presentations, Flash developers need to know how to use the tool, and a whole lot more. This book is unique in that it covers that larger context of Flash development. For example, there are chapters on "Planning Flash Projects" (Chapter 3), "Animation Strategies" (Chapter 10), "Knowing the Nuts and Bolts of Code" (Chapter 24), "Creating a Game in Flash" (Chapter 33), and a whole section on "Expanding Flash" (Part VIII) that covers how to use Flash with applications such as Photoshop, Dreamweaver, Director, and Illustrator. These parts of the book help you successfully apply Flash in real projects.

This book is truly your *Macromedia Flash MX 2004 Bible*, providing a thorough guide to all aspects of the remarkable world of Flash. Read, experiment, learn, think, and design with this book. Above all, make interesting projects that challenge you and effectively communicate in new and creative ways.

Philip van Allen
Graduate Faculty, Media Design Program
Art Center College of Design
Principle, Commotion New Media Inc.
vanallen@artcenter.edu

Preface

In 1997, Macromedia acquired a small Web graphics program, FutureSplash, from a company named FutureWave. FutureSplash was a quirky little program with the astounding capability to generate compact, vector-based graphics and animations for delivery over the Web. With Macromedia's embrace, Flash blossomed. Now Flash has obtained ubiquity. The Flash Player plug-in ships with most major browsers and operating systems. Now Flash graphics appear all over the Web, and the number of Flash users continues to increase at an astonishing pace.

As the Web-surfing public and the development community have continued to demand more of Flash, Macromedia has delivered. The MX 2004 Studio suite offers unparalleled support for multimedia production of all shapes and sizes. The tight integration of specialized programs makes it easier than ever to get the best out of each program, while maintaining a seamless, optimized workflow.

Flash movies can communicate directly with server-side scripts and programs, using standard URL-encoded variables, XML-formatted structures, Web services, or powerhouse data transfers from Flash Remoting MX-enabled servers. Sounds can be imported and exported as MP3 audio, for high-quality music on the Web at the smallest file sizes. Flash now supports nearly every file format you'll ever come across and native JPEG and FLV loading streamlines production and maintenance of dynamic high-volume image sites. The evolution of components, and the addition of custom tools, custom effects, and behaviors have resulted in some exciting possibilities for Flash users of all skill levels.

The Flash MX 2004 interface is consistent with other Macromedia MX 2004 products, with tool options and other editing features contained in streamlined panels and a reorganized application menu. Evidence of the dominance of the Flash format can be found in the wide range of third-party developers creating applications that output to the Flash movie format SWF files). Flash has fulfilled its promise of becoming the central application for generating hot, low-bandwidth, interactive content for delivery on the Web and beyond.

Is there any other Flash book for you?

The *Macromedia Flash MX 2004 Bible* is the most comprehensive and exhaustive reference on Flash. It helps you get started on your first day with the program and will still be a valuable resource when you've attained mastery of the program. When you're looking for clues on how to integrate Flash with other programs so that you can deliver unique and compelling content in the Flash format, you'll know where to turn.

Flash is not just a single tool. You can think of Flash as a multitasking application. It's an illustration program, an image and sound editor, an animation machine, and a scripting engine, all rolled into one. In this book, we look at each of these uses of Flash and explain how all the features work together.

How to get the most out of this book

Here are some things to know so you can get the most out of this book:

First, to indicate that you need to select a command from a menu, the menu and command are separated by an arrow symbol. For example, if we tell you to select the default panel layout from the Flash application menu, the instructions will say to choose Window ➪ Panel Sets ➪ Default Layout.

The first two parts of the book are entirely dedicated to project planning and getting familiar with the Flash interface. Parts III and IV explain how to integrate animations and other media files into your Flash movies. Parts V through VII gradually introduce you to the power of ActionScript. Finally, Part VIII covers other programs and techniques that will enhance your Flash projects. Although this book was written to take a beginner by the hand, starting from page one, you can also use it as a reference. Use the index and the table of contents to find what you're looking for, and just go there, or jump in anywhere. If you already know Flash and want to get some details on sound, for example, just go to the "Integrating Media Files with Flash" section (Part IV).

This is a real-world book: We've worked hard to ensure that our lessons, examples, and explanations are based on professional production conventions. We have also continued the use of expert tutorials to bring you tips and techniques from some of the top names in the Flash industry, so that you can benefit from their specialized expertise.

The CD-ROM that accompanies this book contains many of the source Flash project files (FLAs), with original artwork and ActionScript for the examples and lessons in the book. To help you get started, we've also included trial versions of Flash MX 2004 and Flash MX Professional 2004.

In order to create a forum for the delivery of updates, notes, and additional sample files, we have established an integrated Web site specifically for the *Flash Bible* series: www. flashsupport.com. At the Web site, you'll find new material and corrections that may be added after the book goes to print, and moderated forums where readers can share information or ask questions. We invite you to contribute your comments and suggestions for this edition so that we can continue to improve the material.

We have created a chapter-based evaluation system that makes it easy for you to let us know what parts of this book were most (or least) useful to you. Please visit www.flashsupport. com/feedback and let us know what you think.

Icons: What Do They Mean?

Although the icons are pretty standard and self-explanatory (they have their names written on them!), here's a brief explanation of what they are and what they mean.

Tip   Tips offer you extra information that further explains a given topic or technique, often suggesting alternatives or workarounds to a listed procedure.

Note   Notes provide supplementary information to the text, shedding light on background processes or miscellaneous options that aren't crucial to the basic understanding of the material.

 When you see the Caution icon, make sure you're following along closely to the tips and techniques being discussed. Some external applications may not work exactly the same with Flash on different operating systems and some workflows have inherent risks or drawbacks.

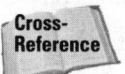 If you want to find related information to a given topic in another chapter, look for the cross-reference icons.

 The New Feature icons point out differences between Flash MX 2004 and previous versions of Flash.

 For related information, resources, or software available online, look for the Web resource icons.

 The RIP icons note features or techniques that are deprecated or no longer relevant to Flash MX 2004.

 This icon indicates that the CD-ROM contains a related file and points you to the folder location.

How This Book Is Organized

This book has been written in a format that gives you access to need-to-know information very easily in every section (or Part) of the book. If you are completely new to Flash, then you'll want to read Parts I through VI. After you have developed a familiarity with the Flash interface, you can proceed to Parts VII and VIII. We've included step-by-step descriptions of real Flash projects to help you "leap" from the intro topics to the advanced topics. These sections of the book guide you through the production process, helping you to apply ActionScript and production techniques that may be new to you.

If you've already used Flash MX, then you may want to review the changes to the Flash MX 2004 interface in Part I, and then jump right into other specific parts to learn more about character animation, ActionScript, creating artwork and content in other applications, and integrating Flash with HTML. Part VIII is especially useful if you have a favorite application such as Dreamweaver or Director in which you want to use Flash movies.

To cover advanced scripting topics and more server-side development issues, Robert coauthored the *Flash MX 2004 ActionScript Bible* with Joey Lott. If you're already adept at creating animation and basic interactive interfaces in Flash and you want to expand your knowledge of more complex coding techniques, you may want to compare the table of contents in this book with that of the ActionScript Bible to determine which book covers the topics you're most interested in.

Part I: An Introduction to Flash Web Production

The first part of this book explores the Flash file format and how Flash MX 2004 fits into the evolution of the program (Chapter 1), explains the context in which Flash movies interact on the Web (Chapter 2), and gives an overview of multimedia planning and some specific techniques and suggestions that will make your Flash project development less painful and more productive (Chapter 3).

Part II: Mastering the Flash Environment

This part gives you all the information you need to feel comfortable in the Flash MX 2004 authoring environment. Get an introduction to, and some tips for customizing, the Flash UI (Chapter 4). Learn where to find your drawing tools and how to use them efficiently (Chapter 5), and then discover all the ways that Flash helps you to organize and optimize project assets (Chapter 6). Learn key color concepts relevant to multimedia production and find out why Flash has the best color tools yet (Chapter 7). Jump into using text editing tools and see how to get the best looking type and the smallest file sizes in your Flash projects (Chapter 8). Finally, learn how to modify text and graphics to get the most out of your Flash artwork (Chapter 9).

Part III: Creating Animation and Effects

After you've learned how to find your way around the Flash interface and to create static graphics, you can get some perspective on animation strategies (Chapter 10). Learn to make things move, work with different symbol types to optimize your animation workflow, and use the new Timeline effects (Chapter 11). Put layers to use for organization and special effects (Chapter 12). Get special production tips for professional character animation and broadcast-quality graphics (Chapter 13). Finally, learn the process for tailoring animation output to a variety of viewing environments (Chapter 14).

Part IV: Integrating Media Files with Flash

Now that you're fluent in the Flash workspace, take your projects to the next level by adding sound, special graphics, and video assets. In Chapter 15, you learn the basics of digital sound, and see which file formats can be imported into Flash and how to import, optimize, and export high-quality sound for different types of projects. Chapter 16 gives an overview of how to bring vector or raster artwork from other programs into Flash and how to protect image quality while optimizing your Flash movies. Chapter 17 introduces the video embedding features of Flash MX 2004.

Part V: Adding Basic Interactivity to Flash Movies

Learn how to start using Flash actions to create interactive and responsive presentations. Get oriented in the Flash MX 2004 Actions panel, which has a new integrated interface (Chapter 18). Use ActionScript in Flash movies to control internal elements on multiple timelines, such as nested Movie Clips (Chapter 19). Use some of the new Flash MX 2004 components to create fast, clean interfaces for multipart presentations that also include some of the Accessibility options (Chapter 20).

Part VI: Distributing Flash Movies

You need to learn how to export (or publish) your Flash presentations to the SWF file format for use on a Web page, or within presentations on other formats. Chapter 21 details options in the Publish Settings of Flash MX 2004, and provides tips for optimizing your Flash movies in order to achieve smaller file sizes for faster download performance. If you prefer to hand-code your HTML, then read Chapter 22, which describes how to use the <embed> and <object> tags, how to load Flash movies into framesets, and how to create plug-in detection systems for your Flash movies. If you want to find out how to create a Flash stand-alone projector, or use the Flash stand-alone player, then check out Chapter 23.

Part VII: Approaching ActionScript

Learn the basic elements of ActionScript syntax (Chapter 24), and how to use ActionScript to control properties and methods of MovieClip objects (Chapter 25). Learn about making functions and arrays (Chapter 26), detecting Movie Clip collisions, and using the Color and Sound objects for dynamic control of movie elements (Chapter 27). Get an introduction to runtime MP3, JPEG, and FLV loading features as well as how to share and load assets in multiple SWF files (Chapter 28). Find out how to use the pre-built components that ship with Flash MX 2004 to enhance your Flash projects (Chapter 29). Start creating Flash forms that send data with the LoadVars object and learn to integrate XML data with Flash movies (Chapter 30). Take control of text fields using new HTML tags and the TextFormat object (Chapter 31). Part VII includes two detailed chapters dedicated to building real Flash projects from the ground up (Chapter 32 and Chapter 33) and finishes with a chapter of troubleshooting tips and suggested best-practices for project architecture (Chapter 34).

Part VIII: Expanding Flash

Every multimedia designer uses Flash with some other graphics, sound, and authoring application to create a unique workflow that solves the problems of daily interactive project development. Part VIII shows you how to manage raster graphics and vector graphics and how create content in popular applications such as Macromedia Fireworks, FreeHand, and Adobe Photoshop. This part also covers topics relevant to Flash production using Dreamweaver MX 2004 and Director.

Part IX: Appendixes

In the appendixes, you'll find a table of common and updated Flash MX 2004 keyboard shortcuts (Appendix A), information on digital sound basics that explains sound sampling rates and bit depths (Appendix B), and information on Digital Video basics (Appendix C). Directions for using the CD-ROM are included in Appendix D and a listing of contact and bio information for the guest experts is available in Appendix E.

Getting in Touch with Us

You can find additional information, resources, and feedback from the authors and other readers at www.flashsupport.com. We want to know what you think of individual chapters in this book. Visit www.flashsupport.com/feedback to fill out an online form with your comments.

If you have a great tip or idea that you want to share with us, we'd like to hear from you. You can also send comments about the book to robert@theMakers.com or snow@theMakers.com.

Also, check Appendix E for more information on contacting this book's various contributors, guest experts, and our technical editors.

Macromedia Wants to Help You

Macromedia has created a Feature Request and Bug Report form to make it easier to process suggestions and requests from Flash users. If you have an idea or feature request for the next version, let the folks at Macromedia know. You can find the online form at www.macromedia.com/support/email/wishform.

The simple fact is this: If more users request a specific feature or improvement, it's more likely that Macromedia will implement it.

To support the Flash community Macromedia has created a searchable registry that allows clients to find Flash developers by location or by services offered. To create a custom developer profile, register yourself at www.macromedia.com/locator.

Regardless of your geographic location, you always have access to the global Flash community for support and the latest information through the Macromedia Online Forums at http://webforums.macromedia.com/flash.

For inspiration and motivation check out the Site of the Day, weekly features, and case studies at www.macromedia.com/showcase.

Acknowledgments

This book would not have been possible without the dedication and talent of many people. Although much of the content in this edition has changed to reflect changes in the tools, there is also a good deal of content from dedicated contributors that has been carried over from the previous edition. We are always grateful for the added breadth and depth the tutorials from our guest experts bring to the content. First and foremost, we would like to thank the Flash development community. In our combined experiences in research and multimedia production, we haven't seen another community that has been so open, friendly, and willing to share advanced tips and techniques. It has been gratifying to be involved as the community keeps expanding and to see the innovators in the first wave of Flash development become mentors to a whole new generation. Thank you all for continuing to inspire and challenge audiences and each other with the possibilities for Flash.

We would like to thank everyone at John Wiley & Sons who supported us as we researched and revised page after page after page. Timothy Borek, our project editor, was resourceful in navigating the many production hurdles that come with a book this size. He almost made it look easy! As always, our endless gratitude goes to Michael Roney, our acquisitions editor. Steadfast, optimistic, and supportive, Mike was willing to trust us even as we pushed deadlines to overhaul a best-selling book.

Damian Burns and Graham Pearson, our technical editors, were dedicated and even cheerful, as they pounded through pages of text and waded carefully through example files in a determined effort to anticipate our readers' perspective. We always prefer to hear "it's broken" *before* the book has gone to print!

David Fugate, our literary agent at Waterside Productions, has been through every revision of the *Flash Bible* series, and honestly none of them could have happened without him — at least, not without loss of life and limb. It's easy to be a good guy when the economy is booming and projects turn on a dime, but we appreciate David's graciousness and resolve even more when the going gets tough.

Of course, this book about Flash wouldn't even exist without the hard work of the people at Macromedia who make it all possible. Many thanks to the developers, engineers, and support staff at Macromedia, especially Lucian Beebe, Gary Grossman, and Erica Norton, who answered our questions during the development of Flash. We would have had a hard time researching this book without software assistance from Heather Hollaender and Henriette Cohn. We're also indebted to all our intrepid fellow developers and authors, who helped us to get our bearings in early versions of Flash MX 2004.

Tutorials at a Glance

Contents at a Glance

Contents

Part IV: Integrating Media Files with Flash   445

Chapter 15: Adding Sound 447

Part V: Adding Basic Interactivity to Flash Movies   559

Chapter 18: Understanding Actions and Event Handlers 561

Chapter 19: Building Timelines and Interactions 591

An Introduction to Flash Web Production

If you're new to Flash or to multimedia production, this section will get you started on the right foot. If you are a veteran Flash user, this section will give you some perspective on the evolution of Flash and the new workflow options brought about by the MX 2004 version of the Macromedia Studio programs.

Chapter 1 provides a comprehensive overview of the strengths and weaknesses of the Flash format and some background on where Flash came from and how it has evolved. Chapter 2 explores the various ways that Flash movies interact with other Web formats and introduces some of the issues that need to be considered when planning for specific audiences. Chapter 3 has expanded coverage of tools and strategies for multimedia project planning, including detailed descriptions of how to create flowcharts, site maps, and functional specification documents.

Understanding the Flash MX 2004 Framework

Since its humble beginnings as FutureSplash in 1997, Macromedia Flash has matured into a powerful tool for deploying a wide range of media content. With every new version released, the possibilities have increased for imaginative and dynamic content creation — for the Web and beyond. Macromedia has responded to the development community's unprecedented embrace of Flash by expanding advanced features and enhancing tools for new users. Never before has Flash incorporated so many new features in a single release.

In this chapter, we introduce Flash MX 2004 and explore the many possibilities that are available for your productions. We also discuss how Flash compares to or enhances other programs that you may be familiar with.

Flash movies are usually viewed in a few different ways. The most common method is from within a Web browser, either as an asset within an HTML page or as a Web site completely comprised of a master Flash movie using several smaller Flash movies as loaded SWF assets. The Flash Player is also available as a standalone application (known as a *projector*), which can be used to view movies without needing a Web browser or the plug-in. This method is commonly used for deployment of Flash movies on CD-ROMs, floppy disks, or other offline media formats.

Cross-Reference You can learn more about projectors and standalones in Chapter 23, "Using the Flash Player and Projector."

It's a (Flash) MX 2004 World

Flash has seen significant development over the years in both capability and design. Consistently proven with each new release is that developers continue to push the technology into new territory. In its current iteration, Flash MX 2004 is advancing the successes of its predecessor, Flash MX. The new version offers more tools to create the latest breed of Web experiences, dubbed Rich Internet Applications (RIAs), and Macromedia has added more authoring features to help the novice user learn the toolset.

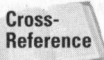
Cross-Reference   We discuss the topic of RIAs in Chapter 2, "Exploring Web Technologies."

However, Flash is no longer a single authoring product. Macromedia has made two versions of the tool available: Flash MX 2004 and Flash MX Professional 2004. Both editions share many core updates to Flash MX, including our following favorites:

✦ **Timeline Effects:** A feature added specifically for new users, Timeline Effects enable you to quickly add motion and visual effects to your Flash artwork or text. Flash MX 2004 automatically creates all the tweens and symbols necessary for the chosen effect. You can change or edit effect settings at anytime while authoring your Flash movie. Learn more about Timeline Effects in Chapter 11, "Timeline Animation and Effects."

✦ **Behaviors:** Another feature added to help novice users, the Behaviors panel adds interactivity to Flash buttons, components, and frames very easily. If you've used behaviors in Dreamweaver, you'll find that using behaviors in Flash is very similar. Several examples throughout this book use the new behaviors in Flash MX 2004.

✦ **Spell checker:** You can now check the spelling of text within your Flash movie, including text in your ActionScript code.

✦ **Document tabs:** If you're using the Windows version of Flash MX 2004, you can quickly switch between multiple Flash documents .fla files) by clicking the document's tab in the authoring environment.

✦ **Improved Actions panel:** The Actions panel has an improved Script navigator, enabling you to edit the actions of any keyframe or instance in your Flash document. You can also pin multiple scripts in the Script pane, so you can quickly switch from one script to another. The Actions panel is discussed throughout Parts V and VII of this book.

✦ **Find and Replace:** A highly requested feature, Find and Replace does exactly what it says: locates and updates elements in your Flash document. Everything from text to font types to colors to imported graphics and sounds can be searched with this tool.

✦ **Better graphics support for imported files:** Macromedia dubs this "high-fidelity import," which now enables you to import Adobe PDF and Adobe Illustrator 10 files with better conversion to Flash-equivalent vector graphics.

✦ **Video Import wizard:** Continuing with Flash MX's video encoding abilities, you have greater control over compression options and in/out points during the video import process. You can find more information about this feature in Chapter 17, "Embedding Video."

✦ **Flash Player detection:** Flash MX 2004 can create fully built HTML and Flash movie detection files for your Flash content. In previous versions, such automation was only available in Dreamweaver. Now, you can setup this detection process directly in the Flash MX 2004 authoring environment.

✦ **ActionScript 2.0:** Perhaps one of the biggest advancements in this new version of Flash is a whole new version of the ActionScript language. While most of the coding conventions remain relatively intact, ActionScript 2.0 adds strict data typing, case sensitivity, and close compliance with ECMAScript 4.0.

If you use Flash MX Professional 2004, sometimes referred to as Flash MX Pro or Flash MX Pro 2004, you can take advantage of the following additional features as well:

✦ **Script editor:** You can edit AS or ASC files (which are external code files for Flash movies or Flash Communication Server applications, respectively) directly in the Flash authoring environment. All of the code support available in the Actions panel is available in the Script editor as well.

✦ **Screen-based visual development environment:** One of the biggest differences between Flash MX 2004 and Flash MX Pro 2004 is the ability to use a new authoring concept: screens. Screens enable you to quickly put together forms or slide shows.

✦ **Advanced components:** Flash MX Pro 2004 ships with more components than the standard version, including data connectors that can tap XML and Web service-based data sources. The standard version of Flash MX 2004 has 13 components, whereas the Professional version has 30 components, including Media components that load Flash Video files (.flv files) or MP3 files. We discuss many of the Standard version components in Chapter 29, "Using Components."

✦ **Data binding:** The Component Inspector panel, available in both editions of Flash MX 2004, has an additional Bindings tab, enables you to easily attach dynamic data to components.

✦ **Project management:** The Project panel, available only in Flash MX Pro 2004, organizes all of the files associated with your Flash projects. You can create and define sites in Flash MX Pro 2004, just as you do in Dreamweaver. The same site definition files are used between the two programs, making it easy to edit files in either application. The Project panel can publish multiple Flash documents (.fla files) at once, and it can be integrated with Microsoft SourceSafe to version-track your source code. You can learn more about the Project panel in Chapter 3, "Planning Flash Projects."

✦ **FLV Exporter:** One of the most amazing aspects of Flash MX Pro 2004 isn't even in the authoring environment! A separate installer ships with Flash MX Pro 2004 that enables you to export Flash Video (.flv files) from professional video applications such as Adobe After Effects, Apple Final Cut Pro, and Apple QuickTime Player Pro. This tool actually installs a QuickTime Component that can be used by most QuickTime-aware programs. The quality of the video produced by this tool is far better than the native Video Import wizard. To learn more about the use of this tool, see Chapter 17, "Embedding Video."

Many enhancements are not directly seen in the authoring environment though. While there are two editions of Flash MX 2004, there's still only one Flash Player 7 that's used to view the movies published from either edition. Flash Player 7 adds the following enhancements, among others:

✦ **Small font size rendering:** You can enable text fields in Flash documents to optimize the display of small font sizes during playback. While it's generally a good idea to anti-alias (or smooth) text in Flash movies, small font sizes can contribute to illegible text — such sizes can be too blurry to read. Now, in Flash Player 7-compatible movies, you can force small text to render *aliased*, with smoothing turned off.

✦ **FLV file playback from standard Web servers:** When streaming audio and video was introduced with Flash Player 6, a new file format, Flash Video (.flv file), was introduced. Prior to Flash MX 2004, this file format could only be served from a regular Web server if it was imported into a Flash document at author-time. Now, you can load FLV files directly into a Flash movie (.swf file) at runtime, using NetStream objects in ActionScript. To learn how to load FLV files in this manner, read Chapter 28, "Sharing and Loading Assets."

Tip

You still need Macromedia Flash Communication Server MX to truly stream Flash Video (.flv files) at runtime. The new FLV loading feature of Flash Player 7 progressively downloads the video file, while Flash Communication Server can stream any portion of a video file.

✦ **Support for Web services:** You can now load data from a Web service running on a remote server. Web services have gained momentum over the last two years as a standard format for sending and receiving data over the Web. Web services access WSDL files (Web Services Description Language) that can tap dynamic data sources such as databases.

Tip

Macromedia Flash Remoting MX remains, however, the fastest and most efficient way to deal with data transactions in Flash movies. Expect to see future updates for Flash Remoting MX for the new version of Flash MX 2004.

✦ **Tougher security restrictions:** Flash Player 7 implements new security policies for data loaded into Flash Player 6 or higher movies. You can only load data from the same domain as that hosting the Flash movie (.swf file), unless a policy file, named crossdomain.xml, exists on the remote domain you are trying to access.

Web
Resource

For the most up-to-date information on the new security policy and crossdomain.xml files, see Macromedia's site at:

www.macromedia.com/support/flash/ts/documents/loadvars_security.htm.

✦ **Better runtime performance:** Macromedia has posted that Flash movie performance has been increased by a factor of two to five times for video, scripting, and general display rendering. In our own tests, we found that even our most complex Flash movies ran better and faster in Flash Player 7.

Tip

This is a relatively simple feature to test. Open one of your most intensive Flash movies created in Flash MX, and publish it as a Flash Player 7 movie from Flash MX 2004. Run the new movie in Flash Player 7 and see if you notice a difference.

✦ **Automatic player updates:** The Windows version of Flash Player 7 can now be updated automatically. This great enhancement means that you can more reliably use enhancements that Macromedia may make available in minor revisions of Flash Player 7, not to mention future major revisions of Flash Player.

For a complete list of features in each edition of Flash MX 2004, see the Help pages in the Help panel's booklet, Getting Started with Flash ➪ Getting Started ➪ What's new in Flash.

Before you buy or upgrade Flash MX 2004, we highly recommend that you take a look at the detailed feature comparison table on Macromedia's site at:

www.macromedia.com/software/flash/productinfo/features/comparison/.

If you're using the trial version of Flash MX 2004 (included on this book's CD-ROM), you can switch to either the Standard or Professional version at anytime by choosing Help ⇨ Switch to Flash MX Professional 2004 or Help ⇨ Switch to Flash MX 2004, depending on which version you're currently running.

Macromedia also released new versions of Dreamweaver and Fireworks, as part of the Studio MX 2004 software bundle. The user interfaces for Flash, Dreamweaver, and Fireworks are nearly identical, each touting a Property inspector, dockable panel sets, and specialized tools to integrate the products with one another.

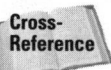

To learn more about enhancing your Flash production with Dreamweaver, Fireworks, FreeHand, and Director, refer to Part VIII, "Expanding Flash."

Although the broad array of Flash work created by Web designers and developers already speaks for itself, the sleek interface and the powerful additional features of Flash MX 2004 surely inspires more challenging, functional, entertaining, informative, bizarre, humorous, beautiful, fascinating experiments and innovations.

There are probably more ways to use Flash than there are adjectives to describe them, but here are just a few examples:

✦ Forms for collecting user information and dynamically loading custom content based on this interaction

✦ Real-time interaction with multiple users on a forum or support site, including live audio/video feeds of connected parties

✦ A video portfolio using native MX 2004 video import capabilities and dynamic loading of content

✦ Animated I.D. spots and loading screens with built-in download detection

✦ A practical Web utility, such as a mortgage calculator or a search tool

✦ Robust chat rooms based on XML and server-socket technology

✦ An audio interface dynamically pulling in requested songs using native MX support for MP3 loading

✦ Interactive conceptual art experimentations involving several users, 3D, or recording and playback of user interaction

✦ Shopping and e-commerce solutions built entirely using Flash and server-side technology

✦ Alternative content or movie attributes based on system capability testing (if a device or desktop doesn't support audio streaming, then a text equivalent of the audio transcript is presented to the user)

✦ Projectors used for creating slide show presentations in the style of PowerPoint, either on either CD-ROM or an alternative storage device

✦ Broadcast quality cartoons, advertising, or titling

✦ Optimized animations for the Web, and for portable devices such as cell phones or Pocket PCs

✦ An interface that addresses accessibility issues by modifying certain elements when a screen reader is active

✦ Flash movies specifically exported for use in digital video projects requiring special effects and compositing

This list is obviously far from complete and is ever-expanding with each new release of the program. As you can probably tell from this list, if you can imagine a use for Flash, it can probably be accomplished.

The topography of Flash MX 2004

Before you attempt to construct interactive projects in Flash, you should be familiar with the structure of the authoring environment. Even if you already know a previous version of Flash, this is advisable. That's because with the release of Flash MX 2004, Macromedia has again added many new features to the interface and either moved or improved other features and functionalities. So, to get a firm footing in the new interface, we strongly suggest that you work your way through this book — from the beginning.

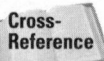
Cross-Reference   Chapter 4, "Interface Fundamentals," introduces the new Flash MX 2004 interface and gives you tips for customizing your workspace and optimizing your workflow.

Moreover, you need to proactively plan your interactive projects before you attempt to author them in Flash. An ounce of preplanning goes a long way during the production process. Don't fool yourself — the better your plan looks on paper, the better it performs when it comes to the final execution.

Cross-Reference   The foundation for planning interactive Flash projects is detailed in Chapter 3, "Planning Flash Projects," and you will find these concepts reiterated and expanded in chapters that discuss specific project workflows. Chapter 20, "Making Your First Flash MX 2004 Project," is a great place to start applying these planning strategies.

In this edition of the *Flash Bible*, we've consolidated the overview of interactive planning in the early chapters of the book. In later chapters, we've included step-by-step descriptions of real-world projects that allow you to see how all the theory and planning suggestions apply to the development of specific projects.

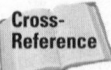
Cross-Reference   Chapter 32, "Creating a Portfolio Site in Flash," describes the process for creating a site that includes a variety of source images. Chapter 33, "Creating a Game in Flash," walks through the logic required to design and script a functional and engaging game.

There are two primary files that you create during Flash development: Flash documents (.fla files) and Flash movies (.swf files). We discuss both of these formats next.

File types in Flash MX 2004

Flash documents (.fla files) are architected to provide an efficient authoring environment for projects of all sizes. Within this environment, content can be organized into scenes, and the ordering of scenes can be rearranged throughout the production cycle. Layers provide easy separation of graphics within each scene, and, as Guide or Mask layers, they can also aid drawing or even provide special effects. The Timeline shows keyframes, motion and shape tweens, labels, and comments. The Library (which can be shared amongst movies at author-time or at runtime) stores all the symbols in your project such as graphics, fonts, animated elements, sounds or video, and components.

Flash documents

 Throughout this book, you will see us refer to Flash documents, which are the .fla files created by Flash MX 2004 when you choose File ➪ Save or File ➪ Save As. Unlike some graphic applications such as Macromedia FreeHand or Adobe Illustrator, the file extension for Flash documents does not reflect the version of the authoring tool. For example, Flash 5, Flash MX, and Flash MX 2004 save Flash documents as FLA files. You cannot open later version documents in previous versions of the authoring tool. You do not use Flash documents with the Flash Player, nor do you need to upload these files to your Web server. Always keep a version (and a backup!) of your Flash document.

Tip   Flash MX 2004 allows you to resave your Flash MX 2004 document (.fla file) as a Flash MX document (.fla file). Choose File ➪ Save As and select Flash MX Document in the Save as type menu. If you save the document in this manner, you can open the Flash document (.fla file) in the Flash MX authoring application.

Figure 1-1 shows how Flash documents are composed of individual scenes that contain keyframes to describe changes on the Stage. What you can't see in this figure is the efficiency of sharing Flash Libraries among several Flash documents, loading other Flash movies into a parent or "master" Flash movie using the loadMovie() action, or creating interactive elements with scripting methods.

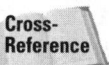
Cross-Reference   Part VII of this book, "Approaching ActionScript," addresses the topic of sharing and loading Flash movies. This part prepares you for taking on more advanced ActionScript development.

Flash movies

 When you publish or test a Flash document, Flash MX 2004 creates a Flash movie file with the .swf file extension. This file format is an optimized version of the Flash document, retaining only the elements from the project file that are actually used. Flash movies are uploaded to your Web server where they are usually integrated into HTML documents for other Web users to view. You can protect your finished Flash movies from being easily imported or edited in the authoring environment by other users.

Caution   The Protect from import option in the Publish Settings does not prevent third-party utilities from stripping artwork, symbols, sounds, and ActionScript code from your Flash movies. For more information, read Chapter 21, "Publishing Flash Movies."

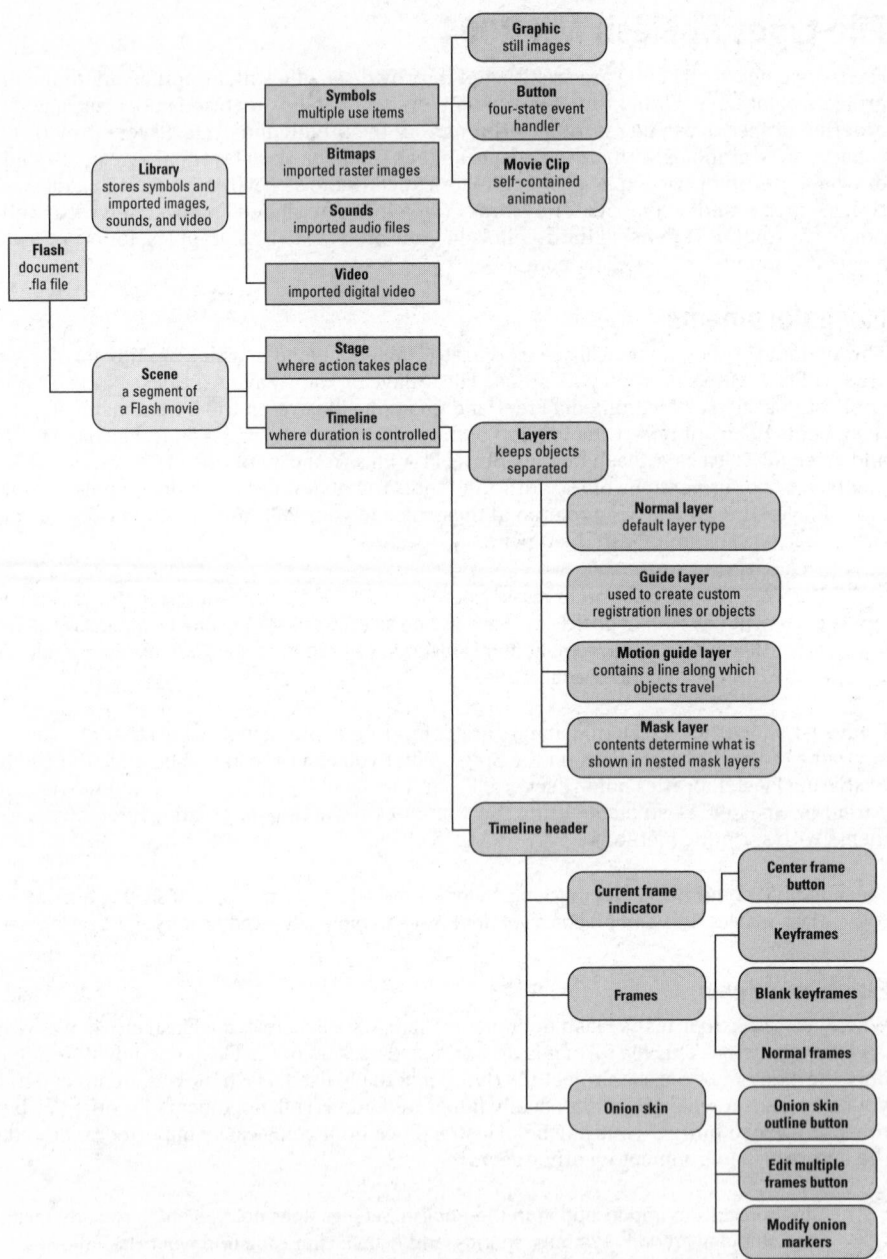

Figure 1-1: Elements of a Flash document (FLA) in the authoring environment

Much of the information contained originally within a Flash document (.fla file) is discarded in the attempt to make the smallest file possible when exporting a Flash move (.swf file). When your movie is exported, all original elements remain but layers are essentially flattened and run on one timeline, in the order that was established in the Flash document. Practically all information originally in the file will be optimized somehow, and any unused Library elements are not exported with the Flash movie. Library assets are loaded into and stored in the first frame they are used in. For optimization, reused assets are only saved to the file once and are referenced throughout the movie from this one area. Bitmap images and sounds can be compressed with a variety of quality settings as well.

Tip   Flash Player 6 and 7 movies can be optimized with a specialized **Compress Movie** option that is available in the Flash tab of the Publish Settings dialog box (File ⇨ Publish Settings). When you apply this option, you will see drastic file-size savings with movies that use a significant amount of ActionScript code.

Refer to Figure 1-2 for a graphic explanation of the characteristics of the Flash movie (.swf file) format.

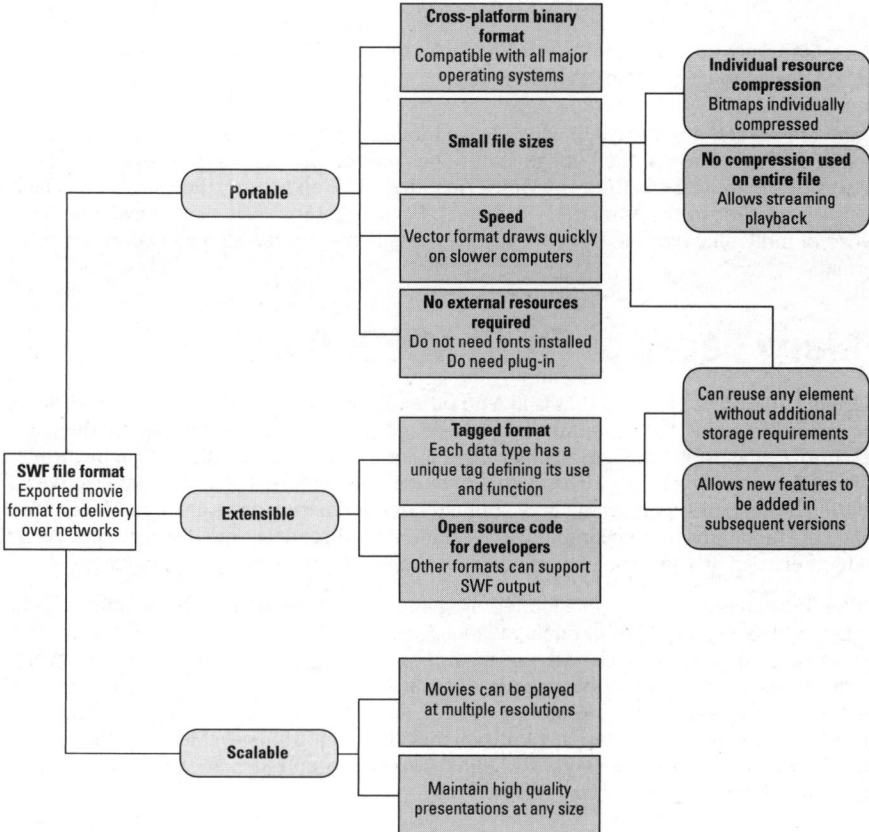

Figure 1-2: Overview of the Flash movie (SWF) format

Introducing Flash Player 7

The difference between the naming conventions of the Flash Player plug-in and the Flash authoring software is potentially confusing. Macromedia refers to its latest release of the player as Flash Player 7, tagging the version number at the end of the name instead of following in the naming convention of its predecessors (that is, "Flash 5 Player"). One probable reason the Flash Player is numbered, rather than dubbed "MX" like the authoring software, is because a standard sequential number is required for plug-in detection.

Flash Player 7 continues to integrate MSAA technology to support assistive technologies, such as screen readers to make Flash content more accessible to people with disabilities. Playback on the Macintosh has been improved, while the file size of the player download has been kept small (despite the additions).

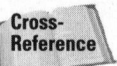

Cross-Reference   Flash Player detection is discussed in detail in Chapter 22, "Integrating Flash Content with Web Pages."

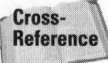

Cross-Reference   Guidelines for creating accessible content for the Flash Player 7 are introduced in Chapter 20, "Making Your First Flash MX 2004 Project."

There are several other ways in which Flash movies, or their parts, can be played back or displayed. Since Flash 4, the Publish feature has offered provisions for the export of movies or sections of movies to either the QuickTime digital video format, the QuickTime Flash layer vector format, or to the Animated GIF format. Parts of movies can also be exported as a series of individual bitmaps or as vector files. Single frames can also be exported to these formats.

The Many Faces of Flash MX 2004

Flash is a hybrid application that is like no other application. On the immediate surface, it may seem (to some) to be a simple hybrid between a Web-oriented bitmap handler, and a vector-drawing program, such as Macromedia FreeHand or Adobe Illustrator. But while Flash is indeed such a hybrid, it's also capable of much, much more. It's also an interactive multimedia-authoring program and a sophisticated animation program suitable for creating a range of animations—from simple Web ornaments to broadcast-quality cartoons. As if that weren't enough, it's also the host of a powerful and adaptable scripting language.

ActionScript has evolved from a limited drag-and-drop method of enabling animation to a full-fledged object-oriented programming language very similar to JavaScript. Flash ActionScript can work in conjunction with XML (eXtensible Markup Language), HTML, and many other applications and parts of the Web. Flash content can be integrated with many server-side technologies including Flash Remoting MX and Flash Communication Server MX, and the Flash Player offers built-in support for dynamically loading images, MP3s, movies, and other data. Flash can work seamlessly with ColdFusion MX 6.1 and XML socket servers to deliver streamlined dynamic interactive experiences.

So, what's this evolving hybrid we call Flash really capable of? That's a question that remains to be answered by developers such as you. In fact, we're hoping that you will master this application and show us a thing or two. That's why we've written this book: to put the tool in your hands and get you started on the road to your own innovations.

Because Flash is a hybrid application capable of just about anything, a good place to start working with this powerhouse is to inquire: What are the components of this hybrid? And if they were separated out, how might their capabilities be described? Those are the questions that we answer in this chapter.

Bitmap handler

In truth, Flash has limited capabilities as an image-editing program. It is more accurate to describe this part of the Flash application as a bitmap *handler*. Bitmap images are composed of dots on a grid of individual pixels. The location (and color) of each dot must be stored in memory, which makes this a memory-intensive format and leads to larger file sizes. Another characteristic of bitmap images is that they cannot be scaled without compromising quality (clarity and sharpness). The adverse effects of scaling an image up are more pronounced than when scaling down. Because of these two drawbacks — file sizes and scaling limitations — bitmap images are not ideal for Web use. However, for photographic-quality images, bitmap formats are indispensable and often produce better image quality and lower file sizes than vector images of equivalent complexity.

Vector-based drawing program

The heart of the Flash application is a vector-based drawing program, with capabilities similar to either Macromedia FreeHand or Adobe Illustrator. A vector-based drawing program doesn't rely upon individual pixels to compose an image. Instead, it draws shapes by defining points that are described by coordinates. Lines that connect these points are called paths, and vectors at each point describe the curvature of the path. Because this scheme is mathematical, there are two distinct advantages: Vector content is significantly more compact, and it's thoroughly scalable without image degradation. These advantages are especially significant for Web use.

Vector-based animator

The vector animation component of the Flash application is unlike any other program that preceded it. Although Flash is capable of handling bitmaps, its native file format is vector-based. So, unlike many other animation and media programs, Flash relies on the slim and trim vector format for transmission of your final work. Instead of storing megabytes of pixel information for each frame, Flash stores compact vector descriptions of each frame. Whereas a bitmap-based animation program (such as Apple's QuickTime) struggles to display each bitmap in rapid succession, Flash quickly renders the vector descriptions as needed and with far less strain on either the bandwidth or the recipient's machine. This is a huge advantage when transmitting animations and other graphic content over the Web.

Video compressor

Flash Player 6 and 7 include a built-in video engine — the Sorenson Spark codec — which means that the Flash Player plug-in can be considered one of the world's smallest video plug-ins. You can import source video files directly into Flash MX 2004 documents (.fla files). Users do not need to have Apple QuickTime, RealSystems RealOne, or Microsoft Windows Media Player installed in order to view video in a Flash movie. Unlike Director Shockwave, which accommodates video but still requires Apple QuickTime to be installed to playback the video, Flash Player 6 and 7 provide a seamless solution.

To learn more about this exciting aspect of Flash authoring, refer to Chapter 17, "Embedding Video." We also discuss the Flash Video Exporter tool and Sorenson Squeeze, applications designed to create the highest-quality Flash video content.

You can manipulate video content and/or include them in your productions, but you could also use Flash MX 2004 to directly export high-quality video content for broadcast video production.

You can learn how to transfer Flash animations to high-quality video in Chapter 14, "Exporting Animation."

Audio player

Since Flash Player 6, Flash movies (.swf files) have had the capability to load MP3 files during runtime. You can also import other audio file formats into a Flash document (.fla file) during author-time. Sounds can be attached to keyframes or buttons, for background tracks or sound effects. A sound file's bytes can be distributed evenly across a timeline, so that the SWF file can be progressively downloaded into the Flash Player, enabling a movie to start playing before the entire sound file has been downloaded.

Multimedia authoring program

If the heart of Flash is a vector-based drawing program, then the body of Flash is a multimedia-authoring program (or authoring *environment*). Flash documents (.fla files) can contain multiple media assets, including sound, still graphics, animation, and video. Moreover, Flash is a powerful tool for creating truly interactive content because it allows you to add (ActionScript) commands to dynamically control movie (.swf file) playback. Whether you are designing simple menu systems or customized and intuitive experimental interfaces, Flash content can be authored to recognize and respond to user-input.

Animation sequencer

Most multimedia-authoring programs have a component for sequencing content as animation, and Flash is no exception. But in Flash, the animation sequencer is the core of the application. The Timeline window controls the display of all content — static or animated — within your Flash project. Within the Timeline window, there are two areas that allow you to organize content in visual space and in linear time.

Layers and layer folders allow you to keep track of content that has been placed into your Flash document. The visibility of each layer can be controlled independently to make it easier to isolate specific elements as you are authoring. Layers are viewed from front to back within each frame of the Timeline — items on upper layers overlay other items on lower layers. Any number of items can be placed on a single layer, but you have less control over the stacking order within a layer. Within the same layer, ungrouped vector lines and shapes will always be on the bottom level, whereas bitmaps, text, grouped items, and symbol instances will be on the upper level.

Tip Flash MX 2004 documents can use Layer folders. This is invaluable for organizing projects that involve many separate elements.

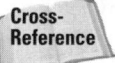

Cross-Reference For a detailed "tour" of the Flash MX 2004 environment, refer to Chapter 4, "Interface Fundamentals." The process of making artwork and managing groups and symbols is discussed in Chapter 5, "Drawing in Flash," and in Chapter 6, "Symbols, Instances, and the Library," respectively.

The structure that creates the illusion of movement in a Flash movie is a series of frames. Each frame represents a still moment in time. By controlling how the Playhead moves through these frames, you can control the speed, duration, and order of an animated sequence.

By changing the content in your layers on each frame, you can manually create frame-by-frame animation. However, one of the things that makes Flash such a popular animation machine is its ability to auto-interpolate or *tween* animation. By defining the content on a beginning and an end keyframe and applying a Motion tween or a Shape tween, you can quickly create or modify animated shape transformations and the movement of elements on the Stage.

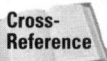

Cross-Reference The many ways of creating Flash animation are discussed in Part III: "Creating Animation and Effects."

Within one Flash document you can also set up a series of separate scenes, each scene is a continuation of the same Main Timeline, but scenes can be named, and reordered at any time. Scenes play through from first to last without interruption unless Flash's interactive commands ("actions") dictate otherwise.

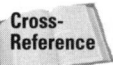

Cross-Reference The steps for using ActionScript for simple control of movie playback are introduced in Part V: "Adding Basic Interactivity to Flash Movies."

Programming and database front end

The past few versions of Flash brought vast expansion of the possibilities for integrating Flash interfaces with server-side technology and dynamic loading of content using XML, ColdFusion, and new server technologies such as PHP, ASP, JSP, Flash Remoting MX and Flash Communication Server MX. These improvements largely came out of the development and maturity of ActionScript as a viable programming language. Flash developed into an alternative front end for large databases, which meant it could serve as an online store, MP3 player, or multi-user game and chat room — an amazing feat for an "animation program"!

With Flash MX 2004 there are even more possibilities at our fingertips. One of the extended functionalities in this version is the incorporation of components supporting advanced data-aware capabilities. You can load JPEGs, MP3s, and Flash Video files into Flash at runtime (or "on the fly"), without having to use a special server technology. Support for XML has been expanded to the use of Web services, a growing standard for data transmission.

There are many other enhancements to the programming environment and functionality of Flash that experienced users will appreciate and new users will come to value. ActionScript 2.0 marks an evolution of Flash's scripting language to a much more-mature format, more closely adhering to ECMAScript 4. These changes support ActionScript's move toward acceptance as a standard, object-oriented programming (OOP) language on its own.

Summary

✦ Flash MX 2004 combines many of the key tools for multimedia authoring into one nimble program. The integration it facilitates with other programs and languages promotes better Web content and more advanced applications.

✦ Flash content is not only found on the Web. For example, it is also used for CD-ROM authoring, broadcast graphics, offline interfaces, and business presentations.

✦ Flash MX 2004 is a multifaceted application that can create a wide range of interactive products for the ever-growing variety of Web-enabled devices that surfers use to access the Internet.

✦ Careful planning of Flash development will undoubtedly save you time and effort in the long run.

✦   ✦   ✦

Exploring Web Technologies

O ver the years, many technologies have been developed to work
in conjunction with Macromedia Flash. Understanding the process of integrating these technologies will no doubt enable you to
create more interactive and complex productions. If you're new to
Flash, or you're looking for new ways to enhance or broaden the
vision or scope of your Flash productions, you'll benefit from reading
this chapter. It explores the placement of Flash within an ever-growing
toolset for universal and "standards-based" Web development in
use today.

 New Feature

Just as Flash 5 and MX added enhanced XML functionality to the
Flash Player, Macromedia continues to expand the use of Flash
with standardized data sources. Flash MX 2004's ActionScript
additions allow Flash movies to consume Web Services. You learn
more about this exciting development later in this chapter.

Contextualizing Flash in the Internet Evolution

If you follow the development of "bleeding edge" technology, you may
have noticed how often software is created, updated, and made obsolete. At times, this cycle seems to happen almost on a daily basis. But
exactly how many practical — and affordable — options exist for Web
development? How can production teams develop consistent frameworks with a variety of server technologies to efficiently build Flash
presentations and applications? In this section, we discuss how Flash
MX 2004 continues to push the direction and limits of the Internet.

High expectations for Web experiences

Despite the devastation to Web production brought about by the
"dotbomb" era (that is, the economic recession that occurred after
many dotcom companies went out of business), the people visiting
your Web sites or using your Web-based applications still want to
experience engaging interfaces with amazing graphics and sound.
Clients who hire you expect that you can produce this type of material. Clients may also believe that everyone will be able to visit the
site and download material instantaneously (regardless of connection speed limitations), and that every visitor will have the same

experience. Before you consider whether Flash is the best tool to meet your clients' goals, let's step back for a moment and consider Flash's history.

With every release of a new version of Flash, Web developers have access to bigger and better capabilities. We've seen a vast evolution from the early days in 1997 of mere vector animations, which vastly reduced file sizes of standard GIF animations. In 1998, Flash 3 made a marked improvement by introducing more control over these animations. At that time, Web sites with small games started to arrive on the development scene. That was also the year when Macromedia Generator was introduced, enabling dynamic graphics and data for Flash movies. Many companies were apprehensive about investing in Flash development because Flash was relatively new, although it was gaining ground as an accepted form of Web delivery.

In 1999, when Flash 4 was introduced, this attitude changed a great deal. The new version was much more powerful, and could accomplish many of the tasks that Generator provided in the past. Database interaction and dynamic content was suddenly possible in real time. However, Flash 4 was still a difficult application for developers to use; the programming interface for ActionScript code was limited by drag-and-drop functionality (which was only avoidable by using third-party software). This problem no longer existed in the 2000 release of version 5. Flash 5 incorporated XML data, and ActionScript "grew up" to come closer to an object-oriented programming (OOP) language that strongly resembled JavaScript.

In 2002, Web designers and developers were handed the sixth version of Flash, dubbed "MX." Flash MX marked Macromedia's success at integrating all of their software products into a universal framework, where ColdFusion, Dreamweaver, Fireworks, Director, and FreeHand could all be used together to produce a new breed of Web experiences, including Rich Internet Applications. With the new software and player, XML data was processed remarkably faster, movies were made accessible to those with physical challenges, and Macromedia Generator was no longer necessary to incorporate dynamic graphics. Flash Player 6 could load JPEG and MP3 files at runtime. Developers could create reusable components that greatly decreased development time. Also, Flash Player 6 introduced support for video playback. Flash movies also become more browser-friendly with named anchors that allow specific sections of Flash movies to be bookmarked. ActionScript continued its development into more of a "real" programming language, as more objects and event handling were exposed in application programming interfaces (APIs). Perhaps most importantly, Flash Player 6 could integrate with new data transfer methods made available by Flash Remoting MX, which allowed serialized data to move more efficiently from application servers (such as ColdFusion MX) to Flash movies. Flash Communication Server MX 1.0 and 1.5, released shortly after Flash MX, enabled Flash movies to synchronize live data among several connected users simultaneously—developers could create live chat rooms, multiplayer games, and shared whiteboards, just to name a few applications. Flash Communication Server also added the capability to stream live or prerecorded audio/video streams to Flash Player 6.

With all of these capabilities, it's hard to imagine that Macromedia could pack anything else into the Flash authoring environment or the Flash Player. But with the release of Flash MX 2004, Macromedia has continued its commitment to pushing the Web to a new definition of excellence. Flash Player 7 has been overwhelmingly optimized for speed. Everything from video playback to text rendering to ActionScript performance has been vastly improved over Flash Player 6. This feature alone will encourage business clients and Web surfers alike to adopt the new player version; everyone loves faster performance. Of course, there's a whole lot more to Flash Player 7. You can now customize the contextual menu (that is, the right-click menu) that's displayed by Flash movies running in the player, and, by default, HTML hyperlinks within Flash text support Open in New Window and Copy Link options in the contextual menu. On the Windows platform, mouse wheel scrolling is now supported for internal Flash elements. Small text sizes can be rendered more cleanly (or crisply). JPEG or SWF content can now be loaded and displayed inline with Flash text. Style sheets and CSS files add new formatting options to Flash text, enabling you to share styles from DHTML documents with your Flash content. Video lovers will be enticed by the ability to load Flash Video (FLV) files directly into Flash movies, without the use of Flash Communication Server MX. Printing control is far superior in Flash Player 7 and Flash MX 2004 ActionScript, with the new `PrintJob` API. Flash MX's UI components have been completely revamped and released as V2 components, and Flash MX 2004 Pro users can enjoy new Data and Streaming Media components.

Note   There's more to Flash Player 7 and Flash MX 2004 than these specific examples, and you'll find more coverage of the new features throughout this book.

In the span of almost seven years, we have seen an incredible evolution of Flash's predecessor FutureSplash to the most widely installed Web-based plug-in technology. When Flash 5 was released, Flash was undoubtedly the key for Web branding, and it seemed as though every company wanted Flash content on their Web sites. Flash has continued to enjoy this popularity, despite opponents calling the technology "unusable." You could almost compare the introduction of Flash to that of the color television. It's difficult to return to largely static HTML pages after the interactivity, animation, eye candy, and innovation Flash sites offer to Web surfers — even those on slow connections or portable devices. Because of Macromedia's efforts to keep the file size of the Flash Player smaller than most browser plug-ins, and the fact that it has been preinstalled on most systems for some time now, Flash remains a widely accessible and acceptable technology for Web deployment.

Note   Currently, the file size of the latest release of Flash Player 7 (r14) is 466 KB for Windows (as an ActiveX control) and 1126 KB (as a BIN file) for Macintosh OS X.

To Flash or not to Flash?

One of the crucial tasks of a Web designer or developer's job is to decide if Flash is the most appropriate tool to achieve the goals of a given project. Consider why you want — or need — to employ Flash in your work, because there are occasions when it may *not* be the best choice. It may not be wise to use this technology merely because it is "the thing to do" or "cool." If you're pitching Flash projects to clients, it's a good idea to be prepared with reasons why Flash is the best tool to use to get the job done. Later in this chapter, we consider the benefits of other technologies, but for now consider what Flash can (and cannot) offer to your projects.

An effective use of Flash

With the Flash MX 2004 authoring tool, you can create a wide range of presentation material or develop fully functional applications that run in a Web browser or on handheld devices:

✦ **Flash generates very small file sizes while producing high-quality animation with optimal sound reproduction.** Even companies making world-renowned cartoons, such as Disney, use Flash for some of their work. Because of these small file sizes, Flash movies (such as cards or announcements) can even be sent via e-mail.

✦ **Nearly any multimedia file format can be integrated into Flash.** Vector images (such as EPS, FreeHand, Illustrator, and PDF files), bitmaps (GIF, PCT, TIF, PNG, and JPG), sound files (such as WAV, AIF, or MP3), and video (such as AVI and MOV) are all importable into your movies. Plug-in technology or third-party software is not required (although it does exist) to accomplish these imports. Nor is it required to play back your movies in Flash Player 7. Significant editing advantages sometimes exist when using imported files, such as symbol and layer formatting from FreeHand and Fireworks files. These features can be beneficial if you will be working with a client's raw resources.

✦ **Precise layouts with embedded fonts are possible with Flash.** Formatting is usually inconsistent when you use HTML to describe page layouts, and formatting can easily vary from one browser to the next. You can be confident your movies will be formatted and displayed consistently when viewed with the Flash Player.

New Feature

Flash Player 7 adds support for crisp-looking text at small point sizes. In previous versions of Flash, most embedded fonts did not display legibly at these sizes. Now you can control how fonts render at small point sizes.

✦ **Text, movies, images, and sound files can be displayed in your movie from a remote data source.** You can incorporate dynamic content into your movie as long as the data source (such as a database or XML file) can be accessed from your host Web server or application server. Flash Player 7 can consume Web Services directly, allowing you to build B2B (business to business) applications that take advantage of public or private data sources such as weather reports and stock information.

✦ **Just as you can receive information from a database in your movie, you can send data from your movie to the database.** Flash movies can accept user input and send the data to a server. Built-in components make it easier and faster than ever before to build interactive elements that do not require an advanced knowledge of ActionScript. Your forms have the potential to be much more engaging with animation or sound additions. You can also use this technology to track user progression throughout your site and send the information to a database.

✦ **With the proper server-side software you can produce multiuser interactivity.** Since Flash 5, you have been able to use XML sockets for transmission of data between a socket server and one or more connected Flash movies. XML operates much faster using Flash Player 6 and 7. Also, with the release of Flash Communication Server MX, developers now have a consistent API to create multiuser applications. Remote Shared Objects, one of the mechanisms employed by Flash Communication Server MX, use an efficient and optimized binary protocol, Real-Time Messaging Protocol (RTMP), to broadcast data updates.

✦ **Several Flash movies can be loaded into one large container movie.** You can create a master Flash movie and then load many Flash assets into it for each individual area of the interface or presentation. Using this method of asset management enables you to delegate tasks in a team production environment, where several designers and developers can work simultaneously. This workflow also enables you to create byte-optimized large Web sites and applications, in which assets are downloaded on an "as needed" basis while the user interacts with the Flash movie.

New Feature

Flash MX 2004 Pro features a Project panel that can tap versioning system software such as Microsoft SourceSafe. The Project panel has several file check-in and check-out features that Dreamweaver users will find familiar.

✦ **You can dynamically load images and MP3 files using Flash Player 6 or 7.** These versions of the Flash Player can load standard JPEG image files and progressively download and play MP3 files. Flash Player 7 can also progressively download Flash Video (FLV) files over the standard Web protocol, HTTP.

Note   A *progressive download* is any file type that can be used before the entire file is actually received by the Flash Player. Progressive downloads are usually cached by the Web browser. You can stream MP3 files with the use of Flash Communication Server MX 1.5. This server uses true streaming of all audio and video content, where nothing is cached by the Flash Player or the Web browser.

✦ **Creating components in Flash** MX **2004 allows developers to form reusable template interfaces or assets for Flash movies.** The components that ship with Flash MX 2004 and Flash MX 2004 Pro greatly reduce the development time of interfaces that require common UI elements such as text input areas and radio buttons. Components can be easily customized in the Property inspector, and many settings can be changed without the use of ActionScript.

New Feature   Flash MX 2004 uses a new format, SWC, for components in Flash documents. Components can now be precompiled, which means that you cannot edit their internal elements or code unless you have access to the original source FLA file used to create them.

✦ **The Flash Player is available on many different platforms and devices including Windows, Macintosh, Solaris, Linux, OS/2, SGI IRIX, Pocket PC, and even some mobile telephones.** Refer to www.macromedia.com/shockwave/download/alternates for the latest version available for these and other alternative platforms. Just about any Web surfer will be able to view Flash content by downloading and installing the latest version of the Flash Player.

✦ **Movies can be developed to run presentations of their own, commonly known as Projectors.** Projectors are Flash movies running from an embedded player, so you do not need a browser to view or use them. They can be burned onto DVDs or CD-ROMs, or saved to any other media-storage device.

✦ **Like HTML pages, content from Flash movies can be sent to a printer.** The new PrintJob API in Flash MX 2004's ActionScript language offers you the capability to precisely control the layout of the printed page. The quality of the printed artwork and text from Flash movies is remarkable. Unlike previous versions of the Flash Player, you can send multiple pages to the printer at once and create content on-the-fly for the printed output.

These are only some of the things that Flash movies can do. Regardless of the intent of your production, verifying the use of this software is usually a good idea during preproduction. In the following subsection, we consider situations in which you may not want to use Flash to develop your content.

Web Resource   We'd like to hear how you've come to use Flash technology in your projects. Post your comments at www.flashsupport.com/howdoyouflash.

When not to use Flash

If you're enthusiastic about Flash and have used Flash for previous Web projects, you can easily develop a bias in favor of Flash. It may even be hard to consider that other options could be better for development. Knowing which technology is best for each solution will assist you in offering the best quality product to your clients.

✦ **Flash movies play in a Web browser using a plug-in.** Despite the near ubiquity of the Flash Player, there are still some users who may need to download it. If you're using Flash MX 2004 to create Flash 7 movies, many Web visitors trying to view your site may need to update their players. It is also important to keep in mind that some workplaces or institutions (such as schools) will not allow their workers or students to install applications, which include plug-ins and ActiveX controls, on the systems.

✦ **The type and version of a Web browser can affect the functionality of a Flash movie.** While internal ActionScript code should largely remain unaffected by browser brand and version, some scripting and interactivity with HTML documents (using JavaScript or VBScript) may be browser-dependent.

New Feature

Later releases of Flash Player 6 and the initial release of Flash Player 7 now support the WMODE (Window Mode) parameter of Flash content across most browsers — previously, this parameter was only supported by Internet Explorer on Windows. If you've ever seen transparent-background Flash ads that whiz across the browser window, then you're already familiar with the use of the WMODE parameter. For more information on this parameter, read Chapter 37, "Working with Dreamweaver MX 2004."

✦ **Web browsers will not automatically redirect to alternative content if the Flash Player is not installed.** You as a developer are required to create detection mechanisms for the Flash Player.

New Feature

Flash MX 2004 has a new detect version option in the Publish Settings. You can learn more about this feature in Chapter 21, "Publishing Flash Movies." To learn how to use this detection feature and other custom detection methods for the Flash Player, refer to Chapter 22, "Integrating Flash Content with Web Pages."

✦ **3D file formats cannot be directly imported or displayed in Flash movies.** To achieve 3D-style effects, frame-by-frame animation or ActionScript is required. Macromedia Director MX, however, has built-in features for importing, creating, and manipulating 3D content.

✦ **Typical search engines (or spiders) have a difficult time indexing the content of Flash movies.** When you make Flash-based sites, you should create some alternative HTML content that can be indexed by search engines. If you simply place Flash movies in an otherwise empty HTML document, your Web site will not likely be indexed.

✦ **Flash sites were never meant to completely replace text-based HTML sites.** For sites largely based on textual information with basic or simple graphics, there is little point to using Flash. Selecting and printing text content from Flash movies is not always as intuitive as that of standard HTML sites. At this time, the Accessibility features of Flash Player 6 and 7 are supported only by Internet Explorer for Windows when used in conjunction with the Windows Eyes reader. A greater number of assistive technologies, however, support HTML pages.

New Feature

You can now add right-click menu support to HTML-styled text containing URL links. For example, this new feature of Flash Player 7 enables a user to open a link in a new browser window.

✦ **In many circumstances, HTML is quicker, easier, and cheaper to develop than Flash content.** There are many established applications supporting HTML development, and clients can tap an ever-increasing designer and developer base for cheaper and competitive pricing.

Of course, there are always exceptions to any rule, and these suggestions should be considered as guidelines or cautions to be examined before you embark on any Flash development. In the following subsection, we examine other tools used to create multimedia content.

Alternative methods of multimedia authoring

Now let's focus on Flash's competition in the multimedia authoring arena. This section is not intended to give you a comprehensive background on these technologies. Rather, we seek simply to give you some context of Flash as it exists in the rest of the multimedia world.

Dynamic HTML

Dynamic HTML (DHTML) is a specialized set of markup tags that tap into an extended document object model (DOM) that version 4 browsers or higher can use. Using `<layer>` or `<div>` tags, you can create animations and interactive effects with Web-authoring tools ranging from Notepad or SimpleText to Macromedia Dreamweaver. You can actually combine Flash content with DHTML to create Flash layers on top of other HTML content. One problem with DHTML is that Netscape and Internet Explorer do not use it in the same way. Usually, you need to make sure you have a specialized set of code (or minor modifications) for each browser type.

New Feature

Flash Player 7 and Flash MX 2004 ActionScript now support the use of cascading style sheets (CSS) to share formatting specifications from DHTML pages with Flash text fields. Refer to Chapter 31, "Applying HTML and Text Field Formatting," for an introduction to this new feature. More comprehensive coverage can be found in Wiley's *Flash MX 2004 ActionScript Bible* (Wiley, 2004), by Robert Reinhardt and Joey Lott.

XML and XSL

XML stands for eXtensible Markup Language. XML looks like HTML, but it's really a language that can manage structured or related data such as pricing information, contact information, or anything else that you would store in a database. XSL stands for eXtensible Stylesheet Language. XSL documents apply formatting rules to XML documents. Together, XML and XSL documents can create interactive data-driven Web sites. While most browsers in use today can read and display XML and XSL documents, some older browsers (prior to 4 browser versions) do not support these formats. The Flash Player can be installed on just about every graphical Web browser available, regardless of the browser's version. As such, you can potentially reach more users with Flash content than you can with XML and XSL content. As you see later in this chapter, XML can also be used to supply data to Flash.

Macromedia Director

Originally, Macromedia's flagship product, Director, was *the* multimedia powerhouse authoring solution. Since its inception in the 1980s, Director has had the benefit of many years to establish its mature interface and development environment. Director can integrate and control many media types, including video, audio, and entire Flash movies. Director also has an Xtras plug-in architecture, which allows third-party developers to expand or enhance Director's capabilities. For example, you can use an Xtra plug-in to tap hardware-specific input and output, such as a motion detector or pressure-sensitive plate connected to the computer's serial port. More recently, Director 8.5 and MX have added true 3D modeling support. You can create Shockwave games with textured models and lighting effects! However, there are two major drawbacks to Shockwave Director: It requires a larger download for the full player installation, and the player is available only for Windows and Macintosh platforms. Director remains a popular authoring tool for CD-ROM and DVD-ROM development.

Macromedia Authorware

Authorware, like Flash, was originally a technology developed by another company and then bought by Macromedia to add to its software lineup. Since this acquisition, Macromedia has significantly developed the features and capabilities of Authorware. It is an authoring application and a companion plug-in technology, with similar audio/video integration capabilities as Macromedia Director. However, Authorware was developed with e-learning in mind. You can use it to structure training solutions and monitor student learning. We mention Authorware as a potential competitor to Flash because many Flash developers use Flash to create Web-training modules that interact with server-side databases.

Scalable Vector Graphics

The Scalable Vector Graphics (SVG) format is widely supported by some of the largest names in the industry, such as Microsoft and Adobe. This format has even been approved as a graphics standard for the Web by the World Wide Web Consortium (W3C), whose purpose is to form universal protocols regarding Web standards. SVG is much more than a graphics format; it is also an XML-based development language. Adobe Illustrator 11, GoLive 6, and LiveMotion 1 create files based on this technology. Adobe also creates the plug-in for using this file format on the Web, but the W3C is pushing for all browsers to provide built-in support for the format so that a third-party download is unnecessary. This may be necessary if SVG is ever to become a viable content format because Web surfers have been quite slow to adopt the SVG plug-in. For more information on this topic, you can refer to www.w3c.org/Graphics/SVG and www.adobe.com/svg.

Note   Even Adobe's support of the SVG format is dubious. The latest release of Adobe LiveMotion 2 does not create SVG files — it outputs Flash movies only (SWF files).

Microsoft PowerPoint

PowerPoint is usually considered a tool for making offline presentations to show in business meetings, conferences, and seminars. What is perhaps not as well-known is how PowerPoint is sometimes used online for presenting such content. A PowerPoint viewer plug-in enables your browser to handle these files, and PowerPoint can export HTML versions of slide shows. While PowerPoint enables anyone from a designer to a programmer to easily create slide-show presentations, Flash can be considered a more robust tool for creating dynamic, high-impact presentations.

New Feature   With Flash MX 2004 Pro, you can create slide-based Flash movies, in which you can create, modify, and reorder slide "structures" instead of typical timelines and keyframes. The left and right arrow keys are also automatically enabled to move you backwards and forwards, respectively, through the slides.

SMIL, Real Systems RealPlayer, and Apple QuickTime

SMIL (Synchronized Multimedia Integration Language) also looks a lot like HTML markup tags. SMIL enables you to layer several media components in SMIL-compatible players such as the RealOne Player and the QuickTime Player. You probably have seen SMIL at work when you load the RealOne Player and see the snazzy graphics that compose the channels interface. With SMIL, you can layer interactive buttons and dynamic text on top of streaming video or audio content. You may not even think of SMIL as a competing technology, but rather a complementary one — Flash can be one of the multimedia tracks employed by SMIL! You can even use Flash as a track type in QuickTime, without the use of SMIL. When Flash 4 was released, Macromedia and Apple announced QuickTime Flash movies, which enable you to create Flash interfaces that layer on top of audio-video content. The RealOne Player will also play "tuned" Flash files directly, without the use of SMIL. A tuned Flash file is weighted evenly from frame to frame to ensure synchronized playback. Note, however, that tuned files usually need to be strict linear animations without any interactive functionality.

 **Note** Several multimedia companies are developing proprietary plug-in-based authoring tools for Web multimedia. To participate in a discussion of multimedia formats, check out the forum at www.flashsupport.com/mediaformats/.

Exploring Companion Technologies

Now that you have a clear understanding of how Flash fits into the current World Wide Web, we can begin to discuss the technologies that contribute to Flash's well-being. In today's world of the Web developer, you not only need to know how to create your Flash movies, but also how to implement Flash into existing environments, such as a Web browser or your business client's Web-ready (or not-so-Web-ready) application servers and related data sources.

HTML is here to stay

HTML is not going anywhere, regardless of the prolific nature of Flash on the Web. Using HTML to your advantage is very important because it is undeniably the best solution for certain forms of Web deployment. In addition, sites constructed entirely in Flash often require HTML to function properly. Here's how HTML works with Flash:

✦ **Displaying and formatting the movie on a Web page requires HTML.** It isn't always easy to hand-code HTML to work with ActiveX for Internet Explorer and the plug-in for Netscape at the same time.

✦ **Placing some content within a Flash movie is not possible, so you will sometimes need to link it from your movie to an HTML page.** For instance, some PDF files cannot be imported into a Flash MX 2004 document and will need to be linked from the Flash movie to be viewed separately with Acrobat Reader. Or, you may need to access video files created for the RealOne Player or Windows Media Player. You can place links to these source files, or link to an HTML document that embeds the source file.

✦ **If your end user is not willing or able to view your Flash content, HTML enables you to provide an alternative version of your Web site.** Despite the addition of accessibility options into Flash Players 6 and 7, which enable screen-reader interaction, not all screen readers are currently able to access this feature. An HTML version of your content is sure to reach most of this potential audience.

Many people find learning, and perhaps even using, HTML, to be painful and tedious. Accommodating the differences among browsers can sometimes be time-consuming and dry work. However, knowing some HTML is highly recommended and well worth the effort. HTML should be understood by any Web professional. If you are uncomfortable with the code, using Macromedia Dreamweaver 2004 will help your transition into the HTML world.

Client-side scripting using JavaScript

ActionScript and JavaScript are similar beasts, especially since Flash 5 and Flash MX. Flash MX 2004 increases the similarity between the two languages, so by learning one language you will be able to translate this knowledge with relative ease. Already knowing some JavaScript when entering the Flash realm definitely puts you at a strong advantage. However, JavaScript itself is frequently used in conjunction with Flash, as discussed in the following:

✦ With JavaScript, you can create customized browser pop-up windows that open from Flash movies. By "customized," we mean browser windows that don't have any scroll bars, button bars, or menu items across the top of the browser window.

✦ JavaScript can pass data into the Flash movie when the Web page containing the movie loads. Some browsers allow you to continually pass data back and forth between Flash and JavaScript. Also, you are able to dynamically pass variables from JavaScript right into the Flash movie.

✦ JavaScript can be used to detect the presence or absence of the Flash Player plug-in in the user's Web browser. Likewise, you can use VBScript on Internet Explorer for Windows to detect the Flash Player ActiveX control. JavaScript (or VBScript) can redirect the Web browser to alternative content if the player is not installed.

✦ Flash movie properties such as width and height can be written on-the-fly using JavaScript. You can also detect various system properties (which is also possible using ActionScript in Flash MX) in JavaScript code, and pass this information into Flash.

The *JavaScript Bible* by Danny Goodman (published by Wiley Publishing) is a highly respected resource on JavaScript. If you require more information on this language, we highly recommend this book. We also explore some uses of JavaScript with Flash movies in Chapter 22, "Integrating Flash Content with Web Pages."

The world of Web Services

If you are using Flash MX 2004 Pro, you'll be able to tap an emerging new world of data transfer directly to your Flash movies. If you've stayed in the loop of Web technologies, you've likely heard of Web Services, which is a generic term to describe a standardized approach to transfer data from one Web application to another. Web Services use a format known as Web Services Description Language (WSDL), which uses a type of XML formatting called Simple Object Access Protocol (SOAP). It's not really important to know these acronyms as much as it is to understand what they do. WSDLs (pronounced "whiz-duhls") enable you to share complex data structures in a uniform, standardized manner. As long as a technology such as Flash Player 7 or ColdFusion MX can interpret a Web Service, it can utilize its data. And because all WSDLs use the same formatting, your Flash movie can easily access data from public services offered by various companies on the Web. Some of these services are free, such as those found at www.capescience.com. Others are more restricted, such as Amazon.com's Web Service program, which is only available to registered associates. You can create your own Web Services with application servers such as Macromedia ColdFusion MX as well. Web Services simply provide a gateway from which your Flash movie can access data over the Internet.

Just about anyone can become an Amazon.com associate. See http://associates. amazon.com for more details about enrolling in Amazon's developer program for Web Services. You don't have to use Amazon.com's Web Service, but it's a fun source of information to keep you engaged while you're learning how to use Web Services with your Flash content. Check www.flashsupport.com/bonus for a tutorial on how to consume a basic Web Service using the Flash MX 2004 Pro component, WebServiceConnector.

Don't forget Flash Remoting! Flash Player 6 and 7 can send and receive data using Flash Remoting gateways, which can be installed on a variety of application servers. Flash Remoting is built into ColdFusion MX and provides a faster and more efficient means of transferring data between a Flash movie and an application server than Web Services can accomplish.

Macromedia server technologies

Nowadays, it's always helpful to have more than just client-side Flash development skills. With the release of Flash Communication Server MX and Flash Remoting MX, more and more business clients are looking for experienced Flash designers and developers to add real-time interactivity to their company's Web sites or Internet-aware applications. Applications created for Flash Communication Server MX use server-side ActionScript (ASC files) to describe and control the interactivity between a Flash movie and the server's resources, including real-time streaming audio/video media and synchronized data updates between multiple Flash clients and the application.

 Web Resource To learn more about creating Flash movies that use Macromedia server technologies, see www.flashsupport.com/ria.

Recognizing Project Potential

In this section, we provide an overview of the categories of Flash projects that you can produce. This is just a starting point to prime your creative juices and break through any self-imposed limiting perceptions that you may have about Flash media. The categories we have devised here are by no means industry standard terms — they're broad, generalized groups into which most Flash development will fall.

Linear presentations

In the early days of Internet growth, Flash shorts (cartoons) were the media buzz. These cartoons generally played from start to finish in a very linear fashion. Generally speaking, these movies load and then play — and count on catching the user's attention through the story and animation. These movies sometimes contain advanced ActionScript for animation, including randomized movement or content.

 **Note** Linear Flash presentations do not necessarily have to be displayed within a Web browser — or even online. Several film-production and advertising companies use Flash to create high-quality animation for use in broadcast TV and feature films.

Interactive presentations

Interactive presentations represent the next step up from linear presentations. They provide the user control over the way information is presented, the flow, or the experience altogether. Usually, Web sites of any construct will be considered an interactive presentation. If you have information or content in a section somewhere in a movie or Web site, then you probably have an interactive presentation. An interactive presentation will enable end users to choose the content they see, by allowing them to navigate throughout a site, bypassing some content while accessing other content. A Flash movie in this category may have all the content viewed stored in a container movie, or across several Flash files linked to a main site.

Data-driven presentations

The data-driven presentations category of Flash development represents any movies that load external data (either dynamic or static) to deliver the presentation to the user. For example, a weather site that uses Flash may download dynamic Flash graphics of precipitation maps to display to the site's visitors. These graphics may be customized for each user of the site, depending on where he or she lives. *Data-driven* may even simply mean that text information within the Flash movie changes from time to time. Simply put, anytime information is separated from the actual Flash movie, you can say it is data-driven.

Data-driven applications (or Rich Internet Applications)

The data-driven applications category is somewhat loosely defined as those Flash movies that allow the user to accomplish some sort of task or enable a transaction from the Flash movie to use an external remote data source. For example, an online Flash ATM (that is, bank machine) could allow a bank customer to log in to the bank's secure server, and transfer funds from one account to another or pay a bill. All of these tasks would require a transaction from the Flash movie to the bank's server. Another example could be an online Flash shopping cart, in which visitors add products to their virtual carts, and check out with their final order. Again, these tasks would require data to be sent from and received by the Flash movie. The term Rich Internet Application, or RIA, was coined during the Macromedia MX product line launch, and implies the use of integrated data and rich media within a graphical user interface (GUI), in or out of a Web browser. Typically, RIAs combine Flash movies with one or more server-side technologies such as Flash Remoting MX and Flash Communication Server MX.

Web Resource   We'd like to know what you thought about this chapter. Visit `www.flashsupport.com/feedback` to fill out an online form with your comments.

Summary

✦ Expectations of Web sites produced by Flash developers and designers grow with every new version of Flash. With an ever-increasing list of features and capabilities included with each version of the Flash Player, sites not facilitating new technology (such as new forms of interaction or media content) can easily become overlooked or considered uninteresting.

✦ Flash MX 2004 has many features that make it a vital piece of authoring software for Web sites and applications. Some of the main reasons to use it include small movie file sizes and the capability to integrate rich media content.

✦ Flash is not always the best tool for the job. End users need a plug-in to view Flash movies, and Flash content is not indexed well by search engines.

✦ There are several multimedia file formats available on the Web today. Although most users have many of the popular plug-ins installed, some users have restricted bandwidth and computer system environments. Flash has the capability to produce small movie files that can play identically across several platforms and devices.

✦ In order to develop advanced Flash projects, you should know the necessary HTML, JavaScript, and data-formatting standards (which now include Web Services) that allow Flash to interact with other environments and data sources. These languages broaden the capabilities for interactivity and access to large amounts of data.

✦ Flash movies loosely fall into several different categories, which are based on the type of experience they provide the end user. These categories provide a basis to visualize future projects for the benefit of your clients.

✦   ✦   ✦

Planning Flash Projects

One of the most important steps — if not *the* most important step — to producing great Flash content is *knowing* what steps you'll have to take to move from the concept or idea of the Flash movie to the finished product. This chapter explores the basics of Flash production and how to use the new Project panel in Flash MX Pro 2004 to organize your files. Whether you're a freelance Web consultant (or designer) or a member of a large creative or programming department, knowing how to manage the Flash content production will save you plenty of headaches, time, and money.

Note   The Project panel is available only in Flash MX Professional 2004 (also known as Flash MX Pro 2004). If you are using the trial version of Flash MX 2004 and want to try out the Project panel, make sure to switch to the Professional edition in the Help menu (Help ⇨ Switch to Flash MX Professional 2004).

Workflow Basics

No matter what the size or scope, every project in which you choose to participate should follow some type of planned workflow. Whether it's for print, film, video, or Web delivery (or all four!), you should establish a process to guide the production of your presentation.

Before we can explore the way in which Flash fits into a Web production workflow, we need to define a holistic approach to Web production in general. Figure 3-1 shows a typical example of the Web production process within an Internet production company.

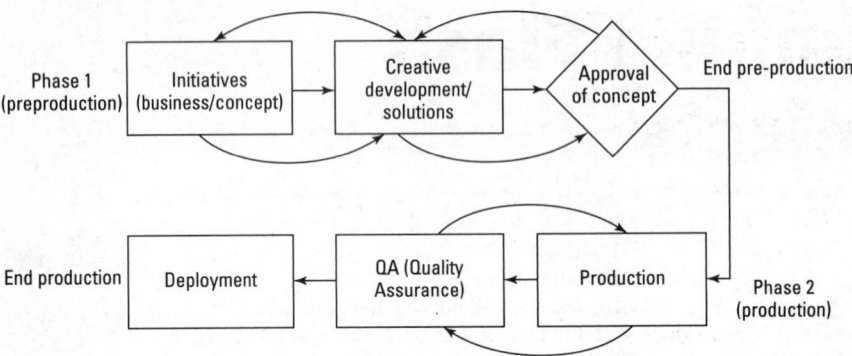

Figure 3-1: Two of the most common phases to generating Web content are preproduction and the actual production phase.

Phase I: Establishing the concept and goals

As a Web developer or member of a creative team, you will be approached by companies (or representatives for other departments) to help solve problems with projects. A problem may or may not be well defined by the parties coming to you. The goal of Phase I is to thoroughly define the problem, offer solutions for the problem, and approve one (or more) solutions for final production.

Defining the problem

Before you can help someone solve a problem, you need to determine what the problem is and whether there is more than one problem. When we say *problem,* we don't mean something that's necessarily troublesome or irritating. Think of it more as a math problem, where you know what you want—you're just not sure how to get there. When you're attempting to define a client's problem, start by asking them the following questions:

✦ What's the message they want to deliver? Is it a product that they want to feature on an existing Web site?

✦ Who's their current audience?

✦ Who's their ideal audience? (Don't let them say, "Everyone!")

✦ What branding materials (logos, colors, and identity) do they already have in place?

✦ Who are their competitors? What do they know about their competitors?

The last question points to a bigger picture, one in which the client may already have several emotive keywords that define their brand. Try to define the emotional heart and feeling of their message—get them to be descriptive. Don't leave the meeting with the words *edgy* or *sexy* as the only descriptive terms for the message.

Tip   Never go into a meeting or a planning session without a white board or a big pad of paper. Documenting everyone's ideas and letting the group see the discussion in a visual format is always a good idea. If all participants are willing, it's often useful to record the meeting with a digital voice recorder or video camera, so that it can be reviewed outside of the meeting.

Information Architects

You may have already been bombarded with the idea of *information architecture*. Information architecture is the method by which sought data is represented and structured. Good information architecture is usually equivalent to intuitive user interface design—visitors to a well-organized Web site won't spend much time finding what they came for.

We mention information architecture because the steps in Phase I are similar to the steps that traditional architects take to build a comprehensive design and production strategy *before* they start building any structure. Although this may seem obvious enough, the sad fact remains that most Internet sites (or projects) are planned as they're constructed. Indeed, we're told that production must move at Internet speed—directives can be given without thorough research into other solutions to the problem.

You can also start to ask the following technical questions at this point:

✦ What type of browser support do you want to have?

✦ Do you have an idea of a Web technology (Shockwave, Flash, DHTML, SVG) that you want to use?

✦ Does the message need to be delivered in a Web browser? Can it be in a downloadable application such as a standalone player? A CD-ROM? A DVD?

✦ What type of computer processing speed should be supported? What other types of hardware concerns might exist (for example, hi-fi audio)?

Of course, many clients and company reps look to *you* for the technical answers. If this is the case, the most important questions are:

✦ Who's your audience?

✦ Who do you *want* to be your audience?

Your audience determines, in many ways, what type of technology to choose for the presentation. If they say that Ma and Pa from a country farm should be able to view the Web site with no hassle, then you may need to consider a non-Flash presentation (such as HTML 3.0 or earlier), unless it's packaged as a standalone player that's installed with a CD-ROM (provided by the client to Ma and Pa). However, if they say that their ideal audience is someone who has a 56K modem and likes to watch mature cartoons, then you're getting closer to a Flash-based presentation. If they have any demographic information for their user base, ask for it up front. Putting on a show for a crowd is difficult if you don't know who's *in* the crowd.

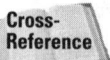 **Cross-Reference**   Stand-alone players are discussed in Chapter 23, "Using the Flash Player and Projector."

Determining the project's goals

The client or company rep comes to you for a reason—they want to walk away with a completed and *successful* project. As you initially discuss the message and audience for the presentation, you also need to get a clear picture of what the client expects to get from you.

✦ Will you be producing just one piece of a larger production?

✦ Do they need you to host the Web site? Or do they already have a Web server and a staff to support it?

✦ Do they need you to maintain the Web site after handoff?

✦ Do they expect you to market the presentation? If not, what resources are in place to advertise the message?

✦ When does the client expect you to deliver proposals, concepts, and the finished piece? These important dates are often referred to as *milestones*. The payment schedule for a project is often linked to production milestones.

✦ Will they expect to receive copies of all the files you produce, including your source FLA files?

✦ What are the costs associated with developing a proposal? Will you do work on speculation of a potential project? Or will you be paid for your time to develop a concept pitch? (You should determine this *before* you walk into your initial meeting with the client.) Of course, if you're working with a production team in a company, you're already being paid a salary to provide a role within the company.

At this point, you'll want to plan the next meeting with your client or company rep. Give them a realistic timeframe for coming back to them with your ideas. This amount of time will vary from project to project and will depend on your level of expertise with the materials involved with the presentation.

Creative exploration: Producing a solution

After you leave the meeting, you'll go back to your design studio and start cranking out materials, right? Yes and no. Give yourself plenty of time to work with the client's materials (what you gathered from the initial meeting). If your client sells shoes, read up on the shoe business. See what the client's competitor is doing to promote their message — visit their Web site, go to a store and compare the products, and read any consumer reports that you can find about your client's products or services. You should have a clear understanding of your client's market and a clear picture of how your client distinguishes their company or their product from their competitors'.

After you (and other members of your creative team) have completed a round of research, sit down and discuss the findings. Start defining the project in terms of mood, response, and time. Is this a serious message? Do you want the viewer to laugh? How quickly should this presentation happen? Sketch out any ideas you and any other member of the team may have. Create a chart that lists the emotional keywords for your presentation.

At a certain point, you need to start developing some visual material that articulates the message to the audience. Of course, your initial audience will be the client. You are preparing materials for them, not the consumer audience. We assume that you are creating a Flash-based Web site for your client. For any interactive presentation, you need to prepare the following:

✦ An organizational flowchart for the site

✦ A process flowchart for the experience

✦ A functional specification for the interface

✦ A prototype or a series of comps

An *organizational flowchart* is a simple document that describes the scope of a site or presentation. Other names for this type of chart are *site chart, navigation flowchart,* and *layout flowchart.* It includes the major sections of the presentation. For example, if you're creating a Flash movie for a portfolio site, you might have a main menu and four content areas: about, portfolio, resume, and contact. In an organizational flowchart, this would look like Figure 3-2.

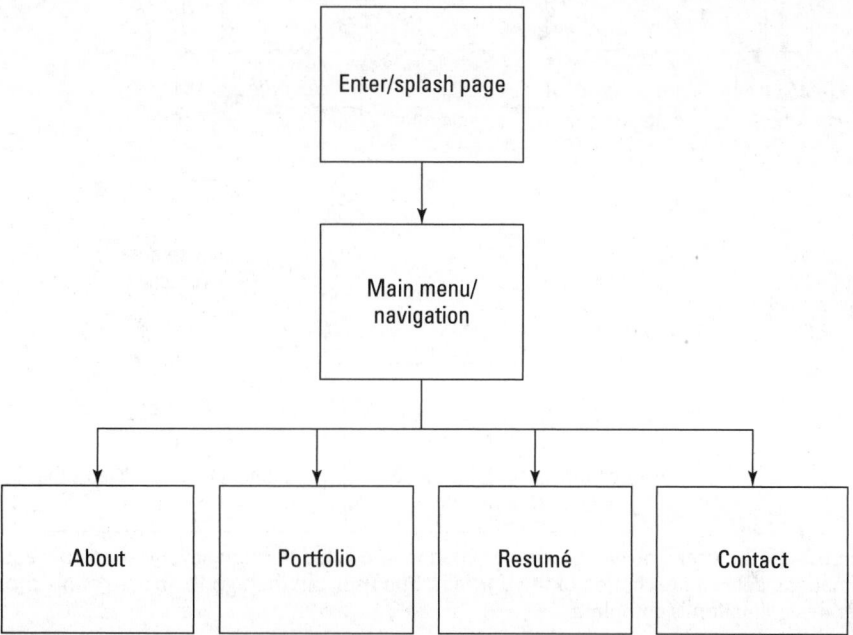

Figure 3-2: A sample organizational chart for a portfolio site

A *process flowchart* constructs the interactive experience of the presentation and shows the decision-making process involved for each area of the site. There are a few types of process charts. A basic process flowchart displays the decision-making of the end-user (for example, what type of options does a user have on any given page of the site?). Another type of flowchart shows the programming logic involved for the end-user process chart. For example, will certain conditions need to exist before a user can enter a certain area of the site? Does he have to pass a test, finish a section of a game, or enter a username and password? Refer to Figure 3-3 for a preliminary flowchart for a section of our portfolio Web site. We discuss the actual symbols of the flowchart later in this chapter.

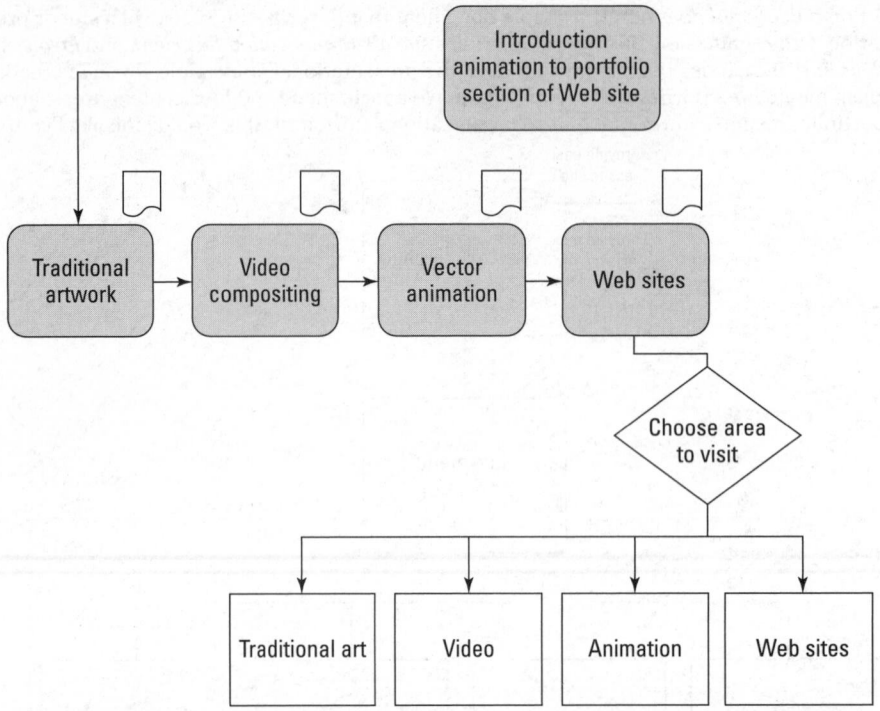

Figure 3-3: The user watches an intro animation and is led through several short subsequent animations detailing each area of the portfolio. The user can then go to an area of his choice after this animation is complete.

A *functional specification* (see Figure 3-4) is a document that breaks down the elements for each step in the organizational and/or process flowchart. This is by far the most important piece of documentation that you can create for yourself and your team. Each page of a functional specification (functional spec, for short) lists all the assets used on a page (or Flash scene, keyframe, Movie Clip) and indicates the following information for each asset:

✦ **Item ID:** This is part of the naming convention for your files and assets. It should be part of the filename, or Flash symbol and instance name. It should also be used in organizational and process flowcharts.

✦ **Type:** This part of the spec defines the name you're assigning to the asset, in more natural language, such as Home Button.

✦ **Purpose:** You should be able to clearly explain why this element is part of the presentation. If you can't, then you should consider omitting it from the project.

✦ **Format:** This column indicates what technology (or what component of the technology) will be utilized to accomplish the needs of the asset. In an all-Flash presentation, list the symbol type or timeline component (frames, scene, nested Movie Clips) necessary to accomplish the goals of the asset.

Project:			Flash interface v2.0	Section:	1 of 5 (Main Menu)
No.	Type	Purpose		Content	Format
1.A	Navigation bar	To provide easier access to site content.			A menu bar fixed at the top left of the browser window.
1.A.1	Directory buttons	To provide a means for accessing any of the portfolio sections.		Names each content area - e.g., video, audio, graphics.	A horizontal row of buttons or a skinned ComboBox component.
1.A.2	Home button	So the user can always jump back to the main page.		The text: "home."	A skinned PushButton component.
1.A.3	Search field	So a specific word can be entered to search site content.		An empty text input area with the label "search."	A Dynamic text field.
1.A.4	Sign up	Captures the user's e-mail address for the site's mailing list.		Text input fields for name and e-mail address.	A PushButton opens a browser window. ColdFusion and Access used for data transfer.
1.A.5	Back button	Allows the user to jump to the previously visited page.		Button labeled with the text "back."	A skinned PushButton component.
1.A.6	Logo or ID	Provides a means of personal branding.		A spider web with the name of the Web site in Arial Narrow text.	Graphics in Flash and Illustrator.

Figure 3-4: This functional spec displays the six components of a Flash-based navigation bar, which will appear on the main menu of our portfolio content site.

Note Functional specs come in all shapes and sizes. Each company usually has their own template or approach to constructing a functional spec. The client should always approve the functional spec, so that you and your client have an agreement about the scope of the project.

Finally, after you have a plan for your project, you'll want to start creating some graphics to provide an atmosphere for the client presentation. Gather placement graphics (company logos, typefaces, photographs) or appropriate "temporary" resources for purposes of illustration. Construct one composition, or *comp*, that represents each major section or theme of the site. In our portfolio content site example, you might create a comp for the main page and a comp for one of the portfolio work sections, such as "Animation." Don't create a comp for each page of the portfolio section. You simply want to establish the feel for the content you will create for the client. We recommend that you use the tool(s) with which you feel most comfortable creating content. If you're better at using FreeHand or Photoshop to create layouts, then use that application. If you're comfortable with Flash for assembling content, then use it.

Caution   Do not use copyrighted material for final production use, unless you have secured the appropriate rights to use the material. However, while you're exploring creative concepts, use whatever materials you feel best illustrate your ideas. When you get approval for your concept, improve upon the materials that inspired you.

Then you'll want to determine the time and human resources required for the entire project or concept. What role will you play in the production? Will you need to hire outside contractors to work on the presentation (for example, character animators, programmers, and so on)? Make sure you provide ample time to produce and thoroughly test the presentation. When you've determined the time and resources necessary, you'll determine the costs involved. If this is an internal project for your company, then you won't be concerned about cost so much as the time involved—your company reps will want to know what it will cost the company to produce the piece. For large client projects, your client will probably expect a project rate—not an hourly or weekly rate. Outline a time schedule with milestone dates, at which point you'll present the client with updates on the progress of the project.

Exploring the details of the workflow process any further is beyond the scope of this book. However, there are many excellent resources for project planning. One of the best books available for learning the process of planning interactive presentations is Nicholas Iuppa's *Designing Interactive Digital Media.* We strongly recommend that you consult the *Graphic Artists Guild Handbook of Pricing and Ethical Guidelines* and the *AIGA Professional Practices in Graphic Design,* edited by Tad Crawford, for information on professional rates for design services.

Approving a final concept and budget

After you have prepared your design documents for the client, it's time to have another meeting with the client or company rep. Display your visual materials (color laser prints, inkjet mockups, and so on), and walk through the charts you've produced. In some situations, you may want to prepare more than one design concept. Always reinforce how the presentation addresses the client's message and audience.

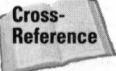

Cross-Reference   See Todd Purgason's tutorial on Flash and FreeHand, in Chapter 36, "Working with Vector Graphics." He offers some excellent suggestions for creating high-impact presentation boards in FreeHand and tips on how to reuse graphics in print and Web projects.

When all is said and done, discuss with the client the options that you presented. Gather feedback. Hopefully, the client prefers one concept (and its budget) and gives you the approval to proceed. It's important that you leave this meeting knowing one of two things:

✦ The client has signed off on the entire project or presentation.

✦ The client wants to see more exploration before committing to a final piece.

In either case, you shouldn't walk away not knowing how you'll proceed. If the client wants more time or more material before a commitment, negotiate the terms of your fees that are associated with further conceptual development.

Designing for Usability, by Scott Brown

As mentioned earlier in this chapter, the first step in developing a Flash site, or any other type of site, is to define the information architecture. In this tutorial, you find out how to define the goals and mission of the site.

Defining the goals and mission of the site

Defining the mission and goals is laying the foundation upon which to build your project. To create a solid project foundation, we must begin by questioning everything, especially the company's business model. Start with these questions:

* What is the mission or purpose of the organization?

* Why does this organization want a Web site?

* Will the Web site support the mission of the organization?

* What are the short and long-term goals of the Web site?

* Who are the intended audiences?

* Why will people come to the site?

* Are we trying to sell a product?

* What is the product or products?

* Do we have a unique service?

* What makes the service different?

* Why will people come to the site for the first time?

* Will they ever come back?

* Why would they come back?

The list of questions can go on forever. After you have gathered a list of questions, you need to get the answers. Ask around the organization, ask your friends, ask strangers, ask anyone. After the answers have been collected, you need to filter through them to create a list of goals that are based on the responses. From this list of goals, you must define further the answer to the question, "Who is the audience?"

Defining the audience

The audience can be defined as the potential users of the site and by their intentions or tasks that they may have when they come to your site. Are they kids or adults? Are they Generation X, Y, or Z? Are they into rave music or country music?

So, who is your audience? It's not an easy question because there are so many possibilities. Start with a list of all the possible audiences that the organization would like to reach, and then rearrange the list in a ranking order of most important audience to least important audience. From the audience-ranking list, create a list of possible goals and needs of each audience.

Creating character scenarios

With the list of possible goals take the process one step further by creating scenarios of the users. Think of it as writing a screenplay for your Web site. Create multiple characters that represent the majority of visitors with hobbies, likes, dislikes, and, most importantly, a task to complete on the site. The object of the scenario game is to get into the characters' heads to learn why and how they would use your site. From their viewpoint you will have an easier time creating a list of needs and wants for the character, a wish list if you will.

After the scenarios are written, the next step in the process is to gather the team together and analyze the Web sites of the competition.

Analyzing the competition

Studying the competition gives you the chance to generate a list of what kind of features they are offering and to determine whether your feature list, the one that you created from the scenarios, is missing anything. If your wish list is lacking anything in comparison to your competition, now is a good time to expand the user's functionality requirements, and to return to the scenarios to determine whether the competition's functionality matches your character's needs. If it does, you should try to elaborate on their functions and create new functions of your own — the classic case of outdoing your competition.

Reaching a consensus on what good design is

At this time in the process, have the team come together to develop a definition of what is "good site design." This step is most beneficial for any contract designer trying to gain an understanding of the client's design viewpoint. To create this "good design" definition, the team should observe a good number of sites and document everybody's likes and dislikes for each site. From the documentation of this exercise, everyone on the team will have a better understanding of what to strive for and what to avoid.

Structuring the content

Now you should have several documents to refer to — the project mission statement, the user functionality needs (wish list), and the organization's definition of good design. With these three documents in hand, the next step is to blend them into one master menu of content inventory. Think of each item on this list as a building block. You now have all the blocks needed to construct the site. The only problem is that these blocks are in a big pile with no organization (structure). Naturally, the next step is to begin creating layouts of the site, providing structure. But before you can begin the page layout process, you need to educate yourself on some Web site usability issues.

Identifying factors of usability

Usability is a much-debated concept, but generally it means creating a site/project/interface that is functional and that your audience understands. A usable site aims to be a natural extension of a user's expectations and needs. A user-friendly site tries to mirror its structure to that of the user's experience and goals. Just to make the task at hand a little more complex, keep in mind that user expectations learned in other areas of life affect how the user will think your site works. So, how can you design a site to meet your user's expectations? Well, if you did your homework on your audience and wrote the character scenarios, you should have a pretty good idea of the target audience's expectations. By knowing the general background of a user, you could include metaphors into the structure of the site. Using metaphors is a great way to help users draw upon knowledge they already have, thereby making the site easier to use. By matching the site structure to the user's experience, the amount of time it takes for the user to learn how to operate or navigate the site is minimized. The shorter the learning curve for the site, the better. If you come to a site when you have a specific goal in mind, and it takes you ten minutes to figure out how to achieve your goal, would you call that a positive experience? Most likely not!

The goal of the designer is to create an attractive site without distracting the users from their goals. Forcing the users to spend a noticeable amount of time trying to learn how to achieve their goals is very taxing on their patience, and is a good way to create a negative experience. If you're trying to sell something, chances are you want customers to be happy not annoyed. One way to make your customers' experience more enjoyable is to make their experience as easy as possible. So, how do you create a positive experience? Let's start with the most basic of user needs: the ability to navigate.

Users need to know at all times where they are in the site, where they have been, and where they can go. When developing a navigation system, be sure to keep the navigation visually consistent. Inconsistency in the navigation can cause the user to be confused and frustrated. A great concept for a navigational aid is the use of a breadcrumb trail. The breadcrumb system is a visual way to show the user the path they took to get to their current position in the site. This navigational convention is used on many resource sites and even in the Flash authoring environment itself — as you click in to edit grouped shapes or symbols, the steps you've taken are shown as text labels on the bar above the Stage. Beyond displaying the path of the user, this system gives the user the ability to backtrack to any page displayed in the path. However, remember that navigation is not the goal of the user, only an aid. The user is there to find or buy something; the user is there for the content. So, make the content the first read on all your pages. Navigational elements are there to support the content, not eclipse it.

Of course, navigation isn't the only factor to consider when designing for usability. Other variables, such as the length of text on a page, can affect the usability of a site tremendously. It's a fact that reading text on a monitor is far more taxing on the eyes than reading text on paper. Therefore, people are less inclined to read large amounts of text on the Web. As designers, we must accommodate these changes in reading patterns. Keep these simple guidelines in mind when writing text for the Web. Try to make the text scannable, because readers skim Web content. Bold the important ideas or put key information in bulleted lists. But most of all, keep the text short.

In addition to the treatment of text, there are several other tips to help improve the usability of a site. The concept of redundant links is an excellent method to support users with different backgrounds and goals. With redundant links, a user has more than one way to get to the desired content. The user may have the option to click a text link, a graphic link, or even a text link that is worded differently. Each redundant link should be designed to accommodate a wide range of users. So, where on the page should all these usability elements go?

I can't tell you where you should place your navigation system or your redundant links. However, I can provide you with some information on eye-tracking studies that will help you make an educated decision. Yes, it is true that usability researchers are able to actually monitor and record what you're looking at when viewing a Web site. Researchers have found that when a Web page loads, our eyes are looking at the center of the page, then move over to the left, and then sometimes to the right. Of course, these findings are dependent on the user's cultural background. Nevertheless, the scary finding is that the users rarely look to the right! This is most likely because most sites use the right side of the page as a place to add sidebar elements, items of lesser importance. This is also a good example of how a user's experience can affect his future experiences. So, how does Flash fit into Web site usability considerations?

Flash is a great design tool to create amazing interfaces. Flash gives the designer the freedom to create almost anything he desires. But the flexibility given to the designer is also Flash's greatest weakness from a usability perspective. Flash is a great tool for creating animation, however, inexperienced Web designers can easily go overboard. Just because you can animate an object doesn't mean that you should. The eye is very sensitive to the smallest amount of animation or movement in its peripheral view, pulling the eyes' attention away from the site's main content. On the plus side, animation used as a transitional element is very beneficial for the user. Animated transitions enable the user to follow the navigation process, gaining a better understanding of how the site might work.

Along with the problems of animation abuse, Flash enables the designers to create their own graphical user interface (GUI) elements. This is great for the designers, but the users are often left out in the cold with all this newfound freedom. This design freedom is forcing the user to learn, almost from scratch, how to operate a scroll bar or a navigation bar. If you recall, earlier we mentioned the importance of a short learning curve for the users. These extreme creative versions of standardized GUI elements might rank high on the "cool" scale, but they really throw a monkey wrench into the user's goal and expectations. GUI standards are developed to help create a consistent experience across all platforms in an effort to eliminate any unpleasant surprises. Again, these usability problems can be avoided in Flash by educating the designers about the issues at hand and finding solutions based on the set standards.

Other usability issues with Flash arise from the actual plug-in nature of Flash. Unfortunately, because Flash requires a plug-in to work in Web browsers, Flash movies are unable to take advantage of some of the browser's built-in capabilities such as the Back button and the capability to display history for the links by changing the color of the links that have been clicked. The problem with the browser's Back button is that when the button is pressed, the browser takes the user back to the previous HTML page, not to the previous state in the Flash movie. It's not a nice surprise for unsuspecting users. One solution to this problem is to pop up the Flash movie in a new browser window (via JavaScript) with all the browser's navigation elements removed (in other words, no toolbar, no location bar, no menus, and so on). No Back button on the browser, no problem right?

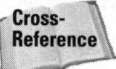

Cross-Reference

Fortunately, ActionScript can often smooth out the discrepancies between the default browser behaviors and Flash movie functionality. For an introduction to some ActionScript solutions, refer to Part VI, "Distributing Flash Movies."

Tip

Named anchor keyframes, available in Flash Player 6 or higher movies, is a feature that makes it easier for users to navigate a Flash movie using keystrokes. For an example of named anchors in action, refer to Chapter 20, "Making Your First Flash MX 2004 Project."

Building mockups of the site

You are now ready to begin mocking up the site structure using index cards, sticky notes, and other common office supplies. Creating these paper mockups saves the development team a large amount of time. The beauty of the paper mockups is that you can quickly create a navigational system and find the major flaws without spending long hours developing a beautiful rendering of a structure that may be flawed. There is nothing worse than spending months developing a product with a faulty structure only to discover the mistake just before launch!

Testing the site on real users

Testing the site is the most important step in creating a usable site. The key to testing the site is *not* to test it on people of the organization, but to test it on people in the target audience. Test the site on the real users. It's usually easier to test the site by using people who are familiar with the project. The problem with that practice is that the people are familiar with the project. You want to test fresh eyes and minds in order to get optimum feedback. For testing purposes, create a list of several tasks to complete on the site. The tasks should be pulled from the list of possible users' goals defined in the early steps of the project. As the test subjects navigate through your project, pay close attention to how long it takes them. How many times did they have to click to find what they were looking for? How many had to resort to using a search feature (or wished that they could)? What elements seemed to cause confusion or delay? What elements attracted or held the users' attention? After each test subject has completed a task, or tried, give her a post-task questionnaire with questions such as:

"How would you rate the quality of the content on this site?"

Unacceptable   −3 −2 −1   0   1   2   3   Excellent

Also, leave some room for the test subject to elaborate on the questions. After the testing is finished, review your findings and determine what needs to be fixed. After the problems are fixed, test the site again, but on new users. Repeat the process until you have a product that meets the defined goals of the organization and the users. Keep asking yourself this question: Is the interface helping the users accomplish their goals? When all else fails, you can always depend on the greatest guideline of the century: keep it simple. Oh, how true.

Tip
If this process is new to you, don't waste time "reinventing the wheel" when there are plenty of resources on this topic that can get you started. Jakob Nielsen has achieved near-celebrity status as a result of his strong opinions on this topic and he has written several books that some consider definitive. Steve Krug and Roger Black have written another popular book on this topic titled *Don't Make Me Think: A Common Sense Approach to Web Usability* (New Riders, 2000).

Phase II: Producing, testing, and staging the presentation

When your client or company executives have signed off on a presentation concept, it's time to rock and roll! You're ready to gather your materials, assemble the crew, and meet an insane production schedule. This section provides a brief overview of the steps you need to take to produce material that is ready to go live on your Web site.

Assembling assets

The first step is to gather (or start production of) the individual assets required for the Flash presentation. Depending on the resources you included in your functional spec and budget, you may need to hire a photographer, illustrator, animator, music composer (or all four!) to start work on the production. Or, if you perform any of these roles, then you'll start creating rough drafts for the elements within the production. At this stage, you'll also gather high-quality images from the client for their logos, proprietary material, and so on.

Making the Flash architecture

Of course, we're assuming that you're creating a Flash-based production. All the resources that you've gathered (or are working to create) in Step 1 will be assembled into the Flash movie(s) for the production. For large presentations or sites, you'll likely make one master Flash movie that provides a skeleton architecture for the presentation, and use `loadMovie()` to bring in material for the appropriate sections of the site.

Cross-Reference
See our coverage on the new Project panel later in this chapter. You can organize several Flash movies with this panel.

Before you begin Flash movie production, you should determine two important factors: frame size and frame rate. You don't want to change either of these settings midway through your project. Any reductions in frame size will crop elements that weren't located near the top-left portion of the Stage — you'll need to recompose most of the elements on the Stage if you used the entire Stage. Any changes in your frame rate will change the timing of any linear animation and/or sound synchronization that you've already produced.

Staging a local test environment

As soon as you start to author the Flash movies, you'll create a local version of the presentation (or entire site) on your computer, or a networked drive that everyone on your team can access. The file and folder structure (including the naming conventions) will be consistent with the structure of the files and folders on the Web server. As you build each component of the site, you should begin to test the presentation with the target browsers (and Flash Player plug-in versions) for your audience.

HTML page production

Even if you're creating an all-Flash Web site, you need a few basic HTML documents, including:

✦ **A plug-in detection page** that directs visitors without the Flash Player plug-in to the Macromedia site to download the plug-in.

✦ **HTML page(s) to display any non-Flash material** in the site within the browser.

New Feature   Flash MX 2004 can create detection pages for you. See Chapter 21, "Publishing Flash Movies," for more information.

You will want to construct basic HTML documents to hold the main Flash movie as you develop the Flash architecture of the site.

Staging a server test environment

Before you can make your Flash content public, you need to set up a Web server that is publicly accessible (preferably with login and password protection) so that you can test the site functionality over a non-LAN connection. This also enables your client to preview the site remotely. After quality assurance (QA) testing has finished (the next step that follows), you'll move the files from the staging server to the live Web server.

We've noticed problems with larger SWF files that weren't detected until we tested them from a staging server. Why? When you test your files locally, they're loaded instantly into the browser. When you test your files from a server (even over a fast DSL or cable modem connection), you have to wait for the SWF files to load over slower network conditions. Especially with preloaders or loading sequences, timing glitches may be revealed during tests on the staging server that were not apparent when testing locally.

Tip   You should use the Simulate Download feature of the Bandwidth Profiler in the Test Movie environment of Flash MX 2004 to estimate how your Flash movies will load over a real Internet connection. See Chapter 21, "Publishing Flash Movies," for more discussion of this feature.

Quality assurance testing

In larger corporate environments, you'll find a team of individuals whose sole responsibility is to thoroughly test the quality of a nearly finished production (or product). If you're responsible for QA, then you should have an intimate knowledge of the process chart for the site. That way, you know how the site should function. If a feature or function fails in the production, QA reports it to the creative and/or programming teams. QA teams test the production with the same hardware and conditions as the target audience, accounting for variations in:

✦ Computer type (Windows versus Mac)

✦ Computer speed (top-of-the-line processing speed versus minimal supported speeds, as determined by the target audience)

✦ Internet connection speeds (as determined by the target audience)

✦ Flash Player plug-in versions (and any other plug-ins required by the production)

✦ Browser application and version (as determined by the target audience)

Tip   If you're a freelance designer or operate a small company, keep in mind that there is no such thing as a useless computer — recycle your older computers as test platforms for target audiences.

Web Resource   It's worthwhile to use an online reporting tool to post bugs during QA. Many companies use the open source (freeware) tool called Mantis, a PHP/MySQL solution. You can find more information about Mantis at `mantisbt.sourceforge.net`.

After QA has finished rugged testing of the production, pending approval by the client (or company executives), the material is ready to go live on the site.

Maintenance and updates

After you've celebrated the finished production, your job isn't over yet. If you were contracted to build the site or presentation for a third party, you may be expected to maintain and address usability issues provided by follow-ups with the client and any support staff they might have. Be sure to account for periodic maintenance and updates for the project in your initial budget proposal. If you don't want to be responsible for updates, make sure you advise your clients ahead of time to avoid any potential conflicts after the production has finished.

You should have a thorough staging and testing environment for any updates you make to an all-Flash site, especially if you're changing major assets or master architecture files. Repeat the same process of staging and testing with the QA team that you employed during original production.

Web Resource   You can find an online archived PDF version of Eric Jordan's tutorial, "Interface Design," on the book's Web site at `www.flashsupport.com/archive`. This tutorial was featured in the last edition of the Bible. Also, look at `www.flashsupport.com/articles` for a future update to the "Using Microsoft Visio to Create Flowcharts" coverage from the last edition as well.

Using the Project Panel in Flash MX Pro 2004

In this final section of the chapter, you learn how to use the Project panel in Flash MX Pro 2004 with some sample files provided to you on this book's CD-ROM. You'll jump right into the Project panel, so you may want to review some of the content in the Help panel of Flash MX 2004 before proceeding. The following pages in the Help panel (Help ⇨ Help) contain useful information about the Project panel:

    ✦ Using Flash ⇨ Working with Projects overview

    ✦ Using Flash ⇨ Creating and managing projects

Tip   You can quickly find these pages in the Help panel by searching with the keyword **project**.

Before you start using the Project panel, let's describe a scenario in which you would *want* to use the feature. The Project panel lets you organize and group all of the files related to a Flash production. You can include any file type you want in the Project panel. All of the asset names and locations are stored in a Flash Project file, which uses a .flp file extension. This file is essentially an XML file that describes the files you want to manage.

Once you have a Flash Project file created, you can quickly open any document directly in Flash or another application. You can publish one or more Flash documents in the project. But more importantly, you can use the Project panel to directly upload content to your FTP server or a local network server. The Project panel can check in and check out files, so that other members on your team know that you're working on them.

The Project file is linked to a site definition in the Project panel. The site definition is exactly the same site you may have created in Dreamweaver MX 2004. If you have made a site in Dreamweaver, it is automatically available to Flash MX Pro 2004 as well.

One important factor to kind in mind when you use the Project panel is that you only ever open a local copy of the project's files on your computer. In this way, everyone working on the project has his/her own copy of the files. In this way, one member can be editing, implementing, and testing changes while other members are doing the same with their copies. When a member is done editing a file, she can check the file back into the server.

Caution   Unless you're implementing a version control system with your project files, you should **not** edit the same file that another person is using. Currently, Flash MX Pro 2004 only ships with support for Microsoft SourceSafe, a version control product. You can develop your own plug-in, though, for your particular version control product. Version control systems have the ability to merge changes to the same document. For example, if two people edit the same ActionScript document (.as file), the version control system merges the changes into one file and even flags potential conflicts during the process. The Project panel can not perform this type of merge without the assistance of a separate software product such as SourceSafe. Also, it's important to note that version control software cannot merge changes in two Flash documents (FLA files) because such files are binary, not ASCII (or Unicode). Usually, only text documents can be merged by version control systems.

In the following exercise, let's quickly review the procedure you follow:

1. Establish a site definition in Flash MX Pro 2004. This definition describes where you'll store your local copy of the project files, and where to upload the master copies of the project.

2. Add the files to the Flash Project file in the Project panel of Flash MX Pro 2004.

3. Open, edit, and test one of the sample files.

4. Create a new blank document to add to the project.

5. Publish an entire project.

In order to easily reference each of these procedures in the exercise, look for the procedure number from the previous list in the respective heading of the following sections.

1. Establishing a project and a site

Before you can start making or editing documents in Flash MX 2004 for a project, you need to define a site that the Project panel can use. In this section, you learn how to define a site and establish a local mirror copy of your site's files on your machine.

1. On your computer, choose a location that you can use to store all of the files with a pro-ject. For example, if you're on Windows, you can create a folder named Sites at the root of your C drive. If you're on a Mac, you can create a folder named Sites at the root of your startup drive, such as Macintosh HD.

2. Inside of the Sites folder, copy the robertreinhardt.com folder from the ch03/starter_files folder located on this book's CD-ROM. As shown in Figure 3-5, the robertreinhardt.com folder has two subfolders, dev and wwwroot.

   The dev folder, short for *development*, will contain any source files, specifications, plan-ning documents, raw assets (images, video, and sound), and so on. The fla folder inside the dev folder holds all Flash documents (.fla files) for the project.

Tip   You could also make an include folder to store ActionScript files (AS files). Feel free to add as many folders in the dev folder as you need.

   The wwwroot folder will contain any and all files that will be part of the final applica-tion, as a publicly accessible Web site or application. All of the Flash movies (.swf files), runtime assets (JPEGs, MP3s, FLVs, and so on), and HTML documents will be kept here. The copy of wwwroot from the CD-ROM includes several subfolders, to store external assets necessarily for the Flash movie (.swf file) at runtime.

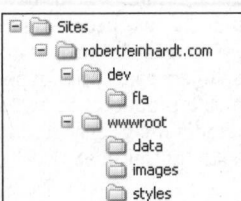

Figure 3-5: The layout of folders for a site named robertreinhardt.com

3. Now you're ready to create a Flash Project file, to put into the project folder you cre-ated in the last step. Open Flash MX Professional 2004. Choose Window ➪ Project (Shift+F8).

4. Click the **Create a new project link** in the Project panel (shown in Figure 3-6).

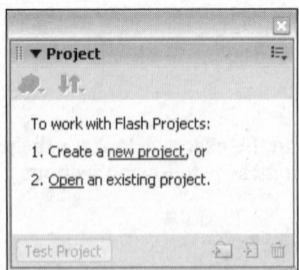

Figure 3-6: The Project panel

5. In the New Project dialog box, browse to the robertreinhardt.com folder on your computer. Save a new project file named `reinhardt_site.flp` in this location, as shown in Figure 3-7.

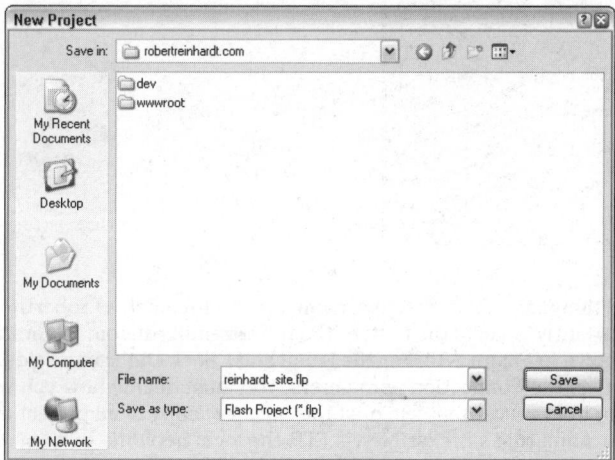

Figure 3-7: The New Project dialog box

6. With a project file created, you're ready to define a site in Flash MX Pro 2004. In the Project panel, click the Version Control button, which features an icon of two arrows pointing in opposite directions. In this menu, choose the Edit Sites option as shown in Figure 3-8.

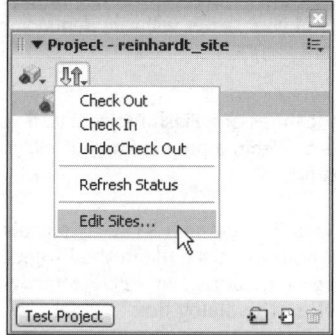

Figure 3-8: The Version Control menu

7. In the Edit Sites dialog box, you may see other sites already defined (as shown in Figure 3-9). If you use Dreamweaver MX or Dreamweaver MX 2004, you can use these sites, or create a new site for the project. For this example, create a new site by clicking the New button.

Figure 3-9: The Edit Sites dialog box

8. In the Site Definition dialog box, specify a name for the site such as robertreinhardt. com. Most importantly, specify the path to the robertreinhardt.com folder in the Local Root field, as shown in Figure 3-10. For the Email and Check Out Name fields, type your own information. In the Connection parameters, you must decide how you will connect to the testing (or live) server that will host the "master" copy of all project documents. You can use a location that's accessible via FTP, the local network, or a SourceSafe database. This location also stores the lock files (.lck files) necessary for members in your team to check in and check out documents. When you are finished specifying the connection details, you may want to click the Test button to make sure that Flash MX Pro 2004 can connect to the location. Click OK to close the dialog box, and click the Done button in the Edit Sites dialog box.

Note The Connection parameters shown in Figure 3-10 are for demonstration purposes only. These parameters will not connect to an actual FTP site. If you use an FTP connection, make sure that the FTP Directory field specifies the path to the *parent* folder of your public HTML or Web folder for the site. The public Web folder of your server will vary depending on your server's operating system and Web server software.

Tip It is entirely optional to use the Version Control features of a Flash Project file. If you simply want a way to quickly access all of the documents within a project for yourself, you do not need to create or link a site to your Flash Project file.

9. Now, you will link the newly defined site to your reinhardt_site.flp project file. Right-click (or Control+click on Mac) the reinhardt_site file in the Project panel, and choose Settings. In the Project Settings dialog box, choose **robertreinhardt.com** in the Site menu. Refer to Figure 3-11. Click OK to close the dialog box.

Figure 3-10: The Site Definition dialog box

Figure 3-11: The Project Settings dialog box

2. Adding files to the project

After you have created a Flash Project file and defined a site for the project, you're ready to start adding files to the project.

1. Begin the process of recreating the folder structure of the local site folders in the reinhardt_site.flp project file. In the Project panel, click the Add Folder icon at the lower right corner of the panel. Name the first folder dev. Repeat this process until you have created all the folder names you had in the robertreinhardt.com folder, including the subfolders. When you are finished, you should have the same folder structure shown in Figure 3-12.

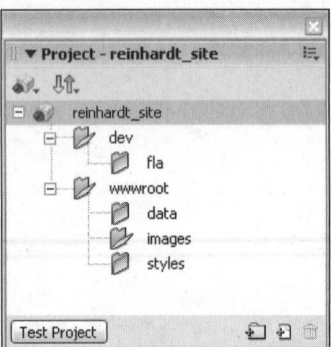

Figure 3-12: The folder structure of the site within the project file

2. Select the fla folder you created in the last step, and click the Add File button in the lower right corner of the Project panel. Browse to the Sites ➪ robertreinhardt.com ➪ dev ➪ fla folder and select the bio_100.fla file located there. Repeat this process for all of the files contained in the robertreinhardt.com folder. Do not add the reinhardt_site.flp file itself. When you are finished, your Project panel should resemble Figure 3-13.

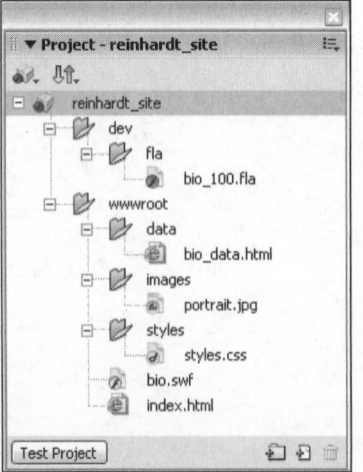

Figure 3-13: The folder and document structure of the site within the project file

3. It is highly likely that you'll have more than one Flash document (.fla file) in a project. As such, you should define the default document for the project. This file should be the master file, the one "most in charge" per se. This could be the Flash document that controls the loading of other runtime assets or the document that contains the most code. In the `dev` folder of the Project panel, right-click (or Control+click on Mac) the `bio_100.fla` document and choose **Make Default Document** in the contextual menu. The icon of the document should change to a downward-pointing green arrow.

3. Committing and editing files in the project

Once you have added files to your project, you should commit the files to your testing server. In this section, you learn how to commit project files and how to open and edit documents from the Project panel.

1. When you are finished creating folders and adding files to your Flash Project file, you should check in the documents to your remote testing server. You can do this procedure only if you have defined a site for the project file. Choose the `reinhardt_site` file at the top of the Project panel. Right-click (or Control+click on the Mac) the filename, and choose **Check In**. Flash MX Pro 2004 then connects to your remote server and checks in the file. When the file has been successfully checked in, a lock appears next to the file (see Figure 3-14).

2. Repeat the process in Step 1 for the `dev` and `wwwroot` folders in the Project panel. When you check in an entire folder, all of the files within the folder will be checked in. When you are finished, you should see locks next to all of your documents, as shown in Figure 3-14.

3. When you're ready to edit a specific file in Flash MX Pro 2004, right-click (or Control+ click on Mac) the file in the Project panel and choose **Check Out** in the contextual menu. Try this step with the bio_100.fla document. Once you have checked out this file, double-click the file to edit it in the Flash authoring environment.

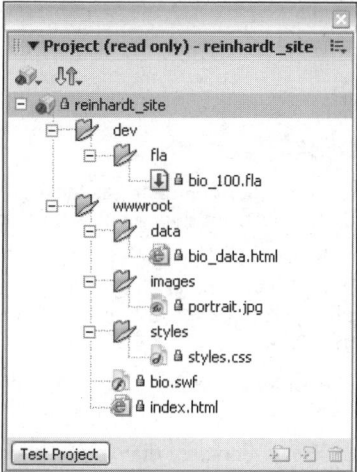

Figure 3-14: A file that is checked in displays a lock icon.

Note   When you have checked out a file, you'll see a green check mark next to the file icon. Other members of your team subscribed to the same project will see a lock next to the same file in their Project panels.

4. With the `bio_100.fla` open, let's take a look at how the `bio.swf` file (located in the `wwwroot` folder) is published. Choose File ➪ Publish Settings. In the Formats tab, notice that relative paths are declared for the `bio.swf` and `index.html` files (see Figure 3-15), in the Flash and HTML fields respectively. The `../../wwwroot/` prefix tells Flash MX 2004 to publish these files two folders above the `fla` folder, inside of the `wwwroot` folder. Click Cancel to close the dialog box. Leave the `bio_100.fla` open for the next series of steps in the following section.

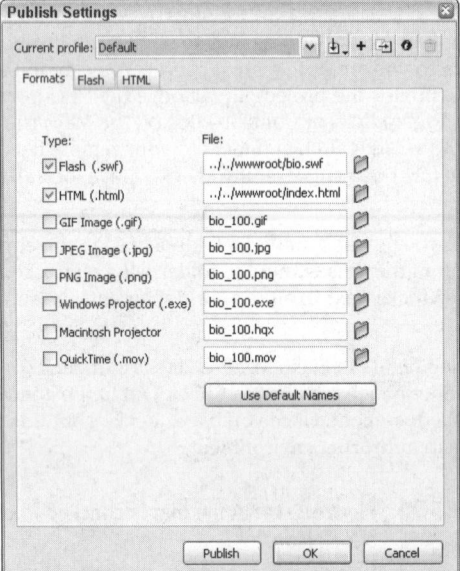

Figure 3-15: You can publish files with relative paths in the Formats tab.

4. Adding new files to the project

In this section, you learn how to create a new ActionScript document (.as file), using code extracted from the `bio_100.fla` document. This ActionScript document will be added to the project file as well.

1. From your desktop, browse to the location of the `dev` folder (for example, `C:\Sites\robertreinhardt.com\dev`). At this location, create a new folder named `includes`. This folder will be used to store ActionScript files.

2. In Flash MX Professional 2004, add the same folder name (`includes`) as a child of the `dev` folder in the Project panel.

3. Choose File ➪ New. In the General tab of the New Document dialog box, choose ActionScript File and click OK. When the new document opens, save the empty file as `functions.as` in the `includes` folder you created in Step 1. Leave the `functions.as` document open.

4. Go back to the `bio_100.fla` document. In the Timeline window, select frame 1 of the actions layer and open the Actions panel (F9). Select lines 1–48 and press Ctrl+X or ⌘+X to cut the code from the frame.

5. Switch back to the `functions.as` document, and choose Edit ⇨ Paste (Ctrl+V or ⌘+V) to move the code into the document. Save and close the `functions.as` document.

6. Now, add the `functions.as` document to the `includes` folder of the Project panel. To do this, you'll need to check out the `reinhardt_site` project file. Then, right-click (Control+click on the Mac) the `includes` folder and choose Add File. Browse to the `includes` folder on your local drive, and add the `functions.as` file. When you are finished, check in the `functions.as` document and the `reinhardt_site` project file.

7. Go back to the `bio_100.fla` document, and select frame 1 of the actions layer and open the Actions panel (F9). Add the following line of code at the top of the Script pane (line 1):

```
#include "../includes/functions.as"
```

This directive tells Flash MX 2004 to insert the contents of the `functions.as` document at the time of publishing or testing.

8. Save and close the `bio_100.fla` document. Leave this document checked out while you proceed to the last section.

5. Publishing the entire project

In this final section, you'll learn how to test an entire project, and upload the updated runtime files to your testing server.

1. Before you can publish or test the project, you'll need to unlock the files that will be published by Flash MX 2004: `bio.swf` and `index.html`. Check out these files in the `wwwroot` folder of the Project panel.

2. Click the Test Project button in the lower-left corner of the Project panel. Flash MX Pro 2004 will publish all of the Flash documents (.fla files) in the project file. In our example, there's only one FLA file, `bio_100.fla`. The newly published `bio.swf` file, located in the `wwwroot` folder, then opens in the Test Movie environment.

3. If everything is working correctly, check in the `bio.swf`, `index.html`, and `bio_100.fla` documents. If there was an error, double-check the code added in the last section for syntax errors. The Output panel will likely provide clues about any errors associated with improper URLs for runtime assets.

On the CD-ROM You can find the final site files in the `ch03/final_files` folder of the *Flash MX 2004 Bible* CD-ROM. If you try to open the `reinhardt_site.flp` document from the CD-ROM (or a copy of it), you'll likely need to relink the documents to the locations of the copies on your system.

Web Resource We'd like to know what you thought about this chapter. Visit `www.flashsupport.com/feedback` to fill out an online form with your comments.

Summary

✦ Your clients rely on you to understand and guide the production process involved with Flash content creation.

✦ Careful planning helps you to create Flash solutions that best meet the goals of your project. The technical issues, such as usability, target audience, and delivery platform, should be balanced with the aesthetic aspects of experience design.

✦ To structure the development of Flash projects many Web developers use a two-phase production model that involves six milestones: Business Initiative, Creative Solutions, Approval, Production, QA, and Delivery.

✦ During the production period, it is helpful to keep six key concepts in mind: asset assembly, a master Flash architecture, a local test environment, HTML page layout, a server staging environment, and proper QA testing. After production is finished, you also need to devise a strategy for systematic maintenance.

✦ You can use the Project panel in Flash MX Professional 2004 to manage all of the Flash documents for a site or application.

✦   ✦   ✦

Mastering the Flash Environment

When you're ready to jump in and get started on the road to efficient and painless production, this section will give you all the information you need to feel comfortable in the Flash authoring environment. Chapter 4 introduces you to the Flash workspace and gives you tips for customizing the UI. You will learn the difference between a window and a panel and discover some of the timesaving features that have been added to Flash MX 2004. Chapter 5 is where you'll find coverage of all the Flash drawing and selection tools. You'll also learn how to control snapping behavior and how to create and edit groups. In Chapter 6, you'll find out what makes Flash so much more powerful than simple vector graphics programs. Symbols and symbol instances are the basis for all optimized Flash projects and the Library gives you all the options you'll need to keep your project assets organized. Chapter 7 includes coverage of color issues specific to Web production and explains how to use the Color Swatches and Color Mixer panels to enhance your projects with custom colors, gradients, bitmap fills and more. Chapter 8 guides you through the various options for creating and editing text in Flash, including Dynamic and Input text and vertical text. You will learn how to control font display and find out how to create and use font symbols. Finally, in Chapter 9, you will be introduced to the more advanced tools for editing graphics and text in Flash, including the Free Transform and Fill Transform tools and the Advanced Color Effects menu.

Interface Fundamentals

This chapter gives you a tour of the Flash workspace and the various methods for organizing and navigating your documents. Fundamental features of the authoring environment are defined, but in some cases the explanation of more-complex functionality is deferred to later chapters. This chapter gets new users oriented in the program and introduces experienced users to some of the new MX 2004 and MX 2004 Professional features.

Cross-Reference

As discussed in the Introduction of this book, Flash is now available in two versions: Flash MX 2004 and Flash MX Professional 2004. The specific differences between the two versions are outlined in Chapter 1, "Understanding the Flash MX 2004 Framework." All of the features available in Flash MX 2004 are also available in Flash MX Professional 2004, so we will only make note of the version of the program if we are introducing a feature available exclusively in Flash MX Professional 2004. In all other cases, assume that the interface feature or functionality described in this chapter will apply in both versions of the program.

Getting Started

When you walk into a studio, the first thing you need to know is where to find your tools. Although you might have an idea of where to start looking based on experience, nothing improves your workflow more than being able to reach for something without hesitation. This kind of familiarity and comfort in a workspace is a prerequisite for the mastery of any craft.

Fortunately, many of the features of the Flash MX 2004 interface will look familiar to you if you've worked in other graphics applications. However, there are many unique features that you will need to understand before you can tackle your Flash projects with the ease of an expert. We begin by introducing the Flash interface and pointing out the tools available for managing and customizing your Flash "studio." We've done our best to keep new terminology consistent with the interface. Where inconsistencies occur, we've tried to choose terms most consistent with other Macromedia products and documentation.

Note   In an effort to maintain consistent terms and UI names across the various programs in the Studio MX family, Macromedia has changed some familiar terms and added some new ones. In some cases, changes to UI terms may not be implemented consistently in all menus, dialog boxes, and Help documents—we hope the context of the term will give you enough clues to sort out what it refers to. Rest assured that you're not imagining things: Flash just has a few growing pains from time to time.

You'll soon notice that there is often more than one way to access an option. As the steps for carrying out a task are described, we include shortcut keys or menu paths in parentheses. You should feel comfortable and ready to get to work in no time.

Welcome to Flash MX 2004 and MX Professional 2004

Whether you've been using Flash since the early days of version 2, or you've just opened the program for the first time, you'll quickly see that the Flash interface has finally matured—enough to remain recognizable from one release to another! As Flash has grown and evolved, the interface has been through a number of variations, but MX 2004 remains true to the streamlined panel system that was introduced with Flash MX. The most significant change in the program with the 2004 release is that it is now offered in two versions. Fortunately, the interface is consistent between MX 2004 and MX Professional 2004. The only difference is that the pro version offers a few extra features that will make developers very happy.

If you are not yet at the level of developing complex rich Internet applications, then rest assured that you will find everything you need in the "basic" version of the program to do everything you have ever done with Flash and more—including creating and animating beautiful graphics or building robust interactive presentations. There have been a few dramatic additions and changes since Flash MX, but this version will make artists and programmers feel equally comfortable and, we hope, more efficient than ever. Some of the most significant changes to Flash MX 2004 are only hinted at by the interface, but we'll give you a peek under the hood in this chapter.

Start Page

Macromedia has replaced the Welcome panel with a new Start Page in Flash MX 2004. The Start Page gives quick access to tutorials and other help features as well as providing a great way to choose the file you want to open or create. The Start Page shown in Figure 4-1 is for the Flash MX 2004 version. The Start Page for Flash MX Professional 2004 includes some other file types in the Create New list, but these are mostly for more advanced development tasks.

Note   Macromedia has added a similar Start Page to the other programs in the Studio MX 2004 suite.

By default, the Start Page should appear when you first launch Flash and any time you close all Document windows while the program is running. After you have opened or created a new file, the Start Page automatically closes to make room on your desktop. If you prefer not to use the Start Page, select the **Don't show again** check box at the bottom of the panel, or change the settings for **On launch** in General Flash Preferences (Edit ➪ Preferences or Flash ➪ Preferences). This leaves you with the more limited, but familiar, option of using the application File menu (or shortcut keys) to create and open files.

The links at the bottom of the Start Page connect you to the built-in Help system in Flash as well as to online content available through the Macromedia Web site. These links are worth investigating if you want to get a quick introduction to Flash:

✦ **Take a quick tour of Flash:** This link launches your default Web browser and loads an orientation presentation from Macromedia. The presentation includes audio and images, so make sure you have your speakers or your headphones on when you connect.

Web Resource

You don't need to have Flash installed to view this presentation. If you would like to introduce other friends or co-workers to the new features of Flash MX 2004, you can direct them to the presentation online at www.macromedia.com/software/flash/productinfo/features/brz_tour/.

✦ **Take a Flash lesson:** This link opens the built-in Flash Help panel, which includes a **Help** tab with a table of contents and searchable reference topics organized under common task headings (shown in Figure 4-3) and a **How Do I** tab with a series of tutorials organized under three main headings (shown in Figure 4-2):

- Quick Start
- Basic Flash
- Basic ActionScript

✦ **Update the Flash Help system:** To ensure that you always have access to the most accurate and comprehensive files available, Macromedia includes an updater that will connect to its Web site and download the most recent documentation. Use the link on the Start page or the **Update** icon on the top of the Help panel to check for new Help content. A dialog box will let you know if new content is available or not and if there is new content you can download it and updates will automatically be integrated with the existing Help files.

Note

If there has been an update to the Help documents available from Macromedia since the last time you were running Flash, you will automatically see the new Help content dialog box when you launch the program. In most cases, the download will be quick and painless, but if you are on a slow Internet connection, you may want to wait until you are ready to take a break from your project before initiating the download.

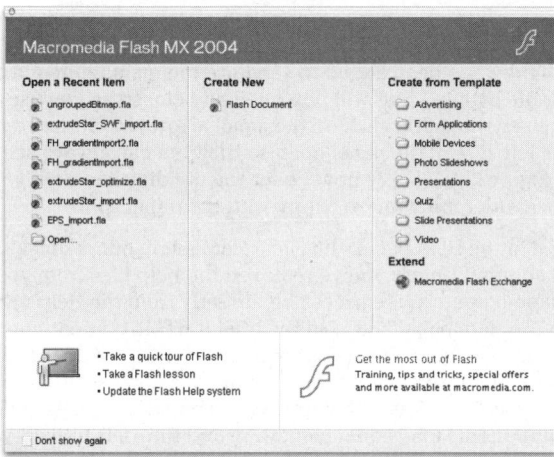

Figure 4-1: The Start Page provides quick access to file lists and resource links.

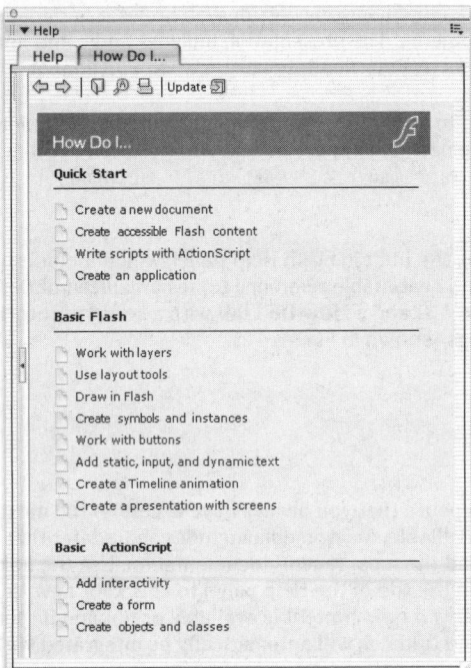

Figure 4-2: To see a list of tutorials in the Help panel, use the **Flash lesson** link from the Start Page or choose **How Do I** from the Help menu.

Help menu options

The Flash MX Answers panel and Reference panel have been consolidated into a new Help panel in Flash MX 2004. To squeeze a comprehensive searchable directory and a window for lessons and documentation into one panel, tabs have been added to separate Help and How Do I content. Also, an accordion divider has been added to separate the main reference content from the table of contents (or file listings) that will pop open and closed as you use the control icons at the top of the panel or when you click on the small arrow tab on the edge of the panel. If you prefer to keep the left side of the panel open so that you can always see the list of available files (as shown in Figure 4-3), simply hover over the dividing line until you see a dual arrow cursor; then drag the divider until you're happy with the panel split.

If you don't want to muddle around in the Help panel, the Flash Help menu offers quick shortcuts to commonly used reference content. Unless you've removed the help files from your Flash installation, a number of offline resources are accessible directly from the Help menu. These resource topics will launch the Help panel and load the offline HTML content you have requested. First, with **What's New**, you can get an overview of the new Flash MX 2004 features. Next, new users may want to browse the tutorial content for general Flash tasks under **Using Flash**. The **ActionScript Dictionary** organizes a vast list of terms and syntax for the ActionScript language alphabetically. **Using Components** loads documentation and tutorials to help you make the most of the new V2 components. **Samples** offers tips on how to learn from example files and directs you to links for samples that you can load into a browser window.

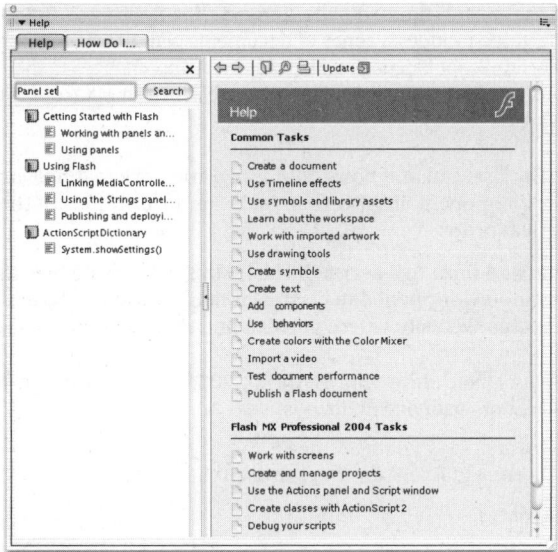

Figure 4-3: Activate the **Help** tab in the Help panel and click the TOC (table of contents) icon to see a list of reference topics or click the Search icon to search for help on a specific topic.

Macromedia has also provided two guided entry points to a vast array of online resources. The **Flash Exchange** is an online resource created to support use and development of Flash extensions. This is a great place to look for new tools, components, and effects that you can download and add to your Flash toolkit. The **Flash Support Center** is Macromedia's original online resource, sometimes also referred to as the Designer's or Developer's (Des/Dev) Resource Center. This is Macromedia's primary vehicle for the distribution of up-to-date information about Flash and Flash-related topics. This is a searchable area with current (and archived) articles on many Flash topics. You can also find links to downloads, documentation, forums, and many other invaluable Flash-related resources and updates.

Finally, the links at the bottom of the Help menu make it easy to take care of administrative tasks such as registering, transferring, or upgrading your Flash software.

Here is a summary list of the reference options available from the main Help menu:

✦ **Help ➪ Help:** Opens the Help panel. Click the Help tab to use the TOC to browse through a comprehensive list of help topics or use the Search button to find a specific term or task.

✦ **Help ➪ How Do I...:** Opens the Help panel to the How Do I tab where you can work through a series of guided lessons on common production tasks.

✦ **Help ➪ What's New:** Summary text introduction to new features of Flash MX 2004 and Flash MX Professional 2004.

✦ **Help ➪ Using Flash:** Background and basic how-to for general Flash MX 2004 tasks.

✦ **Help ➪ ActionScript Dictionary:** Alphabetical listing of ActionScript terms, with definitions, sample entries, and notes on deprecated elements.

Note Although it is not included in the main Help menu, the **ActionScript Reference Guide** is also listed in the Help TOC. The guide includes a series of documents with detailed information on various aspects of the ActionScript language with notes on syntax changes in the latest version and information you need to know if you want to publish Flash MX (or earlier) projects to Flash Player 7.

✦ **Help ⇨ Using Components:** Background and how-to for integrating or creating Flash components with the new v2 component architecture. Includes descriptions of the component APIs, in alphabetical order.

✦ **Help ⇨ Samples:** Introduction and links to a series of Flash MX 2004 sample files that can be viewed in a browser window or opened in Flash and deconstructed. Also includes a link to the Macromedia Web site where you can find more sample files.

Tip The sample files installed on your hard drive with Flash MX 2004 can be found in the Samples folder. The standard directory path on Windows is:

```
C:\Documents and Settings\(username)\Local Settings\Application
Data\Macromedia\Flash MX 2004\en\Configuration\Samples
```

The standard directory path on Mac is:

```
HD\Users: (username)\Library: Application Support\Macromedia\
Flash MX 2004\en\Configuration\Samples
```

✦ **Help ⇨ Flash Exchange:** Macromedia's online resource for extensions. Get or submit extensions and learn how they allow you to add new features to Flash.

✦ **Help ⇨ Manage Extensions:** Loads control panel for managing installed Macromedia extensions.

✦ **Help ⇨ Flash Support Center:** Macromedia's central page for troubleshooting. Searchable TechNotes and a Flash Forum for developers of all skill levels.

Tip The Help panel can be docked with other panels in your workspace, but it is much easier to read or search for help content if you undock the panel and drag the size box horizontally to make it wider. Use the keyboard shortcut (F1) to show or hide the Help panel whenever you need to.

The MX 2004 interface on Macintosh and Windows

Before discussing the various Flash menu items, panels, and miscellaneous dialog boxes that you can use to control and customize your workspace, we begin with a look at the interface with its default array of toolbars and panels as they appear on Macintosh and Windows.

New Feature The default panel set includes two new panels that have been introduced to accommodate Flash MX 2004 features: a Component inspector panel (which replaces the MX Component parameters panel) for working with Component instances and a Behaviors panel for adding prebuilt ActionScript code.

The implementation of panels is consistent across both Mac and Windows. Throughout the book, we discuss each panel in context with the tools and tasks where it is used. As you'll quickly find, there are many ways to arrange these panels for a customized workflow. Your preferred panel layouts for different tasks can be saved as custom Panel Layouts and recalled from the Panel Sets menu.

In addition to the Default Layout, Macromedia has provided a Training Layout panel set (available for a few different monitor resolution settings) that will open the Help panel and the basic interface elements you need to get started with tutorials. Figure 4-4 shows how the default layout (Window ➪ Panel sets ➪ Default Layout) looks on the Mac. Figure 4-5 shows how the same panel set looks on Windows with the Professional version of Flash MX 2004.

Note

Although there are some visible differences between Macintosh and Windows interfaces for Flash MX 2004, these are largely due to differences in the operating systems that are apparent in any application. There are a few additional panels visible in the default layout for Flash MX Professional 2004, but the main features and functionality of the interface are the same. For the sake of clarity, we've compared the two overall interfaces here showing a default panel layout for each version of the program before discussing individual UI items. For the most part, however, we use Macintosh OS X and Windows XP illustrations from both Flash MX 2004 and Flash MX Professional 2004 interchangeably, pointing out differences only when they directly affect workflow.

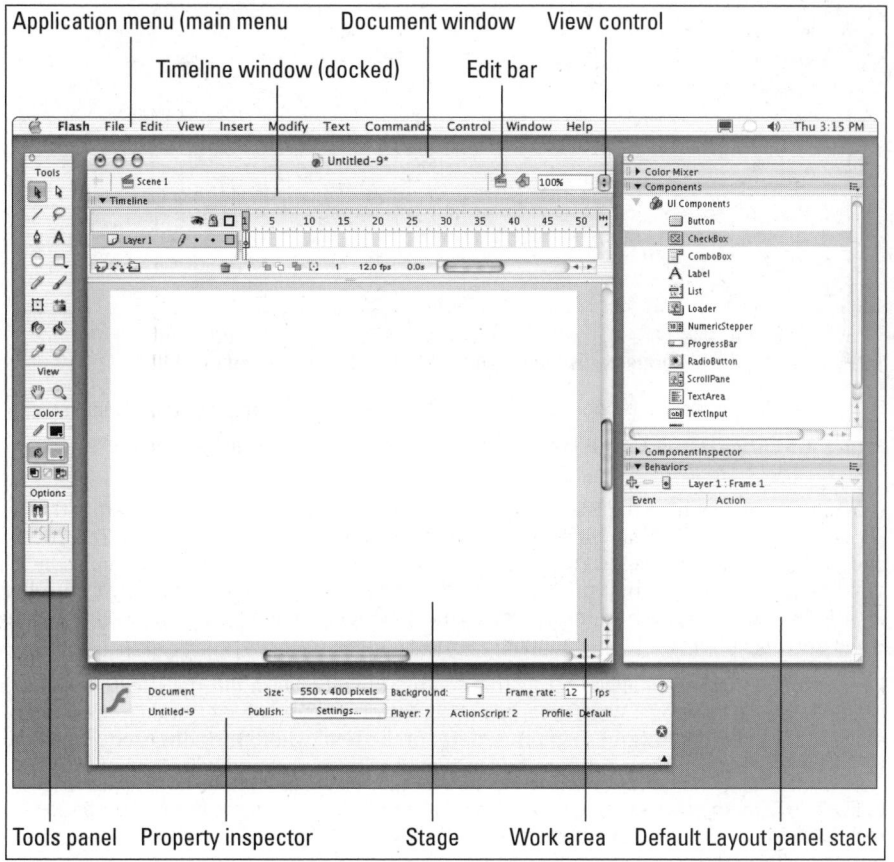

Figure 4-4: The Default Layout for Flash MX 2004 as it appears on Macintosh OS X

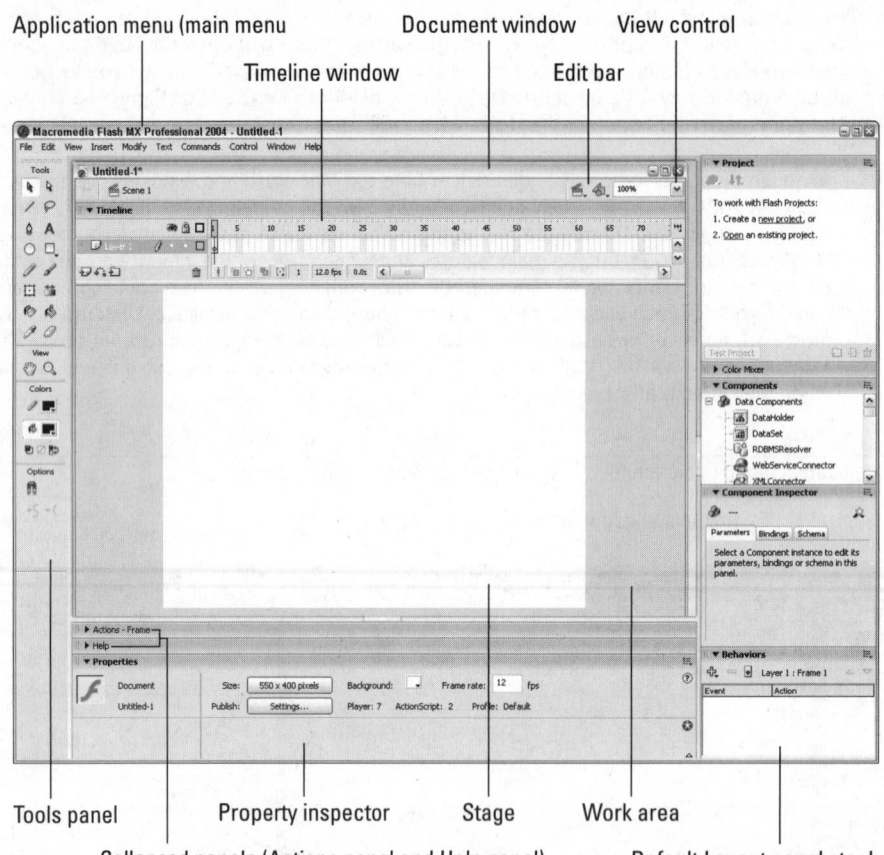

Application menu (main menu   Document window   View control
          Timeline window   Edit bar

Tools panel   Property inspector   Stage   Work area
       Collapsed panels (Actions panel and Help panel)   Default Layout panel stack

Figure 4-5: The Default Layout for Flash MX Professional 2004 as it appears on Windows XP

One minor way in which the Windows version differs from the Mac version is that the Tools panel and the Controller can be docked (or undocked) to the program window. The Tools panel and Controller can be dragged to the edge of the program window to dock seamlessly in the Windows interface. Note that the Tools panel docks only to the sides, while the Controller can also dock to the top and bottom, as well as mesh with other toolbars. To prevent docking while moving either the Tools panel or Controller, press the Control key while dragging.

For clarity, we have capitalized terms that refer to specific Flash interface features such as Document window, Stage, Work area, Timeline, Panel set, Tools panel, and Options area. You may see these words lowercase in other parts of the text, where they are used as general terms rather than as labels for specific parts of the Flash interface.

In Flash MX, all the panels were listed directly in the Window menu, but to accommodate new panels and improve the menu structure in Flash MX 2004, you will now find UI items grouped into logical categories related to production tasks.

The main Window menu includes the most "universal" UI items:

✦ Toolbars (Controller, Edit Bar, and on Windows, Main)

Note The Main toolbar is an optional feature only available on the Windows version of Flash. This toolbar allows quick access to commonly used tool and panel options and should not be confused with the Tools panel. The Controller and the Edit bar options found in the Toolbars menu have the same function on Windows and Mac. The Controller is used to control the position of the Playhead in the Timeline and the Edit bar (which docks to the top of the Document window) includes controls for navigating Scenes, editing symbols, and changing View settings.

✦ Property inspector (listed as "Properties")

✦ Timeline

✦ Tools panel

✦ Library panel

Other commonly used panels are grouped into three main submenus in the Window menu:

✦ **Design panels:**	✦ **Development panels:**	✦ **Other panels:**
• Align panel	• Actions panel	• Accessibility panel
• Color Mixer panel	• Behaviors panel	• History panel
• Color Swatches panel	• Components panel	• Movie Explorer
• Info panel	• Component inspector	• Strings panel
• Scene panel	• Debugger panel	• Common Libraries (Buttons, Classes, Learning Interactions)
• Transform panel	• Output panel	

We describe the actual uses and options for most of these various interface elements in context, as we discuss tasks where the elements are applied. To get started with Flash, we will be introducing the Property inspector, Tools panel, Document window, Scene panel, Timeline, and Controller, along with the related menu items. We discuss the remainder of the panels and windows as they are used in chapters on drawing, animation, interactivity, and other specific production topics.

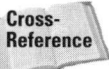

Cross-Reference The use of the new History panel is covered in Chapter 9, "Modifying Graphics." The new Project panel, available only in Flash MX Professional 2004, is described in Chapter 3, "Planning Flash Projects."

The use of the terms *window* and *panel* may also be unclear. For practical purposes, any interface element that can be grouped or nested with other like elements to create a set is considered a panel, while elements that remain independent or can only be docked to the application or Document window are referred to as windows. Unfortunately, the naming conventions used in the UI don't really help to clarify these differences consistently. For example, the Start Page actually behaves more like a dialog box: it cannot be docked with other panels and it disappears as soon as you have used it to make a choice. Also, you'll find that the Property inspector and the Component inspector are actually very different in behavior: the Component inspector is a true panel that can be docked with other panels, while the Property inspector is a unique interface element that can only be docked to the Document window. The Tools panel cannot be docked with other panels either and it does not have any of the display controls that "real" panels have. Fortunately, these semantic issues should only bother you if you're a copy editor and hopefully won't slow you down at all if you're a Flash designer!

What to expect from the Property inspector

The Property inspector has integrated the most common options for various authoring items and allows you to access these and other fundamental features of Flash from one central location. Many options can be selected or modified directly in the Property inspector, but for some items, buttons appear that can be used to launch additional menus or dialog boxes. You will only need to access separate panels for a few specialized editing tasks. Figure 4-6 shows how the Property inspector changes to display options relevant to the currently selected item.

The top figure shows the Property inspector (collapsed), as it appears when the PolyStar tool is active (selected in the Tools panel) — displaying Stroke and Fill colors and options, buttons for launching Settings dialog boxes for line styles and tool options, and the icon for launching the Help panel. The bottom figure shows the Property inspector (expanded), as it appears when a Button component instance is selected on the Stage — displaying instance properties and options. The launcher icon for the Help panel is still available, and icons for launching the Actions panel and the Accessibility panel are also visible when the Property inspector is expanded.

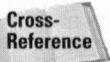

Cross-Reference   Accessibility features available in Flash MX 2004 are explained and applied in Chapter 20, "Making Your First Flash MX 2004 Project."

Notice the tabs at the lower right of the Property inspector for switching between component Properties and component Parameters. The use of these two controls is explained in later chapters where components are introduced in more detail. For now, all you need to know is that you can use the Parameters tab to access component parameters in the Property inspector, but it is actually easier to read and type in the Component inspector, which is designed to handle these parameters more gracefully. Figure 4-7 shows the parameters for a Button component instance displayed in the Property inspector (with the Parameters tab selected) and in the Component inspectors as they appear in Flash MX 2004 and Flash MX Professional 2004.

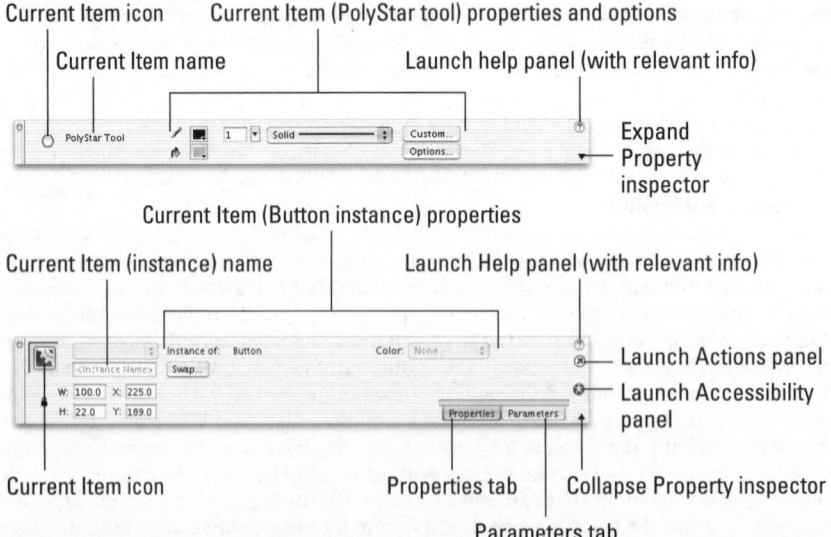

Figure 4-6: The Property inspector, as it appears when the PolyStar tool is active (top), and when a Button component instance is selected (bottom)

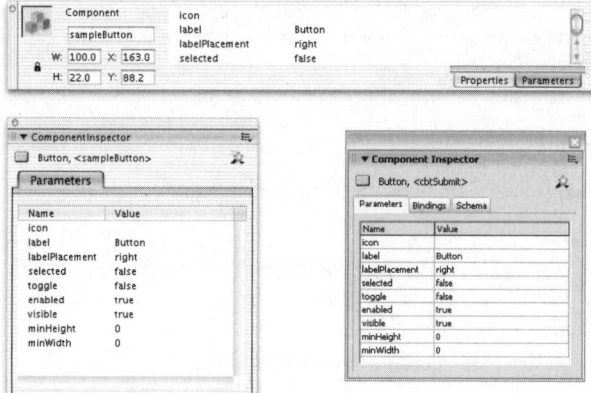

Figure 4-7: Component parameters can be accessed in the Property inspector (top), but can be read and edited more easily in the Component inspector in both Flash MX 2004 (lower left) and Flash MX Professional 2004 (lower right).

New Feature

In both Flash MX 2004 and Flash MX Professional 2004, the Component Parameters panel has been replaced by a Parameters tab in the new Component inspector. This makes room for two additional tabs in Flash MX Professional 2004: *Schema* and *Bindings*. These tabs display settings and information related to data-centric components.

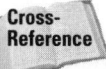
Cross-Reference

The various v2 components that ship with Flash MX 2004 are introduced in Chapter 29, "Using Components."

Depending on what is currently selected, the Property inspector will display relevant attributes for a document, frame, symbol instance, component instance, shape, or text box. Pop-up menus and editable value fields make it quick and easy to make changes without hunting through panel sets or the application menu. As shown in Figure 4-6, when an element is selected that can have code attached to it, a gray arrow appears on the right edge of the Property inspector. Clicking this icon launches the Actions panel for editing code on individual frames or symbol instances.

Tip

Because the Property inspector and the Tools panel provide access to all tool options (with the exception of some drawing and text attributes that are adjusted in the Preferences window), there are only four panels that you might need to open separately for additional options while drawing and editing graphics on the Stage. These are: Color Mixer, for adding alpha, gradients, and custom colors; Align, for accurately arranging elements in relation to each other or to the Stage; Transform, for quickly making exact size or rotation adjustments; and History, for tracking or changing your edits. Simple, right?

Managing Windows and Panels

Most interface elements have built-in display controls (see Figure 4-8 for the controls that you will see on both Mac and Windows panels), but you can also manage what appears in your workspace with the main application menu. Rather than go through a laundry list of all the application menu options, we will note the various features that apply to individual windows and panels as their uses are described.

Tip

To make the interface easier to use, Macromedia kindly made the whole title bar of the panels active so that you can expand or collapse a panel by clicking anywhere in the top gray bar, not only on the expand/collapse arrow.

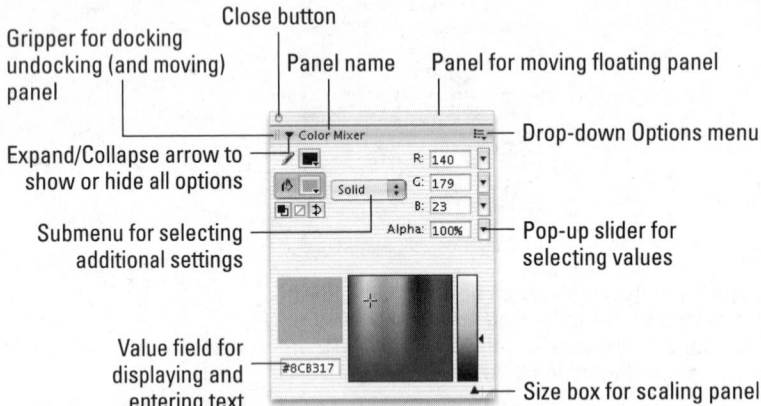

Close button

Gripper for docking undocking (and moving) panel

Panel name

Panel for moving floating panel

Drop-down Options menu

Expand/Collapse arrow to show or hide all options

Submenu for selecting additional settings

Pop-up slider for selecting values

Value field for displaying and entering text

Size box for scaling panel

Figure 4-8: The controls noted here on the Mac Color Mixer panel are consistent with the control icons you will see on other panels for both Mac and Windows.

Contextual menus

As in many other programs, you will find Flash contextual menus pop up in response to a right-click on a selected item in the Timeline, Library panel, or on the Stage. (Control+click for the Mac if you don't have a two-button mouse.) Contextual menus duplicate most functions and commands that are accessible either through the application menu, or through the various panels and dialog boxes, which are discussed in this chapter. Because contextual menus show you only those options relevant to the element you have selected, they provide a handy authoring shortcut that can also help you get familiar with Flash.

Focus: Making panels or windows active

Prior to Flash 4, only one area of the application required users to pay attention to focus — when selecting colors for either the stroke or fill — because it was easy to confuse the two. As the interface has grown to include more panels and windows that can be active at different times within the Flash environment, focus has become an important aspect of the program. What is focus? *Focus* is a term used to describe which part of the application is active, or has priority, at a given time. For example, all panels, such as the Actions panel, do not automatically "have focus" — this means that you have to click within the panel to begin working there. Similarly, to return to the Document window or Stage to edit an element, you must click there to return focus to that aspect of the application. The Property inspector can actually remind you what area or element is active, because it displays the attributes of the currently active item. Otherwise, if a panel or dialog box doesn't seem to respond, just remember to *focus* on what you're doing.

Creating custom Panel Sets

Whether you have chosen a panel set from the Window menu (Window ➪ Panel Sets) or have just opened Flash with the default display, one of the first things you'll want to learn is how to customize the Flash environment to suit your workflow. Whether you're working on an 800 x 600 laptop screen, a 1024 x 768 dual-monitor setup, or a 1,920 x 1,200 LCD, panels give you the flexibility to create a layout that fits your screen real estate and production needs.

To save your current panel layout as a custom set that can be accessed from the Panel Sets menu the next time you open Flash, follow theses simple steps.

1. Open and arrange any panels that you want to include in your custom layout.

2. Go to Window ➪ Save Panel Layout.

3. You will be prompted by a dialog box to name your panel layout. Enter a name that will help you remember why you made that Panel set, such as "animation" or "scripting."

4. Your custom layout will now appear in the list of available Panel sets (Window ➪ Panel Sets). Deleting panel sets is not quite as simple as saving them, but it can be done. Panel sets are stored in a Panel Sets folder on your hard drive. Once you find the Panel set files, you can either add or delete any of these files and the Panel Sets menu in Flash will update to show only the files that you currently have saved there.

✦ The standard directory path on Windows is:

```
C:\Documents and Settings\(username)\Local Settings\Application
Data\Macromedia\Flash MX 2004\en\Configuration\Panel Sets
```

✦ The standard directory path on Mac is:

```
HD\Users: (username)\Library: Application Support\Macromedia\Flash MX
2004\en\Configuration\Panel Sets
```

You can save your Panel set files just as you would project files in order to share them with other people or take them with you when you upgrade to a newer version of Flash (or move to another machine). When you want to add them to your current version of Flash, just place the files in the Panel Sets folder and they'll appear in the Panel Sets menu, ready for you to use. The only limitation is that Panel set files cannot be shared between the Mac and Windows versions of Flash.

On the CD-ROM

Everyone will have a different way of organizing their workspace, but to get you started we have included some of the panel layouts that we use regularly for you to try out. In the ch04 folder on the CD-ROM, you'll find a PanelSets folder with two Mac sets from Snow and a Windows set from Rob. Save these files to your Panel Sets folder and see if you like them. Keep in mind that you can use a panel set as a starting point for your own custom layout — move, close, or add panels as you like, and then use the Save Panel Layout command and give the layout a new name. It will be added to your Panel Sets folder and will be available in the Panel Sets menu.

Tip

If you decide to change or update one of your Panel sets, it is much easier to overwrite the file you have changed than to save a new version of the layout and then dig up and delete the old one. To overwrite an existing Panel set, simply save a new layout with the same name.

Keyboard shortcuts

Keyboard shortcuts allow you to work more quickly, by avoiding the hassle of clicking through a menu to activate a feature with your mouse. This is a workflow trick that many people use even when working in text-editing applications. Instead of browsing to the Edit menu to find the Copy command, you can just press the key combination Ctrl+C (or ⌘+C on Mac). We have included the default keyboard shortcuts for most tools and features as they are introduced by listing them in parentheses after the tool or menu item name. When key options are different on Mac and Windows, we list both. Thus the convention for showing the keyboard shortcut for Copy in both Windows and Mac would be Ctrl+C or ⌘+C. A default set of keyboard shortcuts is available without having to change any settings and these shortcuts are listed after most commands in the various application menus. However, if you would like to use different shortcut keys for certain tasks or add a new shortcut key for a custom Panel set or tool, you can make changes to the default settings in the Keyboard Shortcuts dialog box shown in Figure 4-9.

As shown in Figure 4-9, the Keyboard Shortcuts dialog box enables you to customize your Flash keyboard shortcuts to maintain consistency with other applications or to suit a personalized workflow. Not only can you choose keyboard shortcuts developed from other applications, you can also save your modifications and custom settings. A full explanation of this dialog box follows.

Note   Flash includes a special set of keyboard shortcuts for the Actions panel. This is a boon for coders who may wish to use different shortcuts when editing in the Actions panel than when working in the Document window.

Tip   For the experienced coder, the Actions panel also supports the known keyboard shortcut 'accelerators' such as Ctrl+Arrow key to jump to the next space (end/beginning of words/expressions). You can also click on selected blocks and Ctrl-drag (or Option-drag on Mac) to copy them. There are many of these shortcuts and if you are authoring hundreds of lines of code, they will save you valuable time.

You will find the Keyboard Shortcuts dialog box in the application menu (Edit ➪ Keyboard Shortcuts, or in OS X go to Flash ➪ Keyboard Shortcuts). To create a new keyboard shortcut, you must first duplicate an existing set, from which you can then add or subtract existing shortcuts to form your custom shortcut set. Here's the process:

1. Select a shortcut set from the **Current set** submenu. This is now the active set.

2. Duplicate the active set by clicking the **Duplicate Set** button. The Duplicate dialog box appears. Enter a new name for this set in the **Duplicate name** field and click **OK**.

   A similar procedure is employed to rename a shortcut set. Simply click the **Rename Set** button and enter the new name in the ensuing dialog box. (Note that you can rename all the built-in sets that ship with the program, with the exception of the Macromedia Standard set.)

3. Select a commands list from the **Commands** pop-up menu (Drawing Menu Commands, Drawing Tools, Test Movie Menu Commands, Timeline Commands, Workspace Accessibility, or Actions Panel Commands) either to add a command or to modify it.

4. Next, in the commands list, choose either a grouping or a command from one of the previously chosen commands lists. Note that some lists have sub-lists. Click the plus sign (or small arrow on the Mac) to expand a particular category.

5. Now choose a command that you want to add (or subtract) — a description of the selected command appears in the **Description** area.

6. To delete the existing shortcut click the minus (–) shortcut button.

7. To add a shortcut for this command, click the plus (+) shortcut button; then enter the shortcut key combination in the **Press Key** entry box. Simply press keys on the keyboard, rather than typing the key names. Click **Change** and then **OK** to close the dialog box.

8. Or, to change an existing command, select the command and click the **Change** button.

9. To delete a shortcut set, click the **Delete Set** button, and then select the set to be deleted from the Delete Set dialog box and click the **Delete** button. (Because you cannot delete the built-in sets that ship with the program, they do not appear in the Delete Set dialog box.)

Note

Like Panel set files, Keyboard Shortcut sets are stored on your hard drive. You'll find them in a Keyboard Shortcuts folder in the same Configuration folder location that we listed in the previous section for Panel Sets. You can navigate to this location on your hard drive and copy, back up, restore, delete, or otherwise manipulate any of these files from this folder. Keyboard shortcuts are transferable between machines, although we had no success transferring them across platforms.

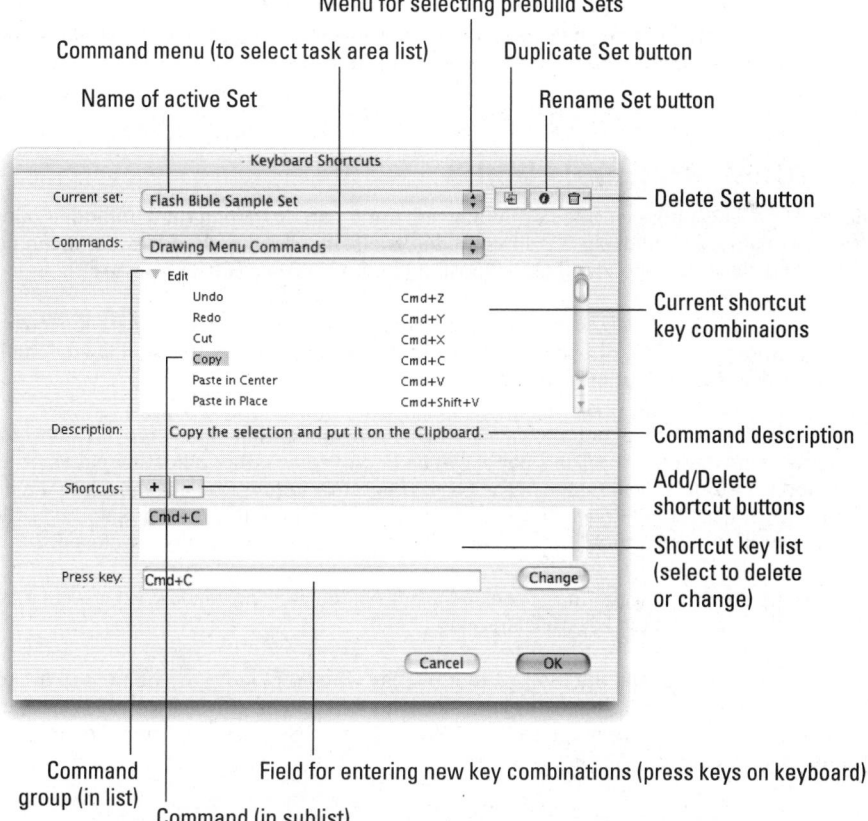

Figure 4-9: The Keyboard Shortcuts dialog box as displayed on Mac OS X. The appearance is slightly different on Windows, but the options available are the same.

Tip   By default, Flash uses the Macromedia Standard set of built-in keyboard shortcuts designed to be consistent on most applications in the MX 2004 Studio family. You can also select a built-in keyboard shortcut set from one of several popular graphics applications, including Adobe Illustrator and Adobe Photoshop. Instead of manually changing a duplicate of the Macromedia Standard set to match your favorite program, simply switch the Current Set using the menu list.

The Tools panel

The vertical bar titled **Tools** that appears by default on the left side of the interface is referred to as the Tools panel. Although it is sometimes also called the Drawing Tools panel, it is used for much more than just drawing. If you haven't just installed Flash, or if someone else has changed the defaults in Flash, you may not see the Tools panel on your screen. You can find it in the main Window menu (Window ⇨ Tools) or invoke it with shortcut keys (Ctrl+F2 or ⌘+F2).

Caution   The official name for the panel that was called the "Toolbox" in Flash MX was changed to "Tools panel" for Flash MX 2004, but at the time of this writing the documentation available in the Flash Help panel had not been updated to match the interface and menu references. Hopefully, by the time you read this text the Help content will have been revised. If not, you may find that you have to search for the term "toolbar" to find information on the Tools panel in the Help files. This first naming convention change was changed again to avoid confusion between the Tools panel and the separate UI items listed in the Window menu under "Toolbars."

Controlling the Tools panel

The Tools panel cannot be scaled or minimized, but it can be hidden (and unhidden) along with other panels by choosing Window ⇨ Hide Panels, by pressing the F4 key, or it can be opened and closed independently by choosing Window ⇨ Tools (Ctrl+F2 or ⌘+F2).

Note   If you're using a Windows machine, don't confuse Tools with the menu item for Toolbars, which refers to a set of optional menus described in the previous section titled, "The MX 2004 interface on Macintosh and Windows."

On Macintosh, the Tools panel is always a free-floating panel that can be moved anywhere on the screen. On Windows, the Tools panel can be deployed as either a floating panel, or as a panel that's docked to either edge of the Flash program window. Docking means that a floating panel is dragged to the edge of the program window, where it then melds to the border of the window. It remains "stuck" there until it is moved to another position or closed.

Tip   On Windows, to drag the Tools panel to the edge of the program window, yet prevent it from docking, press the Ctrl key while dragging.

If you would rather not see the tooltips that display when tool icons are pointed to in the Tools panel, you can turn them off in your General Preferences. (In OS X go to Flash ⇨ ; in OS 9 or earlier and in Windows go to Edit ⇨ Preferences ⇨ General, and under **Selection options** uncheck **Show tooltips**.)

Reading the Tools panel

The Tools panel is organized in four main sections (see Figure 4-10 for tool icons and shortcut keys). The top section contains all 17 Flash tools, as follows from left to right and top to bottom: Selection (arrow), Subselect, Line, Lasso, Pen, Text, Oval, Rectangle (with PolyStar in submenu), Pencil, Brush, Free Transform, Fill Transform, Ink Bottle, Paint Bucket, Eyedropper, and Eraser. The second section contains the Flash View tools: the Hand and Zoom. Beneath the View tools is the Color area, with swatches for assigning Stroke color and Fill color, and buttons for Black and White, No Color, and Swap Color (to reverse stroke and fill colors). The last section of the Tools panel is the Options area, where some of the available tool modifiers appear for any active tool.

Cross-Reference

The application of individual tools and options in the Tools panel will be explained in chapters related to specific production topics that make up the remainder of Section II, "Mastering the Flash Environment."

Using Tool options

Depending on the tool selected, the Options area may display some of the options, or properties, that control the functionality of that particular tool, while other controls may appear in the Property inspector or in a panel that launches separately. Of the options located in the Options area, some appear as submenus with multiple options, while others are simple buttons that toggle a property on or off. (For example, if the Lasso tool is selected, the Magic Wand option can be turned on or off by clicking its toggle button in the Options area.) If an option has more than two settings, these are generally available in a submenu.

Many of the options that appear within the Options area of the Tools panel can also be accessed from the Property inspector, from the application menu, or with keyboard shortcuts.

Caution

The migration of tool options from the Tools panel to the Property inspector is not entirely consistent in this version. For example, the Rectangle Settings dialog box for controlling the corner radius of a rectangle is invoked by clicking the Round Rectangle radius icon in the Options area of the Tools panel (or by double-clicking the icon for the Rectangle tool), but the controls for the PolyStar tool can only be accessed by clicking an Options button in the Property inspector. Although we can hope that options will be more fully integrated into the Property inspector with future versions of Flash, for now you sometimes have to look back in the Options area of the Tools panel for modifiers that you might expect to appear in the Property inspector. Conversely, many tool options do not show up in the Tools panel, so even if the Options area appears empty, look in the Property inspector to be sure you haven't missed anything.

All the tools accessed from the Tools panel have keyboard equivalents, or shortcuts, that are single keystrokes. For example, to access the Selection tool — which is the tool with the black arrow icon, located in the upper-left corner of the Tools panel — you can simply press the **V** key when the Stage or Timeline is in focus. Thus, the V key is the keyboard shortcut for the Selection tool on both Mac and Windows. This is faster than moving the mouse up to the Tools panel to click the Selection tool, and it saves mouse miles on repeated tasks. To help you learn and remember shortcuts, throughout this book when we mention a new tool, the keyboard shortcut for that tool follows in parentheses, like this: Selection tool (V).

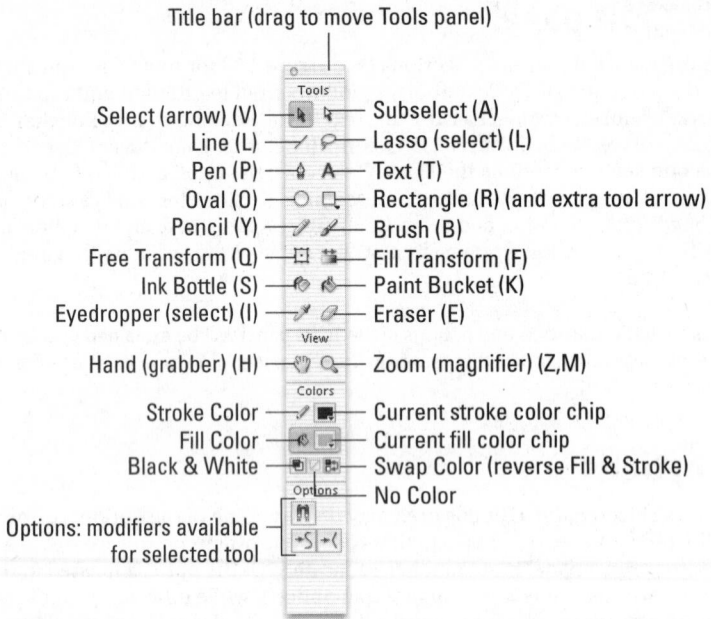

Title bar (drag to move Tools panel)

Select (arrow) (V) —— Subselect (A)
Line (L) —— Lasso (select) (L)
Pen (P) —— Text (T)
Oval (O) —— Rectangle (R) (and extra tool arrow)
Pencil (Y) —— Brush (B)
Free Transform (Q) —— Fill Transform (F)
Ink Bottle (S) —— Paint Bucket (K)
Eyedropper (select) (I) —— Eraser (E)

Hand (grabber) (H) —— Zoom (magnifier) (Z,M)

Stroke Color —— Current stroke color chip
Fill Color —— Current fill color chip
Black & White —— Swap Color (reverse Fill & Stroke)
—— No Color

Options: modifiers available
for selected tool

Figure 4-10: The Mac Tools panel is shown here with the keyboard shortcuts for each tool. Aside from system display characteristics and docking behavior, the Tools panel is identical on both Mac and Windows.

Customizing the Tools panel

Customize Tools Panel is a new Flash MX 2004 option that anticipates an exciting direction for Flash development. There is just one new tool (PolyStar) that has been added to the shipping version of Flash MX 2004, but keep on eye on keen developers who will be creating a whole new generation of Flash tools. Because the Tools panel is the most convenient place to store and access drawing tools, Macromedia has provided a user-friendly interface that makes it possible to add, delete, or rearrange the tools (and icons) that appear in the Tools panel. Open the dialog box shown in Figure 4-11, by choosing Edit ➪ Customize Tools Panel (or Flash ➪ Customize Tools Panel on Mac) from the application menu. A preview of the Tools panel on the left side of the dialog box makes it easy to select any of the squares to add or delete the tools that are stored in each section of the panel. The interface is very flexible, making it possible to put all your tools in one square if you want to, or even add the same tool to multiple squares — unless you enjoy changing things just for the sake of changing them, the main reason to use this option is really to add new tools.

The PolyStar tool is a good example of how you can store new tools that you want to use in Flash. The PolyStar tool was added to Flash MX 2004 and unlike the original Flash Oval tool and Rectangle tool, it did not get its own square in the Tools panel. The PolyStar tool had to move in and share a square with the Rectangle tool. The PolyStar icon is only visible in the Tools panel when the tool has been selected from the drop-down menu triggered by clicking and holding the Rectangle tool icon. Any tool square that has more than one tool stored in it will display a small black arrow below the currently active tool to indicate that a drop-down menu is available. By default, the tool icons will appear in the drop-down list in the order that they are added to the Current selection list in the Customize Tools Panel dialog box. The first tool added to the list will show up in its assigned square in the Tools panel unless one of the other tools in the same square is selected from the drop-down menu. The most recently selected tool in any square will be visible until Flash is restarted or another tool is selected from the same square.

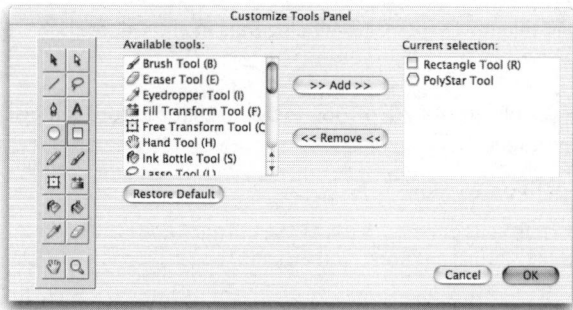

Figure 4-11: Use the Customize Tools Panel dialog box to add or rearrange the tools available in the Tools panel.

All assigned tool shortcut keys remain mapped to individual tools and can be used to activate a specific tool regardless of which square the tool is stored in. If all of the tools are removed from a square, that space on the Tools panel is left blank. Thanks to the Restore Default button in the Customize Tools Panel dialog box, you can have fun moving, grouping, or even deleting tools from different tool squares with the knowledge that you can always go back to the original layout. To illustrate the steps for adding a new Flash tool and storing it in the Tools panel, we have included a brief tutorial on a Grid tool developed by Joey Lott.

Adding New Tools to Flash MX 2004, *by Joey Lott*

Author's Note: Although it is beyond the scope of this book to describe the steps involved in actually scripting your own custom tools for Flash, we can tell you how to use custom tools that other developers have made. Joey Lott has generously agreed to let us include the code for one of his very first Flash MX 2004 tools on the CD-ROM. This brief tutorial is adapted from Joey's notes on how to install and use his "Grid" tool. We hope you will be able to follow these same steps to use other custom tools available from Macromedia or from generous developers in the Flash community.

The first step to using a custom tool is to find the files that Flash needs to make the tool work in the authoring environment and the icon that will be visible in the Tools panel. Unless you happen to know some brainy coders, the best place to look for new custom tools is on the Macromedia Web site.

The three files you will want to find and download are as follows:

✦ An XML file that describes the functionality of the tool and controls any "settings" that can be used to modify the final result

✦ A JavaScript-Flash file that implements required methods for manipulating the Flash authoring tool based on parameters specified by the XML file

✦ A PNG file that will appear in the Tools panel as the icon for the custom tool

On the CD-ROM   We have included `Grid.xml`, `Grid.jsfl`, and `Grid.png` on the CD-ROM in the CustomTool subfolder of the ch04 folder.

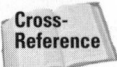

Cross-Reference   To learn more about XML files, refer to Chapter 30, "Sending Data in and Out of Flash."

These files have to be saved in your Flash MX 2004 Tools folder so that the tool can be applied in the authoring environment.

✦ The standard directory path on Windows is:

```
C:\Documents and Settings\(username)\Local Settings\Application
Data\Macromedia\Flash MX 2004\en\Configuration\Tools
```

✦ The standard directory path on Mac is:

```
HD\Users: (username)\Library: Application Support\Macromedia\Flash MX
2004\en\Configuration\Tools.
```

After the three files for the Grid tool are saved to the Tools folder, the Grid tool is added to the list of available tools in the Customize Tools Panel dialog box.

The steps for adding the Grid tool icon to a square on the Tools panel are the same as those used to assign any other tool to a specific location in the panel:

1. Open the Customize Tools Panel dialog box (Edit ⇨ Customize Tools Panel or Flash ⇨ Customize Tools Panel).

2. Select a location square on the Tools panel preview on the left side of the dialog box, select the Grid Tool from the list of Available tools, and click the **Add** button. (As shown in Figure 4-12, we chose to add the Grid tool to the Line tool square.)

3. Click **OK** to apply your changes and close the dialog box.

Now that the Grid tool icon has been added to the Tools panel, you will be able to select it from the square that you chose to store it in. As with the PolyStar tool, you will notice that when the Grid tool is active, an **Options** button appears in the Property inspector. Use this button to launch the **Tool Settings** dialog box (shown in Figure 4-13) where it is possible to control the number of rows and columns that you want to draw with the Grid tool.

After you choose settings for the grid and click **OK** to close the dialog box, you can draw a grid as easily as you would draw a rectangle with the Rectangle tool: Click the Stage and drag horizontally to create width and vertically to create height—the live preview lets you see how the grid looks before you release the mouse. You can select individual lines in the final vector grid, modify them with other drawing tools, group the lines, or convert them into a reusable symbol. This is a simple tool, but it creates perfect grids every time and saves you time and mouse miles, too!

Let's hope there will be many more useful and creative tools available that will open new possibilities for your Flash designs. You can continue to save other custom tool files to your Tools folder and they will be added to the Available tools list in the Customize Tools Panel dialog box.

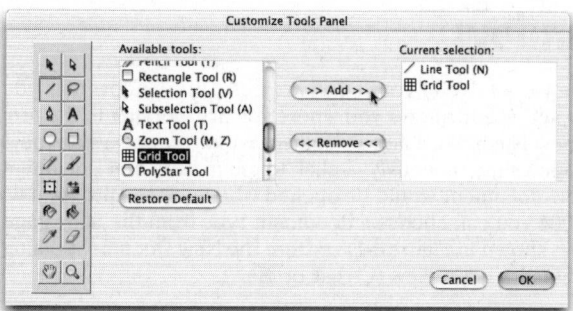

Figure 4-12: Any tool added to the Tools folder — by saving the relevant XML, JSFL, and PNG files there — will appear in the Available tools list in the Customize Tools Panel dialog box.

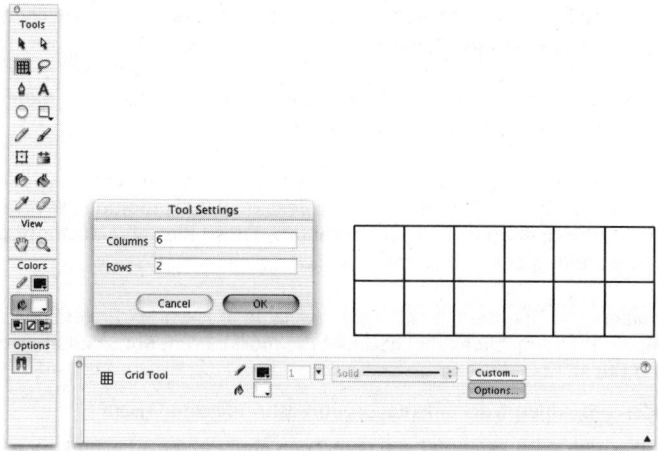

Figure 4-13: After they have been added to the Tools panel, custom tools and options can be used as easily as other standard Flash tools.

Caution

Obviously, it would be a big mistake to save a custom tool file to your Tools folder if it had the same name as an existing tool. Unless you want to overwrite existing Flash tools, make sure you're using unique names for any custom tools that you add. If you'd rather not change the name of a tool, simply add a unique number to the tool name to avoid over-writing other files with the same name.

You can remove tool icons from the Tools panel at any time without actually deleting the files stored in the Tools folder, but if you decide you don't need a tool anymore, or if your available tool list gets too cluttered, simply remove the relevant XML, JSFL and PNG files from the Tools folder (save them somewhere else if you liked the tool, trash them if you didn't).

The Document Window

The Document window is the work table of your Flash project. This window tells you what document (FLA) is currently active and shows you where you are working in the project. When you open or create a new Flash file, a new Document window appears on the screen. You can have multiple files open simultaneously — click to move from one Document window to another. In Flash MX, a new document would be opened whenever the program was launched, but in Flash MX 2004 you can choose a document type from the Start Page (discussed earlier in this chapter, shown in Figure 4-1) or from the New Document dialog box invoked by the New File command: File ➪ New (Ctrl+N or ⌘+N).

Tip   If you prefer to bypass the New Document dialog box, you can create and open a basic Flash document in one step, by using the shortcut command Alt+Ctrl+N (or Option+⌘+N on Mac).

Figure 4-14, shows the New Document dialog box for Flash MX 2004 and for Flash MX Professional 2004. Both dialog boxes include a General tab for opening Flash documents and a Templates tab for opening Flash documents with prebuilt elements that can be used as guides for designing specific kinds of presentations.

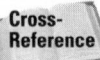

Cross-Reference   Refer to the section later in this chapter on "Working with Flash Templates" for more information about using and modifying Flash templates.

The main difference between the two versions is that, in addition to the basic Flash document (FLA) file type available in Flash MX 2004, Flash MX Professional 2004 includes several specialized file types that can be opened from the General tab. These files give developers more options for application development and script editing.

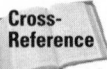

Cross-Reference   For more information on using the new file types available in Flash MX Professional 2004, search Flash Help for the term "slides" or check out the most current documentation on the Macromedia Web site at:

www.macromedia.com/support/documentation/en/flash/index.html#jsapi

Advanced authoring with Flash JavaScript and Flash Form applications is beyond the scope of this book, but if you want to take your Flash development to the next level, the *Flash MX 2004 ActionScript Bible* by Robert Reinhardt and Joey Lott (Wiley, 2004) provides more information on these topics.

Controlling the Document window

Even when you choose to hide all panels (F4), the Document window remains visible — closing the window will close your Flash project. On Macintosh, the Document window is always free-floating and can be moved anywhere onscreen by grabbing the top of the panel with your mouse, or scaled by dragging the size box in the lower-right corner. By default, on Windows, the Document window is maximized to fill the workspace and it cannot be scaled or moved independently, unless you first click the document **Restore Down** button (between the Minimize button and the Close button) in the top-right corner of the window (below the larger buttons that control the application). This will "free" the Document window from other panels in the program window so that you can move it around and scale it.

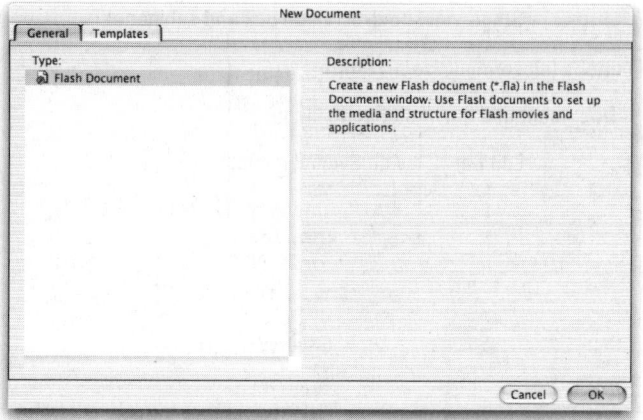

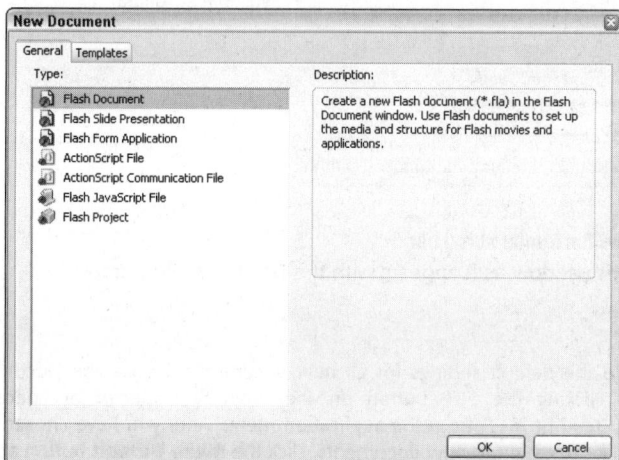

Figure 4-14: Use the New Document panel in Flash MX 2004 (top) or Flash MX Professional 2004 (below) to create new documents or open template files.

The main reason you may want to alter the default placement of the Document window is to organize your panel layouts to suit a dual-monitor workstation. Although you can drastically change the size and location of the Document window, generally you will want it centered in your workspace and scaled to allow you to comfortably work with objects on the Stage. Figure 4-15 shows the Document window on Macintosh as it appears with default settings and with the Document Properties dialog box open.

The default document settings of Flash will automatically create new documents with a size of 550 x 400 pixels, a white background color, and a frame rate of 12. All of these attributes are displayed in the Property inspector and can be changed at any time. Clicking the **Size** button in the Property inspector launches the Document Properties dialog box where you can enter a custom size or use the **Match** options to automatically create a document that fits your current printer page settings (**Printer**), includes all the elements you have placed into your document (**Contents**), or restore the default size setting (**Default**).

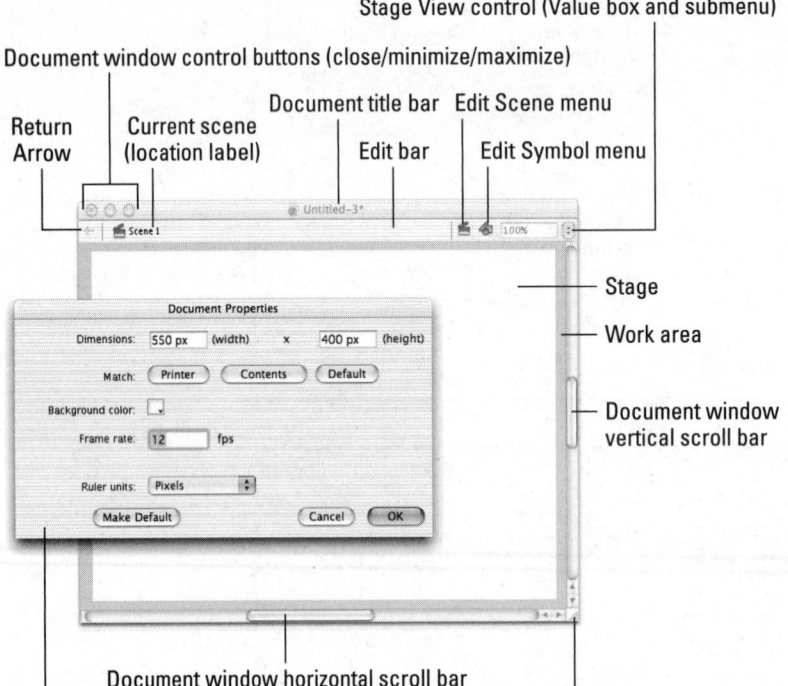

Stage View control (Value box and submenu)

Document window control buttons (close/minimize/maximize)

Return Arrow

Current scene (location label)

Document title bar   Edit Scene menu

Edit bar   Edit Symbol menu

Stage

Work area

Document window vertical scroll bar

Document window horizontal scroll bar

Figure 4-15: The Document window as it appears with the Document Properties dialog box open

Tip   If you wish to change the default settings for all new documents, invoke the Document Properties panel by clicking the Size button on the Property inspector or choosing Modify ⇨ Document (Ctrl+J or ⌘+J) from the application menu. After you have chosen the attributes you would like to assign to new documents, click the **Make Default** button at the bottom of the panel.

Reading the Document window

The white Stage area is the central part of the Document window that becomes the visible area or "screen" of a published Flash movie (SWF). As noted previously, the color and size of this "background" can be changed at any time, but it is best to establish these settings before you begin creating other elements.

The light gray Work area that frames the Stage allows you to place elements into your project while keeping them out of the visible area. This is useful if you want to show only part of an element or to animate it as it moves onto the Stage. A good example of the utility of the Work area feature can be seen in some cartoons in which very large background artwork hangs off the Stage (or View area) until called upon or tweened through to create the effect of a camera pan. The Stage and the Work area are always available in the Document window. The default panel layout also includes the Timeline docked at the top of the Work area, because this is generally the most convenient place to use it.

Tip You can strip the Timeline panel out of the Document window and leave it free floating or you can re-dock it to the top or bottom of the Work area. On Windows, you can also dock the Timeline to either side of the Work area, but this is usually an awkward view.

The narrow bar located above the Stage and Work area is referred to as the Edit bar (shown in context in Figure 4-15). This bar contains three icons and a value box that help you navigate within a document.

New Feature When the Timeline is docked at the top of the Document window in Flash MX 2004, the Edit bar appears above the Timeline. To move the Edit bar below the Timeline (where it appeared in Flash MX), hold down Shift+Ctrl (or Shift+⌘ on Mac) and double-click the Edit bar. Repeat the same steps to move it back above the Timeline at any time.

Stage view control

Although the scale value box is at the end of the bar, we will discuss it first because it can be useful even when you first begin putting artwork on the Stage. This value box, called the Stage View control, shows you the current scale of the Stage area and allows you to type new percentages or select a preset value from a submenu.

Note The view percentages are based on the pixel dimensions of your project, as defined in Document properties, and your screen resolution. For example, if your project size is 500 x 400 pixels and your screen resolution is 800 x 600, then the Stage area would occupy roughly 40 percent of your screen if view scale were set to 100 percent (Ctrl+1 or ⌘+1).

The first three settings in the View submenu list are **Fit in Window**, **Show Frame** (Ctrl+2 or ⌘+2), and **Show All** (Ctrl+3 or @c@md+3); these settings will automatically scale your Stage view to fit your current Document window size in various ways. Fit in Window scales the Stage view to fill the current Document window without cropping the visible area. Show Frame sets the Stage view to a scale that fits the content of a frame in the Document window; if there is nothing on the current frame, the Stage view is set at a scale that shows the entire Stage area within the current Document window size. Show All sets the Stage view to a scale that includes any elements you have placed in the Work area outside the Stage. You can find these same view options from the application menu (View ➪ Magnification).

There are two additional tools available in the Tools panel (see Figure 4-10), which will also control your view of the Stage and Work area within the Document window.

 The Hand tool (H) allows you to move the Stage area within the Document window by "grabbing" it (clicking and dragging). Double-clicking the Hand icon in the Tools panel quickly gives you the same Stage view as choosing the menu item **Show Frame**. To toggle the Hand tool on while using any other tool, without interrupting your selection, hold down the spacebar.

 The Zoom tool, or magnifier (Z, M) does just what the name implies — adjusts the scale of your Stage view. The available magnification range is between 8 percent and 2,000 percent. However you can apply this handy tool in a few ways. With the Zoom tool active, clicking consecutively on the Stage will pull in closer to artwork with the *Enlarge* option (Ctrl+[+] or ⌘+[+]), or move farther away with the *Reduce* option (Ctrl+[–] or ⌘+[–] key). Each click adjusts the Stage view magnification by half. Pressing the Option or Alt key as you click toggles the Zoom tool between *Enlarge* and *Reduce*. Double-clicking the Zoom tool icon in the Tools panel always scales the Stage view to 100 percent (Ctrl+1 or ⌘+1). One last way of applying the Zoom tool while it is active in the Tools panel is to drag a selection box around the area that you want to fill the Document window. Flash will scale the Stage view to the highest magnification (up to 2,000 percent), which fills the Document window with the selected area.

Edit options

Now back to the other icons on the Edit bar. The location label on the top left edge of the window shows you the current scene and what part of the project you are editing. The sequence of labels that display in this area are sometimes referred to as *breadcrumbs* because these labels show the steps, or the path, leading back to the main Timeline from the location you're editing. When in Edit mode, you can use these sequential labels to step your way back to the main Timeline of the current scene, or click the arrow in front of the labels to return to the main Timeline of the first scene in your project. To the right is the **Edit Scene** icon, and at the far right is the **Edit Symbols** icon. Click these icons to evoke menus of scenes or symbols in the document that can be opened and edited within the Document window.

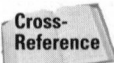

Cross-Reference

For more about symbols, and Edit mode, refer to Chapter 6, "Symbols, Instances, and the Library."

Using scenes

The Scene panel (Shift+F2 or Window ⇨ Design panels ⇨ Scene) allows you to add, name, and sequence scenes. By default, when your Flash movie (SWF) is published, the scenes play in the order in which they are listed, as shown in Figure 4-16. Scenes can help to organize a Flash project into logical, manageable parts. However, with the increasingly robust power of ActionScript, there's been a trend among many developers to move away from scene-based architecture. Using individual Flash movies instead of scenes to organize sections of a project results in files that download more efficiently and that are easier to edit due to their modular organization. It's like the difference between one huge ball of all-purpose twine that's the size of a house, and a large drawer filled with manageable spools — sorted neatly according to color and weight.

Dividing logical project parts into separate documents also facilitates efficiency in team environments, where developers can be working on different pieces of a project simultaneously. Scenes can still be useful for organizing certain types of projects, such as simple presentations without a lot of graphics, or for animators who prefer to organize a cartoon in one file before handing it off for integration into a larger site structure.

Adding named anchor keyframes is another useful option for linear Flash presentations. These allow Forward and Back buttons in a Web browser to jump from frame to frame or scene to scene to navigate a Flash movie. For more on how to set and publish named anchor keyframes, refer to Chapter 20, "Making Your First MX 2004 Project."

New Feature

In Flash MX, the first keyframe of each scene was automatically made a named anchor. In Flash MX 2004, this has been made an option that is turned on or off in the Timeline section of the General Preferences panel (Ctrl+U or ⌘+U).

To navigate and modify scenes from within the Document window:

✦ Click the **Edit Scene** button on the Edit bar and then choose the desired scene from the submenu.

✦ Navigate to a specific scene from the application menu with the View ➪ Go To command.

✦ To add a new scene, either use the Scene panel's Add button — indicated by the plus sign — or, from the Insert menu, use Insert ➪ Scene. New scenes will continue in the same auto-numbering sequence started with Scene 1. Thus, even if you delete Scene 2, the next added scene will be named Scene 3.

✦ Use the Duplicate button on the Scene panel to make a copy of a scene including all content on the scene's Timeline.

✦ To delete a scene, use the Scene panel's Delete button — indicated by the trashcan icon. (To bypass the alert asking if you want to delete the scene, use Ctrl+click or ⌘+click.)

✦ To rename a scene, simply double-click the scene name within the Scene panel and type a new name. Using numbers in scene names will not affect playback order; the scenes will play from the top to the bottom of the list.

✦ To rearrange scene order, simply click and drag a scene to alter its position in the Scene panel list. You can use actions to direct the movie to access scenes outside the default linear order. For more about actions, refer to Chapter 18, "Understanding Actions and Event Handlers."

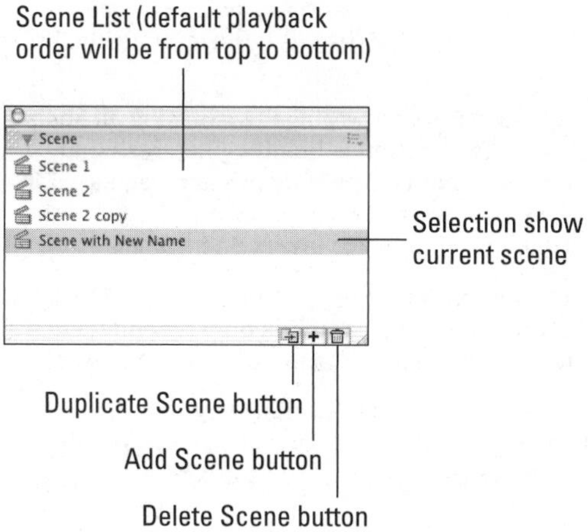

Scene List (default playback
order will be from top to bottom)

Selection show
current scene

Duplicate Scene button

Add Scene button

Delete Scene button

Figure 4-16: The Scene panel showing document scenes in the order they will play back by default

Caution Although scenes give you the visual impression of having a whole new timeline to work on, they are really continuations of the main Timeline that begins in the first scene of your document. If you're using any actions to control your movie playback, it's important to avoid duplicate naming on frame labels or named anchors. Thus, even if it seems logical, it isn't a good idea to label the beginning of each new scene "intro," because you won't be able to differentiate these labels as easily for targeting with ActionScript.

Using Document window menu options

There are several options available from the application menu that control display or editing in the Document window. These can be helpful when creating or placing elements on the Stage. All of these can be accessed from View on the application menu (notice the shortcut key combinations listed after most commands). The basic functions of these various commands are as follows:

✦ **Goto:** Leads to a submenu of scenes in the current movie, including four handy shortcuts to the First, Previous, Next and Last scenes. This menu is also available from the Edit scene icon on the Edit bar in the Document window.

✦ **Zoom In:** Increases the scale of the Stage view by 50 percent.

✦ **Zoom Out:** Decreases the scale of the Stage view by 50 percent.

✦ **Magnification:** Leads to the same view options that are available in the Stage View Control on the top right of the Document window. Note that three of these options also have corresponding keyboard shortcuts.

✦ **Preview Mode:** Leads to a menu of various settings for rendering and displaying content in the authoring environment:

• **Outlines:** Simplifies the view of elements on the Stage by showing all shapes as outlines, and all lines as thin lines. This option is helpful when reshaping graphic elements. It also speeds up the display of complex scenes and can assist in getting the general timing and sense of a movie. It is a global equivalent of the outline options available in the Timeline window for layers and frames.

• **Fast:** Turns off both antialiasing and dithering to speed up display. The default is *Off*, to create the most accurate screen image, and it is only recommended that you turn this option *On* if you need to reduce demand on your processor.

• **Antialias:** Dithers the edges of shapes and lines so that they look smoother onscreen. It can also slow the display, but this is only an issue with older video cards. This is actually a toggle in opposition with the Fast command: turn this On and Fast goes Off.

• **Antialias Text:** As with Antialias, this is also a toggle in opposition to the Fast command. It smoothes the edges of text *only* and is most noticeable on large font sizes. You can only have one Antialias option on at a time, so you can make a choice between smoothing text or smoothing shapes, depending on what content you're working with.

• **Full:** Use this option for the most "finished" or high definition preview. If you are working on intensive animation, it may slow down rendering of the display in the authoring environment.

✦ **Work area:** Makes the light-gray area that surrounds the Stage available for use. When Work area is visible, your Stage area will display centered in the Document window when you apply Show Frame or Show All. If the Work area has been turned off in the View menu, then the Stage will align to the top-left of the Document window.

Caution

Items that are selected and offstage when View ⇨ Work area is toggled off can still be deleted, even if they are not visible. So it's best if you don't have anything selected when you choose to hide the Work area.

✦ **Rulers:** Toggles the reference Rulers (which display at the top and left edges of the Work area) on or off — use Modify ⇨ Document (Ctrl+J or ⌘+J) to change units of measurement. Rulers are a helpful reference for placing guides to align elements in a layout.

✦ **Grid:** Use this option to toggle visibility of the background Stage grid on or off. This grid does not export with the final Flash movie (SWF), but serves as an authoring reference only. You can control the appearance of the Grid and the precision of grid snapping by adjusting the settings in the dialog box invoked with the Edit Grid command. When the Snap to grid option is active, it works even if the Grid is not visible. Edited Grid settings can be saved as the default by clicking the Save Default button, which enables you to have these setting as presets for all subsequent Flash movies.

Note

The default Grid size of 18 pixels is equal to 0.25 inch. Grid units can be changed by entering the appropriate abbreviation for other units of measurement (for example: 25 pt., 0.5", 0.5 in, 2 cm, and so on) in the Grid Spacing entry boxes. Although the specified units *will* be applied to the grid, they will be translated into the current unit of measurement for the Ruler. Thus, if the Ruler is set to pixels, and the Grid units are changed to 0.5 in, then, on reopening the Grid dialog box, the Grid units will be displayed as 36 pix (because pixels are allocated at 72 pix = 1"). Changing Ruler units via Modify ⇨ Document also changes Grid units.

✦ **Guides:** When Rulers are turned on, horizontal or vertical Guides can be dragged onto the Stage from respective rulers. These four commands control the parameters of these Guides.

• **Show Guides:** This is a simple toggle to either show or hide Guides that you have dragged out from the rulers.

• **Lock Guides:** This is a toggle that either locks or unlocks all current Guides. This is useful to prevent Guides from accidentally being moved after you have placed them.

• **Snap to Guides:** This is a toggle that extends snap behavior to Guides. Each snapping behavior works independently of the others — so, regardless of whether Snap to Grid or Snap to Objects is turned on or off, Snap to Guides can still be active.

• **Edit Guides:** This command invokes the Guides dialog box, where Guide Color and Guide-specific snap accuracy can be adjusted. Also included are check boxes for the other three Guide commands: Show Guides, Snap to Guides, and Lock Guides. This enables you to establish Guide settings and then click the Save Default button to have these settings as presets for all subsequent Flash movies. To delete all Guides from the Stage, press the Clear All button.

✦ **Snapping:** Leads to a menu of various options for controlling snapping behavior in the authoring environment. These settings are described in detail in Chapter 5, "Drawing in Flash."

Note   When Snap to Pixels is turned on, a 1-pixel grid appears when the Stage view is magnified to 400 percent or higher. This grid is independent of the Show Grid command.

✦ **Hide Edges:** Hides selection patterns so that you can edit items without the visual noise of the selection pixel "highlight." This only applies to currently selected items and allows a clean view without having to lose your selection. Most useful for seeing colors or fine lines that may appear visually distorted by the selection pattern.

✦ **Show Shape Hints:** This toggles Shape Hints to make them visible or invisible. It does not disable shape hinting. Shape Hints are used when tweening shapes. For more about Shape tweens (or Shape Morphing) refer to Chapter 11, "Timeline Animation and Effects."

Working with Flash templates

The library of predefined Flash documents available in the Templates tab of the New Document dialog box (or in the Create from Template list of the Start Page) is a great starting point for creating many common Flash presentations. The templates shown in Figure 4-17 are listed in both Flash MX 2004 and Flash MX Professional 2004, but some of the templates can only be used in the pro version of the program.

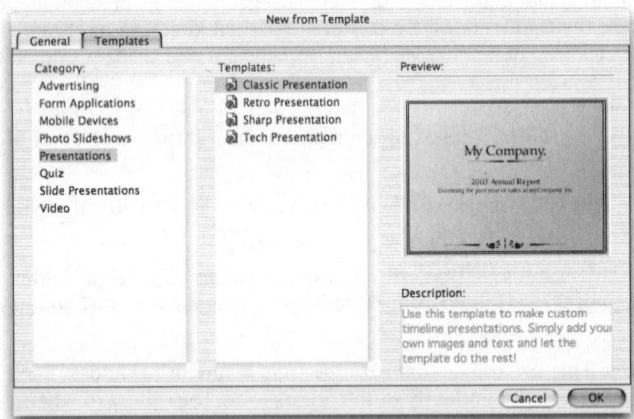

Figure 4-17: The prebuilt templates that ship with Flash provide a good starting point for authoring many common Flash presentations.

To work with a Flash template, open it as you would any other Flash document. You can then add your own content to the Stage or modify the Timeline following the guides in the template and save the finished document with a new name.

Cross-Reference

For descriptions of each of the available templates, do a search for "Using templates" in the Flash Help panel.

You can also create your own reusable template from any Flash document by choosing File ➪ Save As Template. Before the template is saved, you are given options for naming, assigning a category, and description — making it easy to manage a whole library of custom templates. The preview visible for each template is actually just the content on the first frame of the template document. In some cases, this does not provide much visual information for how the template might be used. If you use templates often or if you create your own templates, you may find it helpful to modify the default previews to make them more informative. We have included a tutorial from Bill Perry that will guide you through the steps for modifying a device template preview.

Tip

Although each template type has a different file structure and may contain different content, the preview for any template will include only the visible content in the Stage area on the first frame of the template file. Changing the content in the first frame of a template file will also change the preview for that template.

Caution

If you are not yet comfortable working in the Flash authoring environment to accomplish basic editing tasks, we suggest that you finish reading this chapter before attempting the steps described in Bill Perry's tutorial.

Adding Custom Templates for Devices, *by Bill Perry*

Flash MX 2004 ships with a wide variety of templates; among them are 22 mobile device templates for PDAs and mobile phone platforms. What's great about these templates is that when you open them you'll get a full-size graphic of the actual device with the Stage area shown on the device screen (see Figure 4-18).

This is an improvement over the mobile devices templates found in Flash MX; however, one thing can be improved in Flash MX 2004 — the template previews.

If you take a look at any of the mobile devices templates, you'll notice that the preview doesn't show you the device graphic — it just displays a white rectangle. Figure 4-19 shows the information and preview visible for a selected device template.

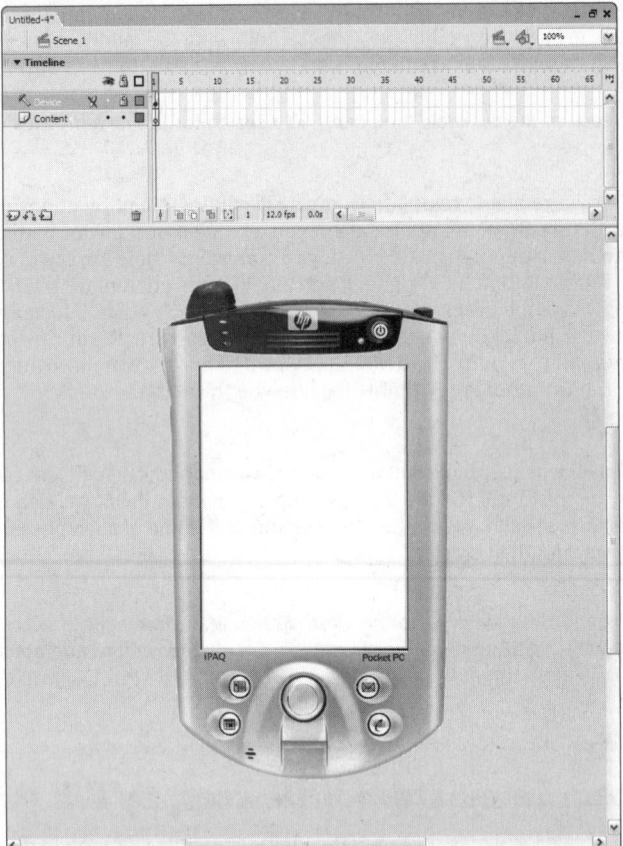

Figure 4-18: Notice how the Stage area fits the screen of the iPAQ 5440 – this gives you a good idea of how your Flash content will look on the device.

Template previews are based on the content (graphic or other items) visible on the Stage of the template document. For the mobile device templates, the graphic image of each device is in a guide layer and is outside of the Stage. Because of this, the preview window only shows a white rectangle, which is, in fact, the empty Stage in the template document

Wouldn't it be nice to actually get a preview of the device in the template preview area? It's easy and I'm going to tell you how.

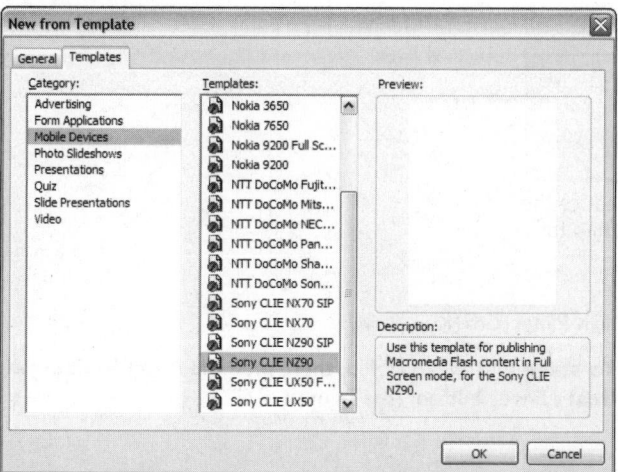

Figure 4-19: There is a description of the template, but the preview area is a blank white rectangle.

All you need is either Flash MX 2004 or Flash MX Professional 2004 to complete this tutorial:

1. Launch Flash MX 2004.

2. From the Start Page, select the Mobile Devices template folder and then select the **iPAQ 5440 Full Screen** template from the New document dialog box.

3. Create a new layer and name it ** **Delete this** **. The Timeline should now look like Figure 4-20.

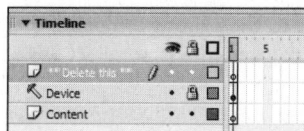

Figure 4-20: A new layer is added to the template Timeline.

4. Unlock the **Device** guide layer so the iPAQ graphic can be selected.

5. Select the iPAQ bitmap and copy it (Ctrl+C or ⌘+C).

6. Lock the **Device** guide layer so you won't accidentally modify it.

7. Select the first frame in the ** **Delete this** ** layer and paste the copied bitmap (Ctrl+V or ⌘+V).

8. Select the pasted bitmap and open up the Transform Panel (Ctrl+T or ⌘+T).

9. Make sure the Constrain check box is selected the Transform panel; then type **50** percent into either the horizontal or vertical scale value boxes, as shown in Figure 4-21.

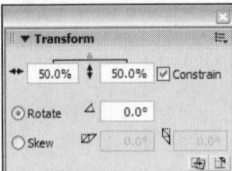

Figure 4-21: Reduce the
scale of the bitmap to
50 percent.

10. Open up the Align Panel (Ctrl+K or ⌘+K).

11. Make sure the **To stage** button is enabled; then, press the **Align horizontal center**
    and **Align vertical center** buttons (see Figure 4-22).

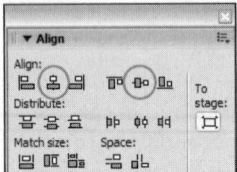

Figure 4-22: Align the
bitmap to the center of
the Stage.

Now it's time to save your template:

1. Go to File ➪ Save as Template.

2. Because we're just adding a preview image to the existing template, there's no reason
   to rename the template. We're just going to overwrite it, so select **Save,** as shown in
   Figure 4-23.

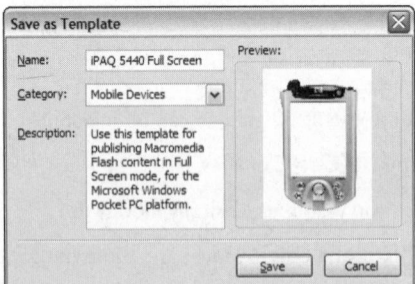

Figure 4-23: Save the modified template
with the same name.

3. A pop-up window appears, asking if you want to replace the existing template. Select **OK**.

4. Close the template.

Let's take a look at the template we just modified:

1. From the start page, select the **Mobile Devices** template folder; then select the **iPAQ 5440 Full Screen** template.

2. Notice how the preview area now shows the graphic for the iPAQ 5440 (see Figure 4-24).

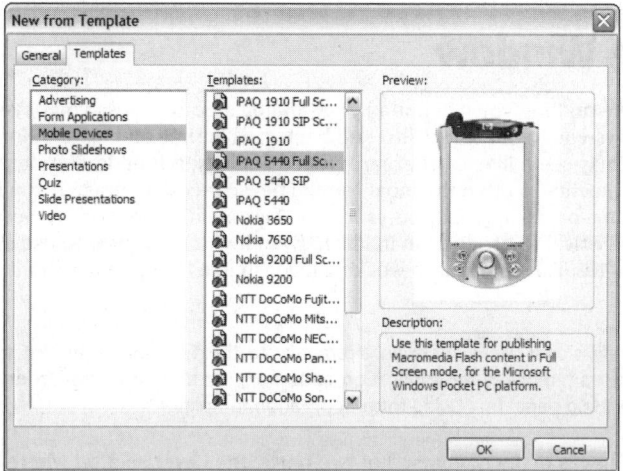

Figure 4-24: The modified template preview with a scaled bitmap of the device

When using these templates be sure to delete the ** Delete This ** layer before saving a new working document. Otherwise it will be a part of your Flash content. By putting a scaled-down version of the device bitmap into this layer it will show up in the preview area for the template — this is the only purpose of this layer. You may have to use different values for reducing the scale of the bitmap in other device templates so the graphic fits in the Stage size defined for each specific device.

As you can see it's fairly easy to add custom templates for devices and these steps can be applied to all of the other existing mobile devices templates.

Authors' Note: You can add or modify the previews for other types of templates with similar steps, but if you modify templates with existing (visible) graphic content, it is advisable to save your custom template with a new name so that you don't overwrite the original template.

The modified template described in this tutorial is included on the CD-ROM in the `CustomTemplate` subfolder in the ch04 folder. You can open the template file directly from the CD-ROM or add it to the `Mobile Devices` subfolder in your Templates folder so that it is available in the Start Page and in the Templates list in the New Document dialog box.

The standard directory path for the Templates folder on Windows is:

```
C:\Documents and Settings\(username)\Local Settings\Application
Data\Macromedia\Flash MX 2004\en\Configuration\Templates
```

The standard directory path on Mac is:

```
HD\Users: (username)\Library: Application Support\Macromedia\
Flash MX 2004\en\Configuration\Templates
```

The Timeline Window

The Timeline is like nothing you will find in your analog studio, unless you have a time machine that allows you to move forward and backward in time and up and down between dimensions. This may seem like a rather far-fetched analogy, but understanding the behavior and purpose of a timeline is often the most foreign new concept to grasp if you have not worked in other time-based applications (such as Macromedia Director). A clear understanding of timelines is critical to production in Flash. Even if you know how to use all your other tools, not knowing the Timeline makes working in Flash like trying to work in a studio with no light.

Flash MX Professional 2004 offers an alternative to the Timeline authoring structure with new form-based templates for application authoring. For more information on this feature, search in the Help panel for "Using form application templates."

The Timeline window is really composed of two parts: the Layer section where content is "stacked" in depth, and the Timeline/Frames section where content is planned out in frames along the duration of your movie, like on a strip of motion picture film. In the Layer section, you can label or organize your "stacks" of frame rows. You can also lock or hide individual layers or just convert their display to colored outlines on the Stage while you are editing. In the Timeline section you can control where and for how long content is visible and how it changes over time to animate when the movie plays back. You can also add actions to control how the Playhead moves through the Timeline, making it start and stop or jump to a specific frame.

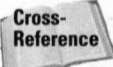

You can find more on animation techniques in Chapter 11, "Timeline Animation and Effects." Actions are introduced in Part V, "Adding Basic Interactivity to Flash Movies."

Controlling the Timeline window

On both Macintosh and Windows, the default position for the Timeline is docked at the top of the Document window, which is often the most logical place to put it. If you don't see the Timeline when you open Flash, go to Window ➪ Timeline (Ctrl+Alt+T or ⌘+Option+T) to bring it up onscreen.

Tip

All panels have a minimize/maximize triangle icon in the top-left corner. Clicking the arrow icon or anywhere within the title bar of the panel expands or collapses a panel faster than finding the menu to hide it completely. This makes it easy to collapse the Timeline window so that it doesn't take up screen space, while still leaving it available to expand again when you need it.

The position, size, and shape of the Timeline can always be adjusted to suit your workflow. The Timeline can be docked to any edge of the Document window, but cannot be grouped with other panels. It can, however, be moved anywhere as a floating window, even exiled to the second monitor — leaving the Document window all for the Stage and Work area.

✦ Move the Timeline by clicking and dragging the title bar at the top of the window. If the Timeline is docked, click anywhere in the gray area above the layer stack to undock the Timeline and reposition it.

✦ If undocked, resize the Timeline by dragging any edge (on Windows), or the gripper/size box in the lower-right corner (Mac). If docked, drag the bar at the bottom of the Timeline that separates the layers from the Stage area, either up or down.

✦ To resize the layer area for name and icon controls (to accommodate longer layer names or to apportion more of the view to frames), click and drag the bar that separates the layer name and icon controls from the Timeline frame area.

Tip

To permanently prevent the floating Timeline from docking to the Document window, use Edit ➪ Preferences (or Flash ➪ Preferences on OS X) and in the General section, under Timeline Options, check Disable Timeline Docking.

Using the Timeline Controller toolbar

The Controller (Window ➪ Toolbars ➪ Controller) is a small bar of buttons that provides basic control of the Playhead. Access to the Controller can be helpful if you need to pan back and forth along an extended section of the Timeline. You can keep it onscreen as a floating bar, and on Windows you can also dock it anywhere along the top or bottom of the Document window. Some developers prefer using the Controller to using shortcut keys for moving the Playhead. Along with the commands available on the Controller bar, the application Control menu also lists some more advanced options, which we discuss in following chapters as they relate to animation and actions.

Caution

Playback speed within the document (FLA) is not as accurate as it is in the movie file (SWF), so the Controller is not intended as a replacement for the Test Movie command (Control ➪ Test Movie or Ctrl+Enter or ⌘+Return).

As you can see in Figure 4-25, the buttons on the Controller will be familiar to anyone who has used a remote control. The only special function to note is that the Play button toggles to start and stop without having to use the Stop button.

Tip

Using shortcut keys is often the preferred way to move along the Timeline. On both Windows and Mac, pressing the Enter/Return key will work as a toggle to start and stop the Playhead. If you prefer to move along the Timeline frame by frame, pressing the period key (.) moves forward one frame and pressing the comma (,) moves back one frame. These keys are more intuitively remembered by looking for the less than (<) and greater than (>) symbols.

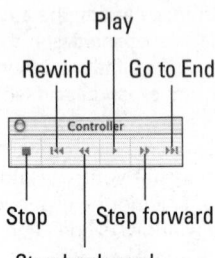

Play

Rewind   Go to End

Controller

Stop   Step forward

Step backward

Figure 4-25: The Controller showing callouts for the buttons as they are used to control movement of the Playhead

Reading the Timeline

The Timeline graphically orders Flash content across two dimensions — time and depth — and provides you with some options for how this content is displayed on the Stage and within frames on the Timeline.

Visual display of time

The order of time is displayed by the sequence of frames arranged horizontally, from left to right, as they appear within the duration of your project. Thus, if your movie is set to 20 frames per second, frame 40 occurs at the 2-second point of your animation.

Note   Although they say that time and space are without limits, the Flash authoring environment supports about 32,000 frames, and the SWF format only officially supports around 16,000, which is actually so long that you might never find your way from one end of the Timeline to the other. Organizing your work with scenes and Movie Clips, or even in multiple documents, should save you from ever having to use a Timeline even a tenth of this length.

Web Resource   For more details on the limits of Flash, refer to the Macromedia Tech Note Index:

    www.macromedia.com/support/flash/ts/documents/bigflash.htm.

You can insert, delete, copy, paste, and reorder frames as well as convert them to various specific frame types that control how elements will animate. Current frame settings display in the Property inspector when a frame is selected, and you can also add/change a frame name or tween type here. The main controls for editing frames are found in the contextual menu (right-click on Windows or Control+click on Mac) or from the Timeline submenus under Edit, Insert, and Modify in the application menu.

Tip   As you work with frames, you'll find shortcut keys invaluable. These shortcut keys are listed in the application menu following most commands. For a complete list of common Timeline editing tasks and the shortcut keys used for these, refer to Appendix A, "Keyboard Shortcuts."

Visual display of depth

The Timeline layers enable you to separate content onto individual "transparent" work surfaces within the Document window. This allows elements to be animated or edited individually even if they occupy the same Timeline (or frame) space as other elements in the

document. These layers are arranged vertically, from bottom to top. They enable you to organize content, actions, comments, labels, and sounds so that you will be able to quickly find
the parts of the project that you want to edit.

Tip   Layer folders are a huge help to organizing multilayered documents. With layers moved
inside a folder, they can be opened up for editing or hidden away to reduce the number of
layers you have to navigate.

You can insert, delete, move, or rename layers and folders, as well as adjust how content is
displayed in the editing environment. Items placed on layers above can visually obscure
other items in layers beneath them, without otherwise affecting each other. With the layer
control icons shown at the top of the layer stack, you can set layer visibility (the Eye icon),
editability (the Lock icon), and the display mode (the Square icon) to regular or outline only.
Note, however, that these settings are visible within the editing environment only and do not
affect the appearance of the final movie (SWF).

Timeline window features

Figure 4-26 shows the Timeline window, as it appears when it is undocked or floating. The various controls of the window interface are labeled here, but detailed explanation of some of
these controls will be deferred to the drawing and animation chapters where they are
applied.

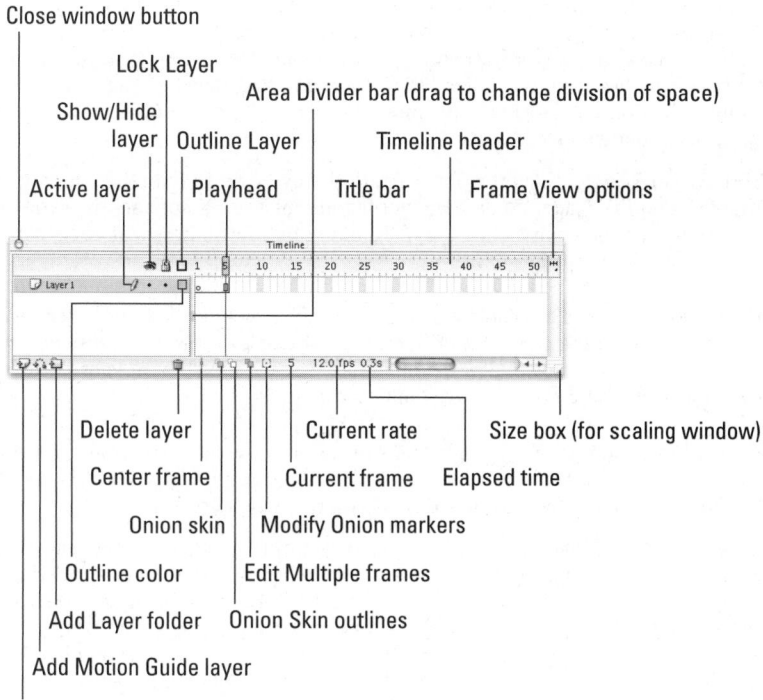

Figure 4-26: The floating Timeline window with callouts showing the principal
features and control elements

As shown in Figure 4-26, the principal features and controls of the Timeline are:

Window features

✦ **Title bar:** This identifies the Timeline and allows it to be collapsed or expanded by clicking anywhere in the bar.

✦ **Timeline Header:** The Timeline Header is the ruler that shows frame numbers and measures the time of the Timeline — each tick is one frame.

✦ **Playhead or Current Frame Indicator:** The red rectangle with a line extending down through all layers is the Playhead. The Playhead indicates the current frame. Drag it left or right along the Timeline to move from one area of the Timeline to another. Push it beyond the visible area to force-scroll the Timeline. You can also drag the Playhead at a consistent rate for a preview of your animation; this is called "scrubbing the Timeline."

Tip

On Windows, if you have a mouse with a scroll wheel, you can scroll up and down through the layers or by holding down the Shift key while you scroll, you can move the Playhead forward and backward along the Timeline. If all of your layers (or layer folders) are already visible in the Timeline window, then the scroll wheel will just scroll you forward and backward along the Timeline without moving the Playhead.

Layer controls

✦ **Active Layer icon:** To make a layer active, either click the layer's name, or select a frame or group of frames. Then the pencil icon appears, indicating that the layer is now active. That's in addition to this more obvious clue: The Layer bar of the active layer is darker gray than inactive Layer bars. Although you can select multiple layers or content on multiple layers, only one layer will be marked as active at a time. For more about frame selection and editing behaviors, please see the heading "Editing frames and layers," that follows in this section.

✦ **Show/Hide Layer Toggle:** Click the dot beneath the eye icon to hide the contents of a layer from view on the Stage. When the layer is hidden, a red X appears over the dot. To return the layer to visibility, click the X. To hide or show all layers at once, simply click on the eye icon directly.

Caution

Hidden layers do export, and any content on the Stage within a hidden layer will become visible upon export. Even if the content is offstage and not visible, it may add considerably to the file size when a Flash movie (SWF) is published, so you should save your document (FLA) and then delete these layers before your final export.

✦ **Lock/Unlock Layer Toggle:** This toggle locks or unlocks the layer to either prevent or enable further editing. When the layer is locked, a padlock icon appears over the dot. To lock/unlock all layers at once, click directly on the lock icon.

✦ **Outline Layer Toggle:** This toggles the colored layer outlines on or off. When on, the filled square icon changes into an outline, and all elements in that layer appear as colored outlines in the Document window. The outline color for the layer can be changed with the Outline Color control of the Layer Properties dialog box, which can be accessed by double-clicking the square Outline color icons in the layer stack or by choosing Modify ⇨ Timeline ⇨ Layer Properties from the application menu.

Tip

Alt-clicking (or Option-clicking on Mac) the Eye, Lock or Outline icons on any layer will apply the command to all *other* layers. For example, Alt-clicking the Lock icon on a layer will lock all other layers and leave the currently active layer unlocked.

✦ **Frame View options:** This button, at the far-right end of the Timeline, accesses the Frame View options menu, which affords many options for the manner in which both the Timeline header and the frames are displayed.

✦ **Add Layer:** Simply click this button to add a new layer above the currently active layer. By default, layers are given sequential numeric names. Double-click the layer name in the Layer bar to change the name. Click and drag any part of the Layer bar to move it to a new position in the stack, or drag it on top of a folder layer to place it inside the folder.

✦ **Add Motion Guide Layer:** Motion guide layers are used to move elements along a path. This button adds a Motion guide layer directly above (and linked to) the currently active layer. To learn about using Motion guide layers, refer to Chapter 12, "Applying Layer Types."

✦ **Add Layer Folder:** This button allows you to create folders for storing groups of layers. New folders will automatically be placed above the currently selected layer and labeled in the same number sequence as layers. They can be renamed or moved in the same way as other layers.

✦ **Delete Layer:** This button deletes the currently active layer, regardless of whether it is locked. Flash always retains one layer in the Timeline, so if you only have one layer in your document, you can't delete it unless you add another layer to the Timeline.

Tip

Because using the Delete key on your keyboard does not remove an active layer or folder, but rather removes all of the content from those frames, it can be helpful to get in the habit of right-clicking (Windows) or Control+clicking (Mac) a layer that you want to remove and choosing Delete from the contextual menu. You can always click the trash icon to dump a selected layer or folder, but sometimes the contextual-menu click is a work habit that can be easily applied.

Frame controls

✦ **Center Frame:** Click this button to shift the Timeline so that the current frame is centered in the visible area of the Timeline.

✦ **Onion Skin:** The Onion Skin feature enables you to see several frames of animation simultaneously.

✦ **Onion Skin Outlines:** This enables you to see the outlines of several frames of animation simultaneously.

✦ **Edit Multiple Frames:** In general, Onion skinning permits you to edit the current frame only. Click this button to make each frame between the Onion Skin Markers editable.

✦ **Modify Onion Markers:** Click this button to evoke the Modify Onion Markers pop-up. In addition to manual adjustments, the options are used to control the behavior and range of Onion skinning.

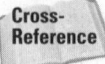

Cross-Reference   Onion skinning is further described in Chapter 11, "Timeline Animation and Effects."

Timeline Status displays

✦ **Current Frame:** This indicates the number of the current frame.

✦ **Frame Rate Indicator:** This indicates the frame rate of the movie, measured in fps, or frames per second. The program default of 12 fps is usually a good starting point. Ideally, some testing in the final playback environment should be done before deciding on an optimal frame rate. You can double-click the Frame Rate Indicator to invoke the Document Properties dialog box (Modify ➪ Document or Ctrl+J or ⌘+J), or set the frame rate directly in the Property inspector.

Note   The fps setting is not a constant or absolute — it really means "maximum frame rate." The actual frame rate is dependent upon a number of variables, including download speed, processor speed, and machine resources — these are variables over which you have no control. However, another factor, over which you do have control, is the intensity of the animation: Complex movement with multiple elements or many layers of transparency is more processor intensive than simple movement. Previewing real-world playback speed at different frame rates — on various machines — early on in your development process is *very* important.

✦ **Elapsed Time:** This indicates the total movie time, measured in fps, which would elapse from frame 1 to the current frame — provided that the movie is played back at the optimal speed.

Editing frames and layers

After much heated debate among developers as to whether the frame selection and display behavior was better in Flash 4 or in Flash 5, Flash MX created the ultimate solution by combining the best of both. This hybrid system offers many useful options, but it may at first result in some confusion for new and experienced users alike. After you learn to recognize the visual conventions of the Timeline and how it displays different types of frames, you will be able to learn a lot about what is happening in an animation just by reading the Timeline. Figure 4-27 illustrates the MX 2004 conventions for frame and layer display.

The Timeline features noted in Figure 4-27 are defined as follows:

✦ **Keyframe:** A keyframe is any frame in which the contents of the frame may differ from the contents of either the previous or subsequent frames. Filled (black) circles on the Timeline mark keyframes with content.

✦ **Blank keyframe:** A keyframe that does not contain any content has the same behavior as any keyframe, but it is marked by an empty (white) circle on the Timeline.

✦ **Frame span:** Frame spans are the sections from a keyframe to an endframe (up to, but not including, the next keyframe to the right). Note that these spans can now be selected by double-clicking and dragged as a whole to a different location.

- **Filled frame(s):** The intermediate frames in a span, following to the right of a keyframe (with content), are shaded gray.

- **Empty frame(s):** The intermediate frames in a span, following to the right of a blank keyframe, are white. A black line also outlines the entire span.

- **Endframe:** The final frame of a span, marked with a small white rectangle and a vertical line to the right of the rectangle.

✦ **Frame-by-frame animation:** Frame-by-frame animation is animation composed entirely of keyframes. In a frame-by-frame animation, the content on every frame is changed manually (rather than tweened).

✦ **Tweened animation:** Tweened animation is movement or change in an element interpolated by Flash over a range of frames that extend between two keyframes. An arrow stretching across a colored frame span designates a tween, of which there are two varieties:

  • **Motion tweens:** Motion tweens are indicated by a blue tint and can be applied only to groups or symbols.

  • **Shape tweens:** Shape tweens are indicated by a green tint and can be applied only to primitive (non-grouped) shapes.

Cross-Reference

For more on making frame-by-frame animation and using tweens and Timeline Effects, refer to Chapter 11, "Timeline Animation and Effects."

✦ **Layer folder:** These folders are used to organize other layers and they can be named and repositioned in the layer stack the same way as layers. Layer folders do not have individual frame settings and thus show up in the Timeline display as a continuous gray bar. To expand (open) or collapse (close) folders, click the arrow toggle at the left of the folder name or use the contextual menu. Note that dragging a folder inside another folder creates subfolders.

✦ **Motion guide layer:** A Motion guide layer is used to guide an animated item along a vector path. For more about Motion guide layers, refer to Chapter 12, "Applying Layer Types."

✦ **Mask layer:** A Mask layer is a layer that is used to selectively obscure the layers beneath it. For more about Mask layers, refer to Chapter 12, "Applying Layer Types."

✦ **Label:** Labels are used to give frames meaningful names, rather than using frame numbers. The advantage of this is that named keyframes can be moved without breaking ActionScript calls assigned to them. Upon export, labels are included as part of the SWF. Use the field in the Property inspector to add a label to a selected frame. Press Enter/Return after typing a frame label or comment to ensure that the label takes.

✦ **Comment:** Comments are special labels, preceded by a double-slash (//). Comments do not export, so you can be as descriptive as you need to be without adding to the SWF size. However, you won't be able to read long comments unless you leave a lot of space between keyframes. Add comments in the Property inspector in the same way as labels; just be sure your text is preceded by two forward-slash characters.

New Feature

The Property inspector in Flash MX 2004 includes a new menu for selecting a frame text Type. After you type into the Frame text field, you can select from three options in the **Type** menu: **Name**, **Comment**, or **Anchor**. Note: A frame "name" is generally referred to as a *label*.

✦ **Waveform:** This squiggly blue line in the "sounds" layer is the waveform of a placed sound. This visual reference for your sound makes it easier to synchronize animated elements to a soundtrack.

✦ **Frame actions:** The small *a*s in frames 10, 20, and 58 of the "actions" layer designate the presence of frame actions.

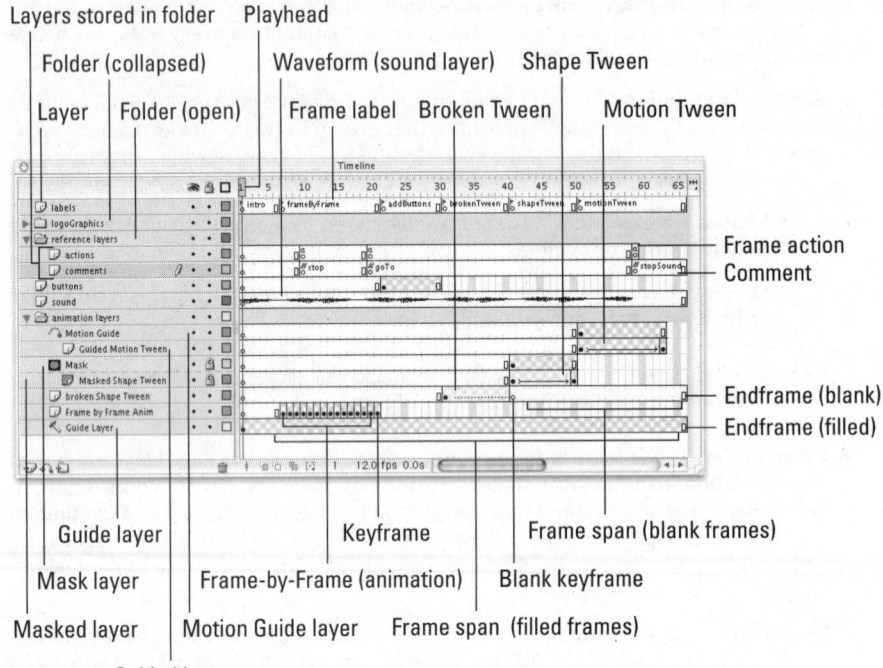

Figure 4-27: Flash MX 2004 conventions for naming and display of various frame and layer types

Frame specifics

Flash users familiar with previous versions may notice that in MX 2004, empty keyframes are marked with an empty circle (white dot), as they were in Flash 4. The last frame of a span is marked with the empty bar icon that was added in Flash 5. As always, keyframes with content are marked with a filled circle (black dot).

Flash MX 2004 offers the option of using either Flash 4 or Flash 5 frame-selection behavior. In Flash 4, individual frames could be selected just by clicking on them, even if they were part of a *span* (a series of frames following a keyframe). With Flash 5, span-based selection was intro-duced as the default behavior — all the frames in a span would be selected just by clicking one frame. In Flash MX (and MX 2004), the default went back to Flash 4 selection style, but double-clicking a frame selects a span. For the option of going back to the Flash 5 selection style, go to Edit ⇨ Preferences (or Flash ⇨ Preferences on OS X) and in the General section, under Timeline Options, select the **Span based selection** check box.

> **Note**
>
> Although double-clicking a frame in the default selection style will select a span of frames, if the span is moved, it will automatically extend along the Timeline until it meets another keyframe. This can be helpful or annoying depending on what you are trying to accomplish. With Span-based selection behavior enabled, when you relocate a span, it does not auto-extend and the original span length is preserved.

So that you can better understand the various frame-editing options available, we have listed them here with notes on the ways you can accomplish your intended result. Some of the methods differ depending on whether you have enabled Span-based selection as described previously. For users of previous versions of Flash, this may take a little getting used to. For new users, deciding on a preference will be a matter of testing out both selection style options. The default methods are listed here first, followed by the methods that differ when Span-based selection is turned on.

The default MX 2004 selection methods are as follows:

✦ **Selecting frames:** The methods for selecting single frames and spans of frames have been simplified since Flash 5.

- **Frame spans:** To select a span of frames extending between two keyframes, double-click anywhere between the keyframes.

- **Single frames:** To select a single frame within a span, or a keyframe outside of a span, simply click to select it.

- **Multiple frames or spans:** To select multiple frames along the Timeline (within a span or independent of a span), click and drag in any direction until you have selected all the frames you want to include in the selection. You can also use Shift+click to add to a selection of frames.

Note

The difference between selecting a frame by dragging over it, and moving a frame by selecting it and then dragging can be hard to differentiate. At first, you may find yourself moving frames that you only wanted to select. The trick is to be sure that you don't release the mouse after you click a frame before you drag to select other frames. Conversely, if your intention is to move a frame or a series of frames, you have to click and release the mouse to select them first and then click again and drag to move them.

✦ **Moving frames:** Select the frame(s) that need to be moved and then drag them to the new location.

✦ **Extending the duration of a span:** There are two ways to change the duration of a span, which is the same result as inserting frames (F5) or removing frames (Shift+F5) after a keyframe. To change where a span begins, select the keyframe and then drag the keyframe to the position where you want the span to begin. To change where a span ends, Ctrl+click or ⌘+click the endframe and drag it to where you want the span to end, or select a blank frame beyond the endframe where you want the span to end and insert a frame (F5) — this automatically extends the span and moves the endframe to the frame you have selected.

Note

If you click and drag any non-keyframe (frame or endframe) without pressing the Ctrl key (or the ⌘ key on Mac), the frame is automatically converted into a keyframe as it is dragged to the new location.

✦ **Copying frames:** Select the frame(s) that you want to copy. Choose Edit ➪ Timeline ➪ Copy Frames from the main menu and then Paste Frames into a new location, or press the Alt or Option key while clicking and dragging to copy selected frames to another location in the Timeline.

✦ **Pasting frames:** Select the frame where you want the copied or cut frames to be inserted (Flash automatically adds frames or layers below and to the right of the selected frame to accommodate the pasted content), and select Edit ➪ Timeline ➪ Paste Frames from the menu.

Caution   Edit ➪ Copy (Ctrl or ⌘+C) is not the same as Edit ➪ Timeline ➪ Copy Frames (Alt+Ctrl+C or Option+⌘+C). Using Copy will only "remember" and copy the content from a single keyframe, while Copy Frames "remembers" and copies content from multiple keyframes and even from multiple layers. To insert this content correctly in a new location, you have to remember to use the corresponding Paste commands: Paste (Ctrl+V or ⌘+V), or Paste Frames (Alt+Ctrl+V or Option+⌘+V). You may notice that the contextual menu offers only the plural options (Copy Frames or Paste Frames). This is because the plural command will safely work to move content from a single frame or from multiple frames. The singular command is just a simpler shortcut key to use if you know that you only want the content from one keyframe.

✦ **Inserting frames:** Select the point at which you would like to insert a new frame, and select Insert Frame (F5) from the contextual menu or from the application menu (Insert ➪ Frame). The visual "clue" that frames have been inserted is that the endframe of a span is moved to the right—this will also push any following keyframes further along the Timeline.

✦ **Inserting keyframes:** Select the point at which you would like to insert a new keyframe, and select Insert Keyframe (F6) from the contextual menu or from the application menu (Insert ➪ Timeline ➪ Keyframe). Note that keyframes can be inserted within a span without extending the span (or pushing the endframe to the right). Thus, inserting a keyframe actually converts an existing frame into a keyframe. So unlike frames, keyframes can be inserted without pushing other frames further down the Timeline.

✦ **Inserting blank keyframes:** Select the point at which you would like to insert a new blank keyframe, and select Insert Blank Keyframe (F7) from the contextual menu or from the application menu (Insert ➪ Timeline ➪ Blank Keyframe). Inserting a blank keyframe within a span clears all content along the Timeline until another keyframe is encountered.

Note   If you already have content in the current layer and you insert a keyframe, a new keyframe will be created that duplicates the content of the endframe immediately prior. But if you insert a blank keyframe, the content of the prior endframe will cease and the blank keyframe will, as its name implies, be void of content.

On the CD-ROM   For a hands-on example, refer to the file frames_example.fla in the ch04 folder of the CD-ROM that accompanies this book.

✦ **Removing frames (to shorten a span):** Select the frame(s) that you want to remove, and then choose Remove Frames (Shift+F5) from the contextual menu or from the application menu (Edit ➪ Timeline ➪ Remove Frames). This does not work for removing keyframes; instead, it will remove a frame from the span to the right of the keyframe, causing all the following frames to move back toward frame 1.

✦ **Clearing a keyframe:** To remove a keyframe and its contents, select the keyframe and choose Clear Keyframe (Shift+F6) from the contextual menu or from the application menu (Modify ➪ Timeline ➪ Clear Keyframe). When a keyframe is cleared, the span of the previous keyframe is extended to fill all frames until the next keyframe on the Timeline. The same thing happens if you insert a keyframe in a span and then Undo it (Ctrl+Z or ⌘+Z). Apply Undo (Edit ➪ Undo) twice—the first Undo deselects the keyframe, and the second Undo clears it.

✦ **Cutting frames (leaves blank frames or keyframes):** To replace selected frames in a span with blank frames, while keeping content in the remainder of the span intact, select the frame(s) you want to "blank" and then choose Cut Frames (Alt+Ctrl+X on Windows or Option+⌘+X on Mac) from the contextual menu or from the application menu (Edit ➪ Timeline ➪ Cut Frames). This "pulls" the content out of only the selected frames, without interrupting content in surrounding frames or shifting any keyframes on the Timeline. The content that you cut can be pasted into another position on the Timeline (as described previously).

Caution

Selecting a frame or keyframe and using the Delete key will remove the content from the entire span, but will not remove the keyframe itself, or change the length of the span. You can delete content from multiple layers this way, but it will leave all the empty frames and keyframes on the Timeline.

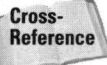

New Feature

Flash MX 2004 includes a new command called **Clear Frames** (Alt+Delete or Option+ Delete). This is a flexible command that will eliminate the content on a selected frame, keyframe, or span of frames without changing the number of frames in a span. If you select a keyframe and apply Clear Frames, the keyframe will be cleared and the content of the keyframe will be removed. If you select a normal frame and apply Clear Frames, the selected frame will be converted into a blank keyframe to eliminate the content in that frame while preserving the content in other frames within the same span. This command is also listed in the contextual menu and in the application menu under Edit ➪ Timeline ➪ Clear Frames.

✦ **Editing the contents of a keyframe:** Select the keyframe where you want to edit content. This moves the playhead to the selected frame so that its content is visible in the Document window, where it can be edited. Note that if you edit content on a keyframe or frame within a span, the changes will apply to the current frame and the span it is part of.

Cross-Reference

Numerous techniques for editing content are detailed in later chapters of this book that address specific types of content. For the most relevant information, look for chapters that describe the types of content you are working with—vector art, bitmaps, sound, video, and so on.

The span-based selection methods are as follows:

✦ **Frame spans:** To select a span of frames extending between two keyframes, simply click anywhere between the keyframes.

✦ **Single frames within a span:** To select a single frame within a span, press the Ctrl key (on Windows) or the ⌘ key (on Mac) and click a frame. Keyframes or endframes can usually be selected with a simple click.

✦ **Single frames not within a span:** To select a single frame that is not implicated with a span, simply click to select it.

✦ **Multiple frames or spans:** To select multiple frames along the Timeline (within a span or independent of a span), use Shift+click to add to a selection of the frames.

Figure 4-28 shows a Timeline that illustrates some editing points. The top layer shows the "original" layer, with content starting on a keyframe on frame 1, followed by a span of 19 frames, putting the endframe on frame 20. This layer was copied into all three lower layers, with the result that the initial content of all four layers was the same. When a frame was inserted at frame 10 of the "insert frame" layer, the content was extended, pushing the end-frame of the span to frame 21. When a keyframe was inserted at frame 10 of the "insert keyframe" layer, the content was maintained in the new keyframe, but the span was not extended, as indicated by the gray filled frames in the span from frame 10 to frame 20. When a blank keyframe was inserted at frame 10 of the "insert blank keyframe" layer, the content was cleared following the new blank keyframe, as indicated by the white frames extending from frame 10 to frame 20.

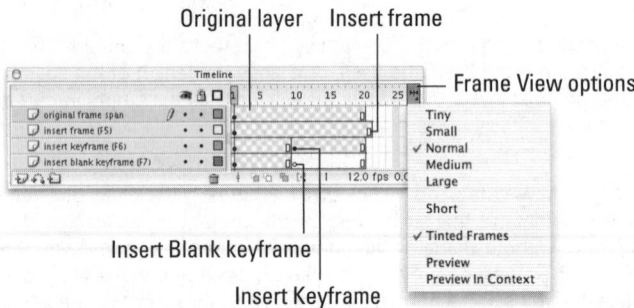

Figure 4-28: Editing on the Timeline

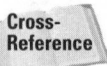

Cross-Reference

For more information about how frames are used to author and control animation, refer to Chapter 11, "Timeline Animation and Effects."

Layer specifics

Knowing how to work with layers makes all the difference between a well-ordered project and a chaotic mess of elements that you may never be able to sort out if you have to come back to edit later on. The necessity of a logical folder structure and consistent naming conventions is even more crucial in a team environment, where someone else may have to try to find her way around in your document. Like most good production habits, this may seem like extra work at first, but over time it pays off. As your projects get more complex and your archive of Flash documents grows, the few additional steps taken early on will be invaluable down the road.

Being organized doesn't mean you have to always put every layer into a folder, but rather that you just try to find the most efficient way of keeping track of where you've placed different elements. To make it easier to remember what content is on different layers it's a good habit to give your layers meaningful names. It can also be helpful to use consistent abbreviations that help you to recognize what type of content is described by the name (such as "MC" for Movie Clip or "Anim" for animation). To edit a layer name, simply double-click the layer's name on the Layer bar and type into the text field.

Tip   With all Flash projects in our studio, we begin the layer structure by creating three layers titled "actions," "labels," and "functions" — these are always kept at the top of the layer stack. On projects that we want to document very carefully, we also add a "comments" layer where the type of action or function added on the other layers can be noted. Although these layers don't hold content that is visible on the Stage, they make it easy to quickly find any actions placed on the Timeline and to see labels and comments that give an indication of how the movie is structured.

Cross-Reference   For detailed methods and suggestions on organizing Flash documents, see Chapter 20, "Making Your First Flash MX 2004 Project," and Chapter 32, "Creating a Portfolio site in Flash."

By default, new layers are stacked on top of the currently active layer. To rearrange layers, click in the area between the layer name and the layer toggle icons, and drag the Layer bar to the desired position in the layer stack and release. To move layers into a folder, click and drag the Layer bar onto any layer with a folder icon. To move a layer back out of a folder, drag it to a position above the folder name bar or below all the other layers contained in the folder.

The Layers contextual menu

Because many of the controls for layer options are built into the Timeline window, layer properties are one of the few attributes that are not displayed in the Property inspector (frame properties are visible when any layer is selected). The contextual menu (right-click on Windows or Control+click on Mac) provides convenient access to most of the commands you will need when editing layers — including commands otherwise found in the Layer Properties dialog box or in the application menu:

- ✦ **Show All:** Shows all layers. If some layers have had their visibility turned off, this makes them all visible.

- ✦ **Lock Others:** Unlocks the active layer and locks all other layers.

- ✦ **Hide Others:** Makes the currently active layer visible, if it is not visible, and hides all others.

- ✦ **Insert Layer:** Inserts a new layer above the currently active layer with an auto-numbered name that continues the number sequence of existing layers and folders.

- ✦ **Delete Layer:** Deletes the active layer and all content stored on that layer.

- ✦ **Guide:** Transforms the current layer into a Guide layer — a reference layer that will only be visible in the authoring environment (FLA).

- ✦ **Add Motion Guide:** Inserts a new Motion guide layer directly above the current layer and automatically converts the current layer into a guided layer.

Note   A Guide layer differs from a Motion guide layer. A Motion guide layer is linked to a guided layer, which usually contains a tweened animation that follows a path drawn on the Motion guide layer. A Guide layer is not linked to a guided layer and is most often used for placing a bitmap design composition, or other items used for design reference that should not be visible in the final movie (SWF). Neither Guide layers nor Motion guide layers export with the project.

✦ **Mask:** Transforms the current layer into a Mask layer.

✦ **Show Masking:** Use this command on either the Mask or the masked layer to activate the masking effect — essentially, this command locks both layers simultaneously, which makes the masking effect visible.

✦ **Insert Folder:** Inserts a new folder above the currently active layer or folder with an auto-numbered name that continues the number sequence of existing layers and folders.

✦ **Delete Folder:** Deletes the currently active folder, along with all the layers stored in that folder.

✦ **Expand Folder:** Opens the current folder to make any layers stored inside visible in the layer stack and on the Timeline.

✦ **Collapse Folder:** Closes the current folder to hide any layers stored in the folder. The elements existing on these stored layers will still be visible in the Document window and in the movie (SWF), but the keyframe rows will not show up along the Timeline.

✦ **Expand All Folders:** Opens all folders to show any stored layers visible in the layer stack and on the Timeline.

✦ **Collapse All Folders:** Closes all folders to hide any layers that have been placed in folders. The elements existing on these stored layers will still be visible in the Document window and in the movie (SWF), but the keyframe rows will not show up along the Timeline.

✦ **Properties:** Invokes the Layer Properties dialog box for the currently active layer. The Layer Properties dialog box can also be invoked directly by double-clicking the "page" icon or the colored square icon on any layer, and is always available in the application menu (Modify ⇨ Timeline ⇨ Layer Properties).

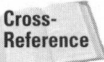
Cross-Reference   For in-depth coverage of using layer types, refer to Chapter 12, "Applying Layer Types."

Using Frame View options

The main place to find options for controlling the appearance of the Timeline within the window is in the submenu available from the Frame View options button, shown in Figure 4-28. This is sometimes referred to as the "train track button" because the icon looks similar to the symbol used on maps to show railroads.

As noted previously, the Frame View options menu is used to customize the size, color, and style of frames displayed within the Timeline. These features can prove very helpful when you're working with cartoon animation and want to see each frame previewed. Or, if you're working on an extremely long project with a huge Timeline, it can be helpful to tweak the size of the individual frames, so that you can see more of the Timeline in the Timeline window.

When used in conjunction with the Layer Height option of the Layer Properties dialog box, you can customize your Timeline display in several ways to better suit your particular project. Your options include:

✦ **Tiny, Small, Normal, Medium, Large:** These options afford a range of sizes for the width of individual frames. When working on extremely long animations, narrower frames facilitate some operations. Wider frames can make it easier to select individual frames and to read frame labels or comments.

✦ **Short:** This option makes the frames shorter in height, permitting more layers to be visible in the same amount of space. When working with many layers or folders, short layers help speed the process of scrolling through the stack.

✦ **Tinted Frames:** This option toggles tinted frames on or off. With Tinted Frames on, the tints are as follows:

- **White:** Empty or unused frames (for any layer). This is the default. The white color of empty or unused frames is unaffected regardless of whether Tinted Frames is on or off.

- **Gray:** There are two kinds of gray frames: (a) The evenly spaced gray stripes in the default (empty) Timeline are a quick visual reference that indicates every fifth frame, like the tick marks on a ruler. These stripes appear regardless of whether Tinted Frames are enabled. (b) The solid gray color with a black outline, which appears when Tinted Frames are enabled, indicates that a frame contains content, even if it isn't visible on the Stage.

- **Blue:** Indicates a Motion tween span.

- **Green:** Indicates a Shape tween span.

Note   Regardless of whether Tinted Frames is enabled, Flash displays tween arrows (and keyframe dots) across a tween. However, with Tinted Frames disabled, tweened spans are indicated by colored arrows that also show the type of tween.

- **A red arrow:** Indicates a Motion tween, when Tinted Frames are off.

- **A green arrow:** Indicates a Shape tween, when Tinted Frames are off.

✦ **Preview:** As shown in composite Figure 4-29, the preview option displays tiny thumbnails that maximize the element in each frame. Thus, the scale of elements is not consistent from frame to frame.

✦ **Preview in Context:** As shown in the lower frame preview of composite Figure 4-29, when previewed in context, the same animation is seen with accurate scale from frame to frame (because elements are not maximized for each frame).

Note   The preview in frames option only shows content in keyframes. Thus, if you use this option to view a tweened animation, you will only see images displayed on the Timeline for the first and last frames of the animation.

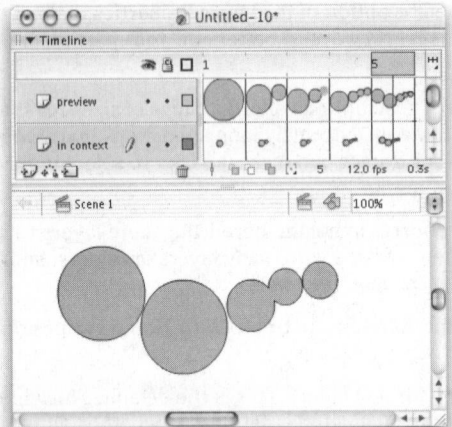

Figure 4-29: In this composite screenshot, the Timeline is displayed with the two preview options—**Preview** (top) and **Preview in Context** (middle)—for the same frame-by-frame animation sequence (bottom).

Printing

Although Flash is considered a Web and animation program, it fully supports printed output. The functionality and specific dialog boxes vary slightly from the Mac to the PC—while other variations are subject to which printers and printer drivers are installed on your machine. The File ➪ Page Setup dialog box is the most standard aspect of the program and the choices for paper size, margins, center positioning, and orientation are pretty intuitive.

However, the options available in the Layout area of the Page Setup dialog box on Windows or in the Print Margins dialog box on Mac (File ➪ Print Margins) deserve a little more attention. The options here are:

✦ **Frames:** Use this drop-down menu to choose to print either All Frames of the animation or the ecological default, which is to print the First Frame Only.

✦ **Layout:** There are three basic options:

 • **Actual Size:** This prints the Frame at full size, subject to the accompanying Scale setting: At what scale do you want to print your frames? Enter a percentage.

 • **Fit on One Page:** This automatically reduces or enlarges the Frame so that it fills the maximum printable area, without distortion.

 • **Storyboard:** This enables you to print several thumbnails per page in the following arrangements: Boxes, Grid, or Blank. There are accompanying settings for Frames Across, Frame Margin, and Label Frames. This is a great tool for circulating comps and promotional materials.

Tip   When printing Storyboard layouts, use File ➪ Print Preview on Windows (or File ➪ Print ➪ Preview on Mac) to ensure optimal results.

✦ **Print Margins** (Mac only): Note the Disable PostScript check box. When printing single large areas of color surrounded by complex borders, problems may occur on PostScript printers. If you encounter such problems, try using the Disable PostScript check box in the Mac Print Margins dialog box (Edit ➪ Print Margins) or in the Windows Preferences dialog box (Edit ➪ Preferences ➪ General ➪ Printing Options). Otherwise, divide the complex area into several simpler areas and use the Modify commands (Modify ➪ Shape ➪ Smooth/Straighten/Optimize) to reduce the complexity of these areas (which may, however, drastically alter your artwork — so save first!).

✦ **Print Preview:** On Windows, use the Print Preview command to see an onscreen preview of how the printed output looks, based upon the options you've chosen in the Page Setup dialog box. On Macintosh, the Preview button is found in the Print dialog box (File ➪ Print) and will generate a PDF to give a preview of how the final page looks, based upon the options you've chosen in the Print Margins dialog box.

✦ **Print:** Just print it! (The Mac option for Preview is found here as well.)

✦ **Send** (PC only): This command invokes the default e-mail client so that you can readily send the Flash file as an attachment.

It is important to note that the Document background color (or Stage color) will not be included on printed output. If you want the background color to appear in your printed output, you must create a filled rectangle of the color that you want in the background and place it on a layer behind the other elements. The printer will then recognize this as artwork and include it in the output.

Summary

✦ Flash MX 2004 retains the familiar interface of Flash MX, while making room for some additional authoring tools and enhanced features.

✦ Although Flash is now available in two versions, the interface is consistent between Flash MX 2004 and Flash MX Professional 2004. Flash MX 2004 will support all of the authoring tasks that were possible in Flash MX. Flash MX Professional 2004 offers some additional templates, components, and specialized features that support development of rich Internet applications.

✦ The new Start Page and robust Help features get you started quickly, while the options for saving custom panel sets and custom keyboard shortcut sets makes it easy to optimize your workspace for specific production needs.

✦ The Property inspector and the streamlined panel structure make the interface intuitive and consistent with other programs in the Studio MX 2004 family.

✦ Layer folders and the expanded frame-editing options make it easy to organize and navigate your document structure.

✦ Although Flash is mainly used to produce Web content, it fully supports printed output.

✦ If you need a quick reminder on any of the fundamental interface elements, this chapter will be your reference.

Now that you know where to find your main tools and how to get comfortable in your workspace, you should be feeling more at home in your Flash MX 2004 studio. So it's time to get down to the business of *creating*.

✦　　　✦　　　✦

Drawing in Flash

This chapter introduces the primary tools for creating and manipulating vector graphics in Flash, as well as some features of the Flash environment that affect how elements behave. The primary drawing tools have nearly self-explanatory names: the Line, Oval, Rectangle, PolyStar, Pencil, Brush, and Eraser. However, these tools all have a variety of options and modifiers that make them more sophisticated than they may at first appear. In this chapter, you learn to apply the primary options of these tools to create shapes and line art.

The selection tools — Selection (arrow), Lasso, and Subselect — are found in the top section of the Tools panel and these work as your "hands" within the drawing space of Flash, enabling you to select elements or grab and adjust specific parts of a shape or line.

The Pen is a powerful tool that draws lines by laying down editable points. Both the Pen and Subselect tools are used to manipulate the points, and can also be used to select and edit all lines and shapes to manually optimize artwork.

The built-in shape-creation tools of Flash and the adjustable shape-recognition settings make it easy even for people who "can't draw a straight line" to create usable elements for Flash interfaces.

In addition to drawing, in this chapter, you also learn to apply some of the terrific tools Flash provides to help you organize and align elements as you create layouts.

Cross-Reference If you're comfortable using the core Flash drawing tools and design panels, you can skip to Chapter 9, "Modifying Graphics" for a deeper look into the options available for editing artwork, including the Free Transform tool, the Envelope modifier, and the exciting new Commands feature that can be used to record and repeat authoring steps.

The primary drawing tools — Line, Oval, Rectangle, PolyStar, Pencil, Brush, and Eraser — can be divided into two groups: geometric shapes and freehand lines and strokes. Line, Oval, Rectangle, and the new PolyStar tool fall into the first category; Pencil, Brush, and Eraser fall into the second. The PolyStar tool is a valuable Flash MX 2004 addition to the default Tools panel. You can find it in the Rectangle tool submenu and use it to create a variety of shapes, from triangles to fancy starbursts.

✦   ✦   ✦   ✦

In This Chapter

Using shape and drawing tools

Setting Brush and Eraser modes

Creating optimized lines and curves

Choosing fill and stroke styles

Using selection tools and options

Controlling snapping behavior

Aligning, scaling, and rotating artwork

Knowing the Edit menu commands

✦   ✦   ✦   ✦

Note   By default, Flash loads a blue fill color and a black 1-pixel stroke. These are sufficient to get started with any of the drawing tools, but many more inspiring choices are introduced in the "Using Fill and Stroke Controls" section, later in this chapter.

Using Geometric Shape Tools

The prebuilt geometric shapes available for creating graphics in Flash are easy to access from the Tools panel. The Line, Oval, and Rectangle tools are straightforward but infinitely useful. The PolyStar tool creates a wide variety of geometric shapes defined by the Tool Settings dialog box—available from the Options button in the Property inspector. Custom stroke styles and the various fill options (described later in this chapter), can be used with these basic shapes to create nearly any graphic you may need. Geometric shapes are already optimized and can be combined or modified in multiple ways to create more complex artwork.

Note   In other parts of this book, the term *primitive shape* is used to refer to any shape that is not grouped or converted into a symbol. Creating and using symbols is covered in Chapter 6, "Symbols, Instances and the Library."

The Line tool

Drawing with the Line tool (N) creates a perfectly straight line that extends from a starting point to an endpoint, simply by clicking a start position and dragging to the end position before releasing the mouse. Just select the Line tool in the Tools panel and start drawing in the Document window. You can select various Line styles and stroke heights from the Property inspector, as well as set the color with the pop-up Color Swatches panel accessible from the Stroke color chip on either the Property inspector or the Tools panel. The various options for Line styles and colors are described later in this chapter. Snapping settings and Guides can be used to help control where a line is placed and how precisely it connects to other lines. The Line tool conforms to the snapping settings described later in this chapter, in the "Simplifying snapping settings" section.

Tip   To restrict the line to 45-degree-angle increments, hold down the Shift key as you drag out the line.

Figure 5-1 shows how a line previews as you drag, and how it appears when the mouse is released and the current line style and stroke height settings are applied.

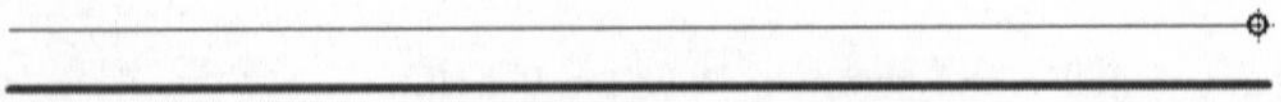

Figure 5-1: Line tool preview (top) and the final line (bottom), displayed when the mouse button is released

The Oval tool

Drawing with the Oval tool (O) creates a perfectly smooth oval. Ovals are drawn by clicking and then dragging diagonally from one "corner" of the oval to the other—dragging more vertically creates a taller oval, whereas dragging more horizontally creates a wider oval.

Tip
To constrain the shape to a perfect circle, hold down the Shift key before releasing the mouse.

The Oval tool has no unique options, but it can be filled with any of the fill colors available in the Color Swatches panel (described in the "Choosing Colors" section later in this chapter) as well as "outlined" with any of the stroke styles or colors. Figure 5-2 shows some of the huge variety of shapes you can create using the Oval tool with different stroke and fill settings.

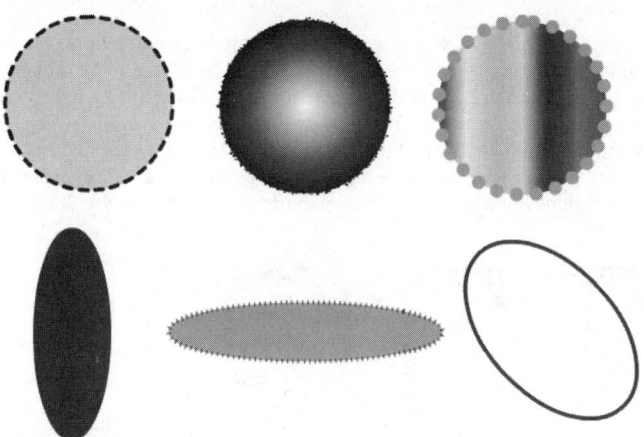

Figure 5-2: Shapes created with the Oval tool, using different stroke and fill settings

The Rectangle tool

The Rectangle tool (R) creates perfect rectangles, which means that all four sides are parallel, regardless of the length or width of the shape. Draw rectangles by clicking to place a starting corner and then dragging toward the opposite corner of your shape until you have the size and shape that you want.

Tip
To constrain the rectangle to a perfect square, hold down the Shift key before releasing the mouse.

Aside from choosing the stroke and fill to apply to a shape drawn with the Rectangle tool, an option on the Tools panel launches the Rectangle Settings dialog box for choosing the radius for corners on the rectangle. The radius is set to 0 pt by default, to create rectangles with square or 90 degree corners. The maximum radius setting is 999 pt, but anything higher than 35 pt produces almost the same kind of shape as the Oval tool, unless the shape is drawn very large, or elongated to create the classic "pill button" shape.

Tip
A quick way to launch the Rectangle Settings dialog box is to double-click the Rectangle tool button in the Tools panel.

Caution   The Round Rectangle Radius button is not a toggle, so if you change the radius setting, you have to set it back to 0 in the Rectangle Settings dialog box to return to drawing standard rectangles.

Choosing a more moderate radius setting creates rounded rectangles or squares with softened corners (see Figure 5-3). You'll want to choose this setting before you create a shape with the Rectangle tool because the radius cannot be reapplied or easily modified after the shape is drawn.

Tip   To adjust the corner radius while you're dragging out your rectangle shape, there is a handy shortcut. Before you release the mouse, use the Up arrow key (↑) to decrease the radius setting (making the corners more square), or use the Down arrow key (↓) to increase the radius setting (making the corners more rounded). The relationship between the arrow keys and the radius settings is counter-intuitive, but just think "Up arrow = more square, Down arrow = less square." After you release the mouse, the radius setting will stick and the arrow keys will go back to their usual behavior of moving selected items up or down on the Stage.

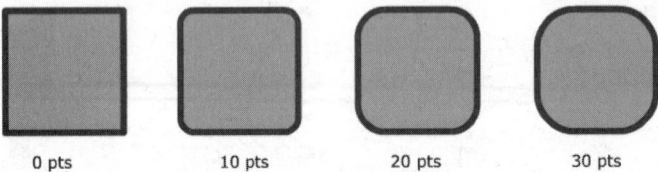

0 pts   10 pts   20 pts   30 pts

Figure 5-3: Rectangles drawn with different radius settings create different degrees of roundness on the corners.

The PolyStar tool

We can't count the number of times we've had to modify a rectangle manually just to create a simple triangle in Flash — fortunately, Flash MX 2004 offers a painless way to create a variety of geometric shapes! The PolyStar tool is so named because it is a multipurpose tool that can make polygons and stars. If you're using the default Tools set in Flash MX 2004, you'll find the PolyStar as a subset of the Rectangle tool — click and hold your mouse over the Rectangle button on the Tools panel to invoke the drop-down menu with the PolyStar tool as shown in Figure 5-4.

Note   The PolyStar tool does not have a shortcut key assigned to it, but the shortcut key for the Rectangle tool (R) will always activate the Rectangle tool, even if the PolyStar tool is visible in the Tools panel because it was the last tool used from that Tools panel location.

When the PolyStar tool is active, an Options button appears in the Property inspector to invoke a Tool Settings dialog box that enables you to control the type of shape you want to draw. The composite in Figure 5-5 includes the Property inspector as it appears when the PolyStar tool is active and the Tool Settings dialog box with the two shape styles available: polygon or star. You can set the number of sides for either shape by entering a value between 3 and 32 in the Number of Sides field. As shown at the top of Figure 5-5, a polygon with three sides is a triangle and a star with three sides is...the beginnings of a Mercedes logo, perhaps?

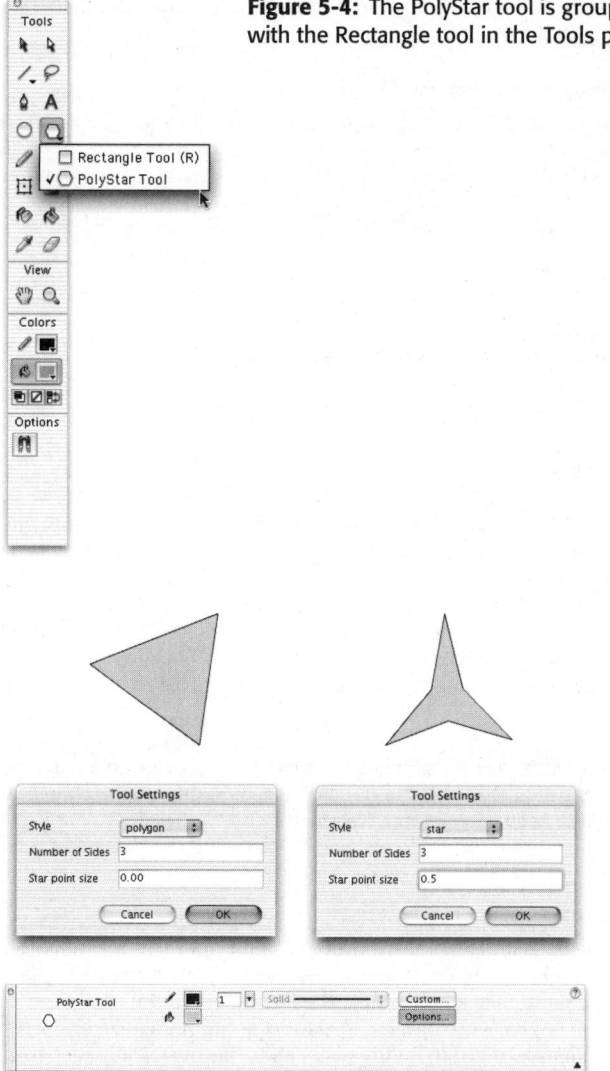

Figure 5-4: The PolyStar tool is grouped with the Rectangle tool in the Tools panel.

Figure 5-5: A composite figure showing the Options button in the Property inspector (bottom) that launches the Tool Settings dialog box (center), used to create different shape styles (top)

The fields in the Tool Settings dialog box look the same whether you select polygon or star in the Style menu, but Star point size does not affect polygon shapes. If you are drawing a star, enter any number between 0 and 1 to control the depth of the star points. This might not look like much of a range, but you can enter decimal numbers, so you actually have 99 possible settings! As shown in Figure 5-6, numbers closer to 0 create sharper stars and numbers closer to 1 create blockier shapes.

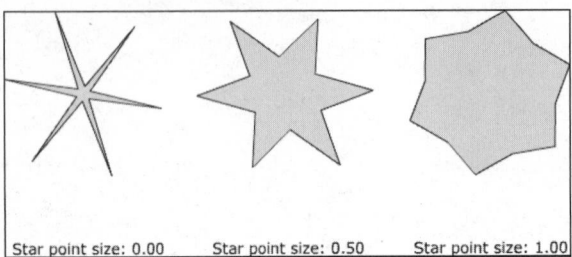

Star point size: 0.00   Star point size: 0.50   Star point size: 1.00

Figure 5-6: Star point size settings between 0 and 1 create various star shapes.

Using Drawing Tools

The tools for drawing freehand lines and strokes in Flash come with options for applying different combinations of line processing and shape recognition. So, what does that mean exactly? These are general terms for a class of options that can be set to assist accurate drawing and manipulation of basic shapes. These options can be applied dynamically as you draw with the Pencil or Brush tool or applied cumulatively to an item selected with the Selection tool to clean up a shape or line that you've already drawn. These are some of the Flash assistants that can help even a drafting-challenged designer create sharp-looking graphics with ease.

Note   The biggest challenge of drawing in Flash is finding a happy medium between the degree of line variation and complexity required to get the graphic look you want, and the optimization and file size that you need to keep your artwork Web-friendly.

The Pencil tool

The Pencil tool is used to draw lines and shapes. At first glance, it operates much like a real pencil. You can use the Pencil tool with different line styles as you draw a freeform shape. But a deeper examination reveals that, unlike a real pencil, the Flash Pencil tool can be set to straighten lines and smooth curves as you draw. It can also be set to recognize or correct basic geometric shapes. For example, a crude lumpy oval can be automatically recognized and processed into a true, or *perfect,* oval. These shapes and lines can be modified further after they've been drawn using the Selection and Subselect tools.

When the Pencil tool is active, one option appears in the Tools panel. This is actually a button for the Pencil Mode pop-up menu, which sets the Pencil tool's current drawing mode. The three modes, or drawing styles, for the Pencil are: Straighten, Smooth, and Ink. These settings control the way that line processing occurs as you draw.

Figure 5-7 shows the same freehand drawing done with the different Pencil modes. The drawing on the left was done with the Straighten mode, the drawing in the middle was done with Smooth mode, and the drawing on the right was done with Ink mode. As you can see, each mode is more effective for certain types of lines and shapes. To create a pleasing finished result, you'll most likely use different Pencil modes when working on individual elements of your drawing.

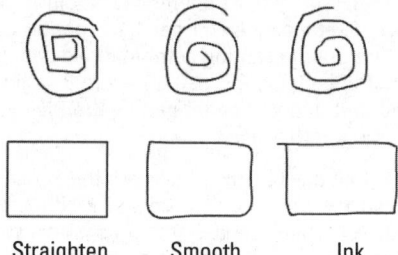

Straighten   Smooth   Ink

Figure 5-7: Similar sketches made using the three different Pencil modes to show how line processing affects various shapes. Straighten (left), Smooth (center), and Ink (right).

Straighten

Drawing with the Straighten option processes your drawings while taking into account both line and shape recognition. This means that nearly straight lines are straightened, and wobbly curves are smoothed. Approximate geometric shapes, such as ovals, rectangles, and triangles are recognized and automatically adjusted.

Smooth

Drawing with the Smooth option reduces the zeal with which Flash automatically processes your drawings. With the Smooth option, line straightening and shape recognition are not applied, but curved lines are smoothed. Additionally, a line that ends near another line is joined automatically, if the **Connect Lines** tolerance is set to **Can be Distant**.

Ink

Drawing with the Ink option turns off all line processing. Lines remain as you've drawn them. Your lines are *not* smoothed, straightened, or joined.

The Brush tool

The Brush tool is used to create smooth or tapered marks and to fill enclosed areas. Unlike the Pencil tool, which creates a single, solid line, the Brush tool actually creates marks using filled shapes. The fills can be solid colors, gradients, or fills derived from bitmaps. Because the Brush paints only with a fill, the Stroke color chip does not apply to the marks drawn with the brush. The Brush tool is especially well suited for artwork created using a drawing tablet. A number of settings and options are available when the Brush tool is active, giving you precise control over the type of marks that it makes.

Adjusting Drawing Settings

The degree to which shape recognition processes your drawings as you create them with the Pencil may be adjusted with the Drawing Settings found in Edit ➪ Preferences ➪ Editing (or Flash ➪ Preferences ➪ Editing). By default, all the Drawing Settings are Normal. Each option can be adjusted to make it more specific or more general. The optimal setting combinations depend on the style of drawing that you're trying to achieve, but in general, the default Normal settings for these controls really only need to be adjusted if you find that you aren't getting the look you want using the Straighten, Smooth, or Ink modes with the Pencil tool.

You can also choose to further simplify lines and shapes that have been drawn with the Pencil in Ink mode by using the Selection tool to select what you've drawn and then using either the Smooth or Straighten modifiers. Or, for maximum control, manually edit extraneous points with either the Pen or the Subselect tool (as described in the Pen and Subselect sections later in this chapter). Here are the various Drawing Settings and options available in Preferences:

✦ **Connect Lines:** The Connect Lines setting adjusts how close lines or points have to be to each other before Flash automatically connects them into a continuous line or shape. This setting also controls how close to horizontal or vertical a line has to be for Flash to set it at an exact angle. The options are **Must be Close**, **Normal**, and **Can be Distant**. This setting also controls how close elements need to be to snap together when Snap to Objects is turned on.

✦ **Smooth Curves:** Smooth Curves simplifies the number of points used to draw a curve when the Pencil is in Straighten or Smooth mode. Smoother curves are easier to reshape and are more optimized, whereas rougher curves will more closely resemble the original lines drawn. The options are **Off**, **Rough**, **Normal**, and **Smooth**.

✦ **Recognize Lines:** This setting controls how precise a line has to be for Flash to recognize it as a straight line and automatically align it. The options are **Off**, **Strict**, **Normal**, and **Tolerant**.

✦ **Recognize Shapes:** This setting controls how accurately you have to draw basic geometric shapes and 90-degree or 180-degree arcs for them to be recognized and corrected by Flash. The options are **Off**, **Strict**, **Normal**, and **Tolerant**.

✦ **Click Accuracy:** Click accuracy determines how close to an element the cursor has to be for Flash to recognize it. The settings are **Strict**, **Normal**, and **Tolerant**.

These drawing settings do not modify the Straighten and Smooth options for the Selection tool, which only reduce point complexity with each application to a shape or line that has already been drawn.

New Feature   In response to feedback from animators who draw directly in Flash, Macromedia has added more precise drawing controls for the Brush tool. In Flash MX 2004, you will notice a Smoothing setting in the Property inspector when the Brush tool is active. Use the value field or the slider menu to select a Smoothing setting between 0.25 and 100. The default value is 50, which was the built-in setting for Flash MX. Values closer to 0.25 add more points to the shape as you draw and make more precise strokes. Values closer to 100 add fewer points to the shape and create "looser" strokes. You can use the Smoothing setting whether you are drawing on a tablet or with your mouse.

The Brush mode menu

The Brush tool includes options for controlling exactly where the fill is applied. The Brush mode option menu reveals five painting modes that are amazingly useful for a wide range of effects when applying the Brush tool: Paint Normal, Paint Fills, Paint Behind, Paint Selection, and Paint Inside, as shown in Figure 5-8.

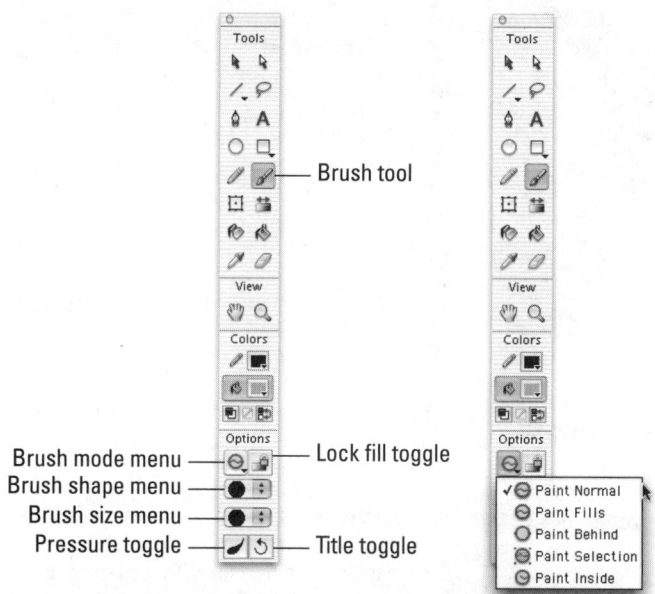

Brush tool

Brush mode menu ——— Lock fill toggle
Brush shape menu ———
Brush size menu ———
Pressure toggle ——— Title toggle

Paint Normal
Paint Fills
Paint Behind
Paint Selection
Paint Inside

Figure 5-8: The Brush tool and options (left); the Brush mode settings menu (right)

The following images depict various ways in which the Brush modes interact with drawn and painted elements. The base image is a solid white rectangle drawn with a black outline. The boat outline is drawn with the Pencil tool in dark gray on top of the rectangle.

Caution

Painting with the background color (such as white) is not the same as erasing. Although painting with a background color may appear to accomplish something similar to erasing, you are, in fact, creating a filled item that can be selected, moved, edited, deleted, and erased. Even if you can't see it, it adds to your file size. Only erasing erases!

Paint Normal mode

Paint Normal mode, shown in Figure 5-9, applies brush strokes over the top of any lines or fills.

Paint Fills mode

Paint Fills mode, shown in Figure 5-10, applies brush strokes to replace any fills, but leaves lines untouched.

Figure 5-9: In Paint Normal mode, a dark-gray brush mark covers all elements: background, outline, fill, and drawn lines.

Figure 5-10: In Paint Fills mode, a dark-gray brush mark covers the white background and fill without painting over any of the lines.

Paint Behind mode

Paint Behind mode applies brush strokes only to blank areas and leaves all fills, lines, or other items untouched. As shown in Figure 5-11, the only areas the brush mark covers are those in the background, outside the frame of the picture. Effectively, the brush has gone behind the entire shape. If the stroke had originated within the frame, it would have covered the white fill and gone behind the drawn gray lines and the black outline.

Figure 5-11: In Paint Behind mode, the gray brush mark is only visible on the background outside the frame because it has gone behind the white fill and the lines.

Paint Selection mode

Paint Selection mode applies brush strokes only to selected fills. In Figure 5-12, a selection was made by Shift+clicking both the white fill inside the boat and inside the sail. The same gray brush marks drawn on the previous figure are now visible only inside the selected fills.

Paint Inside mode

Paint Inside mode, shown in Figure 5-13, applies brush strokes only to the singular fill area where the brush stroke was first initiated. As the name implies, Paint Inside never paints over lines. If you initiate painting from an empty area, the brush strokes won't affect any existing fills or lines, which approximates the same effect as the Paint Behind setting.

Figure 5-12: With Paint Selection mode, only the selected white fills have been covered by the brush marks.

Figure 5-13: With Paint Inside mode, the brush marks only cover the area where the stroke is first started. Lines separate the white fills inside the sail and the boat shape from the background where the stroke was initiated, so those areas are not painted.

The Lock Fill option is common to both the Brush tool and the Paint Bucket tool (which is discussed in Chapter 9). Although similar to Stroke height and style, the Brush size and Brush shape settings are unique to the Brush tool.

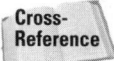

Cross-Reference   For coverage of using the Lock Fill option with the Brush tool and the Paint Bucket tool, refer to Chapter 9, "Modifying Graphics."

In Flash, the size of applied brush marks is always related to the Zoom setting. Therefore, using the same brush diameter creates different sized brush marks depending on what Zoom setting you work with in the Document window (see Figure 5-14). You could paint over your whole stage in one stroke even with a small brush diameter, if your Zoom was at a low setting such as 8 percent. Or you could use a large brush diameter to make detailed lines if your Zoom was at a high setting such as 1500 percent.

Figure 5-14: Marks made using the same brush size applied with the View at different percentages of Zoom

The Brush Shape option is a drop-down menu with nine possible brush shapes that are based on the circle, ellipse, square, rectangle, and line shapes. (Refer to Figure 5-8.) The oval, rectangle, and line shapes are available in various angles. You can combine these stock brush shapes with the range of brush sizes available in the Brush Size menu to generate a wide variety of brush tips. When using shapes other than circles, note that the diameter sizes chosen in the Brush Size menu apply to the broadest area of any brush shape.

Brush options for drawing tablets

If you use a pressure-sensitive tablet for drawing, two extra options appear in the Tools panel when the Brush tool is active. (The Pressure and Tilt toggles are shown at the bottom of the Tools panel in Figure 5-8.) The Pressure toggle enables you to use pen pressure on a tablet to vary the thickness of brush marks as you draw. Working on a tablet with this option you can create organic-looking strokes that taper or vary in width as you change the amount of pressure applied to the tablet surface.

Tip   The Pressure and Tilt options can also be used when the Eraser tool is active.

Figure 5-15 shows a series of tapered marks created with a pressure-sensitive tablet using a single Brush size and a consistent Zoom setting.

Figure 5-15: Drawing with the Brush tool on a pressure-sensitive tablet (with the Pressure option turned on in the Tools panel) creates tapered, calligraphic marks.

If you're drawing on a tablet that supports this feature, activating the Tilt toggle enables you to control the thickness and direction of strokes with the movement of your wrist. The degree of tilt is determined by the angle between the top of your stylus (or pen) and the top edge of the drawing tablet. This is a very subtle control that you'll most likely notice if you're using a large, tapered (or "flat") brush style — and if you spend hours drawing on a tablet! I didn't include a figure to illustrate this feature because it is hard to tell from finished artwork how it affects your drawings, but experienced artists will appreciate the "feel" that this option adds to the drawing environment.

Note　Support for the Tilt feature varies on different drawing tablets. If you have a Wacom tablet, you can get current drivers and feature documentation from www.wacom.com. It is beyond the scope of this book to describe different types and features of drawing tablets, but the drawing options available in Flash MX 2004 have been tested on a wide range of tablets so the chances are good that they will work for you.

The Eraser tool

The Eraser tool (E) is used in concert with the shape and drawing tools to obtain final, usable art. As the name implies, the Eraser tool is primarily used for rubbing out mistakes. When the Eraser tool is active, three options appear on the Tools panel, as shown in Figure 5-16. Erase mode and Eraser Shape are both drop-down menus with multiple options. For Eraser Shape, you can select rectangular or oval erasers in various sizes. Erase modes are similar to Brush modes described previously.

Note　If you have a drawing tablet with compatible drivers installed, you will also see the Tilt and Pressure options (described in the "Brush options for drawing tablets" section).

The Eraser tool's one unique option, the Faucet toggle, is used to clear enclosed areas of fill. Using the Faucet is the equivalent of selecting a line or a fill and then deleting it, but the Faucet accomplishes this in one easy step. Select the Eraser tool, choose the Faucet option, and then you can click on any line or fill to instantly erase it. Clicking on any part of a selection with the Faucet deletes all elements in the selection.

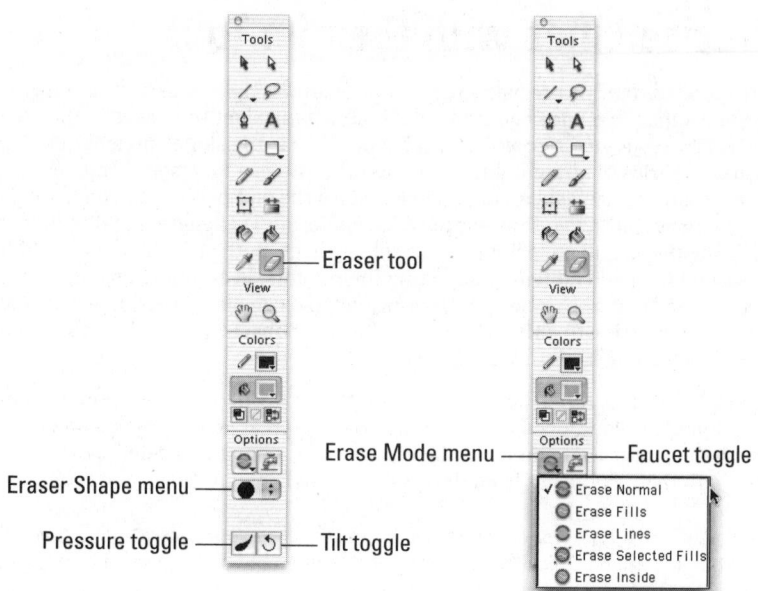

Figure 5-16: The Eraser tool has three basic options: Eraser mode, Eraser Shape, and Faucet.

The interaction of Eraser modes and artwork are consistent with the Brush modes available for the Brush tool. The only difference is that, instead of adding a mark to a specified part of a drawing, the Eraser removes marks in a specified part of a drawing. Aside from Erase Normal, Erase Fills, Erase Selected Fills, and Erase Inside, which you will recognize from the previous descriptions of Brush modes, there is also an Erase Lines mode that enables you to remove any lines without disrupting fills.

Note

The Eraser tool erases only lines and fills that are in the current frame of the scene. It won't erase groups, symbols, or text. When you need to erase a part of a group, you have two options: Select the group and choose Edit ➪ Edit Selected from the application menu (or double-click the group), or select the group and choose Modify ➪ Ungroup from the application menu (Ctrl+Shift+G or ⌘+Shift+G).

The only alternative to using the Eraser tool to remove graphic elements or areas of drawings is to select them with the Selection, Subselect, or Lasso tool, and then delete them by pressing the Delete (or Backspace) key.

Tip

To quickly erase everything in the current keyframe (even from multiple layers), double-click the Eraser tool in the Tools panel. Don't double-click on the Stage with the Eraser selected, but just double-click the Eraser button on the Tools panel. And — poof! — everything in the keyframe is gone.

Creating Precise Lines with the Pen Tool

The Pen tool (P) is used to draw precision paths that define straight lines and smooth curves. These paths define adjustable line segments, which may be straight or curved — the angle and length of straight segments is completely adjustable, as is the slope and length of curved segments. To draw a series of straight-line segments with the Pen tool, simply move the cursor and click successively: Each subsequent click defines the end point of the line. To draw curved line segments with the Pen tool, simply click and drag: The length and direction of the drag determines the depth and shape of the current segment. Both straight and curved line segments can be modified and edited by adjusting their points. In addition, any lines or shapes that have been created by other Flash drawing tools can also be displayed as paths (points on lines) and edited with either the Pen tool or the Subselect tool (described in the section on Putting Selection Tools to Work).

Creating shapes with the Pen tool takes a little practice, but it will produce the most controlled optimization of artwork. Because no points are auto-created, every line and curve is defined only with the points that you have placed. This saves having to delete points from an overly complex path that may result from drawing with the Pencil or the Brush tool.

Tip   If you're working on a background color that is too similar to your Layer Outline Color, the points on your line will be difficult to see and adjust. Remember that you can always change the Layer Outline Color to contrast with the background.

The Preferences for the Pen tool are located in the Pen tool section of the Preferences dialog box. (Choose Edit ➪ Preferences ➪ Editing, or on OS X, Flash ➪ Preferences ➪ Editing.) There are three settings to control preview, point display, and cursor style:

✦ **Show pen preview:** With this option checked, Flash displays a preview of the next line segment, in response to moving the pointer, prior to clicking to make the next endpoint and complete the line.

✦ **Show solid points:** Check this option to display selected anchor points as solid points, and unselected points as hollow points. The default is for selected points to be hollow and for unselected points to be solid.

✦ **Show precise Cursors:** This option toggles the Pen tool cursor between the default Pen tool icon and a precision crosshair cursor. This can make selecting points much easier and is recommended if you're doing detailed adjustment on a line.

Tip   You can also use a keyboard shortcut to toggle between the two Pen cursor displays: Caps Lock toggles between the precise Crosshair and the Pen icon when the Pen tool is active.

As Figure 5-17 shows, the Pen tool displays a number of different icons to the lower right of the cursor. These Pen *states* tell you at any given time what action the Pen can perform on a line. The Pen states are shown in this composite image, which is a detail of a path describing a white line over a light-gray background, shown at a Zoom setting of 400 percent.

Pen Icons
A: Empty state area (x)
B: Complete to End Point (o)
C: Remove Point (-)
D: Add Point (+)
E: Convert Point (^)

Pen/Subselect Icons
F: Adjust Line
G: Adjust Point

Point Icons
H: Selected (Filled)
I: Unselected (Empty)
J: Single tangent handle
K: Double tangent handle

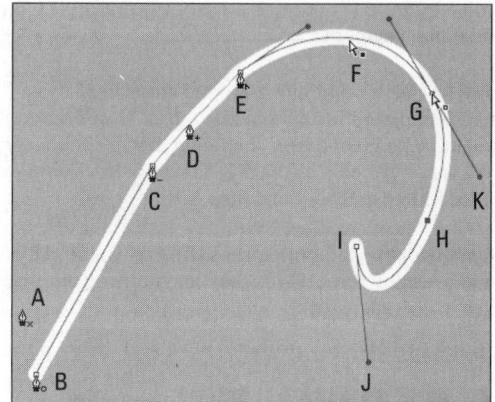

Figure 5-17: In addition to the choice between the cursor icon and crosshair, the Pen tool displays seven Pen states that indicate the Pen's function under various circumstances.

The seven Pen states are as follows:

✦ The Pen displays a small *(x)* when it's simply over the Stage (A).

✦ When the Pen is hovered over an endpoint, it displays an *(o)* to indicate that this is an endpoint (B). Click this point to connect a continuation of this path or, when making a closed shape, to close the path.

✦ When the Pen hovers over a corner point, it displays a minus (–) sign to indicate that clicking this corner point deletes it (C).

✦ When the Pen is over a path (a line between two points), it displays a plus (+) sign to indicate that clicking there adds a point to the path (D).

✦ When the Pen hovers over an existing point, it displays a carat (^) to indicate that clicking that point turns it into a corner point (E).

✦ With the Ctrl (or ⌘) key pressed, the Pen behaves like the Subselect arrow, so it switches to the hollow arrow icon with a filled black box (F) over lines, or a hollow white box (G) over points.

✦ When adjusting a path with either the Pen tool or the Subselect arrow, the default for selected points is a filled circle (H), whereas unselected points display as hollow squares (I). Note that the unselected points display a single tangent handle (J), bound toward the selected point, which displays two tangent handles (K).

Now that you've toured the various Pen tool icons and Pen states, it's time to start drawing and see how these actually apply as you work. To draw and adjust a straight-line segment with the Pen tool, follow these steps:

1. With the Pen tool active in the Tools panel, click to place the first point of your line on the Stage (wherever you want the line to start).

2. Then choose the next point and continue to click to create subsequent points and define individual line segments.

3. Each subsequent click creates a corner point on the line that determines the length of individual line segments.

Note   Each click will be a point along a continuous line. To end one line and begin a new line, double-click to place the final point in a line. This "breaks" the line so that the next click will place a starting point for a new line rather than a continuation of the same line. A line should be ended or completed — by double-clicking or by closing your shape — before using the editing keys described in Step 4 and Step 5.

4. To adjust straight segments, press the Ctrl (or ⌘) key and click a point to select it. Continue pressing the Ctrl (⌘) key as you drag and move the point to change the angle or length of the segment.

5. Or, with the Ctrl (⌘) key pressed, click and drag on the tangent handles of the point to adjust the line. Remember that corner points occur on a straight segment or at the juncture of a straight segment and a curved segment.

Tip   When creating straight lines with the Pen tool, press the Shift key to constrain lines to either 45-degree or 90-degree angles.

To draw and adjust a curved line segment with the Pen tool, follow these steps:

1. Click to create the first anchor point and without releasing the mouse, continue to step two.

2. Drag the Pen tool in the direction you want the curve to go.

3. When the preview of the line matches the curve that you want in the final line, release the mouse and then move to click and place the next point in the segment. Repeat this process to create subsequent curve points for curved segments.

4. Or simply click elsewhere without dragging to place a point and make the subsequent segment a straight line with a corner point.

5. As when adjusting straight segments, press the Ctrl (⌘) key and click a point to select it, continue pressing the Ctrl (⌘) key as you drag and move the point to change the angle or length of the segment.

6. Or, when the Ctrl (⌘) key pressed, click and drag the tangent handles of the point to adjust the depth and shape of the curve.

Although both corner points and curve points may be adjusted, they behave differently:

✦ Because a corner point defines a corner, adjusting the tangent handle of a corner point only modifies the curve that occurs on the same side as the tangent handle that is being adjusted.

✦ Because a curve point defines a curve, moving the tangent handle of a curve point modifies the curves on both sides of the point.

✦ To convert a corner point into a curve point, simply select the point with the Subselection arrow and while pressing the Alt (Option) key, drag the point slightly. A curve point with two tangent handles will appear, replacing the original corner point.

✦ To adjust one tangent handle of a curve point independent of the other handle, hold down the Alt (Option) key while dragging the tangent handle that you want to move.

✦ Endpoints cannot be converted into curve points unless the line is continued or joined with another line. To join two endpoints, simply click one endpoint with the Pen tool and then move to the point you want to connect it with and click again. A new line segment will be created that joins the two points.

✦ You can also use the arrow keys, located on your keyboard, to nudge selected corner and curve points into position. Press the Shift key to augment the arrow keys and to make them nudge 10 pixels with each click.

Note   You can also reshape any lines or shapes created with the Pen, Pencil, Brush, Line, Oval, Rectangle, or PolyStar tools as described in the section on Putting Selection Tools to Work, later in this chapter.

Using Fill and Stroke Controls

Now that you know where to find and use the drawing tools, it's time to get more creative with color and line styles. In the following sections, you're introduced to the controls for setting the Fill and Stroke applied to artwork drawn in Flash.

Choosing colors

The Stroke and Fill Colors that will be applied with any of the drawing tools are determined by the current settings of the color swatches located in the Flash Tools panel and in the Property inspector. The chips in the Tools panel display the most recently selected colors and are always visible regardless of which tool is being used. The Property inspector shows the color chip of the currently active item, and only displays the chips if they can be applied with the tool you have active or to the item you have selected. Thus, if you select the Line tool, both stroke and fill color chips will be visible on the Tools panel, but the Property inspector will display only a stroke color chip. Although these chips indicate the current color, they're really also buttons: Click any color chip to select a new color from the pop-up Swatches menu. The Swatches menu is shown in Figure 5-18 as it pops up from the Tools panel (top) or from the Property inspector (lower).

Tip   The Colors section of the Tools panel includes three buttons, arrayed beneath the Fill color swatch. These are, from left to right, Black and White, No Color, and Swap Colors. The Black and White button sets the Stroke to black and the Fill to white. The No Color button sets the active chip to not apply a color. The Swap Colors button swaps the current colors set in the Stroke and Fill chips.

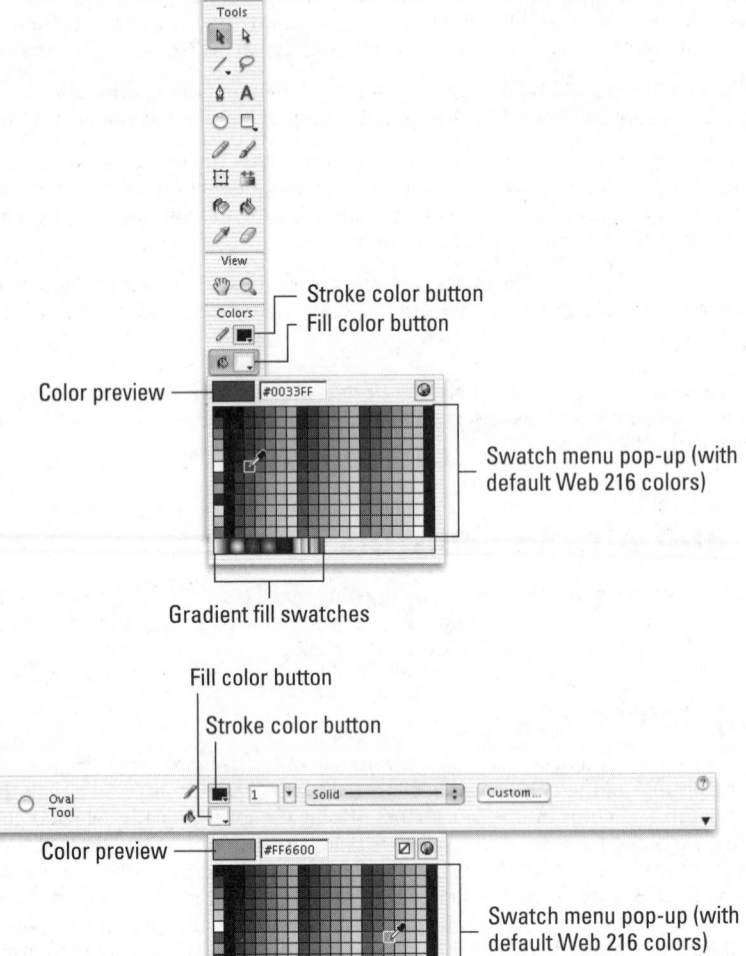

Figure 5-18: The current Swatches pop-up invoked by clicking the Stroke or Fill color chip in the Tools panel (top), or by clicking a color chip on the Property inspector (lower)

The pop-up Color Swatches display the same color options as the main Color Swatches panel shown in Figure 5-19. Use shortcut keys (Ctrl+F9 or ⌘+F9) or look in the Window ➪ Design panels menu to launch the Color Swatches panel. It includes a Hexadecimal color value box, another iteration of the No Color button (when it applies), and a button that launches the Color Picker. The Swatches menu evoked with the fill color chip includes the same solid colors available for stroke, as well as a range of gradient fill styles along the bottom of the panel.

Swatch panel options menu

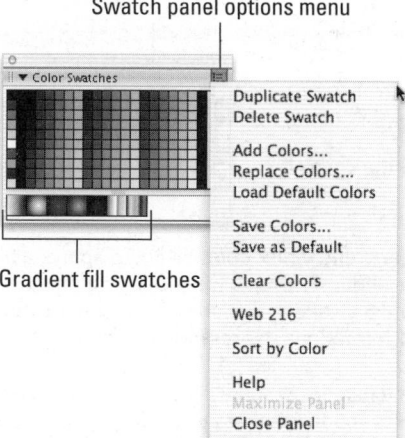

Figure 5-19: The default palette as displayed in the main Color Swatches panel

Gradient fill swatches

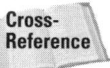

Cross-Reference

The custom palette options available in the Color Swatches panel are discussed in detail, along with the Color Mixer panel, and other colorful issues in Chapter 7, "Applying Color."

You can set the fill and stroke colors before you draw something, or select an element on the Stage and adjust it by choosing a new color from the stroke or fill Swatches. The Oval, Rectangle, PolyStar, Brush, and Paint Bucket tools all rely upon the fill settings to set or customize the type and color of fill that will be applied to a new shape that is about to be drawn, or when changing the color of a selected shape (or shapes).

Choosing line styles

In Flash, for all tools that draw or display a line or outline, the thickness of the line — or stroke — is controlled by either dragging the Stroke Height slider or by entering a value in the Stroke Height numeric entry box. These controls are both available in the Property inspector, as shown in Figure 5-20. The stroke options are only visible when they can be applied — if a drawing tool that creates lines is active in the Tools panel or if an element with a stroke has been selected.

Note

Generally, in Flash, lines that are independent or not attached to any fill are referred to as *lines,* whereas lines or outlines on a filled shape are referred to as *strokes.* Lines and strokes are created and edited with the same tools.

Changes to stroke color and style apply to lines or curves drawn with the Pen, Line, Pencil, Oval, Rectangle, and PolyStar tools. For shapes, the changes apply only to the outline, not to the fill. As with fill color settings, you can select a stroke color and style before you create any artwork (as long as the tool you're going to use is active in the Tools panel), or you can select a line in the Document window with the Selection tool and change it's appearance with the settings in the Property inspector.

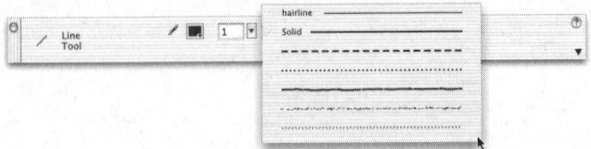

Figure 5-20: The Property inspector gives you all the controls
you need to select stroke height, color, and style.

When dragging the Stroke height slider, the numeric entry box updates and displays a height
read-out analogous to the current position of the slider. This also functions as a precise
numeric entry field. Simply enter a value to create a stroke with a specific height, or thickness. Permissible values range from 0.1 to 10, with fractions expressed in decimals.

Note   Depending upon the level of zoom, the height difference of some lines may not be visible on
screen — even though zooming in closer enables you to see that the stroke height is correct.
Lines set to a height of 1 pixel or lower appear to be the same thickness unless the Stage
view is zoomed to 200 percent or closer. However, all line heights still print correctly on a
high-resolution printer and will be visible in your final Flash movie (.swf) to anyone who
zooms in close enough.

The Stroke Style drop-down menu available on the Property inspector (as shown in Figure
5-20), offers the choice of Hairline or six standard, variable-width strokes. Hairline strokes
always have the same 1-pixel thickness, whereas the other six line styles can be chosen and
combined with any stroke height. If these styles do not deliver the line look you need, the
Custom button on the Property inspector invokes a Stroke Style dialog box (Figure 5-21),
which can be used to generate custom line styles by selecting from a range of properties for
each preset line. Basic properties include Stroke Thickness and Sharp Corners. Other settings
vary depending on what style of stroke is chosen.

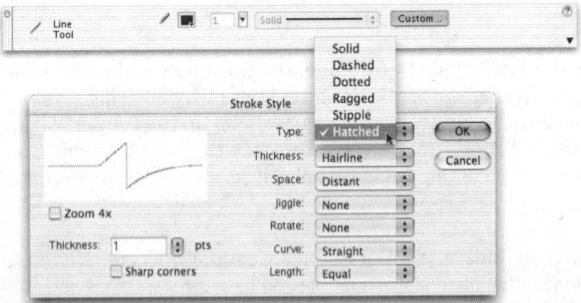

Figure 5-21: The Stroke Style dialog box available from the
Custom button on the Property inspector. The properties
displayed vary depending on the style of line selected for
adjustment.

Note   Points are the default unit of measurement for determining the spacing and thickness of line
segments in the Stroke Style dialog box.

To closely examine a custom line before you begin drawing with it, select the Zoom 4x check box beneath the preview area of the Line Style dialog box. Note the Sharp Corners check box, which toggles this Line Style feature on or off—select the check box to turn Sharp Corners on.

Tip Although there is no way to save custom line styles within the Stroke Style dialog box, you can create a separate document (.fla) and save samples of your favorite lines there. This will ease your workflow if you want to reuse custom line styles extensively. You can apply these styles quite easily to other lines by opening the document and using the Eyedropper tool in conjunction with the Ink Bottle tool. For more information, see the sections on the Eyedropper and the Ink Bottle tools in Chapter 9, "Modifying Graphics."

Of course, the best way to get an idea of the variety of possible strokes is to experiment with settings and sizes for each style, but the following samples and brief descriptions will give you an overview of the different properties for each of the six standard styles.

Hairline

The Hairline line style provides a consistent line thickness that doesn't visually vary at different zoom levels. This is the best line style to choose if you're creating artwork that you want to scale without losing the original line width. Regardless of whether an object with this stroke is enlarged or reduced in size, the hairline stroke always displays as 1-pixel wide.

Solid

The Solid line style draws a smooth, unbroken line. The customization variables for this style are limited to Thickness and Sharp Corners. These two variables can also be adjusted on all line styles.

Note The Solid line style is the optimal style for Web viewing because it requires fewer points to describe it and is consequently less file-intensive. The smaller file sizes theoretically translate into faster download times when the artwork is transmitted over the Web. This really only becomes an issue if you're making extensive use of complex line styles.

Dashed

The Dashed line style draws a solid line with regularly spaced gaps. Customization variables specific to this style are Dash Length and Gap Length. By adjusting these variables individually, it is possible to get a wide range of line patterns.

Dotted

The Dotted line style draws a row of circles with evenly spaced gaps. At first glance, this style appears to have only one variable—Dot Spacing. Change the numeric entry in this field to control the gaps between the dots, and remember that changing the thickness of the line changes the size of the actual dots.

Ragged

The Ragged line style draws a ragged line with various gaps between uneven strokes. The quality of both the raggedness and the gaps are adjustable. This style has three unique parameters: Pattern, Wave Height, and Wave Length. Each of these has a drop-down menu with options that can be combined to create a range of wild possibilities.

Stippled

The Stippled line style creates a line from a series of small irregular "patches" that goes a long way toward mimicking an artist's hand-stippling technique. The qualities of stippling are adjustable with three variables unique to the nature of stippled lines: Dot Size, Dot Variation, and Density. Each of these variables has a drop-down with multiple settings that can be adjusted to create a wide array of stroke densities and patterns.

Hatched

The Hatched line style draws a textured line of amazing complexity, which can be used to mimic an artist's hand-drawn hatched-line technique. This line style has six parameters unique to hatched lines: Thickness (hatch-specific), Space, Jiggle, Rotate, Curve, and Length.

> **Note**   The Hatched line style thickness settings are different from the point size thickness settings that are available for all lines. The default thickness setting (measured in points) defines the thickness or height of the overall hatched line, whereas the hatch thickness setting defines the width of the individual vertical strokes that create the density of the hatched line texture.

Optimizing Drawings

Aside from making a drawing more geometric, the main advantage of simplifying a shape or line is that it reduces the number of points that Flash has to remember and thus reduces the final file size. This is especially important for projects such as cartoons or animations that include a large number of hand-drawn shapes.

The most powerful tool for optimizing artwork precisely is found in the Optimize Curves dialog box invoked by selecting Modify ➪ Shape ➪ Optimize. This feature gives you a slider control to set the amount of smoothing applied between **None** and **Maximum**. You can also choose to apply optimization repeatedly for greater reduction in points. Selecting the **Use multiple passes** check box repeats the smoothing process until no further optimization can be achieved. The totals message notifies you how many points have been removed and what percentage reduction has been achieved each time you apply the modification. Figure 5-22, shows a sketch drawn with the Pencil tool in Ink mode, before and after multiple passes of Optimize Curves were applied. The reduction in points is displayed in the dialog box. For illustration purposes, I made a drastic adjustment by applying Optimize Curves set at Maximum. For practical purposes, a balance between optimization and drawing complexity should be found by testing a range of settings.

Figure 5-22: Before (left) and after (right), Optimize Curves is used to reduce the complexity of a drawing made with the Pencil tool in Ink mode. The reduction in points translates directly into smaller file size.

Putting Selection Tools to Work

Selection tools enable you to choose items that you want to edit in the Document window, as well as move or reshape specific elements. The three main selection tools — Selection, Subselect, and Lasso — provide different selection styles used for different editing tasks. The Subselect arrow is used primarily as a companion to the Pen tool.

Tip

When you are busy with another tool, you can temporarily toggle to the Selection tool by pressing the Ctrl or ⌘ key.

The Selection tool

The Selection (arrow) tool (A) is used most commonly to select and move items — or multiple items — on the Stage. The Selection tool is also used to reshape lines and shapes, in a way that is familiar to users who have worked in other vector graphics applications. The Selection tool's neighbor, which is differentiated by having a white rather than a black arrowhead, is the Subselect tool. The Subselect tool is most useful for moving and editing anchor points created with the Pen tool and adjusting tangents on Bezier curves.

Use the Selection tool to reshape a line or shape by pulling on the line (or shape) itself, or on its endpoints, curves, or corners. You can also use the Selection tool to select, move, and edit other Flash graphic elements, including groups, symbols, buttons, and text. When you click a line or item, a mesh pattern appears, to indicate that the line has been selected. If the item is either a Symbol or a Group, a thin colored line (called the *Highlight*) indicates selection status. This highlight color may be set in the General Preferences dialog box found under Edit ⇨ Preferences, (or in OS X under Flash ⇨ Preferences).

Tip   To temporarily turn off the selection mesh while editing an element, use View⇨Hide Edges (Ctrl+H or ⌘+Shift+ E). To toggle it back on, enter the same key shortcut again. Even if you have toggled the selection off on one element, it will be visible on the next element that you select.

Figure 5-23 shows a shape, a group, and a symbol as they look when unselected (top) and as they appear when selected with the Selection tool. The first oval—a primitive shape—displays a mesh pattern when selected (left), whereas the second oval—with the stroke and fill combined in a group—displays a thin rectangular border when selected (center) and the third oval—which was converted into a Graphic symbol—displays a thin rectangular border with a small crosshair icon in the center when selected (right). Groups and symbols can be moved but not otherwise edited directly on the Stage with the Selection tool, unless you go into Edit mode.

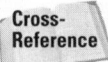

Cross-Reference   The various ways of using grouped shapes in graphics is explained in Chapter 9, "Modifying Graphics," while a discussion of using and editing symbols is included in Chapter 6, "Symbols, Instances and the Library."

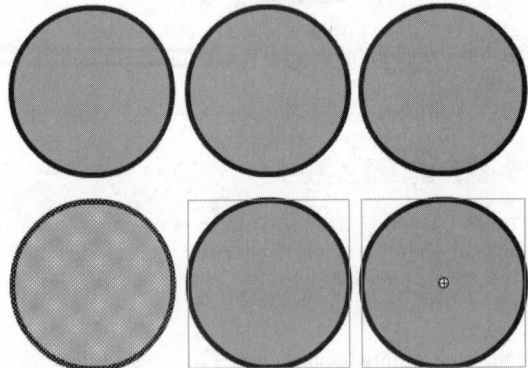

Figure 5-23: Selection tool selection Highlights (L-R) for a shape, a group, and a symbol

In addition to clicking a line to select it, you can select one or more items by dragging a marquee around them when the Selection tool is active. This operation is called *drag-select*. Additional items can be added to a current selection by pressing the Shift key and clicking the items in sequence. When you drag-select to make a selection, previously selected items are deselected and excluded from the selection. In order to include previously selected items, press the Shift key as you drag-select. When a group is selected and you drag to move them on the Stage, holding down the Shift key constrains the movement range of the elements to 45 degrees. This is helpful if you need to move an element up or down while keeping it on the same axis or baseline.

Note   Prior to Flash 4, additional elements were added to a selection simply by clicking them. To use this older selection style, go to Edit⇨Preferences and under General⇨Selection Options, clear the Shift Select check box.

Deselect one or more items by using any of the following methods:

✦ Pressing the Escape key

✦ Choosing Edit ➪ Deselect All

✦ Using the keyboard shortcut Ctrl+Shift+A (or ⌘+Shift+A)

✦ Clicking anywhere outside all the selected items

The Selection tool can also be used for duplicating items. Simply select an item (or line segment) with the Selection tool and press the Alt (Option) key while dragging the item to a new location. The original item remains in place, and a new item is deposited at the end of your drag stroke.

Caution   Selecting a line with the Selection tool and then holding down the Alt (Option) key while dragging it to a new location will duplicate it. Holding down the Alt (Option) key before dragging a line segment (that has not been selected) with the Selection tool will add a new Corner point.

Moving multiple elements with the Selection tool

Text boxes and Groups are selected as single elements and move as a single unit. After you create text in a text box (text features are discussed in Chapter 8, "Working with Text"), Flash treats the text as one block, or group, meaning that all the individual letters move together when the box is selected. Similarly, a group of graphic elements — such as lines, outlines, fills, or shapes — can be grouped and moved or manipulated as a single element. However, when you move an item that is not grouped, only the selected part is moved. This situation can be tricky when you have ungrouped fills and outlines because selecting one without the other could unintentionally break up your shape. To Group elements, select them all and apply the Modify ➪ Group command (Ctrl+G or ⌘+G). If necessary, they can be ungrouped later using Modify ➪ Ungroup (Ctrl+Shift+G or ⌘+Shift+G). Grouping is further discussed in Chapter 9, "Modifying Graphics."

Tip   Double-clicking the fill of a shape that has an outline stroke and a fill will select both. This strategy can also be used on lines with multiple sections. Double-clicking one section selects all the connected parts of a line, rather than just the closest segment.

Using Selection-tool arrow states to adjust or move drawings

In addition to the actions accomplished by selecting a line (or line section) and clicking an option, three arrow states — Move Selected Element, Reshape Curve or Line, and Reshape Endpoint or Corner — enable you to reshape and move parts of your drawings. It works like this: As you move the Selection tool over the Flash Stage, the arrow curser changes state to indicate what tasks it can perform in context with various items (the line or fill) closest to the Selection tool's current position.

Tip   When reshaping brush strokes or other filled items with the Selection tool, make sure that you don't select both the stroke and fill before trying to reshape the outline. If you do, you'll be able to move only the entire brush stroke — you won't be able to reshape it.

Figure 5-24 shows a series of images that demonstrate the various arrow states as they appear and are applied. On the left, the original shape is shown with the arrow states displayed as the cursor is moved over the center of the shape (A), over a corner (B) and over a line (C). The center image shows the preview as the Reshape Corner arrow is used to extend the corner of the square and the Reshape Curve arrow is used to stretch the curve. The final image on the right shows the resulting changes to the original square.

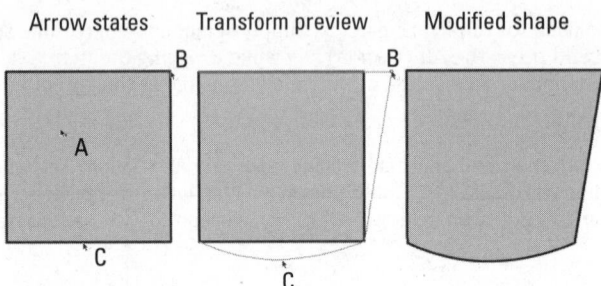

Arrow states   Transform preview   Modified shape

Figure 5-24: Selection tool arrow states used to reshape and reposition an element: Move Selected Item arrow (A), Reshape Corner arrow (B), Reshape Curve arrow (C)

Figure 5-25 shows the various Selection tool arrow states used to modify a line. The lower images show the arrow state cursors, the center images show the preview as the mouse is dragged, and the top images show the resulting changes to the line when the mouse is released. You will notice that lines have to be selected in order to be moved without changing their shape with the Selection tool — if the line is not selected, the arrow only displays Reshape Corner or Reshape Curve states. If you want to add an angle to a line rather than adding a curve, switch from Reshape Curve to Add Corner Point by holding down the Alt (or Option) key before clicking and dragging a line segment.

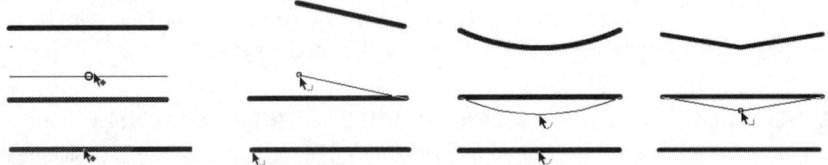

Figure 5-25: Using Selection tool arrow states to reshape and reposition a line. (Left to Right) Move Selected Item, Reshape Corner, Reshape Curve, Add Corner Point.

Tip   Some brush strokes are easier to reshape if you view them as Outlines (as described in Chapter 4: "Interface Fundamentals").

Knowing your Selection tool options

Figure 5-26, shows the three options that appear at the bottom section of the Tools panel when the Selection tool is active: Magnet (or Snap to Objects), Smooth, and Straighten. Because the various snap controls can be confusing at first, the Magnet tool is compared with the other snap settings available in Flash in the "Simplifying snapping settings" section, later in this chapter.

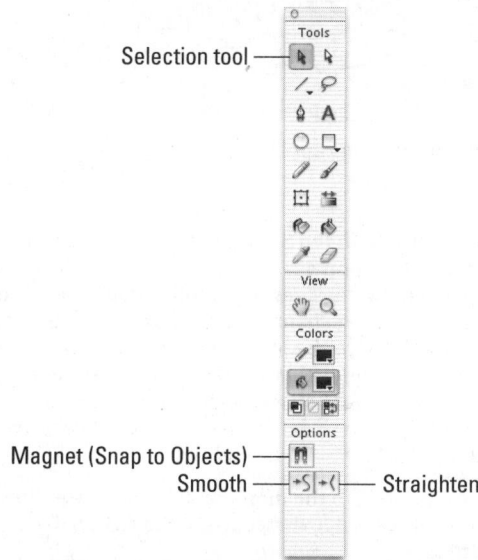

Figure 5-26: The Selection tool options available on the Tools panel

The Smooth and Straighten options available with the Selection tool are best used to clean up drawings by smoothing irregular curves or straightening crooked lines. Smoothing or Straightening reduces the number of bumps and variations (or points of transition) in a complex shape or line by reducing the number of points. The simplest curve or line will only be described by one point at each end.

To simplify a shape or line, click the Selection tool and select the item you've just sketched. Then click the Straighten or Smooth button in the Tools panel (or use Modify ➪ Shape ➪ Straighten or Modify ➪ Shape ➪ Smooth) to begin shape recognition. For hard-edged items such as a polygon, click the Straighten button repeatedly until your rough sketch reaches the level of angularity that you like. For smooth-edged items that approximate an oval or an arc, click the Smooth button repeatedly until your rough sketch has the amount of desired roundness. As shown in Figure 5-27, the simplified shape usually needs some further adjustment to get the result that you want after some of the points have been removed. The tools used for adjusting individual curves and points are the Pen tool and the Subselect tool.

Original   Smooth   Straighten

Figure 5-27: The Arrow Smooth and Straighten modifiers applied to simplify a freehand drawing

The Smooth and Straighten options can be applied with the Selection tool to any selected shape or line to reduce the number of points and simplify the form. The specific effect that these options have on your graphics is dependent on the Drawing Settings that were used to create the original lines. By minimizing complexity in freehand drawings or shapes, Smooth and Straighten gradually reduces an erratic graphic into the most simplified form that can be described with the fewest points possible. You will notice that the Smooth and Straighten options won't have a visible effect on a perfect geometric shape, such as a square, circle, or triangle — this is because Flash uses shape recognition to determine that these forms are already optimized and cannot be simplified any further.

Although these assistants nudge a sketch or line style in the direction that you want, they don't add information; so don't be surprised if it takes a few tries to get the right balance between rough drawing and shape recognition.

The Lasso tool

The Lasso (L) is a flexible tool, somewhat resembling the selection equivalent of the Pen tool crossed with the Pencil tool. The Lasso is primarily used to make freeform selections and to group-select odd or irregular-shaped areas of your drawing. After areas are selected, they can be moved, scaled, rotated, or reshaped as a single unit. The Lasso tool can also be used to split shapes, or select portions of a line or a shape. As shown in Figure 5-28, it has three options in the Tools panel: the Polygon mode button, the Magic Wand, and the Magic Wand properties.

The Lasso tool works best if you drag a loop around the area you want to select. (Hence, the tool name Lasso!) But if you slip or if you don't end the loop near where you started, Flash closes the loop with a straight line between your starting point and the endpoint. Because you can use the Lasso tool to define an area of any shape — limited only by your ability to draw and use the multiple selection capabilities of Flash — the Lasso tool gives you more control over selections than the Selection tool.

Tip   To add to a previously selected area, hold down the Shift key before initiating additional selections.

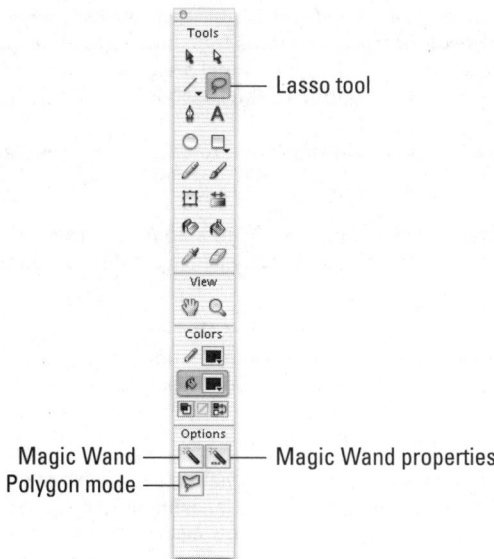

Figure 5-28: The Lasso tool and options

Polygon mode

Polygon mode affords greater precision when making straight-edged selections, or—in mixed mode—selections that combine freeform areas with straight edges. To describe a simple polygon selection, with the Lasso tool active, click the Polygon mode button to toggle on Polygon selection mode. In Polygon mode, selection points are created by a mouse click, causing a straight selection line to extend between mouse clicks. To complete the selection, double-click.

Mixed mode usage, which includes Polygon functionality, is available when the Lasso tool is in Freeform mode. To work in Freeform mode, the Polygon option must be in the off position. While drawing with the Freeform Lasso, press the Alt (Option) key to temporarily invoke Polygon mode. (Polygon mode continues only as long as the Alt (Option) key is pressed.) As long as the Alt (Option) key is pressed, a straight selection line extends between mouse clicks. To return to Freeform mode, simply release the Alt (or Option) key. Release the mouse to close the selection.

Note

Sometimes aberrant selections—selections that seem inside out, or that have a weird, unwanted straight line bisecting the intended selection—result from Lasso selections. That's usually because the point of origination of a Lasso selection is the point to which the Lasso snaps when the selection is closed. It takes a little practice to learn how to plan the point of origin so that the desired selection is obtained when the selection is closed.

The Magic Wand option and Magic Wand properties

The Magic Wand option of the Lasso tool is used to select ranges of a similar color in a bitmap that has been broken apart. After you select areas of the bitmap, you can change their fill color or delete them. Breaking apart a bitmap means that the bitmap image is subsequently seen by Flash as a collection of individual areas of color. (This is not the same as tracing a bitmap, which reduces the vast number of colors in a continuous-tone bitmap to areas of solid color.) After an image is broken apart, you can select individual areas of the image with any of the selection tools, including the Magic Wand option of the Lasso tool.

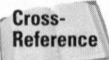

Cross-Reference   To learn more about using and modifying bitmaps in Flash, refer to Chapter 16, "Importing Artwork."

The Magic Wand option has two modifiable settings: Threshold and Smoothing. To set them, click the Magic Wand settings button to launch the Magic Wand Settings dialog box while the Lasso tool is active.

The Threshold setting defines the breadth of adjacent color values that the Magic Wand option includes in a selection. Values for the Threshold setting range from 0 to 200: The higher the setting, the broader the selection of adjacent colors. Conversely, a smaller number results in the Magic Wand making a narrower selection of adjacent colors. A value of zero results in a selection of contiguous pixels that are all the same color as the target pixel.

The Smoothing setting of the Magic Wand option determines to what degree the edge of the selection should be smoothed. This is similar to antialiasing. (Antialiasing dithers the edges of shapes and lines so that they look smoother on screen.) The options are Smooth, Pixels, Rough, and Normal.

The Subselect tool

The Subselect arrow (A) is the companion tool for the Pen and is found in the Tools panel to the right of the Selection tool. The Subselect tool has two purposes:

✦ To either move or edit individual anchor points and tangents on lines and outlines.

✦ To move individual objects.

When moving the Subselection tool over a line or point, the hollow arrow cursor displays one of two states:

✦ When over a line it displays a small, filled square next to it, indicating that the whole selected shape or line can be moved.

✦ When over a point, it displays a small, hollow square, indicating that the point will be moved to change the shape of the line.

Note   If you use the Subselect tool to drag a selection rectangle around two items, you'll find that clicking and dragging from any line of an item enables you to move only that item, but clicking on any point on an item enables you to move all items in the selection.

Figure 5-29 shows the use of the Subselection tool to move a path (A), to move a single point (B), to select a tangent handle (C), and to modify a curve by adjusting its tangent handle (D). Note that a preview is shown before releasing the handle.

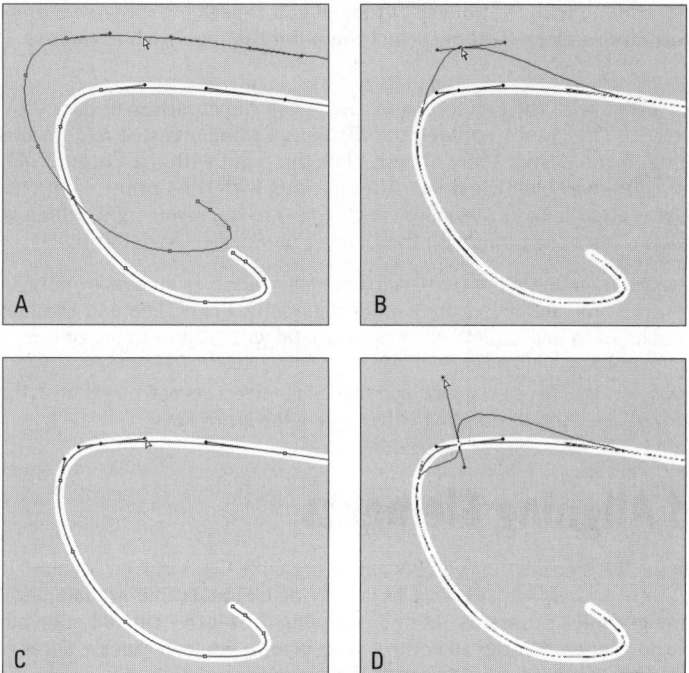

Figure 5-29: Using the Subselect tool to modify lines and curves

The Subselect tool is most useful for modifying and adjusting paths. To display anchor points on a line or shape outline created with the Pencil, Brush, Line, Oval, or Rectangle tools, simply click the line or shape outline with the Subselect tool. This reveals the points that define the line or shape. Click any point to cause its tangent handles to appear. If you have a shape that is all fill, without any stroke, you'll need to position the cursor precisely at the edge of the shape in order to select or move it with the Subselect tool.

To convert a corner point into a curve point, follow these steps:

1. Click to select the point with the Subselect tool.

2. While pressing the Alt (Option) key, click and drag the point.

3. A curve point with tangent handles appears, replacing the original corner point.

Note By holding down the Ctrl (or ⌘) key, the Pen tool can be used to mimic the function of the Subselect tool for moving lines or points but not for converting a curve point into a corner point.

An important use of the Pen tool/Subselect tool combo is editing lines for optimal file size. The simpler your shapes, the smaller your file size and the faster your movie downloads. Most often, this involves deleting extraneous points. There are a couple of ways to delete points:

✦ Select the line or outline with the Subselect tool, which causes the individual points to appear as hollow circles along the line. Select the point that you wish to remove. Press the Delete key.

✦ Select a line or outline with the Pen tool, and then move the cursor over the point that you want to remove. The cursor updates and displays a small inverted v (^) to the lower right, which is the Corner Point cursor. Click the point with the Corner Point cursor, and continue to hover over the point. After clicking with the Corner Point cursor, the cursor updates and displays a small minus sign (–) to the lower right, which is the Delete Point cursor. Click the point with the Delete Point cursor to delete it.

✦ When deleting more than one point from a closed shape, such as an oval or polygon, use the Subselect tool to drag and select any number of points. Press Delete to eliminate the selected points. The path heals itself, closing the shape with a smooth arc or line.

Tip   If you use the Subselect tool to select a path and then Shift+select several points on it, those points can be moved in unison by dragging or by tapping the arrow keys.

Designing and Aligning Elements

After you've drawn some lines or shapes, you'll want to organize them in your layout. Flash provides some useful tools to help with moving or modifying elements that are familiar if you've worked in other graphics programs. Aside from using the Flash Grid and manually placed Guides with various snap settings to control your layout, you can quickly access the Align panel or the Info panel to dynamically change the placement of elements on the stage. The Transform panel is the most accurate way to modify the size, aspect ratio, rotation, and even the vertical or horizontal "slant" of an element.

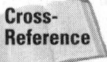

Cross-Reference   Snapping is discussed in this section, but there is additional coverage of controlling the Flash Grid and placing Guides in Chapter 4, "Interface Fundamentals."

The precise alignment possible with panels and snapping controls is especially helpful if you're working with detailed artwork or multiple shapes that need to be arranged in exact relation to each other.

Simplifying snapping settings

There are now five independent snapping settings in Flash. Snapping is a feature that gives you guidance when moving elements on the Stage and helps to align elements accurately in relation to each other, to the drawing grid, to guides, or to whole pixel axis points. You can tell that an item is snapping by the appearance of dotted guide lines as shown in the Snap Align example (Figure 5-30), or by the appearance of a small circle beside the Selection tool arrow cursor as shown in the Snap to Object and Snap to Pixel examples (Figure 5-31, Figure 5-34). For best control of snapping position, click and drag from the center point or from an outside edge of an element. The five different snapping controls are adjusted and applied as follows:

Snap Align

This is a new feature in Flash MX 2004 that gives you relative visual alignment guides as you move elements on the Stage. You'll either love or hate this option because it is the most "interactive" of all the snapping settings. The controls for Snap Align are in the Snap Align Edit dialog box available from the View menu (View ➪ Snapping ➪ Edit Snap Align). By default, Snap Align is set to display visual guides to alert you when an element is within 18 pixels of the Movie border (aka the Stage edge), or within 10 pixels of another element in your layout.

As you move an element around on the Stage you will see dotted lines (see Figure 5-30) that alert you when the edge of the element is exactly 18 pixels from the edge of the Stage, or 10 pixels from the next closest fixed element. If you move the element closer than 10 pixels to the fixed element, you will see another dotted guide to let you know when the edges of the two elements are touching (or perfectly aligned), either vertically or horizontally. Modify the Movie border settings to change the alert or alignment distance between elements and the edge of the Stage. Modify the Horizontal or Vertical Snap tolerance settings to change the alert distance between elements. If you also want to see guides when elements are aligned to the center point of other elements, select the Horizontal or Vertical Center alignment check boxes.

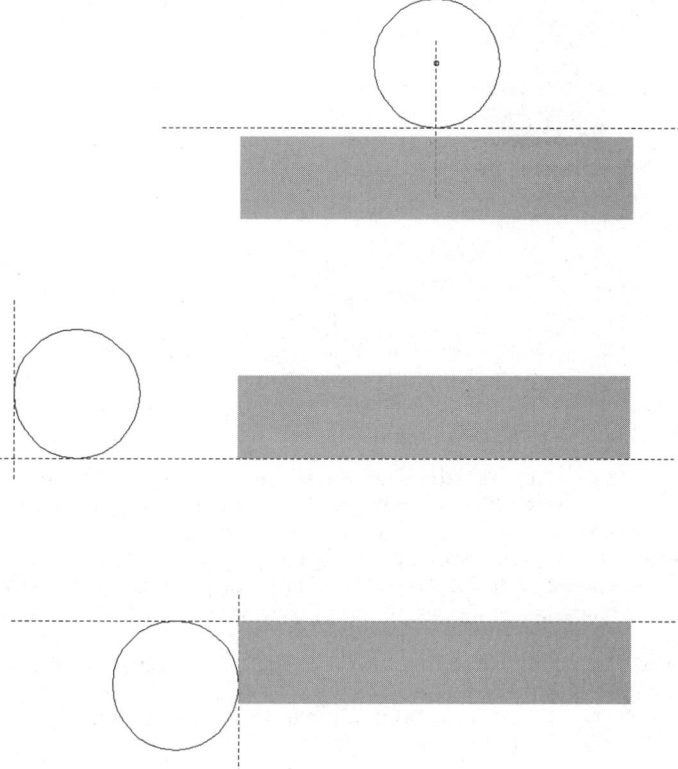

Figure 5-30: Snap Align guides give visual feedback for various alignment settings.

Snap to Object

The Snap to Object setting is a toggle that causes items being drawn or moved on screen to snap to or align with other items on the Stage. Click the magnet icon in the Tools panel to turn snapping on or off, or choose View ➪ Snapping ➪ Snap to Objects (a check mark is displayed next to the command if it's on). To control the tolerance of the magnet or the "stickiness" of the snap, use the Connect Lines setting found in Edit ➪ Preferences ➪ Editing (or in OS X, Flash ➪ Preferences ➪ Editing). By default, the Connect Lines tolerance is set at Normal. To make the magnet stronger, change the tolerance to Can be distant; to make it less strong, use Must be close. The Connect Lines control will help you to connect lines cleanly when drawing shapes or outlines.

As shown in Figure 5-31, Object snapping is indicated by the "o" icon near the center point as an item is moved from its original position (left). When the item is dragged close enough to another item to snap to it, the "o" icon gets slightly larger, which indicates to you to release the mouse (right).

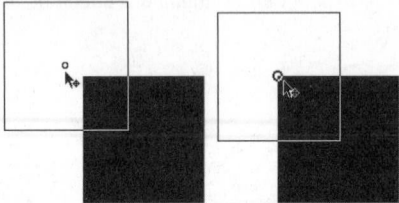

Figure 5-31: Snap to Object indicated by a change in the size of the centerpoint "o" icon as an item is moved to overlap with another item

Snap to Grid

Snap to Grid (Ctrl+Shift+' [apostrophe] or ⌘+Shift+' [apostrophe]) is an option available under View ➪ Snapping ➪ Snap to Grid, which will help to align elements to guides or to the background grid. If Snap to Grid is turned on, elements show the snap icon by the Arrow cursor when you drag them close to a line in your grid, whether the grid is visible or not.

To control the tolerance of this snapping feature, use the settings found under View ➪ Grid ➪ Edit Grid (Ctrl+Alt+G or ⌘+Option+G). The Grid Settings dialog box also includes check boxes for Snap to Grid and View Grid — these just give you another way to turn these tools on or off. Adjust the default horizontal and vertical spacing of the grid lines, by entering new pixel values in the text fields. To preview changes to the grid, select the Show grid check box. (By deselecting and reselecting the check box you can reset the preview when you make a change in the text fields.) The first three settings in the Snap Accuracy menu are the same as those for Snap to Object, but there is an additional setting, Always Snap, which constrains elements to the grid no matter where you drag them. Figure 5-32 shows the default 18 px gray grid as it displays when made visible (View ➪ Grid ➪ Show Grid), with the Stage view zoom at 400 percent.

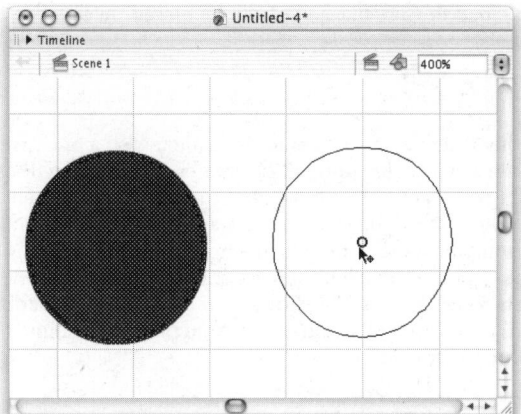

Figure 5-32: The snap icon as it appears when an element is dragged onto a grid line with Snap to Grid turned on (snapping works regardless of whether the grid is visible or not)

Snap to Guide

As described in the previous chapter, Guides are vertical or horizontal visual alignment tools that can be dragged onto the Work area or Stage when Rulers are visible, View ⇨ Rulers (Ctrl+Alt+Shift+R or ⌘+Option+Shift+R). If Snap to Grid is turned on when you drag guides out, they will be constrained to the grid; otherwise you will be able to place guides anywhere. After guides are set, they will be visible even if you turn Rulers off, to toggle guide visibility use View ⇨ Guides ⇨ Show Guides (Ctrl+; [semicolon] or ⌘+; [semicolon]). As shown in Figure 5-33, Snap to Guide enables you to align an element to a guide, even if it is not aligned with the grid.

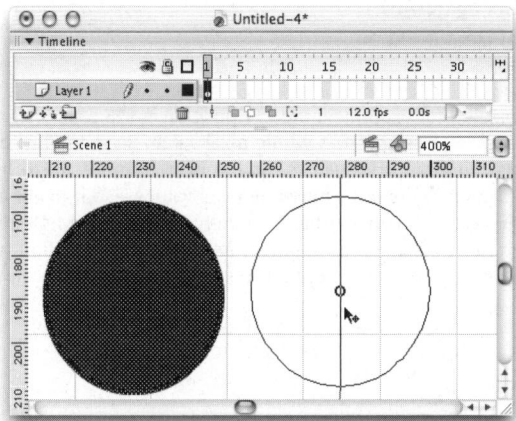

Figure 5-33: The snap icon as it appears when an element is dragged onto a guide with Snap to Guide turned on

Note   Snap to Guide is independent of Snap to Grid, but guides can be placed outside the Grid only when Snap to Grid is turned off.

Snap to Pixel

Snap to Pixel is the only "global" setting that causes all elements to align with a one-pixel grid that is only visible when the View scale is set to 400 percent or greater. This setting does not necessarily help you to align elements with each other, but it does help to keep elements from being placed "between pixels," by constraining movement of elements on the X and Y axis to whole pixels, rather than allowing decimals. There is no shortcut key for turning Snap to Pixel on, but it can always be toggled on and off from the View menu by checking or unchecking View ⇨ Snapping ⇨ Snap to Pixel. Figure 5-34 shows how the pixel grid displays when the View scale is at 400 percent. Items are constrained to whole pixel axis points if they are dragged from the center or from an outside edge.

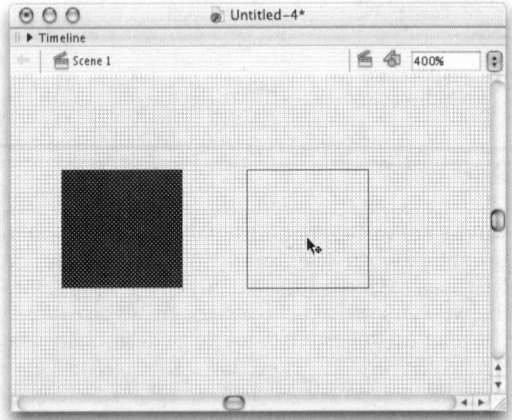

Figure 5-34: The pixel grid visible when View scale is at 400 percent or higher with Snap to Pixel turned on

Note   If an item is positioned between pixels — for example if the X, Y position is 125.5, 200.5 — the Snap to Pixel feature will not *correct* the position to a whole pixel value. Snap to Pixel only constrains the movement of items to whole pixel values. So the item example given here could only be dragged to a new location by *moving* in whole pixel values — so it might end up at a new location such as 130.5, 225.5. If you want to keep items aligned to whole pixel values, use the text fields in the Property inspector to manually enter a starting location with whole pixel X, Y values — then use the Snap to Pixel option to *keep* items aligned with the one pixel grid.

Design panels

When drawing in Flash, the design panels — Align, Info, and Transform — can be your best friends. Use the Align panel to align, *regularize* (match the sizes of), or distribute several items on Stage, either relative to each other or to the Stage area. Use the Info panel to modify the coordinates and dimensions of an item. Or use the Transform panel to scale, rotate, and skew an item.

Cross-Reference The Free Transform tool is detailed in Chapter 9, "Modifying Graphics." This tool offers powerful options for modifying artwork, including an Envelope modifier not available from the Transform panel.

You will find the Align panel (Ctrl+K or ⌘+K), the Info panel (Ctrl+I or ⌘+I), and the Transform panel (Ctrl+T or ⌘+T) in the Window ⇨ Design panels menu.

The Align panel

The Align panel (Ctrl+K or ⌘+K), shown in Figure 5-35, is one of many features for which you'll be grateful every time you use it. It enables you, with pixel-perfect precision, to align or distribute items relative to each other or to the Stage.

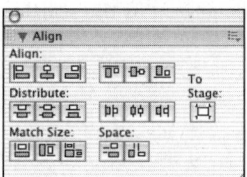

Figure 5-35: Use the Align panel to both size and arrange items with ease.

The Align panel has five controls. The icons on the buttons show visually how the selected items can be arranged:

✦ **To Stage:** On the right, you will also notice a To Stage button. When this button is selected, all adjustments are made in relation to the full Stage. To Stage is actually a toggle that can be turned on or off at any time — it will retain the last chosen state even if the panel is closed and reopened.

✦ **Align:** There are six buttons in this first control. The first group of three buttons is for horizontal alignment, and the second group of three is for vertical alignment. These buttons align two or more items (or one or more items with the Stage) horizontally (top, middle, bottom) or vertically (left, middle, right).

✦ **Distribute:** This control also has six buttons, three for horizontal distribution and three for vertical distribution. These buttons are most useful when you have three or more items that you want to space evenly (such as a row of menu items). These buttons distribute items equally, again vertically or horizontally. The different options enable you to distribute from edge to edge, or from item centers.

✦ **Match Size:** This control enables you to force two or more items of different sizes to become equal in size; match items horizontally, vertically, or both.

✦ **Space:** This option enables you to space items evenly, again, vertically or horizontally. You may wonder how this differs from Distribute. Both are similar in concept, and if your items are all the same size, they will have the same effect. The difference becomes more apparent when the items are of different sizes:

• Distribute evenly distributes the items according to a common reference (top, center, or bottom). For example, if one item is larger than the others, it may be separated from the other items by less space, but the distance between its top edge and the next item's top edge will be consistent with all the selected items.

• Space ensures that the spacing between items is the same; for example, each item might have exactly 36 pixels between it and the next.

To align an item to the exact center of the Stage, do the following:

1. Click to select the item that you want to center.

2. Click the **To Stage** toggle in the Align panel.

3. Click the **Align horizontal center** button.

4. Click the **Align vertical center** button.

The Info panel

Use the Info panel (Ctrl+I or ⌘+I), shown in Figure 5-36, to give precise coordinates and dimensions to your items. Type the values in the fields provided, and by default your item will be transformed relative to its top-left corner. To adjust the transform center point, use the Alignment Grid to choose any side or corner of your selected element as the starting point before applying changes.

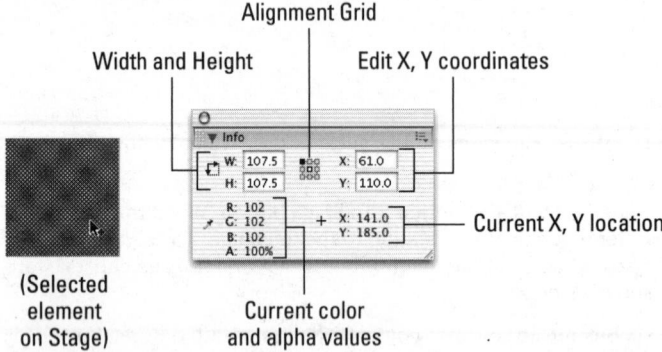

Alignment Grid

Width and Height   Edit X, Y coordinates

— Current X, Y location

(Selected element on Stage)

Current color and alpha values

Figure 5-36: Use the Info panel options to change the location and appearance of an item.

The Info panel has these controls:

✦ **Width:** Use this numeric entry field to alter the width of a selected item.

✦ **Height:** Use this numeric entry field to alter the height of a selected item.

Tip

Units for both Width and Height are measured in the units (pixels, inches, points, and so on) set in Ruler Units option of the Document Properties dialog box found under Modify ⇨ Document (Ctrl+J or ⌘+J). Note, however, that upon changing the unit of measurement, the item must be deselected and then reselected in order for these readouts to refresh and display in the current units.

✦ **Alignment Grid:** The alignment grid is located just to the left of the numeric entry fields that are used for adjusting the X and Y location of any selected item. This alignment grid consists of nine small squares. Together, these squares represent an invisible bounding box that encloses the selected item. Every shape created in Flash, even circles, resides within an imaginary rectangular bounding box that includes the extremities of the shape. The alignment grid enables you to position the selected item relative to either the upper-left corner or to the center of its bounding box. Click either square to define which origin point to use for position or size adjustments.

Note The X (horizontal) and Y (vertical) coordinates are measured from the upper-left corner of the Flash Stage, which is the origin with coordinates 0,0.

✦ **X:** Use this numeric entry field to either read the X coordinate of the item or to reposition the item numerically, relative to the center point on the X (or horizontal) axis.

✦ **Y:** Use this numeric entry field to either read the Y coordinate of the item or to reposition the item numerically, relative to the center point on the Y (or vertical) axis.

✦ **RGBA:** This sector of the Info panel gives the Red, Green, Blue, and Alpha values for graphic items and groups at the point immediately beneath the cursor. Values for symbols, the background, or interface elements do not register.

✦ **+ X: / + Y:** This sector of the Info panel gives the X and Y coordinates for the point immediately beneath the cursor — including offstage or Work area values. A negative X value is to the left of the Stage, whereas a negative Y is located above the Stage.

To scale or reposition an item, select the item and then open the Info panel with shortcut keys or from Window ➪ Design Panels ➪ Info:

✦ Choose to scale or reposition the item relative to either the center, or to the upper-left corner. (The selected square turns black to indicate that it is selected.)

• To work relative to the center, select the center square of the Alignment Grid.

• To scale relative to the upper-left corner, click the top-left square of the Alignment Grid.

✦ To scale the item numerically, enter new values in the Width and Height fields, and then click elsewhere or press Enter to apply the change.

✦ To reposition the item numerically, enter new values in the X and Y fields (located in the *upper* half of the panel); then either press Enter or click outside the panel to apply the change.

The Transform panel

The Transform panel (Ctrl+T or ⌘+T) gives precise control over scaling, rotation, and skewing of an item. With this panel, instead of making adjustments "by eye" — that may be imprecise — numeric values are entered in the appropriate fields and applied directly to the selected item. As shown in Figure 5-37, the value fields in the Transform panel make it easy to modify the size and position of an element. However, once transformations are applied to an ungrouped shape or line, these numbers reset when the shape is deselected.

New Feature If you're using the Property inspector to resize an item by pixel values, you'll appreciate the new constrain option. When an item is selected on the Stage, a small lock icon appears beside the Width and Height fields in the Property inspector. Click the lock to preserve the aspect ratio of an element as you enter a new value for width or height.

Rotate button   Height scale

Width scale   Constrain aspect ratio button

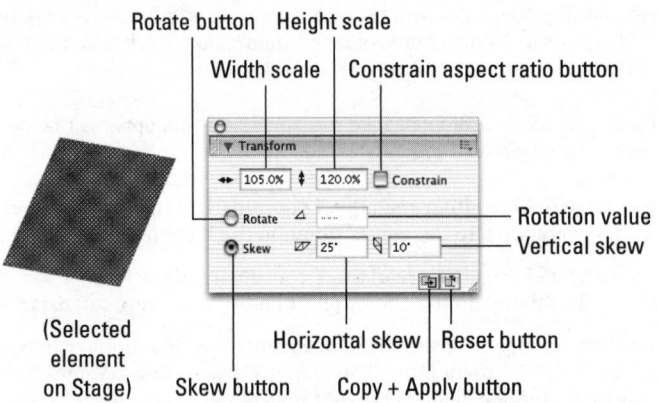

Rotation value

Vertical skew

(Selected element on Stage)

Horizontal skew | Reset button

Skew button   Copy + Apply button

Figure 5-37: Use the Transform panel to scale, rotate, and skew items.

Some other powerful transform options are available from the Tools panel and from the Transform submenu of the Modify menu. These more-complex editing tools are explained in Chapter 9, "Modifying Graphics." However, the best place to start with transform options is the Transform panel, and these options are applied as follows:

✦ **Scale:** Use this to size the selected item by percentage. Enter a new number in the Scale field and press the Enter key. The shape scales to the specified percentage of its original scale. To constrain the shape to its current proportions, click the Constrain check box. After a line or shape is deselected, the values in the Transform panel reset. The quickest way to get back to the original settings is to immediately use Edit ➪ Undo (Ctrl+Z or ⌘+Z) until it is reset. You can also get back to the original size mathematically by applying a new percentage that compensates for the changes you made before deselecting the item.

Tip   When using the Transform panel with groups and symbol instances, the original settings can be referenced or reset even after the item has been deselected. Making and using symbols is explained in Chapter 6, "Symbols, Instances, and the Library."

✦ **Rotate:** Click the radio button and then specify a rotation for the selected item by entering a number in the Rotate field. Press the Return or Enter key to apply the change to the selected item. The item will be rotated clockwise around its center point. To rotate an item counterclockwise, enter a negative number in the Rotate field.

✦ **Skew:** Items can be *skewed* (slanted in the horizontal or vertical direction) by selecting the Skew radio button, and then entering values for the horizontal and vertical angles. Press the Return or Enter key and the item will be skewed to the values entered.

✦ **Copy and Apply transformation:** Press this button and Flash makes a copy of the selected item (including shapes and lines), with all transform settings that have been applied to it. The duplicate is pasted in the same location as the original — select it with the Selection tool and to move it to a new position to separate it from the original. Your original is left unchanged.

✦ **Reset:** This button, at the bottom-right corner of the panel, removes all transformation settings for a selected object. You can always use the Reset button for instances, groups, or type blocks to get back to 100 percent scale with no rotation or skew. However, after a shape or line is deselected, this button does not work. For shapes, this is really more like an "Undo All" button than a Reset button.

The Edit menu

Many of the commands in the Edit menu are discussed in Chapter 4, "Interface Fundamentals," but some of these commands can be helpful for creating or modifying graphics and are worth mentioning again here:

✦ **Undo:** When you make a mistake, before you do anything else, apply this command to get back to where you started. The default number for combined Undos that Flash remembers is 100; the maximum number is 9999. Because Undo "memory" occupies system memory, you can set this level much lower if you find you don't rely on it. This setting is controlled in the General tab of the Flash Preferences dialog box.

Note

Flash generates an Undo stack for several different parts of the interface: Each timeline (main Timeline and Movie Clip timelines) has its own undo stack, as does the ActionScript panel. Furthermore, Undo does not transcend Focus: You cannot Undo work on the Stage from the ActionScript panel — you must first return focus to the Stage to exercise Undo.

✦ **Redo:** The anti-Undo, this redoes what you just undid.

✦ **Repeat:** If you have not just used Undo, you will see this as an option that enables you to "double" whatever edit you may have made, or to apply it to another item.

Cross-Reference

The History panel provides a flexible, non-linear option for backtracking or repeating steps as you create and edit graphics. The History panel can also be used in conjunction with the Commands menu to track and save authoring steps that can be archived and reused. These powerful new features are discussed in Chapter 9, "Modifying Graphics."

✦ **Cut:** This removes any selected item(s) from the Document window and places it on the clipboard.

✦ **Copy:** This copies any selected item(s) and places it on the clipboard, without removing it from the Document window.

✦ **Paste in Center:** Disabled if nothing has been copied or cut, this command pastes items from the clipboard into the currently active frame on the currently active layer. You can also paste text into panel value fields.

Note

The Paste in Center command places items in the center of the *currently visible* area in the Document window, not in the center of the Stage. Double-click the Hand icon in the Tools panel to center the Stage in the Document window before using Paste in Center if you want the pasted item to be placed in the center of the Stage.

✦ **Paste in Place:** This is like Paste, except that it pastes the object precisely in the same area of the Stage (or Work area) from which it was copied (but it can be on a new Layer or Keyframe).

✦ **Paste Special (PC only):** This is a Windows only menu that enables some specialized copying of content into Flash. This is not recommended when working in a cross-platform environment because it is platform-specific and limits how the document can be edited on other platforms.

✦ **Clear:** This removes a selected item(s) from the Stage *without* copying it to the Clipboard.

✦ **Duplicate:** This command duplicates a selected item or items, without burdening the Clipboard. The duplicated item appears adjacent to the original.

✦ **Select All:** Selects all items in the Document window in the currently active keyframe of the project.

✦ **Deselect All:** Deselects all currently selected items.

✦ **Find and Replace:** This command launches a powerful new option that enables you to specify elements in a current Flash document or Scene and modify them with settings you choose in the Find and Replace dialog box. For more detailed information on using the Find and Replace command, refer to Chapter 9, "Modifying Graphics."

✦ **Find Next:** A shortcut that searches through a Flash document or Scene and finds the next item that matches the criteria set in the Find and Replace dialog box.

✦ **Edit Symbols:** Select an instance of a symbol and choose this command to modify the content of the symbol in Edit mode, an edit space that is independent from the Stage. For more about symbols and editing symbols, refer to Chapter 6, "Symbols, Instances, and the Library."

✦ **Edit Selected:** This command is only enabled if a group or symbol is selected on the Stage. It makes a selected group or symbol available in Edit mode. This same kind of edit space is invoked for symbols by choosing Edit Symbol.

✦ **Edit in Place:** This command opens a selected group or symbol in a separate tab of the Document window (shown in the location label area of the Document window), and enables you to edit this group or symbol while still seeing the other elements on the Stage, dimmed in the background for reference.

Tip   Double-clicking a group or symbol on the Stage with the Selection tool has the same result as choosing the Edit in Place command.

✦ **Edit All:** From Edit mode, Edit All is used to go back to editing the main Flash scene. You can always do this also by clicking on the Scene location label of the Document window.

Summary

✦ The geometric shapes available from the Tools panel are a quick, accurate way of creating basic elements that can be customized with various fill and stroke styles.

✦ Shape recognition and line processing provide variable levels of correction to hand-drawn shapes and strokes that can make it easier to create "perfect" graphics.

✦ The Pencil, Brush, and Pen tools enable you to draw freeform or Bezier lines that can be edited using the Selection tool arrow options and the Subselect tool.

✦ By using specific modes for the Brush and Eraser tools, you can choose exactly what areas of artwork are modified.

✦ Enhanced Smoothing controls, a new Tilt toggle and a Pressure toggle give artists who use tablets more options to customize the Flash drawing environment.

✦ The color controls in the Tools panel, Property inspector and Color panels enable you to pick the fill and stroke colors for artwork created with any of the drawing tools.

✦ Line styles can be modified in the Property inspector to create a huge variety of textures and widths.

✦ Optimizing artwork manually by editing points with the Subselect tool, or automatically by using the Optimize Curves option, can greatly reduce file size by simplifying lines and curves.

✦ By adjusting and applying the various snapping modifiers, you can control how "auto" alignment behavior affects elements as you work.

✦ The Align, Info, and Transform panels give you several precise options for arranging and modifying elements on the Stage.

✦ The Edit menu and History panel give you options for copying, pasting, and undoing or redoing steps in your drawing process.

✦   ✦   ✦

Symbols, Instances, and the Library

Symbols are the key to file-size efficiency and interactive power in Flash. A *symbol* is a reusable element that resides in the current movie's project Library, which is accessed with Window ➪ Library (Ctrl+L or ⌘+L). After you convert an item in your Flash movie into a symbol, each time you use that item on your main Timeline or within a Movie Clip timeline, you're working with an *instance* of the original symbol. Unlike using individual graphic elements, you can use many instances of a symbol, with little or no addition to the file size.

Using symbols helps reduce the file size of your finished movie because Flash needs to save the symbol only once. Each time a given symbol is used in the project, Flash refers to its original profile. To support the variations of an instance, Flash needs to save information about the *differences* only — such as size, position, proportions, and color effects. If a separate graphic were used for each change, Flash would have to store a complete profile of all the information about that graphic — not just the changes, but also all of the points that specify what the original graphic looks like.

Furthermore, symbols can save you a lot of time and trouble, particularly when it comes to editing your movie. That's because changes made to a symbol are reflected in each instance of that symbol throughout the movie. Let's say that your logo changes halfway through production. Without symbols, it might take hours to find and change each copy of the logo. However, if you've used symbol instances, you need only edit the original symbol — the instances are automatically updated throughout the movie.

In this chapter, you learn to create and edit basic symbol types stored in your document Library. You also learn to use symbol instances, both within the main Timeline and within other symbols, and to modify individual instances of a symbol. We'll briefly introduce special symbol types associated with Components and Timeline Effects in Flash MX 2004.

Cross-Reference

Applying and editing Timeline Effects is discussed in detail in Chapter 11, "Timeline Animation and Effects." Using and modifying Components is covered in Chapter 29, "Using Components."

Understanding the Document Library

The Library (Ctrl+L or ⌘+L) is the storehouse for all reusable elements, known as *symbols,* which can then be placed as symbol *instances* within a Flash movie. Imported sounds and bitmaps are automatically placed in the Library. Upon creation, Graphic symbols, Button symbols and Movie Clips are also stored in the Library. It's a good practice to convert nearly every main item within a Flash document into a symbol, and to then develop your project from instances derived from these original symbols.

As shown in Figure 6-1, the Document Library (Window ➪ Library) is separate from the three Common Libraries (Window ➪ Other Panels ➪ Common Libraries). However, these libraries are related. When you choose Window ➪ Library, you open a Library specific to the current Flash document (.fla), whereas Common Libraries are available whenever Flash is open and provide elements that you can drag into any document Library to use in your own projects. All of the Library panels can be docked in a vertical panel stack or accessed individually as floating panels. In Figure 6-1, the document Library is shown in Wide state, whereas the Common Libraries are shown in Narrow state. All Library panels can be toggled between these two view options (or scaled manually by dragging the lower-left corner of the panel).

Choose Window ➪ Other panels ➪ Common Libraries to open the submenu of common libraries that ship with Flash. The Buttons and Learning Interactions Libraries contain a selection of pre-built Flash elements that can be reused in any Flash project. The Classes Library contains compiled scripts that are used with the new components that ship with Flash MX 2004. Macromedia stores these elements in the Classes Library as Compiled Clips to protect the code. All of the common libraries files are stored in the Libraries folder of the Configuration folder for Flash MX 2004.

✦ The standard directory path on Windows is:

```
C:\Documents and Settings\(username)\Local Settings\Application
Data\Macromedia\Flash MX 2004\en\Configuration\Libraries
```

✦ The standard directory path on Mac is:

```
HD\Users: (username)\Library: Application Support\Macromedia\Flash MX
2004\en\Configuration\Libraries
```

Tip   To add your own buttons, symbols, or even complete libraries for specific projects, first save them in a Flash document (.fla) with a descriptive name; then place that Flash file in the Libraries folder within the Configuration folder for Flash MX 2004 on your hard drive.

Document Library

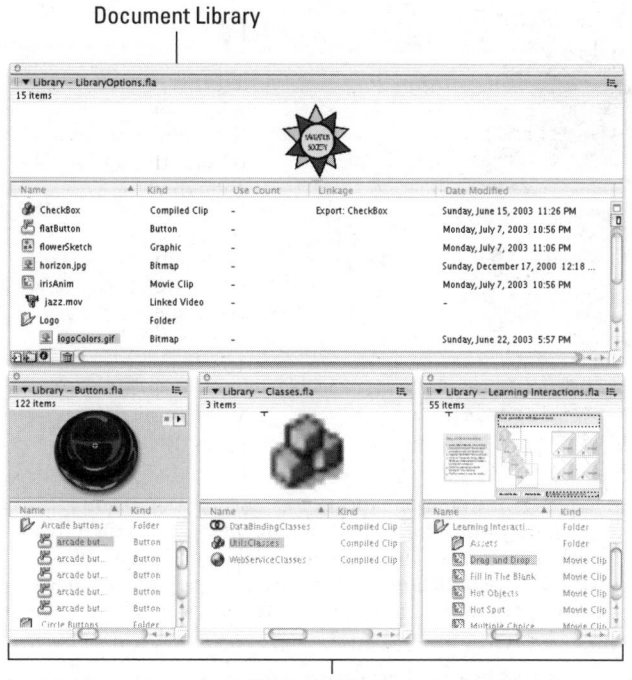

Common libraries

Figure 6-1: The Document Library is specific to the current project file (.fla), whereas Common Libraries contain elements that can be used in any Flash movie.

The Sounds Library is no longer shipped with Flash, but you can create your own Library of sounds if you have a collection of optimized files that you plan to reuse in future projects. Simply load the sounds into one Flash document (.fla) and save the file in the Libraries folder within the Flash MX 2004 Configuration folder on your hard drive. If you have the sounds that were available in the Flash MX Sounds Library, you could also move that folder to the new Libraries folder to use them in Flash MX 2004.

You can access elements stored in the Library of any other Flash document by choosing File ➪ Import ➪ Open External Library from the application menu and browsing to a FLA file. The Library will open next to the Document window of your current project, but it is visually differentiated from the Library for your currently active Document because it displays with gray text in the Library list, as shown in Figure 6-2.

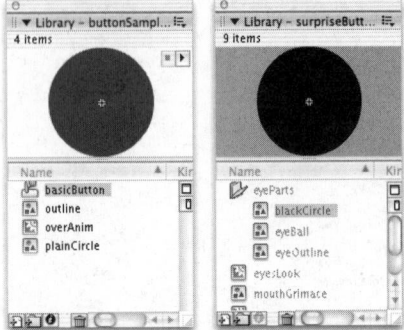

Figure 6-2: The Library for the current document lists items in black text (left), whereas other libraries that may be opened will list items in gray text (right).

You can copy assets from an External or Common Library to a current Document Library by dragging items from the source Library onto the current document Stage, or directly into the Library panel. This will also work if you have two documents open, and you want to move assets between the two Libraries. It is also then possible to drag or copy and paste elements directly from one document Stage onto another, or drag an item from a source document Stage into a current document's Library.

The shared Library feature, introduced in Flash MX, makes it possible to link assets between project (.fla) files during production using *Authortime* sharing, or to link multiple published movie (.swf) files on the server with *Runtime* sharing. Shared libraries create a more optimized workflow than saving individual copies of assets in multiple documents. You can learn more about linking symbols in your project files in the "Using Authortime Shared Libraries" section later in this chapter.

Cross-Reference   The workflow for creating and using Runtime Shared Libraries is fully explained in Chapter 28, "Sharing and Loading Assets."

Reading the Library

Every Flash document has its own Library, which is used to store and organize symbols, sounds, bitmaps, and other assets such as video files. As shown in Figure 6-3, the item highlighted — or selected — in the Sort window is previewed in the Preview window. Each item in the Library has an icon to the left of the name to indicate the asset type. Click any heading to sort the window by Name, Kind (type), Use Count, or Date Modified (all headings shown in Figure 6-1).

If the item selected in the Library is a Button symbol, or a Movie Clip or sound file with more than one frame on its timeline, a controller appears in the upper-right corner of the Preview window. This Preview Stop/Play controller pops up to facilitate previewing these items. It's equivalent to the Play command in the options menu. As shown in Figure 6-4, the Library options pop-up menu lists a number of features, functions, and controls for organizing and working with items in the Library.

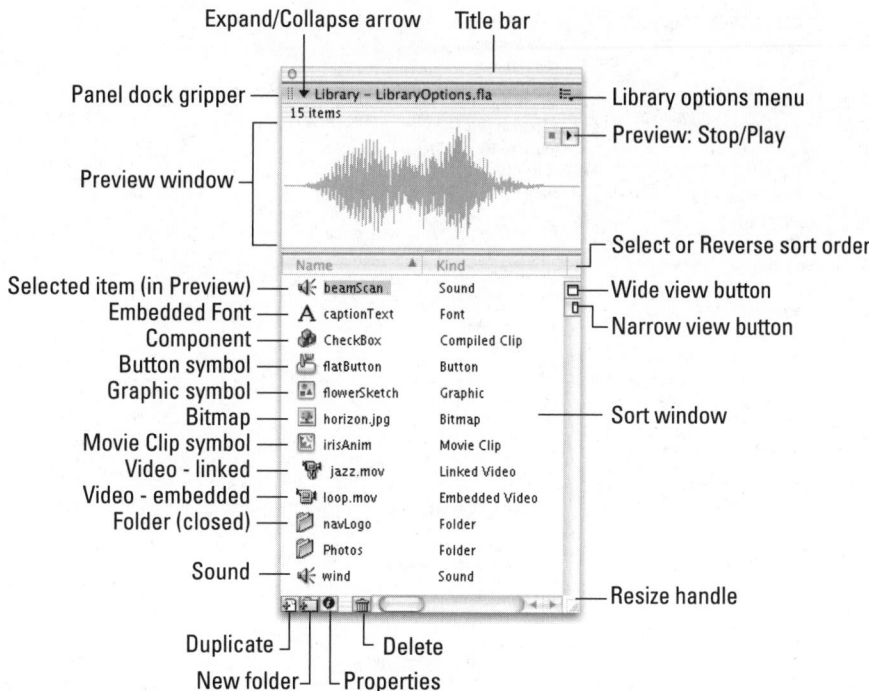

Figure 6-3: The Document Library in Narrow view

The following commands, found in the Library options menu, enable you to add or modify content stored in your document Library.

✦ **New Symbol:** Choose this command to launch the Create New Symbol dialog box where you can name and choose Properties for a symbol. Then click OK to open Edit mode and place or create graphics on the symbol timeline. When a new symbol is created, it is stored at the root of the Library Sort window. You can drag it inside of any existing Library folders.

✦ **New Folder:** Items in the Library can be organized in folders. The New Folder command simply creates a new folder within the Sort window. New folders are "untitled" by default ⌘ double-click the folder text to type a custom folder name. This menu command is equivalent to the New Folder button at the bottom of the Library panel.

✦ **New Font:** Use this command to invoke the Font Symbol Properties dialog box, which is the first step in creating a Font Symbol for use within a Shared Library.

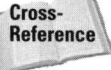
Cross-Reference

For more information about Shared Libraries and Font symbols, refer to the section "Using Authortime Shared Libraries" in this chapter, as well as to Chapter 28, "Sharing and Loading Assets."

Figure 6-4: The Library window and the options pop-up menu

✦ **New Video:** Creates a new empty Video object in the Library.

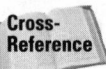

For more on using Video objects with ActionScript, refer to Chapter 28, "Sharing and Loading Assets."

✦ **Rename:** Use the Rename command to rename the currently selected item in the Sort window. Double-click on any item title in the list to achieve the same thing.

✦ **Move to New Folder:** Use the Move to New Folder option to open the New Folder dialog box. Click OK to automatically insert the new folder in the Library Sort window. The currently selected item in the Library is stored in the new folder.

Library items can also be moved to folders by dragging them onto any Folder icon.

✦ **Duplicate, Delete:** Select Duplicate to create a copy of an item and Delete to delete an item in the Sort window.

✦ **Edit:** Choose Edit to access the selected symbol in Edit mode.

Double-clicking a symbol on the Stage takes you into Edit in Place mode, which is a variant of Edit mode, which enables you to see other elements on the Stage dimmed in the background for layout reference as you modify the symbol.

✦ **Edit With:** Provided that you have appropriate external applications installed, most imported assets (such as sounds, bitmaps, and vectors) will have this command available to jump to the external editing environment of your choice.

✦ **Properties:** This command invokes the related Properties dialog box for the particular symbol type—Sound, Bitmap, Symbol, Component, or Video Properties. The Properties dialog box is a central control that enables you to rename an element, access Edit mode, or access the Linkages dialog box from one location. This is also where you can define or edit the Source for any element.

✦ **Linkage:** Use this command to invoke the Linkage options dialog box. Linkage means that you can assign an identifier string to a Movie Clip symbol, a Font symbol, a sound, or a Video object so that it can be accessed with ActionScript. This is an aspect of Shared Libraries.

Cross-Reference

For more information about Shared Libraries and Linkage, refer to Chapter 28, "Sharing and Loading Assets."

✦ **Component Definition:** This Library option invokes the Define Component dialog box, which is used to assign variables to Movie Clips to create your own Components. (Components are Movie Clips with customizable behavior that can be reused in projects.)

New Feature

A library of pre-compiled components is available in the Components panel. To set parameters for the compiled Components that ship with Flash, you must use the new Component Inspector panel or the Parameters tab in the Property inspector.

Cross-Reference

The features and uses of Flash Components are discussed in Chapter 29, "Using Components."

✦ **Select Unused Items:** Select Unused Items to find any items stored in the Library that have not been used in the current project.

Tip

Unused items will not be included in your published movie file (.swf), but they will add weight to your project file (.fla). Select Unused Items is a handy way to find these files so you can delete them to streamline your project file. Use Save and Compact or Save As to save your FLA file minus the extra weight of the unused items that you have deleted from the Library.

✦ **Update:** Use this option if you've edited items subsequent to importing them into Flash. Items will be updated without the bother of reimporting. This option can also be used to swap in a new element of the same kind to replace an item already used in your project.

✦ **Play (or Stop, if currently playing):** If the selected asset has a timeline or is otherwise playable (such as a sound), click this to preview the asset in the Library Preview window. If the asset is currently playing, this option is updated to Stop—in which case, click to stop playing.

✦ **Expand Folder/Collapse Folder:** Use this command to toggle the currently selected folder in the sort window open or closed.

✦ **Expand All Folders/Collapse All Folders:** Use this command to toggle all folders and subfolders in the sort window open or closed.

✦ **Shared Library Properties:** Use this command to invoke the Shared Properties dialog box, which is another aspect of runtime Shared Libraries.

For more information about Shared Libraries, refer to the section "Working with Authortime Shared Libraries" later in this chapter, as well as to Chapter 28, "Sharing and Loading Assets."

✦ **Keep Use Counts Updated:** Use this command to tell Flash to continuously keep track of the usage of each symbol. If you're working with multiple, complex graphics and symbols, this feature can slow down your processor.

✦ **Update Use Counts Now:** Use this option to tell Flash to update the usage of each symbol. This command is a one-time check and is probably less of a drain on system resources than the previous command, which checks continuously.

Selecting New Symbol, Duplicate, or Properties from the options menu launches the Symbol Properties dialog box, shown in Figure 6-5. Use this dialog box to give the symbol a unique name and assign it a behavior (as a symbol type — Graphic, Button, or Movie Clip). However, if the Properties option is chosen for a sound asset, then the Sound Properties dialog box appears.

For more information on Sound Properties, refer to Chapter 15, "Adding Sound."

Assign symbol behavior   Launch Symbol Edit mode

Figure 6-5: The Symbol Properties dialog box. Note the button for Advanced options — this expands the dialog box to include Linkage and Source information for the selected element.

Organizing the Library

When your movies start to become complex, you'll find that the Library gets crowded, and it can be hard to find symbols. When this happens, you'll appreciate the capability to create and name folders for your symbols. You can organize your Library folders however you like, but here are a few suggestions for greater productivity:

✦ Create a separate folder for each Scene.

✦ Create folders for certain kinds of symbols, such as buttons, sounds, or bitmap imports.

✦ Store all symbols or graphics that relate to a specific element (such as a logo or an animated element) together in one folder.

When you build complex layered structures in your movie — a Movie Clip symbol on the first frame of a Button symbol, with a text symbol on the layer above it, and a sound on the layer above that — the Library doesn't visually track this hierarchy. But you can indicate this — just put all the associated symbols in a folder with a name that describes the final element. You can also nest folders within other folders. Working with folders in the Library is almost exactly the same as working with folders in the Layers area of the Timeline window, as follows:

✦ To create a folder, click the folder icon at the bottom-left corner of the Library.

✦ To move a file or folder into another folder, simply drag it over the target folder icon.

✦ To move a folder that's been nested within another folder back to the top level of the Library, drag the folder until it is just above the Library list and over the word Name and release.

Note   Putting symbols in different folders does not affect the links between them and their instances (as opposed to the way moving a graphic file into a new folder breaks an existing link on a Web page). Flash tracks and updates all references to Library items whenever they are renamed or moved into separate folders (within the same Library).

The Movie Explorer is a great way of getting a visual overview of the nested relationship of symbols, Movie Clips, and other items within your document. Refer to the end of this chapter for more on the Movie Explorer.

Caution   For one Library action, there is neither an undo nor escape: Delete. Any item that is deleted from the Library is gone forever, including all instances throughout the current document (.fla). If you decide that you shouldn't have deleted an item, the only cure is to close the file without saving any changes. When you reopen the file, the Library should be intact as it was the last time the file was saved.

Tip   Flash offers an option to Import to Library that is especially useful when you want to bring in a series of items. Instead of having all the items dumped onto the Stage in your Document window, you can load them directly into the project Library.

Resolving Conflicts Between Library Assets

Importing or copying an asset into your current project Library will occasionally invoke a Resolve Library Conflict alert box asking if you want to Replace Existing Items and Instances. This alert box appears when you are trying to add a new asset to your Library with the same name as an asset already present in your current document. If you choose not to replace the existing item, the newly added items will have the word *copy* added to their filenames. For example, if you have an item named *photo* in your current Library and attempt to add another item to the Library with the same name, the new item would be given the name *photo copy* in the Library. To rename the added item, simply double-click on the item name in the Library list and type a new name.

If you choose to replace the existing item in your Library, all instances will be replaced with the content of the newly added item. If you choose to cancel the import or copy operation, the selected items will not be added to your current document and the existing items stored in the Library will be preserved.

Defining Content Types

Understanding the behavior of various media types and learning to streamline asset management unlocks the true potential of Flash for combining compelling content with small file sizes. The basic structures for storing, reusing, and modifying content within a Flash project are not complicated, but the reason for using various symbol types does deserve explanation.

Raw data

When you create graphics directly in Flash, using the shape tools, text tool, or any of the other drawing tools, you produce raw data or *primitive shapes*. These elements can be copied and pasted into any keyframe on the Timeline, but they do not appear in the project Library. Each time the element appears Flash has to read and render all the points, curves, and color information from scratch because the information is not stored in the Library. Even if the shape looks exactly the same on keyframe 10 as it did on keyframe 1, Flash has to do all the work to recreate the shape every time it appears. This quickly bloats the size of the SWF file. Also, because each element is completely independent, if you decide to make any changes, you have to find and edit each appearance of an element manually. This is a daunting task if your project involves animation or nested symbols.

New Feature   The new Find and Replace feature (Alt+F or Option+F) built-in to Flash MX 2004, makes it much easier to accomplish mundane editing tasks on multiple items within your Flash project file. The myriad uses for Find and Replace are introduced in Chapter 9, "Modifying Graphics."

Groups

The first step toward making raw data more manageable is to use groups. By grouping a filled shape with its outline stroke, for example, it becomes easier to select both parts of the shape to move around in your layout. If you added a text element that you also wanted to keep aligned with your artwork, you could add this to the group as well. Groups can be inclusive or cumulative, so that you can select multiple elements and create one group (Ctrl+G or ⌘+G) that can be accessed on the same edit level by double-clicking the whole group once. If you add another element (even another group) to the first group, you will find that you have to click in to a deeper level to edit individual elements. In this way, groups can grow more and more complicated, which is helpful if you're trying to keep multiple elements in order.

The important thing to remember about groups, however, is that they are *not* symbols. Although groups have a similar selection highlight to symbols, you will notice that they don't have a crosshair icon in the center, and that the group information won't appear in your project Library. No matter how careful you are about reusing the same raw data and grouping elements to keep them organized, when it comes to publishing your movie (.swf) or trying to update any single element, you will be no better off than if you had just placed raw elements wildly into your project. Flash still treats each shape and line as a unique element and the file size grows exponentially each time you add another keyframe containing any of your raw data, even if it is grouped. The best way to use groups in your project is for managing symbols, or to organize elements that you plan to keep together and convert into one symbol.

 **Caution** Using groups will help organize raw shapes or other elements in your FLA files, but it will not help to optimize the final SWF file. Using a lot of groups in your project file can actually *add* weight to the final published SWF.

Native symbols

Imported sound, video, bitmap, or font symbols are stored automatically in the Library to define *instances* of the asset when it is used in the project. In addition, three basic *container* symbol types can be created in the Flash authoring environment. Movie Clip symbols, Graphic symbols, and Button symbols all have timelines that can hold images, sounds, text, or even other symbols. Although it is possible to make the behavior of a symbol instance different from the behavior of the original symbol, it is generally best to decide how you plan to use a certain element and then assign it the symbol type that is appropriate to both its content and expected use in the project.

 Tip Dragging a primitive shape or group into the Library panel from the Stage automatically invokes the Convert to Symbol dialog box so that you can name and assign a symbol type to the element before it is added to your Library.

To make a decision on what type of symbol to use, it helps to have a clear understanding of the benefits and limitations of each of the symbol types available in Flash. Each symbol type has specific features that are suited to particular kinds of content. Each symbol type is marked with a unique icon in the Library, but what all symbols have in common is that they can be reused within a project as symbol instances, all defined by the original symbol. A Flash project Library may contain any or all of the symbol types in the following sections, all created directly in Flash.

 **Note** If you use Timeline Effects to auto-create animation or visual effects, the symbols added to the Library to contain the animation are Graphic symbols by default (rather than Movie Clips), so that you can view the final effects just by scrubbing the Timeline.

Graphic symbols

 Graphic symbols are used mainly for static images that are reused in a project. Flash ignores any sounds or actions inside a Graphic symbol. Graphic symbols do not play independently of the main Timeline and thus require an allocated frame on the main Timeline for each frame that you want to be visible within the symbol. If you want a Graphic symbol to loop or repeat as the main Timeline moves along, you have to include another whole series of frames on the main Timeline to match the length of the Graphic symbol timeline for each loop.

Movie Clip symbols

 Movie Clips are actually movies within a movie. They're good for animations that run independently of the movie's main Timeline. They can contain actions, other symbols, and sounds. Movie Clips can also be placed inside of other symbols and are indispensable for creating interactive interface elements such as animated buttons.

Movie Clips can continue to play even if the main Timeline is stopped. Thus, they need only one frame on the main Timeline to play back any number of frames on their own timeline. By default, Movie Clips are set to loop. So, as long as there is an instance of the Movie Clip visible on the main Timeline it can loop or play back the content on its own timeline as many times as you want it to, without needing a matching number of keyframes on the main Timeline.

Button symbols

Button symbols are used for creating interactive buttons. Button symbols have a timeline limited to four frames, which are referred to as *states.* These states are related directly to user interaction and are labeled Up, Over, Down, and Hit. Each of these button states can be defined with graphics, symbols, and sounds. After you create a Button symbol, you can assign independent actions to various instances in the main movie or inside other Movie Clips. As with Movie Clips, Button symbols only require one frame on any other timeline to be able to playback the three visible states (frames) of their own timeline.

Components

Components are prebuilt Movie Clips for interactive Flash elements that can be reused and customized. Flash MX-style, or *uncompiled*, Components are visible in the root folder of the Library along with a folder that holds the elements used to build the component. Flash MX 2004-style, or *compiled*, Components are represented by a single generic icon in the Library. Each Component has its own unique set of ActionScript methods that enable you to set options at runtime.

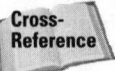

Cross-Reference   Refer to Chapter 29, "Using Components," for more details.

Imported media elements

A Flash project Library also stores certain types of imported assets to define instances of the asset when instances are used in the movie. You can place these imported assets into native Flash symbol structures by converting a bitmap into a Graphic symbol or placing a Sound inside a Button symbol, for example.

Bitmaps

Bitmaps are handled like symbols, the original image is stored in the Library and any time the image is used in the project it is actually a copy, or an *instance,* of the original. To use a bitmap asset, drag an instance out of the Library and onto the Stage. Export settings for individual bitmaps are managed from within the Library by choosing Properties from either the contextual menu or the Library options menu. However, you will not be able to apply Color or Alpha effects to the symbol instance unless you convert it into a native Flash symbol type (Graphic Symbol, Button, or Movie Clip).

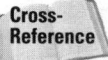
The topic of importing and using bitmaps in Flash is covered in detail in Chapter 16, "Importing Artwork," and in Chapter 34, "Working with Raster Graphics."

Vector graphics

Vector graphics, upon import from other applications, arrive on the Flash Stage as a group, and unlike bitmaps, may be edited or manipulated just like a normal group drawn in Flash. These elements will not be stored in the Library until they have been converted to a native symbol type.

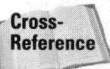
Vectors are discussed in greater detail in Chapter 16, "Importing Artwork," and Chapter 36, "Working with Vector Graphics."

Sounds

The Library also handles Sounds like symbols. However, they can be assigned different playback behavior after they are placed on a timeline. Flash can import (and export) sounds in a range of sound formats. Upon import, these sound files reside in the Library. To use a sound, drag an instance of the sound out of the Library and onto the Stage. Export settings for sound files are managed from within the Library by choosing Properties from either the contextual menu or the Library options menu. Playback behavior and effects can be defined with the Property inspector after a sound is placed on a timeline.

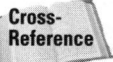
Importing and using sounds effectively is a critical topic covered in Chapter 15, "Adding Sound."

Video assets

Video assets, as with Font symbols, can be embedded or linked. Embedded video assets, like bitmaps, can have Color and Alpha effects applied if they are first converted to a native Flash symbol type.

Font symbols

A Font symbols are symbols created from font files to make them available for use in dynamic text fields. Font symbols can also be defined as shared fonts to make them available to multiple movie files (.swf) without the file size burden of embedding the font into each file individually.

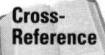
Refer to Chapter 28, "Sharing and Loading Assets," for more details.

Graphic Symbols versus Movie Clips,
by Robin and Sandy Debreuil

Graphic symbols are a quick and tidy way of placing static information into a timeline, whereas Movie Clips animate independently on their own timeline. Graphic symbols should be used to hold single frames of raw data, or multiple frames when it is important to preview your work while designing it, as with linear animation. Movie Clips must be used when ActionScript is involved, or when an animation must run regardless of what is happening around it. However, the use of one type of symbol instead of the other may not always involve clear-cut choices, because often, either works. Consequently, to use symbols effectively, it's important to know the pluses, minuses, and absolutes of both Graphic symbols and Movie Clips. Here are some tips to keep in mind:

✦ Instance properties of Graphic symbols (height, color, rotation, and so on) are frozen at design time, whereas Movie Clips can have their instance properties set on the fly with ActionScript. This makes Movie Clips essential for programmed content such as games.

✦ Scrubbing the main Timeline (previewing while working) is not possible with Movie Clips, although it is possible with Graphic symbols. This makes Graphic symbols essential for animating cartoons. Eyes open, eyes closed — it's that big of a difference.

✦ Movie Clips can't (easily) be exported to video or other linear mediums. This is only significant if you plan to convert your SWF files to another time-based medium.

✦ A Graphic symbol's instance properties are controlled (modified) at design time, with the options available in the Property inspector. One advantage is that this is simple and sure because you have an instant preview of what's happening. In addition, this information is embedded right in that particular instance of the Graphic symbol — meaning that, if it is either moved or copied, all of this information comes with it.

✦ A Movie Clip's instance properties can be controlled at design time or set with ActionScript. This gives it great flexibility, although it's a little more abstract to work with ActionScript. One advantage is that the actions do not need to be directly linked to the Movie Clip, which has the concurrent disadvantage that care must be taken when moving Movie Clips that have visual qualities defined with ActionScript.

✦ Graphic symbols that are animated (have more than one frame), and are nested with other animated Graphic symbols, may have problems with synchronization. For example, if you have a pair of eyes that blink at the end of a ten-frame Graphic symbol, and you put the Graphic symbol containing those eyes within a five-frame Graphic symbol of a head . . . the eyes will never blink. The head Graphic symbol will run from frame 1 to frame 5, and then return to frame 1, only displaying the first five frames of the eyes Graphic symbol. Or, if you nest the eyes Graphic symbol into a fifteen-frame head Graphic symbol, they will blink on frame 10, and then every fifteen frames. That's ten frames, then blink, and then they loop back to frame 1; however, when reaching frame 5 this time, the movie they are in loops back to frame 1 (it's a fifteen-frame movie), and thus resets the eyes to frame 1.

✦ Movie Clips do not have the problem/feature described in the preceding bullet point. They offer consistent, independent timeline playback.

Editing Symbols

Because every instance of a symbol is linked to the original, *any* edit applied to that original is applied to every instance. There are several ways to edit a symbol, covered in the following sections.

Modifying a symbol in Edit mode

Edit mode opens the Stage and timeline of the selected symbol into the Document window, replacing the view of the current keyframe in the main Timeline with a view of the first keyframe in the symbol's timeline. To open a symbol in Edit mode, do one of the following:

✦ Select an instance on the Stage and choose Edit ⇨ Edit Symbols, or Edit Selected from the application menu.

✦ Select an instance on the Stage and right-click (Control+click). Then choose **Edit** from the contextual menu.

✦ Select an instance on the Stage and use the shortcut key Ctrl+E (or ⌘+E).

✦ Double-click a symbol in the Document Library. (Double-clicking Bitmaps, Sound, Video and other non-native symbol types launches the Properties dialog box instead of opening Edit mode.)

Editing a symbol in a new window

This method is useful if you're working on two monitors and want to quickly open a new window to edit in while keeping a view of the main Timeline open and available. On Macintosh these two windows are always separate, but you can click on either window to switch back and forth. On Windows, you can switch between these windows by choosing from the Window menu.

To edit a symbol in a new window, select an instance on the Stage and right-click (Control+click); then select **Edit In New Window** from the contextual menu.

Editing a symbol in place

The advantage of Edit In Place is that, instead of opening the Symbol in a separate edit space, you can edit your symbol in context with the surrounding movie. Other elements present on the current keyframe are visible but dimmed slightly and protected from any edits you make on the selected symbol. To edit a symbol in place, do one of the following:

✦ Select an instance on the Stage and chose Edit ⇨ Edit in Place from the application menu.

✦ Select an instance on the Stage and right-click (Control+click). Then select Edit In Place from the contextual menu.

✦ Double-click the instance on the Stage.

Editing symbols from the Library

You might not have an instance of your symbol available to select for editing in the Document window, but you can still edit it. Just edit it from the Library. Open your movie's Library with Window ⇨ Library from the application menu (Ctrl+L or ⌘+L). Select the symbol in the Library that you want to edit and do one of the following:

✦ Double-click the symbol's icon (not its name), in the Library list.

✦ Right-click (Control+click) and then select **Edit** from the contextual pop-up menu.

✦ If you have opened the Symbol properties dialog box (see Figure 6-5), you can move to Edit mode by clicking the Edit button.

Returning to the main Timeline or scene

After you've edited your symbol, you'll want to go back to the scene to make sure that your changes work properly. Just do one of the following:

✦ Select Edit ⇨ Edit Movie from the application menu or use the shortcut keys — Ctrl+E or ⌘+E.

✦ Double-click in any empty area of the Edit Stage.

✦ Select the scene name in the left corner above the Stage view in the Document window, as shown in Figure 6-6.

Working with Timeline Effect symbols

Timeline Effects are a new addition to Flash MX 2004. They offer some long-awaited shortcuts to making animation and effects on the Timeline. Although you can still create your own animation and effects by manually altering graphics and creating custom tweens, you may be able to get the result you want faster and more easily with Timeline Effects.

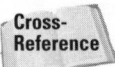

Cross-Reference   The application of various Timeline Effects and settings are discussed in detail in Chapter 9, "Modifying Graphics."

In most production workflows in this book, we advise you to use Movie Clip symbols to contain animation. However, you will find that Timeline Effects automatically create a Graphic symbol to hold the visual effect or animation. We refer to these animated Graphic symbols as Timeline Effect symbols.

You can apply Timeline Effects to raw shapes or to any of the native Flash symbol types, but the symbols generated by the Effect settings will always be Graphic symbols by default. Macromedia chose this symbol type because it enables you to view the animation in the authoring environment just by scrubbing the Timeline. Timeline Effects are rendered based on the options chosen in various Timeline Effects dialog boxes, rather than on the basic tween settings available in the Property inspector.

After you apply a Timeline Effect to an item, you have the option of going back and changing the settings to modify and re-render the Effect so long as the Timeline Effect symbol is not opened in Edit mode. If you try to apply any of the standard symbol-editing techniques listed in the previous section to a Timeline Effect symbol, you will get a warning box. As shown in Figure 6-7, directly editing a Timeline Effect symbol will disable the Timeline Effect Settings option.

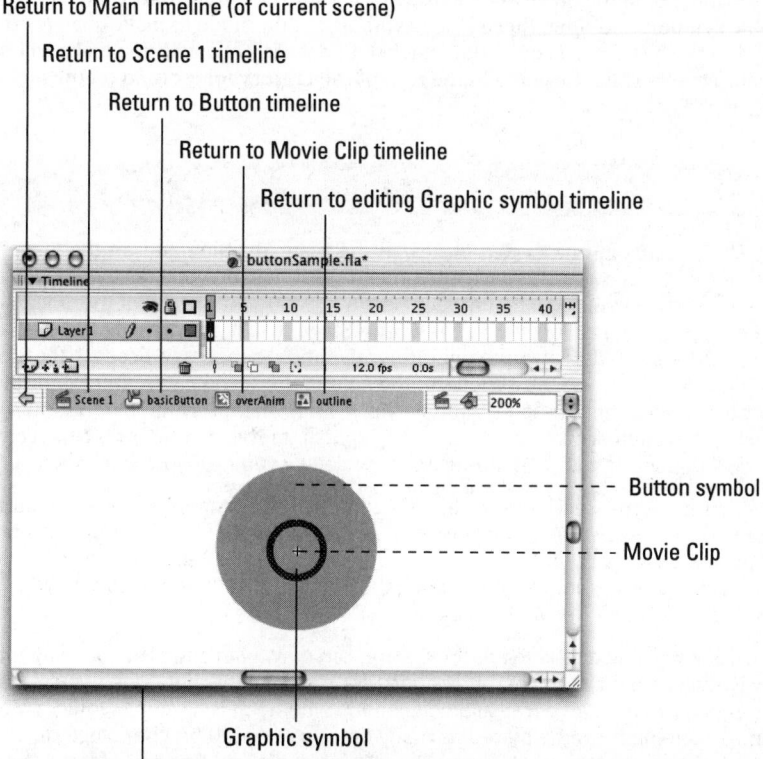

Return to Main Timeline (of current scene)

Return to Scene 1 timeline

Return to Button timeline

Return to Movie Clip timeline

Return to editing Graphic symbol timeline

Button symbol

Movie Clip

Graphic symbol

Symbol edit space for Graphic symbol seen in Edit in Place mode

Figure 6-6: The location label of the Document window is used to identify the current edit space and to return to the main Timeline of the current scene.

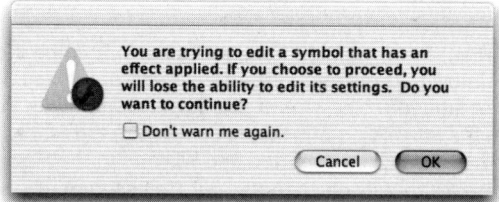

You are trying to edit a symbol that has an effect applied. If you choose to proceed, you will lose the ability to edit its settings. Do you want to continue?

☐ Don't warn me again.

Cancel   OK

Figure 6-7: The warning box triggered by trying to edit directly a Graphic symbol with a Timeline Effect applied

It *is* possible to change the contents of the nested symbols in an animation or effect created with a Timeline Effect, but the only way to access these symbols, while preserving the settings option, is through the project Library. Rather than selecting the symbol with the visible

Timeline Effect applied on the Stage, look in the Library for the folder that contains the nested Graphic symbols and open these static symbols in Edit mode to make changes that will be applied to the instances used in the Timeline Effect. Any changes you make will be visible in the main Timeline Effect symbol in the root of the Library folder (and on the main Timeline).

Editing and Developing

Development in Flash occurs in one of two places: in the main Timeline and on the Stage; or within a symbol, which has its own edit space and timeline. But how do you know when you are on the Scene Stage or when you are in Edit mode? Here's one clue: At the top of the Document window is the Edit bar. If you're working on the Scene Stage, you'll see a single tab with the name of the scene. Unless you name your scenes, this tab should simply say, Scene 1 (or Scene 2). However, in Edit mode, a second tab appears to the right of the scene name: This tab displays the name and icon of the current group or symbol (Movie Clip, Graphic symbol, or Button symbol). If you're editing a nested symbol, more tabs may appear. In this manner, you have convenient access to the hierarchy of your files, no matter how deeply you nest your symbols.

In Flash MX, the Edit bar appeared between the Timeline and the Stage/Work area when the Timeline was docked to the Document window. In Flash MX 2004, the Edit bar appears above the (docked) Timeline by default, but you can move it below the Timeline by holding down Shift+Alt (Win) or Shift+⌘ (Mac) and double-clicking the Edit bar. Use the same command again to move the Edit bar back to the default location.

Edit mode is much like working on the regular Stage. You can draw with any of the drawing tools; add text, place symbols, import graphics, and sound, and use ActionScript. When you're done working with a symbol, you have an encapsulated element, whether it is a static Graphic, a Movie Clip, or a Button. This element can be placed as many times as needed on your Stage or within other symbols. Each time you place it, the symbol's entire contents and timeline (if it is a Button or a Movie Clip) will be placed as well, identical to the original symbol stored in the Library. Remember that even if you access Edit mode from an instance on the Stage, all changes that you make will propagate to every other instance derived from the original symbol in the Library. The only color changes that can be made to one instance at a time without affecting the other instances of the same symbol are those applied using the Color menu on the Property inspector, as explained in the following section on Modifying Instance Properties.

The Stage (if it is not Zoomed to fill the screen) is surrounded by a gray area. This is the Work area, which indicates the edges of the final movie, as defined in the Document properties. The dimensions of any symbol, however, are not limited to the size of the Stage. If you make your symbols too large, when you place them on the Stage, portions that fall outside of the Stage will not be visible in the final movie (.swf), but they will still be exported and will add to the file size. Remember that it is always possible to scale a symbol instance to make it smaller than the original symbol if necessary.

Modifying Instance Properties

Every instance of a symbol has graphic variables that can be modified. These properties only apply to the specific instance—not to the original symbol. Display properties such as brightness, tint, and alpha (transparency) can all be modified without creating a new symbol. An instance can also be scaled, rotated, and skewed. With the behavior menu in the Property inspector, you can change the symbol type behavior of an instance without changing the original symbol. As previously discussed, any changes made to the original symbol in Edit mode will be updated in each instance—this still holds true even if some of the instances also have properties that are modified individually.

Note   Properties can be modified for Timeline Effect symbol instances without losing the ability to adjust the original Effect settings.

Applying basic color effects to symbol instances

Each instance of a symbol can have a variety of color effects applied to it. The basic effects are changes of brightness, tint, and *alpha* (transparency). Tint and alpha changes can also be combined for special effects. To apply color effects to a symbol instance:

1. Select the instance in the Document window that you want to modify.

2. Select one of the options from the Color drop-down menu in the Property inspector. Figure 6-8 shows the basic color effect options.

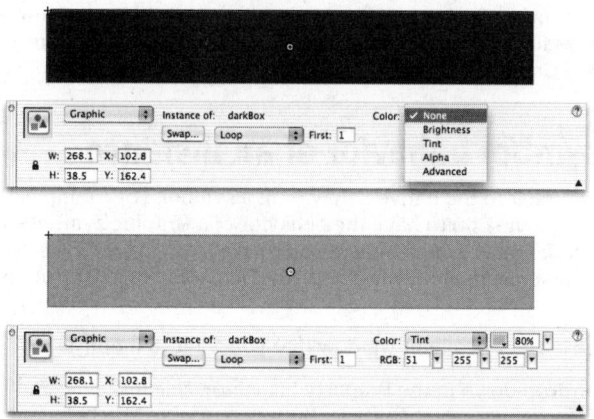

Figure 6-8: The Color menu has basic options to choose from (top). After a color effect is selected, the settings for that effect are available in the Property inspector (bottom).

The options available from the Color menu are as follows:

- **None:** No effect is applied.

- **Brightness:** Adjusts the relative brightness or darkness of the instance. It ranges from 100 percent (white) to –100 percent (black); the default setting is 0 percent (no visible change to instance appearance). Use the slider to change the value or just type a numeric value into the entry field.

- **Tint:** Enables you to shift the color of an instance. Either select a hue with the color picker, or enter the RGB values directly. Then, select the percentage of saturation (Tint Amount) by using the slider or by entering the percentage in the entry field. This number ranges from 0 percent (no saturation) to 100 percent (completely saturated).

- **Alpha:** Enables you to modify the transparency of an instance. Select a percentage by using the slider or by entering a number directly. The Alpha percentage (or visibility setting) ranges from 0 percent (completely transparent) to 100 percent (no transparency).

- **Advanced:** When you select the Advanced option from the Color menu, a Settings button appears to the right of the menu. The Settings button invokes the Advanced Effect dialog box that enables you to adjust both the tint and alpha settings of an instance. The controls on the left reduce the tint and alpha values by a specified percentage, whereas the controls on the right either reduce or increase the tint and alpha values by a constant value. The current values are multiplied by the numbers on the left, and then added to the values on the right.

Cross-Reference The Advanced option includes a range with negative alpha values. Potential uses for this capability, together with more information about using the Color menu, are detailed in Chapter 9, "Modifying Graphics."

Changing the symbol behavior of an instance

You don't need to limit yourself to the native behavior of a symbol. For example, there may be times when you want a Movie Clip to have the behavior of a Graphic symbol so that you can preview animation on the main Timeline. You don't have to go through the extra effort of creating a new symbol — just use the following steps to change the behavior of the instance as needed:

1. Select the instance in the Document window that you want to modify.

2. From the Behavior drop-down in the Property inspector, select the desired behavior. As shown in Figure 6-9, you can select Graphic, Button, or Movie Clip behavior.

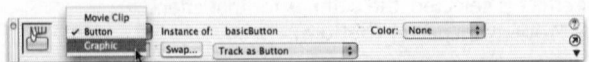

Figure 6-9: Using the menu on the Property inspector, you can change the behavior of a symbol instance at any time.

 **Cross-Reference**   The more-complex uses of symbol instances are covered in Parts V, "Adding Basic Interactivity to Flash Movies," and VII, "Approaching ActionScript."

Swapping symbols

There may be times when you need to replace an instance of one symbol with an instance of another symbol stored in your project Library. Luckily, you don't have to go through and re-create your entire animation to do this — just use the Swap Symbol feature, illustrated in Figure 6-10. This feature only switches the instance of the symbol for an instance of another symbol — all other modifications previously applied to the instance will remain the same. Here's how to swap symbols:

1. Select the instance that you want to replace.

2. Click the Swap symbol button on the Property inspector, choose Modify ➪ Symbol ➪ Swap Symbol from the application menu, or right-click (Control+click) and choose Swap Symbol from the contextual menu.

3. Select the symbol that you want to put into the place of your current instance from the list of available symbols in your project Library.

4. Click OK to swap the symbols.

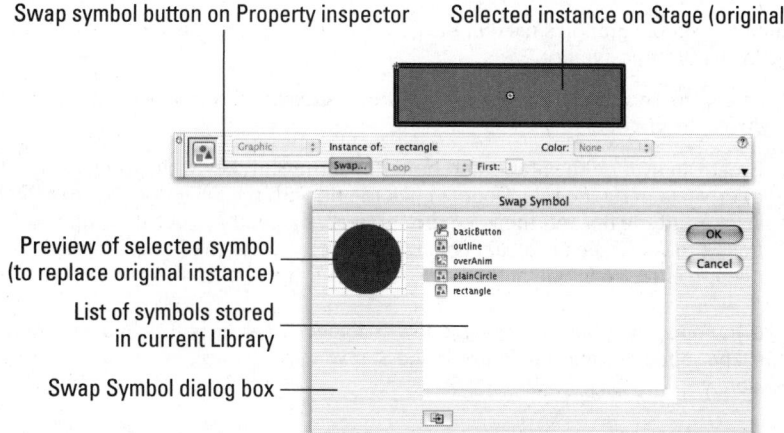

Figure 6-10: With a symbol selected in the Document window, click the Swap symbol button in the Property inspector to invoke the Swap Symbol dialog box.

Building Nested Symbol Structures

Understanding the various symbol types individually is the first step, but the next step is integrating these building blocks to create organized, optimized Flash projects that will be extensible, easy to edit, and fast to build. Although the workflow for different types of Flash projects are covered in depth in other parts of this book, we can synthesize the overview of different symbol types by walking through the steps of creating a Button symbol with some nested animation and Graphic symbols.

To demonstrate building an animated Flash movie from various symbol types, we made a Button symbol called basicButton that uses some raw shapes, some Graphic symbols, and some Movie Clips, all nested inside a Button symbol timeline.

On the CD-ROM

The completed source file (sampleButton.fla) for this series of demonstrations is on the CD-ROM that accompanies this book in the ch06 folder.

Converting a raw shape into a Graphic symbol

The best way to begin creating any graphic element is to first consider the final shape that you need and to try to find the most basic primitive shapes that you can use to build that element. Keep in mind that instances can be scaled, skewed, and adjusted with Color effects. Instead of drawing three circles to make a snowman, you would make just one circle and convert that into a symbol so that you could build your snowman from scaled instances of just one symbol stored in the Library. A resourceful animator we know built a Christmas tree by reusing instances of a symbol he had made for a dog's tail in the same animation — a wagging tail and a tree all built from just one Graphic symbol stored in the Library! Raw graphics can be converted into Graphic symbols after they have been drawn, or you can first create a new Graphic symbol and then draw the raw shapes directly inside the Graphic symbol in Edit mode — either way, the end result is a contained visual element that is stored in the Library to define any instances that you need to place in your movie.

To build the simple graphics used in basicButton, we can begin by converting a primitive shape into a Graphic symbol:

1. Select the Oval tool and set the fill color to green and the stroke color to black with a stroke height of 3.

2. Create an oval on the Stage, and hold down the Shift key while dragging out the shape to create a perfect circle. Double click the fill with the Selection tool to select both the stroke and the fill, and then use the Property inspector to set the width to 75 and the height to 75. (If the constrain check box is selected in the Property inspector, you only need to enter **75** in one of the value fields and the circle will scale evenly.)

Note

If you open the Library panel — Window ➪ Library (Ctrl+L or ⌘+L) — you will notice that the shape you've drawn is not visible in the Sort window because raw data is not stored in the Library.

3. While the stroke and the fill are both still selected, press F8 or choose Modify ➪ Convert to Symbol from the application menu.

4. In the Convert to Symbol dialog box, choose Graphic for the behavior and give the symbol the name **plainCircle.** Then click OK. You should now see the plainCircle symbol with the Graphic symbol icon next to it in the Library.

Instances of this Graphic symbol can now be reused in your document in as many places as you need it just by dragging an instance onto the Stage from the Library panel. For the basicButton example, you will want to use an instance of plainCircle inside of a new Button symbol rather than on the main Stage, so you can delete the instance of plainCircle that is now on the main Timeline.

Using Graphic symbols in a Button

Button symbols are similar to Movie Clips that have a special timeline structure linked to mouse states. For a Button to take us to a new point on the main Timeline or to load any other elements, ActionScript needs to be added to the Button instance.

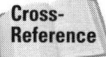

Cross-Reference Adding actions to buttons for more advanced interactivity is discussed in Chapter 18, "Understanding Actions and Event Handlers."

In this example the button simply works as a structure for an animation that reacts to the mouse. Begin by inserting a new Button symbol.

1. Click the New Symbol button in the Library panel, choose Insert ➪ New Symbol from the application menu or use the shortcut keys (Ctrl+F8 or ⌘+F8).

2. In the Create New Symbol dialog box, choose **Button** as the behavior and for our example, give this symbol the name **basicButton.** Then click **OK.**

3. This Button symbol is now stored in the Library and automatically opens in Edit mode in the Document window, so you can add some content to the button.

4. You will notice that the Timeline shows four keyframes with labels that define the button state by mouse behavior: Up, Over, Down, and Hit. These various keyframes can have multiple layers and contain any visual element or sound that you want. The button states function as follows:

   - **Up:** Any elements placed in the Up keyframe will be associated with the button as it appears on the Stage when it is present but not activated by any mouse interaction.

   - **Over:** Any elements placed in the Over keyframe will be associated with the button when the mouse rolls over it on the Stage, but as soon as the mouse rolls off the button it will revert to its Up state.

   - **Down:** Any elements placed in the Down keyframe will be associated with the button only when the mouse is over it and clicked and held down—as soon as the mouse is released, the button will revert to its Over state.

   - **Hit:** The Hit keyframe is actually never visible on Stage, but this instead defines the area of the button that is "sensitive" to the mouse. Whatever shape is present on this frame will be considered part of the button's *hit area.* It is important to note that it is better not to have holes or gaps in the hit area unless it is intended. For example, if you have text as a button, it is best to use a solid rectangle that matches the width and height of the total text area. Using the actual text would result in an irregular button hit area—whenever the mouse rolled into the space between letters the button would revert to its Up state and could not be clicked.

Tip If you ever need an "invisible" button in your project, you can create one by adding artwork to the Hit keyframe only of a Button symbol. The button will be visible in the authoring environment as a pale green preview shape, but when the SWF is published the only indication that a button is on the Stage is the change in the mouse cursor when it enters the Hit area. You can add ActionScript to an invisible button to trigger events in your animation or to control the behavior of other elements in your movie. Invisible buttons are discussed in more detail in Chapter 18, "Understanding Actions and Event Handlers."

For this example, we will be creating animation to be placed into the various visible states, but the main shape of the button will always be consistent so we can begin by creating a layer to define the main shape of the button.

5. Rename Layer 1 as **buttonOutline** and insert two frames (F5) after the first keyframe to create a span of three frames (visible for Up, Over, and Down).

6. With the Playhead set on the first keyframe, drag an instance of plainCircle onto the Button Stage and make sure that it is now visible in the Up, Over, and Down states of the button, but not on the Hit state.

7. Center the instance on the button Stage by using the Align panel (Ctrl+K or ⌘+K). Select the instance of plainCircle and copy it to the clipboard (Ctrl+C or ⌘+C).

8. Create a new layer and name it **hitArea.** Insert a blank keyframe (F7) on frame 4 (Hit). To paste the copy of plainCircle instance into the center of the blank Hit keyframe, use Paste in Place (Ctrl+Shift+V, or ⌘+Shift+V.) If you have done a straightforward paste instead, make sure that the instance of plainCircle is centered to the button Stage.

9. The Timeline of your Button symbol should now look like Figure 6-11.

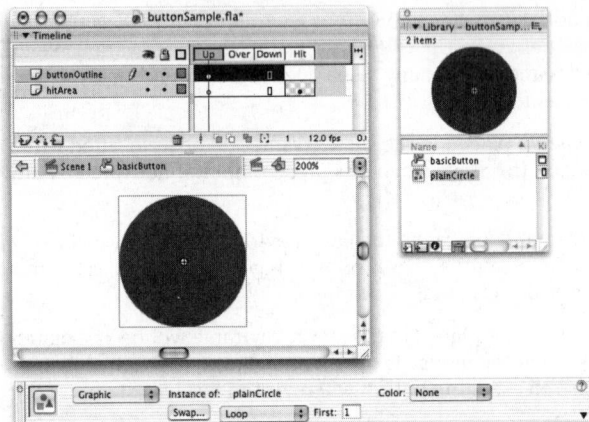

Figure 6-11: The Edit mode view of the basicButton Timeline, with Up, Over, Down, and Hit states defined with instances of the plainCircle Graphic symbol

10. Return to the main Timeline by using the Edit bar or by double-clicking in an empty area of the Stage.

11. If you don't see an instance of your basicButton on the Stage of the main Timeline, drag an instance out of the Library and place it on the first frame of the main Timeline.

Animating Graphic symbols in a Movie Clip

After you have created some Graphic symbols to define your basicButton, you can now start building some animation to add to it. Animation can be built by placing artwork in keyframes on the main Timeline, but this limits how the animation can be used, and can make it difficult to add more elements to your project without disturbing the keyframe structure of the animation. If you need animated elements that can be reused, and quickly moved to different parts of the main Timeline or placed into a Button symbol timeline, it is best to begin by creating a Movie Clip.

1. Click the New Symbol button in the Library panel, choose Insert ⇨ New Symbol from the application menu or use shortcut keys (Control+F8 or ⌘+F8).

2. In the Symbol Properties dialog box, choose Movie Clip as the behavior and give this symbol the name **overAnim.**

3. Create a new circle on the first frame of the Movie Clip timeline with a black stroke (with a height of 3) and no fill. Select the outline with the Selection tool and use the Property inspector to set its width and height to 25. Then use the Align panel to center it on the Stage.

4. Convert this raw shape into a Graphic symbol (F8) with the name **outline.**

5. Insert a keyframe (F6) on frame 10 of the Movie Clip timeline so that you have a span of frames from frame 1 to frame 10 with the outline Graphic symbol visible.

6. Select the instance of outline on keyframe 10 and use the Property inspector to scale it up to 50 high and 50 wide.

7. Now select keyframe 1 and use the Property inspector to set a Motion tween. This creates an animation of the outline Graphic symbol scaling up from its original size to the larger size that you gave it in frame 10.

8. The Timeline of your Movie Clip should now look like Figure 6-12.

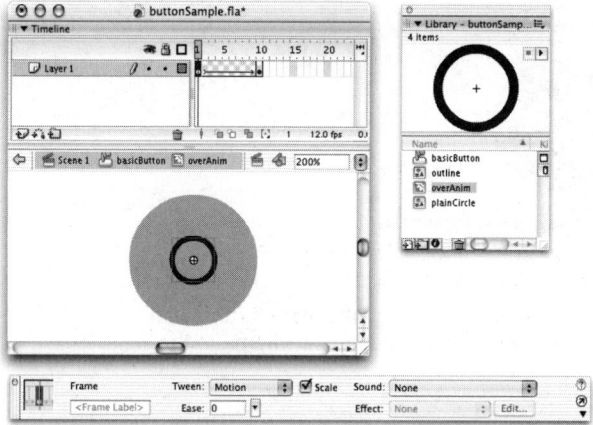

Figure 6-12: The Timeline of the Movie Clip overAnim, showing a Motion tween of the Graphic symbol "outline," from frame 1 to frame 10

Adding a Movie Clip to a Button symbol

The final step in our example is to add the overAnim Movie Clip to the basicButton symbol. This is the secret to animated Button symbols — by nesting multiframe Movie Clip animations into the single frames assigned to the Up, Over, and Down states of the Button symbol timeline, you can create different animated "reactions" as the mouse rolls over or clicks the button.

1. To go back inside your button and add animation in Edit mode, double-click the instance of basicButton on the Stage or the symbol in the Library.

2. Create a new layer in the Button Timeline and name it **outlineAnim.** Make sure that this new layer is above the original buttonOutline layer.

3. On the outlineAnim layer, insert a new keyframe (F6) on frame 2 (Over).

4. Drag an instance of overAnim from the Library onto the button Stage in the keyframe you just created, and use the Align panel to center it.

5. To ensure that the animation is only visible on the Over state of the button, make sure that the content on the overAnim layer only occupies one frame on the Timeline. If the overAnim symbol extends into frame 3, either insert a blank keyframe (F7), or remove a frame (Shift+F5) to keep it contained on frame 2.

6. Your Button symbol Timeline should now look like Figure 6-13.

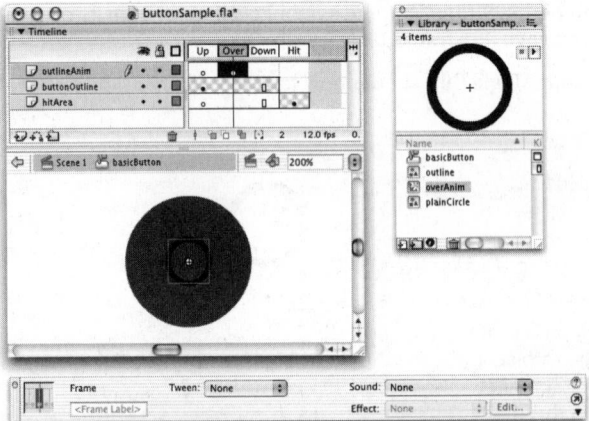

Figure 6-13: The Timeline of Button symbol basicButton with the Movie Clip overAnim placed on the Over keyframe of the outlineAnim layer

You can test your Button symbol with this animation added to see how it is working, by pressing Ctrl+Enter (⌘+Return) on the keyboard to view the movie (.swf) in the Test Movie environment. Now when you roll over the green button with your mouse, you should see the outline circles animate. Remember that you still only have one keyframe on your main Timeline, so this demonstrates how both a Button symbol and a Movie Clip symbol will play back their own timelines even if they are placed into a single frame on another timeline. You still need to add some animation for the Down state of the basicButton, so close the .swf window to go back to the Button timeline.

Modifying a Movie Clip instance

Instead of creating an entirely new animation to display on the Over state of our basicButton, we can reuse the overAnim Movie Clip and change its appearance by adding a Color effect to the instance.

1. Add a new layer to the Button symbol and name it **outlineAnimTint.**

2. Insert a blank keyframe on frame 3 (Down).

3. Drag an instance of the overAnim Movie Clip from the Library, or just copy the Over frame on the outlineAnim layer and paste it into the blank keyframe you just created.

4. Select the instance of the overAnim Movie Clip that you placed on the Down keyframe and with the Property inspector, select Tint from the Color effect menu. Choose white as the tint color from the Swatches that pop up from the color chip and then enter a tint value of 100 percent by using the slider or by typing into the value box.

5. Your Button symbol Timeline should now look like Figure 6-14.

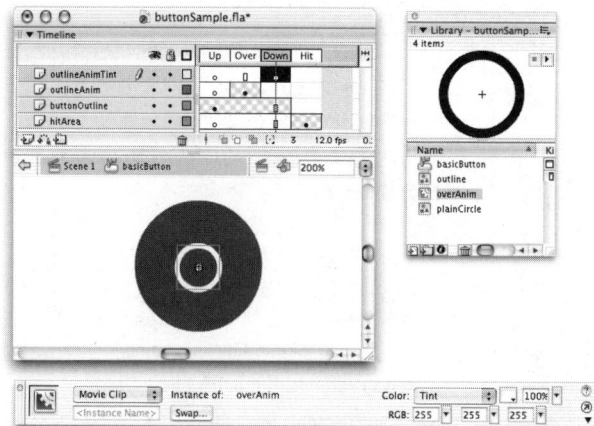

Figure 6-14: The basicButton Timeline with an instance of the overAnim Movie Clip placed on the Down keyframe and modified with a Color Tint

Test your animated button again (Cntrl+Enter, or ⌘+Return) and you will see that animation now appears when you click the button. But instead of the original black that appears on the Over state, the animation for the Down (click) state is white. The three visible states of your button should now resemble Figure 6-15.

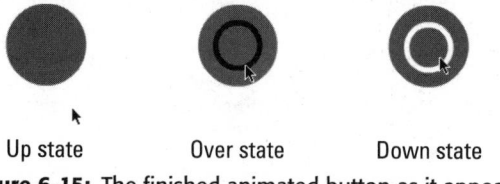

Up state   Over state   Down state

Figure 6-15: The finished animated button as it appears in the Up, Over, and Down states

You have seen how symbols are created, nested, and modified and you are probably realizing that this basic animated Button symbol was only the beginning.

On the CD-ROM

If you would like to deconstruct another layered symbol structure, we have included a silly, but slightly more complex animated Button on this book's CD-ROM. You will find the source file, `surpriseButton.fla`, in the `ch06` folder. Figure 6-16 shows the three visible button states and diagrams the basic symbol nesting.

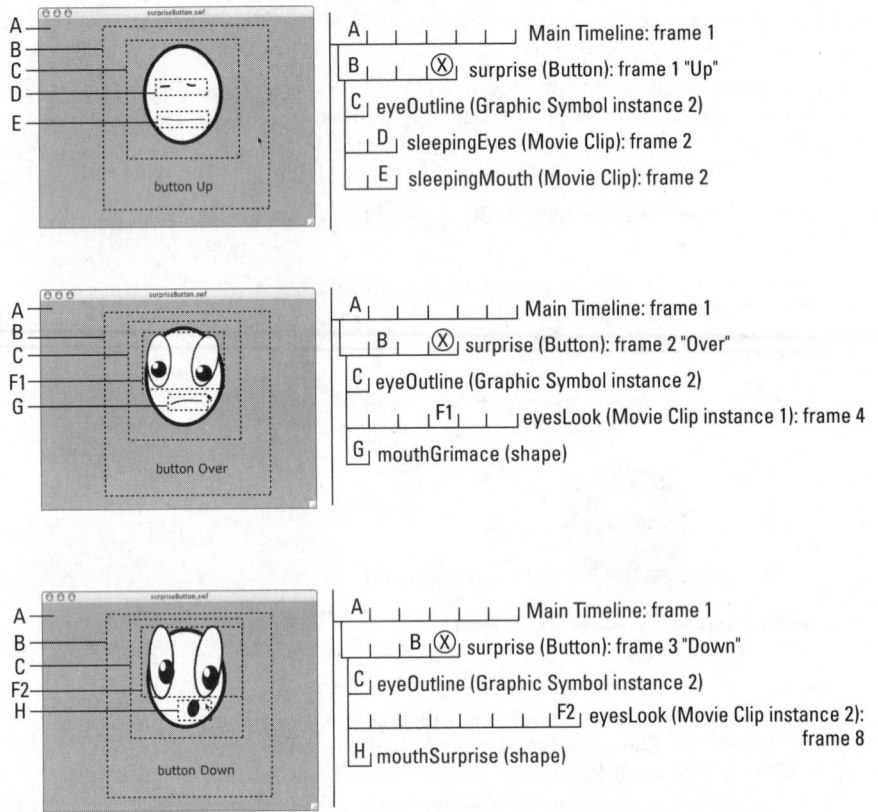

Figure 6-16: The animation as it appears in the three visible button states, Up, Over, and Down (left), with a diagram of the basic nested elements visible in each state (right)

As your symbol structures get more layered and complex, it can be helpful to have some guidance when you are trying to navigate to a specific item in your project, or just trying to remember exactly how you organized things as you were building. Although careful use of layer names, frame labels and symbol names will be indispensable, the Movie Explorer introduced in this next section provides a great assistant for finding your way through the structure of any Flash document.

Using the Movie Explorer

The Movie Explorer panel is a powerful tool for deciphering movies and finding items within them. It can be opened from the application menu by choosing Window ⇨ Other panels ⇨ Movie Explorer (Alt+F3 or Option+F3).

Note
Flash MX 2004 has introduced a fantastic new Find and Replace command that will be a much more efficient choice if your goal is to dig up specific elements such as fonts or colors that you wish to replace in your project file. The many uses of the Find and Replace feature is discussed in Chapter 9, "Modifying Graphics." We include coverage of the Movie Explorer here because it is still the best tool for discovering the structure of a file.

The Movie Explorer is an especially useful tool for getting an overview and for analyzing the structure of a Flash movie. This means that you can see every element in its relationship to all other elements, and you can see this all in one place. However, it's also useful for troubleshooting a movie, for finding occurrences of a particular font, and for locating places where you refer to a certain variable name in any script throughout a movie. As an editing tool, you can use it as a shortcut to edit any symbol, for changing the properties of an instance, or even for doing multiple selections and then changing the attributes of the selected items. Furthermore, the Find function is an incredible timesaver when working on complex project files.

Figure 6-17 shows the Movie Explorer as well as the Movie Explorer Settings dialog box, which you can open by clicking the Customize Which Items to Show button in the Movie Explorer.

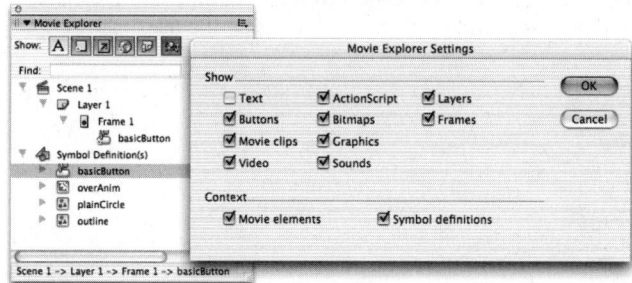

Figure 6-17: The Movie Explorer displaying the file structure for the button example created in the previous section

Filtering buttons

As shown in Figure 6-17, there are several icon buttons across the top of the Movie Explorer panel. These are called Filtering Buttons and they have icons representative of their function. Click any button to toggle the display of those elements in your file. Note, however, that the Movie Explorer's display becomes more crowded as you select more buttons — and that it performs more slowly because it has to sift more data. From left to right, the buttons filter the display of the following kinds of content:

✦ Text

✦ Button symbols, Movie Clips, and Graphic symbols (placed instances)

✦ ActionScript

✦ Video, Sounds, and Bitmaps (placed instances)

✦ Frames and Layers

✦ The Movie Explorer Settings dialog box

Note also the Find field, which enables you to search through all items currently displayed in the Movie Explorer to find specific elements by typing in the name of the symbol, instance, font name, ActionScript string or frame number.

The Display list

Below the icons is a window with the Display list. Much like Windows Explorer, or the Mac Finder, the Movie Explorer displays items hierarchically, either by individual scene or for all scenes. These listings are expandable, so if you have selected the Text button, an arrow (or on Windows, a plus [+] sign), will appear beside the name of any scene that includes text. Clicking the arrow (or plus sign) displays all the selected items included in that scene. This type of visual data display is also referred to as a "tree structure." Clicking a plus sign (or arrow) expands a "branch" of the tree. At the bottom of the Display list, a status bar displays the full path for the currently selected item.

In Figure 6-18, the Text filter button has been selected. As shown, clicking the arrow sign beside the Text icon in the Display list shows the complete text, including basic font information.

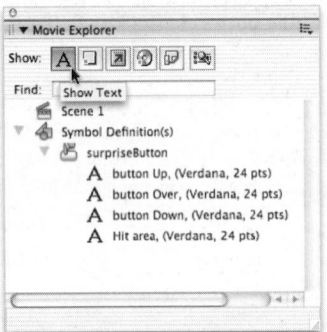

Figure 6-18: The Movie Explorer for the surpriseButton example that is included on the CD-ROM, with the Text filter button chosen to view text and font information inside the file

The Movie Explorer Options menu

The Options menu is accessed by clicking the options triangle, in the upper-right corner of the Movie Explorer panel. These commands enable you to control how much detail is shown in the Display list and also to perform edits or revisions after you've found the specific items that you want to modify:

✦ **Goto Location:** For a selected item, this transports you to the relevant layer, scene, or frame.

✦ **Goto Symbol Definition:** This jumps to the symbol definition for the symbol that's selected in the Movie Elements area. (For this to work, both Show Movie Elements and Show Symbol Definitions must be toggled on.)

✦ **Select Symbol Instances:** Jumps to the scene containing instances of the symbol that is selected in the Symbol Definitions area. (For this to work, both Show Movie Elements and Show Symbol Definitions must be toggled on.)

✦ **Find in Library:** If the Library window is not open, this opens the Library and high-lights the selected item. Otherwise, it simply highlights the item in the Library.

✦ **Rename:** Enables you to easily rename selected items.

✦ **Edit in Place:** Use this to edit the selected symbol in context on the Stage.

✦ **Edit in New Window:** Use this to edit the selected symbol in Edit mode in a separate window from the main Document window.

✦ **Show Movie Elements:** One of two broad categories for how filtered items are viewed in the Display List, Show Movie Elements displays all elements in the movie, organized by scene.

✦ **Show Symbol Definitions:** This is the other category of the Display List, which shows all the items that are related to each symbol. Both Show Movie Elements and Show Symbol Definitions may be displayed simultaneously.

✦ **Show All Scenes:** This toggles the display of Show Movie Elements between selected scenes and all scenes.

✦ **Copy All Text to Clipboard:** Use this command to copy text to the clipboard. Text may then be pasted into a word processor or into another editing application. This command used to be helpful for taking text out of Flash for spell checking, but Flash MX 2004 offers built-in spell checking.

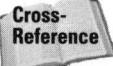

This great new tool and other text-related features are discussed in Chapter 8, "Working with Text."

Unfortunately, getting text back into Flash is not as easy as copying it to the Clipboard. If you copy a large amount of text out to another application, you have to manually update individual text blocks in your Flash document to integrate any changes that were made to the text outside of Flash.

✦ **Cut:** Use this command to cut selected text.

✦ **Copy:** Use this command to copy selected text.

✦ **Paste:** Use this command to Paste text that has been copied from Flash or another application.

✦ **Clear:** Use this command to clear selected text.

✦ **Expand Branch:** This expands the hierarchical tree at the selected location; it's the menu equivalent of clicking the tiny plus (+) sign or right-facing arrow.

✦ **Collapse Branch:** This collapses the hierarchical tree at the selected location; it's the menu equivalent of clicking the tiny minus (–) sign or down-facing arrow.

✦ **Collapse Others:** This collapses the hierarchical tree everywhere except at the selected location.

✦ **Print:** The Movie Explorer prints out, with all the content expanded, displaying all types of content selected.

You can also access the commands found in the Movie Explorer options menu via the contextual menu.

The contextual menu

Select an item in the Movie Explorer and right-click (Ctrl+click) to invoke the contextual menu related to that particular item. Nonapplicable commands are grayed-out, indicating that these are not available in context with the item selected.

Figure 6-19 shows the contextual menu of the Movie Explorer. Among the most useful commands is the Goto Location option at the top. When you can't find an item (because it's on a masked layer or is invisible), this command can be a lifesaver.

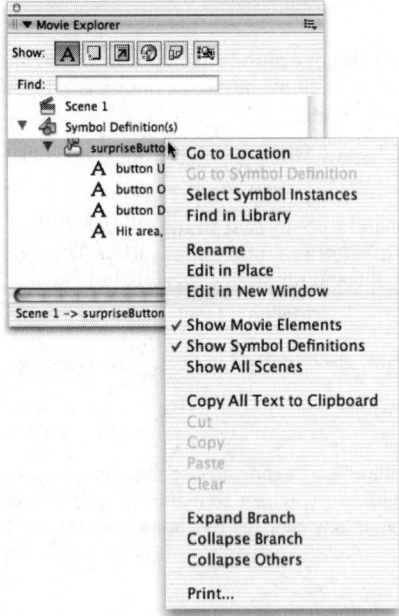

Figure 6-19: The Movie Explorer's contextual menu

When planning or looking for ways to improve a project, the Movie Explorer can provide an excellent map to the structure and function of what you've already accomplished. Whenever relevant, print out the Movie Explorer; this document can function as a project file for finished work, providing a reference of all scripting and Movie Clip placement. As such, it can make it much easier to return to a project months later. It can also facilitate collaboration amongst developers, whether they share the same studio or need to communicate long distance. Finally, for all the reasons listed in this chapter, the Movie Explorer can also be used as a tool for both learning and teaching.

Now that you have a handle on working with symbols in one project file, let's go to the next step and see how you can work with symbols in multiple Flash files.

Using Authortime Shared Libraries

Flash gives you two options for working with shared assets; Authortime and Runtime shared Libraries. Authortime sharing enables a development team to maintain consistency during production on multiple versions of a file or on various project files that use the same symbols by using a centralized internal source FLA file for fonts or other assets. Runtime sharing reduces file sizes and makes it easier to dynamically update content in projects that involve multiple SWFs without having to republish all the files. In Runtime sharing, a Library of assets is created and published as a source movie (.swf) that is uploaded to the server to be shared with multiple linked movies (.swf). Source assets in shared libraries can include any element that is normally created in a Flash movie, as well as assets such as bitmaps, fonts, sounds, or video that are imported and usually embedded in individual project (.fla) files.

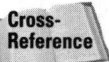

Cross-Reference   For more information about creating and using runtime shared assets and libraries, refer to Chapter 28, "Sharing and Loading Assets."

Runtime sharing involves URLs and linkage info, but authortime sharing is relatively simple and can be accomplished without even publishing any SWF files. You can update or replace a symbol in your current project (.fla) with any other symbol accessible on your local network. Any transformations or effects applied to instances of the symbol in your project file will be preserved, but the contents of the symbol stored in the project Library will be replaced with the contents of the new (or modified) source symbol that you choose to link to.

Note   For clarity, we will refer to the currently open FLA file as a *project file*, and the FLA that contains symbols that you want to link to, as the *source file*. In real-world production you can give the files any name you like. However, adding a special identifier such as "Library" or "Source" to the filenames of FLAs that you plan to use for sharing can help you (and your team) minimize confusion.

On the CD-ROM   We have included two sample files with some basic symbols that you can use to try out the symbol-linking feature. Both shapeProject.fla and shapeSource.fla are in the ch06 folder on this book's CD-ROM.

To link a symbol from one project Library to another, you need a source file and a project file. Open the project file and follow these steps.

1. In the current project Library panel, select the symbol (Graphic symbol, Button, or Movie Clip), that you want to link to a source symbol.

2. Choose **Properties** from the contextual menu or from the Library options menu and under Source in the Symbol Properties dialog box, click the **Browse** button to find the FLA file that contains the symbol you want use as a source. After you find the FLA that will be your source, select it in the file list and click the **Open** button (as shown in Figure 6-20).

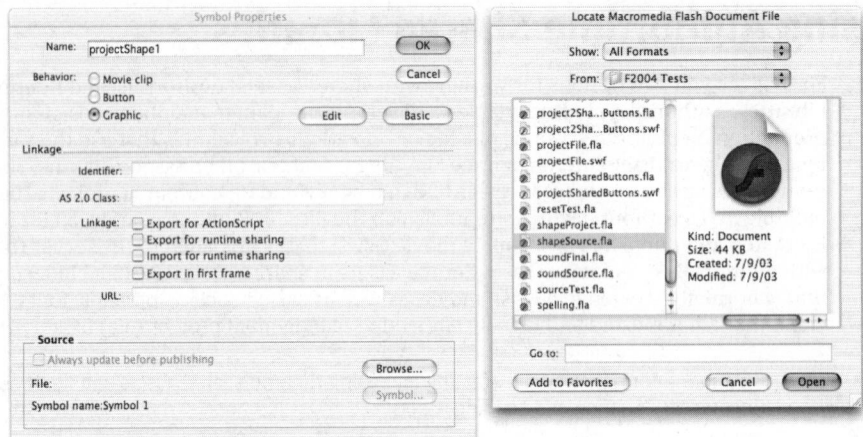

Figure 6-20: Browsing for a source file in the Symbol Properties dialog box

Tip   You can also click the Advanced button in the Create New Symbol dialog box to access Source options and set linkage when you first create a symbol in your project.

3. The Select Source Symbol dialog box (shown in Figure 6-21), will open automatically to allow you to choose the specific symbol in the source Library that you want to link to the symbol in your current project file. Select a symbol in the source Library file list and click **OK** to close the Select Source Symbol dialog box.

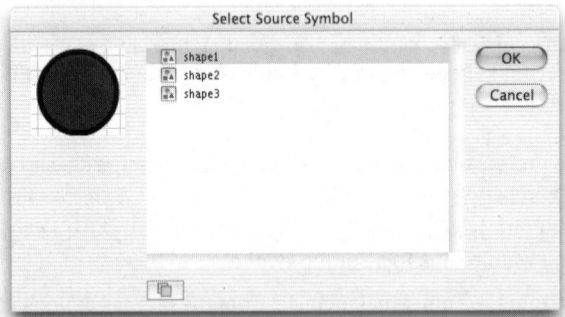

Figure 6-21: Select Source Symbol dialog box where you specify a linked symbol

4. Before you close the Symbol Properties dialog box, notice that the path to the source file is now listed and that you can select a check box for **Always update before publishing** (as shown in Figure 6-22). Select this check box if you want Flash to check for changes in the source file and automatically update all linked symbols each time you publish a SWF from the project file.

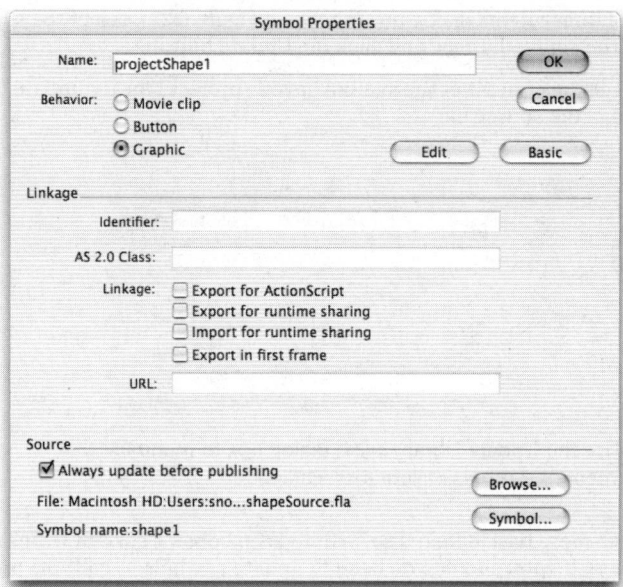

Figure 6-22: Source path shown in Symbol Properties dialog box with the Always update check box

5. Click **OK** to close the Symbol Properties dialog box.

6. The symbol name in your project Library will remain the same, but the content of the symbol in all instances used in your project file should now contain the updated content that will match the content of the symbol you chose in the source file.

7. Save your project file to preserve the linkage information for your symbol.

Should any changes be made to the content of the symbol in the source FLA, you can either publish a SWF from the project file to see Flash automatically check for changes and update all linked symbols (with the Always update before publishing check box selected in the Symbol Properties dialog box), or you can use the Update command to manually get the most recent version of the symbol into your project file before you publish a SWF. To see how this works, follow these steps:

1. Open the source FLA and make some changes to the symbol (using Edit mode) that you originally linked to and then save and close the file. You can change the appearance of the symbol, but don't change the symbol name.

2. Open a project file that contains the symbol you wish to update and either ensure that the Always update check box is selected in Symbol Properties before publishing a SWF to force Flash to check for changes to the source symbol and automatically update your project Library, or go to Step 3.

3. Select the symbol in the Library and use the options menu or the contextual menu to select the **Update** command.

4. In the Update Library Items dialog box (shown in Figure 6-23), select the symbol that you edited in the source Library and click the **Update** button.

5. You will now see the content of the symbol in your project Library update to reflect the changes made in the source file.

Figure 6-23: Use the Update Library Items dialog box to manually update the content of symbols in your project file.

It probably seems like more hassle than it's worth to keep content current in one or two files, but you will find it very helpful should you need to update symbols in multiple project files consistently.

Summary

✦ The Library can be organized with folders and symbols, and assets can be rearranged without breaking their linkage to instances deployed within the project.

✦ Symbols are the building blocks of Flash. They save you time, reduce your file size, and add flexibility to your movies. When ActionScript is used to control symbol behavior or display, symbols are considered as objects within an object-oriented authoring environment.

✦ Flash handles imported sounds, bitmaps, and video assets as symbols. They reside in the Library, and instances of these assets are deployed within a Flash project.

✦ In addition to imported assets, there are three other kinds of symbols that can be created within Flash: Graphic symbols, Movie Clips, and Button symbols.

✦ Movie Clip symbols and Button symbols have timelines that play independently from the main Timeline. Although Graphic symbols also have their own timelines, they are still tied to the main Timeline and require a frame for every frame of their own timeline that will be visible.

✦ Timeline Effects create Graphic symbols by default, even if they contain animation. This makes it easier for you to preview the final result in the authoring environment.

✦ Using symbols within a project is as easy as dragging an asset or symbol from the Library and onto the Stage, although it's usually best to have a new layer ready and to have the appropriate keyframe selected.

✦ Symbols can be edited in a number of ways. Any edits to a symbol in Edit mode are reflected by all instances of that symbol throughout the project.

✦ Timeline Effect symbols cannot be edited directly in Edit mode without disabling the option to adjust the original Effect Settings.

✦ The Property inspector offers a central control for modifying individual symbol instances. The color and transparency of instances of a symbol can be modified, via the Color effect controls. Furthermore, symbol types can be reassigned using the behavior drop-down menu, and specific instances can even be replaced with other symbol instances by using the Swap symbol button.

✦ The Movie Explorer is a powerful tool for navigating movies and finding specific items within them.

✦ Shared Libraries streamline your workflow if a project involves multiple files that use assets that may need to be updated. Shared libraries are also useful for keeping files current and consistent in a team production environment.

✦   ✦   ✦

Applying Color

Before we get into the specifics of applying color with Flash, we want to discuss some of the fundamental theory behind working with color that's destined for display on the Web. Limited color displays are not as common as they were in the early days of Web graphics, but it is useful to have a basic understanding of the various contexts and limitations of digital color. This chapter introduces some resources that may be helpful to you for Flash work and as a reference for color issues that may come up in other productions. Whether you're designing corporate graphics or creating a photo album to share online, consistent and accurate color is a key factor in the quality of your projects. I offer an overview of the reasons and methods for using Web-safe color. We then explore the options available in Flash for choosing and modifying your color palette using the Color Swatches panel and how colors can be accessed from the Tools panel. We also show you how to work with the Property inspector menus, Color Swatches panel, and Color Mixer panel to select, change, mix, and apply solid colors, gradients, and even bitmap fills.

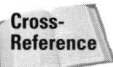
Cross-Reference

Flash symbol instances can be tweened so that they will change color over time. Although this involves color, the selection of colors for the original symbol used in the keyframes of the tween is merely a rudimentary application of fill and line color, as described in this chapter. Applying the Color Effect controls available in the Property inspector to symbol instances is discussed in Chapter 9, "Modifying Graphics." Methods for controlling color with ActionScript and the Flash Color Object are covered in Chapter 25, "Controlling Movie Clips."

Introducing Color Basics

Computer monitors display color by using a method called *RGB color*. A monitor screen is a tightly packed array of pixels arranged in a grid, where each pixel has an address. For example, a pixel that's located 16 rows down from the top and 70 columns over from the left might have an address of 70,16. The computer uses these addresses to send a specific color to each pixel. Because each pixel is composed of a single red, green, and blue dot, the colors that the monitor displays can be "mixed" at each pixel by varying the individual intensities of the red, green, and blue color dots. Each individual dot can vary in intensity over a range of 256 values, starting with 0 (which is *off*) to a maximum value of 255 (which is *on*). Thus, if red is *half-on* (a value of 127), while green is *off* (a value of 0), and blue is fully *on* (a value of 255), the pixel appears reddish-blue or purple.

The preceding paragraph describes unlimited, full color, which is sometimes referred to as *24-bit color.* However, older computer systems are still incapable of displaying full color. Limited color displays are either 8-bit or 16-bit displays. Although a full discussion of bit-depth is beyond the scope of this book, it is important to note several points:

✦ 24-bit color is required to accurately reproduce photographic images and smooth color transitions in gradients.

✦ Because 8-bit and 16-bit systems are color challenged, they can display only a limited number of colors, and they must dither-down anything that exceeds their *gamut,* which is their expanse of possible colors. *Dithering* means that, in order to approximate colors that are missing from the palette, the closest colors available are placed in proximity to each other to fool the eye into seeing a blended intermediate color. This can result in unwanted pixel patterns.

✦ Some image formats, such as GIF, use a color palette that limits them to 256 colors. This is called *indexed color.* Indexed color is ideally suited for reproducing vector graphics that have solid fills and strokes, but will often create noticeable *banding* (uneven color) when applied to photographic images.

✦ Bitmap (or photographic) images will not accurately translate an indexed color palette, so matching color between GIF images and JPEG images can be unpredictable because the JPEG will expand the original indexed palette of a GIF file to include colors that may not be within the Web-safe color palette.

✦ Calibration of your monitor is essential for accurate color work. For more information, check out the ColorVision Web site at `www.colorpar.com`.

Discussing Web-safe color issues

Web-safe color is a complex issue, but what it boils down to is this: The Macintosh and Windows platforms handle their color palettes differently, so browsers don't have the same colors available to them across platforms. This leads to inconsistent, unreliable color — unless you're careful to choose colors for Web design from the Web-safe palette. The Web-safe palette is a selection of 216 colors that's consistent on both the Mac and Windows platforms for Netscape, Explorer, and Mosaic browsers. The Web-safe palette contains only 216 of 256 possible indexed colors, because 40 colors vary between Mac and Windows displays. Use the Web-safe palette to avoid color shifting and to ensure greater design (color) control.

By default, the Color Swatches panel (Ctrl+F9 or ⌘+F9) loads with Web 216 colors, and if the swatches are modified, this swatch palette can always be reloaded from the Options menu at the upper right of the panel. Web 216 restricts the color palette to Web-safe colors. However, *intermediate colors* (meaning any process or effect that generates new colors from two Web-safe colors) — such as gradients, color tweens, transparent overlays, and alpha transitions — will not be constrained to Web-safe colors.

When there are over 16 million possible colors, why settle for a mere 216? Consider your audience. Choose a color strategy that will enable the majority of your viewers to view your designs as you intend them to appear. For example, if you're designing an e-commerce site for a very broad audience on a mix of platforms, then you might seriously consider limiting your work to the Web-safe palette. (If you choose this route, then hybrid swatches may enable you to access colors that are technically unavailable, while remaining within the hardware limitations of your audience.) On the other hand, if you're designing an interface for a stock photography firm whose clients are mainly art directors with high-end Mac machines, then color limitations are probably not an issue. In either case, keep in mind that no one will see the exact same colors that you see. The variables of hardware, calibration, ambient light, and environmental influences are unavoidable. If you do settle for 216 colors, remember that the value of color in Web design (or any design or art for that matter) has to do with color perception and design issues, and numbers have little to do with that.

Using hexadecimal values

Any RGB color can be described in hexadecimal (hex) notation. This notation is called *hexadecimal* because it describes color in base-16 values, rather than in base-10 values like standard RGB color. This color value notation is used because it describes colors in an efficient manner that HTML and scripting languages can digest. Hex notation is limited to defining *flat color,* which is a continuous area of undifferentiated color. In HTML, hexadecimal notation is used to specify colored text, lines, backgrounds, image borders, frame cells, and frame borders.

A hexadecimal color number has six places. It allocates two places for each of the three color channels: R, G, and B. So, in the hexadecimal example 00FFCC, 00 signifies the red channel, FF signifies the green channel, and CC signifies the blue channel. The corresponding values between hexadecimal and customary integer values are as follows:

16 integer values: 0 1 2 3 4 5 6 7 8 9 10 11 12 13 14 15

16 hex values: 0 1 2 3 4 5 6 7 8 9 A B C D E F

The Web-safe values in hexadecimal notation are limited to those colors that can be described using combinations of the pairs 00, 33, 66, 99, and FF. White is described by the combination FFFFFF, or all colors *on* 100 percent. At the other end of the spectrum, black is described by the combination 000000, all colors on 0 percent, or *off.* A medium gray would be described by the combination 666666, or all colors on 40 percent.

Using custom Web-safe colors

The basic Web-safe color palette will be broad enough for most project needs, but if you feel too limited by these colors, you can create custom-mixed Web-safe colors. There are tools that will help you to build patterns composed of Web-safe colors that fool the eye into seeing a new color. These are essentially blocks of preplanned dithers, built out of the Web-safe palette, that augment the usable palette while retaining cross-platform, cross-browser color consistency:

✦ **ColorSafe:** An Adobe Photoshop filter plug-in that generates hybrid color swatches with this logic. ColorSafe (Mac and Windows) is available directly from BoxTop Software at www.boxtopsoft.com.

✦ **ColorMix:** An easy online utility that interactively delivers hybrid color swatches, much like ColorSafe. It is free at www.colormix.com. After you mix a custom dithered swatch, you can download it and save it as a GIF for import into Flash.

After you've created some custom swatches and saved them to a folder on a local machine, you can use them in your Flash projects by importing the GIF directly to your document library and using the Color Mixer panel to apply the GIF as a bitmap fill. Figure 7-1 shows two Web-safe colors used to create a custom-dithered swatch and the mixed custom color as it displays when imported to Flash.

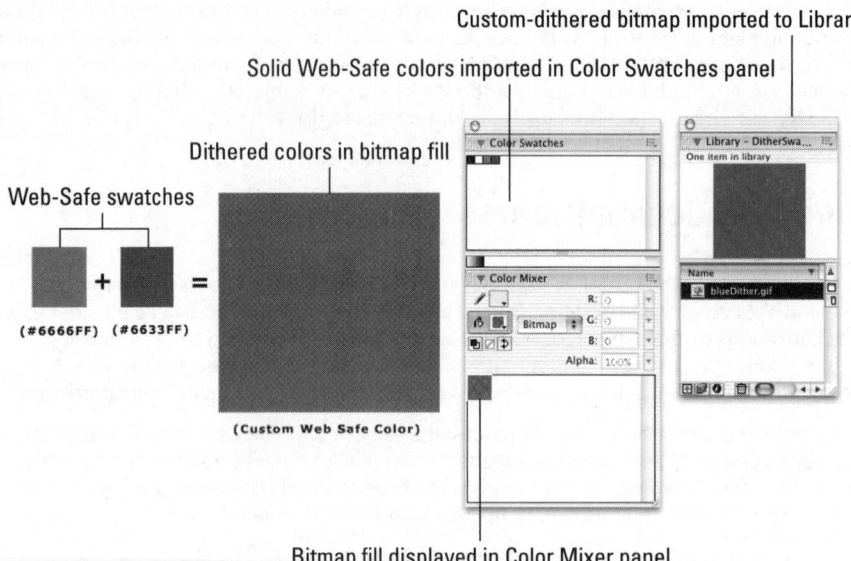

Custom-dithered bitmap imported to Library

Solid Web-Safe colors imported in Color Swatches panel

Dithered colors in bitmap fill

Web-Safe swatches

(#6666FF) (#6633FF)

(Custom Web Safe Color)

Bitmap fill displayed in Color Mixer panel

Figure 7-1: Two Web-safe colors mixed to create a custom-dithered color. The dithered GIF file was imported to the Flash Library and the solid Web-safe colors used in the GIF were added to the Color Swatches panel.

Note that the dithered GIF color is displayed only in the Mixer panel under the Bitmap fill option, whereas the solid Web-safe colors can be added directly to the Color Swatches panel. The steps for adding colors from a GIF file to the Color Swatches panel are described in the "Importing custom palettes" subsection later in this chapter, and the steps for applying a bitmap fill are described in the subsection "Selecting bitmap fills."

Using color effectively

According to some developers, the issue of color on the Web has been seriously confused by the misperception that people can set numbers to give them Web-safe colors, and that, if they do that, they will have *good* color. Have you ever noticed that as soon as someone starts designing on-screen, it's as if he's forgotten anything he may have learned about legibility and design on the printed page? While getting caught up in the excitement of layered patterns and multicolored text, there is a tendency to overlook the obvious problem that the result is entirely illegible. Although we all want to be creative and unique, there are certain color rules that can actually be more liberating than they are restrictive.

Although unconventional design choices can add an element of surprise, a touch of humor, or just a visual punch that will help your layout stand out from the rest, it is vital that you don't compromise your end goal. When you get noticed, you want to deliver your message success-fully—whether that message is "Buy this product" or just "Hey, this is a cool site." If you start to carefully deconstruct the layouts that grab your attention, you will probably find that there are consistencies to the choices that were made in the design, regardless of the content. You'll begin to notice that even the most bizarre or cutting-edge designs share certain features that make them eye-catching and memorable.

Much of the underlying strategy in a design may be transparent, or not *consciously* perceived by the viewer. But don't make the mistake of thinking that individual preference is completely unpredictable. The secret to successful design is leveraging the unconscious visual language that your audience is physically and culturally conditioned to respond to. Individual viewers may have specific preferences for certain colors or styles, but they will all recognize and understand many of the same visual conventions.

Although learning to apply all these conventions and to integrate them into your own design style can take years of study and practice, there are some fundamental "truths" that will serve you well, no matter how long you've been designing:

✦ **Color is relative:** Humans perceive color relative to the context of other colors in which the color is set. Most art schools offer at least one course about color. They often start with color experiments that are conducted with pieces of colored paper. An early assignment is to make three colors look like more than three colors — by placing small scraps of the same color on larger pieces of different colors. Students are always amazed to learn how much a person's perception of a single color is influenced by placing it on those different-colored backgrounds. Figure 7-2 shows how the same shade of gray can appear lighter or darker depending on the background color. The lesson is that color is *not* an absolute — it never was before computers, and it never will be to the human eye.

Figure 7-2: The same gray circle displayed on different background values will appear to be darker or lighter by comparison.

✦ **Contrast is king:** Only one thing is more important than color: contrast. Contrast is the relative difference in lightness or darkness of items in a composition. Here's a good test: Take a colorful design that you admire and reduce it to grayscale. Does it still work? Contrast is a major factor in good color composition. Figure 7-3 shows different amounts of contrast created by relative differences in value.

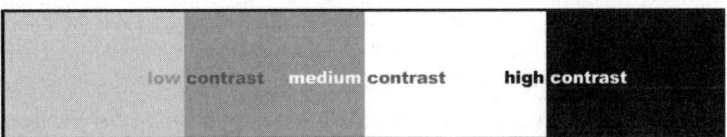

Figure 7-3: Varying levels of color contrast determine legibility and emphasis.

To ensure a strong design, it can be helpful to work on your initial layouts in grayscale. When you have contrast working for you, then you can start to add color with the confidence that the design will not be visually *muddy*—or hard to read—because of poor contrast. Often, the same color scheme can be a disaster or a huge success, all depending on the contrast created in the design. The concept of contrast also applies to other characteristics of your design—size, texture, even mood. Try to use contrast wherever you want to create emphasis or add drama. But remember: If you make everything huge and flashing red, or extra-small and pale gray, you will no longer have any contrast. The strength of contrast is in variety. Figure 7-4 shows how contrast can be achieved by varying the size and style of your text.

low   **MEDIUM**   **HIGH**
contrast   c o n t r a s t   c o n t r a s t

Figure 7-4: Variety in the size and shape of elements will also add visual contrast.

✦ **Less is more:** Keep in mind that the power of contrast should always be used in moderation. White text on black backgrounds can be great for headlines, but after more than a few paragraphs, it will make the reader feel as though her retina is actually being burned by the text on the page—one of the best ways to keep someone from actually reading your copy. Also, don't be afraid of empty space; the impact of individual elements is often dependent on having a little room to breathe. One element in a striking color will be much more effective than a whole page filled with competing colors.

✦ **Start at the beginning:** Visual hierarchy is the best secret weapon in any designer's arsenal. Although you may not be sure what the most important element is in your design, if you don't give your reader a place to start, chances are you'll lose his attention. By deciding on the order of importance for elements in your design and then using contrast, size, and color to guide the reader through your layout, you'll create motivation for him to actually stick around long enough to absorb your message. Think of your content as the elements of a good story: In order to make the narrative compelling, you have to have a catchy intro, a juicy middle, and a rewarding ending or payoff. You might argue that you want to let readers make their own choice about where to start (like starting at the back of a novel), but if you don't create a visual structure, the reader won't feel empowered to make any choices. Presented with a big muddle of uncertain order, he will most likely move on to a design where he can find the beginning, middle, and end at a glance, before deciding what he wants to read first. Figure 7-5 shows a layout with poorly defined visual hierarchy compared to an example with stronger contrast and clearer hierarchy. The page with more clearly defined hierarchy gives the reader more clues about the order of importance of each element on the page. Of course, these examples don't even use color, but as mentioned earlier, it can be best to plan the structure of your layout before adding color to support it.

Here's the bottom line: Color can help a good design look *great,* and when used with strategy it can help to engage the viewer and sell your message. But no amount of color can save a poorly planned design, so consider the underlying structure, contrast, and visual hierarchy of your layout before adding color.

Weak contrast = muddy visual hierarchy   Strong contrast = clear visual hierarchy

Figure 7-5: Adding contrast to a design improves the visual hierarchy and orients readers in your layout.

There are innumerable books on color theory and many different software solutions that can provide inspiration and take the guesswork out of choosing color schemes. These are just two sources that can help you create harmonious color families for your designs:

✦ **Color Schemer:** A handy utility that will generate a palette of harmonious colors for any key color that you want to start with. Although the full version of the software is for Windows only, the online version is helpful regardless of what platform you use. Try it out at www.colorschemer.com/online.html.

You can generate lists of RGB or hexadecimal colors from the Web-safe palette and choose to darken or lighten all colors in the palette until you find the exact color set you like. Color Schemer also offers a basic color tutorial that will help you understand how to generate harmonious palettes. You can find it at www.colorschemer.com/tutorial.html.

✦ ***Pantone Guide to Communicating with Color:*** A wonderful reference book by color guru Leatrice Eiseman (published by Design Books). This colorful book includes a wealth of information about the science and psychology of color, as well as a guide to a whole range of color families, grouped according to mood. Get inspired to add meaningful color to your projects.

Tip   The Pantone system for specifying ink color is the industry standard for communication between designers and printers. Pantone swatch books are indispensable and well worth the investment if you do any print work. Visit www.pantone.com to learn more. Pantone has also developed systems to help designers and retailers who need to specify and display color consistently in a digital environment. Visit www.therightcolor.com to learn more if you are developing online catalogues or other projects that require precise color matching.

Working in the Color Swatches Panel

The most commonly used source for selecting colors as you work in Flash is the Color Swatches panel (Ctrl+F9 or ⌘+F9). Although the controls for loading or modifying specific palettes are available only on the main Color Swatches panel, both the Tools panel and the Property inspector give you quick pop-up menus to access whatever colors are currently loaded. The Color Swatches panel is included in all the default Flash panel sets, but if it isn't visible, you can always find it in the application menu under Window ⇨ Design Panels ⇨ Color Swatches. Figure 7-6 shows the Fill Swatches for the default Web 216 colors as they display in the pop-up menu in the Tools panel (A) and the Property inspector (B) and on the main Color Swatches panel (C). The Color Swatches panel is shown with the Options menu that is invoked by clicking the top-right corner of the panel.

Tools that create fields of color, or fills, include the Brush, the Paint Bucket, and the various Shape tools. Each of these tools is accompanied by the Fill color button, which appears in the Tools panel and in the Property inspector. Although the Fill Swatches pop-up is similar to the Stroke pop-up, it has one significant difference: It includes another row of swatches at the bottom, which are gradient swatches — click one to fill with a prebuilt gradient style.

Tools that create lines, or strokes, include the Line, Pencil, Ink Bottle, Pen, and — because they create outlines around fills — any of the Shape tools. These tools rely upon the Stroke color button, which appears in both the Tools panel and on the Property inspector.

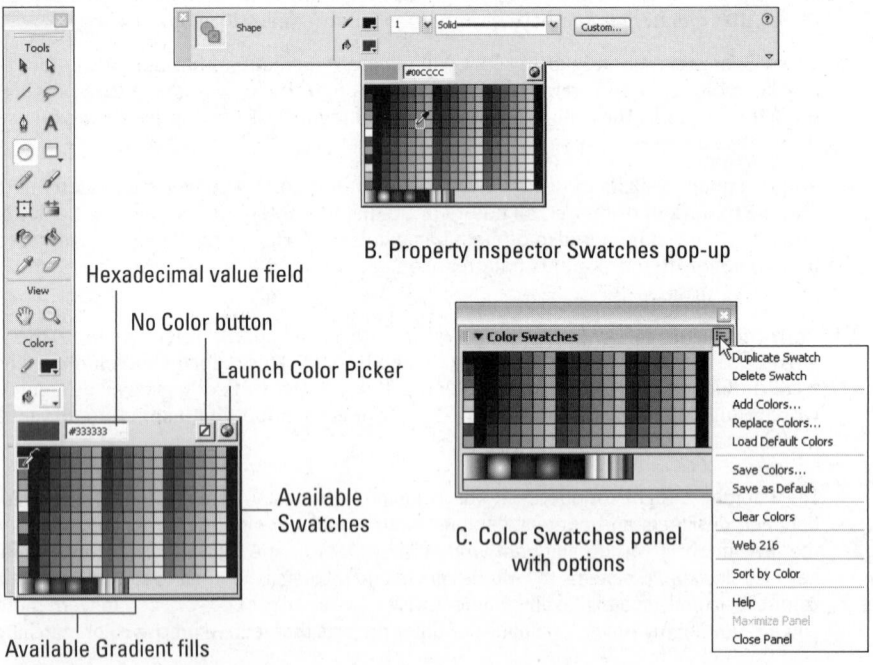

B. Property inspector Swatches pop-up

Hexadecimal value field

No Color button

Launch Color Picker

Available Swatches

Available Gradient fills

A. Tools panel Swatches pop-up

C. Color Swatches panel with options

Figure 7-6: The default color palette as it displays in the Tools panel (A), Property inspector pop-up menus (B), and on the Color Swatches panel (C)

For all drawing tools, basic color selection is accomplished by clicking either the Stroke or Fill color buttons, and then choosing a color from the Swatches pop-up. This pop-up displays the same swatch set that is currently loaded in the Color Swatches panel. It also includes a hexadecimal color-entry box—which facilitates keyboard entry, as well as cut-and-paste of hex values. Depending upon the tool selected, the Swatch menu available from the Tools panel may display a No Color button above the solid swatches as well as a button that launches the Color Picker.

Note   You cannot apply a fill or stroke of None (or No Color) to an item that has already been drawn. Instead, remove the fill or stroke by selecting it with the Selection tool and using Edit⇨ Clear or pressing the Backspace (Delete) key.

The color chips displayed on the Tools panel will always display the most recently selected Stroke and Fill colors, while the Property inspector will display the color chips relevant to the active tool or the currently selected item.

If the color you want is not available in the current Swatches menu, you may opt to invoke the Color Picker by clicking the Color Picker button. Alternatively, you may also open the Color Mixer panel to create a new color and add it to the currently loaded selection of swatches. The Color Swatches panel enables you to load, add, delete, and modify various color sets for individual documents. Whatever changes are made to the Color Swatches panel will be saved with the document (.fla) that is currently active.

Color Swatches panel options

Think of the Color Swatches panel (refer to Figure 7-6) as a paint box or a way to organize your existing swatches and to manipulate the display of colors that are available in the other panels. Use the Color Swatches panel to save color sets, import color sets, and reorder or change selected colors. The options menu of the Color Swatches panel provides the controls used to sort or modify individual swatches as well as various color sets:

✦ **Duplicate Swatch:** Use this to duplicate a selected swatch. This can be useful when you want to make a range of related color swatches by duplicating and then editing a series of swatches with the Color Mixer panel.

Tip   You can duplicate a selected swatch with just two clicks. First, select a swatch with the Selection tool or use the Dropper tool to pick a color from any item on the Stage. As you move the pointer into the space below the current solid swatches set (above the gradient swatches), the pointer icon changes from a dropper into a paint bucket. Just click and a new swatch is added to the color set.

✦ **Delete Swatch:** Botched a swatch? Select and delete it here.

Tip   Another way to remove a swatch with just a click is to hold down Shift+Ctrl or Shift+⌘ and then move the pointer over the swatch you want to remove. You will see the icon change into a pair of scissors. Click and the swatch is "snipped" out.

✦ **Add Colors:** Opens the Import Color Swatch menu, which is a simple dialog box used to locate, select, and import color sets. Add Colors retains the current color set and appends the imported color set at the bottom of the panel.

Be careful about creating huge color sets! In some cases, the Swatch color pop-ups may extend beyond the visible screen and you'll have to use the Color Swatches panel to be able to scroll to choose colors that are hidden off-screen. This can happen if you add colors from a complex GIF image to the default Web 216 set.

✦ **Replace Colors:** Also opens the Import Color Swatch menu. However, Replace Colors replaces the current color set when it loads the selected color set. If the current set has not been saved, it will be lost.

✦ **Load Default Colors:** Clears the current color set and replaces it with the default Web 216 swatch palette. Again, if the current set has not been saved it will be lost. Flash MX 2004 allows you to change the specification for your default color palette if you prefer not to use Web 216. (See Save as Default.)

✦ **Save Colors:** Opens the Export Color Swatch menu, which is used to name and save color sets to a specific location on your hard drive. Color sets may be saved in either the Flash Color Set (.clr), or Color Table (.act) format, which can be used with Macromedia Fireworks and Adobe Photoshop. Gradients can only be imported and exported from Flash using the .clr format.

✦ **Save as Default:** Saves the current swatch set as the default set to be loaded in the Color Swatches panel for all new Flash documents.

✦ **Clear Colors:** Removes all colors currently loaded in the Color Swatches panel, leaving only the black and white swatches and a grayscale gradient.

✦ **Web 216:** Loads the Web-safe palette. This option makes it safe to mess with the swatches in Flash because no matter what you do, you can always just reload this original default color set.

You can override the default Web 216 color set by switching the Color Mixer panel to either the RGB or HSB (hue, saturation, brightness) color spaces. You can then mix your own fresh colors, add them to the Color Swatches panel, and save that palette as the default. Another alternative is to locate the Photoshop Color Tables on your hard drive (or download a specialty color table from the Web) and replace the default set with a broader gamut.

✦ **Sort by Color:** This organizes the swatches by hue rather than by mathematical number and can visually be a more logical way to find colors in your current set. Note, however, that once you apply this sort there is no way to toggle back to your original swatch order. So it is best to save any custom palette first before sorting so that you have the option of going back to the other display if you prefer it. Figure 7-7 shows the Web 216 palette as it appears sorted numerically (left) and as it appears sorted by hue (right).

Importing custom palettes

The option of loading custom swatches is helpful if you're developing a Flash project that you want to match with a predefined palette — whether this is out of necessity or just for inspiration. For example, you can match your Flash elements to a corporate logo or to the range of hues in a photo that you love. In addition to loading the colors in a specific GIF file, Flash allows you to load RGB color palettes from other graphics applications, which have been saved as Color Tables (in the .act format).

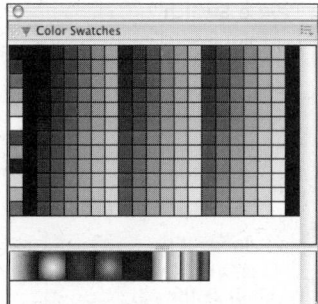   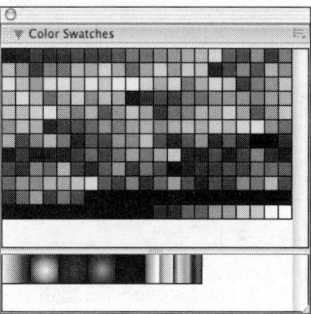

Web 216 swatches in default order   Web 216 swatches sorted by color

Figure 7-7: The default Web 216 palette as it appears sorted by number (left), and as it appears when sorted by hue (right) using the Sort by Color option

Loading a custom GIF color palette

To simplify your Flash swatch selection to match the colors in a company logo or other GIF image, follow these steps:

1. Clear the currently loaded color set by choosing Clear Colors in the Color Swatches panel options menu.

2. Choose Add Colors from the Color Swatches panel options menu and, in the Import Color Swatch dialog box, specify the GIF file that you want to define the imported color set.

3. Flash will load the colors from the GIF image into the Color Swatches panel and you can then save the document (.fla) to keep these colors as the loaded set.

4. To organize the loaded color set in the Color Swatches panel by hue, choose the Sort by Color option. You can always add or delete swatches from this new set.

5. If you want to use your custom color set in other files, use the Save Colors command in the Color Swatches panel options menu to save a Color Table (.act) or Flash Color Set (.clr).

The sample source GIF image and the resulting imported Swatches palette are shown in Figure 7-8.

Tip   The color settings defined in the original authoring environment (such as Adobe Illustrator or Photoshop) for saved GIF files will affect the colors available for loading to the Flash swatches. For the widest range of colors, use 256 colors and an adaptive palette. To get only the exact colors used in a graphic, manually restrict the number of colors that can be included by typing in a number that matches the number of colors in the original graphic. For example, if a logo that you plan to use as a source file for your swatches is red, blue, yellow, black, and white, restrict the GIF to 5 colors when you export it from the original authoring application.

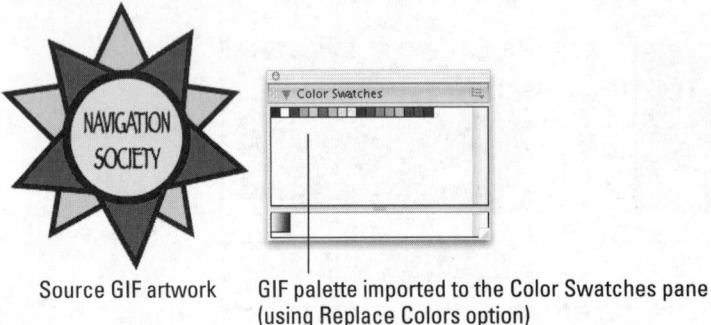

Source GIF artwork   GIF palette imported to the Color Swatches pane
                            (using Replace Colors option)

Figure 7-8: The simple logo GIF file that we specified as the source for
a custom Swatches palette. The resulting swatches match the colors in
the logo.

Creating and loading a custom Color Table

If you want to save a color palette that will match the hues in a photograph, you can also generate a Color Table in Adobe Photoshop or Macromedia Fireworks.

To create a Color Table in Adobe Photoshop (or Illustrator), follow these steps:

1. Open a source bitmap image (.jpeg, .tif, or .psd)

2. Use the Save for Web command to access the settings that allow you to choose the file type and color space that you wish to export. To create a Color Table, set the file type to GIF, choose adaptive color and choose the number of colors you wish to include in the color table. Although you can include anywhere from 2 to 256 colors in your Color Table, you will not likely need more than 16. Preview the swatches with the Color Table tab in the lower left of the interface (next to Image Size).

Note   Although Photoshop includes a menu option for creating a Color Table (Image ➪ Mode ➪ Color Table), this option is available only if the source image is first converted to Indexed color. Also, the Color Table dialog box only offers limited control of the swatches that will be exported, so we prefer to use the Save for Web workflow.

3. When you have a set of swatches that you are happy with, choose Save Color Table from the Color Table options menu. The settings used for the sample file are shown in Figure 7-9.

4. Give the Color Table a name that you will remember (such as airplaneColors) and save the .act file to a folder where you can find it again. Creating a Custom Palettes folder on your system, where you can store and organize any of the Color Tables or source GIFs that you may want to use again, is a good idea.

5. Open a Flash document (.fla) and from the Color Swatches panel options menu choose Add Colors if you want new colors added to the currently loaded set (or Replace Colors if you want to use only your new colors).

6. From the Import Color Swatch dialog box, browse to your Color Table (.act) file and select it. Flash will load the new colors into the Color Swatches panel and you can then sort and save this set with your document.

Figure 7-9: Use the Save for Web command and the Color Table settings in Adobe Photoshop to create a custom color set from a photograph.

The sample source bitmap image and the resulting Color Table loaded into the Color Swatches panel are shown in Figure 7-10.

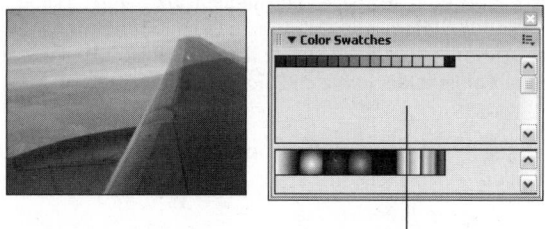

Source bitmap image   Color Table (.act) imported to the
Color Swatches panel
(using Replace Colors option)

Figure 7-10: A photo used to generate a Color Table (.act), and the resulting color set loaded into the Flash Color Swatches panel

To create a Color Table in Macromedia Fireworks, follow these steps:

1. Open a source bitmap image (.jpeg, .tif, or .psd).

2. Open the Optimize panel (Window ⇨ Optimize) to access the settings that allow you to choose the file type and color space that you wish to export. To create a Color Table, set the file type to GIF, choose adaptive color, and choose the number of colors you wish to include in the color table. To preview the swatches, select the Preview (or 2-Up) tab in the main image window.

3. When you have a set of swatches that you are happy with, choose Save Palette from the Optimize panel options menu. The settings used for the sample file are shown in Figure 7-11.

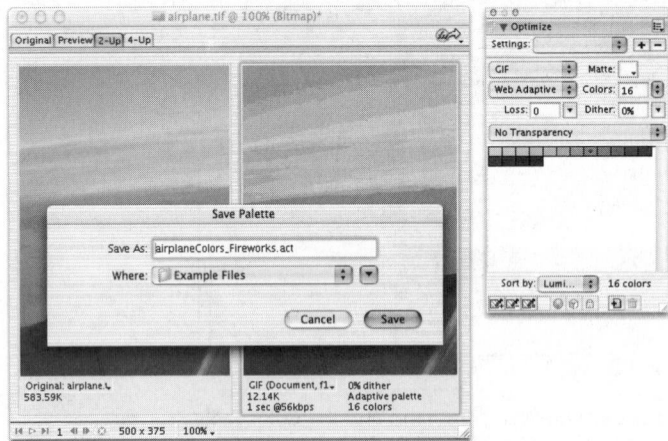

Figure 7-11: Use the Optimize panel in Fireworks to create a custom color set from a photograph.

4. Continue with Steps 4 through 6 in the previous instructions.

In the example, we created a Color Table from an image of an airplane wing. You can find the source bitmap (`airplane.tif`) and the Photoshop Color Table (`airplaneColors.act`) file, along with a Flash document (`photoSource.fla`) that has the TIF imported and the color palette loaded in the Airplane Colors folder in the ch07 folder on the CD-ROM.

Refer to the color insert pages to see the Web 216 and airplaneColors swatch samples discussed in this section printed in color.

Using the Color Mixer Panel

Think of the Color Mixer panel as the "boss" of the Color Swatches panel. The Color Swatches panel handles the color inventory and serves up the available colors, but the Mixer panel has the power to modify those colors and add the variations to the current set. The Color style menu available on the Color Mixer panel allows you to choose the type of color pattern that you want to work with—including solid colors, linear and radial gradients, and bitmap fills.

As shown in Figure 7-12 and Figure 7-13, the Color Mixer panel enables you to create new colors, with settings in any of three color spaces—RGB, HSB, or hex—using either the condensed Color bar or the expanded "rainbow" color selection field. All colors are handled with four channels, which are RGBA (red, green, blue, alpha); these values can be individually adjusted using the Color value fields and slider controls. The Tint slider control allows you to dynamically shift your current color darker or lighter. A Fill or Stroke color selected in any of the Swatch menus will be displayed in the Mixer panel where it can be modified.

Fill color chip (has focus)

Stroke color chip

Color style menu   Color value fields   Color Mixer panel Options menu

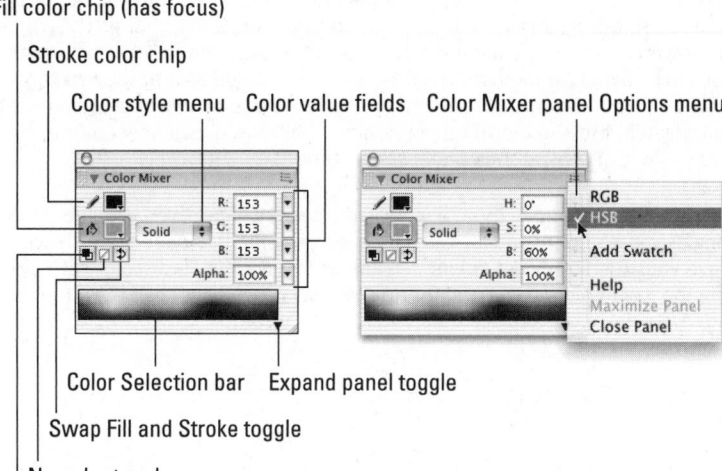

Color Selection bar   Expand panel toggle

Swap Fill and Stroke toggle

No color toggle

Default color toggle (Black & White)

Figure 7-12: The Color Mixer panel and the Options menu

As shown in Figure 7-13, colors modified in the Color Mixer panel can be added to the palette loaded in the Color Swatches panel — just select Add Swatch from the Color Mixer panel options menu and the color will be added below the colors currently loaded in the Color Swatches panel.

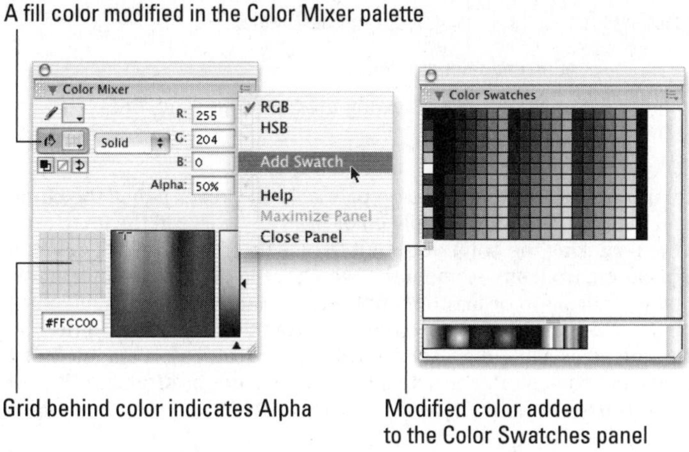

A fill color modified in the Color Mixer palette

Grid behind color indicates Alpha   Modified color added
to the Color Swatches panel

Figure 7-13: Colors modified in the Mixer panel can be added to the Color Swatches panel.

Any color swatch selected in the Color Swatches panel will be loaded into the Mixer panel as a starting point only — modifications made in the Mixer panel will not change the original color in the Color Swatches panel. The new color or gradient that you create using the controls in the Color Mixer panel (shown in Figure 7-14) will be added as a new swatch only when you select Add Swatch from the options menu. You can always edit your custom color by selecting the new swatch, but the modified version will be treated as a new color and will also have to be added to the Color Swatches panel separately.

Caution   The colors you create and add to the Color Swatches panel will be saved with the document (.fla) as long as you do not reload the default set or overwrite the loaded swatch set. If you want to save your custom mixed colors, remember to save the Flash color set (.clr) to a folder using the Save Colors command in the Color Swatches panel before you reload the default Web 216 color set or Replace Colors with a new palette.

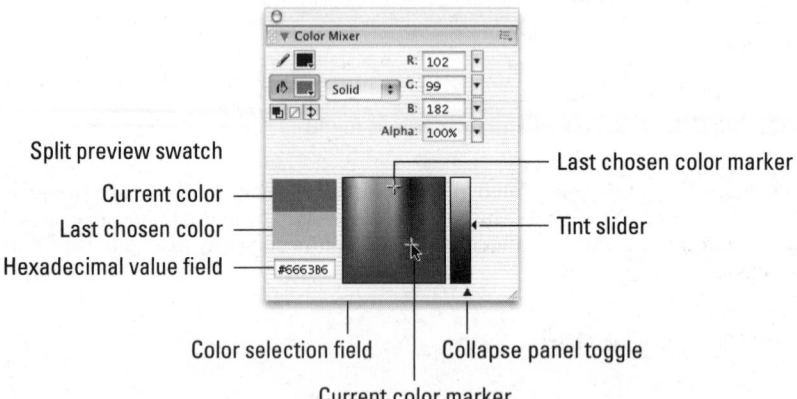

Expanded Color Mixer panel

Figure 7-14: The expanded Color Mixer panel showing the Hex value field, the split preview swatch, and the Tint slider control

When you select a color from the Swatches pop-up palette in the Mixer panel, the cursor converts to a Dropper tool that allows you to sample color from anywhere in the interface just by dragging the dropper and clicking the color you want to pick up. You can pluck colors from icons in the Flash application, from any element that you have in the Document window, and even from elements on your desktop or in other application windows that are currently open. Figure 7-15 shows the Dropper tool picking up the yellow from the Scene icon in the Flash Document window to be used as a fill color. The same Dropper feature is available from any of the Swatches pop-ups, but the colors you select this way will not be stored in the Color Swatches panel unless you use the Color Mixer panel menu's Add Swatch option.

Caution   To pick up colors with the Dropper tool outside of the Flash application itself, be careful not to release the mouse button while you move the mouse from the Swatches in the Color Mixer panel to the other color that you want to sample. If you release the mouse button before moving it to the color you want to sample, you will be able to pick up colors from inside the Flash application only.

Dropper used to sample color from the Flash scene icon

Document window

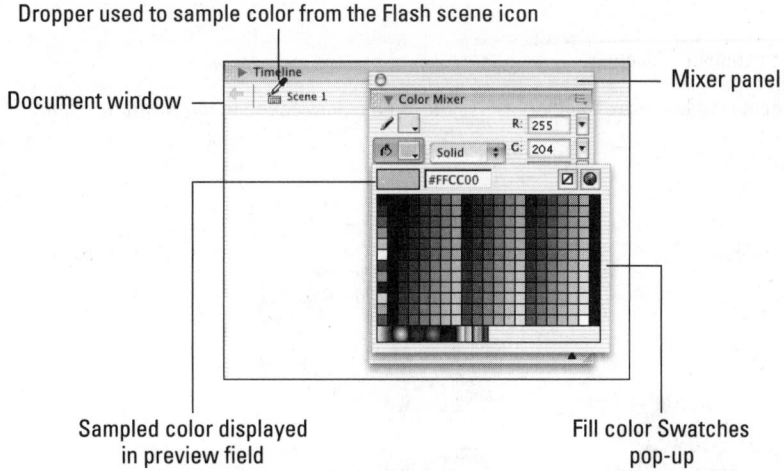

Mixer panel

Sampled color displayed
in preview field

Fill color Swatches
pop-up

Figure 7-15: When the Swatches pop-up is active in the Mixer panel, the cursor converts to a Dropper tool that can pick up colors from any visible element on your desktop.

Adjusting fill and stroke transparency

The Alpha control in the Color Mixer panel is used to adjust the transparency of stroke and fill colors, either to modify a selected graphic or to create a new color that can be added to the Color Swatches panel.

Cross-Reference

The Color Mixer panel Alpha control is used only to adjust stroke and fill colors. To dynamically change the transparency of individual symbol instances, the Color effect options in the Property inspector are used as described in Chapter 9, "Modifying Graphics." The color and transparency of Movie Clips can also be controlled with ActionScript using the Color object, as described in Chapter 25, "Controlling Movie Clips."

There are two ways to change the Alpha value for a selected color: Either drag the Alpha slider until the preview display looks right, or enter a numeric value directly in the Alpha value box. Numeric entry is useful when you already know what level of transparency is required, while the slider is useful for tweaking the transparency by eye to get it just right — as indicated in either the stroke or fill color chip. To see a larger preview of your alpha adjustments, expand the Mixer panel so that you can see the large preview box to the left of the expanded Color selection field. The larger preview display also gives you a split view that allows you to compare the last chosen setting with the current setting.

In Figure 7-16, a stroke color and a fill color have both been adjusted to 50 percent alpha and then added to the Color Swatches panel. While the Alpha slider is being dragged to a new setting, the preview displays the original 50 percent Alpha value (at the bottom) as well as the current 25 percent Alpha value (at the top). The rectangle below the panels shows the 50 percent alpha stroke and fill applied to a shape. The Flash grid has been turned on (View ⇨ Grid ⇨ Show Grid), so that the alpha is easier to see — on a flat white background, the color just looks lighter rather than transparent.

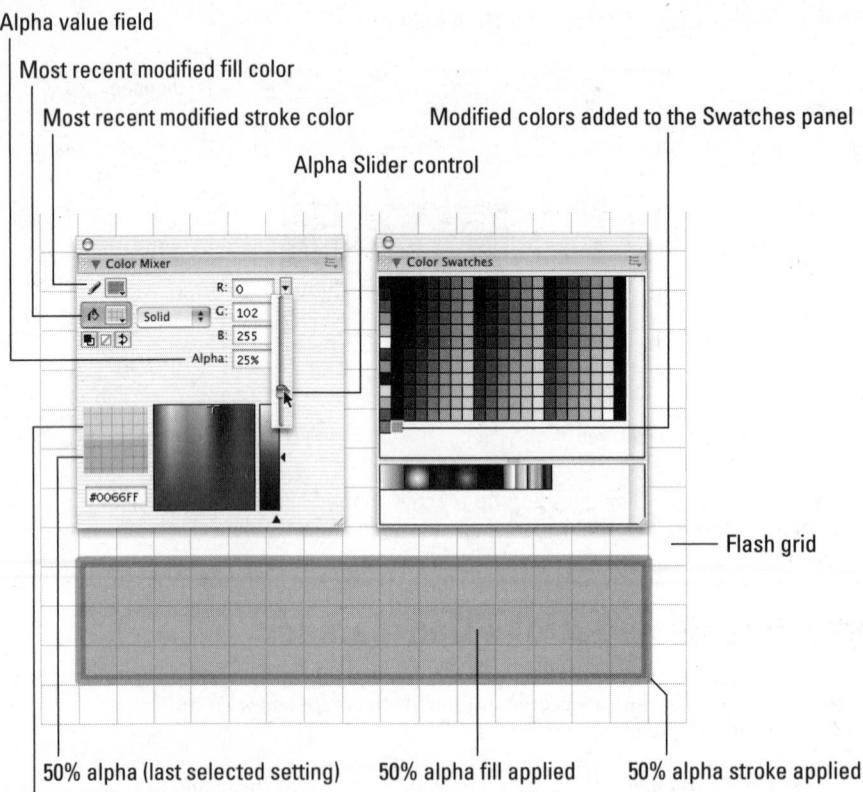

Alpha value field

Most recent modified fill color

Most recent modified stroke color

Modified colors added to the Swatches panel

Alpha Slider control

Flash grid

50% alpha (last selected setting)   50% alpha fill applied   50% alpha stroke applied

25% alpha preview (current setting)

Figure 7-16: The Color Mixer panel expanded to show the large preview swatch. The adjusted Stroke and Fill colors that are added to the Color Swatches panel are shown below the other solid fill colors in the current palette.

Tip

Alpha transparency will result in more of a performance hit than a color tint, especially if there are a lot of overlapping animated transparencies. If you can achieve the effect that you want by using a tint instead (fading to a solid color), then save the Alpha effect for graphics that you need to layer on top of other elements or textured backgrounds.

Working with gradient fills

Gradients are composed by blending two or more colors together in bands across a plane (*a linear gradient*) or from the center to the edge of an object in concentric circles (*a radial gradient*). You can modify these two basic styles of gradient fill to create virtually unlimited variations.

Figure 7-17 shows the gradient editing controls in the Mixer panel, with the preview display for a linear gradient on the left, and for a radial gradient on the right. When working with linear gradients, the position of the color pointers on the Edit bar will correspond to control points on the blend from left to right. When used in conjunction with radial gradients the Gradient Edit bar corresponds to the *radius,* or a slice from the center out to the edge, of the circular gradient. Color pointers at the left end of the Gradient Edit bar represent the center — or inside — of the radial gradient, while color pointers at the right end represent the outside border. The active color pointer is identified by a black fill in the pointer, and unselected color pointers have a white fill in the pointer.

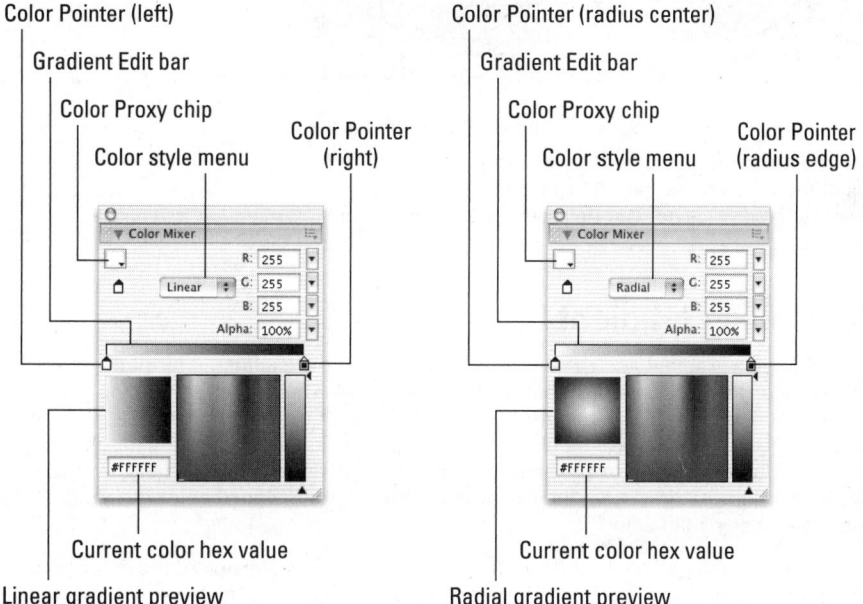

Figure 7-17: The Mixer panel displaying edit controls and preview for a linear gradient (on the left) and for a radial gradient (on the right)

The main Color Swatches panel and any of the fill Swatches pop-ups display the prebuilt linear and radial gradients that are included in the default palette. To edit an existing gradient swatch, just select it from the any of the fill Swatches pop-ups or select it from the main Color Swatches panel, and it will be loaded into the Mixer panel where the relevant controls will be displayed automatically. The other option is to start by choosing a gradient style from the central Color style menu on the Mixer panel to load a basic linear or radial gradient. After you create a custom gradient in a document, your settings will appear when you go back to the Mixer panel menu. To start with an unmodified default gradient, just select one from the fill Swatches palette. Figure 7-18 shows the two methods of selecting a gradient style to modify.

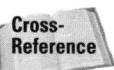

Cross-Reference
The Fill Transform tool is independent and used to scale, rotate, and skew gradient or bitmap fills after they have been applied to an item. This tool is introduced in Chapter 9, "Modifying Graphics."

Color style menu   Fill color Swatches pop-up

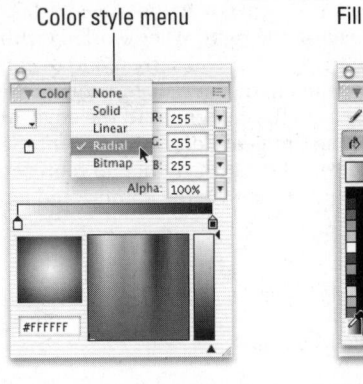

Default gradient swatches

Figure 7-18: Default gradient styles can be selected from any of the fill Swatches pop-ups, or one of the basic grayscale gradient styles can be selected from the Color style menu.

Controlling gradient fill colors

The colors in a gradient and the distribution of blending are adjusted by sliding the color pointers along the Gradient Edit bar in the Mixer panel. These pointers are the access points to the key colors that define the gradient. After you click on a pointer to make it active, you can assign the color that will be blended in its range, either by using the Swatches pop-up from the color proxy chip or by choosing a color in the Color Selection field. You can also use the value fields and the color slider controls to modify an assigned color in a gradient the same way as any solid color.

You can adjust the pattern of the blend by clicking and dragging any of the color pointers to slide them to new positions along the Gradient Edit bar. You can add additional color pointers to the gradient range by clicking anywhere along the Gradient Edit bar. These additional pointers will create new control points in the gradient that can be dragged to new positions or assigned new colors to define the gradient pattern. To remove color pointers, simply drag them downward away from the Gradient Edit bar; they will detach and disappear, taking their assigned color and control point with them. Figure 7-19 shows a basic radial gradient modified with the addition of a new color pointer. To save a custom gradient to your Color Swatches panel, choose Add Swatch from the Mixer panel options menu.

By selecting an element on the Stage, you can also apply or dynamically modify its gradient fill using the Mixer panel. When an item is selected in the Document window, you will see the current fill displayed in the fill color chip in the Property inspector. To load the fill into the Mixer panel, select it from the Swatches pop-up preview in the Property inspector. After the selected fill is loaded in the Mixer panel, any changes you make will be updated on the item dynamically. Remember to select Add Swatch from the options menu if you want to store the new gradient in the Color Swatches panel. Figure 7-20 shows the display of the Mixer panel when a shape is selected with a solid fill (on the left). Modifying the fill in the Mixer panel applies changes directly to the selected shape (shown in the center and on the right).

Added Color Pointer

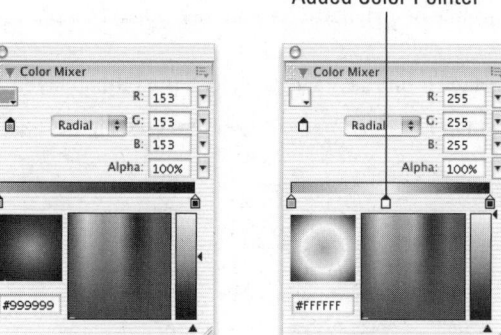

Two point gradient   Three point gradient

Figure 7-19: A radial gradient from gray to black (on the left), modified with the addition of a central color pointer assigned a color of white (on the right)

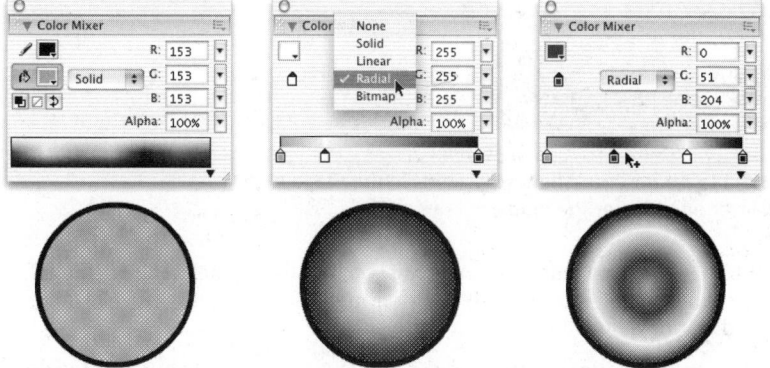

Figure 7-20: Selecting a filled shape (on the left), changing the fill style in the Mixer panel (in the center), and dynamically editing the fill (on the right)

Tip   To make it easier to see how a gradient looks in a selected shape, you can toggle off the display of the selection mesh by using Shift+Ctrl+E (Shift+⌘+E).

Using Alpha settings with gradients

As mentioned previously, all the normal Color sliders and value fields will apply to control points on a gradient. You may have noticed already that this means you can add alpha to the blend range of any gradient. To create a soft transition between a bitmap or a patterned background and a solid color, you can create a gradient from a 0 percent alpha to a 100 percent alpha of the same solid color. To demonstrate just one application of this feature, we will walk through the steps of adding the appearance of a vignette (or softened edge) to a photograph imported into Flash:

1. Import a bitmap into Flash and place it on the Stage; then lock the bitmap layer.

2. Create a new layer above the bitmap layer and name it **gradient** (see Figure 7-21).

Figure 7-21: An imported bitmap placed on the Stage with a new layer above it for the gradient

3. Open the Mixer panel and set the gradient style to radial, or select the default grayscale radial gradient from the fill Color Swatches panel. Set the stroke color to black, with a stroke height of 2.

4. Select the gradient layer and then use the Rectangle tool to drag out a rectangle on the Stage that is the same size as the photograph on the layer below (see Figure 7-22).

5. Select the fill of the rectangle and then select the left (white) color pointer on the Gradient Edit bar and assign it a color of black and an Alpha value of 0 percent (see Figure 7-23).

6. Press Shift+Ctrl+E (Shift+⌘+E) to hide the selection mesh and adjust the position of the color pointer by sliding it along the Gradient Edit bar, until you like the way the blend looks on top of the photo (see Figure 7-24).

Note   As you read through the steps in this example, you might have wondered why we assigned the same color to both color pointers — since one of the pointers is set to an alpha value of 0 percent, perhaps it doesn't matter which color is used? The answer is that you *can* create a "fade" effect with a radial gradient made from two different colors, but the blend will not be clean unless you use only one color. Although the end point of the gradient assigned an alpha value of 0 percent will be "clear," the interstitial bands of the gradient will be tinted by whatever color you have assigned to the color pointer before changing the alpha value.

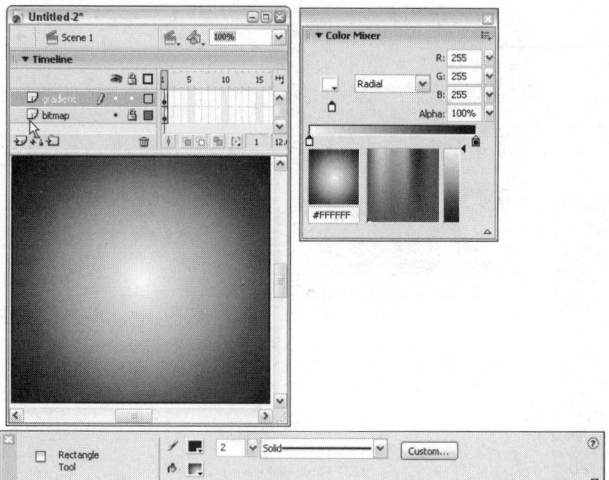

Figure 7-22: Drawing a rectangle with a radial gradient fill and a black stroke of 2. The rectangle is dragged out to match the size of the photograph on the layer below.

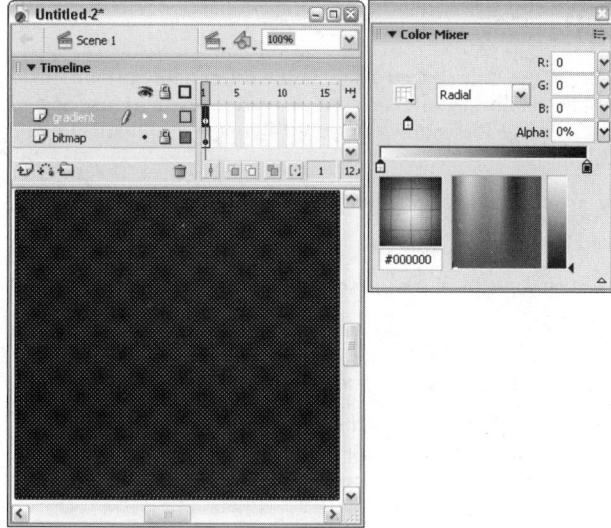

Figure 7-23: Both color pointers assigned a color of black for the selected gradient fill

Figure 7-24: The final gradient can be previewed as the color pointer is moved to adjust the edges of the alpha blend.

Selecting bitmap fills

Another handy feature available in the Color Mixer panel is the Bitmap fill option. This option allows you choose any bitmap, in the library or elsewhere on your system, to use as a fill for shapes drawn in Flash. When the image loads into a selected shape, it automatically tiles at 100 percent scale to fill the shape.

To apply a bitmap fill directly to an existing shape, perform the following steps:

1. Select the shape fill with the Selection tool.

2. Open the Mixer panel and choose Bitmap from the Color style menu.

3. If you have bitmaps stored in your current document library, they will be available from the Bitmap Preview area of the Mixer panel. Simply click on the thumbnail of the bitmap that you want to apply and it will automatically fill the selected shape.

4. If you do not have any bitmaps available in the current document, selecting Bitmap from the Color style menu in the Mixer panel will launch the Import to Library dialog box, where you can browse your system and specify a bitmap to be imported and applied as a fill.

Figure 7-25 shows a selected shape with a bitmap fill applied, chosen from the available thumbnails in the Mixer panel Preview area.

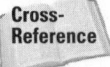

Cross-Reference   The Fill Transform tool can be used to scale, rotate, or skew the bitmap fill as described in Chapter 9, "Modifying Graphics."

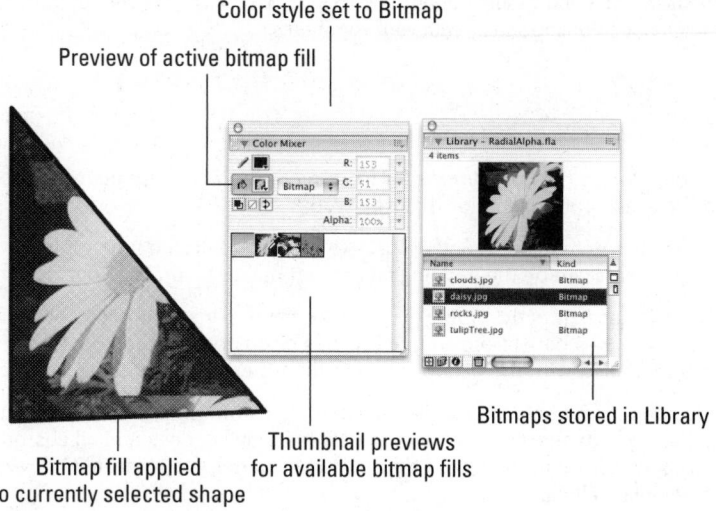

Color style set to Bitmap

Preview of active bitmap fill

Bitmaps stored in Library

Bitmap fill applied
to currently selected shape

Thumbnail previews
for available bitmap fills

Figure 7-25: A bitmap fill applied to a selected shape. The bitmap is chosen from images stored in the library, displayed as thumbnails in the Mixer panel Preview area.

Working with Droppers, Paint Buckets, and Ink Bottles

So far in this chapter, we've introduced the various ways of controlling your palette and setting stroke and fill colors on items selected with the Selection tool. There is one other set of tools used for applying colors and fills that will make modifying existing artwork even easier. You have already seen the Dropper tool in action when selecting a color from any of the Swatches pop-ups—where the Arrow pointer automatically converts to a dropper and allows you to pick up a color from any visible element to be loaded into the active fill or stroke color chip.

This same tool can be summoned at any time by clicking on the Eyedropper tool (I) icon in the Tools panel. You will notice that when the Eyedropper tool is used to pick up a fill color or bitmap, it immediately converts into the Paint Bucket tool (K). This tool will allow you to dump the selected fill into any other shape just by clicking on it. If you have a fill or stroke selected when you invoke the Eyedropper tool, any other fill or stroke that you pick up with the Dropper tool will be applied instantly to the selected item.

When you sample a stroke with the Eyedropper tool, it converts into an Ink Bottle tool (S), which can be used to apply the stroke to any other item. If the item already has a stroke, it will be modified and if the item did not previously have a stroke, the Ink Bottle will add one.

Cross-Reference   We cover the various options and methods for putting these tools to best use in Chapter 9, "Modifying Graphics," where you will also find information about the Fill Transform tool and the Free Transform tool.

Web Resource   We'd like to know what you thought about this chapter. Visit www.flashsupport.com/feedback to fill out an online survey with your comments.

Summary

✦ The science of color on the computer is far from accurate. There are many variables involved in the presentation of color over the Web.

✦ Web-safe color does not ensure "good color"—many strategies go into applying color skillfully, but contrast can be the defining factor that makes or breaks your design.

✦ Although Flash doesn't directly support color scheme plug-ins, colors can be loaded into the Color Swatches panel from source GIF files or custom Color Table (.act) files, or they can be sampled with the Dropper tool to load them into the active color chip.

✦ The Swatches pop-up available from the Tools panel or from the Property inspector gives immediate, intuitive access to the currently loaded swatches and all custom colors that have been added to the main Color Swatches panel. It also permits direct insertion of hexadecimal values.

✦ The Color Swatches panel is used to save out color sets, import color sets, and reorder or change selected colors and gradients.

✦ The Color Mixer panel is used to create and modify gradients and select bitmaps to be used as fills, in addition to adjusting the alpha and tint of new or existing colors. Custom colors added to the current swatches will be available in any of the Swatches pop-ups.

✦ The Eyedropper, Paint Bucket, and Ink Bottle tools work together to select and apply fill and stroke colors. The options for these tools are discussed along with the Transform Fill and Free Transform tools in Chapter 9, "Modifying Graphics."

✦ Advanced color capabilities of Flash include color tweening, scriptable color, and negative alpha. These topics are discussed in depth in subsequent chapters.

✦   ✦   ✦

Working with Text

For designers who love fonts, Flash is a dream come true. Even if you never plan to animate anything, you may want to use Flash simply to see your fonts displayed how you want them, wherever and whenever you need them on the Web. Of course, there are a few exceptions to this unequivocal freedom, but Flash has options that give you text styles to meet nearly any project criteria.

Because Flash is a vector program, it enables the integration of most fonts within the movie without any fuss. For standard text content, this means that fonts don't have to be rendered into bitmap elements — the .swf files that Flash publishes (or exports) will include all the necessary information for the font to display properly on every browser.

In this chapter, we introduce the various text types available in Flash and explain how and why they are used. This chapter also covers some basic font management issues and offers strategies for handling fonts in your project files (FLA) as well as in your published movies (SWF).

Flash includes some nifty Static text options for handling vertical and right-to-left reading text. You will look at these options along with the other character and paragraph controls available in the Property inspector. This chapter also touches on some new features for optimizing text and working with international character sets in Flash MX 2004.

Cross-Reference

For coverage of the new `TextArea` component used to control scrolling text, refer to Chapter 20, "Making Your First Flash MX 2004 Project." For a detailed explanation of using the `TextField` object for controlling editable text with ActionScript, refer to Chapter 31, "Applying HTML and Text Field Formatting."

Considering Typography

Typography is the formal term for the design and use of text. Although Flash offers the capability to deliver finely designed typography to your audience, too many Flash artists are typography challenged. Unfortunately, no matter how well Flash renders text, it can't disguise bad design or make up for a designer's lack of knowledge about working with type. As with color, sound, animation, or any other specialized area of production, the amount you can learn about typography is really only limited by your interest.

Although many people can get by without ever studying typography formally, they are missing the chance to leverage one of the most powerful and complex tools of graphic design. Although computers have changed the way that final designs are created, they have not changed the fundamental principles and uses of typography. The best part about studying typography is that your knowledge will be equally useful no matter what medium or digital tool you are working with.

Because type is such an important and long-standing aspect of design, there are innumerable resources available to guide and inspire you. Just wander through the graphic design section of any bookstore or do a search online for *typography,* and you will find something that can introduce you to the basics or help develop the skills you already have.

This chapter includes some common typography terms that are familiar to most people who have designed with text. Although a more detailed explanation of the source and meaning of these terms is beyond the scope of this book, you will be able to follow visually how things like *tracking* and *leading* apply to text in Flash.

If you are unfamiliar with typography, here are some excellent resources to get you started:

✦ *The Non-Designer's Type Book* **by Robin Williams:** This is a classic must-read (and study) for anyone who really wants to take Flash-type designs to the next level.

✦ *The Elements of Typographic Style* **by Robert Bringhurst:** This is a manual of typography and book design that concludes with appendices of typographic characters and currently available digitized fonts [and] a glossary of terms.

✦ *Jan Tschichold: A Life in Typography* **by Ruari McLean:** This is an inspiring and informative biography of the life and work of one of the most influential masters of modern typography.

✦ *Type in Use* **by Alex W. White:** This book offers a concise primer on the history of publication design and includes many useful examples of effective strategies for designing pages with type.

✦ *The End of Print* **by Lewis Blackwell and David Carson:** This colorful book charts the creative evolution of one of the most legendary mavericks of contemporary graphic design.

Text Field Types in Flash

Flash allows you to include text in your projects in a variety of ways. Often one Flash project will contain several different text types, each suited to a specific kind of content. The steps for creating text boxes and editing type are described later in this chapter, but we will begin here with an overview of the three main text types used in Flash:

✦ **Static:** Static text boxes are used for display type or text content created at author-time (in the .fla), that won't change at runtime (in the SWF).

✦ **Dynamic:** Dynamic text fields are used to hold text content that is generated at runtime from a live data source, or text that will be updated dynamically, such as weather or sports scores.

✦ **Input:** Input text fields are exactly what they sound like, fields created for text that is entered at runtime by users. Input text fields are used whenever you need users to do things such as entering passwords or answering questions.

Note   For the purpose of brevity I often refer to both Dynamic and Input text fields as *editable text fields* because both of these text-field types can be modified at runtime (unlike Static text boxes, which can be modified only at author-time.)

On the CD-ROM   You will find examples of each style of text field in the `textSamples.fla` file in the `ch08` folder of the CD-ROM.

The Text tool is used to create text boxes and to enter and modify type. When a text box is first created in Flash, the default text type is Static, but it can be assigned a different text type in the Property inspector at any time. Subsequent text boxes are automatically assigned the most recently selected type style. This makes it quicker to create a series of text boxes of the same type, but it means you should double-check the settings if you need text boxes of different types.

Figure 8-1 shows the basic controls that appear in the collapsed Property inspector when the Text tool is selected from the Tools panel.

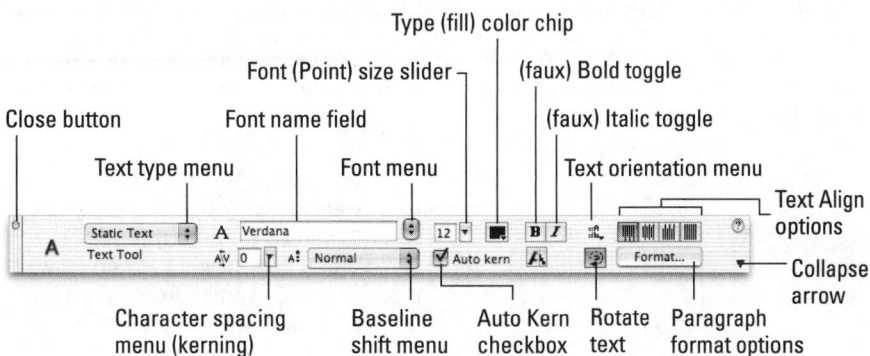

Figure 8-1: The basic text options that appear in the (collapsed) Property inspector when the Text tool is active or a Static text box is selected with the Selection tool

Static text boxes

Although the term *Static text* sounds limiting, this type of text box actually offers the most design options at author-time. Static text boxes can be scaled, rotated, flipped, or skewed, and they can be assigned a variety of colors or alpha levels while preserving individual editable text characters. Static text can also be animated or layered like any other graphic element in Flash. By default, Flash embeds the outlines for any fonts used in Static text for display on other machines, but you may also choose to specify a generic device font to reduce the size of your final movie or to eliminate antialiasing (or smoothing) on small text.

New Feature   Flash MX 2004 includes a new Alias text button in the Property inspector that will render an "unsmoothed" outline of characters in any selected text field for export with the final SWF. The benefits and limitations of this feature are described in more detail later in this chapter.

The Link entry field is another helpful feature in the Property inspector that allows you to select sections of Static or Dynamic (horizontal) text and enter a URL to create a text link to a Web page or to an e-mail address in your Flash movie without any additional coding.

By default, Static text boxes are horizontal, and they can be either *expanding* boxes, which allow you to keep typing along one line as it extends to fit the type, or fixed-width boxes, which constrain your text box to a set width and auto-wrap the text to fit. These two types of text fields look the same when selected by clicking once with the Selection tool, but by double-clicking you can see the text box handle icon that indicates the current behavior of the box. Figure 8-2 shows the respective icons for expanding or *label* text and for fixed-width or *block* horizontal Static text.

static text box: expanding   static text box: fixed width

Figure 8-2: The handle icons for expanding (left) and for fixed-width (right), horizontal Static text boxes

Static text boxes in Flash include the option for left-to-right- or right-to-left-reading vertical text boxes. Have you ever wanted a line of text characters to stack vertically, but found it tedious to use a hard return between each letter? Thanks to vertical text, you can now easily switch your type alignment from horizontal to vertical, with characters either stacked or rotated. This eliminates the headache of trying to read sideways while editing type — with a simple menu choice you can switch from vertical to horizontal and back again with no hard returns or freehand rotations required. Figure 8-3 illustrates how the vertical text option changes the orientation of Static text.

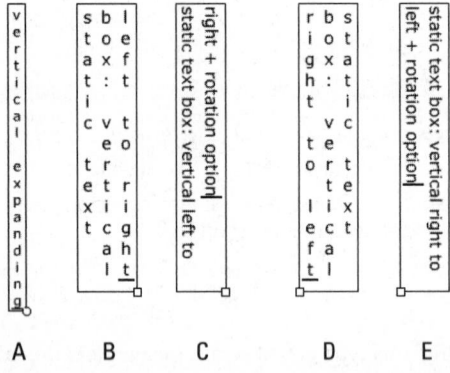

A   B   C   D   E

Figure 8-3: Vertical text box orientations: (A) Vertical expanding, (B) Vertical fixed-height L-R, (C) Vertical fixed-height L-R with rotate option, (D) Vertical fixed-height R-L, (E) Vertical fixed-height with rotate option

Aside from giving developers authoring in English more options for cool layouts, this feature makes Flash much friendlier for developers authoring in language sets that require vertical or right-to-left character flow. As described in the "Vertical text options" section later in this chapter, the alignment of vertical text can also be modified to anchor it to the top, center, or bottom of the text box.

Although the default orientation for text in Flash is horizontal and left to right, you can modify the Vertical text settings in the Editing tab of the Flash Preferences dialog box, as shown in Figure 8-4 (File ⇨ Preferences or, in OS X, Flash ⇨ Preferences.) To make all new Static text boxes automatically orient vertically, select the Default text orientation check box, and to change the default text flow, select the Right to left text flow check box. You also have the option of disabling kerning on vertical text by selecting the No kerning check box.

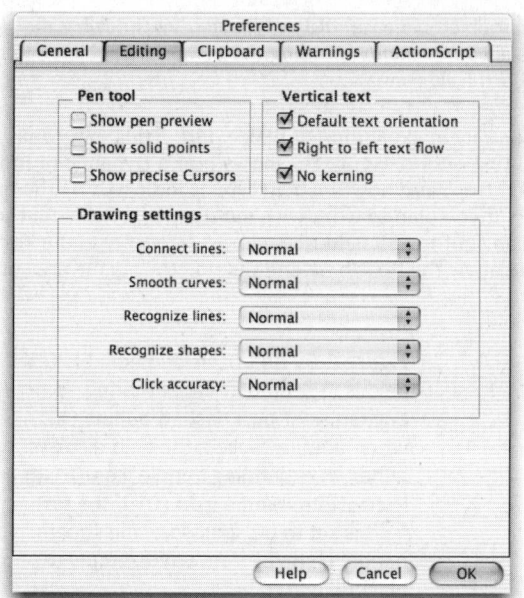

Figure 8-4: Changing the default Vertical text settings in the Preferences dialog box

Editable text fields: Dynamic and Input

Editable text begins like Static text as a *block,* but when converted to Dynamic or Input behavior, these editable text boxes are referred to as *text fields* — probably because they are often used as empty fields in which users can input text, as with a form or a password entry. Think of an editable text field as an empty window with a name attached to it. When text or data is sent to the Flash movie (.swf), it is sent to a specific named text instance, which ensures that it will be displayed in the proper window or editable text field. Dynamic text fields can display information supplied from a database, read from a server-side application, or loaded from another Flash movie (or another part of the same Flash movie).

Because Dynamic text fields are generated or edited on the fly (at runtime), there are limitations on how much you can control the appearance of the text at author-time. You cannot apply special formatting or shape modifications (such as skewing or kerning) directly to Dynamic text fields. However, Flash recognizes Dynamic text field instances in the same way as other Movie Clip instances, so you can assign a name to a Dynamic text field instance and use ActionScript to control its appearance.

Note

The Flash 5 convention of naming editable text fields using a variable name only was modified by the introduction of the TextField object in Flash MX. In Flash MX and in Flash MX 2004, all editable text fields are recognized as nameable instances of the TextField object. It is important to differentiate these two naming conventions. Variable names should only be used to identify editable text fields for backwards compatibility with older versions of the Flash Player, and the variable name or `var` attribute of a text field should not be the same as its instance name.

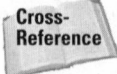
Cross-Reference

For an introduction to ActionScript objects, please refer to Chapter 24, "Knowing the Nuts and Bolts of Code," and for a detailed explanation of using the `TextField` object, refer to Chapter 31, "Applying HTML and Text Field Formatting."

Dynamic text can be authored horizontally in expanding or fixed-width fields, but cannot be rotated or modified with the Vertical text option. Figure 8-5 shows how a Dynamic or Input text field will display when unselected (top) and how the field type is indicated by the handle icons when the text is double-clicked. If you plan to work with multiline text fields, but you have limited space for the text you can set the text field behavior to *scrollable* in the Text menu (Text ➪ Scrollable) and this will allow the text to extend outside the visible area of the text box.

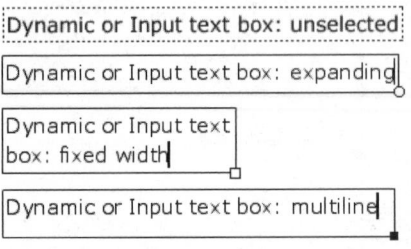

Figure 8-5: An unselected editable text field is indicated in the authoring environment by a dashed outline (A); when double-clicked, the field displays either an expanding handle icon (B), or a fixed-width handle icon (C). If the text field is set to be *scrollable*, the square handle changes from white/empty to black/filled (D).

When the Render text as HTML button in the Property inspector is toggled on, rich text formatting such as links and font styles indicated in Dynamic text with HTML tags will be recognized by Flash and applied when the text is rendered in the Flash movie (.swf).

The Text Tool and the Property Inspector

Although Flash is neither an illustration program like Freehand, nor a traditional page-layout program like Quark, its text-handling capabilities are robust and easy to use. Although nearly any style of text can be created directly in Flash, you can also import text created in other applications as vector artwork. With applications such as Macromedia Freehand, you can even preserve your type as editable text boxes when it is imported to Flash.

Cross-Reference

For more information on importing vector graphics, refer to Chapter 16, "Importing Artwork." For coverage of some of the vector graphics applications that can be used to create Flash-friendly artwork, including text, refer to Chapter 36, "Working with Vector Graphics."

Working with the Text tool

The Text tool, shown in Figure 8-6, delivers a broad range of control for generating, positioning, and modifying text. Although the basic Text tool is located in the Flash Tools panel, when the tool is active, the controls for working with text are in the Property inspector.

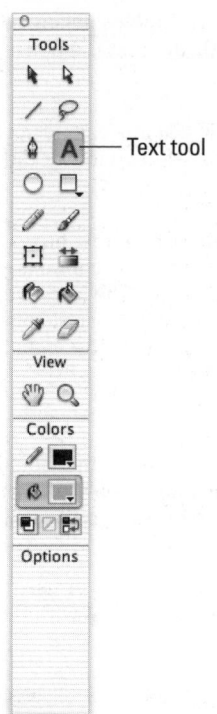

Figure 8-6: The Text tool is used to create all text boxes and text fields in Flash.

— Text tool

Creating Static text boxes

To create text in your current Flash document, click the Text tool in the Tools panel to activate it. You may choose to create new text in your Document window with either of two methods:

✦ **Label text:** To enter text on one extending line click on the Document Stage and begin typing. To control the width of a line of label text, you can either enter hard returns with the Enter or Return key as you type, or you can convert the label text into block text by dragging the round corner handle to a specific width — it will change to a square handle to indicate that the box is now constrained instead of expanding. Refer to Figure 8-2 (left image) for an illustration of the round label text handles.

Tip

If your text continues beyond the viewable area of the Document window, you can add some line breaks, click and drag to move the label text box, or select View ➪ Work Area to make the entire text label visible.

✦ **Block text:** To define the width for an area of text that will constrain your type by auto-wrapping as you enter more characters, click on the Document Stage and drag the box to the width that you want. You can change the width of your block text at any time by double-clicking the box to invoke the square corner handle and then dragging the handle to set a new width. Refer to Figure 8-2 (right image) for an illustration of the square box text handles. You can convert a text block into label text by double-clicking on the square corner handle, which changes to a round handle to indicate that the box is now extending instead of constrained.

Tip   The handles on text boxes or fields are visible only when the text is in Edit mode. To return an existing text box to Edit mode, either double-click the item with the Selection tool or click it once with the Text tool.

One characteristic of the Flash text tool that might surprise you is that Static text boxes that do not contain any text are cleared from the Stage. As long as a Static text box contains even one character, it remains on the Stage until you delete or move it manually. The latest version of Adobe Illustrator has adopted this same behavior because it eliminates the hassle of a project cluttered by empty invisible text boxes. Editable text fields *will* remain visible even if you have not entered any text characters at author-time.

Modifying or deleting text

Flash handles text as a group, which allows you to use the Text tool to edit the individual letters or words inside a text area at any time by clicking on the text box and then typing or drag-selecting specific characters. To select the whole block or group of text, you can click once anywhere on the text with the Selection tool.

To delete individual characters, click and drag to select them with the Text tool or use the Backspace key (the Delete key on Mac). To delete a whole group of text, select it with the Selection tool and then use the Backspace key (or Delete key).

Tip   Double-clicking a text block with the Selection tool also activates the Text tool — this allows you to modify the individual characters or to change the text box style, without having to go to the Tools panel. The shortcuts used to navigate in the Actions panel can also be used in an active text box. For example, the Ctrl+arrow key (⌘+arrow key on Mac) shortcut will move the cursor to the beginning or end of a word and holding down the Shift key at the same time will select the word.

You can use most common text editing/word processing commands in Flash. Cut, Copy, and Paste work to move selected text within Flash and also between Flash and other applications that handle type. Flash MX 2004 finally provides the built-in Spell Check and Find & Replace features that so many of us have been waiting for.

The Spell Check settings are quite sophisticated and you can customize them using the Spelling Setup dialog box available from the application menu (Text ➪ Spelling Setup). As shown in Figure 8-7, these options enable you to work with language-specific features and to control what areas of your Flash document to include when Spell Check is applied.

After you choose your settings, you can select Text ➪ Check Spelling from the application menu and Flash opens the Check Spelling dialog box (shown in Figure 8-8). You can then go through various text elements in your Flash document and modify or replace errors (with the help of suggestions), as you would in any other program with a spell check feature. This seems simple enough, but it is a huge improvement over the workaround required in older versions of Flash.

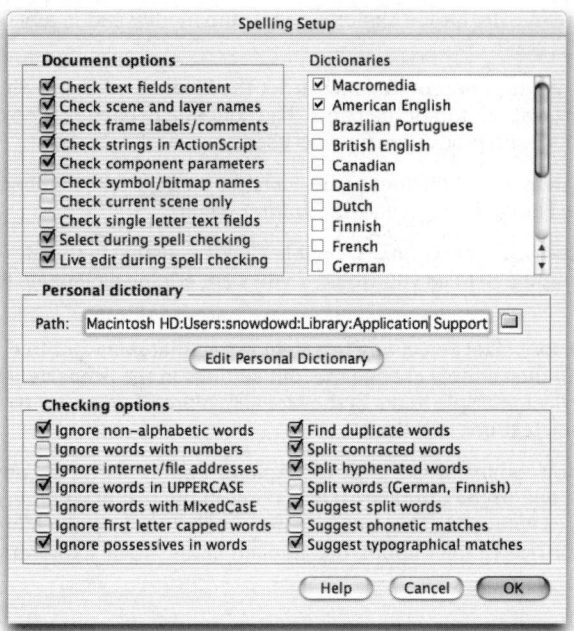

Figure 8-7: The Spelling Setup dialog box gives you a range of settings to control how the Spell check command is applied to your documents.

Figure 8-8: Check spelling with ease in Flash MX 2004

The Movie Explorer panel (which also opens when Spell Check is applied) makes it easier to find and modify text if you are working with a complex document. To access this feature if it is not already open, use the application menu (Window ➪ Movie Explorer) or the Alt+F3

(Option+F3) shortcut keys to invoke the Movie Explorer panel, and modify text in any of the following ways:

✦ **To see all the text used in your current document:** Set the Movie Explorer to Show Text with the option button at the top of the panel. The contents of each text box will be listed along with the font and point size that was used.

✦ **To search for a specific item:** Enter the font name, instance name, frame number, or ActionScript string in the Find field of the Movie Explorer panel.

✦ **To edit the contents of individual text boxes:** Double-click any listing in the Movie Explorer panel, and type in the field as you would if you were editing a filename in any other list.

✦ **To specify a new font or font size:** Select any text item listing that you want to change in the Movie Explorer and then simply change the font settings in the Property inspector. Use Shift+select to select multiple items in the Movie Explorer if you want to apply a change to more than one text box at a time.

✦ **To copy text:** Use the Copy command in the Movie Explorer options menu to copy a currently selected line of text to the Clipboard. Or to copy all the text in your current document to the Clipboard without having to select items individually in the Movie Explorer, use the Copy All Text to the Clipboard command in the Movie Explorer options menu.

Setting text attributes in the Property inspector

The Text tool does not include options in the Tools panel because the extensive text controls are centrally located in the Property inspector. All Flash text is created with the same Text tool in text blocks or boxes, but when a text block is created, it can be assigned specific behavior with the Property inspector.

Although font style and size menus can always be accessed from the application menu (Text ⇨ Font, Text ⇨ Size and Text ⇨ Style), the options for controlling text are not visible in the Property inspector unless the Text tool is active or a text box is selected with the Selection tool. The options available in the Property inspector vary slightly, depending on the kind of text selected.

Static text options

When working with Static text, you can modify both the font and paragraph attributes with the following options, shown in Figure 8-9:

✦ **Text type menu:** This drop-down enables you to specify Static, Input, or Dynamic for your text box type. Set this behavior first to invoke the relevant options in the Property inspector.

✦ **Font field (and menu):** When the Text tool is active this displays the name of the current font. Click the arrow button to invoke a scrolling menu of available fonts. Choose a font from this scrolling menu to set the font for the next text element that you create. Or, to change the font of existing text in the Document window, first select individual characters with the Text tool or select the whole group with the Selection tool, and then choose a different font from the scrolling menu. When selecting a font from the Property inspector menu, the currently highlighted font is previewed in the style or typeface that will display.

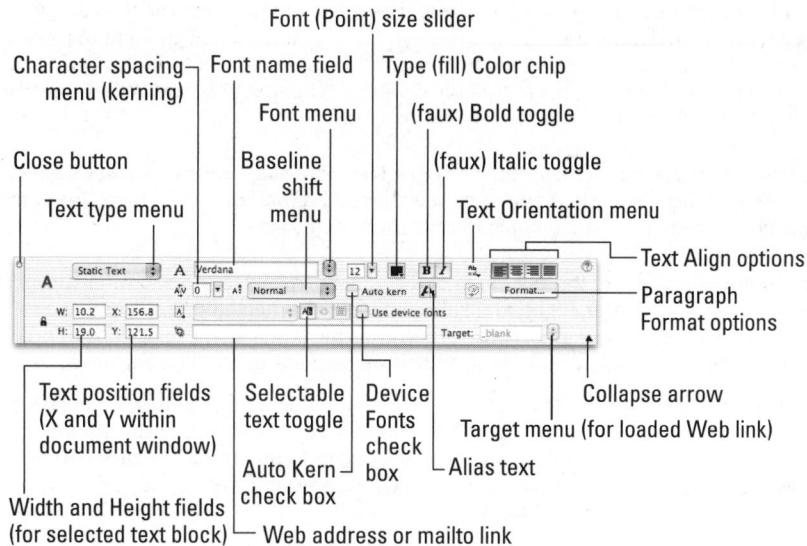

Font (Point) size slider

Character spacing— Font name field Type (fill) Color chip
menu (kerning)

Font menu (faux) Bold toggle

Close button Baseline (faux) Italic toggle
shift
Text type menu menu Text Orientation menu

Text Align options

Paragraph
Format options

Text position fields Selectable Device Collapse arrow
(X and Y within text toggle Fonts Target menu (for loaded Web link)
document window) check
Auto Kern box Alias text
check box

Width and Height fields
(for selected text block) Web address or mailto link

Figure 8-9: The main options available for Static text in the (expanded)
Property inspector

Tip

The font assigned to existing text can also be changed from the application menu with Text ➪
Font. The advantage of this method is that the list is more expansive and easier to scan. The
disadvantage of this list is that it doesn't give you a visual preview of the fonts.

✦ **Font size:** You can select the size of your type with either a pop-up slider or a point size
entry field. When the Text tool is active, it displays the current font size in the entry
field. You can change the font size by typing a specific point size number in the field. If
you click the arrow button to the immediate right of the text entry field, a pop-up slider
enables you to select a font size — as you move the slider, the font size number updates
in the entry field.

✦ **Type Color chip:** Click this button to invoke the current Swatches, which in addition
to current and temporary swatches also enables you to acquire a color from anywhere
within the interface by sampling with the dropper arrow.

✦ **Bold and Italic:** The Bold option is a radio button that toggles selected text between
Normal and faux Bold. The Italic option is another radio button. It toggles selected text
between Normal and faux Italic.

Note

Many computer programs (including Flash) that handle type permit you to approximate a
bold and/or italic version of a font, even if this style is not available in the original installed
font; this has led to some confusion about font styles. If a font was originally designed to
include a bold or italic version, it will be appropriately named in the font menu (such as
Century Schoolbook Bold), and will be selected as a *separate* typeface. With many fonts,
the faux bold or italic style may display very similarly to the designed Bold or Italic style, but
with well-designed fonts, the shapes and proportions of individual characters are designed
separately for each style. Theoretically, the original designed letter shapes for each style
should look better than a normal letter shape thickened with an outline to create a faux
bold style, or slanted to create a faux italic style.

✦ **Text Orientation menu:** This pop-up menu enables you to select the flow direction for your text. The default is Horizontal, which orients text from Left to Right in rows along a horizontal baseline. The vertical text options are Vertical Left to Right, and Vertical Right to Left — these options automatically orient the text in columns that progress from left to right or from right to left, respectively.

Note   If you select a Vertical text orientation, the other text formatting options will apply slightly differently than they do to Horizontal text. See the section "Vertical text options" for descriptions of the controls that are relevant to vertically oriented type.

✦ **Text Align options:** The top-right area of the panel displays four buttons for the arrangement of text: Left, Center, Right, and Full Justification. When editing, alignment affects the currently selected paragraph(s) only. When entering text, use these options to predetermine the alignment before text entry, and all subsequent text will be aligned accordingly.

✦ **Character spacing menu:** This value field and slider are used to change the space or tracking between individual letters. The default setting of 0 applies the built-in tracking and kerning of the font, while any setting between +1 and +60 adds space between characters and any setting between –1 and –60 decreases space between characters (extreme settings cause the letters to overlap).

Tip   With a section of text selected, you can use Ctrl+Alt+arrow keys (⌘+Option+arrow keys on Mac) to increase or decrease spacing between characters. The higher the Zoom setting, the smaller the spacing increments will be.

✦ **Baseline shift:** Three options are in this drop-down menu. Normal resets text to the baseline. Superscript shifts Horizontal text above the baseline and Vertical text to the right of the baseline. Subscript sets Horizontal text below the baseline and Vertical text to the left of the baseline.

✦ **Alias text:** Use this button to convert text in a selected text box from anti-aliased (or smoothed) text to unsmoothed or aliased outlines that will be embedded with the final SWF. This option is best applied to make medium-sized text more crisp — between 12 pt and 24 pt — smaller text will become illegible and larger text will just look "jaggy."

Note   Embedding aliased outlines for text below about 36 pt can make your final SWF file smaller. However, embedding aliased outlines for text at larger point sizes can make your file larger than if you just embed the standard anti-aliased font. Embedding aliased outlines for a large number of different fonts can bloat your final file, so apply this option only when it makes a significant improvement to the legibility of specific text.

✦ **Auto Kern check box:** If the font includes built-in kerning information, which evens out the spaces between letterforms, select this to activate automatic kerning.

✦ **Paragraph Format options:** The Format button invokes the paragraph Format Options dialog box shown in Figure 8-10, for the following additional text controls:

   • **Right margins:** Use this numeric entry field (or click the arrow button to invoke the interactive slider) to define the space between the text and the right border of the text box. By default, this space is described in pixels.

- **Line spacing:** Use this numeric entry field or associated slider to adjust line spacing. By default, Line Spacing is described in points. Regardless of settings for individual fonts, the largest font on a line will always determine line spacing for that line.

- **Indentation:** Use this numeric entry field or associated slider to adjust the indent, measured in pixels, of the first line of a paragraph. The indent is relative to the left margin.

- **Left margins:** Use this numeric entry field (or click the arrow button to invoke the interactive slider) to define the space between the text and the left border of the text box. By default, this space is described in pixels.

Note   The default units of measurement for both the Margin and Indentation entries of the paragraph Format Options dialog box are determined by the Ruler Units for the movie. Ruler Units can be reset in the Document Properties dialog box, which is accessed from the application menu with Modify ⇨ Document or from the keyboard by pressing Ctrl+J (⌘+J).

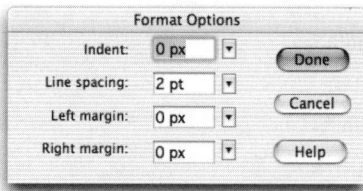

Figure 8-10: The paragraph Format Options dialog box for Horizontal text invoked with the Format button in the Property inspector

✦ **Selectable:** Use this toggle button to make selected text, or text that's entered subsequently, selectable when displayed on users' machines. This allows users to copy and paste your text into other text-editing applications or browser windows. Type in Vertical text boxes cannot be made selectable.

✦ **Use Device Fonts:** This little check box is the secret to keeping more control of your font display while taking advantage of device fonts for file size savings. *It is not a substitute for selecting one of the three device fonts that appear at the top of the Font menu.* Rather, it's an innovative way in which Flash enables you to rely on commonly installed fonts without embedding all the font information in your Flash movie (.swf), as described later in this chapter.

✦ **Link entry:** This option is only available for Horizontal Static or Dynamic text. (To apply this option to Dynamic text, you must first select the Enable HTML button.) By selecting a text box or an individual word in the Document window, and then entering a URL in this Link entry field, you can add a hyperlink to selected text. The text link will be identified in the authoring environment with a dotted underline—the underline will not be visible in the published .swf file, but the mouse pointer will change to indicate a link when it is over the text.

✦ **Target menu:** This menu is accessible after you enter a URL in the Link field and it allows you to select a destination for the loaded URL. The options will be familiar to anyone who has worked with HTML page structures. For more information, refer to the description of the getURL() action in Chapter 18, "Understanding Actions and Event Handlers."

Application menu commands

Some of the text settings in the Property inspector are also available from the application Text menu:

✦ Under Text ➪ Font, you can select from the same available fonts listed in the Property inspector Font menu, but the list is slightly larger so it is easier to read.

✦ Under Text ➪ Size, you can select a specific font point size from a list, instead of using the Font size slider in the Property inspector.

✦ Under Text ➪ Style, the commands include:

  • **Plain:** Ctrl+Shift+P or ⌘+Shift+P

  • **Bold:** Ctrl+Shift+B or ⌘+Shift+B

  • **Italic:** Ctrl+Shift+I or ⌘+Shift+I

  • **Subscript**

  • **Superscript**

✦ Under Text ➪ Align, the commands include:

  • **Align Left:** Ctrl+Shift+L or ⌘+Shift+L

  • **Align Center:** Ctrl+Shift+C or ⌘+Shift+C

  • **Align Right:** Ctrl+Shift+R or ⌘+Shift+R

  • **Justify:** Ctrl+Shift+J or ⌘+Shift+J

✦ Under Text ➪ Tracking, you will find a list of options that offer an alternative way to adjust the space between characters. If you have the Property inspector open as you apply these commands manually, you will see the Character spacing or Tracking value field update. Manual tracking has the advantage that it can be applied either to selected (highlighted) text characters or to the pair of text characters on either side of the cursor:

  • **Decrease:** To decrease text character spacing by one half-pixel, press Ctrl+Alt+← (⌘+Option+←). To decrease text character spacing by two pixels, press Shift+Ctrl+Alt+← (Shift+⌘+Option+←).

  • **Increase:** To increase text character spacing by one half-pixel, press Ctrl+Alt+→ (⌘+Option+→). To increase text character spacing by two pixels, press Shift+Ctrl+Alt+→ (Shift+⌘+Option+→).

  • **Reset:** To reset text character spacing to normal, press Ctrl+Alt+↑ (⌘+Option+↑).

✦ **Scrollable:** The final item in the Text menu is an option that is only available when an editable text box is selected. When applied to a Dynamic text field, this option makes it possible to enter and scroll through text that extends beyond the frame of the text box. Apply this option by choosing Text ➪ Scrollable from the application menu or from the contextual menu when a Dynamic text box is selected, or by Shift+double-clicking the handle of a Dynamic text box.

Vertical text options

Some of the options that are visible in the Property inspector change slightly when you choose a Vertical orientation for your text box. Figure 8-11 indicates some of the options that are different from those described previously for Horizontal Static text.

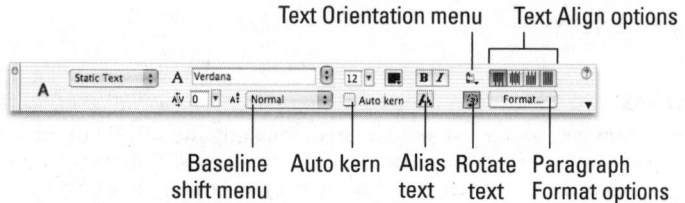

Figure 8-11: The formatting options available in the Property inspector for Vertical text

- ✦ **Text Align options:** These buttons now function to align the arrangement of text in a vertical text box to Top, Middle, Bottom, and Full Justification. When entering text, use these options to predetermine the alignment before text entry, and all subsequent text will be aligned accordingly.

- ✦ **Auto kern check box:** If the font includes built-in kerning information, which evens out the spaces between letterforms, check this to activate automatic kerning. On Vertical text, this setting can be overridden by the Vertical text settings in the Flash Preferences dialog box (refer to Figure 8-4). When No Kerning is selected in Preferences, then the Auto-Kerning toggle in the Property inspector will only apply to Horizontal text.

- ✦ **Rotate toggle:** This very handy button flips the characters in your Vertical text box so that the type is turned sideways — or actually resting on the vertical baseline. This is an effective alternative to creating Horizontal text and then using Free Transform to rotate the text box 90 degrees.

- ✦ **Paragraph Format options:** The Format button invokes the paragraph Format Options dialog box (see Figure 8-12) with the following additional text controls:

  - • **Indent:** Use this numeric entry field or associated slider to adjust the space between the top border of the text box and the first character in a column of type. This setting is described in pixels.

  - • **Column spacing:** Use this numeric entry field or associated slider to adjust space between columns of type. By default, Column Spacing is described in points. Regardless of settings for individual characters, the largest character in a column will always determine the calculation of line spacing for that line. This setting is described in points.

  - • **Top margin:** Use this numeric entry field or associated slider to adjust the space between the text and the top border of the text box. This setting is described in pixels.

  - • **Bottom margin:** Use this numeric entry field (or click the arrow button to invoke the interactive slider) to define the space between the text and the lower border of the text box. This setting is described in pixels.

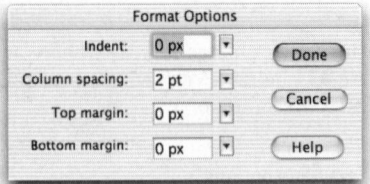

Figure 8-12: The paragraph Format Options dialog box for Vertical text invoked with the Format button in the Property inspector

Editable text options

The options available for Dynamic and Input text are predominantly the same, but there are a few important options that are unique for these two Editable text types. Figure 8-13 shows the Property inspector as it displays when you specify Dynamic behavior for your text. Only the additional options not shown in Figure 8-9 are labeled here.

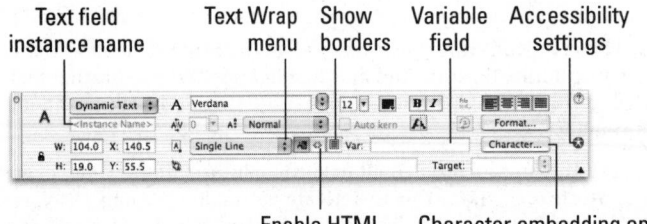

Figure 8-13: The additional options available in the Property inspector when Dynamic text behavior is selected.

The following options are common to both Dynamic and Input text:

✦ **Text field instance name:** As described previously, this identifier allows the Flash Player to put your dynamic data in the correct field.

✦ **Text Wrap:** Use this drop-down menu to choose how your text will be organized in the text field. Choose between Single Line, Multiline (with line breaks), and Multiline with no text wrap.

✦ **Enable HTML:** When this toggle is turned on, Flash preserves rich text styles when displaying Dynamic text. This includes font, font style, hyperlink, paragraph, and other formatting consistent with permissible HTML tags. You can also enable HTML so that the entry field will accept formatting that has been assigned to it in the Actions panel. For more information on this, refer to Chapter 31, "Applying HTML and Text Field Formatting."

✦ **Show border:** Use this to draw the text field with a border and a white background that will be visible in your published movie (.swf).

✦ **Variable:** This field is now redundant with the Instance name field, but if used for backwards compatibility it should be assigned a different name than your instance to avoid confusion in Flash MX or MX 2004.

✦ **Character Options:** When preparing a file for export, you can control how much font information is included with the SWF. The Character button invokes the Character Options dialog box (shown in Figure 8-14), in which you can specify that no characters are embedded by selecting the No characters radio button, or you can select the Specify Ranges radio button to pick from a long list of character or *glyph* sets to be embedded. The first four items in the Ranges field are most commonly used to specify standard characters in the English alphabet. You can also enter a more selective range of characters by typing them directly into the field at the bottom of the dialog box (under "Include these characters"). The Auto Fill button automatically loads all the unique glyphs or characters in the currently selected text box into the Include field to be embedded with the final SWF. The Total Number of Glyphs counter at the bottom of the dialog box updates based on your settings to show the total number of unique glyphs that will be embedded with the final exported file.

The Character Options have been expanded in Flash MX 2004 to include international language sets and specialized sets such as music symbols. These glyph sets can be very large, but this is a useful feature if you are creating dynamic text fields that will need to display specialized characters.

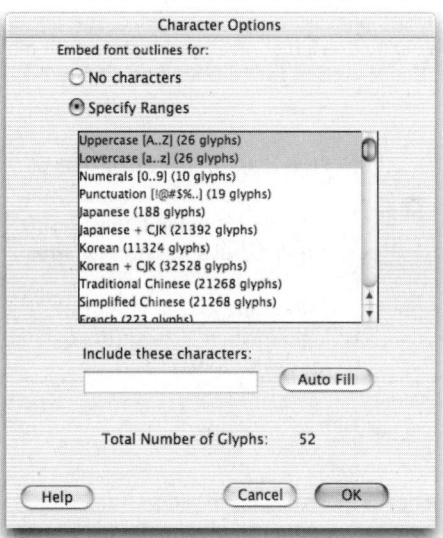

Figure 8-14: The dialog box for specifying characters to include in embedded font information to be exported with your final SWF

The Link and Target value fields are not available in the Property inspector when Input text behavior is selected, because you cannot add links to text that users will be entering. The only additional control available in the Property inspector for Input text fields is the Maximum Characters value field. Use the Maximum Characters value field to specify the maximum number of characters that a user can enter in this particular text field. The number of characters can be limited to any number between 0 and 65,535. This feature is generally used for controlled content, like passwords.

Font Export and Display

By default, Flash embeds all fonts used in Static text boxes in order to deliver WYSIWYG display in the published movie (.swf.) As long as font outlines are available for text used in your Flash document (.fla), the published movie (.swf) displays consistently, regardless of what fonts the user has installed on his machine.

In order to edit a Flash project (.fla) you need to have the original fonts available, unless you are willing to view the document with a substitute font in the authoring environment. If you select a text box that is displayed with a substitute font, you should still see the name of the original font listed in the Property inspector, although it will be marked by parentheses. As long as the font formatting is not modified, Flash preserves all the original font information so that when the document (.fla) is opened again on a machine that has the original font, any edits that were made using the default font are rendered correctly. Although you can make text edits while working with a default font, you need to have the original font installed in order to publish the final movie (.swf) with the design intact.

The consistent text display of embedded fonts is what endears Flash to type-obsessed designers, but there is a small price to pay: Every embedded font adds to the final file size, and embedded type is anti-aliased or smoothed by default. For many projects the additional weight is not an issue. For text at larger sizes, anti-aliasing is usually needed. But if you are trying to keep your files lean and mean and your text crisp at small point sizes, you may want to consider some of the alternatives to default anti-aliased font embedding. Figure 8-15 compares aliased with anti-aliased text.

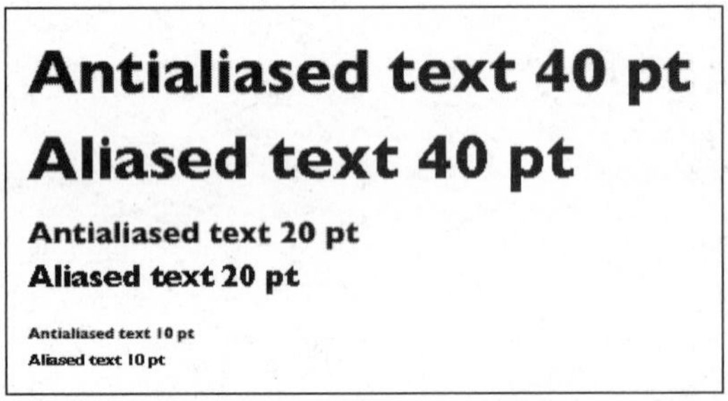

Antialiased text 40 pt

Aliased text 40 pt

Antialiased text 20 pt

Aliased text 20 pt

Antialiased text 10 pt

Aliased text 10 pt

Figure 8-15: Text characters at large point sizes look smoother with Flash's default anti-aliasing applied, but smaller point sizes can look too blurry with smoothing and will be most legible when aliased (the default for device fonts).

Caution   If you are working on OS X, you may not notice as much difference between aliased and anti-aliased text because the system applies automatic smoothing on any screen text, even on application menu lists. Although this feature cannot be turned off completely, the text smoothing menu in your General Preferences panel allows you to specify between the lowest setting (only smoothes text larger than 12 point) and the highest setting (smoothes all text larger than 8 point.) The default anti-alias setting smoothes any text larger than 9 point.

Understanding device fonts

Device fonts are three basic font style designators identified by a preceding underscore in your font menu. These fonts will be familiar to anyone who has worked with HTML text. Although not as exciting as some custom fonts, there are nevertheless whole design styles based on these "generic" fonts—think minimal and unpretentious. You will find the three device font designations: _sans, _serif, and _typewriter, in either the Property inspector font menu or in the application menu under Text ➪ Font. These device font labels tell the Flash Player to use any equivalent font available on a viewer's system. The formatting that you have applied to the text in your Flash document (.fla), such as bold or italic style and point size, will be preserved and applied to the font selected by the Flash player from the viewer's system to render the text in your Flash movie (.swf).

To give you an idea of how device fonts relate to installed fonts sans usually becomes Arial or Helvetica, while serif usually becomes Times or Times New Roman, and typewriter becomes Courier. Because these settings utilize the default fonts on the user's machine, Flash doesn't have to include their outlines in the exported .swf and the final movie file size is reduced.

Device fonts are always available and always quick to render, but they cannot be rotated and occasionally they will vary slightly in their metrics from player to player and across platforms. Another important difference between standard embedded fonts and device fonts is that embedded fonts will be anti-aliased or smoothed by Flash, while device fonts will be unsmoothed or aliased. This makes device fonts ideal for small type such as image captions or menu items because when text is smoothed it can make it harder to read at small point sizes.

Rendering outlines with the Alias text button

The new Alias text button in the Property inspector is a good addition to the authoring environment. This handy little button makes it possible to quickly convert any selected text from anti-aliased to a pre-rendered aliased outline that will be embedded with the final SWF. The aliased outline will actually add less to your file size than the anti-aliased font information, if the font is at a point size below about 24. Despite the benefits of the Alias button, we can't say it is a *great* addition yet because it doesn't always give the crisp, clean results you might hope for. In fact, this feature is only really useful when applied to fonts in the mid-size range. Applied to fonts between 12 and 24 point, the Alias text feature will render a fairly crisp outline and will eliminate the "blur" associated with anti-aliased text smoothing. Unfortunately, when we tried the Alias text feature on smaller text (between 6 and 11 point), most fonts completely fell apart and became illegible blocky pixel shapes. On text larger than 24 point, the Alias text feature not only made the text look rough, but it also bloated file size more than including standard font outlines.

The advantage of using the Alias text button is that you can create a "custom" aliased outline from any font on your machine, which gives you many more creative options than the three basic device fonts. Unlike device fonts, text converted to aliased outlines using this button can also be rotated or scaled—although it doesn't always look that great, at least it does display in the published SWF.

Working with the Property inspector Use Device Fonts option

You will notice that even if you have not used one of the device fonts from your font menu, you can still select the Use Device Fonts check box in the Property inspector. This is a terrific "compromise" option if you strive for more specific control over the Flash Player's font choices, but still want to take advantage of the file size savings afforded by device fonts. When the Use Device Fonts option is checked in the Property inspector, the font is not embedded—only the Font Name, Font family/style (serif/sans serif/monospace), and other information are added to specify the font—which adds no more than 10 or 15 bytes to the final .swf file. This information is used so that the Flash player on the user's system will know if the font is installed or not. If the original font is available, it will display exactly as you designed it. If the original font is not present, then the Flash Player will still know whether the substitute font should be serif or sans serif.

The Use Device Fonts option also works as a toggle to turn off anti-aliasing. This means that even if the user has all the fonts used in your Flash movie installed, Use Device Fonts changes how the type displays:

✦ **When Use Device Fonts is selected:** Text displays better at small point sizes. That's because there is no anti-aliasing or smoothing applied to any device font, regardless of its presence on your system.

✦ **When Use Device Fonts is *not* selected:** The font outline is embedded and all characters are smoothed (even if the font is available). Smoothed text can be illegible at small point sizes.

To accurately preview the Use Device Fonts setting on your machine, if you have a font manager (as most Web designers do), you need to make sure you're careful about your font activation settings. Make sure Global activation is turned *off* to limit the number of fonts that the Flash player can find for rendering the movie (.swf).

For best results with this specific Use Device Fonts option, we suggest that you limit your font selection to those fonts that most of your audience is likely to have (all those common fonts that come installed with their machines), or those that will translate into one of the default device fonts without wreaking havoc on your design. It is better to be conservative and design your layout using Times, Arial, and Courier than to go wild with custom fonts that will most likely be substituted very differently when the movie is viewed on someone else's machine. Otherwise, for unusual fonts, we suggest that you either embed the full font outline information (Device Font option cleared) or, for limited areas of text (such as headlines), that you use the Alias text button to generate a custom aliased outline or break the text apart to manually create vector shapes, as described later in this chapter.

Troubleshooting font display

Although Flash does an amazing job of displaying fonts consistently and cleanly, even on different platforms, the success of your font export is entirely dependent on the quality and completeness of the font information available when the Flash document is created (.fla). Because Flash can access font information on your system while you are working in the authoring environment, many of the font display problems that can come up during production will only be visible when the Flash movie (.swf) is published.

To display fonts in the published movie (.swf), the Flash Player relies on the font information embedded in the movie, or else on the fonts installed on the user's system. If there are discrepancies between the information available to the Flash Player and the font information that was available to the Flash authoring application when the document was created, you will run into font display problems.

When you encounter problems with fonts (as you almost always do at some point), a good guide to font management is indispensable. We can't describe everything that can go wrong when working with fonts here, and solutions will often vary depending on how you are storing and managing your fonts. Ideally, you should find resources that are specific to the platform and programs you are using.

Tip

A good general guide to some basic font-management techniques for Macintosh users is *How to Boss Your Fonts Around* by Robin Williams. Even if you are a Windows user, this book can give you some basic background on how fonts and font management utilities work.

TrueType, Type 1 PostScript, and bitmap fonts (Mac only) can be used in Flash. Although Flash exports the system information about the fonts that are used, a damaged or incomplete font may still display correctly in the authoring environment (.fla). However, the exported movie (.swf) will appear incorrectly on other systems if the end user doesn't have the font installed. This is due to the fact that Flash can display the font within the editor by using the screen font; it does not recognize that particular font's outline and can't export information needed to display the text in the .swf. In order to check for this problem in the authoring environment, switch your view to View ➪ Antialias Text. If the text appears jaggy, that's a problem font. These font display problems can be avoided by using device fonts (_sans, _serif, or _typewriter fonts).

Controlling font substitution

If Flash cannot find font information on your machine to match what is specified in a file (.fla) when you open it in the authoring environment, you will be notified by the Missing Fonts alert box shown in Figure 8-16, and prompted to select fonts installed on your system to substitute for display.

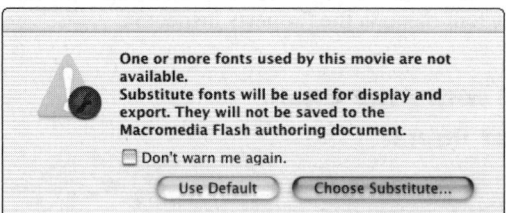

Figure 8-16: The Missing Fonts alert box used to control font substitution

Note

If you publish or export a document without viewing any of the scenes containing missing fonts, the alert box only appears when Flash attempts to publish or export the .swf.

The first time that a scene with missing font information is displayed in the authoring environment, you will be prompted by the Missing Fonts alert box to choose one of the following options:

✦ **Choose Substitute Fonts:** To specify individual substitutions from the fonts available on your system for each missing font, click this button to invoke the Font Mapping dialog box shown in Figure 8-17. This dialog box lists all fonts specified in the document that Flash can't find on your system. To choose a substitute font for a missing font, select the font name in the Font Mapping list and then choose a font installed on your machine from the Substitute Font pop-up menu. Click OK to close the dialog box.

✦ **Use Default:** This option substitutes all missing fonts with the Flash system default font and dismisses the Missing Fonts alert box.

✦ **Turn Alert off:** To disable the Alert box in the current document, select Don't Show Again for this Document, Always Use Substitute fonts.

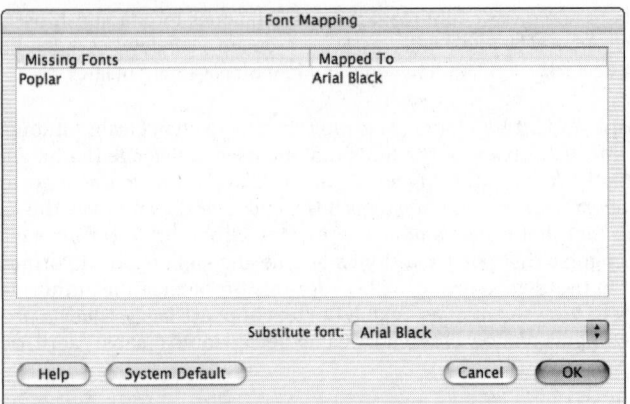

Figure 8-17: The Font Mapping dialog box is used to view missing fonts and to modify mapping of substitute fonts.

Even though the text is displayed in a substitute font, Flash includes the name of the missing font in the Property inspector font menu, as shown in Figure 8-18. Flash preserves the original font specification when the file is saved so that the text displays correctly when the document (.fla) is opened on a system with the missing fonts installed. You can even apply the missing font to new text by selecting it from the font menu in the Property inspector.

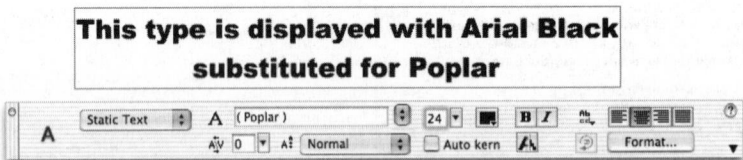

Figure 8-18: The missing font name is displayed in the font menu even when text is displayed in a substitute font in the authoring environment.

Because appearance attributes such as size, leading, and kerning may render differently with a substitute font, any modifications made while viewing text in a substitute font may have to be adjusted when the document is opened on a machine with the original font available.

Tip   To turn the Missing Fonts alert box off for all documents, clear the Warn on missing fonts check box in the Warnings tab of Flash Preferences (Edit ⇨ Preferences or Flash ⇨ Preferences for OS X). To turn alerts on again, reselect the check box.

To view all the missing fonts in the currently active document or to reselect font mappings, select Edit ⇨ Font Mapping (or in OS X, Flash ⇨ Font Mapping) from the application menu and repeat the same steps described previously to choose new substitute fonts. To view all the font mapping settings saved on your system or to delete font mappings, close all Flash documents before opening the Font Mapping dialog box or making changes to the listed mapping.

Using Miniml Fonts in Flash, **by Craig Kroeger**

For those of you who are not familiar with Miniml fonts, these are fonts designed to remain crisp (aliased) in Flash and they can be used as an alternative to generic device fonts. These aliased fonts are particularly useful at small sizes, where anti-aliasing can reduce legibility. This is a real concern when designing Flash applications for devices.

ALIASED TEXT
ANTIALIASED TEXT

Crisp aliased text (top) compared to blurry anti-aliased text (lower)

There are free versions of the Miniml fonts, included on this book's CD-ROM in the ch8 folder — you may use these to test what you can do with them. Professional versions of these fonts are available at www.miniml.com.

There is also a sample source file (Miniml.fla) on the CD-ROM that shows how the fonts are used in various text field examples. In order for the Miniml fonts to work properly, consider these guidelines:

✦ **Select Font:** When the Miniml fonts have been installed on your system, you can select them from the Font menu in the same way as any other available font. However, the font must be a Miniml font to display properly as aliased text. Other pixel fonts will not work because they will be anti-aliased.

✦ **Font Size:** Miniml fonts must be set to 8 points or any multiple of 8 (16, 24, 32, and so on) The numbers in the font name refer to the font style, not what point size it should be set to.

✦ **Vertical Static text:** Miniml fonts can now be used on a vertical axis when they are rotated with the rotate option in Flash.

✦ **Spacing Static text:** Only Static text can have adjusted character spacing. When adjusting the character spacing, use whole-pixel values to keep the text aliased. Professional Miniml fonts have versions with increased letter spacing for use with Dynamic or Input text fields.

✦ **Paragraph Alignment:** Do not use Center paragraph alignment — only use Left or Right.

✦ **Embed Font:** You must embed the Miniml fonts when using Dynamic or Input text fields. In Character Options, select the Select All Characters check box to embed the complete font. To reduce overall fill size, only embed the characters you need in your text. Static text is automatically embedded.

✦ **Snap to Pixel:** Use the Snap to Pixel feature under View in the application menu to keep fonts clear. When the fonts are not on whole _x and _y values, the fonts will appear blurry. If you are not using Snap to Pixel, make sure to check your Info panel to set the text box _x and _y values to whole pixels, using the top-left corner

as the registration point. To ensure consistent placement of text after you have converted a text box into a symbol, reposition the registration point of the symbol by
dragging it from the center to the top-left corner of the text box.

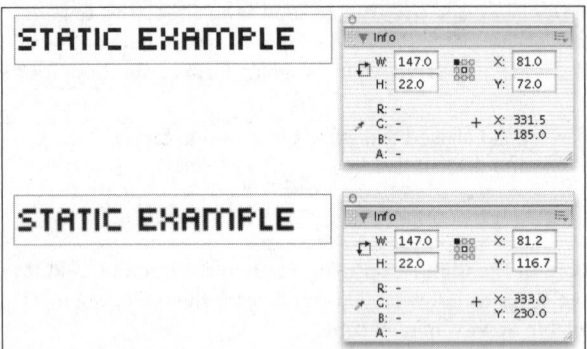

To keep text crisp (aliased), use Snap to Pixel or the Info
panel to set X,Y values to whole pixels (top). If text boxes
are not aligned to whole X,Y values then the font will be
anti-aliased (bottom).

* **Using Miniml fonts in motion:** When you are using Miniml fonts in animation,
  you need to round the _x and _y values to whole values to keep them crisp. Use
  the following ActionScript to round the numbers down to the closest integer:

  ```
  _x = Math.floor(_x);
  _y = Math.floor(_y);
  ```

* **Preview in the Flash Player:** Preview your finished movie in the Flash Player
  (.swf), to see the aliased text displayed correctly because it may appear anti-aliased
  in the authoring environment (.fla).

This may seem like a lot of rules, but I think you will find the results well worth the effort.

Font Symbols and Shared Font Libraries

Using Font symbols and Shared libraries in your Flash authoring workflow offers several benefits that can make it worth the little time it takes to set them up. Although you can nest a
Static text box inside any other symbol type if you want to reuse a specific text element in
your movie, this does not change how the text is published in the Flash document. Using
instances of a symbol to place repeated text elements such as logos or taglines offers the
same benefits as converting artwork into symbols — you can make changes to the symbol
stored in the Library and it will be propagated to every instance in your document, and you
can also modify the appearance of individual instances without changing the original symbol.

The difference between text nested in another symbol type and a real Font symbol is that Font symbols can actually be used to store the display information for an entire font. When placed into a runtime Shared library, Font symbols can be used to link text in one movie to the font display information in a source movie; this allows you to use custom fonts without having to embed the font information in every Flash movie (.swf) individually. This workflow is especially effective on projects that involve multiple .swf files using the same custom fonts. The bonus is that if your client suddenly decides that they prefer "Leonardo script" to "Chickenscratch bold" (or whatever font switcheroo they might come up with), you can make the change in your source Font symbol without even opening any of the other files (as long as the new font is given the same name and it still fits in your layouts).

This all sounds great so far, right? Now for the reality check: Because you are storing font information in a separate file from your layouts, there is one more factor that you have to manage. The source font library (.swf) can be in the same directory as your other movie (.swf) files or it can be stored on a completely different server. It is very important to decide on the storage location of your source font files (.fla and .swf) before you begin linking text in your other Flash documents (.fla) to shared Font symbols because the URL that defines the relative or absolute path is stored in each .fla file and your font links will be broken if you later change the source movie's location.

Note   Runtime shared assets do not need to be available on your local network when you are editing .fla documents that rely on linked assets, but the shared asset .swf must be available at your specified URL in order for the published movies (.swf) to display the linked assets at runtime.

As you can imagine, having your font links fail is a major disaster, so many developers believe that relying on an external font source isn't worth the risk. On the other hand, there is always an element of uncertainty with Web delivery, so it might not be fair to eliminate what is otherwise an excellent way to optimize font management in your Flash layouts. As with any Web production, just be sure to test early and often as you develop a Flash project that uses shared fonts.

Shared libraries can be used to store other symbol types, but it is best to organize different kinds of assets in separate FLA files. This chapter focuses on making Font symbols and creating a source file for a Shared font library.

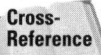

Cross-Reference   For a description of using Shared libraries for other assets as well as an explanation of how to load external .swf files, refer to Chapter 28, "Sharing and Loading Assets."

Creating a Font symbol

Font symbols can be integrated in your workflow in two ways. If you plan to use Font symbols within a Flash document (.fla) simply as a way to make edits faster in that one document, and you don't mind exporting the font information with every .swf, you can create a Font symbol directly in the main Library of your current document and rely on author-time sharing to update instances of the font. However, if you want to save file size by linking to the Font symbol information for runtime sharing, you should open a new Flash document before creating your Font symbols. In either case, the initial steps for creating a Flash Font symbol are the same:

1. Open the Library panel where you want to store the Font symbol.

2. From the Library options panel choose New Font, as shown in Figure 8-19.

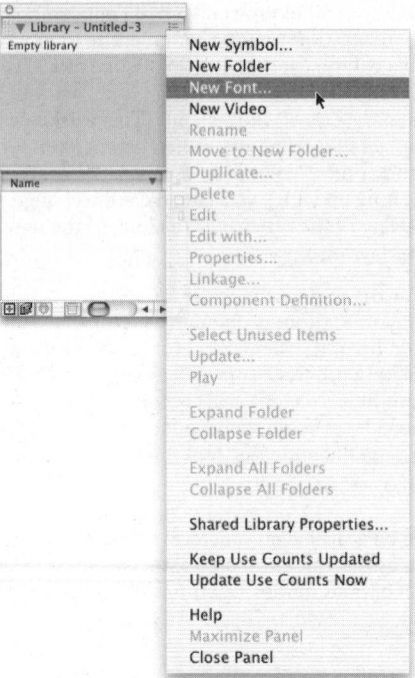

Figure 8-19: Choosing to insert a new Font symbol from the Library panel options menu

3. The Font Symbol Properties dialog box appears so that you can enter a name for your Font symbol and select the font you want to embed in the file (see Figure 8-20). The name that you enter shouldn't be the same as the original font name but rather should indicate how the font is being used in your project. For example, if you are using Impact font for your titles, instead of naming the Font symbol "Impact" you could name it "myProjectTitle" or some other name that will inform you (and the rest of your team) how the font is being used.

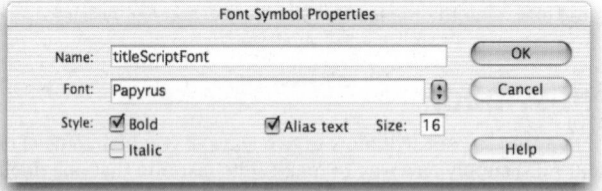

Figure 8-20: Selecting a font to store in the new Font symbol and giving it a reference name

4. If you also want the option to use faux bold or italic style on text linked to your Font symbol, select the Style check boxes for Bold or Italic to include these characters with the embedded font. Flash MX 2004 includes the option to create aliased outlines of any font and you can now select this check box in the Font Symbol Properties dialog box. If

you choose to render an aliased outline of a font, you also need to enter the font size that you want to use by typing it in the value field. This will increase the size of your source .swf only — the additional size will not be passed on to other SWF files that link to the Font symbol for runtime sharing.

Caution   If you create a Font symbol without the Bold or Italic options selected in the Font Symbol Properties dialog box and then try to apply the options in the Property inspector to create faux Bold or Italic style on text that is linked to the symbol, you will encounter one of two problems. If the text you are modifying is in a Static text box, then the applied styles will display, but the additional font information for the modified characters will be exported with your published file, thus increasing the size of the SWF. If the text you are modifying is in a Dynamic or Input text field, the text will not display in the published .swf file because the font information needed to render the Bold or Italic type on-the-fly will not be found by the Flash Player. These same rules apply to Aliased outlines rendered at a specific font size.

5. Now when you browse the font menu available in the Property inspector or from the application menu (Text ⇨ Font) you will see your new font listed with the other fonts installed on your system. Font symbols are also differentiated from regular fonts in the menu with an asterisk (*) following the name it has been given (see Figure 8-21).

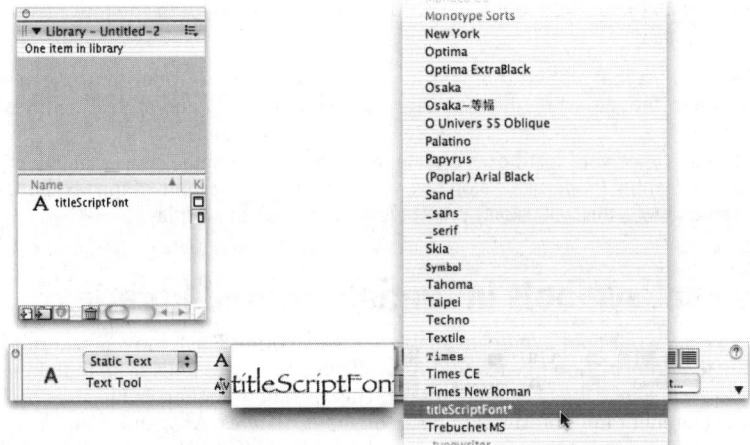

Figure 8-21: Font symbol names are followed by an asterisk in the Property inspector font menu (or in the application Text menu). Font symbols are also added to the Library list.

The next step that you need to take to use the Font symbol in your project depends on how you choose to integrate Font symbols into your workflow. As mentioned earlier in this chapter, using symbols for author-time asset sharing can make it easier to propagate changes throughout a document, but any assets used in your document will still be embedded in each movie (.swf) that you publish. Creating a separate library for storing symbols and linking these as runtime shared assets in multiple movies takes a little more work, but it gives you the benefit of both streamlined updates and smaller file sizes. The most appropriate workflow depends on the scope and content of your particular project and on how willing you are to manage the risks involved with using runtime shared assets.

Updating Font symbols at author-time

If you intend to use a Font symbol as an author-time shared asset only, you can simply leave it in your current Library so that the font is available in the font menu whenever you want to use it in your project. You will be able to modify any of the text boxes that use your Font symbol in the same way as any other text. There is no limit on the number of colors or sizes that you can use or on what you can type into each text box.

The main reason that this is a more flexible workflow than simply nesting text inside other symbols for reuse is that you can actually change the *characters* used in individual text boxes that reference a Font symbol, while you can only modify the *appearance* of text that is nested in a symbol instance.

The process for updating instances of a Font symbol used within one Flash document (.fla) is much the same as updating any other symbol type or imported asset stored in the Library:

1. Open the current document Library and select the Font symbol that you want to modify.

2. Choose Properties from the Library options menu or from the contextual menu.

3. In the Font Symbol Properties dialog box, simply select a new font from the font menu, but don't change the font name that you had previously chosen. (Now it makes sense why naming your Font symbol with the same name shown in the font menu isn't a good idea, right?)

   You will find that all text that was in your old font will be updated to the new font that you have chosen, while maintaining all other formatting and style attributes.

Tip   If you don't see your text boxes update to the new font immediately after you change it in the Font Symbol Properties dialog box, you may need to click one of the text boxes with the Selection tool — this will usually prompt Flash to refresh the display.

Using Font symbols in runtime Shared libraries

In order to make your Font symbol available for use in other Flash movies without having to embed the font information in each file, you will need to create links from individual *destination* files to your *source* file or Shared library. This workflow optimizes file sizes by eliminating storage of redundant font information between linked movies. As with HTML files, you have to specify a path in order for the Flash Player to locate font information in one movie (.swf) for text display in another. Because the font information is retrieved from a .swf file by the Flash Player and supplied to another .swf for text display, it is referred to as *runtime* asset sharing.

If you have already followed the steps to create a Font symbol in an otherwise empty Flash document (.fla), the next part of the process is to enter an identifier and a location (path) that will "lead" the Flash Player to your Shared library. As mentioned previously, you will need to know where the published source movie (.swf) will be stored before you can create font links to other documents. The location (or path) can be relative or absolute.

Tip   To keep your linkage intact while preserving source file version numbers as you develop your project, you might want to use the Publish Settings dialog box to give your published source .swf a generic name (such as `titleFontSource.swf`) while using a more specific naming convention for your source .fla files (such as `titleFontSource101.fla`). This eliminates the hassle of going back to your destination movies and changing the linkage information if you decide you need to move to a new version name to keep track of modifications to your source file (.fla).

To help clarify how runtime shared fonts are stored and accessed we will walk through the three possible scenarios for Font symbol use and show you how each is displayed in the authoring environment (.fla) and in the published movie (.swf).

On the CD-ROM

The Flash files illustrated in this section are included in the ch8 folder of the CD-ROM. You will find both the `fontSource` files (Shared library file) and the `fontLink` files (destination document). As long as the files are kept together in the same storage location, the font linkage should remain intact. We have also included a `fontEmbed` example file with the same text entered on the Stage, but with embedded font information (including uppercase, lowercase, and punctuation for Papyrus Bold), instead of linked font information to demonstrate the significant difference in file size.

The first file you will be working with is a source document, or the Flash document that contains the Font symbols that you want to use as runtime shared assets.

Caution

If you are using the files from the CD-ROM to follow this example, you may need to modify the Font symbol in `fontSource.fla` to match a font that you have on your system (instead of "Papyrus") before you can use Test Movie to publish the SWF file (Step 5).

1. Open your source document and select your Font symbol in the Library. If you are looking at the files on the CD-ROM, open `fontSource.fla` and select the Font symbol called NewFont in the Library.

2. Open the Linkage Properties dialog box (see Figure 8-22) by choosing Linkage from the Library options menu or from the contextual menu.

3. Enter an identifier that will help you to remember what this Font symbol is used for in your project (such as `titleFont`). When you enter the identifier, you will see it displayed after the Font symbol name in the Library. In our example file, we used the identifier `fontSource` to make the connection more obvious between the document (`fontSource.fla`) and the published movie (`fontSource.swf`). Don't close the Linkage dialog box until you have completed the next step.

4. The URL field is where you enter the path to the storage location for the source movie (.swf) that you will publish after you have finished choosing settings in the source document (.fla.) The link can be relative or absolute depending on how you will be storing your project .swfs:

   • If you are planning to keep the source movie (.swf) in the same folder as your individual destination movies (.swf), then all you need to enter in the URL field of the Linkage Properties dialog box is the name of your source .swf file—as in our example: `fontSource.swf`.

   • If the source .swf file will be stored in a different folder or even on a separate server than the destination (linked) SWF files, you need to enter an absolute path (Web address) in the URL field to specify the exact storage location of your source .swf file, such as: `http://yourserver.com/projectdirectory/ sourceName.swf`.

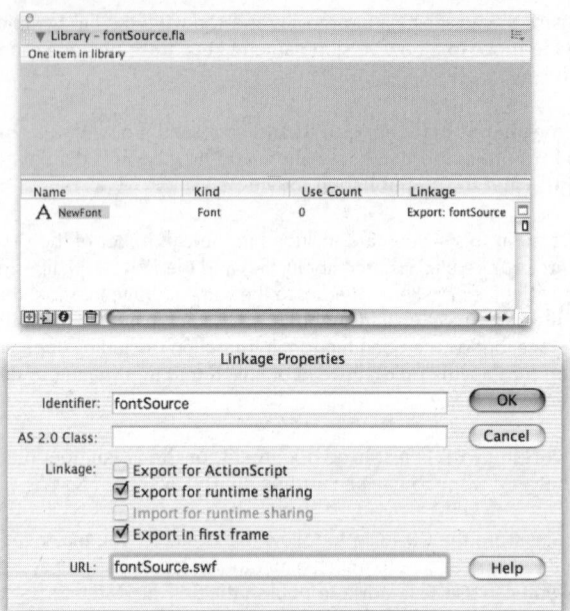

Figure 8-22: Setting up Linkage Properties for a Font symbol in the Flash source document (.fla)

5. Now you can save your source .fla file to the final storage location using File ⇨ Save (Ctrl+S or ⌘+S) and test your source .swf using Control ⇨ Test Movie (Ctrl+Enter or ⌘+Return). Although nothing is displayed in the published .swf, if you turn on the Bandwidth Profiler (from the application menu: View ⇨ Bandwidth Profiler or with shortcut keys Ctrl+B or ⌘+B), you will notice that the file size is probably more than 40K (our example file was 44K). (See Figure 8-23.) This is the size of the font information for all of the embedded characters included in your Font symbol.

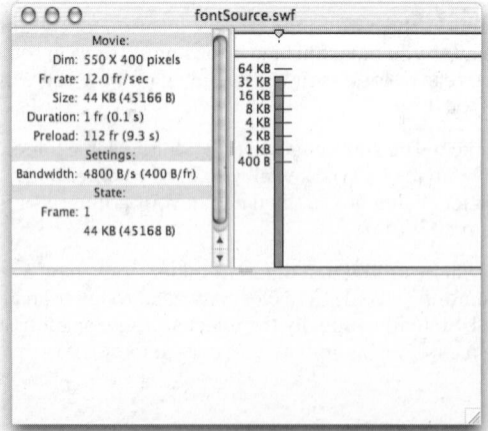

Figure 8-23: The published source movie (.swf) with embedded font information for the Font symbol to be used in other destination movies as a runtime shared asset

You have successfully created and saved a runtime shared asset. Now you can create another Flash document that references the font information stored in `fontSource.swf` so that you can use your custom font without having to embed the font information:

1. Create a new Flash document or open the `fontLink.fla` file from the CD-ROM, and make sure that you have the Library panel for the current document open.

2. There are two ways of linking another document to the font information in your Shared library:

   - If you have already created a document that uses Font symbols as described in the section on author-time sharing and decide to link to a runtime shared asset instead, you can enter the identifier and the URL of the Shared library movie (.swf) in the Linkage properties for any Font symbol in your Library. To enter linkage information manually, you need to have a Font symbol in the document Library selected so that you can access the Linkage properties dialog box from the options menu or from the contextual menu. Enter the identifier and the URL exactly as they appear in your font source file but instead of Export for runtime sharing you will see that Import for runtime sharing is selected (see Figure 8-24). You should now find that all instances of the Font symbol in your current document are updated with the Font information stored in the shared asset movie (.swf) (as long as it is available on your server when you publish the movie for your current document).

   - If you are authoring a document (.fla) that does not yet contain any Font symbols and you want to link to your runtime shared asset, you can simply drag the Font symbol from the source library into the current document Library. With your destination document and Library panel open, select File ➪ Open or File ➪ Import ➪ Open External Library and navigate to the Flash document (.fla) for your shared asset. You can then drag your source Font symbol from the shared asset library and drop it into your destination document Library. If you access Linkage properties for the Font symbol that you dragged into your Library, you will see that Flash automatically inserts the identifier and URL for the shared asset. You can now use the font in your new document and it will be linked to the font information stored in the runtime shared asset movie (.swf).

3. When a Font symbol in your Library has the identifier and URL entered in its Linkage properties, you can use the linked font in your document by selecting it from your font menu and using the Text tool as you normally would. When you publish your movie (.swf), you will notice that your file size is much smaller than it would be with embedded font information. For an example of this, compare the file size listed in the Bandwidth Profiler shown in Figure 8-25 (linked = 198 B), with Figure 8-26 (embedded = 24K).

4. If you decide that you want to disable runtime sharing for a Font symbol in a destination document, you can clear the Import for Runtime Sharing check box in the Linkage Properties dialog box. The font information for the characters used in your file will now be embedded with the .swf file, so the file size will be larger, but the Flash Player will not require access to the shared asset.

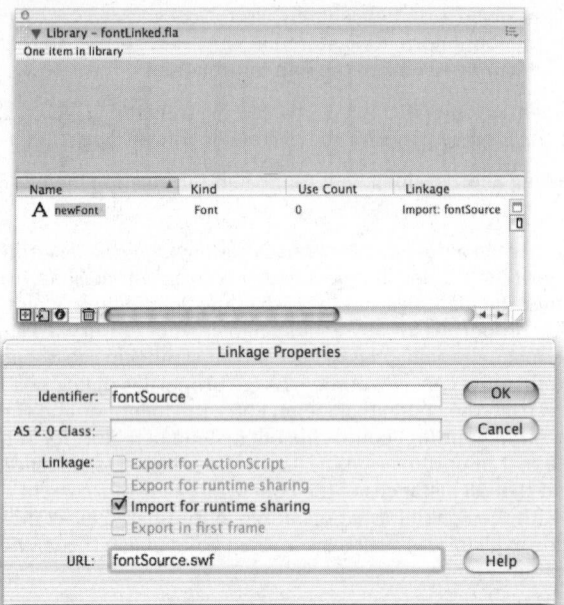

Figure 8-24: Linkage settings for a Font symbol in a destination movie refer to the font information stored in the runtime Shared library.

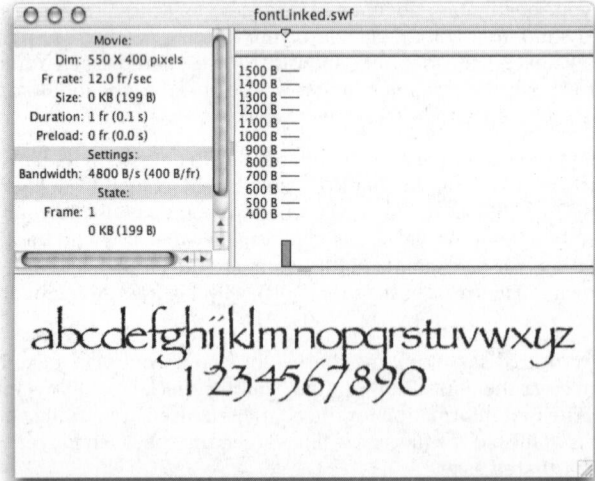

Figure 8-25: The published SWF file from a document using linked font information from a runtime shared asset

Figure 8-26: The published SWF file from a document using embedded font information

Modifying Text

In addition to all of the powerful text-handling capabilities discussed earlier in this chapter, there are some other ways that you can modify the appearance of text to create custom effects. Flash gives you the ability to reshape and distort Static text to suit your taste (or lack thereof). Figure 8-27 illustrates some of the ways that you can modify text after you have finished editing it with the regular text options.

Figure 8-27: Text boxes can be modified with Free Transform options (top). To create individual characters apply Break apart once (middle), and apply it again to create graphic text (bottom). Graphic text can be modified like any other shape in Flash.

Tip

If you plan to animate individual text characters, you can quickly move each letter onto it's own layer by first applying the Break apart command (Ctrl+B or ⌘+B) to a text box and then using the Distribute to Layers command (Shift+Ctrl+D or Shift+⌘+D).

On the CD-ROM

We have included the Flash files for the modified text shown in this section on the CD-ROM. If you want to look at these in the Flash authoring environment, you can open the file `modifyText.fla` in the ch8 folder.

Custom text information adds to your file size, so it is best to reserve these treatments for special text such as titles or graphics. If you are working with longer sections of text (such as an article or a story), it is better to use common fonts or device fonts to help keep your files smaller and to make the text easier to read.

Tip

With long sections of text, you will most likely need to add scrolling, and this is much easier to do if you use Dynamic text. If you use modified Static text or graphic text, it is still possible to add scrolling behavior by creating animation and controls manually, but this is much more time-consuming and requires more information embedded in your final .swf.

Cross-Reference

When text is nested in a Graphic, Movie Clip or Button symbol, you can modify its appearance using the Color Effect controls on the Property inspector as described in Chapter 9, "Modifying Graphics."

By selecting a text box with the Selection tool and activating the Scale option, you can scale your text by dragging the text box handles, but this is not recommended as a way to increase the size of text unless it has been broken into vector shapes. Flash has to interpolate the normal font outlines to scale text this way, so it can result in jagged edges when the movie is published. When sizing text, it is much better to simply choose or enter a larger point size in the font menu to ensure a clean outline when the text is exported.

Sampling and sharing text attributes

If you want to use the same font attributes on a variety of text boxes, it is often best to modify one text box so that it has all the qualities you want — including color, size, font, style, and line or character spacing. You then have two options for transferring these attributes to other text boxes using the Eyedropper tool:

✦ **To modify existing text boxes:** You can select other text boxes with the Selection tool and then activate the Eyedropper tool in the Tools panel and click on your modified text to sample its attributes and transfer them to all the other selected text boxes simultaneously. This is much more efficient and consistent than trying to remember what settings you used and changing them manually on different text boxes.

✦ **To set attributes for new text boxes:** You can load the visual attributes of any text into the Property inspector by activating the Eyedropper tool and clicking on the text to acquire its appearance. The Text tool is automatically activated after text is sampled, so you can immediately begin creating new text with the settings now loaded in the Property inspector.

Converting text into vector shapes

The Break apart command (Ctrl+B or ⌘+B) is used to reduce symbols to grouped shapes, and it can also be used to modify Static text. Applying Break apart once to a text box breaks a line of text into individual characters; applying the command again converts the characters into *graphic text* (vector lines and fills). Individual text characters can be grouped or changed to symbols. To make it easier to use individual characters in Motion tweened animation, you can apply the Distribute to Layers command to automatically place each character on its own layer.

 **Cross-Reference** Breaking apart text and using Distribute to Layers is described in more detail, along with coverage of applying special line and fill effects in Chapter 9, "Modifying Graphics."

Graphic text can be modified using any of the drawing tools, reshaped with the Selection and Subselect tools or distorted with any of the Free Transform options. You can also select special fills such as bitmaps or gradients to create patterned text, or use the Eraser tool to delete pieces of the letter shapes (as shown in Figure 8-28).

Figure 8-28: Using the Eraser tool to delete parts of a graphic letter shape

However, after text characters have been converted to lines and fills, they can no longer be edited as text. Even if you regroup the text characters and/or convert the text into a symbol, you can no longer apply font, tracking, or paragraph options. To streamline your workflow, consider how you can combine graphic text with normal text for some effects — rather than converting all text into graphic shapes. Figure 8-29 shows how a graphic version and a character version of the same text can be combined to create an exaggerated dimensional drop shadow.

Figure 8-29: Combining versions of the same text to create a drop shadow (the foreground text was broken apart once, while the shadow text was broken apart twice)

There are a few tips and guidelines to remember when converting text to shapes in Flash:

✦ To convert text characters to component lines and fills, the text characters that you want to convert must first be selected, or highlighted. Then choose Modify ➪ Break apart from the application menu. To undo, choose Edit ➪ Undo (Ctrl+Z or ⌘+Z) from the application menu.

✦ Rotation and Break apart can only be applied to fonts with available outline information such as TrueType fonts.

✦ On Macs, PostScript fonts can only be broken apart if a type manager is installed that will handle PostScript fonts.

✦ Bitmap fonts disappear from the screen if you attempt to break them apart.

✦ Test whether a font is a bitmapped font by choosing View ➪ Antialias from the application menu. If the text still appears with ragged edges, it is a bitmapped font and will disappear when broken apart.

As you experiment with graphic text you may want to refer to some of the other chapters that cover working with shapes.

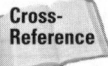

Cross-Reference   For more information on reshaping, and manipulating lines and fills with drawing tools, see Chapter 5, "Drawing in Flash," and for information on animating shapes refer to Part III, "Creating Animation and Effects."

Using Timeline Effects on Static text

Flash MX 2004 includes a new series of "ready-made" effects that can be applied and modified using the Timeline Effect Settings dialog box. To apply these effects, select a Static text box with the Selection tool and use the contextual menu or the Insert menu to browse to Timeline Effects and choose one of the effects in the drop-down menu. When you select an effect to apply, a dialog box pops up to allow you to tweak the settings to get exactly the look you want before Flash renders the final Graphic symbols that create the effect. Figure 8-30 shows the dialog box with a preview of the Drop Shadow effect created by default settings. You can modify the color, and transparency of the shadow, as well as its vertical and horizontal distance from the original text.

You can go back and adjust the settings for your effect by selecting the text and choosing Modify ➪ Timeline Effects ➪ Edit Effect or choosing Timeline Effects ➪ Edit Effect from the contextual menu.

Caution   If you manually edit a Timeline Effect Graphic symbol in Edit mode you lose the option to go back and adjust the settings for the effect.

Although Timeline Effects *can* be applied to Dynamic text or Input text, Flash is not sophisticated enough to magically re-render the effect if the text is changed during runtime—the Graphic symbol rendered in the authoring environment is just exported with the SWF file and if the text is changed, the effect will no longer match up. You can probably create some great looking effects on your own, but Timeline Effects are a great way to get started with making stylized graphic text and it makes it easier to edit the content of your text fields than it would be if you had broken the text into raw shapes.

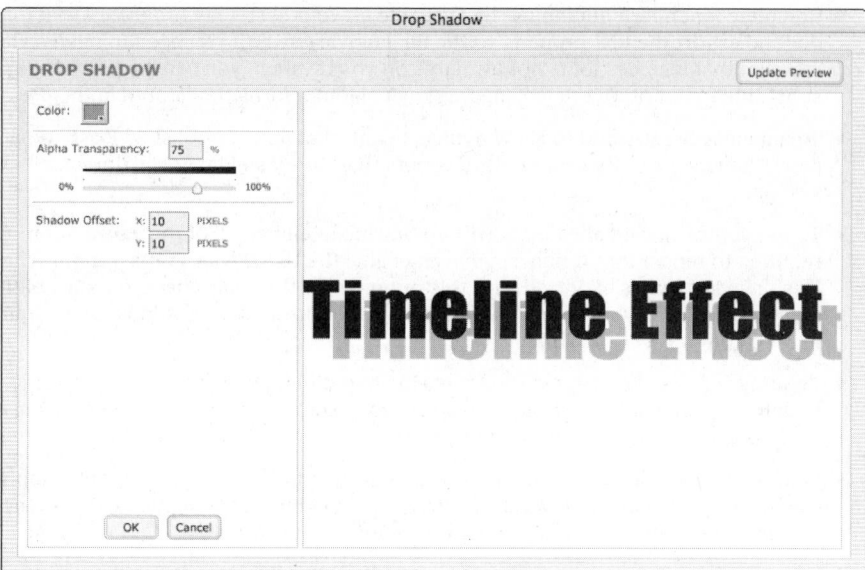

Figure 8-30: Settings and preview window for the Drop Shadow Timeline Effect

We'd like to know what you thought about this chapter. Visit `www.flashsupport.com/feedback` to fill out an online form with your comments.

Summary

✦ Flash offers robust and well-organized text editing controls, but you can make the most of these tools only if you are familiar with at least the basic principles of typography.

✦ Studying the history of type in visual communication is one of the most practical and inspiring things you can do to improve your design skills.

✦ Type controls have been centralized in the Property inspector since Flash MX. This makes working with text more streamlined and intuitive than it was in early versions of Flash.

✦ Although minor issues may come up when working with text in Flash, it is relatively simple to work cross-platform and deliver high-quality presentations to users on many different systems.

✦ Flash offers three text types for various uses in interactive projects: Static text, Dynamic text, and Input text.

✦ Flash MX 2004 has an added option for converting any font into an Aliased outline that can be embedded with the final movie (.swf) — this overrides the default smoothing or anti-aliasing that can make some text look slightly blurry.

✦ Complete font information must be available on your system in order for Flash to render and export the text properly to the final movie (.swf). If you need to open a Flash file (.fla) that includes fonts not available on your system, you can choose temporary substitute fonts without damaging the original font information stored in the file.

✦ To minimize file size and to allow dynamic control of text in published Flash movies (.swf), you may specify generic device fonts that the Flash Player will find on all users' systems.

✦ To use commonly installed fonts without having to embed all of the information required to render font outlines, you can enable the Use Device Fonts option. When the Flash movie (.swf) is exported with this option, only the basic characteristics of the font (name, size, style) are embedded so that the Flash Player can look for an equivalent font on the user's machine.

✦ Creating Font symbols and storing them in Shared libraries for either author-time updates or runtime linkage can help you to manage large projects by centralizing font sources and making updates faster and easier.

✦ Lines of type in text boxes can be broken apart into individual characters by applying the Break apart command. When the Break apart command is applied twice to the same text box, the text outline is converted into vector shapes.

✦ You can add visual interest to your text with Timeline Effects while still keeping options open for editing the content of the text field or for modifying the settings that control the final effect.

✦   ✦   ✦

Modifying Graphics

After becoming familiar with the Flash authoring environment and learning to use the Drawing tools, you are now ready to move on to the really fun part: messing with the basic shapes and text elements you have made to create your own unique effects!

In this chapter, we revisit some of the core tools to learn new ways of applying them. We also introduce some specialized tools that exist only to transform your artwork. Following a look at how the Eyedropper, Paint Bucket, and Ink Bottle work together to modify strokes and fills, we show you how to use the Fill Transform tool to create custom fills.

The Modify Shape submenu offers some special commands you can apply to alter lines and fills, whereas the Modify Transform submenu includes various options for skewing, stretching, rotating, flipping, and rotating shapes.

Before explaining the Flash stacking order and how to create compound shapes, we introduce the powerful Free Transform tool and the Envelope modifier that enables you to warp and distort multiple shapes simultaneously. Other features worth exploring include the stepped Break apart command on text and the indispensable Distribute to Layers command — these two features combined make animating text infinitely easier than it was in early versions of Flash.

The final section on manual editing demonstrates how to alter the appearance of individual symbol instances using the Color Effect controls available in the Property inspector.

Flash MX 2004 now includes some nifty Timeline effects that can be used to modify static graphics. We'll get you started with these and explain how they differ from manually created visual effects.

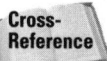

Cross-Reference For coverage of animated Timeline Effects, refer to Chapter 11, "Timeline Animation and Effects."

Last but not least, we'll cover the Find and Replace command and the History panel — both indispensable new features of Flash MX 2004. We introduce the options for these flexible features and demonstrate some ways you can use them to modify your graphics without even using any tools!

As various techniques and tools are introduced, we show you how to apply them for modifying artwork and adding the illusion of depth and texture to your 2D graphics.

In This Chapter

Sampling and swapping fills and line styles

Applying the Fill Transform tool to control gradient and bitmap fills

Using Modify Shape options

Working with the Free Transform tool

Stacking, grouping, and arranging item types

Creating and managing compound shapes

Using Break apart and Trace bitmap

Applying Distribute to Layers to auto-separate items

Working with Advanced Effect settings for symbol instances

Using static Timeline effects

Autopilot editing with Find and Replace

Using the History panel to create custom commands

Sampling and Switching Fills and Strokes

The Selection tool can always be used to select a stroke or fill so that it can be deleted, moved, or modified using any of the Swatches pop-ups or the Stroke Style menu on the Property inspector. But, what do you do if you want to add a stroke or fill to a shape that was not drawn with one? The answer to this dilemma is found in a trio of tools that work nimbly together to provide one of the most unique graphics-editing solutions found in Flash. The Eyedropper tool is used to acquire fill and stroke styles or colors, and the Paint Bucket and Ink Bottle tools are used to transfer these characteristics to other shapes.

Note These tools will only apply changes directly to shapes, so to modify an element that has been grouped or converted into a symbol, you must first access the element in Edit mode.

The Eyedropper tool

As introduced in Chapter 7, "Applying Color," the dropper icon that appears when the Selection tool is used to select colors from any of the pop-up Swatches menus is similar to the Eyedropper tool available in the Tools panel. However, when pulled out of the Tools panel directly, the Eyedropper tool (I) has slightly different behavior. Although the Eyedropper tool cannot be used to sample colors from elements outside the Document window, it can be used to sample line and fill styles or to simultaneously change the stroke and the fill color chips to the same sampled color.

Note When used to acquire colors, the Tools panel Eyedropper tool is limited to acquiring colors from the Flash Stage and Work area. However, the droppers that are accessed from the Swatches pop-ups in the Color Mixer panel, Tools panel, or Property inspector can acquire colors from other visible areas, such as the system background, items on the desktop, or items that are open in other applications. The only "trick" to this is to press and hold the mouse over any of the color chips and only release the mouse when you are hovering over the color that you want to sample. The preview in the Swatches pop-up changes as you roll over different colors and the color chip changes when you release the mouse to load the color that you have selected.

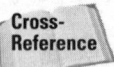

Cross-Reference For more information about this feat, refer to Chapter 7, "Applying Color."

The Eyedropper tool doesn't have any options in the Tools panel because they are all built in. As you hover over an item, the Eyedropper tool displays a small icon to indicate whether it is over a line or a fill that can be sampled by clicking. When a line is sampled, the Eyedropper tool automatically converts to the Ink Bottle tool, and when a fill is sampled, the Eyedropper tool converts to the Paint Bucket tool.

The composite image shown in Figure 9-1 shows the icons displayed when the Eyedropper tool is used to sample a fill (A) and apply it to another shape with the Paint Bucket tool (B), sample a stroke (C), and apply it to another shape with the Ink Bottle tool (D).

Any items already selected when the Eyedropper tool samples a stroke or fill will immediately acquire the applicable stroke or fill style. This is the quickest way to transfer the fill or line styles of one element to a whole group of elements. Figure 9-2 shows the Eyedropper tool used to sample a fill with one (A) or more (B) elements already selected.

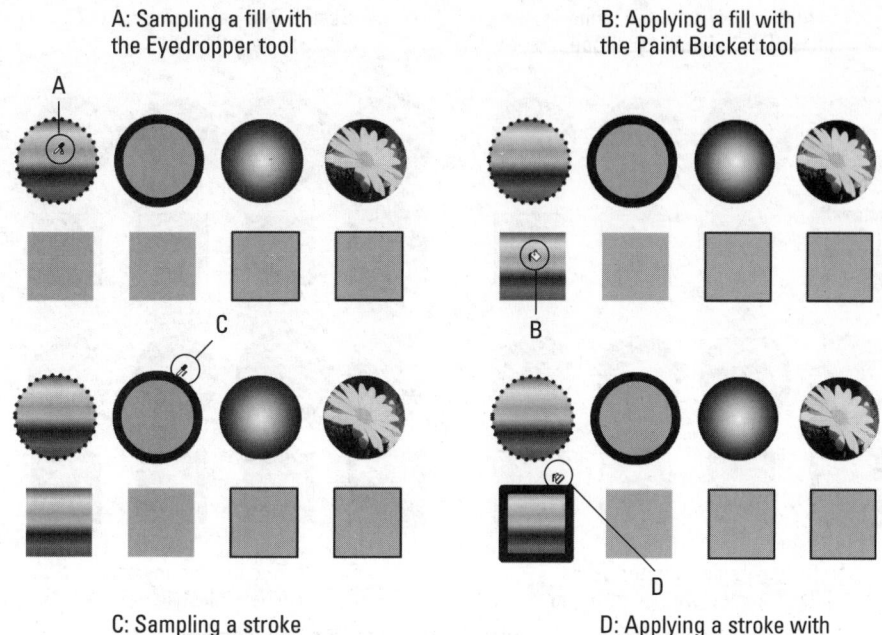

A: Sampling a fill with
the Eyedropper tool

B: Applying a fill with
the Paint Bucket tool

C: Sampling a stroke
with the Eyedropper tool

D: Applying a stroke with
the Ink Bottle tool

Figure 9-1: The Eyedropper tool is used to sample a fill and apply it with the Paint Bucket tool (A, B) and to sample a stroke and apply it with the Ink Bottle tool (C, D).

Note

By holding down the Shift key while clicking a line or stroke color with the Eyedropper tool, the Fill and the Stroke color chips will both be converted simultaneously to the newly selected color so that it can be applied with any of the other drawing tools.

The Ink Bottle tool

The Ink Bottle tool (S) — refer to Figure 9-1 (D) — is used to change the color, style, and thickness of existing outlines. It is most often used in conjunction with the Eyedropper tool. When the Ink Bottle tool is in use, pay attention to the following three options:

✦ The current Stroke Color option on the Tools panel or the Property inspector

✦ The Line Height option of the Property inspector

✦ The Stroke Style option of the Property inspector

The Ink Bottle will apply the current stroke color and line style, either sampled with the Eyedropper tool or chosen from the pop-up in the Tools panel or the controls in the Property inspector.

Caution

When you click to sample a line with the Ink Bottle tool, all other currently *selected* lines are changed simultaneously.

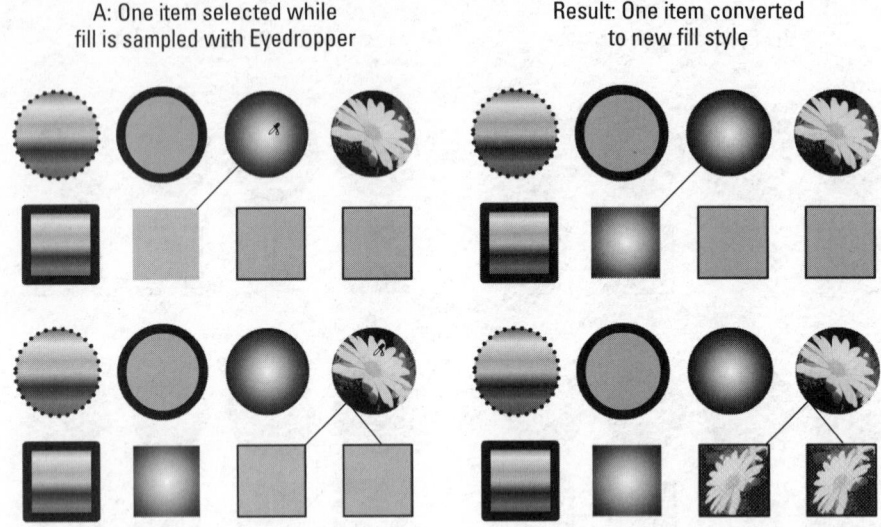

A: One item selected while
fill is sampled with Eyedropper

Result: One item converted
to new fill style

B: Two items selected while
fill is sampled with Eyedropper

Result: Two items converted
to new fill style

Figure 9-2: The Eyedropper tool also instantly converts selected elements to the sampled fill or stroke style.

The Ink Bottle tool is especially useful for applying custom line styles to multiple lines. You can build a collection of custom line styles either off screen or in a special custom line palette that is saved as a single-frame Flash movie. You can then acquire these line styles whenever you want to reuse them.

Caution Depending on the level of zoom, some lines may not display accurately on the screen—although they will print correctly on a high-resolution printer. Stroke Height (or thickness) may also be adjusted in the Stroke Style dialog box invoked by choosing the Custom stroke style option in the Property inspector.

The Paint Bucket tool

The Paint Bucket tool is used to fill enclosed areas with color, gradients, or bitmap fills. Although the Paint Bucket tool is a more robust tool than the Ink Bottle, and can be used independently, it's most often used in conjunction with the Eyedropper tool. As discussed earlier in this chapter, when the Eyedropper tool is clicked on a fill, it first acquires the attributes of that fill and then automatically changes itself to the Paint Bucket tool. When the Paint Bucket tool is active, as shown in Figure 9-3, two options are available from the Tools panel: Lock Fill and Gap size. The Gap size drop-down menu offers four settings to control how Flash handles gaps or open spaces in lines when filling with the Paint Bucket tool.

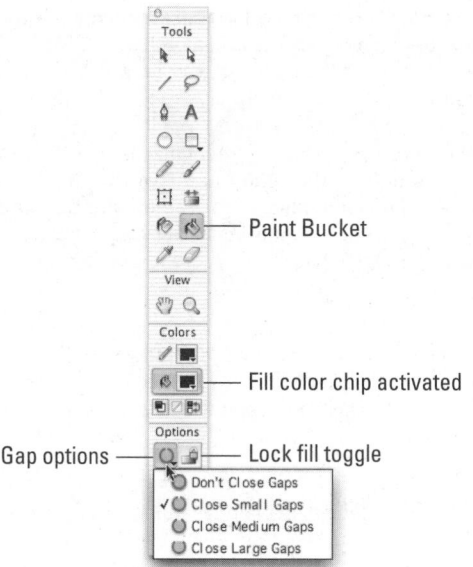

Figure 9-3: The Paint Bucket tool and Gap size options

When the Eyedropper tool is used to acquire a fill that is a broken-apart bitmap, the Eyedropper tool is automatically swapped for the Paint Bucket tool and a thumbnail of the bitmap image appears in place of the fill color chip. This procedure also automatically engages the Paint Bucket Lock Fill option.

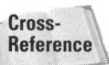

Cross-Reference   For more information about working with bitmaps, refer to Chapter 16, "Importing Artwork."

The final appearance of a bitmap fill can vary greatly depending on how it is applied. Figure 9-4 shows a series of shapes all filled with the same bitmap to illustrate the various results achieved from using different steps to define the fill.

A   B   C   D

Figure 9-4: (A) A shape drawn with the Rectangle tool using a bitmap fill selected in the Mixer panel; (B) a bitmap fill applied with Selection tool selection and Mixer panel fill style menu, after the shape was drawn; (C) a broken apart bitmap sampled with the Eyedropper tool and then applied to the finished shape using the Paint Bucket tool; (D) a shape filled with the Paint Bucket tool, using the color sampled with the Eyedropper tool from the bitmap symbol (not broken apart)

Caution Using the Paint Bucket to fill with white (or the background color) is not the same as erasing. Painting with white (or the background color) may appear to accomplish something similar to erasing. However, you are, in fact, creating a filled item that can be selected, moved, deleted, or reshaped. Only erasing erases!

Another behavior of the Paint Bucket tool that can be helpful to recognize is that the exact location where the Paint Bucket tool is applied defines the center point for the fill. This has no visible effect when filling with solid colors, but when filling with gradients or bitmap fills it will make a difference how the fill is aligned within the boundaries of the shape. Figure 9-5 illustrates how the center point of a gradient fill varies based on where it was "dumped" with the Paint Bucket.

  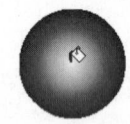

Figure 9-5: The center point of gradient and bitmap fills is defined by the location of the Paint Bucket tool when the fill is applied to a shape.

As with the Ink Bottle tool, the Paint Bucket tool can be especially useful for applying custom fill styles to multiple items. You can build a collection of custom fill styles either off-screen (in the Work area) or in a special, saved, custom-fills-palette, single-frame Flash movie. You can then acquire these fills whenever necessary.

Caution If you click with the Paint Bucket tool on one of several selected fills, *all* of the selected fills will be simultaneously changed to the new fill.

Using the Paint Bucket Gap size option

As shown in Figure 9-3, the Gap size option drop-down offers four settings that control how the Paint Bucket treats gaps when filling. These settings are Don't Close Gaps, Close Small Gaps, Close Medium Gaps, and Close Large Gaps. These tolerance settings enable Flash to fill an outline if the endpoints of the outline aren't completely joined, leaving an open shape. If the gaps are too large, you may have to close them manually with another drawing tool. Figure 9-6 illustrates how the Gap size option settings affect the Paint Bucket fill behavior.

Note The level of zoom changes the apparent size of gaps. Although the actual size of gaps is unaffected by zoom, the Paint Bucket's interpretation of the gap is dependent upon the current Zoom setting. When zoomed in very close, the Paint Bucket tool will find it harder to close gaps; when zoomed out, the Paint Bucket tool will find it easier to close gaps.

Using the Paint Bucket Lock Fill option

The Paint Bucket's Lock Fill option is the same as the Brush Lock Fill option — it controls how Flash handles areas filled with gradient color or bitmaps. When this button is turned on, all areas (or shapes) painted with the same gradient or bitmap appear to be part of a single, continuous, filled shape. The Lock Fill option locks the angle, size, and point of origin of the current fill to remain constant throughout any number of selected shapes. Modifications made to the fill in one of the shapes will be applied to the other shapes filled using the same Lock Fill option.

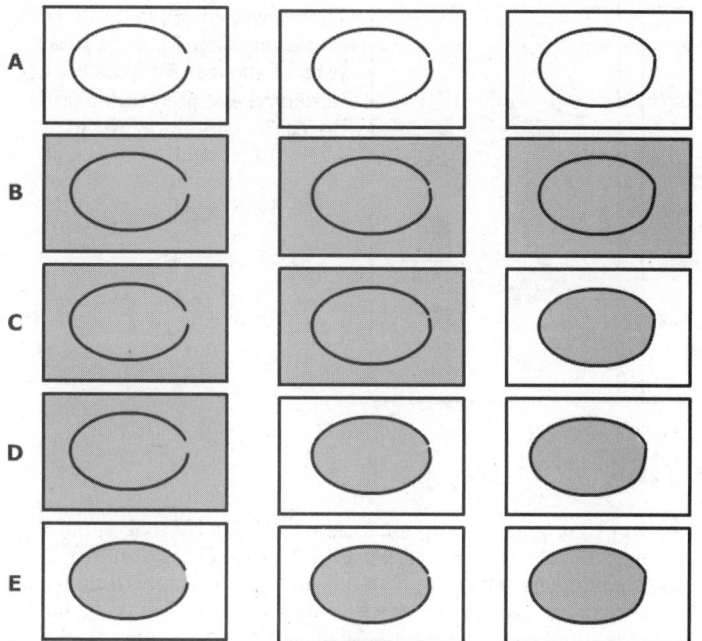

Figure 9-6: Paint Bucket fill applied with various Gap size settings: (A) original oval outline with decreasing gap sizes, left to right, with no fill; (B) gray fill applied with Don't Close Gaps; (C) gray fill applied with Close Small Gaps; (D) gray fill applied with Close Medium Gaps; (E) gray fill applied with Close Large Gaps

Cross-Reference Working with gradient colors is discussed in Chapter 7, "Applying Color."

To demonstrate the distinction between fills applied with or without the Lock Fill option, we created five shapes and filled them with a bitmap with Lock Fill off. As shown in Figure 9-7, on the left, the image is rendered separately from one shape to the next. On the right, those same shapes were filled with the same bitmap, but with Lock Fill on. Note how the image is now continuous from one shape to the next. Bitmap fills are automatically tiled to fill a shape, so the bitmap fill on the right was also scaled using the Fill Transform Transform tool to make it easier to see the continuation of the image between the various shapes.

Tip When the Eyedropper tool is used to pick up a fill or gradient from the scene, the Lock Fill button is automatically toggled on.

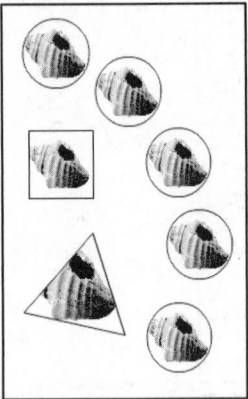 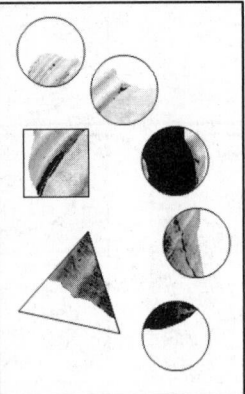

Figure 9-7: Fill applied with Lock Fill turned off (left), compared with fill applied with Lock Fill turned on and then scaled using the Fill Transform tool (right)

Transforming Fills

The Fill Transform tool (F) was originally an option for the Paint Bucket tool, but in Flash MX it was given a home on the main Tools panel, right next to the Free Transform tool. Fill Transform is used only to modify bitmap or gradient fills and will not apply to simple color fills. The Fill Transform does many of the same things as the Free Transform tool, but it only modifies the *fill* of a shape without changing the stroke or outline appearance at all. This is a lot like scooting, rotating, or skewing a larger piece of material behind a frame so that a different portion is visible.

The Fill Transform tool has only one option in the Tools panel, but, as with the Eyedropper tool, it does apply differently depending on the type of fill selected. To use the Fill Transform tool, select it in the Tools panel, and then simply click an existing gradient or fill. A set of three or four adjustment handles appears, depending on the type of fill. The following three transformations can be performed on a gradient or bitmap fill: adjusting the fill's center point, rotating the fill, and scaling the fill. The extra set of adjustment handles displayed on bitmap fills enables them to be skewed. The Magnet option in the Tools panel toggles on Snapping behavior — making it easier to constrain transformations to even adjustment increments.

Figure 9-8 illustrates the various adjustment handles on three types of fills (top) and the icons that display when the pointer is rolled over each of the handles (bottom).

The position of these handles may shift if a fill (or bitmap fill) has been variously copied, rotated, or pasted in any number of ways. The fundamental rules are as follows:

✦ The round center handle moves the center point.

✦ The round corner handle rotates.

✦ The round edge handles skew either vertically or horizontally.

✦ The square edge handles scale either vertically or horizontally.

✦ The square corner handle scales symmetrically.

Fill Transform tool

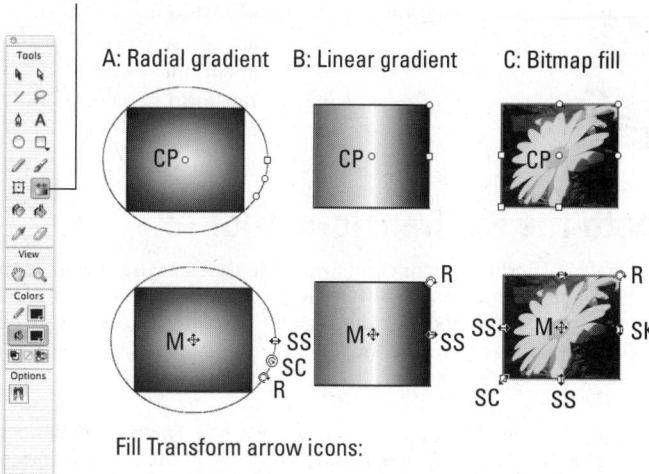

A: Radial gradient   B: Linear gradient   C: Bitmap fill

Fill Transform arrow icons:

CP:	Center point	SC:	Scale Corner arrow
R:	Rotate arrow	SS:	Scale Side arrow
M:	Move arrow	SK:	Skew arrow

Figure 9-8: The Fill Transform tool applied to a Radial gradient, a Linear gradient, and a Bitmap fill. Each handle type displays an icon on rollover to indicate its function (bottom).

Tip

To see all the handles when transforming a large element or working with an item close to the edge of the Stage, choose View ➪ Work Area from the application menu or use the short-cut keys Shift+Ctrl+W (Shift+⌘+W).

Adjusting the center point with the Fill Transform tool

If the fill is not aligned in the shape, as you would like it to be, you can easily move the center point to adjust how the fill is framed by the shape outline. To adjust the center point, follow these steps:

1. Deselect the fill if it has been previously selected.

2. Choose the Fill Transform tool.

3. Click the fill.

4. Bring the cursor to the small circular handle at the center of the fill until it changes to a four-arrow cursor, pointing left and right, up and down, like a compass, indicating that this handle can now be used to move the center point in any direction.

5. Drag the center circular handle in any direction you want to move the center of the fill.

Figure 9-9 shows a radial gradient (left) repositioned with the Fill Transform tool (right).

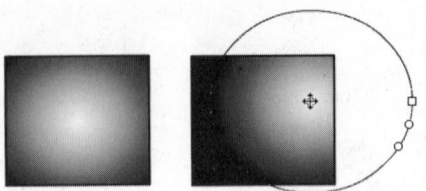

Figure 9-9: Adjusting the center point of a fill with the Fill Transform tool

Rotating a fill with the Fill Transform tool

To rotate a gradient or bitmap fill, find the small circular handle that's at the corner of the fill. (In a radial gradient, choose the middle circular handle.) This circular handle is used for rotating a fill around the center point. Simply click the circular handle with the Rotate cursor and drag clockwise or counterclockwise to rotate the fill. Figure 9-10 shows a bitmap fill (left) as it appears when rotated clockwise (right).

Tip   Activate the Snapping toggle in the Tools panel if you want to use Snapping behaviors to help guide rotation or scaling of a fill. (Turn behaviors on or off in the application menu under View ⇨ Snapping.)

Figure 9-10: Rotating a fill with the Fill Transform tool

Adjusting scale with the Fill Transform tool

To resize a bitmap fill symmetrically (to maintain the aspect ratio), find the small square-corner handle, which is usually located at the lower-left corner of the fill. On rollover, the diagonal arrow icon appears, indicating the direction(s) in which the handle resizes the fill. Click and drag to scale the fill symmetrically. On radial gradients, the center round handle is used to scale with the gradient aspect ratio constrained. Linear gradients only have one handle for scaling, and this handle always scales in the direction of the gradient banding.

To resize a fill asymmetrically, find a small square handle on either a vertical or a horizontal edge, depending on whether you want to affect the width or height of the fill. On rollover, arrows appear perpendicular to the edge of the shape, indicating the direction in which this handle resizes the fill. Click and drag a handle to reshape the fill.

Figure 9-11 shows the three fill types with their respective scale options. Linear gradient fills (left) can only be scaled in the direction of the gradient banding, but they can be rotated to scale vertically (lower) instead of horizontally (upper). Radial gradient fills (center) can be expanded symmetrically (upper) with the circular handle, or asymmetrically (lower) with the square handle. As with Linear gradients, they can be rotated to scale vertically rather than horizontally. Bitmap fills (right) can be scaled by the corner handle to maintain the aspect ratio (upper), or dragged from any side handle to scale asymmetrically (lower).

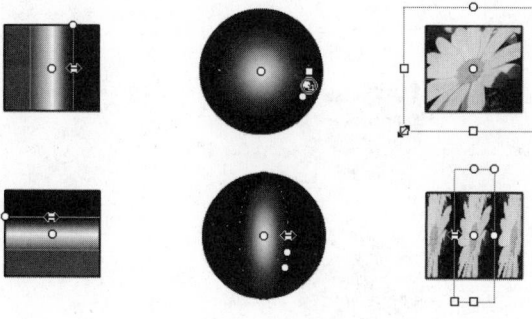

Figure 9-11: Scaling fills symmetrically (top) and asymmetrically (bottom)

The right column of Figure 9-11 is a good example of a situation in which scaling a bitmap fill smaller with the Fill Transform tool causes it to tile — or repeat — and fill the space of the original image.

Skewing a bitmap fill with the Fill Transform tool

To skew a bitmap fill horizontally, find the small round handle at the middle of the right-hand border. Click the handle; arrows appear, parallel to the edge of the fill, indicating the directions in which this handle skews the fill. Drag to skew the image in either direction. Figure 9-12 shows a bitmap skewed horizontally (left) and vertically (right). Note that the skew procedure is still active after it has been applied, meaning that the skew may be further modified—this behavior is common to all functions of the Fill Transform tool.

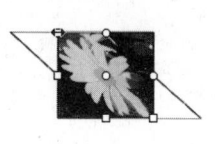

Figure 9-12: Skewing a bitmap fill with the Fill Transform tool

Gradient fills cannot be skewed; they can only be scaled on the horizontal or vertical axis.

Fill Transform Used for Effects

You will apply the Fill Transform tool most often to get a patterned fill or a gradient aligned and sized within its outline shape. A simple way of adding more depth to shapes is to modify gradient fills so that they appear to reflect light from one consistent source. You can choose to emulate a soft light for a more even illumination, or to emulate a hard, focused light that emphasizes dramatic shadows. As you create a composition on the Stage, you can use the Fill Transform tool to modify individual elements so that they appear to share a common light source. Figure 9-13 illustrates how a default radial gradient (left) can be modified to emulate a soft (center) or hard (right) illumination.

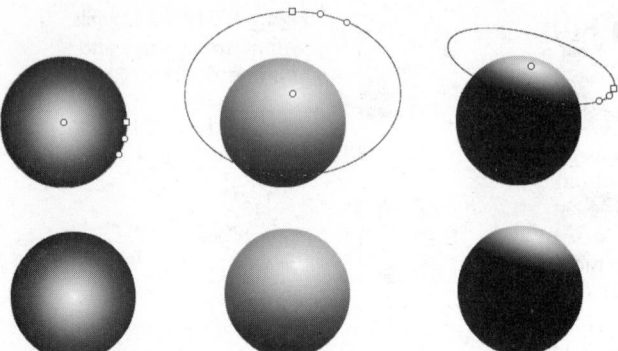

Figure 9-13: Applying Fill Transform to create different illumination effects

To show how these lighting effects can be applied to create the illusion of 3D, we created a little scene using only radial fills that were modified with the Fill Transform tool. Figure 9-14 shows the radial gradients as they appeared when drawn with the default settings (left) and how the scene appeared after the gradients were modified with Fill Transform and some basic shape scaling as described later in this chapter.

On the CD-ROM   If you want to deconstruct this example, we have included the file on the CD-ROM with both the unmodified and the final transformed shapes. You will find the file named `SphereLighting.fla` in the `ch09` folder of the CD-ROM.

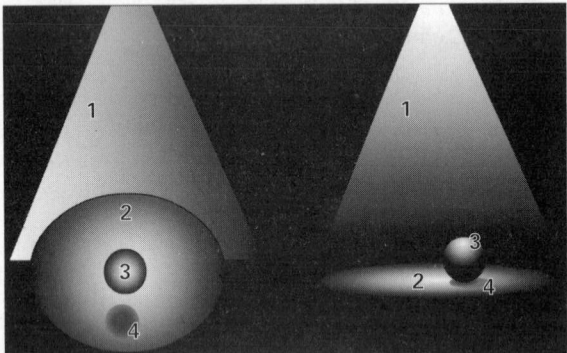

Figure 9-14: The Fill Transform tool used to modify default radial gradient fills (left) to create the illusion of 3D lighting effects (right)

Applying Modify Shape Menu Commands

The three specialized commands found in the application menu (under Modify ➪ Shape), provide modification options that cannot be achieved with any other tools in Flash.

Convert Lines to Fills

Lines to Fills does exactly what its name implies: It converts lines defined by single points into shapes defined by an outline of editable points. To apply the Lines to Fills command, simply select any lines that you wish to convert before choosing Modify ⇨ Shape ⇨ Convert Lines to Fills. After a line has been converted in this way it can be edited like any other filled shape, including adding bitmap or gradient fills or applying the Selection or Subselection tools to adjust the corners and curves of the outlined shape.

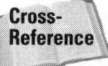

Cross-Reference   The Selection tool and the Subselection tool are discussed in Chapter 5, "Drawing in Flash."

Creating scalable artwork

The Lines to Fills command is especially important because it provides the one solution for maintaining line to fill ratios when scaling artwork that would require lines to display at smaller than 1 point size. Fills do not have the same display limitation as lines and they will maintain visual consistency as they are scaled larger or smaller. In Figure 9-15, the image on the left was drawn using the pencil tool to make lines around the eyes and on the whiskers of the cat cartoon. When it was scaled, the lines were not visually consistent with the fills. The image on the right was modified using the Lines to Fills command before scaling it down to 25 percent size. In this case, the ratio between the outlines around the eyes and the whiskers was consistent with the other filled shapes in the cartoon.

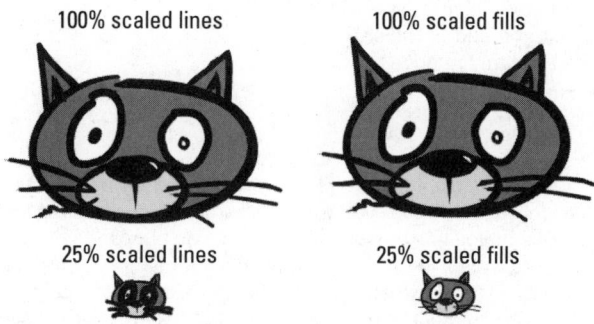

Figure 9-15: Use the Lines to Fills command to ensure consistency when scaling artwork

Note   Remember that in Flash, the smallest line size that can be displayed is 1 point. Lines with a height of less than 1 point will all appear to be the same size on screen when viewed at 100 percent scale. The difference in size is only visible when the View is scaled larger or zoomed in. However, the lines print correctly on a high-resolution printer.

Correcting rounded corners and lines

Another important task that the Lines to Fills command accomplishes is creating true square corners on angled shapes. As you have probably noticed by now, one of the quirks of the Flash drawing tools is that lines over 1 point in thickness have rounded ends and soft corners by default. By converting lines to fills, you can apply the Straighten modifier or edit individual points in the shape to create true sharp corners and squared ends on lines.

Figure 9-16 illustrates the difference between a default rectangle with a 2-point stroke (A), the same rectangle converted with Modify ➪ Shape ➪ Convert Lines to Fills (B), and then modified using the Modify ➪ Straighten command (C).

Figure 9-16: Using the Lines to Fills and Straighten commands to create true square corners

Figure 9-17 illustrates the slightly different process to create squared ends on a line. The original 2-point line (A), is converted using Modify ➪ Shape ➪ Convert Lines to Fills (B), and then because the Straighten command can be unpredictable on multiple curved lines, the extra points in the line are instead removed manually using the Subselection tool (C). After the extra points along the curve of the line are deleted, be certain to convert the final two points that define the end of the line into corner points by Option (Alt)+clicking them with the Subselection tool to ensure a perfectly flat end.

Figure 9-17: After converting a line to a fill, it is possible to manually edit the points that define the end of the shape to eliminate the curve and create a clean, flat edge.

Expand Fill

The Expand Fill command has two options used to size fills up or down evenly on all sides of a shape. To apply the command, select the fill(s) that you want to modify. Then choose Modify ➪ Shape ➪ Expand Fill. The Expand Fills dialog box appears, where you can choose to expand or inset (shrink) the fill by a specific pixel value. Keep in mind that this command applies differently than a normal scale modification. The fill expands or shrinks from all sides evenly, so an extreme modification can cause a shape to bloat to the extent that unfilled areas are obscured, or conversely can cause a shape to shrink to the point that some of the areas are no longer visible. When applied moderately, the Expand Fill command can be very helpful for adjusting multiple filled shapes consistently, without scaling lines in the same area of the artwork.

Figure 9-18 includes a rectangle, a cartoon cat, and a sketch of some grapes. The original shapes are shown on the left, the expanded fills in the center, and the inset fills on the left. As you can see, expanding fills often obscures the strokes surrounding a shape, whereas choosing to inset a fill leaves space between the fill and any surrounding stroke.

The Expand Fill command can also be used to create custom text forms. Figure 9-19 shows how the original text shape (left) can be modified using either the Expand or Inset option. To create bloated balloon-like text (center), or shrunken, eroded text (right), you first have to apply the Modify ➪ Break apart command (Ctrl+B or ⌘+B) twice to reduce the text to simple filled shapes. By selecting all of the letter shapes before applying the Expand Fill command, you can modify the whole word at the same time.

Figure 9-18: Modifying an original shape (left) with the Expand Fill command using the Expand option (center) or the Inset option (right) will respectively bloat or shrink a fill by a specified pixel amount.

Expand **Expand** Expand

A   B   C

Figure 9-19: Text broken apart into letter shapes (A) can be expanded (B), or inset (C) to create custom text effects.

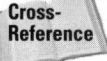

Other text-editing options are discussed in Chapter 8, "Working with Text."

Soften Fill Edges

The Soften Fill Edges command is the closest thing to a static blur filter available in Flash. This command, as with the Expand Fill command, can only be applied to fills and gives you the option to expand or inset the shape by a specific number of pixels. As discussed later in this chapter, the Blur command available in the Timeline Effects menu is used for creating *animated* or directional blur effects.

Flash MX 2004 enables you to select a line and choose the Soften Edges command from the Modify ➪ Shape menu. After you apply the command, however, the line will just disappear from the Stage — surprise! If you make this mistake, you can recover your line by immediately choosing Edit ➪ Undo (Ctrl+Z or ⌘+Z).

The unique effect of Soften Fill Edges is created by a series of banded fills around the original fill that decrease in opacity toward the outermost band. You can control the number and width of these bands by entering values in the Soften Fill Edges dialog box (shown in Figure 9-20) to create a variety of effects, from a very subtle blurred effect to a dramatic stepped appearance around the edges of the fill.

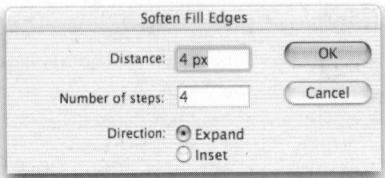

Figure 9-20: The Soften Fill Edges dialog box with settings for controlling the edge effect

The Soften Fill Edges dialog box controls the following features of the fill modification:

✦ **Distance:** Defines the number of pixels the original shape will expand or shrink

✦ **Number of Steps:** Sets the number of bands that appear around the outside edge of the fill

✦ **Expand or Inset:** Controls whether the bands will be added to the outside edge of the fill (expand) or stacked on the inside edge of the shape (inset)

Figure 9-21 shows how the original fill (left) appears after Soften Fill Edges is applied with the Expand option (center), or with the Inset option (right).

Figure 9-21: Applying Soften Fill Edges with the Expand option and with the Inset option

The width of the individual bands equals the total number of pixels set in Distance divided by the Number of Steps. When the edge of the shape is magnified, the individual bands can clearly be seen. Figure 9-22 shows a series of eight bands, each 1-pixel wide, created by using a Distance setting of 8 with a Number of steps setting of 8.

Figure 9-22: A magnified view of the banded edge of a fill created by applying Soften Fill Edges

As with the Expand Fill command, Soften Fill Edges can create interesting text effects when applied to broken-apart letter shapes. Figure 9-23 shows an effect created by combining the original white text with a "shadow" made by applying the Soften Fill Edges command to a broken apart copy of the text that was filled with dark gray.

Figure 9-23: A shadow effect created by layering the original text over a copy that was broken apart, filled with dark gray and modified using Soften Fill Edges

On the CD-ROM   The Soften Fill Edges examples shown in Figure 9-21 and Figure 9-23 are included on the CD-ROM in the ch09 folder. The file is named SoftenEdges.fla.

Free Transform Commands and Options

The commands we have looked at so far in this chapter are generally used for localized modification of lines or fills. In this section, we introduce some commands that are applied to create more dramatic change of whole items or even groups of items.

The basic transform commands can be applied to primitive shapes or to symbols, groups, and text blocks, but it is important to know that any transformations applied to symbols, groups, or text blocks are saved in the Info panel even if they are unselected and then reselected later on. This allows these items to easily be reverted to their original appearance. The transform settings for primitive shapes, on the other hand, are reset to the default values in the Info panel as soon as they are deselected. This means that while a primitive shape is actively being modified, you can revert to the original appearance, but as soon as you apply a change and deselect the shape, its modified appearance will be considered original the next time it is selected.

As shown in Figure 9-24, there are various ways to access the transform commands available in Flash.

The Transform panel

The Transform panel (Ctrl+T or ⌘+T) includes value fields for horizontal and vertical scale percentages, degrees of rotation and degrees of vertical and horizontal skew. These fields can be used as visual reference or as a way to enter precise transform values. The Transform panel also includes two important buttons.

The **Copy and Apply Transform** button is used to duplicate the selected item with all transformations included. When you select this button, you may not notice that anything has happened to your selected item — this is because Flash places the duplicate exactly on top of the original. To see both the original and the duplicate, drag the duplicate to a new position in the Document window.

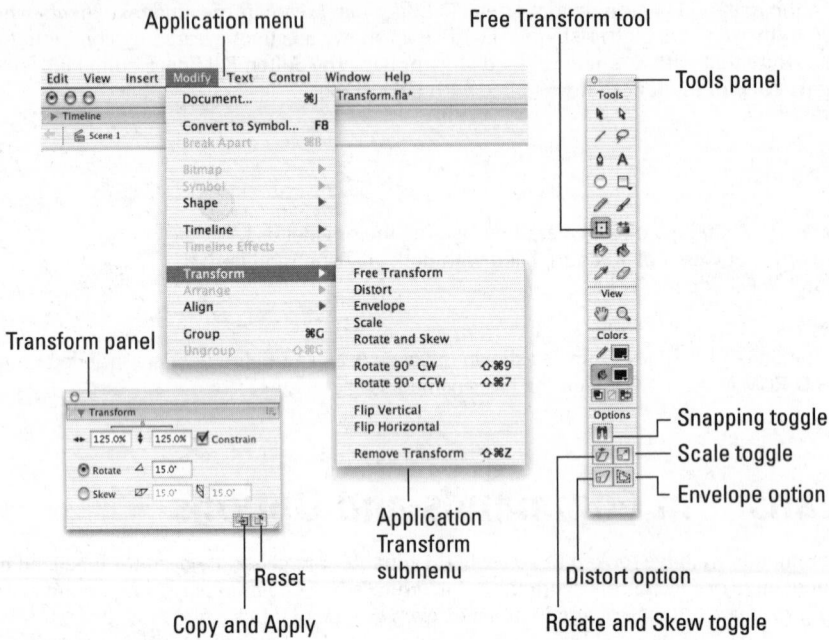

Figure 9-24: The various ways to access transform commands in Flash — the Transform panel (left), the Modify Transform submenu (center), and the Free Transform tool (right)

 The Reset button will revert a transformed symbol, group, or text field to its original appearance and return all values in the Transform panel to the default settings. This can also be achieved by selecting Modify ➪ Transform ➪ Remove Transform. If you only want to remove the most recently applied modification, use Edit ➪ Undo (Ctrl+Z or ⌘+Z).

The Modify Transform menu

The commands found in the application menu under Modify ➪ Transform make it possible to choose specific combinations of transform options as well as a couple of "shortcuts" for commonly needed modifications. Because these shortcuts are unique to the application menu, they deserve a brief description, although they are nearly self-explanatory.

✦ **Rotate 90 degrees CW or Rotate 90 degrees CCW:** Used to rotate any selected items by a half-turn in the chosen direction around the central axis point of the selection.

 You can also use shortcut keys to rotate any selected item in 90-degree increments. To rotate an item 90-degrees clockwise, use Ctrl+9 or ⌘+9. To rotate an item 90-degrees counterclockwise, use Ctrl+7 or ⌘+7.

✦ **Flip Vertical or Flip Horizontal:** Used to place the item in a mirrored position either on the vertical axis (calendar flip) or the horizontal axis (book flip).

The Free Transform tool

The Free Transform tool (Q) available directly from the Tools panel, enables you to apply transform commands dynamically with various arrow icons. These icons appear as the pointer is moved over the control points or handles of the selected item. Various transform states can also be invoked from the contextual menu. Although the position of these arrow icons can vary with the position of the pointer, they provide consistent indication of what transformation will be applied from the closest available handle. To finish any transformation, simply deselect the item by clicking outside of the current selection area.

 Move arrow: This familiar arrow indicates that all currently selected items can be dragged together to a new location in the Document window.

 Axis point or transformation point: By default, this circle marks the center of shapes as the axis for most transformations or animation. On symbols, the axis point is in the top-left corner or at axis 0,0. By dragging the point to a different location, you can define a new axis or transformation point for modifications applied to the item. To return the axis point to its default location, double-click the axis point icon.

 In Flash MX 2004, the axis point of symbols is in the top-left corner by default because it is easier to modify an item mathematically if the origin point is 0,0. However, this means that symbols cannot be scaled towards the top or to the left, unless the axis point is first adjusted. Move the axis point to the center of the symbol to mimic the original Flash MX transform behavior. Shapes can be scaled in any direction, and the scale will always originate from the side opposite the handle that is selected.

 Skew arrow: Generally available on any side of an item between transformation points. By clicking and dragging the outline, you can skew the shape in either direction indicated by the arrows.

Rotate arrow: Generally available near any corner of an item. By clicking and dragging, you can rotate the item clockwise or counterclockwise around the transform axis. Note that if you move the arrow directly over the closest corner handle, the Rotate arrow will usually be replaced with the Scale Corner arrow. To rotate around the opposite corner point without moving the axis point, press the Alt (Option) key while dragging. To constrain rotation to 45-degree increments, press the Shift key while dragging.

 Scale Side arrow: Available from any handle on the side of an item. Clicking and dragging will scale the item larger or smaller, in one direction only, relative to the transform axis.

 Scale Corner arrow: Appears only on the corner handles of an item and is used to evenly scale the item larger or smaller, in all directions from the transform axis. To constrain the aspect ratio of the shape, press the Shift key while dragging.

Transforming shapes, symbols, text, and groups

Figure 9-25 shows how a symbol and a shape display differently after they have been modified, deselected, and then reselected with the Free Transform tool. The symbol (left) displays transform handles that are aligned with the originally modified item and the values of the transformation settings are preserved in the Transform panel. The shape (right), however, displays transform handles aligned to default values unrelated to the original modifications, and the values in the Transform panel are also reset to their defaults.

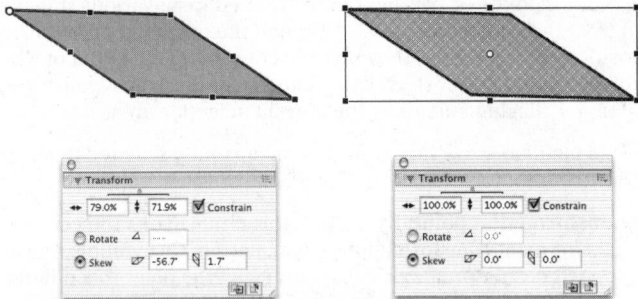

Figure 9-25: The Free Transform handles and Transform panel settings displayed for a symbol (left) and for a shape (right) that have been reselected after an initial modification

Free Transform limit options

The first two options in the Tools panel for the Free Transform tool are toggles to limit the modifications that can be applied to a selected item. It can sometimes be easier to use the Free Transform tool with more specific behavior. When the Rotate and Skew button or the Scale button is toggled on, they will exclude all other modifications.

 The Rotate and Skew toggle protects the selected item from being scaled accidentally while you're rotating or skewing it. This Tools panel option is equivalent to selecting Modify ⇨ Transform ⇨ Rotate and Skew from the application menu.

 The Scale toggle protects the selected item from all other transformations while it is being sized larger or smaller. This Tools panel option is equivalent to selecting Modify ⇨ Transform ⇨ Scale from the application menu.

Free Transform special shape options

The last two options in the Tools panel for the Free Transform tool — Distort and Envelope — are not available for symbols, groups, or text fields. However, when transforming primitive shapes, these two options can be used to create complex modifications not easily achieved using other Flash tools.

 **Note**   Remember that you can access the primitive shapes in a group or symbol by entering Edit mode. It is also possible to convert text fields into primitive shapes by applying the Break apart command (twice).

 Distort works by widening or narrowing the sides of the item, or stretching out the corners. This transform option does not bend or warp the shape; it allows sides of the shape to be scaled individually. To apply Distort, first select a shape with the Free Transform tool in the Tools panel, and turn on the Distort toggle in the Options area of the Tools panel. You will then be able to click and drag handles on the sides or corners of the item to stretch or compress individual sides. This is equivalent to selecting a shape with the Selection tool and choosing Modify ⇨ Transform ⇨ Distort from the application menu or selecting Distort from the contextual menu.

Tip | You can also apply the Distort option to a shape that has been selected with the Free Transform tool, by pressing the Control (⌘) key while dragging a side or corner handle. To taper a shape or move two adjoining corner points an equal distance simultaneously, press the Shift key while dragging any corner handle with the Free Transform tool.

Figure 9-26 shows an original shape being modified with the Distort option (left), and the final shape with distort handles, as they appear when the shape is reselected (right).

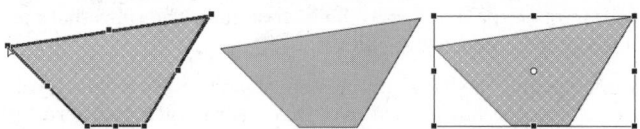

Figure 9-26: Free Transform applied to a shape using the Distort option

The Envelope option for the Free Transform tool may be one of the most engaging transform methods available in Flash. Once you try it, you may be stretching, squashing, bending, and warping for hours. On the other hand, as you get used to working with this nifty little option, you will find it faster than ever to create unique shapes.

The Envelope option enables you to work with control points and handles much the same way you would when editing lines or shapes using the Subselection tool. The powerful difference is that the Envelope can wrap around the outside of multiple items so that the control points and handles will curve, scale, stretch, or warp all of the lines and shapes contained within the Envelope selection.

To apply the Envelope, first select a shape or multiple shapes with the Free Transform tool and then toggle on the Envelope option in the Tools panel. The Envelope offers a series of control points and tangent handles. The square points are used to scale and skew the shape(s), whereas the round points are actually handles used to control the curve and warp of the shape(s). The Envelope option can also be accessed by selecting the shapes you want to transform and choosing Modify ⇨ Transform ⇨ Envelope from the application menu, or selecting Envelope from the contextual menu.

Figure 9-27 shows an original shape being modified with the Envelope option (left), and the final shape with Envelope handles, as they appear when the shape is reselected (right).

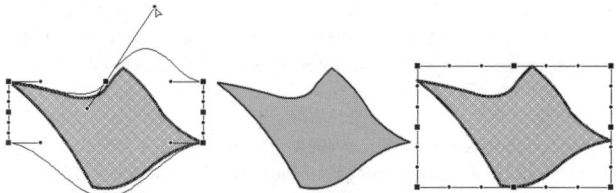

Figure 9-27: Free Transform applied to a shape using the Envelope option

Modifying Item Types

In previous chapters, we have focused on the features of the Timeline and how your Flash projects are ordered in time from left to right. Now we are going to look at the arrangement of items from the front to the back of the Stage, or the stacking order of elements in Flash. In this section we'll explain how multiple items can be moved together, and how the Break apart and Trace bitmap commands are applied to change item types.

Stacking order

Within a single layer, Flash stacks items of the same type in the same order they are placed or created, with the most recent item on top, subject to the *kind* of item. The rules that control the stacking order of various kinds of items are simple:

✦ Within a layer, ungrouped primitive shapes or lines are always at the *bottom* level, with the most recently drawn shape or line at the top of that layer's stack. Furthermore, unless you take precautions, drawn items either compound with, or cut into, the drawing beneath them.

✦ Groups and symbols (including bitmaps) stack above lines and shapes in the *overlay* level. To change the stacking order of several drawings, it's often advisable to group them first, as described in the next section of this chapter.

To change the stacking order within a layer, first select the item that you want to move. Then, do one of the following:

✦ **To move the item to the top of the stacking order,** select Modify ➪ Arrange ➪ Bring to Front (Alt+Shift+↑ or Option+Shift+↑).

✦ **To move an item to the bottom of the stacking order,** select Modify ➪ Arrange ➪ Send to Back (Alt+Shift+↓ or Option+Shift+↓).

✦ **To move the item up one position in the stacking order,** select Modify ➪ Arrange ➪ Bring Forward (Ctrl+↑ or ⌘+↑).

✦ **To move the item down one position in the stacking order,** select Modify ➪ Arrange ➪ Send Backward (Ctrl+↓ or ⌘+↓).

Remember the stacking-order rules: You won't be able to bring an ungrouped drawing above a group or symbol — if you need that drawing on top, group it and then move it, or place it on a separate layer.

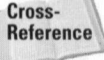
Cross-Reference   The Align panel (Ctrl+K or ⌘+K) used to distribute items in a layout in relation to each other or to the Stage is detailed in Chapter 5, "Drawing in Flash."

To stack an item in a lower layer above an item in a higher layer, you simply change the order of the layer among the other layers: First, activate the layer; then drag the Layer bar to the desired position in the layer stack of the Timeline.

Tip   Regardless of the number of layers in a Flash project (FLA), neither the file size nor the performance of the final SWF file will be adversely impacted because Flash flattens layers upon export.

Grouping

As discussed in Chapter 5, "Drawing in Flash," grouping shapes or lines makes them easier to handle. Rather than manipulating a single item, group several items to work with them as a single unit. Grouping also prevents shapes from being merged with or cropped by other shapes. In addition, the stacking of groups is more easily controlled than ungrouped drawings. Here's how to create groups:

1. Use Shift+click to select multiple items or drag a selection box around everything that you want to group. This can include any combination of items: shapes, lines, and symbols—even other groups.

2. Select Modify ➪ Group (Ctrl+G or ⌘+G). The selected elements are now grouped.

3. To ungroup everything, select the group and then use Modify ➪ Ungroup (Ctrl+Shift+G or ⌘+Shift+G). Ungrouping will only separate grouped items, it will not break apart bitmaps, symbol instances, or text as the Break apart command does.

Caution Be careful when ungrouping. Your newly ungrouped drawings may alter or eliminate drawings below in the same layer.

To edit a group:

1. Select the group and then choose Edit ➪ Edit Selected, or double-click the group. Everything on Stage—except for items in the group—is dimmed, indicating that only the group is editable.

2. Make changes in the same way you would edit individual primitive shapes or symbols. If there are other groups or symbols included in a larger group, you'll have to click-in deeper to edit those items. You can keep double-clicking on compound groups to gradually move inside to the deepest level or primitive shape available for editing. You can use the location labels to move back out level by level, (or double-click an empty area of the Stage), or go to Step 3 to return to the Main Timeline.

3. To stop editing the group, choose Edit ➪ Edit All, or use the location labels to return to the main scene. Other items on Stage return to normal color.

Applying Break apart

The Modify ➪ Break apart command (Ctrl+B or ⌘+B), is rather like an Undo command for groups and symbols as well as a deconstruction tool for text and bitmaps. To use Break apart, simply select an item and then apply the command. Occasionally the Break apart command will need to be applied more than once to reduce a compound group to its core primitive shapes. When applied to a symbol instance, Break apart reduces the instance to primitive shapes that no longer are linked to the original symbol stored in the Library.

Caution Breaking apart is not entirely reversible; when applied to an animated symbol instance, it will discard all but the current frame of the symbol instance Timeline.

Breaking apart text

When text is reduced to shapes using Break apart, it can be filled with gradients and bitmaps and also modified with the shape Transform options. Specific examples of using the Break apart command are shown in Chapter 8, "Working with Text," and in Chapter 16, "Importing Artwork." Figure 9-28 illustrates how text is broken apart in two stages, so that the original block (left) is first separated into individual letters (center), and then when broken apart a second time, reduced to shapes (right).

Break Break Break

Figure 9-28: A text field (left), broken apart once (center) and then once again (right)

Caution   It is not recommended to break apart symbols or groups that are included in a tweened animation because the results may be unpredictable and not easy to undo. Breaking apart complex symbols or large text blocks can also add to the file size of your final movie.

Creating Metallic Type

To demonstrate how text characters can be modified after they've been converted to shapes, we have applied some gradient fills to create the illusion of shiny metal letters. The file for this effect is titled metalType.fla and is included in the ch09 folder of the CD-ROM. Start with a document that has a dark gray background.

1. First type a word or words on the Stage to create a text block. This effect works best if applied to a bold, sans serif font at a fairly large point size. We used Verdana bold set at 50pt.

2. Select the text block and apply the Break apart command (Ctrl+B or ⌘+B), once to break the text block into individual letters, and then a second time to convert the letters into shapes.

3. With the letter shapes still selected, load a default grayscale linear gradient into the Color Mixer panel and then adjust it so the gradient is dark at each end with a highlight in the center. Set the left and far right Color pointers to black (#000000) and then add a new Color pointer in the center of the Edit bar and set it to white (#FFFFFF), as shown in Figure 9-29.

4. Next use the Fill Transform tool to rotate the gradient fill clockwise to a 45-degree angle in each letter shape. You may also scale each fill slightly or adjust individual center points to align the highlight on each letter, as shown in Figure 9-30.

5. Now to create a more three-dimensional look, make a copy of all the letter shapes in a new layer below the current layer. Use the Copy (Ctrl+C or ⌘+C) and Paste (Ctrl+V or ⌘+V) commands. Turn the visibility of the original layer off (click the Eye icon) for now, so you can see only the copied letter shapes.

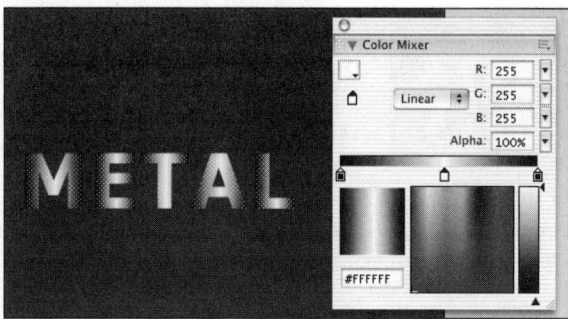

Figure 9-29: Text shapes selected and filled with a custom linear gradient created in the Mixer panel

Figure 9-30: Linear gradients aligned in each letter shape with the Fill Transform tool

6. Select all the copied letter shapes and using the Color Mixer panel, reverse the gradient fill colors. Set the center Color pointer to black and both end Color pointers to white, as shown in Figure 9-31.

Figure 9-31: Copied letter shapes on a new layer with reversed gradient fill applied

7. Next, use the Modify ⇨ Shape ⇨ Expand Fill command to expand the fill in all the selected letters by 2 pixels.

8. If you turn the visibility of both layers back on, you should see that you now have two opposing gradient fills and the copied letter shapes are slightly larger than the original letter shapes. Figure 9-32 compares the letters with the original gradient and the letters with the modified gradient.

Figure 9-32: Original letter shapes with gradient fill (top) and copied letter shapes with reversed and expanded gradient fill (bottom)

9. Select all the copied letter shapes on the lower layer and drag them behind the original letter shapes so that they're aligned just slightly above and to the right of the original shapes. This creates the illusion of a metallic beveled edge on the original letter shapes, as shown in Figure 9-33.

Figure 9-33: Copied letter shapes aligned behind the original letter shapes to create the illusion of a beveled metallic edge

Breaking apart bitmaps

When applied to bitmaps placed in the Document window, Break apart will make it possible to select the bitmap image with the Eyedropper tool to apply as a fill to other shapes. This is not the same as tracing a bitmap, which reduces the vast number of colors in a bitmap to areas of solid color and converts it to vector format, as described in the section that follows. Figure 9-34 shows an imported bitmap placed on the Stage and sampled with the Eyedropper tool to create a colored fill in the rectangle below (left) compared to the same bitmap broken apart and sampled with the Eyedropper tool to create an image fill in the rectangle below (right).

Figure 9-34: A bitmap and the fill that results from sampling it with the Eyedropper tool when it is intact (left) and when it has been broken apart (right)

It isn't necessary to break apart bitmaps to use as fills because they can be specified with the Mixer panel, as described in Chapter 7, "Applying Color." But breaking apart bitmaps enables them to be selectively edited and also allows the visible area of the bitmap to be modified with the shape Transform options.

Caution   Although the Distort and Envelope modifiers of the Free Transform tool can be applied to a bitmap after it has been broken apart, they may not have the result you expect. Instead of distorting or warping the actual bitmap image, you'll find that these modifiers reveal how Flash "sees" bitmap fills. The visible area of the bitmap is not really treated as a shape, but rather as a mask, or shaped window that allows a certain part of the bitmap to be visible. You can distort or warp the viewable area, but the bitmap itself will not be modified, as it is when you apply the Rotate or Skew modifiers.

Figure 9-35 illustrates a bitmap that has been broken apart (left) so that colored areas in the background of the image can be selected with the Magic Wand option of the Lasso tool (center) and then deleted to leave the flower floating on the white Stage (right). Any stray areas of unwanted color can be cleaned up using the Lasso tool or the Eraser tool.

Figure 9-35: A bitmap broken apart and selectively deleted using the Magic Wand option of the Lasso tool

About the Magic Wand option

The Magic Wand option of the Lasso tool is used to select ranges of a similar color in either a bitmap fill or a bitmap that's been broken apart. After you select areas of the bitmap, you can change their fill color or delete them, without affecting the Bitmap Swatch in the Mixer panel.

Cross-Reference   For more information about the Lasso tool, refer to Chapter 5, "Drawing in Flash." Click the Magic Wand option in the Tools panel to invoke the Magic Wand Settings dialog box.

Magic Wand Threshold setting

The Threshold setting defines the breadth of adjacent color values that the Magic Wand includes in a selection. Values for the Threshold setting range from 0 to 200 — the higher the setting, the broader the selection of adjacent colors. Conversely, a smaller number results in the Magic Wand making a narrower selection of adjacent colors.

A value of zero results in a selection of contiguous pixels that are all the same color as the target pixel. With a value of 20, clicking a red target pixel with a value of 55 will select all contiguous pixels in a range of values extending from red 35 to red 75. (If you're familiar with Photoshop, it's important to note that the Flash Threshold is unlike Photoshop, in which a Threshold setting of 20 will select all contiguous pixels in a range of values extending from red 45 to red 65.)

Magic Wand Smoothing setting

The Smoothing setting of the Magic Wand option determines to what degree the edge of the selection should be smoothed. This is similar to anti-aliasing. (Anti-aliasing dithers the edges of shapes and lines so that they look smoother on screen.) The options are Pixels, Rough, Normal, and Smooth. Assuming that the Threshold setting remains constant, the Smoothing settings will differ as follows:

✦ **Pixels:** Clings to the rectangular edges of each pixel bordering similar colors.

✦ **Rough:** With this setting, the edges of the selection are even more angular than with Pixels.

✦ **Normal:** Results in a selection that's somewhere between Rough and Smooth.

✦ **Smooth:** Delivers a selection with more rounded edges.

Tracing bitmaps

The Trace bitmap command is used to convert an imported image from a bitmap to a native Flash vector graphic with discrete, editable areas of color. This unlinks the image from the original symbol in the Library (and also from the Bitmap Swatch in the Color Mixer panel). It is possible to create interesting bitmap-based art with this command. However, if your intention is to preserve the look of the original bitmap with maximum fidelity, you will have to work with the settings — and you will most likely find that the original bitmap is actually smaller in file size than the traced vector image. Figure 9-36 includes a selected bitmap image on the left, and the final vector image that resulted from the settings shown in the Trace Bitmap dialog box.

To trace a bitmap, follow these steps:

1. Use the Selection tool to select the bitmap that you want to trace — it can be in Edit mode or directly on the Stage.

2. Choose Modify ➪ Bitmap ➪ Trace Bitmap to invoke the Trace Bitmap dialog box and set the options according to your needs:

   • **Color Threshold:** This option controls the number of colors in your traced bitmap. It limits the number of colors by averaging the colors based on the criteria chosen in Color Threshold and Minimum Area. Color Threshold compares RGB color values of adjacent pixels to the value entered. If the difference is lower than the value entered, then adjacent pixels are considered the same color. By making this computation for each pixel within the bitmap, Flash averages the colors. A lower Color Threshold delivers more colors in the final vector graphic derived from the traced bitmap. The range is between 0 and 500, with a default setting of 100.

- **Minimum Area:** This value is the radius, measured in pixels, which Color Threshold uses to describe adjacent pixels when comparing pixels to determine what color to assign to the center pixel. The range is between 1 and 1,000, with the default setting being 8.

- **Curve Fit:** This value determines how smoothly outlines are drawn. Select Very Tight if the shapes in the bitmap are complex and angular. If the curves are smooth, select Very Smooth.

- **Corner Threshold:** This setting determines how sharp edges are handled; choose Many Corners to retain edges and Few Corners to smooth the edges.

3. Click OK. Flash traces the bitmap, and the original pixel information is converted to vector shapes. If the bitmap is complex, this may take a while. Depending on the settings you have chosen, the final look of the traced graphic can vary between being very close to the original or very abstracted.

Tip   If your objective is for your traced bitmap to closely resemble the original bitmap, then set a low Color Threshold and a low Minimum Area. You'll also want to set the Curve Fit to Pixels and the Corner Threshold to Many Corners. Be aware that using these settings may drastically slow the tracing process for complex bitmaps and result in larger file sizes. If animated, such bitmaps may also retard the frame rate dramatically.

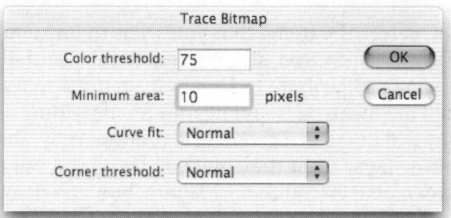

Figure 9-36: Selecting a bitmap (left) and choosing settings in the Trace Bitmap dialog box to define the final vector image (right)

As shown in Figure 9-37, the traced bitmap can vary in how closely it resembles the original bitmap (A). The image in the center (B) was traced with lower settings to achieve a more detailed image: Color Threshold of 25, Minimum Area of 2 pixels, Curve Fit of Pixels, and Corner Threshold of Many Corners. The image on the right (C) was traced with higher settings to create a more abstract graphic image: Color Threshold of 100, Minimum Area of 25 pixels, Curve Fit of Very Smooth, and Corner Threshold of Few Corners.

A   B   C

Figure 9-37: Bitmap images (A) can be traced to create different styles of vector graphics by using low settings (B) or high settings (C).

Caution   If you drag a bitmap from the Library panel onto the Stage and then attempt to acquire the bitmap fill by first tracing the bitmap and then clicking with the Eyedropper tool, be careful of how selection affects the results. If the traced bitmap is still selected, clicking with the Eyedropper tool acquires the nearest color and replaces the entire traced bitmap with a solid fill of the acquired color. If the traced bitmap is not selected, the Eyedropper tool simply acquires the nearest solid color and loads it into the fill color chip.

Using Distribute to Layers

The Distribute to Layers command (Shift+Ctrl+D or Shift+⌘+D) is a great time-saver if you're managing multiple elements that you need to move to animate on individual layers. If you've imported several items to the Document window, or you've created a complex graphic that you decide needs to be split up on different layers, you can use this command to do most of the work for you. Instead of having to manually create new layers and copy and paste items one by one, you can select a number of individual items in the Document window and apply Distribute to Layers to have Flash automatically create a layer for each selected item.

To apply Distribute to Layers, select the items that you want to have moved to discrete layers — these items can be symbols, groups, shapes, text blocks, and even bitmaps or video objects. Select Modify ⇨ Timeline ⇨ Distribute to Layers from the application menu, or choose Distribute from the contextual menu. Strokes and fills for an individual shape will be kept together on the same layer, as will items in a group or a multi-part symbol. The items you select can be on different source layers, but they must all be on the same frame of the Timeline. When items have been distributed to new layers, you can delete any old layers that have been left empty.

The auto-created layers will be stacked from top to bottom below the currently selected layer in the order that the selected items were created. So the most recently created item should be placed on a layer at the bottom of the stack, just above the layer that was formerly below the selected layer, while the item that was created before the others in the selection will be placed at the top of the stack, just below the currently selected layer. If you are completely disoriented by now, have a look at Figure 9-38 to see a file with the layer order before applying Distribute to Layers to the selected items, and look at Figure 9-39 to see how the new layers were stacked and named.

Characters from a broken apart text block will be stacked in layers in the same order that the text block was created (from left to right, right to left, or top to bottom). Flash names auto-created layers with the following conventions:

✦ A new layer made for any asset stored in the Library (a symbol, bitmap, or video clip) will be given the same name as the asset.

✦ A new layer made for a character from a broken-apart text block is named with the text character or letter.

Caution When applying Distribute to Layers to text blocks that have not been broken apart, new layers will be named with the entire text string. It is best to rename these layers because they will usually be difficult to read and may even exceed the 64-character limit for layer names.

✦ A new layer made for a shape (which is not stored in the Library) will be named in the same numeric sequence as other layers in the current document (Layer 1, Layer 2, and so on).

✦ A new layer made for a named symbol instance will be given the instance name instead of the stored symbol name.

Any layer can always be renamed after it has been created.

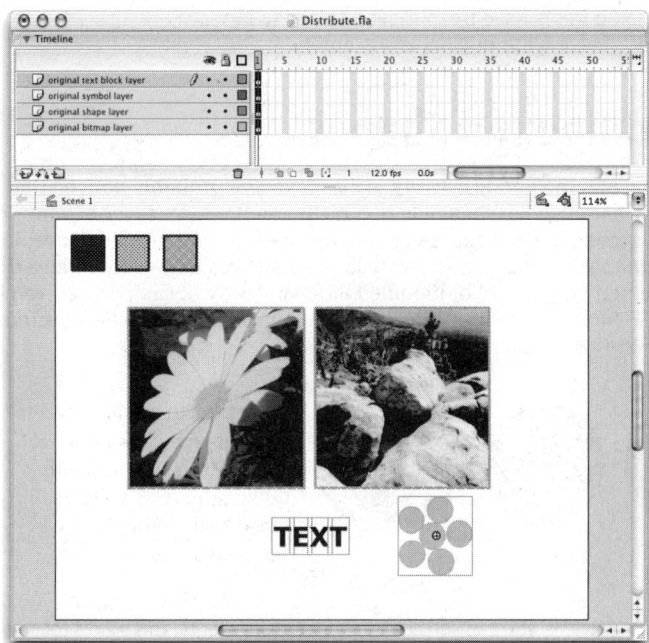

Figure 9-38: A Flash document with the original layer structure for some bitmaps, symbols, shapes and a broken apart text block to be distributed to layers

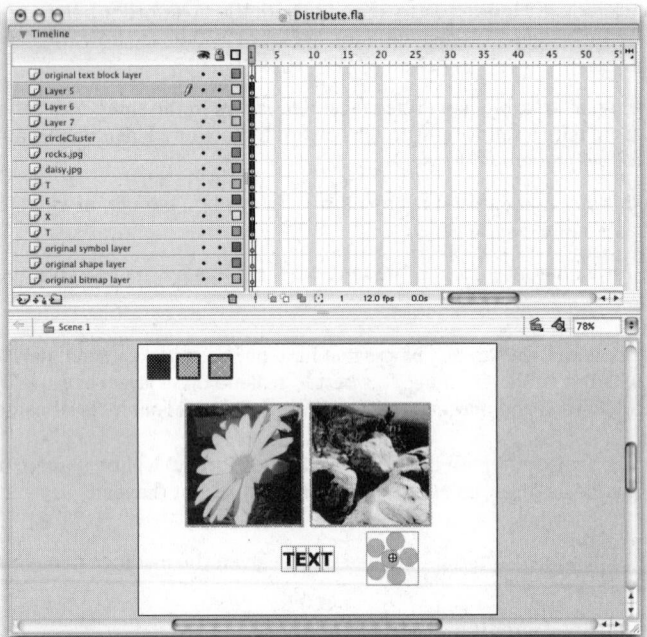

Figure 9-39: The same Flash document after Distribute to Layers has been applied. All selected items have been moved to newly created, auto-named layers, leaving the original layers empty.

Working with Compound Shapes

As you have been drawing and modifying artwork in Flash, you've probably noticed that Flash has a unique way of handling lines and fills that reside on the same layer of your document. Items that are the same color merge, whereas items that are a different color replace or cut out other items where they overlap. Flash treats lines or strokes as separate items than fills, so these can be selected and moved or modified independently of each other, even if they are the same color. Figure 9-40 shows how Flash allows lines and fills to be selected individually, even if they are the same color.

Figure 9-40: A black oval fill with a black stroke may not appear to have a discrete outline, but Flash allows these two elements to be selected separately

Tip   By double-clicking an element, you can select all the related segments. This works for selecting the stroke and fill of a shape or for selecting connected sections of a segmented line (such as the four sides of a rectangle).

Both lines and fills are divided into segments at points of intersection. Figure 9-41 shows a fill split into two independent shapes by drawing a line on top of it (top) or modified by merging with a fill of the same color and being cut-out by a fill of a different color (bottom).

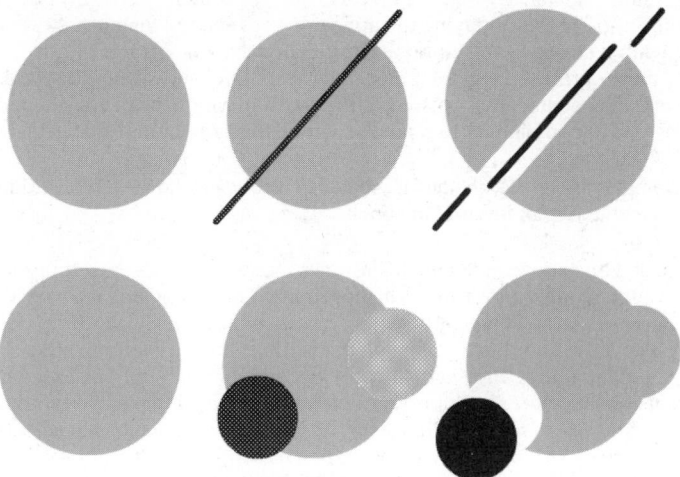

Figure 9-41: A fill split by an overlapping line drawn on the same layer (top). Two fills of the same color merge into a compound shape when they intersect on the same layer (bottom).

These behaviors can be destructive or helpful to your artwork, depending on how you manage individual elements. The key point to remember is that primitive shapes cannot be overlapped on the same layer while deselected without affecting each other. If items are grouped or converted into symbols, they remain independent and will not be compounded or deleted by intersection with other items. Items on layers are also autonomous and will not merge with or erase items that exist on other layers.

Lines or fills can be moved over other primitive shapes without affecting them, as long as they remain selected — as soon as they are deselected they will intersect or merge with adjacent primitive shapes on the same layer. Figure 9-42 illustrates the process of moving a selected shape over and then off of another shape while keeping the two shapes independent (top) and the result if the shape is deselected while it is overlapping another shape, before being reselected and moved, to create a compound shape (bottom).

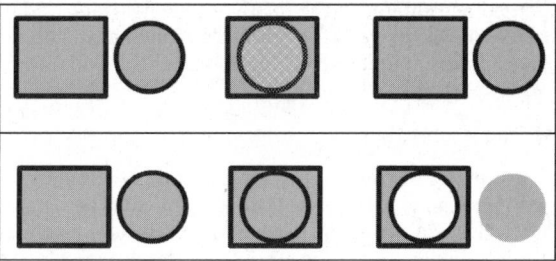

Figure 9-42: A shape moved across another shape while being continuously selected (top), compared to a shape that is deselected while on top of another shape, and then reselected and moved (bottom)

Using Advanced Color Effects for Symbol Instances

Many of the effects discussed in this chapter have been applicable only to shapes, but as intro-duced in Chapter 6, "Symbols, Instances, and the Library," the Color menu in the Property inspector provides some options for modifying the appearance of symbol instances without changing the original symbol stored in the Library. The individual color settings on the Property inspector for most of the items in the Color menu are useful and straightforward. The Advanced option in the Color menu comes with a Settings button, which when clicked opens a dialog box that enables you to combine more than one setting for more complex effects.

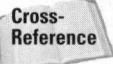 **Cross-Reference**   Because these examples are not very helpful illustrated in black and white, we have included the relevant graphics in the color insert of the book.

The Advanced Effect dialog box shown in Figure 9-43 shows the two columns of settings for Red, Green, and Blue color channels, plus the setting for Alpha. This dialog box is invoked when a symbol instance is selected on the Stage, by selecting Advanced from the Color drop-down menu on the Property inspector, and then clicking on the Settings button. Although these columns may seem redundant at first, they actually provide very different options for control-ling the appearance of instance color. The important difference between these two types of con-trols is that the first column creates *relative* changes by applying percentage-based adjustment, while the second column creates *absolute* change by adding or subtracting integer values.

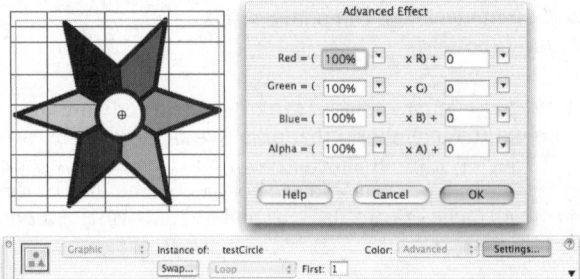

Figure 9-43: The Advanced Effect dialog box shown with the symbol instance testStar, with no effect applied

Other than playing with these settings, the easiest way to understand what some of the possi-ble combinations produce is to dig out your calculator and find a chart of RGB color swatches (with decimal values rather than Hex values). By taking the RGB values in your original instance, multiplying them by the percentage entered in the relative value field, and adding the value shown in the absolute color field you will arrive at the new RGB value that will appear in the symbol instance when the effect is applied. If that doesn't make it all clear, read on.

Relative color control

The first column of values adjusts the color of the instance relative to the percentages of color (or alpha), present in the original with a range of –100 percent to 100 percent. The default or "no effect" setting is 100 percent. With these controls, 100 percent red does not change every-thing to pure red or 255 red, but rather it displays 100 percent of the current percentage of red in the existing colors. For example, yellow (255, 255, 0) cannot be made more orange by increasing the amount of red because 255 x 100 percent is still 255 — the maximum amount of red. However, if you reduce the percentage of green to 45 percent of the original value, the ratio of red will be increased making the visible color shift to orange (255, [255 x 45 percent], 0 or 255, 102, 0).

This process of reducing the amount of the opposite (or *complementary*) color to alter the ratio of colors is called *subtractive* color adjustment, and it can be helpful to remember some basic color theory to predict how it will alter the appearance of your symbol instance. Because the color value changes that you make are applied to all the colors in your symbol, the overall effect can be more complex than just shifting one color in your palette. As shown in our second example of the testCircle instance (printed in the color insert), *reducing* the percentage of red and green to 0, made the gray and white areas shift to blue, whereas the red and green areas shifted to black and the originally black areas were unaltered.

Because the maximum value for relative Alpha is also 100 percent, this control cannot be used to increase the alpha setting of an instance. For example, a symbol that has an alpha fill of 50 percent cannot be made to appear more solid because 100 percent of 50 percent is still only 50 percent alpha.

Absolute color control

The settings in the right column are referred to as *absolute* color controls because they add or subtract color in concrete amounts regardless of the color values in the symbol instance. The scale of absolute color is from –255 to 255 and the default or "no effect" setting is 0. When absolute color is applied to a symbol instance, it is possible to make more drastic global color changes than you can make with relative color adjustments.

The effect of absolute color value changes made in the Advanced Effect dialog box is similar to the effect of using the Tint option of the Color menu. What makes these controls more advanced is that not only can you add a tint by increasing the value of certain colors, but you can also add an *inverse* tint by using negative values. So, for example, you could add a red tint to all the colors present in the symbol instance shown in Figure 9-43, with the exception of white and pure red (which already contain 255 red), by entering a value of 255 Red, or you could add a yellow tint to all colors containing blue by entering a value of –255 Blue, this would make pure blue (0, 0, 255), turn to black (0, 0, 0) and white (255, 255, 255), turn to pure yellow (255, 255, 0).

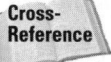
Cross-Reference You can see the original testStar symbol instance and the three modified examples described in this section, printed in the color insert.

Perhaps one of the most unique feats that absolute values can perform is to make a symbol instance that contains alpha fills or strokes appear less transparent. Because the alpha settings are absolute, it is possible to shift an item with an original alpha setting of less than 100 percent, to any opacity level between invisible (–255) and completely solid (255).

If you've entered negative values in the relative alpha setting, it is even possible to make an area with an alpha fill visible while solid areas are made invisible. Consider a shape that has an area of solid fill (100 percent or 255 alpha) and an area of transparent color (40 percent or 102 alpha). If this shape is converted into a symbol and then modified using the Advanced Effect options, you could enter a relative alpha value of –100 percent and an absolute alpha value of 255. When these effect settings were applied, the solid fill in the symbol instance would be invisible with 0 percent alpha (255 × –100 percent + 255 = 0), whereas the originally transparent fill would be visible with 60 percent alpha (102 × –100 percent + 255 = 153).

The confusion that these settings sometimes cause has created debate about whether negative alpha settings can really be applied. As long as you can remember that outside of the absolute settings in the Advanced Effect dialog box, 0 percent alpha is invisible, whereas inside the Advanced Effect dialog box, a 0 alpha setting is equal to no effect, you will be able to prove as we just did, that negative alpha effects can be used to invert alpha values, similar to the way that negative color effects can be used to invert color values.

The Magic and Mayhem of Timeline Effects

Flash MX 2004 has introduced a whole new way of creating animation and visual effects. Rather than manually placing symbol instances on the Stage and inserting tweens on the Timeline, you can simply select an item (shape or symbol) on the Stage and choose a static or animated effect from the Timeline Effect menu. The Timeline effects listed in the application menu under Insert ⇨ Timeline Effects (or in the contextual menu if you have an item selected on the Stage) each invoke their own dialog box. You can tweak settings for these effects and preview the final result before you choose to apply it to a shape or a symbol. After you have chosen your settings and applied the effect, Flash automatically converts your selected item into Graphic symbols and renders the effect, including tweens on the Timeline for animated effects. With just a few selections in the Settings dialog box, you can add animation or effects that would have taken considerable time to create step-by-step. In this section, we look at the Timeline effects that can be used to modify the appearance of static graphics.

Cross-Reference
The animated Timeline effects (those that have settings for duration or number of frames to render motion graphics) are discussed in detail in Chapter 11, "Timeline Animation and Effects."

The magic of Timeline effects is simply that they can save you a lot of time and make it much less painstaking to change the timing or placement of a rendered animation or visual effect. The mayhem of Timeline effects comes in when you look in your project Library. Macromedia has done a great job of organizing this automated process, but you may still be a little confused by all the symbols and folders that show up in the Library panel after you've applied a few Timeline effects. In this section, we give a quick description and show an example of each of the Timeline effects that are used for modifying static graphics. Next, we walk through the steps of adding a Drop Shadow Effect and point out the elements that are added to the project file, so you'll know what to expect when you apply other Timeline effects.

If you're planning to just apply a few effects, publish a SWF file and move on, you needn't worry about understanding the symbol structures and editing "rules" for Timeline effects. However, if you plan to integrate Timeline effects with other animation that you've created, or if you decide you want to edit an item after an effect has been rendered — which of course you will! — we hope this section makes the process a little less mysterious.

Static Timeline effects

Static Timeline effects are those that make a change to an item, but which do not necessarily add a tweened animation span to the Timeline. The nonanimated Timeline effects that are included with Flash MX 2004 include the following:

✦ **Copy to Grid:** Makes it possible to duplicate and distribute multiple copies of an item in rows and/or columns. This effect does not make any change to the appearance of the item, but it gives you the controls you need to create an organized layout of multiples (see Figure 9-44).

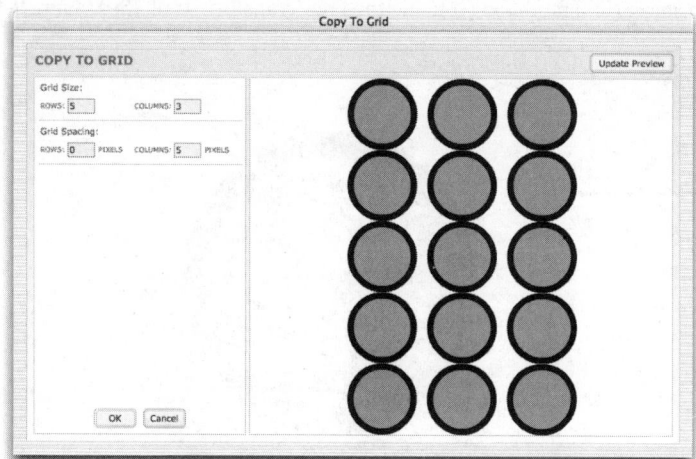

Figure 9-44: Settings and preview for the Copy to Grid Timeline effect

✦ **Distributed Duplicate:** This effect, demonstrated in Figure 9-45, creates a series of copies of an item, distributed along a tangent that can be set by entering the x and y offsets. The copied items can also be shifted in scale, color, and transparency.

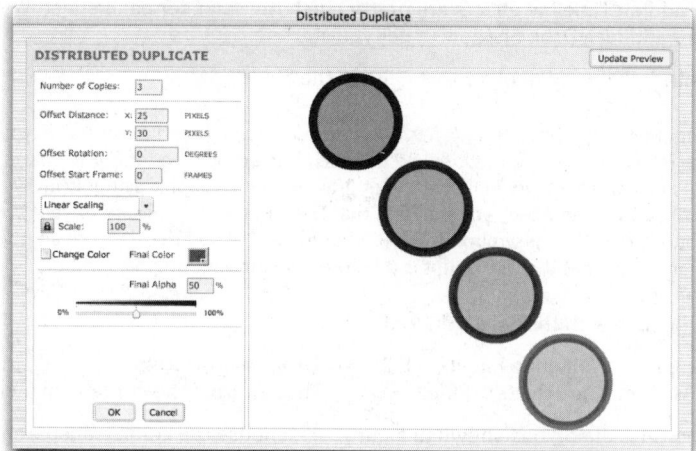

Figure 9-45: Settings and preview for the Distributed Duplicate Timeline effect

✦ **Drop Shadow:** This sounds as if it's an effect that you would use a lot, but the truth is, you will most likely get better-looking drop shadows if you make them yourself. The Drop Shadow effect has controls for the position, color, and transparency of the shadow, but it does not include a scale or a skew control — so, if you want shadows with depth, you'll have to make them the old-fashioned way: by adding a copy of your item (or a custom shape) and modifying it using the Free Transform tool. (See Figure 9-46.)

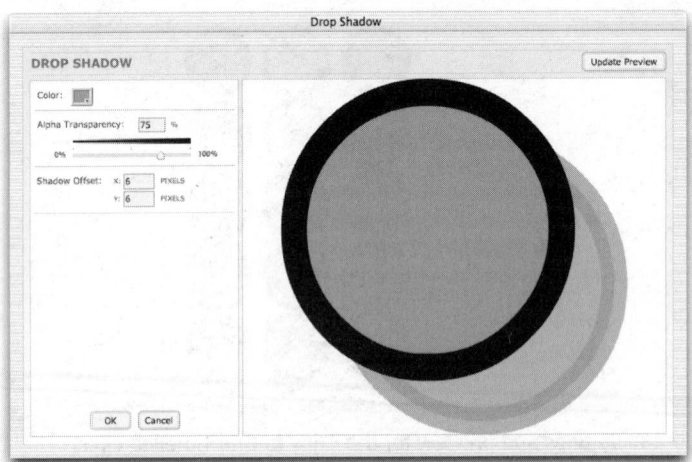

Figure 9-46: Settings and preview for the Drop Shadow Timeline effect

Adding a Drop Shadow Timeline effect

The steps for adding Timeline effects are pretty much the same for each effect. We'll describe the process for adding a Drop Shadow to get you started.

1. Start with a shape, symbol, or text field on the Stage.

Tip   Flash automatically converts any item you select into a Graphic symbol if you apply a Timeline effect, so this is one workflow in which it is actually better *not* to make a symbol before adding an effect. If you convert your artwork into a Graphic symbol (mySymbol) and then apply a Timeline effect, you will find that Flash makes a duplicate of your symbol and does not use the original symbol in the rendered effect. If you decide to clean up your project Library, verify that the Use Count is 0 before deleting your original symbol.

2. Select the item with the Selection tool.

3. Choose Insert ➪ Timeline Effects ➪ Effects ➪ Drop Shadow from the application menu, or choose Timeline Effects ➪ Effects ➪ Drop Shadow from the contextual menu.

4. In the Settings dialog box shown in Figure 9-46, choose the color, transparency, and position for the shadow and click the Update Preview button to see the rendered effect. Make adjustments to any of the settings and click the Update Preview button as many times as you need to get the look you want.

5. Click OK to close the Settings dialog box. You'll see the final effect rendered on the Stage.

Note If there is no other artwork on the layer with the item to which you add a Timeline effect, Flash simply renames the layer when the effect is applied. If there are other symbols or artwork on the layer with the item to which you added the Timeline effect, Flash moves the item to a new layer when the effect is applied. This can lead to duplicate layer names that should be manually changed to keep the structure of your Timeline clear.

6. If you want to reopen the Settings dialog box to make adjustments to the effect, simply select the Graphic symbol instance on the Stage and chose Timeline Effects ➪ Edit Effect from the Modify menu or from the contextual menu. To delete the effect (without deleting the item to which the effect was applied), choose Modify ➪ Timeline Effects ➪ Remove Effect.

Now to analyze what has changed in your project file: Select the item on the Stage and look at the Property inspector. Notice that the item on the Stage with the effect applied is now a Graphic symbol instance with an auto-assigned name — in our example it is Drop Shadow 5. The number designates the symbol order in which the Drop Shadow was created in your current work session. In our example, Drop Shadow was the fifth symbol created in the document. (The other symbols were deleted from the Library because they weren't relevant to this example.) To see the symbols that Flash has created in the Library, open the Library panel (Ctrl+L, or ⌘+L). If you didn't manually add any other symbols to the file, the list of new items would look like those in the Library panel in Figure 9-47.

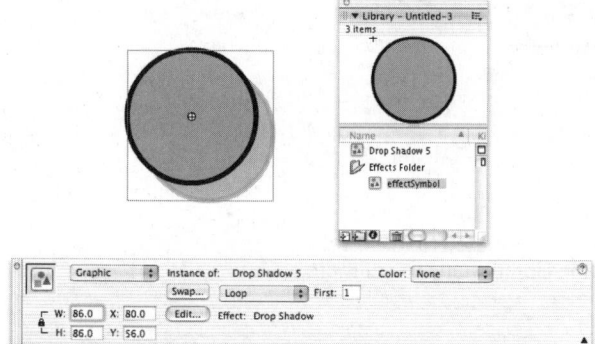

Figure 9-47: A new Graphic symbol instance created by Flash for a Drop Shadow Timeline effect and the nested symbols stored in the project Library

Managing Timeline effect symbols and folders

The nested symbols that are used to "build" a Timeline effect are stored in an Effects Library folder that is automatically created when you apply a Timeline effect. The Graphic symbol visible on the Stage after you apply a Timeline effect is stored in the root of the project Library list. You can rename the automatically created folder or any of the symbols to give them more meaningful names.

Caution

Adding custom symbol and folder names is helpful for keeping your project Library clear and easy to edit in the future. Unfortunately, each time you modify the settings for a Timeline effect (by using the Edit Effect command), Flash renames the symbols in your Library and adds another folder with the default naming convention. It will also rename the layer in your Timeline; so if you plan on adjusting an effect, you may want to make renaming these items your final step.

So what happens if you add another Timeline effect to the same project file? As an example, we added a square shape to the Stage of the same file used in the previous example (shown in Figure 9-47). Without converting the square into a symbol, we applied a Drop Shadow Timeline effect — in the same way that we applied the effect to the first item in the project file. As shown in Figure 9-48, Flash converts the shape into a nested Graphic symbol to create the final Drop Shadow effect and adds another symbol to the Effect folder.

Note

If you rename the folder added to your Library list with the first Drop Shadow Timeline effect that you apply (`Effects Folder`), Flash will add a new folder to your Library when you add additional Drop Shadow effects. The top-level Graphic symbols (with the completed effect) always appear in the root (or main) Library list when they are rendered.

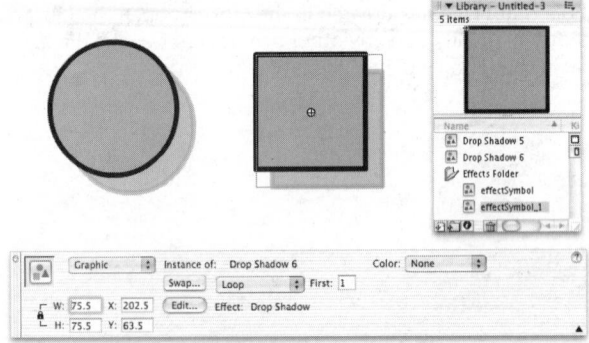

Figure 9-48: When a Timeline effect is added to a second shape in the same project file, the Library starts to get more cluttered.

When you apply other Timeline effects, the symbol and folder names that are added to your Library panel may be different, but the default file structure will be the same.

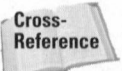

Cross-Reference

Samuel Wan's tutorial in Chapter 11, "Timeline Animation and Effects," explains how to install and use a custom Timeline effect. The script files for Sam's "Jitter" effect are included in the ch11 folder of the CD-ROM.

Modifying Timeline effect symbols

If you are accustomed to working with tweened animation or compound symbol structures that you have made manually, there are a few differences that will come up when you start working with Timeline effects. Although the symbols added to your Library when you apply a Timeline effect have the same icon as any other Graphic symbol, there are some special rules about how they can (or cannot) be modified.

Flash renders an effect based on the settings you enter in the Timeline Effect dialog box, so once the Graphic symbols for the effect have been rendered you cannot edit the top-level Graphic symbol directly. If you try to open the symbol in Edit mode, you will see the Effect Warning box as shown in Figure 9-49.

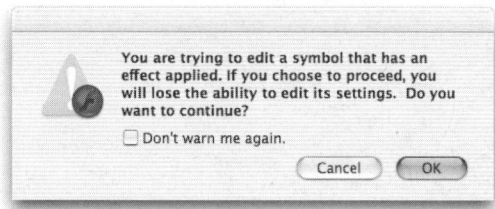

Figure 9-49: The Warning dialog box that lets you know if you are trying to edit a symbol with a Timeline effect applied. If you proceed to open the symbol in Edit mode, you will no longer be able to use the Edit Effect menu option to access the settings panel to modify the Timeline effect.

Although the top-level Graphic symbol (with the final rendered effect) can't be opened in Edit mode without disabling the Edit Effect option, you *can* edit the nested Graphic symbols that are stored in the Effect folder. In most cases, the changes you make to the nested Graphic symbol are passed on to all instances used in the final rendered effect. However, in cases where the effect required incremental mathematical adjustments (such as on a Color Change), you have to use the Edit Effect command to open the Settings dialog box so that the effect can be re-rendered in the Preview window (it will automatically update to include any changes you made to the nested symbols in the Library). You can make additional changes to the effect using the options in the Settings dialog box, or you can simply click OK to close it and go back to the Stage — where you should now see the changes passed on to all of the instances of the effect.

Tip   Rather than trying to access nested Timeline effect symbols by double-clicking the symbol instance on the Stage — which triggers the warning box — double-click the nested symbol names listed in the Effect folder in the Library (or use the Edit command in the Library options menu).

You can also use the instance-editing options available in the Property inspector and the Transform panel to adjust the appearance of a rendered (or top-level) Timeline effect symbol without disabling the Edit Effect option. With the Free Transform tool added to the mix, you should be able to squish, stretch, rotate, tint, and otherwise adjust rendered Timeline effect symbols to suit your fancy.

Editing with Find and Replace

This may be the feature that some designers needed to see to believe that Flash is finally all grown up. Although you can use the Movie Explorer to search for some elements in a project file so that they can be modified, it doesn't automate updates in the same speedy way that the Find and Replace panel, shown in Figure 9-50, does.

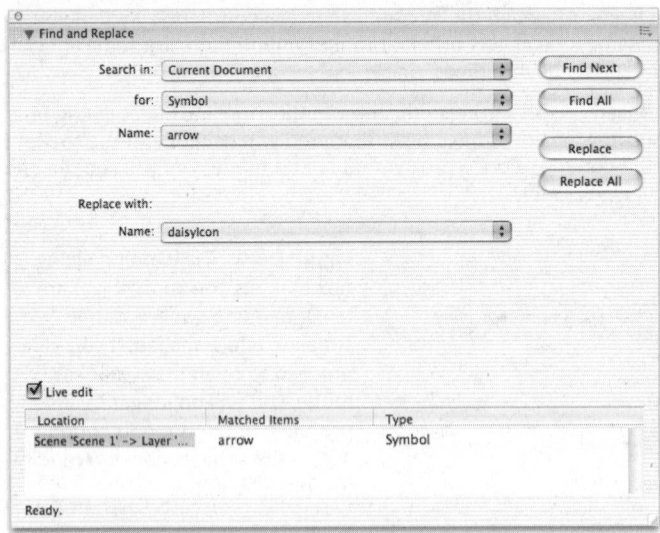

Figure 9-50: The Find and Replace panel makes revisions so easy, they're almost fun.

Note　Although the Find and Replace item in the Edit window does invoke a real panel and not just a dialog box, it is not included with the other panels listed in the Window menu. The logic for this is not exactly clear, but we can guess that Macromedia believed it would be more intuitive to find it in the Edit menu. Although the Find and Replace panel takes up a lot of room on your desktop, you could dock it with other panels for quick access if you prefer that to using the menu or shortcut keys.

If you have used the Find and Replace feature in any other application (even in a basic text-editing program), you will be familiar with the main buttons in the Find and Replace panel (Find Next, Find All, Replace, and Replace All). Open the Find and Replace panel by choosing Edit ➪ Find and Replace in the application menu (Alt+F or Option+F). The real benefits of this Flash MX 2004 addition to the authoring environment become clearer when you look at the items you can select to search for, these include:

✦ **Text:** Search for words, partial words, or whole paragraphs in text fields, frames, layers, parameters, strings or in ActionScript in your current project or current scene.

✦ **Font:** Search for fonts by name, style, and even size, within your current project or scene.

✦ **Color:** Pick a color from the pop-up swatches (or enter a hexadecimal value in the field) to search for fills, strokes, or text where a specific color is used in the current project or scene.

✦ **Symbol/Sound/Video/Bitmap:** Use the handy drop-down list that lists all symbols (or sounds, or video, or bitmaps) used in your current project to pick a symbol to search for and a symbol to use as a replacement.

As you select each item in the for: drop-down list, options relevant to that item become available in the panel. These options give you very precise control over the type of edits that you want to make. Now that replacing a color or font or even a specific word in your entire project file, is as easy as making a few quick selections in the Find and Replace panel, those dreaded last-minute revisions might almost seem fun.

Caution   Although any effects or transformations that have been applied to a symbol instance (and any formatting you have applied to text), should be preserved if you change it using the Find and Replace panel, you will have to verify that the newly inserted content displays as you expect it to. If a font is much larger it might not fit into your layout, or if a replacement bitmap is much larger or smaller than the original, you may have to make some manual adjustments to get everything polished. These are the same kinds of adjustments you would expect to make if you used the Swap symbol feature.

Using the History Panel

Another long-awaited feature added to Flash MX 2004 is the History panel (Alt+F10 or Option+F10), which makes it possible to escape the linear limitations of Undo/Redo. As you work in your project file, the History panel records your editing steps in a sequential list (refer to Figure 9-51). The History panel only stores steps taken in the active project file during the current editing session. It does not store steps from the last time you had a project file open or from other files edited during the same session. You *can* save and move steps from one file or session to another, but it requires you to use some of the special features of the History panel, described later in this section.

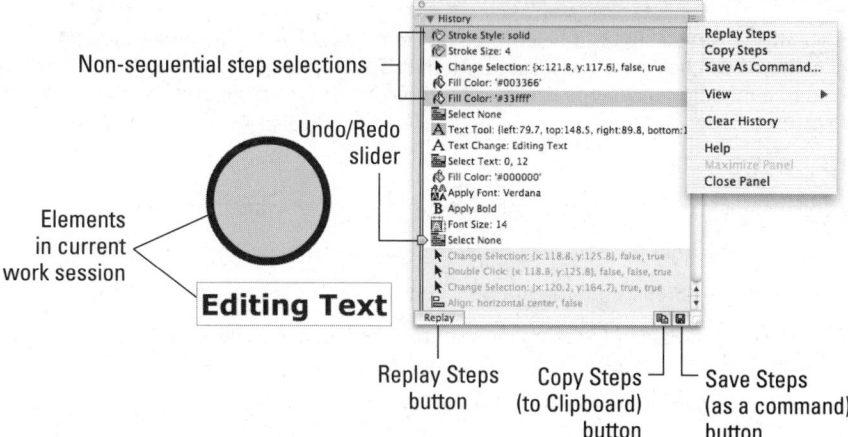

Figure 9-51: The History panel lists steps taken as a file is authored or edited.

The History panel can be used as a reminder of the steps taken to create a special graphic effect, or it can be used as a nonlinear authoring control. Should you need to get back to a specific step in your authoring session, you can use Undo (Ctrl+Z or ⌘+Z), over and over and over . . . or you can simply open the History panel and drag the edit pointer on the left side of the panel upwards to go back in time until you reach the point at which you want to jump back into authoring. As long as you don't make any edits at an earlier point in the History list, you can easily scroll forwards again if you need to Redo your steps — without wearing out the Ctrl+Y or ⌘+Y keys! However, if you Undo a step (or a series of steps) and then make changes to your project file, you can no longer redo the steps in the History panel. This is where the History panel does behave a little like a time machine — as long as you don't change anything, you can jump backwards and forwards in time, but as soon as you change something, you lose the option of going "back to the future."

Tip   Click to the left of a step in the History panel to jump to that point without scrolling. All steps listed after the point that you click will be undone and grayed out until you scroll forward again (or click to the left of an item closer to the bottom of the list).

The options menu and the buttons along the bottom of the History panel are the keys to the more advanced editing tasks that you can accomplish when you take your steps a step further. (Refer to Figure 9-51 for call-outs on the location of History panel controls.)

Replay Steps

The Replay Steps control will repeat or reapply a series of sequential or nonsequential steps in your current History list.

1. Select sequential items by dragging or by Shift+clicking the text labels in the list. Select nonsequential items by Ctrl+clicking (⌘+clicking on Mac).

2. With a step (or series of steps) selected, you can apply the step(s) to a new item — by selecting the item with the Selection tool and clicking the Replay button or choosing Replay Steps from the options menu.

All currently selected steps will be applied (in order) to the item and a new step labeled "Replay Steps" will be listed in the History panel. The Replay Steps item in the History list can be used to apply the same steps again without having to select the original steps individually.

Copy Steps

This command makes it possible to move steps from one document to another.

1. Select steps from your History panel list (as described in the previous section).

2. Choose Copy Steps from the options menu.

3. In the Flash document where you want to reuse the steps, select an item that you want to apply the steps to.

4. Use Edit ⇨ Paste in Center (Ctrl+V or ⌘+V).

The editing steps copied from your original file will be applied to the item in your current file and a new item will be added to the History panel, labeled "Paste Steps."

Clear History

This is a helpful command to use if you want to start from a clean slate before performing a series of editing steps that you plan to save. Clear History deletes all the listings in the

History panel of your current document. You can't undo this choice, but you will see a Warning dialog box (see Figure 9-52) that gives you the chance to change your mind before it's too late. (Closing a Flash document will also clear the History list.) The number of steps listed in the History panel can be limited by the *Undo levels* set in the General Flash Preferences dialog box. The default setting is 100, but it can be set as high as 9,999. Every item recorded in the History panel eats up some memory and disk space, so choose the lowest setting that suits your authoring style.

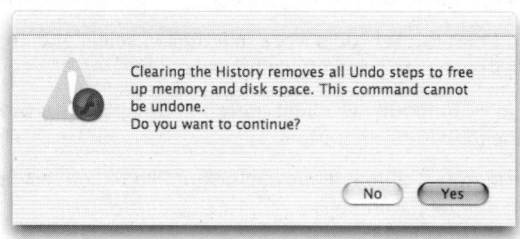

Clearing the History removes all Undo steps to free up memory and disk space. This command cannot be undone.
Do you want to continue?

No   Yes

Figure 9-52: The Warning dialog box that appears before the History list is cleared

History View

You want to leave this setting on Default unless you plan to use the History panel as a tool for helping you write new JavaScript commands. This is a very exciting potential use of the History panel, but it is beyond the scope of this book. If you are familiar with JavaScript, you can try different View settings to get more information that helps you to deconstruct the steps in an editing workflow.

Save As Command

If you're not quite ready to start writing your own JavaScript from scratch, this is a terrific shortcut that makes it easy to save and reuse custom editing workflows.

1. Select the step(s) from the History panel that you want to save and reuse.

2. Choose Save As Command from the options menu (or click the small disk icon at the bottom right of the History panel).

3. In the Save as Command dialog box, give the command a meaningful name — you might call the steps used to create a fancy custom type treatment Headline style.

4. By the magic of Flash MX 2004, your custom command now appears in the Command menu list.

5. You can apply your specific editing steps in any document by selecting an item and choosing Commands ➪ Headline style (or whatever commands you have created and named).

The options at the top of the Command menu give you some controls for managing your custom commands and for using commands from other sources. The Get More Commands menu item loads a link to the Macromedia Exchange where you can find new commands contributed by other Flash developers (look for JSFL files). If you download a custom command script, you can use the Run Command menu option to browse to the JSFL file and apply it to an item in your current project. The possibilities are wide open.

We'd like to know what you thought about this chapter. Visit www.flashsupport.com/feedback to fill out an online form with your comments.

Summary

✦ After you've mastered the basic drawing tools in Flash, there are innumerable methods for modifying artwork to create custom effects.

✦ The Eyedropper, Ink Bottle, and Paint Bucket tools work together to select and apply fill and stroke styles to multiple items or to swap styles between items.

✦ The Fill Transform tool can be used to modify gradient fills and bitmap fills for precise alignment and appearance inside individual shapes.

✦ The commands available in the Modify ⇨ Shape menu can be applied to convert lines into fills and to modify fills with unique parameters.

✦ The Free Transform tool has two powerful options that can be applied to shapes only, as well as two options that restrict the Free Transform behavior to make it easier to achieve specific tasks.

✦ Flash organizes artwork with specific parameters and the Modify ⇨ Arrange commands can be used to help define the stacking order when you're working with similar items on the same layer.

✦ The Break apart command can be used to convert bitmaps and text so that they can be edited like shapes to create special effects.

✦ The Trace bitmap command is used to convert imported bitmaps into vector graphics with varying degrees of detail.

✦ Distribute to Layers is a time-saving command that can be very helpful when preparing artwork for animation on separate layers.

✦ The Advanced Effect dialog box for Color settings on symbol instances enables you to make dramatic changes to the appearance of individual instances without modifying the original symbol. The absolute value fields make it possible to invert or override both color and alpha settings of an instance without editing the source symbol.

✦ Timeline effects provide a whole new range of options for modifying the look of static and animated graphics. However, the final rendered Graphic symbols created by Flash when a Timeline effect is applied cannot be opened in Edit mode without losing the option to change the settings that define the rendered effect.

✦ Flash MX 2004 includes a Find and Replace command that makes it easy to modify almost any element in any part of a project.

✦ The new History panel and Commands menu make it possible to move beyond Undo and Redo. You can save and reuse authoring or editing steps and even share these steps (as custom Commands) with other Flash developers.

✦   ✦   ✦

Creating Animation and Effects

Now that you're comfortable with the Flash tools and making static Graphic symbols and groups, it's time to move on to creating animated elements and dynamic effects. Chapter 10 introduces some of the fundamental production and planning issues that you need to consider when designing animated elements. Chapter 11 will give you all the information you need to start working with time-based content. Learn to create frame-by-frame and tweened animation and how to use Movie Clips to control display of content on multiple timelines. This chapter also introduces the creative possibilities of the new Timeline Effects in Flash MX 2004. Chapter 12 introduces the various layer tools that will make your production easier and allow you to add more advanced effects. If you are interested in character animation, Chapter 13 provides comprehensive coverage of character animation and the tricks that professional animators use to create engaging and optimized cartoons. When you're ready to transfer your Flash content to the Web or to a tape format, Chapter 14 will help you to tailor your content to specific viewing environments and will walk you through the steps for exporting final content from the Flash authoring environment.

Animation Strategies

Have you ever wondered what makes some animation so compelling and other animation so dull? Regardless of the content of a site, or even the style of the site's graphics, some animation is engaging, whereas other animation is just annoying or even pathetic — we've all seen it, limping or flashing across our screens at one time or another.

Of course, your response to animation is partly determined by what you're expecting from an interface (sometimes you want diversion, and other times you just want to find information — fast!). Most designers are aware of the issues of usability and relevance that should be considered when adding animation to an interface (whether they decide to ignore them or not). But, what happens after you've done all your audience research and content planning and you decide that animation would be appropriate for your project?

The next step should be fun, right? Unfortunately, unless you have the privilege of working with a skilled animator, you're actually entering one of the most complex and challenging areas of visual design. Although most people recognize "good" animation when they see it, the leap from *appreciating* motion to *designing* motion is difficult, even for people who have natural aptitude.

The good news is that you possess an innate understanding of physics, even if you've never taken a science class in your life — you know what to expect when you bounce a ball. But can you interpret the ball's motion and recreate it frame-by-frame in an animation? The challenge of designing motion is translating daily experience into a time-based, 2D environment. Your eyes and brain will tell you if something isn't right, but how do you know what can be done to correct it? The ability to analyze perceptions that we normally take for granted is the true skill of animation and motion graphics design.

With experience, animators can intuitively finesse the many visual factors that effectively communicate motion — even bending the rules to suit their personal animation styles or to convey specific atmospheres and characters. But, the first step toward making better animation is to become familiar with some of the fundamental concepts and laws that govern matter in the real world.

Establishing Ground Rules

No matter what the style or purpose your animation ultimately has, you'll need to establish guidelines for yourself if you want to create an engaging and convincing experience for the user. This may feel limiting at first, but these self-imposed ground rules make content more meaningful to your audience. The most commonly recognized example of structured, shared expression is music. Even the wildest music is based on an underlying structure of notes and timing (or else it isn't exactly music).

Structure is also one of the key characteristics that shape great books or even movies. Consider the difference between a private journal and a well-crafted story, or the difference between a home movie and an engrossing film. This doesn't mean that you're stuck repeating the same old narrative over and over again or that you have to follow someone else's rules. But if you have free license to create any experience for your audience, it's even more important to decide on the rules that will guide your designs so that all the elements and animations support your idea.

Artists who prefer not to follow the most commonly used conventions must work even harder to establish their own signature style—or to create content defined by the consistent choices they make. As in music, the possible choices for the basic aspects of animation are practically infinite—a little faster, a little slower, spinning or bouncing or wiggling or jumping or fading or . . . you get the idea. The guidelines that you establish for each project help you make the right decisions. There isn't an exact formula for "good animation," the variables are too broad, but once you create some rules for yourself, you'll be able to make the choices that best support your goals for a specific animation.

Defining Variables

To establish guidelines that support your design process, you first have to analyze the choices that are relevant to the content. Is the tone of the project peaceful, quiet, fast, slick, funny, scary? Try to be as specific as you can about the approach that best suits your content. Then try to make consistent choices that support that description. Some of the questions that may help you to frame the basic elements of your project include:

> What kind of motion suits the style of the project or personality of a character?
>
> How does color communicate your theme or idea?
>
> How does sound support the atmosphere or character?

If you try to make a design that is "all of the above," it will end up being too vague and confusing to keep anyone interested. One of the hardest things to learn as a designer (and to communicate to clients) is that if you try to make a site (or story) that is a little bit of everything in an attempt to suit all audiences, you'll only weaken your message and your branding and/or dilute the experience for everyone. The very best designs are consistent enough that they allow anyone to understand them (or at least get what they're about), and specific enough in style that they have a memorable personality and attitude.

Of course, there are some things that do appeal to many people—humor or surprise, well-executed visual complexity, engaging and functional navigation. But even these elements can be too generic; they need to be added to your design with a specific (and hopefully original) style. After you've decided what style is appropriate for the project, you can begin to plan the elements that will create the experience for the audience.

Although it may seem as if you're overthinking to consider these kinds of factors for every project, try to see how often you can apply at least some of the questions outlined in this section to really focus your design strategy.

The environment

What planet are you on? As you begin to plan and build a virtual environment, even in a 2D space, thinking of it as a real place is helpful. Decide what kind of place you want it to be and what characteristics will help the audience to understand where they are.

Is this a soft, fuzzy world where everything floats gently as it moves, or is this a hard, metallic world where things are heavy and make fast, abrupt movements, or maybe even a liquid world where things are very smooth and quiet, with organic movement? These are extreme examples; obviously, the possibilities are endless. Try to include all the factors that define an environment as you experience it visually:

> How light or dark is it?
>
> Is everything very distinct or blurred and layered?
>
> How crowded or open is the space?
>
> How quickly can things move?
>
> How much does gravity affect objects?
>
> Is space (depth) limited or endless?

The main thing to keep in mind is that all the elements and movement that you add to the design should help the audience to locate themselves in the environment that you want. Aside from natural environmental analogies, try to consider historical and cultural context, too. Is this meant to have a retro feel or a post-modern feel? Is it an environment influenced by multicultural elements, or is it defined only by a very specific subculture?

If you find yourself thinking, "Well, all I really want is to make a cool site that the audience will like," then remember the point made previously: the more specific you can be about the kind of environment you want to create, the better chance you have of making a design that the audience will be interested in. Most people are pretty jaded viewers by now, and something that looks trendy or resembles a jumble of many other things they've seen before is not likely to hold their attention very long.

The materials

As you consider the overall environment that you want to create, you also have to decide on the smaller details that will be consistent with your idea. Even if you're working purely with Flash strokes and fills, trying to imagine the kinds of materials that would be most appropriate for your graphic elements can be helpful. Do you want elements to be jagged and hard or fuzzy or squishy? How much volume do shapes or graphic elements have? Are any of the items transparent? Considering these questions will help you to make decisions about line styles and perhaps even colors, but most importantly these decisions will help you to design motion that will be convincing and appropriate for each item.

If your materials are soft, motion will include a lot of stretching and squashing and maybe even jiggling. If you want materials to seem hard, motion will probably be smoother, with sharper, cleaner transitions. If objects are heavy, they will have a lot more inertia. If objects are very light, they will need to move in a way that conveys weightlessness. Some of these types of motion are hard to describe, but if you can visualize them clearly (or even better, find examples in real life), you'll have an easier time planning and making your animation.

Even if you decide that your "materials" are actually best kept very flat and graphic (such as construction paper or felt cutouts), then you can still focus on that kind of look and avoid throwing in gradient fills or shiny highlights. The most important thing is to simply have a clear concept in mind that allows you to make (and explain) the design choices that best support your content.

The motion

Choosing to add animation to an item can be a quick decision, but finding the right kind of motion to add can take a lot more time. If you've made some of the decisions suggested so far in this chapter, then you will have a much easier time narrowing down the style of motion that you want to add.

Flash provides some great options for controlling the speed and pattern of motion, but until you have a clear "flight path" mapped out, you won't be able to use these tools effectively. There are few things worse than spending a lot of time creating an animation, only to realize that the motion lacks personality or seems meaningless. Most ineffective animation is the result of poor planning. This is one area of design where endless options can work against you. It can be fun, and helpful for learning, to just play with different kinds of movement in Flash, but this is not the best way to develop a project, unless you're already an experienced animator. "Designing" animation by simply throwing together some random tweens and time-line effects is the visual equivalent of whistling tunelessly or absentmindedly strumming a guitar — entertaining for the person doing it, very annoying for everyone else.

Although experienced animators develop an intuitive sense of timing and rhythm, designers who are just starting to experiment with motion will have a better chance of success if they have a very specific example to refer to. Reference for animation (or styles of movement) can be found almost anywhere in the real world — you just have to observe carefully, and if possible document the motion with video or a sequence of stills. Often, documentation of motion will surprise you. It wasn't until cameras were used to photograph horses running that artists realized there were moments during the horse's run cycle that all four feet were tucked under their stomachs. Before this motion was captured on film, it had become a convention to illustrate running horses with their legs stretched out forwards and backwards, like a rocking horse.

These are some resources that we have found inspiring as motion references:

✦ **Eadweard Muybridge:** A photographer who did some of the first "stop-motion" images ever made. His classic photographic sequences can be found in books published in the Pictorial Archive series by Dover Publications. The California Museum of Photography provides some background for and examples of Muybridge's work on its Web site, `http://photo.ucr.edu/photographers/muybridge/contents.html`

✦ **Lawrence Jordan:** Lawrence Jordan created strange and wonderful animated films using cutout graphics and stop-frame animation. In his 40-year career, he produced a body of work that has been influential for many artists working in new media. You can

learn more about him in an essay in the Bright Lights Film Journal at www.
brightlightsfilm.com/30/lawrencejordan.html.

✦ **Bruce Conner:** Bruce Conner is a visionary and groundbreaking artist who works
in a variety of mediums. He was honored with an exhibit at the Walker Art Center in
1999–2000, and it has produced the most comprehensive catalogue on his work to date.
You can find out more about Bruce Conner on the Walker Art Center Web site at
www.walkerart.org/programs/vaexhibconner.html.

Of course, you probably also have examples in mind of animation that you've seen and
admired. This can be a great way to analyze "how it's done," but you should always aspire to
develop a unique style rather than to copy someone else's directly. The history of animation
is rich and full of many examples of diverse styles that have been effective. By looking back at
the work done by great animators and filmmakers, you're likely to find something that will
inspire you and offer new possibilities for the ways that images and motion can be rendered
on a 2D screen.

Adding Personality

As many great animations have shown, any object can be given its own personality. There is
really no medium quite as effective as animation for enabling you to give life to the characters
that would otherwise stay in your imagination. Even if you don't aspire to be a character animator in the strictest sense, any element that is animated within your Flash projects should
have some recognizable personality. You don't have to add eyes and a mouth to an object in
order for it to be expressive. In fact, the main expression of any animated element should be
conveyed by the way it moves, even more strongly than by the exact composition of the
graphic.

You can add personality to a line or a letter as easily as you can add personality to a cartoon
character. A common exercise done in art schools to help students realize the expressive
power of abstract lines and shapes is to give the students a list of atmospheres or emotions
that they have to interpret and communicate with purely abstract lines and forms. The most
surprising thing about this exercise is how similar most people's drawings turn out to be.
Although the drawings do not include any concrete symbols or signs, students realize how
concise their shared visual language really is (even if they aren't always conscious of it).

As an animator, you can draw on the common visual vocabulary to communicate a great deal
to your audience without having to spell it out. Most people would probably recognize angry
movement or joyous movement if they saw it. Certainly, some personal and cultural variations in interpretation exist, but the basic recognition is usually very consistent. As with
some of the other topics described so far in this chapter, this is an aspect of motion design
that may not at first seem relevant to every project. However, if you take the time to consider
how you want to connect with your audience, you'll probably be able to pin down a fairly specific emotional tone or personality that you want your animation to have.

The next step is to observe and experiment to find the kinds of motions that best represent
the personality or tone that you want the audience to recognize. Some of the factors that you
can consider in designing expressive motion include the following:

✦ **Speed:** How fast or how slowly does an object move? Does it accelerate or decelerate?

✦ **Timing and rhythm:** How does the object's movement loop or change over time?
Finding music to help with the timing and pace of an animation is often helpful.

✦ **Consistency or irregularity:** How much variety is there in an object's movement? Does it follow a repeated pattern, or a random path of motion?

✦ **Anticipation or surprise:** Does the object give some visual foreshadowing as it moves, or does it make sudden, unexpected movements?

✦ **Freedom or constraint:** How large or small are the movements that the object can make? Does it move all around your composition or stay in a very restricted area? How much of the object moves at any one time?

The "meaning" of these various kinds of movement may be debated as much as the "meaning" of various colors. However, it is safe to assume that overall there is enough consistency among viewers on the meaning of certain kinds of motion for this to be an effective way of communicating the character of an object. If you're not sure how a certain motion will be read by your audience, just test it out on a few people — show them what you're working on, and then ask them what emotion or personality *they* think the object has. If enough people recognize the mood that you want your animation to have, you've succeeded! If most people are confused or have very different responses, you probably need to simplify and clarify what you're trying to communicate. It's not likely that most people read that an object has slightly low self-esteem but is feeling optimistic. However, most people recognize movement consistent with extreme shyness or joy (or any other simple and exaggerated emotion).

Exaggeration is the foundation of the art of animation. Define the kind of movement that may communicate a particular emotion to your audience, and then see how far you can push it. In some cases, you may want very overt movements, and in other cases you may want more conservative or subtle movements, but by pushing the boundaries you can assess your options and find the right balance for a particular character or object.

Keeping Ideas Fresh

Some of the greatest modern works of art and music are based on the concept of permutation — the process of exploring all the possibilities within a specific, usually limited, group of elements. Permutation of a limited set of options can yield more surprising or unique results than unlimited options because forcing yourself to work within defined boundaries allows the content of your work to influence the final result in ways that you may not have previously considered.

For example, if you allow yourself to choose any colors from a full palette, this may seem very liberating. But the truth is you'll probably choose colors (or at least color combinations) that are familiar or comfortable for you, without even giving some new options a real chance. A much more inventive use of color can be achieved by forcing yourself to work with a truly random selection of colors (or to create an effective design with a more limited palette), you may be surprised by how well pink and brown go together, or by how much you can do with just a few colors. At the very least, experimenting with randomness or intentional limitation in a design can help open up new possibilities to keep your work from getting stale.

Manipulating Perception and Illusion

As you spend time analyzing motion in the real world and motion in more stylized animations, you will become more aware of some of the tricks that your eyes can play on you. Animators, like magicians, know how to take advantage of people's often-unreliable perception to create illusions. By understanding how the audience's eyes and minds put visual information together to "see" things, clever performers and designers are able to convince the audience that they're seeing something that may not actually be happening.

Another interesting phenomenon that makes an animator's job a little easier is referred to as *suspension of disbelief.* This is something you participate in whenever you really *want to believe* you're seeing something—children are often the best at this. When you push doubt aside, your eyes can be very forgiving as your brain works even harder to compensate for any gaps that may spoil the illusion or the spectacle that you want to believe in.

Some visual tricks in animation have been used so consistently that people now expect them as conventions, instead of seeing them as poorly rendered versions of a real-life motion. Most people recognize that a swirling cyclone of lines, with hands and feet or other objects occasionally popping out of it, is usually a fight. An oval blur or circular scribble at the bottom of a character's legs is not a cloud, but is, in fact, their feet spinning extra fast. Lines radiating from an object don't mean that it is spiky, but can instead mean that it is shiny or hot or even smelly. (Our favorite cartoon convention is the light bulb appearing over a character's head when they've suddenly gotten an idea.) Figure 10-1 shows a sequence by animator Richard Bazley that uses the simple but effective technique of blurred lines to simulate motion that is faster than the eye can see. This classic device can be modified to show rockets blasting off or wind rushing by or any object moving so quickly that it becomes a blur.

© 2002 Richard Bazley

Figure 10-1: Blurred lines effectively communicate the idea of wind or fast-moving elements rushing by in an animation.

On the CD-ROM We have included SWF files for most of the examples discussed in this chapter on the CD-ROM. Because the figures only show a few frames from an animation, you can get a better idea of how a motion plays by reviewing the files in the `ch10` folder of the CD-ROM. We thank animators Richard Bazley, Tom Winkler, and Sandro Corsaro for kindly sharing some of their expert examples with us.

There are innumerable examples of cartoon tricks, but the main thing to keep in mind is that you don't have to draw every detail of a movement to make it convincing. Instead, it's better to find ways that you can exaggerate the motion to make it more *expressive*. A well-executed illusion will save you time drawing and will also make your animation more fun to watch.

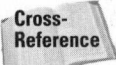

Cross-Reference Several examples of cartoon-motion tricks that you may be familiar with are discussed in Chapter 13, "Character Animation Techniques."

Viewpoint, framing, and depth

By thinking of the Flash stage area as a camera viewfinder rather than as a sketch pad, you'll be able to start crafting the various scenes in your animation to have some of the same expressive qualities as shots from a well-edited film. The ability to manipulate viewpoint is one of the strongest storytelling devices available to filmmakers and animators alike. Audiences have come to accept (and expect) seeing things from new angles and perspectives. Screen images have evolved from the basic wide-angle, theater-audience perspective of early film to the spinning, time-defying 360-degree *Matrix* views of action — don't be afraid to push your "camera" beyond the limits of normal human perception. Choosing how you will frame animation can have as much effect on your audience as the actual content in each scene. The traditional bird's-eye or mouse's-eye reconsideration of viewpoint is as effective in a digital design as it is in sketches or drawings. Try to use your content to inspire a framing strategy that adds both interest and meaning to your designs.

Depth is another key element to consider when composing a scene and choosing a viewpoint. Traditional animators are cautious to avoid awkward line intersections caused by overlapping elements. When the lines from two different elements bump into each other unintentionally, it can make a drawing look flat — this is known as a *tangent*. Tangents interrupt the illusion of depth created by scaling and layering elements in a composition. The main thing to avoid is an overly busy layout that may confuse the viewer's understanding of the picture plane. Try to keep elements that are meant to be behind or in front of other elements from looking as though they are joined or existing uncomfortably in the same space. Add a little more separation between elements to maintain visual clarity.

With careful planning, overlapping elements add depth to your designs. Notice in Figure 10-2 that the overlapping of the larger figure on the right with the border helps it jump into the foreground, whereas the overlapping of the smaller figure on the left makes it hard to tell which element is supposed to be in front.

Another common device used to add depth to a scene is to choose a viewpoint that enables you to add a natural frame or border around the image. By giving the viewer a reference point for where they are located in the plane of the image, you can exaggerate the feeling of depth. In drawing or painting, windows are often used to frame a view in the distance, but in animation you can find more original frames by choosing unique viewpoints. In a scene from Richard Bazley's animated film "The Journal of Edwin Carp," he uses the view from the back of a police van to add depth to a simple composition of two characters talking. Imagine how much flatter and less interesting the scene shown in Figure 10-3 would be if the characters were not framed by the outline of the van.

Figure 10-2: Overlapping should be planned (as shown in the example on the right) to avoid tangents that may flatten out the depth of the composition (as shown on the left).

© 2002 Richard Bazley

Figure 10-3: By using a clever but logical framing device, Richard Bazley has added a great deal of depth to this animated scene.

In another scene, Bazley uses the convention of a character running into the camera to enhance the feeling of panic as Edwin Carp's mother runs down a hallway. As shown in Figure 10-4, by using an extreme viewpoint, Bazley makes a simple scene more humorous and dramatic while still being very efficient with his artwork.

© 2002 Richard Bazley

Figure 10-4: By using an extreme viewpoint, an otherwise simple Motion tween can add drama and humor to a scene.

Anticipation

Anticipation is one of the primary techniques used to give animation personality and life. If you haven't spent much time studying animation, it's easy to overlook, but animation without anticipation appears robotic. Anticipation communicates the organic tension that exists in real life motion. Visualize a baseball pitcher winding up before he throws a fastball. If the ball just flew out of his hand without his body first coiling back to gather force, you wouldn't have the visual information to understand that the force was transferred from the pitcher's body to the ball. It would appear that the ball just suddenly had the ability to fly on its own. Figure 10-5 shows a classic example of anticipation as a character gathers force before launching into a run.

The principle of anticipation can be used to add extra life to almost any motion. Picture how an element would gather force before jumping into the main movement and then add a draw-ing or two to exaggerate that movement in your animation. Generally, anticipation can be communicated by reversing the main motion for a few frames before and after a tween (or frame-by-frame sequence). For example, if an item is going to move to the left, have it back up a little to the right first, and then after it stops moving to the left, have it stagger back a little to the right before reaching its final resting point. If an item is going to suddenly get larger, have it shrink just a little first before popping up to the larger size, and then allow the item to grow just a little beyond the final size so that it can appear to settle into the final size at the end of the animation. These inverted motions at the beginning and ending of an animated sequence are also referred to as *bounces,* because they can be compared to the motion of a ball bouncing. Depending on the effect you're trying to achieve, bounces can be very small and subtle or extremely exaggerated. Figure 10-6 illustrates how a small bounce can be added to give anticipation and follow-through to an animated head turn. This same kind of bounce works equally well on eye blinks and on almost any other small movement that needs a little extra life.

Figure 10-5: By winding up before taking off in a run, a character communicates the urgency and force behind his movement.

character designs © www.sandrocorsaro.com

Figure 10-6: Subtle bounces add anticipation and follow-through to head turns and other movements.

Although you may not at first be conscious of these extra movements when you watch a cartoon, it is one of the conventions that an audience associates with polished, professional animation. If you start to watch carefully for anticipation and follow-through motions, you'll see them on nearly every movement in well-crafted animations.

Secondary motion

Of course, some items don't need to bounce like a ball, but instead should flap or float as they move. It's still helpful to keep the pattern of a bounce in mind, but the modified patterns that you apply to items to visually show the forces of acceleration or gravity in motion is called *overlapping action*. A single object or character can have multiple overlapping actions — overlapping action added to smaller details of an item are sometimes called *secondary motion*. After you've planned the basic motion pattern of your main element, consider how you may add life and detail to your animation with overlapping action and secondary motion.

Figure 10-7 shows an example of an animation with overlapping action added to a character's belly as he runs. Secondary motion has been added by also animating the character's hat with overlapping action. The combination of these smaller motion patterns with the pattern of the basic run cycle makes the animation dynamic and gives the character personality.

Figure 10-7: Overlapping action and secondary motion add life and personality to animation.

Expert animator Richard Bazley provided suggestions for efficient and engaging animation in a tutorial he contributed to the *Macromedia Flash MX Bible.* This tutorial is archived online for readers who wish to learn more about specialized animation techniques. Go to www. flashsupport.com/archive. One of the things you will notice about his work is that he often adds frame-by-frame secondary motion to make simple tweened animation more dynamic and lifelike.

Understanding the Laws of Nature

Depending on your learning style, you may find it easier to simply observe and copy patterns of movement or to analyze the underlying principles of force that cause these patterns. Either approach can be effective. Even if you're more of a visual person than a theory-oriented person (as many animators are), an overview of some of the basic principles of physics can help to give you a framework for understanding the limitless variations of animated motion. The stylized interpretations of movement found in motion graphics and cartoons often deny the laws of nature—that's what makes them so entertaining. However, if you don't know the basic physics that dictate motion in reality, it can be more difficult to extrapolate convincing motion to fantastic lengths.

Advanced interactive motion can be designed using physics formulas to define the behavior of objects controlled with ActionScript. Although the math may look a little bit intimidating at first, it's often easier to understand when you can get visual feedback on how the numbers directly affect motion patterns. In fact, more than a few top designers claim to be math-impaired, but the beauty of motion controlled by numbers has given them the incentive to learn (or relearn) some of those scary calculus and physics equations. Spending a little time polishing up your math skills can enable you to efficiently script realistic, organic motion that would be insanely time-consuming or even impossible to render manually. Even if you never intend to use ActionScript to define the patterns of motion in your animations, a basic understanding of how physics and math can be used to calculate motion makes it much easier to plot movement and plan your drawings. Math and physics, as with color and type, are a powerful part of the vocabulary of motion graphics. Regardless of how you choose to apply them, these principles can be helpful for planning and modifying animation.

Almost all animated motion can be analyzed or designed using Newton's Laws. If you sat through a science class in high school, these scientific descriptions of how objects interact with force will sound familiar. Of course, in animation you aren't required to obey these laws. In fact, you'll probably create more interesting animations by pushing these laws to the limits or even by inverting them to create objects with unexpected behavior.

Law #1: Inertia

Objects that are at rest will stay at rest and objects in motion will stay in motion unless acted upon by an unbalanced force. In animation terms, objects should show a change in force if they're going to have a change in motion. This is communicated visually with anticipation and with overlapping actions, as described earlier in this chapter. Most animation seems much more lifelike with forgiving transitions. Enable objects to ease in and out of motion and to settle into new positions in your composition. Unless you want them to appear robotic, objects don't just change behavior suddenly without showing some anticipation and delayed secondary animation. You can add an element of surprise to an object's movement by intentionally disregarding inertia. For example, if an object stops cold without any visual indication of a change in force, it will appear jarring and hard, or if a very small object takes a long time to accelerate it will seem hesitant.

Law #2: Acceleration

The acceleration of an object as produced by a net force is directly proportional to the magnitude of the net force, in the same direction as the net force, and inversely proportional to the mass of the object. In animation terms, speed is dependent on a combination of mass and force; increasing force increases speed, whereas increasing mass decreases speed. An important related concept is *terminal velocity*. Although most people have heard this term, not everyone can explain what it means. Basically, once an item is falling fast enough for air resistance to be strong enough to prevent gravity from increasing the speed, then it has reached terminal velocity or the maximum speed of its fall. Objects with greater mass take longer to reach terminal velocity so they accelerate for longer, generally hitting the ground while still accelerating. An object with less mass quickly reaches terminal velocity and appears to float to the ground, because it doesn't gain any more speed. Figure 10-8 shows an animation of the classic acceleration test — two objects dropped from the same height.

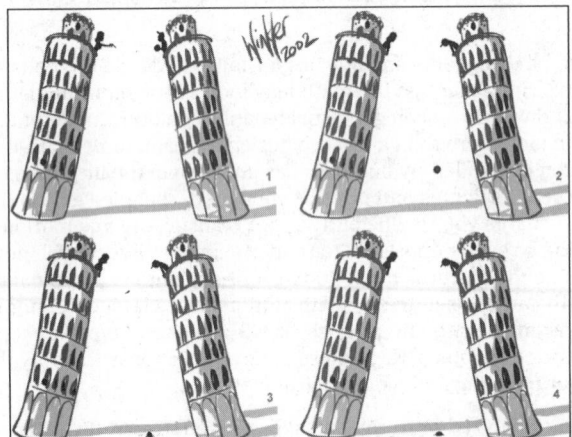

Figure 10-8: Acceleration is determined by mass, and objects with more mass take longer to reach terminal velocity.

By modifying the principles of acceleration, you can create whimsical environments where cannonballs might float and feathers crash to the ground (or any other variation you can think of).

Law #3: Action/reaction force pairs

This is the most commonly quoted of Newton's Laws: "For every action there is an equal and opposite reaction." Although this law is often used as a metaphor for human behavior, it was originally intended to explain how forces interact and affect objects. This is the law that explains how far backwards a character may fall when pulling on a rope that breaks. The force is directed along the rope and acts equally on objects at either end of the rope — the end result is that a character literally pushes himself backwards by pulling on the rope, as shown in Figure 10-9.

This is also the law that explains why a ball bounces back into the air when it strikes the ground. If there weren't any gravity or friction acting on the ball, it would bounce back to the exact height that it originally fell from. The actual result is that the ball reaches only a percentage of its original height with each bounce; this percentage depends on how hard the surface is and how heavy and/or bouncy the ball is. You can plan a realistic series of bounces by using a consistent percentage to calculate the descending height of each bounce. The bounce shown in Figure 10-10 was calculated by using a multiple of 0.5 (or 1/2) for the distance traveled in each bounce.

Figure 10-9: The force of pulling on a rope causes the character to fly backward when the rope breaks.

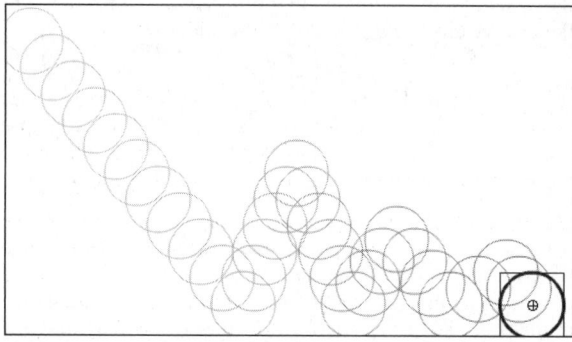

Figure 10-10: A starting pattern for a bounce can be plotted using a consistent multiple to calculate the height of each bounce.

On the CD-ROM

This bounce will be much improved by adding some easing to make the acceleration more realistic. To see the final result animated, open the `bounce50percent.swf` file in the `ch10` folder of this book's CD-ROM. Ideally, a convincing bounce also includes some *stretch 'n squash*—one of the most common animation tricks used to make motion look more realistic. This is discussed in more detail in Chapter 13, "Character Animation Techniques."

If you're interested in exploring the formulas for more advanced motion patterns, any basic physics textbook will help you get started. Two useful sources that we recommend for motion designers are:

✦ *Physics for Game Developers,* by David M. Bourg (O'Reilly & Associates, 2001)

✦ Jack's Page, a Web site created by physics teacher Jack Orb to provide information on basic physics and optics for computer-rendered graphics (with sample JavaScript): `www.kw.igs.net/~jackord/j6.html#p1`

We'd like to know what you thought about this chapter. Visit `www.flashsupport.com/feedback` to fill out an online form with your comments.

Summary

✦ To engage an audience, it's important for motion to have meaning. Meaning is derived when an animation includes visual cues that are part of our common vocabulary.

✦ Motion should support the underlying concept and content of your project. If motion is simply added as decoration without having some connection to the ideas in the content, it distracts from your design instead of enhancing it.

✦ Motion can communicate mood, emotion, and personality as effectively as text or color. Although the meaning of certain styles of motion can have a different personal or cultural impact, the way that core emotions are linked to styles of motion is remarkably similar for most people.

✦ To convey a strong message or establish a convincing mood, you must first evaluate the variables and then make consistent design choices to support your original concept.

✦ Careful observation and documentation of motion in daily life will help you to build a reference library to draw from when creating animation. Exaggeration and interpretation are crucial for developing a personal style. However, your animation will not be convincing unless you can build on a core understanding of motion in the real world.

✦ There are many useful tricks or conventions that you can learn to give your animation a more professional look. Overlapping action and secondary motion add life and personality to basic animated movements. Anticipation and follow-through also help to make an animation more convincing and entertaining to watch. Without these finishing touches, animation appears flat and lifeless no matter how many tweens you use.

✦ Physics equations can be invaluable for designing advanced motion patterns. Even if you don't have a propensity for numbers, spending some time exploring how basic equations explain force makes it easier to analyze and recreate organic motion. A little math and science combined with your graphics can help to create magic.

✦   ✦   ✦

Timeline Animation and Effects

I n this chapter, we discuss the basic methods and tools used to create animations in Flash. Animation is the process of creating the illusion of movement or change over time. Animation can be the movement of an item from one place to another, or it can be a change of color over a period of time. The change can also be a morph, or change, from one shape to another. Any change of either position or appearance that occurs over time is animation. In Flash, changing the contents of successive frames (over a period of time) creates animation. This can include any or all of the changes mentioned previously, in any combination.

Basic Methods of Flash Animation

In Flash, there are three basic methods of animation:

+ **Frame-by-frame animation** is achieved by manually changing the individual contents of each of any number of successive keyframes.

+ **Tweened animation** is achieved by defining the contents of the start and end points of an animation (with keyframes) and allowing Flash to interpolate the contents of the frames in between. There are two kinds of tweening in Flash:

  • Shape tweening

  • Motion tweening

+ **Timeline Effects** are a new Flash MX 2004 feature. Timeline Effects give you "automated" animation and visual effects that can be applied to shapes or symbols. Timeline Effects are created by prebuilt scripts that you can control by choosing settings in a preview dialog box before the Effect is rendered. After you choose settings and apply an Effect, Flash generates Graphic symbols and adds a new layer to the Timeline to hold the frames needed to display the Effect. You don't even have to make any keyframes!

There's a growing trend among advanced Flash developers to animate almost exclusively by controlling Movie Clips with ActionScript. Although this might seem intimidating to illustrators or animators who are more comfortable using analog tools, this programmatic approach to creating motion (and even artwork) dynamically makes sense. After all, computer animation is the art of orchestrating items according to various properties over time — and in the digital realm numbers describe all properties, even color. The Timeline Effects feature of Flash MX 2004 is a big step toward making this type of authoring more accessible. Coders now have an easy way to distribute or reuse scripted animation and effects and designers can take advantage of these without having to learn how to write or edit advanced ActionScript.

New Feature

Although the methods for authoring custom Timeline Effects are beyond the scope of this book, the basic process for adding and using a custom Timeline Effect is described later in this chapter. In a quick tutorial we'll show you how to install and use Samuel Wan's "Jitter" Effect. We look forward to seeing many other creative and useful Effects from Flash developers. The Timeline Effects shipping with Flash MX 2004 are only the beginning.

Flash components and Timeline Effects make it easier than ever for beginning programmers to integrate ActionScripted elements into Flash projects. But, before you jump into scripted animation, it helps to know how to animate on the Main Timeline with simple groups and graphics.

Cross-Reference

If you need to review the features of Flash timelines, please refer to Chapter 4, "Interface Fundamentals." The characteristics and uses of the various symbol types in Flash are described in Chapter 6, "Symbols, Instances, and the Library."

Frame-by-Frame Animation

The most basic form of animation is frame-by-frame animation. Because frame-by-frame animation employs unique drawings in each frame, it's ideal for complex animations that require subtle changes — for example, facial expressions. However, frame-by-frame animation also has its drawbacks. It can be very tedious and time-consuming to draw unique art for each frame of the animation. Moreover, all those unique drawings contribute to a larger file size. In Flash, a frame with unique art is called a *keyframe*. As shown in Figure 11-1, frame-by-frame animation requires a unique drawing for every movement or change, which makes nearly every frame a keyframe.

Figure 11-1: When you use keyframes to gradually add to the artwork, the text appears to be written out letter by letter in the final animation.

The example shown in Figure 11-1 (`keyframeText.swf`) was created by inserting keyframes (F6) with the same text repeated in every frame and then working backwards to erase the letters in sequential keyframes. In the final effect, the text appears letter by letter until the whole word is written out in keyframe 10. This process of modifying your original artwork to create a sequence is one use of frame-by-frame animation. Another approach is to create completely unique artwork in a series of blank keyframes (F7).

As shown in Figure 11-2, the changes in the lines from frame to frame can add a lot more motion to the final animation. If you are a skilled illustrator you will be able to keep enough consistency from keyframe to keyframe that it will seem to be the same shape or figure moving to a new position. If you are an aspiring illustrator (like this author), you will end up with a lot more variation among your drawings. As long as you are not trying to get a very precise sequence, this variation can actually be a lot of fun to watch — every line will dance and move in your final animation. Keep in mind that you are not restricted to just one series of frames; you can keep adding elements with their own keyframe sequences on separate layers.

On the CD-ROM The source files for the examples in this section are included on the CD-ROM — they're in the Keyframe folder of the ch11 folder.

The images shown in Figure 11-2 are from the file `faceFramebyFrame.fla`. This sequence of drawings was originally done on top of a short video clip of a real person. If you're learning to draw motion, video can be a good starting point — place it in a guide layer so it won't add to the file size of your final movie. If you work in a loose style, the roughness of the individual traced drawings can add more life to the final animation.

Figure 11-2: A loosely sketched sequence can be paced by adding more "repeater" frames between the unique keyframe images.

Adding keyframes

To add a keyframe to the Timeline, select the frame that you would like to convert into a keyframe. Then do one of the following:

✦ Convert a frame into a keyframe:

  • Right-click (or Control+click on Mac) the frame and select **Insert Keyframe** from the contextual menu.

  • Select Insert ➪ Timeline ➪ Keyframe from the application menu.

  • Press **F6** on the keyboard.

✦ Convert a frame into a *blank* keyframe:

- Right-click (or Control+click on Mac) the frame and select **Insert Blank Keyframe** from the contextual menu.

- Select Insert ⇨ Timeline ⇨ Blank Keyframe from the application menu.

- Press **F7** on the keyboard.

Note

If you select a frame in a span, the selected frame will be converted to a keyframe without adding to the length of the span. If you insert a keyframe at the end of a span, the keyframe will add to the length of the sequence. If you convert a frame in a span to a blank keyframe, all content will be cleared from the keyframe and the following frames of the span.

Tip

If you need to make a sequence of keyframes, but you would rather not have to press F6 or F7 repeatedly to create individual keyframes, you can select a range of frames and use the Modify ⇨ Timeline ⇨ Convert to Keyframes (F6) or Modify ⇨ Timeline ⇨ Convert to Blank Keyframes (F7) command to quickly convert all selected frames to keyframes or blank keyframes.

Creating frame-by-frame animation

The basic steps for creating a frame-by-frame animation are as follows:

1. Start by selecting the frame in which you'd like your frame-by-frame animation to begin.

2. If it's not already a keyframe, use Insert ⇨ Timeline ⇨ Keyframe (F6) to convert it.

3. Then either draw or import the first image for your sequence into this keyframe. Wherever possible, use symbols and flip, rotate, or otherwise manipulate them for reuse to economize on file size.

4. Select the next frame and either carry the artwork from the previous keyframe forward for modification by adding a keyframe (F6), or, if you want to create a completely new image from scratch or place an imported image, make the next keyframe a blank keyframe (F7).

5. Continue to add keyframes and change the contents of each keyframe until you've completed the animation. Finally, play back your animation by returning to the first keyframe and then selecting Control ⇨ Play from the application menu (Enter or Return key), or preview the animation in the test movie environment by choosing Control ⇨ Test Movie (Ctrl+Enter or ⌘+Return).

Modifying Multiframe Sequences

To control the pacing of your animation, you can add more frames (F5) between the keyframes, or add more keyframed (F7) images to the sequence to extend its length. Adding more frames between keyframes will "hold" or pause the animation, until the Playhead hits the next keyframe with changed content. In the example shown in Figure 11-2, the face holds on some frames while the butterfly continues to move in keyframed drawings on its own layer. To speed up (or shorten) animation you can remove frames (Shift+F5) or keyframes (Shift+F6) to shorten the sequence. You can make changes in the length of a span by selecting a frame in the span that you want to modify and using the application menu commands (or shortcut keys), or you can simply drag the endframe of the span to change its position on the Timeline.

Tip   If you drag the endframe of a span to a new position, Flash will automatically insert a new keyframe in the endframe's original location. If you want to change the length of a span without adding more keyframes, hold down the Ctrl or ⌘ key while clicking and dragging the endframe to a new position.

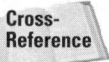

Cross-Reference   For a review of the methods used to edit frames and keyframes, refer to Chapter 4, "Interface Fundamentals."

Inserting more frames does work to slow down an animated sequence, but generally if you insert more than two frames between keyframes the movement will be interrupted and the animation will start to look too choppy. Try adding more keyframes to the sequence with very subtle change to the content in each keyframe if you want to create a slower, smoother animation.

By default Flash will loop the content on your Timeline, so if you want a sequence to be repeated, you don't need to draw it over and over again. If you notice that your animation disappears before it loops to play again, check to make sure that there are no extra empty frames at the end of the sequence, or that the endframe of one of your sequences is not further down the Timeline than the endframe of the element that disappears. Although you won't see anything on the Stage in these frames, Flash will still play those frames if they exist on the Timeline. Obviously, blank frames can be used in an animation whenever you want to empty the Stage — either as a pause between sequences or to create the illusion that your artwork has disappeared.

Frame Rate and Animation Timing

An underlying factor that will affect the playback of all animation is the project frame rate. The frame rate is displayed in the Document Properties dialog box (Modify ➪ Document) or in the Property inspector if you click in the Document window of an open file without selecting any items on the Stage. The default setting is 12 frames per second (fps), but you can adjust the frame rate of a project file at any time. The allowable frame rate range is between 0.01 and 120 fps. The most commonly used range is somewhere between 12 fps (for most Web sites and for low-bandwidth animation) and 24 fps (for subtle animation and complex effects intended for broadcast).

It might seem like a good idea to push the frame rate higher to get smoother-looking animation, but the reality of Web delivery is that you can't be sure that your audience will have the bandwidth or the processor speed to play back the animation as you intended. There is nothing worse than seeing your gorgeous animation stuttering and dropping frames. In most cases, 12 fps provides all the momentum you need to drive your animation and effects — you can create quick cuts, smooth fades or anything in between, just by adjusting your artwork and pacing your frames appropriately.

Although you can always change the frame rate after you've authored a file, it makes sense to decide on a final frame rate *before* you start designing and testing complex animation sequences. Re-timing animation by inserting or removing frames and changing the duration of tweens is always an option, but it is painful to go back and try to match the original pacing of a file that was created using a different frame rate.

To illustrate how blank frames play back in an animation, we've created a silly example with a face and a rectangle that persist in every frame and some text that only exists on some frames (see Figure 11-3).

Figure 11-3: You can insert blank keyframes to clear artwork from the Stage. Remember that the Playhead will continue along the Timeline if there are frames on any one of the layers, even if the artwork on other layers is no longer present.

Onion skinning

Traditional animators worked on layers of transparent cels using a light table. This made it possible for them to create consistent drawings and to plan the pacing of movement in a sequence of cels. As you move from keyframe to keyframe in Flash, you might feel that you are working blind because you can only see the artwork on the current frame. If you are creating artwork for a sequence of related keyframes, it is crucial to have some visual indication or "map" of the changes from frame to frame. Fortunately Flash has an effective digital version of the traditional light table—this handy feature is called *Onion skinning*. In Flash, Onion skinning allows you to see several frames of your artwork displayed at one time. The Onion markers on the Timeline determine the number of frames that are visible. Onion skinning can be turned on or off whenever you need it using the toggle buttons at the bottom of the Timeline window. As shown in Figure 11-4, there are actually two options for Onion skinning: **Onion Skin** or **Onion Skin Outlines**.

Tip   Layers that are locked will not be visible when Onion skinning is active.

The current frame (indicated by the position of the Playhead) is displayed at 100 percent opacity, while the other frames in the sequence are displayed at a slightly reduced opacity or as outlines, depending on the Onion Skin button you have selected.

Tip   If you don't like the color of the outlines that display when you turn on Onion Skin Outlines, you can change the setting for Outline color in the Layer Properties dialog box. (Double-click the layer icon or choose **Properties** from the contextual menu.)

Figure 11-4: Onion Skin will show grayed-out or ghosted artwork on multiple frames, while **Onion Skin Outlines** will show colored outlines of the artwork on multiple frames. It's hard to see the "color" here, but notice that the lines are thinner with Onion Skin Outlines (right).

The number of frames that are included in the Onion skin display can be controlled either by choosing a setting from the **Modify Onion Markers** menu (shown in Figure 11-5), or by selecting the round marker handles with the Selection tool and sliding them to a new position on the Timeline. The number of frames that you select from the Modify menu will be shown before and after the current frame—so in our example with **Onion 2** selected, the Onion markers actually span five frames (the current frame, plus two frames on each side).

Figure 11-5: You can control the number of frames visible when Onion skinning is turned on with the **Modify Onion Markers** menu, or by dragging the Onion skin markers to a new position on the Timeline.

Editing multiple frames

One of the drawbacks of manually creating unique artwork on every frame is that changes can be very time-consuming. If you decide to change the color or size of an element or perhaps edit out a feature of your artwork, repeating this edit on every frame of a sequence will be tedious and labor-intensive.

New Feature The Find and Replace panel (Edit ⇨ Find and Replace) makes it much easier to replace colors and text in Flash MX 2004, but erasing or moving an element that appears in a multiframe sequence can still be time-consuming.

Fortunately, Flash provides a shortcut that can make repeated edits on multiple frames much more efficient. **Edit Multiple Frames** allows you to see and select items on multiple frames for simultaneous modification. As shown in Figure 11-6, the Edit Multiple Frames option is turned on with the toggle button at the top of the Document window. When this feature is active you can use any of the selection methods (Selection tool, Lasso, application menu, or shortcut keys) to select the parts of your artwork that you wish to move, modify or delete. This feature is especially helpful for edits that need to be consistent from frame to frame, such as moving all of your artwork to a new position in your layout.

Tip Using the Lock feature to protect layers that you don't want to edit makes it much easier to select and edit multiple elements on specific layers. If you use the Lasso tool or the Selection tool to drag-select items on the Stage, only items on unlocked layers will be included in your selection.

Figure 11-6: With Edit Multiple Frames toggled on, you can select elements on individual keyframes in a sequence (left) to be modified simultaneously (right).

The frames visible and available for selection are marked by a gray span on the Timeline with start and end handles. The number of frames included in the span can be adjusted with the Selection tool by clicking and dragging the round handles on the Timeline to a new position.

Using Tweens for Animation

Tweening is one of the most powerful Flash animation features. Whether you are creating character animation or motion graphics, or even the most basic button effect, you will find tweening indispensable. Once you have planned your animation and created the initial artwork, you can use Flash tweening to generate the transitional images between one keyframe and another. This is the tool that makes it possible for an artist to quickly generate smooth, precise animation—without spending half their life manually filling in unique graphics on every frame. Instead, you can establish a beginning point and an end point, and only make drawings, or key art, for each of those points. Then you let Flash interpolate and render, or *tween,* the changes between the keyframes. Tweening can be used to render changes in size, shape, color, position, and rotation. Unlike Timeline Effects, manual tweens are limited only by your imagination—anything is possible with the keyframed artwork that you set up.

Tweening also minimizes file size because you don't have to include unique information on each frame in the animation. Because you define the contents of the frames at the beginning and end point (keyframes), Flash has to save only those graphics, plus the values needed to make the *changes* on the frames in between. Basically, Flash has to store only the difference between the beginning frame and the endframe so that the images on the frames in between can be calculated and rendered.

The other significant benefit of using tweens to generate an animated sequence is that if you want to make a change, you only need to modify the beginning or end point and Flash will instantly update the images in between. Two kinds of tweens can be created in Flash—shape tweens and Motion tweens—each applied for specific purposes. Both tween types are represented on the Timeline by a colored fill with a continuous arrow on the span between the start keyframe and the end keyframe of the animation. Shape tweens are represented by a green fill and Motion tweens by a blue fill. If a tween is incomplete, either because the wrong tween type has been applied or because information on one of the defining keyframes is missing, the continuous arrow will be replaced with a dashed line.

The type of tween that you want to apply is selected from the Tween menu in the Property inspector. As shown in Figure 11-7, the options available for controlling the playback of the final tween depend on the type of tween selected.

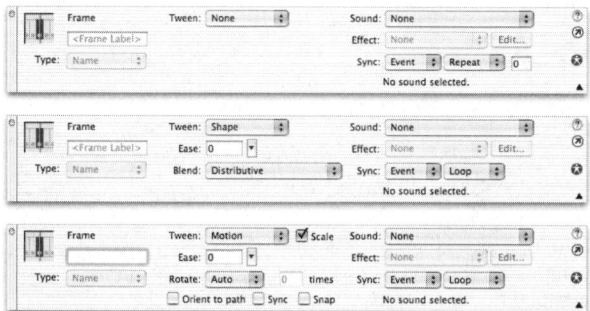

Figure 11-7: When you specify a tween type in the Property inspector, the relevant options for controlling the tween appear.

Shape tweening

Shape tweening is useful for morphing basic shapes — for example turning a square into a circle, or animating the drawing of a line by tweening from a dot to a finished line. Flash can only shape tween primitive *shapes,* so don't even try to shape tween a group, symbol, or editable text — it won't work. You can tween multiple shapes on one layer, but for the sake of organization and animation control, it's best to put each shape on its own layer. This allows you to adjust the speed and length of Shape tweens individually and also makes it much easier to figure out what's going on if you need to edit the file later.

On the CD-ROM

The `smileTween.fla` example file is located on the CD-ROM in the `ShapeTween` subfolder of the `ch11` folder.

Figure 11-8 shows an animated "smile" created by interpolating the graphics between a dot and a curved stroke with a Shape tween. Flash nimbly handles this simple transition, rendering a gradually extending line on the frames between the dot of the pursed mouth and the final curve of the smile.

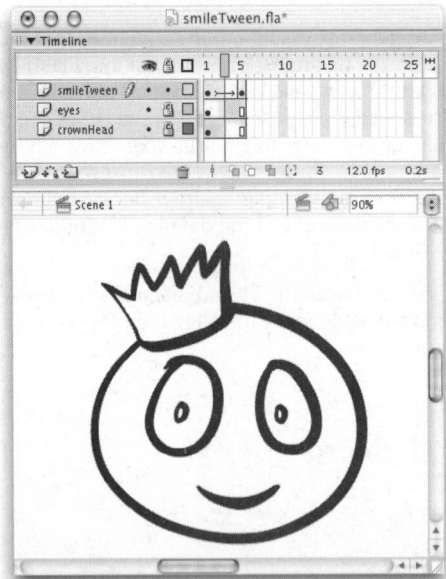

Figure 11-8: After a dot is drawn on keyframe 1 and an arc is drawn on keyframe 5, a Shape tween is applied to render the shapes on the frames in the span between — creating an animation.

Here are the steps for creating a Shape tween:

1. Select the frame in which you'd like to start the animation. If it's not already a keyframe, convert it to one (F6).

2. Then draw your starting image on the Stage (see Figure 11-9). Always remember that Shape tweening only works with *shapes* — not groups, symbols, or editable text. To Shape tween these items, you first need to break them into shapes (Modify ⇨ Break Apart).

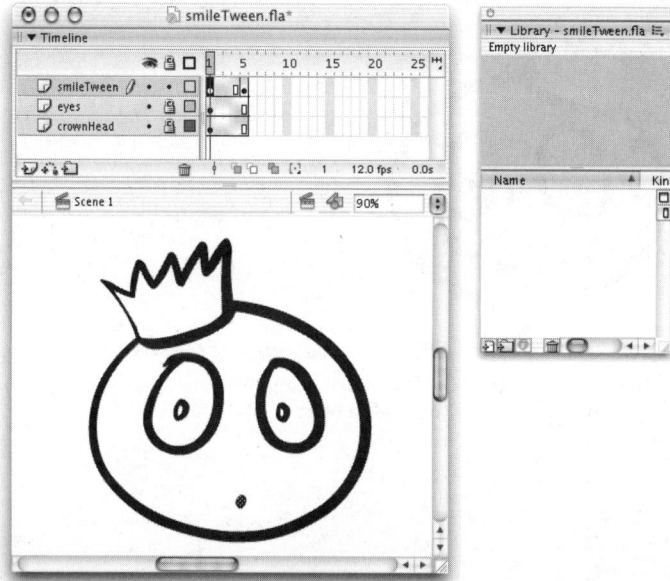

Figure 11-9: The contents of the first keyframe in your span will define the starting point for the Shape tween.

3. Next, insert a keyframe (F6) on the Timeline where you want the animation to end and modify the artwork to define the end point of the animation (see Figure 11-10). If you want to create the artwork in the final frame from scratch then insert a blank keyframe (F7) instead of a keyframe that includes the artwork from the first keyframe.

4. Select the keyframe at the beginning of the span that you want to interpolate with a Shape tween. Remember that results will be easiest to control and modify if you tween only one shape per layer.

5. Open the Property inspector if it is not already available by selecting Window ⇨ Properties from the application menu (Ctrl+F3 or ⌘+F3), as shown in Figure 11-11.

6. Choose **Shape** from the **Tween** drop-down menu. The span between the start keyframe and the end keyframe of your animation will display with a green fill and an arrow to indicate that a Shape tween has been applied.

Figure 11-10: The contents of the final keyframe after your span will define the ending point for the Shape tween.

Figure 11-11: On the first keyframe, specify Shape as the tween type with the Property inspector Tween menu

7. As shown previously in Figure 11-7, the Property inspector panel updates to present two options for modifying the Shape tween:

   - Set the **Ease** slider if you want to vary the rate or speed of the animation. This is useful if you want to create the effect of acceleration or deceleration. If you want your animation to start slowly and progressively speed up, push the slider down to add an Ease In. This will cause **In** to display adjacent to the slider and will update the value field with a negative number (between –1 and –100). For an animation that starts fast and progressively slows, push the slider up to add an Ease Out. The word **Out** will appear and a positive number (between 1 and 100) will display in the value field. If you want the rate of your animation to stay constant, leave the slider in the middle (0). You can also type any number between –100 and 100 directly into the Ease value field.

   - Select a **Blend** type: **Distributive** blending creates smoother interpolated shapes, whereas **Angular** blending creates interpolated shapes that preserve corners and straight lines. If your end points contain shapes with corners and lines, select **Angular** blending. Otherwise, use the default **Distributive** blending.

8. Preview the animation by selecting Control ➪ Play (Enter) from the application menu, or use Control ➪ Test Movie (Ctrl+Enter or ⌘+Return) to publish a an SWF file.

Note

If you accidentally assign the wrong tween type to the start keyframe of your animation or if you delete the artwork on the start or the end keyframes, you will notice that the arrow icon on the Timeline is replaced with a dashed line and a yellow warning icon appears in the Property inspector. This indicates that the tween is broken or incomplete. To restore the tween, it is usually best to select the first keyframe and choose **None** from the Tween menu in the Property inspector. Then check your Timeline and your artwork to make sure that you have shapes on both a beginning and an end keyframe for Flash to interpolate. When you think all the elements are in place, select the first keyframe and choose **Shape** from the Tween menu in the Property inspector to reapply the tween.

Adding Shape Hints

Because Flash calculates the simplest way to interpolate from one shape to another, you occasionally get unexpected results if the shapes are complex or extremely different from one another. Shape tweening becomes less reliable the more points there are to be calculated between the defined keyframes. In our example, we have added a keyframe at the end of the span with the eyes of the character changed from circles to stars. We want the animation to be a smooth transition from the rough circle to the star shape in each eye. As shown in Figure 11-12, a basic Shape tween results in some odd inbetween shapes.

One way of making the inbetween artwork more precise is to insert keyframes in the middle of the Shape tween so that you can manually adjust the shapes that Flash has generated. Another option that allows you to control a tween without modifying any artwork is to add *Shape Hints* for Flash to follow when rendering the inbetween shapes. Shape Hints allow you to specify points on a starting shape that should match with specified points on the final shape. This helps Flash to "understand" how the shapes are related and how the transitional images should be rendered. Compare Figure 11-12 with Figure 11-13 to see the improvement that Shape Hints can make in the precision of inbetween shapes.

Figure 11-12: When a Shape tween is added to create an animation from one keyframe to another, the transition artwork that Flash generates may not look how you expect it to.

On the CD-ROM

To compare the difference made by adding Shape Hints to the animation, open `eyeTween.fla` (or .swf) and `eyeTweenHints.fla` (or .swf) from the `ShapeTween` subfolder in the `ch11` folder on the CD-ROM.

Figure 11-13: Placing shapes on individual layers and adding Shape Hints to control the way that Flash renders inbetween shapes improves the precision of Shape tweens.

Caution

When copying and pasting a span of frames into a new Timeline — such as from the Main Timeline to a Movie Clip timeline — Flash disconnects the Shape Hints from the shape. When pasting is confined to a single timeline, hints stay as you placed them.

Shape Hints can only be added to artwork on keyframes that define the beginning and ending points of a Shape tween. To add Shape Hints to the artwork in a Shape tween, follow these steps after you have created a basic Shape tween:

1. Begin by selecting a shape on the starting keyframe and choosing Modify ⇨ Shape ⇨ Add Shape Hint from the application menu (Shift+Ctrl+H or Shift+⌘+H).

2. Flash places a small red circle, labeled with a letter *a*, onto the Stage — this is your first Shape Hint. Additional Hints can be added and they will also be identified alphabetically.

3. To specify a point on your starting shape, use the Selection tool to select and move the first Hint (a) — position it on an area of the shape (for example, a corner or a curve) that you want to match up with an area on the final shape, as shown in Figure 11-14.

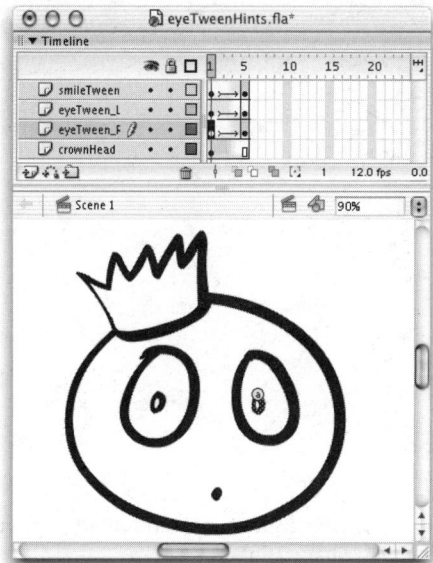

Figure 11-14: Shape Hints positioned on a shape in the starting keyframe for a Shape tween

4. When you move the Playhead to the final keyframe of your Shape tween, you will see a lettered Hint that matches the one that was placed on the starting keyframe. Position this Hint with the Arrow key so that it marks the area of the final shape that should match up with the area specified on the starting shape. The Hint will only be recognized by Flash if it attaches correctly to the artwork. You will know that your Hints are positioned properly when their fill color changes from red to green on the final keyframe (see Figure 11-15) and from red to yellow on the starting keyframe.

5. Preview the new inbetween shapes by *scrubbing* the Timeline (dragging the Playhead with the Selection tool to review frames in the tweened sequence.).

6. Continue to add or reposition Hints until Flash renders the inbetween shapes correctly.

7. To remove an individual Hint, drag it off the Stage with the Selection tool. To remove all Hints from an active keyframe, select Modify ➪ Shape ➪ Remove All Hints from the application menu. A shortcut is to right-click (Control+click on Mac) any of the Hints to invoke the contextual menu, as shown in Figure 11-16, for these and other options as you are working.

Tip

If the Shape Hints are not visible after you have placed them, make sure that the Show All Hints option in the contextual menu is toggled on, or use the application menu to select View ➪ Show Shape Hints (Alt+Ctrl+H or Option+⌘+H) — this option is only available if the layer and keyframe that contain the Hints is currently active.

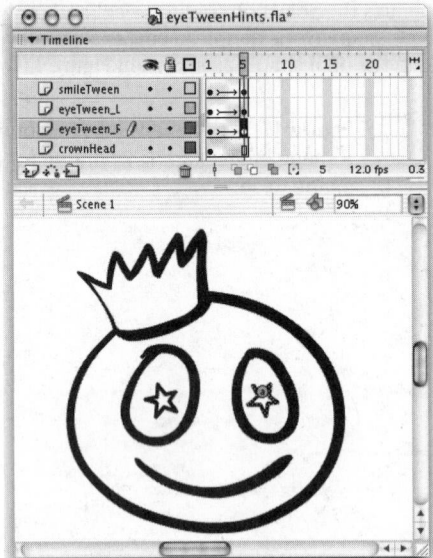

Figure 11-15: Shape Hints aligned to points on a shape in the ending keyframe of the tween

Figure 11-16: The contextual menu offers some options for working with Shape Hints.

Motion tweening

Motion tweening is useful for animating groups, symbols, and editable text; however, it cannot be used to animate primitive shapes. As the name suggests, Motion tweening is applied to move an item from one place to another, but it's capable of much more. Motion tweening can also be used to animate the scale, skew, or rotation of items; as well as the color and transparency of a symbol.

Note   Motion tweening can only be applied to one item per layer — use multiple layers to Motion tween multiple items in the same span of the Timeline.

The pacing of a Motion tweened sequence can be modified at any point — simply insert a keyframe for each phase of the animation. In addition to the scale and Color effect settings applied directly to the symbol instance, the settings in the Property inspector that control Easing and rotation can be adjusted on each keyframe of a Motion tween. So, if you use a tween to move a symbol from frame 1 to frame 10 and stop the tween on frame 11, you can have the symbol sit still for 10 frames (no tween), and then start a new tween (of this same symbol on the same layer) with rotation or an alpha fade from frames 20 to 30. The possibilities are almost endless.

Like a Shape tween, a Motion tween is more efficient than frame-by-frame animation because it doesn't require unique content for each frame of animation. Yet it is *not* appropriate for all effects — sometimes you'll need to use either frame-by-frame animation or Shape tweening to create the kind of inbetweens you need in a sequence.

On the CD-ROM

Create your own file from scratch, or open `motionTween_start.fla` from the `MotionTween` subfolder of the `ch11` folder on the CD-ROM. To view the final animation, open `motionTween_final.fla` (or .swf) from the same location.

Here's how to create a Motion tween:

1. Select the frame in which you'd like to start your animation. If it's not already a keyframe, make it one by selecting Insert ⇨ Timeline ⇨ Keyframe (F6.)

2. Draw or import the image that you want to tween. Just remember that you can only Motion tween groups, symbols (including imported bitmaps — which are, by default, symbols), and editable text (a text block).

   • If you are using an image, group it or turn it into a symbol.

Cross-Reference

Refer to Chapter 6, "Symbols, Instances, and the Library," for a review of creating symbols.

   • If you already have the element as a symbol in your current Library, you can just drag an instance from the Library onto the Stage. Place each symbol that you want to animate on a separate layer, as shown in Figure 11-17.

   • If you are using editable text, you don't have to do anything — it's already an element that can be Motion tweened.

3. Select the frame where you want the tween to end and make it a keyframe by selecting Insert ⇨ Timeline ⇨ Keyframe (F6.)

4. Make any modifications to the symbols that you want animated on the beginning and end keyframes, as shown in Figure 11-18. Remember that you can move tweened elements, as well as scale, skew, and rotate them. If your end-point images are symbols, you can also use the Color Effect menu to modify Tint, Alpha, and Brightness.

Cross-Reference

Refer to Chapter 9, "Modifying Graphics," for a review of Color effects and other possible symbol modifications.

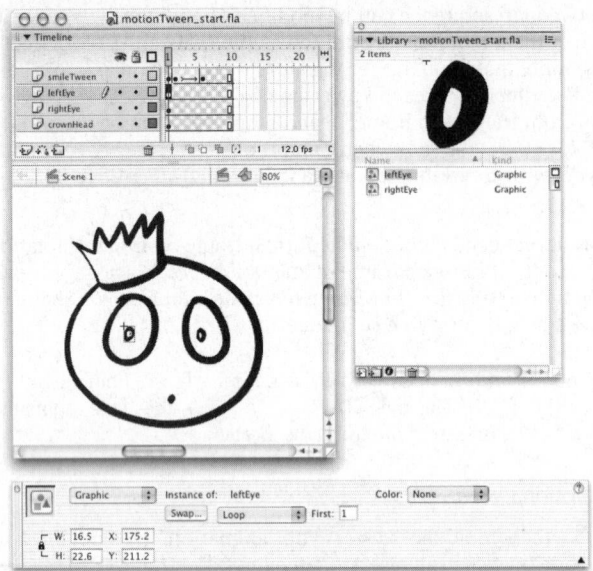

Figure 11-17: The artwork on the first keyframe of the span you want to Motion tween should be a text box, a group, or a symbol on its own layer.

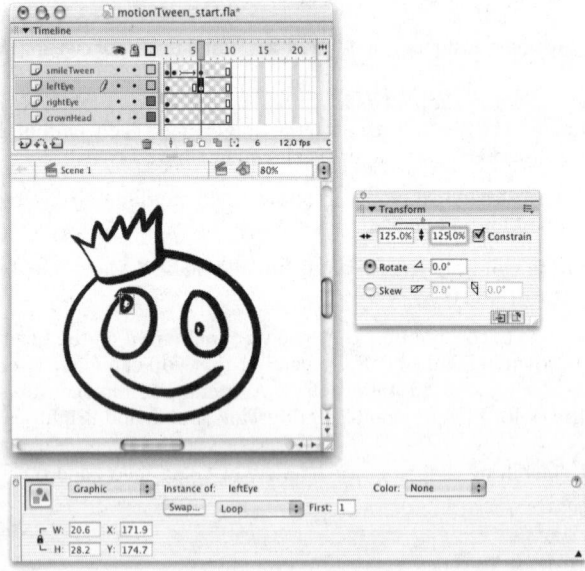

Figure 11-18: Modify the features of the symbol on the end keyframe that you want to interpolate with a Motion tween.

Read This Before Using Create Motion Tween

If you have not converted your artwork into symbols before using the Create Motion Tween command, Flash automatically converts any item in the selected keyframe into a symbol with the generic name of Tween followed by a number (Tween1, Tween2). Although this might seem like a handy shortcut, it actually creates a mess that you will need to clean up later.

Because the symbols are auto-created and named, you will not have the same control over how your Library is organized and how your artwork is optimized. It is much better to analyze the most efficient way to convert your artwork into symbols and to reuse those symbols as much as possible than to allow Flash to make generic symbols that may be redundant. As with all elements in your Flash project, it is also much more useful to assign meaningful names to your symbols that will help you navigate the project when you need to make edits.

Manually creating and naming your own symbols before assigning a tween to specific keyframes helps avoid redundant or confusing items being added to your document (.fla) Library. If you make a habit of using the Property inspector to assign tweens, you will always be reminded if you haven't converted an element into a symbol.

Tip   Alpha effects in Motion tweens will slow most fps (frames per second) settings. The only way to make sure that the fps is honored, no matter how intensive the animation might be, is to use a stream sync sound that loops over the course of any critical fps playback. For more on the relationship between streaming sounds and fps rate, see Chapter 15, "Adding Sound."

5. There are three different ways that you can apply a basic Motion tween to a span between two keyframes:

   - Select the beginning keyframe, and then open the Property inspector (Window ⇨ Properties) and use the Tween menu to specify a Motion tween.

   - Right-click (Control+click on Mac) any frame between the two keyframes and select **Create Motion Tween** from the contextual menu.

   - Select the beginning keyframe or any frame in the span and choose Insert ⇨ Timeline ⇨ Create Motion Tween from the application menu.

6. Select the first keyframe of your Motion tween and use the options in the Property inspector to add more control to the final tween, as shown in Figure 11-19.

   - **Rotate:** You can rotate tweened items using this option. Select a rotation type from the drop-down menu and then type the number of rotations in the value field. **Automatic** rotation rotates your item in the direction that requires the least amount of motion, while **Clockwise** and **Counterclockwise** rotate your item in the indicated direction. In both cases, the rotation will be completed as many times as you specify in the value field. If you type **0** in the entry field, or select **None** from the drop-down menu, no rotation will occur (other than rotation that has been applied to the symbol with the Transform panel).

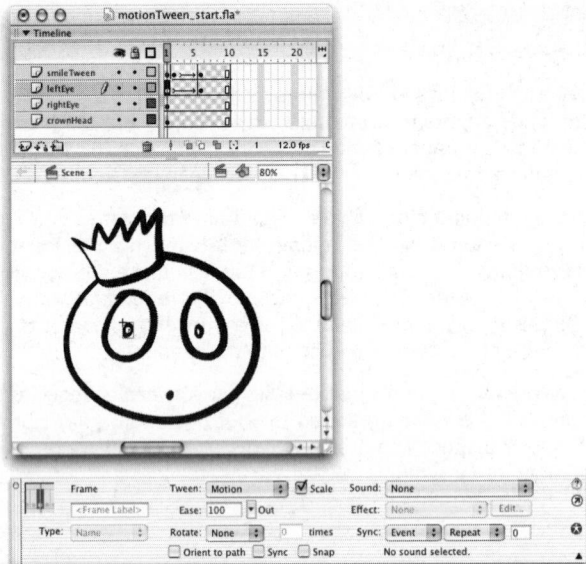

Figure 11-19: There are several options for Motion tweens available in the Property inspector.

- **Orient to path:** When your item follows a path (or Motion guide), turning this selection on forces the item to orient its movement to that path. We discuss paths in the next chapter.

- **Sync:** When this setting is activated on a tween, you can replace the symbol in the first keyframe and it will automatically be updated in the remaining frames and in any other synchronized keyframes that follow. This setting is also important if your animation is contained within a Graphic symbol. Flash recalculates the number of frames in a tween on a Graphic symbol's Timeline so that it matches the number of frames available on the Main Timeline. Sync ensures that your animation loops properly when the animated symbol is placed in the Main Timeline, even if the frame sequence in the Graphic symbol is not an even multiple of the number of frames assigned to the symbol in the Main Timeline.

Tip

You can tell if a tweened sequence is synchronized by observing that the vertical lines separating the keyframes from the span are not visible when this setting is applied.

- **Snap:** This option snaps your animated item into alignment with a Motion guide. Motion guides are discussed in Chapter 12.

7. Other elements can be Motion tweened on the same span of the Timeline, as long as they are on separate layers (see Figure 11-20). You can interpolate different features on each tween and also apply any control settings that you wish — Flash reads and renders the Motion tween on each layer independently.

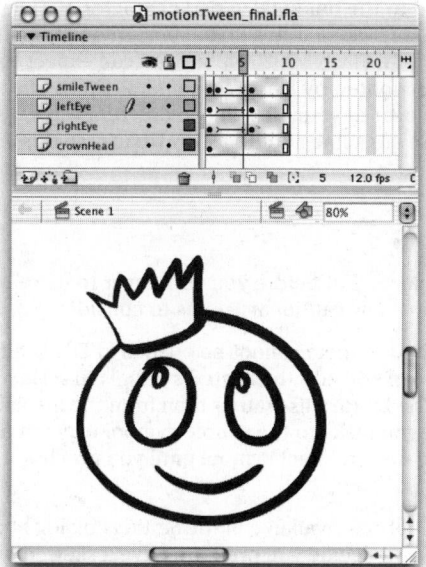

Figure 11-20: Multiple items can be animated simultaneously by creating tweens on individual layers.

 As with Shape tweens, the arrow icon on the Timeline span of your Motion tween will be replaced with a dashed line if the tween is broken or incomplete. A common mistake with Motion tweens is to try and animate multiple elements on the same layer. To restore the tween, it is usually best to select the first keyframe and choose **None** from the Tween menu in the Property inspector. Then check your Timeline and your artwork to make sure that you have only a single group or symbol (not a shape) on a layer with both a beginning and an end keyframe for Flash to interpolate. When you think all the elements are in place, select the first keyframe and chose **Motion** from the Tween menu in the Property inspector to reapply the tween.

Using Timeline Effects for Animation

The specific functionality of manual tweens and the differences between Shape tweens and Motion tweens are relatively easy to explain. Timeline Effects are a bit more of a muddle. They can be used for effects on static graphics or for adding multiframe animation. Some Timeline Effects can only be added to symbols, but most can be added to either shapes or symbols. By default, most Timeline Effects render as Graphic symbols on the Timeline, but if they're applied to a Movie Clip symbol they will inherit that behavior. The only definitive thing we can say about Timeline Effects is that they offer some very intriguing possibilities for non-coders to add more sophisticated effects to their projects. With prebuilt JavaScript-Flash code, Timeline Effects make it possible to select an item on the Stage and control its appearance and motion by simply making selections in a Settings dialog box. After you preview and apply your chosen settings, Flash automatically converts the selected item to a Graphic symbol and renders a nested symbol on the Stage and frames on the Timeline to hold the finished Effect or animation. Easy so far, right?

There are other special features that add to the uniquely varied character of Timeline Effects. Each Effect comes with different options that appear in a dialog box unique to that Effect. A basic set of Timeline Effects is included with Flash MX 2004, but you can expect to see many more custom Effects being made and distributed by Flash developers. These Effects may generate different symbol structures and appear in your Timeline in different ways. As discussed in Chapter 9, "Modifying Graphics," there are some additional drawbacks to this automated authoring process.

Timeline Effect limitations

You *can* do great things with Timeline Effects. But before you vow never to use a manual Motion tween again, we'd like to give you a few cautionary notes to consider:

✦ Symbols with Timeline Effects added to them cannot be opened in Edit mode without breaking the settings option. You can still edit the nested symbols in a Timeline Effect, but you have to open them from the Library list rather than from the instances on the Stage. Unfortunately, the changes you make to the source symbol may not always be carried over to all instances in the nested Effect symbol until you preview it again in the Settings dialog box.

✦ Practically, you are limited to the options available in the Settings dialog box for each Timeline Effect. So for example, if you decide you prefer to have a skewed drop shadow, you will either have to break the settings option to edit the symbols individually, or you'll have to make your own layered symbol instances.

✦ In order to layer multiple Timeline Effects (such as adding a fade Transition to an item with a Drop shadow), you have to manually nest the Timeline Effect Graphic symbols inside of other symbols.

✦ Timeline Effects are generally rendered as nested Graphic symbol structures. The benefit is that you can see animated Effects by scrubbing the Timeline. The drawback is that you will end up with redundant symbols in your Library if you apply a Timeline Effect to an existing symbol. Also, your animation will be tied to the Timeline unless you nest it inside a Movie Clip symbol.

✦ Timeline Effects add auto-named symbols and layers to your project file, which can make it harder to keep your naming systems consistent and meaningful.

✦ You *can* rename generic symbols and folders in your Library and layers in your Timeline that have been generated by a Timeline Effect. However, if you edit the settings on any of your Timeline Effects, these items will revert to the generic naming sequence.

✦ You must apply (or reapply) Behaviors *after* you have added Timeline Effects. Timeline Effects added to an item with an assigned Behavior will nullify the action controlled by the Behavior because it changes the symbol type of the item.

Now, if that wasn't enough to dissuade you from using Timeline Effects—and it shouldn't be, unless you are a symbol structure and naming purist—we'll move on to investigate some of the animated Timeline Effects that are included with Flash MX 2004.

Timeline Effect options

The Timeline Effects that ship with Flash MX 2004 are organized into three categories in the Timeline Effects menu (under **Insert** in the application menu or in the contextual menu for items selected on the Stage):

✦ **Assistants:** These Effects give you a more streamlined way to complete authoring tasks that could otherwise be accomplished using the Transform and Align panels with Color effects.

- **Copy to Grid:** Gives you the option to create multiple symbol instances and renders them in rows or columns on the Stage.

- **Distributed Duplicate:** Makes it possible to render multiple symbol instances, with changes in alpha or color and with consistent spacing between each instance.

✦ **Effects:** These Effects modify the graphic content of your original item.

- **Blur:** Adds something similar to an animated soften fill edges effect with settings for duration, scale, resolution, and direction. Could also be described as a "glow" or "drag" effect.

- **Drop shadow:** Adds a static duplicate "shadow" with settings for color, alpha and offset.

- **Expand:** This is hard to describe, but the best analogy I can give in print is filling a balloon with water. You can specify the direction and amount for an item to stretch and/or squash over a given span of frames.

- **Explode:** If you've been waiting to blow up some logos in Flash, now's your chance! You can specify the size and direction of the pieces and even how far and how fast they fly.

✦ **Transform/Transition:** These Effects are used to add animated changes to the display or position of your original item over a specified range of frames. The most subtle and flexible group of Effects, these are the two that I expect to use most often to save production time.

- **Transform:** Change position, scale, rotation, color, and/or alpha.

- **Transition:** Wipe and/or Fade an item in or out.

Cross-
Reference

The steps for applying static Timeline Effects to modify non-animated items are described in Chapter 9, "Modifying Graphics." The static Timeline Effects include those listed in the Assistants category, plus the Drop shadow Effect.

Applying an animated Timeline Effect

The specific result of frames and symbols rendered by different Timeline Effects will vary, but the steps for adding an Effect are consistent.

On the
CD-ROM

We have included examples of various Timeline Effects, including a Transition Effect applied to a bitmap image in the TimelineEffects subfolder of the ch11 folder on the CD-ROM.

To add an animated Timeline Effect to a shape or symbol, follow these steps:

1. Select an item on the Stage—it can be a shape or a symbol. In our example, we used an imported bitmap. As with Shape or Motion tweens, it is best to apply Effects to items that exist on their own layer.

Caution   Although you can select an item in the first keyframe of an existing Motion or Shape tween and apply a Timeline Effect to it, in most cases the tween will be broken when the Timeline Effect is rendered because the item will be moved to a new layer. As discussed later in this section, it is best to render the Timeline Effect on a separate timeline if you want to combine animation methods.

2. Use the Insert menu (or the contextual menu) to access **Timeline Effects**. Choose a category and select the Effect you want to apply. For this example, we'll apply the **Transition** Effect (as shown in Figure 11-21).

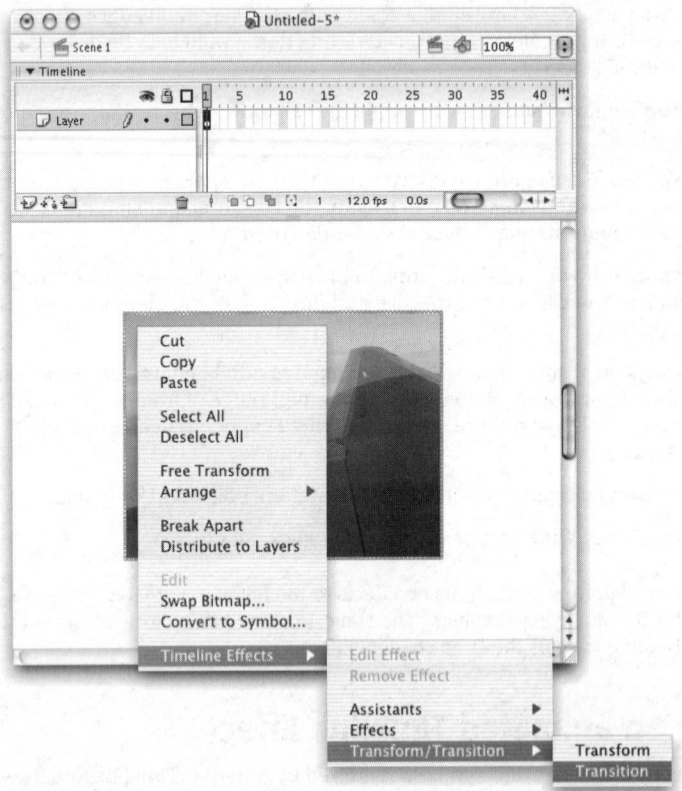

Figure 11-21: The various Timeline Effects that ship with Flash are organized in categories in the Timeline Effects menu.

3. In the Settings dialog box, a preview of the animation will be rendered with the default settings. Modify the settings and use the Update Preview button to test the result, until you achieve an effect that you like. (Our Transition example is shown in Figure 11-22.)

4. Click **OK** to close the Settings dialog box and render the Effect.

5. If you have applied a complex Timeline Effect, it may take a few seconds for Flash to render the symbols and insert the frames on your Timeline to hold the Effect.

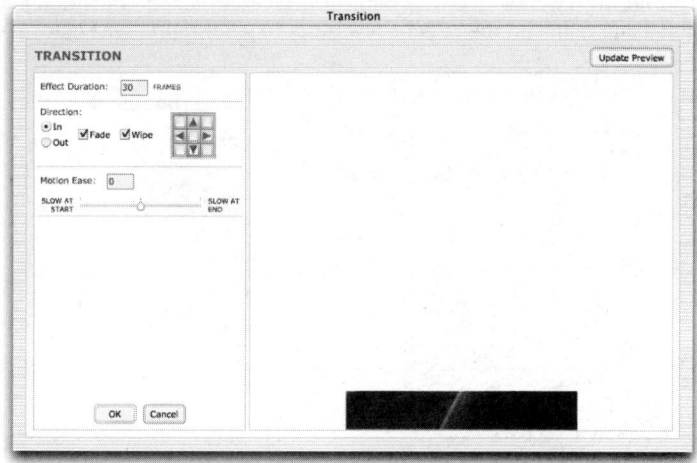

Figure 11-22: The default settings for a Transition Timeline Effect (top) can be adjusted to achieve the final result that you like (bottom).

Note   If there is no other artwork on the layer with the item to which you add a Timeline Effect, Flash simply renames the layer when the Effect is applied. If there are other symbols or artwork on the layer with the item to which you added the Timeline Effect, Flash moves the item to a new layer when the Effect is applied. This can lead to duplicate layer names that should be manually changed to keep the structure of your document clear.

   6. After the Effect is finished, you will see a new layer in your Timeline auto-named to indicate the Effect that was rendered and the sequence that it was rendered in during your project authoring process. In our example, the layer is named Transition 4 because we had applied and removed the Effect a few times to get it right (see Figure 11-23).

Figure 11-23: After a Timeline Effect is rendered, you will see a newly named layer for the animated frame span and you will find symbols in the Library that were generated by Flash to create the Effect from your original item.

Tip   If you have created an animation that starts with an alpha setting of 0, you won't see anything on the Stage in the first frame of the new animated frame span. However, if you click the *frame*, you will see the blue selection box on the Stage to indicate the position of your "invisible" artwork.

   7. A frame span will extend on the Main Timeline for the duration of the animation if you applied an animated Effect to a shape, bitmap, Graphic symbol, or Button symbol. You can preview the animation by scrubbing the Timeline in the authoring environment.

Note   If you apply an animated Effect to a Movie Clip symbol, the animation span is rendered on a Movie Clip timeline, so you will not see frames added to the Main Timeline and you will have to preview the animation in Test Movie mode.

8. As shown in Figure 11-23, you will also find new symbols that Flash rendered to create the Effect added to your Library list. These symbols are given default names that will indicate the type of Effect applied and the sequence that it was created in during an edit session.

Caution   This is the only time in this book that we will advise you not to change the default symbol and layer names right away. If you decide to edit the settings for your animated Effect, the symbols and layers rendered by Flash will be renamed anyway. The best approach is to rename these items only as a final step in your editing process.

And there you have it — a lovely fade transition that can be adjusted without touching the Timeline or moving any keyframes. If you want to change the pacing or the look of the Timeline Effect, use the **Edit Effect** option in the Timeline Effects menu to open the Settings dialog box again. If you decide that the Effect is not really what you wanted, use the **Remove Effect** option in the Timeline Effects menu to get rid of it without deleting your original item.

All you have to remember is that the symbols and the frame span rendered with a Timeline Effect can't be edited manually without breaking the option to use the Settings dialog box. If you try to change the frame span in the Timeline or try to open the symbols on the Stage in Edit mode, you will see a warning dialog box that gives you the option to proceed with the action or to cancel it. Proceed only if you don't think you will need to adjust the rendered animation again using the Settings dialog box and if you cannot achieve your authoring task in any other way.

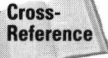

Cross-Reference   Notes on managing Timeline Effect symbols and folders and specific steps for editing Timeline Effect symbols are covered in Chapter 9, "Modifying Graphics."

Using Custom Timeline Effects, by Samuel Wan

Author's Note: Although it is beyond the scope of this book to describe the steps involved in actually scripting your own Timeline Effects, we can tell you how to use custom Effects that other developers have made. One of the developers making cool new Effects is Samuel Wan. He has kindly agreed to let us include the code for one of his very first Flash MX 2004 Effects on the CD-ROM. This brief tutorial is adapted from Sam's notes on how to install and use his "Jitter" Effect. We hope you will be able to follow these same steps to use other custom Effects available from Macromedia or from generous developers in the Flash community.

The first step to using a custom Timeline Effect is to find the files that Flash needs to make the Effect Settings appear in the authoring environment and to render the final Effect. Unless you happen to know some brainy coders, the best place to look for new Timeline Effects is on the Macromedia Web site.

The two files you will want to find and download are:

✦ An XML file that describes the parameters or "properties" of the Effect and how the parameters can be customized. These files can be recognized by the .xml file extension.

✦ A JavaScript-Flash file that implements required methods for manipulating the Flash-authoring tool based on parameters specified by the XML file. These files can be recognized by the .jsfl file extension.

On the CD-ROM

We have included `Jitter.xml` and `Jitter.jsfl` on the CD-ROM in the `CustomEffect` subfolder of the `ch11` folder. To see the rendered Effect, open `JitterSample.fla` (or .swf) from the same location.

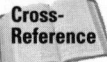

Cross-Reference

To learn about other uses for XML files, refer to Chapter 30, "Sending Data In and Out of Flash."

Both of these files have to be saved in your Flash MX 2004 Effects folder so that a custom Effect can be applied in the authoring environment.

✦ The standard directory path on Windows is:

```
C:\Documents and Settings\(username)\Local Settings\Application
Data\Macromedia\Flash MX 2004\en\Configuration\Effects
```

✦ The standard directory path on Mac is:

```
HD\Users: (username)\Library: Application Support\Macromedia\Flash
MX 2004\en\Configuration\Effects
```

After you save the XML file and the JSFL file to the Effects folder on your system, you will need to restart Flash to see the custom Effect in the Timeline Effect menu.

The steps for applying a custom Timeline Effect are the same as the steps for applying a built-in Timeline Effect, but the settings available for the Effect will be unique. To apply the Jitter Effect, follow these steps:

1. Select an item on the Stage (a shape or a symbol).

2. Access the Timeline Effect menu from the Insert menu or from the contextual menu. As shown in Figure 11-24, a new category of effects has been added — **Sam's Super Duper Effects** are now listed along with the other categories that were described earlier in this chapter. Select Sam's **Jitter** Effect.

3. A Settings dialog box appears on Stage so that you can enter values to control the rendered Jitter Effect. (Refer to Figure 11-25.)

Note

As shown in Figure 11-25, the Settings dialog box for the Jitter Effect looks quite different than the Settings dialog box used to apply the Transition Timeline Effect earlier in this chapter (shown in Figure 11-22). This is one of the quirks of custom Timeline Effects. Some developers will include SWF control for the settings that generates a dynamic preview of the Effect, while others will only build the JSFL and XML files, which results in a more generic-looking Settings dialog box — similar to the dialog box for drawing tool settings. The purpose and effect of the settings are the same in either interface. The main difference is that you can't preview the Effect before you apply it unless you're using SWF settings dialog box. Fortunately, it is easy to remove an Effect at any time, so the generic settings box is not a huge problem — most custom Effects will be worth the extra trouble of testing and removing a few different settings before you decide what works best.

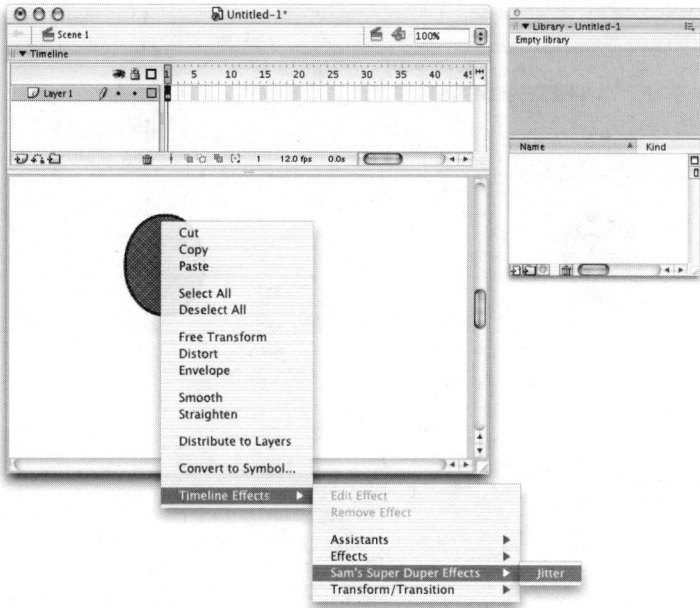

Figure 11-24: After you save the XML and JSFL files for a custom Timeline Effect in the Effects folder, and you restart Flash, the custom Effect is added to the Timeline Effects menu.

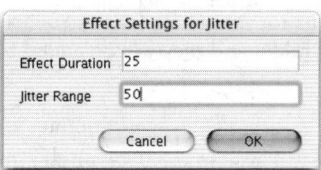

Figure 11-25: The Settings dialog box for custom Effects may have a more generic appearance than the Settings dialog box for built-in Timeline Effects.

4. After you enter values for the frame duration of the Effect and the pixel offset, or the amount of jitter, click **OK**.

5. The animation will be rendered on the Timeline in a layer called "Jitter 1." If you look in the project Library, you will see that the original selected shape has been converted to a Graphic symbol ("symbol 1") and nested in an animated Graphic symbol ("Jitter 1"), both now stored in the Library. (Refer to Figure 11-26.)

On the CD-ROM

To see the final animated Jitter Effect, have a look at the JitterSample.swf file in the Custom Effect subfolder of the ch11 folder on the CD-ROM.

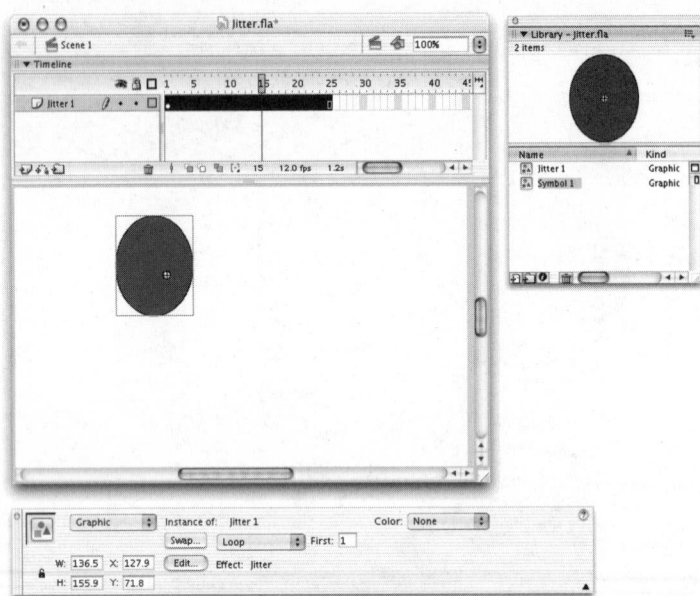

Figure 11-26: The applied Jitter Effect adds new symbols to the Library and renders a span of frames on the Timeline.

That seems like a lot of steps, but it certainly takes less time to install a custom Effect than it does to make one from scratch! We hope there will be many more useful and creative Effects available that will open new possibilities for your Flash designs. You can continue to save other custom Effects files to your Effects folder and they will be added to the Timeline Effects menu.

Caution   Obviously, it would be a big mistake to save a custom Effect file to your Effects folder if it had the same name as an existing Effect. Unless you want to overwrite existing Timeline Effects, make sure you're using unique names for any custom Effects that you add. If you'd rather not change the name of an Effect, simply add a unique number to the Effect name to avoid overwriting other files with the same name.

If you decide you don't need an Effect anymore, or if your Timeline Effect menu gets too cluttered, simply remove the relevant XML and JSFL files from the Effects folder (save them somewhere else if you liked the Effect, trash them if you didn't). The next time you restart Flash the Effect will no longer show up in the menu.

Integrating Multiple Animation Sequences

So far in this chapter, we've looked at creating different types of animation on the Main Timeline. As you can tell, even with the simple examples that we've used, adding multiple tweens to the Main Timeline can soon result in a jumble of colored spans and keyframes that might be hard to navigate when you need to make edits. Authoring all animation sequences on the Main Timeline also puts you at risk of unintentionally displacing multiple sequences as you make edits.

The best solution for keeping your project (FLA) files manageable as you continue to add animation is to move animation sequences off the Main Timeline and organize them instead on individual symbol timelines. This makes it much easier to move or reuse animation and will also ensure that any edits you make to individual animation sequences will not disrupt sequences on other symbol timelines. Graphic symbols and Movie Clip symbols can both be used to hold multiple layers of animation, but they have different uses.

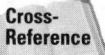

Cross-
Reference

For a review of how various symbol timelines relate to the Main Timeline, please refer to Chapter 6, "Symbols, Instances, and the Library."

As discussed in Chapter 6, all symbols have their own timelines, so you could just as easily store an animation in a Graphic symbol as in a Movie Clip. However, there are some important differences to keep in mind:

✦ A Graphic symbol timeline must still be tied to frames on the Main Timeline, while a Movie Clip timeline will play back independently, regardless of how many frames it is assigned on the Main Timeline.

✦ The benefit of using a Graphic symbol to store an animated sequence is that it can be previewed frame by frame directly in the authoring environment, even if it is nested. You *can* preview animation on a Movie Clip timeline in Edit mode, but you will not be able to see how the animation on the Movie Clip timeline syncs with animation on other symbol timelines or with the Main Timeline until you publish the movie or use the Test movie command.

✦ Another significant limitation of Graphic symbols is that they cannot be targeted with ActionScript. Movie Clip symbols can be targeted with ActionScript to control the playback of each symbol instance independently, as opposed to having all animation tied to frame sequences on the same (main) Timeline.

The extent to which you separate and nest animated elements will depend on the complexity of the project and also on how you intend to reuse animation. In general, any elements that will always be linked together on playback can be stored in the same symbol. If you want to have the option of altering playback speed or placement of certain elements independently, then these should be stored in discrete symbols. For example, if you have an animated logo that may be used in a project separately from an animated title, then these two elements should be in individual symbols. On the other hand, if the logo always appears in the same way with the title, then these two elements can be stored in a single symbol (on separate layers, if necessary).

Note

As discussed earlier in this chapter, Timeline Effects generally render an animated sequence as a multiframe Graphic symbol on the Main Timeline. Although this is not always the recommended symbol type for Flash animation, it does make it possible to view the animation just by scrubbing the Timeline. This was intended to make Timeline Effects more user-friendly for people learning Flash.

Tip

It is always possible to use the Property inspector to change the behavior (or symbol type) of a symbol instance on the Stage. If you are working with multiple Movie Clips and you need to sync some parts of the animation, it can be helpful to temporarily assign a Movie Clip instance Graphic symbol behavior so that you can see the animation on its timeline in the main authoring environment. Don't forget to switch the instance back to Movie Clip behavior before you publish your movie.

Moving tweens onto symbol timelines

Certainly, it is more efficient to plan your project structure before you begin adding animation so that you can nest animation in symbols as you create it, but Flash is flexible enough to allow you to optimize the organization of your animation sequences even after you have strewn them around on the Main Timeline.

Caution

The only exception to this flexible authoring rule is caused by Timeline Effects. You must create a holder symbol for the Timeline Effect and render the Effect on the symbol timeline rather than on the Main Timeline, unless you are willing to "break" the Timeline Effect settings option when you try to re-architect your project file.

To illustrate how tweens are moved from the Main Timeline to symbol timelines, we will modify a file called tweensTimeline.fla, which includes multiple layers with Shape tweens and Motion tweens on the Main Timeline.

On the CD-ROM

We have included two files in the Integrate subfolder of the ch11 folder on the CD-ROM for you to refer to: the original tweensTimeline.fla with tweens on the Main Timeline and the modified tweensNested.fla, with tweens moved onto symbol timelines.

To reorganize a file (FLA) that has animation built on the Main Timeline, follow these steps:

1. Analyze the Main Timeline carefully to see how the various animated sequences need to relate to each other in the final SWF file. Decide which frame spans and layers you need to keep tied together and which should be independent.

2. Pay close attention to how the transitions between different animated sequences are handled on the Main Timeline. If two different phases of a tween share a common keyframe (for example if you have scaled an element in one tween and then rotated the same element in another tween that continues from the final keyframe of the first tween), you must keep these tweens together or else insert an additional keyframe before you separate them in order to keep both tweens intact.

Tip

To be certain that linked sequential tweens can be separated without getting messed up, it can be helpful to remove the tween from the end keyframe of the first tweened sequence after inserting another keyframe (F6) to maintain the beginning of the tween that follows. This ensures that there is no interpolation between the end keyframe of the first tween and the start keyframe of the second tween.

3. Double-click the span or Shift-select the beginning and end keyframes of the sequence that you want to move off the Main Timeline.

Tip

To select multiple layers, drag-select or click the top-left keyframe in the series; then Shift-click the lowest-right keyframe in the series.

4. With all frames in the sequence selected, choose **Copy Frames** from the contextual menu (see Figure 11-27), or Edit ⇨ Timeline ⇨ Copy Frames from the application menu (Alt+Ctrl+C or Option+⌘+C).

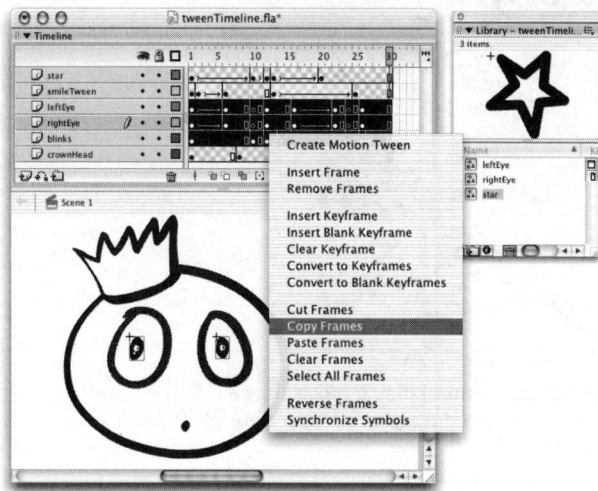

Figure 11-27: You can select frame spans on multiple layers to move at one time. Be sure to use **Copy Frames** rather than simply **Copy** to move all the frames to the Clipboard.

5. Create a new symbol by selecting Insert ⇨ New Symbol from the application menu (Ctrl+F8 or ⌘+F8). Assign the symbol **Movie Clip** or **Graphic** behavior and give it a name that will be useful for identifying the animation, as shown in Figure 11-28.

6. After you click **OK** to close the New Symbol dialog box, the symbol is automatically opened in Edit mode. Select the first frame of the symbol Timeline and choose **Paste Frames** from the contextual menu, as shown in Figure 11-29. Or choose Edit ⇨ Timeline ⇨ Paste Frames from the application menu (Alt+Ctrl+V or Option+⌘+V).

7. Flash automatically inserts enough layers and frames to accommodate the content you paste into the symbol Timeline (see Figure 11-30). Your animation sequence is now stored inside the symbol and can easily be accessed from the Library for reuse or editing.

Flash even preserves the original layer names when content is pasted into a new Timeline.

Create as many new symbols as you need to hold all of the individual animation sequences that you want to work with in your project. When you are finished, you should have a set of named Movie Clip symbols in your Library that are easy to identify, containing animated elements that will now be efficient to edit or reuse.

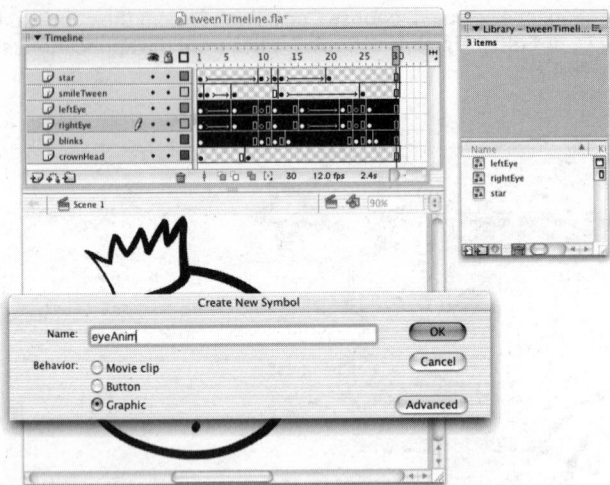

Figure 11-28: In the Create New Symbol dialog box, select a symbol behavior and enter a meaningful name for your new symbol.

Figure 11-29: Select the first frame in your new symbol timeline and use **Paste Frames** to insert the frames and layers from the Clipboard.

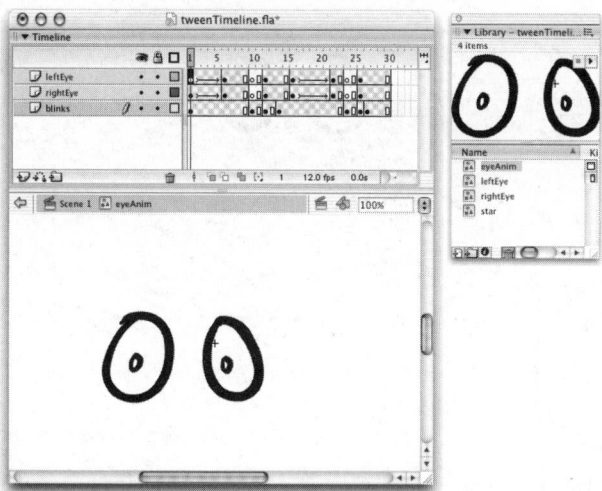

Figure 11-30: When you use **Paste Frames** to place the content from the Clipboard into your symbol, you will keep the layers and keyframes intact.

Organizing Symbol Instances on the Main Timeline

You may have noticed in the last section that we suggested *copying* your animation sequences from the Main Timeline to be pasted into individual symbol timelines — even though this results in redundant content. The rationale for leaving the original sequences on the Main Timeline, rather than cutting them, as you move content into separate symbols, is that they provide a useful reference for where the symbol instances should be placed on the Stage and how they should be arranged on the Main Timeline. The simplest way to "rebuild" your animation, using the nested symbols you have created, is to insert a new layer for each symbol on the Main Timeline directly above the original sequence that was copied. As you drag each symbol instance onto the Stage, you will be able to align the artwork with the original sequence on the Stage and also to determine how many frames the symbol should occupy on the Main Timeline.

Using the example from the previous section, we will proceed to replace the tweened sequences on the Main Timeline with our nested symbol instances.

1. Insert a new layer on the Main Timeline directly above the original tweened sequence by selecting the original layer and using the **New Layer** button in the Timeline window or choosing Insert ➪ Timeline ➪ Layer from the application menu (or the contextual menu).

2. Drag an instance of your nested animation symbol onto the Stage in the new layer and align it with the content on the other layers (see Figure 11-31).

Tip

Use the Lock Others command to protect content on your original layers while you drag in and position the symbol instance on your new layer.

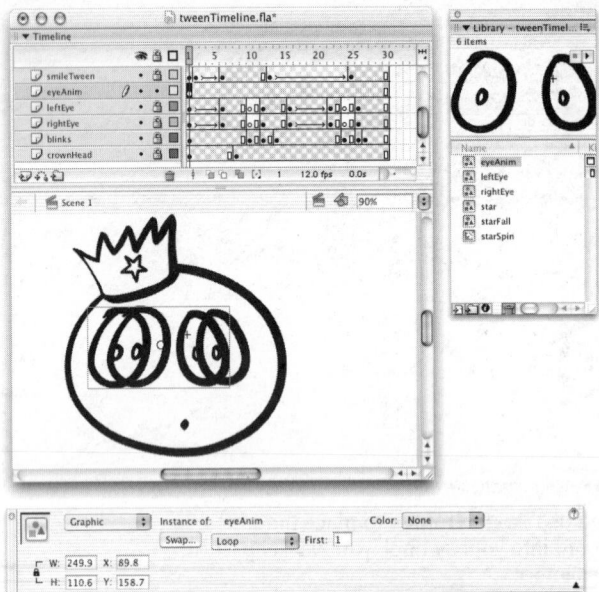

Figure 11-31: The original animation layers can help you to sequence and visually align the new symbol instances as you rebuild your project.

3. After you finish placing the new symbol instance in the Main Timeline, you can delete the layers containing the original tweened sequences (which are now redundant). You will quickly see how much cleaner and easier to modify the Timeline becomes when the tweened and frame-by-frame sequences are replaced with nested symbol instances, as shown in Figure 11-32.

Movie Clip timelines will loop automatically, so you can repeat an animation sequence as many times as you like, either by holding on a single frame of the Main Timeline, or by extending the span of the Movie Clip so that it remains visible as the Main Timeline continues to play. You can quickly change the order of your animation by moving the integrated symbol instances to new positions on the Main Timeline — without having to worry about breaking any tweens.

Reusing and Modifying Symbol Instances

Although you won't be able to preview the animation in your Movie Clip instances by scrubbing the Main Timeline, you can now easily move or reuse your animated elements. In the **tweensNested** example, we have placed additional instances of the **starSpin** Movie Clip on a new **bkgrndStars** layer to create some animated background elements (see Figure 11-33).

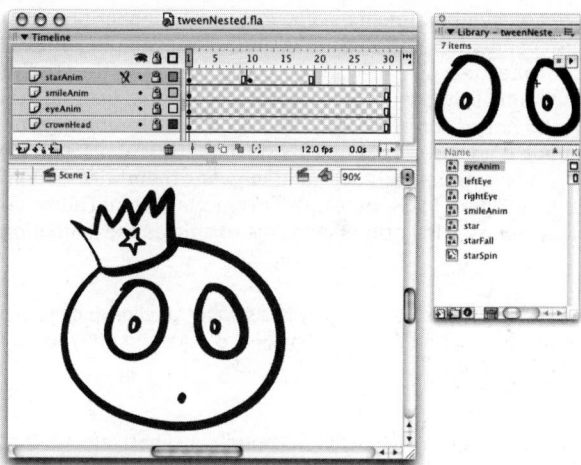

Figure 11-32: The Main Timeline becomes easier to manage as you replace the tweened and frame-by-frame sequences with nested symbol instances.

To follow this example, you can start with the tweensNested.fla that we referred to in the last section, or you can open the tweensModified.fla file from the Modify subfolder in the ch11 folder on the CD-ROM to see the final result of adding and modifying symbol instances.

On the CD-ROM

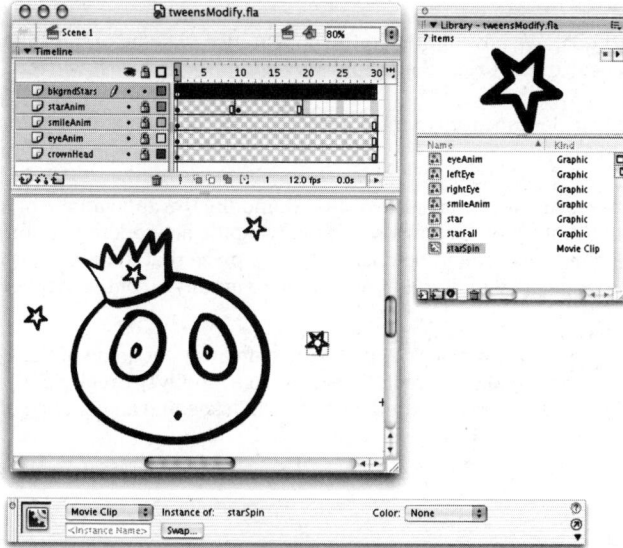

Figure 11-33: Movie Clips make it easy to place multiple instances of your animated elements.

Now that your animation is stored on symbol timelines, you can use ActionScript to control the playback of each element independently of the Main Timeline. For example, rather than stopping everything on the Main Timeline, you can place a `stop()` action on the starSpin symbol timeline to hold the animation of the stars while the other elements continue to play (as shown in Figure 11-34, top). Any ActionScript placed directly on the symbol timeline will apply to all instances of the symbol. If you are working with Movie Clip symbols, you have the additional option of naming individual symbol instances and *targeting* them with ActionScript from the Main Timeline (as shown in Figure 11-34, bottom). This method would allow you to stop the animation on some stars, while letting others continue to spin as the animation on the Main Timeline plays.

On the CD-ROM   To see the difference between adding ActionScript directly to a symbol timeline and targeting a named symbol instance with ActionScript on the Main Timeline, compare `stopSymbol.fla` (or .swf) with `stopInstance.fla` (or .swf).

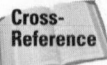

Cross-Reference   For a more detailed introduction to using ActionScript to control timelines, refer to Chapter 19, "Building Timelines and Interactions."

As discussed in previous chapters, the appearance of symbol instances can be modified without having to edit the contents of the original symbol. This can be helpful when working with static elements, but it really becomes indispensable when working with animated elements. Imagine the time it would take to copy and paste a series of tweens or a frame-by-frame sequence on the Main Timeline and then to edit the artwork on each keyframe just to change the scale or the color of your animated element each time you want to use it. Now be very happy that the little extra time spent moving your animated sequences off the Main Timeline and into symbols makes it possible to drag and drop your animated elements and then to scale, rotate, or apply Color effects to get endless variations without ever having to edit the original keyframe artwork.

In our example (see Figure 11-35), we have modified the appearance of some of the animated stars by transforming instances of the original starSpin Movie Clip.

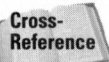

Cross-Reference   For a review of the options for modifying symbol instances, refer to Chapter 9, "Modifying Graphics."

The beauty of symbols is that you always have the option to modify the appearance of individual symbol instances or to make global changes by modifying the artwork in your original symbol. If you decide that an element should be changed every place that it appears, it will be much quicker to edit the original symbol than it would be to modify all of the symbol instances individually.

If you decide that you want to keep the artwork, but not the animation for some of the symbol instances you have placed on the Main Timeline, you can use Modify ➪ Break Apart (Ctrl+B or ⌘+B) to "break" the link to the animated symbol, while keeping an instance of the original artwork (or static symbol) on the Stage.

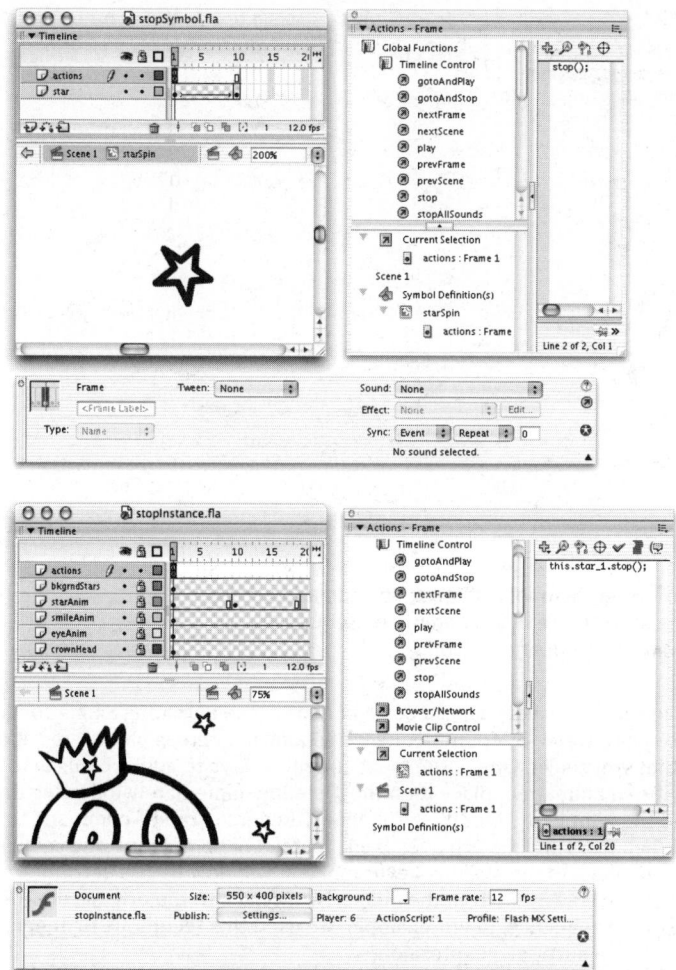

Figure 11-34: ActionScript can be added to symbol timelines (top) or used to target symbol instances (bottom) to control the playback of animated elements, independent of the Main Timeline.

We have included different versions of our example file so that you can see how the structure of the file was altered with the steps explained in this section. The files are located in the Modify subfolder in the ch11 folder of the CD-ROM.

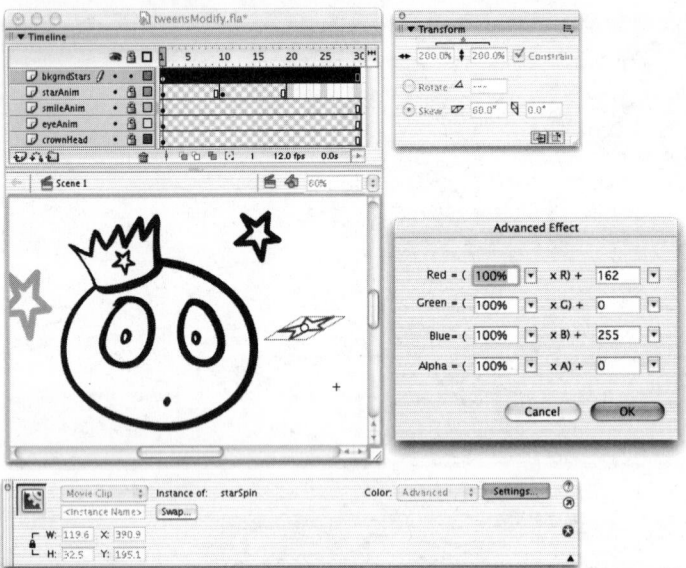

Figure 11-35: By transforming symbol instances, you can add almost endless variation to the appearance of your animated sequences without having to modify any keyframe artwork.

The option of reversing a sequence of frames comes in handy when creating animation loops. You can reverse a tween or a frame-by-frame sequence as long as there is a keyframe at each end of the sequence that you select. One of the most common ways to achieve this is to copy a sequence of frames for an animation, place it on the Timeline immediately following the original sequence, and then apply the Modify ➪ Timeline ➪ Reverse Frames command to create a seamless loop. When the Timeline is played back, instead of completing one sequence and then jumping directly back to the starting keyframe, you will now have a second sequence that smoothes the transition from the final artwork back to the original artwork on the starting keyframe of the sequence. In our example, we used this technique to animate the mouth from a smile back to a surprised expression.

1. The first step is to copy and paste the frames for the smile animation (you can place them on the same layer, but for clarity we have placed them on a layer directly under the original smile).

   You can select all the frames in the sequence and use the Copy Frames command, or hold down the Option (Alt) key while dragging the selected span to a new layer (or position on the Timeline). Make sure that the copied sequence is placed immediately following the original sequence (either on the same layer or on a new layer), as shown in Figure 11-36.

2. With all of the frames (and keyframes) of the copied sequence selected, choose Modify ➪ Timeline ➪ Reverse Frames from the application menu or from the contextual menu. Flash will automatically rearrange the order of the selected frames so that the animation is reversed, as shown in Figure 11-37. You can also make adjustments to the length of the sequence or apply different tween settings (for example, you may want to change Easing from In to Out).

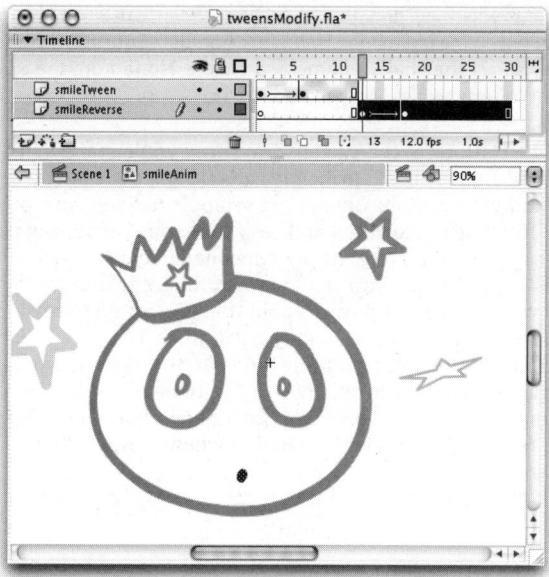

Figure 11-36: Place the copied sequence immediately following the original sequence on the Timeline.

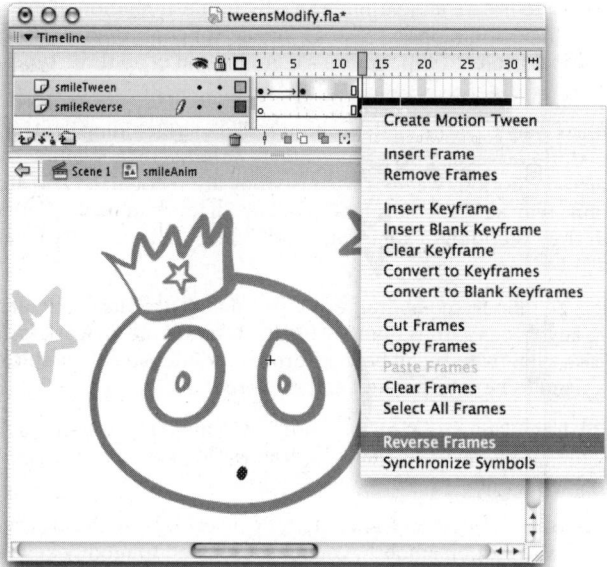

Figure 11-37: After the sequence is reversed, you can make adjustments to polish the loop.

 **Note**   After the animation is reversed, you may find that a broken tween exists on the final keyframe in the reversed sequence. The animation will work fine as-is, but to make your tween Timeline cleaner, simply select the final keyframe and choose **None** from the Tween menu in the Property inspector to remove the "broken end" of the tween.

We could fill an entire book with illustrations of the various ways that you can move, edit, and recombine your animated sequences, but the basic principles are always the same. Use symbols to keep your files optimized and your options open. Nest symbols to keep your project organized. Try to keep your Main Timeline uncluttered and easy to modify by putting frame-by-frame animation and tweens on symbol timelines. Apply Timeline Effects on symbol timelines or as the last step in your editing process if you want to layer different animation techniques. Let Flash do as much work for you as possible, but don't be afraid to manually tweak animated sequences by inserting keyframes or modifying artwork. Use layers to keep elements organized and when you need to animate multiple items on the same span of the Timeline. Plan and design your animation in logical sections rather than in complex groups — complexity can be added by nesting multiple symbols. Avoid redundant work and keep your files small and easy to manage by reusing artwork and animation whenever possible.

Summary

✦ The Flash authoring environment includes several features that have been adapted from tools that are used for creating traditional animation. Onion skinning, keyframes, and tweens are the digital equivalents of layered transparent cels, keyart, and manual inbetweens.

✦ There are three basic ways to create animation: frame-by-frame animation, two types of interpolated animation (Shape and Motion tweens), and script-controlled, auto-rendered Timeline Effects. Most projects will require a combination of all three types of animation.

✦ You can use Shape tweens only to interpolate primitive shapes (including broken apart text), and you can use Motion tweens only to interpolate editable text, symbols, or groups. Bitmaps can also be Motion tweened because they are recognized and stored in the Library in the same way as symbols. Most Timeline Effects can be applied to any item on the Stage, with the exception of some animated Effects that can only be applied to groups or symbols.

✦ Tweens add less to file size than frame-by-frame animation because Flash calculates the difference between the keyframes rather than having to store unique artwork for every frame in a sequence. However, tweens can be very processor intensive if complex transitions or alpha layers need to be interpolated and rendered.

✦ You can create frame-by-frame animation by inserting keyframes (F6) and modifying the artwork in each frame, or by inserting blank keyframes (F7) and creating completely new artwork in each frame.

✦ You can modify the pace of frame-by-frame animation by inserting or deleting frames; however, in order to keep the motion smooth, you may also need to modify keyframes.

✦ You can modify the pace of tweened animation by extending or shortening the span of the tween and also by adjusting the Easing settings to create acceleration or deceleration in a sequence.

✦ Timeline Effects can be modified and re-rendered from the Settings dialog box that is invoked with the Edit option, unless they have been opened in Edit mode or the rendered frame span has been manually adjusted. Manually editing a symbol or frame span rendered by a Timeline Effect will "break" the Edit option, but leave you with all the editing options that can be used to modify standard symbols and tweens.

✦ Symbols are an integral part of creating optimized Flash animation. Primitive shapes or artwork must be grouped or converted into symbols before they can be Motion tweened. Most animation should be organized in Graphic or Movie Clip symbols instead of on the Main Timeline.

✦ By temporarily converting a symbol instance's behavior from Movie Clip to Graphic symbol, it is possible to preview animation that would otherwise not be visible when scrubbing the Main Timeline.

✦ By nesting artwork and animation in symbols, you can create sophisticated and complex animated effects while keeping your project structure easy to modify and your Main Timeline uncluttered. The Main Timeline should not be considered a space to author animation, but rather a place to integrate all of the nested elements that you have created and stored in the Library as symbols.

✦   ✦   ✦

Applying Layer Types

Besides storing and organizing the contents of your project (.fla), Flash layers offer some special features that help you create more advanced animation. Standard layers can be locked, hidden, or displayed as outlines, but they can also be converted into Guide layers, Motion guides, or Mask layers. Each of these layer types can be used to accomplish specific authoring tasks.

 ActionScript can also be used to guide or control animation and to apply dynamic masking. For an introduction to these more advanced alternatives to Mask layers and Motion guides, refer to Chapter 27, "Interacting with Movie Clips."

Flash gives you the flexibility to quickly change the behavior of layers at any time in the authoring environment, so that you can take advantage of the special characteristics of each of these layer types as needed.

With the layer buttons at the lower-left corner of the Timeline window, you have the option of creating standard layers, Motion guide layers, and Folder layers. If you have already created a standard layer, it can be converted into any of the special layer types by using the contextual menu (invoked by right-clicking or Ctrl+clicking the layer bar), or by changing settings in the Layer Properties dialog box (invoked by double-clicking the layer icon or by choosing Modify ➪ Timeline ➪ Layer Properties from the application menu).

Flash automatically converts layers if they are dragged into specific positions in the stacking order with other layer types — although this sounds a bit cryptic, it will make sense as you read about each layer type and how they affect other layers. Each layer type has a unique icon, as shown in Figure 12-1.

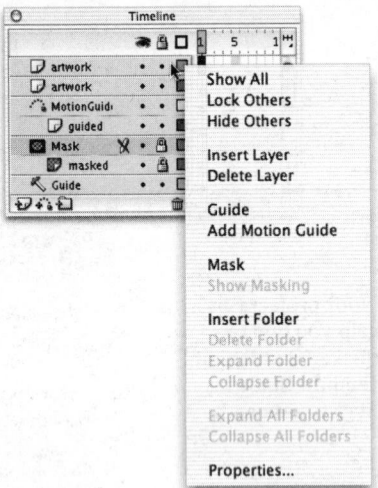

Figure 12-1: A unique icon in the layer stack identifies each of the layer types. The behavior of a layer can quickly be assigned or changed using the contextual menu.

Guide Layers

Guide layers are the only layer types that are not exported with your final Flash movie (.swf). Guide layers are used primarily when you need to use an element as a reference in the authoring environment (.fla), but you don't want it to be part of the finished movie (.swf). To convert an existing layer into a Guide layer, you can use the contextual menu and select Guide. Alternatively, you can invoke the Layer Properties dialog box (shown in Figure 12-2) by double-clicking the layer icon (or choosing Modify ⇨ Timeline ⇨ Layer Properties from the application menu), and then selecting the Guide check box.

Tip   As you are developing a project, it can be helpful to "turn off" certain layers while you're testing content on other layers. For example, by temporarily turning a layer that contains a large background graphic into a Guide layer, the movie (.swf) will render more quickly for preview in the test movie environment. Remember to turn all layers that you want exported back into normal layers before publishing your final movie (.swf) — either by unchecking Guide in the contextual menu or by selecting the Normal check box in the Layer Properties dialog box.

Bitmaps and video sequences can be placed in Guide layers if you want to use them as references for drawings or animated sequences that are drawn in Flash — think of it like working with tracing paper to redraw images. The content on a Guide layer adds to the file size of the Flash document (.fla), but it won't be included with or add to the file size of the exported movie (.swf). Guide layers are also useful when organizing layouts in Flash that require special alignment, such as a circular or diagonal arrangement of multiple elements.

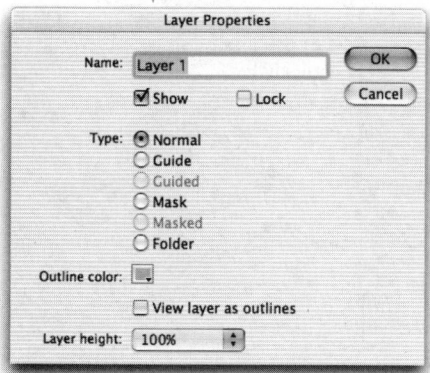

Figure 12-2: Use the Layer Properties dialog box to convert a standard layer into a Guide layer, Mask layer, or even a layer folder.

To create a Guide layer that serves as a reference for aligning a custom layout follow these steps:

1. Add a new layer to your Flash document (.fla) and make it a Guide layer. You have a couple of options for adding a Guide layer:

   • Use the contextual menu or the Layer properties dialog box to convert a standard layer into a Guide layer.

   • Use the Add Motion Guide Layer button to insert a Motion guide layer and then drag the guided layer above the Motion guide layer in the stacking order to revert the Motion guide to a (static) Guide layer.

Note   Guide layers are actually just Motion guide layers that don't have any guided layers nested below them.

2. Drag the Guide layer below your art layers in the stacking order, or add a new layer above the Guide layer if you need a fresh layer for arranging artwork.

3. Place an imported image on the Guide layer for reference, or use the Flash drawing tools to create any guide image needed (such as a circle or a diagonal line).

4. Make sure that Snap to Objects is active by toggling on the Magnet option in the toolbox or selecting View ⇨ Snapping ⇨ Snap to Objects in the application menu.

5. Use the Arrow tool to drag elements on the art layers into alignment with the reference on the Guide layer (see Figure 12-3).

Figure 12-3: Use snapping to align the center point of elements on your art layers with a reference shape or line on your Guide layer.

6. When you test your movie (Ctrl+Enter or ⌘+Return), you won't see the content of the Guide layer displayed in the .swf (see Figure 12-4).

7. Add to or modify the reference content on the original Guide layer or add additional Guide layers if needed. Use the Visibility toggle button (Eye icon) to control which layers display as you're working on different elements.

Figure 12-4: The content of the Guide layer is not visible when the movie is viewed in the test movie environment.

Motion Guides

The graphics on Motion guide layers, as on Guide layers, are not exported with the .swf file. But it is important to note that Motion guides will actually control the path of movement for an animated element on another layer, rather than simply serving as a visual reference for static content. A Guide layer is automatically converted to a Motion guide layer if another layer is nested below it to become a *guided* layer. To describe it simply, Guide layers suggest only what can be done, whereas Motion guide layers dictate what something on another layer will do.

On the CD-ROM The files shown in these Motion guide examples are included on this book's CD-ROM for your reference. You will find the source FLA files in the `motionGuide` subfolder located in the `ch12` folder.

Applying a Motion guide

To define the path for an animated element using a Motion guide, follow these steps:

1. Define a Motion guide layer that contains the guide (or path) and a guided art layer that contains your animated element(s):

   • Select the layer that contains the elements that you want to animate, and then use the Add Motion Guide button to insert a Motion guide layer above your art layer. You can also use the contextual menu or select Insert ➪ Timeline ➪ Motion Guide from the application menu to add a Motion guide layer.

   • If a Guide layer is already present and you want to convert it into a Motion guide layer, simply drag your art layer below the Guide layer in the stacking order (see Figure 12-5).

   • If you have added a Motion guide layer but your art layer is not nested below it as a guided layer, simply rearrange your layer stack by moving layers until the art layer is indented below the Motion guide layer indicating that it will be guided.

Note Dragging a Guide layer above a normal layer will not convert it into a Motion guide layer, but dragging a *normal* layer *below* a Guide layer will convert the normal layer into a guided layer and the Guide layer into a Motion guide.

2. Create a stroke that will define the path of the animation. You can use the Shape tools or any of the other drawing tools that create raw graphics. Although you can snap your animated elements to the edge of a filled shape, paths are usually defined by a stroke only.

Caution Although you can snap artwork to align with a grouped shape or an object on your Motion guide layer, the tween will not stick to the path correctly unless the grouped artwork on the Motion guide is ungrouped or the object is broken apart to simplify the elements that define the animation path into raw graphics (strokes and/or fills).

3. Add a Motion tween to the graphics (symbols) on your art layer. Make sure that Snap to Objects is active, and use the Arrow tool to snap the registration point of the animated element to the path on both the beginning and end keyframes of the tween, as shown in Figure 12-6.

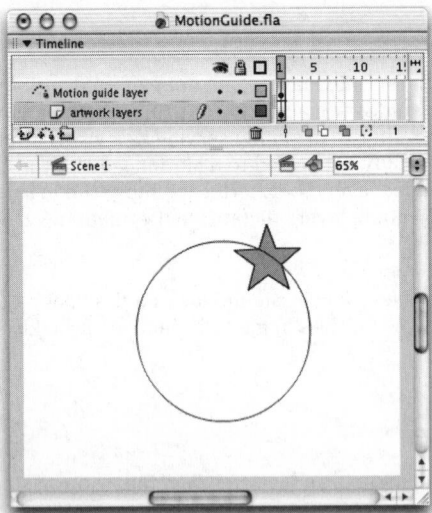

Figure 12-5: One or more art layers can be nested below a Motion guide layer.

Caution

If you apply a Timeline Effect directly to a symbol in a guided tween, the tween will be broken and the symbol will no longer animate along the path defined in the Guide layer. Nest your artwork inside of a Movie Clip symbol before applying a Timeline Effect if you plan to use Timeline Effect animations in other tweens. For example, before you add a Timeline Effect to spin or fade a graphic that will be tweened along a path defined by a Motion guide, you must place the graphic on its own Movie Clip Timeline. And then apply the Timeline Effect there, rather than on the Timeline where the Motion guide and guided Motion tween is created.

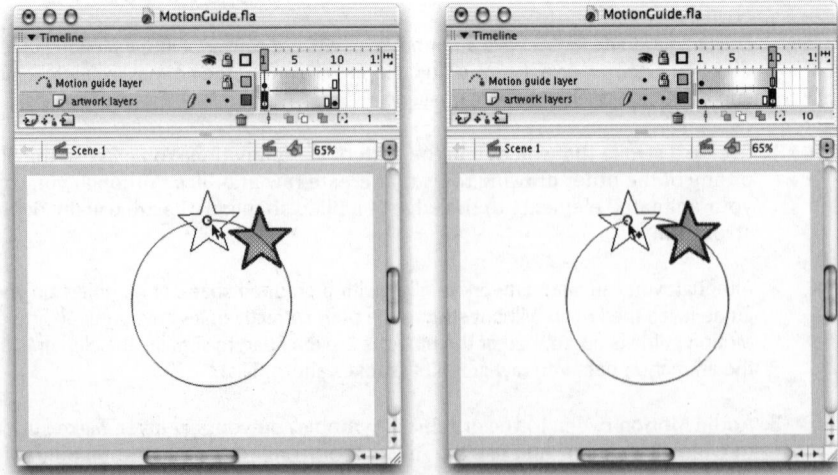

Figure 12-6: Snapping the registration point of the animated item to the Motion guide on the beginning (left) and end (right) keyframes of the tween

Tip Flash will always choose the most efficient path to animate tweened elements, interpolating the shortest route from the position defined in the starting keyframe to the position defined in the end keyframe. Occasionally, you may want to override this default efficiency. To force Flash to animate an element the "long way around" a closed path, add a gap to the stroke, as shown in Figure 12-6. Although the gap can be very, very small, it should cut the stroke that defines your path, creating a space between the starting point and the ending point of your animation. Flash does not jump gaps in a motion path. Instead, it tweens your animated element the long way around the shape.

4. Scrub the Timeline to preview the animated element; it should now follow the path defined in the Motion guide. You can reposition your artwork in the beginning or end keyframes to adjust where the animation starts and stops on the path. The path can be adjusted by modifying the stroke on your Motion guide layer. Use the Lock layer toggle to protect other layers as you make adjustments to specific elements. You can also use the settings in the Property inspector to apply easing and rotation to the Motion tween layer and preview the interpolation by turning on onion skinning (see Figure 12-7).

5. When the movie (.swf) is published, the stroke on the Motion guide layer will not be exported, but the animation will still be rendered to tween along the path that was defined in the authoring environment (.fla).

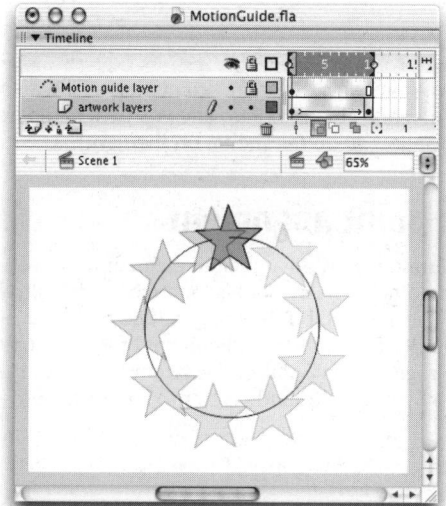

Figure 12-7: Guided tween previewed with onion skinning turned on

Adding control to animation along a path

Even after you have succeeded in getting your tweened animation to follow the path defined in your Motion guide layer you may find that the movement of the animated element is not exactly as you would like. Fortunately, there are a few different ways that you can modify how a tweened element follows a Motion guide.

Using Orient to Path

The first control to consider is found in the Property inspector when the first keyframe of your Motion tween is selected—the Orient to Path check box (shown in Figure 12-8) forces an item to rotate as it follows a curved path so that it stays aligned or headed along the path. When Orient to Path is not active, an animated item maintains the same orientation throughout the tween, with no relation to the curves or loops in its Motion guide.

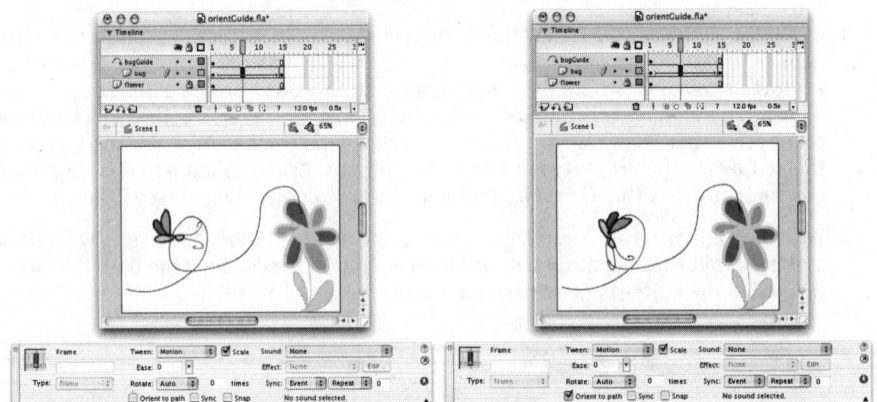

Figure 12-8: By default, a tweened item maintains the same orientation as it tweens along a curved path (as shown on the left). Selecting Orient to Path keeps an animated item headed along the curves or loops in a Motion guide (as shown on the right).

Registration and center point alignment

The second important factor that determines how an animated element moves along a Motion guide is where the registration point of the symbol is located. By default, the registration point is generally at the center of the symbol, but this may not be the point of the item that you want to snap to the Motion guide. To modify the alignment of a guided symbol, you have two options: You can modify the registration point of the symbol (refer to Figure 12-9) or change the alignment of the artwork in Symbol Edit mode (refer to Figure 12-10).

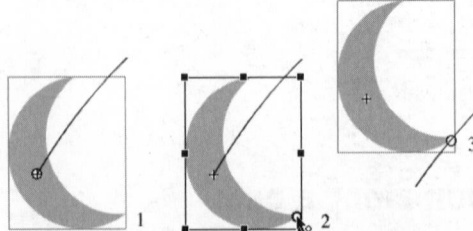

Figure 12-9: When Free Transform is active, you can modify the registration point of a symbol without changing the alignment of the artwork in relation to the center point.

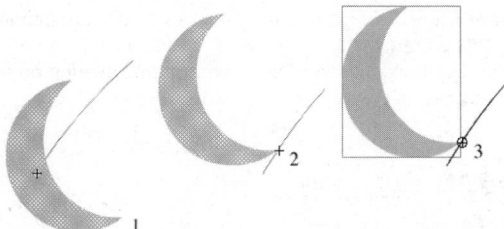

Figure 12-10: By changing the position of artwork in Symbol Edit mode, you can alter its alignment relative to both the center point and the registration point.

To modify the registration point of the symbol, follow these steps:

1. Click the Arrow tool on the stage to select the symbol on the first keyframe of the tween.

2. Activate the Free Transform tool in the toolbox and drag the registration point to a new location.

3. Use the Arrow tool to snap the newly positioned registration point to the Motion guide.

To change the alignment of the artwork in Symbol Edit mode, follow these steps:

1. On the first keyframe of the tween, double-click the symbol with the Arrow tool.

2. Reposition the artwork in relation to the center point of the stage in Symbol Edit mode so that the center point crosshair is located where you want the registration point to be.

3. Return to the main Timeline, and you should see the artwork in your symbol positioned differently in relation to the registration point, but the registration point is still aligned with the center point of the symbol and snapped to the Motion guide.

Mask Layers

In the real world, a mask is used to selectively obscure items beneath it. In Flash, a mask layer is used to define the *visible* area of layers nested beneath it. Multiple layers can be nested as *masked* layers beneath a single Mask layer. As with Motion guide layers, the content on Mask layers is not visible in the final SWF because it is intended only to modify how content in nested masked layers is rendered.

On the CD-ROM

The various examples discussed in this section can be found in the mask subfolder of the ch12 folder. You may find it helpful to examine the structure of these files to understand the many ways that Mask layers can be applied.

Almost any symbol or filled shape (excluding strokes) may be used to create a mask. However, Flash ignores bitmaps, gradients, transparency, colors, and line styles in a Mask layer. Masks may be animated or static. The only other limitations are that you cannot apply a mask to content in another mask layer and mask layers cannot be placed within Button symbol timelines.

Caution   Although groups, text boxes, and Movie Clips or Graphic symbols can all be used to define a mask, only one such item will be recognized on a single Mask layer. Multiple primitive shapes can be used to define a mask, but they will override all other items existing on the same Mask layer.

Masking with a filled shape

Here's how to create the simplest form of mask:

1. Make sure that the content that will be visible through the mask is in place on its own layer, with visibility turned on. This will become the masked layer.

2. Create a new layer stacked above the masked layer. This will become the Mask layer.

3. In the Mask layer, create the "aperture" through which the contents of the masked layer will be viewed. This aperture can be any filled item, text, or placed instance of a symbol that includes a filled item. (Of course, lines can be used as masks if they are first converted to fills with the Modify ⇨ Shapes ⇨ Convert Lines to Fills command.)

4. Now, position your mask content over the content on the masked layer (see Figure 12-11), so that it covers the area that you will want to be visible through the mask.

Figure 12-11: The content on the upper layer defines what is visible in the lower layer(s).

5. Right-click (or Ctrl+click) the layer bar of the Mask layer to invoke the contextual menu (see Figure 12-12), and choose Mask from the menu (or use the Layer Properties dialog box to change the layer behavior from Normal to Mask).

6. The layer icons change to indicate that the masked layer is now subordinate to the Mask layer and both layers are automatically locked to activate the mask. The contents of the masked layer are now visible only through the filled portion(s) of the Mask layer, as shown in Figure 12-13.

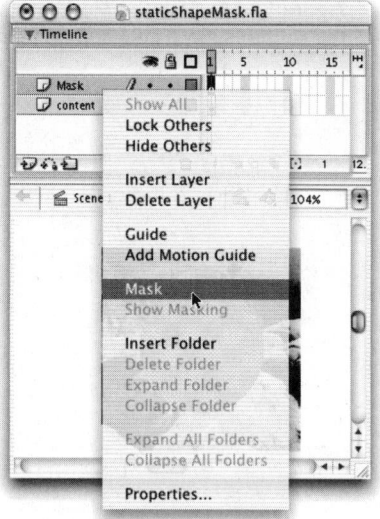

Figure 12-12: Convert the upper layer into a Mask layer by selecting Mask from the contextual menu.

Figure 12-13: When the mask is active, the content on the Mask layer is no longer visible, but it will define the visible area of the content on the masked layer underneath.

7. To reposition, or otherwise modify, the mask layer, temporarily unlock it (see Figure 12-14).

8. To reactivate masking, lock the Mask layer again (and confirm that the masked layer is also locked). The contextual menu for Mask layers and masked layers includes Show Masking—this handy command locks the Mask layer and all nested masked layers for you.

Figure 12-14: With the Mask layer unlocked, the contents are visible and editable.

 **Caution**   When you first start working with Mask layers it is easy to forget to lock both the Mask layer and the masked layer to make the mask effect visible. If you are ever having trouble editing or viewing your masked effect, just remember that when the layers are unlocked the mask art is visible and editable and that when the layers are locked the final masked effect is "turned on."

Masking with a group

Grouped filled shapes can also be used as a mask, as long as the Mask layer doesn't also contain primitive ungrouped shapes. If a mask is composed of multiple items, using a group makes it easier to position the mask, as shown in Figure 12-15.

Figure 12-15: Grouped filled shapes make it easier to position complex masks.

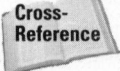 **Cross-Reference**   For coverage of working with groups and shapes, refer to Chapter 5, "Drawing in Flash."

Masking with a symbol instance

As you are reminded in nearly every chapter of this book, working with symbols is working smart because doing so helps to reduce file size. Because symbols composed of filled shapes can be used as masks, there's no reason not to use a symbol from your Library to make a mask. (If you've already made a shape on your Mask layer, go ahead and convert it into a symbol so that you can use it again without adding to the final file size.) Reusing symbol instances to define masks is especially logical if you are making multiple masks that all have the same basic shape. For example, if you need a rectangular or oval mask, you will often find a symbol in your Library that was created to define the active area of a button or some other basic element. It is smarter to modify an instance of an existing symbol so that it works as a mask than to add redundant elements that increase your file size.

Note
Although in theory you can use a Button symbol instance as mask artwork, note that a Button symbol instance placed into a Mask layer will no longer function as a button. The result of this workflow is similar to selecting a Button symbol instance and assigning it Graphic symbol behavior in the Property inspector.

To illustrate the way that symbols can be reused as both graphic content and as mask elements, I have used instances of a symbol as static content on a masked layer and then Motion tweened another instance of the same symbol on a Mask layer to create an animated oval reveal. Figure 12-16 shows the symbol instance used on the Mask layer (on the left), the symbol instances used on the art layer (in the center), and the final mask effect visible when both layers are locked (on the right).

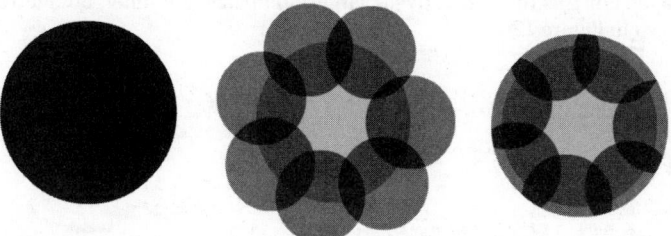

Figure 12-16: Instances of one oval symbol combined to create a graphic and a mask effect

On the CD-ROM
Open the symbolMask.fla example from the mask folder inside the ch12 folder on this book's CD-ROM to see the animated effect.

Masking text

Not only can text be masked, but it can also be used to mask other graphics. To mask text, simply set up your mask and art layers as described in the previous section, with the text to be masked on the lower layer, and the filled item that you'll use for your aperture on the Mask layer, as shown in Figure 12-17.

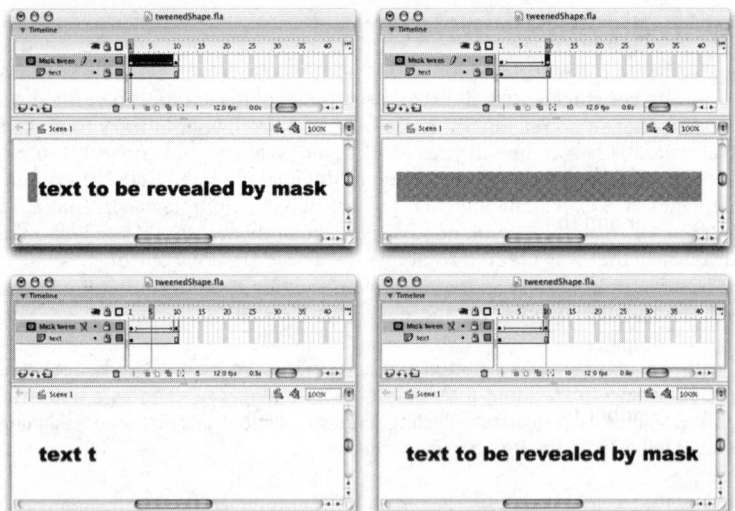

Figure 12-17: Masking a text block with a tweened shape (shown on top) and the final reveal effect (shown on the bottom)

To use text as a mask, the layers should be set up as described previously. In this situation, the text (which goes on the mask layer) will look as though it were filled by whatever is placed on the lower layer. For this to be effective, a larger point size and fuller, bold letter-forms are best, as shown in Figure 12-18.

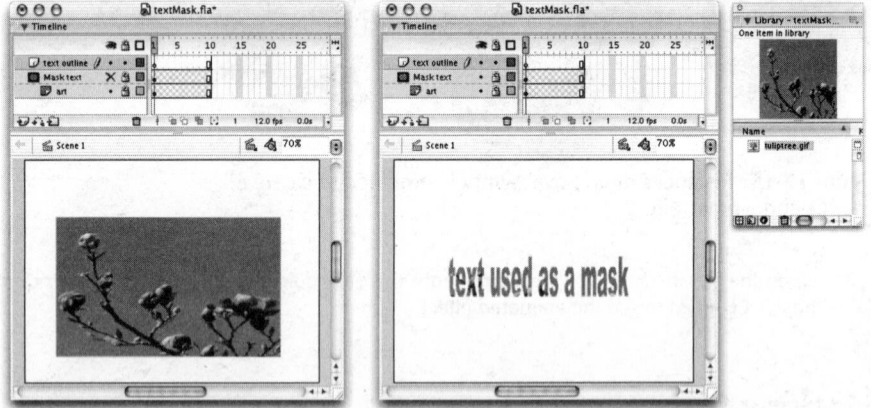

Figure 12-18: A photo (on the left) placed on the art layer and masked with text (on the right)

Caution

Although you can type as much text as you like in a single text box to apply as a mask, you can have only one text box per Mask layer. To use multiple text boxes as mask elements, add separate Mask layers for each text box.

Because the edges of mask letterforms may be hard to discern if the image underneath is not a solid color, it can be helpful to add an outline to make the mask letters more legible. However, a stroke added to the text on the Mask layer is not visible, so it is necessary to copy the text onto a normal layer stacked above the Mask layer as follows:

1. To keep the text copy aligned with the text mask, use Copy (Ctrl+C or ⌘+C) and Paste in Place (Shift+Ctrl+V or Shift+⌘+V) to place a copy of the text into the normal layer exactly on top of the mask text. After you have copied the text in the Mask layer, lock both the Mask layer and the masked layer to protect them while you are working on the normal layer.

2. The solid copied text completely obscures the masked image below, so create an outline of the text. To do so, first use Break apart (Ctrl+B or ⌘+B) to reduce the text to primitive letter shapes (see Figure 12-19).

3. Use the Ink Bottle tool to add a 1- or 2-pixel stroke to each letter shape, as shown in Figure 12-20. Remember to add a stroke to the counter spaces of any letters with internal openings (such as *O*s or *B*s).

Figure 12-19: Apply the Break apart command twice to reduce the copied text block to primitive letter shapes.

Figure 12-20: Use the Ink Bottle tool to add a thin stroke to the edges of all the letter shapes.

4. Next use the Selection tool or the Eraser tool to select and delete the fills in each letter shape, leaving only the outline stroke, as shown in Figure 12-21.

Figure 12-21: Use the Selection tool to delete the fills in each letter shape.

5. When you are finished, and the visibility is toggled back on for all layers, the text should show the image through the mask letters but now also have an outline that makes the text easier to read (see Figure 12-22). You can use the Ink Bottle tool to modify the outline on the normal layer at any time by applying a different color, style, or thickness of stroke.

Figure 12-22: The final letter shape outlines on the normal layer help to make the mask text more legible over the image on the masked layer.

Motion Guides and Movie Clip Masks

As you have seen in the examples so far, you can Shape tween primitive shapes or Motion tween symbol instances directly on the main Timeline in Mask layers to create animated masks. But what if you want to add more control to the movement of a mask? Unfortunately, one of the limitations of Mask layers is that they can't be nested below Motion guide layers to become guided elements. However, by using a Movie Clip symbol instance as the content of your Mask layer, you have the option of adding a Motion guide to the Movie Clip timeline to control the movement of the element that defines your mask.

To create a mask that contains an element controlled by a Motion guide, follow these steps:

1. Set up an art layer and a Mask layer on the main Timeline as in previous examples. Because the animation of your mask exists on a Movie Clip timeline, you need only one frame on each layer.

2. Unlock the Mask layer and, on the first keyframe of the main Timeline, insert a new symbol (Ctrl+F8 or ⌘+F8). In the Symbol Properties dialog box, specify Movie Clip behavior and name the symbol (circleAnim in this example), as shown in Figure 12-23.

Figure 12-23: Insert a Movie Clip symbol that will contain the Motion guide to control the animated mask content.

3. After you click OK in the Symbol Properties dialog box, Flash automatically opens the symbol timeline in the Document window.

4. Add a Motion guide layer that contains the path for the animation and a guided layer that contains a Motion tween of the symbol that you want to define the final mask, as shown in Figure 12-24.

5. When you return to the main Timeline, you will see only the first frame of the animation that you just created in the Movie Clip (as shown in Figure 12-25). You can select the Movie Clip instance on the Mask layer to alter its position on the Stage.

6. If you want to see how the whole Motion guide aligns with the content on the masked layer, double-click the Movie Clip symbol instance on the Mask layer to enter Edit mode (see Figure 12-26). You will now be able to scrub the Movie Clip timeline and see how the animation lines up with (the dimmed out) content on the main Timeline. You can make adjustments as needed to the Motion guide layer or to the tweened symbol that will define the mask.

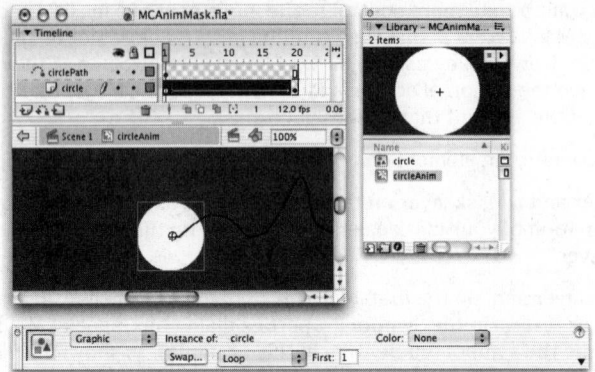

Figure 12-24: A Motion guide and a Motion tween layer added to the Movie Clip timeline

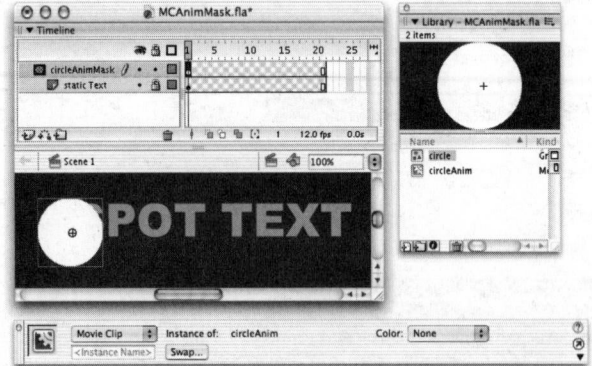

Figure 12-25: The first frame of the Movie Clip animation visible on the Mask layer in the main Timeline

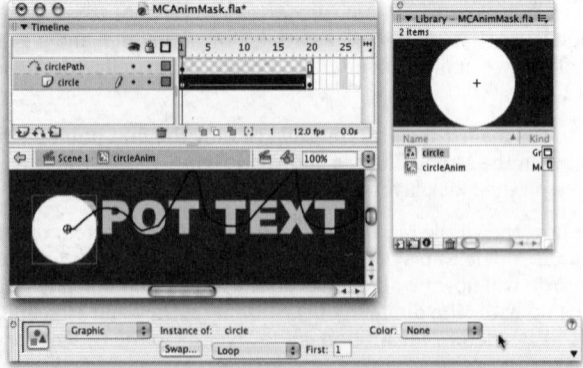

Figure 12-26: Use Edit-in-Place mode to align the Motion guide on the Movie Clip timeline with the content on the masked layer of the main Timeline.

7. After you have all the elements aligned and edited, lock both the Mask layer and the masked layer and test the movie (Ctrl+Enter or ⌘+Return) to see how the guided animation in the Movie Clip on the Mask layer reveals the content on the masked layer. Figure 12-27 shows one frame of the Motion tween in the example as it displays in the final SWF.

Figure 12-27: The final SWF previewed in the test movie environment

To see how the finished animated Movie Clip mask example looks, open `MCAnimMask.swf` from the `mask` folder in the `ch12` folder on this book's CD-ROM.

Of course, content on masked layers can also be animated separately from the content on Mask layers. But the endless possibilities for layering masks and masked content starts to get confusing when the additional variable of animation is thrown in. To make the best use of these features, take the extra time to carefully consider the most efficient way to achieve the final effect that you want. First consider what you would like to see on the Stage and then plan any animation of visible elements. The next step should be adding a mask if needed, and finally adding animation to the mask itself. Try to create your effects with the fewest possible animated elements — you will waste less production time and end up with a more optimized file.

When working on multiple nested layers, it can be visually confusing to work on animation while all layers are displayed. Use the Eye toggle to hide or show specific layers in the Timeline so that you can concentrate on only the elements that you are currently editing. Also, to avoid changing the wrong items, lock all layers that you are not currently modifying.

Keeping some basic principles in mind as you are working with multiple masks and animated elements will help you to follow the logic of masking in Flash:

✦ The mask always goes above the item that is revealed by it.

✦ Filled items on Mask layers function as windows that reveal content on the masked layers nested beneath them.

✦ The content on Mask layers is only visible in the authoring environment if the Mask layer is unlocked. For the applied mask to preview properly in the authoring environment, both the Mask layer and the masked layer(s) must be locked.

✦ Mask layers will only apply to layers that are nested below them as masked layers. Normal layers or Guide layers that may be lower in the layer stack (but not nested with the Mask layer) won't be affected by the mask.

✦ Multiple layers can be nested below a single Mask layer, but masks cannot be applied to other Mask layers, and each Mask layer can contain only one masking item (with the exception of multiple primitive shapes).

✦ Content on Mask layers is not visible in the final movie (.swf).

Summary

✦ The four layer types available in the Flash authoring environment are normal, Mask, Guide, and Motion guide. Mask layers apply to nested masked layers and Motion guide layers apply to nested guided layers. A unique layer icon identifies each layer type.

✦ Layer types can be assigned or modified in the Layer Properties dialog box, which is invoked by double-clicking any layer icon.

✦ Guide layers are used to hold content that is only needed for reference in the authoring environment, or to speed up movie testing as you develop a project — by temporarily keeping the content on specific layers from being exported with the .swf.

✦ To move a tweened element along a specific path, you can add a Motion guide layer to control the animation.

✦ Motion guide layers are actually Guide layers that have another layer nested below them as a guided layer.

✦ Timeline Effects cannot be directly applied to a symbol that is animated along a path with a guided Motion tween — to combine Timeline Effects with Motion guides; you must use nested Movie Clip timelines.

✦ Any content that you create in a Flash document can be masked with a static or animated Mask layer.

✦ Filled shapes, text, and symbol instances can be used to define the mask area (or window) on a Mask layer, but this content will not be visible in the final movie (.swf).

✦ You can animate the content of a Mask layer by creating a Motion tween or a Shape tween directly on the main Timeline, but Motion guides cannot be applied to Mask layers. To control the animation of a mask with a Motion guide, use a Movie Clip instance to define the area of the mask. The Motion tween and the Motion guide layer can then be created on the Movie Clip timeline.

✦ The linkage between various layers can be modified at any time by rearranging the order of the layer stack.

✦   ✦   ✦

Character Animation Techniques

Flash is a powerful tool that continues to grow in popularity as a professional production option for creating high-quality cartoons and animated graphics. The best thing about Flash cartoons is that you don't always *know* they were created in Flash when you see them. Flash allows artists to create characters in nearly any style they can dream up. Although Flash makes it especially easy to produce clean, geometric designs, it can also be used for sketchy hand-drawn styles or even for collage animation that uses source material from photos or video. This is the result of Flash's unique drawing tools, media-friendly authoring environment, and scalability. By "scalability," we mean that a Flash cartoon can be scaled down for delivery on the Web or scaled up to the size and resolution needed for video or film presentation. Creating broadcast cartoons can be extremely complex — specialized techniques are covered in many books and classes — so we focus on some basics to get you started.

Although there are some special techniques used in Flash, most of the basic principles of animation apply regardless of the authoring environment or production process you choose. You can often learn more about animation principles by watching classic animated films than by looking at toons online — at least those examples created by "animators" who know how to Motion tween but have not spent any time learning techniques for effective character animation.

A growing number of artists with traditional animation skills are making the transition to working directly in Flash, and there are even a few Flash experts who have taken the time to study animation. Individuals able to combine knowledge of classic animation principles with technical aptitude in Flash have the best chance of finding success in this challenging field.

Working with Large File Sizes

Because Flash output is usually intended for the Web, Flash file size is often a dominant concern. But when creating cartoons for broadcast output, this concern is thrown to the wind. In cartoon land, you create for digital video output via QuickTime or AVI and these file sizes can be huge. It's common for such projects to expand into the gigabytes, so it's important to have the equipment to handle this kind of work. This means the more RAM and hard drive space you have, the happier you will be. If you tried to build a full-length animation masterpiece in one Flash file, you would be setting yourself up for a rocky and inefficient production process. As you continue to add artwork and animation to your Flash file, it takes longer to render an SWF for preview and it takes even longer to render a sequence for raster output. There are several strategies you can use to make your animation more manageable. As we describe in this section, start with a good storyboard and follow through with a series of separate Flash files organized into scenes.

You'll spend many hours working on your animation so back it up as often as you can! The project file is precious. Make a habit of keeping incremental backups on various hard drive volumes or on removable storage, such as Zip or Jaz disks so that you won't lose everything when disaster strikes (it will). A good plan is to make a new copy on a different hard drive volume or removable disk after each major change, rotating through two or three different storage locations. This way, if Flash eats your project file or a disk or drive fails, you can always go back to the version you saved an hour ago (which should be on a different disk) without losing much time. The same versioning logic used in other documents can be applied to your Flash animation files: start with `myFile_100`, go to `myFile_101`, `myFile_102`, and so on as you make small adjustments and revisions. When you get to a significant change or a semifinished version of your file, save it `as myFile_200`, and so on. This makes it easy to find your way back to a specific phase of the project at any time.

Storyboarding scenes and shots

Let's assume that you already have characters and a story and you want to build a cartoon based on that inspired beginning. Although it's okay to experiment and develop characters, never start a serious cartoon project without a storyboard. The storyboard is your roadmap, your plan, your menu of things needed and your best friend when your project gets complicated. The storyboard can be loose and roughly sketched out, but it should help you start to see the flow of your story and to make decisions about how best to communicate it visually.

On the CD-ROM   You'll find a storyboard template on the CD-ROM, in the `ch13` folder. It's an EPS (`storyboardMAC.eps` or `storybPC.eps`) template form that includes all the essentials of a basic storyboard. Print it out as is, or import it into FreeHand, Illustrator, or Flash, and modify it to suit your needs.

As you sketch out the overall story, you can break up the narrative into workable cartoon scenes. Long before Flash, cartoonists used the term "scene" to describe something quite different than a Flash Scene. By cartoon scenes, we mean phases in a narrative, similar to any movie or TV scene. Remember that cartoons are fast-paced adventures—most cartoon scenes last less than 30 seconds. Generally, a cartoon scene can stand alone, but it needs other scenes to complete the story. Fast-paced as it is, 30 seconds of animation still requires between 360 and 720 frames in the Flash Timeline. It becomes unruly if you rely solely upon Flash's Scene feature—you'd do a lot of scrubbing, just trying to cover one scene.

After your cartoon scenes are in order, you can start to establish the camera angles or "shots" for key moments. A shot is a break or change in the camera framing or viewpoint. For example, in a soap opera dialogue scene, the camera will cut back and forth between characters to show each person talking—one scene will include many shots. Although the art of cinematography is beyond the scope of this book, the same tricks used to add drama to live action are involved when deciding shots in a cartoon scene. Always try to introduce variety in the viewpoint; think of ways to add interest with close-ups or extreme angles. If you're looking at a series of shots with characters all in the same basic position within the frame, keeping the same distance from the viewer, you're looking at a scene that will turn out to be pretty dull. If you can cut some visual contrast into the scene while still pushing your narrative forward, you will have a better chance of keeping your viewers hooked in long enough to connect with your characters and to appreciate your story.

Flash Scenes and project files

Never create an entire cartoon in one Flash project file (.fla)! Even trying to load the huge files can cause problems for Flash. Instead, create a separate Flash project file for each storyboard scene and use Flash's Scene function to organize shots within a cartoon scene. (This may seem confusing at first, but the utility of this method will become clear as you work on your masterpiece.) In other words: The Flash project file (.fla) is a storyboard scene and the shots, or Flash Scenes, are nested within the project file.

Voices, sound effects, and ambient sound

The single most important work you'll do in your cartoon is not the drawing, but the voices of your characters; the voices give the characters heart and depth. In fact, some animators prefer to record the voices first and then use the performance of the voice actors as inspiration for the animated characters' movement and expression. Obtaining a voice can be as simple as speaking into a microphone in front of your computer or as complex as having a highly paid professional acting into a microphone in a studio. The key here is not the type of voice, but the emotion put into it. If you capture a unique voice with the right emotion, it can be taken into an editing program, such as Sound Forge or Acid, and tweaked with effects to render the exact cartoon sound that you're looking for. Audio effects, including adjustments to pitch and timing, can always be added digitally; human emotion cannot. Some online voice resources are:

- ✦ www.voicecasting.com
- ✦ www.voicetraxwest.com
- ✦ www.world-voices.com

Another important part of cartoons is the use of *sound effects*. Try to imagine Tom and Jerry or Road Runner without them. There's nothing like a good CLANK, followed by the tweeting of birds, when the old anvil hits Wile E. Coyote's head. Many good sound effects collections are available on CD-ROM and online. You can even find sound effects CDs in bargain bins at your local music store. A couple of the collections that we keep on hand are: *The Ultimate Digital Sound Effects Library* from The Sound Effects Company, and *Crashes, Collisions & Catastrophes* from Madacy Music Group. We also recommend any of the *Loops for Acid* CDs from Sonic Foundry. The sounds included in these collections can be imported into any sound-editing program to be mixed into your own original soundscapes.

 Web Resource
One online source that offers a variety of effects at a broad range of prices, and RealAudio links that allow you to audition them online, is www.radiomall.com. Another popular site that has a subscription-based system for thousands of royalty-free sounds is www.platinumloops.com.

Sometimes, you just can't find the sound you need. Fortunately, it's not difficult to set up your own little *Foley stage* or sound effects recording area. A good shotgun microphone (highly directional for aiming at sound) and DAT recorder are ideal, although you can get by with less.

Tip   If you have to scrimp, don't pinch pennies on the microphone. A good microphone can make an average capture device sound better.

The capture device (audio tape, DAT, miniDV, MD, and so on) should be portable not only in order to get it away from the whirring sound of hard drives and fans but also to enable you to take it on location when needed. Another advantage of a battery-powered portable device is that static from power line voltage won't be a problem. After you get started and begin playing around, you'll be surprised at the sounds that you can create with ordinary objects. Squeeze your dish soap bottle, and you might notice that when amplified, it will make a nice whoosh. Great for the fast limb movement of that character doing a karate chop. Crumpled paper can sound like fire — once you get started, you never know what you might put to use around the house. Be creative — innovate!

The voices and the sound effects in a cartoon grab your attention and punctuate action, but listen more closely when you watch an engaging animated piece (or any film), and you will gain appreciation for the subtle art of *ambient* sounds. These background noises add tone and atmosphere, making a scene rich and believable. Ambient sound should almost be "felt" more than heard so it doesn't distract from your main narrative. Because it is layered behind the more dominant sounds, you can often get away with looping a short sample of ambient sound — think of wind or water sounds or distant city noises, they have some variation but they also tend to have a repetitive rhythm. And of course, don't overdo it. Well-timed silence can be a powerful narrative device, too!

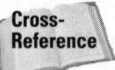

Cross-Reference   For coverage of importing and editing sound in Flash, please refer to Chapter 15, "Adding Sound."

Web Resource   There are also many great resources available online for further study of sound and sound effects — one tutorial that we found useful was through the webmonkey site at `http://hotwired.lycos.com/webmonkey/98/33/index0a.html`.

Some Cartoon Animation Basics

In the world of film, movies are shot at 24 frames per second (fps); in video and 3D animation, 30 fps is the norm. But for cartoons, 12 to 15 fps is all that's needed. The cartoon language of motion that we've all learned since childhood has taught our minds to expect this slightly jumpy quality of motion in a cartoon. As an animator, this is good for you, because 15 fps means half the amount of hand-drawing work that 30 fps requires. It also means that you can get your cartoon done within your lifetime and maybe take a day off here and there. Actually, there are a lot of scenes in which as few as three drawings per second will suffice — depending on how well you can express motion with your art or drawing. The rule of motion here is that things that move quickly require fewer frames (drawings), while things that move slowly require more frames. This is the main reason you'll hardly ever see slow-motion sequences in cartoons. Broadcast cartoons have lots of fast-paced motion. Fewer drawings are produced more quickly making the production less costly. These are very significant factors when battling tight budgets and scary deadlines.

Cross-Reference   We introduced some of the techniques described in this section in Chapter 10, "Animation Strategies." To review those examples, check out the SWF files in the `ch10` folder on the CD-ROM. We hope that by showing various examples and contexts for these animation tricks, you'll get inspired to find your own way of adding them to your cartoons.

Expressing motion and emotion

The hardest part of animation is expressing motion and emotion. Learning to do this well saves time and makes your work more effective. One of the best exercises you can do in this respect is to simply watch the world around you. Videotaping cartoons and advancing through them at single-frame speed can give you insight on different ways that the "real world" is translated to cartoon-land. (If you have digitizing capabilities, you can get a more stable frame by capturing a cartoon to your hard drive and then analyzing the results.) Another good learning trick is to import raster video to your Flash Timeline, so that you can use a live action sequence as your guide and practice drawing on top of it. While this can help you get a feel for the mechanics of motion, it's really just a start. Cartoons are engaging *because* they so often deviate from or even defy the predictable motion we see every day.

Exaggerate everything! After all, this is what makes it a cartoon.

 Tex Avery was a pioneering animator who created cartoons with overblown and hilarious motion, which revolutionized animation. You can read about him at www.brightlights film.com/22/texavery.html.

Anticipation

Anticipation is a technique used to indicate that characters are about to do something, like take off running. Before lunging into the sprint, characters slowly back up, loading all their motion into their feet until their motion reverses and sends them blasting off in the other direction. In a more subtle form, this is shown in Figure 13-1, when Weber the pelican crouches before he takes flight from his perch on the pier.

Figure 13-1: Anticipation is used to accentuate Weber's take-off.

Weight

Keep the weight of objects in mind. This helps to make your cartoon believable. A feather falls more slowly than an anvil. The feather also eases out (slows down) before landing gently on the ground, while the anvil slams into the ground with such force as to make a gashing dent in it. Humor can play a role here by giving extreme weight to things that do not have it (or vice versa) thereby causing a surprise in the viewer's preconceived notion of what should happen—and this is the seed of humor.

Overlapping actions

Visualize a jogging Santa Claus, his belly bouncing up and down with each step. Because of its weight, his belly is still on a downward motion when the rest of his body is being pushed upward by the thrust of his leg. This opposing motion is known as overlapping actions. Overlapping action does not only happen in an up-and-down motion, it can happen in any direction. An example of side-to-side overlapping actions is shown in Figure 13-2. Note that, as the bully thrusts forward, Weber's body reacts in the opposite direction . . . only to catch up just in time for the thrust to reverse and go the other way.

Figure 13-2: Overlapping actions can accentuate movement in any direction.

Blurring to simulate motion

Blurring is a technique or device that animators use to signify a motion that's moving faster than the frame rate can physically show. In film, this manifests itself as a blurred out-of-focus subject (due to the subject moving faster than the camera's shutter can capture). You may have already employed this effect in Photoshop, with the motion blur filter. In cartoon animation, blurring is often (and easily) described with blur lines. Blur lines are an approximation of the moving subject utilizing line or brush strokes that trail off in the direction that the subject is coming from. When used properly, this great device can save hours of tedious drawing. An example of animated motion blur used to indicate a spinning motion is shown in Figure 13-3, which shows a sequence in which the *word* "Weber" turns into Weber the pelican.

Figure 13-3: Blur lines simulate the effect of motion that is "faster than the eye can see."

On the CD-ROM   To see animated examples of the blurred line effect, look in the R_Bazley folder inside the ch13 folder on the CD-ROM. Richard Bazley has used blur lines effectively to create a collapsing ceiling and a rush of wind.

Animator's Keys and Inbetweening

In Chapter 11, "Timeline Animation and Effects," you learned about two Flash animation methods: frame-by-frame and tweening. This section focuses on traditional cartoonist frame-by-frame techniques together with traditional cartoonist's keys and inbetween methods to accomplish frame-by-frame animation. Despite the similarity of terminology, this topic heading does not refer to a menu item in Flash. Instead, it should be noted that animation programs such as Flash have derived some of their terminology (and methods) from the vintage world of hand-drawn cel animation. Vintage animators used the methods of keys and inbetweening to determine the action a character will take in a given shot. It's akin to sketching, but with motion in mind. In this sense, keys are the high points, or ultimate positions, in a given sequence of motion. Thus, in vintage animation:

✦ Keys are the pivotal drawings or highlights that determine how the motion will play out.

✦ Inbetweens are the fill-in drawings that smooth out the motion.

In Flash, the usual workflow is to set keyframes for a symbol and then to tween the intervening frames, which harnesses the power of the computer to fill the inbetweens. Although this is fine for many things, it is inadequate for many others. For example, a walk sequence is too subtle and complex to be created simply by shape or motion tweening the same figure — each key pose in the walk requires a unique drawing. So, let's take a look at the traditional use of keys and inbetweens for generating a simple walk sequence that starts and ends according to a natural pace, yet will also generate a walk loop.

Walk cycles (or walk loops)

Humans are incredibly difficult to animate convincingly. Why? Because computers are too rigid — too stiff. Human movement is delightfully sloppy — and we are keenly aware of this quality of human movement, both on a conscious and a subconscious level. (Another term for this is body language.) Experienced animators create walk cycles with life not by using perfectly repeating patterns, but rather by using the dynamic quality of hand-drawn lines to add just the right amount of variation to basic movements.

The most difficult aspect of creating a walk cycle is giving the final walk distinctive qualities that support the role that the character plays. This again is something that only gets easier with practice. There is no substitute for drawing skill and time spent studying human movement, but to get started it can be helpful to study a basic walk pattern.

On the CD-ROM The three walk cycle examples shown in this section are included on the CD-ROM for you to open and analyze. The frame-by-frame pattern of the different walks can be a good starting point for designing your own walk cycle. You will find the files in the `Walks` folder inside the `ch13` folder of the CD-ROM.

Many 3D programs have pre-built walk cycles that you can modify. We started with a basic walk made in Poser (a popular 3D character animation program from Curious Labs) and output it as an image sequence that could be traced in Flash. As you can see in Figure 13-4, this walk cycle was composed of 10 different poses, but the final result is fairly generic.

Figure 13-4: A traced sequence from a basic walk cycle that was created in Poser

Notice that the main pivot points of the figure create a balanced pattern that can be used as a basis for many other kinds of figures. Also notice that as the figure moves through the cycle, there is a slight up and down movement that creates a gentle wave pattern along the line of the shoulder. This wave motion is what will keep your figure from looking too mechanical. It is important to remember that the final pose in the cycle is not identical to the first pose in the cycle — this is crucial for creating a smooth loop. Although it might seem logical to create a full cycle of two strides and then loop them, you will get a stutter in the walk if the first and last frames are the same. Whatever pose you *begin* the cycle with should be the next logical "step" after the final pose in your cycle, so that the pattern will loop seamlessly.

Although the figures are shown here with the poses spaced horizontally, you will actually draw your poses on individual frames (best done on a Movie Clip timeline), but align the drawings on top of each other so that the figure "walks in place" as if on a treadmill. Once you have established your walk cycle, the horizontal movement is added by tweening the walk cycle Movie Clip. As shown in Figure 13-5, by using a Motion tween to scale the walk cycle Movie Clip and move it from one corner of the Stage to another, you can create the illusion that the figure is walking toward the viewer.

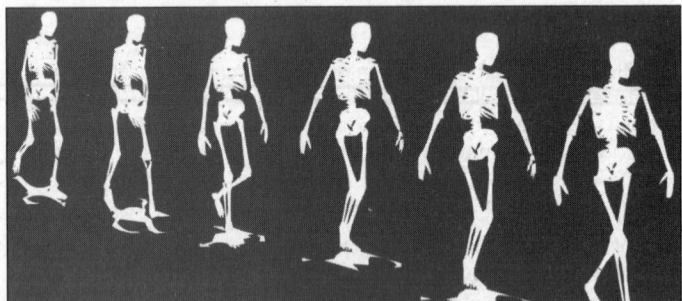

Figure 13-5: A series of angled poses in a walk cycle work well to create the illusion that the figure is walking toward the viewer if the final Movie Clip is scaled as it is Motion tweened from the far corner to the near corner of the Stage.

The speed of the Motion tween has to match the speed of the walk cycle. If the tween is too slow (too little distance or too many frames), the figure will seem to be walking in place. If the tween is too fast (too much distance or too few frames), the figure will seem to be sliding over the ground. Play with the ratio of your Motion tween, and if the figure needs to walk faster or slower, then make adjustments to the walk cycle itself rather than just "pushing" or "dragging" the figure with your Motion tween. Also keep in mind that a figure should seem to walk more quickly as it gets closer to the viewer. In the skeleton walk example, the Motion tween is eased-in so that as the figure gets closer (larger), the walk appears to cover more ground.

Achieving realistic human walk cycles can take hours of work and require very complex walk cycles (often 30 or more poses.) Fortunately, many cartoons actually have more personality if they use a simplified or stylized walk cycle that suits the way they are drawn. Figure 13-6 shows a walk cycle that only required three drawings to create a serious but child-like stride for an outlined character.

Notice that the legs, arms, torso, and head of the character are all animated on separate layers. This allows you to reuse the same drawings for both sides of the body — by simply offsetting the pattern so that the legs swing in opposition to each other, with the leg on the far side layered underneath the leg on the near side. This economy of effort is helpful not only because it is faster, but also because it makes it easier to maintain the symmetry of your character if you are trying to keep the motion simple and stylized.

Figure 13-6: A stylized walk cycle created by flipping and reusing the same three drawings for both legs of an outlined character

Repeaters

You may notice some blank, nonkeyed frames (repeaters) in the Timeline for the cartoon walk. These were used to economize drawing time and to slow the walk of the character. If a speedier walk were called for, we would simply delete these repeater frames. A good basic rule about repeaters is to add no more than one repeater frame between keys; adding more causes the smoothness of motion to fall apart. If the motion must proceed more slowly, then you have to draw more inbetweens.

Fortunately, with Flash Onion skinning (the capability to see before and after the current time in a dimmed graphic), which is discussed in Chapter 11, "Timeline Animation and Effects," the addition of a few more inbetweens is not an enormous task. In fact, Onion skinning is indispensable for doing inbetweens, and even for setting keys. One pitfall of Onion skinning is the tendency to trace what you're seeing. It takes practice to ignore the onion lines and use them only as a guide. You need to remember that the objective is to draw frames that have slight, but meaningful, differences between them. Although it can mean a lot more drawing, it's well worth it. Because you'll use your walk (and running) cycles over and over during the course of your cartoon, do them well.

Tip
One real time-saver in creating a walk cycle is to isolate the head and animate it separately via layers or grouping. This trick helps to prevent undesirable quivering facial movements that often result from imperfectly traced copies. Similarly, an accessory such as a hat or briefcase can be isolated on a separate layer. Finally, if the character will be talking while walking, make a copy of the symbol and eliminate the mouth. Later, the mouth will be added back as a separate animation. We cover this later in this chapter in the section on lip-syncing.

Types of walks

So far, we've covered the mechanics of a walk cycle. But for animators, the great thing about walking — in all its forms — is what it can communicate about the character. We read this body language constantly every day without really thinking about it. We often make judgments about people's mood, mission, and character based on the way that they carry themselves. Picture the young man, head held high, briskly striding with direction and purpose: He is in control of the situation and will accomplish the task set before him. But if we throw in a little wristwatch checking and awkward arm movements, then that same walk becomes a stressful "I'm late." Or, witness the poor soul — back hunched, arms dangling at his sides. He moves along, dragging his feet as if they each weigh a thousand pounds. That tells the sad story of a person down on their luck. Finally, what about a random pace, feet slipping from side to side, sometimes crisscrossing, other times colliding, while the body moves in a stop-and-start fashion as if it were just going along for the ride? Is that someone who couldn't figure out when to leave the bar? Of course, these are extreme examples. Walks are actually very subtle and there are limitless variations on the basic forms. But if you begin to observe and analyze these details as they occur in everyday life, you'll be able to instill a higher order in your animations. Simply take time to look. It's all there waiting for you to use in your next animation. Then remember that because it's a cartoon, *exaggerate!*

Coloring the Art

In traditional animation, characters were first inked in as outlines and then filled with color and shading. Coloring was the most tedious and time-consuming job of all: endless thousands of cels to be hand painted and dried. Most often, armies of low-paid workers in far away lands did it. But with Flash it's a snap! That's because of Flash's wonderful (and sometimes mysterious) gap-jumping fill tool, the Paint Bucket. With Flash, you never run out of paint, and it dries instantly — a real time-saver to be sure!

The model sheet

Here's a coloring time-saver that you can use for yourself within Flash: Use a fully colored model of your character at the start of a cycle or scene. This will serve as a color model and will be discarded when the cycle or shot is finished. It's very important to keep a model sheet, which is an archive of color models — finished, fully colored characters — to maintain consistent color across the span of the project. (It's also quite useful at the start of future projects.)

Cross-Reference   Sandro Corsaro includes an excellent example of a fully colored model sheet in his tutorial on "Flash Character Design Strategies." To see the animated version of the model sheet, open modelSheet.swf from the S_Corsaro folder in the ch13 folder on the CD-ROM.

Although Flash has the capability to save color sets, it's still difficult to remember which yellow was used on a certain area of the character, especially when there are ten different yellows in the palette. Making such a color mistake — even a slight shade off — will cause unsightly flicker on playback. The Eyedropper tool makes no mistakes. So, to develop good animation habits, start a model sheet. When you begin a scene, copy the appropriate color model and paste it into the cycle, setting it off to the side of the active art in the first frame (if needed, ungroup it). Acquire the color that you need with the Eyedropper tool and then set about the business of filling.

When filling, we've found that the most efficient method is to go through the entire cycle with one color, filling all objects of that color. Then go back to the beginning and sweep through again, doing the next color. This method saves you the tedium of continually having to change the Paint Bucket's color and also minimizes the possibility of mistakes. If some places fill while others don't, you'll probably need to adjust the Paint Bucket Gap size modifier.

Gap problems

There are, however, times when you can't find the gaps and the Paint Bucket tool just won't work. In this case, keep looking because the gaps are there. But if it just doesn't work, no matter how much you zoom in and click with the Paint Bucket tool, you may need to zoom in and use the Selection tool to close the gap by adjusting a stroke. In a situation in which it's not aesthetically pleasing to do that, use the Brush tool (set to the same fill color and to paint fills only) to fill the gaps manually. Perhaps this would be the case on a head and neck that you don't want connected to the body (remember earlier about the advantages of animating the head separately). You would use the Brush tool to paint a stroke of fill connecting the inked lines and then fill the larger areas with the Paint Bucket tool.

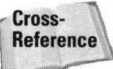

For a review of working with the Paint Bucket tool and using the Gap size modifier, refer to Chapter 9, "Modifying Graphics."

Speed coloring

A good way to speed up the coloring process is to allocate one of the mouse buttons (if you have a programmable mouse) to perform the keyboard shortcut for step forward advancing (which is the > key). If you have a pressure-sensitive graphics tablet, you can allocate a button on the pen to do the same. With a setup like this, you can leave the cursor in pretty much the same place and click-fill, click-advance, click-fill, click-advance, and so on.

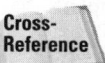

The process for creating custom shortcut keys is discussed in Chapter 4, "Interface Fundamentals."

Temporary backgrounds

Another problem that's easily solved is the process of filling areas with white. If you're like most people, you most likely work on the default background color of white, which makes it impossible to distinguish when filling white areas. In this case, it's helpful to create a very light color that you don't plan to use in the final art, something like a light pink. While coloring, temporarily change the background color in the Property inspector or in the Movie Properties dialog box (Modify ➪ Document) to the substitute color for the background of the entire movie. This makes it much easier to see what you're doing when using white as a fill color for objects such as eyeballs, teeth, and clouds. Then, when you're done coloring, you can set the background color back to white.

Flash Character Design Strategies, *by Sandro Corsaro*

Flash offers a cheaper, faster, and more malleable approach to creating animation than anything in the history of animation. While traditional animation production can be unforgiving, the Flash authoring environment offers animators a variety of starting points in fulfilling their visions. Many creative types who are experienced with Flash can delve into projects with simple thumbnail sketches or even with just concepts in their heads. Purists, and developers working with larger teams, generally prefer the traditional story-board route. Whether it is intended for Web or broadcast, creating an efficient Flash animation begins and ends with the strategy of your initial design. That design can be on paper, in Flash, or even in your head. What is crucial is that on some level, there is a clear and concise plan in the design. For the purposes of this tutorial, we will look at two simple examples involving design strategy.

By now you should be are familiar with the concept of breaking elements into reusable parts or pieces. For Web purposes, this keeps the file small and saves the artist production time. This systemized approach to animation is the evolution of *limited animation* — the cut-out system that hasn't changed since it was first applied by Hanna-Barbera for televi-sion shows like *The Flintstones* and *Scooby Doo*. When Fred would talk, his mouth would be on one layer, while his head and body would be on another. If Fred tilted his head dur-ing a rant, his mouth and head would tilt during the animation, while his upper body would be held. Why do you think all those great Hanna-Barbera characters always had some sort of accessory (like a tie or necklace) around their necks? This design strategy was effective even with a constrained budget because it allowed for maximum animation with minimal artwork.

Today, Flash has the potential to revolutionize the production process by building on the animation techniques used in the past. Just like the traditional cel method, inactive Flash layers can be "held" while action layers continue with additional frames of movement. The newest feature of this evolution is that symbols, unlike old-school painted cels, can be flipped, stretched, and squashed without having to redraw the artwork. A traditional painted animation cel of a left arm could not be reused for the right arm. On the simplest level, appendages can be flipped, rotated, and scaled to complete character designs. The model sheet created in Flash of Da Boss (shown in Figure 13-7) is an example of effective reuse of artwork.

Figure 13-7: By designing the character in reusable pieces, you can simplify your workflow while increasing the options for how the character can be animated.

On the CD-ROM

To see the animated Flash version of the model sheet for Da Boss, open the `modelSheet.swf` from the `S_Corsaro` folder in the `ch13` folder on the CD-ROM.

The script called for this character to be constantly pacing his office. When I designed the character, I broke him into three distinct parts, each with their own animation. The first part was the combed-over hair—I kept it as a separate piece from the head, so it could undulate up and down as he paced. This provides a nice secondary action to his walk. Although the hair is a small detail, without the initial planning, attempting to add it later in the animation process would have proven frustrating and time-consuming. The second animation was the inertia of the heavy upper body. As Da Boss walked, his body needed to convey a sense of weight and power. Utilizing the animation principle of stretch and squash, the symbol of his upper body cycles through various shapes in conjunction with his walk.

The final and most dynamic component of the character's movement is the leg cycle taking place on the layer underneath his upper body. Only one leg has actually been drawn—the other is offset and placed on a lower layer to create a looped walk. As the legs move into each keyframe, the first two elements described previously are adjusted to create the secondary animation. On the low points of the walk, his weight squashes down, while his hair holds (or pauses) for a momentary beat. A progression of movement follows in the next few keyframes to get to the inverse position of this low point.

Besides the basic model movement, a turnaround was also needed for the animators to work with this character. Obviously some of the views can be flipped, but what about the front and back? Copy and paste your front view to create your back view. Build on your finished artwork to create the new artwork. Figure 13-8 illustrates how the front view of the Da Boss was modified to create the back view. Unlike the traditional animation process, which travels in distinct and separate stages from point A to B to C, think of Flash animation as a more integrated progression as point A *becomes* B which *transforms* into C. Always try to build on your work, rather than starting from scratch each time you need a new movement or character.

Figure 13-8: With small modifications, the same artwork can be used for the front and back of the character.

Perhaps the most convincing example of the benefits of strategizing your design can be understood by referring to Figure 13-9. These were three different characters intended to be used for broadcast purposes, but the actual animation only had to be created once.

To see how the motion is actually reused in the example shown in Figure 13-9, open `reuseWalk.swf` from the S_Corsaro folder in the ch13 folder on the CD-ROM.

Figure 13-9: When a character is designed strategically, you can reuse your animation as well as your artwork to quickly create other characters.

Because of the strategy involved in the original character design, I was able to transform him into the other two characters, reusing both his Graphic symbols and the actual animation. By tweaking the timing of one leg on the run cycle, and obviously making some other artistic changes, the skateboarder character was created from the same artwork as the character running to catch a bus.

Flash is a very sophisticated authoring environment for animation, but nonetheless there is no substitute for knowledge of motion. To create truly compelling and intriguing animation in any genre, you must understand the scientific fundamentals of this art. The best place to learn about the principles of animation is in the daily environment around you. Observe the way things move; then strategize how to translate that movement efficiently using the tools available in Flash.

Flash Tweening

You can use Flash tweening to help your cartooning. Now that you've created some symbols, such as the walk cycle, here's where you can save a great deal of time making them slink and prance across the view without drawing every tedious frame. The hard manual drawing work is done; now you'll choreograph the character. Once you've built a library of various walks, runs, turnarounds, and standstills (a piece of walk cycle that ends with the character just standing still), you can use computer power to help you tell a story. Remember that you can always create more symbols of the character as needed — you can even steal from other symbols to create new ones.

Panning

Use the techniques discussed earlier in this chapter to get your walking symbol looping, stationary in the middle of the view. Then move the background elements to give the illusion of the camera following alongside the walking character, a sort of dolly. The trick for creating extra long pans is described later in this chapter. It usually requires a little experimentation to get the motion of the background to match the stride of the step. If the timing isn't correct, you'll notice that the feet will seem to skate across the ground. To fix this, adjust the speed of the background by either increasing or decreasing the number of frames in the tween of the background. Another trick is to set the walking symbol to start at one end of the view and to move to the other by tweening the symbol itself. What's really cool is to use a mixture of both. Again, to get it just right, experiment.

Instance swapping

There comes a time when the star of your show must stop walking (or running, or whatever he's doing) and reach into his pocket to pull out a hot rod car and make his getaway. This is where instance swapping comes in. At the end of the tween, create a keyframe on the next frame (the frame immediately following the last keyframe in the tween), and then turn off Motion tweening for that keyframe in the Property inspector. This causes the symbol to stop at whichever frame the cycle ended on in the Timeline. To swap the symbol, follow these steps:

1. Click the symbol to select it on the Stage.

2. Open the Property inspector.

3. Click the Swap Symbol button.

4. In the Swap Symbol dialog box, select the symbol that you want to replace it with (in this case, the one where he reaches into his pocket).

5. Click OK.

If you loop the play of the symbol, you can also choose the frame on which the symbol's cycle will start. Other choices are limiting the symbol to play once and playing just a single frame (still).

Caution

When you swap a symbol instance on a Motion tween, if the Synchronize box is checked, the old symbol instance will not be replaced with the new one, which is Swap Symbol failure. If you turn off tweening on the frame where you swap the symbol, synchronization is not an issue.

Finally, unless you've drawn all your symbols to perfect scale with each other, this new symbol may not fit exactly. No problem! To fix this, simply enable onion skinning from the Main Timeline, and set it to show the previous frame (the frame the tween ended on). Now you can align and scale the new symbol to match the ghosted image. We can't begin to tell you how much you'll use this simple instance-swapping function when you create your cartoon. This is one of the unique functions that set Flash apart from all other cel-type animation programs. After you have a modest library of pre-drawn actions, the possibilities for combining them are endless.

Motion guides

Although not terribly useful for tweening a walking character, the Flash Motion Guide feature is tops for moving inanimate objects. If your character needs to throw a brick, a straight tween between points and some blur lines will do fine. If he needs to lob that brick over a fence to clang a pesky neighbor, then motion guides are the ticket. Here's how:

1. Turn the brick into a Graphic symbol if you haven't already. This makes it easier to make changes to the brick later.

2. Create a Motion Guide layer.

3. Draw an arc from start to destination. This is best done by drawing a line with the Line tool and then retouching it with the Selection tool until you have bent it into the desired arc. This method keeps the motion smooth. (Using the Pencil tool to draw the Motion guide would create too many points and can cause stuttering in the motion.)

Although your brick is flying smoothly, something's wrong. Again, the computer made things too darned smooth. You could insert a few keyframes in the tween and rotate slightly here and there to give it some wobble. But that's still not convincing. You want this brick to mean business! Here's what to do: Because the brick is already a symbol, go back to the brick symbol and edit it, adding a few more frames. Don't add more than three or four frames; doing so will slow it down. At each of these new frames, mess up the brick a little here and there; differ the perspectives a little from one frame to another. Then, when you go back to your main Timeline, the brick should be twitching with vengeance as it sails toward its target.

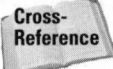 **Cross-Reference**   For more information on creating and using Motion guides, refer to Chapter 12, "Applying Layer Types."

Lip-syncing

Now here's the part we've all been waiting for . . . a word from our character. If done properly, lip-syncing is where a character can really spring to life. This is accomplished by drawing the various mouth positions that are formed for individual *phonemes,* which are the basic units of sound that make up a spoken word. Then these phonemes are melded together into *morphemes,* which are distinct units of a word, like a syllable. Morphemes are then strung together over the course of a sentence to present the illusion of a talking, animated character. Most languages, although populated with thousands of words, are really made up from around 30 to 60 distinct sounds, or phonemes. For cartooning, these phonemes can be reduced to about 10 basic mouth positions. Some of these positions can be repeated for more than one sound because many sounds share roughly the same mouth positions. Although there are more subtleties in the real world, for cartoons, reliance upon transitions between mouth positions is convincing enough.

Earlier, we suggested that the face in an action (walk) cycle should be drawn without a mouth. That's because this method facilitates the use of layers (in the Timeline) for the addition of lip-syncing. To do this, create a layer above the character so that you can freely draw in the mouth positions needed to add lip-syncing. It's also very helpful to put the voice track on another separate layer directly above the Mouth layer. This makes it easy to see the waveform of the sound while you draw, giving important clues to where and when the sound occurs visually.

Since version 4, Flash has had the capability to scrub the Timeline, which means that you can drag the Playhead, or current frame indicator, and hear the sound as you drag. This functionality is limited to streaming sounds, which means that the sounds have their Sync option in the Property inspector set to Streaming. The capability to hear the sound and see the animation in real time is an important tool for lip-syncing. This real-time feedback is critical for getting the timing just right. There's nothing worse than being plagued with O.G.M.S. (Old Godzilla Movie Syndrome), in which the mouth doesn't match the sounds coming from it.

Tip   To scrub most effectively, here's a hint: If you're working with a complex animation file with lots of moving bitmaps, you might have a hard time getting smooth playback in the authoring environment. To overcome this drag and to get real-time playback at the full-frame rate, simply hide all layers except the mouth layers and turn off anti-aliasing.

Shape morphing is not for lip-syncing

You may be asking, "What about using shape morphing to save time in lip-syncing?" Well, shape morphing is a wonderful tool but, for lip-syncing, it's more hassle than it's worth. Your mouth drawings will become very complicated because they consist of lips, tongue, teeth, and facial features. Furthermore, because shape morphing only seems to work predictably on the simplest of shapes out of the box, shape hinting is required. Thus, by the time you've set all hinting (and even hinting heavily still leaves you with a mess at times), you might have had an easier time and obtained a better result (with greater control) if you had drawn it by hand.

Expression and lip-syncing

In terms of control and expression, it's important to remember to use the full range of expression when drawing the talking mouths. Happy, sad, or confused — these give life to your character. Furthermore, always emphasize mouth movements on those syllables that correspond with spikes of emotion in the voice track. These sections usually have a spike in the waveform that's easily recognized in the voice track. This device helps to convince the viewer that proper sync is happening.

Lip-sync tricks

There are a few more tricks to help ease the load. When characters talk, they do not always have to be looking you square in the face. Try lip-syncing the first few words to establish that the character is speaking, and then obscure the character's mouth in some natural way. (Refer to Figure 13-10.) The head and body of a character can move with the words being said, but the mouth can be hidden by changing the angle of the head, or with a prop such as a microphone, or even with a moustache — think about this when designing your character's features. A bit of design savvy can save time without detracting from a character's purpose in the story line.

Many animators use a mirror placed nearby and mouth (act out) the words they're trying to draw. This is extremely helpful when learning to do lip-sync. It is also of great help in mastering facial expressions. Just try not to get too wrapped up in drawing every nuance you see. Sometimes less is more. Another trick that you can use to ease the load is to reuse lip-sync. Do this by copying frames from previous stretches of mouth movements to new locations where the words are the same, and then tweak the copied parts to fit the new dialogue. Still, there is no magic lip-sync button. Even with all these tricks, effective lip-syncing is hard work. It's also one of the more tedious tasks in animation and takes practice to get it right.

Figure 13-10: Lip-syncing tricks include economy of effort, such as having a character begin to speak and then turn away naturally (left). Appropriate props and even moustaches can also be used to hide mouths (right).

Syncing with music and sound effects

Because our brain works to create connections between sound and visual input, it is relatively easy to make movement in your animation match up with audio elements in your soundtrack. If you've already succeeded with lip-syncing work, then this type of syncing is easy. All that's required is a bit of instance swapping set to the beat of the music. If you study your music waveform for visual clues and then scrub it for the sound, you're sure to find the exact section where the change in action (instance swap) needs to go. You don't have to make your sync tight to every note. To keep the shot engaging, sync to the highlights, or hard beats.

Adding sound effects is really the fun part. It's easy and highly effective. Either working from your storyboard, or as you're animating, you'll know where you want to insert a sound effect. For example, when the anvil hits the head, a CLANK is needed there. If the effect you need is on hand, great! Just make sure it has the necessary duration, and then plug it in at the frame where it should start. For broadcast animation you'll set the sound sync to Streaming for the soundtrack exclusively. In addition to using separate layers for each voice track, it's wise to confine your sound effects to a layer or two. This leads to less confusion; yet using two layers enables more than one sound effect to occur at a time.

On the CD-ROM

For the following Expert Tutorial, we've supplied a short track for your use, `lip_track.wav` or `lip_track.aif`, which you'll find in the `B_Turner` folder inside the `ch13` folder of the CD-ROM. These tracks include the major sounds used in the English language.

Lip-Syncing Cartoons, by Bill Turner

For animated characters to really come alive, you need to know how to do lip-sync. To get quality lip-sync effects, you either need to draw them yourself or hire someone else to do it for you. Although this tutorial can't possibly cover every circumstance known to human communication, it can get you started on the road to lip service. There are some prequalifications: First, you must be able to draw in Flash, which usually means drawing with a tablet, preferably a pressure-sensitive graphics tablet (such as a Wacom tablet), and second, you need to have a recorded voice track on its own layer in Flash.

Because lip-sync can't be described in a simple a, b, c routine tutorial, you'll be required to improvise — in your style of drawing. I can't tell you how to do that. Style comes from years of practice and experimentation. But if you do know how to draw and you do have a style, then the intention here is to provide a context in which you might discover the basic trick of lip-sync.

The major sounds, known as phonemes, are less numerous than you might think. It's how these sounds meld together to become words and sentences that add an aura of complexity. Although one might surmise, from the alphabet, that there are 26 sounds, there aren't nearly that many. That's because many letters have the same basic mouth shape, movement, and pronunciation. And because we're now in the land of cartoons, we can simplify even further — the really great cartoons are often the simple ones built of tireless simple reinterpretation.

In this tutorial, to keep it simple, we'll deal with the two dominant views of talking heads: profile and face forward. A face forward talking head is probably the easiest to animate in Flash because the mouth can be animated on a layer that's situated in the layer stack above a drawing of a mouthless head. A talking head in profile is more difficult because of the need to redraw the portion of the face that extends down from the nose, to and including the chin, for *every* frame. Of course, including nose-to-chin movements can also enhance the animation of a face forward talker, and doing so would make for a more expressive animation. But we want to move quickly here.

In Figure 13-11, you see a mouthless head (provided on the CD-ROM in the B_Turner folder for both demonstration and practice) in both of the basic orientations: face forward and profile.

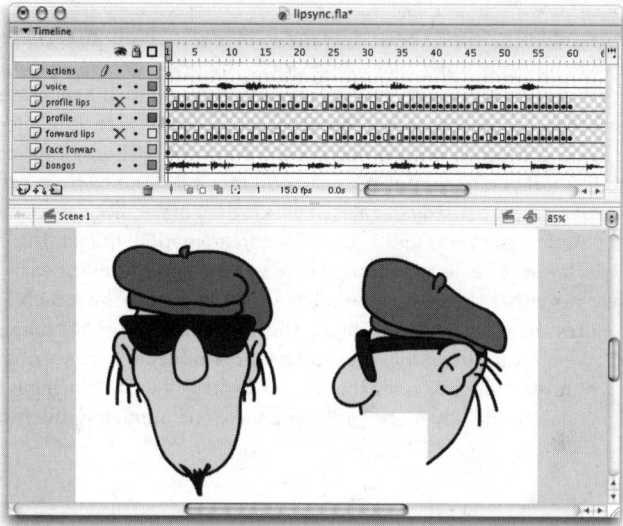

Figure 13-11: A mouthless head in both of the basic orientations: face forward and profile with sound and animation layers for adding lip sync.

The spoken test line reads, "Zinkle Meyers is very talented on the bongo drums. Flip Flap beats his hands on the smooooth skins. Dig the rhythm. Excellent!" Creating lip-sync for this line requires a number of mouth positions. To demonstrate the concepts, the first sentence of this test line is supplied, already drawn to lip-sync. Your task is to draw the mouth positions for the remainder of the spoken text.

On the
CD-ROM

To help get you started, Bill Turner supplied a fully functional FLA file for you to work on, with the base character already drawn (`lipsync.fla`.). You can find the file in the `ch13/B_Turner` folder on the CD-ROM.

The Sync option

If you were setting this file up from scratch, you'd want to start by placing the voice soundtrack on its own layer on the Timeline. You'd rename this layer with a meaningful name, such as voice, and then, in the Property inspector, you'd set the Sync option to Stream.

Never use Event as the Sync option for any sound that must sync to the Flash Timeline. Otherwise, the timing of the voice will not be locked to the frame rate, meaning that the mouth drawings may not appear simultaneously with their appropriate sounds, thus losing sync.

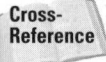

Cross-
Reference

For a full explanation of the Streaming versus Event sound settings, refer to Chapter 15, "Adding Sound."

Getting into sync

The best way to understand lip-sync is to have the sample file open. Note that there is a visible waveform (the little squiggly stuff) that shows where the peaks and valleys of the sound occur across the Timeline. Note, too, that the voice is brought in as a separate asset. It's on its own layer, separate from background sounds or music. Otherwise, it would be impossible to see the voice within the waveform if it were premixed with other sounds before bringing it into Flash. If you're producing a cartoon show, it's best to have each character recorded separately, particularly in cases in which they may talk over each other simultaneously. This separation gives you more control when animating. In fact, the entire animation is broken into layers for ease of editing. There's at least one layer for each major element. You might also note that the bongo soundtrack is set to event. This is useful while authoring because it mutes the track when scrubbing the Timeline to listen for timings in the voice track. If both were set to streaming, it would be more difficult to concentrate on the voice alone. (You must remember to reset this option to Stream when syncing is completed, or you could just delete that layer until after you are done animating the mouth.)

The phonemes

Now for the phonemes, there are several standard mouth positions for most of the major sounds, as shown in Figure 13-12. Although this is not a rigid rule, it does provide a good basis from which to expand into greater mastery of lip-sync. First, you'll note that the word *Meyers* begins on frame 12 of the animation. The mmmm sound is best represented with the bottom lip tucked slightly under the top lip. Try saying mmmm to see for yourself. In the word *Meyers*, this mmmm sound lasts two frames and is then followed by the long *I* sound. Notice that we didn't sync the word as it is spelled, e-y-e, because that's more complicated than it needs to be. The word *Meyers* is usually pronounced M-I-ER-Z, with the *ER* being just an *ease-out* (mouth holds shape but gets slightly smaller as phoneme trails off) of the long *I* sound. The word ends with the Z phoneme, which is simply drawn with the mouth slightly open, and the tongue at the top of the mouth.

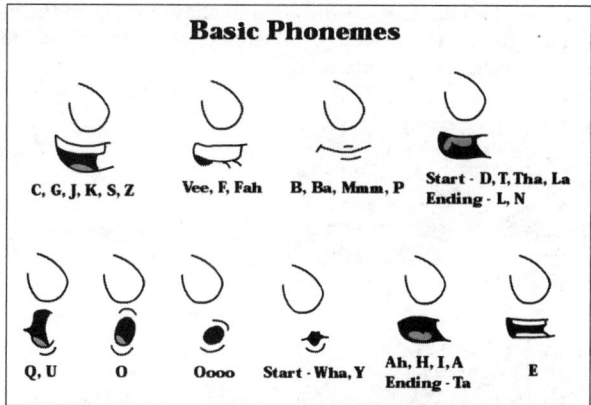

Figure 13-12: You can combine a few basic phonemes to create lip-synced speech.

In the next section of speech, the "very talented" part is a fast-moving set of syllables, so every available frame is needed to represent it. Here, you'll notice that most of the movement occurs when the tongue engages the roof of the mouth for both the *T* and *L* phoneme. Now, because the *T* and *L* are nearly the same mouth position, you can use the luxury of duplicating frames. Similarly, the *V* sound requires the same basic mouth formation as the *M* sound, so you could copy this one as well from the Meyers word. Although the *B* sound, in *bongos*, uses nearly the same mouth as M and V, we don't copy that one. Here, we draw a new mouth to add a bit of chaos because we don't want the mouth to look like a machine. The logic behind deciding which part to copy and which part to make new drawings for is a large part of the art of lip-sync. In short, it's all about balancing how much new artwork you really want to do, while avoiding obvious repetition.

Now that I've given you an insight into how this is done, I've left the rest of the phrase for you to complete. To accomplish this, you'll probably want to reuse many of the supplied mouth positions to sync the remaining voice. Remember that timing is the most crucial part. You can determine where a new mouth position is needed, or where the mouth needs work, by slowly scrubbing the Timeline. Then, if you need new mouths, simply draw them in. We highly recommend doing this drawing yourself because this practice will start you on your way to becoming a master of lip-sync.

Backgrounds and Scenery

As you have learned in previous chapters, in Flash you work in an area that is called the Stage area. For broadcast animation (or any other kind, for that matter) it is better to think of it as the viewfinder of a camera. The main difference between this camera and the traditional kind, or even those used in 3D animation, is this: *You can't move it.* So, to give the illusion of camera movement, everything within the view must move. This is not as hard as it might seem with Flash's capability to use animated graphic symbols. A good example is in Richard Bazley's animated short, *The Journal of Edwin Carp*.

In a scene where the view seems to pan up from Edwin's bed to show a crack in the ceiling, all of the elements on the Stage have to move to create the illusion of a camera move. Here are the steps for creating this effect, as shown in Figure 13-13:

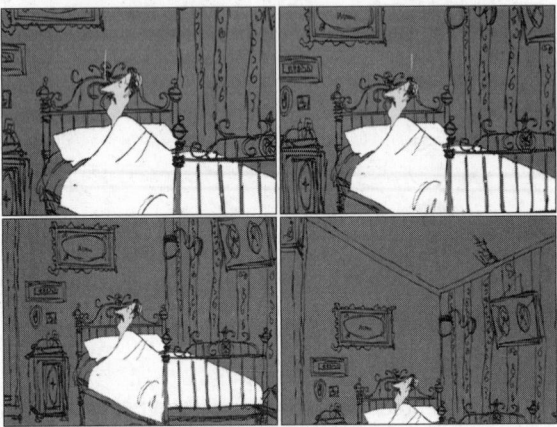

Figure 13-13: A few shots from the bedroom scene in *The Journal of Edwin Carp*

1. A Graphic symbol of the entire scene of animation that was larger than the camera's view was made (so that white space wouldn't show at the edges).

2. The symbol was placed in the Main Timeline.

3. The symbol was scaled and placed on the first keyframe to frame the medium view of Edwin in his bed.

4. The symbol was then scaled and placed on a later keyframe to frame the view of the cracked ceiling.

5. By tweening between these two keyframed views, the illusion of a camera zoom out and pan up is created as the whole scene moves on the Stage.

On the CD-ROM

This scene and several others from *The Journal of Edwin Carp*, an animated feature film that was done entirely in Flash, are included on the CD-ROM in the R_Bazley folder inside the ch13 folder.

 Richard Bazley described some of his other clever animation techniques in his tutorial for the Flash MX Bible on "2D Character Animation". This tutorial is archived online for readers who wish to learn more about specialized animation techniques. Go to www.flashsupport. com/archive.

Bitmaps

As mentioned previously, when designing with Flash for the Web, raster (bitmap) images should be used with a careful eye on their file size. But for broadcast output, there's no limit. Not only can you use as many images as you'd like (within system constraints), but doing so will make a richer, far more attractive finished product. And, unlike the SWF format, when output as raster video, even animations built with a lot of bitmaps will play at the proper frame rate. So move, animate, scale, and rotate them — even play sequences of them. The sky and RAM are the only limits.

QuickTime limitations

Beginning with Flash 4, Flash expanded its import capabilities to include raster video — QuickTime and AVI. When using video output for broadcast you can export to these formats, too, and video that has been embedded in a Flash project file (.fla) will show up when output to SWF format. Unfortunately, Flash does not recognize alpha channels embedded in the QuickTime 32-bit animation codec (which supports traveling mattes, or alphas). However, you can use Mask layers on the video in Flash. Remember that you also have the option to link the video file rather than saving it within the Flash project file (thank goodness) — it makes a pointer to it instead. This will keep your file sizes much more manageable. The only drawback to linking video instead of embedding it is that it won't show up when output to the SWF format.

The option of combining video with vector animation has brought tremendous functionality to Flash because animations can be keyed (composited) over (or behind) live video without having to recomposite in After Effects. To take advantage of this, keep your live video at the same frame rate as the Flash project. Note, however, that Flash will export only the audio from the video clip in some formats, so you may need to reapply sound in a video-editing application. An alternate solution is to bring the video and audio tracks into Flash separately and to synchronize them there before exporting to your chosen format.

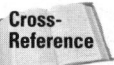 For more detailed information about the various options for exporting animation and audio, refer to Chapter 14, "Exporting Animation."

Building layered backgrounds in Photoshop

By using layers in Photoshop to create artwork, multiplane shots are easily accomplished in Flash. Using layers is very important to the organization of the animation. It is not uncommon for a single shot to require more than 20 layers to keep things where they need to be in the visual stacking order. When designing backgrounds (or *scenery,* to be more precise) remember that, at some point, background elements may need to be foreground elements. For instance, the sky will always be in the background, so it is on a layer furthest down in the stack. Other background elements, however, may sometimes need to be in the foreground to facilitate movement of the character either in front of or behind them. To allow flexibility in how your various elements interact, they should be kept on separate layers.

When creating layered backgrounds, use of Photoshop and alpha channels delivers the most versatility. When using Photoshop for scenery elements, it's mandatory to work in layers and to save a master file with all layers intact. Elements can then be exported to individual files (with alpha channels) as needed. (Retaining the master layered Photoshop file gives you maximum options later, if edits or changes occur. It can also be used as a resource for subsequent animations, so don't flatten or discard your master layered Photoshop file. Instead, number and archive it!) Why the alpha channels? When translating the Photoshop elements into Flash vector scenery, they automatically mask themselves — so a little preplanning in Photoshop can save lots of time later.

Cross-Reference

For guidelines on importing raster artwork to Flash, refer to Chapter 16, "Importing Artwork." More suggestions for preparing raster artwork in Photoshop are included in Chapter 35, "Working with Raster Graphics."

Flash Mask layers

Whoops! You got to a point where you didn't use layers and now you need a mask. Some situations may be either too complicated or else unforeseeable in the original design. Flash Mask layers can come to the rescue. Here's the good news: You can mask (and animate the mask) interactively with the other elements while in Flash. The bad news is that it may be more difficult to create a precise mask in Flash than it would have been to export an alpha channel from the original Photoshop file. A classic example of masking used in character animation is the black circle that closes in on a scene at the end of an animated episode — this simple animated shape mask is easy to add in Flash.

Cross-Reference

For detailed explanation of creating various mask types in Flash, refer to Chapter 12, "Applying Layer Types."

Long pans

Long pans are a standard device of animated cartoons, as when Fred Flintstone runs through the house and furniture keeps zipping past (that must be one looooong living room). This can be done in a couple of ways in Flash. For landscape backgrounds, it's usually best to first create a very wide graphic (bitmap or vector) of the landscape and then to Motion tween it horizontally, with keyframes for stopping and starting as needed within the tween. If something is either falling or ascending, use a tall graphic and Motion tween vertically. Another solid technique is to create art of the objects that will pan (such as clouds) and then loop them as the background layer, across the view. To get smooth results when using looping, don't use easing in or out with the tween setup. Also, to maintain constant speed, maintain the exact number of frames between the keyframes. Then, copy the tween by Alt (Option) dragging the selected tween frames to the desired area in the Timeline. Repeat copying until you've covered the time needed.

Caution

For Web animation, it is best to use Movie Clips for looping animation, but if you are planning to output your animation to video, all animation has to be laid out in keyframes on the main Timeline (or in Graphic symbols.) When exported to video, only the first frame of any Movie Clips will display, unless you use After Effects to translate the SWF file before final output.

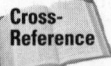

Cross-Reference

For more information on exporting animation, refer to Chapter 14, "Exporting Animation."

In the Weber cartoon scene of a chase along the beach, a camera pan was created by tweening a symbol of the whole beach scene horizontally. As shown in Figure 13-14, the "camera view" reveals only a small area of the larger background scene.

Figure 13-14: The chase scene from the Weber cartoon is created with a looping pan.

Multiplane pans

To provide 3D-motion depth during the pan, keep this rule in mind: An object that is farther away appears to move slower (than a nearer object) as it moves across the view. This takes some experimenting to get it right, but once mastered, this will add a professional touch to your animations. For example, in a 100-frame pan:

✦ The sky moves very slowly at 100 pixels total.

✦ The water moves more quickly at 125 pixels total.

✦ The character on the beach moves more quickly than the water at 150 pixels total.

✦ A parked car in the immediate foreground moves most rapidly at 250 pixels total.

Blurring to simulate depth

The multiplane camera was used in early Disney films to give a feeling of depth in the animation of flat artwork. There was physical space between the individual cels when photographed. By using a short depth of field lens, the artwork that was further away from the lens lost focus slightly. (You may have noticed this in still photography yourself.) If you set up your scenery using bitmaps, you can recreate this effect. A good example of this is the pier scene from the Weber cartoon, which is shown in Figure 13-15. In Photoshop, it's a simple case of using incrementally higher doses of Gaussian blur on the layers of your scenery that are further way. The further the object is, the more blur that is applied — just be sure that the blur is applied to the alpha channel that Flash will use in compositing. Photographers use this technique to bring attention to the element in the shot that is in focus. Using it in animation enhances the illusion of depth. However, using it in the foreground can also portray various elements such as fog.

Figure 13-15: The opening pier scene from the Weber cartoon has a feeling of depth created by using Photoshop blur on the background layers.

Finishing Up

When you have a shot done, it's often helpful to see it play at full speed. Unfortunately, Flash is unable keep up with all of the sounds, bitmaps, and complicated vectors that go into broadcast-quality animation. Plus, it's impossible—even with the most macho of processors—to play the shot at full speed without hiding a bunch of elements. But, hey, you're the director of this masterpiece—it's time for dailies, and you need to see it all.

The best way to do this and to cut down on file size is to export a raster video at 320 x 240 pixels, using the standard QuickTime Video codec (Mac) or the Microsoft Video 1 codec. These codecs are for draft purposes only, so it may have banding and artifacts from compression, but the point is to generate something that even a machine that's ill-equipped for high-end video output can display easily at full frame-rate speed. This method will be of great help in revealing those areas of the animation that still need further tweaking and work before going out to the final published version. The general movement and pace of the shot will make itself known. Look for errors such as unintended jumpiness in frames, and color shifts or inconsistencies between views. Furthermore, your lip-syncing efforts will either be a glory to behold or a disaster in need of medical attention. Other things, such as sound clipping (pops in high volume sound) also become apparent here. To put it bluntly, if the preview makes you cringe, then it needs work—if not, you're on your way to final output.

Final output

Now, after checking endlessly you're ready for the final video file of the shot to be rendered. Back it up one more time. Then, when you've safely archived your final project file, it's time to choose the codec that your playback equipment can use and render one out for the tube. Then, when you have rendered all your shots at full screen, you can take them into Premiere or After Effects for more detailed editing and tweaking, utilizing all the power that these applications offer. For example, you might want music to play gently in the background across all of your scenes. Although this would be impossible to piece together with separate Flash project files, it's a snap in Premiere. Again, the possibilities are endless.

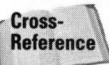

Cross-Reference

Some suggested workflows for output of character animation are described in detail in Chapter 14, "Exporting Animation."

Filter Effects for "Classic" Broadcast Animation, by Evan & Gregg Spiridellis

If you've made it to this section of the book, you are by now well aware that Flash is an amazing tool not only for online animation, but also for broadcast animation.

There is one pitfall with using Flash animation for broadcast purposes: Time and time again, we hear that Flash looks too "Flashy" — meaning that it is too "digital" or "perfect" when transferred. The perfectly flat colors that you get from Flash work great in some circumstances, but when transferred for broadcast they come across as a bit cold and lifeless. Looking at big, even blocks of color on a computer monitor is one thing, but traditional animation needs to look more organic.

We've found the solution in DigiEffects CineLook 1.5 plug-in for Adobe AfterEffects. The software is a bit expensive at US$695, but if you do a lot of this kind of work, it is worth every penny! It takes your perfect digital files and adds enough imperfection to give your Flash animation a more organic look and feel. In this tutorial we will explain our process for adding filter effects to a Flash animation file in preparation for broadcast delivery. Although many of the filter effects are very subtle, you can see some of the differences between the original Flash artwork and the final filtered animation in Figure 13-16.

Web Resource

For more information and demo versions of the CineLook plug-in go to www.digieffects.com.

Figure 13-16: Flash artwork that looks too "clean" for broadcast (top) can be modified with filters in AfterEffects to look more organic (below).

Setting up the file

After installing the CineLook plug-ins you're ready to begin. Start by exporting your Flash movie as a Quicktime or AVI.

Cross-Reference   For coverage of the options for exporting Flash files for broadcast, refer to Chapter 14, "Exporting Animation."

Open After Effects and set up a new Composition. The dimensions and duration should match your Flash file. Import your Quicktime or AVI file and drag your movie to the Timeline. Select the movie in the Timeline by clicking its layer and now you can begin to add filters.

Softening with Gaussian Blur

The first thing that we recommend is adding an ever-so-slight Gaussian blur to take the hard "edge" off of the lines in your Flash movie. Go to **Effect** ➪ **Blur & Sharpen**. Apply a **0.1** or **0.25 Gaussian blur** depending on the style you are trying to achieve.

Caution

It is very easy to get carried away with these filters! It is important to find the filter effect that bests compliment your movie and not go overboard with the effects. After all, you want people to congratulate you on your movie, not your filters!

After the initial Gaussian softening, we can proceed with our "film look" filters.

Adding DE CineLook filters

Make sure that your movie is still selected in the Timeline, go to Effects ➪ DigiEffects CineLook and select **DE CineLook**.

The CineLook plug-in allows us to add and control film grain, adjust color temperatures and view whether our colors are NTSC safe. There is nothing worse then spending hours perfecting your animation only to find that when it's transferred to television your colors bleed all over the screen.

The first thing we do is run the **NTSC Gamut Warning**. This will block out any colors that are not NTSC safe and allow us to make the appropriate adjustments. You can adjust your saturation and color levels until non-safe colors enter the NTSC spectrum. Cinelook gives you seven layers of adjustment for your Red, Green, Blue and White channels or you can transform your entire file to Black and White.

Next we tackle the **film grain**. This is by far the biggest advantage of the CineLook plug-ins. Color film is processed in three layers: red, green and blue. CineLook allows you to control the amount of grain and the softness of the grain in each color field. Adding a slight grain effect will help activate the big, flat shapes that Flash is notorious for. If done well, this adjustment may not be overtly noticeable to the average viewer but will simply add a more organic feel to your movie. Of course, if it fits the style of your movie, you can go overboard!

Once you find the right grain level for your current animation, you have the option of saving your settings. This makes it possible to get a uniform look throughout an entire project or apply the same effects to multiple projects.

Adding DE FileDamage filters

After polishing your Flash movie with a "film look" you might want to take it one step further and "damage" the film a bit. The FileDamage plug-in is a great tool for making a perfect digital file look more weathered. The descriptively named main categories for adjustment are **Flicker**, **Vertical Scratches**, **Hair**, **Dust** and **Dirt**.

In the old days, shooting film was by no means a precise art form and it seems that no two consecutive frames ever received the same amount of light. **Flicker** makes it possible to control the difference in exposure between frames. Select the movie in the timeline then go to **Effects ⇨ DigiEffects CineLook** and select **DE FileDamage**.

The first effect we add is Flicker. FileDamage allows you to control the **Amount**, **Speed** and **Variation** of exposure differences. This might be difficult to see in side-by-side illustrations but when the movie plays in real time Flicker is a very natural effect.

Another disadvantage of traditional film developing (in the early days) was that the celluloid was exposed to the elements at almost every stage of the process. FileDamage allows you to control the amount of hair, dust and dirt that has mucked up the film along the way.

The **Vertical Scratches** effect is the perfect "Old Time" filter and FileDamage allows you to control the **Number**, **Speed**, **Opacity** and **Thickness** of the scratches.

Finishing up

Once you've gotten the desired look for your movie save your settings in the **Presets** section for future use. If you're all set with your filters, save your After Effects file and go to **Composition ⇨ Make Movie** to test your movie.

 **On the CD-ROM**

To see a "live" comparison of the before and after files described in this tutorial open `JibJab_Willy.swf` (original file) and `JibJab_Willy.mov` (filtered file) from the JibJab folder in the `ch13` folder on the CD-ROM.

Film filters like DigiEffects CineLook give you a range of options to take the digital edge off your Flash animation and, when done properly, will give the impression that you've been scribbling cels in your basement for years!

Summary

✦ Flash can be a powerful tool for the creation of broadcast-quality cartoons. In such cases, many of the usual file-size concerns related to Flash development are set aside because the final output will not have to be Web-friendly.

✦ The task of a cartoon animator is to express motion and emotion. Anticipation and overlapping actions are basic tools used by cartoon animators to add drama to a character's movement.

✦ Coloring the art is critical to the final quality of the cartoon—the model sheet, speed coloring, and the use of temporary backgrounds ease the task and lead to greater consistency.

✦ Flash tweening, including instance swapping and Motion guides, is one of the most useful Flash cartooning tools.

✦ Lip-syncing, which is critical to fine cartoon animation, is not a push-button task—even with Flash, an animator must understand the relationship between expression and lip-sync, and have a working knowledge of phonemes, and syncing with music and sound effects.

✦ There are many ways to create effective backgrounds and scenery. These techniques include the use of bitmaps, layers, multiplane pans, blurring to simulate depth, and innumerable combinations of these basic techniques.

✦ Sandro Corsaro has honed the skill of reusing both artwork and animation in Flash to optimize production. By sketching directly in Flash and reusing artwork, Sandro is able to keep the spontaneity of hand-drawn strokes, while saving hours of redundant work.

✦ After a cartoon is created in Flash, final output may include using either Premiere or After Effects for the final polish.

✦ Veteran animator Richard Bazley has compiled a number of insightful tricks from his use of Flash to create his animated short, *The Journal of Edwin Carp*. These tricks include the judicious reuse of drawings, knowing when and where to "cheat," the advantages of simplicity, the power of layers, and the process of making a stagger.

✦ The key point of this entire chapter is this: Computers can save time, but artists animate!

✦   ✦   ✦

Exporting Animation

Flash MX 2004 isn't just a vector graphics tool for the Web. Using Flash, you can create amazing video effects for your home videos or professional productions. This chapter explains how to use digital video with Flash. It also shows you how to export high-quality material from Flash to use in your video-editing applications.

As more developers learn how flexible and powerful the Flash MX 2004 authoring environment is, Flash graphics will be seen on screens in every possible context. With a bit of tweaking, animations originally designed for the Web can be repurposed for stand-alone presentations, broadcast, high-resolution digital projection, or even for transfer to film.

In this chapter, we go over the main factors that need to be considered when preparing Flash content for output to various linear formats.

High-Quality Video Output from Flash

Although Flash is primarily used to create interactive animations and presentations on the Web, you can also generate high-quality output for other media uses. Macromedia began as a company called MacroMind, specializing in frame-by-frame video animation tools for desktop computers. Their flagship product, VideoWorks, eventually became Director, which was the first widely used Macromedia authoring product. Like Director, Flash also has some "hidden" video animation capabilities. You can use Flash to create spinning logos for your own corporate, creative, or home videos. Or you can export those shape morphs — so difficult to create elsewhere — to layer over other video content. Flash can output the content of a FLA file as a QuickTime multimedia file. Flash can also generate numbered still sequences for use in other video-editing applications.

In previous Mac versions of Flash, 100 percent video-based (a.k.a. raster-based) QuickTime (QT) files could be directly rendered via the Export Movie command. Macromedia has added a more robust solution — based on QuickTime 4 — that exports Flash material directly to a Flash track for use in conjunction with video and audio tracks from other sources. This is wonderful if you want to create QTs for QuickTime 4-enabled applications.

Note   All references to QuickTime 4 can also be applied to QuickTime 5 or 6 — QuickTime 4 is just the earliest version that is integrated with Flash.

Most Mac and Windows applications that use the QuickTime architecture — such as Adobe Premiere and Adobe After Effects — will import QuickTime Flash movies. Some NLE (nonlinear editing) software, such as Discreet Cinestream, will not allow you to import QuickTime Flash movies. For the best video results, you will want to export still image sequences from Flash instead of using QuickTime Flash files, or export traditional QuickTime Video files (available only on the Macintosh version of Flash) or AVI files (available only on the Windows version of Flash).

Note Because the export process for sequences uses generic vector or raster formats, you lose all interactivity that you have created in Flash. But that's perfectly fine because you're transferring your Flash movie to a linear viewing environment such as video — you're simply making something to watch on a television or on a computer monitor without any interaction required from the audience.

Flash artwork is completely scalable and flexible for just about any media use. Combined with the QuickTime architecture, Flash artwork can be output to DV tape or motion picture film. If you think your project looks good in Flash, you should be able to repurpose that hard work into another format very easily.

A Quick Video Primer

If you're a neophyte to digital video, you need to know some basic terms and procedures involved with digital video. The following section will be useful if you've never used digital video or used it without really knowing what you were doing.

A brief history of digital video

In the past, viewing or editing digital video on a desktop computer was almost impossible. It required expensive hardware such as super-fast processors, huge hard drives, video-capture boards, and professional-quality video decks and cameras. Beginning at $15,000, such systems were out of reach for most users. But like most technology after it has been around for a while, digital video equipment has become much more affordable for the average user. Although digital video still requires fast and efficient computers to work well, it isn't nearly as expensive as it was in the past. You can get 200GB hard drives for under $200! Since the advent of the DV (Digital Video) format (a.k.a. DVCAM or MiniDV), consumer-level video cameras and decks are catching up to the quality of their professional-level counterparts.

The need for space

Why does digital video require so many resources? To begin with, digital video is entirely *raster-based*. This means that, unlike Flash and other vector file formats, each frame of digital video requires almost every pixel on the screen to be remembered and stored individually. *Vector* formats, on the other hand, use mathematical descriptions of objects on the screen and compute any differences or movement from frame to frame very efficiently. The resolution of an average television set is roughly equivalent to a 640x480 resolution at 24-bit color depth on your computer monitor. Mathematically speaking, one frame of digital video at this resolution is nearly 1MB!

$$640 \times 480 \times 3^* = 921,600 \text{ bytes} = 900 \text{ KB} = 0.88\text{MB}$$

---

*Each byte has 8 bits. Therefore, 24 bits is equivalent to 3 bytes.

If that isn't bad enough, consider that 1 second of video contains 30 frames. That's 26MB for just 1 second of video! Only the fastest systems and hard drives on the market could deliver such performance. One solution to this performance bottleneck was to compress the data. Thus, most digital video now employs some form of compression (for storage) and decompression (for playback). The short form of this expression is *codec* (compression and *decompression*). You may have already heard of many codecs in use today, but what you probably don't know is that there are three kinds of codecs: software, hardware, and hybrid.

Note

Cinepak, Indeo, RealVideo, and Sorenson are all software-based codecs, meaning that the computer processor has to decompress each frame of compressed video. These differ from hardware-based codecs, such as MJPEG (Motion JPEG, based on the Joint Photographic Experts Group compression scheme), which need video-capture cards to compress and decompress each frame of video.

The latest breed of codecs today is hybrids, both software and hardware based, such as the MPEG (Moving Picture Experts Group) and DV codecs. MPEG currently has two versions, MPEG-1 and MPEG-2. Originally, MPEG-1 and MPEG-2 video needed special hardware to playback, but as computer processors got faster, software-based players could handle the decompression tasks. Today, MPEG-2 is standard for DVD.

DVD, or digital versatile/video disc, is a new storage medium that can handle feature-length movies in a snap. DVD should not be confused with DV, which refers to true Digital Video, in which the source video originates as binary (zeros and ones) data. Furthermore, the general term *digital video* should not be confused with *DV*. *Digital video* usually refers to the any video that has been stored as binary data, although it most likely originated from an analog source such as a regular VHS or BetaCam video camera. *DV* refers to video that originated from a digital (a.k.a. *binary*) source and that remains digital through any number of edits on a digital system. With the current implementation of DV, using IEEE-1394 (a.k.a. *FireWire* or *i.LINK*) technology, video is transferred from digital tape to your computer hard drive with no loss of quality. The DV footage is not recompressed unless the image in the footage is changed during editing by adding effects or transitions. But like any digital video, DV still requires a lot of hard drive space — about 2GB for every 9 minutes.

Note

Older operating systems have a maximum file-size limit of 2GB. This means that you cannot have more than 9 minutes of DV-compressed footage in one QuickTime or AVI file. However, you can string many movies together during playback for continuous recording. New versions of the Mac OS (version 9.0.4 or higher) and of the Windows OS support files that are larger than 2GB. Even so, some applications may not be capable of using these larger files unless they've been updated to do so.

Codec, frame size, and frame rate: The keys to manageable video

Before you begin any digital video project you should have a clear understanding of codecs. Most software-based codecs are intended for computer playback and distribution, while hardware-based codecs are intended for capturing and editing original footage to be used for television broadcast or feature films. You can repurpose hardware-based codec video by compressing it with a software-based codec. Most video developers take high-quality video and shrink it, in both frame and file size, to fit onto multimedia CD-ROMs or the Web.

Three variables can be applied to digital video to make it more manageable for most consumer computer systems: frame size, frame rate, and compression. Developers often use all three variables to shrink huge 9GB video projects down to 3–5MB, which may lead to undesirable results.

First, let's talk about frame size. Although most professional video uses a 640 x 480 or greater frame size, you may have noticed that most video on multimedia CD-ROMs only takes up a quarter or less of your entire computer monitor. Most video on the Web or CD-ROMs is rendered at 320 x 240 resolution, half the resolution of broadcast video. Actually, this is only slightly less than the horizontal-line resolution of your VHS recordings.

What about frame rate? You may have also noticed that video on multimedia CD-ROMs often looks a little jerky or choppy. Although this may be due to a slow processor, it's more likely that — in order to cut the file size — the frame rate of the video was reduced. It's not uncommon to find CD-ROM frame rates as low as 12 or 15 fps (frames per second) — about half of the original frame rate of broadcast video. This slower frame rate is also the default frame rate of a new Flash movie, to ensure consistent playback on slower machines. Despite the drop in video quality, the lower frame rates result in much smaller file sizes with fewer frames for the processor to play within each second, which delivers better CD-ROM performance.

Finally, how does compression affect video? You've probably noticed that Web and multimedia CD-ROM video is often blocky looking. This is due to the software-based compression that has been used on the video. Codecs look for areas of the frame that stay consistent over many frames, and then log those areas and drop them from subsequent frames. The result is that no unnecessary repetition of data exists that needs to be continually decompressed. But, depending on the level of compression used, the properties of the codec itself, and the settings used in running that codec, the video varies in quality.

Keeping with the trend of better and faster, digital video continues to improve dramatically. This is well illustrated by the fact that many popular Web sites, such as Apple's QuickTime Web site (www.apple.com/quicktime), now enable visitors to download larger, higher-quality videos (upwards of 15MB) for playback on newer, faster systems.

Playback bottlenecks

Digital video needs to be kept small for two reasons: storage and playback. So far, we have largely discussed storage issues. But playback (or transfer rate) further complicates the creation of digital video. Despite the relatively large capacity of CD-ROMs (650MB), most CD-ROM readers have limited transfer rates of about 600 KB/second. It's important to note that each second of video cannot exceed the transfer rate; otherwise the video will drop frames to keep up with the audio. So if the video is distributed via CD-ROM, this factor results in serious limitations.

Let's look at some of the math involved under ideal (choppy) playback conditions: If you use 15 fps for compressed video, you are limited to a maximum of roughly 40 KB per frame. (Remember, however, that the playback stream usually includes an audio track as well, which means that less than 40 KB is available for the video component of each individual frame.)

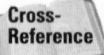 **Cross-Reference**   For more information on audio formatting and compression, see Chapter 15, "Adding Sound."

Unfortunately, the Web still affords less than ideal playback conditions for video. On the Web, transfer rates can be as slow as 500 bytes/second. On average, a 56 KB modem downloads around 4 KB/second. The ideal Web video should stream to the user while loading the page. If you intend to stream video quickly, you have to keep this very small transfer rate in mind. Large videos simply will not stream! This is why most Web sites offer larger videos as a download file. But you do have an alternative. Later in this section, you can learn how to extract a minimal number of frames in order to simulate digital video motion with Flash, yet keep your Flash files streaming quickly. As modem technologies get faster, however, we'll most likely see bigger and better video delivered across the Web. The ADSL (Asymmetrical Digital Subscriber Line) modem was developed with the MPEG-1 and -2 standards in mind.

Adjusting Flash Movies for Video Output

By default, Flash MX 2004 uses a frame rate of 12 fps for all new movies. Unless you have changed this setting with the Modify ➪ Document command (Ctrl+J or ⌘+J), this is the setting for any Flash document you have created so far. As mentioned earlier in this chapter, broadcast (NTSC) video needs 30 fps (29.97 fps to be exact) for motion to be smooth and fluid. It may be necessary for you to add more blank frames between each of your tweened keyframes to accommodate a faster frame rate. Your 5-second intro to your Web site may have been possible with 70 or fewer frames, but now you need 300 frames for the same amount of time in full-motion video. Flash doesn't support interlacing (or field-ordering) with any export method (see the "What Is Interlacing?" sidebar for an explanation of interlacing). As a result, you need twice the number of frames (double the frame rate) used for every second of NTSC video — 59.94 fps to be exact — to properly render full-motion video from Flash. It's easier to use 60 fps in Flash and then alter the rendered sequence to 59.94 fps in the video-editing application.

However, 60 fps may be an unrealistic frame rate to time your animation. Several hundreds (if not thousands) of frames are necessary for this frame rate. As you will see later in this chapter, you can achieve high-quality video using 30 fps for your Flash documents. If you have the flexibility and skill to animate at 60 fps, you may want to do so.

Caution If you are using the PAL or SECAM video systems, which are video systems used outside of North America, then you need to use different frame sizes and frame rates to accurately render Flash content. Use the same methods described here, but adjust any values to fit within PAL or SECAM specifications.

If possible, restrict your Flash movie to one scene for video-editing purposes. Flash exports all scenes within a Flash movie into a sequence or QT/AVI movie, which may complicate the editing process later. It's easier to make more Flash movies and render them independently of each other.

Frames stored in Movie Clips do not export with sequences. Make sure that you have either removed any Movie Clip symbols or that you have replaced them with the actual frames contained within the Movie Clip.

To replace a Movie Clip symbol with the actual frames contained within it:

1. Open the Movie Clip in the Library, and select the frames in the Timeline window.

2. Copy the frames with the Copy Frames command (Ctrl+Alt+C or ⌘+Option+C) in the Edit menu.

3. Go back to the scene and paste the frames with the Paste Frames command (Ctrl+Alt+V or ⌘+Option+V). Paste the frames on their own layer, so that they won't conflict with any tweens or settings in other layers.

Caution Remember that, unlike regular Flash movies, the exported sequence will not have any interactivity. The sequence is simply a collection of still images that will be compiled later in your video-editing application. (So don't mistakenly overwrite or delete your original Flash document!)

What Is Interlacing?

Most computer monitors are non-interlaced, which means that each "frame" of video is fully displayed with each screen refresh. Most TV sets, however, are interlaced displays, which means that each frame of video consists of two fields: one upper and one lower, and each screen refresh shows one field and then the other. Therefore, each second of video contains 60 fields, or 30 frames. Because Flash doesn't export field-ordered sequences, you have to compensate for the lack of individual fields by using two Flash frames for every regular frame of video.

You may also need to adjust your Flash document's pixel width and height. Depending on the type of video-editing software and hardware you are using, this setting needs to be 640 x 480, 640 x 486, 720 x 534 (DV), 720 x 540 (D1), or something else. Again, use the Modify ⇨ Document command to adjust the size of your Flash document. You may notice that adjusting pixel sizes of the Flash document doesn't have the same effect as changing pixel heights or widths of raster-based images. Usually, adjusting pixel sizes will distort or change the shape of elements. With Flash, the document's pixel size is independent of the pixel sizes of any elements it may contain. You're simply adding or subtracting space to the area of the Stage. If you intend to bring the sequence into another video-editing application such as Adobe Premiere and you are outputting with the DV format, a movie size of 720 x 534 should be used. Why? The DV format uses nonsquare pixels delivering the same 4:3 aspect ratio with 720 x 480 as other video formats do with only 640 x 480 square pixels. By using 720 x 534 movie sizes, the frame can be stretched to fit a 720 x 480 DV workspace without losing any resolution quality. It's better to adjust the size before you export any material intended for broadcast video delivery (or for transfer to any NTSC recording media), especially with raster formats. Not only does this ensure optimal quality; it could easily lessen the video rendering time needed in other applications.

Note   The movie sizes just listed should work equally well for MJPEG video hardware and DV hardware. If you use these baseline settings, you can accommodate either MJPEG or DV specifications in your video-editing application.

Not only do you need to have the proper frame size for high-quality video output, but you also need to be aware of overscanning. TV sets overscan video images, which means that information near the edges of the frame may be cropped and not visible. Because the amount of overscan is inconsistent from TV to TV, some general guidelines have been developed to make sure vital information in the frame is not lost. The crux of the guidelines is simple: Don't put anything important (such as text) near the edges of the frame. Video has two safe zones: title-safe and action-safe. To see these zones in a sample document in Flash, refer to Figure 14-1.

On the CD-ROM   You can find the document shown in Figure 14-1, `Video SAFE Exp DV.fla`, in the `ch14` folder of this book's CD-ROM.

The action-safe zone is approximately 90 percent of the 720 x 534 (or 640 x 480) frame size we're using in Flash, which calculates into 648 x 480 (or 576 x 432). All of your Flash artwork should be contained within the limits of the action-safe zone. The title-safe zone is about 80 percent of the total frame size. For a 720 x 534 frame size, any text on the Flash stage should fall within the borders of a 576 x 427 centered frame. With a 640 x 480 frame size, this centered frame size would be 512 x 384.

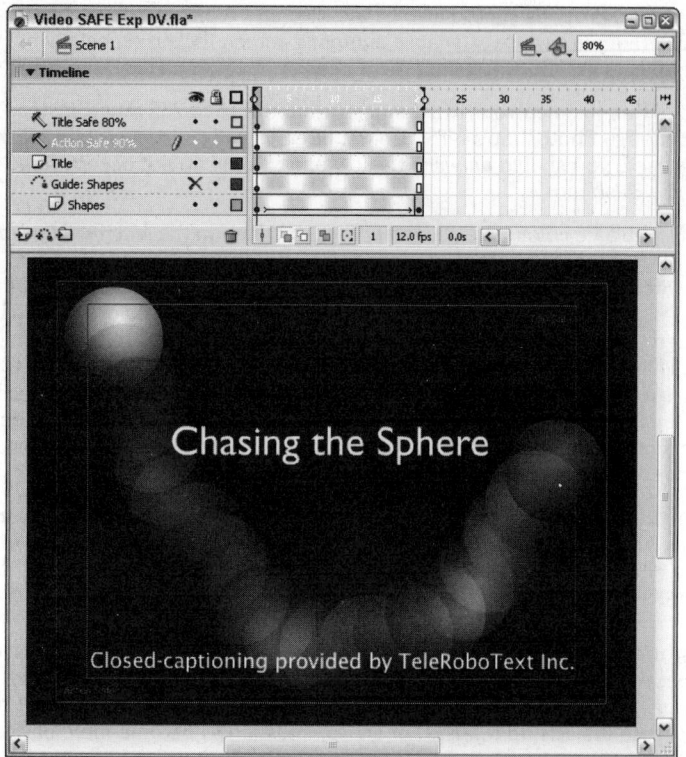

Figure 14-1: While designing for broadcast content in Flash MX 2004, you should always be aware of the safe-zone boundaries for NTSC video playback.

Finally, you may need to adjust the colors and artwork you used in your Flash document. NTSC video, while technically 24-bit, doesn't display some colors very well. In general, bright and saturated RGB colors tend to bleed on regular TV sets. Here are some guidelines for using broadcast (and WebTV)-safe color:

✦ Avoid one-pixel-wide horizontal lines. Because NTSC is interlaced, this line flickers constantly. If you need to use thin lines, try blurring a one-pixel line or simply never use anything less than a two-pixel stroke width.

Tip You can convert a one-pixel or hairline stroke to a fill by choosing Modify ➪ Shape ➪ Convert Lines to Fills. Use Modify ➪ Shape ➪ Soften Fill Edges on the converted line to blur it.

✦ Do not use very fine textures as they may flicker and bleed at the edges. Because most NTSC monitors have low-quality resolutions, the fine details are lost anyway.

✦ Avoid using any color that uses a color channel's maximum intensity. Use an NTSC color filter on any bitmap art, such as the NTSC Colors filter in Adobe Photoshop:

  • Full red (R: 255, G: 000, B: 000) displays horribly on TV sets. Replace a full red with R: 181, G: 000, B: 000.

- Pure white backgrounds should also be avoided and replaced with R: 235, G: 235, B: 235. Like red, pure white can cause annoying screen flicker, especially if high contrast objects are placed against the white.

- As a rule of thumb, keep your RGB values within the 16 to 235 range, instead of 0 to 255. Although Photoshop's NTSC Colors filter actually allows certain 255 values to be used, you should *only* use these values if they do not occupy large solid areas in the Flash movie.

✦ Use the NTSC & Web Safe color set (ntsc_web_179.act file) on the *Macromedia Flash MX 2004 Bible* CD-ROM (see Chapter 7, "Applying Color," for more information on importing or switching color sets). Of the 216 Web-Safe color palettes, only 179 of them are NTSC/WebTV safe. NTSC TV sets are capable of displaying more colors than that, but if you're used to working with Web color palettes, then you may find this optimized palette handy. There's another color set file, ntsc_213_colors.act, on the CD-ROM that you can use if you're just taking Flash content to video, which has 213 NTSC-safe colors, converted from the 216 Web-Safe colors. Because 35 colors in this set are outside of the Web-Safe colors, you should not use this palette for Web and broadcast work.

✦ If you're using video-editing software that allows both color and levels corrections on imported clips, then you can avoid making time-consuming adjustments to your original Flash movie. After you've generated a Flash sequence and imported the sequence into your video-editing application, restrict the gamut of the sequence clip using the values in the preceding tips.

Tip   In After Effects, use the Broadcast Colors filter to perform NTSC color adjustments on imported sequences or movies. This filter can adjust either luminance or saturation values to bring out-of-gamut colors into the NTSC color gamut. Use caution, however, as reducing the luminance may cause artifacts from MJPEG or DV compression to become more obvious. Reducing saturation is the preferred method for using the Broadcast Colors.

Refer to Table 14-1 to see how Photoshop's NTSC Colors filter remaps the saturated values of the Web-Safe color palette.

Table 14-1: NTSC Color Conversion Chart

Original Web HEX Value	Original RGB Web Value			Converted RGB NTSC Value		
	R	**G**	**B**	**R**	**G**	**B**
FF0033	255	000	051	227	000	045
CC6699	204	051	153	204	102	153
FF00FF	255	000	255	210	000	210
	R	G	B	R	G	B
FF00CC	255	000	204	219	000	175

Original Web HEX Value	Original RGB Web Value			Converted RGB NTSC Value		
	R	G	B	R	G	B
FF0099	255	000	153	226	000	136
FF0066	255	000	102	230	000	092
CC00FF	204	000	255	199	000	248
00CCCC	000	204	204	000	170	170
00FFFF	000	255	255	000	170	170
33FFFF	051	255	255	045	225	225
66FFFF	102	255	255	101	253	253
00CCFF	000	204	255	000	160	201
0099FF	000	153	255	000	147	245
00FFCC	000	255	204	000	178	143
33FFCC	051	255	204	047	237	190
00FF99	000	255	153	000	188	113
33FF99	051	255	153	050	249	150
00CC66	000	204	102	000	193	096
00FF00	000	255	000	000	210	000
00FF33	000	255	051	000	210	042
00FF66	000	255	102	000	198	079
33FF00	051	255	000	047	234	000
66FF00	102	255	000	088	220	000
99FF00	153	255	000	122	203	000
99CC00	153	204	000	142	190	000
FFFF66	255	255	102	252	252	101
CCCC00	204	204	000	170	170	000
CCFF00	204	255	000	148	185	000
FFCC00	255	204	000	191	153	000
CC9900	204	153	000	197	148	000
FF9900	255	153	000	216	130	000
FF6600	255	102	000	248	099	000
FF0000	255	000	000	181	000	000
CC0000	204	000	000	181	000	000

Creating Sequences from Flash Movies

A *sequence* is a series of still images that simulate full-motion video when played back continuously. Think of a sequence as a regular QuickTime or AVI broken down into individual frames. Another analogy would be that of a flipbook made of individual sketches that animate when you thumb through the pages quickly. Flash MX 2004 can export a scene or movie as a series of still images as well, with quite a bit of flexibility.

Because Flash artwork is vector-based, it supports all the major vector formats used in other applications: EPS 3.0 (or higher), Illustrator, and DXF formats. On the Windows version of Flash, you can also export metafile sequences in the WMF and EMF formats. Generally, all of these vector formats will retain the scalable quality that Flash offers for the Web; that is, you can shrink or expand the size of vector formats, displaying equal smoothness and quality at all sizes. Most vector formats can also embed raster content, and any raster content will have a finite resolution capacity. You will notice degradation on any embedded raster elements if you scale the entire vector graphic beyond its original fixed pixel size.

You can also export a still sequence in raster-based formats such as PICT (Mac only), BMP (Windows only), GIF, JPEG, or PNG. We can review the benefits of each format and the particular uses each can have, but first, we should look at how the exporting of individual frames is accomplished in Flash.

Export process in Flash

After you have opened a Flash document that you wish to export, make sure that your document falls within the guidelines described in the last section. All of these settings are critical for flawless video playback: 30 or 60 frames per second, 640 x 480 (or greater) movie dimensions, integration of scenes and Movie Clips, and color gamut restrictions. When you're all ready to go, the actual export process is quite simple. You will export your Flash document as a series of still images that can later be compiled by a video application.

On the CD-ROM
You can use the `characterAnim.fla` document from the `ch14` folder of the *Macromedia Flash MX 2004 Bible* CD-ROM. Sandro Corsaro (`www.sandrocorsaro.com`) provided this excellent sample of his Flash animation.

1. Open your Flash document and select File ➪ Export ➪ Export Movie.

2. Browse to (or create) the folder where you want to store the sequence. Choose an empty folder — you don't want to have several files from the sequence mixed with other files. See Figure 14-2.

3. In the Format menu (Mac) or Save as type menu (Windows), choose the type of file you want Flash to create. If you're using the sample Flash document on the book's CD-ROM, use the PICT format if you're using the Macintosh version of Flash MX 2004 (see Figure 14-3 for specific settings). Use the BMP format if you're using the Windows version (see Figure 14-4 for specific settings). Later, you can use the exported PICT or BMP sequence in the Adobe After Effects section.

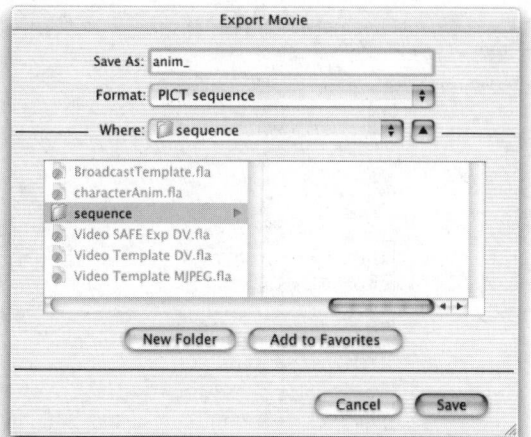

Figure 14-2: The Export Movie dialog box in the Mac version of Flash MX 2004

Figure 14-3: The Export PICT dialog box on the Mac

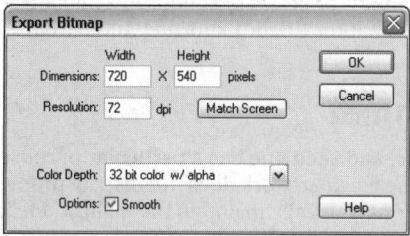

Figure 14-4: The Export Bitmap dialog box on Windows

4. Specify a filename and click **Save**. Flash MX 2004 will automatically append a series of numbers to the end of the filenames, such as `anim_0001`, `anim_0002`, and so on. Flash generates a still image for each frame in the Flash timeline. This process can be quite lengthy if you have several hundreds of frames in the timeline. When you browse the directory where the files were saved, you should see a listing similar to that of Figure 14-5.

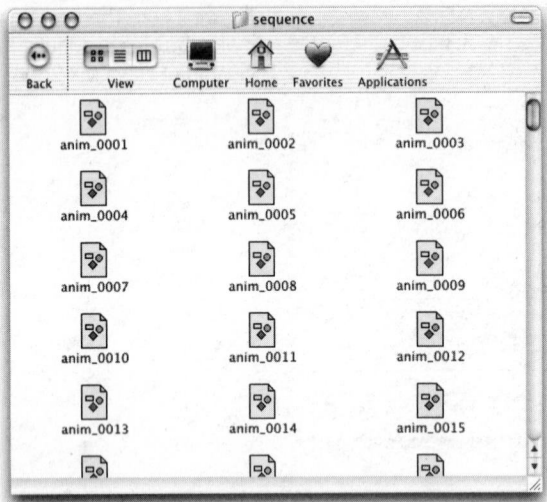

Figure 14-5: When you export a Flash movie as a sequence, Flash generates a still image (that is, one file) for each frame in the Flash movie.

Tip

For the highest quality video rendering, use a vector file format for export. The next section details each file type and its particular uses. However, if you export a raster image at the full size of the video frame (such as 720 x 540), you will not experience any resolution loss as long as you don't scale the exported artwork in the video application.

If you want to jump right into After Effects to output this footage to DV video, then proceed to the "Importing Image Sequences into After Effects" section at the end of this chapter. If you need to export an accompanying Stream sound (or series of sounds in a soundtrack on the Main Timeline), jump to the section of this chapter titled "Exporting Audio from Flash Documents."

Uses of each sequence format

Flash can export in a variety of file formats, and each one has a particular purpose. While vector formats allow the most scalability, some Flash artwork does not display properly when converted from vector to raster. Raster formats usually maintain the highest fidelity to original Flash artwork, but the file sizes can be rather large.

Vector sequence formats

Use a vector format type for your sequences when you want the highest quality image translation in applications such as Adobe After Effects or Premiere (see Table 14-2 for a list of formats that can be exported from Flash). Flash exports vector sequences very quickly, but these files may take longer to re-render in your video-editing application than raster formats. Once you see the smooth edges of vector-rendered sequences, however, you can see that it is worth the extra time. Vector formats automatically matte out the Flash background color, making it quick and easy to superimpose Flash graphics with other content.

Caution   You may want to test a single EPS or AI file export (using File ➪ Export Image) from Flash MX 2004 in your target video application. The EPS format natively uses CMYK (Cyan, Magenta, Yellow and blacK) color space. Flash artwork uses RGB (Red, Green and Blue) color space. If the RGB colors are converted to the CMYK color space during the export, you may notice extreme color shifts with your Flash artwork when you view it in your video application.

Table 14-2: Flash-Compatible Vector Sequence Formats

Export Format	Extension	Description
EPS (6.0 or earlier); Encapsulated PostScript	.eps	Universal vector format recognized by most editing or design applications. This is the preferred format for high-quality vector export. However, any gradients created in Flash will not export well with this format.
Illustrator; Adobe Illustrator	.ai	Proprietary file format mainly used by Adobe applications. Any gradients created in Flash will not export well with this format.
DXF; Drawing eXchange Format	.dxf	AutoCAD 2D/3D file format. Because this format does not support fills, it is mainly used for drafting plans or schematic drawings. This format is used by most CAD, 3D, and modeling programs for transferring drawings to other programs.
WMF/EMF; Windows Meta File/Enhanced Meta File	.wmf, .emf	There's no reason to use these formats over the other vector formats. While some non-Microsoft applications support them, they aren't widely used on either Mac or PC systems.

Caution   Mask layers (and the artwork that they mask) will not export properly in EPS sequences. The artwork in the Mask layer will show up in the exported EPS file(s). If you use Mask layers in your Flash document, export raster image sequences instead of vector.

Raster formats

All raster formats can export at variable pixel widths, heights, and resolutions. As long as your Flash document (.fla file) is in the proper aspect ratio for video (usually 4:3), you can scale up your Flash movie on export (see Table 14-3 for a list of raster formats that Flash supports). This will save time during the rerendering process in the video-editing application. Not all raster file formats support alpha channels, which are necessary if you intend to superimpose exported Flash graphics on top of other video content.

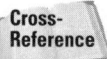
Cross-Reference   Refer to Chapter 35, "Working with Raster Graphics," for more detailed information on the options associated with each raster file format.

Table 14-3: Flash-Compatible Raster Sequence Formats

Flash Export Format	File Extension	Description
PICT (Mac only); Picture	.pct (or .pict)	Can be used with many PC and all Mac programs. Variable bit-depths and compression settings with support for alpha channels. Allows for lossless compression.
BMP (PC only); Windows Bitmap	.bmp	Can be used with all PC and some Mac programs. Variable bit-depths and compression settings with support for alpha channels. Allows for lossless compression.
GIF; Graphics Interchange File	.gif	Limited to a 256-color palette. Not recommended for full-motion NTSC video.
JPEG; Joint Photographic Experts Group	.jpg (or .jpeg)	Only supports 24-bit RGB color. No alpha channel support. Recommended for full-motion NTSC video, but this format does throw out color information due to its lossy compression method.
PNG; Portable Network Graphic	.png	Supports variable bit-depth and compression settings with alpha channels. Lossless compression schemes make it ideal for projects intended for NTSC video output.

Creating AVI Files on Windows

If you want a quick-and-dirty 100-percent raster-based video version of your Flash document, and you use the Windows version of Flash MX 2004, you can export your Flash document as a Video for Windows movie (.avi file). If you want the best video quality for output to video-tape, you shouldn't use this method for rendering video. Flash doesn't support interlaced video and won't create the smoothest possible video content directly. This export file format is used primarily for digital video intended for computer playback, not NTSC playback.

Note   You can render a Flash movie at twice the frame rate of NTSC video (29.97×2 = 59.94 fps) using the necessary codec for your video hardware. If you want to play the AVI through your IEEE-1394 (a.k.a. *FireWire, i.Link*) hardware, you need to resize the 720 x 534 AVI movie to 720 x 480 in a video-editing application or by using the Dimensions property of the Export AVI Settings dialog box. Do not change the properties of the original Flash document (.fla file) via Modify ➪ Document! DV uses non-square pixels, and shapes will be stretched if you use a 720 x 480 movie size in Flash.

Choose **Export Movie** from the File menu. Select a folder (or create one) to store the AVI file, type the filename, and click **Save**. You will then see the Export Windows AVI dialog box with the following options (see Figure 14-6).

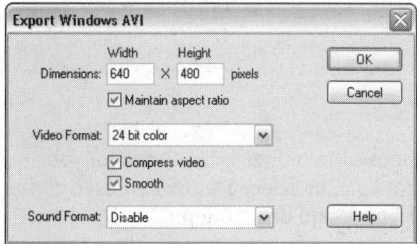

Figure 14-6: Adjust the values of the Windows AVI settings to accommodate your playback needs.

Dimensions

This property enables you to scale your AVI movie. If you wish to scale the movie's width separate from the height, clear the **Maintain Aspect Ratio** check box for this property. This may be necessary if you have to accommodate non-square pixel formats such as DV or D1.

Video format

The drop-down menu associated with this property enables you to choose a bit-depth for the AVI movie. For serious video work, you'll want to choose 24-bit color or greater.

+ **8-bit color:** Limits the rendered movie to 256 colors that are determined on the fly by Flash.

+ **16-bit color:** Limits the movie to 65,536 colors; also known as High Color in Windows or Thousands of Colors on the Mac.

+ **24-bit color:** Enables the movie to use full RGB color (16.7 million colors); also known as True Color on the PC or Millions of Colors on the Mac.

+ **32-bit color w/ alpha:** Enables the movie to use full RGB color and store an alpha channel for compositing effects. Not all video codecs can store alpha channel information.

+ **Compress video:** If this option is checked, you are given the option to select a video compressor (codec) after you click **OK** on the Export Windows AVI dialog box. If you don't select this check box, Flash generates uncompressed video frames, which can take over 1MB of file space per frame. In general, you don't want to use uncompressed video; it takes a lot more time to rerender uncompressed video into the hardware codec used by your video setup.

Caution

Even if you want to use uncompressed video, we recommend that you select the Compress video option and choose None for the compressor.

+ **Smooth:** Using the smooth option anti-aliases the Flash graphics. This adds more time to the export process, but your AVI file looks much more polished. If you just want faster exporting, and you need only a rough AVI movie, clear the **Smooth** check box.

Sound format

This drop-down list enables you to specify the audio sampling settings. If you didn't use any audio in your Flash movie, choose **Disable**. For a description of each of the sampling rates and bit-depths, refer to Appendix B, "Digital Audio Basics."

Video compression

When you've chosen the options you need, click **OK**. If you specified **Compress Video**, you'll see the dialog box shown in Figure 14-7:

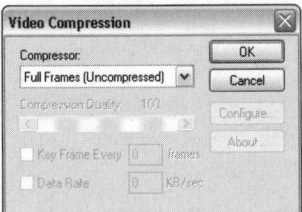

Figure 14-7: Choose the proper video codec for your video output hardware, or select a software-based codec for computer playback and distribution.

In the Video Compression dialog box, you can select a software- or hardware-based codec to use for the AVI movie. By default, Flash chooses **Full Frames** (Uncompressed). This option is the same as deselecting **Compress Video**, which forces Flash to render full-frame video. Because you probably want manageable file sizes, choose the codec that will be compatible with your video hardware. If you want to simply review your Flash work as an AVI movie, use Cinepak or Indeo codecs. Adjust the codec settings as necessary for your needs. Smaller files and lower quality will result from using compression qualities less than 100 percent, exporting selective keyframes, and limiting data rates. For high-quality rendering using hardware-based codecs, make sure that the hardware codec (such as MJPEG or DV) is set to 100 percent compression quality with no keyframes or data-rate limiting. When you have chosen all the appropriate settings, click **OK**.

Flash then exports an AVI movie file to the folder you specified. Depending on the length of your Flash movie and the video codec used, the export process could take less than a minute or many hours. Unfortunately, Flash doesn't give you an estimated time for completion as Adobe Premiere or After Effects does. When Flash has finished exporting the file, you can view the video with Windows Media Player or with the software that your video hardware uses.

Exporting Audio from a Flash Document

If you created a Flash animation with Stream sounds that are synchronized to the animation of the artwork, you may want to export the audio as a separate file to combine with exported image sequences in a video application such as Adobe After Effects. If you created QuickTime Video or Windows AVI files, then you can export audio directly in the export options of these file formats. This section describes how to export audio separately from the animation within a Flash document.

On the CD-ROM

Open the characterAnim.fla document from the ch14 folder of the *Macromedia Flash MX 2004 Bible* CD-ROM. You can export the audio track of this document to use with the matching image sequence that was exported earlier in this chapter.

1. Open the Flash document. Make sure any and all sounds that you want to include in the exported audio file are located on the Main Timeline (that is, Scene 1). Each sound on a keyframe should be set to the Stream sync option in the Property inspector.

2. Choose File ⇨ Export ⇨ Export Movie. On Windows, choose **WAV audio** in the Save as file type menu, and specify **soundtrack.wav** as the filename. See Figure 14-8 for the WAV settings that follow the Export Movie dialog box. On the Mac, choose **QuickTime Video** in the Format menu, and specify **soundtrack.mov** as the filename. With the Mac version of Flash MX 2004, you cannot export a sound file — you can, however, export a QuickTime Video and simply disregard the video track when you import the .mov file into your video-editing application. See Figure 14-9 for the QuickTime Video settings that follow the Export Movie dialog box.

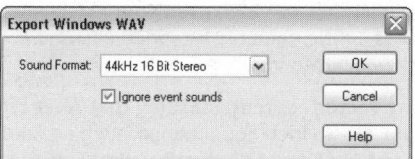

Figure 14-8: The Export Windows WAV dialog box

Figure 14-9: The Export QuickTime Video dialog box

Caution

Though you can export Event sounds with the WAV file format on the Windows version of Flash MX 2004, we recommend that you only use Stream sounds for exact synchronization of sound and image in your Flash animations.

Once you have exported the sound from the Flash document, you're ready to combine the exported image sequence with the sound file. In the next section, you learn how to combine these sources in Adobe After Effects 6.

Importing Image Sequences into After Effects

Now that you've created an image sequence (and supporting audio track, if necessary) with Flash MX 2004's Export Movie command, you can bring the newly generated material into most video-editing applications. Not all video-editing applications will accept still image sequences and will automatically treat them as one video clip (as Adobe After Effects and Premiere do). In this section, you see how to prepare an image sequence for video output.

Adobe After Effects is the video production equivalent of Photoshop. After Effects allows you to modify moving images in ways similar to how you modify still images in Adobe Photoshop.

With powerful native tools and filters, as well as a vast array of custom effects plug-ins, After Effects is a program with enough depth to keep many motion graphics designers happy for years. Although After Effects is a complex program with innumerable settings, you can certainly use it for simple tasks as well.

Note At the time of this writing, Adobe After Effects 6 was the latest version of the product. You can download a trial version of this software at www.adobe.com/support/downloads/main.html.

Using After Effects, you can achieve the highest quality video from your Flash-generated image sequence. That's because After Effects offers subtle controls for video clip and composition settings that deliver crisp, interlaced, frame-accurate video.

After Effects can continuously rasterize any vector content, meaning that After Effects can re-render each vector frame into a raster frame. Most video applications, such as Adobe Premiere, rasterize the first frame of a vector image and continue to reuse that first rasterized version for the entire render process.

What does that mean? Simply put, if you have a small vector circle in the first frame of a project that grows larger in subsequent frames, then the circle appears very jagged at the larger sizes. Although both Premiere and After Effects render a Flash-generated image sequence at the same quality, please note that if you want to do special effects with just one frame (or still) from a Flash movie (not an entire image sequence), then After Effects does a much better job. Also note that this can be confusing because there are two potential uses of material imported from Flash into either After Effects or Premiere. These are either single-frame imports or multi-frame imports. The general point is this: After Effects does a consistently high-quality job with both types, whereas Premiere handles only the latter type (multiframe) well.

Caution While EPS and AI image sequences offer the most scalability for digital video production, Flash poorly translates gradients in these formats into common PostScript-defined colors. As a result, gradients appear as solid color fills in After Effects. If you're using gradients in your Flash artwork, it's best to export the movie as a raster sequence. After Effects can import a PNG, BMP, or PICT sequence, which has less degrading compression than JPEG.

The following steps show you how to import a sequence into After Effects 6. If you exported an image sequence from the exercise earlier in this chapter, then use that sequence for this exercise.

1. Open an existing After Effects project (.aep file) or create a new project (Ctrl+Alt+N or ⌘+Option+N).

2. Double-click in the Project window to import the image sequence. In the Import File dialog box, browse to the folder containing the image sequence. Select the first file of the sequence (for example, anim_0001) and select the appropriate **Sequence** check box (such as PICT Sequence, JPEG Sequence, EPS Sequence, and so forth), as shown in Figure 14-10. Click **Import**.

3. If After Effects detects an alpha channel in the imported file(s), then an Interpret Footage dialog box opens, as shown in Figure 14-11. You must tell After Effects how to treat the alpha channel. For any image (or image sequence) with an alpha channel imported from Flash, use the **Straight — Unmatted** setting.

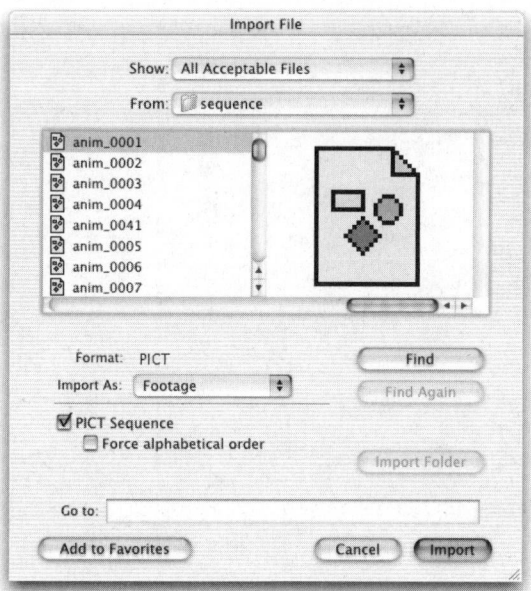

Figure 14-10: The Import File dialog box

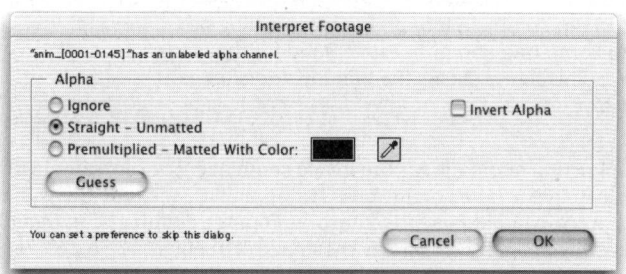

Figure 14-11: After Effects automatically detects the presence of an alpha channel in imported file(s). For alpha channels that Flash creates, use the Straight—Unmatted setting.

4. Select the imported sequence (now shown as one footage item) in the Project window and choose File ⇨ Interpret Footage ⇨ Main. This time, the Interpret Footage dialog box (see Figure 14-12) displays the complete settings for the selected footage file. In the Frame Rate section, enter the correct frame rate in the **Assume this frame rate** field. If you followed the guidelines given earlier in this chapter, then you used a 30 or 60 fps for your Flash document. Enter that value here. Also, make sure **Square Pixels** is selected for the Pixel Aspect Ratio setting. If you are using the image sequence from the earlier exercise, use a frame rate of **30 fps**.

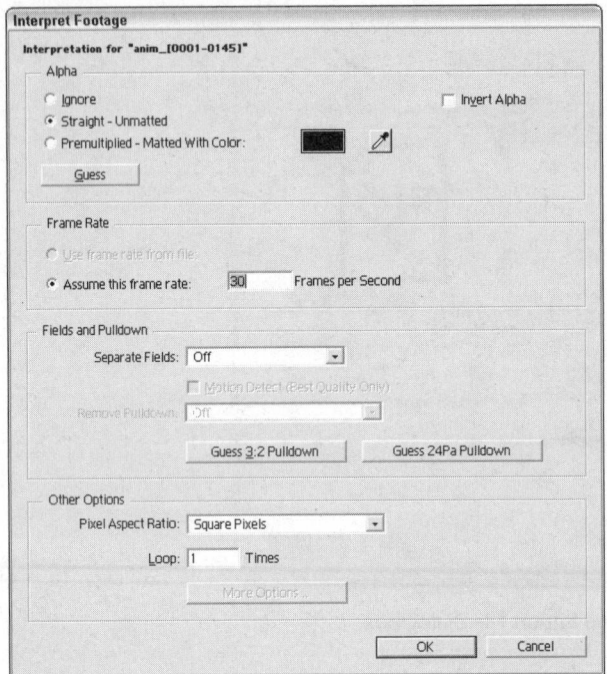

Figure 14-12: In the complete Interpret Footage dialog box, you can set the frame rate and pixel aspect ratio for the Flash image sequence. This figure shows the Windows version of this dialog box.

5. Import any supporting audio file for the image sequence. For our sample image sequence, you can import the soundtrack.wav or soundtrack.mov file you created in an earlier section. You should use the Interpret Footage command on this file as well — make sure it has the same frame rate as the image sequence.

6. Create a new composition via the Composition ➪ New Composition command (Ctrl+N or ⌘+N). Name the composition **Flash Animation**. Depending on your video hardware, the settings for a new composition will vary. For the **Duration** section, enter a value greater than or equal to the length of the imported Flash sequence. See Figure 14-13 for a DV-specific composition. For the sample image sequence, use a duration of 4 seconds and 25 frames (0;00;04;25), as shown in Figure 14-13.

7. Drag the Flash sequence footage file (such as anim_[0001-0145]) from the Project window to the Timeline window for the Flash Animation composition. The footage will automatically center in the composition.

8. Because you are using square pixel footage (from Flash MX 2004) in a DV composition using non-square pixels, you need to size the footage file appropriately. Use the fit-to-comp shortcut (Ctrl+Alt+F or ⌘+Option+F) to rescale the footage to the size of the comp. The borders of the footage should now match the borders of the comp.

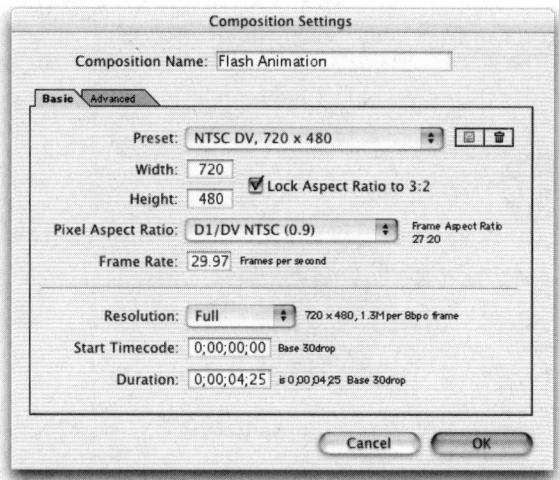

Figure 14-13: Composition settings for DV-format (for example, MiniDV, DVCAM) video

9. Check the **Frame Blending** option for the image sequence layer in the Timeline window. Alternatively, you can select the layer in the Timeline window and choose Layer ➪ Switches ➪ Frame Blending.

10. Drag the imported soundtrack file to the Timeline window of the Flash Animation composition. If you are using a QuickTime Video from the Mac version of Flash MX as your soundtrack, turn off the video track by clicking the eye icon to the left of the layer name. Alternatively, you can select the layer in the Timeline window and choose Layer ➪ Switches ➪ Video. The Timeline window should match the one shown in Figure 14-14.

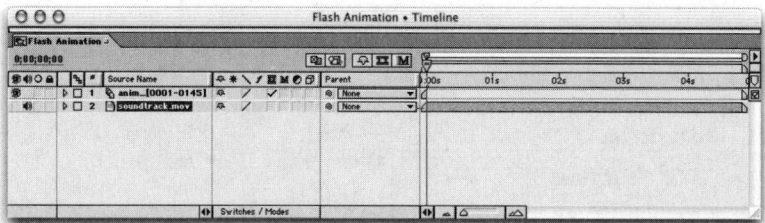

Figure 14-14: The After Effects Timeline window with the two imported Flash assets

11. Change the background color of the composition by choosing Composition ➪ Background Color. For this example, try a legal NTSC white value, with an RGB value of 235, 235, 235. When you're finished, your composition window should look like Figure 14-15.

Figure 14-15: The Flash Animation composition window

12. Save your project as **flashAnimation.aep**.

13. Now, you're ready to render the composition to a final DV file. With the Flash Animation composition selected in the Project window, choose Composition ⇨ Add to Render Queue. The Render Queue window will appear, as shown in Figure 14-16.

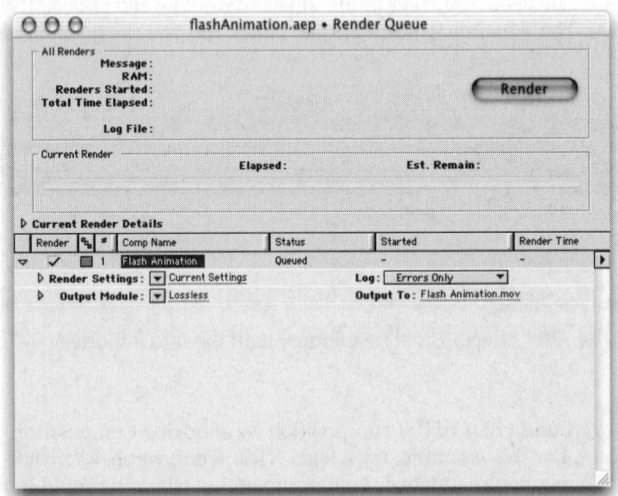

Figure 14-16: The After Effects Render Queue window

14. Click the **Current Settings** text to the right of the Render Settings option in the Render Queue window. In the Render Settings dialog box, choose the settings shown in Figure 14-17 for DV-formatted output. Click **OK** when you are finished.

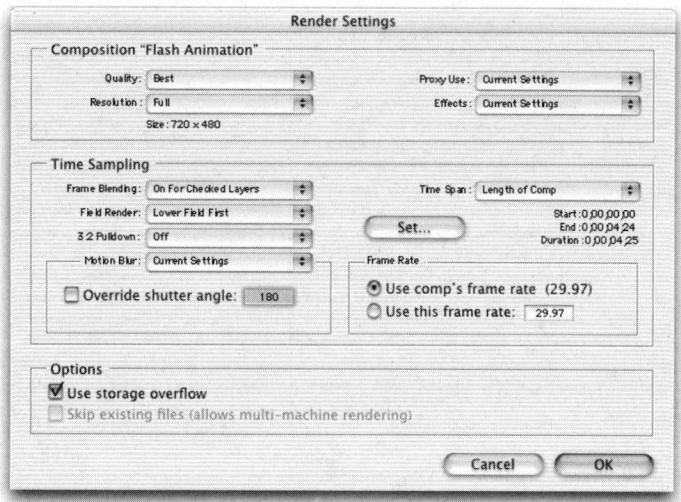

Figure 14-17: The Render Settings dialog box

15. Click the **Lossless** text to the right of the Output Module option in the Render Queue window. This opens the Output Module Settings dialog box, shown in Figure 14-18. Choose **QuickTime Movie** in the Format menu. In the Video Output section, click the **Format Options** button. This opens the Compression Settings dialog box, shown in Figure 14-19. Choose **DV/DVCPRO — NTSC** for the Compressor, and click **OK**. Select the **Audio Output** check box of the Output Module Settings dialog box, and make sure the audio is set to 48.000 kHz at 16 Bit Stereo. Click **OK** to close the dialog box.

16. Click the filename text to the right of the Output To option in the Render Queue window. Choose a location to store the QuickTime movie, and specify a filename, such as `flashAnimation.mov`.

17. Finally, click the **Render** button in the Render Queue window. After Effects examines the composition and creates a DV-formatted file.

On the CD-ROM You can find the files associated with this project in the `ch14` folder of this book's CD-ROM. After you copy the source files to your local drive, you may need to relink the media files in the After Effects project file.

You can output the DV file to your DV camcorder or deck using another video application such as Adobe Premiere or Apple Final Cut Pro. Or you can use the DV file in another project file in After Effects or your preferred video-editing application.

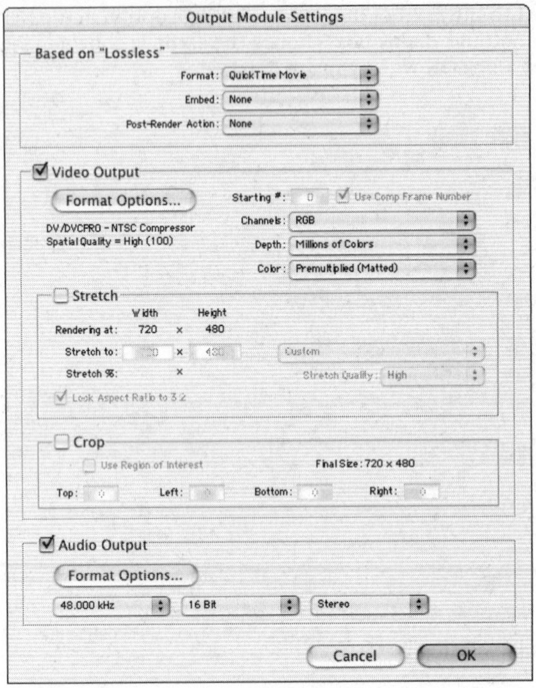

Figure 14-18: The Output Module Settings dialog box

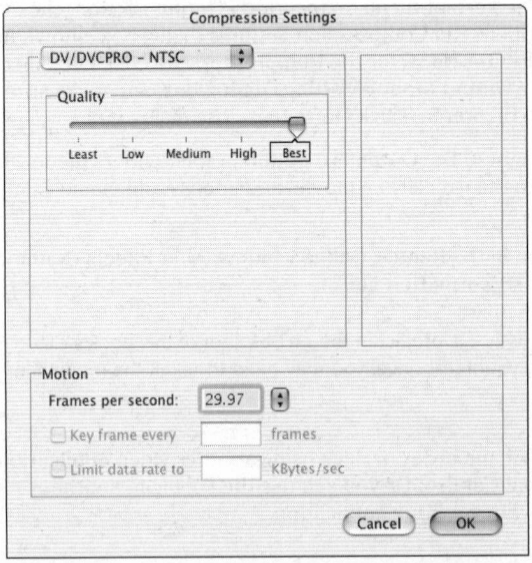

Figure 14-19: The Compression Settings dialog box

Tip

Try using the Broadcast Colors filter on the image sequence layer in the Flash Animation composition. This filter can replace illegal NTSC colors with less-saturated versions of the offending colors.

Web Resource

We'd like to know what you think about this chapter. Visit www.flashsupport.com/ feedback to fill out an online form with your comments.

Summary

✦ You can use Flash to export animations as high-quality image sequences. An image sequence is a series of numbered still images. Certain video-editing applications, such as Adobe Premiere and After Effects, can import both raster and vector sequences. These sequences can be composited with other video tracks and output to film or to the video format of your choice — which opens up a whole new realm of motion techniques for content generated in Flash!

✦ You can use Flash also to export high-quality raster-based AVI and QuickTime movies. It should be noted, however, that these movie files will not contain any Flash interactivity or Flash tracks.

✦ Desktop digital video systems have become more affordable with the advent of the DV format, used by MiniDV and DVCAM camcorders and decks. Because DV material is binary from start to finish, there is virtually no loss of video quality during the editing process.

✦ Because Flash is designed for optimal playback on the Web, Flash movie properties (frame size, frame rate, and the number of total frames) need to be adjusted to work with high-quality digital video.

✦ NTSC television sets and WebTV displays have color signal limitations. Avoid using highly saturated colors and thin lines in Flash movies intended for interlaced video delivery.

✦   ✦   ✦

Integrating Media Files with Flash

Y ou can create a wide range of graphic elements directly in Flash, but most projects will also require imported assets. This section covers the three main media types that you can use to enhance your Flash projects. Chapter 15 introduces the process for importing and controlling sound in Flash. This chapter also covers various compression options and how to edit and export sound from Flash. Learn techniques that help you to get the most bang per byte in your final Flash movies. Chapter 16 addresses the specific workflow and optimization issues related to importing vector and bitmap artwork (and text) from other programs to the Flash authoring environment. Find out how to maintain color consistency and how to preserve layers and vector outlines when moving graphics from other programs, including Adobe Illustrator, Macromedia FreeHand, Fireworks, and Adobe Photoshop. Flash MX 2004 offers a whole range of possibilities for video content. Chapter 17 focuses on the process for embedding video directly in Flash movies.

Adding Sound

One of the more neglected — or perhaps understated — aspects of multimedia development is sound. Because the majority of people who use Flash or create multimedia come from graphic-arts backgrounds, it's no surprise that sound is often applied as the last effect to an otherwise visually stunning presentation — there may be little or no consideration for the soundtrack in early stages of development. Moreover, it's the one element that is usually taken from a stock source, rather than being original work by the Flash designer. (Exceptions exist, of course, as many Flash designers have demonstrated time and time again.)

Note It goes without saying that as Web projects or applications grow in scope, production teams tend to include specific members responsible for unique tasks from graphic design to user interface design to sound design.

You can use sound in Flash movies to enhance interactive design with navigation elements such as buttons, to layer the visitor's experience with a background soundtrack, to add narration, or for more experimental uses. This chapter focuses on the fundamentals of importing and integrating sound files into your Flash project. We also discuss the intricacies of controlling audio output, with particular attention to MP3 bit rates. You'll learn how to use the Publish Settings dialog box and compare that with the enhanced control that is available for customizing compression from within the Sound Properties dialog box of the Library. This chapter guides you through the use of audio within a Flash document and suggests tips for getting the most bang per byte in the final Flash movie (.swf file).

Cross-Reference You read more about sound in Appendix B, "Digital Audio Basics." To learn how to load external MP3 files into a Flash movie at runtime, read Chapter 28, "Sharing and Loading Assets."

Identifying Sound File Import and Export Formats

Flash MX 2004 can work with a wide variety of sound file formats. In this section, you learn which sound file types you can bring into a Flash document (.fla file) and how Flash can compress audio in a variety of formats in the final Flash movie (.swf file).

Import formats

You can import most sound file formats in either the Windows or Macintosh version of Flash. All major sound file types, such as MP3 and WAV, are compatible on both versions. Once a sound file is imported into a Flash document, the resulting .fla file can be edited on either platform.

Flash MX 2004 can import the following sound file formats:

✦ **MP3 (MPEG-1 Audio Layer 3):** Among the many advantages of MP3 sound files for Flash users, the most obvious is that they are cross-platform. Flash MX 2004 can import MP3 files on either the PC or the Mac. This single advantage improves Flash workflow in cross-platform environments. Other advantages are the efficiency of MP3 compression, the increasing availability of MP3 files, as well as the ease of creating MP3 files with common players such as Windows Media Player or Apple iTunes. For more information about MP3s, see the sidebar at the end of the section.

✦ **WAV (Windows Wave):** Until the relatively recent support for MP3, WAV files reigned for nearly a decade as the standard for digital audio on Windows PCs. Still, the WAV format remains the primary acquisition sound format, the format in which you record sound from a microphone or other sound source on your computer. Flash can import WAV files created in sound applications and editors such as SoundForge or ACID. The imported WAV files can be either stereo or mono and can support varying bit depths and frequency rates. WAV files can be directly imported into Flash MX 2004 on a Mac.

✦ **AIFF or AIF (Audio Interchange File format):** Much like WAV on the PC, the AIF format is the most commonly used digital audio format for sound acquisition on the Mac. Flash can import AIFF sounds created in sound applications and editors such as Peak, DECK II, or SoundEdit. Like WAV, AIFF supports stereo and mono, in addition to variable bit depths and frequency rates. Unassisted, the Windows version of Flash MX 2004 cannot import this file format. But with QuickTime 4 or later installed, AIFF files can be imported into Flash MX 2004 on Windows. The Windows version of Flash MX 2004 recognizes, properly opens, and can edit Flash documents created on the Mac that contain AIFF sounds.

✦ **Sun AU:** This sound format (.au file) was developed by Sun Microsystems and Next, and it is the native sound format on many Solaris and UNIX systems, just as WAV and AIF are native to Windows and Macintosh, respectively. The Sun AU format is frequently used with sound-enabled Java applets on Web pages.

✦ **QuickTime:** QuickTime audio files (.qta or .mov files) can be imported directly into Flash MX, provided that you have QuickTime 4 or later installed. Once a QuickTime audio file is imported into a Flash document, the sound file appears in the Library just as any other sound would.

✦ **Sound Designer II:** This proprietary audio file format created by Digidesign is used with its signature professional audio suite, Pro Tools. Sounds saved in this file format can be imported into the Macintosh version of Flash MX 2004. If you need to use a Sound Designer II file (.sd2 file extension) with the Windows version of Flash MX 2004, you can import the file directly if you have QuickTime 4 or later installed.

Note
With Flash MX Professional 2004, you can link proxy sound files to MIDI and MFI files that can be played back on mobile devices with Flash Lite. You learn more about this feature later in this section.

Tip
Don't rely upon the imported sound that's embedded in the Flash document (.fla file) as your master or backup sound file. Always retain your original master sound file as a backup or for reuse in other multimedia projects.

These sound file types are structural or "architecture" based, meaning that they simply indicate the wrapper used to encode digital audio. Each of them can use a variety of compression techniques or a variety of audio *codecs*. A codec is a *co*mpression and *dec*ompression module for digital media. Sound and video is encoded (compressed) with a specific technique by an application or device. After it is encoded, it can be played back (decompressed) by a media player that has access to the codec module. In order for a sound file to play on your computer, you must have the audio codec used in that file installed on your system. MP3 files, for example, can be compressed in a variety of bit rates and frequencies, as can WAV and AIF files. Once Flash imports a sound file, the wrapper type (AIF, WAV, AU, and so on) is stripped. Flash simply stores the sound file as generic PCM (Pulse Code Modulation) digital audio. Moreover, Flash converts any imported 8-bit sound file into a 16-bit sound file. For this reason, it's best not to use any precompression or low bit depths on your sound files before you bring them into Flash MX 2004.

Note
Individual MP3 sound files in the Flash document's Library can be adjusted to retain their original compression. This is the sole exception to the rule we just mentioned in the preceding paragraph. As you'll see later in this chapter, however, Flash MX 2004 may need to recompress all sound files in a Flash movie, depending on their use in the movie's timeline.

MP3s Demystified

MP3 is an amazing compression technology as well as a file format. It excels at the compression of a sound sequence — MP3-compressed files can be reduced to nearly a twelfth of their original size without destroying sound quality. MP3 was developed under the sponsorship of the Motion Picture Experts Group (MPEG) using the following logic: CD-quality sound is typically sampled at a bit depth of 16 (16-bit) at sample rate 44.1 kHz, which generates approximately 1.4 million bits of data for each second of sound — but that second of sound includes a lot of data for sounds that most humans cannot hear! By devising a compression algorithm that reduces the data linked to imperceptible sounds, the developers of MP3 made it possible to deliver high-quality audio over the Internet without excessive *latency* (the delay between loading a sound and playing it). Another way of describing this is to say that MP3 uses perceptual encoding techniques that reduce the amount of overlapping and redundant information that describe sound. As you learn later in this chapter, the Flash Player can actually buffer Stream sounds (which can be created from any sound file imported into Flash), which means that the sound begins to play in the Flash movie before the sound file has been downloaded in its entirety. Shockwave Audio, the default audio compression scheme for Macromedia Director-based Shockwave movies, is actually MP3 in disguise.

Export formats

You can decide which sound encoding to use for audio when publishing Flash document files to Flash movies (.swf files). Although the default Publish Settings in Flash MX 2004 is to export all audio with the MP3 format, sound can be exported in several other audio formats. The benefits and drawbacks of each format are noted in the list that follows.

New Feature   Flash MX 2004 Professional allows you to export device sounds in a Flash movie, for playback on mobile devices that use file formats such as MIDI and MFI. We provide an overview of this feature in this section, and provide more in-depth coverage in Chapter 42, "Making Movies for the Pocket PC and Mobile Devices."

Regardless of the format that you choose in your document's Publish Settings for exporting your sounds, you can individually specify a compression scheme for each sound in the Flash document's library. Furthermore, each format has specific options and settings that we'll examine later in this chapter.

✦ **ADPCM (Adaptive Differential Pulse-Code Modulation):** ADPCM is an audio compression scheme that converts sound into binary information. It is primarily used for voice technologies, such as fiber-optic telephone lines, because the audio signal is compressed, enabling it to carry textual information as well. ADPCM works well because it records only the difference between samples and adjusts the encoding accordingly, keeping file size low. ADPCM was the default setting for older versions of Flash, such as Flash 2 and 3. It isn't as efficient as MP3 encoding but is the best choice for situations in which compatibility is required with *all* older Flash Players.

✦ **MP3 (MPEG-1 Audio Layer 3):** Over the last three years, MP3 has become the standard for digital audio distributed on the Internet. Although MP3 compression delivers excellent audio quality with small files, it's much more processor-intensive than other compressors. This means that slower computers — and we mean slow, as in Pentium I or pre-PowerMac G3 processors — may gasp when they encounter a high bit-rate MP3 audio while simultaneously processing complex animations. As always, it's wise to know your audience. When in doubt, test your Flash movie with MP3 audio on slower computers. Flash Players 4 and higher support MP3 playback.

Note   Flash Player 4 for the Pocket PC does not support MP3 sound. With Flash Player 6 and higher, you can use ActionScript's `System.capabilities.hasMP3` property to determine if the hosting player device supports MP3 audio. You can learn more about this use of ActionScript in the *Flash MX 2004 ActionScript Bible* (Wiley, 2004).

✦ **Raw (Raw PCM):** Flash can export sound to .swf files in a raw audio format. If you use this setting, Flash won't compress any audio. However, uncompressed sound makes very large files that would be useless for Internet-based distribution. As uncompressed sound, audio in the imported sound file retains its original fidelity. We recommend that you use the Raw format only for Flash movies that you intend to distribute on fixed media, like CD-ROM or DVD-ROM, or for Flash movies that you intend to export as linear animation for video-editing purposes.

✦ **Speech (Nellymoser):** This new audio codec in Flash MX is specifically designed for audio sources that contain mostly human speech, such as narration or instructional content. Macromedia licensed audio technology from Nellymoser, Inc., which specializes in the development of voice-only audio codecs. All sounds that use the Speech codec will be converted to mono sounds. The real power of this codec can be seen in live streaming audio delivered by Flash Communication Server MX, as this codec is incredibly efficient and a fast encoder with a low server and client processor overhead. For example, if you want to use a `NetStream` object in ActionScript to stream live audio from a microphone, the Speech codec will optimize the audio information very efficiently. Flash Player 6 must be used to play sounds encoded with this format.

✦ **Device sound:** If you use Flash MX 2004 Professional, you can link device sound files to imported sounds in your Flash movie. Device sounds are used specifically for playback of Flash movies on mobile devices enabled with Flash Lite, a version of the Flash Player. Because the desktop Flash Player cannot play device sound files formats, you import regular sound files such as MP3s into your Flash document. These sounds are then used in a proxy fashion — you add the sound to event handlers (keyframes, buttons, and so on) just as you would any other sounds. Before you publish the Flash movie (.swf file), however, you change the settings of the sound file in the Library panel to point to a device sound. When the Flash movie is published, the device sound is embedded and used within the Flash movie, not the original imported sound.

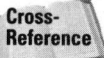

We'll examine the specific export options for each audio format later in this chapter. This section will help you determine which format you should use for your specific needs.

Table 15-1 shows the compatibility of Flash's audio export formats with various platforms.

Table 15-1: Audio Export Formats for Flash Players

Export Format	Flash 3 or Earlier	Flash 4 and 5	Flash 6 and 7	Comments
ADPCM	Yes	Yes	Yes	Good encoding scheme; compatible with all Flash players, and works well for short sound effects such as button clicks.
MP3	No	Yes	Yes	Best general use encoding scheme, and ideal for music tracks. *Not compatible with Flash Player 4 for the Pocket PC.
Raw	Yes	Yes	Yes	No compression; lossless; large file sizes.
Speech	No	No	Yes	Excellent compression for human speech; avoids "tinny" sounds for voices. Ideally suited for real-time compression with Flash server-side applications.
Device sound	No	No	No	New sound export feature from Flash MX 2004 Professional, for use with MIDI and MFI files for playback on mobile devices with Flash Lite.

Importing Sounds into Flash

In the preceding section, we discussed the various sound formats that Flash MX 2004 can import and export. In addition to our discussion of the merits of the MP3 and Speech codecs, we also explained the uses of platform-specific AIF (Mac) and WAV (Windows) audio files. But we didn't delve into the process of importing sound into Flash MX 2004. So, let's get started.

Note   When working with sound, you may encounter some interchangeable terminology. Generally, these terms—*sound file, sound clip,* or *audio file*—all refer to the same thing, a single digital file in one of several formats, which contains a digitally encoded sound.

Unlike other imported assets, such as bitmaps or vector art, Flash doesn't automatically insert an imported sound file into the frames of the active layer on the timeline. In fact, you don't have to select a specific layer or frame before you import a sound file. That's because all sounds are sent directly to the Library immediately upon import. At this point, the sound becomes part of the Flash document (.fla file), which may make the file size balloon significantly if the sound file is large. The sound does not become part of the Flash movie (.swf file), nor will it add to the size of the Flash movie *unless* it is assigned to a keyframe, as an instance of that sound, or it is set to export for use in ActionScript.

Tip   Flash Players 6 and 7 allow a Flash movie to load MP3 files directly. Earlier versions of the Flash Player required Macromedia Generator (or an equivalent server-side application) to transform sound files into Flash movies (.swf files) on the fly. We'll show you how to load and attach sounds with ActionScript in Chapter 28, "Sharing and Loading Assets."

To import a sound file into the Flash MX 2004 authoring environment follow these steps:

1. Choose File ➪ Import (Ctrl+R or ⌘+R), or File ➪ Import to Library.

   For sound assets, these commands work identically.

Note   File ➪ Import to Stage achieves the same result as using File ➪ Import or File ➪ Import to Library.

2. From the Files of type list (Windows) or Show list (Mac) in the Import dialog box, select All Sound Formats.

Caution   On the Mac OS X version of Flash MX 2004, you may need to choose All Files in the Show menu in order to select an appropriate sound file.

3. Browse to the sound file that you want to import.

On the CD-ROM   If you're looking for a sample audio file, you can import the `atmospheres_1.mp3` file found in the `ch15` folder of this book's CD-ROM.

4. Click Open.

   The selected sound file is imported into your Flash document (.fla file) and arrives in the document's library with its filename intact. If the Library panel is closed, you can open it by choosing Window ⇨ Library, or by using the keyboard shortcut (Ctrl+L or ⌘+L). With the Library panel open, locate the sound, and click it to highlight the name of the sound file where it appears in the Library list. The waveform appears in the Library preview pane, as shown in Figure 15-1. Click the Play button above the waveform to audition the sound.

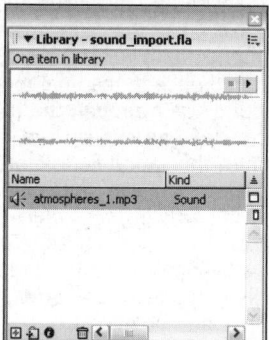

Figure 15-1: This is a stereo sound in the Flash document's library.

Refer to the section "Fine-Tuning Sound Settings in the Library" later in this chapter for an explanation of how unique compression settings can be specified for each sound in a document's library.

Sounds may also be loaded from a shared library. Refer to Chapter 28, "Sharing and Loading Assets," to learn more about shared libraries. Chapter 28 also shows you how to preload an MP3 file into a Flash movie (.swf file). To learn how to assign a linkage identifier string to an asset, such as a sound file, refer to Chapter 27, "Interacting with Movie Clips."

You can also import sound files into a Flash document by dragging the sound file from the desktop to the Timeline window or the Library panel. On the Macintosh, you can drag the sound file to the Stage as well. This method can be especially useful when you have searched for a sound file using the operating system's search tool (Start ⇨ Search in Windows, or Sherlock in the Mac OS), and want to quickly bring the found file into Flash MX 2004.

When you import a sound file using this method on the Windows version of Flash MX 2004, the sound file is placed in its own Flash document (.fla file). If you want to use it in another document, then drag it from the new document's Library panel to the other document's Library panel. Remember that Windows users cannot drag sound files to the Document window (or Stage area) — doing so may result in an OLE error dialog box instructing you to use File ⇨ Import instead.

Assigning a Sound to a Button

The interactive experience can be enhanced by the addition of subtle effects. The addition of sounds to correspond with the various states of a button is perhaps the most obvious example. Although this effect can be abused, it's hard to overuse an effect that delivers such meaningful user feedback. Here, we show how different sounds can be added to both the Over (rollOver) and the Down (press) states of a button.

How Sound Is Stored in a Flash Movie

Earlier in this chapter, we mentioned that when you import a sound file into a Flash MX 2004 document (.fla file), an entire copy of the sound file is stored within the document. However, when you place a sound on a Timeline, a reference is made to the sound in the library. Just as symbol instances refer to a master or parent symbol in the Library, sound "instances" refer to the master sound resource in the Library. Throughout this chapter, we use the term "instance" for sound assets with this understanding in mind. When the Flash document is published as a Flash movie, the master sound in the Library is compressed and stored *once* in the final movie (.swf file), even though there may be several instances of that sound used through the movie (for example, in multiple frames on multiple timelines). This type of efficient storage, however, applies to Event sounds only. Whenever you use Stream sounds, the sound file is stored in the Flash movie each time you refer to the sound in a Timeline. For example, if you compressed a sound to export from Flash as a 3K sound asset in the final movie (.swf file), you could reuse that sound as an Event sound several times without adding significant bytes to the file size. However, that same compressed sound (at 3K) would occupy 12K in the final movie if it were placed four times as a Stream sound on keyframes within the movie. We'll discuss Event and Stream sounds later in this chapter, so you may want to refer to this sidebar at a later point.

It is also worth mentioning that Flash MX 2004 must have enough available RAM on the computer system to accommodate imported sound files. For example, if you import a 30MB WAV file into a Flash document, then you must have an additional 30MB of RAM available to the application. On 32-bit Windows operating systems and Mac OS X, you will not likely experience problems with memory usage, where virtual memory exists alongside the physical RAM within the computer.

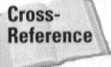

Cross-Reference   For more general information about creating the buttons themselves, see Chapter 6, "Symbols, Instances, and the Library," and see Chapter 18, "Understanding Actions and Event Handlers," to learn how to add code to buttons.

Because buttons are stored in the Library, and because only instances of a Button symbol are deployed within the Flash movie, sounds that are assigned to a button work for all instances of that Button symbol. However, if different sounds are required for different buttons, a new Button symbol must be created (see the following New Feature note for an exception to this "rule"). You can create a new Button symbol from the same Graphic symbols as the previous button (provided it was built out of symbols) or duplicate it in the Library panel using the Duplicate command in the Library's options menu.

New Feature   With the new Behaviors panel, you can quickly assign different sounds to the various instances of the same Button (or Movie Clip) symbol. You learn about behaviors related to sound use later in this chapter.

To add a sound to the Down state of a Button symbol, follow these steps:

1. Create a new Button symbol (Insert ⇨ New Symbol) or choose a symbol from the Buttons Library (Window ⇨ Other Panels ⇨ Common Libraries ⇨ Buttons).

2. Drag an instance of the button from the Library (or the document's Library) to the Stage.

3. Edit the Button symbol by double-clicking it on the Stage, or by choosing Edit from the Library options menu.

Both methods transfer the working environment into Edit mode.

4. Add a new layer to the button's timeline, label the new layer sound, and then add keyframes to this layer in the Over and Down columns.

Your timeline should look similar to Figure 15-2.

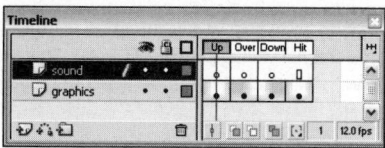

Figure 15-2: The timeline for your button should resemble this one.

5. Select the frame of the button state where you want to add a sound for interactive feedback (such as a clicking sound for the Down state), and then access the Property inspector by doing one of the following: (a) right-click/Control+click the selected frame, choose Properties from the contextual menu; or (b) choose Window ➪ Properties.

An alternative method (with the frame selected) is to simply drag the sound from the Library panel onto the Stage.

You should now have the Property inspector open, as shown in Figure 15-3. Click the arrow in the lower-right corner of the Property inspector to see all of the options.

Cross-Reference For more information about using the Flash MX 2004 interface, refer to Chapter 4, "Interface Fundamentals."

Sound attributes

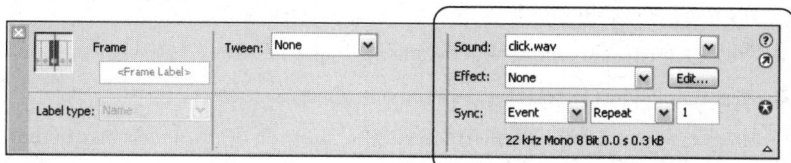

Figure 15-3: The Property inspector houses the options for sound usage.

6. Choose the sound clip that you want to use from the Sound menu.

This menu lists all of the sounds that have been imported and that are available in the library of the current movie. In this example, we used the click.wav sound found in the ch15 folder of the book's CD-ROM.

7. Use the Sync menu to choose *how* you want the sound to play.

For this lesson, simply use the default, which is the Event option. We'll defer our exploration of the other options in the Sync menu for a later section.

You have now added a sound to your button state. Remember that you're still in Edit mode, so to test the button, return to the Scene 1 timeline (that is, the Main Timeline) either by clicking the Scene 1 location label at the upper-left corner of the Document window, or by pressing Ctrl+E (⌘+E). Then choose Control ⇨ Enable Simple Buttons, or Control ⇨ Test Movie.

To add a sound to the Over state of a Button symbol, simply retrace the preceding steps, referencing the Over state of the button wherever appropriate. Remember that different sounds can be assigned to the Up, Over, and Down states of a Button symbol. A sound that is added to the Up state will play whenever the mouse rolls out of a button's hit area.

On the CD-ROM

For a completed example of this button, refer to the Flash movie `button_sound_100.fla` located in the `ch15` folder of the *Macromedia Flash MX 2004 Bible* CD-ROM. This movie has a button with sounds attached and was made with the same technique described in this section.

Adding Sound to the Timeline

In addition to the use of sounds to enhance the interactivity of buttons, another popular use of sound in Flash is to provide a background score. The simplest way to achieve this is to place the sound within its own layer in the Main Timeline (Scene 1), at the precise frame in which you want the sound to begin. To do this, you must first import the sound (as described earlier in this chapter) and create a new layer for it.

On the CD-ROM

If you don't have access to sounds, you can use the sample sound `atmospheres_1` to practice. This sound is in the `ch15` folder of the *Macromedia Flash MX 2004 Bible* CD-ROM. It is available in both WAV and AIF formats.

Adding sound files to the timeline is similar to assigning sound to a button. To add sounds to a timeline, follow these steps:

1. Add a new layer in the Timeline window and label the layer with the name of the sound.

   You can use a name such as "sound" or "background track."

2. Create a keyframe on the sound layer at the frame where you want the sound to begin.

3. With that keyframe selected, open the Property inspector.

   Make sure you have expanded the view to show all of the sound attributes.

4. If you remembered to import the sound that you want to use, you can now choose that sound clip from the Sound drop-down menu.

   If you find yourself stuck at this point, review the preceding steps and/or retrace your steps through the methodology for adding sound to a button.

5. From the Effect menu, choose how the sound should be handled by Flash.

   The Effect menu offers several preset fading and panning treatments, plus custom, which invokes the Edit Envelope dialog box. For no special effect, choose None. For more about the Effect presets and the Edit Envelope dialog box, refer to the subsequent section, "Editing Audio in Flash."

6. From the Sync menu, choose one of four options — Event, Start, Stop, or Stream — to control how you want to the sound to be synchronized.

   See the next section for a detailed explanation of Sync options.

7. Specify how many times you want the sound to loop.

   To loop the sound indefinitely (for example, as a background track), choose Loop in the second drop-down menu in the Sync parameters. If you want the sound to loop only for a specific number of times, choose Repeat in the menu and enter a number in the text field to the right of the menu. For specific information about looping stream sounds, refer to the next section.

8. Perform any last-minute editing or finessing of the sound file (see "Editing Audio in Flash" later in this chapter).

   Then return to the Main Timeline and save your work.

Your sound is now part of the timeline. Its waveform is visible on the layer to which it was added. Test your sound by pressing the Enter key on your keyboard, which plays the timeline. Or, for sound with a Sync setting of Stream, manually "scrub" the sound by dragging the Playhead across the timeline. To perform the most accurate test of the sound, use either Control ➪ Test Scene or Control ➪ Test Movie to see and hear it as a Flash movie (.swf file).

Tip   If you sync a sound to the timeline using the Stream feature, you should test your Flash movie (.swf file) on various platforms and machines with different processor speeds, especially if the timeline is always playing animation. What looks and sounds good on a fast Pentium IV might be less impressive on an underpowered legacy machine, like a first- or second-generation Pentium machine.

Organizing Sounds on the Timeline

There is no technical limit to the number of sound layers; each layer functions like a separate sound channel, and Flash mixes them on playback. (This capability of Flash might be considered a built-in economy sound mixer.) There is, however, a practical limit because each sound layer potentially increases the movie's file size, while the mix of multiple sounds may burden the computer it's being run on.

Tip   If you can't recall the *name* of a particular sound in the timeline, remember that with ToolTips enabled from the Preferences dialog box (Edit ➪ Preferences in Windows, Flash ➪ Preferences in Mac OS X), the filename of the sound will pop up whenever the mouse pointer is over the waveform.

Enhanced viewing of sound layers

Because sound is different from other types of Flash content, some users find that increasing the layer height of the sound layers eases working with multiple sounds in the timeline. That's because a taller layer height provides a better visual cue due to the unique waveforms of each sound. To increase the layer height for individual layers, follow these steps:

1. Right-click (or Control+click on the Mac) the layer in the Timeline window, and then choose Properties from the contextual menu.

2. At the bottom of the ensuing Layer Properties dialog box, change the layer height from the default 100 percent to either 200 or 300 percent.

   Note that these percentages are relative to the settings chosen in the Frame View options menu.

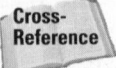

For more information on the Timeline window, see Chapter 4, "Interface Fundamentals." For an actual example of this enhanced viewing, open the file `enhanced_view.fla`, located in the `ch15` folder on the CD-ROM.

Your movie's frame rate, as specified in the Document Properties dialog box (Modify⇨ Document), affects the number of frames that a sound occupies on the timeline. For example, at Flash's default setting of 12 frames per seconds (fps), a 30-second sound clip extends across 360 frames of the timeline. At 18 fps, the same 30-second clip expands to 540 frames — but in either case, the time length of the sound is unchanged.

Organizing sound layers with a layer folder

Flash MX introduced a new organization tool for layers in any timeline: Layer folders. To nest sound layers in a layer folder, create a new layer folder and then drag each of the sound layers to the folder. As you drop each layer on the folder, it will nest within the folder.

We discuss Layer folders in Chapter 4, "Interface Fundamentals."

Synchronizing Audio to Animations

In film editors' lingo, to *synchronize*, or *sync*, means to precisely match picture to sound. In Flash, sound can be synchronized to the visual content of the timeline. Flash sync affords several options for the manner in which the audio clip is related to graphics or animation on the timeline. Each of these sync options is appropriate for particular uses, which the following sections discuss.

The Sync options in the sound area of the Property inspector control the behavior of sound in Flash movies, relative to the timeline in which the sound is placed. The Sync option you choose depends on whether your sound is intended to add dimension to a complex multimedia presentation or to add interactivity in the form of button-triggered sound, or whether it is intended to be the closely timed soundtrack of an animated cartoon.

Event

Event is the default Sync option for all sounds in Flash, so unless you change this default to one of the other options, the sound automatically behaves as an Event sound. Event sounds begin with the keyframe in which they occur and then play independently of the timeline. If an Event sound's duration is longer than the remaining frames of its timeline, it continues to play even though playback on the timeline has stopped. If an Event sound requires considerable time to load, the movie pauses at that keyframe until the sound has loaded completely. Event sounds are the easiest to implement and are useful for background sound scapes and other sounds that don't need to be synced. Again, Event is the default Sync setting in the Sound menu of the Property inspector.

Event sounds can degrade into a disturbing inharmonious round of out-of-tune sound loops. If the timeline holding the Event sound loops before the sound has completed, the sound begins again — over the top of the initial sound that has not finished playing. After several loops, the resulting effect can become intolerable. To avoid this effect, use the Start Sync option.

Start

The Start Sync option is similar to an Event option, but with one crucial difference: If any instance of that sound is already playing, then no other instance of that sound can play. In other words, the Start Sync tells the sound to begin playing only if other instances have finished playing or if it's the first instance of that sound to play. This option is useful if you want to avoid the layering problem discussed in the previous caution note for Event sounds.

Note   Start sounds are actually a type of Event sound. Later in this chapter, when we refer to Audio Stream and Audio Event settings in the Publish Settings dialog box, realize that Start sounds belong to the Audio Event category.

Stop

The Stop Sync option is similar to the Start Sync option, except that any and all instances of the selected sound stop playing when the frame containing the Stop Sync option is played. This option comes in handy when you want to mute a specific sound in a crowd of others. For example, if you created a sound mixer with an arrangement of Button instances, you could assign the Stop Sync to a mute button for each of the sounds in the mixer.

Stream

Stream sounds are similar to a traditional soundtrack in a video-editing application. A Stream sound locks to the timeline and has priority over visual content. When Stream sound is chosen, the Flash Player attempts to pace the animation in sync with the sound. However, when animations either get too complex or are run on slower machines, the Flash Player skips — or drops — the frames as needed to stay in sync with the Stream sound. A Stream sound stops when the Playhead reaches the last frame that includes the waveform of the Stream sound. A Stream sound can be *scrubbed*; by dragging the Playhead along the layer's frames in the Timeline window, the Stream sound plays in direct relationship to the content as it appears, frame by frame. This is especially useful for lip-sync and coordinating the perfect timing of sound effects with visual events.

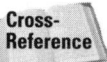

Cross-Reference   See Chapter 13, "Character Animation Techniques," for more information on lip-sync.

To use sound effectively, it's important to understand how Stream sounds work. When a Flash document is published as a Flash movie (.swf file) and the Sync option for a sound is set to Stream, Flash breaks the sound into chunks that are tied to the timeline. The bytes within the movie are arranged according to the linear order of the Main Timeline (that is, Scene 1). As such, if you have a Stream sound that stretches from frames 1 to 100 of the Main Timeline and the movie contains a total of 200 frames, the Stream sound's bytes will be evenly distributed over the first 50 percent of the file's bytes.

Tip   When adding sounds to the timeline, no matter how many times you tell a Stream sound to loop, a Stream sound will stop playing wherever the visual waveform in the Timeline window ends. To extend a Stream sound's duration, add as many frames as necessary to a Stream sound's layer.

Stopping Sounds

The default behavior of Event sounds is for them to play through to the end, regardless of the length of the timeline on which they exist. However, you can stop any sound, including Event sounds. Place another instance of the same sound at the keyframe where the sound should stop and assign this instance as a Stop sync option. This Stop setting can be on any layer, and it will stop all instances of the specific sound. Let's give this a try.

Stopping an Event sound

In this section, we'll show you how to stop an Event sound using two different methods. The first method uses a Stop sound on a keyframe in the Main Timeline (Scene 1). The second method uses a Button instance with a Stop sound on its Down state.

1. Create a Flash document that has an Event sound placed on the first keyframe and has enough frames on the timeline to display the entire waveform of the sound.

   You can use the `enhanced_view.fla` file from the book's CD-ROM as a practice file.

2. Create a new layer in the Timeline window, and name this layer stop sound.

3. On the stop sound layer, pick a frame that's about five seconds into the sound displayed on the original layer.

4. Create a keyframe on this frame in the stop sound layer.

5. With this keyframe selected, open the Property inspector.

6. In the Sound menu, choose the same sound file that was used in the original sound layer.

7. In the Sync menu of the Property inspector, choose Stop.

   As a Stop sound, this setting will tell the Flash Player to stop any and all instances of the sound that is specified in the Sound menu.

8. Save your Flash document, and test it (Control ➪ Test Movie).

   When the Playhead reaches the keyframe with the Stop sound, you should no longer hear the Event sound.

Now, we'll show you how to play and mute an Event sound by clicking buttons. Let's place an Event sound on one Button symbol instance, and then a Stop sound on another Button symbol instance.

1. In a new Flash document, create a copy of the Play and Stop buttons from the Circle Buttons folder in the Buttons Library (Window ➪ Other Panels ➪ Common Libraries ➪ Buttons).

   To do this, drag each of the buttons from the Buttons Library panel to your document's Stage. Close the Buttons Library when you are done. Rename Layer 1 to **buttons**. Your document's Stage should resemble Figure 15-4.

2. Import a sound file to use as your Event sound.

   You can use the `atmospheres_1.mp3` sound from the book's CD-ROM.

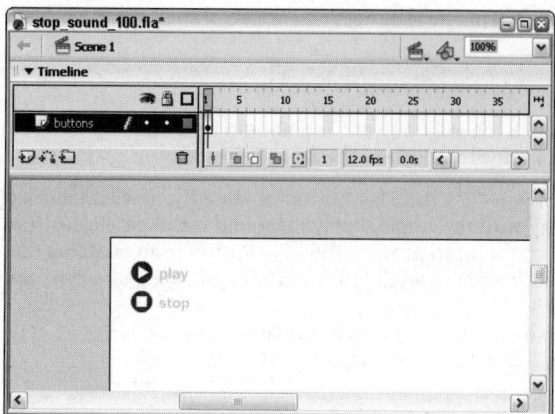

Figure 15-4: The Play and Stop buttons on the Stage

3. In the document's Library panel, double-click the Play button to edit the symbol.

4. In the Timeline window, create a new layer and name it sound.

5. Insert a keyframe on the Down state of the sound layer.

6. Select the keyframe made in Step 4, and open the Property inspector.

7. Select the imported sound's name in the Sound menu, and leave the Sync menu at the default Event setting.

   When you are finished, your document should resemble Figure 15-5.

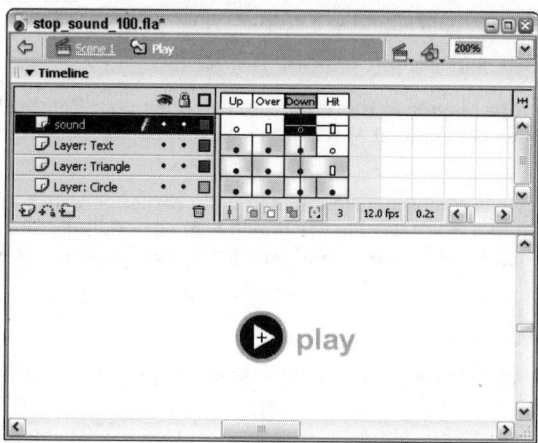

Figure 15-5: This sound will play when the Play button is clicked.

8. Double-click the Stop button in the Library panel.

9. Repeat Steps 3 through 7. This time, however, choose Stop in the Sync menu for the atmospheres_1 sound.

10. Save your document and test it (Control ⇨ Test Movie).

In Test Movie mode, click the Play button. You should hear the imported sound begin to play. When you click the Stop button, the sound should stop playing.

You may have noticed that, if you click the Play button repeatedly, new instances of the sound will begin to play, overlapping with the original playing sound instance. Regardless, the Stop Sync will stop all of them. If you want to prevent the Play button from enabling this type of overlap, go back to the sound keyframe on the Play button and change its Sync option to Start.

On the CD-ROM

You can find a completed example of the Play and Stop buttons exercise as stop_sound_100.fla, located in the ch15 folder of the book's CD-ROM.

Stopping a single instance of a Stream sound

A single instance of a Stream sound can also be stopped. To do this, simply place an empty keyframe in the sound layer at the point where the sound should stop.

1. Open the enhanced_view.fla file, located in the ch15 folder of the book's CD-ROM.

2. Switch the layer view of the atmospheres_1 layer back to 100% in the Layer Properties dialog box.

3. Select the first frame of the atmospheres_1 layer.

4. In the Property inspector, switch the Sync option to Stream.

5. Select frame 60 of the atmospheres_1 layer, and insert a blank keyframe (F7).

This is the point where the Stream sound will stop playing.

6. Save your Flash document, and test it (Control ⇨ Test Movie).

Notice that the sound stops playing at frame 60. You can open your Bandwidth Profiler (View ⇨ Bandwidth Profiler) in the Test Movie mode to see the Playhead move as the movie plays.

The Bandwidth Profiler also reveals something we touched upon earlier: Stream sounds export only the actual portion of the sound that's used in the timeline. In our example, 60 frames' worth of the atmospheres_1 sound was about 12K (at default MP3 compression, 16 Kbps).

Stopping all sounds

You can stop the sounds that are playing in all timelines (including Movie Clips) at any point by doing the following:

1. If there isn't already an actions layer on your timeline, add a layer, label it **actions**, and select the frame that occurs at the point where you want all sounds to stop. Make this frame into a keyframe.

2. With the keyframe selected, open the Actions panel by pressing the F9 key, or by navigating to Window ⇨ Actions.

The title bar of the Actions panel should read Actions — Frame.

3. Click the Global Functions booklet in the left pane of the panel, and then click the Timeline Control booklet.

4. Double-click the `stopAllSounds` action.

The following ActionScript code,

```
stopAllSounds ();
```

appears in the Script pane of the Actions panel, as shown in Figure 15-6.

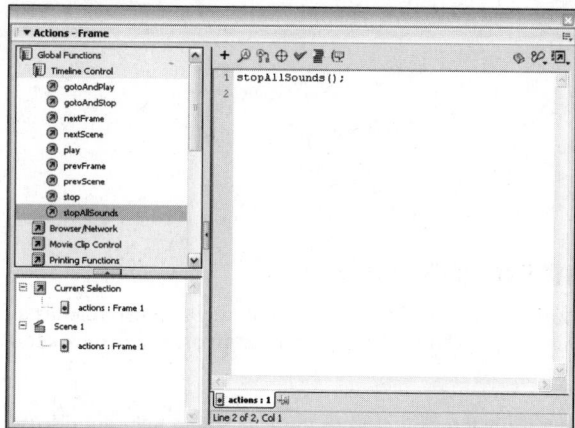

Figure 15-6: Any sound that's currently playing stops when the movie reaches a keyframe with a stopAllSounds() action.

5. Save your Flash document, and then test it with Control ➪ Test Movie.

When the movie's Playhead reaches the frame with the `stopAllSounds()` action, every sound that is currently playing stops.

The `stopAllSounds()` action stops only sounds that are playing at the time the action is executed. It will not permanently mute the sound for the duration of the movie. You can proceed to re-initialize any sounds any time after the `stopAllSounds()` action has executed. If you want to stop playback again, you will have to enable another `stopAllSounds()` action or use a Stop sound.

Applying Behaviors That Control Sound

One of the new features of Flash MX 2004 is the Behaviors panel, which allows you to quickly add interactive functionality to elements of your Flash movie. There are five behaviors in the Sound category of the Behaviors panel. In this section, you learn how each of these behaviors works.

Note

Behaviors are essentially prewritten ActionScript code blocks that appear on event handlers such as keyframes, Button instances, and Movie Clip instances. Just as Dreamweaver behaviors add JavaScript code to HTML documents, Flash behaviors add ActionScript code to your Flash documents.

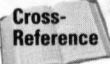

Cross-Reference For more information on how to access the Behavior panel and other panels, see Chapter 4, "Interface Fundamentals."

You can see all of the Sound behaviors by clicking the Add Behavior (+) button in the top-left corner of the Behaviors panel and choosing the Sound menu item (see Figure 15-7).

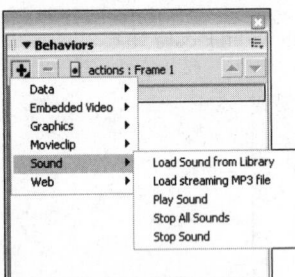

Figure 15-7: The Sound behaviors in the Behaviors panel

Load Sound from Library

This behavior locates a sound item in the Flash movie's library and establishes a reference to that sound, so that the sound can be later played. This behavior can also be used to play the sound as well.

Caution You must use this behavior before you can use the Play Sound behavior discussed later in this section.

In practice, you will use this behavior to set up references to any sounds that you wish to use the Play Sound behavior. For example, if you have three sounds in your Library and you want to prepare all three for later use in your Flash movie, you would add three Load Sound from Library behaviors to the first frame of a layer in your Flash document. In the following steps, you learn how to add this behavior to a Flash document.

On the CD-ROM In the following exercise, you can use the atmospheres_1.wav or atmospheres_1.aif sound file from the ch15 folder of this book's CD-ROM.

1. Create a new Flash document by choosing File ➪ New.

2. In the New Document dialog box, select Flash Document and click OK.

3. Import a sound file into the Flash document. Choose File ➪ Import to Library and browse to a sound file on your local computer.

   You can import one of the sound files from the book's CD-ROM. For this example, we refer to the atmospheres_1.wav file.

4. Once the sound is imported into the document's library, open the Library panel (Ctrl+L or ⌘+L).

   You need to create a linkage identifier for the newly imported sound in order for the Load Sound from Library behavior to locate the sound in the library.

5. Select the sound file in the panel, and right-click (or Control+click on the Mac) the sound file.

6. Choose the Linkage option in the contextual menu.

7. In the Linkage Properties dialog box, select the Export for ActionScript check box.

   The sound filename automatically populates the Identifier field. You can leave the name as is, or rename the identifier term. For this example, use the term **song**, as shown in Figure 15-8. Click OK to close the dialog box.

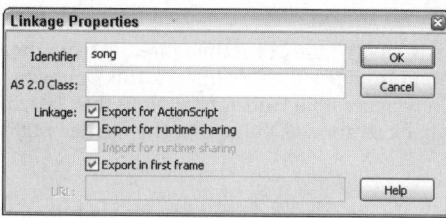

Figure 15-8: The Linkage Properties dialog box

Now, you are ready to access the linked sound in a behavior.

8. In the Timeline window, rename Layer 1 **behaviors**.

9. Select frame 1 of this layer, and open the Behaviors panel (Shift+F3).

10. In the top-left corner of this panel, click the Add Behavior (+) button, and choose Sound ➪ Load Sound from Library.

    A dialog box opens, in which you can enter the parameters for the behavior.

11. In the Linkage ID field, type the identifier you specified in Step 7.

    In the sample, we used the term "song." In the Identifier field, type a unique instance name for this sound. For this example, use **song_sound**. Refer to Figure 15-9. The **Play this sound when loaded** check box is checked by default. As such, the atmospheres_1.wav sound will play as soon as frame 1 is loaded.

Figure 15-9: The Load Sound from Library parameters

12. Save your Flash document (File ➪ Save) as loadsound_behavior.fla.

13. Choose Control ➪ Test Movie (Ctrl+Enter or ⌘+Enter).

    As soon as the Flash movie starts, you will hear the atmospheres_1.wav sound begin to play.

Note   The audio options in the Publish Settings dialog box (File ⇨ Publish Settings) are automatically compressing the sound file to MP3 audio at 16 Kbps.

On the CD-ROM   You can find the completed file, `loadsound_behavior.fla`, in the `ch15` folder of this book's CD-ROM.

Load streaming MP3 file

This behavior, as the name implies, loads an MP3 file at runtime directly from the Flash Player environment. Instead of attaching a sound from the movie's library, this behavior can access an external MP3 file residing on a publicly accessible Web server. Note that "streaming" here means that the MP3 file will begin playback as soon as enough of the file has buffered into the Flash Player.

Note   Technically, this type of loading is called a progressive download — it's not true streaming like audio or video from a Flash Communication Server application.

In the following exercise, you learn how to use this behavior to play an MP3 file from a remote Web server.

1. Create a new Flash document by choosing File ⇨ New.

2. In the New Document dialog box, select Flash Document and click OK.

3. Rename Layer 1 to **behaviors**.

4. Select this layer's first frame, and open the Behaviors panel (Shift+F3).

5. In the top-left corner of this panel, click the Add Behavior (+) button, and choose Sound ⇨ Load streaming MP3 file.

   When this behavior's dialog box opens, there are two options: Sound Location and Identifier.

6. In the Sound Location, type the URL to an MP3 file that has been copied to a publicly accessible folder on your Web server.

   You can use the following URL to test this example: **http://www.flashsupport.com/ mp3/atmospheres_1_short.mp3**

7. In the Identifier field, type **bg_sound**.

   This identifier allows you to target the sound with another behavior or in your own ActionScript code.

8. Click OK to close the dialog box.

   See Figure 15-10 for more details.

9. Save your Flash document as loadmp3_behavior.fla.

10. Test your movie by choosing Control ⇨ Test Movie (Ctrl+Enter or ⌘+Enter).

As soon as the movie loads, the MP3 begins to stream into the Flash Player. When enough of the sound has buffered, the MP3 file automatically plays.

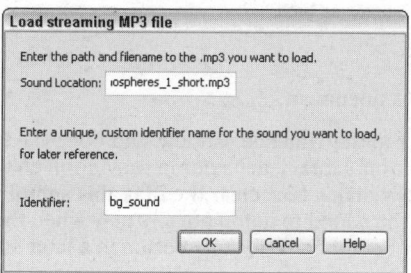

Figure 15-10: The Load streaming MP3 file behavior parameters

Note You need to have a connection to the Internet in order for this example to work. If you would like to test this example with a local MP3 file, make a copy of the MP3 file directly to the same location as your Flash document. Then, change the URL in the behavior's parameters to `atmospheres_1_short.mp3`, omitting the `http://www.flashsupport.com/mp3/` portion.

On the CD-ROM You can find the completed file, `loadmp3_behavior.fla`, in the `ch15` folder of this book's CD-ROM.

As indicated by the previous note, you can specify relative URLs (or file locations) in the Sound Location field for this behavior's parameters. For example, if you save your Flash movie (.swf file) in the same location or folder as your MP3 file, you can simply specify the MP3 filename in the Sound Location field. You can also use relative path notation. For example, `../myfile.mp3` would load the myfile.mp3 file located one directory above (that is, the parent folder) the Flash movie's location.

Note With the Load streaming MP3 file behavior, the sound does not loop. If you want to replay the sound, you need to use the Play Sound behavior or target the sound with further ActionScript code.

Play Sound

The Play Sound behavior plays a sound that has been set up with the Load Sound from Library or Load streaming MP3 file behaviors. Remember that the Load streaming MP3 file behavior automatically begins playback of the MP3 file, and the Load Sound from Library behavior has an optional parameter that automatically begins playback as well. You can use the Play Sound behavior to:

✦ Play a sound that was only set up by the Load Sound from Library behavior, where the Play this sound when loaded option was not selected.

✦ Replay a sound that finished playing or was stopped by the Stop Sound behavior (discussed later in this section).

In the following steps, you learn how to add a Play Sound movie to a Button instance.

On the
CD-ROM

Use the `loadsound_behavior.fla` file you created earlier in this section. You can find this file in the `ch15` folder of the book's CD-ROM as well.

1. Open the `loadsound_behavior.fla` document.

2. Select frame 1 of the behaviors layer in the Timeline window, and open the Behaviors panel. Double-click the Load Sound from Library behavior in the Action column of the panel. In the Load Sound from Library dialog box, clear the **Play this sound when loaded** checkbox. You do not want the sound to automatically play when the sound loads because you will assign a Play Sound behavior to a button in a later step. Click OK to accept the new setting.

3. Create a new layer named **buttons**, and place this layer below the existing behaviors layer.

4. Save your Flash document as `playsound_behavior.fla`.

   It's always good practice to resave an older document with a new name whenever you are changing the scope of your document.

5. Open the Buttons library by choosing Windows ⇨ Other Panels ⇨ Common Libraries ⇨ Buttons.

6. In this Library, navigate to the Circle Buttons folder, and drag an instance of the Play symbol to the Stage.

   Make sure you have selected the first frame of the buttons layer before you drag the symbol.

7. Select the new Play instance on the Stage, and open the Behaviors panel (Shift+F3).

8. In the top-left corner of this panel, click the Add Behavior (+) button, and choose Sound ⇨ Play Sound.

9. In the Play Sound dialog box, type **song_sound** in the Identifier field.

   Remember that the sound loaded in the `loadsound_behavior.fla` file had this same identifier. See Figure 15-11.

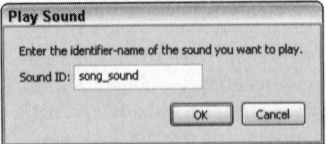

Figure 15-11: The Play Sound behavior parameters

10. Save your Flash document, and test the movie (Control ⇨ Test Movie).

    When you click the Play button, you hear the `song_sound` instance play.

You can find the completed file, `playsound_behavior.fla`, in the `ch15` folder of this book's CD-ROM.

The Play Sound behavior is the first Sound behavior discussed in this section that has different events from which you can choose in the Behaviors panel, as shown in Figure 15-12.

Figure 15-12: The event options available for behaviors attached to buttons

If you prefer the Play Sound behavior to activate with a different mouse event, you can choose another option in the Event combo box.

Stop All Sounds

This behavior inserts the `stopAllSounds()` function into the code of the selected event handler (that is, a keyframe, a Button instance, or Movie Clip instance). As we discussed earlier in this chapter, the `stopAllSounds()` function halts the playback of any and all playing sounds.

In the next exercise, you learn how to stop the playback of multiple sounds with the Stop All Sounds behavior.

Use the `loadmp3_behavior.fla` document as a starting point for this exercise. You can find this document in the `ch15` folder of this book's CD-ROM. This exercise also requires the `robert_video.flv` file located in the same folder of the CD-ROM. Make a copy of this file to your local hard drive.

1. Open the `loadmp3_behavior.fla` document, and create a new layer named **video**.
2. Place this layer below the existing behaviors layer.
3. Save your Flash document as `stopallsounds_behavior.fla`.

   The video file that you import in the next step has a frame rate of 24 fps. As such, you need to change the frame rate of this Flash document to match.
4. Click anywhere on the Stage of your document, and press the Esc key to deselect any selected objects.
5. In the Property inspector, change the frame rate from 12 fps to 24 fps.

Remember that this document already plays the streaming MP3 file located on the `flashsupport.com` Web server. Now, you will add a video to the Flash movie, to act as a second sound source.

6. Select the first frame of the video layer, and import the `robert_video.flv` video file by choosing File ➪ Import to Stage.

During the import process, you'll see a dialog box alerting you to the number of frames required by the video file on the current timeline, as shown in Figure 15-13. Click Yes, and Flash automatically inserts the required frames.

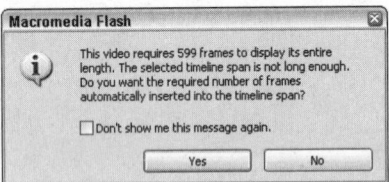

Figure 15-13: When you import video files to the Stage, Flash asks you if frames should be added to accommodate the length of the video file.

7. Create a new layer, and rename it **buttons**.

8. Place this layer at the bottom of the layer stack.

9. On frame 1 of the buttons layer, drag an instance of the Stop button from the Circle Buttons folder of the Buttons Library (Window ➪ Other Panels ➪ Common Libraries ➪ Buttons) to the Stage.

10. Place the instance below the video object.

11. Select the new Stop instance, and open the Behaviors panel.

12. Click the Add Behavior (+) button in the panel, and choose Sounds ➪ Stop All Sounds.

When you choose this behavior, you see a dialog box describing this behavior (see Figure 15-14).

Figure 15-14: The Stop All Sounds behavior dialog box

13. Click OK.

14. Save your Flash document, and test the movie (Control ➪ Test Movie).

As the movie plays, you hear the streaming MP3 file and the video's audio track play. If you click the Stop button, all of the sounds stop playing.

On the CD-ROM

You can find the completed file, `stopallsounds_behavior.fla`, in the `ch15` folder of this book's CD-ROM.

You may have noticed that if you allow the movie to continue to play, the movie eventually loops back to the first frame and repeats. You can add a stop() action to the last frame of the timeline to prevent the Flash movie from looping.

Cross-Reference   You learn how to apply basic actions to Flash timelines in Chapter 18, "Understanding Actions and Event Handlers."

Tip   To decrease publishing (or testing) time, change the Audio stream compression option to Speech in the Flash tab of the Publish Settings dialog box (File ➪ Publish Settings). The Speech codec is particularly suited to the audio track of the sample video clip, but it does add more weight, in bytes, to the final SWF file.

Stop Sound

The Stop Sound behavior stops the playback of a specific sound that has been set up by the Load Sound from Library behavior or the Load streaming MP3 file behavior. In the following steps, you add the Stop Sound behavior to a Button instance.

On the CD-ROM   Use the stopallsounds_behavior.fla document from the previous section for the next exercise. You can find this file in the ch15 folder of the book's CD-ROM.

1. Open the stopallsounds_behavior.fla file, and resave it as stopsound_behavior.fla.

2. In the first frame of the buttons layer, select the Stop button on the Stage.

3. Open the Behaviors panel (Shift+F3), and choose the existing Stop All Sounds behavior in the Action column of the panel.

4. Press the Delete key, or click the Delete Behavior (-) button.

5. With the Stop button selected, click the Add Behavior (+) button in the Behaviors panel and choose Sound ➪ Stop Sound.

6. In the Stop Sound dialog box (shown in Figure 15-15), type the identifier for the sound used in the Load streaming MP3 file behavior, **bg_sound**.

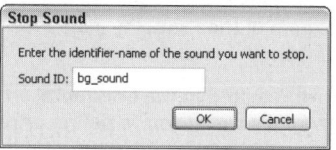

Figure 15-15: The Stop Sound behavior dialog box

7. Save the Flash document, and test it (Control ➪ Test Movie).

When the movie begins to play, you hear both the video's audio track and the streaming MP3 audio play. If you click the Stop button, only the streaming MP3 audio sound (bg_sound) stops playing.

You can find the completed file, `stopsound_behavior.fla`, in the `ch15` folder of this book's CD-ROM.

Editing Audio in Flash

Although Flash was never intended to perform as a full-featured sound editor, it does a remarkable job with basic sound editing. If you plan to make extensive use of sound in Flash, we recommend that you consider investing in a more robust sound editor. You'll have fewer limitations and greater control over your work.

Web Resource You can find an archived version of the "Working with Audio Applications" chapter from the *Macromedia Flash MX Bible* (Wiley, 2002) at `www.flashsupport.com/archive`. That chapter discusses several popular sound editors that are commonly used in concert with Flash.

Sound-editing controls

Flash MX 2004 has basic sound-editing controls in the Edit Envelope dialog box, which is accessed by clicking the Edit button in the Property inspector. (As you may recall from previous sections, you must first select the keyframe containing the sound, and then open the Property inspector.) The Time In control and the Time Out control, or Control Bars, in Edit Envelope enable you to change the In (start) and Out (end) points of a sound. The envelope handles are used to create custom Fade-in and Fade-out effects. The Edit Envelope dialog box also allows you to edit each sound channel separately if you are working with a stereo (two-channel) sound.

Note Edits applied to a sound file in the Edit Envelope dialog box affect only the specific instance that has been assigned to a keyframe. The original file that resides in the Flash document's Library panel is neither changed nor re-saved.

A sound's In point is where the sound starts playing, and a sound's Out point is where the sound finishes. The Time In control and the Time Out control are used for setting or changing a sound's In and Out points. Here's how to do this:

1. Start by selecting the keyframe of the sound you want to edit; then access the Property inspector.

2. Click the Edit button in the sound attributes area of the Property inspector to open the Edit Envelope dialog box, shown in Figure 15-16.

3. Drag the Time In control and Time Out control (located in the horizontal strip between the two channels) onto the Timeline of the sound's waveform to define or restrict which section will play.

4. Use the envelope handles to edit the sound volume by adding handles and dragging them up or down to modulate the volume.

5. Click the Play button to hear the sound as edited before returning to the authoring environment.

6. Rework the sound if necessary.

Property inspector   Click the Edit button to open the Edit Envelope dialog box

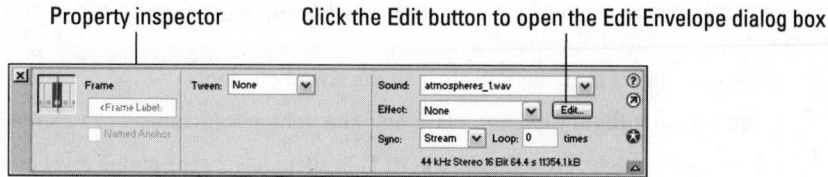

Left channel   Envelope handles

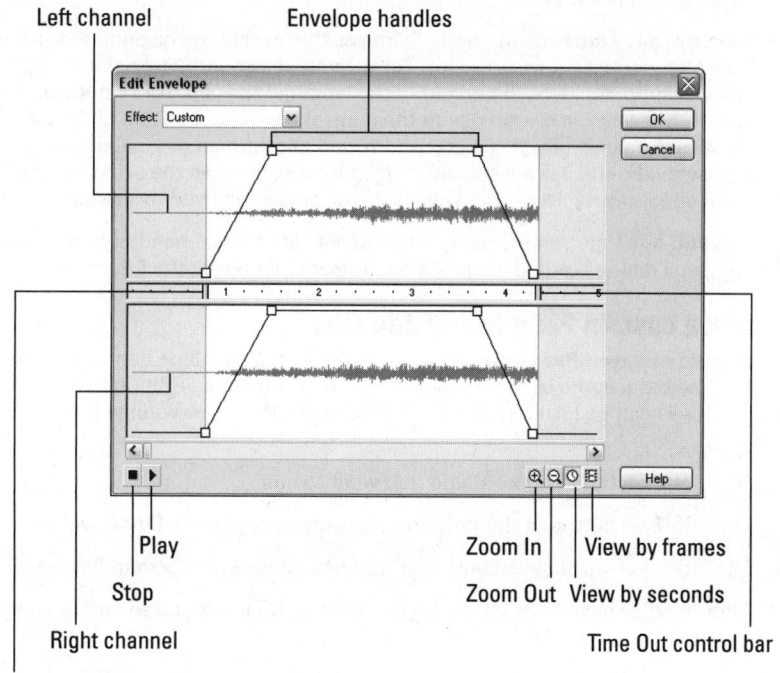

Play   Zoom In   View by frames

Stop   Zoom Out View by seconds

Right channel   Time Out control bar

Time In control bar

Figure 15-16: The sound-editing tools and options of the Edit Envelope dialog box, which is accessed from the Property inspector

7. When you've finessed the points and are satisfied with the sound, click OK to return to the Property inspector.

8. Save your Flash document.

Applying effects from the Effect menu of the Property inspector

You can apply a handful of preset fades and other effects to a sound by selecting the effect from the Effect menu located in the sound attributes area of the Property inspector. For many uses, the Flash presets will be more than sufficient, but if you find yourself feeling limited, remember that more subtle effects can be created in an external sound editor. Flash's preset effects are described in detail here:

✦ **None:** No effect is applied to either of the sound channels.

✦ **Left Channel/Right Channel:** Plays only the right or left channel of a stereo sound.

✦ **Fade Left to Right/Fade Right to Left:** This effect lowers the sound level of one channel while raising the level of the other, creating a panning effect. This effect occurs over the entire length of the sound.

✦ **Fade In/Fade Out:** Fade In gradually raises the level of the beginning of a sound clip. Fade Out gradually lowers the level at the end of a sound. The default length for either effect is approximately 25 percent of the length of the clip. We've noticed that even if the size of the selection is edited with the control bars, the duration of the Fade In/Fade Out remains the same. (Thus, a 35-second sound clip with an original default Fade In time of nine seconds, still has a 9-second Fade In time even when the selection's length is reduced to, say, 12 seconds.) This problem can be resolved by creating a custom fade.

✦ **Custom:** Any time you manually alter the levels or audio handles within the Edit Envelope dialog box, Flash MX 2004 automatically resets the Effect menu to Custom.

Creating a custom Fade In or Fade Out

For maximum sound-editing control within Flash, use the envelope handles to create a custom fade or to lower the audio levels (or amplitude) of a sound. In addition to creating custom fades, the levels can be lowered creatively to create subtle, low-volume background sounds. Here's how:

1. Select the keyframe of the sound you want to edit.

2. Click the Edit button of the Property inspector to open the Edit Envelope dialog box.

3. Click the envelope lines at any point to create new envelope handles.

4. After handles have been created, you can drag them around to create your desired volume and fading effects.

   The lines indicate the relative volume level of the sound. When you drag an envelope handle downward, the line slopes down, indicating a decrease in the volume level, while dragging an envelope handle upward has the opposite effect. The Edit Envelope control is limited to eight envelope handles per channel (eight for left and eight for right).

Tip   Envelope handles may be removed by dragging them outside the Edit Envelope dialog box.

Other controls in the Edit Envelope control

Other useful tools in the Edit Envelope dialog box warrant mention. See Figure 15-7 for their locations.

✦ **Zoom In/Zoom Out:** These tools either enlarge or shrink the view of the waveform, and they are particularly helpful when altering the In or Out points or envelope handles.

✦ **Seconds/Frames:** The default for viewing sound files is to represent time in seconds. But viewing time in frames is advantageous for syncing Stream sound. Toggle between viewing modes by clicking either the Seconds or Frames button at the lower right of the Edit Envelope dialog box.

The Repeat/Loop option

This option appears in the Property inspector, yet a measure of its functionality occurs in conjunction with the Edit Envelope dialog box. The Repeat/Loop drop-down menu and field is used to set the number of times that a sound file will repeat (or loop indefinitely). A small looping selection, such as a break beat or jazz riff, can be used for a background soundtrack. A short ambient noise can also be looped for an interesting effect. To test the quality of a looping selection, click the Edit button, which takes you to the Edit Envelope dialog box, where you can click the Play button for a preview of your loop. If the loop isn't perfect or has hiccups, use the In and Out control bars and envelope handles to trim or taper off a blank or adversely repeating section.

Tip

Flash links looped sounds and handles them as one long sound file (although it's really one little sound file played repeatedly). Because this linkage is maintained within the editing environment, the entire expanse of a looped sound can be given a custom effect in the Edit Envelope dialog box. For example, a simple repeating two-measure loop can be diminished over 30 loops. This is a subtle effect that performs well, yet is economical in terms of file size. Note, however, that this applies only to Event sounds.

Sound Optimization Overview

There are several considerations to be aware of when preparing Flash sound for export. For Web-based delivery, the primary concern is to find an acceptable middle ground between file size and audio quality. But the concept of acceptability is not absolute; it is always relative to the application. Consider, for example, a Flash Web site for a record company. In this example, sound quality is likely to be more important than file size because the audience for a record company will expect quality sound. In any case, consideration of both your audience and your method of delivery will help you to determine the export settings you choose. Luckily, Flash MX 2004 has capabilities that enhance the user's experience both by optimizing sounds more efficiently and by providing improved programming features to make download delays less problematic.

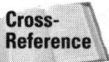

Cross-
Reference

We'll talk more about Flash MX 2004's MP3 loading features in Chapter 28, "Sharing and Loading Assets."

There are two ways to optimize your sound for export. The quickest, simplest way is to use the Publish Settings dialog box and apply a one-setting-optimizes-all approach. This can work well if all of your sound files are from the same source. For example, if all of your sound material is speech-based, then you may be able to use global settings to encode all of your Flash sound. However, if you have a variety of sound sources in your movie, such as a combination of musical scores along with narrative tracks, then the Publish Setting dialog box may not deliver the highest possible level of optimization.

If you demand that your Flash movie has the smallest possible file size, or if your Flash project includes audio from disparate sources, or uses a combination of audio types — such as button sounds, background music, speech — it's better to fine-tune the audio settings for each sound in the Library. This method gives you much better control over output.

Cross-
Reference

This chapter discusses only the audio-centric Publish features of Flash MX 2004. General Publish Settings features are explained in greater detail in Chapter 21, "Publishing Flash Movies."

Publish Settings for Audio

To take a global approach to the control of audio output quality, choose File ⇨ Publish Settings (Ctrl+Shift+F12 or Shift+⌘+F12) to access the Publish Settings dialog box. Then choose the Flash tab of the Publish Settings dialog box, shown in Figure 15-17. This tab has three areas where the audio quality of an entire Flash movie can be controlled *globally*.

Tip
You can also access the Flash tab of Publish Settings using the Property inspector. Click the document's Stage or Work Area, and in the Property inspector click the Flash Player button to the right of the Publish: text.

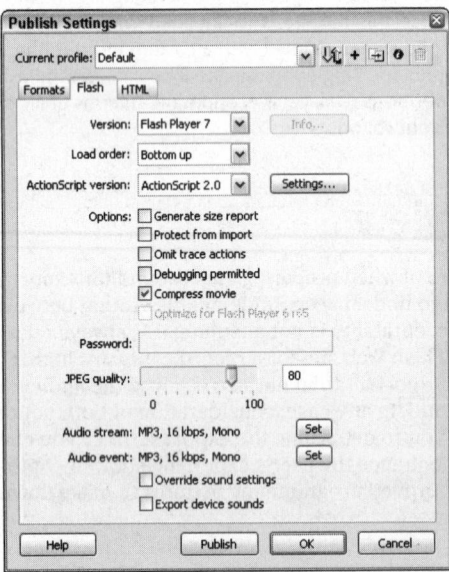

Figure 15-17: The Flash tab of the Publish Settings dialog box has several options to control audio quality.

The Flash tab of the Publish Settings dialog box has three options for controlling audio quality:

✦ **Audio Stream:** Controls the export quality of Stream sounds. To customize, click Set. This gives you a number of options, which are described in the section that follows. Flash MX supports MP3, which is the optimal streaming format, as well as a new Speech codec.

✦ **Audio Event:** Controls the export quality of Event sounds. To customize, click Set. This gives you the same number of options as the Set button for Audio Stream. These options are described in the section that follows.

✦ **Override Sound Settings:** If this box is checked, Flash uses the Publish Settings rather than the individual audio settings that are fine-tuned in the Library panel for the current document. For more information, see the section "Fine-Tuning Sound Settings in the Library" later in this chapter.

Note Flash MX 2004 Professional also has an Export Device Sounds option. For more information on the device sounds, see www.flashsupport.com/articles.

The Set options

Audio Stream and Audio Event have individual compression settings, which can be specified by their respective Set button options. If you click either Set button on the Flash tab, the same Sound Settings dialog box appears — it is identical for both Audio Stream and Audio Event, which means that the same options are offered for both types of sound. The Sound Settings dialog box, shown in various permutations in Figure 15-18, displays numerous settings related to the control of audio quality and audio file size. The type of compression chosen governs the specific group of settings that appear.

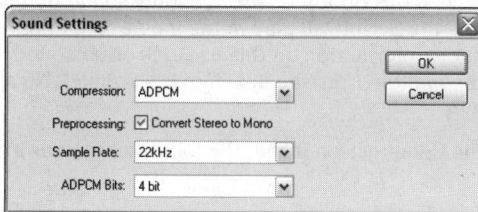

Figure 15-18: The various options in the Sound Settings dialog box

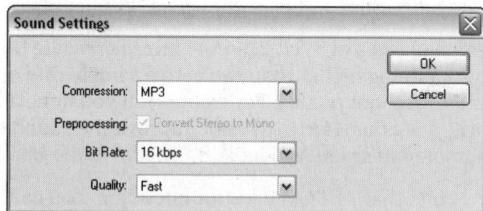

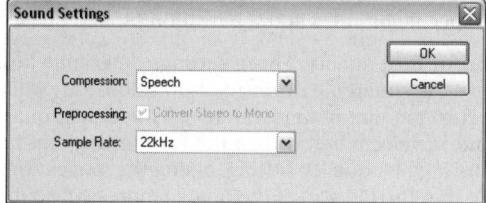

Note The impact of individual sound settings may be overridden by another setting. For example, a Bit Rate setting of 160 Kbps may not result in good sound if the Quality is set to Fast. Optimal results require attention to *all* of the settings. It's like a set of interlinked teeter-totters: A little experimentation will reveal the cumulative or acquired impact of each setting on the others. However, the need to experiment here is hobbled by the lack of a preview mechanism. By contrast, tuning a sound in the Library is much more serviceable because there's a sound preview button adjacent to the settings controls. For more about this workflow, refer to the following section of this chapter, "Fine-Tuning Sound Settings in the Library."

The specific options that are available in the Sound Settings dialog boxes are always related to the compression, or audio-encoding scheme, selected in the Compression drop-down menu. That's because different compression technologies support different functionalities:

✦ **Disable:** This option turns off all sounds that have been assigned in the Property inspector to keyframes in any timeline. If this option is selected, only sound that has been linked and attached for use in ActionScript will play in the movie (see Chapter 27, "Interacting with Movie Clips," for more information on this use). All other sound sources assigned in the movie will be omitted from the final movie (.swf file). No additional options accompany this setting.

✦ **ADPCM:** With ADPCM selected in the Compression menu, the following options are available:

  • **Convert Stereo to Mono:** Mixes the right and left channel of audio into one (mono) channel. In sound-engineer parlance, this is known as "bouncing down."

  • **Sample Rate:** Choose from sampling rates of 5, 11, 22, or 44 kHz. Increasing the sample rate of an audio file to something higher than the native sample rate of the imported file simply increases file size, not quality. For example, if you import 22 kHz sounds into the Flash movie, selecting 44 kHz will not improve the sound quality. For more information on sample rates, see Appendix B, "Digital Audio Basics."

  • **ADPCM Bits:** Set the number of bits that ADPCM uses for encoding. You can choose a rate between 2 and 5. The higher the ADPCM bits, the better the audio quality. Flash's default setting is 4 bits.

✦ **MP3:** If you select MP3 in the Compression menu, you can set the following options:

  • **Convert Stereo to Mono:** Mixes the right and left channel of audio into one (mono) channel. This is disabled at rates below 20 Kbps because the lower bit rates don't allow stereo sound.

  • **Bit Rate:** MP3 measures compression in kilobits per second (Kbps). The higher the bit rate, the better the audio quality. Because the MP3 audio compression scheme is very efficient, a high bit rate still results in a relatively small file size. Refer to Table 15-2 for a breakdown of specific bit rates and the resulting sound quality.

  • **Quality:** Choose Fast, Medium, or Best quality. These settings determine how well Flash MX 2004 will analyze the sound file during compression. Fast will optimize the audio file in the shortest amount of time, but usually with less quality. Medium will analyze the sound waveform better than the Fast setting, but takes longer to compress. Best is the highest quality setting, taking the longest time to compress the sound file. Note that the file size of the final compressed sound will not be affected by any Quality setting — it simply instructs Flash how well it should analyze the sound during compression. The longer Flash takes to analyze a sound, the more likely the final compressed sound will capture the high highs and the low lows. If you have a fast computer processor, then we recommend you use the Best setting during your final Flash movie publish. During development and testing, you may want to use Fast to avoid long waits.

✦ **Raw:** When Raw (also known as Raw PCM audio) is selected in the Compression menu, there are two options:

- **Convert Stereo to Mono:** Mixes the right and left channel of audio into one (mono) channel.

- **Sample Rate:** This option specifies the sampling rate for the Audio Stream or Audio Events sounds. For more information on sample rate, please refer to Appendix B, "Digital Audio Basics."

✦ **Speech:** When the Speech codec is selected in the Compression menu, there is only one option available: Sample Rate. Any sound compressed with the Speech codec will be converted to mono (one-channel) sound. Even though the Speech codec licensed from Nellymoser was designed for 8 kHz, Flash MX 2004 "upsamples" this codec to those frequencies supported by the Flash Player. See Table 15-3 for an overview of these sampling rates and how they affect sound quality.

Table 15-2: MP3 Bit Rate Quality

Bit Rate	Sound Quality	Good For
8 Kbps	Very bad	Best for simulated moonwalk transmissions. Don't use this unless you want horribly unrecognizable sound.
16 Kbps	Barely acceptable	Extended audio files where quality isn't important, or simple button sounds.
20, 24, 32 Kbps	Acceptable	Speech or voice.
48, 56 Kbps	Acceptable	Large music files; complex button sounds.
64 Kbps	Good	Large music files where good audio quality is required.
112–128 Kbps	Excellent	Near-CD quality.
160 Kbps	Best	Near-CD quality.

Table 15-3: Speech Sampling Quality

Sample Rate	Sound Quality	Good For
5 kHz	Acceptable	Sound playback over extremely limited data connections, such as 19.2 Kbps wireless Internet modems used by mobile devices.
11 kHz	Good	Standard telephone-quality voice audio.

Continued

Table 15-3 *(continued)*

Sample Rate	Sound Quality	Good For
22 kHz	Excellent	Not recommended for general Internet use. While this setting produces higher fidelity to the original sound, it consumes too much bandwidth. For comparable sound, we recommend using a midrange MP3 bit rate.
44 kHz	Best	See description for 22 kHz.

Tip

As a general rule, if you use the Publish Settings to control audio export globally, we recommend choosing MP3 at 20 or 24 Kbps. This will result in moderate to good sound quality (suitable for most Flash projects), and the ratio of file size-to-quality will give reasonable performance.

Supporting Audio and MP3 Playback

Although this is becoming less of an issue with the release of Flash MX 2004 and Flash Players 6 and 7, it may still be important to consider that MP3 is not supported by Flash Player 3 (or earlier), as well as some device players, such as Flash Player 4 for the Pocket PC. There may be a number of users in your audience that haven't upgraded their Flash Player plug-in to version 4, much less to versions 5, 6, or 7. Although it would be nice to assume that your audience will eventually upgrade, it's more realistic and advisable to consider implementing a transitional solution. For example, you could provide both a Flash 3 movie with ADPCM-encoded audio and a Flash 6 movie with MP3-encoded audio. Include information on the splash page about the benefits of Flash Player 7: reduced download time and increased audio quality. This is an incentive for you users to upgrade. You'll also want to provide a link to Macromedia to download the new plug-in. Another, more "invisible" solution is to add intelligence to your splash page with a plug-in detection script that automatically serves users the movie that corresponds to the version of the Flash Player they have installed.

Cross-Reference

To add plug-in detection to your Flash movies, use one of the HTML templates installed with Flash MX 2004. HTML templates are discussed in the "Using the HTML settings" section of Chapter 21, "Publishing Flash Movies." For custom plug-in detection solutions, refer to Chapter 22, "Integrating Flash Content with Web Pages," and Chapter 37, "Working with Dreamweaver MX 2004."

In addition, you can use some Flash Player 6 and 7 features in the ActionScript language to check the capabilities of the Flash Player installed on a user's system. Using the System.capabilities object, you can check to see whether an MP3 decoder is installed. The specific property is:

```
System.capabilities.hasMP3
```

More importantly, though, you can script your movies to check whether the Flash Player has access to general audio output. Some devices with the Flash Player may not have any audio output. This property is:

```
System.capabilities.hasAudio
```

Caution These new additions to the ActionScript language are only available in Flash Player 6 and 7. Earlier versions of the Flash Player will not recognize these objects or properties.

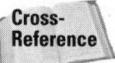

Cross-Reference You can find more detailed coverage of the System and Capabilities objects in the *Flash MX 2004 ActionScript Bible*.

Fine-Tuning Sound Settings in the Library

The Publish Settings dialog box is convenient because it permits you to tweak a minimal set of sound adjustments, whereupon Flash exports all of your "noncustomized" Stream sounds or Event sounds at the same rate and compression. However, if you have many sounds and you are seriously concerned about obtaining the ideal balance of both optimal sound quality and minimum file size, you will need to export them at different rates and compressions. Consequently, for the fullest level of control over the way in which Flash compresses sound for delivery, we recommend that each sound be optimized, individually, in the Library panel. In fact, it would be impossible for us to overemphasize this bit of sound advice: *We recommend that each sound be optimized, individually, in the Library.*

Tip As you become more advanced with Flash MX 2004, particularly with ActionScript, you will likely want to store sound files in separate Flash movies (.swf files) that are individually loaded into a master Flash movie on your Web site. Also, Flash Players 6 and 7 allow you to load MP3 files directly into movies, as they play in the Web browser. We'll discuss these features in Chapter 28, "Sharing and Loading Assets."

Settings for audio in the Library

Audio settings in the Library panel are similar to those discussed previously for the Publish Settings dialog box. These settings appear in the Sound Properties dialog box, shown in Figure 15-19. To access these settings, either (a) double-click the icon of the sound in the Library, or (b) select the sound as it appears in the Library and (i) click the Properties button, or (ii) choose Properties from the Library panel's options menu.

Tip Flash MX 2004 also allows you access the compression settings alone for a sound file by right-clicking (or Control+clicking on the Mac) the sound file in the Library panel. Choose Export Settings from the contextual menu, and the Sound Settings dialog box appears. These are the same compression settings that we'll be discussing in this section.

The top half of the Sound Properties dialog box displays status information about the sound file: To the far left is a window with the waveform of the selected audio; to the right of the waveform is an area that displays the name of the file together with its location, date, sample rate, channels, bit depth, duration, and file size.

Note The file location will indicate the full absolute path to the sound file (for example, C:\ Inetpub\wwwroot\mysound.mp3) if you save your Flash document (.fla file) in a volume or hard drive that is different than the location of the sound file.

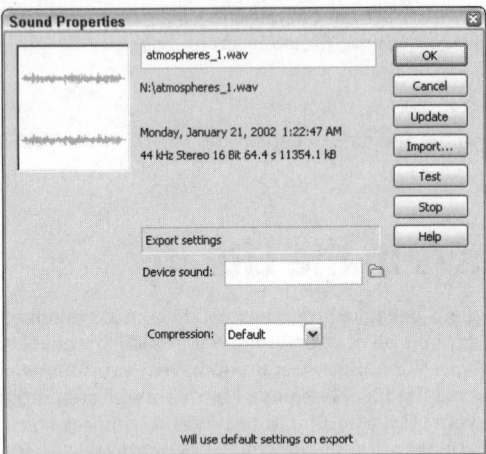

Figure 15-19: The Sound Properties dialog box enables you to control the compression settings and to precisely balance all other related settings for each individual sound in the Library.

The lower half of the dialog box is titled Export Settings. The first setting is a menu used to select the Compression scheme. The Compression options, and the subsequent compression-related options that appear in the other settings, are exactly the same as the sound options of the Publish Settings dialog box, discussed earlier in this chapter.

Note   Flash MX 2004 Professional also includes a Device sound option in this dialog box, as shown in Figure 15-19. For more information on device sounds for Flash movies on mobile devices, see www.flashsupport.com/articles.

Estimated results are displayed beneath the Export Settings. Here, the estimated final file size (after compression) of the clip is displayed, together with the compression percentage. This is an extremely important tool that is easily overlooked.

Caution   The estimated final file size is just that, an estimate. In our tests, the file size reported in the Sound Properties dialog box was consistently different from the actual file size reported by the size report generated during publishing. You can generate a text file containing detailed information about your final movie by enabling Generate size report in the Flash tab of the Publish Settings dialog box. Once enabled, you can view the size report in the Output window in Test Movie mode.

The buttons to the right of the Sound Properties dialog box offer the following options:

✦ **Update:** Click this button to have Flash check for an update of the audio file, if the original MP3, WAV, or AIFF file has been modified, and update it accordingly. Generally, this works only on the machine on which the audio file was originally imported. If you stored your files on a network server, then all the members of your Flash production should be able to use this feature.

✦ **Import:** This enables you to import another audio file into the Flash environment. The imported audio file will overwrite the existing sound displayed in the Sound Properties dialog box, but will retain the original sound's name. This feature is useful if you originally imported a placeholder or low-quality sound and need to specify a new file to be used in its place.

✦ **Test:** This excellent feature enables you to audition the export quality of the sound based on the options that you've selected from the Compression menu (and supporting options in the Export Settings).

✦ **Stop:** Click this button to stop (silence) the sound that has been auditioned using the Test button.

✦ **Help:** This launches the Flash Help system within your default Web browser.

Fine-tuning your audio in the Sound Properties dialog box of the Library panel has three benefits. Foremost of these benefits is the ability to set specific compressions and optimizations for each individual sound. Another benefit is the Test button—this is an excellent way to audition your audio file and to know what it will sound like when it is exported with different compression schemes and bit rates; hearing is believing. Finally, the estimated results, which display how each setting will affect the compressed file size, is a powerful tool that helps to obtain the desired balance of quality and file size. In contrast, optimizing sounds with the Publish Settings is more of a blind process—it is not only more global; it's also more of a painful trial-and-error method.

Combining methods for controlling sounds

One of the coolest things about Flash audio is that you can combine the two methods of controlling sounds, using both the Publish Settings and the Library panel's Sound Properties dialog box to streamline your work flow while still maintaining a relatively high degree of control over sound quality. (This method works best if you already have some experience with sound behavior in Flash.)

For example, let's assume that you have three different Event sounds in your Flash project. Two of these are simple button sounds. You decide that you won't require specialized compression for the sound used with the buttons. So, based on your prior experience of sound behavior in Flash, you go directly to the Publish Settings and set Event sounds to publish as MP3 at 48 Kbps with Best Quality.

Note   We assume that you have left the sounds used for the buttons untouched in the Library panel, leaving the Compression setting in the Sound Settings dialog box at Default. The Default option tells Flash to handle the compression for these sounds with the Publish Settings.

But the third sound is a loop of background jazz music that you want to be heard at near-CD quality. For this sound, you access the Sound Properties dialog box and try a number of combinations—and test each one—until you find a balance between file size and audio quality that pleases your ears. For example, you may decide to assign this sound to export as an MP3, stereo at 64 Kbps, with Quality set to Best.

Final Sound Advice and Pointers

Here are a few final notes about sound and some pointers to more complex sound-related topics that may help your work with sound files in Flash MX 2004.

VBR (Variable Bit Rate) MP3

Macromedia has licensed the Fraunhofer MP3 codec, which supports streaming MP3 with a constant bit rate. However, neither Flash MX 2004 nor any Flash Player supports Variable Bit Rate (VBR), or VBR MP3, encoding for Stream sounds. VBR MP3 is a variant of MP3 that utilizes specialized algorithms to vary the bit rate according to the kind of sound that is being compressed. For example, a soprano solo would be accorded a higher bit rate than a crashing drum sequence, resulting in a superior ratio of quality to file size. There are a number of sound applications, such as Apple iTunes, MusicMatch Jukebox, and the MP3 creation packs available for Windows XP Media Player, that export VBR MP3. If you have access to a sound application that exports VBR MP3, you'll be happy to know that you can import your VBR MP3 sound files, which are (theoretically) optimized for file size and quality beyond the compression capabilities of Flash MX 2004, and that the compression of such files can be maintained by doing the following:

✦ In the Flash tab of the Publish Settings dialog box, leave the option to Override Sound Settings unchecked.

✦ In the Sound Properties (or Export Settings) dialog box, which is accessed from the Library panel, choose Default for the Compression option in Export Settings.

✦ The Sync option (located in the Property inspector) for the sound cannot be set to Stream.

If you choose to use VBR MP3 files in your Flash documents, you may need to test the following options of VBR compression in your MP3 creation software:

✦ **Bit rate:** Test the minimum bit rate that VBR will use for the MP3 file. Regular MP3 files use CBR, or Constant Bit Rate, which keeps the sound's bit rate steady through the entire sound file. With VBR, the bit rate can vary in ranges that you specify. Some higher bit rates, such as 320 Kbps, may not import well into the Flash MX 2004 authoring tool.

✦ **Quality:** Most VBR-enabled MP3 software allows you to also pick an arbitrary quality setting for VBR MP3 files. Using terminology like Lowest, Medium Low, and High (and several in between) or percentages (1–100%), you can alter the quality of the bit rate. Note that this "quality" is not necessarily used in the same manner that Flash MX 2004 refers to quality for MP3 compression.

You may find that Flash MX 2004 will give you an import error for some VBR- (and CBR-) encoded MP3 files. If a particular setting created an MP3 file that couldn't import into Flash MX, then try another bit rate and/or quality combination. However, we have found that Flash MX 2004 has strange inconsistent behavior when it comes to importing MP3 files. For example, you may find that one VBR setting/combination does not work for a particular sound file, but that it works fine for others. Even more strangely, MP3 files that won't import into the Flash MX 2004 authoring environment will load just fine into Flash Player 6 or 7 at runtime via ActionScript.

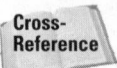

Cross-Reference

You can find more information about VBR encoding at the following URL:

    www.fezguys.com/columns/057.shtml

We also recommend reading the "null sound" Flash tutorial at:

    www.vrprofessionals.com/html/whitepaper/nullsound.htm

This tutorial shows you how to use a Stream sound to kick other Event sounds into streaming mode. Robert Reinhardt contributed a chapter to August de los Reye's *Flash Design for Mobile Devices* (Hungry Minds, 2002) covering this technique.

Optimizing sounds for bandwidth usage

It goes without saying that every Internet developer strives to make every file and data transaction as small and efficient as possible to accommodate the majority of slow network connections in use today. As a Flash developer incorporating sound into your projects, you'll want to properly plan sound usage in an effort to avoid 1MB .swf file downloads.

Table 15-4 explores many of the available network bandwidths that are in use on the Internet. However, as you've likely experienced, it's highly unusual to actually get the full download (or upload) speed out of your network connection. Variables such as network congestion, server load and phone line conditions affect the quality of your network speed. Using the same "formula" that Macromedia uses to determine approximate download speeds in the Bandwidth Profiler (within Test Movie mode), we calculated estimated bandwidth speeds for the connection speeds shown in Table 15-4. Because Flash MX 2004 displays compressed sound information in Kbps units, we converted these connection speeds into Kbps bit rates. More important, though, we also provided a 50-percent portion of this bit rate, as you'll likely need to save room for other Flash material, such as vector artwork, bitmap graphics, and animations.

Table 15-4: Bit Rates for Flash Movies

Hardware Support	Theoretical Bandwidth	Estimated Bandwidth	Percent of Theoretical	100% Bit Rate	50% Bit Rate
14.4 Kbps	1.8 KB/s	1.2 KB/s	67	9.6 Kbps	4.8 Kbps
19.2 Kbps	2.4 KB/s	1.6 KB/s	67	12.8 Kbps	6.4 Kbps
28.8 Kbps	3.6 KB/s	2.3 KB/s	64	18.4 Kbps	9.2 Kbps
33.6 Kbps	4.2 KB/s	2.8 KB/s	67	22.5 Kbps	11.2 Kbps
56 Kbps	7 KB/s	4.7 KB/s	67	37.6 Kbps	18.8 Kbps
64 Kbps	8 KB/s	5.4 KB/s	67	43.2 Kbps	21.6 Kbps
128 Kbps	16 KB/s	10.7 KB/s	67	85.6 Kbps	42.8 Kbps
256 Kbps	32 KB/s	21 KB/s	67	168 Kbps	84 Kbps
384 Kbps	48 KB/s	32 KB/s	67	256 Kbps	128 Kbps
768 Kbps	96 KB/s	64 KB/s	67	512 Kbps	256 Kbps
1.5 Mbps	192 KB/s	129 KB/s	67	1,032 Kbps	516 Kbps
11 Mbps	1,408 KB/s	943 KB/s	67	7,544 Kbps	3,772 Kbps

Using Table 15-4 as a guide, try to plan your Flash project for your target audience. Actually, you may have more than one target audience. As such, you may need to develop several versions of your sound assets, with each version targeted to a specific connection speed.

Once you've decided your target audience(s), you can determine the maximum Kbps that your sound files should use. Table 15-5 shows you the bit rates of Raw, Speech, and ADPCM mono sounds. We don't include MP3 bit rates here because they're already calculated (and available) for you in the Compression menu of the Sound Properties dialog box: 8, 16, 20, 24, 32, 48, 56, 64, 80, 112, 128, and 160 Kbps. In Table 15-5, bit rates that are suitable for analog modem connections (14.4, 28.8, 33.6, and 56 Kbps) are shown in bold.

Note   If you'd like to see the actual sample rate used by Flash MX 2004's MP3 compression options, see Table 15-7.

Table 15-5: Mono Bit Rates for Streaming Sound

Sampling Rate	Raw	Speech	ADPCM 2-Bit	ADPCM 3-Bit	ADPCM 4-Bit	ADPCM 5-Bit
5 kHz	80 Kbps	**10 Kbps**	**10 Kbps**	**15 Kbps**	**20 Kbps**	**25 Kbps**
11 kHz	176 Kbps	**22 Kbps**	**22 Kbps**	**33 Kbps**	44 Kbps	55 Kbps
22 kHz	352 Kbps	44 Kbps	44 Kbps	66 Kbps	88 Kbps	110 Kbps
44 kHz	704 Kbps	88 Kbps	88 Kbps	132 Kbps	176 Kbps	220 Kbps

In Tables 15-6 and 15-7, we calculate the file sizes that one second of mono (one-channel) sound occupies in a Flash movie (.swf file). Use the values in these tables as multipliers for your sound file's actual length. For example, if you know that you have a 30-second soundtrack file, the final Flash movie file size (containing just the audio) would be about 60K with ADPCM 3-bit, 5 kHz compression. Regardless of the actual content of the digital audio, these encodings will produce consistent file sizes based on length and resolution.

Table 15-6: File Sizes in Bytes (KB) for One Second of Mono Audio

Rate Sample	Raw	Speech	ADPCM 2-bit	ADPCM 3-bit	ADPCM 4-bit	ADPCM 5-bit
5 kHz	11,037 (10.8)	1,421 (1.4)	1,397 (1.4)	2,085 (2.0)	2,774 (2.7)	3,463 (3.4)
11 kHz	22,061 (21.5)	2,829 (2.8)	2,777 (2.7)	4,115 (4.0)	5,532 (5.4)	6,910 (6.8)
22 kHz	44,109 (43.1)	5,581 (5.5)	5,541 (5.5)	8,296 (8.1)	11,051 (10.8)	13,806 (13.5)
44 kHz	88,205 (86.1)	11,085 (10.8)	11,065 (10.8)	16,576 (16.2)	22,086 (21.6)	27,597 (27.0)

Table 15-7: File Sizes in Bytes (KB) for One Second of Mono MP3 Audio

Bit Rate	Size	Output Sample Rate	Bit Rate	Size	Output Sample Rate
8 Kbps	1,263 (1.2)	11 kHz	56 Kbps	5,605 (5.5)	22 kHz
16 Kbps	2,511 (2.5)	11 kHz	64 Kbps	8,543 (8.3)	44 kHz
20 Kbps	3,135 (3.1)	11 kHz	80 Kbps	10,716 (10.5)	44 kHz
24 Kbps	3,369 (3.3)	22 kHz	112 Kbps	14,980 (14.6)	44 kHz
32 Kbps	4,487 (4.4)	22 kHz	128 Kbps	17,112 (16.7)	44 kHz
48 Kbps	5,605 (5.5)	22 kHz	160 Kbps	17,112 (16.7)	44 kHz

Note   You may notice that some bit rate settings in Table 15-7 create the same file size for the MP3 compression. This is a known bug of Macromedia Flash MX 2004. You may also find that the Convert Stereo to Mono option for MP3 compression does not affect the outcome of some settings.

Extracting a sound from a Flash document

Sometime you may be handed a Flash document (.fla file) that has sound embedded within it and told that the original sounds have either been lost or are no longer available. Here's how to extract a sound from such a file:

1. Back up the file.

   If the original file is named sound.fla, you might resave it as sound_extraction.fla. If you want to start with an exercise file, save a copy of the enhanced_view.fla file on the book's CD-ROM. You can skip Steps 2 through 7 if you are using this file.

2. Add a new layer in the Timeline window, at the top of the layer stack.

3. Label this layer **sound extraction**.

4. With the first frame of this layer selected, open the Property inspector.

5. In the Sound menu, specify the sound file from the Library that you wish to export.

6. Add enough frames to the sound extraction layer so that you can see the entire waveform of the sound file.

7. Delete all other layers.

8. Open the Library panel and locate the sound that needs to be extracted from the file.

In the example file, the sound is named `atmospheres_1.wav`. Note that any other assets within this file are irrelevant to this process. That's because Flash will utilize only Library items that have been actually used within the movie.

 9. Double-click the sound icon for `atmospheres_1.wav` in the Library panel to invoke the Sound Properties dialog box.

10. Set the Compression to Raw.

   This ensures that the sound will be exported as uncompressed audio.

11. Select a sample rate that matches the one listed to the right of the waveform display, near the top of the Sound Properties dialog box.

   If the sound is specified as a Stereo sound, make sure the Convert Stereo to Mono option is unchecked.

12. Access the Flash tab of the Publish Settings dialog box, and make sure that the Override Sound Settings check box is *not* checked.

   Now we're ready to extract the sound file from the Flash document (.fla file). We've created a movie that will ignore all other assets in the library except this sound, and we've told Flash to export the sound with the original sample rate of the sound, as uncompressed (Raw) audio.

13. Choose File ➪ Export Movie, and specify a file location, name, and file type.

   If you're using the Windows version of Flash MX 2004, choose WAV Audio as the file type. If you're on a Mac, choose QuickTime Video.

14. For Windows users, the Export Windows WAV dialog box appears with those sound specifications. In the Sound Format menu, make sure the audio specifications match those of your audio source in the Library panel; then click OK. For Mac users, the Export QuickTime Video dialog box appears. Ignore all of the options except Sound Format. In this menu, select the sound setting that matches the specifications of the sound file. For our example, this setting should be 44 kHz 16 Bit Stereo. Click OK.

15. For Windows users, the process is complete. You now have a WAV copy of your Flash movie sound asset. For Mac users, you still have a couple of steps to complete:

   1. Open the exported QuickTime movie in the QuickTime Pro Player. You must have the Pro version installed.

   2. Choose File ➪ Export.

   3. Select Sound to AIFF in the Export menu.

   4. Click the Options button, and in the Sound Settings dialog box, set the Compressor to None and choose a sample rate, bit depth, and channel type that match the sound from the Flash document. For our example sound, this should be 44.1 kHz, 16 bit, and Stereo. Click OK.

   5. Finally, specify a filename and location for the exported file, and click Save.

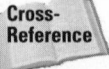
Cross-Reference
Several sound-related topics must be deferred until after our discussion of Flash MX 2004's enhanced ActionScripting capabilities. Work your way to Chapter 27, "Interacting with Movie Clips," and Chapter 28, "Sharing and Loading Assets."

Summary

✦ Flash movies (.swf files) can use four types of audio compression: ADPCM, MP3, Raw, and Speech. ADPCM is compatible with all versions of the Flash Player. MP3 is compatible with most versions of Flash Player 4, 5, 6, and 7. The Speech codec is compatible only with Flash Player 6 and 7.

✦ When sound is imported to a Flash document, it's added and displayed in the Library panel. You can assign sounds from the Library panel to a keyframe on a timeline. You can also use sounds with ActionScript.

✦ Sounds can be assigned to the Up, Over, and Down states of a Button symbol.

✦ The Sync options control how a sound will play in relation to the rest of the timeline.

✦ Use the Loop setting in the Property inspector to multiply the length of the original sound.

✦ Stream sounds force the Flash Player to keep playback of the timeline in pace with the sound.

✦ Use a `stopAllSounds()` action to stop all sounds that are currently playing in the movie.

✦ The Effect menu in the Property inspector contains useful presets for sound channel playback. You can perform custom edits with the Edit Envelope dialog box.

✦ Global audio compression is controlled in the Flash tab of the Publish Settings dialog box.

✦ Use the Sound Properties dialog box in the Library panel to customize the audio compression schemes of individual sounds.

✦ The Sound Properties dialog box enables you to test different compression settings and to hear the results. Useful file size information is also provided in the Export Settings section of this dialog box.

✦ Variable Bit Rate (VBR) MP3 sound files can be brought into Flash and exported without degrading the encoding; however, Flash itself cannot encode using VBR.

✦   ✦   ✦

Importing Artwork

Although Flash gives you powerful options for creating and modifying a variety of graphics, you don't have to limit yourself to the Flash authoring environment. That's because Flash also has the capability of importing artwork from a wide range of sources. You can import both vector and raster graphics, and you can use both formats in a variety of ways.

In this chapter, we discuss the differences between vector graphics and raster or bitmap images. We also show you how to import external artwork so that it can be used in a Flash movie, as well as tell you about the Flash features that can be used to handle imported bitmap images and vector graphics.

We define all the formats that Flash supports and go over some of the issues to consider when preparing artwork for import from various programs. We also introduce some new Flash MX 2004 features that are helpful for managing imported assets and give some insight into optimizing your final file size.

Cross-Reference

This chapter focuses on *importing* bitmap and vector artwork. For information on creating and *exporting* Flash-friendly artwork in other applications, refer to Part VIII, "Expanding Flash."

Defining Vectors and Bitmaps

In addition to various sound and video formats, Flash supports two types of image formats: vector and bitmap. *Vector* graphic files consist of an equation that describes the placement of points and the qualities of the lines between those points. Using this basic logic, vector graphics tell the computer how to display the lines and shapes, as well as what colors to use, where to put them on the Stage, and at what scale.

Flash is a vector program. Thus, anything that you create with the Flash drawing tools will be described in vector format. Vector graphics have some important benefits: They're small in file size and they scale accurately without distortion. However, they also have a couple of drawbacks: Highly complex vector graphics may result in very large file sizes, and vectors aren't really suitable for creating continuous tones, photographs, or artistic brushwork.

Bitmap (also referred to as *raster*) files are described by an arrangement of individual pixels, which are mapped in a grid-like a piece of graph paper with tiny squares. Each square represents a single pixel, and each of these pixels has specific color values assigned to it. So, as the name implies, a bitmap image maps out the placement and color of each pixel on the screen. A line is "drawn" by filling each unique pixel, rather than simply using a mathematical formula to connect two points as is done with vectors.

Note   Do not be confused by the name *bitmap*. You might already be familiar with the bitmap format used by Windows, which has the file extension .bmp. Although *bitmap* may refer to that particular image format, it's frequently applied to raster images in general, such as GIF, JPEG, PICT, and TIFF files, as well as many others.

Although bitmap images aren't created in Flash, they can be used within Flash projects. To do this, you need to use an external bitmap-editing application and then import the bitmaps into Flash. Figure 16-1 shows a vector image and a bitmap image of the same logo, scaled at 100 percent.

Figure 16-1: A vector image drawn in Flash (left) and the same image imported as a bitmapped GIF graphic (right)

Although these vector and bitmap images are of similar quality at their original size, their differences become more apparent when the same images are scaled to a larger size. Unlike vector graphics, bitmap images become more pixilated as they are scaled larger because there is a finite amount of information in the image and Flash has to spread this information over more pixels. As explained later in this chapter, Flash is able to interpolate the pixel information by using Smoothing to reduce the jagged appearance of the scaled pixel pattern, but this can also cause the image to look blurred. Figure 16-2 shows the difference between vector and bitmap graphics when scaled in Flash with Smoothing turned off.

Figure 16-2: The same vector (left) and bitmap (right) image scaled to 200 percent in Flash to illustrate the difference in image quality

Simple bitmap images are often larger in file size than simple vector graphics, but very complex bitmap images (for example, a photograph) can be smaller and display better quality than vector graphics of equal complexity. Figure 16-3 shows a bitmap image compared to a vector image of equal complexity (created by tracing the bitmap). The original bitmap is a smaller file and better suited for reproducing the photographic image.

Original bitmap 16KB   Traced vector image 198 KB

Figure 16-3: File size comparison of an imported bitmap image (left), and a traced vector image of equivalent complexity (right)

The rule of thumb is to use scalable, bandwidth-efficient vector graphics as much as possible within Flash projects, except for situations in which photographs — or photographic-quality, continuous-tone images — are necessary for special content.

Tip Most 8-bit raster images are GIFs, and they are most frequently used for images with large areas of solid color, such as logos and text. Rather than use this image type in Flash, consider re-creating or tracing this artwork with Flash drawing tools. The final Flash movie (.swf) will not only be smaller; it will also look cleaner and be scalable.

Knowing the File Formats for Import to Flash

You can import a variety of assets (in compatible formats) directly into your Flash project Library, or you can import or copy and paste from another application into the Flash Document window. Assets can also be dragged from one Flash Document window or library to another. Files must be a minimum size of 2 pixels by 2 pixels for import into Flash.

Caution Copying and pasting bitmap images into Flash from other applications does not always transfer transparency settings, so it may not be the best workflow for some assets. Using the Import dialog box and specifying that the artwork be imported as an editable object will preserve transparency settings from Macromedia Fireworks.

The import menu (Ctrl+R or ⌘+R) gives you the option to limit imports to a specific format or to choose broad media categories. Unless you find it helpful to have some files grayed out when you dig through lists to find items to import, you will most likely be happy just using the most inclusive menu setting: All Files.

New Feature

One setting that may not be self-explanatory on the Mac is the new All PostScript setting that was added to Flash MX 2004 to include PDF (as well as AI and EPS) files created in Adobe Illustrator 9 or higher. The specific options available for integrating PDF files into your Flash documents are described later in this chapter.

Cross-Reference

For a full discussion of importing and handling sound assets, refer to Chapter 15, "Adding Sound." Flash-compatible video formats are documented in Appendix C, "Digital Video Basics." For coverage of other bitmap and vector applications, refer to Chapter 35, "Working with Raster Graphics," and Chapter 36, "Working with Vector Graphics," respectively.

For now, let's focus on a brief summary of the image formats for Flash import, as shown in Table 16-1.

Table 16-1: Image Formats for Flash Import

File Type	Extension	Description	Platform
Adobe Illustrator (v. 9 or 10 files are most compatible)	.ai, .eps	Adobe Illustrator files are imported into Flash as vector graphics (unless they contain bitmap images). The importer plug-in is required to import files from Adobe Illustrator 8 and earlier. The importer for Flash MX 2004 does not preserve layers in EPS files. To preserve layers, import in AI, PDF, or SWF format.	Windows Macintosh
AutoCAD DXF	.dxf	Drawing eXchange format is the original inter-program format for AutoCAD drafting software. Because this format does not support fills, it is mainly used for drafting plans or schematic drawings. This format is used by most CAD, 3D, and modeling programs for transferring drawings to other programs.	Windows Macintosh
(Windows) Bitmap	.bmp, .dib	Although Bitmap is a Windows format for bitmap images, don't be confused by the format name—not all bitmap images are Windows Bitmaps. Can be used with all Win and some Mac applications. Allows variable bit depths and compression settings with support of alpha channels. Supports lossless compression. Ideal for high-quality graphics work.	Windows Macintosh (only with QuickTime 4 or later)
Enhanced Metafile	.emf	Enhanced Metafile is a proprietary Windows format that supports vectors and bitmaps internally. This format is occasionally used to import vector graphics, but for most professional graphics work this is not a recommended format.	Windows
Flash Movie	.swf, .spl	Flash Player files are exported Flash movies. The movie is flattened into a single layer and scene, and all animation is converted to frame-by-frame animation.	Windows Macintosh
FreeHand	.fh	This is the vector-based format of Macromedia's FreeHand (v.7 or later).	Windows Macintosh

File Type	Extension	Description	Platform
GIF image or animated GIF	.gif	Graphic Interchange Format (GIF) was developed by CompuServe as a bitmap image type that uses lossless compression. Limited to a 256-color (or less) palette. Not recommended as a high-quality Flash export format, even for Web use.	Windows Macintosh
JPEG image	.jpg	Joint Photographic Experts Group (JPEG) images are a bitmap type that uses lossy compression. Supports 24-bit RGB color. Recommended for Web-friendly compression of photographic images. Because of small file size, JPEG is often the native format for digital still cameras. No support for alpha channels.	Windows Macintosh
MacPaint image	.pntg	This is a legacy format for the old MacPaint program.	Windows (with QT4) Macintosh (with QT4)
PDF file (included in the All PostScript import menu option)	.pdf	Portable Document Format is a multipurpose, cross-platform format that preserves fonts, formatting, vector graphics, and bitmap images. Compression is variable and can be chosen when the file is created. PDF files are generally created or edited with Adobe Acrobat and read with the free Adobe Acrobat Reader. Adobe Illustrator and Adobe Photoshop also support PDF import and export. The new importer plug-in for Flash MX 2004 uses the GhostScript technology to support PDF files from Adobe Illustrator, with options for handling layers and multi-page documents. Photoshop PDF files can also be imported, but text is converted into masked shapes.	Windows Macintosh
PICT image	.pct, .pict	Compatible with many Win and all Mac applications. Allows variable bit depths and compression settings with support of alpha channels (when saved with no compression at 32 bits). Supports lossless compression. Can contain vector or raster graphics. Ideal for high-quality graphics work.	Windows (with QT4) Macintosh
PNG image	.png	The Portable Network Graphic (PNG) format is another type of bitmap image that supports variable bit depth (PNG-8 and PNG-24) and compression settings with alpha channels. PNG files imported to Flash from Macromedia Fireworks as editable objects (unflattened), will preserve artwork in vector format. Lossless compression schemes make it ideal for high-quality graphics work. The recommended media type for imported images with alpha channels.	Windows Macintosh

Continued

Table 16-1 *(continued)*

File Type	Extension	Description	Platform
Photoshop image (2.5 or higher)	.psd	This is the layered format for most versions of Photoshop—from version 2.5 through version 6. Although it is possible to import PSD files, it's not the best alternative. If you have the PSD, open it in Photoshop, optimize it for use in Flash, and then export it as either a JPEG or a PNG for ideal import into Flash.	Windows (with QT4) Macintosh (with QT4)
QuickTime image	.qtif	This is the static raster image format created by QuickTime. Not commonly used.	Windows (with QT4) Macintosh (with QT4)
Silicon Graphics image	.sgi	This is an image format specific to SGI machines.	Windows (with QT4) Macintosh (with QT4)
TGA image	.tga	The TGA, or Targa, format is a 32-bit format that includes an 8-bit alpha channel. It was developed to overlay computer graphics and live video.	Windows (with QT4) Macintosh (with QT4)
TIFF image	.tif or .tiff	TIFF is a lossless, cross-platform image type used widely for high-resolution photography and printing.	Windows (with QT4) Macintosh (with QT4)
Windows Metafile	.wmf	Windows Metafile is a proprietary Windows format that supports vectors and bitmaps internally. This format is generally used to import vector graphics.	Windows
Toon Boom Studio file	.tbp	Vector format for files created with Toon Boom Technologies proprietary animation software. Preserves layers, scenes, sound, and so on. Imported with support from the Toon Boom Studio Importer plug-in (TBSi) shipped with Flash MX 2004.	Macintosh (with TBSi) Windows (with TBSi)

Tip Although you can export to the GIF format from Flash, this should be considered an option for raw-information transfer only, not as a means for creating final GIF art. For optimal quality and control, GIFs exported from Flash should be brought into Fireworks for fine-tuning and optimization. A preferable workflow is to export a PNG sequence from Flash that can be brought into Fireworks for fine-tuning and final GIF output.

Preparing Bitmaps

Flash is a vector-based application, but that shouldn't stop you from using bitmaps when you *need* them. There are many situations in which either the designs or the nature of the content require that photographic images be included in a Flash project. You can import a wide variety of bitmap image types, including JPEG, GIF, BMP, and PICT using the methods described in the next section.

Considering that it's a vector-based program, Flash supports bitmap graphics extraordinarily well. However, because the most common use of Flash movies is for Web presentations, you always need to keep file size in mind. Here's what you can do to limit the impact of bitmap images on Flash playback performance:

✦ Limit the number of bitmaps used in any one frame of a Flash movie.

✦ Remember that, regardless of how many times the bitmap is placed on the Stage, the actual bitmap (or its compressed version in the SWF file) is downloaded before the first occurrence of the bitmap (or its symbol instance).

✦ Try spreading out bitmap usage, or hide a symbol instance of the bitmap in an earlier frame before it is actually visible, so that it will be loaded when you need it.

Tip If you need to include several high-resolution bitmap images in your Flash movie, consider using an ActionScript preloader or try breaking up the project into several linked Flash movies.

Cross-Reference For an example of an optimized Flash movie structure that uses an ActionScript preloader, see Chapter 32, "Creating a Portfolio Site in Flash."

When you want to bring raster images into Flash documents, you should know what portion of the Flash Stage the image will occupy. Let's assume that you're working with the default Flash document size of 550 x 400 pixels. If you want to use a bitmap as a background image, it won't need to be any larger than 550 x 400 (as long as your movie will not be scalable.) So, assuming that you're starting with a high-resolution image, you would downscale the image to the largest size at which it will appear in the Flash movie *before* you import it into Flash; for our example, that would be 550 x 400.

Tip Use an image-editing program such as Macromedia Fireworks or Adobe Photoshop to downsize the pixel width and height of your source image if necessary.

If you mask bitmaps with a Mask layer in the Flash Timeline, the entire bitmap is still exported. Consequently, before import you should closely crop all images that will be masked in Flash. For example, if all you need to show is a face, crop the image so that it shows the face with as little extraneous background information as possible.

Be aware that Flash doesn't resize (or resample) an image to its viewed or placed size when the Flash movie (.swf) is created. To illustrate how the size of an imported bitmap can impact the size of a final Flash movie (.swf), we compared two different image resolutions used in identical layouts. Using the same source image, we sized the JPEG at two different pixel dimensions, and then placed it in two identical Flash documents (.fla). The first source version of the image had a 400 x 600 pixel dimension, while the second source version had a 200 x 300 pixel dimension — exactly half the size of the first. In both Flash documents, the final image was displayed at 200 x 300 pixels.

Raster Images: Resolution, Dimensions, and Bit Depth

Resolution refers to the amount of information within a given unit of measurement. Greater resolutions mean better quality (or more image information). With respect to raster images, resolution is usually measured in pixels per inch (when viewed on a monitor) or dots per inch (when output on film or paper).

What is resolution?

The resolution of an original image changes whenever the scale of the image is changed, while the pixel dimensions remain fixed. Thus, if an original photograph is scanned at 300 pixels per inch (ppi) with dimensions of 2" x 2", subsequently changing the dimensions to 4" x 4" will result in a resolution of 150 ppi. Although a 4" x 4" image at 300 ppi could be interpolated from the original image, true resolution will be *lost* as an image is scaled larger. When an image is digitally enlarged, the graphics application simply doubles existing pixel information, which can create a softened or blurred image. Reducing the scale of an image has few undesirable side effects — although a much smaller version of an original may lose some fine details.

Because all raster images consist of pixels, and because resolution simply describes how many pixels will be arranged in a given area, the most accurate way of referencing raster images is by using the absolute pixel width and height of an image. For example, a 4,000 x 5,000-pixel image could be printed or displayed at any size with variable resolutions. This image could be 4" x 5" at 1000 ppi, or it could be 8" x 10" at 500 ppi — without any loss of information. Remember that resolution simply describes how much information is shown per unit. When you reduce the pixel width and height of an image, the resolution is lowered accordingly and after any pixels are thrown out, discarded, or interpolated, they're gone for good.

Raster images: Bit depth

Bit depth is an important factor that influences image quality and file size. *Bit depth* refers to the amount of information stored for each pixel of an image. The most common bit depths for images are 8-bit and 24-bit, although many others exist. An 8-bit image contains up to 256 colors, while a 24-bit image may contain 16.7 million color values. Depending on their file format, some images can also use an 8-bit alpha channel, which is a multilevel transparency layer. Each addition to an image's bit-depth is reflected in a considerable file size increase: A 24-bit image contains three times the information per pixel as an 8-bit image. Mathematically, you can calculate the file size (in bytes) of an image with the following formula (all measurements are in pixels):

```
widthxheightx(bit depth ÷ 8) = file size
```

Note: You divide bit depth by 8 because there are 8 bits per byte.

When importing 8-bit images in formats such as GIF, BMP, and PICT, it is preferable to use the default Lossless (PNG/GIF) compression setting in Bitmap Properties to avoid adding Flash's default Publish Settings Quality 24-bit JPEG compression. Eight-bit images that use Web-safe color palettes will ensure greater display predictability for people viewing your Flash artwork on older systems with 8-bit video cards.

In the first Flash document (we'll call it Movie A), the larger JPEG was imported and resized by 50 percent (using the Info panel) to match the smaller image. In the second Flash document (Movie B), the smaller JPEG was imported and placed at its original size, occupying the same portion of the Flash Stage as the image in Movie A. Although both Flash movies exported a bitmap of the same display size on the Flash Stage, the resulting SWF files (using the same level of JPEG compression on export) had drastically different file sizes. Movie A was 44.1 KB, whereas Movie B was 14.8 KB! Movie A is nearly three times larger than Movie B. The difference in image resolution could be seen when a view magnification greater than 100 percent was used within the Flash Player; the larger JPEG in Movie A was much less pixilated than the smaller JPEG in Movie B.

Preserving Bitmap Quality

When you choose to use bitmap images, remember that they won't scale as well as vector drawings in the authoring environment. Furthermore, bitmaps will become degraded if the viewer scales your final movie so that the bitmap is displayed larger than its original size. Here are a few points to consider that will help you maintain the quality of your presentation when using bitmaps:

✦ Know your audience and design for the largest screen (at the highest resolution) that your audience may have. Or, if you deviate from this, remember that audience members with optimal equipment will see a low-quality version of your work. If you're using ActionScript to load image assets, consider having low-res and high-res versions of the images available.

✦ Measure your largest hypothetical image dimensions in pixels. One way to determine these dimensions is to use the Flash Info panel to read the size of a placed image or a place-holder shape. Another way is to take a screen capture of your mock-up, and then measure the intended image area in Photoshop.

✦ Create or resize your bitmap image to the maximum hypothetical dimensions. If there are any rotations or skews required, it is better to do these within your image-editing application — prior to importing bitmaps into Flash.

✦ Import images into Flash at the maximum required size, and then scale them down to fit into your layout.

The advantage of using this approach is that the movie can be scaled for larger monitors without causing the bitmap image to degrade. The disadvantage is that it requires sending the same large bitmap to all users. A more sophisticated solution is to use JavaScript to detect browser dimensions and then send the appropriately scaled bitmaps to each user. Other workaround solutions that may help preserve the quality of your final presentation without adding file size include the following:

✦ Restrict scaling capability of your published movie. This can be done using HTML options in the Publish Settings or using ActionScript.

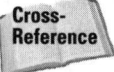
Cross-Reference

For coverage of Publish Settings refer to Chapter 21, "Publishing Flash Movies." For coverage of advanced options for controlling Flash movies including the `Stage` object, refer to the *Flash MX 2004 ActionScript Bible* by Robert Reinhardt and Joey Lott (Wiley, 2004).

✦ Set the bitmap's compression to Lossless (GIF/PNG) if it is already optimized in GIF format.

✦ Trace the bitmap to convert it to a vector graphic (covered later in this chapter).

✦ Never apply double JPEG compression to your images. If you have compressed and saved images in JPEG format outside of Flash, be certain to select the Use imported JPEG data check box when importing the images to Flash.

Before sizing and importing bitmaps, you need to consider how you will set the dimensions for the Flash movie (.swf) in the HTML tab of the Publish Settings dialog box. You also need to know whether the bitmap is to be scaled in a Motion tween. If the Flash movie scales beyond its original pixel width and height (or if the bitmap is scaled larger in a tween), then bitmap images will appear at a lower resolution with a consequent degradation of image quality.

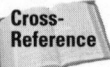 **Cross-Reference** Scaling of Flash movies is discussed in Chapter 21, "Publishing Flash Movies," and Chapter 22, "Integrating Flash Content with Web Pages."

If you're uncertain of the final size that you need for a bitmap in Flash, it may be best to import a temporary low-resolution version of the image — being careful to store your original high-resolution version where you can find it later. Whenever you need to place the bitmap, drag an instance of the symbol onto the Flash Stage. Then, during final production and testing, after you've determined the required pixel size for the maximum scale of the final bitmap, create and swap-in a higher-resolution image, as follows:

1. Double-click the icon of the original low-resolution bitmap in the Flash Library to access the bitmap's properties.

2. In the Bitmap Properties dialog box, click the Import button and select the new, higher-resolution version of the bitmap.

After import of the high-res image, all instances of the bitmap will update automatically, with the scaling, animation, and placement of the image maintained.

Importing and Copying Bitmaps

When importing bitmaps, Flash supports all the formats that QuickTime supports — as long as QT4 or later is installed (refer to Table 16-1). However, this reliance upon QuickTime can be confusing the first time you try it. If you attempt to import any previously unsupported format, the dialog box shown in Figure 16-4 appears. If you click Yes, the image is imported as a bitmap. According to Macromedia, you will always get this warning so you'll be aware when QuickTime is used to complete the import, and there are no adverse consequences to importing files in this manner.

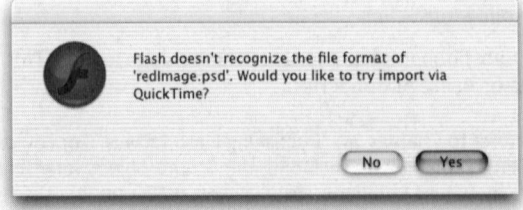

Flash doesn't recognize the file format of 'redImage.psd'. Would you like to try import via QuickTime?

No   Yes

Figure 16-4: This warning dialog box appears when a file format that requires QuickTime support is imported to Flash.

Importing a bitmap file into Flash

Flash has the option to import directly to the document Library, in addition to the standard option of importing to the document Stage. When a bitmap file is imported to the Stage, it will be added to the Library as well. To import a bitmap into Flash, follow these steps:

1. If you want to import an item to the Stage, make sure that there's an active, unlocked layer.

   If no layer is available for placement of the imported item, the Import to Stage command is dimmed and you will only be able to use the Import to Library option.

2. Select File ➪ Import to Stage (Ctrl+R or ⌘+R) or File ➪ Import to Library.

   The Import (or the Import to Library) dialog box opens (shown in Figure 16-5).

3. Navigate to the file that you'd like to import, select it, and click the Import or Import to Library button.

The important difference between Import and Import to Library is that the latter option places the asset directly into the document Library without placing an instance on the Stage. Remember that any file that requires QuickTime support will invoke the warning dialog box shown in Figure 16-4 — in that case, it's okay to click Yes; the file should import correctly.

Figure 16-5: The Import dialog box as it appears on Mac OS X. Multiple files can be imported in the same batch by selecting them from the file list before clicking Import.

Because Flash offers full support for the PNG image format (including lossless compression and multilevel transparency), PNG is an ideal format for images that you intend to import into Flash. The PNG format has two types, PNG-8 and PNG-24. Generally, only PNG-24 images support 24-bit color and an alpha channel, but the file sizes can often be prohibitive. Macromedia Fireworks makes it possible to create PNG-8 files with transparency for import to Flash.

Cross-Reference

The PNG format is discussed in depth in Chapter 35, "Working with Raster Graphics."

Caution

When using bitmap images with transparent areas, display problems can occasionally occur with certain color settings and file types. For troubleshooting assistance, refer to the Macromedia TechNote on "Transparency Support in Flash" at: www.macromedia.com/support/flash/ts/documents/transparent_bitmaps.htm.

Importing sequences

When using the Import to Stage option, if you select an image from a series of images in the same storage location that include sequential numbers at the end of their filenames, Flash prompts you to import the files as a sequence. If that's what you want to do, select Yes from the dialog box (shown in Figure 16-6) to have Flash import all the files and place them in numeric sequence on successive keyframes of the current Timeline. Otherwise, select No, and only the single file that you've selected will be placed on the Stage.

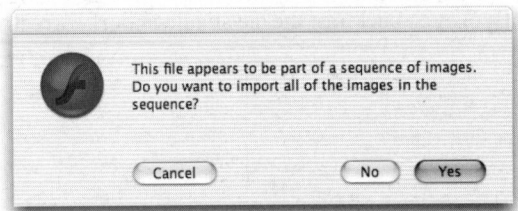

Figure 16-6: Images in a numbered sequence can be imported and placed on successive keyframes automatically using the Import to Stage option.

If you are importing a series of stills to be used sequentially to create animation (stills from a video sequence for example), this feature can save a lot of the time you would spend placing and ordering images manually. The most efficient workflow is to create a Movie Clip symbol before importing the images, so that the sequence can be placed directly on the Movie Clip timeline. This method creates an animated element that can easily be placed anywhere in your Flash project. If you have already imported a sequence to the main Timeline and decide that it would be more easily managed as a symbol, simply create a Movie Clip, and then cut the images from the main Timeline and paste them into the Movie Clip timeline.

Web Resource

For more coverage on how to create bitmap sequences from QuickTime video, go to the archived *Flash MX Bible* Chapter 41, "Working with QuickTime" available online at: www.flashsupport.com/archive

Although sequential import is not an option when using Import to Library, it is possible to manually select multiple images for import while using either of the Import dialog boxes. In order to bring more than one file into Flash in the same batch, Shift+click to select multiple items in sequence or use Ctrl+click (or ⌘+click) to select multiple nonsequential items in the file list of the Import dialog box.

Copying and pasting a bitmap into Flash

Here's how to use the Clipboard to import a bitmap into Flash:

1. Copy the bitmap from your image-editing application to your Clipboard.

   Most programs support the Ctrl+C or ⌘+C shortcut key.

2. Return to Flash and make sure that you have an active, unlocked layer that you can paste the bitmap into; this can be on the main Timeline or on any symbol timeline.

3. Paste the bitmap onto the Stage by selecting Edit ➪ Paste in Center from the menu (Ctrl+V or ⌘+V).

Note   When you are pasting a selected area from Photoshop, any transparency (alpha channel) is ignored.

Setting Bitmap Properties

The Bitmap Properties dialog box, shown in Figure 16-7, has several options that are used to control the quality of your imported bitmaps. Settings in the Bitmap Properties dialog box will override the default JPEG compression setting for the document that is controlled in the Flash tab of the Publish Settings dialog box (File ➪ Publish Settings).

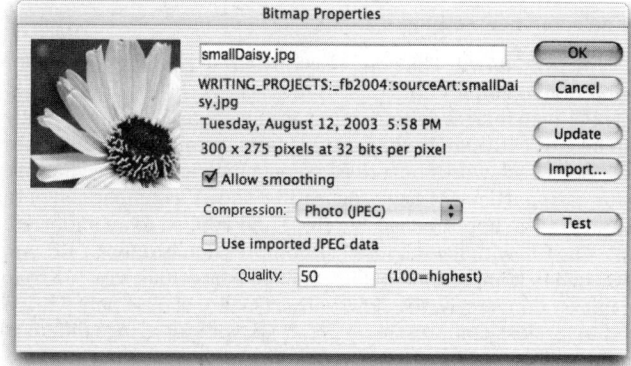

Figure 16-7: The Bitmap Properties dialog box controls the compression settings applied to bitmaps imported into Flash.

Follow these steps to use the Bitmap Properties dialog box:

1. Open the Library panel with Window ➪ Library (F11) to access bitmaps in your current project (.fla).

2. Double-click one of the bitmap's icons, or use the contextual menu to open the Bitmap Properties dialog box.

   You can also select Properties from the Library options menu or, with the bitmap highlighted, click the Properties button.

3. Now, set the properties of your bitmap as needed:

- **Preview Window:** This displays the bitmap according to the current settings.

Tip

Although the preview window in the Bitmap Properties dialog box may show only a small portion of your image, you can move the picture around within the preview window by clicking and dragging the image to view different areas.

- **Name:** This is the name of the bitmap, as indicated in the Library. To rename the bitmap, highlight the name and enter a new one.

- **Image Path, Date, Dimensions:** Beneath the filename, Flash lists the local path, dimensions, and date information for the source of the imported image (not available if you pasted the image from the Clipboard).

- **Update:** This feature enables you to reimport a bitmap if it's been altered outside of Flash. Flash tracks the original location of the imported bitmap and will look for the original file in that location when the Update button is clicked.

- **Import:** This opens the Import Bitmap dialog box. When using this button, the new imported bitmap will replace the current bitmap (and all instances, if any), while retaining the original bitmap's name and all modifications that have been applied to the image in Flash.

- **Test:** This button updates the file compression information, which appears at the bottom of the Bitmap Properties dialog box and the image in the Preview window. Use this information to compare the compressed file size to the original file size after you have selected new settings.

- **Compression Type drop-down:** The compression setting enables you to set the bitmap's compression to either Photo (JPEG) or Lossless (PNG/GIF). Photo is good for very complex bitmap images (photographs for example); Lossless is better for graphic bitmap images with simple shapes and fewer colors. Play around with these settings to see which works best to give you a balance between file size and image fidelity for each particular image. Figure 16-8 shows a comparison of these two settings applied to an imported GIF file (top) and applied to an imported JPEG image (bottom). The GIF with default lossless compression is only 4.7 KB. Applying a reduced JPEG Quality compression of 50 results in a larger file size (7 KB) for a worse-looking image. Conversely, the JPEG with a Quality of 50 is only 9 KB, while the JPEG forced to lossless compression is 145.6 KB, without a huge difference in display quality.

- **Use imported JPEG data/Use Document default quality:** If the imported image is a JPEG, the first option will appear — select this check box to avoid double-JPEG compression. If the image is not a JPEG, the second option will appear — select this check box to apply the global JPEG Quality setting defined in the Publish Settings dialog box for your current document. To select a new compression setting for an image, clear the check box beside "Use imported JPEG data" or "Use Document default quality" and enter a new setting between 1 and 100 in the Quality value field. This is not recommended for imported JPEGs because it will result in double JPEG compression. On uncompressed source files, higher Quality settings produce better quality images but also larger file sizes. Figure 16-9 includes a JPEG published with imported data and a JPEG published with a reduced Quality setting (double JPEG compression).

Figure 16-8: *Top:* A GIF file imported to Flash using PNG/GIF (Lossless) compression (left) and imported with forced JPEG (Lossy) compression (right). *Bottom:* A JPEG file imported to Flash using JPEG (Lossy) compression (left) and imported with forced PNG/GIF (Lossless) compression (right).

Figure 16-9: The same bitmap image as it displays in the published Flash movie (.swf) using imported JPEG data (left) and using a reduced Quality setting of 25 (right)

Note   The Quality settings applied in the Bitmap Properties dialog box will not be visible in the authoring environment. The quality for images displayed on the Stage will appear the same regardless of the Flash JPEG settings. You will see a difference in the image (and the file size) only when you publish the movie (.swf).

- **Allow Smoothing (antialiasing):** Select this check box to enable Flash to antialias, or smooth, the edges of an image. Results may vary according to the image. Generally, this is not recommended because it blurs an image. However, smoothing can be beneficial for reducing jagged edges on low-res images scaled in an animation. Figure 16-10 shows the effect of smoothing applied to a GIF image (top), and smoothing applied to a JPEG image (bottom).

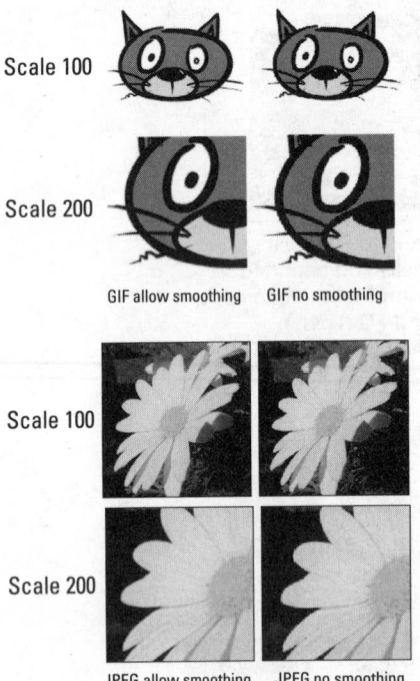

Scale 100

Scale 200

GIF allow smoothing   GIF no smoothing

Scale 100

Scale 200

JPEG allow smoothing   JPEG no smoothing

Figure 16-10: Compare the images with Flash smoothing (left) to the images with no smoothing (right).

4. Click OK.

All copies of this bitmap used in Flash are updated to the new settings.

For specific bitmap compression recommendations for different types of source files, please refer to the section on "Making Sense of Bitmap Compression" later in this chapter.

Being Prepared for Common Problems

Flash retains existing JPEG compression levels on any imported JPEG image, but, if specified in the Bitmap Properties dialog box, it applies additional JPEG compression (set in the Quality field) when the movie is published or exported. Recompressing an image that has already been compressed usually leads to serious image degradation, due to the introduction of further compression artifacts. When importing JPEGs, you'll note that the Use imported JPEG data check box is selected by default in the Bitmap Properties dialog box. This is the preferred setting because Flash has a relatively generic JPEG compression engine, which is usually less effective than Fireworks or Photoshop, and because recompressing a JPEG is generally detrimental to image quality.

Tip If you import JPEG images, make sure that you either test the results of further JPEG compression or select the Use imported JPEG data check box in the Bitmap Properties dialog box, which is accessible from the Flash Library.

You can apply compression settings to each individual bitmap in the Library with the Flash Bitmap Properties dialog box to determine the quality that you need before you use the general JPEG settings in the Export Movie or Publish Settings dialog box. Any Quality defined in the Bitmap Properties dialog box will override the JPEG Quality in Publish Settings. To apply the Publish Settings compression to an image, you must select the Use document default check box in the Bitmap Properties dialog box.

Cross-Reference You'll find JPEG export settings for Flash movies (SWF files) discussed in greater detail in Chapter 21, "Publishing Flash Movies."

RIP There was a known problem in Flash MX, referred to as *bitmap shift*, in which the position (and even colors) occasionally shifted slightly from one instance to another of the same image. Flash MX 2004 has thankfully resolved this small but important workflow issue.

Cross-browser consistency

We've received more than a few queries about image formats and Flash's capability to transcend issues of browser inconsistency, so here's the answer. Many image formats, such as PNG, are not supported across all browsers. When you import such an image format into Flash and publish or export to the SWF format, you have accomplished browser independence—because the Flash movie (.swf) is browser independent and the image has been encapsulated within the SWF format. (The image is not being sent to the browser in the imported format and then magically empowered to display.) Conversely, if you export any Flash document (.fla) to PNG or to any other format that's subject to cross-browser inconsistency, browser independence is lost.

JPEG rotation

This is perhaps the trickiest problem to analyze. When animation that includes a bitmap is resolved and the image is displayed at an angle, it can be distorted. Regardless of whether it was rotated in Photoshop and imported with the angle, or if it was imported into Flash on the square and subsequently rotated, the manner of the distortion changes, but not the perception of distortion!

✦ When rotated in Flash, hard edges, such as text or high-contrast areas of an image, may appear choppy—as if they had been cut out with pinking shears. Yet, when zoomed, this effect is less problematic.

✦ When rotated in Photoshop, prior to import into Flash, hard edges are less choppy. Although the file will increase (to accommodate the larger overall shape), the background will become a fixed color, and a certain flutter may occur along the edges of the transition between the background and the image. Yet, other straight lines and text will appear smoother and more acceptable. However, at 200 percent zoom, text looks worse than the same image rotated in Flash.

Before rotating a bitmap in Flash, you should perform a few tests to see how your specific bitmap will be affected by the combination of compression, zoom, smoothing, and rotation (either in or out of Flash). Your choices and your decision will vary, subject to the content of the bitmap and the manner in which it will be used within Flash.

Applying Alpha and Color Effect settings to bitmaps

A bitmap has some of the same advantages as the native Flash symbol types: It is automatically added to the Library when you import it, and instances can be dragged onto the Stage and even used in Motion tweens. However, the Color (and Alpha) Effects are not available in the Property inspector when you select a bitmap instance. If you wish to change the alpha settings or color tint of an imported image, you have two easy options:

✦ Convert the bitmap into a Flash symbol type (F8). You can even use the same name for the symbol instance as the original bitmap image. Color Effect settings will be available in the Property inspector when you select the new (converted) symbol instance. Unfortunately, not all of the instances of the bitmap will be automatically linked to the symbol you create, and you cannot use the Swap button to insert a Flash symbol instance in place of a bitmap instance.

Tip

Library folders are very helpful for managing large sequences of images that need to be converted into symbols. We usually create a "Bitmap source" folder and an "Image symbol" folder to make it easy to keep track of where all the assets are. Keep in mind that edits to the bitmap will be visible in the Flash symbol, but changes to the Flash symbol will not change the original bitmap.

✦ You can use Timeline Effects to add alpha or color changes to a bitmap instance. Flash still converts the image into a Graphic symbol before the Effect is applied, but you don't have to worry about doing it as a separate step.

Of course, using an external image-editing program is always an option, too. The features described in the next section can assist you if you plan to edit images outside of Flash.

Using the Bitmap Buttons in the Property Inspector

When a bitmap is selected in the Document window, the Property inspector displays the bitmap's name, symbol type, current size, and X, Y location. In addition to these basic bitmap properties, the Property inspector offers two useful options — the Swap button and the Edit button.

Swap

The Swap button invokes the Swap Bitmap dialog box (shown in Figure 16-11), allowing you to specify a different bitmap from the current project Library to replace the bitmap selected in the Document window. This can be considered a localized equivalent of the Import option of the Bitmap Properties dialog box. Rather than replacing the original bitmap symbol in the Library and all instances of the image, the Swap button will simply replace the currently selected bitmap instance without altering the symbols in the Library or any of the other instances of the bitmap that may occur in your project. (This feature is also available from the application menu under Modify ➪ Bitmap ➪ Swap bitmap.)

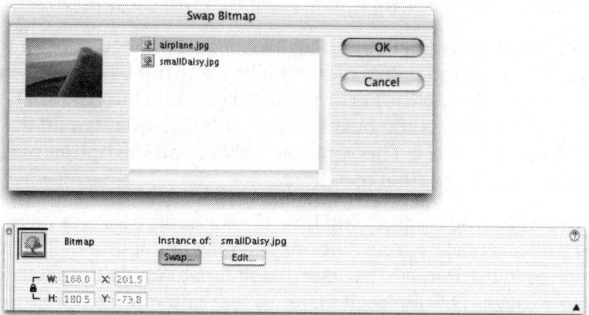

Figure 16-11: The Swap Bitmap dialog box lists all the bitmap symbols available in your current project Library.

Edit

The Edit button of the Property inspector will open the selected bitmap for editing outside of Flash, either in your default image editing application or the application that was used to save the bitmap file, if it is installed on your system. After you edit the image and choose Save, it will automatically be updated in the Flash document. If you prefer to select a specific application for editing a bitmap, select the bitmap in the Library before choosing Edit With from the options menu or the contextual menu. The Edit With menu item launches the Select External Editor dialog box that allows you to browse or search for a specific application installed on your system (or network). When you have selected the application of your choice, it will be launched and the bitmap is opened for editing.

Note   Bitmaps imported from Fireworks as PNG files specified as editable objects cannot be edited in an external image editor.

Making Sense of Bitmap Compression

Although we did some sample testing to try to show you all the possible image-compression combinations and the final results, the truth is that the optimal settings are entirely dependent on the quality of the original image and the final appearance needed in the context of your design. The main goal when testing various compression strategies should always be to find a balance between image quality and file size. The ideal balance will vary depending on the purpose the image serves in your presentation. For example, when using bitmap images in animation sequences, you may find that you can get away with using higher compression settings because the detail in the image may not be as important as it would be if the image was used in a catalogue or some other presentation where the detail and color would be more critical.

The following compression workflows are intended to serve only as general guidelines. You will have to experiment with the specific value settings in each case to find the best results for your particular content and project needs.

24-bit or 32-bit lossless source files

If you have 24-bit (or 32-bit including an alpha channel), high-resolution source images saved without compression in PNG-24, PICT, or TIFF format, you have two workflow options:

✦ **Set JPEG compression in Bitmap Properties dialog box:** If you want to control the compression applied to each imported image individually, clear the Use document default quality check box in the Bitmap Properties dialog box and choose a JPEG compression (Quality) setting that achieves the best balance of image quality and file size for each imported image in your Library. This approach gives you the option of applying more compression to some images than to others.

✦ **Set JPEG compression in Publish Settings dialog box:** If your source images have similar color and content, as well as consistent resolution, you may find it more efficient to use the compression settings in the Publish Settings dialog box to apply the same JPEG compression to all of your images. This makes it faster to test different compression settings on all the images in your project at once. If this is the workflow that you choose, make sure that the Use document default quality check box is selected in the Bitmap Properties dialog box for each imported image — this ensures that the Quality settings in the Publish Settings dialog box will be applied when the Flash movie (.swf) is published.

The main benefit to importing uncompressed source files is that you will not be tied to a specific resolution and thus will maintain the option of changing compression settings at any time in the development process. The main drawback is that your project files (.fla) will be much larger, and each time you test your movie (.swf), you will have to wait for Flash to apply JPEG compression on the images. This might not seem important at first, but the cumulative time loss over the course of developing a project does add up.

Tip   As mentioned previously, it can be helpful to work with lower resolution place-holder images as you develop a project. You can use the Import option in the Bitmap Properties dialog box to load your high-resolution images in the final stages of the project.

The image formats PNG-24, PICT, and TIFF also support alpha channels when saved with 32-bit color. Alpha channels allow import of complex masks that might otherwise be difficult to create in Flash. You may be surprised to see that even after you apply Flash JPEG compression to an imported PNG, PICT, or TIFF image, the transparency is maintained. You might say that Flash lets you have your alpha and eats the file size, too.

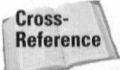
Cross-Reference   The process for creating alpha channels in PICT and TIFF files is slightly different from that used for PNG files. For more information on creating alpha channels in source bitmaps, refer to Chapter 35, "Working with Raster Graphics."

Caution   Although Macromedia Fireworks files are saved with the .png file extension, the options for importing Fireworks PNG files are different from those for importing PNG files saved from Photoshop or other image-editing programs. For more information about importing Fireworks PNG files, refer to the section "Importing Vector Artwork" later in this chapter.

8-bit lossless source files

Source files in 8-bit formats are restricted to 256 (or fewer) colors and are optimized to a file size that is Web-friendly. These files are usually saved in GIF or PNG-8 format and are best suited for graphics that have simple shapes and limited colors, such as logos or line drawings. PNG-8 and GIF files can still support an alpha channel, but unlike 24-bit images, you will not want to apply any JPEG compression to these files when they're brought into Flash.

Caution To avoid display problems, when exporting GIF files with transparency for use in Flash, the index color and the transparency color should be set to the same RGB values. If these settings are not correct, transparent areas in the imported GIF may display as solid colors in Flash. For more information on this issue, refer to the Macromedia TechNote on Transparency support in Flash at `www.macromedia.com/support/flash/ts/documents/transparent_ bitmaps.htm`.

Applying JPEG compression to 8-bit files generally results in larger files and degraded image quality (refer to Figure 16-8). To preserve the clean graphic quality of 8-bit images, follow these steps:

1. In the Bitmap Properties dialog box, make sure that Lossless (PNG/GIF) compression is selected.

   This is the default for imported 8-bit images, but it never hurts to double-check to ensure that it hasn't been changed by mistake.

2. Decide whether to leave the default setting for Allow Smoothing in Bitmap Properties.

   The image will have sharper edges if this option is unchecked, so it is best to make a decision on this setting depending on whether you prefer smoothed edges when the image is scaled larger.

Remember that the JPEG Quality specified in Publish Settings will not apply to imported images that have been set to Lossless compression in the Bitmap Properties dialog box.

Source files with lossy compression

Although JPEG is the native bitmap compression format in Flash, it is generally advisable to use an alternative application for optimal JPEG compression on images. In our experience, JPEG compression from either Macromedia Fireworks or Adobe Photoshop produces smaller file sizes and more consistent image quality than JPEG compression applied in Flash. If you have created an optimized Web-ready JPEG using your preferred lossy compression method, you will want to avoid adding additional compression to the image when it is imported to Flash.

New Feature JPEG images saved with the option for progressive download selected could not use imported JPEG data when brought into Flash MX. Flash MX 2004 gives you the option to use imported JPEG data for JPEG images saved with or without the progressive download option.

If you find that a JPEG file size is not reduced enough to fit the parameters of a particular project, it is better to go back to the uncompressed source file to redo the JPEG compression than it is to apply additional compression in Flash. As in all media production, double JPEGing images in Flash produces diminishing returns — by the time you get the file down to a size that you want, it has so many compression artifacts that it is generally unusable. By going back to the uncompressed source file and adjusting your compression settings to produce a new JPEG file, you end up with a cleaner image and a smaller file size than you would by compounding the JPEG compression in Flash.

For optimal results when importing JPEG images to Flash projects, the main settings to consider are the Use imported JPEG data and the Allow Smoothing check boxes in the Bitmap Properties dialog box.

✦ To maintain the original JPEG compression of your imported image, simply select the check box to Use imported JPEG data from the Bitmap Properties dialog box. When this check box is selected, the original compression will be preserved and the JPEG Quality specified in Publish Settings will not be added to your imported JPEG image.

✦ Smoothing is only advised if you will be scaling the JPEG image in Flash and you want to minimize the jagged edges with aliasing. The compromise of Smoothing is that the image will also appear slightly blurred — this may or may not be desirable depending on the detail in the original image.

Although you can clear the Use imported JPEG data check box and choose a setting in the Quality field, remember that this compression will be added to the compression on the original image and will cause inferior results.

Converting Rasters to Vectors

Have you ever wanted to take a scan of a "real" pen-and-ink drawing that you made and turn it into a vector graphic? It's not incredibly hard to do, and the results are usually pretty close to the original (see Figure 16-12). You can also turn continuous tone or photographic images into vector art, but the converted version will not likely bear much resemblance to the original. However, this can be useful for aesthetic effects.

Figure 16-12: Compare the raster version (left) of the sketch to its traced vector version (right).

As described in Chapter 9, "Modifying Graphics," bitmap images can be traced in Flash to convert them to vector shapes. Figure 16-3 illustrated why this is not recommended for complex photographic images — the file size will be huge and the image quality will not be as satisfactory as the original bitmap. However, converting rasters to vectors allows you to create some unique visual effects in Flash. After an image has been traced, you can use any of the Flash tools available for shapes, including the Distort and Envelop options of the Free

Transform tool. You can also select parts of the image individually to modify colors, or even add custom gradient or bitmap fills.

The Trace bitmap command is different from using the Break apart command on a bitmap. When an image is broken apart, it is perceived by Flash as areas of color that can be modified or sampled for use as a fill in other shapes. Break apart actually duplicates the automatic conversion handled by the Mixer panel to show bitmaps from the Library in the bitmap fill menu. Although images that are broken apart can be modified with the drawing and painting tools, you cannot select individual parts of the image with the Arrow tool or apply the Optimization command, Smooth/Straighten options, or Distort and Envelop modifiers as you can with a traced vector image.

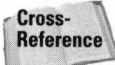

Cross-Reference For more information on using the Break apart command, refer to Chapter 9, "Modifying Graphics."

To apply Trace bitmap, select a bitmap image that has been imported to Flash (ideally with lossless compression and no Smoothing) and placed on the Stage; then select Modify ⇨ Bitmap ⇨ Trace bitmap from the application menu to invoke the Trace Bitmap dialog box, as shown in Figure 16-13.

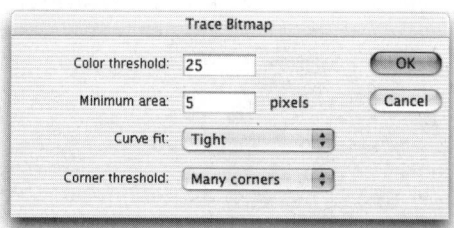

Figure 16-13: Use the Trace Bitmap dialog box to select settings for converting a raster image into vector shapes.

The settings for the Trace bitmap command are detailed in Chapter 9, but the default settings can be a good place to start. Higher Color Threshold and Minimum Area values reduce the complexity of the resulting Flash artwork, which means smaller file sizes. This process is most effective when applied to simple images with strong contrast. In these cases tracing a bitmap graphic can actually reduce the file size and improve the appearance of the scaled image. The settings shown in Figure 16-13 were used to trace the GIF image shown in Figure 16-14. When viewed at a scale of 200 percent, the difference in image quality can clearly be seen, and this difference will be exaggerated the more the images are scaled — the vector image will remain smooth, while the bitmap will break apart and look increasingly jagged.

Tip The traced vector lines and fills created from an imported bitmap are not always exact, but you can use the Smooth and Straighten modifiers or any of the other drawing tools to "touch up" the artwork.

In order to get the best results from using Trace bitmap, we advise reducing the number of colors in the original image before importing it to Flash. Figure 16-15 shows an imported image that was converted to indexed color and reduced to four colors in Photoshop before saving as a GIF image for import to Flash. After the image is traced, you can simplify the shapes further by applying the Optimize command (Modify ⇨ Shape ⇨ Optimize), which cleans up the image and reduces the final file size. You can also use any of the drawing tools to further modify the image.

Figure 16-14: Images with simple shapes and limited colors can be cleaner and more scalable when converted from bitmap (left) to vector art (right) using the Trace bitmap command.

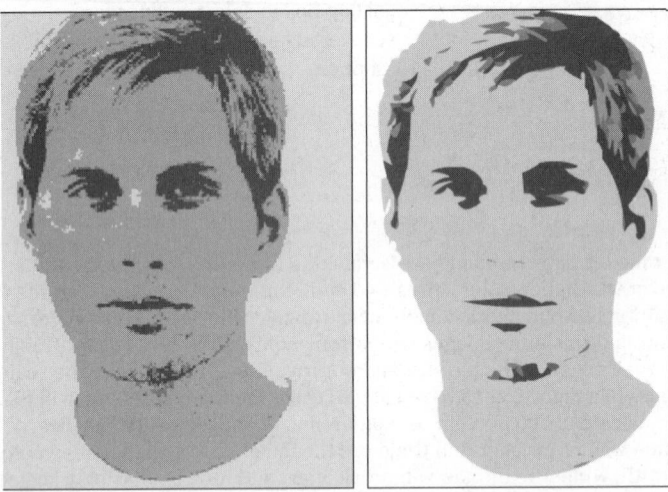

Imported 4 Color GIF image   Traced and Optimized vector image

Figure 16-15: A reduced-color GIF image (left) can be traced and then simplified using the Optimize command in Flash (right).

Using External Vector Graphics

All artwork drawn in Flash is vector-based and, as shown in Table 16-1, Flash also offers robust support for external vector formats, including Macromedia FreeHand and Adobe Illustrator. However, not all vector graphics are created the same. Some vector graphics may be simple objects and fills, whereas others may include complex blending or paths that add significant weight to a Flash movie. Although most vector graphics are by nature much smaller than raster graphic equivalents, don't assume that they're optimized for Flash use.

Importing vector graphics from other applications is fairly simple and straightforward. However, because most vector graphics applications are geared for print production (for example, publishing documents intended for press), you need to keep some principles in mind when creating artwork for Flash in external graphics applications:

✦ **Limit or reduce the number of points describing complex paths.**

✦ **Limit the number of embedded typefaces (or fonts).** Multiple fonts add to the final movie's (.swf) file size. As described later in this chapter, converting fonts to outlines is one way to avoid adding extra fonts to your Flash file.

✦ **To ensure color consistency between applications, use only RGB colors (and color pickers) for artwork.** Flash can only use RGB color values, and automatically converts any CMYK colors to RGB colors when artwork is imported. Color conversions can produce unwanted color shifts.

Note When Flash imports a vector file with any placed grayscale images, the images will be converted to RGB color, which will also increase the file size.

✦ **Unless you're using Macromedia FreeHand or Fireworks, you may need to replace externally created gradients with Flash gradients, or accept the file size addition to the Flash movie.** Gradients created in other drawing applications are not converted to editable Flash gradients when the file is imported; instead they will be rendered as complex banded graphics with clipping paths or as rasterized, bitmap images.

✦ **Preserve layers where possible to help keep imported artwork organized**. Some vector formats use layers, and Flash can recognize these layers if the graphic file format is correctly specified. Layers keep graphic elements separate from one another and can make it easier to organize items for use in animation.

✦ **If the artwork you are importing includes large areas of solid color, such as a plain background, consider excluding those parts of the graphic from import.** They can easily be replaced in Flash after the more complex parts of the artwork are brought in.

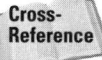

Cross-Reference For coverage of using other applications to create vector artwork for Flash, refer to Chapter 36, "Working with Vector Graphics."

Importing Vector Artwork

Vector graphics from other applications can be imported into Flash with relative ease using the Import to Stage or Import to Library command. Browse for files using the All Files or All PostScript setting to make most vector file formats selectable. Vector files in most formats, including EPS, PDF, and AI will invoke the new Import Options dialog box (shown in Figure 16-16). Use the settings to control how your file will be handled in the Flash authoring environment. So long as you do *not* choose Rasterize everything, vector graphics are generally imported as groups, and can be edited just like a normal group drawn in Flash.

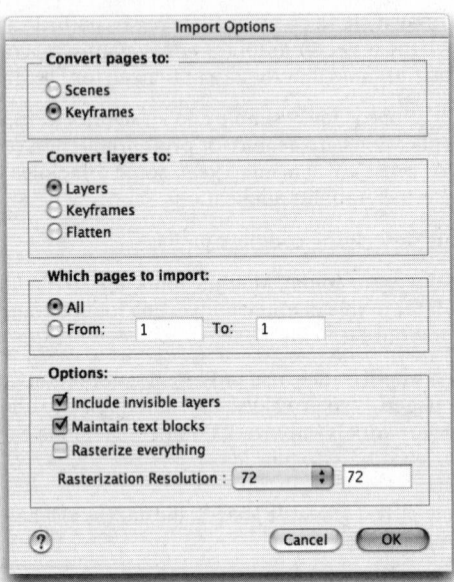

Figure 16-16: The Import Options dialog box used for setting conversion options for most imported graphics files

New Feature   Flash MX 2004 supports import of PDF and EPS files created with Adobe Illustrator. With PDF files, you have the option to preserve layers and to convert multi-page documents into Flash scenes or keyframes. Both the PDF and EPS formats are included in the All PostScript file import option.

Vector artwork will only be saved in the Library on import if it includes clipping paths or gradients that cannot be converted to editable Flash fills. In these cases, Flash automatically adds nested Graphic symbols with masks or bitmap symbols to the Library to preserve the appearance of elements that cannot be converted to basic grouped shapes.

Tip   Adobe Illustrator 6.0 is the only version that can be imported to Flash in AI format with placed bitmap images. If you are importing Adobe Illustrator layouts with placed bitmap images and you also need to preserve editable text and vector graphics, the best option is to save the layout as an Adobe PDF file before importing it to Flash. Although EPS files will import to Flash with placed bitmaps and editable text, you will not be able to preserve layers and placed bitmaps will be converted to nested PNG files with layer masks.

You can also copy and paste or even drag and drop artwork from external applications, but this gives you less control over how the vector information will be translated in Flash — for example, transparency or special fill types may be lost and any layers will be flattened into the currently selected Flash layer.

Because generic numbered layer names, such as Layer 1, may be redundant with layers already present in your Flash document, it is helpful to give layers meaningful names in the original file before importing to Flash. To avoid unexpected color shifts, it is recommended that you convert your color space to RGB in any external application before saving files that will be imported to Flash.

Caution You must specify Illustrator 7 or higher in the Adobe Illustrator document options when saving AI files to ensure color consistency for artwork imported to Flash. If you choose Illustrator 6 or lower format, then RGB values will not be saved and color shifts may result. When saving EPS files from Illustrator for import to Flash, be sure to *deselect* the CMYK PostScript option to avoid color shifts when the file is converted to RGB on import to Flash.

To import a vector file to Flash, simply follow these steps:

1. To import a file to the Stage of your Flash document, make sure that you have an empty, unlocked layer selected and chose File ⇨ Import ⇨ Import to Stage.

2. In the Import dialog box, choose a file format to browse using the Files of Type (Win) or Show (Mac) menu.

Note EPS files saved from FreeHand will not be selectable in the file list with Show: FreeHand. Use Show: All PostScript or Show: All Files to import EPS files from most applications.

3. Find the vector file that you wish to import and select it from the file list. Then choose Import.

4. If the application you are importing from includes options for how the artwork will be placed in Flash, you will be prompted to make choices from the Import Options dialog box.

   Depending on your options, the artwork will be imported to a single layer or to multiple layers or keyframes in your Flash document after you click OK.

Note If you choose to rasterize the vector artwork into a bitmap image when importing to Flash, remember to apply JPEG compression using the Quality setting in the Bitmap Properties dialog box, or if the Use document default quality check box is selected, set JPEG Quality in the Publish Settings dialog box before exporting your Flash movie (.swf).

5. To edit the imported graphic with Flash shape tools, ungroup the elements (Shift+Ctrl+G or Shift+⌘+G) or double-click parts of the group until you are able to select strokes and fills in Edit mode.

Tip Double-clicking a grouped item takes you into Edit mode, but if the item is in a compound group, you may have to continue double-clicking until you are able to isolate the stroke and fill of one part of the group for modification.

6. To store elements in the Library so they are reusable, convert them to Graphic symbols.

   If you have imported a layered sequence into multiple Flash keyframes, consider cutting and pasting the frames into a new Movie Clip symbol.

Although you can scale, move, or rotate the grouped elements, to modify individual parts of the graphic you must either ungroup the elements or go into Edit mode until you are able to select the strokes and fills of a particular element.

Any small inconsistencies in fill style are easy to fix once the elements are ungrouped in Flash. Remember that you can delete fills, add strokes, scale, or otherwise modify the imported artwork with any of the Flash tools.

To make the artwork efficient to reuse and update, it is best to convert the whole graphic into a symbol. If you intend to animate parts of the graphic individually, then convert these into discrete symbols and place them on separate layers.

Cross-Reference

For more information on working with grouped artwork in Flash refer to Chapter 9, "Modifying Graphics." For more information on using symbols refer to Chapter 6, "Symbols, Instances, and the Library."

Tip

If you use a program such as Macromedia FreeHand that allows you to define Flash-compatible symbols and layers in your graphic files, you can save some time when the file is imported to Flash.

Here's how to use the Clipboard to import a vector image into Flash:

1. Select all vector elements that you wish to include.

2. Copy the selected items from your vector drawing application to the Clipboard.

   Most programs support Ctrl+C or ⌘+C.

3. Return to Flash and make sure that you have an active, unlocked layer that you can paste the vectors into. This can be on the Main Timeline or on any symbol Timeline.

4. Paste the graphics onto the Stage by selecting Edit ⇨ Paste in Center from the menu (Ctrl+V or ⌘+V).

5. You may want to group or move parts of the pasted graphic onto new layers in your Flash document for better organization and for animation.

Importing Macromedia Fireworks files

Macromedia Fireworks offers one of the most flexible file formats for import into Flash. Fireworks PNG files can contain bitmap and vector artwork, as well as text, layers, guides, and even frames. Fireworks PNG files can be imported into Flash as either flattened images or as editable objects, with various options for handling the contents of the file. When importing images exported from Fireworks into Flash, you will be prompted by the Fireworks PNG Import Settings dialog box (shown in Figure 16-17) to make selections for the following import options:

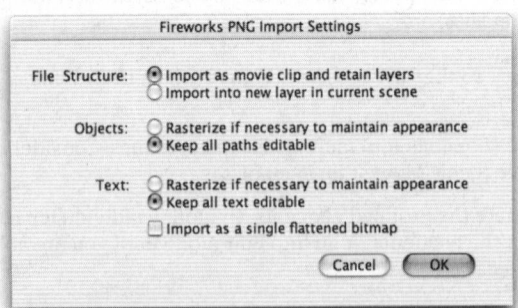

Figure 16-17: Use this special import dialog box to choose conversion settings for Fireworks PNG files.

✦ To import the PNG as one rasterized image to the current layer or to the Library, select **Import as single flattened bitmap**. When this option is selected, all other options will be unavailable. If you choose this option, you may want to apply Flash JPEG compression to the bitmap image either in Bitmap Properties or in Publish Settings. To edit a flattened image, you can launch Fireworks from inside Flash and edit the original PNG file (including any vector data or text).

✦ To import more complex files, select one of the following File Structures:

   • **Import as movie clip and retain layers** to import the PNG file to a new Movie Clip timeline with all frames and layers intact inside a Movie Clip symbol.

   • **Import into new layer in current scene** to import the PNG file into a single new layer in the current Flash document at the top of the stacking order. All Fireworks layers will be flattened, but not rasterized unless specified, and any frames in the Fireworks file will be included on the new layer.

✦ For Objects, select either "Rasterize if necessary to maintain appearance" to rasterize Fireworks fills, strokes, and effects in Flash as part of a bitmap image, or select "Keep all paths editable" to preserve vector paths in Flash. Some Fireworks fills, strokes, and effects may be lost on import.

✦ For Text the same options can be chosen as those listed for Objects.

As with most files created in external applications, you will find that rasterized and flattened Fireworks vector artwork and text will import more consistently to Flash, but you also lose all the benefits of having editable vector art and text. Although the option for launching Fireworks at any time to edit the original PNG file does make rasterized Fireworks images less limiting than other bitmaps, it is usually worth the little extra time you might need to spend simplifying your artwork to get it to import to Flash with vectors and editable text intact. Any special fills or textures that have been applied to your text in Fireworks will be lost if you choose to preserve editable text on import Flash.

Note   While gradients imported from FreeHand are converted to raw Flash shapes with gradient fills, gradients imported from Fireworks are converted to Movie Clip symbols that will appear in the Library in a folder labeled "Fireworks Objects" — it is still possible to edit the gradient fill just by opening the symbol in Edit mode (or double-clicking the symbol instance).

Caution   If you import a Fireworks PNG file by cutting and pasting into Flash, all vector elements will be rasterized into a flattened bitmap image.

Importing Macromedia FreeHand files

FreeHand is one of the most compatible applications for transferring vector artwork into Flash. When importing FreeHand files, you can preserve library symbols and pages in addition to layers and text blocks. You may also choose a specific page range to import. Figure 16-18 shows the options available from the FreeHand Import dialog box, which is invoked when importing files with the FreeHand (.fh) extension into Flash. Although FreeHand can export a variety of file formats, including .swf and .eps, the native .fh format will give you the most editing options for files imported to Flash.

Cross-Reference

For more information on working with FreeHand files, refer to Chapter 36, "Working with Vector Graphics." You will also find some sample FreeHand files in the ch36 folder on the CD-ROM.

Figure 16-18: The FreeHand Import dialog box used to specify how the vector file will be handled when placed into Flash

Remember to convert your FreeHand file to RGB color mode. If the file is in CMYK, it will be converted automatically on import to Flash and this may cause unexpected color shifts. There are some other special considerations when importing FreeHand artwork. To ensure seamless translation of FreeHand elements imported into Flash observe the following guidelines:

✦ Any placed grayscale elements in FreeHand will be converted to RBG color when imported to Flash, which may increase file size.

✦ EPS files placed in FreeHand will not be viewable when imported to Flash, unless you select the Convert Editable EPS when Imported option in FreeHand Import Preferences before you place an EPS into FreeHand. Regardless of the settings used, Flash will not display information for any placed EPS imported from FreeHand.

✦ Strokes with square caps will be converted into rounded caps in Flash.

✦ Be cautious with compound shapes: When importing overlapping elements that you want to keep intact in Flash, place them on separate layers in FreeHand and import the layers into Flash. If items on a single layer are overlapping when imported, they will be divided or merged at intersection points in the same way as primitive shapes created in Flash.

✦ Flash only supports up to eight colors in an imported gradient fill. If a gradient created in FreeHand contains more than eight colors, Flash uses clipping paths to interpret the gradient. Clipping paths increase file size. To work around this issue, use gradients that contain eight or fewer colors in FreeHand or replace the imported gradient with a Flash gradient fill as described later in this chapter.

✦ Imported FreeHand blends also increase Flash file size because Flash interprets each step in a blend as a separate path.

As shown in Figure 16-19, Flash recognizes text and even limited-color gradient fills imported from FreeHand and Fireworks, making it easy to edit these elements directly in Flash.

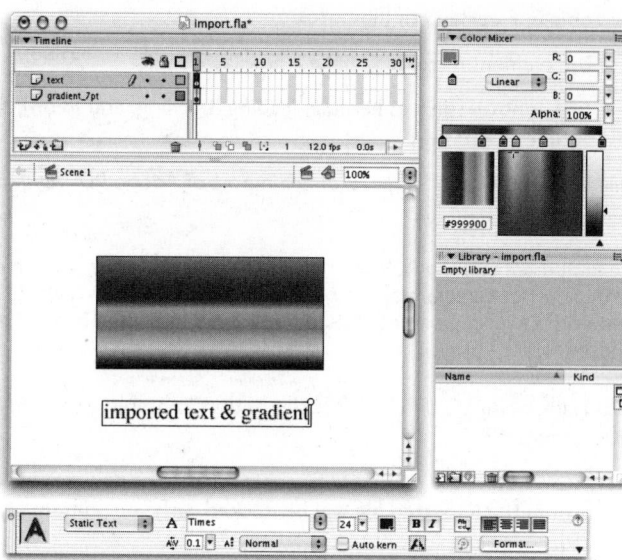

Figure 16-19: FreeHand and Fireworks files can be edited directly in Flash, but shapes and text elements still need to be converted into symbols to store in the Library for reuse.

Tip   Remember that gradients created in Macromedia FreeHand or Adobe Illustrator can be directly exported to SWF format as Flash gradients. However, if the gradient contains more than eight colors, Flash adds clipping paths when it is imported. Also, remember that FreeHand blends will always be interpreted by Flash as a series of paths, which can increase file size and sometimes add banding to the blend.

Animating Imported Vector Graphics

A handy feature of many popular illustration programs is support for layers. Just like layers in a Flash document (.fla), layers in illustration programs enable you to keep individual groups of graphics separate from one another. A simple technique with animating vector graphic files is to animate or tween each layer separately in the Flash authoring environment.

An example of an easily converted illustration movie is a logo. If you have created artwork in FreeHand or Illustrator and have kept the elements separated by layers, then you can quickly create an interactive Flash graphic.

For this exercise you can use the sample logo, `daisyLogo.ai` or `daisyLogo.pdf`, in the `ch16` folder of the CD-ROM. If you use the example file, start at Step 4.

1. Create a layered graphic in FreeHand or Illustrator.

   Before each part of the element is created, make a new layer for it.

2. If you use extensive text controls (such as kerning, leading, tracking, and so on), then convert the text to outlines (or paths).

3. Save the layout. Flash MX 2004 now supports direct import of Adobe PDF files, in addition to Illustrator or FreeHand files.

Caution   CMYK colors shift when imported into the RGB color space of Flash. Moreover, some masking and cropping information (for bleeds) may not be interpreted correctly by Flash. To see the color difference between CMYK import and RGB import for the logo used in this example, refer to the color insert.

4. Import the file into Flash, being certain to select the option to preserve your artwork in layers and vector format.

   You may want to create a new scene or symbol to contain the imported graphic(s). Otherwise, the layers from the imported file will be stacked with your current layers (as shown in Figure 16-20).

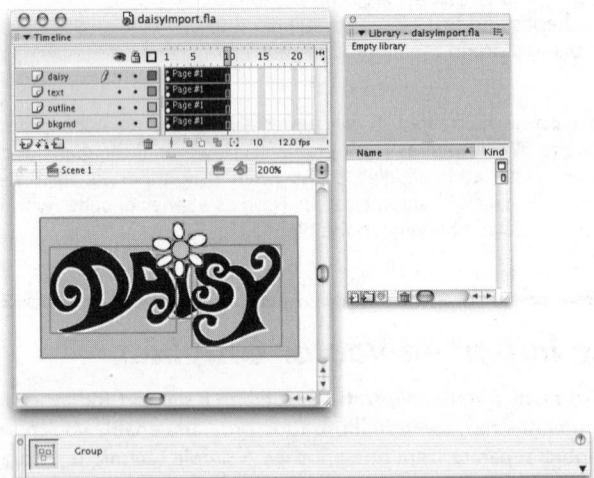

Figure 16-20: Layered vector graphic imported as grouped artwork in Flash layers on the main Timeline

5. You may convert the layered elements into symbols for reuse or easier modification later.

   You will need to make button symbols for any element that you want to use interactively (such as the flower animation triggered by the mouse). Repeat this step for every layer.

6. Now add any Flash tweens or actions to the groups or symbols in each layer.

At this point, you could continue creating a full Flash project with other components, or export a Flash movie (.swf). The project Timeline for the finished animated example on the CD-ROM is shown in Figure 16-21.

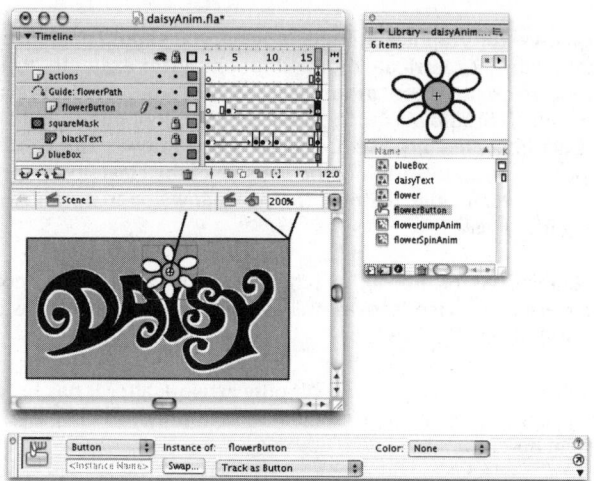

Figure 16-21: Imported artwork converted to Flash symbols and tweened to create an animated logo

As you can see, in just six straightforward steps, you can create an animated logo and many other translations of vector graphics into interactive presentations that could be included in other projects or in e-mail. Whenever you're developing complicated layered work in an illustration application such as FreeHand or Illustrator, you can take advantage of those layers in Flash.

On the CD-ROM

Check out the completed interactive logo, `daisyAnim.fla` or `daisyAnim.swf`, located in the `ch16` folder of the CD-ROM.

Optimizing Vectors

All vector graphics are made up of paths in one shape or another. A path can be as simple as a straight line with two points, a curved line with two points, or 500 or more points along an irregular shape or fill. For this reason vector graphics are best suited for graphic images such as logos, architectural drawings, and clip art that do not include continuous tones. Fonts are also made up of paths. As you've seen with Flash-drawn graphics, you can scale them to any size without any loss of resolution, unlike raster (bitmap) artwork, which cannot scale larger than its original size without loss of resolution.

Note   Vector graphics are eventually *rasterized,* so to speak. The vector formatting for drawn shapes and text is more of a simplified storage structure that contains a mathematical description (that is, smaller than a bit-for-bit description) of an object or set of objects. When the vector graphic is displayed, especially with anti-aliasing, the video card needs to render the edges in pixels. Likewise, the PostScript RIP (Raster Image Processor) of a laser printer needs to convert the vector information, or an EPS (Encapsulated PostScript) file, into printer "dots."

When you use imported vector graphics in Flash movies, you should minimize the number of points describing curved lines or intricate outlined graphics (for example, "traced" raster images). The problem with creating cool graphics in vector-based applications such as Illustrator, FreeHand, and 3D Studio Max is the large number of points used to describe lines. When these graphics are imported into Flash, animations are slower and harder to redraw (or refresh) on the computer screen. In addition, the file size of the Flash movie grows considerably. Most vector applications include features that will allow you to optimize or simplify artwork before importing it to Flash.

Cross-Reference   For tips on optimizing vector artwork in other applications, including Adobe Illustrator, Streamline, and Macromedia FreeHand, as well as coverage of export options refer to Chapter 36, "Working with Vector Graphics."

There are also a number of ways that you can simplify artwork after it has been imported to Flash. Many of these Flash features have been discussed in previous chapters, but we will briefly summarize them here.

Tracing complex vector artwork

Many graphics programs, such as Discreet 3D Studio Max and Adobe Dimensions can create some astonishing vector-based graphics. However, when you import EPS versions of those graphics into Flash, they either fall apart (display horribly) or add unrealistic byte chunks to your Flash movie. But, this doesn't mean that you can't use these intricate graphics in your Flash movies. You can try several different procedures with intricate vector artwork, including smoothing as described previously, to make complex graphics more Flash-friendly.

Depending on the specific use of the artwork, you may also be able to output small raster equivalents that won't consume nearly as much space as highly detailed vector graphics. However, in some instances, the best solution is a bit more labor-intensive. To get just the right "translation" of a complex vector graphic in your Flash movie, you may need to try redrawing the artwork in Flash. Sound crazy and time-consuming? Well, it's a bit of both, but some Flash designers spend hour after hour getting incredibly small file sizes from "hand-tracing" vector designs in Flash.

For example, if you made a highly detailed technical drawing of a light bulb, and wanted to bring it into Flash, you could import the original EPS version of the drawing into Flash, place it on a locked layer, and use Flash drawing tools to recreate a simplified sketch version of the object (see Figure 16-22).

Tip   Many other Flash SWF tools can help to speed up the work of optimizing vector artwork — for example, Electric Rain's Swift 3D, which can simplify 3D models and output SWF files. The art and science of creating 3D Flash graphics is a complex topic that is beyond the scope of this book. If this is an area that you would like to learn more about, we suggest you refer to *The Flash MX 3D Graphics Bible* from Wiley Publishing, Inc.

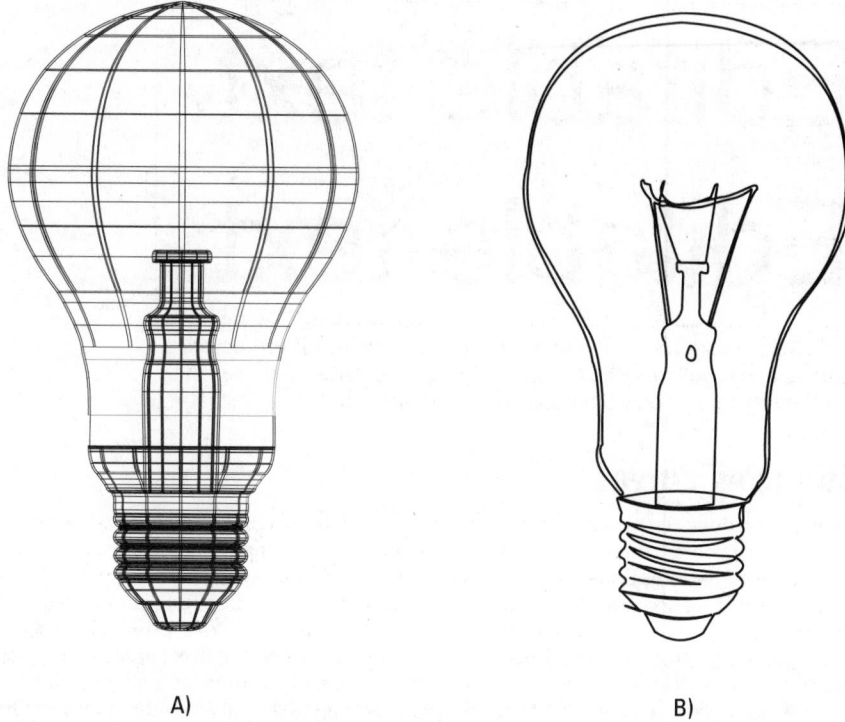

A)   B)

Figure 16-22: Compare the original imported vector artwork of the light bulb (left) with the simplified version drawn in Flash (right).

Converting text to outlines

Another aspect of vector graphics that you need to keep in mind — especially when working with other designers — is font linking and embedding. With most vector file formats, such as Illustrator, FreeHand, or EPS, you can link to fonts that are located on your system. However, if you give those files to someone who doesn't have those fonts installed, then he won't be able to see or use the fonts. Some formats enable you to embed fonts into the document file, which circumvents this problem. However, whether the fonts are linked or embedded, you may be unnecessarily bloating the size of the vector graphic.

You can break apart imported text in Flash by using the Modify ⇨ Break apart command (Ctrl+B or ⌘+B). You have to first break the text into letters and then break them apart a second time to get basic shapes.

You can also convert any text into outlines (or *paths*) in most drawing or illustration programs (see Figure 16-23). In Macromedia FreeHand, select the text as a text block (with the Arrow tool, not the Text tool) and choose Text ⇨ Convert to Paths. In Adobe Illustrator, select the text as an object and choose Type ⇨ Create Outlines.

If you have a lot of body text in the graphic, you may want to copy the text directly into a Flash text box and use a _sans, _serif, or other device font. These fonts do not require additional file information (as embedded fonts do) when used in a Flash movie.

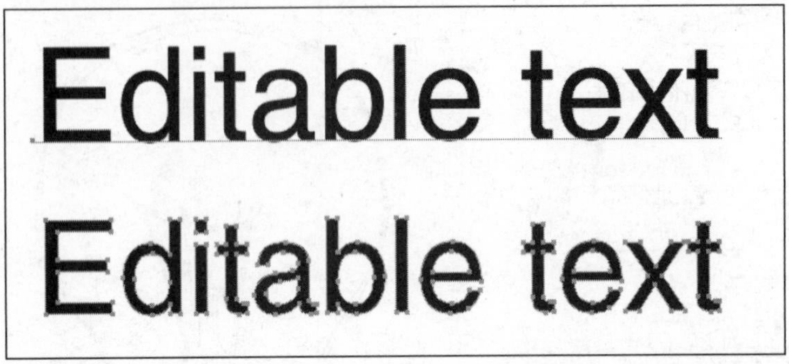

Editable text

Editable text

Figure 16-23: Make sure that you have finished editing your text before converting it into outlines. The text at the top can be edited, whereas the text at the bottom can only be modified as individual shapes.

Optimizing curves

You can also reduce the complexity of paths within Flash, by using the Modify ➪ Shape ➪ Optimize curves command. This has the same effect as the Simplify command in FreeHand, with a couple of extra options. When working with bitmaps or symbols, be sure to use the Modify ➪ Break apart command, and if you are working with a group, ungroup it (Modify ➪ Ungroup) before you use the Optimize command (Alt+Shift+Ctrl+C or Option+Shift+⌘+C) — you can't optimize groups or symbols. The Optimize Curves dialog box enables you to specify multiple passes, which means that Flash will optimize the graphic at a given setting as much as it possibly can. Figure 16-24 shows the effect of maximum smoothing on a complex seashell graphic.

Figure 16-24: A complex vector graphic simplified with maximum smoothing

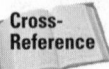

For a more detailed description of the Optimize curves options, refer to Chapter 5, "Drawing in Flash."

We'd like to know what you thought about this chapter. Visit www.flashsupport.com/ feedback to fill out an online form with your comments.

Summary

✦ Flash can use a variety of external media, which enables you to select the most effective format for various types of content.

✦ Bitmaps are best suited for photographic images or images that contain detailed shading and/or complex color blends.

✦ Bitmaps can be optimized or compressed in your image-editing application or in Flash, but it is important to follow a workflow that will avoid double JPEGing on any artwork.

✦ Bitmaps can be converted to vector artwork in a variety of ways. This process works best on simplified bitmap images or when used to create special image effects.

✦ Vector graphics are most often used for logos, line drawings, and other artwork that does not include complex patterns and blends.

✦ Flash supports import of layers and editable text and gradients from some graphics applications including Macromedia FreeHand, Fireworks, and Adobe Illustrator. Some care is needed in preparing files to get the best results, but being able to reuse your file structure and editable elements created in other applications can save a lot of time.

✦ Although the native file format of Flash is vector and this format is very efficient by design, often vector graphics still need to be optimized.

✦ Most graphics applications include their own options for reducing the complexity of vector art. However, using Flash's various tools for optimizing vector artwork can also be an effective way to reduce your final file size.

✦   ✦   ✦

Embedding Video

One of the most exciting features introduced with Macromedia Flash MX was the power to add digital video footage to a Flash movie (.swf file), playable within Flash Player 6! Designers and developers alike had long awaited this feature. Flash MX 2004 continues to improve the video capabilities and performance of the Flash Player. Macromedia has added tools to make it easier for you to integrate video into your Flash movies. With Flash Player 6 or higher, video can be played without relying upon additional browser or system plug-ins such as Apple QuickTime or Real Systems RealOne player. In this chapter, we show you how to embed a video file into a Flash MX 2004 document, specify import quality of the video, and control playback of the video within the Flash movie.

Note   This chapter explores the Flash Video Exporter, which is only available with Flash MX Professional 2004. If you are using the trial version of Flash MX 2004, make sure you have switched it to Flash MX Pro 2004 in the Help menu.

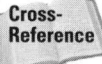

Cross-Reference   We've moved our coverage of digital video basics from the last edition of the Flash Bible to Appendix C, "Digital Video Basics."

Importing the Video

Digital video, as with other external media assets that Flash can import, is something that you need to create before working with it in a Flash document. In today's economic climate, you might not only be a Web designer or developer; you might also wear the part-time hat of a videographer. Be sure to read our coverage of video in Appendix C, "Digital Video Basics," for a primer on shooting and producing better-looking video. The appendix also discusses the various video formats that you can import into Flash MX 2004.

After you have created a video file in the desired import format, you're ready to bring it into Flash MX 2004. This section introduces you to the Sorenson Spark codec options available in Flash MX 2004. In the latter half of this section, we walk you through the process of importing one of the sample files on the *Macromedia Flash MX 2004 Bible* CD-ROM.

Integrating video: The solutions

In Flash MX 2004, there are four methods in which Flash content can interact with video content. In the following sections, we provide a high-level overview of these methods.

Linking video with QuickTime Flash

When Flash 4 was released, QuickTime movies could be imported into the Flash authoring environment. There, you could animate and develop Flash content that interacted with the QuickTime movie. However, in Flash 4 and 5, you could only export QuickTime Flash movies (.mov files) that required the Apple QuickTime 4 (or higher) Player to view. The QuickTime video files were linked to the Flash document (.fla file), which meant that the Flash document didn't store the actual video content. You can still use linked video files in Flash MX 2004 to create QuickTime Flash movies.

Cross-Reference   You can learn more about QuickTime Flash movies by reading our online PDF archived version of the *Flash MX Bible*'s Chapter 41, "Working with QuickTime." This chapter can be found online at www.flashsupport.com/archive.

Embedding video into a Flash movie

The second method that you can use to view video in Flash Player 6 or 7 is to embed the video file in the Flash document (.fla file), where it is then published directly inside the Flash movie (.swf file). This method enables Flash MX 2004 to encode your video with the Sorenson Spark codec (discussed in the next section). It's important to understand that this codec does not require additional plug-ins for playback—the Web user needs only to have Flash Player 6 or higher installed on her/his browser. Spark does not use any system-level video codecs; the Spark codec is built into Flash Player 6 or higher.

If you select a QuickTime movie to import into either the Windows or Macintosh version of Flash MX 2004, you will see the QuickTime-specific screen of the Video Import Wizard, as shown in Figure 17-1. To use the QuickTime video file as an embedded video playable by Flash Player 6, choose the first option. To use the video file for a QuickTime Flash movie, choose the second option.

When you import a video clip as an Embedded Video object, the video is stored in the Library as Flash Video (.flv file). This chapter discusses the embedding video features of Flash MX 2004. Later in this chapter, we explore the compression options available for the Sorenson Spark codec in Flash MX 2004.

Tip   You can also use a third-party application to create Flash movies (swf files) with embedded video. These utilities produce better quality video than the native encoder used by Flash MX 2004. Some examples of these applications are mentioned in the next section.

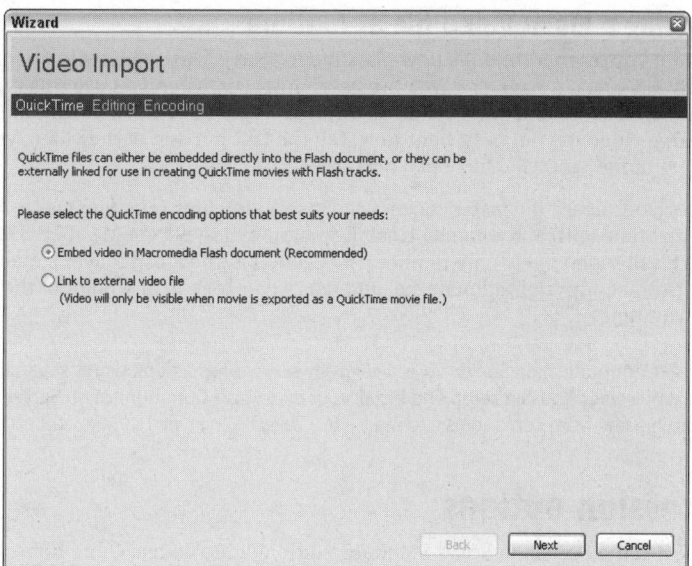

Figure 17-1: The Video Import Wizard appears when you import a QuickTime video file into Flash MX 2004.

Loading a Flash Video file at runtime

Starting with Flash Player 7-compatible movies, you can now load Flash Video files (.flv files) at runtime. When we say "runtime," we mean that you can create a separate Flash Video file (.flv file), upload it to your Web server, and use ActionScript code or a component to load the video directly into your Flash movie (.swf file) as it plays in the Web browser. With the following, you can create Flash Video files by:

✦ Importing a video file into a Flash document, and then exporting the Embedded Video symbol from the document's Library panel as a Flash Video file (.flv file).

✦ Exporting a Flash Video file (.flv file) from a QuickTime-compatible application and the new Flash Video Exporter that ships with Flash MX Pro 2004.

✦ Using a third-party video compression tool designed to export Flash Video files (.flv files) such as Sorenson Squeeze 3 for Flash MX, Sorenson Squeeze 3 Compression Suite, or Wildform Flix.

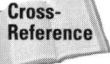

Cross-Reference

You learn how to load a Flash Video file using the `NetStream` class in ActionScript in Chapter 28, "Sharing and Loading Assets."

Real-time streaming a Flash Video file at runtime

In the previous section, you learned that it's now possible to load a Flash Video file directly into a Flash movie (SWF file) as it plays in a Web browser. However, when you use this type of loading, the Flash Video file is loaded and cached as any other asset accessed at runtime. As such, if you have a large video file but only want to watch the last portion of the video, you'll have to wait until most of the video file has been downloaded.

One way you can offer your users the fastest access to Flash Video files (FLV files) is to stream the video in real-time with Macromedia Flash Communication Server MX. With this server technology, a Flash Video file is only temporarily cached in the Flash Player's memory. You can more easily protect copyrighted material, and users can seek to any point in the video with minimal wait times.

Note   Macromedia Flash Communication Server MX is a specialty server product that works separately from a standard Web server. You can setup and install your own Flash Communication Server, or you can purchase hosting from companies such as `MediaTemple.net` or `Influxis.com`.

Spark compression options

Flash MX 2004 ships with the Sorenson Spark Standard edition video codec. Quite honestly, this codec is among the better codecs we have ever used. In this section, we discuss the options of the Spark Standard edition. Before we do that, we offer a quick review of video compression schemes.

Video codecs can compress image data in two different ways — temporally and spatially. A temporal compression algorithm, or interframe compressor, compares the data between each frame and stores only the differences between the two. A spatial compression algorithm, also known as intraframe compression, compresses the data in each frame, just as the JPEG format compresses data in a still image. Most video codecs designed for Web playback, including Sorenson Spark, do not use a lossless compression technique with either temporal or spatial algorithms. Rather, some color and detail information is thrown out in an effort to minimize the amount of data saved with each frame. For example, if the original video source recorded a sunset with 80 shades of orange, the compressed version of the sunset may only include 50 or fewer shades of orange. You may have noticed the extremes of lossy compression in Web videos where a person's face is hardly distinguishable, looking more blocky than human.

Note   Historically speaking, most new codecs developed in the last few years rely upon the ever-increasing computer processor speeds to efficiently decompress each frame of video on playback. For this reason, you may want to test video playback on a number of machines and devices that support the Flash Player 6 and video decoding.

Sorenson Spark uses interframe (temporal) compression, but it also uses intraframe compression when making keyframes. (You see how tricky keyframes can be in just a moment.) A keyframe in video footage is similar to a keyframe in a Flash timeline. A keyframe defines a moment in time where a significant change occurs. For example, if a section of video has three hard cuts from one scene to another to another, the compressed version of that video should have a keyframe at the start of each scene. A keyframe then becomes the reference for subsequent frames in the video. When the following frame(s) are compared to the keyframe, only the differences are remembered (or stored) in the video file. As soon as the scene changes beyond a certain percentage, a new keyframe is made in the video. If you use the Video Import Wizard, video keyframes are created while the movie is being compressed (or imported) into Flash MX 2004.

> **Caution**   Video keyframes are the reason you should be careful with special effects or filter use in transitions from scene to scene in your video. The more frequently your video changes from frame to frame, the more keyframes your video file needs. Keyframes take up more file size than interframes between the keyframes.

Now that you have had an introduction to compression concepts, let's look at the options available in the Standard edition of the Sorenson Spark codec. Create a new Flash document in the Flash MX 2004 authoring environment, and use File ⇨ Import ⇨ Import to Stage to select a video file. For this example, you can use the sample_high.avi file from the ch17/source folder of the *Macromedia Flash MX 2004 Bible* CD-ROM. When you choose this Windows AVI file for import, select the **Import the entire video** option in the first screen (dubbed Editing) of the Video Import Wizard. After you click the Next button, you'll see the Encoding screen of the Video Import Wizard, as shown in Figure 17-2.

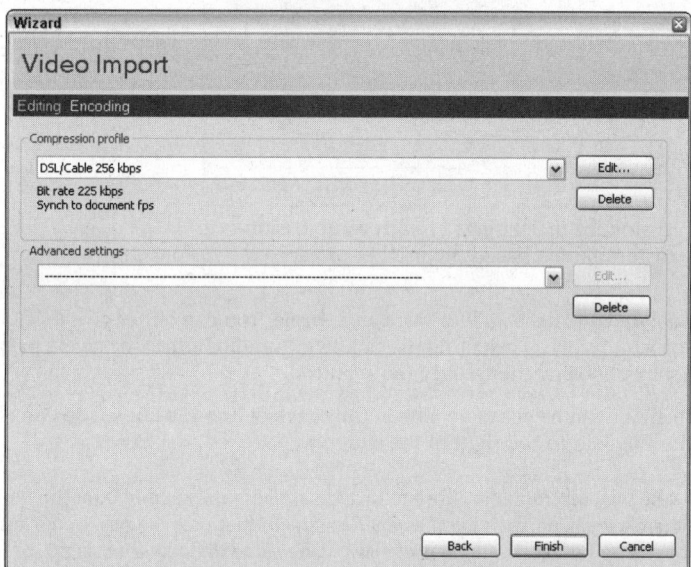

Figure 17-2: The Import Video Settings dialog box controls the compression options for the Sorenson Spark codec.

The Encoding screen of the Flash MX 2004's Video Import Wizard offers you simpler options than Flash MX did. In the Compression Profile menu, you can quickly choose a target bitrate for your embedded video. Let's take a look at the parameters that can be set for a profile. Make sure the default DSL/Cable 256 kbps profile is selected, and press the Edit button. The Video Import Wizard moves to the Encoding (Compression Settings) screen, shown in Figure 17-3.

New Feature Flash MX 2004's Video Import Wizard includes a live preview of the compression settings. You can now more easily determine which settings produce the results you want. You can also drag the playhead on the video control bar below the video window to see how a compression applies to a specific frame.

Figure 17-3: You can customize the settings of each compression profile or save a new custom profile based on another profile.

✦ **Bandwidth and Quality:** These sliders work as a toggle. You can either give a priority to bandwidth consumption by selecting the Bandwidth radio button, or give a priority to image quality by choosing the Quality radio button.

The Bandwidth slider can be set to a value in the range of 0 to 750 kbps. You can also type a value into the field to the right of the slider.

Note We're not quite sure why Macromedia chose to include a minimum value of 0 for the bandwidth scale, as there's really no such thing as a video stream that uses 0 Kbps. In our tests, choosing a 0 Kbps value for bandwidth was effectively the same thing as choosing 0 for the quality setting.

The Quality slider and text field allow you to enter a value from 0 to 100. This scale is similar to JPEG quality, where 100 is maximum quality and 0 is least quality. For most video, you will find that 60 is the minimum acceptable quality. Anything lower than this may be too compressed and appear blocky.

Tip

If you use the Bandwidth slider, be sure to factor in the bandwidth necessary for the audio track. The bandwidth setting here only applies to the video stream. As you learn later, you control the audio compression of the video's audio track in the Publish Settings. To use the DSL/Cable 256 Kbps profile as an example, the bandwidth setting is 225 Kbps, implying that you should only use a 31 Kbps or lower bitrate for the audio track in the Publish Settings.

✦ **Keyframes:** This slider and text field control how often the Spark codec creates keyframes in the video. A value of 0 inserts no keyframes. Lower values (except 0) insert more keyframes, whereas higher values insert fewer keyframes. One sample file set to use 0 as a keyframe interval (with all other settings equal) compressed to 42 KB, whereas the same file set to use 1 as a keyframe interval compressed to 219 KB. The same file set to use 48 as a keyframe interval compressed to 45 KB.

On the CD-ROM

Compare the visual quality of the `sample_0kf_50qu.swf`, `sample_1kf_50qu.swf`, and `sample_48kf_50qu.swf` files, located in the `ch17/keyframe_interval` folder of the book's CD-ROM. In this case, fewer keyframes (0 keyframe interval or 48 keyframe interval) produce a cleaner video image — the background behind Robert does not display as much video noise. Each sample used a Quality value of 50.

✦ **High quality keyframes:** This check box option produces better-looking video, especially if you are using the bandwidth setting (instead of the quality setting). Make sure you select this option for consistent image quality in keyframes.

✦ **Quick compress:** Selecting this option decreases the amount of time required to compress the stream, at the potential expense of reduced image quality. Use this option only to import placeholder (or temporary) video, to mock up a composition, or draft a layout.

✦ **Synchronize video to Macromedia Flash document frame rate:** When this check box is selected, Flash MX 2004 adjusts the source video file's frame rate to match the frame rate of the current Flash document. For example, if a source file has a frame rate of 15 fps and the Flash document has a rate of 12 fps, this selected option will drop three frames from each second of the imported video. If you clear this option, Flash MX 2004 assigns each frame of video to one frame of the Flash timeline. As such, the video may play slower than real time because it's keeping the same number of frames but being played back at a slower frame rate. You can see this "delay" effect by watching the Length value change in the Output properties area as you clear the check box and/or select it.

✦ **Number of video frames to encode per number of Macromedia Flash frames:** This menu controls the ratio of video frames to Flash frames. This option works hand-in-hand with the Synchronize option to reduce the number of frames that are actually imported into the Flash document. By default, a 1:1 ratio is selected, which preserves the original frame rate of the source video. You can use this control to reduce the frame rate of your source video by choosing an appropriate ratio. Whenever possible, we recommend that your final video frame rate be at least 12 fps for smooth video playback.

Let's look at another area of the Video Import Wizard. From the Encoding (Compression Settings) screen, click the Back button. In the Advanced settings area of the Video Import Wizard, choose **Create new profile** in the drop-down menu. The Video Import Wizard moves to the Encoding (Advanced settings) screen, as shown in Figure 17-4.

Figure 17-4: The Advanced settings enable you to control finer details of the import process.

In this screen, you can adjust various aspects of the image's color, dimensions, and track control.

✦ **Color:** In this area of the wizard, you can control the hue, saturation, gamma, brightness, and contrast of your video image. We recommend that you only use this feature to make subtle changes to the video image. You can do some interesting "easy" effects such as making color footage black-and-white by reducing the saturation value. If you make a change that you don't like, click the Reset button to revert the color settings to their default values.

✦ **Dimensions:** You can use these settings to change the scale and cropping of the video. You can reduce the scale with percentage values, and you can clip unwanted areas of the video with the crop fields You can use the scale control to effectively resize larger full-frame video files (that is, with frame sizes of 640 x 480 or larger) to more Web-friendly sizes such as 320 x 240 or 160 x 120.

Note   Unfortunately, you cannot independently resize the width from the height to correct the pixel aspect ratio of DV format video files. After import, your video's image will appear stretched horizontally. If you're importing video that uses a non-square pixel aspect ratio, we highly recommend that you use a tool such as Sorenson Squeeze to compress your video for Flash use.

✦ **Track options:** Perhaps one of the better features added to Flash's video import capabilities, these parameters affect the way Flash handles the video and audio tracks.

  • **Import:** This menu controls how the Flash Video is brought into the current Flash document. The default value, Current timeline, imports the Flash Video on to the timeline of the active object (or symbol) at the time of import. If you choose Movie Clip or Graphic symbol, then the importer automatically nests the Flash Video asset into a Movie Clip or Graphic symbol, respectively, in the Library panel. The symbol's name will be the same as the imported file.

Note If you use the File ➪ Import ➪ Import to Library, the Current timeline option is disregarded.

- **Audio track:** This menu controls how the audio track (if it exists) of the video asset is handled. The default value, Integrated, keeps the audio track bound inside of the embedded video symbol after import. When you use this option, you control the compression of the audio track via the audio stream settings in the Flash tab of the Publish Settings dialog box (File ➪ Publish Settings). The Separate option tells Flash MX 2004 to store the audio track as a separate Sound asset in the Library panel. If you use this option, you must physically place this Sound asset on the starting keyframe of the video layer in the Timeline window. (You can put the sound on another layer on the same timeline as well.) Be sure to set this sound to use a Stream sync, to ensure proper playback. If you choose None in the menu, the audio track is stripped from the video asset; the audio, then, is not imported into the Flash document.

Tip If you use the Separate option for the Audio track, you can scrub the video track *and* the audio track in the Timeline window. If you use the Integrated option, you will not be able to scrub the audio track in the Timeline window.

Last, but by no means least, you can now specify multiple in and out points for a video file in the new Video Import Wizard of Flash MX 2004. To see this feature, cancel any currently open Video Import Wizard, and choose File ➪ Import ➪ Import to Stage. Choose the same sample Windows AVI file mentioned earlier in this chapter. On the Editing screen of the Video Import Wizard, choose **Edit the video first** and click the Next button. The wizard moves to the Editing (Customize) screen, shown in Figure 17-5.

Figure 17-5: The Editing (Customize) screen can create multiple clips from a single video file.

Here, you can drag the in and out markers to specific sections of your video file. Click the Create clip button to add a new segment to the editing list (on the left side of the wizard). You can click the text area of segment names in the editing list to rename the clips — these names translate to the names of the imported video symbols in the document's Library panel.

You can change the in and out points of a segment in the editing list by choosing the segment in the list, altering the in and/or out markers, and clicking the Update clip button. You can even reorder clips in the editing list by selecting a clip and clicking the up or down arrow at the top right corner of the editing list.

You can also enable the **Combine list of clips into a single library item after import** option. This feature stitches all of your edits into one video asset in the Library panel. Otherwise, each clip is imported as its own video asset.

Note   You cannot apply different compression profiles to individual clips. You can choose only one profile, which is applied to all clips.

Now that you're familiar with the new Video Import Wizard, the next section walks you through the steps of using the wizard with one of the sample files on the book's CD-ROM.

Cross-Reference   This section covered the settings available for the Basic edition of the Sorenson Spark codec. Later in this chapter, we explore the extended options offered by the Pro edition of the Spark codec, available in the Flash Video Exporter, Sorenson Squeeze, and other third-party tools. Squeeze is a separate encoding application that offers superior compression over the native encoding found in Flash MX 2004.

We discuss data rate and bandwidth concerns in the "Publishing Flash Movies with Video" section later in this chapter.

Adjusting audio compression

As strange as it may sound, the audio track of a digital video file is imported and retained in its original source format. Flash MX 2004 uses the global audio settings found in the Publish Settings dialog box to control the compression applied to your imported video's audio track. Most importantly, audio linked to an embedded video is treated as Stream sound so that it will be properly synched to the playback of the video. Therefore, you must specify the video's audio compression in the Audio Stream options of the Publish Settings dialog box.

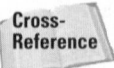

Cross-Reference   For more information on audio compression, read Chapter 15, "Adding Sound." Flash MX 2004 features a Speech codec that can also be used for the audio track of a video clip.

Note   You can use the new Separate option in the Audio track menu of the Advanced settings area of the Video Import Wizard to extract the audio of a video file to its own Sound asset in the Library. See our prior coverage of this feature in this chapter.

Compressing video with Flash MX 2004

In this section, we show you how to go through the process of selecting a video file and embedding it in a Flash MX 2004 document. Remember, embedded video can be played only with Flash Player 6 or higher.

For this example, make a copy of the `sample_high.avi` to a local folder or your desktop.

1. Open a new Flash document (File ➪ New).

2. Open the Document Properties (Modify ➪ Document), and make sure the frame rate is set to 12 fps. Alternatively, you can change the frame rate in the Property inspector. Click any empty area of the Stage or Work area to show the document properties in the Property inspector.

3. Using File ➪ Import ➪ Import to Stage (Ctrl+R or ⌘+R), browse to the sample_high.avi file that you copied to your system. With the file name selected, click Open in the Import dialog box.

4. In the Video Import Wizard dialog box, choose **Import the entire video**. Click the Next button.

5. In the next screen of the Video Import Wizard, choose **Corporate LAN 150kbps** in the Compression profile menu. This setting produces a video image quality that doesn't appear too lossy. Click Finish at the bottom of the wizard.

6. When the Importing progress bar is finished, Flash MX 2004 displays the dialog box shown in Figure 17-6. One feature of video import in Flash MX 2004 is that it automatically expands a timeline (if necessary) to accommodate the length of the video file. Because video is a streaming asset (such as Stream sound), the timeline that holds the video needs to be as long as the video clip. In this example, the Flash document needs 87 frames to display the entire clip. Click Yes in this dialog box.

Figure 17-6: Flash MX 2004 asks you if you want to add more frames to the timeline to display the full video clip.

7. The video clip appears on the Main Timeline of the current Flash document. Flash MX 2004 automatically centers the video clip as well. At this point, rename Layer 1 to **sample video**.

8. Because the original digital video file was recorded with a DV camcorder, the aspect ratio is not appropriate for computer display. Select the video object on the Stage, and in the Property inspector, change the width to **320** pixels and the height to **240** pixels.

Tip

Even though you resized the width to put the video in the proper aspect ratio, the Flash movie will still contain the extra "weight" of the pixels imported in the original 360 x 240 dimensions. For this reason, you should make sure that your original video clip is compressed at the proper dimensions and pixel aspect ratio before importing it to Flash. We intentionally used this example to demonstrate what needs to be done to "raw" DV footage in Flash MX 2004.

9. With the video clip selected on the Stage, open the Align panel and recenter the object on the Stage.

10. Save your Flash document as `sampleVideo_100.fla`, and test it (Ctrl+Enter or ⌘+Enter). The Flash movie (swf file) is only 155 KB. Not bad for seven seconds of Web video! That's roughly a data rate of 20 KB/s, or 160 Kbps.

11. You can further modify the quality of the video clip's audio track by adjusting the Audio Stream settings in the Publish Settings. By default, Flash MX 2004 uses MP3 compression at 16 Kbps, mono, with Fast quality. Open the Publish Settings dialog box (File ➪ Publish Settings), and click the Flash tab. Click the Set button for the Audio Stream option, and choose a new codec and/or bitrate. For example, you can choose MP3 compression at 20 Kbps, mono, with Best quality. This will produce a slightly larger file size with better audio quality than the default. Close the Publish Settings dialog box, and retest your movie.

You may want to repeat this exercise, experimenting with a different compression profile or even creating a custom profile of your own. Try other sample video files on the book's CD-ROM as well.

Using Video in a Timeline

In the preceding section, you learned how to import video into a Flash document. Now, we'll get into practical use of the `Video` objects. When you embed video into your Flash document, you add an Embedded Video symbol to the Library, as shown in Figure 17-7.

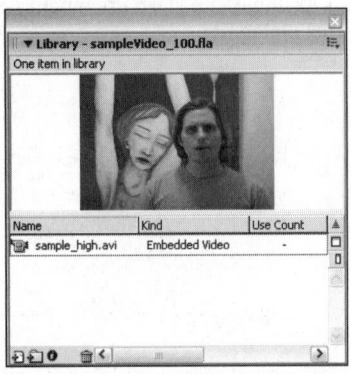

Figure 17-7: An Embedded Video symbol in the Library panel

As with other symbols in the Library, you can reuse the same Embedded Video symbol as several instances throughout the Flash document, but you may notice significant file size gains. Keep in mind, though, that video on a Flash timeline is treated just like Stream sound — only the frames of video that you can view within the Timeline window are exported with your Flash movie.

Tip   You can effectively trim your video by removing frames at the tail of the clip.

Controlling playback of embedded video

You can control the playback of your Embedded Video object by controlling the playback of the timeline in which it is contained. In the following steps, you add Play and Stop buttons to the Main Timeline to control the video.

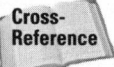

Cross-Reference   To learn more about basic actions and Button instances, read Chapter 18, "Understanding Actions and Event Handlers."

For this example, open the `sampleVideo_100.fla` file from the `ch17` folder of this book's CD-ROM. Alternatively, you can start a new file and embed a new video file into the Flash document. You should have an Embedded Video object on a layer in the Main Timeline (that is, Scene 1) before you proceed with the steps.

1. Add a new layer, and rename it *buttons*.

2. Open the Buttons library (Window ➪ Other Panels ➪ Common Libraries ➪ Buttons). From this library's Circle Buttons folder, drag instances of the Play and Stop buttons to the Stage. Position them under the video, as shown in Figure 17-8.

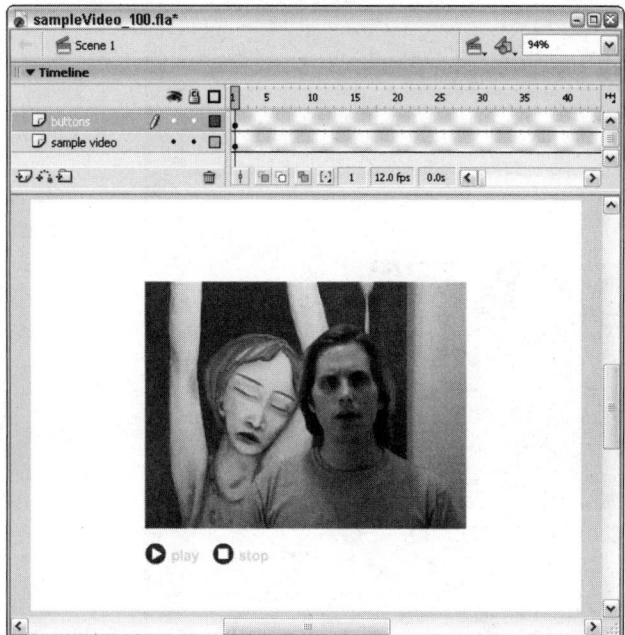

Figure 17-8: The Play and Stop buttons positioned under the video

3. Select the Play button instance on the Stage, and open the Actions panel (F9). Type the following actions into the Script pane:

```
on (release){
    play();
}
```

4. Select the Stop button instance, and open the Actions panel (F9). Type the following actions into the Script pane:

```
on (release) {
    stop();
}
```

5. Save your Flash document as `sampleVideo_200.fla`, and test it (Ctrl+Enter or ⌘+Enter). Click the Stop button to stop the video, and click the Play button to resume play.

6. Now, let's stop the video from playing at the beginning at the movie. Create a new layer named **actions**, and select frame 1 of this layer. Open the Actions panel, and type the following action in the Script pane:

```
stop();
```

7. Open the Buttons library once again, and select the Buttons layer in the Timeline window. Drag instances of the Rewind, Step Ahead, and Step Back buttons onto the Stage. Position these instances below the video, as shown in Figure 17-9.

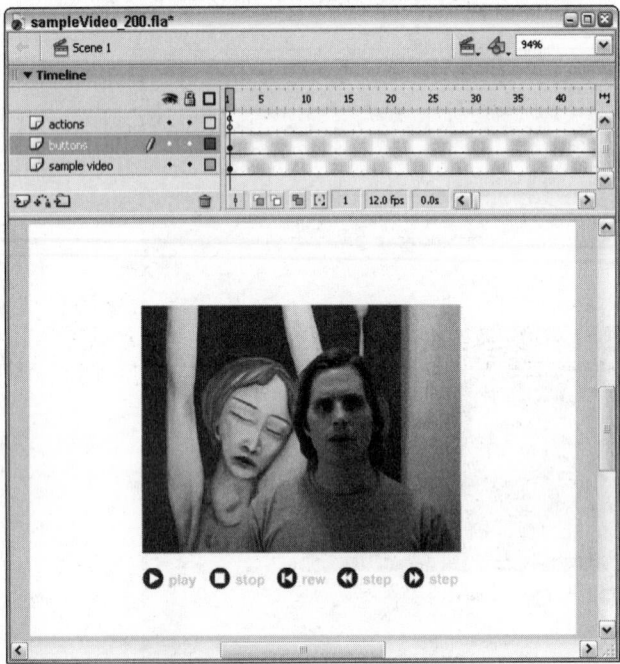

Figure 17-9: These buttons add more playback control to the video clip.

8. With the Rewind instance selected, open the Actions panel (F9) and type the following actions into the Script pane:

```
on (release){
    gotoAndStop(1);
}
```

9. With the Step Back instance selected, type the following actions into the Script pane of the Actions panel:

```
on (release){
    prevFrame();
}
```

10. With the Step Ahead instance selected, type the following actions into the Script pane of the Actions panel:

```
on (release){
    nextFrame();
}
```

11. Save your Flash document again, and test it (Ctrl+Enter or ⌘+Enter). Try out each of your control buttons. If one didn't work, go back and check its code in the Actions panel.

On the CD-ROM

You can view the completed Flash document, sampleVideo_200.fla, located in the ch17 folder of the book's CD-ROM. This document has additional background graphics.

Placing and controlling video within a Movie Clip

While you can place Embedded Video objects on the Main Timeline of a Flash movie, you may find it useful to place video within a Movie Clip symbol, and reuse instances of that Movie Clip throughout the document. In the following steps, you change the structure of the sampleVideo_200.fla to make a control bar MovieClip object, as well as a video MovieClip object. For this example, open the sampleVideo_200.fla file from the ch17 folder of this book's CD-ROM.

1. In the Timeline window, expand the contents of the background folder. Lock the following layers: sample video, video frame, and video background. Then, select all of the Button instances and remaining background element by choosing Edit ⇨ Select All (Ctrl+A or ⌘+A). Your document should resemble Figure 17-10.

2. With these items selected, choose Modify ⇨ Convert to Symbol (F8). In the Symbol Properties dialog box, type the name **controlBarClip**. Select the Movie Clip behavior as well, and click OK.

3. With this new MovieClip object selected on the Stage, open the Property inspector and assign the instance name controlBar_mc. Rename the buttons layer to **controlBar_mc**, and delete the empty button background layer.

4. Unlock the sample video layer, and select the Embedded Video instance on the Stage. Press the F8 key to convert this object to a Movie Clip symbol. In the Symbol Properties dialog box, name this symbol **myVideoClip**. When you click OK, you see a message asking if you want to assign more frames to the symbol's timeline. Choose Yes on this dialog box.

5. With the new symbol selected on the Stage, open the Property inspector and give the instance the name myVideo_mc. Now that the instance is named, you can target this Movie Clip instance with ActionScript. Rename the sample video layer to **myVideo_mc** as well.

6. Now you need to update the ActionScript code on each of the Button instances within the controlBar_mc instance. Double-click the controlBar_mc instance on the Stage to edit the symbol in place.

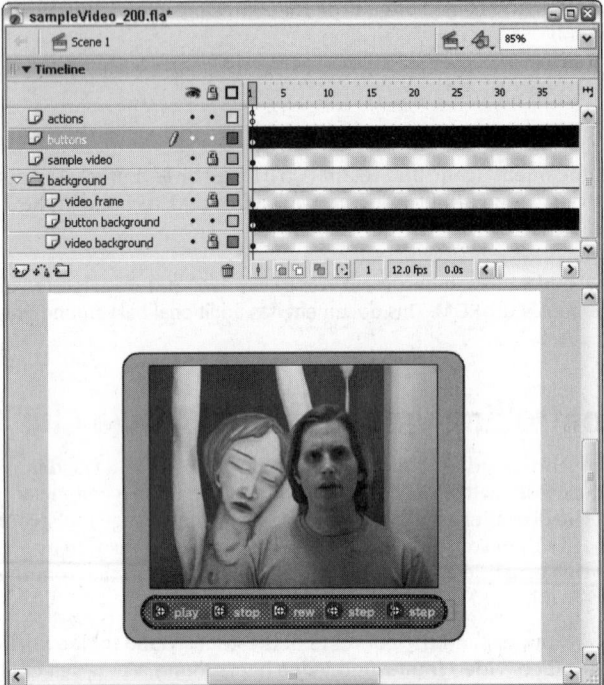

Figure 17-10: Select all of the Button instances and the artwork behind them.

7. For each of the buttons, insert the path `this._parent.myVideo_mc.` in front of each navigation action. For example, for the Play button, the code in the Script pane should be changed to:

```
on (release){
    this._parent.myVideo_mc.play();
}
```

8. Save your Flash document as `sampleVideo_300.fla`, and test it (Ctrl+Enter or ⌘+Enter). Notice that the video automatically starts to play. You can control the playback of the video by using the buttons in the `controlBar_mc` instance.

On the CD-ROM

You can find the completed file, `sampleVideo_300.fla`, in the `ch17` folder of the *Macromedia Flash MX 2004 Bible* CD-ROM.

You can tidy the Main Timeline of the Flash document by deleting frames 2 through 87. Also, if you want to stop the video from playing when the movie first loads, place a `stop();` action on frame 1 of the `myVideo_mc` timeline.

By placing your video in a Movie Clip, you can more easily reuse this control bar with other video clips. Simply create a new Flash document, import the video source file, and nest it in a

Movie Clip symbol. Name the instance `myVideo_mc`, and copy and paste the `controlBar_mc` instance from this exercise's document to your new document. Make sure that the `control Bar_mc` and `myVideo_mc` instances are on the same timeline; otherwise, the target path assigned in the Buttons' actions will not work.

Tip   To stop the video from automatically looping, place a `stop()`; action on the last frame of the `myVideoClip` timeline.

Publishing Flash Movies with Video

When you use Embedded Video objects in a Flash movie, you're making the decision to use rather large file sizes on the Web. One of Flash's original claims to fame is the ability to stream lightweight animation, graphics, and sound over the Web. While it may seem contrary to use video for lightweight graphics, video can be streamed into Flash Player 6 or higher. Careful attention must be given to the data rate of the Flash movie containing the video. Use the following guidelines for matching a target data rate to a specific video frame size:

✦ **Dial-up modem:** This connection speed includes 28.8, 33.6, and 56 Kbps modems. For these data rates, we recommend that you use video at 160 x 120 (or smaller), at 6 fps or slower.

✦ **Broadband or LAN connection:** If your target audience has a fast Internet connection such as DSL, cable, high-speed wireless, T1, or T3, you have much more flexibility with your data rate options for Flash video. A common video size for this connection type is 320 x 240, with a frame rate of 15 fps or higher. However, because the video frame rate is tied to the frame rate of the Flash movie, you may want to stick with 12 fps, the default frame rate for documents in Flash MX 2004.

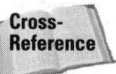

Cross-Reference   The Flash Video Exporter and third-party tools such as Sorenson Squeeze offer several output settings for Flash Video, to use with various connection speeds. We discuss some of these tools later in this chapter.

In truth, Macromedia Flash movies do not stream into the Flash Player — they download progressively. Video streaming, as it is referred to by QuickTime, RealOne, and Windows Media Players, means that the video file is never downloaded as one single file to the end-user. Rather, a streaming video server delivers the video in real-time, sending the video frame by frame to the player.

Note   Macromedia Flash Communication Server MX is the only server-side solution that can deliver Flash audio and video streams in real-time.

A progressive download, on the other hand, is downloaded to the player. However, the term *progressive* means that the video can start playback as soon as a certain percent of the video has downloaded into the player. So, while a 5MB file size may sound large for the Web, the user may not have to wait for the entire 5MB to download in order to begin his/her viewing of the video. Macromedia offers the following formula to determine the average wait time for a given video clip:

wait time = total download time – clip duration + 10% of clip duration

So, if you have a Flash movie (SWF file) that's 300 KB with a duration of 20 seconds, a user with a 56 Kbps modem with an average download rate of 4.7 KB/s will wait an estimated 64 seconds for the entire file to download (300 KB ÷ 4.7 KB/s = 63.8 seconds). However, using the formula, you can calculate how long the user must wait before the movie begins playback:

64 seconds − 20 seconds + 2 seconds = 46 seconds

During longer wait times, you may want to offer some interim activity while the user waits, such as some important news to read, a simple game, or an interesting animation.

Many dial-up users are willing to wait for larger high-quality digital video files. Therefore, you may want to offer visitors the choice to select which video file they want to download.

We show you how to build preloaders for Flash movies and assets in Chapter 28, "Sharing and Loading Assets." In that chapter, you also learn how to progressively download Flash Video files (FLV files) at runtime.

Storing video in a separate Flash movie

Anytime you have a very large asset (in file size) that you want to use in a Flash movie on the Web, your best bet is to make it its own Flash movie (SWF file) that loads into your "master" Flash movie for the Web site (or page). This idea holds true for sound files, video files, and bitmap graphics. In this section, we show you how to put an Embedded Video object into a timeline, make it a Flash movie (SWF file), and load it into another Flash movie.

Now that Flash Player 7 can load Flash Video files (FLV files) directly into Flash movies (SWF files), you may want to explore the loading of Flash Video (FLV files) at runtime , as discussed in Chapter 28. One caveat, though, to the use of FLV files is that you can't retrieve the length (in seconds or bytes) of the FLV file. As such, it can be cumbersome and difficult to make dynamic playback bars.

For this example, make a copy of the `sampleVideo_300.fla` file, located in the `ch17` folder of the *Macromedia Flash MX 2004 Bible* CD-ROM.

1. Open the `sampleVideo_300.fla` file, and double-click the `myVideo_mc` instance on the Stage. Inside of the myVideoClip symbol, select the Embedded Video object and delete it. You should have nothing in the myVideoClip symbol.

2. Delete frames 2 through 87 of the myVideoClip timeline.

You can click and drag a selection across frame 2 through 87 and press Shift+F5 to remove the selected span of frames.

3. Go back to the Main Timeline (that is, Scene 1). You will now see a small white dot at the top left corner of the video frame artwork, as shown in Figure 17-11. The X and Y coordinates of this position are 115, 80, respectively. In later steps, you will load the video file (as another SWF file) into this empty instance.

4. Now create a new Flash document while leaving the `sampleVideo_300.fla` open. Open the Library for the `sampleVideo_300.fla` document, and drag the `sample_high.avi` Embedded Video asset to the Stage of the new document. When the message box appears asking if you want to add 87 frames to the timeline, click Yes.

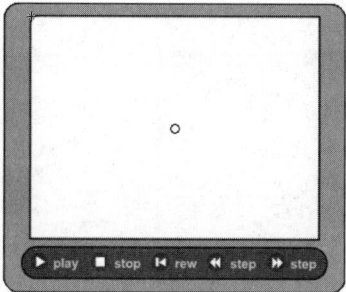

Figure 17-11: The empty Movie Clip holds the external video SWF file.

5. Save the new Flash document as **video.fla**.

6. In the Property inspector, change the width of the Embedded Video instance on the new document's stage to 320 pixels. Remember that this clip was imported from DV format footage, with a nonsquare pixel aspect ratio.

7. Change the width and height of the video.fla document to match the dimensions of the Embedded Video instance. In this example, the width of the video is 320 pixels, and the height is 240. Choose Modify ➪ Document to change these dimensions.

8. Center the Embedded Video instance on the Stage, using the Align panel. Alternatively, you can use the Flash MX 2004 shortcut, Ctrl+Alt+2 or ⌘+Option+2 to center vertically, and Ctrl+Alt+5 or ⌘+Option+5 to center horizontally.

9. Resave the `video.fla` document, and test it (Ctrl+Enter or ⌘+Enter). Close the Test Movie window after you've verified that the Embedded Video instance plays.

10. Close the `video.fla` document, and go back to the `sampleVideo_300.fla`. In the next few steps, you add the ActionScript to load the `video.swf` file you created in Step 9. The `myVideo_mc` instance will be the target of a `loadMovie()` action.

11. On the Main Timeline of the `sample_300.fla` document, create a new layer and name it **myText_txt**. In the next steps, you will add a Dynamic text field to this layer, and the text "Load video" will appear in the field. You will add a link to this text to initiate a `loadMovie()` action into the `myVideo_mc` instance, using the `video.swf` as the movie to be loaded.

12. Select the Text tool, and click once on the Stage. Make sure you create this text on the myText_txt layer. In the field, type **Load video**.

13. With the text field selected, open the Property inspector. Give this field an instance name of **myText_txt**, and enable the HTML button. (If you are unfamiliar with text fields, see Chapter 8, "Working with Text.")

14. Select the "Load video" text in the text field, and in the Property inspector, type the following ActionScript code in the URL field. This code uses the `asfunction` available for HTML text fields in Flash movies. We discuss the `asfunction` in Chapter 31, "Applying HTML and Text Field Formatting." This code links the "Load video" text to execute the `loadMovie()` action with the `myVideo_mc` instance, specifying the `video.swf` file to load into the `myVideo_mc` instance. When you are finished, your document will resemble Figure 17-12.

```
asfunction:myVideo_mc.loadMovie,video.swf
```

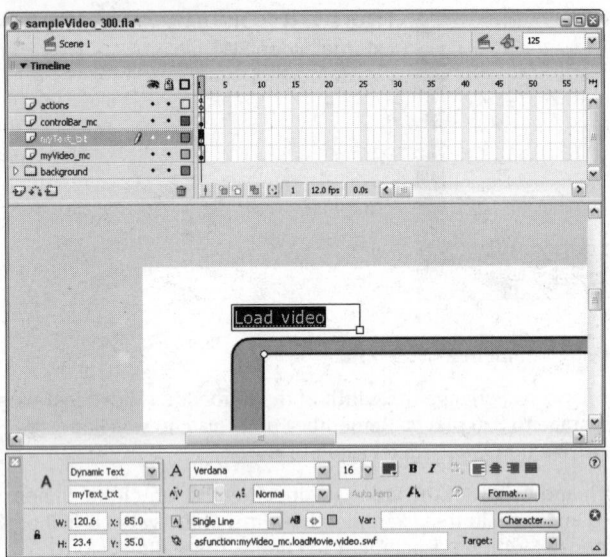

Figure 17-12: The "Load video" text is linked to ActionScript code.

15. Save your Flash document as **sampleVideo_400.fla**, and test it (Ctrl+Enter or ⌘+Enter). Click the "Load video" text, and the `video.swf` loads into the `myVideo_mc` instance and begins to play.

On the CD-ROM   You can find the completed Flash documents, `sampleVideo_400.fla` and `video.fla`, in the `ch17` folder of the *Macromedia Flash MX 2004 Bible* CD-ROM.

With this workflow, you can create several video documents and publish them as individual Flash movies (SWF files). Then change the URL for the "Load video" text to point to the new file, replacing the existing filename.

Tip   If you have extraordinarily long video content which reaches the 16,000 frame limit of a Flash movie (SWF file), you will likely want to load a Flash Video file (FLV file) directly with ActionScript, as discussed in Chapter 28.

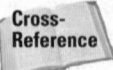

Cross-Reference   In Chapter 28, "Sharing and Loading Assets," you learn how to display a loading progress bar for assets such as video and sound files.

Using named anchors with video timelines

Flash Player 6 introduced a new Web browser feature: named anchors. A named anchor is a special frame label on the Main Timeline of a Flash movie that registers in the browser's history. The history remembers all of the Web pages that a user has visited during the current browser session. (Depending on the browser preferences, the histories can store months of

Web page URLs.) One major complaint with previous versions of the Flash Player was that pressing the Back button on the Web browser would take the user to a different Web page instead of a prior scene or frame label in the Flash movie. For example, if a Web visitor came to your all-Flash site and clicked one menu, and then went somewhere else in the movie, he/she would have no way of pressing the Back button on the browser to get to that last "place" seen in the Flash movie; the Web browser would simply refresh to the very beginning of the Flash movie, or go to the last HTML page visited. You can also bookmark specific sections of a Flash movie—the named anchor appends a label to the end of the file's URL.

Caution

Named anchors are supported in Flash Player 6 only on browsers that support the fscommand with JavaScript, such as Internet Explorer for Windows or Netscape 3.x to 4.x and Netscape 7 or higher. Netscape 6 does not support the fscommand action. To learn more about named anchors and browsers that support them, read Chapter 20, "Making Your First Flash MX 2004 Project."

In this section, you learn how to add named anchors to a Flash movie with an Embedded Video object. You will make an anchor at any defining moment in your video clip. Then, you will publish the Flash movie with an HTML document and watch the video play in Internet Explorer for Windows. You can also test the movie in Netscape 3.x–4.x or Netscape 7 or higher on either Mac or Windows. As each named anchor plays, you will be able to hit the browser's Back button to go back to the previous named anchor.

On the CD-ROM

Open the video_anchors_starter.fla file, located in the ch17/anchors folder of the *Macromedia Flash MX 2004 Bible* CD-ROM.

1. Create a new layer in the starter document, and name the layer **labels**.

2. Insert a keyframe on frame 2 of the labels layer. In the Property inspector, assign the frame label **marker_1** to this keyframe. In the Label type menu, choose **Anchor** (see Figure 17-13).

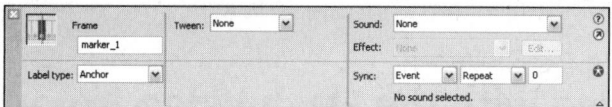

Figure 17-13: Frame labels can also be named anchors.

3. Place more keyframes and named anchors along the Main Timeline. Place them wherever you'd like to tag an area of the video. For example, you can add frame labels marker_2, marker_3, marker_4, and marker_5 at frames 130, 210, 280, and 435, respectively. Again, make sure you select the Anchor option in the Label type menu.

4. Create a new layer, and name it **actions**. On frame 1 of the actions layer, add a stop(); action in the Actions panel. Also add a stop(); action to frame 435 of the actions layer. These are the first and last keyframes of the movie, respectively.

5. Save your Flash document as **video_anchors.fla**. Open the Publish Settings (File ➪ Publish Settings) and click the HTML tab. In the Template menu, choose Flash with Named Anchors. This template inserts a JavaScript function into the HTML document that will catch the named anchors as they play in the browser.

6. Preview the Flash movie within an HTML document by choosing File ➪ Publish Preview ➪ HTML. When the Flash movie loads into the Web browser, the video clip will be paused. Click the Play button, and the video will play. As the video plays, the URL of the HTML document will change. For example, when the marker_1 frame plays, you'll see the document URL change to video_anchors.html#marker_1. When you reach the end of the movie, press the browser's Back button. If the last anchor that played was marker_5, pressing the Back button will take you to the marker_4 label.

Tip

You can reduce your wait times for publishing lengthy video clips by setting the audio codec in the Audio stream settings (found in the Flash tab of the Publish Settings dialog box) to Raw. This codec requires no compression and greatly reduces your wait times. However, only use this codec for testing purposes while you're developing the Flash movie. When you're ready to produce the final Flash movie (SWF file), make sure you choose a more optimal codec such as MP3 and an appropriate bitrate for your target audience.

On the CD-ROM

You can find the finished example file, video_anchors.fla, in the ch17/anchors folder of the *Macromedia Flash MX 2004 Bible* CD-ROM. This file includes an additional action on frame 1 to keep the Stage of the Flash movie from scaling in the browser: Stage.scaleMode = "noScale";. The HTML tab of the Publish Settings is also set to use 100% of the width and height of the browser window. Combined, these two changes allow the movie to appear centered in the browser window without scaling.

You can go back to the Flash document and adjust the placement of your named anchors. You can also use named anchors to create bookmarks. When you view a specific anchor that you'd like to go to straight away, create a bookmark. Named anchors work only with the Main Timeline (that is, Scene timelines) of the current movie loaded in the browser. This means you can't make named anchors inside of Movie Clip timelines or in timelines of movies loaded into Level 1 or higher of the Flash Player.

Note

If you access a bookmarked Flash movie (or HTML page) in the browser, you need to wait for all prior frames of the Flash movie to load into the browser. The browser can't request an individual portion of a Flash movie (SWF file) to download.

Optimizing Video with the Flash Video Exporter

Flash MX Professional 2004 ships with an awesome new utility called the Flash Video Exporter tool. This tool is not accessible from any menu or command in the Flash MX Pro 2004 authoring environment. Rather, the tool works with other video applications such as Adobe After Effects or Apple Final Cut Pro to export high-quality Flash Video files (FLV files) that use the Sorenson Spark Pro codec. Once you have created an .flv file, you can import the file into a Flash MX 2004 document. Or, you can load the FLV file into a Flash movie (SWF file) at runtime in Flash Player 7, using ActionScript or a component.

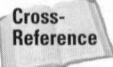

Cross-Reference

Learn more about the Sorenson Spark Pro codec in our coverage of Sorenson Squeeze later in this chapter.

Installing the Flash Video Exporter

The Flash Video Exporter is not automatically installed when you run the installer for Flash MX Pro 2004. You need to run the Flash Video Exporter installer separately. You can find this installer on this book's CD-ROM, or you can find it on your Macromedia Flash MX Professional 2004 installation CD-ROM. If you downloaded the trial version from the Macromedia site, the Flash Video Exporter installer is included.

You should be running Apple QuickTime 6.1.1 or higher on your system in order to use the Flash Video Exporter tool. You can download the QuickTime 6 at www.apple.com/quicktime. You do not need the Pro version of QuickTime Player to use the Flash Video Exporter in most applications. In the next section, though, we demonstrate the use of the Flash Video Exporter from QuickTime Player Pro. You can't export video (of any type) in the basic version of QuickTime Player.

Note   Not much happens during the installation process, which doesn't take very long. The installer simply places a new QuickTime component on to your system. Be sure to reboot your machine after you run the installer.

Caution   You must install the Flash Video Exporter on a computer system that is running a licensed or trial version of Flash MX Professional 2004. Otherwise, the Exporter will not work.

Using the Flash Video Exporter

Most applications that support QuickTime output can utilize the new Flash Video Exporter tool. In this section, you learn how to export a high-quality Flash Video file (FLV file) from Apple QuickTime Player Pro. You must be using the Pro edition of QuickTime Player to complete this exercise. If you don't have QuickTime Player Pro, we suggest that you read through these steps and see if you can apply the same procedure in your preferred video application. Usually, you will find the Flash Video Exporter in the File ➪ Export option (or some variation thereof) in your video editing application.

On the CD-ROM   You'll need a source video file to use in QuickTime Player Pro. You can use the sample_high.avi file found in the ch17/source folder of this book's CD-ROM.

1. Open QuickTime Player Pro on your Windows or Mac computer.

2. Choose File ➪ Open Movie in New Player, and browse to the location of the video file you want to compress in Flash Video format. For this example, we use the sample_high.avi file from this book's CD-ROM.

3. Once the file has opened in the player, choose File ➪ Export. In the Save exported file as dialog box, choose Movie to Macromedia Flash Video in the Export menu, as shown in Figure 17-14. Do not click any other options at this time.

4. Now click the Options button. As you can see in Figure 17-15, here's where the magic happens. The extra options you see in this dialog box are more precise than those in the Video Import Wizard. Furthermore, most of the options cannot be replicated in the Video Import Wizard, such as VBR encoding. You learn more about VBR encoding in the Sorenson Squeeze coverage later in this chapter. To quickly show you the power of the Flash Video Exporter tool, choose the options shown in Figure 17-15 and click OK.

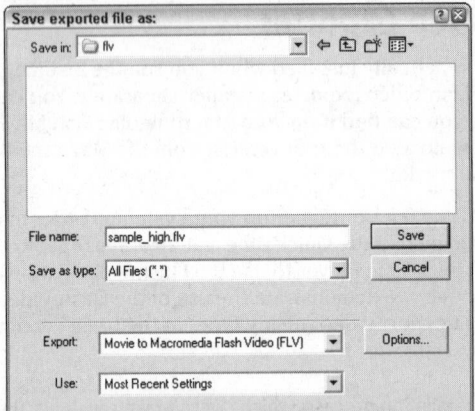

Figure 17-14: The Export menu option in QuickTime Player Pro, shown in the Windows version

Note

Regardless of the video application you use, the dialog box shown in Figure 17-15 is exactly the same. You always have access to these options from any compatible video-editing program.

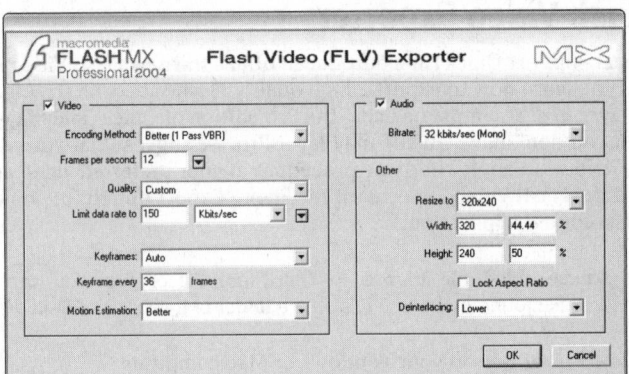

Figure 17-15: The Flash Video Exporter options

Cross-Reference

For a complete description of each setting in the Flash Video Exporter options, search the Flash MX 2004 Help panel for "Flash Video Exporter," and expand the "To export an FLV file from a supported application" section.

5. In the export dialog box of QuickTime Player, click the Save button. (If you want to specify a new location and/or filename, do so before clicking the Save button.) QuickTime then exports the FLV file from the source video file.

On the CD-ROM

You can see the output file from this example, sample_high.flv, in the ch17/flv folder of this book's CD-ROM.

After you have created an FLV file, you can import it into a Flash document. Try comparing the quality and file size of the FLV created in this exercise with that of file from an earlier exercise. We're sure you'll be pleasantly surprised with the results.

Tip   You can also use the FLV files produced by the Flash Video Exporter (or a third-party application such as Sorenson Squeeze or Wildform Flix) with Flash Communication Server applications. With Flash Communication Server, FLV files can be streamed in real-time.

Using Sorenson Squeeze for Flash Video

Needless to say, the plain fact Macromedia Flash MX 2004 can import and embed video files playable by Flash Player 6 or higher is truly remarkable. Just when you thought you've seen everything, we need to tell you that your journey with Flash video doesn't end with the Flash MX 2004 authoring tool or the Flash Video Exporter tool. The native video compressor in Flash MX 2004's Video Import Wizard is Sorenson Spark Basic edition. As you've already seen, the compressor options within the wizard are much more limited than those in the Flash Video Exporter tool. What you can't see in Video Import Wizard is that the Basic edition of Sorenson Spark encodes only in CBR, or constant bitrate. CBR encoding means each frame of the video is uniformly compressed, consuming the same (or constant) data rate throughout the entirety of the clip. If you're familiar with MP3 sound, you may already be aware of CBR encoding with music. The same principle applies to video compression as well.

We all know, however, that each frame of video may not require the same amount of data to describe. For example, a solid field of blue (such as a big blue sky) may not need as much data as a field of multi-colored flowers, where several pixels in the frame have a different color. If your video footage contains a mixture of compositions and subject matter, it could benefit from another type of encoding known as VBR, or variable bitrate. VBR encoding enables the compressor to change the rate of compression applied to each frame of video. Therefore, one frame may need only 200 bytes, whereas another may need as many as 400 bytes. In practice, just about all video footage can benefit from VBR encoding. One of the drawbacks to encoding with VBR is that it takes longer to compress a video clip than it does with CBR encoding.

Unfortunately, Flash MX 2004's Video Import Wizard does not allow you to apply VBR encoding to imported files. However, the Flash Video Exporter tool can compress video in CBR and VBR encodings. Macromedia has also teamed up with Sorenson to offer an application that does: Sorenson Squeeze 3. This application, which is sold separately from Flash MX 2004, comes in two editions:

✦ **Flash MX only:** This version of Squeeze creates Flash FLV and SWF files using the Sorenson Spark Pro codec, which we describe later in this section.

✦ **Compression Suite:** This version can output several multimedia audio/video formats, including DVD MPEG2, VCD MPEG1, QuickTime video movies (.mov files), Windows Media files, RealPlayer files, Flash Video files (FLVfiles), and Flash movies (SWF files). For the purposes of our coverage, we discuss this version in the remainder of the chapter, but we only use features that are available in both the Flash MX and Compression Suite editions.

Note   At the time of this writing, Sorenson Squeeze was in release version 3.5 for Windows and 3.1 for Macintosh.

Sorenson Squeeze enables you to compress video files with Sorenson Spark Pro, which can use 2-pass VBR encoding, which means that Squeeze carefully examines each frame of video — twice. On the first pass, Squeeze analyzes the content of each frame. On the second pass, Squeeze performs the actual encoding, using the information it gathered from the first pass. The following list describes the added functionality Sorenson Squeeze offers beyond the native capabilities of Flash MX 2004's Video Import Wizard:

✦ **Superior encoding control:** Sorenson Squeeze can use either CBR or 2-pass VBR compression with your digital video. You can adjust audio and video data rates independently, and specify other codec options not available in Flash MX. We discuss these options in a later section.

✦ **Batch processing:** You can create several output versions of your digital video files with Sorenson Squeeze. Using the compression presets (discussed later), you can make a variety of low- and high-bandwidth movies all in one go.

✦ **DV capture:** Sorenson Squeeze can capture video directly from a DV source, over an IEEE 1394 (also known as FireWire or iLink) connection. Just connect your DV camcorder or deck to the computer and capture a live feed from the camera.

✦ **Multiple output formats:** Sorenson Squeeze can open several file formats and output several popular audio/video formats, including QuickTime Sorenson Video 3.0, Flash movie (SWF file), or Flash video (FLV file) formats. As such, you can make different movie formats for all of your Web video needs. You can use the Flash movie or Flash video formats with your Flash-based Web material and use other formats for non-Flash Web pages.

✦ **Filter settings:** You can adjust the contrast, brightness, gamma, white restore, and black restore of the video image. Squeeze can also de-interlace your video footage, reduce video noise, crop the video frame, and fade the footage in and/or out. You can even normalize the audio track of the video file.

✦ **Compression Presets:** Perhaps the most useful feature of Sorenson Squeeze is the ability to use bandwidth presets for your video compression. Squeeze has predefined compression options for the following connection speeds: Modem, ISDN, Broadband Low, Broadband, Broadband High, LAN CD, and CD High Quality. You can adjust the compression settings of each preset, but you cannot add your own custom presets.

 You can download a trial version of Sorenson Squeeze at www.sorenson.com.

Choosing a Flash output file type

After you install the demo version of Sorenson Squeeze 3.5 (or 3.1 on Mac), go ahead and launch the application. The Sorenson Squeeze interface is shown in Figure 17-16. The output formats are represented as three file icons in the application's toolbar.

For any given video file, you can enable one or more of these formats to be exported in a batch.

Flash SWF output

Flash FLV output

Figure 17-16: You can choose from several output formats in Sorenson Squeeze 3 Compression Suite.

Flash Video

As you learned throughout this chapter, a Flash Video file (FLV file) is a video file that has been compressed with the Sorenson Spark codec. As such, it can be quickly imported into a Flash MX 2004 document — no further video encoding is necessary. Just like regular video files (such as AVI or MOV files), Flash Video files have a frame rate, frame size (dimensions), and an optional audio track. Once you import the Flash Video file into your Flash document, you can add further interactivity to it with ActionScript. We show you how to import a Flash Video file later in this chapter. You can also dynamically load Flash Video files into a Flash Player 7-compatible movie, or with a Flash Player 6-compatible movie connected to a Flash Communication Server application.

Caution

If you are importing a Flash Video file into a Flash document, make sure your Flash Video file uses the same frame rate as the Flash document that will be hosting it. If your Flash movie's frame rate is slower than the Flash Video's frame rate, the video will play at the slower frame rate and lose sync with its audio track. Alternatively, you can match the frame rate of your Flash movie to that of the Flash video file. This cautionary note does not apply to FLV files that are loaded at runtime.

Flash Movie

Squeeze can also create fully functional Flash movies (.swf files) from your digital video files. If you don't need to add anything to your video in Flash MX 2004, you can simply choose your digital file and specify a compression setting for the Flash movie (.swf file) to be output from Squeeze. Voila! You have an instant Flash movie that can be loaded into an existing Flash movie with the `loadMovie()` action, or viewed independently in a separate HTML document.

Tip

You can create Flash movies (SWF files) containing video with frame rates different from Flash movies that load them. This means that you can create a 15 fps Flash movie from Sorenson Squeeze and load it into a slower playing 12 fps Flash movie. As soon as the Flash movie with video starts to play, both movies will play at the speed of the Flash movie with video. Video content is treated just like Stream sound in the Flash Player—it will govern the player's frame rate.

Compressing video with Sorenson Spark Pro

In this section of the chapter, we walk you through the process of encoding video with Sorenson Spark Pro and using either Flash FLV or SWF output in other Flash presentations. While you will create one Flash FLV file and one Flash movie (.swf file), you do not need to create both file types to incorporate video into your Flash project. Flash Video files can be imported into existing Flash MX 2004 documents or loaded directly into Flash Player 7. Flash movies can be loaded directly into Flash Player 6.

On the CD-ROM

Make a copy of the `sample_high.avi` file, located in the `ch17/sources` folder of the *Macromedia Flash MX 2004 Bible* CD-ROM.

1. Open Sorenson Squeeze 3.5 (or 3.1 on Mac), and choose File ➪ Open. Browse to the `sample_high.avi` file that you copied from the book's CD-ROM.

2. Press the Flash FLV Output and Flash SWF Output buttons on the Squeeze toolbar.

3. Now press the Filter Settings button (that is, the one with wrench icon) on the toolbar. Select the Contrast check box, and drag the slider to the first tick mark left of the center. Check the Normalize Audio option as well, as shown in Figure 17-17. Click OK.

Figure 17-17: Boosting the contrast of the image improves this video's appearance on computer monitors, especially if the original source footage was captured with a camcorder.

4. Choose the **300k** option in the Streaming compression menu in the right half of the toolbar, shown in Figure 17-18. This adds two files to the Output Files queue, as shown in Figure 17-19. These files will be saved in the same folder as the original source video file.

Figure 17-18: Sorenson Squeeze has several compression presets available in the toolbar.

Figure 17-19: The Output Files queue lists the files that are waiting to be encoded.

5. Squeeze is ready to encode the Flash Video file (FLV file) and Flash movie (SWF file) from the original source video. Press the Squeeze It button in the lower right corner of the application window. Squeeze starts the encoding process for the output files. You can preview the compression by clicking the Preview On button in the Squeezing dialog box. When the compression is finished, click the Close button and quit the Squeeze application.

You can find the `sample_high_300k.flv` and `sample_high_300k.swf` files in the `ch17/squeeze` folder of the *Macromedia Flash MX 2004 Bible* CD-ROM.

We'd like to know what you thought about this chapter. Visit `www.flashsupport.com/feedback` to fill out an online form with your comments.

Summary

✦ Flash MX 2004 encodes video with the Sorenson Spark Basic edition codec, which uses CBR (constant bitrate) encoding. You have limited control over the compression options in Flash MX 2004, but the new Video Import Wizard offers many editing options than the previous release of Flash.

✦ The Sorenson Spark codec is built into Flash Player 6 or higher. Web users will not need to download additional software to view video in Flash 6 movies.

✦ The Flash Video Exporter tool can be used any computer with a licensed (or trial) version of Flash MX Professional 2004. This utility creates higher quality video files, in the FLV format, than Flash MX 2004's Video Import Wizard can create.

✦ The Flash Video Exporter tool can use one of several encoding techniques, including VBR encoding with the Sorenson Spark Pro codec.

✦ Sorenson Squeeze can compress Flash Video files (FLV files) or Flash movies (SWF files) with the Sorenson Spark Pro edition codec. Squeeze is a separate application that is not included with the Flash MX 2004 (or Professional) installation.

✦ Pay attention to the frame rate you use for Flash Video and Flash movie output from Sorenson Squeeze.

✦   ✦   ✦

Adding Basic Interactivity to Flash Movies

So far you've been learning how to make *things*–drawing shapes, creating symbols, and working with frames and adding special assets. In the next three chapters you learn how to integrate these various elements and how to make things *happen*. Chapter 18 introduces the concepts you need to understand when adding interactivity to presentations. Chapter 18 also gives you an orientation in the Flash MX 2004 Actions panel, where you will find some changes from Flash MX. Chapter 19 gives you the skills needed to control playback of multiple timelines. Find out how easy it is to use ActionScript to control display of internal elements in your Flash movies, including nested Movie Clips. See how Flash MX 2004 Behaviors can be applied to control sound playback. If you want to apply these concepts and techniques to real Flash production, Chapter 20 has just what you need – a step-by-step explanation of how to build a basic Flash presentation with a non-linear interface. The project introduces some other important Flash MX 2004 features such as components, named anchor keyframes, and accessibility options.

Understanding Actions and Event Handlers

Interactivity in a Flash movie can broadly be thought of as the elements that react and respond to a user's activity or input. A user has many ways to give input to a Flash movie, and Flash has even more ways to react. But how does interactivity actually work? It all starts with actions and event handlers.

Actions and Event Handlers

Even the most complex interactivity in Flash is fundamentally composed of two basic parts: the *behavior* (what happens), and the *cause* of the behavior (what makes it happen). Here's a simple example: Suppose you have a looping soundtrack in a movie and a button that, when clicked, turns the soundtrack off. The *behavior* is the sound turning off, and the *cause* of the behavior is the mouse clicking the button. Another example is stopping an animation when it reaches a certain frame on its timeline. When the last keyframe of the animation is played (the *cause*), an action on that keyframe stops the animation (the *behavior*). In Flash, the building blocks of behaviors are referred to as *actions*.

New Feature   Flash MX 2004 introduces a new interactive authoring tool, the Behaviors panel. Our usage of the term *behaviors* in the preceding description should not be confused with this new feature. The Behaviors panel, which you learn about later in this chapter, enables you to quickly add an action or series of actions to a Flash object or keyframe.

The first step in learning how to make interactive movies is becoming familiar with the list of possible actions. However, actions can't act without being told to act *by* something. That something is often the mouse pointer coming in contact with a button, but it can also be a keystroke, or simply a command issued from a keyframe. We refer to any occurrence that can cause an action to happen (such as the button click in the preceding example) as an *event*. The mechanism we use to tell Flash what action to perform when an event occurs is known as an *event handler*. This cause-and-effect relationship seems obvious, but it is an extremely important concept. For the purposes of creating basic interactivity, the difference between an action and the cause of an action is merely a practical detail. As the set of Flash actions, collectively know as *ActionScript*, continues to grow with each release of the Flash authoring tool (and therefore the interactive capabilities that they provide), understanding the relationship between actions and the things that cause them can be the key to adding more sophisticated behavior to your movies with traditional programming techniques. Every interactive framework, whether it is Macromedia Flash or Macromedia Director or Apple DVD Studio Pro, has unique handlers for specific events. Table 18-1 relates interactive events with Flash handlers.

Table 18-1: Events and Flash Handlers

Event	Type	Event handler	Example
Playback	Time-based	Keyframes `MovieClip` object `NetStream` object	Timeline plays until it reaches a certain frame; a Movie Clip instance monitors the amount of time that has passed in a movie; when a video stream stops playing, another stream begins playback.
Mouse	User input	`Button` object `MovieClip` object `Mouse` object	Visitor clicks a button; mouse movement detected over a Movie Clip instance.
Key press	User input	`Button` object `MovieClip` object `Key` object	User presses the Enter key to submit a form; an alert appears if the Caps Lock key is enabled.
Microphone or Webcam activity	Audio/video input	`Microphone` object `Camera` object	When a user stops talking into a microphone, a graphic turns red; a stream starts to record audio and video when movement is detected in front of a Webcam.
Data	System-based	`MovieClip` object data objects	Search results display in the Flash movie when the results have fully loaded.

While the breadth and depth of ActionScript involved with the interactions described in Table 18-1 may seem overwhelming, don't worry—we're taking it one step at a time. First, you learn about what the new Behaviors panel can do. Then you learn how to set up the Actions panel, whose look and feel has changed from Flash MX. Later, we'll look at actions that control movie playback. Later in this chapter, you'll learn how to call these actions in various ways with three kinds of event handlers: button manipulation, keyframes, and keystrokes.

What are behaviors?

Flash MX 2004 includes a brand new Behaviors panel, which is a tool designed to help a novice who is just starting to use Flash for design and development. You can open the Behaviors panel, shown in Figure 18-1, by choosing Window ⇨ Development Panels ⇨ Behaviors (Shift+F3).

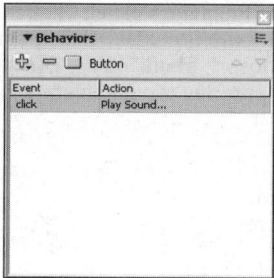

Figure 18-1: The Behaviors panel showing a Button component with a behavior applied

If you create a new Flash document and select the first frame of Layer 1, you can click the Add Behavior (+) button at the top left corner of the Behaviors panel to see a list of categories (Figure 18-2).

Figure 18-2: The categories in the Add Behavior menu

These categories represent a variety of objects you can control with one or more behaviors. So what do behaviors do? In the simplest sense, a behavior is automated scripting. When you add a behavior to an event handler, Flash MX 2004 generates the necessary ActionScript code to make that behavior happen. Let's take a quick look at a Web behavior.

1. Create a new Flash document by choosing File ⇨ New. In the New Document dialog box, double-click the Flash document item.

2. Rename Layer 1 to **button**.

3. Open the Components panel (Ctrl+F7 or ⌘+F7). Expand the UI Components set, and drag an instance of the Button component to the Stage.

4. Select the Button component instance on the Stage, and open the Property inspector. In the <Instance Name> field, type **webButton_mc**. In the Label field, type **web site**. See Figure 18-3.

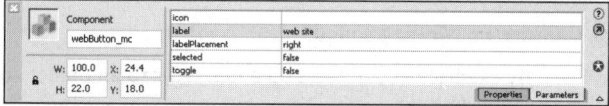

Figure 18-3: The settings for the Button component

5. With the Button instance selected on the Stage, open the Behaviors panel. Click the Add Behavior (+) button, and choose Web ⇨ Go to URL. In the Go to URL dialog box, type **http://www.flashsupport.com** in the URL field. Choose **"_blank"** in the Open in menu. Refer to Figure 18-4. Click OK when you are done entering the parameters.

Figure 18-4: The Go to URL settings

6. Now look at the code that Flash MX 2004 created for the behavior. Select the webButton_mc instance, and choose Window ⇨ Development Panels ⇨ Actions (F9). You'll see the following code:

```
on (click) {

    //Goto Webpage Behavior
    //copyright Macromedia, Inc. 2003
    getURL("http://www.flashsupport.com","_blank");
    //End Behavior

}
```

The heart of this code is the event handler, on(), and the getURL() action. When the user clicks the Button component instance, the on() handler detects the click and executes (or *invokes*) the getURL() action. You'll learn more about these actions later in this chapter.

Note   The click event is new to Flash MX 2004, and specific to the UI components. This event is not used for standard mouse events on Button symbol instances.

7. Save your Flash document (File ⇨ Save) and choose Control ⇨ Test Movie. When the Flash movie loads, click the button. Your Web browser should open to the FlashSupport.com Web site, the official support site for this book.

We won't discuss any other behaviors in this chapter, as you can find specific categories of behaviors explained in other parts of the book:

Embedded Video behaviors, Chapter 17, "Embedding Video"

MovieClip behaviors, Chapter 19, "Building Timelines and Interactions"

Projector behavior, Chapter 23, "Using the Flash Player and Projector"

Sound behaviors, Chapter 15, "Adding Sound"

Behaviors allow you to learn by example — you can add a behavior to an object and look at the code used to describe the interaction.

Note   Experienced Flash developers and programmers will be the first to tell you that it's not a good idea to put a lot of code on objects that are on the Stage. Most scripts are placed on one or more keyframes, or the code is stored in a separate .as file. You learn more about programming practices in Part VII, "Approaching ActionScript."

What is ActionScript?

Every interactive authoring system uses a language (or code) that enables elements within the system to communicate. Just as there are several languages that people use to speak to one another around the globe, there are hundreds of programming languages in use today. In an effort to make Flash more usable to computer programmers, Flash's scripting language, called ActionScript, changed much of its formatting in Flash 5 to mirror JavaScript, a fundamental component for DHTML and HTML Web pages. Right now, we focus on using the most basic Flash ActionScript.

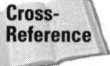

New Feature

In Flash MX 2004, ActionScript has matured to a whole new version, dubbed ActionScript 2.0. ActionScript 2.0 is a different—and more complex—style of coding than what was used in Flash MX and earlier. The ActionScript style used in Flash MX and earlier is now known as ActionScript 1.0. It's still perfectly valid to code in either style. ActionScript 2.0 will feel more familiar to developers who have used other object-oriented programming languages such as C++ or Java.

Cross-Reference

If you're interested in learning the fundamental building blocks of ActionScript programming, check out our advanced coverage of ActionScript in Chapters 24 through 34. The three chapters of Part V are intended to provide a starting point for Flash designers and developers who are new to Flash actions and interactive concepts. Exhaustive coverage of the ActionScript language can be found in the *Flash MX 2004 ActionScript Bible*, by Robert Reinhardt and Joey Lott.

Navigating the Actions panel

Flash MX 2004 has a specific interface element that enables you to add interactive commands to Flash movies—the Actions panel. Unlike behaviors and the Behaviors panel, you don't use menus to add interactive functionality—you type the ActionScript code describing the interactivity in (or out of) of the Actions panel. You can open the Actions panel in a number of ways:

✦ Go to Windows ➪ Development Panels ➪ Actions

✦ Press the F9 key

✦ Alt+double-click (or Option+double-click) a keyframe in the Timeline window

If you have a keyframe selected in the Timeline window, the Actions panel will be titled **Actions - Frame** (see Figure 18-1). If you have a Movie Clip symbol instance selected on the Stage, you'll see the name **Actions - Movie Clip**. If you have a Button symbol instance selected on the Stage, the Actions panel will be titled **Actions - Button**. If you have a component selected, the Actions panel will simply read **Actions**. Don't be confused—there is only one Actions panel. Flash MX simply lets you know the object to which you are assigning actions.

RIP

The Actions panel in Flash MX 2004 no longer features a Normal mode. Normal mode enabled you to code ActionScript by selecting actions and filling in parameters, instead of writing out all the code by hand. If you used Normal mode in Flash MX or earlier, don't fret—the Actions panel still offers automatic code hints, which provide pop-up descriptions of an action's parameters as you type.

As shown in Figure 18-5, the Actions panel in Flash MX 2004 has three distinct areas (counter-clockwise from the left): the Actions toolbox, the Script navigator, and the Script pane. There are two auto-snap dividers, one dividing the Actions toolbox and Script navigator from the Script pane, and another subdividing the Actions toolbox and Script navigator. You may want to practice opening and closing these dividers, as well as dragging each to your preferred width and height, respectively. Figure 18-5 shows a breakdown of the new Actions panel in Flash MX 2004.

✦ The Actions toolbox contains several nested booklets of ActionScript commands. You can select actions to add to the Script pane.

✦ The Script navigator can jump to any script within your Flash document. When you select a keyframe or object in this pane, any code attached to the item is displayed in the Script pane.

 New Feature The Script navigator shows the actions for the entire document, not just for the current time-line (as was the case in Flash MX).

✦ The Script pane displays the current code for an item selected on the Stage, a keyframe selected in the Timeline window, or an item selected in the Script navigator. You can type, copy, cut, and paste code at will into the Script pane. An options bar is located at the top of the Script pane as well. The options bar contains several buttons to modify, search, debug, or format your code in the Script pane. Most of these options can also be found in the panel's options menu, located in the top-right corner of the panel.

New Feature In Flash MX 2004, you can click the pin icon at the bottom tab of the script in the Script pane. You can pin multiple scripts in the Script pane, and quickly tab between them.

Tip When the Actions panel has focus, a highlighted bar shows up on the left side of the Script pane. This highlighted color enables you to know if you can start typing in the Script pane.

For this chapter, you'll work primarily within the Timeline Control booklet, located within the Global Functions booklet in the Actions toolbox.

You can add actions to the Script pane in one of three ways:

✦ Drag an action from the Actions toolbox to the Script pane.

✦ Select an action from the Actions menu, accessed by clicking the plus (+) icon.

✦ Double-click an action in the Actions pane.

To delete actions, select the action line(s) in the Script pane, and press the Delete or Backspace key on the keyboard.

Once you have added an action to the Script pane, you can specify parameters (or arguments) for the action. Depending on the action, you may or may not need to type such parameters. By default, Flash MX 2004 provides code hints as you type actions into the Script pane. The Show Code Hint button enables you to see the parameters for an action, as shown in the `gotoAndPlay` action in Figure 18-5.

You should get in the habit of clicking the Check Syntax button (the blue checkmark) to make sure you didn't mistype an action. If you have an error, the Output panel displays some infor-mation related to the error, indicating the line number where the syntax error occurs.

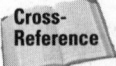 **Cross-Reference** In Chapter 24, "Knowing the Nuts and Bolts of Code," you can also learn about referencing actions in the new Help panel of Flash MX 2004.

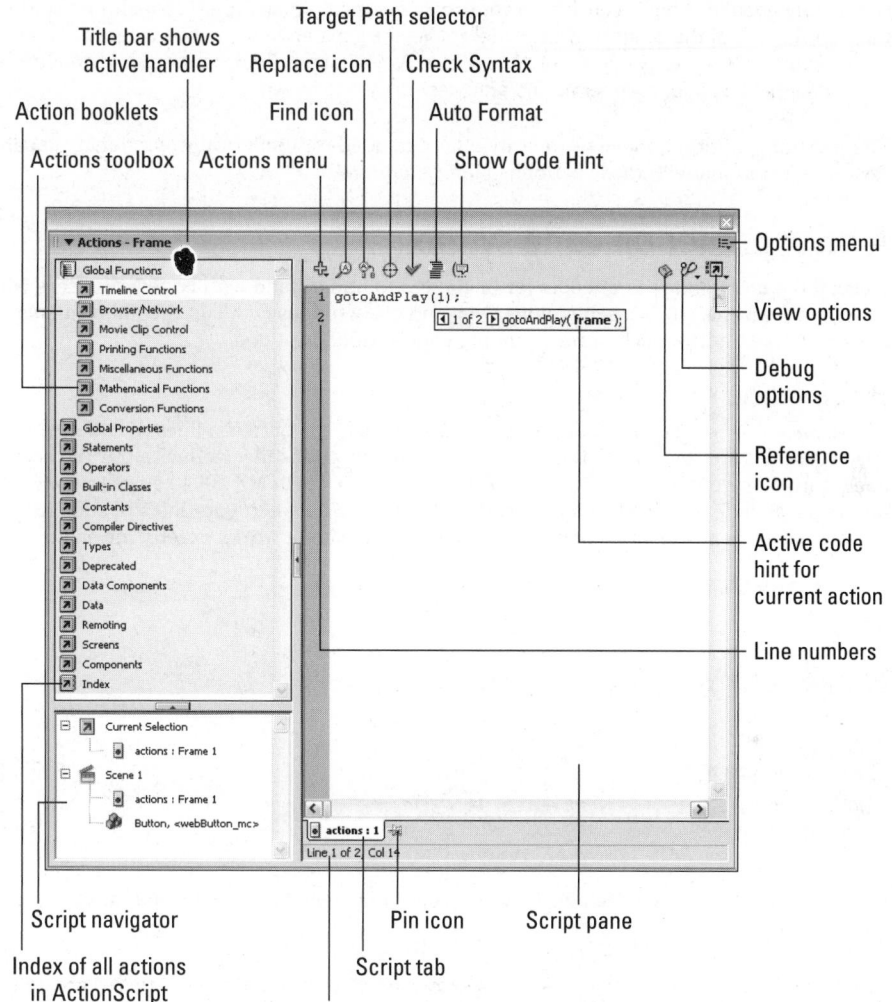

Figure 18-5: The Actions panel enables you to instantly add, delete, or change Flash movie commands.

For now, let's look at two booklets in the Actions toolbox's Global Functions booklet: Timeline Control and Browser/Network. The Timeline Control actions are listed in alphabetical order. The first eight actions in this booklet, including gotoAndPlay, gotoAndStop, play, and stop, control the playback of the movie. The last action, stopAllSounds, is a global command to handle sound playback.

The Browser/Network actions—fscommand, getURL, loadMovie/loadMovieNum, loadVariables/loadVariablesNum, and unloadMovie/unloadMovieNum—enable movies to load external files and communicate with the browser, a Web server, or the standalone player. In this chapter, we'll get you up and running with the getURL action, which enables you to link to other Web resources outside of the Flash movie (such as Web pages and file downloads).

Note   Throughout this book, you'll more commonly see most actions specified with ( ) characters at the end of the action's name. For example, the `gotoAndPlay` action is really a method, and in code, appears as `gotoAndPlay()`. In Part VII of this book, we provide more detailed information about code terms and practices.

The remaining Action booklets primarily offer extended ActionScript programming capabilities. We discuss many of these actions in later chapters.

A brief primer on code syntax

Some of the most difficult concepts for beginners to understand with code writing are white space, parentheses (( )), semicolons (;), and curly braces ({ }). In the following paragraphs, you learn how each of these affects your ActionScript code.

White space

White space is a collective term referring to any blank areas between lines of code. White space includes spaces inserted by the Spacebar, indentations inserted with the Tab key, and line returns inserted with the Enter or Return key. When Flash MX 2004 compiles your ActionScript code into the Flash movie, the white space between your lines of code usually will not generate any errors. For example, the following code works exactly the same:

```
on(release){ getURL("mypage.html"); }
```

or

```
on(release){
   getURL("mypage.html");
}
```

or

```
on        (              release ){
getURL("mypage.html");
}
```

However, white space is an issue when it separates the key terms in the action, such as:

```
get URL("mypage.html");
```

The space between `get` and `URL` will cause an error when Flash MX 2004 tries to create the Flash movie.

Tip   To check if your syntax is correct, click the Check Syntax button in the Actions panel. If you do have any white space errors, the Output panel will display information related to the error.

Parentheses

Many, but not all, actions require parentheses after the action term, such as `on()`, `getURL()`, or even `play()`. A general rule to remember is that if the action requires a parameter, such as `on (release)`, then parentheses are required as well. However, many actions, such `play()` and `stop()`, still required parentheses, even though they do not use any arguments. Another rule for parentheses is that any open parenthesis (( ) must eventually be followed by a closing parenthesis ( )). A habit we like to encourage is counting the number of opening parentheses in a script and then counting the number of closing parentheses. If the numbers don't match, you need to review your code to find the place where you forgot to include a parenthesis.

Deprecated and Incompatible Actions: What Are They?

As the ActionScript language of Flash continues to expand and encompass new functionality, older actions coexist with newer and better actions (or methods, properties, event handlers, and functions, which we discuss later). While Flash Player 7 will continue to support ActionScript 1.0 and earlier actions, it's better not to use older actions if the newest version of Flash has a new way of accomplishing the same task. Older actions that have been replaced with a new action (or new way to perform the same task) are called deprecated actions. The Actions panel in Flash MX 2004 houses all deprecated actions in the Deprecated booklet of the Actions pane. Why shouldn't you use these actions? As we see in more advanced scripting, Flash MX 2004 has specific syntax to target Movie Clips and determine whether certain frames have loaded, among other features of the ActionScript "dot syntax" language. The following figure shows the actions within the Deprecated ⇨ Actions booklet. Note that there are other groups of deprecated actions inside the Deprecated booklet as well.

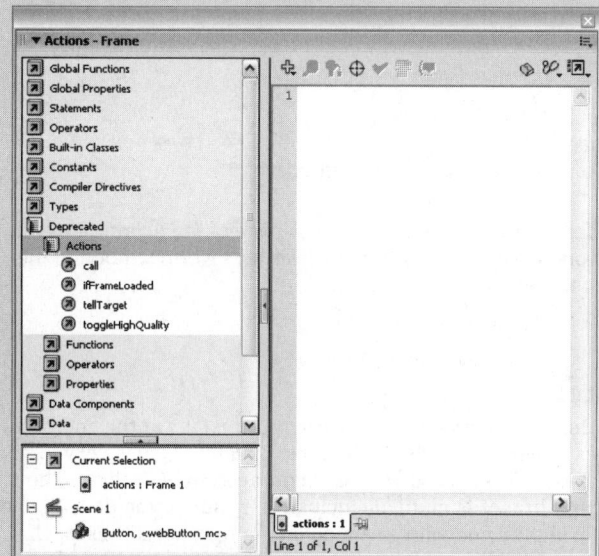

Actions that are highlighted in the Deprecated booklet should be avoided if possible. However, Flash Player 7 continues to support these older actions.

Flash MX 2004 will also let you know if certain actions are not supported with the Player version that is selected in the Flash format's Publish Settings. Note that you can also find the Player version setting in the Property inspector when you click an empty area of the Stage or the Work area. If an action is not supported by the version you have selected, the action is highlighted in yellow. The following figure shows this type of highlighting in the Actions panel for Mac OS X. You will notice that the tooltip (or rollover description) indicates which version of the Flash Player supports the action.

Continued

Continued

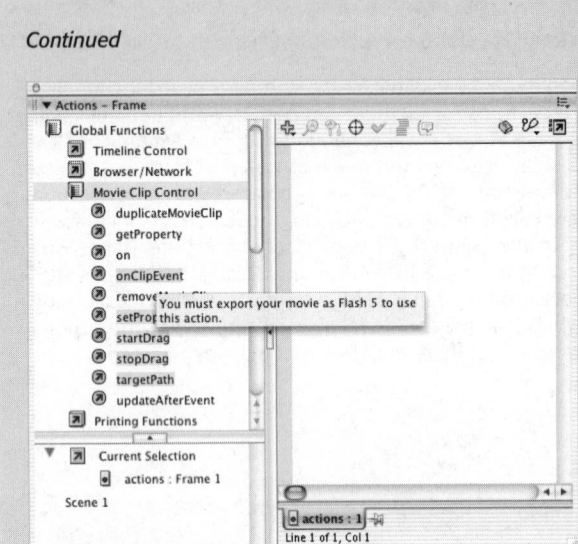

Flash Player 4 (or earlier) will not support the `onClipEvent` or `updateAfterEvent` actions (among others), as these actions were introduced in Flash Player 5.

Note that Flash MX 2004 no longer offers indication within the Script pane of the Actions panel if you have added conflicting actions to one keyframe or object. In Flash MX's Normal mode of the Actions panel, these conflicts were highlighted in red.

Semicolons and curly braces

You've probably already noticed that most actions include a semicolon (;) at the end of the code line. In practice, many coders forget to include semicolons. Usually, Flash is very forgiving if you omit semicolons, but by no means should you be encouraged to omit them. The general rule for semicolons and curly braces is mutually inclusive: if your action doesn't end with an opening curly brace ({), it should end with a semicolon. As with parentheses, all opening curly braces must eventually be followed by a closing curly brace (}). Curly braces are commonly used with actions beginning with on, such on() and onClipEvent(), as well as if and function declarations.

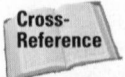

Cross-Reference You learn more about if statements and functions in Part VII, "Approaching ActionScript."

Your First Five Actions

Now that you have a general picture of what actions do, let's look at five common actions in detail. At this point, we're describing only the functionality of each action, not how to add an action to your movie. Information on adding an action is covered in the next section, "Making Actions Happen with Event Handlers."

You will find coverage of further actions (and full-blown ActionScript) in later chapters. For exhaustive coverage of the ActionScript language, be sure to read the *Flash MX 2004 ActionScript Bible* by Robert Reinhardt and Joey Lott.

As they appear in the Flash interface, the actions are alphabetically sorted from top to bottom. In the following sections, complementary actions are grouped together.

gotoAndPlay and gotoAndStop

These "go to" actions change the current frame of the movie to the target frame specified as the actions' parameter. There are two variations:

✦ gotoAndPlay: Changes the current frame to the frame specified, and then executes a play action. gotoAndPlay provides the capability to show animated sequences as preludes to individual content areas. gotoAndPlay also gets frequent use in choose-your-own-adventure style animations, in which the user guides an animated character through different paths in a narrative.

✦ gotoAndStop: Changes the current frame to the frame specified and then halts play-back on that frame. gotoAndStop is often used to produce toolbar-style interfaces where the user clicks buttons to view different areas of content in a movie.

Both actions enable you to jump to certain areas of the Flash movie. The parameters of these actions start with the largest time unit, the scene, and end with the smallest one, the frame.

You can specify frames in other scenes as the target of goto actions with the scene parameter. As shown in the following code, you type the name of the scene first, with double quotes around the name, and then the frame number (without quotes) or frame label. In this example, "Scene 2" is the name of the scene and "animate_in" is the frame label in that scene to jump to.

```
gotoAndPlay("Scene 2", "animate_in");
```

However, if you only specify one parameter in a gotoAndPlay or gotoAndStop action, the parameter is interpreted as a frame label. For example, the following code tells the current timeline to jump to its "menu" frame label.

```
gotoAndStop("menu");
```

While we haven't looked at actions specifically for use in Movie Clip instances, make a note that you can't use a goto action specifying a scene within a Movie Clip instance. In this case, you should target the Main Timeline to go to and stop (or play) the keyframe label in the desired scene, omitting the Scene's name. For example, _root.gotoAndStop ("products"); executed from a Movie Clip Timeline would tell the Main Timeline to go to and stop on the frame label products, which would be located in a different scene.

There are three methods of specifying the frame to which the movie should go when it receives a goto action. The methods for specifying the frame are:

✦ **number:** Specify the target frame as a number. Frame 1 is the beginning of the movie or scene. Number spans scenes, so if you have a movie with two scenes, each containing 25 frames, and you add a goto action with Frame Number set to 50, your action advances the movie to the 25th frame of the second scene. Frame numbers should not use sur-rounding quotes, as frame labels do. The following action tells the current timeline to jump to frame 10 and start playing:

```
gotoAndPlay(10);
```

Caution   Using frame numbers to specify the targets of goto actions can lead to serious scalability problems in Flash movies. Adding frames at the beginning or in the middle of a movie's Timeline causes the following frames to be renumbered. When those frames are renumbered, all goto actions that use frame numbers must be revised to point to the correct new number of their target frames.

In the vast majority of cases, goto actions that use a frame label to specify target frames are preferable to goto actions that use a frame number to specify target frames. Unlike numbered frame targets, goto actions with labeled frame targets continue to function properly even if the targeted frame changes position on the timeline.

✦ **label:** Individual keyframes can be given names via the Label field in the Property inspector. Once a frame is labeled, a goto action can target it by name. To specify a label as the target of a goto action, type the name of the frame as the action's parameter. The following example tells the Flash movie to go to the frame labeled "products" and stop at that frame.

```
gotoAndStop("products");
```

✦ **ActionScript expression:** Specify the target frame as an interpreted ActionScript code segment. Expressions are used to dynamically assign targets of goto actions. Here's a quick example of a string variable being used as a frame label in ActionScript 1.0 style:

```
var targetLabel = "products";
gotoAndPlay(targetLabel);
```

Notice that the term targetLabel does not use quotes, because it is not the actual frame label name. When the Flash Player interprets this action, it looks up the value of targetLabel, which is "products", and inserts that value into the gotoAndPlay action. In ActionScript 2.0, the same action would look like this:

```
var targetLabel:String = "products";
gotoAndPlay(targetLabel);
```

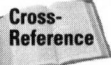

Cross-Reference   Expressions are covered in Chapter 24, "Knowing the Nuts and Bolts of Code."

nextFrame and prevFrame

The nextFrame and prevFrame actions act like a gotoAndStop action, in that they both transport the timeline to a new position and stop.

✦ nextFrame: This action tells the current timeline to move forward one frame and stop playback. nextFrame can be used in conjunction with prevFrame to quickly set up a slide-show-style walkthrough of content, where each of a series of contiguous keyframes contains the content of one "slide." This action does not use any parameters. The following code moves the timeline to the next frame:

```
nextFrame();
```

✦ prevFrame: This action moves the current timeline backward one frame and stop playback. For example, if the timeline is on frame 20 and the movie runs a prevFrame() action, the timeline moves to frame 19. As with the nextFrame action, prevFrame does not use any parameters:

```
prevFrame();
```

nextScene and prevScene

These actions advance the Flash movie to a new scene. Here's how they work:

✦ nextScene: This action tells the current timeline to move to the first frame of the next scene. You can use nextScene for more elaborate slideshows or demonstration movies, where each scene contains animated content with a stop action on the last frame. The last frame of the scene would then contain a button using the nextScene action. This action does not use any parameters. The following code tells the movie to jump to the next scene:

```
nextScene();
```

✦ prevScene: This action jumps the movie to the previous scene. The order of scenes is determined by the Scene panel (Window ⇨ Design Panels ⇨ Scene). If you have two scenes, Main and Products, and the Playhead of the Flash movie is currently in the Products scene, a prevScene action moves the Playhead to the first frame of the Main scene. As with the nextScene action, prevScene does not use any parameters:

```
prevScene();
```

Note The nextScene and prevScene actions do not automatically recycle the scenes when the last or first scene is reached, respectively. For example, if you have three scenes and use a nextScene action while the movie is on the last scene, the movie will not jump back to the first scene.

Tip While you may find it simpler to segment your Flash content across several scenes as you begin to learn Flash, most seasoned Flash designers and developers only use one scene, and separate content across several Movie Clip symbols placed on one or more frames of Scene 1. Scenes are not compatible with standard targeting syntax, as you learn in the next chapter.

On the CD-ROM You can find an example of nextScene and prevScene usage in the document named nextScene.fla in the ch18 folder of this book's CD-ROM.

play and stop

These simple actions are the true foundations of Flash timeline control. play sets a movie or a Movie Clip instance in motion. When a play action is executed, Flash starts the sequential display of each frame's contents along the current timeline.

The rate at which the frames are displayed is measured as frames per second, or fps. The fps rate can be set from 0.01 to 120 (meaning that the play action can cause the display of as little as 1 frame every 100 seconds to as many as 120 frames in 1 second, subject to the limitations of the computer's processing speed). The default fps is 12.

Once play has started, frames continue to be displayed one after the other, until another action interrupts the flow, or the end of the movie or Movie Clip's timeline is reached. If the end of a movie's timeline is reached, the movie either loops (begins playing again at frame 1, Scene 1), or stops on the last frame.

Cross-Reference Whether a movie loops automatically depends on the Publish settings described in Chapter 21, "Publishing Flash Movies."

Once the end of the Movie Clip's timeline is reached, playback loops back to the beginning of the clip, and the clip continues playing. To prevent looping, add a `stop` action to the last frame of your Movie Clip.

Note   A single `play` action affects only a single timeline, whether that timeline is the main movie timeline or the timeline of a Movie Clip instance. For example, a `play` action executed inside a Movie Clip does not cause the Main Timeline to begin playing. Likewise, any goto action on the Main Timeline doesn't migrate to the Movie Clips that reside there. A timeline must be specifically targeted to control playback along that timeline. If there is no specified target, the action is referring to its own timeline. However, this is not the case for animations within Graphic symbol instances. An animation in a Graphic symbol is controlled by actions on the timeline in which the symbol instance is present—Flash ignores actions on a Graphic symbol's timeline.

`stop`, as you may have guessed, halts the progression of a movie or Movie Clip that is in a play state. `stop` is often used with buttons for user-controlled playback of a movie, or on frames to end an animated sequence.

Tip   Movie Clip instances placed on any timeline begin to play automatically. Remember to add a `stop` action on the first frame of a Movie Clip if you don't want it to play right away.

stopAllSounds

A simple but powerful action that mutes any sounds playing in the movie at the time the action is executed, `stopAllSounds` does not disable sounds permanently—it simply cancels any sounds that happen to be currently playing. It is sometimes used as a quick-and-dirty method of making buttons that shut off background looping soundtracks. `stopAllSounds` is not appropriate for controlling whether individual (or specific) sounds are played or muted.

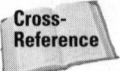

Cross-Reference   For information on more accurate control over sounds, read Chapter 15, "Adding Sound," and Chapter 27, "Interacting with Movie Clips."

getURL

Want to link to a Web page from a Flash movie? No problem. That's what `getURL` is for. You can find the `getURL` action in the Global Functions ⇨ Browser/Network booklet of the Actions panel. `getURL` is simply Flash's method of making a conventional hypertext link. It's nearly the equivalent of an anchor tag in HTML (`<a href="...">`), except that Flash's `getURL` can also send variables for form submission. `getURL` can be used to link to a standard Web page, an FTP site, another Flash movie, an executable, a CGI script, or anything that exists on the Internet or on an accessible local file system.

`getURL` has three parameters that are familiar to Web builders (the first one, URL, is required for this action to work):

✦ **url:** This is the network address of the page, file, script, or resource to which you are linking. Any value is permitted (including ActionScript expressions), but the linked item can be displayed only if the reference to it is correct. URL is directly analogous to the HREF attribute of an HTML anchor tag. You can use a relative or absolute URL as well. Examples:

```
http://www.yoursite.com/
ftp://ftp.yoursite.com/pub/documents.zip
menu.html
/cgi-bin/processform.cgi
/script/form.cfm
```

Since Flash 4, getURL can be used to link to documents on the Web from the stand-alone Flash player. Execution of a getURL action in the standalone player causes the default Web browser to launch and load the requested URL.

Tip   You can specify secure domain URLs by using the https protocol for SSL (Secure Socket Layer) connections.

✦ **window:** This is the name of the frame or window in which you wish to load the resource specified in the URL setting. The window parameter is directly analogous to the target attribute of an HTML anchor tag. In addition to enabling the entry of custom frame and window names, the window parameter can use the following browser-standard target names:

- **"_self":** Loads the URL into the same frame or window as the current movie. If you do not specify a window parameter in the getURL action, this behavior will be the default.

- **"_blank":** Creates a new browser window and loads the URL into it.

- **"_parent":** Removes the current frameset and loads the URL in its place. Use this option if you have multiple nested framesets, and you want your linked URL to replace only the frameset in which your movie resides.

- **"_top":** Loads the URL into the current browser and removes all framesets in the process. Use this option if your movie is in a frame, but you want your linked URL to be loaded normally into the browser, outside the confines of any frames.

Note   Frame windows and/or JavaScript windows can be assigned names. You can target these names by manually typing the name in the Window field. For example, if you had a frame defined as <frame name="main". . .>, you could load specific URLs into a frame named main from a Flash movie.

✦ **method:** This parameter enables getURL to function similarly to an HTML form submission. For normal links, the method parameter should be omitted. But in order to submit values to a server-side script, one of the submission methods, "GET" or "POST", should be specified. For a complete discussion on submitting data to a server from a Flash movie (using the new LoadVars object), see Chapter 30, "Sending Data In and Out of Flash."

Tip   getURL functions in the Test Movie environment. Both the Flash stand-alone player and the Test Movie command give you access to external and/or local URLs.

Let's look at some quick examples of how a getURL action can be written. The following code tells the browser to load the URL, www.wiley.com, into the current browser window:

```
getURL("http://www.wiley.com");
```

Alternatively, you can specify a unique target for the loaded URL. The following example loads an HTML document named menu.html into a frame named menu_frame:

```
getURL("menu.html", "menu_frame");
```

A more advanced usage of the getURL action sends variables from the Flash movie to a Web server's script, which is setup to receive the variables. The following code retrieves the current version of the Flash Player and sends to a script that logs the information:

```
var playerVersion = getVersion();
getURL("http://www.mysite.com/scripts/log.cfm", "_self", "GET");
```

As we mentioned with the goto actions, you can also use expressions with getURL actions. Expressions can be utilized as parameters of any ActionScript action. The following example uses a string variable to specify the URL used by a getURL action:

```
var siteURL = "http://www.flashsupport.com";
getURL(siteURL);
```

You should start familiarizing yourself with the ActionScript notation that Flash uses for each action (see Table 18-2). As you use Flash for more advanced interactivity, you'll need to have a firm grasp of code notation. Part VII, "Approaching ActionScript," teaches you how to start building more advanced code.

Table 18-2: Common Actions and ActionScript Notation

Action	*ActionScript Notation*	*Arguments*
gotoAndStop	gotoAndStop(arguments);	Scene Name (Frame Label, Number, or Expression)
gotoAndPlay	gotoAndPlay(arguments);	Scene Name (Frame Label, Number, or Expression)
nextFrame	nextFrame();	None
prevFrame	prevFrame();	None
nextScene	nextScene();	None
prevScene	prevScene();	None
play	play();	None
stop	stop();	None
stopAllSounds	stopAllSounds();	None
getURL	getURL(arguments);	url, target frame or window, method for form submission

Making Actions Happen with Event Handlers

The ten common actions discussed in the previous sections provide many of the behaviors that you need to make an interesting interactive Flash movie. But those actions can't make your movies interactive on their own. They need to be told when to happen. To tell a Flash movie when an action should occur, you need event handlers. Event handlers specify the condition(s) under which an action can be made to happen. For instance, you might want to mouse-click a button to initiate a `play()` action, or you might want a movie to stop when a certain keyframe in the timeline is reached. Creating interactivity in your movies is simply a matter of deciding what event you want to detect (mouse click, keystroke, and so on), adding the appropriate event handler to detect it, and specifying the action(s) that should be performed when it happens.

Before we describe each event handler in detail, let's see an example of exactly how an event handler merges with an action to form a functioning interactive button.

Combining an action with an event handler to make a functioning button

Imagine that you have a short, endlessly looping movie in which a wire-frame cube rotates. Now imagine that you want to add a button to your movie that, when clicked, stops the cube from rotating by stopping the playback of the looping movie. Here's what you need to do:

For this exercise, you can use the `rotatingCube.fla` file located in the `ch18` folder on the *Macromedia Flash MX 2004 Bible* CD-ROM. The finished file is named `rotatingCube_complete.fla`.

1. Open the example Flash document (FLA file), and make a new layer called **button.**

2. Place a button on the button layer. You can use Flash MX 2004's sample Stop button found in the Circle Buttons folder of the Buttons library (Window ➪ Other Panels ➪ Common Libraries ➪ Buttons). See Figure 18-6 to see this button's placement on the Stage.

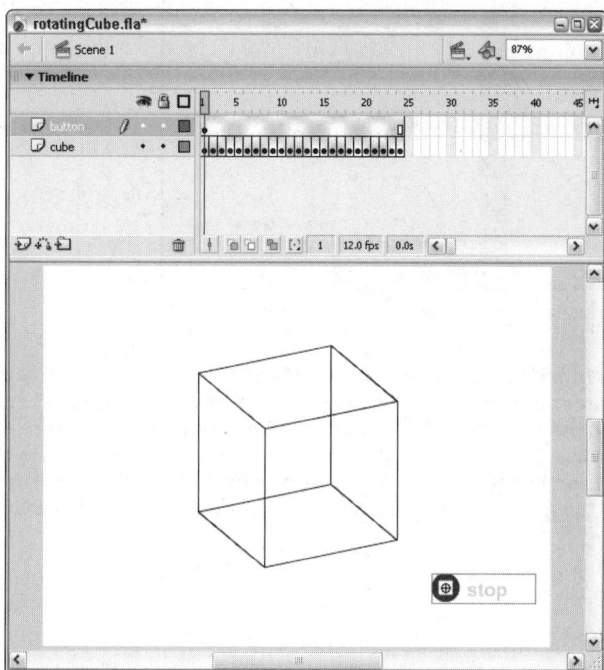

Figure 18-6: The Stop button on the Stage

Tip   Selecting buttons and editing button properties sometimes can be tricky if buttons are enabled in the Flash authoring environment. For easier button manipulation, disable buttons by unchecking Enable Simple Buttons under the Control menu.

3. With the Stop Button instance selected, open the Actions panel (F9); then open the Global Functions ➪ Movie Clip Control booklet in the Actions toolbox.

4. Double-click the on event handler in the Movie Clip Control booklet, or drag it to the Script pane. A list of mouse events for on appears in a code hint menu between the parentheses of the on action.

5. In the event list (shown in Figure 18-7), double-click the release event. The release event is one of several mouse-click events (the other frequently-used event is press; both are described later in this chapter in the section titled "The Flash event handlers"). Notice that the event is specified between the parentheses of the on handler in the Script pane. You've now told Flash that you want something to happen when the mouse clicks the button. All that's left is to tell it what should happen. In other words, you need to nest another action within the on (release){} code.

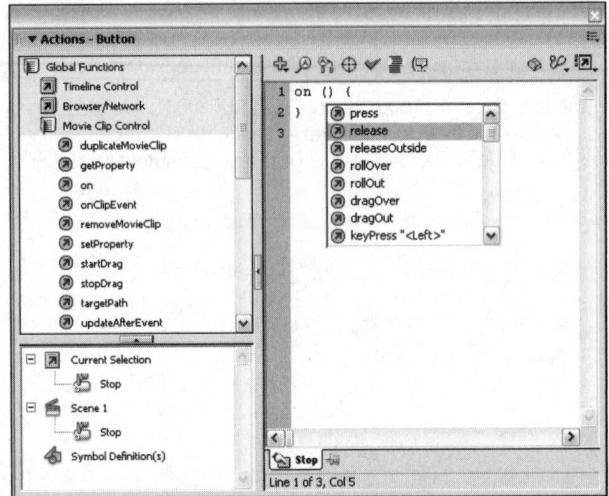

Figure 18-7: Adding a release event to the on handler

6. Now you'll try another method for adding an action to the Script pane. Click once with your mouse pointer to the left of the closing curly brace (}) on line 2. Then click the plus (+) button in the toolbar of the Actions panel. From the menu, choose Global Functions ➪ Timeline Control ➪ stop. A stop action will be placed between the curly braces ({}) of the on handler. To format the code cleanly, click the Auto Format button in the toolbar of the Actions panel. The Script pane should now read as follows:

```
on (release){
  stop();
}
```

The `stop` action, represented by the code `stop();` is contained by the curly braces {
and } that mark the beginning and end of the list of actions that are executed when the
`release` event occurs (there could be any number of actions in this list). Each action
line (handlers excluded) must end with the semicolon (;) character.

7. We now have a button in our Flash movie that stops the movie's playback when it is
   clicked. Save your Flash document ((FLA file) file), and test the movie using Control ⇨
   Test Movie. When you click the button, the rotating cube animation should stop.

To make any interactivity in your movies, you simply have to apply the basic principles you
used to make the stop button: Decide which action (or actions) you want to happen, and indicate when you want that action to happen with an event handler. Let's look now at more
event handlers you can use to make those actions happen.

The Flash event handlers

Three primary event handlers exist in Flash: those that detect mouse activity on Button
instances (button manipulation), those that recognize when a key is pressed on the keyboard
(key presses), and those that respond to the progression of the timeline (keyframes).

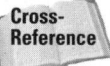

Cross-Reference

As a Flash developer, you have an inordinate amount of control over events and event handlers
with ActionScript. We'll look at other event models in Chapter 25, "Controlling Movie Clips."

Working with mouse events and buttons

Event handlers that occur based on the user's interaction with a button rely entirely on the
location and movement of the mouse pointer. If the mouse pointer comes in contact with a
Button symbol's Hit area, it changes from an arrow icon to a finger pointer icon. At that time
the mouse is described as "over" the button. If the mouse pointer is not over a button, it is
said to be *out* or *outside* of the button. General movement of the mouse *without* the mouse
button depressed is referred to as *rolling*. General movement of the mouse *with* the mouse
button pressed is referred to as *dragging*.

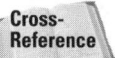

Cross-Reference

If you don't know how to make a Button symbol and its various states, read Chapter 6,
"Symbols, Instances, and the Library."

Caution

Event handlers and actions for buttons must be placed only on Button *instances*, not on the
four frames in the timeline of the original Button symbol. One of the new features in Flash
MX 2004 is that it will not allow you to place *any* actions in a Button symbol timeline.

It's worth mentioning that you can assign one or more mouse events to a Button instance's `on`
handler. For example, the following code will be invoked when the user releases the mouse
button over or outside of the Hit area of the Flash button:

```
on (release, releaseOutside){
    stop();
}
```

As this code demonstrates, multiple events are separated by a comma (,). You can specify
as many events as you need within the parentheses of the `on` handler.

Here are the mouse-based events for Flash buttons:

press

A single mouse click can actually be divided into two separate components: the downstroke (the *press*) and the upstroke (the *release*). A press event occurs when the mouse pointer is over the Hit area of a button *and* the downstroke of a mouse click is detected. Press is best used for control panel-style buttons, especially toggle switches.

Caution

Typically, developers should program reversible decisions for primary navigation so that users can abort their click by rolling the cursor away from the Hit area before releasing the mouse. For example, a user might click a button for more information and decide she would rather not get that information. We do not recommend using the press event for important user moves such as these because it does not give users an opportunity to abort their move.

release

A release event occurs when the mouse pointer is over the Hit area of a button *and* both the downstroke and the upstroke of a mouse click are detected. The release event is the standard button click event.

Tip

If you use the Track as Menu Item behavior for a Button instance in the Property inspector, a button will respond to a release event over its Hit state even if the mouse was pressed outside of the button's Hit area.

releaseOutside

A releaseOutside event occurs in response to the following series of mouse movements:

1. The mouse pointer moves over a button's Hit area.

2. The mouse button is pressed.

3. The mouse pointer is moved off the button's Hit area.

4. The mouse button is released.

The releaseOutside event can be used to react to an aborted button click.

rollOver

A rollOver event occurs when the mouse pointer moves onto the Hit area of a button without the mouse button depressed.

Note

To perform standard rollover button effects, such as graphic art changes or sound events, you can insert graphics and sound on to the Over state of the Button symbol timeline. It's common practice, however, to create Movie Clip instances that use mouse event handlers for specialized rollover effects. You learn more about this advanced usage of Movie Clips in Chapter 25, "Controlling Movie Clips."

rollOut

A rollOut event occurs when the mouse pointer moves off of the Hit area of a button without the mouse button depressed. This event is commonly used for switching an advanced button's graphic state back to its original state when the user rolls off the button.

dragOver

A dragOver event occurs in response to the following series of mouse movements:

1. The mouse button is pressed when the mouse pointer is outside the Hit area of a Flash button.

2. The mouse pointer moves over the Hit area while the mouse button is still depressed.

The dragOver event is rather obscure, but could be used for special cases of interactivity such as revealing a hidden item in a game. For example, when the mouse button is held down and mouse movement occurs over a specific area, ActionScript can detect the coordinates of the mouse movement and reveal a Movie Clip instance that is otherwise invisible on the Stage.

dragOut

A dragOut event occurs in response to the following series of mouse movements:

1. The mouse button is pressed when the mouse pointer is over the Hit area of a Flash button.

2. The mouse pointer moves outside the Hit area of the Flash button, and the mouse button is still depressed.

As with dragOver, you'll likely encounter very few situations where the dragOut event is necessary. Most of the more complicated mouse events are only useful for Flash games and experimental user interfaces.

Capturing keyboard input

You can also use event handlers to detect events that occur on the user's keyboard. You can enable your Flash movies to "capture" a key press (also known as a keystroke) initiated by the user. One way in which ActionScript can detect a keystroke is by using the keyPress event. This event lets you execute an action (or series of actions) when the user presses a key on the keyboard. The implementation method for a keyPress event handler may be confusing, but it's the least code-intensive (and most designer-friendly) route: To add a keyPress event handler, you must first place a button onstage at the frame where you want the keyboard to be active. You then assign the keyPress event to the Button instance's on handler. Keep in mind, though, that the button's Hit area has no effect on the keyPress event detection. As such, even though the keyPress event is defined on a button, any key press that occurs in the Flash movie can be captured by the button, regardless of the user's mouse position.

Tip   If you are using the button only as a container for your keystroke event handler and you do not want the button to appear on Stage, you should make sure that (in Edit mode for the symbol) all the frames of the Button symbol timeline are blank.

For example, if you have a Button instance on the Stage of your Flash document, you can select the Button instance, open the Actions panel, and add the following code to capture an Enter keystroke:

```
on (keyPress "<Enter>"){
    trace("The Enter key was pressed.");
}
```

Note   A `trace` action sends a message to the Output panel in the Test Movie environment. You learn more about `trace` actions in Part VII of this book.

As you can see in this example, you specify the key's name between a set of double quotes, after the `keyPress` term. Some keys, such as Enter and Escape, require less than (<) and greater than (>) characters as well. You can use the `keyPress` event in conjunction with other mouse events. The following example detects when the user clicks the mouse button over the Hit state of the Flash button or presses the spacebar key anywhere within the Flash movie:

```
on (release, keyPress "<Space>"){
    stop();
}
```

The `keyPress` event, which was introduced with Flash Player 4, and the newer `Key` object, introduced with Flash Player 6, open up many possibilities for Flash. Movies can have keyboard-based navigation, buttons can have keyboard shortcuts for convenience and accessibility, and games can have keyboard-controlled objects (such as ships and animated characters). But watch out for some potential "gotchas" to keyboard usage, *specifically with* `on` *handlers and* `keyPress` *events.* If you're planning ambitious keyboard-based projects, you may want to check the following list of potential issues first:

✦ Multiple key combinations are not supported. This scenario rules out diagonals as two-key combinations in the classic four-key game control setup. It also means shortcuts such as Ctrl+S are not available. You can, however, use the Shift key in combination with another key to specify an uppercase letter or symbol. (See the case-sensitive note later in this list.)

✦ If presented in a browser, the Flash movie must have "focus" before keystrokes can be recognized. To "focus" the movie, the user must click anywhere in the space it occupies within the browser window. Keyboard-based movies should include instructions that prompt the user to perform this initial mouse click.

Tip   You can use the JavaScript `focus()` method in HTML documents to automatically draw attention to a Flash movie contained within the page. You can use the `onLoad` event to initiate a JavaScript function that includes the `focus()` method to enable this behavior as soon as the page loads into the browser.

✦ Because the Escape (Esc), Enter, less than (<), and greater than (>) keys are used as authoring shortcuts in the Test Movie environment, you may want to avoid using them as control keys in your movies. If you need to use those keys in your movies, make sure that you test the movies in a browser, or use the Control ➪ Disable Keyboard Shortcuts option in the Test Movie environment.

✦ `keyPress` events are case-sensitive. For example, an uppercase letter "S" and a lowercase letter "s" can trigger two different actions. No case-insensitive keystroke event (that is, one that would enable both cases of a letter to trigger the same action) exists for Button instances and the `on` handler. Achieving case-insensitivity would require two separate `on` handlers (and their contained actions), one for each case of the letter, on the same Button instance. For example, the following code would stop the current timeline when either the s key or Shift+s key (or the s key with Caps Lock enabled) is pressed:

```
on (keyPress "s"){
     stop();
}
on (keyPress "S"){
     stop();
}
```

Note ActionScript's Key object, its methods, and its properties enable you to do much more with keystroke-based events than the on handler does. The Key object is discussed in greater detail in the *Flash MX 2004 ActionScript Bible* by Robert Reinhardt and Joey Lott.

Capturing time events with keyframes

The keyframe event handler depends on the playback of the movie itself, not on the user. Just about any action (except the on( ) and onClipEvent( ) handlers) can be attached to any keyframe on the timeline. An action attached to a keyframe is executed when the Playhead enters the keyframe, whether it enters naturally during the linear playback of the movie or as the result of a goto action. So, for instance, you may place a stop action on a keyframe to pause the movie at the end of an animation sequence.

In some multimedia applications, keyframe event handlers can differentiate between the Playhead *entering* a keyframe and *exiting* a keyframe. Flash has only one kind of keyframe event handler (essentially, on enter). Hence, as a developer, you do not need to add keyframe event handlers explicitly — they are a presumed element of any action placed on a keyframe. As mentioned in an earlier note, ActionScript 1.0 and 2.0 can employ a more advanced event model. You learn about different event models in Chapter 25, "Controlling Movie Clips."

Tip Complex movies can have dozens, or even hundreds, of actions attached to keyframes. To prevent conflicts between uses of keyframes for animation and uses of keyframes as action containers, it is highly advisable to create an entire layer solely for action keyframes. Name the layer **actions** and keep it on top of all your layers for easy access. Remember not to place any symbol instances, text, or artwork on your actions layer. You can also create a labels layer to hold — you guessed it — frame labels.

The process for adding an action to a keyframe is as follows:

1. Create a keyframe on a timeline. This keyframe can exist in the Main Timeline (that is, Scene 1) or a Movie Clip symbol timeline.

2. Select the keyframe in the Timeline window, and open the Actions panel. The Actions panel title should read Actions — Frame.

3. Type your desired actions in the Script pane.

In the next section, you'll get a little more hands-on experience adding actions to both buttons and keyframes.

Creating Invisible Buttons and Using getURL

In this section, you learn how to create an "invisible button" and practice the use of getURL actions. An invisible button is essentially a Button symbol that has only a Hit state defined, with empty Up, Over, and Down states. Once you have created an invisible button, you can use it to convert any type of Flash element into a button. By dragging an instance of the invisible button on top of another piece of artwork or symbol instance on the Stage, you can add interactivity to that element.

On the CD-ROM Make a copy of the `themakers_ad_starter.fla` file, located in the `ch18` folder of the book's CD-ROM. This file contains a sample layout of graphics and text for a mock Flash ad, sized for display on a Pocket PC screen. This document uses a Flash Player 6 version setting in the Publish Settings, which is why some actions in the Actions toolbox's booklets are highlighted in yellow.

With the starter Flash document (.fla file) open in Flash MX 2004, quickly familiarize yourself with the existing content. There are four layers on the Main Timeline (Scene 1). The comments layer indicates what the Flash document is, the border layer contains a black outlined box with no fill, the graphics layer contains a Graphic symbol of branding artwork, and the animText layer contains a Movie Clip instance featuring a tweened animation. Go ahead and test this movie (Control ➪ Test Movie) to see how these elements currently play. When the animation finishes, you should see the artwork displayed in Figure 18-8.

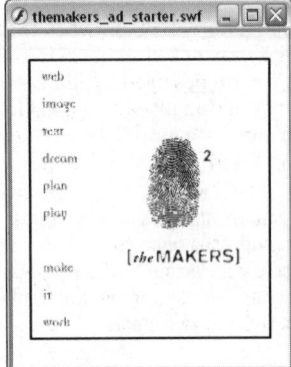

Figure 18-8: The artwork of the Flash movie designed for a Pocket PC screen

In this exercise, you're going to add two invisible buttons to this movie. One is an oval-shaped button that fits over the thumbprint graphic, and another is a rectangular-shaped button that fits over the company's name. The thumbprint button, when clicked, opens the e-mail client to send an email to the company. When the user clicks the name button, a new browser window opens displaying the company's Web page.

1. In the starter Flash document, create a new layer named **actions**. Place this layer just underneath the comments layer.

2. Select the first frame of this layer and open the Actions panel (F9). In the plus (+) menu, choose Global Functions ➪ Timeline Control ➪ stop. This will add a `stop()`; action to the keyframe. Currently, there is more than one frame on the Main Timeline, and if this Flash movie were to be developed further, we wouldn't want the Playhead going past the first frame without some input from the user.

3. With this first frame of the actions layer still selected, open the Property inspector and in the <Frame Label> field, type **//stop.** This will add a frame comment of //stop to the layer in the Timeline window. This comment provides a quick visual cue about the behavior of this keyframe.

4. Now you're going to make your first invisible button. Choose Insert ➪ New Symbol (Ctrl+F8 or ⌘+F8) and make a new Button symbol named **invisibleButton_rect.** This button will be the rectangular button that is placed over the company's name. Flash will take you right inside the symbol's workspace as soon as you press the OK button in the Create New Symbol dialog box.

5. Rename Layer 1 to **hit area graphic.** On this layer of the Button symbol's Timeline, create a keyframe for the Hit state. Move the Playhead in the Timeline window to this new keyframe.

6. Select the Rectangle tool, and draw a uniform square on the symbol's Stage. The square can be any color, although we prefer red for invisible buttons. If you drew the shape with a stroke, delete the stroke. Select the square, and in the Property inspector, give the square a width and height of **50** pixels. Then, using the Align panel, center the square on the Stage. Your Button symbol and Timeline should now resemble Figure 18-9.

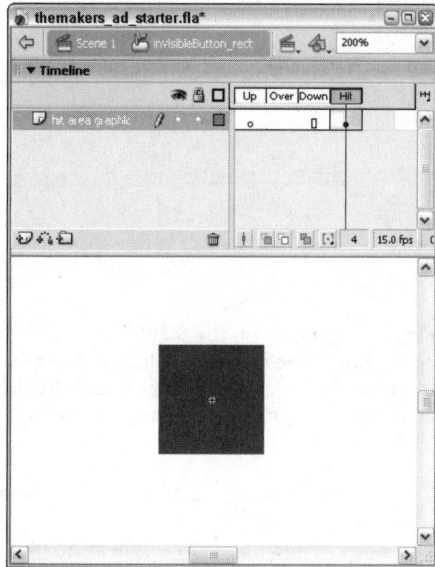

Figure 18-9: The square will act as the active area of the Button symbol.

7. Now, go back to Scene 1 (the Main Timeline), and create a new layer. Rename this layer **linkButton**, and place it above the graphics layer.

8. Open the Library panel (Ctrl+L or ⌘+L), and drag an instance of the `invisible Button_rect` symbol to the Stage. Place this instance over the company's name. Using the Free Transform tool, size the instance to fit the size of the text, without overlapping other elements on the Stage. You'll notice that your Button instance has a transparent aqua blue tint that overlays the underlying elements (as shown in Figure 18-10). This is Flash's way of enabling you to select and manipulate an invisible button. You will not see this color effect for the button when the document is published as a Flash movie (.swf file).

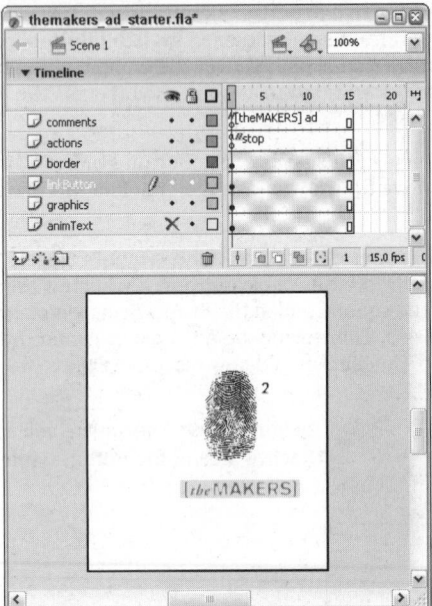

Figure 18-10: The aqua blue tint of the
Button instance indicates the presence
of a button that has only a Hit state.

9. With the Selection tool, select the Button instance on the Stage, and open the Actions
panel (F9). Your Action panel title bar should read **Actions - Button**. Using the booklets
in the Actions toolbox, add an on handler from the Global Functions ⇨ Movie Clip
Control booklet. Inside the on handler, specify a release event. Your Script pane should
show the following code:

```
on (release){
}
```

10. In the Script pane, click the mouse pointer just before the closing curly brace (}) on
line 2. Now add a getURL action from the Global Functions ⇨ Browser/Network booklet.
Specify a URL for the first parameter of the action, and a blank browser window target
for the second parameter, as shown in the following code:

```
on (release){
    getURL("http://www.theMakers.com", "_blank");
}
```

For this example, we used the URL http://www.theMakers.com. When you're linking
to domain names, make sure you specify the transfer protocol (such as http://,
ftp://, and so on). If you are linking to relative URLs, specify the name of the HTML
document (or other resource) that you want to access. This on() handler with the
getURL() action will direct a button click on this instance to [theMAKERS] Web site,
in a new browser window.

11. Save your Flash document as `themakers_ad.fla`, and test it using Publish Preview ➪ HTML (Ctrl+F12 or ⌘+F12). In the browser window, roll over the company's name in the Flash movie. You'll notice that this area is an active button. When you click the button, a new browser window will open, displaying the company's Web page.

12. Now, let's go back to the Flash document and add another invisible button. You'll use a different procedure this time. On the Scene 1 timeline, create a new layer and name it **emailButton.** Place this layer above the linkButton layer.

13. On the first frame of the emailButton layer, select the Oval tool, and draw a perfect circle anywhere on the Stage. Again, you can use any fill color you wish. If the circle has a stroke, delete the stroke. With this circle selected, open the Property inspector and give the circle a width and height of **50** pixels.

14. With the circle selected, choose Insert ➪ Convert to Symbol (F8). In the Convert to Symbol dialog box, make a Button symbol named **invisibleButton_oval** and click OK.

15. Now, edit the new symbol, either by double-clicking the instance on the Stage, or by double-clicking its listing in the Library panel. On this symbol's timeline, rename Layer 1 to **hit area graphic**. Now, select the keyframe for the Up state, and drag it to the Hit state. Note that you may need to click, then click and drag the keyframe for this method to work properly. When you are finished, your circle shape should be on only the Hit area of the button's timeline.

16. Go back to the Scene 1 timeline, and you'll notice that your circle button is now an invisible button, just as our rectangular one. Move the circular invisible button over the thumbprint graphic, and use the Free Transform tool to shape the circle as an oval that closely matches the shape of the thumbprint, as shown in Figure 18-11.

17. With the oval invisible button selected, open the Actions panel. Repeat Steps 9 and 10 of this exercise. This time, however, we'll use a `mailto:` URL, as in `"mailto:info@theMakers.com"`. Type this value as the first parameter of a `getURL` action for this Button instance. For this `getURL` action, however, you do not need to specify a window parameter.

18. Save your Flash document once again, and preview it in a browser. When you click the active area over the thumbprint graphic, the default e-mail client on your system should open, displaying a new message window with the To: field predefined to the URL you typed in Step 17.

Tip   You can specify subject lines and body text in `mailto:` URLs as well, just as you can with HTML documents. For example, the following code will open a new e-mail message window addressed to `info@theMakers.com`, a subject line of "Web Feedback" and body text of "Here are my comments". The following code should be typed as one line of code.

```
getURL("mailto:info@theMakers.com?subject=Web%20Feedback&body=
Here%20are%20my%20comments%3A");
```

Now you know how to make invisible buttons and add `getURL` actions to them. In your own work, you may come to realize the true benefit of invisible buttons: You can quickly drag several instances of either invisible button shape (oval or rectangle) to the Stage to create active areas. This offers two benefits: First, you don't have to make Button symbols from regular graphics that don't need four button states, and second, you can make "hidden" areas in interactive puzzles or games.

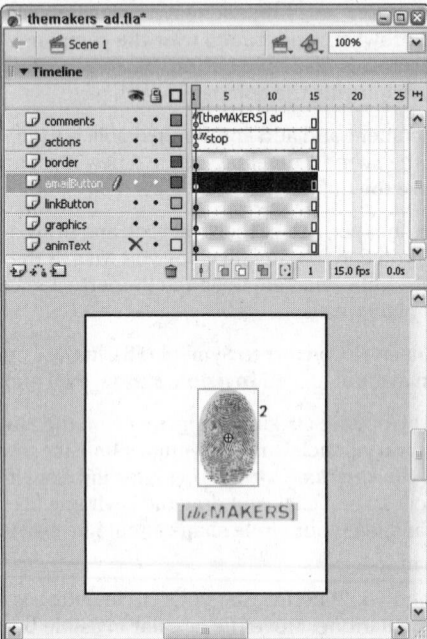

Figure 18-11: The thumbprint graphic now has an invisible button on top of it.

Web Resource

We'd like to know what you thought about this chapter. Visit www.flashsupport.com/feedback to fill out an online form with your comments.

Summary

✦ ActionScript is Flash's interactive language. It is a set of actions that enables Flash to communicate with internal elements (timelines, symbols, sounds, and so on) and external Web pages and scripts.

✦ The Behaviors panel, new to Flash MX 2004, allows the novice user to quickly add interactive commands to Flash movie elements.

✦ Flash interactivity is based on a relatively simple structure: An event handler waits for something to happen (a playback point being reached or the user providing input), and when that something does happen, it executes one or more actions (which alter the movie's playback, behavior, or properties; loads a file; or executes a script).

✦ The Timeline Control booklet contains the fundamental actions for navigating Flash playback through multiple scenes and keyframes, as well as controlling soundtracks. The Browser/Network booklet contains the getURL action, which can direct the browser window to external Web resources such as HTML pages and FTP downloads.

✦ All actions need an event handler to activate them. Event handlers include keyframes on a timeline, button clicks, mouse movements, and key presses. More-advanced event handlers are discussed in later chapters.

✦ Invisible buttons enable you to create interactive areas on top of other Flash artwork or symbols.

✦　　✦　　✦

Building Timelines and Interactions

Unlike most multimedia authoring applications, Flash has the capability to use multiple simultaneous timelines in its movies. So far, most of the examples in this book have only one timeline or have used only one scene. You've seen how to add basic actions to your movies to make them interactive. Now you begin exploring the world of multiple movie timelines using the Movie Clip symbol.

Movie Clips: The Key to Self-Contained Playback

A powerful addition to the Flash format was the Movie Clip symbol, introduced in version 3. Movie Clips enabled Flash developers to create complex behaviors by nesting self-contained sequences of animation or interactivity inside each other. These sequences could then be placed as discrete, self-playing modules on the Main Timeline (that is, Scene 1). Initially, the key to the power of Movie Clips was their ability to communicate with and control each other via the tellTarget action.

In Flash 4, the role of Movie Clips was expanded — they could be used with ActionScript. That capability put Movie Clips at the foundation of advanced interactivity in Flash. In Flash 5, when ActionScript matured into a full-blown scripting language that mirrored JavaScript, Movie Clips became the central object of programming. In Flash MX, Movie Clips could utilize more compiler directives, which allowed them to become full-blown user-interface components. In Flash MX 2004, Movie Clips and components continue to evolve and play a vital role in the organization of a Flash movie's content and interactivity. In this chapter, you'll look at several key features of the Movie Clip symbol.

Cross-Reference   We discuss Movie Clip symbols as the MovieClip object in Part VII, "Approaching ActionScript," where you learn more about the object's methods and properties.

How Movie Clips interact within a Flash movie

Previous chapters dealt with Flash movies as a single sequence of frames arranged along a single timeline. Whether the playback along that timeline was linear (traditional animation) or non-linear (where the Playhead jumps arbitrarily to any frame), our example movies have normally comprised only the frames of a single timeline. Ostensibly, a single timeline may seem to provide everything you'd need to create any Flash behavior, but as you get more inventive or ambitious, you'll soon find yourself conceiving ideas for animated and interactive segments that are thwarted by the limits of a single timeline.

Suppose you want to create a looping animation of a dog with its tail wagging. You decide that the tail should wag every 5 seconds and the dog should bark every 15 seconds. On a single timeline, you'd need a loop of 180 frames to accommodate the timing of the bark (assuming a frame rate of 12 frames per second), and repeating keyframes for the wagging tail artwork every 60 frames. Although animating a dog in that manner would be a bit cumbersome, it wouldn't be impossible — until your dog had to move around the screen as an integrated whole. Making the bark and the wagging tail loop while the whole dog moved around complex paths for extended periods of time would quickly become impractical, especially if the dog were only one part of a larger environment.

Now imagine that you could make the dog by creating two whole separate movies, one for the tail and one for the barking mouth and sound. Could you then place those movies as self-contained, animated objects on the Main Timeline, just like a graphic or a button? Well, you can — that's what Movie Clips are all about. Movie Clips are independent sequences of frames (timelines) that can be defined outside the context of the Main Timeline and then placed onto it as objects on a single frame. You create Movie Clips the same way you create a Graphic symbol in Edit mode. Unlike a Graphic symbol, a Movie Clip (as the name implies) acts in most cases just like a fully functional SWF file, meaning, for instance, that frame actions in Movie Clip timelines are functional. After you have created a Movie Clip as a symbol, you drop instances of it into any keyframe of the Main Timeline or any other Movie Clip timeline. The following are some general Movie Clip principles:

✦ During playback as a Flash SWF file, a Movie Clip instance placed on a timeline begins to play as soon as the frame on which it occurs is reached, whether or not the Main Timeline (or the clip's parent timeline) is playing.

✦ A Movie Clip plays back autonomously, meaning that as long as it is present on the Stage it is not governed by the playing or stopping of the Main Timeline.

✦ Movie Clips can play when the Main Timeline is stopped, or stay halted when the Main Timeline plays.

✦ Like a Graphic or a Button symbol, Movie Clips can be manipulated on the Stage — you can size them, skew them, rotate them, place effects such as alpha blending on them, or tween them, all while the frames within them continue to play.

✦ All timelines play at the frame rate specified by the Document Properties dialog box (Modify ➪ Document) or the Property inspector (when the Document window is focused, and all items on the Stage are deselected). However, it is possible to modify playback behavior of a timeline with ActionScript routines.

In our dog wagging and barking example, the tail and head of the dog could be looping Movie Clips, and then those Movie Clips could be nested inside another Movie Clip symbol (representing the entire dog). This "whole" dog clip could then be tweened around the Stage on the Main Timeline to make the dog move. You could use the same principle to move a Movie Clip of a butterfly with flapping wings along a motion path.

One movie, several timelines

Because a Flash movie can have more than one timeline existing in the same space and time, there must be a way to organize Movie Clips within the Main Timeline (Scene 1) of your Flash document. Just like artwork can be placed inside any symbol, symbol instances can be nested within other symbols. If you change the contents of the nested symbol, the parent symbol (the symbol containing the other symbol) will be updated as well. Although this may not seem special, it's of extreme importance to Movie Clips and Flash interactivity. Because the playback of each Movie Clip timeline is independent from any other timeline, you need to know how to tell Flash which Movie Clip you want to control.

The Flash movie diagram in Figure 19-1 illustrates multiple timelines. This Flash movie has two layers on the Main Timeline: Layer 1 and Layer 2. Layer 1 has a Movie Clip (instance "A") that exists for 19 frames on the Main Timeline. Layer 2 has a Movie Clip (instance "B") that exists for 10 frames on the Main Timeline, but it also contains a nested Movie Clip (instance "C").

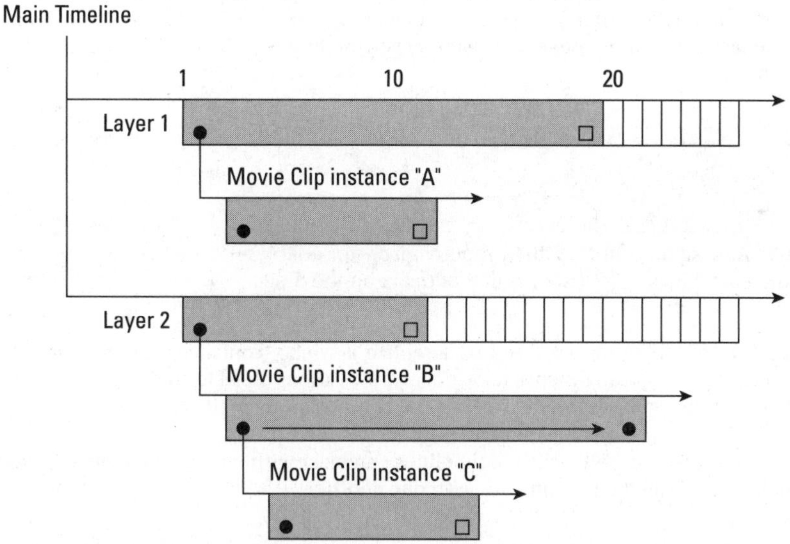

Main Timeline

Figure 19-1: This figure shows one method of diagramming Flash timelines.

In Figure 19-1, if the Main Timeline has a stop action on the first frame, all three Movie Clips will continue to play unless there are stop actions on their first frames or they are told to stop by actions targeted to them. If the Main Timeline plays to frame 20, instance "A" will no longer be on the Stage, regardless of how many frames it may have on its timeline. Figure 19-2 shows a more practical diagram of a timeline hierarchy.

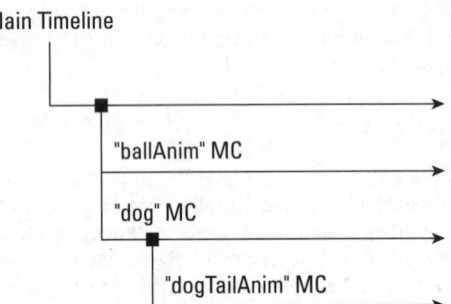

Main Timeline

"ballAnim" MC

"dog" MC

"dogTailAnim" MC

Figure 19-2: Flash movies can be flow-charted in this fashion. This diagram is similar to the Movie Explorer's method of displaying Flash movie information.

In Figure 19-2, you can see three Movie Clips. Two of them, `ballAnim` and `dog`, occupy space on the Main Timeline. The other one, `dogTailAnim`, is nested within the `dog` Movie Clip. Each Movie Clip instance on any given timeline *must* have a unique name — you can't have two or more Movie Clip instances on the same timeline using the same instance name. The instance name is specified in the Property inspector, shown in Figure 19-3. To see the settings for a particular instance, you must have the instance selected on the Stage before referencing the Property inspector.

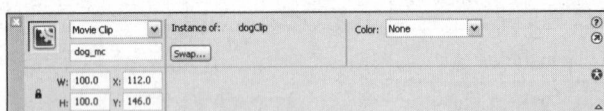

Figure 19-3: Among other things, the Property inspector enables you to name each Movie Clip instance that appears on the Stage.

Tip

The suffix `Anim` is commonly used to designate a symbol containing an animation. Also, using the `_mc` suffix with instance names allows the Actions panel to show code hints specifically for Movie Clip instances. You learn more about this later in the chapter.

Now that you understand how multiple timelines can exist within a Flash movie, let's see how you can make Movie Clips communicate with one another.

Targets and Paths Explained

If you already studied Movie Clips in Chapter 6, "Symbols, Instances, and the Library," you probably know that they provide the solution to our animated dog problem. However, you might not have guessed that Movie Clips can also add logic to animation and Flash interfaces. Let's take our animated dog example a little further: When dogs bark, their tails may stop wagging. Our hypothetical dog may look strange if it is barking and wagging at the same time. Suppose we wanted to stop the tail wagging during every bark. We'd have to have some way for the barking head Movie Clip to control the tail Movie Clip so that we could tell the tail to stop wagging when the dog barks, and then tell the tail to return to its wagging loop again when the bark is over.

What Is Dot Syntax?

Flash 5 introduced a new method of writing all ActionScript called *dot syntax*. Earlier versions of Flash used a natural-language scripting environment that was menu-based, in which actions could be read and understood easily and accessed via pop-up menus and dialog boxes. While most people prefer easy-to-use scripting environments, the production demands of complex interactive projects are often compromised by such menu-driven scripting environments. Computer programmers prefer to create, edit, and debug scripting with a language that can be accessed and modified easily. Consequently, we see the best of both worlds with Flash MX 2004.

ActionScript adheres closely to the ECMA-262 specification that is based on JavaScript, the universal scripting language used by most browsers for interactive HTML and DHTML documents. Therefore, Flash ActionScript uses a dot syntax, also known as Dots notation. What does that mean? It means that all actions are written within a standard formula that is common with object-oriented programming (OOP) languages:

```
Object.property = value;
```

or

```
Object.method();
```

The examples beg four things to be defined: objects, properties, methods, and values. An *object* is any element in a program (in this case, the Flash movie) that has changeable and accessible characteristics. Objects can be user-defined (in other words, you create and name them) or predefined by the programming language. Flash has several predefined objects, also called classes, meaning that they're already built into the ActionScript language. We look at object types in more detail in later chapters. An important object (and perhaps the easiest to conceptualize) is the MovieClip object. Any Movie Clip instance on the Stage is a MovieClip object, such as ballAnim_mc or dogTailAnim_mc. An object has characteristics, or *properties*, that can be updated or changed throughout the movie. An example of a MovieClip property is scale, which is referred to as _xscale and _yscale. We look at MovieClip properties in Chapter 25, "Controlling Movie Clips." Properties always have some data accompanying them. This data is called the property's *value*. Using the previous example, at full size, a MovieClip object's _xscale is 100 (the scale property uses percent as the unit of measure). For a MovieClip object named ballAnim_mc, this would be represented in ActionScript syntax as:

```
ballAnim_mc._xscale = 100;
```

Finally, objects can be enacted upon by procedures that do something to or with the object. These procedures are called *methods*. One method for the MovieClip object is the gotoAndPlay() method, which you used as a basic action in the previous chapter. In Flash 5 or higher movies, methods can be created for your own objects or predefined for existing Flash objects. Any goto action can be used as a method of any MovieClip object, as in:

```
ballAnim_mc.gotoAndPlay("start");
```

The preceding example tells the ballAnim_mc instance to direct its playback head to the frame label start on its timeline. This chapter helps you understand how to use the gotoAndPlay() method for Movie Clips.

Well, you have a few ways to control the tail Movie Clip from the barking head Movie Clip. In Flash 3 and 4, the `tellTarget` action was used to let actions on any timeline (including Movie Clip timelines and the Main Timeline) control what happens on any other timeline. How? `tellTarget` simply provided a mechanism for extending basic actions such as `play` and `stop`, enabling them to specify (or *target*) the Timeline upon which they should be executed. Targets are any Movie Clip instances that are available at the current "state" of a Flash movie — you can't target a Movie Clip that isn't displayed (or existing) on the Stage. For example, suppose you had two Movie Clips, one on frame 1 and another on frame 10 of the Main Timeline. If the Main Timeline was stopped on frame 1, you couldn't target the Movie Clip on frame 10 because the instance is not on the current frame.

Since Flash 5, developers have been able to direct actions to specific timelines by attaching the same actions as *methods* to the `MovieClip` object (we define methods in the following sidebar). As such, the `tellTarget` action is a deprecated action; it's still supported in current Flash Players, but it's been replaced with more versatile actions and syntax that make its use outdated. For an overview of deprecated actions, see the sidebar on deprecated actions in the preceding chapter. In this chapter, you work exclusively with the preferred ActionScript dot syntax to control Movie Clip instances. First, however, you need to understand how targeting works in Flash movies.

Note   If you're new to scripting, please read the "What Is Dot Syntax?" sidebar.

Paths: Absolute and relative modes

Earlier in this chapter, you learned how multiple Movie Clip timelines appear on the Stage. It's entirely possible to nest several Movie Clips within another Movie Clip. To understand how Movie Clips communicate with one other by using actions, you need to have a firm grasp on Movie Clip paths. A path is simply that — the route to a destination, an address *per se*. If you have a Movie Clip instance named `tailAnim_mc` inside a `dog_mc` Movie Clip instance, how is Flash supposed to know? What if there was more than one `tailAnim_mc` in the entire movie, with others nested in other Movie Clips besides the `dog_mc` instance? You can specify a Movie Clip's path in an absolute or a relative mode.

An *absolute path* is the full location information, or target, for a given Movie Clip instance from any other location (or target). Just like your postal address has a street name and number and a ZIP code so that people can find you on a map, all Movie Clips have a point of origin: the Main Timeline (that is, Scene 1). Flash MX 2004 only displays Dots notation with absolute and relative paths.

Flash MX 2004 no longer shows you Dots and Slash notation in the Insert Target Path dialog box. See the sidebar "Paths in Flash 4 or Earlier Movies" for an explanation of Slash notation.

Note   Dots notation and dot syntax are synonymous terms, and are used interchangeably throughout this book.

Dots notation follows the ActionScript language conventions. With Dots notation, the Main Timeline becomes

`_root`

A Movie Clip instance named `dog_mc` on the Main Timeline (or `_root`) would have an absolute path of

`_root.dog_mc`

Notice that a period, or dot, separates the term `_root` from `dog_mc`. The dot denotes a parent-child relationship; the `dog_mc` instance is a "child" of its parent, `_root`. And, following suit, a Movie Clip instance named `tailAnim_mc` that is nested within the `dog_mc` Movie Clip would have the absolute path of

`_root.dog_mc.tailAnim_mc`

A *relative path* is a contextual path to one timeline from another. From a conceptual point of view, think of a relative path as the relationship between the location of your pillow and the rest of your bed. Unless you have an odd sleeping habit, the pillow is located at the head of the bed. You may change the location of the bed within your room or the rooms of a house, but the relationship between the pillow and the bed remains the same. Another example that can illustrate the difference between absolute and relative references is the postal address example we used earlier. An absolute reference to your residence would use your full street address, city, state, and ZIP code. However, if you're giving directions to a friend of yours who lives nearby, you're more likely to tell your friend, "From your house, walk two blocks down A street, and turn right on B street. I'm five houses down on the left side of the street."

With Flash, relative Movie Clip paths are useful within Movie Clips that contain several nested Movie Clips. That way, you can move the container (or parent) Movie Clip from one timeline to another and expect the inner targeting of the nested Movie Clips to work. To refer to a timeline that is above the current timeline in Dots notation, use

`this._parent`

Here, the term `this` refers the current timeline from where the action is being called, and `_parent` refers to the current timeline's parent timeline. You can use relative Dots notation to refer up and down the hierarchy at the same time. For example, if you have two nested Movie Clips, such as `tailAnim_mc` and `barkingAnim_mc`, within a larger Movie Clip named `dog_mc`, you may want to target `tailAnim_mc` from `barkingAnim_mc`. The relative dots path for this task is

`this._parent.tailAnim_mc`

This path tells Flash to go up one timeline from the current timeline, `barkingAnim_mc`, to its parent timeline (the `dog_mc` timeline), and then look for the instance named `tailAnim_mc` from there.

You can also use successive `_parent` references to travel up in the timeline hierarchy multiple times, such as

`this._parent._parent`

Using the `dog_mc` instance example again, if you wanted to control the Main Timeline (which is the parent timeline of the `dog_mc` instance) from the `tailAnim_mc` instance, you could use `_parent._parent` in the target path of an action executed from the `tailAnim_mc` timeline.

Paths in Flash 4 or Earlier Movies

Before Flash 5, the Main Timeline was represented in a Movie Clip path as a starting forward slash (/) character. The absolute path of a Movie Clip instance named `dog_mc` on the Main Timeline is

```
/dog_mc
```

Any nested Movie Clips inside of the `dog_mc` instance would be referenced after that starting path. For example, the absolute path to `tailAnim_mc`, an instance inside the `dog_mc` Movie Clip instance, would be

```
/dog_mc/tailAnim_mc
```

Another / character was put between the two instance names. Think of the / as a substitute for the period or dot (.) in ActionScript target paths. Use of the / character in Movie Clip paths is known as the *Slash* notation.

The equivalent to `_parent` in Slash notation is a double-dot, as in

```
../
```

The two dots here work just like directory references for files on Web servers; use a pair of dots (..) for each timeline in the hierarchy.

Just as `tellTarget` is considered a deprecated action in Flash MX 2004, the Slash notation is deprecated syntax. It will still work with current Flash Players, but subsequent versions of the Flash authoring program will continue to be built upon Dots notation.

Note   You can directly control the Main Timeline using the reference `_root`. However, as you'll see later in Chapter 28, "Sharing and Loading Assets," you may load an entire SWF file into a Movie Clip instance, thereby changing the reference to `_root`. Flash MX 2004 has a new property of `MovieClip` objects, named `_lockroot`, which can help you avoid path problems when loading external SWF files.

As with absolute paths, we recommend that you become familiar with using the Dots notation for relative paths.

Okay, that's enough theory. Now, you're going to practice nesting Movie Clips inside of other Movie Clips, as well as target actions at specific instances using Dots notation.

Targeting Movie Clips in Flash MX 2004

In this section, you'll see how to make Movie Clips interact with one another by using Dots notation and ActionScript. Specifically, you're going to create our barking and wagging dog example. You begin this exercise with a starter Flash document (.fla file) located on the book's CD-ROM.

On the CD-ROM   Open the `stella_starter.fla` file found in the ch19/stella folder of this book's CD-ROM.

With the starter file open in Flash MX 2004, test the movie using Control ➪ Test Movie. You'll see that our dog, Stella, is wagging her tail. At timed intervals, she will bark. Right now, her tail keeps wagging as she barks. In this exercise, we'll show you how to stop the tail from wagging while Stella is barking. Close the Test Movie window and take a look at the Library panel. You'll find the following assets listed:

✦ **bark.wav:** This is the sound file used for Stella's bark. You will find this sound on the bark layer of the barkAnimClip Timeline.

✦ **barkAnimClip:** This Movie Clip symbol contains the animation for Stella's barking head. If you double-click this symbol in the Library panel, you'll see that the timeline has two layers, one for the sound and another for the head animation. This symbol is used in the stellaClip Movie Clip symbol.

✦ **bodyGraphic:** This Graphic symbol is artwork of Stella's body and legs. This is no animation on its timeline. The bodyGraphic symbol is used in the stellaClip Movie Clip symbol.

✦ **headGraphic:** This Graphic symbol is artwork of Stella's head. You'll find a couple of instances of this symbol in the barkAnimClip symbol.

✦ **stellaClip:** This Movie Clip timeline contains instances of the barkAnimClip, bodyGraphic, and tailAnimClip symbols.

✦ **tailGraphic:** This Graphic symbol contains the artwork for Stella's tail.

✦ **tailAnimClip:** This Movie Clip symbol contains two instances of the tailGraphic symbol. Each instance is rotated differently to create the wagging effect.

Tip   As you can see by the names of the symbols, you can adopt naming conventions for your symbol types in the Library panel. All Movie Clip symbols use a "Clip" suffix, and Graphic symbols use a "Graphic" suffix. A naming convention can help you quickly identify the type of asset just by looking at its name.

Now, you're going to add some behaviors to the movie. First, you'll need to name the instances in the movie. ActionScript can find a Movie Clip instance only by its instance name. Using the Property inspector, you'll add instance names to all of the Movie Clip instances. Each instance will be named with a _mc suffix, as in tailAnim_mc, in order to work with Flash MX 2004's code hinting feature.

Once the instances are named, you can then target the instances with ActionScript. In this example, you'll target the tailAnim_mc instance from the barkAnim_mc. When the keyframe containing the barking mouth inside of barkAnim_mc is reached, the movie will tell the tailAnim_mc to go to and stop on a specific frame. When the barking is over, tailAnim_mc will be told to continue playing.

1. With stella_starter.fla open in Flash MX 2004, select the instance of the stellaClip symbol on the Stage, on the Main Timeline. Open the Property inspector, and name the instance stella_mc in the <Instance Name> field, as shown in Figure 19-4. Rename the stella layer to stella_mc as well.

2. Double-click the stella_mc instance on the Stage to edit the stellaClip symbol in the Library. Select the barkAnimClip symbol instance, and again, using the Property inspector, name this instance barkAnim_mc in the <Instance Name> field. Rename the barkAnim layer to **barkAnim_mc**.

Figure 19-4: You can name Movie Clip instances in the Property inspector.

3. Select the tailAnimClip symbol instance located on the tailAnim layer. Name the instance in the Property inspector, using the name tailAnim_mc. Rename the tailAnim layer to **tailAnim_mc**.

4. With all of the Movie Clip instances named, you can now target actions to specific time-lines. Your first goal is to stop the wagging tail while Stella barks. Double-click the barkAnim_mc instance to edit the barkAnimClip symbol's timeline.

5. On the barkAnimClip timeline, create a new layer and rename it **actions**. Place this layer at the top of the layer stack. On frame 14 of this new layer, insert an empty keyframe (F7). Frame 14 is the frame just before the Stream sound on the bark layer begins. On frame 14, you want to tell the tailAnim_mc instance to stop playing. So, let's give this keyframe a frame comment that indicates this behavior. With the keyframe selected, open the Property inspector and, in the <Frame Label> field, type //**stop wagging**, as shown in Figure 19-5.

6. After you have assigned a comment on the frame, you're ready to write the ActionScript to perform the described behavior. With frame 14 selected on the actions layer, open the Actions panel (F9). Click the Target Path selector icon (see Figure 18-1 for its location). The Insert Target Path dialog box will open, as shown in Figure 19-6. Click the plus icon (+) next to the stella_mc instance to reveal the nested instances, barkAnim_mc and tailAnim_mc. Select the tailAnim_mc instance because it contains the wagging anima-tion that you want to stop. Finally, make sure the Absolute option is selected in the Mode setting. Click OK.

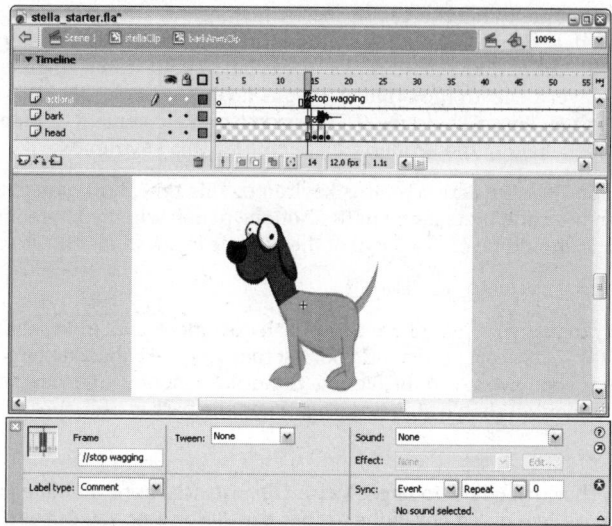

Figure 19-5: Frame comments can be used to describe the actions on a keyframe.

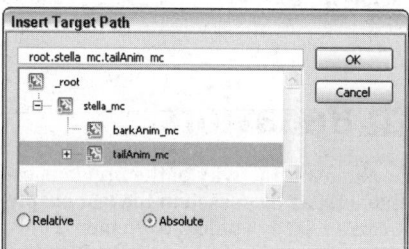

Figure 19-6: The Insert Target Path dialog box can help you build the path to a Movie Clip instance.

7. In the Script pane of the Actions panel, you now see the path to the instance _root. stella_mc.tailAnim_mc. After this name, type a single dot, or period (.). Almost immediately, you'll see the code hints menu appear next to your text. Because you named your instances with a _mc suffix, Flash MX 2004 knows that the code hinting should show actions (or methods and properties) relevant only to Movie Clip instances. In the menu, scroll down to the stop method and double-click it. Then, end the line of code with a semicolon (;). When you are finished, the Script pane should contain the following code:

```
_root.stella_mc.tailAnim_mc.stop();
```

8. Use this same technique to tell the `tailAnim_mc` instance to start playing again once the bark has ended. In the barkAnimClip symbol timeline, create yet another actions layer. You can make more than one to prevent overlap of your frame comments. Place this new actions layer beneath the original actions layer. On frame 20 of this second actions layer, insert an empty keyframe (F7). Assign a frame comment of **//start wagging** in the <Frame Label> field of the Property inspector for this keyframe.

9. Repeat Steps 6 and 7 for the action on this keyframe. This time, however, choose a `play` action from the code hints menu in the Actions panel. When you are finished, the following code should be on frame 20 of the actions layer:

```
_root.stella_mc.tailAnim_mc.play();
```

10. Now you're ready to test your movie. Save the Flash document as `stella_absolute.fla`. You'll use the suffix `_absolute` to remind yourself that you used absolute target paths in this example. After you have saved the file, use Control ⇨ Test Movie to view your movie. When Stella barks, her tail should stop wagging. When the bark is over, the tail should resume wagging.

This example has shown you how to target Movie Clip instances using absolute paths built with the Insert Target Path dialog box in the Actions panel. However, you can also try using relative paths to target the instances. In the ch19/stella folder of the book's CD-ROM, open the `stella_relative.fla` file to see an example of relative path addressing. Note that this example also uses a `gotoAndStop(2)` action on the `//stop wagging` keyframe to make sure Stella's tail is pointed down during the bark. You can also find a completed example file for the exercise you just completed, `stella_absolute.fla`.

Targeting Movie Clips with Behaviors

In this section, you learn how to include the same interactivity of the previous exercise using Flash MX 2004's new behaviors feature. Behaviors, as discussed in the last chapter, are self-contained blocks of ActionScript code that can be easily applied to elements in your Flash movie. In the following steps, you use behaviors instead of hand-coded actions to stop Stella's tail from wagging during the bark cycle.

As the starter file for this exercise, use the `stella_absolute.fla` document in the ch19/stella folder of this book's CD-ROM.

1. Open the `stella_absolute.fla` document, and double-click the `stella_mc` instance on the Stage.

2. On the stellaClip timeline, double-click the `barkAnim_mc` instance (that is, Stella's head).

3. On the barkAnimClip timeline, select frame 14 on the topmost actions layer. Open the Actions panel (F9), select the existing ActionScript code in the Script pane, and press the Delete or Backspace key to erase the code. Close the Actions panel when you're finished.

4. Rename the topmost actions layer to **behaviors**. Re-select frame 14 of this layer, and open the Behaviors panel (Shift+F3). Click the Add Behavior (+) button and choose

Movieclip ➪ Goto And Stop at frame or label. In the dialog box for this behavior, you'll notice a similar interface to that of the Insert Target Path dialog box. Expand the stella_mc node, and choose the tailAnim_mc instance. In the frame field, type the number **2**. See Figure 19-7 for a review of the settings. Click OK to accept the settings.

Figure 19-7: The Goto and Stop at frame or label behavior settings

5. Select frame 20 of the lower actions layer, and erase the existing ActionScript code on this keyframe, as you did in Step 3.

6. Rename the lower actions layer **behaviors**. With frame 20 of the lower behaviors layer selected, click the Add Behavior (+) button in the Behaviors panel, and choose Movieclip ➪ Goto and Play at frame or label. In this behavior's dialog box, expand the stella_mc node, and choose the tailAnim_mc instance. In the frame field, type the number **2**. See Figure 19-8. Click OK to accept the settings.

Figure 19-8: The Goto and Play at frame or label behavior settings

Tip

You can review the ActionScript code that the behavior uses by selecting its keyframe in the Timeline window and opening the Actions panel. Do not edit this code, however, or the behavior will not likely function properly.

7. Save your document as `stella_behaviors.fla`, and choose Control ➪ Test Movie. The Flash movie should operate exactly the same as the movie you created in the last section. When Stella barks, the tail stops wagging. When the bark is finished, the tail resumes wagging.

On the CD-ROM

You can find the completed example, `stella_behaviors.fla`, in the `ch19/stella` folder of this book's CD-ROM.

Integrating Behaviors with Movie Clips

Chapter 15 discussed the ins and outs of sound import and use in Flash documents. In this chapter, we show you how to create a sound library using Flash MX 2004's new Behaviors panel. Once the set of sounds is created, you learn how to stop the sounds from keyframes in another Movie Clip timeline.

On the CD-ROM

You'll find sound files (WAV and AIF formats) in the `ch19/pianoKeys/sounds` folder of the *Macromedia Flash MX 2004 Bible* CD-ROM. Make a copy of the `pianoKeys_starter.fla` file for this exercise. This file is located in the `ch19/pianoKeys` folder.

Overview of the pianoKeys Movie Clip

Open the `pianoKeys_starter.fla` file. A `keys_mc` Movie Clip instance is already on the Stage of the Main Timeline. Double-click the `keys_mc` instance to enter Edit mode, as shown in Figure 19-9. Note that the Timeline window is docked to the left side of the Document window.

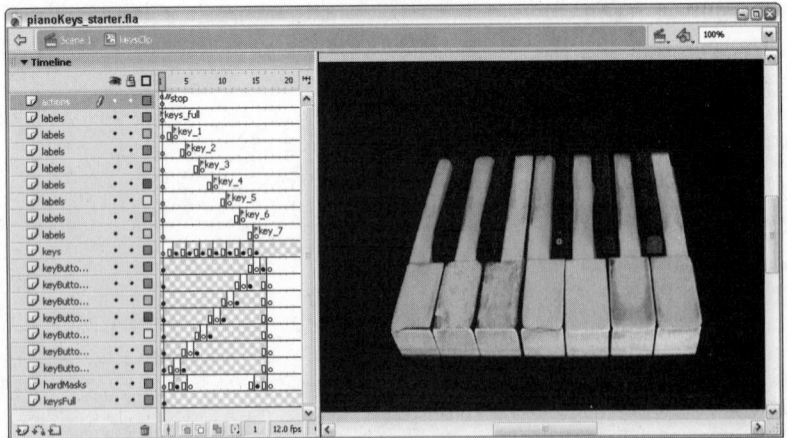

Figure 19-9: The Timeline window showing the frames of the keysClip Movie Clip symbol

The timeline for the keysClip symbol has several layers for individual Button instances and labels. If you test this movie using Control ⇨ Test Movie (Ctrl+Enter or ⌘+Enter), you'll see that the Button instances over each piano key will tell the Playhead of the keysClip timeline to go to that key's frame label. For the first key on the left, the button on layer keyButton_1 has the following action list:

```
on (press, keyPress "a") {
    gotoAndStop ("key_1");
}
on (rollOver) {
    gotoAndStop ("keys_full");
}
```

These actions don't use any Dots notation—they are simple navigation actions that you learned in the last chapter. When the keyButton_1 instance is clicked with the mouse, the Playhead moves to the key_1 label on the current timeline, which is the keysClip timeline. Unless targeting is used, all actions on a Button instance will target the timeline on which the button exists.

When the timeline goes to the key_1 frame label, a new PNG bitmap of a "pressed" piano key (key_01.png on the keys layer) appears on top of the keys_full.png bitmap that is placed on the bottom keysFull layer. Note that the keys_full.png bitmap is present throughout the entire keysClip timeline. Each Button instance in the keysClip Movie Clip sends the Playhead to the appropriate piano key frame label.

Now that you have an understanding of what's happening in this Movie Clip, let's create some sounds with the Behaviors panel. These sounds will be targeted by the keys_mc instance later in this chapter.

Create sound instances with a behavior

Before we start making sound instances, you need to establish *a naming convention* for your sounds. A naming convention is simply a way of consistently identifying components in any project, in or out of Flash. To a member of a Web production team, the importance of naming conventions cannot be overemphasized—everyone involved with the project should know how to give names to images, sounds, symbol names, instance names, and so on. Even if you work by yourself, a naming convention provides a system of integrating elements from project to project and enables you to identify elements much more easily when you open old files.

1. For each key on the piano, you'll make a unique sound. Each sound will be on its own timeline where it can be targeted to play. Because there are seven keys on this odd piano, you need to import seven sounds into the Flash document. Using File ⇨ Import to Library, locate the ch19/pianoKeys/sounds folder on the *Macromedia Flash MX 2004 Bible* CD-ROM. Import each of the key sounds (AIF or WAV files) into your Flash document.

Cross-Reference
If you need to know how to import sound files into Flash, refer to Chapter 15, "Adding Sound."

2. Link each sound in the library, so that the sounds can be referenced by ActionScript (and behaviors). Open the Library panel (Ctrl+L or ⌘+L) and right-click, or Control+click on Mac, the key_1.wav (or key_1.aif) file. Choose Linkage in the contextual menu. When the Linkage Properties dialog box opens, select the Export for ActionScript check box. Change the auto-filled text in the Identifier field to key_1. Refer to Figure 19-10. When you are finished, click OK to accept the settings.

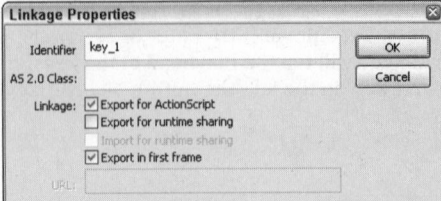

Figure 19-10: The Linkage Properties settings for the key_1.wav (or key_1.aif) file in the Library panel

3. Repeat Step 2 for each sound file in the Library panel, matching the number of the linkage identifier name to the number used in the filename. For example, the `key_2.wav` (or `key_2.aif`) file should be linked as `key_2`. When you are finished, expand the width of your Library panel to reveal the Linkage column. Your sound files should have identifiers displayed, as shown in Figure 19-11.

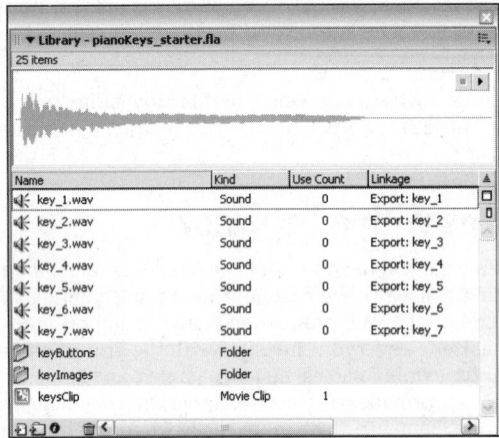

Figure 19-11: The Library panel's Linkage column displays the identifier values for all linked assets.

4. Now you're ready to use behaviors to create ActionScript-ready references to the sounds in the Library. Make sure you are on the Main Timeline (Scene 1) of the `pianoKeys_starter.fla` document. On this timeline, you should see a `keys_mc` layer. Create another layer and rename it **behaviors**.

5. Select the first frame of this new layer, and open the Behaviors panel (Shift+F3). Click the Add Behavior (+) button in the top-left corner of the panel, and choose Sound ⇨ Load Sound from Library from the menu. In the Load Sound from Library dialog box, type **key_1** in the top field, which specifies the linkage ID for the asset you want to load. In the lower field, type keySnd_1. This term will be the ActionScript object to target with behaviors you'll use later in this exercise. Also, clear the **Play this sound when loaded** check box—you *don't* want the sound to start playing when the movie starts. See Figure 19-12 for a review of these settings. Click OK to accept the parameters of the behavior.

Figure 19-12: Each sound requires a unique instance name (the lower field name).

6. Repeat Step 5 for each sound in the Library, matching the instance name's number to the number used in the linkage identifier. For example, the Load Sound from Library behavior for the `key_2.wav` (or `key_2.aif`) file should specify key_2 for the top field and keySnd_2 for the lower field. When you are finished completing this task for every sound in the Library, you should have seven behaviors listed in the Behaviors panel. You can double-click the Action name of each behavior to review that behavior's settings.

7. Save your Flash document as `pianoKeys_sounds.fla`.

On the CD-ROM You can refer to the `pianoKeys_sounds.fla` file located in the ch19/pianoKeys folder of the *Macromedia Flash MX 2004 Bible* CD-ROM. This file has the seven sound files in the Library panel, sorted in the keySounds folder.

Targeting the sounds with more behaviors

Now that you have behaviors set up for the sounds, you're ready to begin controlling the sounds with additional behaviors attached to keyframes in the keysClip timeline. This section of the exercise shows you how to add behaviors to the keysClip timeline that will target the sound instances.

Note There will be more than one actions layer in this timeline. The actions layer in Step 1 is a new layer in addition to the existing actions layer (with the `//stop` comment).

1. Enter Edit mode by double-clicking the `keys_mc` instance on the Main Timeline (Scene 1). On the keysClip Timeline, add a new layer and name it **behaviors**. Move this new actions layer underneath the layer that contains the key_1 frame label, as shown in Figure 19-13.

2. On frame 3 of the new behaviors layer, you need to add a behavior that will play the first Sound instance, `keySnd_1`. Remember that the Button instances on the keysClip timeline already move the Playhead to each key's label. Insert a blank keyframe (F7) on frame 3.

3. With the new keyframe selected, open the Behaviors panel (Shift+F3). Click the Add Behavior (+) button, and choose Sound ⇨ Play Sound. In the Play Sound dialog box, type **keySnd_1**, as shown in Figure 19-14. Click OK to close the dialog box.

4. Now, open the Property inspector. With frame 3 of the second actions layer selected, type **//play sound** into the <Frame Label> field. Your Timeline window should resemble Figure 19-15.

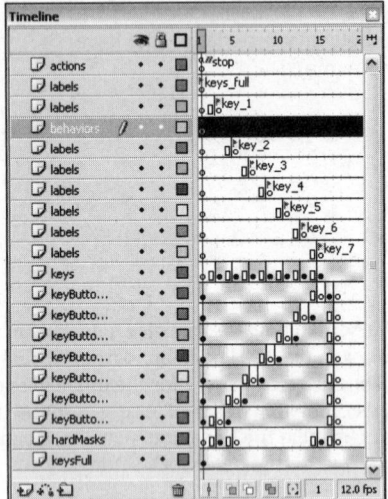

Figure 19-13: Don't be afraid to keep information separated on actions and labels layers. Separating the information will make it much easier for you to access the appropriate sections of your timelines.

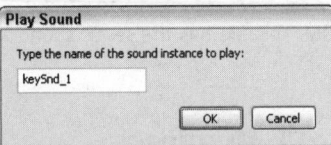

Figure 19-14: The Play Sound behavior can play a sound set up by the Load Sound from Library behavior.

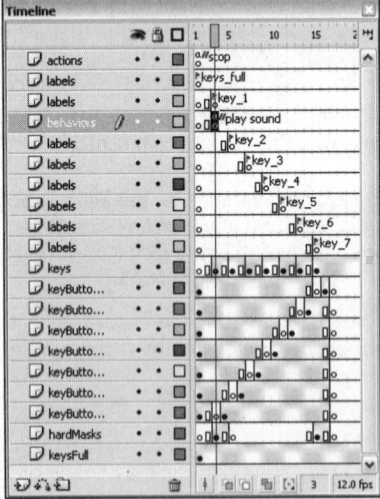

Figure 19-15: The //play sound comment lets you know what the behavior on this keyframe does.

At this point, you will want to test your movie to see if the behavior is finding the target and playing the sound. Save your document, and use Control ➪ Test Movie to create a Flash movie (.swf file). Make sure that the behavior on the keyframe works by clicking the first key on the piano keyboard (from the left), and that you hear a sound.

5. Now, you need to enable all the other sound instances created by your earlier Load Sound from Library behaviors. Create a new layer and name it **behaviors**. Place the new layer underneath the label layer that contains the key_2 frame label. Copy the //play sound keyframe from the previous actions layer, by selecting the keyframe and choosing Edit ➪ Timeline ➪ Copy Frames. Then, paste the copied keyframe to frame 5 of the new behaviors layer. Select frame 5 and choose Edit ➪ Timeline ➪ Paste Frames.

6. Select the new //play sound keyframe in the behaviors layer underneath the key_2 frame label layer. Open the Behaviors panel (Shift+F3). You need to change the copied Play Sound behavior to point to the keySnd_2 instance. Double-click the Play Sound item in the Action column of the panel. In the Play Sound dialog box, change the target to **keySnd_2**, as shown in Figure 19-16.

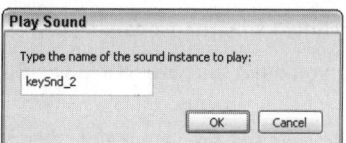

Figure 19-16: This Play Sound behavior targets the keySnd_2 instance.

7. Repeat Steps 5 and 6 for each key and sound. Each key_ frame label should have its own behaviors layer with a //play sound keyframe. Test your movie each time you add a new keyframe with ActionScript. If a particular key doesn't work, check the target's name in the Play Sound settings.

8. When you've finished adding a behavior for every key, save the document as pianoKeys_behaviors.fla and test it. After all's been said and done, you should have a functional Flash piano (well, at least 7 keys' worth!) that plays a sound whenever you click a piano key. If you want to change the sounds, you can either update the sound file in the Library or import new ones.

You can refer to the complete exercise file, pianoKeys_behaviors.fla, located in the ch19/pianoKeys folder of the book's CD-ROM.

We'll discuss more sound-related ActionScript in Chapter 27, "Interacting with Movie Clips," and Chapter 28, "Sharing and Loading Assets."

We'd like to know what you thought about this chapter. Visit www.flashsupport.com/feedback to fill out an online form with your comments.

Summary

✦ Movie Clips are the key to Flash interactivity. Each Movie Clip has its own independent timeline and playback.

✦ Each Movie Clip instance needs a unique name on any given timeline. You cannot reuse the same name on other Movie Clips on a timeline. You can, however, use the same instance name on different timelines.

✦ There are two types of target paths for Movie Clips: absolute and relative. Absolute paths start from the Main Timeline and end with the targeted instance name. Relative paths start from the timeline that's issuing the action(s) and end with the targeted instance name.

✦ The Slash and Dots notations are formats for writing either absolute or relative paths. The Slash notation is considered deprecated, and should be avoided unless you are authoring for Flash Player 4 or earlier. The Dots notation was introduced in Flash 5 and has a more complete syntax for programming in ActionScript.

✦ All Movie Clips and Flash movie elements should adhere to a naming convention.

✦ The Insert Target Path dialog box can help you build the path to a Movie Clip instance, to use with another action.

✦ Behaviors can be used across timelines. For example, an instance of a sound created by a behavior on the Main Timeline can be accessed by another behavior located within another Movie Clip instance.

✦   ✦   ✦

Making Your First Flash MX 2004 Project

Now that you've learned the basic principles behind Flash actions, you probably want to start creating a presentation to put on a Web site. For this edition of the *Flash Bible*, we integrated several basic production principles into one chapter. This chapter teaches you how to make a simple interactive Flash movie that has basic navigation and text functionality, before we get into the nitty gritty of ActionScript in Part VII of the book.

The Main Timeline as the Site Layout

Before you can start creating a Flash project, you need to know what you're communicating—what is the basic concept of the experience? Is this an all-Flash Web site? Is this a Flash animation that introduces some other type of content (HTML, Shockwave Director movies, and so on)? For the purposes of this chapter, you create a Flash movie for a basic all-Flash presentation. In a sense, this project will be the Flash equivalent of a Microsoft PowerPoint presentation. Let's look at the completed project (shown in Figure 20-1) that you will create in this chapter.

**On the
CD-ROM**

In a Web browser, open the `main.html` document, located in the ch20 folder of the *Macromedia Flash MX 2004 Bible* CD-ROM. This movie contains two completed sections of the presentation.

When you load the main.html file into a Web browser with the Flash Player 7 installed, you see the presentation's title, Digital Video Production, along with four navigation buttons that take you to each section of the presentation. The opening section, Introduction, has scrolling text featuring the new TextArea UI component. When you click the Video Equipment button in the navigation bar, a Movie Clip featuring five video items is displayed along with another instance of the TextArea component. The Next and Previous buttons allow you to browse the video items. Each video item uses a custom component that fades the item onto the Stage.

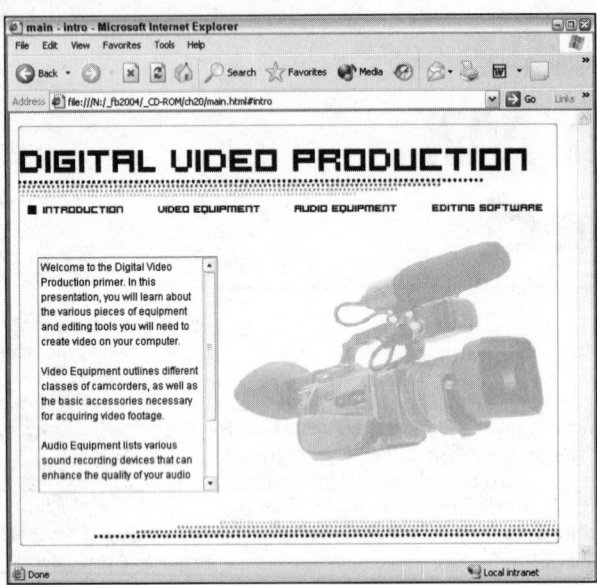

Figure 20-1: The completed presentation

Cross-Reference   In this book, we show you how to use prebuilt or custom components. Read Chapter 29, "Using Components," for more information on the prebuilt components shipped with Flash MX 2004. To learn how to build a custom component like the Fade component used in this chapter, read the *Macromedia Flash MX 2004 ActionScript Bible* (Wiley, 2004) by Robert Reinhardt and Joey Lott.

You will also notice that when you click each navigation button, the browser history updates. You can click the Back button of the Web browser to go directly to the previous section of the presentation. In this chapter, we show you how to create named anchors in the Flash document.

If you have a screen reader installed and are using the Windows operating system, you will hear each item in the Introduction section described by the screen reader. A screen reader is an application that assists visually impaired computer users by speaking text aloud. The Flash Player 7 ActiveX control will only work with screen readers that adhere to the MSAA (Microsoft Active Accessibility) specification built into Windows operating systems. As of this writing, only the Window-Eyes screen reader by GW Micro and JAWS from Freedom Scientific adhere to MSAA. In this chapter, you learn how to add accessibility information to elements in your Flash document.

Creating a plan

Once you know what goals you want to achieve with your Flash content, you should map the ideas on paper (or with your preferred project planning or flowchart software). We create a basic presentation for digital video production that has four areas: introduction, video equipment, audio equipment, and editing software. Our organizational chart for this site has four discrete areas, as shown in Figure 20-2.

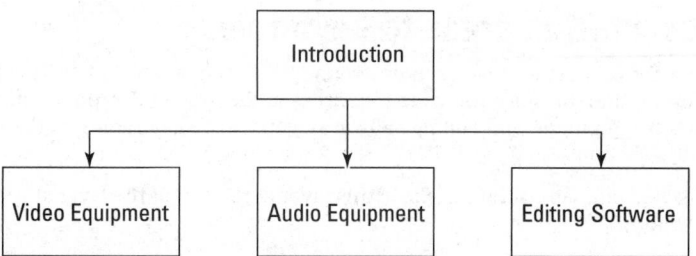

Figure 20-2: Our organizational chart will help us plan our Flash movie architecture.

In this chapter, you create the first two sections: introduction and video equipment. If you prefer, you can continue to develop the presentation with graphics provided on the CD-ROM.

Cross-Reference

Flowchart creation and project planning are discussed in greater detail in Chapter 3, "Planning Flash Projects."

Determining Flash movie properties

After you've made your organizational chart, you'll want to determine the frame rate, size, and color of the Flash document. We've skipped much of the "real-life" planning involved with Flash Web sites, which is discussed in Chapter 3, "Planning Flash Projects." For this example, we have made a starter Flash document for you to use, containing all of the elements necessary to complete the chapter. This document contains some of the basic graphic elements already positioned on the Stage.

On the CD-ROM

Make a copy of the `main_starter.fla` document, located in the ch20 folder of the *Macromedia Flash MX 2004 Bible* CD-ROM. Before you open this file, you should install the Miniml font files from the ch08 folder.

Open the starter document in Flash MX 2004. This document uses a frame size of 640 x 480 (to maintain the aspect ratio of a computer monitor), a standard frame rate of 12 fps, and a white background color. These are set in the Document Properties dialog box, shown in Figure 20-3, which is accessed by Modify ➪ Document (Ctrl+J or ⌘+J).

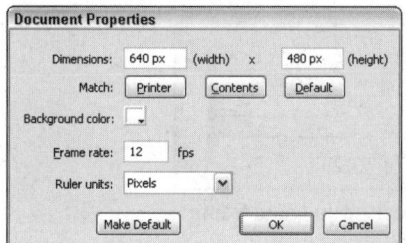

Figure 20-3: The Flash document properties

Mapping presentation areas to keyframes

Once the Flash document properties have been determined, you can create a Main Timeline structure for the presentation. Because there are four areas in the project (introduction, video equipment, audio equipment, and editing software), you'll have keyframes on the timeline that indicate those sections.

1. Create a new layer, and name it **labels**. Place this layer at the top of the layer stack in the Timeline window.

2. With the Selection tool, select frame 10 of the labels layer, and press F7. This creates a keyframe on frame 10.

Tip

It's usually a good idea to leave some empty frame space in front of your "real" Flash content. You can later use these empty frames to add a preloader, as discussed in Chapter 28, "Sharing and Loading Assets."

3. With the keyframe selected, open the Property inspector. In the <Frame Label> field, type **intro**. After you have typed the text, press the Tab (or Enter) key to make the name "stick."

4. Repeat Steps 2 and 3 with frames 20, 30, and 40, with the frame labels **video**, **audio**, and **software**, respectively.

5. Select frame 50 of the labels layer, and press F5. This will enable you to read the very last label, software. Your Timeline window should resemble Figure 20-4.

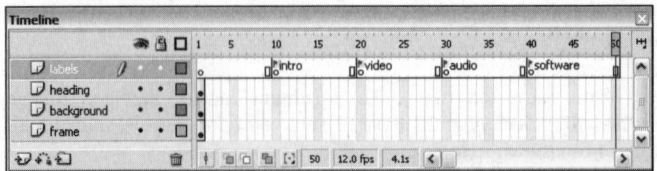

Figure 20-4: Frame labels will be used to differentiate each section of the site.

6. Select frame 50 on all other layers in the Timeline window, and press F5 to extend the content on these layers across the entire timeline, as shown in Figure 20-5.

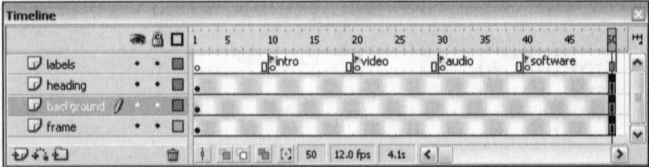

Figure 20-5: The content in the heading, background, and frame layers will be present throughout the entire movie.

7. Save your Flash document as **main_100.fla**.

8. Make a new layer, and rename it **actions**. Place this layer below the labels layer. Add a keyframe on frame 10 of the actions layer, and open the Actions panel (F9).

9. In the Actions toolbox (located in the left-hand column of the Actions panel), open the Global Functions ➪ Timeline Control booklet contained there. Double-click the stop action. This adds the following code to the Script pane in the right column of the Actions panel:

```
stop();
```

10. Close the Actions panel, and open the Property inspector. Make sure frame 10 of the actions layer is selected. In the <Frame Label> field, type **//stop**. The // characters assign a frame comment instead of a frame label. Although this step isn't necessary for the functionality of the movie, frame comments can provide quick and easy access to the designer's or programmer's notes. Your Timeline window should now look like Figure 20-6.

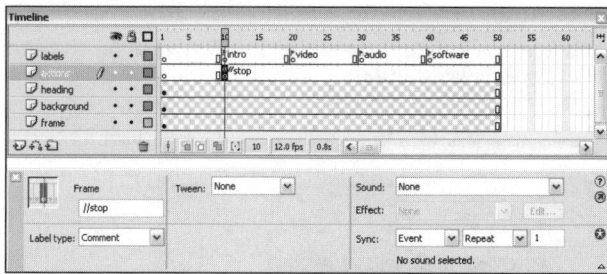

Figure 20-6: Unlike labels, frame comments cannot be used in ActionScript. Comments can provide quick visual references for ActionScript code.

11. Save the Flash document again.

At this point, the Flash document has a skeleton architecture (a blueprint) for our interactive functionality. Now let's add some content to each section of the movie.

On the CD-ROM   You can find the main_100.fla document in the ch20 folder of this book's CD-ROM.

Creating content for each area

In this section, you create navigation artwork for each area of the presentation. You also build some content for the video section.

1. In the Flash document you created in the last section, create a new layer named **menu**. Place this layer beneath the actions layer. Insert a keyframe on frame 10 of the menu layer.

2. On frame 10 of the menu layer, use the Text tool to add a Static text block with the text **Introduction**. For this example, we use the Miniml font hooge 05_53 at 12 points with bold formatting. Use the Property inspector to set these options. Place the text near the left edge of the Stage below the heading, as shown in Figure 20-7.

Main Timeline versus Scene Structure

Arguably, you might be wondering why you are using keyframes to delineate each section, instead of new scenes. There are two reasons to use one scene (in other words, one Main Timeline):

✦ You can see the entire layout of our site very easily on one timeline.

✦ You can blend interstitials (transitions between each area of the site) over two sections more easily. It's much easier to have one Movie Clip instance span the area between two section keyframes on the Main Timeline.

Ultimately, the decision is yours. Make sure that you determine your Flash architecture well before you start production within the Flash MX 2004 authoring environment. It's not a simple task to re-architect the layout once production has begun.

On the CD-ROM

If you don't have this font installed, copy the Miniml font files from the ch08 folder of the *Macromedia Flash MX 2004 Bible* CD-ROM.

Figure 20-7: Use the Text tool to add the Introduction text to the Stage.

3. Repeat Step 2 for the text **Video Equipment**, **Audio Equipment**, and **Editing Software**. Space these text blocks across the Stage beneath the heading, as shown in Figure 20-8. Again, all of these text blocks should be on frame 10 of the menu layer. Later, you will convert each of these text blocks to a Button symbol.

Now, you add a graphic that lets the user know which section is currently active. To do this, a black square will appear next to the appropriate text block. When the presentation starts, the black square will be next to the Introduction text. When the user navigates to the Video Equipment section, the black square will appear next to the Video Equipment section. Open the Library panel, and expand the graphics folder. There, you will find a Graphic symbol named marker. You will use this symbol in a moment.

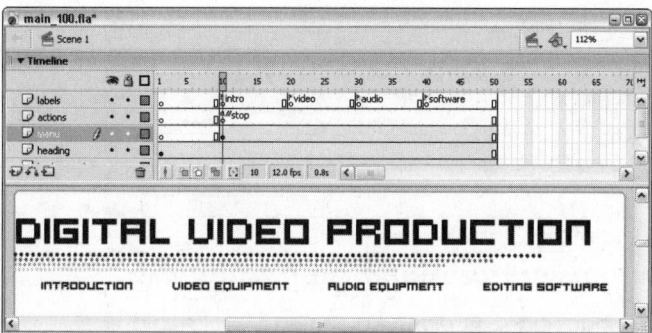

Figure 20-8: Add text that describes each section of the presentation.

4. Create a new layer on your Main Timeline (that is, Scene 1), and name it **marker**. Place this layer underneath the menu layer.

5. On frame 10 of the marker layer, insert a keyframe. Drag the marker symbol from the Library panel to the Stage. Position the instance of the marker to the left of the Introduction text, as shown in Figure 20-9.

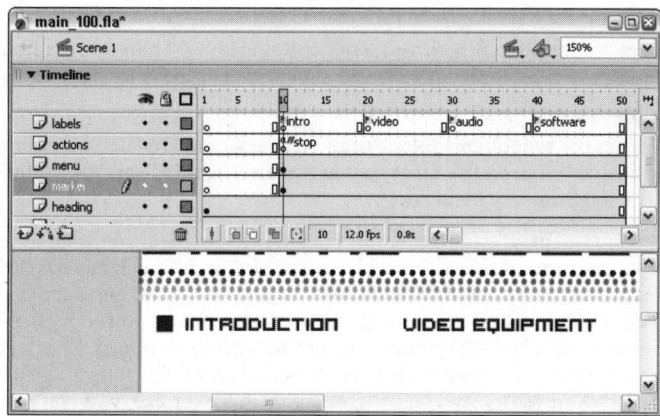

Figure 20-9: This marker designates the active section.

6. Insert another keyframe (F6) on frame 20 of the marker layer — make sure you do not insert empty keyframes. Move the instance of the marker at frame 20 to the left of the Video Equipment text, as shown in Figure 20-10.

7. Repeat Step 6 from frames 30 and 40 of the marker layer, moving the marker instance to the left of the Audio Equipment and Editing Software text, respectively. You now have the marker changing its position for all sections of the timeline.

Now let's add a slide show of the video equipment that can be used for digital video production. This slide show will appear in the Video Equipment section of the presentation. For this, you create a Movie Clip symbol that has each product graphic on a separate keyframe.

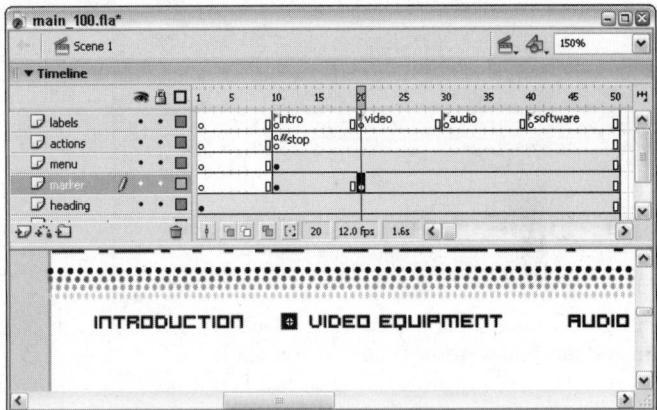

Figure 20-10: When the user goes to the Video Equipment section, the marker will appear next to the Video Equipment text.

8. Create a new symbol using Insert ➪ New Symbol (Ctrl+F8 or ⌘+F8). Make sure the Behavior option is set to Movie Clip, and give it a name of **videoEquip**.

9. Flash MX 2004 automatically switches to Edit mode, on the videoEquip timeline. Rename Layer 1 to **items**.

10. Add keyframes to frames 2, 3, 4, 5, and 6 of the items layer. There are six items in the videoItems folder of the Library panel, and each item is put on its own keyframe.

11. Move the playhead to frame 1 of the videoEquip timeline, and drag the dvTape movie clip symbol from the videoItems folder of the Library panel to the Stage. Once an instance of the symbol is on the Stage, name the instance **dvTape_mc** in the <Instance Name> field of the Property inspector.

12. Continue moving the playhead to the next frame, dragging another item to the Stage for each frame. Place cameraLow on frame 2, cameraMid on frame 3, cameraHigh on frame 4, dvDeck on frame 5, and dvCable on frame 6. Make sure you name each instance in the Property inspector, using the same name as the symbol followed by the _mc suffix. When you're finished, press the < and > keys to review your frames. Check Figure 20-11 to compare your work. You may want to center each graphic on the Stage using the Align panel (Ctrl+K or ⌘+K). As you progress with this exercise, you can adjust the exact placement of each item. Before you proceed to the next step, check that each instance is named in the Property inspector.

13. Now you need to insert an actions layer for this Movie Clip symbol. Create a new layer, and rename it **actions**. Select frame 1 of the actions layer, and open the Actions panel. Add a stop action to make sure the items don't automatically loop when the movie loads:

```
stop();
```

14. Return to the Main Timeline (Scene 1) by clicking the Scene 1 tab in the upper-left corner of the document window.

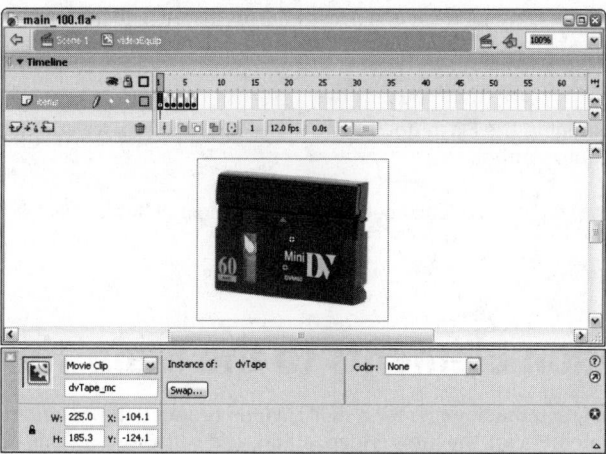

Figure 20-11: You should have six filled keyframes on the item layers of the videoEquipment timeline.

15. Create a new layer, and rename it **content**. Place this layer underneath the marker layer. Insert a new keyframe on frame 20 of the content layer.

16. Open the Library panel, and drag the **videoEquip** symbol from the Library to the Stage. Place it just left of the center of the Stage, as shown in Figure 20-12. In the Property inspector, name this instance videoEquip_mc.

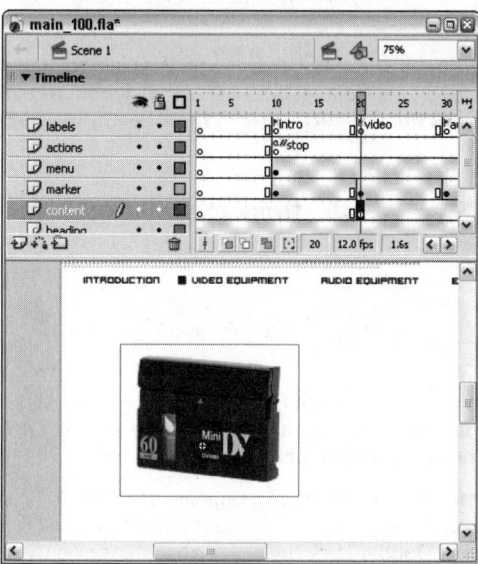

Figure 20-12: The videoEquip_mc instance will only be present in the video section of the timeline.

17. Select frame 30 of the content layer, and press F7. This inserts a blank keyframe. Now, the videoEquip_mc instance will show only in the Video Equipment area of the timeline.

18. Save your Flash document as **main_200.fla**.

Now we have some content in the Flash document. In the next section, we add navigation controls to the videoEquip symbol.

On the CD-ROM You can find the main_200.fla document in the ch20 folder of this book's CD-ROM.

Adding Navigation Elements to the Main Timeline

In the last section, you created a timeline for a digital video production presentation. We inserted content placeholders for the intro, video, audio, and software sections of the timeline, and you made a Movie Clip with video item graphics to place in the video section. However, the user has no way of actually getting to any section except the intro frame. In this section, you convert the text blocks in the menu to Button instances, whose actions will control the position of the playhead on the Main Timeline.

Creating text buttons for a menu

In this part of the exercise, you make menu buttons that will enable the user to navigate to the different areas of the Flash movie.

1. On the Main Timeline of your main_200.fla document, select frame 10 of the menu layer.

2. With the Selection tool, select the Introduction text block. Press F8 to convert this text into a symbol. In the Convert to Symbol dialog box, name the symbol **introButton**. Assign it a Button behavior. Click the top-left corner of the Registration box, as shown in Figure 20-13.

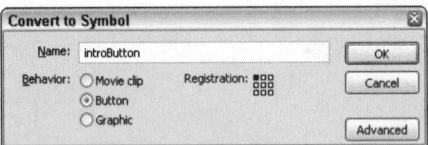

Figure 20-13: The introButton symbol settings

3. Select the Button instance on the Stage, and in the Property inspector, type **btIntro** in the <Instance Name> field. You will not target the button in any ActionScript for this project, but naming your instances is a good habit to get into.

4. Now you need to add a Hit state to the introButton timeline. By default, Flash MX 2004 uses the last frame of a Button symbol timeline for the Hit state, unless content is added to the Hit state keyframe. Double-click the btIntro instance on the Stage to switch to Edit mode.

5. On the timeline of the introButton symbol, select the Hit frame of Layer 1. Press F7 to insert an empty keyframe.

6. Click the Onion Skin Outlines button in the Timeline window toolbar. This enables you to view the previous frames of the introButton timeline, as shown in Figure 20-14.

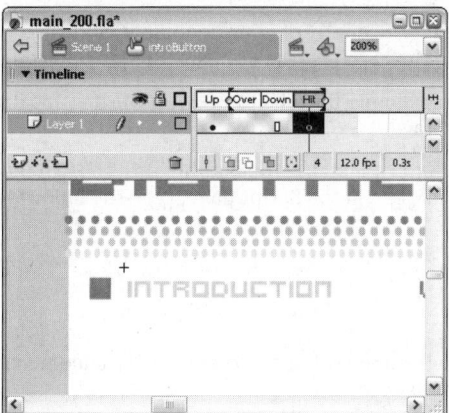

Figure 20-14: Onion skinning enables you to align the contents of several keyframes accurately.

7. Select the Rectangle tool, and draw a filled rectangle that covers the same area of the Introduction text block. You can use any fill color because the user never sees the Hit state. Make sure you turn off the stroke, or delete the stroke after the shape is drawn. Your button's timeline should resemble the one shown in Figure 20-15.

Figure 20-15: The Hit state defines the "active" area of the Button instance in the movie. When the user's mouse pointer enters this area, the Over frame of the button is displayed.

8. Select the shape you drew in Step 7, and press F8 to convert it to a Graphic symbol named **hitArea**. As with the introButton symbol, make sure the Registration icon is active in the top-left corner. You will reuse this shape for the other buttons in this section.

9. Next you add an Over state to the introButton, so that the user has a visual indication that it's an active button. Select the Over frame of Layer 1, and press F6. This copies the contents of the previous keyframe into the new one. Select the Introduction text block with the Selection tool, and change the fill color to a shade of blue such as #0099CC in the Tools panel or the Property inspector. You can also turn off Onion Skin Outlines at this point.

10. Return to the Main Timeline (that is, Scene 1) of your document, and save your Flash document. Select Control ⇨ Test Movie to test the states of the introButton.

   You can also use Control ⇨ Enable Simple Buttons to preview the graphical states of a Button instance directly on the Stage.

11. Now you put an action on the btIntro instance. Select the btIntro instance on the Stage, and open the Actions panel (F9). In the Script pane, type the following ActionScript code:

```
on (release) {
    this.gotoAndStop("intro");
}
```

   With these actions, the btIntro instance will move the Main Timeline playhead to the intro frame label when the user clicks the button.

12. If you test our movie at this point, your btIntro instance won't do anything—the play-head already stops on the intro frame label when the movie starts. Add a button for each section on the site. Repeat Steps 2 to 9 for each section name in our movie. Note that you should reuse the hitArea Graphic symbol from Step 8 for the remaining buttons—use the Free Transform tool to size each new instance of hitArea to match the size of the text block in the Button symbol. You should end up with four Button instances on the Stage: btIntro, btVideo, btAudio, and btSoftware.

Tip   When you're finished making all the buttons, make a folder in the Library panel named **buttons**, and move the Button symbols and the hitArea graphic into the new folder.

13. Repeat Step 11 for each new Button instance. For each Button instance, change the frame label parameter in the gotoAndStop() action to match the name of the button's area (for example, this.gotoAndStop("video"); on the btVideo instance).

14. Save your Flash document as **main_300.fla**, and test it (Ctrl+Enter or ⌘+Enter).

On the CD-ROM   You can find the main_300.fla document in the ch20 folder of this book's CD-ROM.

When you test your Flash movie, you should be able to click each button to go to each area of the movie. If a button isn't functioning, double-check the code on the instance. Make sure that each Button instance has a Button behavior in the Property inspector. In the next section, you add buttons to the videoEquip Movie Clip symbol, so that the user can browse the pictures of the video items.

Browsing the video items

In this section, you go inside the videoEquip symbol and add some navigation buttons for the video items.

1. From the Main Timeline of your main_300.fla document, double-click the videoEquip_mc instance on frame 20 of the content layer. Flash MX 2004 switches to Edit mode.

2. Make a new layer on the videoEquip timeline, and rename the layer **buttons**.

3. Open the Buttons Library (Window ⇨ Other Panels ⇨ Common Libraries ⇨ Buttons). In the Buttons Library panel, double-click the Circle Buttons folder. Drag the **circle button — next** Button symbol to the Stage. Place the Button instance below and to the right of the dvTape_mc instance. Name the new Button instance **btNext** in the Property inspector.

4. With the btNext instance selected, open the Actions panel. In the Script pane, type the following code. This time, try using keyboard shortcuts to type the code. Type Esc+O+N, in succession — not simultaneously. That is, press the Esc key, release the key, press the O key, release, and then press the N key, and release. This sequence adds an on(){} handler to the Script pane. Type the keyword **release** between the ( ) of the on handler, and between the { }, type Esc+n+f. This sequence adds a nextFrame() action. Finally, press the Auto Format button in the toolbar of the Actions panel. When you are finished, the Script pane should show the following code:

```
on (release){
    nextFrame();
}
```

5. With the **circle button — next** instance selected, press Ctrl+D (⌘+D) to duplicate the instance on the Stage. Name the duplicate instance **btPrev** in the Property inspector. Move the duplicate instance to the left of the original arrow button. With the Free Transform tool selected, enable the Rotate modifier in the Tools panel. Rotate the duplicated button 180 degrees. Press the Shift key while rotating, to lock in 45-degree steps.

6. Select both arrow buttons, and align them horizontally to each other by using the Align panel. Insert some descriptive text next to the instances, as shown in Figure 20-16.

7. Select the btPrev instance, and open the Actions panel. Change the nextFrame action to a prevFrame action. The Script pane should show the following code:

```
on (release){
    prevFrame();
}
```

8. Save your Flash document as **main_400.fla**, and test it. Click the Video Equipment button, and try the new navigation arrows for your video items catalog.

You can enhance your presentation by adding information in the videoEquip Movie Clip symbol. In the next section, you add a scrolling text window that displays descriptions of the video items.

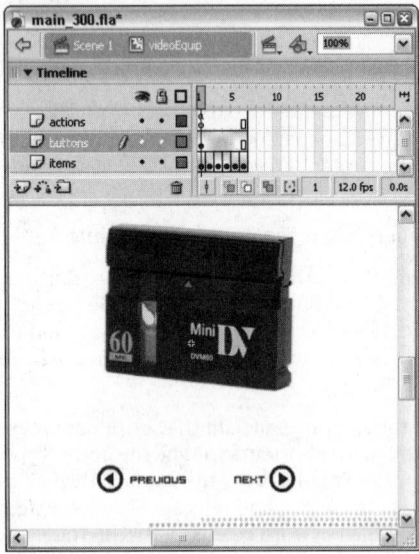

Figure 20-16: Add text to the buttons to describe their functionality.

On the
CD-ROM
You can find the `main_400.fla` document in the `ch20` folder of this book's CD-ROM.

The topic of Flash usability has received a lot of press, particularly because many Flash interfaces are considered experimental or nonintuitive to the average Web user. In December 2000, Macromedia created a special section in its Web site: Macromedia Flash Usability. You can read usability tips and view examples of interface design at `www.macromedia.com/software/flash/productinfo/usability`.

Closely related to usability is accessibility: How easily can someone with a disability access the content within your Flash movie? You look at Flash movie accessibility options in the final section of this chapter.

Text Scrolling with the TextArea Component

Continuing from the previous Flash movie example with the digital video production presentation, you learn how to create basic scrolling text using the new TextArea component in Flash MX 2004. Unlike Flash MX, you do not need to bind a ScrollBar component to a dynamic text field. In fact, Flash MX 2004 doesn't even include a ScrollBar component. We demonstrate the use of the TextArea component for one item in the videoEquip symbol to get you started.

Cross-
Reference
Components are a special type of Movie Clip symbol that have custom properties and values that can be easily changed in the Property inspector. To learn more about components, read Chapter 29, "Using Components."

1. In the Flash document you created from the previous section, double-click the videoEquip_mc instance on the Stage, at frame 10 of the content layer. Flash MX 2004 switches to Edit mode.

2. Add a new layer, and rename it **ctaDescription**. (We use the prefix cta to designate a TextArea component.) Move this layer beneath the buttons layer, and select frame 1 of the ctaDescription layer. Now, open the Components panel (Ctrl+F7 or ⌘+F7). In the UI Components nesting, drag an instance of the TextArea component to the Stage, to the right of the dvTape_mc instance.

3. Use the Free Transform tool to stretch the component instance. This instance should accommodate several lines of text, as shown in Figure 20-17. The size of the instance should match the size of the text area you wish to display in the scrolling text window. In the Property inspector, name the TextArea instance **cbtDescription**. In the Parameters area of the inspector, change the html setting from false to true. The html setting controls whether or not the instance should interpret HTML tags.

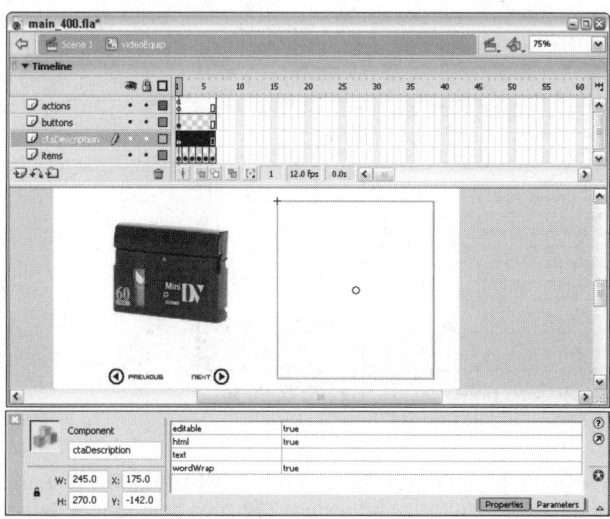

Figure 20-17: This text field will display the text associated with the first video item.

Now, some text needs to be supplied to the ctaDescription instance. You can specify text directly in the text parameter of the instance in the Property inspector, but for this project, you'll learn how to format HTML text that is assigned in ActionScript to the TextArea component. Open the item_1.rtf document in a text editor such as WordPad or TextEdit. This file is located in the ch20/text folder of the *Macromedia Flash MX 2004 Bible* CD-ROM. Now, open the item_1_formatted.txt document on the CD-ROM, and compare it to the item_1.rtf version. (You may want to enable word wrapping in your text editor so that you can see all of the text in the TXT file.) You'll notice that all of the text in the TXT file is specified in one continuous non-breaking line. Moreover, any carriage returns in the item_1.rtf have been replaced with

tags in the TXT version. Some characters, such as the double quotes around the word "data," have been escaped in the TXT file—that is, the character is preceded by a backslash (\ ). These special formatting characters ensure that ActionScript will correctly display the text.

4. Select all of the text in the item_1_formatted.txt file, and copy it. Later in this exercise, you'll paste the text into your own ActionScript code.

5. On the videoEquip timeline, create a new layer and rename it **actions - text**. Place this layer at the top of the layer stack. Select frame 1 of the new layer, and open the Actions panel (F9). In the Script pane, type the following code:

```
ctaDescription.text = "";
```

6. Between the pair of double quotes you typed in Step 5, paste (Ctrl+V or ⌘+V) the copied text into the Script pane. Initially, the text should be displayed on one line, but you can choose Word Wrap in the options menu of the Actions panel to see all of the text, as shown in Figure 20-18.

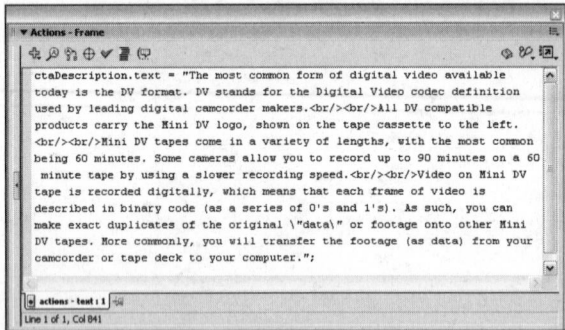

Figure 20-18: The Actions panel displaying the code to assign text to the TextArea component

7. Save the Flash document as **main_500.fla**, and test it (Ctrl+Enter or ⌘+Enter). Click the Video Equipment navigation button, and try the TextArea component. If the text is not displaying or scrolling, go back to the authoring environment and double-check the ActionScript code on frame 1 of the actions - text layer. Do not proceed with any steps until the TextArea component is functioning properly.

8. Now, you're ready to set up the text for the second item on the videoEquip timeline. Select frame 2 of the actions - text layer, and press F7 to insert an empty keyframe. Add the same actions and text as shown in Steps 5 and 6, but this time, copy and paste the text from the item_2_formatted.txt file (located in the ch20/text folder of this book's CD-ROM).

9. Save your Flash document again, and test it (Ctrl+Enter or ⌘+Enter). When you navigate to the Video Equipment section, you should be able to click the next button to see the text for item 2.

10. Repeat Step 8 for frames 3, 4, 5, and 6 of the actions - text layer. When you are finished you should have six separate action keyframes, one per item on the timeline.

11. Save your Flash document again, and test it (Ctrl+Enter or ⌘+Enter). When you go to the Video Equipment section, you should be able to click the Next button to reach each video item's description field, and the field should be scrollable.

The next step in real production would be to finesse the artwork and to add transitional effects between each video item. In the next section, you can add a custom Fade component that we created for your use in this exercise.

You can find the completed document, main_500.fla, in the ch20 folder of the *Macromedia Flash MX 2004 Bible* CD-ROM.

Using the Custom Fade Component

So far, much of the material and artwork used in this presentation could have been accomplished with a traditional HTML page layout in Macromedia Dreamweaver with GIF or JPEG graphics. In this section, you will add a fade effect to each of the video items in the videoEquip symbol. We created a custom component that can be applied to any Movie Clip instance on the Stage. This component will fade in or out a Movie Clip instance, based on settings in the Property inspector. To see this fade effect in action, open the main.swf file from the ch20 folder in Flash Player 7. When you go to the Video Equipment section, each item will fade in. In other words, the alpha of the each Movie Clip instance animates from 0 to 100 percent.

To learn how to build your own custom components, read the component coverage in the *Macromedia Flash MX 2004 ActionScript Bible* (Wiley, 2004), by Robert Reinhardt and Joey Lott.

The Fade component snaps to Movie Clip instances. Because we built the Fade component for you, you won't find the Fade component in the Component panel along with the Flash MX 2004 components. The Fade component is located in the starter document's Library and has been saved in each version of the main_ document that you've created in previous sections. Let's add the Fade component to the video items in the videoEquip symbol.

1. Open your saved Flash document from the previous section. On frame 20 of the content layer, double-click the videoEquip instance on the Stage to edit the symbol.

2. Select frame 1 of the items layer, and open the Library panel. Drag the Fade component to the dvTape_mc instance on the Stage. When you release the mouse button, the Fade component should snap to the top-left corner of the dvTape_mc instance, as shown in Figure 20-19. We made a custom icon for this Fade component: a little gradient box with a capital F. This icon will not show up in the actual Flash SWF file — it is displayed only in the authoring environment.

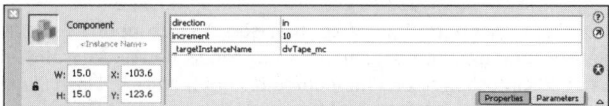

Figure 20-19: The Fade component snaps to the top-left corner of the Movie Clip instance.

3. The default settings for the Fade component instance can be viewed in the Property inspector. Select the Fade component instance at the top-left corner of the `dvTape_mc` instance, and open the Property inspector. This component has three options, as shown in Figure 20-20: `direction` (**in** to fade in the targeted instance, **out** to fade out the targeted instance), `increment` (how much should the alpha change per frame execution), and `_targetInstanceName` (the Movie Clip instance that the Fade component instance has snapped to).

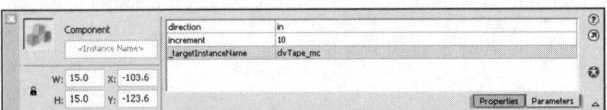

Figure 20-20: This custom component has three settings.

4. Save the Flash document as **main_600.fla**, and test it (Ctrl+Enter or ⌘+Enter). When you click the Video Equipment button, the first video item will fade into the Stage.

5. Repeat Step 2 for the other Movie Clip instances on frames 2, 3, 4, 5, and 6 of the items layer.

6. Save the Flash document again, and test it. After you click the Video Equipment button, click the Next button. Each video item will fade into the Stage.

If you want to use the Fade component in other Flash documents, simply drag the Fade component from one Library to another document's Library. Alternatively, you can copy and paste the Fade component instance from one document to another. Try different increment values for the Fade component (in the Property inspector) to see how the fade animation is affected in the Flash movie.

On the CD-ROM

You can find the completed document, `main_600.fla`, in the `ch20` folder of the *Macromedia Flash MX2004 Bible* CD-ROM.

Adding Named Anchors

Flash Player 6 and 7 give Flash movies extended functionality in some Web browsers, allowing the Back and Forward buttons of the browser to navigate to areas *within* the Flash movie. In earlier versions of the Flash Player, the Web browser's Back button would reset the position of the Flash movie to the first frame every time the movie reloaded into the browser. Now, you can add named anchors to Flash movies. Named anchors, when played, alert the browser's history to the location of the current anchor within the Flash movie. When another anchor is played, you can click the browser's Back button to go back to the previous named anchor.

Caution

Named anchors are only supported in Web browsers that support `fscommand` and JavaScript interactivity. Currently, Internet Explorer 4 (or higher) on Windows or Netscape 3.x to 4.x on Windows or Macintosh supports the named anchor feature of Flash Player 6 and 7. Netscape 6 (on any platform) or Internet Explorer on Mac (any version) does not support named anchors.

You can add named anchors to Flash movies in two ways:

✦ Enable the Named Anchor on Scene option in the Preferences dialog box. On Windows, you can access the preferences by choosing Edit ➪ Preferences. On Mac OS X, choose Flash ➪ Preferences. You will find the Named Anchor on Scene option in the General tab of the Preferences dialog box.

✦ Choose the Anchor option in the Label type menu of the Property inspector. Select a frame in the Timeline window, assign a frame label, and choose the Anchor option in the Property inspector.

In the presentation you're building in this chapter, you do not use any scenes. Therefore, you will add named anchors to all of the frame labels you created in previous sections.

1. Open the last Flash document you created from the previous section. Select frame 10 of the labels layer, and open the Property inspector. Select the Anchor option in the Label type menu, underneath the Frame Label field.

2. Repeat Step 1 for frames 20, 30, and 40 of the labels layer.

3. Open the Publish Settings (File ➪ Publish Settings). Click the HTML tab, and choose the **Flash with Named Anchors** option in the Template menu. Click OK to close the Publish Settings dialog box.

4. Save the Flash document as **main_700.fla**, and preview the presentation by choosing File ➪ Publish Preview ➪ HTML. Flash MX 2004 creates the Flash SWF file and HTML file, and opens the default Web browser. If you have a supported Web browser, you can click each navigation button (that is, Introduction, Video Equipment, and so on) and see the browser's history update. After you have clicked into one section, you can visit the previous section by clicking the browser's Back button.

On the CD-ROM

You can find the `main_700.fla` document in the `ch20` folder of this book's CD-ROM.

Cross-Reference

In Chapter 17, "Embedding Video," we show you how to use named anchors for embedded video in a Flash movie.

Making the Movie Accessible

This final section of the chapter shows you how to add accessibility information to your Flash presentation. As we mentioned earlier in this chapter, screen readers on the Windows operating system, working in concert with the Flash Player 6 or 7 ActiveX control, can read aloud the content inside of Flash movies. Window-Eyes 4.2 from GW Micro was engineered to work with Flash Player 6 and 7 through the use of MSAA (Microsoft Active Accessibility) technology. As of this writing, Window-Eyes 4.2 is one of two screen readers capable of accessing Flash content.

Note

You can download a demo version of Window-Eyes for the Windows operating system at `www.gwmicro.com`. This version will only work for 30-minute durations—you will need to restart your computer to initiate a new session.

We recommend that you review the Accessibility information in the new Help panel that ships with Flash MX 2004. Choose the Help ⇨ Help command in the Flash MX 2004 application. We provide a quick overview of the Accessibility features of Flash MX 2004 in this section.

Note Flash MX 2004 added accessibility support to the authoring environment as well. This feature allows designers and developers with disabilities to more easily use Flash MX 2004 to author Flash movies. To find out more information about this feature, search with the term "accessibility" in the Help panel.

Screen readers will access information within the Flash movie differently, depending on the features of the specific screen reader. Here we discuss Accessibility options as they relate to Window-Eyes 4.2. You will add some content to the Introduction section of the presentation that can be read aloud by Window-Eyes.

1. In the last Flash document you created in the previous section, insert an empty keyframe at frame 10 of the content layer on the Main Timeline (that is, Scene 1).

2. On frame 10 of the content layer, drag an instance of the TextArea component to the left side of the Stage. In the Property inspector, name this instance **ctaIntro**. Change the `html` setting from `false` to `true` as well.

3. Open the `introduction_formatted.txt` document in the ch20/text folder of the *Macromedia Flash MX 2004 Bible* CD-ROM. Copy the text in this document. Select the `ctaIntro` instance in your Flash document, and paste the copied text into the `text` setting of the Property inspector. Click any area of the Stage, and you should see an automatic preview of the copied text, as shown in Figure 20-21.

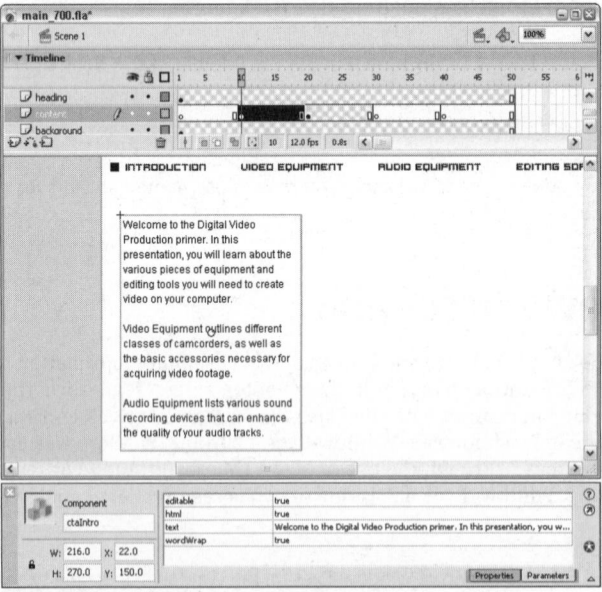

Figure 20-21: The TextArea component can show a live preview of formatted text in the authoring environment. The screen reader can read aloud this text field's contents.

4. With frame 10 of the content layer active, drag an instance of the cameraHigh Movie Clip symbol (located in the videoItems folder) from the Library panel to the Stage. In the Property inspector, change the alpha of this instance to **30** percent. Name the instance **cameraHigh_mc** as well.

Now you will use the Accessibility panel to add information to specific elements in the Introduction section of the presentation. You can open the Accessibility panel in two ways: select the Movie Clip, Button, Component, or text field instance and click the Accessibility icon in the Property inspector; or choose Window ➪ Accessibility.

You can add general information about your Flash movie by deselecting all elements on the Stage (you can press the Esc key to do this quickly) and opening the Accessibility panel.

The Make Movie Accessible option allows the screen reader to see elements inside the Flash movie. If this option is cleared, the screen reader will not be able to read any elements of the Flash movie.

The Make Child Objects Accessible option allows elements other than the current Name and Description in the Accessibility panel to be accessed by the screen reader.

5. Clear the Auto Label option. Auto Labeling will tell Flash Player 6 to describe buttons and other elements by associating the closest text object to the element. For example, if you had some text underneath a Button instance, Auto Label would assign this text to the Button instance for the screen reader.

The Name field allows you to assign a title to the Flash movie, while the Description field allows you to add a quick summary about the Flash movie. Window-Eyes will read the Name contents, but not the Description contents. Let's add some general information to the current Flash document.

6. Deselect all of the elements on the Stage, and open the Accessibility panel. Select the Make Movie Accessible and Make Child Objects Accessible options, and clear the Auto Label option. In the Name field, type the presentation's title, **Digital Video Presentation**. In the Description field, type the following text: **A primer for digital video equipment and accessories**. Refer to Figure 20-22.

Figure 20-22: The Accessibility panel controls options for the Flash movie and its elements.

7. Now select the Introduction button on frame 10 of the menu layer. In the Accessibility option, enter the options shown in Figure 20-23. Note that you will not assign a keyboard shortcut description for this example. The Name and Description for this button

will be read after the general information you added in the previous step. Window-Eyes will say the word "button" before it reads the name. For this example, Window-Eyes will say, "Button. Introduction. Access the introduction section of the presentation."

Note   If you do want to have a keyboard shortcut read by the screen reader, then you should type out the text for any modifier key or combination including the + character, such as Ctrl+E. You will also need to add ActionScript to the Button (or Movie Clip) instance to make the movie respond to the key press that you described in the Accessibility panel.

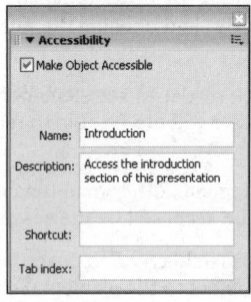

Figure 20-23: The Name and Description contents for buttons can be read by Window-Eyes.

8. Repeat Step 7 for each Button instance in the menu layer.

9. Select the ctaIntro instance on frame 10 of the content layer, and make sure the Make Object Accessible and Make child objects accessible check boxes are selected in the Accessibility panel. It is not necessary to add a description to this text field — the text inside of the field will be read automatically by the screen reader.

10. Select the cameraHigh_mc instance on frame 10 of the content layer, and clear the Make Object Accessible option in the Accessibility panel. Not all elements need to be read by the screen reader, and this graphic does not need to be revealed to visually impaired users.

11. Save your Flash document as **main_800.fla**, and preview it in Internet Explorer for Windows. Make sure the Window-Eyes application is active. As soon as the movie loads into the browser, Window-Eyes reads the information for the movie and then reads the name and descriptions of the buttons. Then it will read the text inside of the description text field. After Window-Eyes reads the last Flash element, it speaks the word "bottom," indicating the end of the Web page has been reached. If you added body text to the HTML document, Window-Eyes would read that text as well.

On the CD-ROM   You can find the completed Flash presentation, main_800.fla, in the ch20 folder of the *Macromedia Flash MX2004 Bible* CD-ROM. This document contains the first two sections of the presentations — on your own, try adding your content to the remaining sections using techniques you learned in this chapter. You can also find a sample version of this same project using the new Button component in the main_cbt.fla document, located in the ch20 folder of this book's CD-ROM.

You can continue to add more accessibility information to other elements in the Flash document. You can even add information to elements within Movie Clip symbols. Try adding descriptions to the buttons inside of the videoEquip symbol.

 **Note** Screen reader technology can only interface with Flash movies played by the Flash Player 6 or 7 ActiveX control. Screen readers cannot access Flash movies played by the stand-alone Flash Player 6 or 7.

 **Cross-Reference** You can learn more about ActionScript and accessibility from the *Macromedia Flash MX 2004 ActionScript Bible*, by Robert Reinhardt and Joey Lott.

 **Web Resource** We'd like to know what you thought about this chapter. Visit www.flashsupport.com/feedback to fill out an online form with your comments.

Summary

✦ Before you can start to create an interface in Flash, you need to have a plan for your Flash movie timeline. Create an organizational chart outlining the sections of the presentation.

✦ Determine your Flash movie properties (frame size, frame rate, and background color) before you undergo production in Flash.

✦ If you don't have final art for a Flash production, you can still create a functional prototype of the presentation using placeholder graphics. When the final artwork is ready, replace the placeholder graphics with the final artwork.

✦ You can create simple slide shows or product catalogs using sequential keyframes and buttons with nextFrame() and prevFrame() actions.

✦ The Hit area of a text-based Button symbol should always be defined with a solid shape.

✦ You can achieve basic text scrolling by adding the new Flash MX 2004 TextArea component to your Flash movie.

✦ You can apply time-based alpha effects to artwork with the custom Fade component.

✦ You can add accessibility information to Flash movies. Windows-based screen readers designed to work with Flash Player 6 or 7, such as GW Micro's Window-Eyes 4.2, can read this information.

✦　✦　✦

Distributing Flash Movies

◆   ◆   ◆   ◆

◆   ◆   ◆   ◆

When you finally have your project assembled in the Flash authoring environment and you're ready to prepare it for final presentation, this section will explain all the options available for delivering Flash content to your audience. Chapter 21 details every option and setting in the Publish Settings of Flash MX 2004 that will control your final file size and format. This chapter also includes tips for optimizing your file sizes for faster downloads and better performance. Chapter 22 covers all the HTML techniques relevant to integrating Flash content on Web pages. Learn how to create plug-in detection systems for your Flash movies. This chapter also introduces the new Detect Flash Version feature. If you are planning to distribute Flash content offline or you want to avoid plug-in problems, Chapter 23 will walk you through the various methods for creating Flash standalone projectors and using the Flash standalone player.

Publishing Flash Movies

If you have read Parts I through V of the book, you're probably more than ready to get your Flash movies uploaded to your Web server to share with your visitors. This chapter shows you how to create Flash movies (.swf files) from Flash MX 2004 so that your Flash movies can be played with the Flash Player plug-in or ActiveX Control for Web browsers. We show you how to test your Flash movies, prepare Flash movie options, and adjust other output formats from Flash MX 2004, such as HTML documents and image formats.

New Feature

In this chapter, you also learn how to take advantage of Flash MX 2004's new Publish profile and Flash Player detection options.

Cross-Reference

If you have Flash MX Professional 2004, you can also publish documents directly from the Project panel. Read Chapter 3, "Planning Flash Projects," for more information about the Project panel.

Testing Flash Movies

You have four ways to test your Flash documents: in the Timeline window using the Play command, in the authoring environment using the Test Movie and Test Scene commands, in a browser using the Publish Preview command, or in the stand-alone Flash Player using Flash movies (.swf files) made with the Publish or Export Movie commands. There are several reasons why you should test your Flash movie (.swf file) before you transfer Flash movies to your Web server (or to the intended delivery medium):

✦ Flash documents (.fla files) have much larger file sizes than their Flash movie (.swf file) counterparts. To accurately foretell the network bandwidth that a Flash movie requires, you need to know how large the final Flash movie will be. If the download demand is too overwhelming for your desired Internet connection speed (for example, a 28.8 Kbps modem), you can go back and optimize your Flash document.

✦ The Control ⇨ Play command in the Flash authoring environment does not provide any streaming information. When you use the Test Movie or Scene command, you can view the byte size of each frame and how long it will take to download the SWF file from the Web server.

✦ Movie Clip animations and actions targeting Movie Clip instances cannot be previewed using the standard Control ➪ Play command (or the Play button on the Controller) in the Flash authoring environment.

Tip

You can temporarily preview Movie Clip symbol instances within the Flash authoring environment (for example, the Timeline window) by changing the Symbol instance behavior to Graphic instead of Movie Clip. Do this by selecting the instance, opening the Property inspector, and choosing Graphic in the Behavior drop-down menu. However, if you switch the behavior back to Movie Clip, you will have lost the original instance name of the Movie Clip.

✦ Most scripting done with Flash actions, such as `loadMovie()`, `loadVariables()`, and `startDrag()`, cannot be previewed with the Play command. Enabling Simple Frame Actions or Simple Buttons in the Control menu has no effect with newer scripting actions. You need to use Test Movie to try out most interactive functions in a Flash movie.

Tip

Any actions that require the use of remote server-side scripts, Flash Remoting, or Flash Communication Server MX connections to load variables, movies, or XML data, will work in the Test Movie environment. You do not need to view your SWF files in a browser to test these actions.

✦ Accurate frame rates cannot be previewed with the Play command (Control ➪ Play) in the authoring environment. Most complex animations appear jerky, pausing or skipping frames when the Play command is used.

Using the Test Scene or Movie command

You can test your Flash movies directly within the Flash MX 2004 interface by using the Control ➪ Test Movie or Test Scene command. When you choose one of these commands, Flash MX 2004 opens your Flash document in a new window as a Flash movie (.swf file). This file format, SWF, is usually pronounced "swiff." Even though you are only "testing" a Flash movie, a new SWF file is actually created and stored in the same location as the Flash document (.fla file). For this reason, it is a good idea to always save your Flash document before you begin testing it.

Caution

If your movie is currently titled Untitled1, Untitled2, and so on in the application title bar, it usually indicates that the document has not yet been saved. Make sure you save your Flash movie with a distinct name before testing it.

Before you use the Test Scene or Movie command, you need to specify the settings of the resulting Flash SWF file. The Test Scene or Movie command uses the specifications outlined in the Publish Settings dialog box to generate SWF files. The Publish Settings dialog box is discussed later in this chapter. For the time being, we can use the Flash MX 2004 default settings to explore the Test Scene and Movie commands.

Test Movie

When you choose Control ➪ Test Movie (Ctrl+Enter or ⌘+Enter), Flash generates a SWF file of the entire Flash document that is currently open. If you have more than one Flash movie open, Flash MX 2004 creates a SWF file for the one that is currently in the foreground and that has "focus."

 **New Feature** If you use Flash MX Professional 2004, you can publish multiple FLA files at the same time by using the Project panel. To learn more about this feature, read Chapter 3, "Planning Flash Projects."

Test Scene

If you are working on a lengthy Flash document with multiple scenes, you may want to test your scenes individually. You can do this by using Control ➪ Test Scene (Ctrl+Alt+Enter or ⌘+Option+Enter). The process of exporting large movies via Test Movie may require many minutes to complete, whereas exporting one scene will require a significantly smaller amount of time. Movies that require compression for several bitmaps and MP3 sounds usually take the most amount of time to test. As you see in the next section, you can analyze each tested scene (or movie) with the Bandwidth Profiler.

One Reason to Use Imported MP3 Files

If you have imported raw audio files such as WAV or AIF files into your Flash document, you may notice lengthy wait times to use the Test Movie or Publish commands in Flash MX 2004. Why? The default MP3 encoding process consumes much of the computer processor's power and time.

Flash MX 2004 has three MP3 compression qualities: Fast, Medium, or Best. Fast is the default MP3 quality setting — this is by far the fastest method of encoding MP3 sound. Because MP3 uses perceptual encoding, it compares a range of samples to determine how best to compress the sound. Fast compares a smaller range of samples than either Medium or Best. As you increase quality, the sampling range increases.

This process is similar to building 256-color palettes for video files; it's best to look at all the frames of the video (instead of just the first frame) when you're trying to build a palette that's representative of all the colors used in the video. While MP3 doesn't quite work in this fashion, the analogy is appropriate. So, at Best quality, the MP3 encoding scans more of the waveform to look for similarities and differences. However, it's also more time intensive.

As strange as it may seem, the quality does not affect the final size of the Flash movie (.swf file). The bit rate of the MP3 sound is the same regardless of the quality setting. Again, we'll use an analogy — consider the file sizes generated by three different digital cameras that have the same number of pixels in the pictures. The best camera, which will have the highest quality lens and recording mechanism, produces better-looking pictures that capture detail *and* produces the same file size as the others. This is one of the few times where it's not about the amount of information stored in the compressed file — it's a matter of the accuracy and quality of the information within that quantity.

If you want to avoid the wait for Flash MX 2004 to publish Flash movies that use MP3 compression, we recommend that you compress your source audio files to the MP3 format (including support for VBR — Variable Bit Rate — compression) and import those MP3 files into Flash MX 2004. Unless the MP3 sound file is used for Stream Sync audio, Flash MX 2004 will export the audio in its original MP3 compressed format.

For more information on sound in Flash movies, read Chapter 15, "Adding Sound."

Tip
You can use the Test Scene command while you are in Edit mode to export a SWF file that contains the current symbol timeline. The movie will not contain anything else from your Flash document. Note that the symbol's center point will become the top-left corner of the playback stage.

Using the Bandwidth Profiler

Do you want to know how long it will take for a 28.8 Kbps modem to download your Flash movie or scene? How about a 36.6 Kbps modem? Or a 56 Kbps modem? Or a cable modem? The Bandwidth Profiler enables you to simulate any download speed.

On the CD-ROM
See the ch21 folder of the *Macromedia Flash MX 2004 Bible* CD-ROM for a Flash document named bandwidth.fla. We use that Flash document for this section.

To use the Bandwidth Profiler, you first need to create a movie or scene to test. When you create a Flash movie with the Control ⇨ Test Movie or Scene commands, Flash opens the SWF file in its own window.

Note
In Flash MX 2004, Macromedia has rearranged many of the options in the Test Movie environment. If you have used Flash MX or earlier, you should review the new layout as discussed in the following section.

View menu

The Test Movie or Test Scene viewing environment changes the application menu bar in Flash MX 2004, specifically the View and Control menus. The first three commands in the View menu are the same as those of the Flash Player plug-in viewing controls, while the others are specific to the testing environment:

✦ **Zoom In:** Selecting this option enlarges the Flash movie. The shortcut key for this command is Ctrl+= or ⌘+=.

✦ **Zoom Out:** Selecting this option shrinks the Flash movie. The shortcut key for this command is Ctrl+-or ⌘+-.

✦ **Magnification:** This submenu enables you to change the zoom factor of the movie. The Flash movie is displayed at the original pixel size specified in the Modify ⇨ Document dialog box when 100 percent (Ctrl+1 or ⌘+1) is the setting. For example, if the movie size is 500 x 300 pixels, it takes up 500 x 300 pixels on your monitor. If you change the size of the viewing window, the movie may be cropped. The lower section of this submenu enables you to change the viewable area of the Flash movie. Show Frame (Ctrl+2 or ⌘+2) will show only the frame boundary area in the Player window. Show All (Ctrl+3 or ⌘+3) shrinks or enlarges the Flash movie so that you can view all the artwork in the Flash movie, including elements off-stage.

✦ **Bandwidth Profiler:** To view the Bandwidth Profiler in this new window, use View ⇨ Bandwidth Profiler (Ctrl+B or ⌘+B). The viewing window will expand to accommodate the Bandwidth Profiler. Here's a breakdown of each section of the profiler:

- The left side of the profiler displays three sections: Movie, Settings, and State. Movie indicates the dimensions, frame rate, size (in KB and bytes), duration, and preload (in number of frames and seconds). The Settings area displays the current selected connection speed (which is set in the View ⇨ Download Settings menu). State shows you the current frame playing and its byte requirements, as well as the percent of the movie that has loaded.

- The larger right section of the profiler shows the timeline header and graph. The lower red line beneath the timeline header indicates whether a given frame streams in real-time with the current modem speed specified in the Control menu. For a 28.8 Kbps modem, any frame above 200 bytes may cause delays in streaming for a 12 fps movie. Note that the byte limit for each frame is dependent on frame rate. For example, a 24 fps movie has a limit of 120 bytes per frame (for a 28.8 Kbps modem connection).

- When the Bandwidth Profiler is enabled, two other commands are available in the View menu: Streaming Graph (Ctrl+G or ⌘+G) and Frame By Frame Graph (Ctrl+F or ⌘+F).

✦ **Streaming Graph:** By default, Flash opens the Bandwidth Profiler in Streaming Graph mode. This mode indicates how the Flash movie streams into a browser (see Figure 21-1). Alternating light and dark gray blocks represent each frame. The size of each block indicates its relative byte size. For our bandwidth.swf example, all the frames will have loaded by the time our Playhead reaches frame 13 when the movie is played over a 56 Kbps connection. The shortcut key for Streaming Graph is Ctrl+G or ⌘+G.

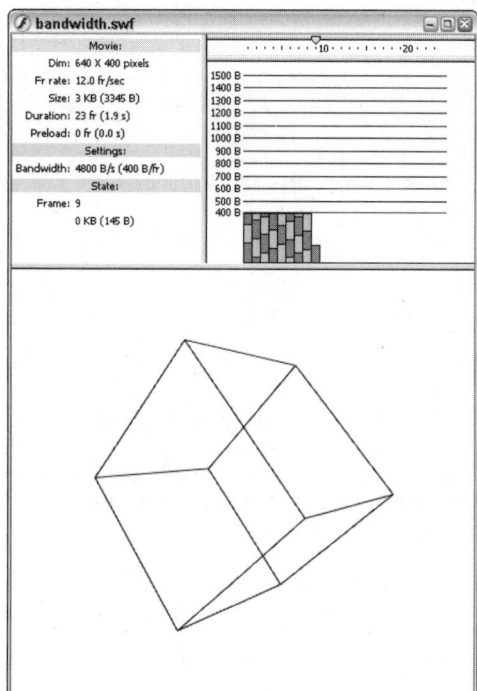

Figure 21-1: The Streaming Graph indicates how a movie will download over a given modem connection. Shown here is our bandwidth.swf as it would download over a 56 Kbps modem.

✦ **Frame By Frame Graph:** This second mode available to the Bandwidth Profiler lays each frame side by side under the timeline header (see Figure 21-2). Although the Streaming Graph enables you to see the real-time performance of a Flash movie, the Frame By Frame Graph enables you to more easily detect which frames are contributing to streaming delays. If any frame block goes beyond the red line of the graph (for a given connection speed), then the Flash Player halts playback until the entire frame downloads. In the bandwidth.swf example, frame 1 is the only frame that may cause a very slight delay in streaming when the movie is played over a 28.8 Kbps connection. The remaining frames are right around 200 bytes each—right at the threshold of 200 bytes per frame for a 28.8 Kbps modem connection playing a 12 fps Flash movie. The shortcut key for Frame By Frame Graph is Ctrl+F or ⌘+F.

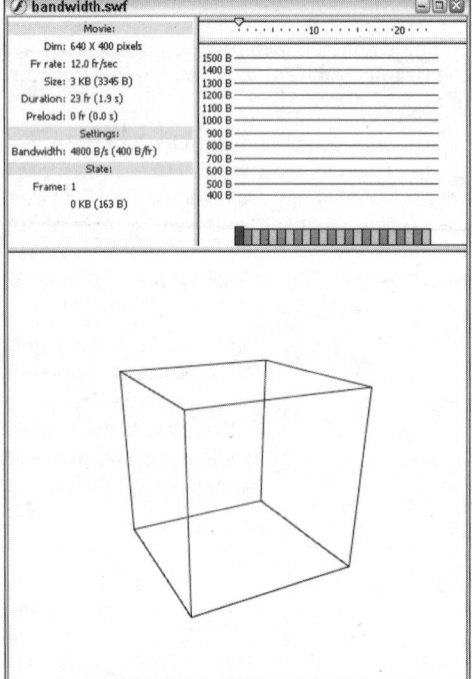

Figure 21-2: The Frame By Frame Graph shows you the byte demand of each frame in the Flash movie.

✦ **Simulate Download:** When the Simulate Download option is enabled, the Bandwidth Profiler emulates the chosen modem speed (in the View ➪ Download Settings menu) when playing the Flash movie. The Bandwidth Profiler counts the bytes downloaded (displayed in the Loaded subsection of the State heading), and shows the download/play progress via a green bar in the timeline header.

Note   In previous versions of Flash, the Simulate Download feature was called Show Streaming.

The Simulate Download command also applies to loaded runtime assets, such as SWF, JPEG and MP3 files. For example, when a `loadMovie()` action begins to load another file, the left side of the Bandwidth Profiler shows the progressive download at the simulated download speed.

✦ **Download Settings:** The View menu also features a submenu of connection speeds, which work in tandem with the Streaming and Frame By Frame Graphs:

- **14.4, 28.8, 56K, DSL, T1:** These settings determine what speed the Bandwidth Profiler uses to calculate estimated download times and frame byte limitations. Notice that these settings use more practical expectations of these modem speeds. For example, a 28.8 modem can theoretically download 3.5 kilobytes per second (KB/s), but a more realistic download rate for this modem speed is 2.3 KB/s.

- **User Settings 6, 7, and 8:** These are user-definable speed settings. By default, they are all 2.3 KB/s.

- **Customize:** To change the settings for any of the modem speeds listed previously, use the Customize command to input the new value(s).

✦ **Quality:** The Quality submenu controls the visual appearance of graphics within the Flash movie. By default, all graphics are displayed at High quality. You can choose from Low, Medium, or High quality in this menu.

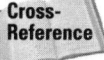

For more a detailed explanation of Quality settings, refer to the Quality descriptions later in this chapter.

Control menu

Use the Control menu to play (Enter key) or rewind (Ctrl+Alt+R or ⌘+Option+R) the test movie. Rewinding pauses the bandwidth.swf movie on the first frame. Use the Step Forward (. or > key) and Step Backward (, or < key) commands to view the Flash movie frame by frame. If a Flash movie doesn't have a `stop()` action on the last frame, the Loop command forces the player to infinitely repeat the Flash movie.

You can use the Disable Keyboard Shortcuts command to turn off the shortcut keys for all of the commands available in Test Movie mode. This is especially useful if you have enabled interactive key presses within ActionScript for your movie. For example, if you enable the Return or Enter key for a button, it will conflict with the Play command (Control ➪ Play). As such, when you press the Enter key while you test your movie, the movie will play to the next frame and the button actions will be ignored.

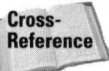

We discuss the debugging features of the Control menu in Chapter 34, "Managing and Troubleshooting Flash Movies."

Debug menu

The Debug menu contains List Objects and List Variables commands. List Objects can be used to show the names of Movie Clip instances or ActionScript Objects in the Output window, while the List Variables command displays the names and values of any currently loaded variables, ActionScript objects, and XML data.

A Word About the Export Movie Command

Even though Flash streamlines the process of creating Flash movies with the Publish commands (discussed in the next section), it is worth mentioning that the File ➪ Export Movie command provides another route to creating a SWF file. Although the Publish command is the quickest way to create HTML-ready Flash movies, the Export Movie command can be used to create updated SWF files that have already been placed in HTML documents, or Flash movies that you intend to import into Macromedia Director movies (see Chapter 38, "Working with Director MX").

Cross-Reference   We'll discuss how these features can be used in Chapter 34, "Managing and Troubleshooting Flash Movies."

Using the size report

Flash also lets you view a text file summary of movie elements, frames, and fonts called a size report. In addition to viewing Frame By Frame Graphs of a Flash movie with the Bandwidth Profiler, you can inspect this size report for other "hidden" byte additions such as font character outlines. You can enable the size report to be created by accessing the Publish Settings dialog box (File ➪ Publish Settings), clicking the Flash tab, and checking the Generate size report option. Once enabled, you can view the size report in two ways:

✦ After you publish, publish preview, or export a Flash movie, go to the folder where the SWF file was created. In that folder, you'll find a text file accompanying the Flash movie. On Windows, this file is named after your Flash movie's name, followed by "Report" and the .txt file extension, as in `bandwidth Report.txt`. On the Macintosh, this file is named after your Flash movie's name, followed by the word "Report," as in `bandwidth.swf Report`.

✦ When you test your Flash movie using the Control ➪ Test Movie command, open the Output panel before you view the Flash movie. You can open the Output panel by going to Window ➪ Development Panels ➪ Output (F2). Once the Output panel is open, choose Control ➪ Test Movie and the report automatically loads into the Output panel.

On the CD-ROM   A sample size report, called `bandwidth Report.txt`, is included in the `ch21` folder of the *Macromedia Flash MX 2004 Bible* CD-ROM.

Publishing Your Flash Movies

After you've made a dazzling Flash movie complete with Motion tweens, 3D simulations, and ActionScripted interactivity, you need to make the Flash movie usable for the intended delivery medium—the Web, a CD-ROM (or floppy disk), or a QuickTime Flash movie, to name a few. As we mentioned in the introduction to this book, you need the Flash MX 2004 application to open FLA files. Because the majority of your intended audience won't have the full Flash MX 2004 application, you need to export or publish your FLA file in a format that your audience can use. More importantly, Flash documents are authoring documents, while Flash movies are optimized for the shortest delivery times and maximum playback performance.

You can convert your Flash document (.fla files) to Flash movies (.swf files) by using either the File ➪ Export Movie, Control ➪ Test Movie, or File ➪ Publish/Publish Settings commands. You can specify just about all file format properties in one step using the File ➪ Publish Settings command. After you've entered the settings, the File ➪ Publish command exports any and all file formats with your specified parameters in one step—all from the Flash MX 2004 application.

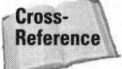

The Export Movie command is discussed throughout the book. For more information on exporting still images in raster/bitmap formats, see Chapter 35, "Working with Raster Graphics." To export vector formats, see Chapter 36, "Working with Vector Graphics." To export QuickTime or AVI files, see Chapter 14, "Exporting Animation."

Three commands are available with the Publish feature: Publish Settings, Publish Preview, and Publish. Each of these commands is discussed in the following sections.

Publish Settings

The Publish Settings command (File ➪ Publish Settings) is used to determine which file formats are exported when the File ➪ Publish command is invoked. By default, new Flash documents created with Flash MX 2004 use Publish Settings that will export a Flash movie (.swf file) and an HTML file with the proper markup tags to utilize the Flash Player 7 plug-in or ActiveX Control. If you want to customize the settings of the exported file types, you should familiarize yourself with the Publish Settings before you attempt to use the Publish command.

The Publish Settings dialog box has many new features in Flash MX 2004. You should be aware that the default ActionScript language version is AS2.0 for new Flash documents. You learn more about ActionScript and the implications of ActionScript 2.0 in Part VII, "Approaching ActionScript."

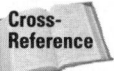

To learn how to use the new Profiles feature in the Publish Settings, jump to the "Using Publish Profiles" section later in this chapter.

Selecting formats

Select File ➪ Publish Settings to access the Publish Settings dialog box, which is nearly identical for both the Windows and Macintosh versions of Flash MX 2004. The dialog box opens to the Formats tab, which has check boxes to select the formats in which your Flash document will be published (see Figure 21-3). For each Type that is checked, a tab appears in the Publish Settings dialog box. Click each type's tab to specify settings to control the particulars of the movie or file that will be generated in that format.

If you click the Use Default Names button, all of the File fields fill in with the name of your Flash document, followed by the file format's suffix. For example, if your movie is named intro.fla and you click the Use Default Names button, this is the base from which the names are generated in publishing. Thus, intro.swf, intro.html, intro.gif, and so on would result.

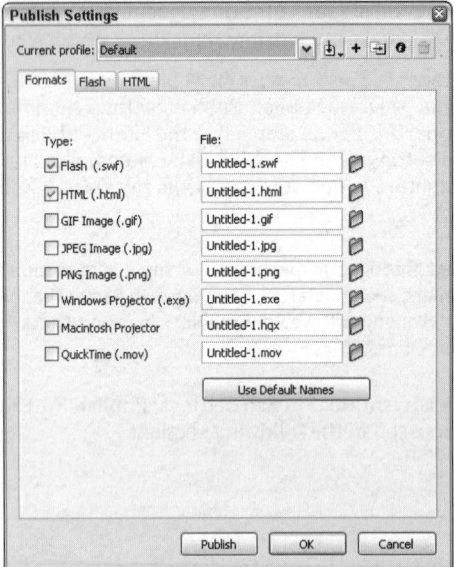

Figure 21-3: The Formats tab of the Publish Settings dialog box enables you to select the published file formats and to use default or custom names for these published files.

Tip   You can enter nonversion–specific filenames for Flash documents that you incrementally save as you work. For example, if you have a Flash document named main_100.fla, set the Flash movie filename to main.swf, and then every new Flash document version you save (for example, main_101.fla, main_102.fla, and so on) will still produce a main. swf file. This way, you can consistently refer to one Flash movie (.swf file) in your HTML code and incrementally save your Flash documents.

New Feature   One of the new Publish Settings features in Flash MX 2004 offers the ability to specify which folder a publish document is created and stored in. All of the file formats have a folder icon to the right of the File field. If you click the folder icon, you can browse to a specific location where your published file will be created.

Using the Flash settings

The primary and default publishing format of Flash MX 2004 documents is the Flash movie SWF format. Only Flash movies retain full support for Flash actions and animations. To control the settings for the Flash movie, choose the Flash tab of the Publish Settings dialog box as shown in Figure 21-4.

Here are your options in the Flash tab:

✦ **Version:** This drop-down menu provides the option to publish movies in any of the Flash movie formats. To ensure complete compatibility with all of the new Flash MX 2004 features, select Flash Player 7. If you haven't used any Flash 5, MX, or MX 2004-specific ActionScript commands, you can use Flash 4. Flash 1 and 2 support only basic animation and interactive functions. Flash 3 supports just about all animation and artwork created in Flash MX, but it doesn't recognize any actions introduced with either Flash 4 or 5, editable text fields (such as form elements), or MP3 audio. If in doubt, you should test your choice of version in that version's Flash Player.

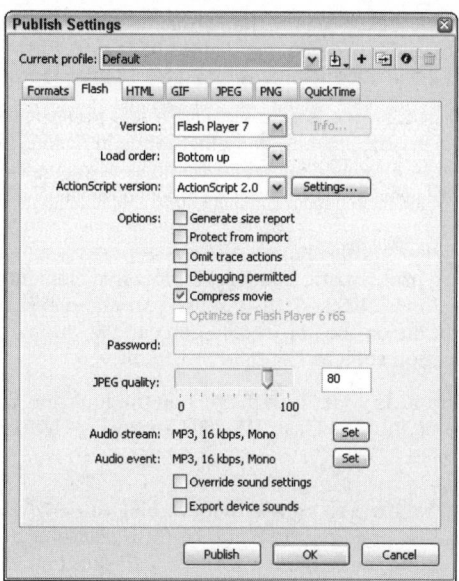

Figure 21-4: The Flash tab of the Publish Settings dialog box controls the settings for a movie published in the Flash format.

New Feature

Flash MX Professional 2004 has a Flash Lite 1.0 option in the Version menu. Flash Lite 1.0 is a new Flash Player shipping with DoCoMo phones. With this option selected, make sure you are using a Stage size that is compatible with the screen size of a DoCoMo handset. There are several templates available for this device in the Mobile Devices category of the Template tab of the File ➪ New dialog box.

Tip

You can download older versions of the Flash Player from the Macromedia site at www. macromedia.com/support/flash/ts/documents/oldplayers.htm.

✦ **Load order:** This option determines how the Flash Player will draw the first frame of the Flash movie as it is downloaded to the plug-in or player. When Bottom up (the default) is chosen, the layers load in ascending order: the lowest layer displays first, then the second lowest, and so on, until all of the layers for the first frame have been displayed. When Top down is selected, the layers load in descending order: the top-most layer displays first, then the layer underneath it, and so on. Again, this option affects the display of only the first frame of a Flash movie. If the content of the first frame is downloaded or streamed quickly, you probably won't notice the Load Order's effect.

Note

Load Order does **not** affect the order of actions spread across layers for the same frame. ActionScript will always execute in a top-down fashion; the actions on the top-most layers will execute before actions on lower layers.

✦ **ActionScript version:** This new option in Flash MX 2004 controls how ActionScript is compiled in a Flash movie (.swf file). You can choose ActionScript 1.0 or ActionScript 2.0. By default, ActionScript 2.0 is selected. Only use ActionScript 2.0 if you use the new ActionScript 2.0 coding features introduced with Flash MX 2004. If you code ActionScript the same way that you did in Flash MX or Flash 5, then choose ActionScript 1.0.

Tip

Flash MX 2004 can actually compile ActionScript 2.0 code so that it is compatible with Flash Player 6. If you choose ActionScript 2.0 and set the Version menu to Flash Player 6, Flash MX 2004 automatically compiles ActionScript 2.0 in a format that Flash Player 6 understands.

Also, keep in mind that ActionScript 1.0 or 2.0 code is case-sensitive *if* it is published for Flash Player 7. In Flash Player 7, variables, instance names, and other terms in ActionScript are case-sensitive. If you accidentally refer to a variable named myName as myname, Flash Player 7-compiled movies will not be as forgiving as Flash Player 6-compiled movies.

✦ **Generate size report:** As discussed earlier in this chapter, the size report for a Flash movie can be very useful in pinpointing problematic bandwidth-intensive elements, such as font characters. When this option is checked, the Publish command exports a text (.txt) file on Windows or a TextEdit file on the Macintosh. You can view this document separately in a text-editor application such as Notepad or BBEdit.

✦ **Protect from import:** This option safeguards your Flash movies on the Internet. When enabled, the SWF file cannot be imported into the Flash MX 2004 authoring environment or altered in any way.

Caution

The Protect from import option will *not* prevent a Web browser from caching your SWF files. Also, Macromedia Director can import and use protected Flash movies. Flash utilities such as SWF-Browser from www.swifftools.com can break into any SWF file and extract artwork, symbols, and sounds. There's even an application called ActionScript Viewer from www.buraks.com/asv that can extract ActionScript from your SWF files! For this reason, you should always use server-side scripts to verify sensitive data such as password entries in Flash movies, rather than internal ActionScripted password checking with if/else conditions. Don't store sensitive information such as passwords in your source files!

✦ **Omit trace actions:** When this option is selected, Flash MX 2004 removes any trace() actions used in your Flash document's ActionScript code. trace() actions will open the Output panel in Test Movie mode for debugging purposes. In general, if you used trace() actions, you will want to omit them from the final Flash movie — they can't be viewed from the standard version of the Flash Player anyway.

Cross-Reference

We discuss the use of trace() actions in Chapter 24, "Knowing the Nuts and Bolts of Code," and Chapter 34, "Managing and Troubleshooting Flash Movies."

✦ **Debugging permitted:** If this option is checked, you can access the Debugger panel from within the Debug Movie environment, or from a Web browser that is using the Flash Debug Player 7 plug-in or ActiveX control. To install the Flash Debug Player plug-in or ActiveX control, go to the Players folder in your Macromedia Flash MX 2004 application folder. There, you will find a Debug folder. With your browser applications closed, run one (or more) of the following files:

- **Install Flash Player 7 AX.exe** to install the ActiveX control for Internet Explorer on Windows 95/98/ME/NT/2000/XP.

- **Install Flash Player 7.exe** to install the plug-in for Netscape on Windows 95/98/ME/NT/2000/XP.

- **Install Flash 7 Player** to install the plug-in for Netscape and/or Internet Explorer for Macs running OS 9.x or earlier.

- **Install Flash Player 7 OSX** to install the plug-in for Netscape and/or Internet Explorer for Macs running OS X 10.1 or greater.

Note Flash MX 2004 creates an SWD file along with the SWF file when the Debugging permitted option is checked. You must upload both the SWD and SWF files to your Web server for remote debugging to function properly. We discuss remote debugging in Chapter 34, "Managing and Troubleshooting Flash Movies."

✦ **Compress movie:** This option compresses Flash Player 6 or Flash Player 7 movies only. When enabled, this compression feature will greatly reduce the size of text or ActionScript-heavy Flash movies. However, you may see little or no size difference on other Flash elements, such as artwork and sounds. Compression cannot be used on Flash 5 or earlier movies.

✦ **Optimize for Flash Player 6 r65:** If you decide to publish your Flash movie for Flash Player 6, you can select this check box to further optimize the SWF file. The r65 release of Flash Player 6 introduced enhancements for Flash movie playback that were not available in prior releases of Flash Player 6.

Note If you select the Optimize for Flash Player 6 r65 option, Flash MX 2004 prompts you with a warning dialog box when you publish the Flash movie. If you use this option, you should use the new version detection features in the Publish Settings' HTML tab to ensure that visitors trying to view the movie will be redirected to the proper plug-in download page if they are using an earlier version of the player.

✦ **Password:** If you selected the Debugging permitted option, you can enter a password to access the Debugger panel. Because you can debug movies over a live Internet connection, you should always enter a password here if you intend to debug a remote Flash movie. If you leave this field empty and check the Debugging permitted option, Flash MX 2004 will still prompt you for a password when you attempt to access the Debugger panel remotely. Simply press the Enter key when this prompt appears if you left this field blank.

✦ **JPEG quality:** This slider and text-field option specifies the level of JPEG compression applied to bitmapped artwork in the Flash movie. The value can be any value between (and including) 0 to 100. Higher values apply less compression and preserve more information of the original bitmap, whereas lower values apply more compression and keep less information. The value entered here applies to all bitmaps that enable the Use document default quality option, found in the Bitmap Properties dialog box for each bitmap in the document's Library panel. Unlike the audio settings discussed in a moment, no "override" option exists to disregard settings in the Library.

✦ **Audio Stream:** This option displays the current audio compression scheme for Stream audio. By clicking the Set button (see Figure 21-4), you can control the compression applied to any sounds that use the Stream Sync setting in the Sound area of the Property inspector (when a sound keyframe has focus). Like the JPEG quality option discussed previously, this compression value is applied to any Stream sounds that use the Default compression in the Export Settings section of each audio file's Sound Properties dialog box in the document's Library. See Chapter 15, "Adding Sound," for more information on using Stream sounds and audio compression schemes.

✦ **Audio Event:** This setting behaves exactly the same as the Audio Stream option, except that this compression setting applies to Default compression-enabled Event sounds. See Chapter 15, "Adding Sound," for more information on Event sounds.

Tip Flash MX 2004 supports imported MP3 audio that uses VBR (Variable Bit Rate) compression. However, Flash cannot compress native sounds in VBR. If you use any imported MP3 audio for Stream Sync audio, Flash will recompress the MP3 audio on export.

✦ **Override sound settings:** If you want the settings for Audio Stream and Audio Event to apply to all Stream and Event sounds, respectively, and to disregard any unique compression schemes specified in the document's Library, check this option. This is useful for creating multiple SWF file versions of the Flash movie (hi-fi, lo-fi, and so on) and enabling the Web visitor to decide which one to download.

✦ **Export device sounds:** If you are using Flash MX Professional 2004, you have the option of exporting device sounds with your Flash movie. This option is used only if you are using the Flash Lite 1.0 option in the Version menu. To learn more about the use of this feature, use the search phrase "device sound" in the Help panel (Help ➪ Help) in Flash MX Pro 2004.

When you are finished entering the settings for the Flash movie, you can proceed to other file type settings in the Publish Settings dialog box. Or you can click OK to return to the authoring environment of Flash MX 2004 so that you can use the newly entered settings in the Test Movie or Scene environment. You can also export a Flash movie (and other file formats currently selected in Publish Settings) by clicking the Publish button in the Publish Settings dialog box.

Using the HTML settings

HTML is the language in which most Web pages are written. The HTML tab of the Publish Settings dialog box (see Figure 21-5) has a number of settings that control the way in which Flash MX 2004 publishes a movie into a complete Web page with HTML tags specifying the Flash Player.

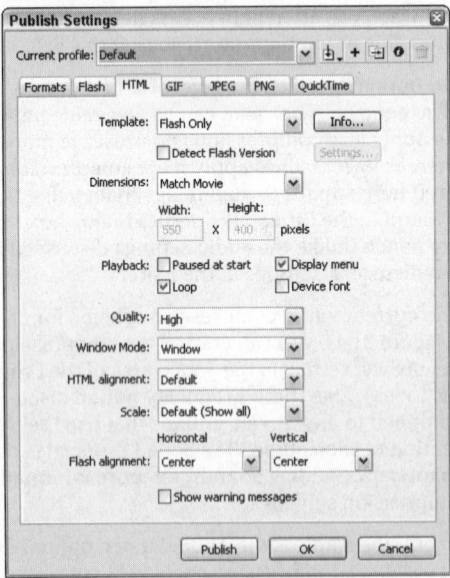

Figure 21-5: The HTML tab controls flexible Flash movie options—you can change these options without permanently affecting the Flash movie.

The settings available in the HTML tab include:

✦ **Template:** Perhaps the most important (and versatile) feature of all Publish Settings, the Template setting enables you to select a predefined set of HTML tags to display your Flash movies. To view the description of each template, click the Info button to the right of the drop-down list (shown in Figure 21-5). All templates use the same options listed in the HTML tab—the template simply places the values of those settings into HTML tags scripted in the template. You can also create your own custom templates for your own unique implementation of Flash movies.

You can view the "source" of each template in the HTML folder found inside of the en\ FirstRun\HTML folder of the Flash MX 2004 application folder. Although these template files have .html extensions, you can use Macromedia Dreamweaver MX 2004, Notepad (Windows), or TextEdit (Mac) to view the files. All of the preinstalled templates include HTML tags to create an entire Web page, complete with <head>, <title>, and <body> tags. The following templates are available in the HTML tab:

Note The Template option in this HTML tab has nothing to do with the New from Template option (File ➪ New and Template tab). For more information on Flash MX 2004 templates, please read Chapter 4, "Interface Fundamentals." Also, the Detect for Flash templates included with previous Flash versions have been replaced by the new Detect Flash Version feature of Flash MX 2004. By themselves, these templates do not perform any true version-checking functionality. We encourage you to use the new Detect Flash Version feature with any entry page into your Flash-driven Web site.

● **Flash For Pocket PC 2003:** With this template, Flash creates an HTML document that can display the Flash movie within the Pocket IE application running on a Pocket PC. This template also creates the necessary tags to display the same Flash movie in the regular desktop versions of Internet Explorer and Netscape. At the time of this writing, Flash Player 6 was the latest public release available for the Pocket PC.

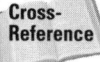

Cross-Reference If you are designing Flash movies for the Pocket PC, be sure to check out the Pocket PC document templates. Choose File ➪ New, click the Templates tab, and choose the Mobile Device category.

● **Flash HTTPS:** This template looks nearly identical to the Flash Only template (discussed next). The only difference with this template is that the download locations for the ActiveX control and plug-in page use https:// instead of http://. If you are loading your Flash movie (.swf file) from a secure URL and page, it's recommended that any and all URLs used within that document use secure URLs as well. A secure URL always starts with https://.

● **Flash Only:** This default template simply inserts the <object> and <embed> tags for a Flash movie. It does not perform any browser or plug-in detection. If the user does not have the Flash Player plug-in or ActiveX control, the browser may produce an error message, a missing plug-in icon, or a prompt to download the latest plug-in or ActiveX control, depending on the browser configuration. The HTML produced by this template may allow an earlier Flash Player (such as Flash Player 4) to attempt playback of your newer Flash movie. Keep in mind that any version of the Flash Player will try to render any Flash movie file. However, you may get unpredictable results when a newer-version Flash movie loads into an older player.

- **Flash with AICC Tracking:** Use this template if you are creating Flash movies that incorporate components from the Learning Interactions Library (Window ➪ Other Panels ➪ Common Libraries ➪ Learning Interactions). Use this template if you want the components in the Flash movie to comply with the AICC (Aviation Industry CBT Committee) training guidelines. The template will create JavaScript/VBScript functions that can work with the ActionScript of the learning components. For more information on AICC guidelines, see `www.aicc.org`. Note that this template will function only in Web browsers that support the `fscommand()` action from Flash movies.

- **Flash with FSCommand:** Use this template if you are using the `fscommand()` action in your Flash movies to communicate with JavaScript in the HTML page. The `fscommand()` is discussed in Chapter 22, "Integrating Flash Content with Web Pages." The necessary `<object>` and `<embed>` tags from the Flash Only (Default) template are also included.

- **Flash with Named Anchors:** If you are using named anchors in the Main Timeline of your Flash document, you will want to use this template for your published HTML document. This template creates the necessary JavaScript to enable the Back button on your Web browser with named anchors within your Flash movie. Named anchors allow you to designate specific keyframes (and scenes) that register in the browser's history when played.

Cross-Reference   For an example of named anchors in action, read Chapter 20, "Making Your First Flash MX 2004 Project."

- **Flash with SCORM Tracking:** This template will create the HTML and JavaScript/VBScript functions to enable communication between Flash movies that use the components from the Learning Interactions Library and the HTML page. SCORM, which stands for Shareable Content Object Reference Model, is a set of guidelines for learning systems created by the U.S. Department of Defense Advanced Distributed Learning (ADL) Initiative. Both SCORM and AICC guidelines aim to promote interoperability among learning and training systems. Note that this template will only function in Web browsers that support the `fscommand()` from Flash movies.

- **Image Map:** This template does not use or display any Flash movie. Instead, it uses a GIF, JPEG, or PNG image (as specified in the Publish Settings' Format tab) as a client-side image map, via an `<img>` tag with a `USEMAP` attribute. Use a frame label of `#map` in the Flash document (.fla file) to designate which frame is used as the map image. See the section "Using the GIF settings" later in this chapter for more details.

- **QuickTime:** This template creates both the `<object>` and `<embed>` tags to display QuickTime Flash movies. You need to enable the QuickTime file type in the Publish Settings' Format tab. A QuickTime Flash movie is a special type of QuickTime movie, playable with QuickTime 4 or higher. QuickTime 4 can recognize Flash 3 features only, QuickTime 5 can play Flash 4, and QuickTime 6 can play Flash 5 movies. Be careful to only use ActionScript features that are compatible with each respective version. You must choose Flash Player 3, Flash Player 4, or Flash Player 5 as the Version option in the Flash tab. Depending on the options selected in the QuickTime tab of Publish Settings, the Flash movie may or may not be stored within the QuickTime movie file.

The "Working with QuickTime" chapter, found in previous editions of the *Flash Bible*, has been moved to an online-only location. You can download the PDF file at `www.flashsupport.com/archive`.

✦ **Detect Flash Version:** This new feature of Flash MX 2004 enables you to add version detection to your Flash content. Select this check box and click the Settings button to open the Version Detection Settings dialog box, as shown in Figure 21-6. Note that you need to select Flash Player 6 or earlier to detect specific minor revision releases of the player. The Detect Flash Version feature creates a flash_detection.swf movie along with several HTML files to direct the user to the appropriate content on your site. The Version Detection Settings dialog box includes the following options:

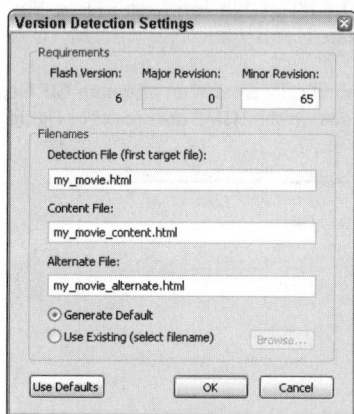

Figure 21-6: The Version Detection Settings dialog box accepts the parameters for your own custom Flash Player detection mechanism.

- **Flash Version:** This area of the dialog box displays the version of the Flash Player selected in the Version menu of the Flash tab. You cannot edit the value directly in this dialog box.

- **Major Revision:** This text field controls the major version revision number you want to require. Note that, to date, there have been no major revisions to existing Flash Players.

- **Minor Revision:** This text field displays the minor revision number of the Flash Player you want to require. If you have selected Flash Player 6 or earlier, you can edit this value directly in the dialog box. For example, if you chose the Optimize for Flash Player 6 r65 option in the Flash tab, you could enter the number 65 in this field. The detection script would then check for r65 or higher.

- **Detection File (first target file):** In this field, you type the name of the HTML document that will contain the auto-generated `flash_detection.swf` file. This document will be the first page accessed by the user. If the user has any version of the Flash Player installed, the page will load the flash_detection.swf and check the parameters you specified in this dialog box. If the user does not have any version of the Flash Player installed, a `<meta http-equiv="refresh" ... >` tag in this HTML document redirects them to the Alternate File document.

- **Content File:** This field specifies the name of the HTML document displaying the actual Flash movie you are currently publishing. If the user passes the detection test, he/she sees this HTML page along with your Flash content.

- **Alternate File:** This field specifies the name of the HTML document that is displayed to users who do not have the version of the Flash Player you specified, or to those users who do not have any version of the Flash Player installed.

- **Generate Default/Use Existing (select filename):** These radio buttons work in tandem with the Alternate File option. If you choose Generate Default, Flash MX 2004 creates the alternate HTML document for you. This generated page, shown in Figure 21-7, instructs the user to download the latest version of the Flash Player plug-in from the Macromedia site. If you choose the Use Existing (select filename) option, you must specify the HTML file you wish to use. You can click the Browse button to find the alternate HTML file.

Tip   The auto-generated default alternate file automatically creates an alternate GIF file, which is the "Get Macromedia Flash Player" button shown in the HTML document of Figure 21-7.

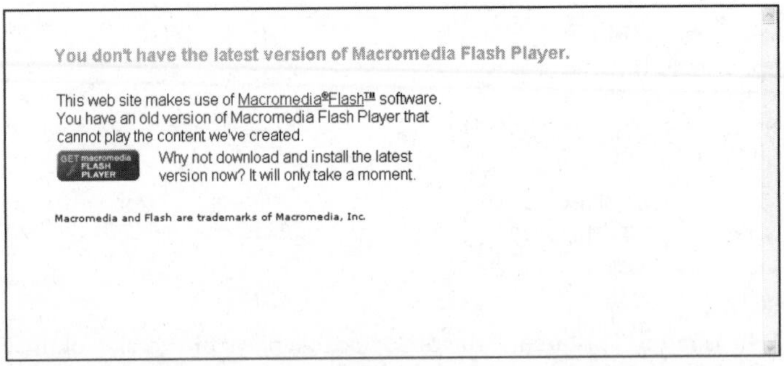

You don't have the latest version of Macromedia Flash Player.

This web site makes use of Macromedia®Flash™ software.
You have an old version of Macromedia Flash Player that
cannot play the content we've created.
GET macromedia FLASH PLAYER   Why not download and install the latest
version now? It will only take a moment.

Macromedia and Flash are trademarks of Macromedia, Inc.

Figure 21-7: The auto-generated alternate HTML document created by Flash MX 2004 instructs users to download the latest version of the Flash Player plug-in.

- **Use Defaults:** If you click this button in the dialog box, the filename fields are reset to the default values.

Cross-Reference   To learn how to create a sample set of detection pages, read Chapter 22, "Integrating Flash Content with Web Pages."

✦ **Dimensions:** This setting controls the width and height values of the <object> and <embed> tags. The dimension settings here do not change the original Flash movie; they simply create the area through which your Flash movie is viewed on the Web page. The way that the Flash movie "fits" into this viewing area is determined with the Scale option (discussed later). Three input areas exist: a drop-down menu and two text fields for width and height. The options here are:

- **Match Movie:** If you want to keep the same width and height that you specified in the Document Properties dialog box (Modify ➪ Document), then use this option in the drop-down menu.

- **Pixels:** You can change the viewing size (in pixel units) of the Flash movie window by selecting this option and entering new values in the Width and Height text fields.

- **Percent:** By far one of the most popular options with Flash movies, Percent scales the movie to the size of the browser window—or a portion of it. Using a value of 100 on both Width and Height expands the Flash movie to fit the entire browser window. If Percent is used with the proper Scale setting (see the description of the Scale setting later in this chapter), the aspect ratio of your Flash movie will not be distorted.

Tip

The ActionScript `Stage` object and its supporting methods allow you to disable or override automatic scaling of the Flash movie. For example, the following action added to frame 1 of your Flash movie will disable scaling: `Stage.scaleMode = "noScale";`

- **Width and Height:** Enter the values for the Flash movie width and height here. If Match Movie is selected, you shouldn't be able to enter any values. The unit of measurement is determined by selecting either Pixels or Percent from the drop-down menu.

✦ **Playback:** These options control how the Flash movie plays when it is downloaded to the browser. Each of these options has an `<object>` and `<embed>` attribute if you want to control them outside of Publish Settings. Note that these attributes are not viewable within the Publish Settings dialog box—you need to load the published HTML document into a text editor to see the attributes.

- **Paused at start:** This is equivalent to adding a `stop()` action on the first frame of the first scene in the Flash movie. By default, this option is off—movies play as soon as they stream into the player. A button with a `play()` action can start the movie, or the Play command can be executed from the Flash Player shortcut menu (by right-clicking or Control+clicking the movie). Attribute: `play="true"` or `"false"`. If `play="true"`, the movie will play as soon as it is loaded.

- **Loop:** This option causes the Flash movie to repeat an infinite number of times. By default, this option is on. If it is not checked, the Flash movie stops on the last frame unless some other ActionScripted event is initiated on the last frame. Attribute: `loop="true"` or `"false"`.

- **Display menu:** This option controls whether the person viewing the Flash movie in the Flash Player environment can access the shortcut menu via a right-click (Windows) or Control+click (Mac) anywhere within the movie area. If this option is selected, the visitor can select Zoom In/Out, 100 percent, Show All, High Quality, Play, Loop, Rewind, Forward, and Back from the menu. If this option is not selected, the visitor can only select About Flash Player from the menu. Attribute: `menu="true"` or `"false"`.

- **Device font:** This option applies to Flash movies played only in the Windows version of the Flash Player. When enabled, this option replaces fonts that are not installed on the Player's system with anti-aliased system fonts. Attribute: `devicefont="true"` or `"false"`.

✦ **Quality:** This menu determines how the Flash artwork in a movie will render. While it would be ideal to play all Flash movies at high quality, slower processors may not be able to redraw anti-aliased artwork and keep up with the frame rate. The options for this setting include the following:

- **Low:** This setting forces the Flash Player to turn off anti-aliasing (smooth edges) completely. On slower processors, this may improve playback performance. Attribute: `quality="low"`.

- **Auto Low:** This setting starts in Low quality mode (no anti-aliasing) but will switch to High quality if the computer's processor can handle the playback speed. Attribute: `quality="autolow"`.

- **Auto High:** This setting is the opposite of Auto Low. The Flash Player starts playing the movie in High quality mode, but if the processor cannot handle the playback demands, it switches to Low quality mode. For most Web sites, this is the optimal setting to use because it favors higher quality first. Attribute: `quality="autohigh"`.

- **Medium:** This quality produces anti-aliased vector graphics on a 2 x 2 grid (in other words, it will smooth edges over a 4-pixel square area), but it does not smooth bitmap images. Artwork will appear slightly better than the Low quality, but not as smooth as the High setting. Attribute: `quality="medium"`. This quality setting will only work with the Flash 5 or higher Player.

- **High:** When this setting is used, the Flash Player dedicates more of the computer's processor to rendering graphics (instead of playback). All vector artwork is anti-aliased on a 4 x 4 grid (16-pixel square area). Bitmaps are smoothed unless they are contained within an animation sequence such as a Motion tween. By default, this setting is selected in the HTML tab of the Publish Settings dialog. Attribute: `quality="high"`.

- **Best:** This mode does everything that High quality does, with the addition of smoothing all bitmaps — regardless of whether they are in Motion tweens. This mode is the most processor-intensive. Attribute: `quality="best"`.

✦ **Window Mode:** The Window Mode setting works only with any version of the Flash ActiveX control on Internet Explorer for Windows 95/98/ME/NT/2000/XP or with Flash Player 6 r65 and higher for Netscape on Windows browsers or any Mac OS X browsers. If you intend to deliver to one of these browsers and/or this version of the Flash Player, you can animate Flash content on top of DHTML content. One of the following values can be selected from this menu:

- **Window:** This is the "standard" player interface, in which the Flash movie plays as it would normally, in its own rectangular window on a Web page. Attribute: `wmode="window"`.

- **Opaque Windowless:** Use this option if you want the Flash movie to have an opaque (that is, non-transparent) background and have DHTML or HTML elements behind the Flash movie. Attribute: `wmode="opaque"`.

- **Transparent Windowless:** This option "knocks out" the Flash background color so that other HTML and DHTML elements can show through. You have likely seen this type of Flash movie and effect used on several commercial Web sites, where Flash ads animate across the screen on top of the HTML document. Note that the Flash movie's frame rate and performance may suffer on slower machines when this mode is used because the Flash movie needs to composite itself over other non-Flash material. Attribute: `wmode="transparent"`.

✦ **HTML Alignment:** This setting works much like the `ALIGN` attribute of `<img>` tags in HTML documents, but it's used with the `ALIGN` attribute of the `<OBJECT>` and `<embed>` tags for the Flash movie. Note that these settings may not have any effect when used within a table cell (`<td>` tag) or a DHTML layer (`<div>` or `<layer>` tag). The options for this setting include the following:

- **Default:** This option horizontally or vertically centers the Flash movie in the browser window. If the browser window is smaller than a Flash movie that uses a Pixel or Match Movie dimensions setting (see Dimensions setting earlier in this section), the Flash movie will be cropped.

- **Left, Right, Top, and Bottom:** These options align the Flash movie along the left, right, top, or bottom edge of the browser window, respectively.

✦ **Scale:** This setting works in tandem with the Dimensions setting discussed earlier in this section, and it determines how the Flash movie displays on the HTML page. Just as big-screen movies must be cropped to fit the aspect ratio of a TV screen, Flash movies may need to be modified to fit the area prescribed by the Dimensions setting. The settings for the Scale option include the following:

- **Default (Show all):** This option fits the entire Flash movie into the area defined by the Dimensions setting without distorting the original aspect ratio of the Flash movie. However, borders may appear on two sides of the Flash movie. For example, if a 300 x 300-pixel window is specified in Dimensions and the Flash movie has an aspect ratio of 1.33:1 (for example, 400 x 300 pixels), then a border fills the remaining areas on top of and below the Flash movie. This is similar to the "letterbox" effect on widescreen video rentals. Attribute: `scale="showall"`.

- **No border:** This option forces the Flash movie to fill the area defined by the Dimensions setting without leaving borders. The Flash movie's aspect ratio is not distorted or stretched. However, this may crop two sides of the Flash movie. Using the same example from Show All, the left and right sides of the Flash movie are cropped when No Border is selected. Attribute: `scale="noborder"`.

- **Exact fit:** This option stretches a Flash movie to fill the entire area defined by the Dimensions setting. Using the same example from Show All, the 400 x 300 Flash movie is scrunched to fit a 300 x 300 window. If the original movie showed a perfect circle, it now appears as an oval. Attribute: `scale="exactfit"`.

- **No scale:** This options prevents the Flash movie from scaling beyond its original size as defined in the Document Properties dialog box (Modify ⇨ Document). The Flash Player window size (or the Web browser window size) has no effect on the size of the Flash movie. Attribute: `scale="noscale"`.

✦ **Flash Alignment:** This setting adjusts the `salign` attribute of the `<object>` and `<embed>` tags for the Flash movie. In contrast to the HTML Alignment setting, Flash Alignment works in conjunction with the Scale and Dimensions settings, and determines how a Flash movie is aligned within the Player window. This setting has the following options:

- **Horizontal:** These options — Left, Center, and Right — determine whether the Flash movie is horizontally aligned to the left, center, or right of the Dimensions area, respectively. Using the same example from the Scale setting, a 400 x 300-pixel Flash movie (fit into a 300 x 300 Dimension window with `scale="noborder"`) with a Flash Horizontal Alignment setting of Left crops only the right side of the Flash movie.

- **Vertical:** These options—Top, Center, and Bottom—determine whether the Flash movie is vertically aligned to the top, center, or bottom of the Dimensions area, respectively. If the preceding example used a Show All Scale setting and had a Flash Vertical Alignment setting of Top, the border would occur only below the bottom edge of the Flash movie.

✦ **Show Warning Messages:** This useful feature alerts you to errors during the actual Publish process. For example, if you selected the Image Map template and didn't specify a static GIF, JPEG, or PNG file in the Formats tab, Flash returns an error. By default, this option is enabled. If it is disabled, Flash suppresses any warnings during the Publish process.

Using the GIF settings

The GIF (Graphics Interchange File) format, developed by CompuServe, defined the first generation of Web graphics and is still quite popular today, despite its 256-color limitation. In the context of the Publish Settings of Flash MX 2004, the GIF format is used to export a static or animated image that can be used in place of the Flash movie if the Flash Player or plug-in is not installed. Although the Flash and HTML tabs are specific to Flash movie display and playback, the settings of the GIF tab (see Figure 21-8) control the characteristics of a GIF animation (or still image) that Flash MX 2004 will publish.

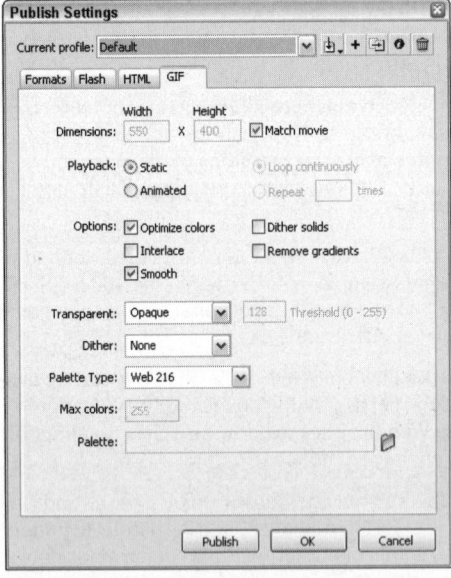

Figure 21-8: Every subtle aspect of a GIF animation or still image can be finessed with these settings of the GIF tab of the Publish Settings dialog box.

The settings in the GIF tab include the following:

✦ **Dimensions:** This setting has three options: Width, Height, and Match Movie. As you might surmise, Width and Height control the dimensions of the GIF image. These fields are enabled only when the Match Movie check box is unchecked. With Match Movie checked, the dimensions of the GIF match those of the Flash Movie that is being published.

✦ **Playback:** These radio buttons control what type of GIF image is created and how it plays (if Animated is chosen):

- **Static:** If this button is selected, then Flash exports the first frame of the Flash movie as a single still image in the GIF format. If you want to use a frame other than the first frame, use a frame label of #Static on the desired frame. Alternatively, you could use the File ⇨ Export Image command to export a GIF image from whatever frame the Current Frame Indicator is positioned over.

- **Animated:** If this button is selected, Flash exports the entire Flash movie as an animated GIF file (in the GIF89a format). If you don't want to export the entire movie as an animated GIF (indeed, a GIF file for a Flash movie with over 100 frames would most likely be too large to download easily over the Web), you can designate a range of frames to export. Use a frame label of #First on the beginning frame of a given range of frames. Next, add a frame label of #Last to the ending frame of the desired sequence of frames. Flash actually is pretty good at optimizing animated GIFs by saving only areas that change over time in each frame—instead of the entire frame.

- **Loop Continuously:** When the Animated radio button is selected, you can specify that the animated GIF repeats an infinite number of times by selecting the Loop Continuously radio button.

- **Repeat __ times:** This option can be used to set up an animated GIF that repeats a given number of times. If you don't want the animated GIF to repeat continuously, enter the number of repetitions here.

✦ **Options:** The options in the Options settings control the creation of the GIF's color table and how the browser displays the GIF:

- **Optimize Colors:** When you are using any palette type other than Adaptive, this option removes any colors preexisting in the Web 216 or custom palettes that are not used by the GIF image. Enabling this option can only save you precious bytes used in file overhead—it has no effect on the actual quality of the image. Most images do not use all 216 colors of the Web palette. For example, a black-and-white picture can use only between 3 and 10 colors from the 216-color palette.

- **Interlace:** This option makes the GIF image download in incrementing resolutions. As the image downloads, the image becomes sharper with each successive "scan." Use of this option is usually personal preference. Some people like to use it for image maps that can provide basic navigation information before the entire image downloads.

- **Smooth:** This option anti-aliases the Flash artwork as it exports to the GIF image. Text may look better when it is anti-aliased, but you may want to test this option for your particular use. If you need to make a transparent GIF, smoothing may produce unsightly edges.

- **Dither Solids:** This option determines whether solid areas of color (such as fills) are dithered. In this context, this type of dithering would create a two-color pattern to mimic a solid color that doesn't occur in the GIF's color palette. See the discussion of dithering later in this section.

- **Remove Gradients:** Flash gradients do not translate or display very well in 256 or fewer colors. Use this option to convert all Flash gradients to solid colors. The solid color is determined by the first color prescribed in the gradient. Unless you developed your gradients with this effect in mind, this option may produce undesirable results.

✦ **Transparent:** This setting controls the appearance of the Flash movie background, as well as any Flash artwork that uses alpha settings. Because GIF images support only one level of transparency (that is, the transparent area cannot be anti-aliased), exercise caution when using this setting. The Threshold option is available only if Alpha is selected. The options for this setting include the following:

- **Opaque:** This option produces a GIF image with a solid background. The image has a rectangular shape.

- **Transparent:** This option makes the Flash movie background appear transparent. If the Smooth option in the Options setting is enabled, Flash artwork may display halos over the background HTML color.

- **Alpha and Threshold:** When the Alpha option is selected in the drop-down menu, you can control at what alpha level Flash artwork becomes transparent by entering a value in the Threshold text field. For example, if you enter 128, all alphas at 50 percent become completely transparent. If you are considering an animated GIF that has Flash artwork fading in or out, you probably want to use the Opaque transparent option. If Alpha and Threshold were used, the fade effect would be lost.

✦ **Dither:** Dithering is the process of emulating a color by juxtaposing two colors in a pattern arrangement. Because GIF images are limited to 256 colors (or fewer), dithering can often produce better-looking images for continuous tone artwork such as gradients. However, Flash's dithering seems to work best with the Web 216 palette. Dithering can increase the file size of a GIF image.

- **None:** This option does not apply any dithering to the GIF image.

- **Ordered:** This option applies an intermediate level of dithering with minimal file size overhead.

- **Diffusion:** This option applies the best level of dithering to the GIF image, but with larger file size overhead. Diffusion dithering only has a noticeable effect when the Web 216 palette is chosen in Palette Type.

✦ **Palette Type:** As mentioned earlier in this section, GIF images are limited to 256 or fewer colors. However, this grouping of 256 is arbitrary: Any set of 256 (or fewer) colors can be used for a given GIF image. This setting enables you to select predefined sets of colors to use on the GIF image. See Chapter 7, "Applying Color," for more information on the Web color palette. The options for this setting include:

- **Web 216:** When this option is selected, the GIF image uses colors only from the limited 216 Web-color palette. For most Flash artwork, this should produce acceptable results. However, it may not render Flash gradients or photographic bitmaps very well.

- **Adaptive:** With this option selected, Flash creates a unique set of 256 colors (or fewer, if specified in the Max Colors setting) for the GIF image. However, these adapted colors fall outside of the Web-Safe Color Palette. File sizes for adaptive

GIFs are larger than Web 216 GIFs, unless few colors are chosen in the Max Colors setting. Adaptive GIFs look much better than Web 216 GIFs, but they may not display very well with 8-bit video cards and monitors.

- **Web Snap Adaptive:** This option tries to give the GIF image the best of both worlds. Flash converts any colors close to the 216 Web palette to Web-Safe colors and uses adaptive colors for the rest. This palette produces better results than the Adaptive palette for older display systems that used 8-bit video cards.

- **Custom:** When this option is selected, you can specify a palette that uses the ACT file format to be used as the GIF image's palette. Macromedia Fireworks and Adobe Photoshop can export color palettes (or color look-up tables) as ACT files.

✦ **Max Colors:** With this setting, you can specify exactly how many colors are in the GIF's color table. This numeric entry field is enabled only when Adaptive or Web Snap Adaptive is selected in the Palette Type drop-down menu.

✦ **Palette:** This text field and the ". . ." browse button are enabled only when Custom is selected in the Palette Type drop-down menu. When enabled, this dialog box is used to locate and load a palette file from the hard drive.

Using the JPEG settings

The JPEG (Joint Photographic Experts Group) format is just as popular as the GIF format on the Web. Unlike GIF images, however, JPEG images can use much more than 256 colors. In fact, JPEG files must be 24-bit color (or full-color RGB) images. Although GIF files use lossless compression (within the actual file itself), JPEG images use lossy compression, which means that color information is discarded in order to save file space. However, JPEG compression is very good. Even at its lowest quality settings, JPEG images can preserve quite a bit of detail in photographic images.

Another significant difference between GIF and JPEG is that GIF images do not require nearly as much memory (for equivalent image dimensions) as JPEG images do. You need to remember that JPEG images "uncompress" when they are downloaded to your computer. While the file sizes may be small initially, they still open as full-color images in the computer's memory. For example, even though you may get the file size of a 400 x 300-pixel JPEG image down to 10 KB, it still requires nearly 352 KB in memory when it is opened or displayed.

Flash publishes the first frame of the Flash movie as the JPEG image, unless a #Static frame label is given to another frame in the Flash movie. The limited settings of the JPEG tab of the Publish Settings dialog box (see Figure 21-9) control the few variables of this still photo-quality image format:

✦ **Dimensions:** This setting behaves the same as the GIF Dimensions setting. Width and Height control the dimensions of the movie. But these fields are enabled only when the Match Movie check box is unchecked. With Match Movie checked, the dimensions of the JPEG match those of the Flash Movie.

✦ **Quality:** This slider and text field work exactly the same way as the JPEG Quality setting in the Flash tab of Publish Settings. Higher values apply less compression and result in better quality, but they create images with larger file sizes.

✦ **Progressive:** This option is similar to the Interlaced option for GIF images. When enabled, the JPEG image loads in successive scans, becoming sharper with each pass.

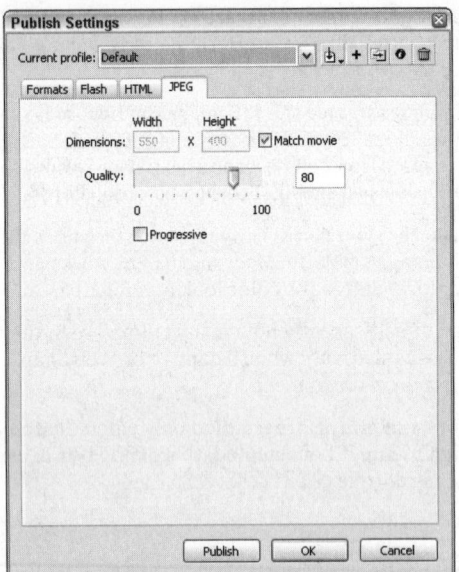

Figure 21-9: The settings of the JPEG tab are limited because JPEGs are still images with relatively few variables to be addressed.

Using the PNG settings

The PNG (Portable Network Graphic) format is another still-image format. The PNG specification was developed in 1996 by the W3C (World Wide Web Consortium), and the format is an improvement over both the GIF and JPEG formats in several ways. Much like JPEG, it is excellent for transmission of photographic quality images. The primary advantages of PNG are variable bit-depths (images can be 256 colors or millions of colors), multilevel transparency, and lossless compression. However, some browsers do not offer full support for all PNG options without some kind of additional plug-in. When in doubt, test your PNG images in your preferred browser.

The settings of the PNG tab (see Figure 21-10) control the characteristics of the PNG image that Flash will publish.

The PNG tab options are:

✦ **Dimensions:** This setting works just like the GIF and JPEG equivalents. When Match Movie is checked, you cannot alter the Width and Height of the PNG image.

✦ **Bit Depth:** This setting controls how many colors are created in the PNG image:

- **8-bit:** In this mode, the PNG image has a maximum color palette of 256 colors, similar to the palette function of GIF images. When this option is selected, the Options, Dither, Palette Type, Max Colors, and Palette settings can be altered.

- **24-bit:** When this option is selected, the PNG image can display any of the 16.7 million RGB colors. This option produces larger files than 8-bit PNG images, but it renders the Flash artwork most faithfully.

- **24-bit with Alpha:** This option adds another 8-bit channel to the 24-bit PNG image for multilevel transparency support. This means that Flash will treat the Flash movie background as a transparent area, so that information behind the PNG image (such as HTML background colors) shows through. Note that, with proper browser support, PNG can render anti-aliased edges on top of other elements, such as HTML background images!

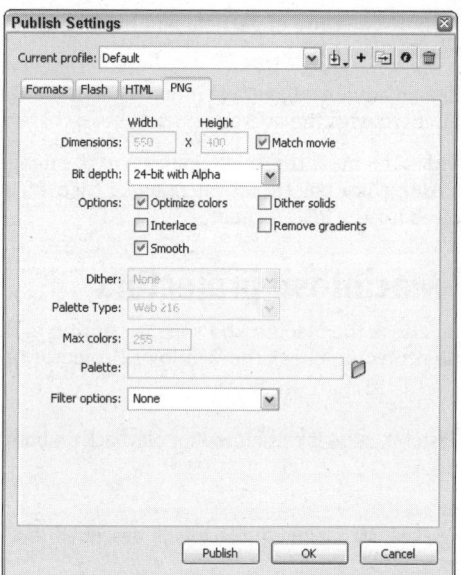

Figure 21-10: The settings found on the PNG tab closely resemble those on the GIF tab. The PNG was engineered to have many of the advantages of both the GIF and JPEG formats.

Note   Flash MX 2004's PNG export or publish settings do not reflect the full range of PNG options available. PNG can support transparency in both 8-bit and 24-bit flavors, but Flash enables transparency only in 24-bit with Alpha images.

✦ **Options:** These options behave the same as the equivalent GIF Publish Settings.

✦ **Dither, Palette Type, Max Colors,** and **Palette:** These settings work the same as the equivalent GIF Publish Settings. Because PNG images can be either 8- or 24-bit, these options apply only to 8-bit PNG images. If anything other than 8-bit is selected in the Bit Depth setting, these options are disabled. Please refer to the previous section for more information.

✦ **Filter Options:** This drop-down menu controls what type of compression sampling or algorithm the PNG image uses. Note that this does not apply an art or graphic "filter effect" as the filters in Adobe Photoshop do, nor does it throw away any image information — all filters are lossless. It simply enables you to be the judge of what kind of compression to use on the image. You need to experiment with each of these filters on your Flash movie image to find the best filter-to-file size combination. Technically, the filters do not actually look at the pixel data. Rather, they look at the byte data of each pixel. Results vary depending on the image content, but here are some guidelines to keep in mind:

   • **None:** When this option is selected, no filtering is applied to the image. When no filter is applied, you usually have unnecessarily large file sizes.

   • **Sub:** This filter works best on images that have repeated information along the horizontal axis. For example, the stripes of a horizontal American flag filter nicely with the sub filter.

- **Up:** The opposite of the sub filter, this filter works by looking for repeated information along the vertical axis. The stripes of a vertical American flag filter well with the up filter.

- **Average:** Use this option when a mixture of vertical and horizontal information exists. When in doubt, try this filter first.

- **Paeth:** This filter works like an advanced average filter. When in doubt, try this filter after you have experimented with the average filter.

- **Adaptive:** This filter provides the most thorough analysis of the image's color and creates the most accurate color palette for the image. However, it usually provides the largest file sizes for the PNG format.

Creating Windows and Macintosh projectors

To export a Mac stand-alone projector, check the Macintosh Projector option in the Formats tab. To publish a Windows stand-alone projector, check the Windows Projector option in the Formats tab.

Note The Mac projector published by Flash MX 2004 is carbonized for playback on both Mac OS X and Mac OS 9.*x* (or earlier) systems.

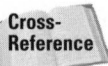

Cross-Reference The process of creating and using Flash standalone projectors is described in Chapter 23, "Using the Flash Player and Projector."

Using the QuickTime settings

Now that Apple QuickTime 4 or higher includes built-in support for Flash tracks and SWF files, you may want to publish QuickTime movies (MOV files) in addition to your Flash movies. If you want to enable QuickTime movie output via the Publish command, make sure that it is selected in the Formats tab of the Publish Settings dialog box.

Web Resource The QuickTime publish settings are discussed at length in an online PDF, "Working with QuickTime." This content, found in previous editions of the *Flash Bible,* has been moved to an online-only location. You can download the PDF file at www.flashsupport.com/archive.

Publish Preview and Publish Commands

After you have entered the file format types and specifications for each in the Publish Settings dialog box, you can proceed to preview and publish the file types you selected.

Using Publish Preview

The Publish Preview submenu (accessible from File ➪ Publish Preview) lists all of the file types currently enabled in the Publish Settings dialog box. By default, HTML is the first file type available for preview. In general, the first item enabled in the Formats tab of the Publish Settings dialog box is the first item in the submenu and can be executed by pressing Ctrl+F12 or ⌘+F12. Selecting a file type in the Publish Preview menu launches your default browser and inserts the selected file type(s) into the browser window.

Note   When you use Publish Preview, Flash MX actually creates real files in the same location as the saved Flash document (.fla file). In a sense, previewing is the same as running the Publish command, except that Publish Preview will save you the steps of opening the browser (or player) and loading the files manually.

Using Publish

When you want Flash to export the file type(s) selected in the Publish Settings dialog box, choose File ➪ Publish (Shift+F12). Flash creates the new files wherever the Flash movie was last saved. If you have selected an HTML template in the HTML tab of the Publish Settings dialog box, you may receive a warning or error message if any other necessary files were not specified. That's it! After you've tested the files for the delivery browser and/or platforms of your choice, you can upload the files to your Web server.

Tip   We highly recommend using Macromedia Dreamweaver MX 2004 for managing file uploads to your Web server. Dreamweaver has a cloaking feature that can hide specific file extensions (such as .fla) from site file lists—preventing them being accidentally uploaded to your Web server.

Using Publish Profiles

Flash MX 2004 introduces a new profiling feature to the Publish Settings. You can now save the settings from all of the enabled format tabs in Publish Settings to a custom profile. You can create as many profiles as you need. The profiles that you create are document-specific. They are saved with the Flash document (.fla file), and by design, you cannot access the profiles of one document directly from another. However, you can export a profile from a Flash document and import it into another.

To choose, create, modify or delete profiles, open the Publish Settings dialog box (File ➪ Publish Settings). At the top of the dialog box, you will find the Profile features available in Flash MX 2004. Refer to Figure 21-11 and the following description list.

   ✦ **Profile Name:** This drop-down menu displays the currently active profile. Every new Flash MX 2004 document has a Default profile. If you open a Flash MX document in Flash MX 2004 and resave it as a Flash MX 2004 document, the original MX document publish settings are stored in a Flash MX Settings profile.

   ✦ **Import/Export Profile:** If you click this button, you can choose Import or Export from this option's menu. If you want to use one document's publish settings in another document, you need to first export the current profile. Profiles are exported as XML documents. In the other document, you can then import the XML profile document.

   ✦ **Create New Profile:** This button adds a new profile name to the Profile Name menu, using the current profile's settings as a starting point. If you click this button, the Create New Profile dialog box appears, prompting you to enter a new profile name.

   ✦ **Duplicate Profile:** This button makes a copy of the currently active profile. If you click this button, the Duplicate Profile dialog box appears, prompting you to enter a new profile name for the copy.

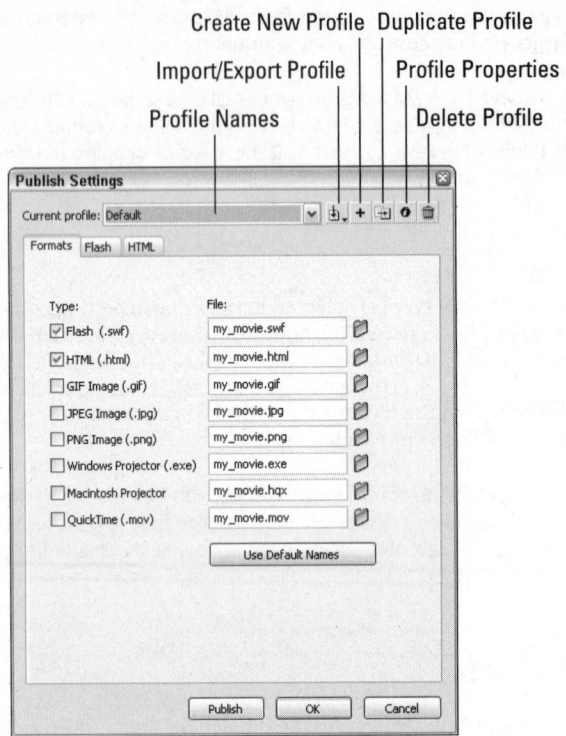

Figure 21-11: The Profile features in the Publish Settings dialog box

✦ **Profile Properties:** This button opens a dialog box wherein you can change the name of the currently active profile. No other properties are associated with a profile.

✦ **Delete Profile:** Clicking this button removes the currently active profile from the document.

Changes to profiles do not need to be saved. When you choose a profile from the Profile Name menu, any settings that you change, enable, and so on are automatically saved to the current profile as long as you click OK to close the Publish Settings dialog box. If you click the Cancel button, any changes you make will not be saved to the current profile.

Summary

✦ To minimize your wait during publishing or testing Flash movies, you may want to use MP3 files for all of your Event Sync sounds.

✦ Test your Flash movies and scenes within the Flash authoring environment. The Bandwidth Profiler can provide vital information about frame byte requirements and can help you find problematic streaming areas of the Flash movie.

✦ The size report that can be generated from the Export Movie or Publish commands for Flash movies lists detailed information regarding any and all Flash elements, such as audio, fonts, and frame byte size.

✦ The Publish Settings dialog box enables you to pick any number of file formats to export at one time. You can control just about every setting imaginable for each file type and use HTML templates to automate the insertion of Flash movies into your Web pages.

✦ Flash MX 2004 offers a new Flash Player version detection feature in the Publish Settings dialog box. With this feature, you can create HTML pages that detect which version of the Flash Player a user has and direct them to appropriate content on your site.

✦ Publish Preview automatically launches your preferred browser and loads the selected publish file(s) into the browser window.

✦ The new profiles feature in Flash MX 2004 enables you to quickly load publish presets that you can apply to one or more Flash documents.

✦   ✦   ✦

Integrating Flash Content with Web Pages

If you're not one for automated HTML production using templates, this chapter is for you. This chapter teaches you the ins and outs of the ⟨object⟩ and ⟨embed⟩ tags, as well as some tips on how to check for the Flash Player with Flash MX 2004's new detection features. At the end of this chapter, we examine how Flash movies can interact with JavaScript and DHTML by using fscommand actions from Flash.

Writing Markup for Flash Movies

In Chapter 21, you learned how to use the Publish feature, which included automated HTML templates. These templates created the necessary HTML tags to display Flash movies on Web pages. This section discusses the use of Flash movies in your handwritten HTML documents. You can also use this information to alter HTML documents created by the Publish feature.

Note

In the following code examples, we use an asterisk (*) when displaying optional parameters that are not in the default options that are enabled in the Flash Only HTML template. We also use the term *plug-in* to mean both the Netscape plug-in and the ActiveX control for Flash Player 7.

You can use two tags to place Flash movies on a Web page (such as an HTML document): ⟨object⟩ and ⟨embed⟩. You need to include both of these plug-in tags in HTML documents, as each tag is specific to a browser: ⟨object⟩ for Internet Explorer on Windows, and ⟨embed⟩ for Netscape on Windows and Mac (and Internet Explorer and Safari browsers on Mac). Each tag works similarly to the other, with some slight differences in attribute names and organization. Remember that if both sets of tags are included with the HTML, only one set of tags is actually read by the browser, depending on which browser is used to view the Web page. Without these tags, the browser cannot display Flash movies with other HTML elements such as images and text.

Web Resource

You can, however, directly link to Flash movies (.swf files) as an alternative method for displaying Flash content. That method, however, precludes the use of parameters to control the look and playback of the Flash movie—it would be the same as loading the Flash movie straight into the standalone Flash Player. For more information on direct linking, see Colin Moock's tutorial, "Filling the Browser Windows Using the <frameset> Tag," found at the book's Web site, www.flashsupport.com/archive.

Using the <object> tag

Microsoft Internet Explorer for Windows uses this tag exclusively to enable the Flash Player ActiveX control. When the Flash Only HTML template is used in Publish Settings, the HTML document that is published uses the <object> tag in the following way. Some of these options (marked with an asterisk) are created only if you enable/disable specific options in the HTML tab of the Publish Settings dialog box.

Note

Flash MX ActionScript introduced a Stage object that allows you to control or override many of the same properties that the Player HTML tags specify. For more details on the Stage object, refer to the *Macromedia Flash MX 2004 ActionScript Bible* by Robert Reinhardt and Joey Lott (Wiley, 2004).

```
A. <object
B.      classid="clsid: clsid:d27cdb6e-ae6d-11cf-96b8- ⊃
        444553540000"
C.      codebase="http://download.macromedia.com/pub/ ⊃
        shockwave/cabs/flash/swflash.cab#version=7,0,0,0"
D.      width="550" height="400"
E.      id="home"
F.      align="middle">
G.      <param name="allowScriptAccess" value="sameDomain" />
H.      <param name="movie" VALUE="home.swf" />
I.*     <param name="play" VALUE="false" />
J.*     <param name="loop" VALUE="false" />
K.*     <param name="menu" VALUE="false" />
L.      <param name="quality" VALUE="high" />
M.*     <param name="scale" VALUE="noborder" />
N.*     <param name="salign" VALUE="LT" />
O.*     <param name="wmode" VALUE="transparent" />
P.*     <param name="devicefont VALUE="true" />
Q.      <param name="bgcolor" VALUE="#FFFFFF" />
R.*     <param name="flashvars" VALUE="title=My%20Movie" />
S. </object>
```

New Feature

Flash MX 2004's HTML templates now use XHTML-compliant code. Notice that all the tags use lowercase, and that all <param> tags end with a />.

A. <object: This is the opening tag containing the ID code and locations of the ActiveX control for the Flash Player. Note that this opening tag includes the attributes lettered B through F.

B. `classid`: This lengthy string is the unique ActiveX identification code. If you are inserting the `<object>` tag by hand in a text editor, make sure that you copy this ID string exactly.

C. `codebase`: Like the `codebase` attribute of a Java `<applet>` tag, this attribute of the `<object>` tag specifies the location of the ActiveX control installer (.cab file) as a URL. Notice that the `#version=7,0,0,0` portion of the URL indicates that the Flash Player version 7 should be used. You can also specify specific minor releases, such as `#version=6,0,65,0`, which would require Flash Player 6.0 r65 ActiveX control or higher. If the visitor doesn't have the ActiveX control already installed, Internet Explorer automatically downloads the control from this URL.

Tip If you want to make a secure Web page with Flash content, make sure the `codebase` URL uses `https://` instead of `http://`.

D. `width` **and** `height`: These attributes control the actual width and height, respectively, of the Flash movie as it appears on the Web page. If no unit of measurement is specified, these values are in pixels. If the % character is added to the end of each value, the attribute adjusts the Flash movie to the corresponding percent of the browser window. For example, if 100 percent was the value for both `width` and `height`, the Flash movie fills the entire browser, except for the browser gutter. See Colin Moock's tutorial at the Web archive for this book to learn how to minimize this gutter thickness.

E. `id`: This attribute of the `<object>` tag assigns a JavaScript/VBScript identifier to the Flash movie, so that it can be controlled by DHTML JavaScript/VBScript functions. By default, this attribute's value is the name of the actual .swf file, without the .swf extension. Each element on a DHTML page should have a unique `id` or `name` attribute. The `name` attribute is discussed in the next section.

F. `align`: This attribute of the `<object>` tag determines how the Flash movie will align on the HTML document. The acceptable values for this attribute are `left`, `right`, `top`, or `bottom`. As with `<img>` tags in HTML, the `align` attribute gives very loose layout control. It's likely that you'll want to rely on the `align` attribute of table cell tags such as `<td>` to position a Flash movie with other HTML elements.

G. `<param name="allowScriptAccess" value="sameDomain" />`: This is the first set of `<param>` subtags within the `<object></object>` tags. Each parameter tag has a unique `name=` setting, not to be confused with JavaScript `name`s or `id`s. `allowScriptAccess` controls how the Flash movie can access JavaScript or VBScript functions contained within the HTML document. A Flash movie can try to invoke a JavaScript or VBScript function by using an ActionScript `fscommand()` or `getURL()` line of code. There are two values supported: `always` and `never`. The value `always` allows the Flash movie to access scripts on the page, while `never` prohibits the Flash movie from accessing scripts. The value `sameDomain`, which is the default value, enables a Flash movie to access scripts on the page *only* if the Flash movie resides on the same domain as the HTML page containing the movie. The `allowScriptAccess` attribute is supported by Flash Player 6 r40 and higher.

H. `<param name="movie" value="home.swf" />`: This parameter determines which Flash movie (.swf file) is loaded into the document. The `value` attribute specifies the filename of the Flash movie, as a relative or absolute URL. Note that you can pass Flash variables to the movie directly by specifying them after the filename. For example, `home.swf?firstName=Joey` will pass a variable named `firstName` with a string value of Joey to the _root timeline (that is, _level0). You can use the newer flashvars (item R) HTML attribute to do this type of data transfer as well.

I. <param name="play" value="false" />: This optional parameter tells the Flash Player whether it should start playing the Flash movie as it downloads. If value equals false, the Flash movie loads in a "paused" state, just as if a stop() action was placed on the first frame. If the value equals true, the Flash Player starts playing the movie as soon as it starts to stream into the browser. If this tag is omitted, the Flash Player behaves as if play equals true.

J. <param name="loop" value="false" />: This optional setting tells the Flash Player whether the Main Timeline (any scene timeline, for instance) should repeat when the playhead reaches the last frame. If value equals false, the playhead will not loop. If value equals true, the playhead will loop. If this parameter tag is omitted, the Flash Player by default will loop playback of the Main Timeline.

Note If you have a stop() action on the last frame of the Main Timeline, the Flash movie will not loop, regardless of the HTML loop value.

K. <param name="menu" value="false" />: This setting controls the display of the Flash Player contextual menu that can be invoked by right-clicking (Windows) or Control+clicking (Mac) the Flash movie in the Web browser. If you set this option to false, the menu displays the options shown in Figure 22-1. If you set this option to true, all of the options are available to the end user, as shown in Figure 22-2. Also, the player's Settings option is available in both modes of the menu.

RIP The Play, Stop, and Rewind options that were available in Flash Player 6 and earlier are no longer available in Flash Player 7.

Note If you have installed the Debugger version of Flash Player 7, the contextual menu displays a Debugger option in both modes (true and false).

Figure 22-1: The Flash Player menu with control options disabled

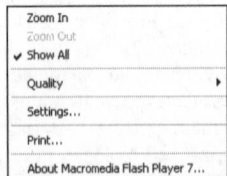

Figure 22-2: The Flash Player menu with control options enabled

Tip You can override the HTML menu attribute by setting the Stage.showMenu property to true or false. This property, which can be set in client-side ActionScript, supercedes the HTML menu attribute.

Note   Flash Player 7 supports additional items that you can script into the contextual menu, using the new `ContextMenu` class. For more information on the usage of this class, refer to the *Macromedia Flash MX 2004 ActionScript Bible* by Robert Reinhardt and Joey Lott.

L. `<param name="quality" value="high" />`: This parameter controls how the Flash movie's artwork renders within the browser window. `value` can be `low`, `autolow`, `autohigh`, `high`, or `best`. Most Flash movies on the Web use the `high` value, as this forces the Flash Player to render the movie elements antialiased. For a full description of each of the `quality` settings, please refer to the section "Using the HTML settings" in Chapter 21, "Publishing Flash Movies."

M. `<param name="scale" value="noborder" />`: This optional parameter controls how the Flash movie scales in the window defined by the `width` and `height` attributes of the opening `<object>` tag. Its value can be `showall`, `noborder`, `exactfit`, or `noscale`. If this entire subtag is omitted, the Flash Player treats the movie as if the `showall` default setting was specified. The `showall` setting fits the Flash movie within the boundaries of the `width` and `height` dimensions without any distortion to the original aspect ratio of the Flash movie. Again, refer to "Using the HTML settings" section of Chapter 21 for a complete description of the `scale` settings and how they work within the dimensions of a Flash movie.

N. `<param name="salign" value="lt" />`: This parameter controls the alignment of the Flash movie within the space allocated to the viewing area of the movie in the browser window. For example, if you size your Flash movie to use 100 percent of the width and height of the browser window, a `value` of `lt` aligns the Flash movie to the left and top of the browser window. The acceptable values for this parameter are shown in the following list. For more information, refer to our coverage in Chapter 21.

- `l` : left edge, centered vertically
- `r` : right edge, centered vertically
- `t` : top edge, centered horizontally
- `b` : bottom edge, centered horizontally
- `lt` : left and top edge
- `rt` : right and top edge
- `lb` : left and bottom edge
- `rb` : right and bottom edge

O. `<param name="wmode" value="transparent" />`: This Player option works with all versions of the Flash Player if you are using Internet Explorer (version 3 or higher) for Windows, or with Flash Player 6 r65 or higher on Internet Explorer, Netscape, and most Mac OS X browsers. If you are only targeting an audience that uses these browsers, you can control how the Flash movie's background color appears on top of the HTML or DHTML elements on the Web page. There are three acceptable values:

- `window`: This value is the default appearance of movies playing in the Flash Player on Web pages. With this value, movies play within the area specified by the `width` and `height` attributes (discussed in item D), and the background color of the Flash movie's stage (as defined by Document Properties or item Q later in this section) displays.

- opaque: This value provides the same visual appearance of the movie's stage as window does. However, if you want to animate other DHTML objects in front of or behind a layer containing the Flash movie, it is recommended that you use the opaque value.

- transparent: This value allows the stage of the Flash movie to act like an alpha channel. When enabled, the Flash movie appears to float on the HTML page, without any background color to reveal the corners of the Flash movie's stage. Again, while this feature is somewhat extraordinary, it will function only with specific browsers and later versions of the Flash Player plug-in. Also, because the browser must antialias the Flash artwork on top of other HTML elements, playback of Flash animations may suffer.

P. <param name="devicefont" value="true" />: This feature controls how Flash text appears in the browser window and works only on the Windows operating system. Like the device fonts with the Flash MX authoring environment (_sans, _serif, and _typewriter), this option can display any and all embedded text to system fonts such as Times and Arial. To do this, set value to true. To disable device font rendering in this fashion, set value to false. If this tag is omitted from the HTML, the value defaults to false. Finally, the rules of Flash device fonts apply to system device fonts as well. For example, device or system fonts cannot be masked, rotated, or manipulated with the Transform panel or the Property inspector.

Note   This seldom-used setting does not work predictably from use to use. In our tests, we could not get devicefont to work consistently from movie to movie, nor could we propose any reasonable use for it. It's likely that this is a legacy setting, meaning that it was made available for machines that had slow video or computing performance when the Flash Player was first introduced to the market.

Tip   If you use ActionScript to create the masks over device font text, you can avoid the issues of masking mentioned in item P.

Q. <param name="bgcolor" value="#FFFFFF" />: This parameter name, bgcolor, controls the background color of the Flash movie. If you published an HTML document via the Publish command, the value is automatically set to the background color specified by the Modify ➪ Document command in Flash. However, you can override the Movie setting by entering a different value in this parameter tag. Note that this parameter, like all HTML tags and attributes concerning color, uses hexadecimal code to describe the color. For more information on color, see Chapter 7, "Applying Color."

R. <param name="flashvars" value="title=My%20Flash%Movie" />: This Flash Player 6 and higher attribute allows you to declare variables within the Flash movie when it loads into the Web browser. flashvars stands for "Flash Variables." This feature allows you to circumvent the browser URL length limitation for declaring variables in the Flash movie's filename, as discussed in item H of this list. For example, you can use client-side (for example, JavaScript) or server-side (for example, ColdFusion, ASP, PHP) scripting to dynamically write the value for this tag in your HTML, passing information from databases into the Flash movie at load time.

Tip

If you use Flash Remoting services with your Flash movie, be sure to declare the `gatewayUrl` variable in `flashvars`. The `gatewayUrl` variable specifies the location of the Flash Remoting gateway, such as: `<param name="flashvars" value="gatewayUrl=http://mydomain.com/flashservices/gateway" />`.

S. `</object>`: This is the closing tag for the starting `<object>` tag. As shown later in this chapter, you can put other HTML tags between the last `<param>` tag and the closing `</object>` tag for non-ActiveX–enabled browsers, such as Netscape or Apple Safari. Because Internet Explorer for Windows is the only browser that currently recognizes `<object>` tags, other browsers simply skip the `<object>` tag (as well as its `<param>` tags) and only read the tags between the last `<param>` and `</object>` tags.

Tip

We recommend that you consistently apply quotes around names and values, such as `<param name="bgcolor" value="#FFFFFF" />`. This syntax is especially important for the `flashvars` attribute.

Using the <embed> tag

Netscape, Mozilla-based browsers, and browsers on a Macintosh use the `<embed>` tag to display nonbrowser native file formats that require a plug-in, such as Macromedia Flash and Shockwave Director or Apple QuickTime. Following is a sample listing of attributes and values for the `<embed>` tag. Again, attributes with an asterisk are generally optional for most Flash movie playback.

```
A. <embed
B.      src="home.swf"
C.*     play="false"
D.*     loop="false"
E.      quality="high"
F.*     scale="noborder"
G.*     salign="lt"
H.*     wmode="transparent"
I.*     devicefont="true"
J.      bgcolor="#FFFFFF"
K.      width="550" height="400"
L.*     swLiveConnect="false"
M.      name="home"
N.*     id="home"
O.      align="left"
P.      allowScriptAccess="sameDomain"
Q.      flashvars="name=Lucian"
R.      type="application/x-shockwave-flash"
S.      pluginspage="http://www.macromedia.com/go/ ⤵
        getflashplayer">
T. </embed>
```

A. `<embed`: This is the opening `<embed>` tag. Note that lines B through Q are attributes of the opening `<embed>` tag, which is why you won't see the > character at the end of line A.

B. `src`: This stands for *source,* and it indicates the filename of the Flash movie. This attribute of `<embed>` works exactly like the `movie` parameter of the `<object>` tag.

C. `play`: This attribute behaves in the same manner as the `play` parameter of the `<object>` tag. If you omit this attribute in your HTML, the Flash Player assumes that it should automatically play the Flash movie.

D. `loop`: This attribute controls the same behavior as the `loop` parameter of the `<object>` tag. If you omit this attribute in your HTML, the Flash Player automatically loops playback of the movie's Main Timeline.

E. `quality`: This attribute controls how the Flash movie's artwork will display in the browser window. Like the equivalent `quality` parameter of the `<object>` tag, its value can be `low`, `autolow`, `autohigh`, `high`, or `best`.

F. `scale`: This attribute of `<embed>` controls how the Flash movie fits within the browser window and/or the dimensions specified by `width` and `height` (item K). Its value can be `showall` (default if attribute is omitted), `noborder`, `exactfit`, or `noscale`.

G. `salign`: This attribute controls the internal alignment of the Flash movie within the viewing area of the movie's dimensions. See the description for the `salign` parameter of the `<object>` tag for more information.

H. `wmode`: This attribute controls the opacity of the Flash movie's background color and works only with specific browser and Flash Player version combinations. See the `wmode` parameter description in the `<object>` tag for more details.

I. `devicefont`: This attribute controls the appearance of any text within a Flash movie and functions correctly only on the Windows operating system. See the description for `devicefont` in the `<object>` tag section.

J. `bgcolor`: This setting controls the Flash movie's background color. Again, this attribute behaves identically to the equivalent `<param>` subtag of the `<object>` tag. See that tag's description in the preceding section.

K. `width` and `height`: These attributes control the dimensions of the Flash movie as it appears on the Web page. Refer to the `width` and `height` descriptions of the `<object>` tag for more information.

L. `swLiveConnect`: This is one attribute that you won't find in the `<object>` tag. This unique tag enables Netscape's LiveConnect feature, which enables plug-ins and Java applets to communicate with JavaScript. By default, this attribute is set to `false`. If it is enabled (the attribute is set to `true`), the Web page may experience a short delay during loading. The latest versions of Netscape don't start the Java engine during a browsing session until a Web page containing a Java applet (or a Java-enabled plug-in such as the Flash Player) is loaded. Unless you use `fscommand()` actions in your Flash movies, it's best to omit this attribute or set its value to `false`.

M. `name`: This attribute works in tandem with the `swLiveConnect` attribute, allowing the Flash movie to be identified in JavaScript. The value given to the `name` attribute will be the Flash movie object name that can be used within your JavaScript programming.

N. `id`: This attribute is also used for JavaScript functionality. It's uncertain whether this value is necessary if the name attribute exists, but Flash MX 2004's Flash with FSCommand HTML template (in the Publish Settings) includes both the `name` and `id` attributes. The `id` attribute should use the same value as the `name` attribute.

O. `align`: This attribute behaves exactly the same as the `align` parameter for the `<object>`. See its description in the preceding section for more information.

The new Flash MX 2004 interface for Mac OS X

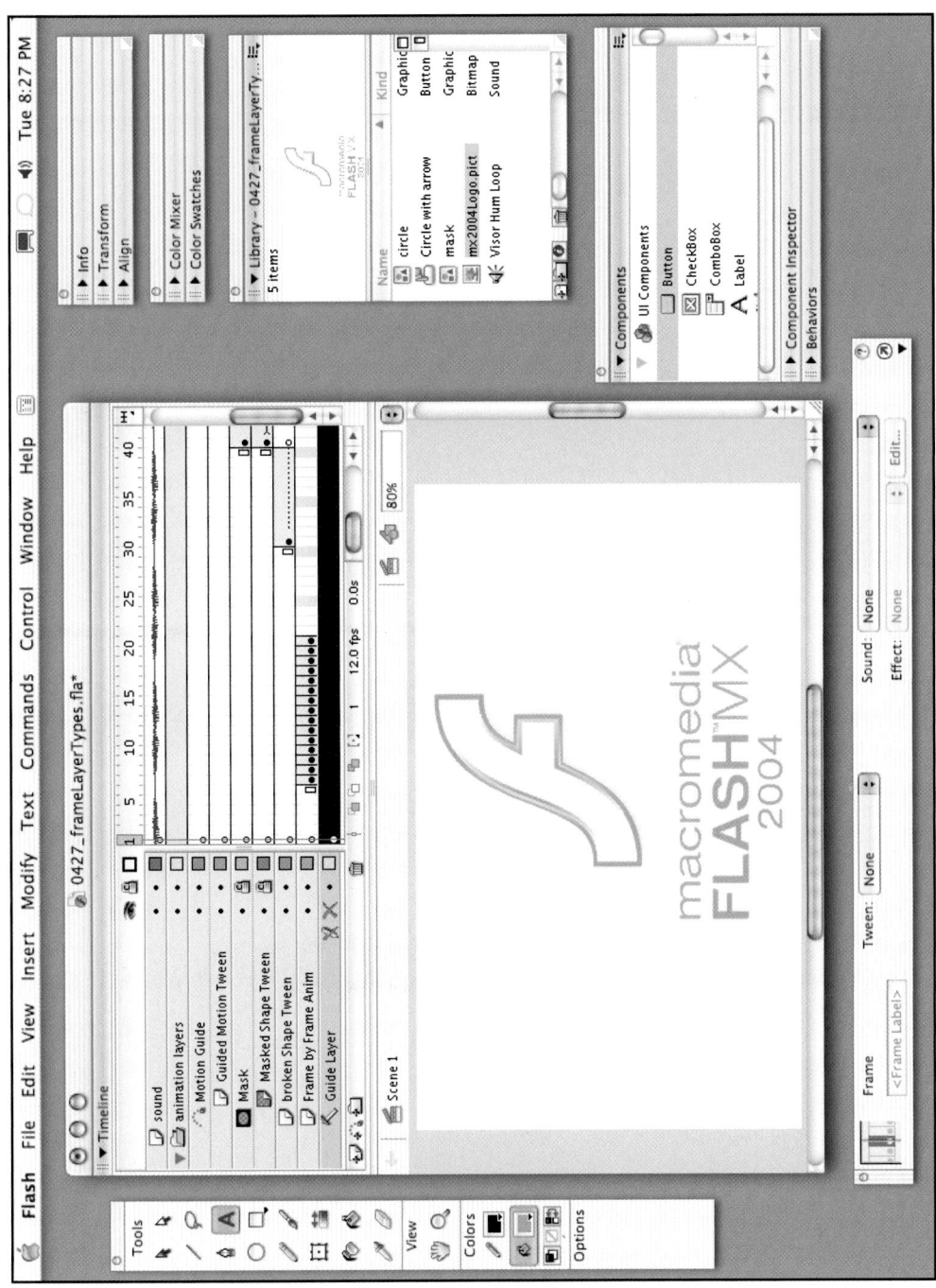

Learn to customize your Flash workspace in Chapter 4

The new Flash MX 2004 interface for Windows XP

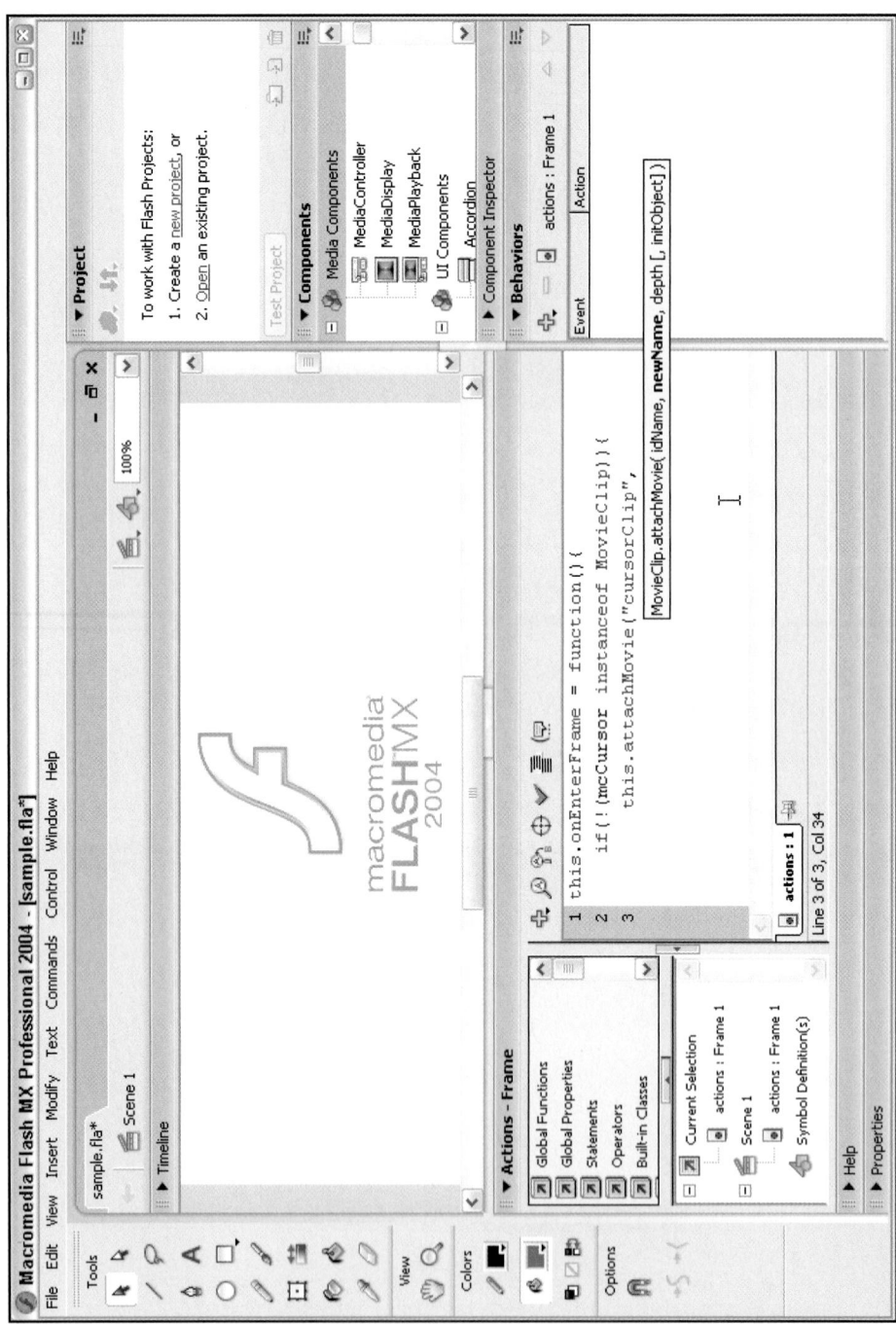

Learn to customize your Flash workspace in Chapter 4

Working with color

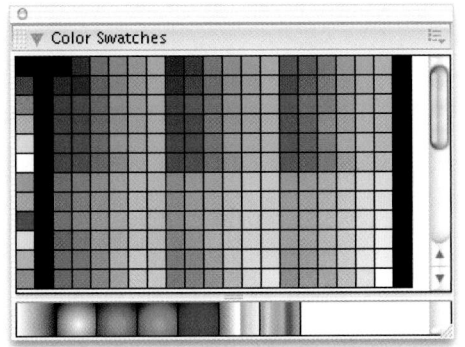

Default Web 216 swatches

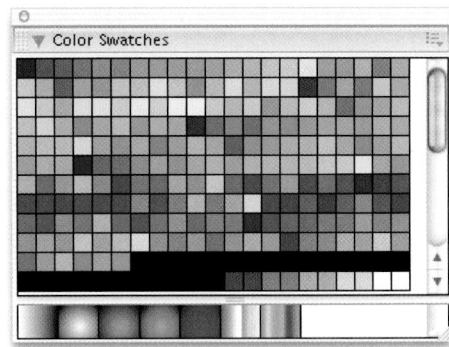

Web 216 Sort by Color

Source GIF image for loaded colors

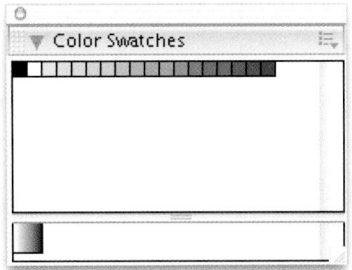

custom color swatches

Learn to customize your Flash Color Swatches panel in Chapter 7

Use Timeline Effects to quickly modify or animate graphics

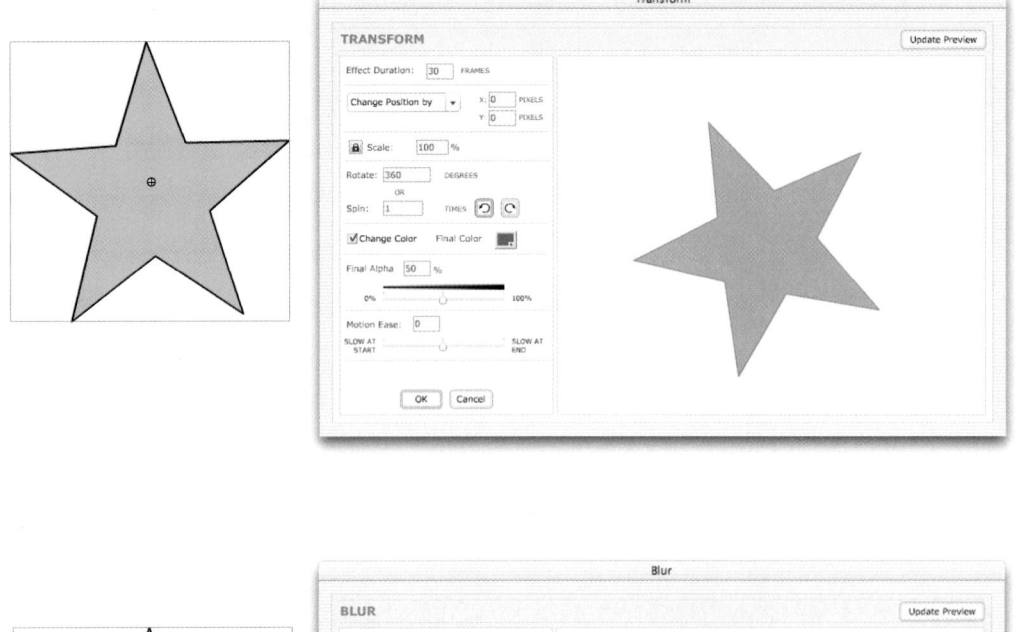

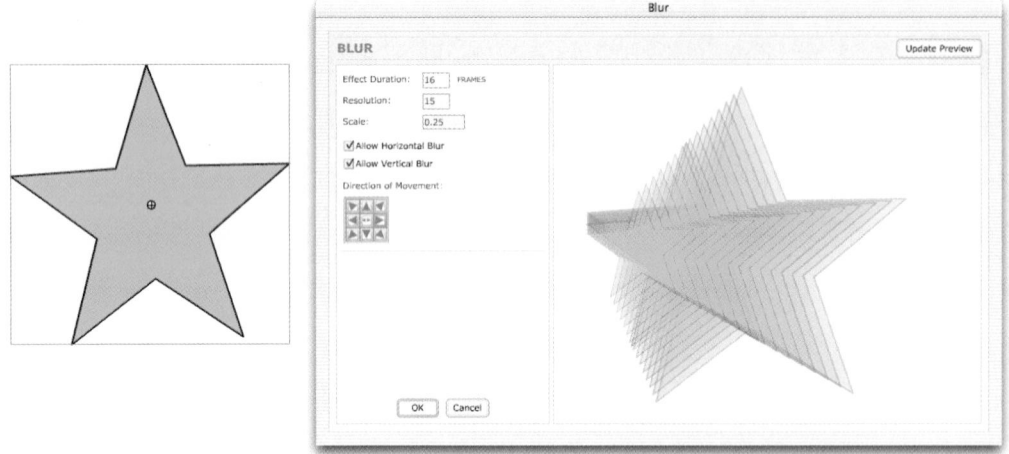

Learn to use Flash MX 2004 Timeline Effects in Chapter 11

Build custom applications with interactive components

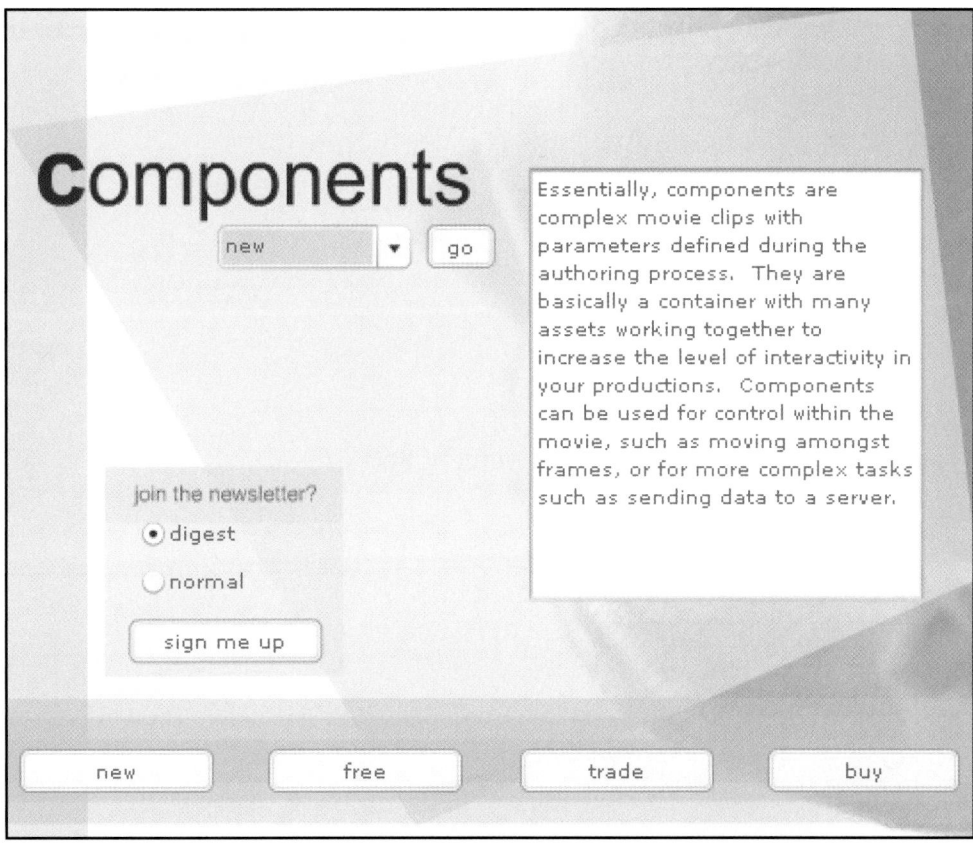

Learn to use built-in Flash MX 2004 components in Chapter 29

Relative Color Adjustment with Advanced Effect Settings

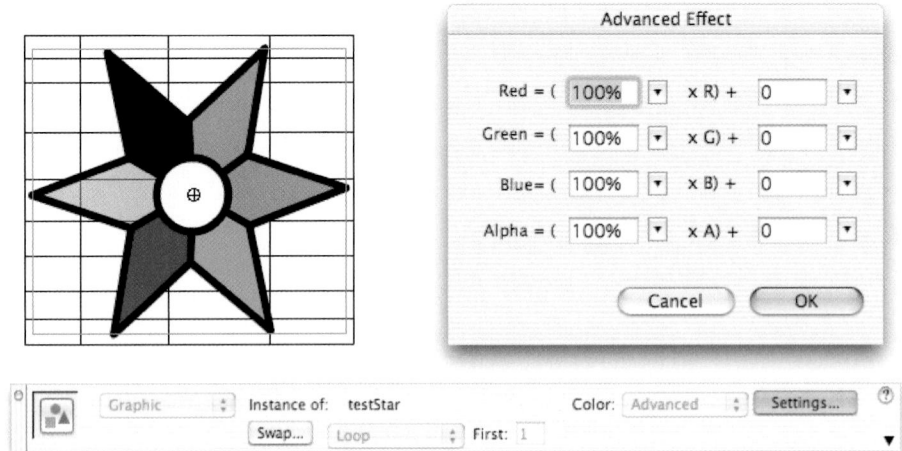

Original color symbol: 100 percent Red, Green, Blue, Alpha

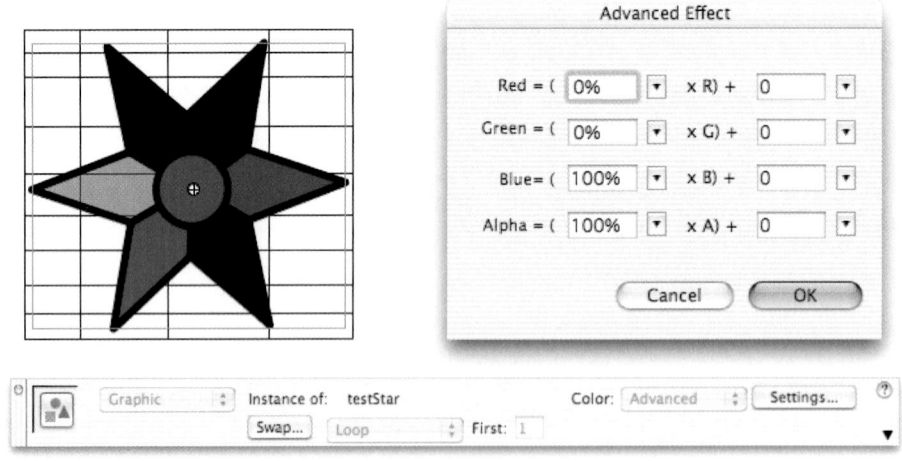

Relative color: 0 percent Red and 0 percent Green

Learn to modify symbol instances with Advanced Color Effects in Chapter 9

Absolute Color Adjustment with Advanced Effect Settings

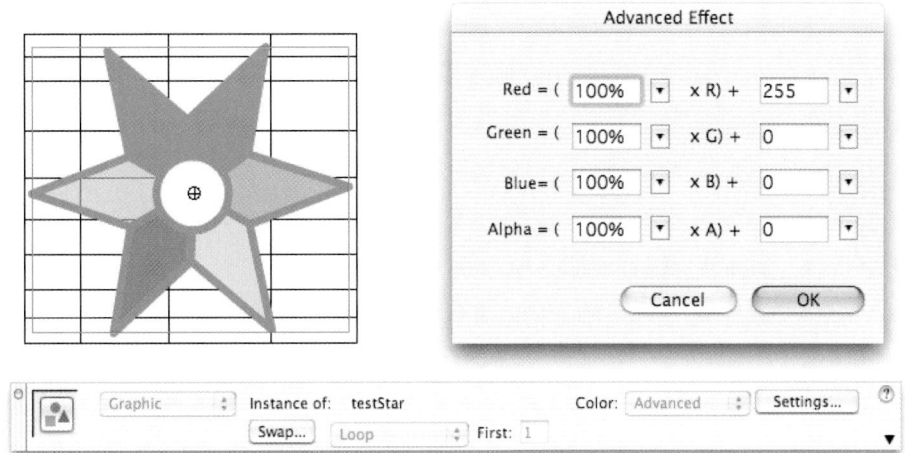

Absolute color: +255 Red

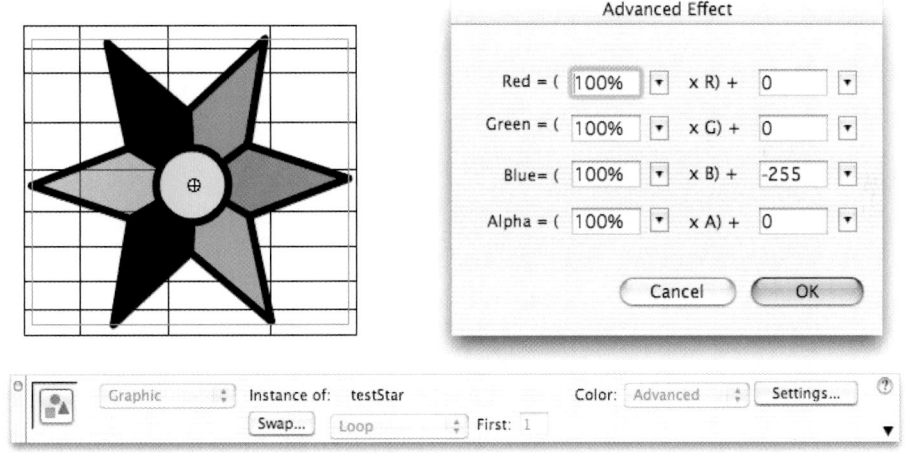

Absolute color: −255 Blue

Learn to modify symbol instances with Advanced Color Effects in Chapter 9

Create artwork with Flash drawing and effects tools

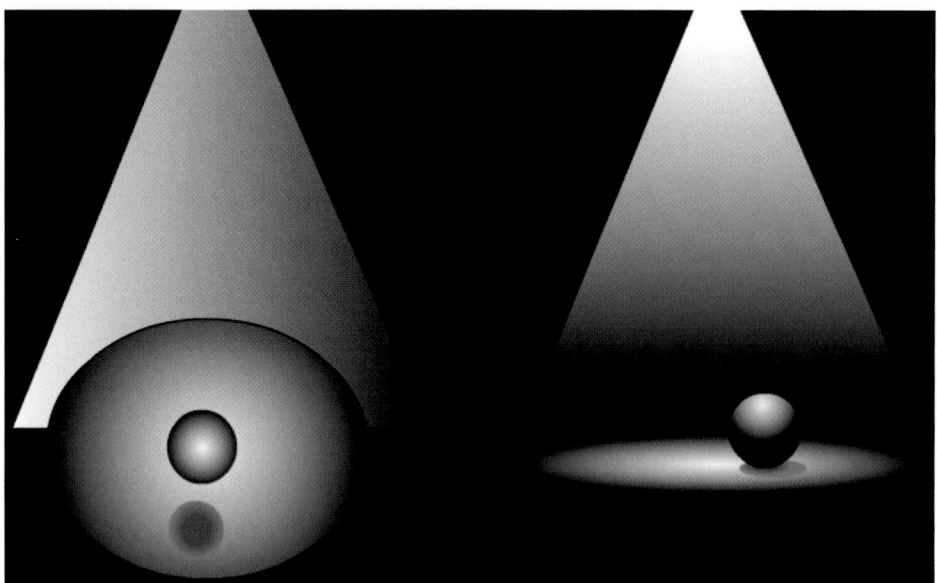

Create and modify custom gradients for lighting effects in Chapter 9

Import and optimize vector artwork in Flash MX 2004

Original vector artwork

Imported EPS in RGB color space

Imported EPS in CMYK color space

For guidelines on importing artwork refer to Chapter 16

Animation fundamentals and character animation techniques

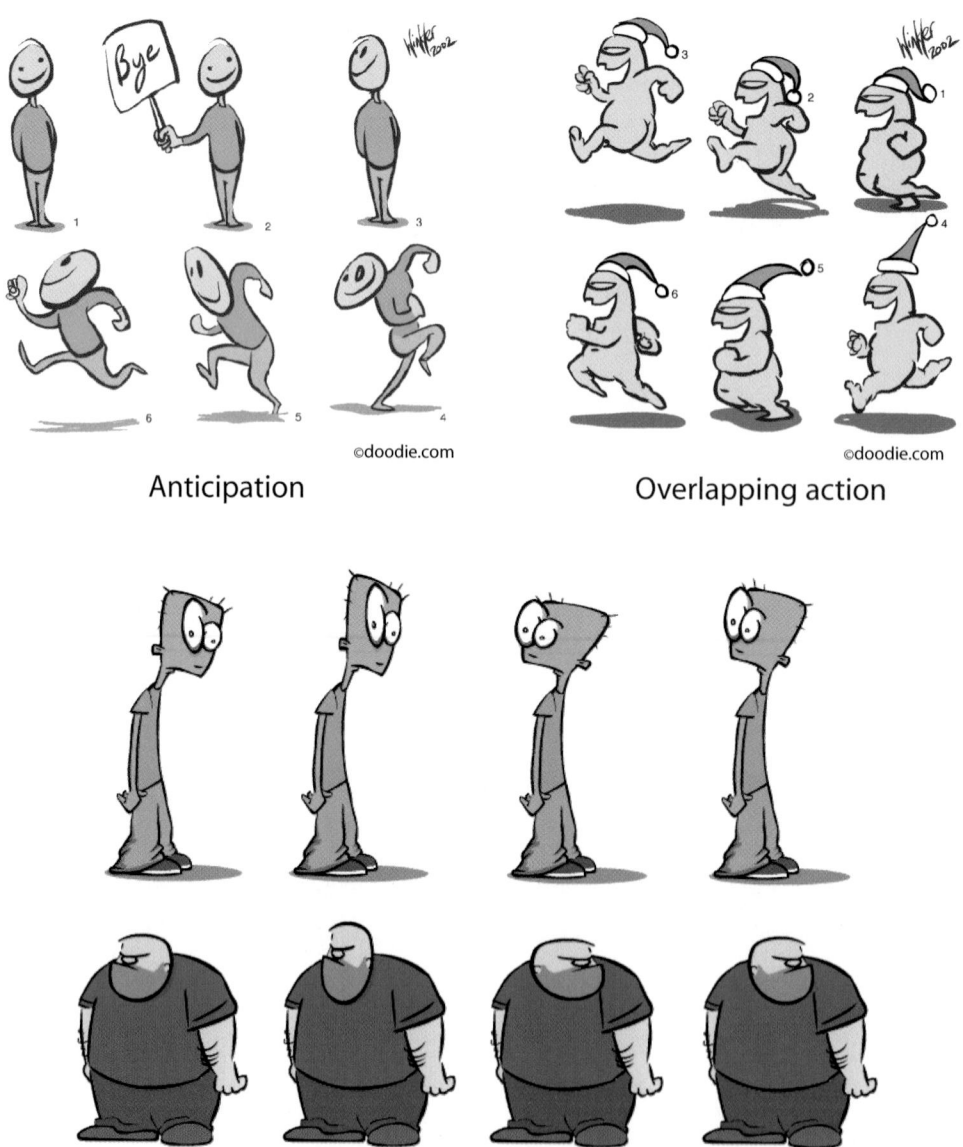

Anticipation

Overlapping action

©doodie.com

character designs © www.sandrocorsaro.com

Bounces for head turns

Learn from examples by expert animators in Part III

Advanced animation strategies and special effects

Richard Bazley's illustrative animation drawn directly in Flash

JibJab.com's filter techniques for broadcast animation

Learn from examples by expert animators in Part III

Work with digital video source files

Low-quality sample:
from a digital still camera

Mid-quality sample:
from a DV camcorder

High-quality sample:
from a DVCAM camcorder

Review digital source comparisons in Appendix C

Optimize raster images for Flash

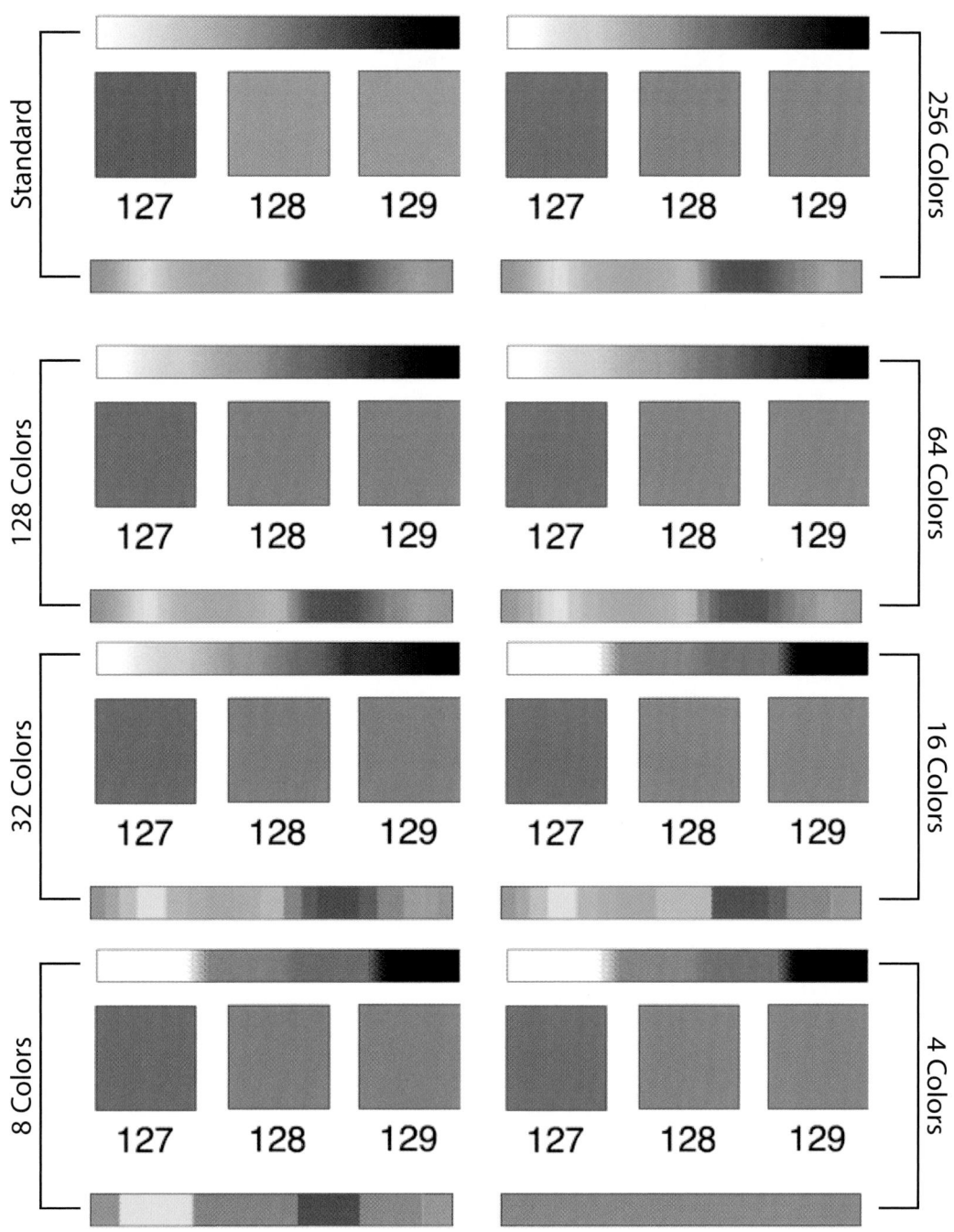

Compare GIF compression settings in Chapter 35

Build complete Flash MX 2004 projects

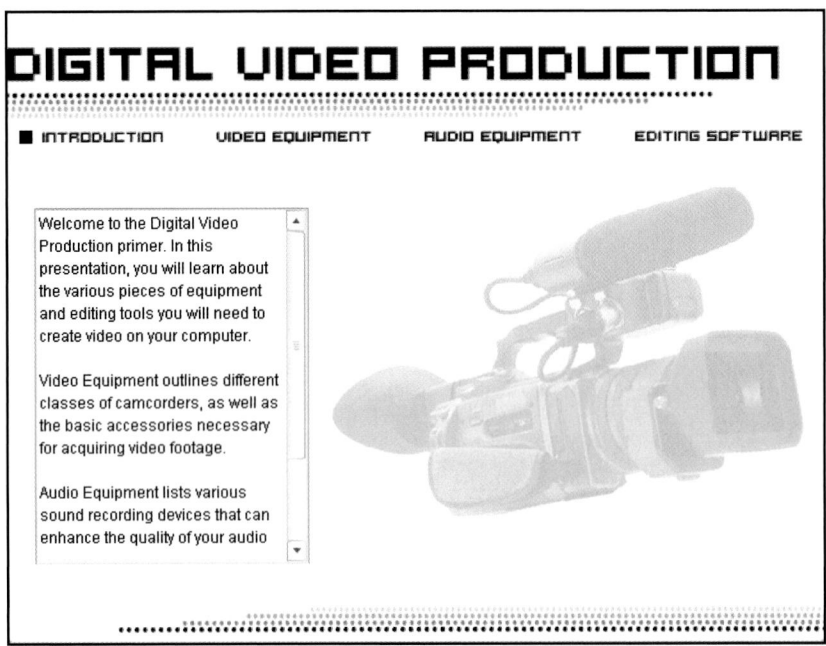

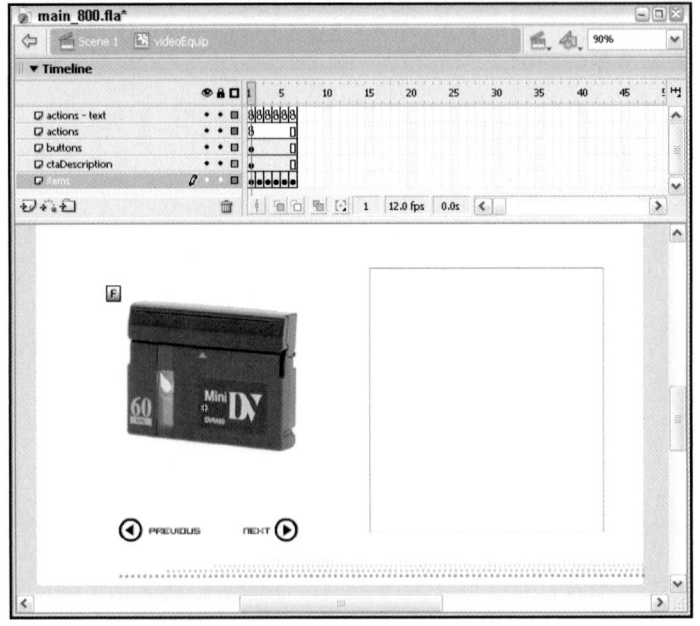

"Making Your First Flash MX 2004 Project" in Chapter 20

Build complete Flash MX 2004 projects

"Creating a Portfolio Site in Flash" in Chapter 32

"Creating a Game in Flash" in Chapter 33

Concepts and examples apply to real-world workflow

Optimize artwork from other applications for Flash projects

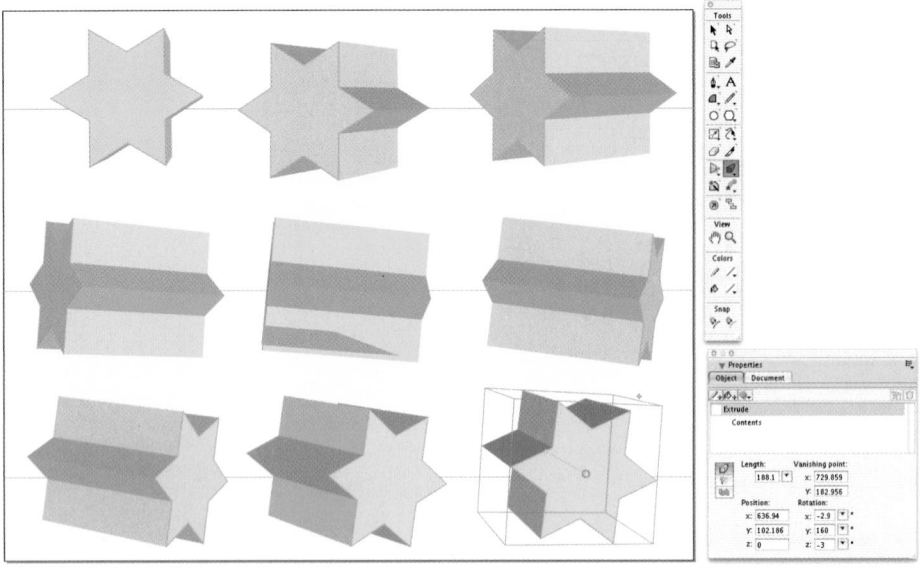

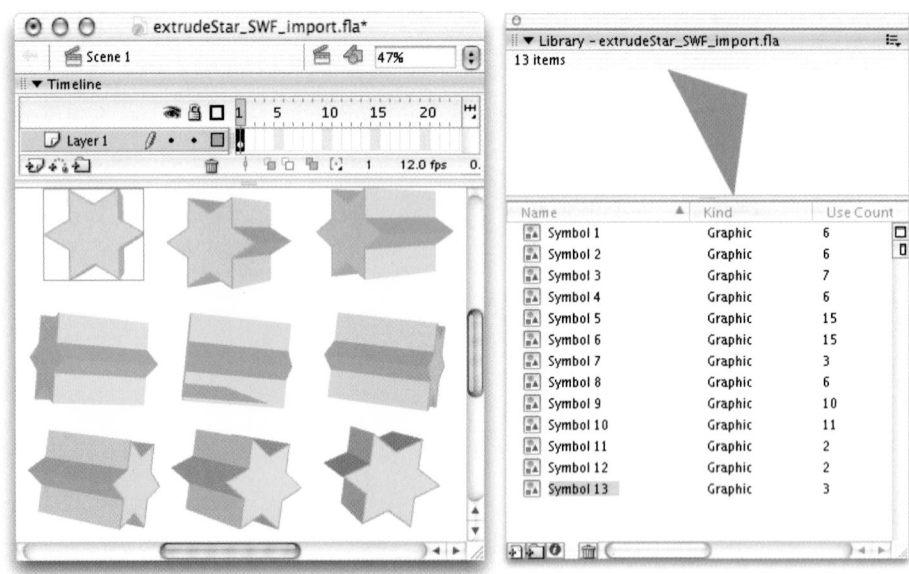

Import extruded artwork from FreeHand to Flash in Chapter 36

P. `allowScriptAccess:` This attribute controls how the Flash movie can access JavaScript from `getURL()` and `fscommand()` actions. See the description of `allowScriptAccess` in the `<object>` tag coverage earlier in this chapter.

Q. `flashvars:` This attribute assigns variables to the Main Timeline of the Flash movie at runtime. See the description of `flashvars` in the `<object>` tag coverage earlier in this chapter.

R. `type="application/x-shockwave-flash":` This attribute tells the browser what MIME (Multipurpose Internet Mail Extension) content-type the embedded file is. Each file type (TIF, JPEG, GIF, PDF, and so on) has a unique MIME content-type header, describing what its content is. For Flash movies, the content-type is `application/x-shockwave-flash`. Any program (or operating system) that uses files over the Internet handles MIME content-types according to a reference chart that links each MIME content-type to its appropriate parent application or plug-in. Without this attribute, the browser may not understand what type of file the Flash movie is. As a result, it may display the broken plug-in icon when the Flash movie downloads to the browser.

S. `pluginspage:` Literally "plug-in's page," this attribute tells the browser where to go to find the appropriate plug-in installer if it doesn't have the Flash plug-in already installed. This is not equivalent to a JavaScript-enabled autoinstaller. It simply redirects the browser to the URL of the Web page where the appropriate software can be downloaded.

T. `</embed>:` This is the closing tag for the original `<embed>` tag in line A. Some older or text-based browsers such as Lynx are incapable of displaying `<embed>` tags. You can insert alternate HTML (such as a static or animated GIF image with the `<img>` tag) between the `<embed> </embed>` tags for these browsers. Some browsers may require that you insert these alternate tags between a `<noembed></noembed>` set of tags within or after the `<embed></embed>` tags.

Caution You may be surprised to learn that all versions of Internet Explorer (IE) for the Macintosh cannot read `<object>` tags. Rather, IE for Mac uses a Netscape plug-in emulator to read `<embed>` tags. However, this emulator does not interpret all `<embed>` tags with the same level of support as Netscape. As a result, the `swLiveConnect` attribute does not function on IE for Mac browsers. This means that the `fscommand()` action is not supported on these browsers.

Detecting the Flash Player

What good is an awesome Flash experience if no one can see your Flash movies? Because most Flash content is viewed with a Web browser, it's extremely important to make sure that your HTML pages check for the existence of the Flash Player plug-in before you start pushing Flash content to the browser. There are a variety of ways to check for the Flash Player, and this section provides an overview of the available methods.

New Feature As mentioned in the previous chapter, Flash MX 2004 includes a new Flash Player detection feature within the Publish Settings. You learn how to create a set of detection pages with this new feature later in this chapter.

Plug-in versus ActiveX: Forcing content without a check

The Flash Player is available for Web browsers in two forms: the Flash Player plug-in (as a Netscape-compatible, or Mozilla-compatible, plug-in) and the Flash Player ActiveX control (for use only with Microsoft Internet Explorer on Windows 95/98/ME/NT/2000/XP).

If you directly insert a Flash movie into a Web page with the `<embed>` tag (for Netscape browsers), one of two scenarios will happen:

✦ The browser has the Flash Player plug-in and will load the Flash movie.

✦ The browser does not have the Flash Player plug-in and displays a broken plug-in icon.

If the second scenario occurs and the `pluginspage` attribute of the `<embed>` tag is defined, the user can click the broken plug-in icon and go to the Macromedia site to download the Flash Player plug-in. If the `pluginspage` attribute is not specified, clicking the broken plug-in icon will take you to a generic Netscape plug-in page.

If you insert a Flash movie into an HTML document with the `<object>` tag (for Internet Explorer on Windows only), one of two scenarios will happen:

✦ The browser has the Flash Player ActiveX control and will load the Flash movie.

✦ The browser does not have the Flash Player ActiveX control and will autodownload and install the ActiveX control file from the Macromedia site.

The ActiveX control will autodownload and install only if the `classid` and `codebase` attributes of the Flash movie's `<object>` tag are correctly specified. Depending on the user's security settings, the user needs to grant permission to a Security Warning dialog box (shown in Figure 22-3) to commence the download and install process.

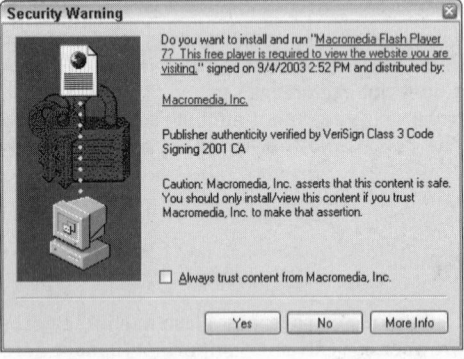

Figure 22-3: The Flash Player 7 ActiveX control will automatically download if Microsoft Internet Explorer for Windows encounters an HTML page with Flash content.

Although using the `<object>` and `<embed>` tags by themselves is by far the simplest method for integrating Flash content into a Web page, it's not the most user-friendly method of ensuring that the majority of your Web visitors can view the Flash content. One of the best methods is to use a Flash sniffer movie, which is exactly what the new Detect Flash Version feature of Flash MX 2004's Publish Settings uses.

Detecting the Flash Player with Flash MX 2004

Since Flash Player 4 was released, many seasoned Flash developers have used small Flash movies known as *sniffers* to detect the presence of the Flash Player in a user's Web browser. Sniffers are virtually hidden from the visitor to a Web site, and they direct an entry HTML page to a new location (using a getURL() action) where the real Flash content (or site) exists. If the Player is not installed, the sniffer movie won't be able to play and direct the HTML page to a new location. If this happens, a special <meta> tag in the <head> of the HTML document directs the browser location to a screen that informs the visitor to download the plug-in or ActiveX control. In Flash MX 2004, Macromedia has made the process of using a sniffer methodology incredibly simple. In the following steps, you learn how to use the new Detect Flash Version feature to properly direct a user to Flash Player 6 r65 content.

Note   You can check for Flash Player 4 or higher with the Detect Flash Version feature. For demonstration purposes, we chose Flash Player 6 r65 because Flash MX 2004 introduced a new optimization feature for .swf files generated for this version (or higher) of Flash Player 6.

Cross-Reference   For an introduction to the Detect Flash Version settings, see Chapter 21, "Publishing Flash Movies."

1. Create a new Flash document, by choosing File ➪ New. In the New Document dialog box, choose Flash Document and click OK. Alternatively, open an existing .fla file that you have created and skip to Step 4.

2. Save the new Flash document as detection_test.fla.

3. Add some placeholder text to the stage using the Text tool. As this example is checking for Flash Player 6 r65, you can type the **This is Flash Player 6 r65 content.**

4. Choose File ➪ Publish Settings. By default, both the Flash and HTML formats are selected in the Formats tab of the Publish Settings dialog box. The filenames for these formats should reflect the current .fla filename, such as detection_test.swf and detection_test.html, respectively.

5. To keep the new version settings in a separate profile, click the Create New Profile (+) button at the top of the Publish Settings dialog box. Name the profile **FP6 r65 Detection**, as shown in Figure 22-4. Click OK to close the dialog box, but leave the Publish Settings dialog box open.

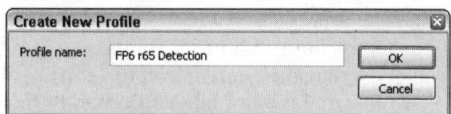

Figure 22-4: The Create New Profile dialog box, showing the new profile name

6. Click the Flash tab. In the Version menu, choose Flash Player 6. In the ActionScript version menu, choose ActionScript 1.0. Select the Optimize for Flash Player 6 r65 check box. Refer to Figure 22-5 for a review of these settings.

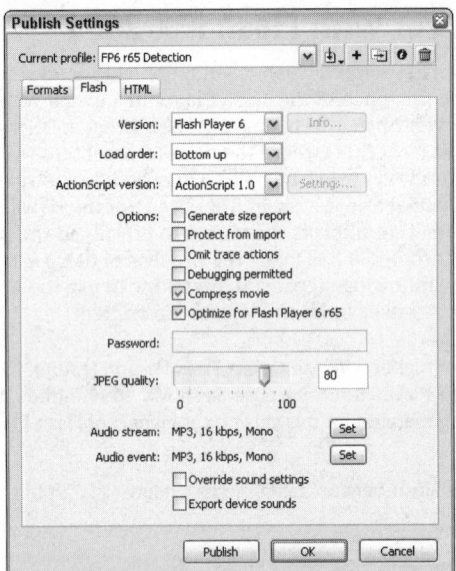

Figure 22-5: The Flash Player 6 r65 settings in the Flash tab

7. Click the HTML tab of the Publish Settings dialog box. Select the Detect Flash Version check box, and click the Settings button to the right of the check box. In the Version Detection Settings dialog box, review the automatic default values Flash MX 2004 has created for you. The Minor Version field should display the value 65 — if it doesn't, you can manually type 65 into the field. If you wanted to check for a different minor version of Flash Player 6, you could enter that value instead. Keep the default filenames for the Detection, Content, and Alternate File fields. The Detection File, detection_test.html, will contain a pre-built Flash movie sniffer (.swf file). If the user has the desired version of the Flash Player, he or she is directed to the Content File, detection_test_content. html, which contains the detection_test.swf published from the current .fla file. If the user doesn't have Flash Player 6 r65 or higher, the browser is directed to the Alternate File, detection_test_alternate.html. If you want to use a different alternate HTML document, you have the option of clicking the Browse button to select a custom HTML document that you have already created. Refer to Figure 22-6 to compare your settings. Click OK to close the dialog box, and go back to the HTML tab of the Publish Settings dialog box.

8. In the Publish Settings dialog box, click the Publish button. You may see an alert box, as shown in Figure 22-7, letting you know that the content .swf file you are about to publish is only compatible with Flash Player 6 r65 or higher. Click OK to this alert box. Flash MX 2004 generates all of the necessary .html and .swf files for your content movie and the detection mechanism. Click OK to close the Publish Settings dialog box.

9. On your desktop, navigate to the folder where you saved your original .fla file. If you created the sample document in Step 1, you want to find the location of detection_test. fla. In this location, you will see the three HTML files for the detection, content, and alternate files. You will also find an alternate.gif file, which is the "Get Macromedia Flash Player" button graphic, as well as a flash_detection.swf file, which is the Flash movie embedded on the detection_test.html page. This page is the first page that your potential Web user should load.

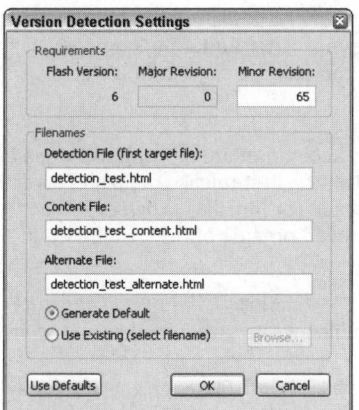

Figure 22-6: The Version Detection Settings dialog box

Figure 22-7: The Optimize for Flash Player 6 r65 alert box

10. In your own Web browser, load the `detection_test.html` page. If your browser has Flash Player 6 r65 or higher, the browser should instantly jump to the `detection_test_content.html` page, displaying your `detection_test.swf` movie. This process works because the `detection_test.html` passes variables to the `flash_detection.swf` file embedded with it. These variables contain the major and minor version values that were entered into the Version Detection Settings dialog box. The `flash_detection.swf` compares these passed values to the version of the Flash Player that loaded the movie. If the Flash Player matches (or exceeds) the version requirements, the content page, `detection_test_content.html`, is loaded into the browser window with a `getURL()` action. Otherwise, the `detection_test_alternate.html` document is loaded.

11. To accurately test your pages over an Internet connection, upload all of the files (except the .fla file) to your Web server and load the `detection_test.html` document from the Web server URL to redo the test.

On the CD-ROM You can find all of these files created for this detection example in the `ch22/mx2004_detection` folder of this book's CD-ROM.

If you want to test the detection mechanism with an older version of the Flash Player, we recommend that you use an older Flash Player installer with Netscape or a Mozilla-compatible browser. The process of uninstalling an ActiveX control used by Internet Explorer is much more difficult to do.

You can find just about every past version of the Flash Player at www.macromedia.com/support/flash/ts/documents/oldplayers.htm, for testing purposes. As mentioned previously, we recommend that you install the older versions with a Netscape or Mozilla-compatible browser.

You can set up your Netscape plug-ins folder to accommodate multiple versions of the Flash Player plug-in. When you installed Flash MX 2004, the first release of Flash Player 7 should have automatically been installed to your Netscape (or Mozilla) browser's Plugins folder. The plug-in file, named NPSWF32.dll, can be moved outside of the Plugins folder, into a new parent folder that you create.

We prefer to create a Flash Players folder in the C:\Program Files\Netscape\Netscape 7 folder, and put each Flash Player version plug-in file into its own folder, as shown in Figure 22-8.

Regardless of the Flash Player version you install, all Flash Player plug-in files for Netscape (or Mozilla) have the same name, NPSWF32.dll. For this reason, you must isolate multiple installations of the Flash Player into their own folder.

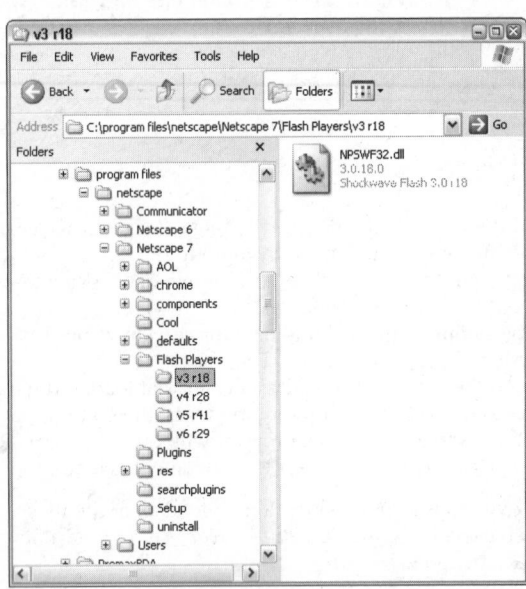

Figure 22-8: A sample Flash Players folder structure for use with Netscape 7 on Windows

You can do the same procedure on Mac OS X, where all browsers share the same plug-in folders. That's right! Netscape, Internet Explorer, and Apple Safari all refer to the same plug-ins folder. On your boot disk, such as Macintosh HD, browse to the Library\Internet Plug-Ins\ folder. In this location, you will find the Shockwave Flash NP-PPC plug-in file. As Figure 22-9 shows, you can create a Library\Internet Plug-Ins (DISABLED) folder to store other versions of this plug-in file.

On Mac OS X, you may need to recreate the same plug-in structure with the Users\[Your User Name]\Library\Internet Plug-Ins\ folder. Or, you may just want to remove any Flash Player plug-in files within this folder. Mac OS X should then default to the main Library\Internet Plug-Ins\ folder.

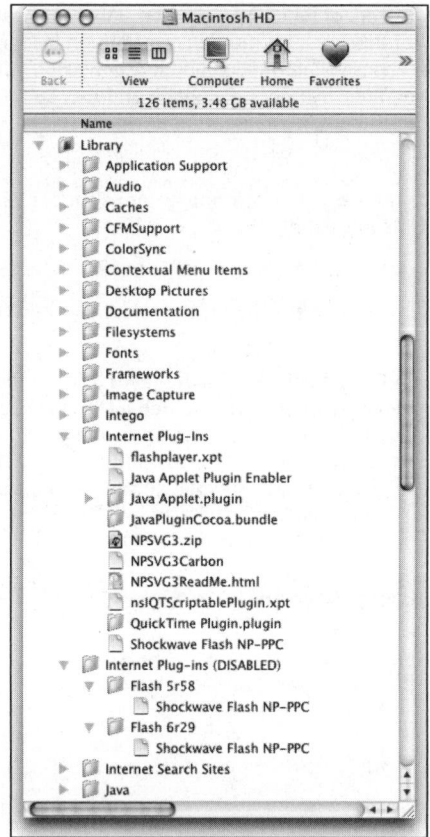

Figure 22-9: A sample Flash Players folder structure for use with Netscape 7 on Windows

This process takes some time, as you have to download and run each installer, from the URL mentioned in the previous note, and move the NPSWF32.dll file from the Plugins folder to its own folder in the Flash Players folder. When you're done, however, you'll have an efficient system for checking your content against older version of the Flash Player. Simply move the current NPSWF32.dll file into its appropriate Flash Players folder, and move the desired test version from its Flash Players folder into the Plugins folder.

Building your own Flash sniffer movie

While the Macromedia Flash MX 2004 detection features work wonderfully, you may want to know how to build your own custom Flash detection sniffer. In this section, you learn how to build a Flash movie that uses client-side ActionScript to direct the browser window to the appropriate content. Unlike the Flash MX 2004 version, this sniffer directs each version of the Flash Player to its own unique HTML page. Meaning, Flash Player 3 (or earlier) is directed to a flash3.html page, Flash Player 4 is directed to a flash4.html page, Flash Player 5 jumps to a flash5.html page, and so on.

Cross-
Reference This exercise uses ActionScript code, some aspects of which you may be unfamiliar with. Refer to Part VII, "Approaching ActionScript," of this book for more information on learning the basics of ActionScript. For the most comprehensive information about ActionScript, refer to the *Macromedia Flash MX 2004 ActionScript Bible*, by Robert Reinhardt and Joey Lott.

Making the Sniffer movie

The sniffer movie is a small Flash movie that has the same background color as the HTML document. We do not need any artwork or symbols in this movie.

1. Open Flash MX 2004, and in a new Flash document (.fla file), rename Layer 1 to **actions**.

2. Add a keyframe on frame 2 of the actions layer. With this keyframe selected, open the Actions panel (F2).

3. In the Actions panel, add some ActionScript that checks for Flash Player 3 (or earlier). If Flash Player 3 is detected, then the movie will stop here and launch a URL for Flash 3 movies. If a later version of the player is detected, a separate keyframe labeled checkPlayer is called. We can direct each version of the Player to a unique URL. The basic principle of this ActionScript is to use Flash version-specific actions to determine which Player is displaying the movie. Refer to Listing 22-1.

Listing 22-1: **The Detection Script on Frame 2 of the actions Layer**

```
// create a Flash variable, whose value is equal to the
// $version environment variable in Flash Player 4, 5,
// or 6. This action line will not be read by Flash
// Player 3(or earlier).

player = eval("$version");

// The $version value will be in the format:
//
// abc 1,2,3,4
//
// where abc is the operating system (e.g. WIN, MAC)
// and 1 and 2 are the major version designations
// (e.g. 4.0, 5.0, etc.) and 3 and 4 are the minor and
// sub-minor version designations (e.g. r20, r27, etc.)
//
// By default, Flash MX 2004 ships with a Player version equal
// to WIN 7,0,0,0 or MAC 7,0,0,0. However, the Flash
// Player is available on other platforms like UNIX and
// POCKETPC as well.
//
// We just need the major version designation at
// placeholder 1. Using a while loop and substring(), we
// can extract this number, searching for the space (" ")
// between the platform text and the version numbers. The
// major version starts just after the space (" "). The
// Flash Player 3 will disregard this section of code.
```

```
playerLength = length(player);

i=1;

while (i<=playerLength) {
   currentChar = substring(player, i, 1);
   if (currentChar eq " ") {
      platform = substring(player, 1, i-1);
      majorVersion = substring(player, i+1, 1);
      break;
   }
   i = i+1;
}

// This code will check the value of majorVersion.
// Flash Player 3 will not be able to execute the
// call() action, but Flash Player 4 or higher will.

if (majorVersion == " ") {
   // Flash Player 3 will execute this code
   // automatically, because it will not interpret
   // the if action.
   getURL("flash3.html");
} else {
   call("checkPlayer");
}

// We will prevent the movie from accidentally looping.

stop ();
```

4. Now you need to create a keyframe with actions that will be executed by Flash Player 4, 5, or 6. Add a keyframe on frame 5, and in the Property inspector assign a label of **checkPlayer** in the <Frame Label> field. Press the F5 key on frame 20 to add more empty frames to the layer so that you can read the frame label.

5. Select frame 5, and open the Actions panel (F9). In Expert mode, type the following code into the Script pane. The code in Listing 22-2 checks to see if the Flash Player is version 4, 5, or 6 (or higher).

Listing 22-2: **The Script on the checkPlayer Frame of the actions Layer**

```
// majorVersion will be equal to either 4, 5, 6, or 7 in
// Flash Player 4, 5, 6, or 7 (or higher) respectively.

if (Number(majorVersion) == 4) {
   // Flash Player 4 will execute this code.
   getURL("flash4.html");
```

Continued

Listing 22-2 *(continued)*

```
} else if (Number(majorVersion) == 5) {
    // Flash Player 5 will execute this code.
    getURL("flash5.html");
} else if (Number(majorVersion) == 6) {
    // Flash Player 6 will execute this code.
    getURL("flash6.html");
} else if (Number(majorVersion) >= 7) {
    // Flash Player 7 or higher will execute this code.
    getURL("flash7.html");
}
```

6. Change the size of the movie frame to 18 px x 18 px, in the Document Properties dialog box (Modify ➪ Document). This is the smallest size a Flash movie can have. Change the background color of the movie to match the background color of the HTML document. Click OK.

7. Save the Flash movie as `sniffer.fla`.

8. Open the Publish Settings dialog box (File ➪ Publish Settings). Make sure the Flash and HTML options are selected in the Formats tab. Rename the HTML file `sniffer_start.html`.

9. In the Flash tab, select Flash Player 4 in the Version drop-down menu.

Note We are using the Flash Player 4 format because Flash Player 3 ignores all Flash 4 or higher actions, and Flash Player 4 or higher recognizes the formatting of the variable and ActionScript structures. Flash Player 5 SWF files restructure variables and ActionScript (even Flash 4-compatible code) in a manner that doesn't work consistently in the Flash Player 4.

10. In the HTML tab, select the Flash Only template. Click the Publish button located at the bottom of the Publish Settings dialog box.

11. When the files have been published, click OK to close the Publish Settings dialog box. Save your document again.

You now have `sniffer_start.html` and `sniffer.swf` files in the same folder as your `sniffer.fla` file. In the next section, you add some additional HTML tags to the `sniffer.html` document.

Integrating the sniffer movie into an HTML document

After you have made the `sniffer.swf` and the `sniffer.html` files, you can modify the HTML document to guide the browser to a unique URL where plug-in information and a download screen are shown. Remember that the ⊃ indicates a continuation of the same line of code. Do not insert this character into your HTML document.

1. Open the `sniffer_start.html` file in your preferred HTML document editor. Macromedia Dreamweaver, Notepad (Windows), SimpleText (Mac), or BBEdit (Mac) will do just fine.

2. Somewhere between the `<head>` `</head>` tags, insert the following HTML `<meta>` tag as one line of code:

```
<meta http-equiv="Refresh" content="8; ↺
url=download.html" />
```

This `<meta>` tag has two attributes, `http-equiv` and `content`. The `http-equiv` attribute instructs the hosting Web server to add the value of `http-equiv` as a discrete name in the MIME header of the HTML document. The value of the `content` attribute becomes the value of the MIME entry. Here, the Web browser will interpret the META tag as

```
Refresh: 8; URL=download.html
```

in the MIME header. This name/value pair tells the browser to reload the browser window in 8 seconds with the file `download.html`. After testing, you may decide to increase the time the browser waits before reloading a new URL. On slower connections (or during peak Internet hours), you may find that 8 seconds is not long enough for the initial HTML and Flash movie to load into the browser.

Caution   Some older browsers may require an absolute URL in the content attribute. This means that you may need to insert a full path to your HTML document, such as `http://www.yourserver.com/download.html`, as the URL in the content attribute.

3. You may want to create some text on this HTML document that indicates its purpose. If the user does not have the plug-in installed, he or she will be staring at a blank white page until the refresh is activated. For the purposes of this example, create an HTML table that centers the text "Checking for Flash Player . . ." on the page.

4. Save the HTML file as `sniffer.html`. If you want this to be the default page for your Web site, you may need to rename this file to index.html, idex.htm, index.cfm, or to whatever filename your Web server is configured to use as a default page. At this point, you need to create a `download.html` file. You also need to create `flash3.html`, `flash4.html`, `flash5.html`, `flash6.html`, and `flash7.html` files for the `getURL()` actions in the sniffer.swf movie.

On the CD-ROM   We have included sample `sniffer.html`, `download.html`, `flash3.html`, `flash4.html`, `flash5.html`, `flash6.html`, and `flash7.html` files in the `ch22/custom_sniffer` folder on the *Macromedia Flash MX 2004 Bible* CD-ROM. The Flash movie placeholder documents (for example, `flash3.html`, `flash4.html`, and so on) do not contain any Flash content. Note that the `download.html` sample file uses the JavaScript and VBScript player detection discussed in the next section.

When you have your HTML documents ready, you can load the `sniffer.html` document into a browser. If the Flash Player is not installed, then the `meta` tag should transport the browser location to the `download.html` URL. If the Flash Player is installed, then the Flash ActionScript directs the browser to the appropriate page.

Detecting the Flash Player with JavaScript and VBScript

The use of scripts written into an HTML document is also popular for Flash Player detection. If you're getting familiar with ActionScript syntax, you'll find that JavaScript detection code isn't all that complex. JavaScript is a universal scripting language that most 3.0 or higher Web browsers can employ to some capacity. Microsoft's implementation of JavaScript, called JScript, isn't exactly the same as Netscape's JavaScript. For this reason, you can translate some JavaScript functionality into Microsoft's proprietary Web-scripting language, VBScript.

On the CD-ROM   You'll find the HTML, Flash documents, movies, and GIF files for this section in the `ch22/ javascript_detection` folder of the *Macromedia Flash MX 2004 Bible* CD-ROM.

In this section, we look at how to create an HTML document that checks for the presence of the Flash Player plug-in with JavaScript, and the Flash ActiveX control with VBScript. We use two images of a traffic light — one Flash movie with a green light animating on and off, and one GIF image with a red light on — to display the results of our plug-in and ActiveX detection. Many Web sites employ a similar mechanism: Before an HTML page with Flash content can be accessed, visitors are presented with a splash screen telling them whether they have the Flash Player installed. If they don't have it, they can click a link to get the plug-in or ActiveX control. As a backup, many splash pages also include a link to bypass the detection in case the detection fails. This link would take the visitor straight to the HTML document that contains the Flash content.

Caution   The Flash Player can be detected with most JavaScript-enabled Web browsers by using the JavaScript array `navigator.mimeTypes`. The value for this array is always empty for Internet Explorer browsers, including IE 4.5 on Macintosh. IE 5.0 (or higher) for Macintosh now supports this array. While we can use VBScript to detect for IE on Windows, there is no script plug-in detection available for IE 4.5 on Macintosh. You can however, use the Flash sniffer method, discussed in the previous sections, to detect Flash on IE 4.5 on Macintosh.

Detecting the plug-in with JavaScript

By rearranging the JavaScript code that was created by the Flash MX's original Detect for Flash 6 HTML template in the Publish Settings, we can set up a testing mechanism that delivers one of two graphics to the visitor's Web browser.

Note   Flash MX 2004 no longer uses the same JavaScript detection templates. The code we are using here originated from Flash MX, not Flash MX 2004.

Copy the `script_detection.html` document located in the `ch22/javascript_detection` folder of the *Macromedia Flash MX 2004 Bible* CD-ROM and open it in your preferred text editor (TextEdit, Notepad, BBEdit, and so on), or, even better, in Macromedia Dreamweaver MX 2004. Look at lines 12 through 17 in the following listing.

Note   The ⤸ indicates a continuation of the same line of code. It should not be written in the actual JavaScript code in the HTML document.

```
12. var plugin = 0;
13. var activeX = 0;
14. var plugin = (navigator.mimeTypes && ⤸
    navigator.mimeTypes["application/x-shockwave-flash"]) ⤸
    ? navigator.mimeTypes["application/x-shockwave- ⤸
    flash"].enabledPlugin : 0;
15. if ( plugin ) {
```

```
16.    plugin = parseInt(plugin.description.substring ⊃
       (plugin.description.indexOf(".")-1)) >= 7;
17. }
```

Line 12 initializes a variable `plugin` to save a value that indicates the presence of the Flash Player 7 plug-in on Netscape (or Mozilla, IE 5.0 Mac, or Apple Safari). Line 13 initializes a variable called `activeX` to save a value that indicates the presence of the Flash Player 7 ActiveX control. At this point, we assign a value of 0 to these variables, meaning that the plug-in and ActiveX Control are not installed. This is used for worst-case scenarios in which the user may be using a version of JavaScript that doesn't interpret the detection code correctly.

Line 14 is borrowed from the Detect Flash 6 HTML template output from Flash MX (not Flash MX 2004). It uses the `mimeTypes` array of the `navigator` JavaScript object to determine whether the Flash Player (in any version) is installed. If the Flash Player plug-in is installed, the variable `plugin` is now equal to the value [object Plugin]. If this is true, lines 15 and 16 will execute. Using the `description` property of the `Plugin` object, we can determine whether the Flash Player is the correct version. In this example, we check whether it's greater than or equal to 7. Notice that we can use a comparison as the value of the `plugin` variable. If Flash Player 7 (or higher) is installed, `plugin` will equal `true` (or 1); if a lower version is installed, `plugin` will equal `false` (or 0).

Creating a test object in VBScript

At this point, if the visitor is using Netscape (or a Mozilla-based browser, on any operating system) or Internet Explorer on the Macintosh, the variable `plugin` will have a value of either 0 or 1. However, we still need to check for the ActiveX control if the visitor is using Internet Explorer for Windows. Line 13 already initialized a variable called `activeX`. Lines 18 through 23 check to see if VBScript can create a Flash object in the document:

Note   The ⊃ indicates a continuation of the same line of code. It should not be written in the actual JavaScript code in the HTML document.

```
18. else if (navigator.userAgent && ⊃
       navigator.userAgent.indexOf("MSIE")>=0 && ⊃
       navigator.userAgent.indexOf("Windows")>=0){
19.    document.write('<SCRIPT LANGUAGE=VBScript\> \n');
20.    document.write('on error resume next \n');
21.    document.write('activeX = ( IsObject(CreateObject ⊃
       ("ShockwaveFlash.ShockwaveFlash.7")))\n');
22.    document.write('<' + '/SCRIPT>');
23. }
```

Line 18 determines whether the visitor is using Internet Explorer on Windows. If that's the browser the visitor is using, lines 19 to 23 will execute. These lines of code create the VBScript that is necessary to check for the existence of the Flash Player 7 ActiveX control. Using the `IsObject()` and `CreateObject()` methods, VBScript can determine whether the ActiveX Control is installed. If it is installed, the variable `activeX` equals `true` (or 1). Note that this variable is available to both JavaScript and VBScript.

Inserting the graphics

After the variables `plugin` and `activeX` have been set appropriately, we can use these variables to either display a Flash movie (.swf file) or a GIF image graphic. In the body of the HTML document, we can reuse the `plugin` and `activeX` variables to insert either the Flash or GIF graphics. Lines 33 through 38 of the HTML document will write the tags to display the Flash movie or the GIF image for Netscape (on any platform) or IE on the Mac.

Note   The ⟳ indicates a continuation of the same line of code. It should not be written in the actual JavaScript code in the HTML document.

```
31. if ( plugin ) {
32.    document.write('<embed src="trafficlightgreen.swf" ⟳
       width="105" height="185" swliveconnect="false" ⟳
       quality="high"></embed><br><font ⟳
       face="Verdana,Arial,Geneva" size="2">Flash ⟳
       Player 7<br/>Plug-in detected.</font>');
33. } else if (!(navigator.appName && ⟳
       navigator.appName.indexOf("Netscape")>=0 && ⟳
       navigator.appVersion.indexOf("2.")>=0)){
34.    document.write('<a href="http://www.macromedia.com ⟳
       /go/getflashplayer/">');
35.    document.write('<img src="trafficLightRed.gif" ⟳
       width="105" height="185" border="0" /></a><br> ⟳
       <font face="Verdana,Arial,Geneva" size="2">Flash ⟳
       Player 7<br/>Plug-in not installed.</font>');
36. }
```

If the `plugin` variable is not equal to `false` (line 31), line 33 executes. Line 33 uses the `<embed>` tag to insert a Flash movie (.swf file), depicting a green light that animates to a full green color, and the HTML text "Flash Player 7 Plug-in detected." If the `plugin` variable is equal to `false` and the browser is Netscape 2.0 or higher (line 33), then lines 34 and 35 create `<a href>` and `<img>` tags, depicting a static GIF image of a red traffic light that links to the Macromedia download area. Then, JavaScript creates the HTML text "Flash Player 7 Plug-in not installed."

Note   The following discussion refers to lines not shown in the code listings for this section. Please refer to these lines (and line numbers) within your preferred text editor.

Lines 45 through 54 perform the same functionality for Internet Explorer for Windows. If the `activeX` variable is `true`, then an `<object>` tag is written and a green traffic light animates on. If it's not installed, then a static GIF image of a red traffic light is displayed. Finally, we should do two more things:

✦ Tell IE 4.5 (or earlier) Mac users that we can't detect the Flash Player 7 plug-in

✦ Tell other users that they can either proceed to the main Flash site, or click the appropriate traffic light to download the plug-in or ActiveX control

Lines 62 to 65 tell IE 4.5 (or earlier) Mac users that we can't detect their plug-in settings. We can either leave it to them to decide whether they should download the plug-in, or we could direct them to a sniffer movie (discussed in the next section) to determine whether the plug-in is installed.

Lines 66 to 68 check whether either the plug-in or the ActiveX control is installed. If it is, we tell the visitor to proceed to the main Flash site. Note that you would want to insert more JavaScript code here that includes a link to your Flash content.

Lines 69 to 77 check whether the plug-in and the ActiveX control are both absent. If neither is installed, we tell them which traffic light (lines 70 to 77) to click.

Although you'll most likely want to spruce up the look and feel of this page to suit your particular site, you can use this scripting layout to inform your visitors about their plug-in or ActiveX control installations.

Using Flash Movies with JavaScript and DHTML

The ActionScripting features of Flash MX 2004 have once again increased the range of interactive and dynamic possibilities for Flash movies on the Web. Prior to Flash Player 4, Flash movies could interact with external HTML or scripts only through the `fscommand()` action. This meant mapping commands and variables to JavaScript, which, in turn, passed information to the document object model of DHTML, Java applets, or CGI (Common Gateway Interface) scripts. Now that Flash movies can directly send and receive data to server-side CGI scripts, just about anything can be done within the Flash movie. However, if you want to directly communicate with the Web browser or the HTML document, you need to use `fscommand()` actions or `getURL()` actions with `javascript:` statements. Because not all JavaScript-capable browsers support these methods, we're limiting this discussion to `fscommand()` actions and JavaScript-controllable Flash movie properties.

A word of caution to Web developers

This section covers `fscommand` actions, which, when used in Flash movies on Web pages, are supported by only a handful of browsers. Currently, not one version of Internet Explorer for Macintosh (up to version 5.1) can interpret `fscommand()` actions directed to JavaScript functions (see the Caution note in "Using the <embed> Tag" section earlier in this chapter). Only Netscape browsers versions 3.0 through 4.x offer cross-platform support for `fscommand()` actions. Internet Explorer 3 and higher for Windows 95/98/ME/NT/2000/XP also support `fscommand()` actions. Our coverage of the `fscommand()` actions assumes that you have basic knowledge of JavaScript and Flash ActionScript. If you don't know how to add actions to frames or buttons, please read Chapter 18, "Understanding Actions and Event Handlers.". If you don't know JavaScript, you can still follow the steps to the tutorials and create a fully functional Flash-JavaScript movie. However, because this isn't a book on JavaScript, we don't explain how JavaScript syntax or functions work.

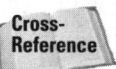

Cross-Reference We'll gladly refer you to the *JavaScript Bible* by Danny Goodman (Wiley, 2001) for more information on the JavaScript language.

Understanding how Flash movies work with JavaScript

As mentioned earlier, Flash has an action called `fscommand()`. `fscommand()` actions are used to send a command (and an optional argument string) from a Flash movie to its hosting environment (such as a Web browser or standalone Flash Player). What does this mean for interactivity? The `fscommand()` offers the capability to have any Flash event handler (Button instance, `onClipEvent()`, frame actions, and so on) initiate an event handler in JavaScript. Although this may not sound too exciting, you can use `fscommand()` actions to trigger anything that you would have used JavaScript alone to do in the past, such as updating HTML-form text fields, changing the visibility of HTML elements, or switching HTML background colors on-the-fly. Most Flash-to-JavaScript interactivity works best with dynamic HTML (DHTML) browsers such as Netscape 4 or higher and Internet Explorer 4 or higher. We look at these effects in the next section.

Caution   Netscape 6 and 6.1 do not support `fscommand()` interactivity from Flash movies with JavaScript. Netscape 6.2 requires Flash Player 6 r40 or higher to support `fscommand()` actions. Apple Safari 1.0 does not support `fscommand()` interactivity.

Flash movie communication with JavaScript is not a one-way street. You can also monitor and control Flash movies with JavaScript. Just as JavaScript treats an HTML document as an object and its elements as properties of that object, JavaScript treats a Flash movie as it would any other element on a Web page. Therefore, you can use JavaScript functions and HTML hyperlinks (`<a href>` tags) to control Flash movie playback.

Note   For JavaScript to receive Flash `fscommand()` actions, you need to make sure that the attribute `swLiveConnect` for the `<embed>` tag is set to `true`. By default, most Flash MX 2004 HTML templates have this setting omitted or set to `false`.

Changing HTML attributes

In this section, we show you how to dynamically change the `bgcolor` attribute of the `<body>` tag with a `fscommand()` action from a Flash movie while it is playing in the browser window. In fact, the background color will change a few times. Then, after that has been accomplished, you learn how to update the text field of a `<form>` tag to display what percent of the Flash movie has been loaded.

On the CD-ROM   Before you start this section, make a copy of the Flash document `countdown_starter.fla` located in the `ch22/fscommand` folder of the *Macromedia Flash MX 2004 Bible* CD-ROM. This is a starter document to which you will add ActionScript code.

Adding fscommand() actions to a Flash movie

Open the `countdown_starter.fla` Flash document from the *Macromedia Flash MX 2004 Bible* CD-ROM, and use Control ⇨ Test Movie to play the Flash .swf file. You should notice that the filmstrip countdown fades to white, and then to near-black, and then back to its original gray color. This countdown continues to loop until the entire first scene has loaded into the Flash Player. When the first scene has loaded, playback skips to a Movie Clip of two dogs (in "negative") and a title sequence. There's more to the Flash movie, but for now, that's all we need to deal with.

Our goal for this section of the tutorial is to add `fscommand()` actions to specific keyframes in the `countdown_starter.fla` document. When the Flash Player plays the frame with the `fscommand()` action, the Player sends a command and argument string to JavaScript. JavaScript then calls a function that changes the background color to the value specified in the argument string of the `fscommand()` action (see Figure 22-10). To be more exact, you add an `fscommand()` action to the frames where the color fades to white, black, and gray. When the Flash movie changes to these colors, so will the HTML background colors.

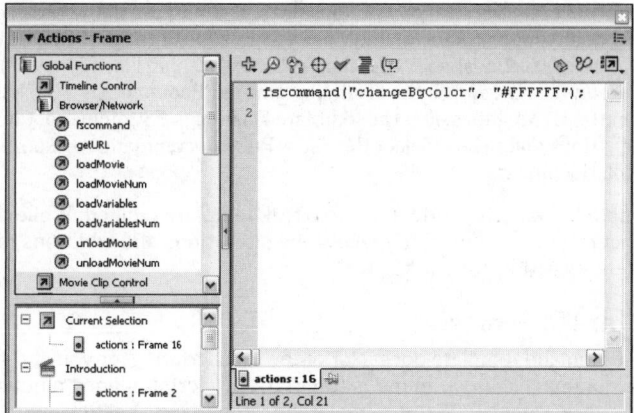

Figure 22-10: Frame 16: An fscommand() with a command of changeBgColor and with an argument of #FFFFFF (the hexadecimal code for the color white)

Here's the process:

1. On frame 16 of the Main Timeline, add a keyframe on the actions layer. With the keyframe selected, open the Actions panel (F9). Open the Global Functions ⇨ Browser/Network actions booklet, and double-click the `fscommand()` action. In the script pane, between the parentheses of the `fscommand()` action, type `"changeBgColor", "#FFFFFF"`. The complete line of code, shown in Figure 22-9, is:

   ```
   fscommand("changeBgColor", "#FFFFFF");
   ```

   The command `changeBgColor` is mapped to a JavaScript function called `changeBgColor` later in this tutorial. The argument string `#FFFFFF` is passed to that function, changing the HTML background color to white.

2. On frame 20, add another `fscommand()` action to the corresponding keyframe on the actions layer. With frame 20 selected, open the Actions panel and type another `fscommand()`:

   ```
   fscommand("changeBgColor", "#333333");
   ```

   The argument `"#333333"` will be used to change the HTML background color to a dark gray.

3. On frame 21 of the actions layer, follow the same instructions as you did for Step 2, except use `"#9E9E9E"` for the argument string. This changes the HTML background color to the same color as the Flash movie countdown graphic.

4. On frame 66 of the actions layer, add another `fscommand()` action with a `changeBgColor` command. (Add this action after the existing action on this frame.)This time, use an argument string of `"#000000"`, which changes the HTML background color to black.

5. Now that you've added several `fscommand()` actions, let's try them out in the browser. Save the document as `countdown_100.fla`, and open the Publish Settings dialog box (for more information on Publish Settings, refer to Chapter 21, "Publishing Flash Movies"). In the Formats tab, type `countdown.swf` as the Flash filename, and `countdown_100.html` as the HTML filename. In the HTML tab, select the template Flash with FSCommand. Click OK to close the Publish Settings dialog box. Select the File ➪ Publish command to export the Flash movie and HTML document.

Next, we look at the automated JavaScript code that the HTML template created. While the basic code structure has been set up, we need to make some alterations and additions to the JavaScript for our `fscommand()` actions to work.

Enabling JavaScript for Flash movies

Although the Flash with FSCommand template does a lot of the JavaScripting for you, it doesn't automatically map out the commands and arguments (args) to JavaScript-defined functions. In this section, you add the necessary JavaScript to make the `fscommand()` actions work in the browser. What follows in Listing 22-3 is the JavaScript code that Flash MX 2004 generates, along with the custom function `changeBgColor` that we have created for you.

Note   The line numbers reflect the actual line numbers in the HTML document. Any numbered line of code marked with an asterisk (*) is custom JavaScript code that Flash MX 2004 does not create. Also, remember that the ⊃ indicates a continuation of the same line of code. Do not insert this character into your HTML document.

Listing 22-3: The JavaScript Code to Enable the fscommand() Actions

```
8.    <script language="JavaScript">
9.    <!--
10.   var isInternetExplorer = ⊃
      navigator.appName.indexOf("Microsoft") != -1;
11.   // Handle all the FSCommand messages in a Flash movie
12.   function countdown_DoFSCommand(command, args){
13.     var countdownObj = isInternetExplorer ? ⊃
      document.all.countdown : document.countdown;
14.*    eval(command)(countdownObj, args);
15.   }
16.*  function changeBgColor(fMovie, hexColor){
17.*    document.bgColor = hexColor;
18.*  }
19.   // Hook for Internet Explorer.
20.   if (navigator.appName && ⊃
      navigator.appName.indexOf("Microsoft") != -1 ⊃
      && navigator.userAgent.indexOf("Windows") != -1 ⊃
      && navigator.userAgent.indexOf("Windows 3.1") ⊃
      == -1){
21.     document.write('<script language=\"VBScript\"\> \n');
22.     document.write('on error resume next \n');
23.     document.write('Sub countdown_FSCommand(ByVal ⊃
      command, ByVal args)\n');
```

```
24.     document.write('  call ⊃
        countdown_DoFSCommand(command,ù args)\n');
25.     document.write('end sub\n');
26.     document.write('</script\> \n');
27.     }
28.     //-->
29.     </script>
```

The following is a line-by-line explanation of the code:

8. This HTML tag initializes the JavaScript code.

9. This string of characters is standard HTML comment code. By adding this after the opening `<script>` tag, non-JavaScript browsers ignore the code. If this string wasn't included, text-based browsers such as Lynx might display JavaScript code as HTML text.

10. This variable simply condenses the JavaScript code that detects Internet Explorer into a single term, `isInternetExplorer`.

11. This is comment code added by the Macromedia team to let us know that the following JavaScript code is designed to catch the `fscommand()` actions from a Flash movie.

12. This is the initial JavaScript function that works exclusively with Flash `fsommand()` actions. The function's name is the value of the `name` attribute of the `<embed>` tag (or the value of the `id` attribute of the `<object>` tag) followed by an underscore and `DoFSCommand(command,args){`. In this example, the Flash movie `name` is `countdown`. Notice that the command and arguments that were specified in Flash are passed to this function as (`command, args`), respectively.

13. This is a handy optional variable that the Flash with FSCommand template created. This variable, `countdownObj`, refers to the Flash movie object. Due to the differing document object models between Internet Explorer and Netscape, a conditional check using the `?` and `:` operators is done. You can insert the `countdownObj` variable in your own JavaScript code, which is exactly what is done in line 14.

*14. This line utilizes the JavaScript `eval()` function to take the string value of the command argument passed by Flash and evaluate it to the same-named JavaScript function, which is defined in lines 16–18. The `countdownObj` reference is passed as the first argument to the `changeBgColor()` JavaScript function, while the argument passed from the Flash `fscommand()` action is passed as the second argument to the `changeBgColor()` function.

15. This curly brace ends the function defined in line 12.

*16. This is where the function `changeBgColor()` is defined. Remember that line 14 invokes this function when Flash passes the "changeBgColor" command to the `counter_DoFSCommnad()` JavaScript function. There are two arguments defined for the function, `fMovie` and `hexColor`. The function `fMovie` evaluates to the `countdownObj` variable passed in line 14, while `hexColor` evaluates to the `args` argument, representing the hexadecimal value passed from the Flash movie.

*17. This line of code passes the argument `hexColor` to the `document.bgColor` property, which controls the HTML background color. When the Flash `fscommand()` action sends the command "changeBgColor", the JavaScript `changeBgcolor()` function is invoked, which passes the argument string from the Flash `fscommand` action to `document.bgColor`.

*18. This line of code ends the function defined in line 16.

19.–27. This section of code detects the presence of Internet Explorer for Windows and maps the JavaScript functions to VBScript (which is used exclusively by Windows-only versions of Internet Explorer).

28. This end comment closes the comment started in line 11.

29. The closing `</script>` tag ends this portion of JavaScript code.

That's it! We also added `<center>` tags around the `<object>` and `<embed>` tags to center the Flash movie on the HTML page. Once you've manually added the custom lines of JavaScript code, you can load the HTML document into either Internet Explorer or Netscape (see the caveats mentioned at the beginning of this section). When the Flash Player comes to the frames with `fscommand()` actions, the HTML background should change along with the Flash movie. Next, you add a `<form>` element that displays the percentage of the Flash movie that has loaded into the browser window.

**On the
CD-ROM**

You can find this version of the `countdown_100.fla` document in the `ch22/fscommand` folder on the *Macromedia Flash MX Bible* CD-ROM. You will also find `countdown.swf` and a fully JavaScripted HTML document called `countdown_100.html`.

Using the percentLoaded() method

JavaScript can control several Flash movie properties. It's beyond the scope of this book to describe each JavaScript method for Flash movies. If you want to see a complete list of Flash JavaScript methods, see the Macromedia Flash tech support page:

```
www.macromedia.com/support/flash/ts/documents/tn4160.html
```

In this section, you use the `PercentLoaded()` method to display the Flash movie's loading progress update as a text field of a `<form>` element. First, you add the necessary `fscommand()` action to the Flash movie, then HTML `<form>` elements, and then you add the appropriate JavaScript.

1. Open the `countdown_100.fla` movie that you modified in the previous section. There should already be an empty keyframe present on frame 1 of the actions layer. Add an `fscommand()` action to this keyframe in the Actions panel:

   ```
   fscommand("percentLoaded", "");
   ```

   This command has no arguments. Add the same `fscommand()` action to keyframes on frames 10, 20, 30, 40, 50, 60, and 67 of the actions layer. If a keyframe exists at a given frame number, add the `fscommand()` after the existing action(s).

2. Save your Flash document as `countdown_complete.fla`, and open the Publish Settings dialog box. In the Formats tab, uncheck the HTML file format, and change the Flash movie filename to `countdown_complete.swf`. Then publish your Flash movie.

3. In a text editor such as Macromedia Dreamweaver MX 2004, Notepad, or TextEdit, open the `countdown_100.html` document from the previous section. Immediately resave this document as `countdown_complete.html`.

4. Add the following HTML after the `<object>` and `<embed>` tags:

```
<form method="post" action="" name="flashPercent" ⤸
style="display:show">
  <input type="text" name="textfield" size="5" ⤸
  style="display:show" />
</form>
```

The code in Step 4 uses two `name` attributes so that JavaScript can recognize them. Also, the DHTML `style` attribute assigns a `display:show` value to both the `<form>` and `<input>` tags.

Caution

Netscape 4's implementation of the document object model (DOM) doesn't allow styles to be updated on the fly unless the page is reformatted (for example, the user resizes the window). It could be possible to write more JavaScript code that would insert JavaScript styles for the `<form>` elements, but that's beyond the scope of this section.

5. Add the JavaScript code shown in Listing 22-4 to your HTML document after the `function changeBgColor()` section. The following `percentLoaded` function tells the browser to update the `<form>` text field with the percent of the Flash movie currently loaded. When the value is greater than or equal to 99, then the text field reads 100 percent and disappears after two seconds. As mentioned earlier, Netscape is unable to change the `style` of the `<form>` elements on-the-fly. (The ⤸ indicates a continuation to the same line of code. Do not type this character in your code.)

Listing 22-4: The JavaScript Code for the percentLoaded() Function

```
function percentLoaded(fMovie, args){
  var mPercent = fMovie.PercentLoaded();
  if(mPercent >= 99 ){
    document.flashPercent.textfield.value="100 %";
    if (navigator.appName.indexOf("Microsoft") != -1){
      setTimeout("document.flashPercent.textfield.style.⤸
      display = 'none'", 2000);
      setTimeout("document.flashPercent.style.display ⤸
      = 'none'", 2000);
    }
  } else {
    document.flashPercent.textfield.value = mPercent + " %" ;
  }
}
```

---

6. Save the HTML document and load it into a browser. If you run into errors, check your JavaScript syntax carefully. A misplaced ; or } can set off the entire script. Also, the function names specified in the Flash `fscommand()` actions and the JavaScript code are case-sensitive and must be exactly the same. If you continue to run into errors, compare your document to the `countdown_complete.html` document on the *Macromedia Flash MX 2004 Bible* CD-ROM. We also recommend that you test the preloading functionality from a remote Web server. If you test the file locally, the Flash movie loads 100 percent instantaneously.

Caution   Remember that this type of interactivity won't work on Netscape 6 or 6.1. If you want to test with a Netscape browser, use Netscape versions 3 through 4.x or 6.2 or higher.

Okay, that wasn't the easiest task in the world, and, admittedly, the effects might not have been as spectacular as you may have thought. Now that you know the basics of Flash and JavaScript interactivity, however, you can take your Flash movie interactivity one step further.

Web Resource   We'd like to know what you thought about this chapter. Visit www.flashsupport.com/ feedback to fill out an online form with your comments.

Summary

+ You can customize many Flash movie attributes by adjusting the attributes of the `<object>` and `<embed>` tags in an HTML document. Scaling, size, quality, and background color are just a few of the Flash movie properties that can be changed within HTML without altering the original .swf file.

+ You can detect the Flash Player plug-in or ActiveX control in a variety of ways: by using the `<object>` and `<embed>` tags alone, by using JavaScript and VBScript to check for the presence of the plug-in or the ActiveX Control, or by inserting a Flash sniffer movie into an HTML document with a special `<meta>` tag.

+ Flash MX 2004 includes a new Detect Flash Version feature in the Publish Settings. This feature automatically creates a series of HTML pages and a Flash sniffer movie to check for a version of the Flash Player that you specify.

+ You can use JavaScript and VBScript to check for the existence of the Flash Player plug-in or ActiveX control. This method requires more attention to HTML and JavaScript coding than the Flash MX 2004 Detect Flash Version method.

+ Flash movies can interact with JavaScript and DHTML elements on a Web page. This type of interactivity, however, is limited to the 3.0 or higher versions of Internet Explorer (on 32-bit Windows versions) and Netscape (on Windows and Macintosh). Currently, Netscape 6.0 and higher do not support Flash and JavaScript interactivity.

+ Flash movies can send commands to JavaScript with the Flash action, `fscommand()`. An `fscommand()` action consists of a user-defined command and argument (or parameter) string.

+ Although the Flash with FSCommand HTML template will set up the initial JavaScript to enable support for `fscommand()` actions, it won't find the `fscommand()` actions you specified in the Flash movie and map them to JavaScript functions. You have to do this manually.

+ `fscommand()` actions can be used to change HTML document attributes or styles.

+ The Flash Player plug-in has JavaScript-specific methods that can be used to send or receive information to or from a Flash movie. For example, JavaScript can query a Flash movie to determine how much of it has downloaded to the browser.

✦   ✦   ✦

Using the Flash Player and Projector

This chapter, the last in Part VI, explores alternative means of distributing your Flash movies as self-contained executable applications for CD-ROMs or floppy disks. We also look at the broad support available for the Flash Player plug-in for Web browsers.

The Stand-Alone Flash Player and Projector

The stand-alone Flash Player and projector enable you to take your Flash right off the Web and onto the desktop without having to worry whether users have the plug-in. In fact, you don't even need to worry about them having browsers! Stand-alone players and projectors have similar properties and limitations, although they're slightly different.

✦ **Stand-alone player:** This is an executable player that comes with Flash MX 2004. You can open any SWF file in this player. The stand-alone player can be found in the `Macromedia/Flash MX 2004/Players/Release` folder (Windows) or the `Macromedia Flash MX 2004:Players:Release` folder (Mac) on the volume where you installed Flash MX 2004.

✦ **Projector:** A projector is an executable copy of your movie that doesn't need an additional player or plug-in to be viewed. It's essentially a movie contained within the stand-alone player. The projector is ideal for distribution of Flash applications on CD-ROMs or DVD-ROMs. Figure 23-1 shows a Flash movie played as a Projector.

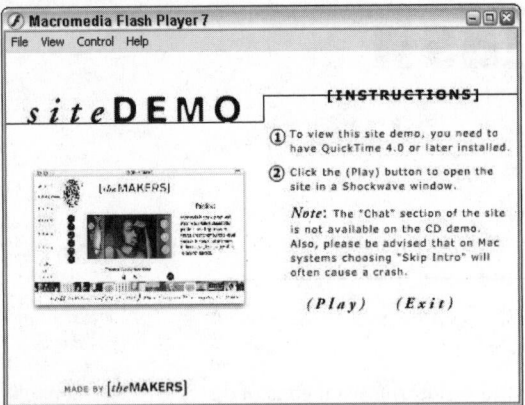

Figure 23-1: A movie playing as a projector

For the sake of simplicity, we refer both to projectors and movies played in the stand-alone Flash Player as *stand-alones* in this discussion. Because both the projector and stand-alone player have the same properties and limitations, you can apply everything discussed here to either one you choose to use.

Note   Due to the differences in operating systems, Flash stand-alones on the Mac have the application menu listed in the system bar at the top of the Macintosh desktop area. On Windows, the application menu bar is part of the stand-alone window, as shown in Figure 23-1.

Creating a projector

When you have finished producing a Flash movie, it's fairly simple to turn it into a projector. You have two ways to create a stand-alone projector. Turning your Flash movies into Flash Player 7 stand-alone projectors typically adds 973 KB (Windows projectors) or 1.3MB (Mac projectors) to the final file size. If you create a Mac projector from the Windows version of Flash MX 2004, the projector will add about 1.7MB to the size of the .hqx file.

Note   As each new version of Flash is released, the projector size will likely increase. Flash 4 projectors added 280 KB (316 KB Mac) to a movie's file size, Flash 5 added 368 KB (500 KB Mac) to the file size, Flash MX added 800K (1MB Mac) to a Flash movie's file size, and Flash MX 2004 added 973 KB (1.3MB Mac) to the movie's size. As the Flash Player's features are expanded, we'll likely see the size of the player continue to increase with each release of Flash.

Method 1: Using the Publish command

The simplest way to make a Flash projector file is to use the Publish feature of Flash MX 2004. In three short steps, you can have a stand-alone Flash movie presentation.

1. Select File ⇨ Publish Settings from the application menu.

2. When the Publish Settings dialog box opens, select the Formats tab and check the projector formats. Publish both Windows and Macintosh projectors using this method. Figure 23-2 shows the Publish Settings dialog box with the appropriate formats selected.

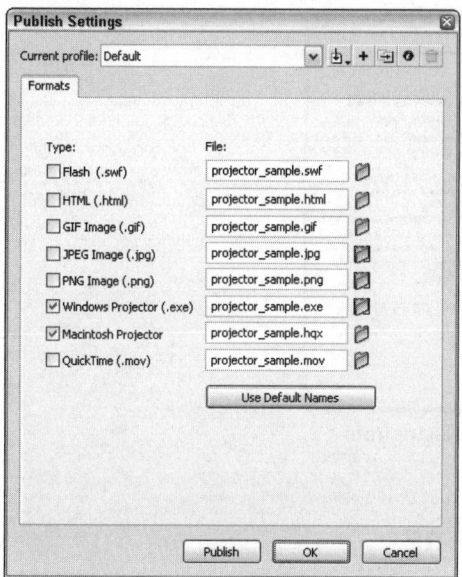

Figure 23-2: Select the projector formats in the Publish Settings dialog box.

3. Click the Publish button in the Publish Settings dialog box, and your Flash movie will be published in all of the formats (for example, SWF, GIF, JPEG, and projector formats) specified with Publish Settings.

Method 2: Using the Stand-alone Flash Player

You can also create a Flash projector file using the stand-alone Flash Player executable file that ships with Flash MX 2004. You can find the stand-alone Flash Player in the `Players/Release` folder of the Flash MX 2004 application folder.

Note If you use this method to create a projector, you can make a projector for the current platform only. Thus, if you are using the Windows version of the stand-alone Flash Player, you can create a Windows projector only.

1. Export your Flash movie as a .swf file using File ⇨ Export Movie. Alternatively, you can use the Publish feature to create the .swf file.

2. Open the exported Flash movie (.swf file) in the stand-alone Flash Player.

3. Choose File ⇨ Create Projector from the stand-alone player's application menu, as shown in Figure 23-3.

4. When the Save As dialog box opens, name the Projector and save it.

Tip If your movie is set to play at full screen (see `fscommand` coverage later in this chapter), press the Esc key to make the stand-alone player menu bar appear. If the Flash movie is set to play without the application menu, you should use the Publish method to create a projector.

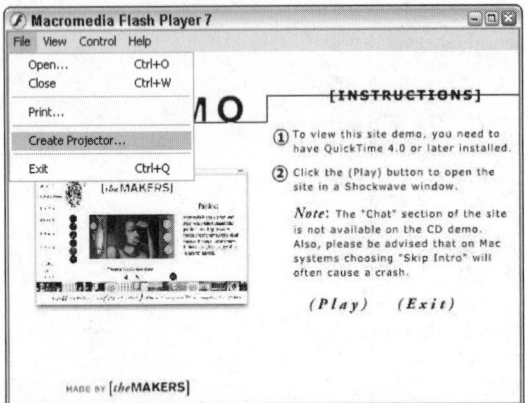

Figure 23-3: Choose File ➪ Create Projector from the stand-alone player menu.

Distribution and licensing

Distribution of stand-alone projectors or the Flash Player is free; you don't have to buy a license to distribute either the stand-alone Flash Player or projector. However, according to Macromedia, you need to follow specific guidelines for distributed Flash Players and projectors. The runtime license agreement and Macromedia logos can be downloaded from the Macromedia Web site. For more information, check out `www.macromedia.com/support/shockwave/info/licensing/`.

Distribution on CD-ROM or DVD-ROM

Flash has become increasingly popular for use on multimedia CD-ROMs or DVD-ROMs, especially as embedded .swf files in larger Macromedia Director projectors. Stand-alones can be used as front-ends for installations, splash screens for other programs, or even as complete applications. When you combine the good looks of a Flash interface with a few `fscommand` actions (see the next section for more information) and put them together on a CD-ROM (or DVD-ROM) that's programmed to start automatically on insertion, you have a first-class product.

Caution   As a general rule, don't try to send projector files (as EXE files) as attachments e-mail messages. Most current e-mail clients such as Microsoft Outlook will not allow you to open an e-mail containing an executable file, protecting you against computer-virus infections.

fscommand actions

The `fscommand` actions can be used to provide greater functionality to your stand-alones. These actions can turn a simple Flash movie into something spectacular! When combined with additional scripting and executables, you can make fully functional applications. Table 23-1 lists `fscommand` actions for stand-alones.

Table 23-1: `fscommand` **Actions for Stand-Alones**

FSCommand	Arguments	Function
`"fullscreen"`	`"true"` or `"false"`	The argument `"true"` sets the stand-alone to full-screen mode, without a menu. The argument `"false"` sets it to the size specified by the Movie Properties.
`"allowscale"`	`"true"` or `"false"`	Allows for scaling of the movie. The argument `"false"` sets the movie to the size specified by the Document Properties dialog box (Modify ⇨ Document). This doesn't actually keep the stand-alone from being resized; it only keeps the movie inside of it from being scaled.
`"showmenu"`	`"true"` or `"false"`	Toggles the menu bar and the right-click/Control+click menu. The argument `"true"` enables them; `"false"` turns them both off.
`"trapallkeys"`	`"true"` or `"false"`	Captures all key presses, including those that would normally control the player. If you have turned off the menu with the `"showmenu"` command, you will need to manually create a `"quit"` command to exit the player or projector.
`"exec"`	Path to executable (BAT, COM, EXE, and so on)	Opens an executable from within the stand-alone player. The application opens in front of the projector.
`"quit"`	No argument	Closes the stand-alone.

When an `fscommand` action is added in the Actions panel, you can access stand-alone-specific commands from a drop-down menu (see Figure 23-4). Refer to Chapter 18, "Understanding Actions and Event Handlers," for more information on adding actions to Flash frames or buttons.

Flash 5 offered an undocumented save command for use in `fscommand` actions. This command enabled a Windows projector to save variables from the Flash movie to a text (.txt) file on the end-user's system. Although Flash MX and Flash MX 2004 no longer offers this feature, you can combine Flash movies with Director projectors and the FileIO Xtra to write text files on either Mac or Windows systems. Even better, Flash ActionScript contains a `SharedObject` object that enables local storage of information from Flash movies. We demonstrate the `SharedObject` object in Chapter 33, "Creating a Game in Flash." Both `SharedObject` objects and the FileIO Xtra methods are discussed in the *Flash MX 2004 ActionScript Bible* by Robert Reinhardt and Joey Lott (Wiley, 2004).

Make sure you list the commands and arguments for `fscommand` actions as strings, not as expressions (unless you purposely want to refer to an ActionScript variable). If you do not encapsulate the command and argument in quotes, as in `fscommand("allowscale","true");`, it may not be interpreted by the stand-alone.

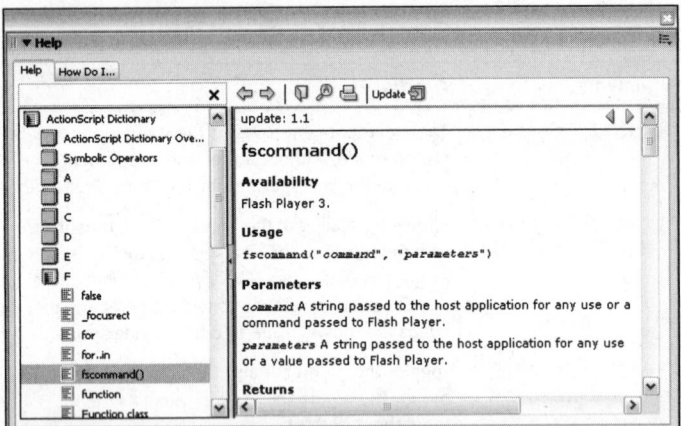

Figure 23-4: The Help panel gives you access to the entire ActionScript dictionary. Choose ActionScript Dictionary ➪ F ➪ fscommand() to see the details for this action.

You can also open HTML documents (even ones stored on a distributed CD-ROM) in the system's default Web browser by using the getURL() action. The following getURL() action opens a file named start.html that's in the same location as the stand-alone movie:

```
getURL("start.html");
```

Or, alternatively, you can display remote content in the Web browser by specifying absolute URLs, such as:

```
getURL("http://www.theMakers.com/index.html");
```

Although fscommand actions are relatively simple to use, Flash ActionScript has a Stage object that enables you to control many of the same features of the Flash Player. Refer to the coverage of the Stage object in the *Flash MX 2004 ActionScript Bible* by Robert Reinhardt and Joey Lott.

Using a behavior to toggle the screen mode

One of the behaviors included with Flash MX 2004 is the Toggle Full Screen mode behavior, to be used for Flash stand-alone projectors. When you run a Flash projector, you can have the projector take over the user's desktop, getting rid of the application window and menus. This mode is similar to a presentation mode for a PowerPoint file or a QuickTime or Windows Media movie. In the following steps, you learn how to quickly apply this behavior to a Button component.

1. In Flash MX 2004, create a new document.

2. Rename Layer 1 to **button**.

3. Open the Buttons library by choosing Window ➪ Other Panels ➪ Common Libraries ➪ Buttons. In this library, open the Component Buttons folder. With frame 1 of the button layer selected, drag an instance of the pill button component from the library to the Stage. Place the instance in the upper-left corner of the Stage.

4. Select the new instance on the Stage. In the Property inspector, name the instance **btnToggle**. In the parameters area of the inspector, type **Toggle Screen** in the Label field and select the auto-width check box above the field, as shown in Figure 23-5.

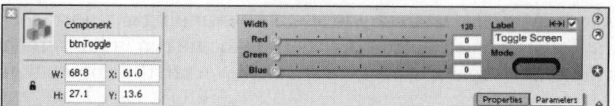

Figure 23-5: The settings for the pill button instance

5. With the instance selected on the Stage, open the Behaviors panel (Shift+F3). Click the Add Behavior (+) button in the panel, and choose Projector ⇨ Toggle Full Screen mode. Flash MX 2004 presents a confirmation dialog box, telling you what the behavior does (see Figure 23-6). Click OK.

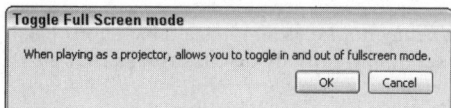

Figure 23-6: The Toggle Full Screen mode behavior dialog box

6. Save your Flash document as projector_behavior.fla.

7. Choose File ⇨ Publish Settings to open the Publish Settings dialog box. In the Formats tab, choose Windows Projector and Macintosh Projector, as shown in Figure 23-7. Click the Publish button to create the projector files; then click OK to close the dialog box.

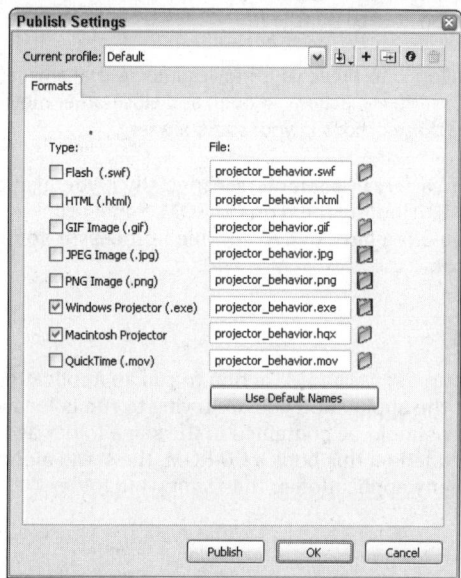

Figure 23-7: The Publish Settings dialog box

8. On your desktop, browse to the location where you saved the Flash document in Step 6. Double-click the projector file that corresponds to the operating system you are using. For example, if you're using Windows, double-click the projector_behavior.exe. If you're on a Mac, double-click the projector_behavior application file.

9. When the projector starts, the Flash movie should be running in a normal application window. Click the Toggle Screen button to make the movie run in full-screen mode. When you click the button again, the movie should revert to the application window mode.

On the CD-ROM   You can find the completed Flash document, `projector_behavior.fla`, in the `ch23` folder of this book's CD-ROM.

Stand-Alone Limitations and Solutions

When you create a stand-alone, the task may not be as simple as taking your Flash document and exporting it as a projector. In this section, we briefly discuss issues that may affect the performance of your projector.

File sizes

When you distribute your Flash movies as stand-alones, you may think that you won't have to worry about streaming and download. As a consequence, stand-alones are often made considerably larger than a typical Flash movie — which can be a mistake! Very large movies (1MB or more) may not play well on slower computers with Pentium II (or PowerMac G3) or older processors. Remember that Flash movies require the computer processor to compute all of those vector calculations, especially for rich animation. When you try to give a slower computer 1MB of Flash at once, it may not be able to handle it.

Tip   One way to get around this limitation is to break your movies into several smaller movies. You can use the `loadMovie`/`unloadMovie` actions to open and close other movies within the original movie. You should use these actions in your stand-alones.

You should also test your movies on a variety of computers, especially if you plan to put a lot of development time and money into distributing them on CD-ROM. Some processors handle the movies better than others, and you often have to decide which processor you want to target as the lowest common denominator.

File locations

If you use the `"exec"` parameter with an `fscommand()` action to run an application from the projector, you need to make sure that the application you are trying to run is located within a folder named `fscommand`. This folder should be contained in the same folder as the stand-alone projector file. In the sample included on this book's CD-ROM, the stand-alone projector named `start.exe` is allowed to open any application in the `fscommand` folder.

On the CD-ROM

You can find a sample projector structure and file setup in the ch23/exec folder of this book's CD-ROM.

Macromedia implemented this security feature with Flash Player 6 stand-alones, and continues to implement the policy with Flash Player 7 stand-alones. By restricting access to executables (that is, application files), users can trust that a Flash movie or projector won't be able to run system-level applications that could potentially corrupt their computer or install a virus.

Caution

As a Web user, you should always be careful of running any type of application file, especially if you received it in an e-mail or downloaded it from an unknown company's Web site. A malicious user could easily disguise a virus within any executable. Make sure you run applications only, including projectors, from trusted sources.

Using the Flash Player Plug-in for Web Browsers

Flash movies can be played only in Web browsers that have the Flash Player plug-in or ActiveX control installed. Macromedia has made huge strides in making the plug-in prepackaged with newer Web browsers and operating system installation programs, eliminating the need for users to manually download and install the plug-in themselves. Unfortunately, the Flash Player 7 version of the plug-in will likely only be included in future releases of Web browsers and operating systems. Remember that earlier versions of the plug-in can *try* to play Flash movies published for Flash Player 7; however, new features in Flash Player 7-based movies (such as image support in text fields and loading Flash Video, or FLV files, over HTTP) will not be available.

Note

For up-to-date information on the Flash Player plug-in, see Macromedia's download page at www.macromedia.com/shockwave/download/alternates.

Supported operating systems

Since Flash 3, Macromedia has greatly expanded its platform support for the Flash Player plug-in. At the time of this writing, you can download Flash Players for Windows 95/98/ME/NT/2000/XP and for Mac Power PCs. By the time this book is published, version 7 players should be available for Sun Solaris and Linux *x*86. At conferences worldwide, Macromedia has demonstrated that Flash graphics can be ported to a variety of GUIs (graphical user interfaces) and operating systems. We've also seen Flash graphics showing up in add-on applications for entertainment consoles such as the Sega Dreamcast and set-top boxes from Motorola.

Supported browsers

The Flash Player plug-in works best with Netscape and Internet Explorer browsers. Any browser compliant with Netscape Navigator 2.0's plug-in specification or Internet Explorer's ActiveX technology can support the Flash Player plug-in or ActiveX control, respectively.

The Flash Player on the Pocket PC and Other Devices

The development for the Flash Player is so demanding that Macromedia dedicates an entire department's worth of resources to the job. The Flash Player has been made available for Pocket PC devices using the Pocket PC 2002 and 2003 operating systems from Microsoft. Computer hardware manufacturers such as Hewlett-Packard/Compaq and Casio currently manufacture a wide range of PDAs (personal data assistants) that can use the Flash Player via the Pocket Internet Explorer Web browser or a stand-alone player. At the time of this writing, Flash Player 6 was available for most Pocket PCs. As the computer processing power of Palm, Handspring, and Sony devices (that implement the Palm OS) increases, we see Flash Player support being extended to these devices.

Nokia and DoCoMo have released phones in Japan that can play full-color Flash animations as well! These phones use a version of the Flash Player called Flash Lite. With this player, you can create Flash movies that use Flash 5 objects and Flash 4 ActionScript. For more information on Flash Lite and DoCoMo, visit the following page on Macromedia's site:

`www.macromedia.com/devnet/devices/i-mode.html`

It's no surprise that the Flash Player is being adopted so widely by computer and device manufac-turers. The SWF format allows rich media such as animation, sound, and video to be transmitted over incredibly slow (or congested) networks. Until high-speed wireless access becomes more available, we'll likely need to keep wireless connection speeds such as 19.2 Kbps (CDPD-based networks) or 25 to 60 Kbps (GPRS-based networks) in mind while we develop Flash movies that can be accessed by a universal audience.

Note that Mac versions of Internet Explorer or Apple Safari use a Netscape plug-in emulator to use the Flash Player plug-in rather than an ActiveX control.

For AOL subscribers, any version of AOL's 3.0 through 8.0 browsers (except for the earliest 3.0 release that used a non-Microsoft Internet Explorer shell) will support Macromedia plug-ins.

Caution   The Flash action `fscommand`, when used to communicate with JavaScript, works only with certain browser versions. Currently, no versions of Internet Explorer on the Macintosh (up to version 5.1) or Apple Safari support the `fscommand` action. Netscape 3.01 through 4.x (on both Macintosh and Windows) or Internet Explorer 3.0 or greater for Windows 95/98/NT/ 2000/XP is necessary for `fscommand` implementation. Netscape 6.0 or 6.1 do not support `fscommand` interactivity with JavaScript.

For a comprehensive list of supported browsers (and Flash compatibility), please see the Macromedia tech note at `www.macromedia.com/support/flash/ts/documents/ browser_support_matrix.htm`.

Plug-in and Flash movie distribution on the Web

Anyone can download the Flash Player plug-in for free from the Macromedia Web site. You can direct visitors at your Web sites to Macromedia's Flash Player download page, `www. macromedia.com/go/getflashplayer`. In fact, according to Macromedia's licensing agree-ment, if you're publishing Flash movies on your Web site, you need to display the "Get Shockwave Player" logo or "Get Flash Player" logo on your Web site. This logo should link to Macromedia's download page, just listed. However, you need to license the right to distribute any plug-in installer from Macromedia. For more details on licensing, see www.macromedia. com/support/shockwave/info/licensing/.

You can find the official Macromedia button graphics at www.macromedia.com/support/ programs/mwm/swb.html.

Plug-in installation

In Chapter 21, "Publishing Flash Movies," we discuss the Publish feature of Flash MX 2004 and the use of preformatted HTML templates to deliver your Flash movies to your Web site. The template and/or handwritten HTML that you use for your Flash-enabled Web pages will determine the degree of difficulty your visitors will have upon loading a Flash movie.

We devote extensive coverage to plug-in detection in this book. See Chapter 22, "Integrating Flash Content with Web Pages," for more information. This chapter includes details on using the new Detect Flash Version feature of Flash MX 2004.

Using the Settings in Flash Player 6 and 7

Flash Player 6 introduced the Settings option from the Flash Player's contextual menu, which can be accessed by right-clicking (or Control+clicking on the Mac) a Flash movie. When you choose the Settings option, the Macromedia Flash Player Settings dialog box opens. This dialog box has four tabs, which are discussed in the following sections.

Privacy

This tab, shown in Figure 23-8, controls the access of the current Flash movie to your Webcam and microphone. Whenever a Flash movie tries to access your Webcam or microphone, the Flash Player opens this tab to ask you for permission. You can choose Allow, which gives the Flash movie access to your camera and microphone, or Deny, which stops the Flash movie from gaining access to these devices. You can also select the Remember check box so that the Flash Player remembers the choice you made, preventing the dialog box from opening during subsequent visits to the same Flash movie (or Web site hosting the Flash movie). If you click the Advanced button in the Privacy tab, a new Web browser opens and loads the help page for the Settings options on Macromedia's site.

Flash movies can stream live audio and video to Flash Communication Server applications by using the Camera, Microphone, and NetStream objects.

The Privacy option applies to any and all Flash movies hosted on the domain listed in the Privacy tab.

For the most up-to-date information on the Privacy tab, refer to the following page on Macromedia's site:

www.macromedia.com/support/flashplayer/help/privacy/

You can also access the Global Settings manager on Macromedia's site, which enables you to control the privacy settings for all sites you have visited. Go to the following URL:

www.macromedia.com/support/flashplayer/help/settings/global_ privacy.html

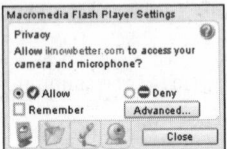

Figure 23-8: The Privacy tab

Local Storage

As shown in Figure 23-9, the Local Storage tab controls how much information can be stored on your computer from the Flash Player. Since Flash Player 6, Flash movies can be engineered to store data on the user's machine, with the use of local Shared Objects. The SharedObject class in ActionScript allows you to remember customized information on a user's machine, just like JavaScript cookies can store information from a Web browser.

Figure 23-9: The Local Storage tab

By default, a Web site and Flash movies hosted on that site can allocate as much as 100 KB of data on a user's machine. If a Flash movie hosted from a Web site requests more than this amount, the Flash Player automatically opens this tab asking for the user's permission to store more data. You can click the Never Ask Again option to prevent the Flash Player from automatically opening this tab when a site requests to store more data than its allotted amount.

You can find the latest information about the Local Storage tab at:

www.macromedia.com/support/flashplayer/help/localinfo/.

To learn more about using the SharedObject class, refer to the *Flash MX 2004 ActionScript Bible* by Robert Reinhardt and Joey Lott.

Microphone

The Microphone tab, shown in Figure 23-10, controls the source of audio input to a Flash movie. Depending on your computer system, you may have several audio capture devices listed in this tab's menu. If you don't have an audio capture device on your system, then you may not see any options available in this panel. You can use this tab to control the sensitivity of the microphone (or capture device) by adjusting the slider position. The tab provides real-time audio monitoring with a bar graph. You can click the Reduce Echo check box to minimize the echo or feedback from a speaker that is located near your microphone.

Figure 23-10: The Microphone tab

For more information on Microphone settings, see www.macromedia.com/support/flashplayer/help/microphone/.

Camera

The Camera tab, shown in Figures 23-11 and 23-12, controls the camera source used by the Flash Player. If your computer does not have a camera (or digital video capture card, which includes Firewire, or IEEE 1394, cards), then you may not see a camera source listed in this tab. If you have multiple video capture sources, you can use this tab to control which source is used for live streams going out of the Flash movie into a Flash Communication Server application.

Figure 23-11: The default view of the Camera tab

You can click the camera icon in the Camera tab to see live video from your chosen capture source, as shown in Figure 23-12. If you do not see any picture in this area after you click the camera icon, you may have a problem with your capture driver or the Flash Player may be incompatible with the driver.

Tip

Restarting your computer or reconnecting the camera to the computer may help reinitialize the camera. If you need to do this, you'll have to close the Flash movie and reload it.

Figure 23-12: An active preview of a camera's output in the Camera tab

For more information on the Camera tab and its settings, see the following page on Macromedia's site:

www.macromedia.com/support/flashplayer/help/camera/

Alternative Flash-Content Players

Macromedia has teamed up with RealSystems and Apple to enable Flash content in the RealOne Player and the QuickTime Player, respectively. By enabling Flash content in other players, Macromedia is promoting the acceptance of Flash as the de facto vector standard for Web graphics. Moreover, with so many alternatives for Flash playback, it is more likely that your Web visitors can see your Flash content.

RealOne Player with Flash playback

With a little effort, you can repackage your Flash movies as RealFlash presentations over the Web. Web visitors can use the RealPlayer G2, RealPlayer 8, or the new RealOne Player to play Flash, RealAudio, or RealVideo (among a long list of RealMedia types) content. RealMedia movies stream from a RealServer (special server software running concurrently with Web server software) into the RealPlayer plug-in (Netscape) or ActiveX control (Internet Explorer).

Note   Since Flash MX, you can no longer publish Flash movies tuned for RealPlayer. You can find more information about Flash and RealPlayer at `service.real.com/help/library/guides/ realone/ProductionGuide/HTML/realpgd.htm?page=htmfiles/flash.htm`.

QuickTime Player

Apple introduced playback support for Flash movies with QuickTime 4. Better yet, Macromedia has included QuickTime Flash export options with Flash 4, 5, and MX. A QuickTime Flash movie (.mov file) is essentially a Flash movie (.swf file) packaged as a QuickTime media type.

Web Resource   The QuickTime architecture and QuickTime Flash format are discussed at length in the archived, "Working with QuickTime," available on the book's support site at `www.flash support.com/archive`.

You can use the QuickTime HTML template in Publish Settings to create an instant Web page that uses the QuickTime Player plug-in. It uses the `<object>` and `<embed>` tags to prescribe the name, width, height, and plug-in download location.

QuickTime 4 can support only Flash 3 graphics and actions, QuickTime 5 can support Flash 4 SWF format features, including `loadVariables` actions, and QuickTime 6 supports Flash Player 5-based features and ActionScript. Flash movies can act as a timeline navigator for other QuickTime media, such as video or audio. For interactive Flash content, you should limit yourself to Flash 4- or 5-compatible actions.

Note   At the time of this writing, there was not an upgrade to the QuickTime Player that supported Flash Player 6 or 7 SWF features.

Tip   For a demo of QuickTime Flash, check out Apple's QuickTime Sprites overview page at `www.apple.com/quicktime/overview/sprites.html`.

Shockwave Player

Since Director 6.5, you can include Flash movies (.swf files) in your Director movies, either as stand-alone Director projectors or as part of Shockwave movies (.dcr files) on the Web. The Flash Asset Xtra is automatically included as part of the default Shockwave plug-in installation process. Among other benefits, Shockwave movies enable you to integrate Flash movies with dynamic 3D models and graphics and use Flash assets with third-party Xtra capabilities.

Cross-Reference
For more information on Director and Flash interactivity, please read Chapter 40, "Working with Director MX."

Player Utilities

You can also reformat and modify stand-alones for both Windows and Macintosh. A few software companies create applications specifically designed to modify Flash movies and stand-alones. Here is a list of Web site URLs for those companies:

✦ www.flashjester.com

✦ www.northcode.com

✦ www.screentime.com

✦ www.alienzone.com/screensaver_features.htm

✦ www.screenweaver.com

✦ www.goldshell.com

Some of these companies offer more than just one utility for Flash movie development, such as the JTools of FlashJester. For updates to this list, check out the book's Web site, listed in the Preface of the book.

Tip
You can find directories of Flash utilities at www.flashmagazine.com and graphics soft.about.com/cs/flashtools.

One of our favorite utilities is Versiown, created by Goldshell Digital Media. This handy utility allows you to modify the properties of a Flash (or Director) projector file, specifically .exe versions for Windows. With Versiown, you can:

✦ Add or modify the version information that shows up in the Properties dialog box, accessible by right-clicking the .exe file and choosing Properties.

✦ Add a custom icon for the .exe file of the projector. Together with an icon utility such as IconBuilder from Iconfactory (which is a filter plug-in for Adobe Photoshop), you can make custom .ico files to be used as icons for your Flash projectors.

You can download trial versions of Versiown at www.goldshell.com/versiown. A trial of IconBuilder is available at www.iconfactory.com/ib_home.asp.

Future Players, Future Features

Who can predict where Flash content will show up next? While the Flash Player plug-in has made its way into browser installations all over the world, there are still other possible avenues for Flash content. Currently, there is no SVG output from the Flash authoring environment. (If you'd like to experiment with Flash SWF to SVG conversion, check out www.eprg.org/projects/SVG/flash2svg/swfsvganim.html.) Or, maybe you would like to see Flash content supported in some other authoring application as an additional asset. If you have feature requests or general comments regarding the Flash authoring application or the Flash SWF format, you can send feedback to Macromedia at www.macromedia.com/support/email/wishform..

Note   You can use the Show Info dialog box (Mac OS X) on Mac files to easily replace the icon image for Flash projector files on the Mac. Open the .ico file made from IconBuilder in an image editor such as Adobe Photoshop, use Edit ➪ Select All to select the entire image, copy it to the clipboard (Edit ➪ Copy) and paste it into the picture area of the Get (or Show) Info dialog box.

Web Resource   We'd like to know what you think about this chapter. Visit www.flashsupport.com/feedback to fill out an online form with your comments.

Summary

✦ Flash movies can be viewed in Web pages with the Flash Player plug-in or ActiveX control. You can also play Flash movies (.swf files) with the stand-alone Flash Player included with the Flash MX 2004 application, or you can publish a Macintosh or Windows projector that packages the stand-alone Flash Player and .swf file into one executable file.

✦ You can freely distribute a Flash movie projector or stand-alone Flash Player as long as you adhere to the guidelines outlined at Macromedia's Web site.

✦ Flash movies can be distributed with other multimedia presentations such as Macromedia Director projectors. Your Flash movies can be distributed on a CD-ROM or DVD-ROM.

✦ The Actions panel of Flash MX 2004 has a stand-alone–specific submenu for the fscommand action. fscommand actions can control playback and execute external applications from a stand-alone.

✦ Flash movies can be viewed best with the Macromedia Flash Player plug-in or ActiveX control. However, you can also view Flash movies with third-party products, such as the RealOne Player or the Apple QuickTime Player.

✦ You can enhance your Flash movies with third-party tools such as FlashJester's JTools for Flash.

✦   ✦   ✦

Approaching ActionScript

Chapter 24 introduces the basic syntax of ActionScript code so that you understand why all those brackets, dots, and quote marks are used. In Chapter 25 you learn how to control methods and properties of `MovieClip` objects. If you thought animating Movie Clips was fun, wait until you start to apply more sophisticated control to multiple elements with ActionScript! Chapter 26 covers using functions and arrays, two of the most crucial techniques for organizing and controlling dynamic data. Chapter 27 takes you to the next level of Movie Clip control with an overview of how to detect collisions, and how to use the `Color`, `Sound` and `PrintJob` objects to control dynamic movie elements. One of the most powerful features of Flash is the capability for dynamic data loading. Chapter 28 introduces you to MP3, JPEG, and FLV loading, and covers how to share and load assets between multiple SWF files. Chapter 29 gets you starting using many of the new UI components that ship with Flash MX 2004.

If you've made it this far, you will be surprised to find in Chapter 30 how easy it is to create a dynamic Flash movie that sends data with the `LoadVars` object and to integrate XML data with your Flash movies. Chapter 31 gives you the tools you need to take control of Flash text fields using HTML tags and the `TextFormat` object. This chapter also introduces the new CSS features in Flash MX 2004. The final two chapters in this section give you an opportunity to work through complete Flash projects. You can apply your new ActionScript know-how to build a portfolio site in Chapter 32, and an interactive game in Chapter 33. Chapter 34 is an overview of the most common issues that may come up in your Flash production and the best practices for resolving problems and optimizing your workflow.

Note: If you're hungry for more ActionScript, you will find everything you need for more advanced code in the *Flash MX 2004 ActionScript Bible* by Robert Reinhardt and Joey Lott (Wiley Publishing, 2004).

Knowing the Nuts and Bolts of Code

✦ ✦ ✦ ✦

In This Chapter

Describing interactive problems

Speaking the ActionScript language

Understanding the value of variables

Working with conditionals

✦ ✦ ✦ ✦

For many serious Web developers, Flash's enhanced programming capabilities are the most important new feature of each product release. Now, more than ever, elements inside Flash movies can be dynamic, have properties calculated on the fly, and respond to user input. Movies can communicate with server-side applications and scripts by sending and receiving processed and raw data. What does this mean for your movies? It means you have the capability to produce truly advanced movies (such as Flash asteroids, a multiplayer role-playing adventure game, or a navigational interface with a memory of the user's moves). It also means that Flash can be used to produce many complex Web applications (such as database-driven e-commerce product catalogs) without the need for proprietary server-side applications.

While many of the individual actions have not changed in Flash MX 2004, the structure of ActionScript programming has changed dramatically. Macromedia has officially graduated ActionScript to version 2.0, wherein programming jumps to a whole new level, more closely adhering to ECMA 4-compliant standards. The Actions panel has been reorganized and improved to facilitate faster and more efficient coding. Components have also graduated to use ActionScript 2.0, using complex event handling. Components, now more than ever, make it simpler for you to add interface elements and integrate data into your Flash projects. Flash MX 2004 continues to push the advancement of Rich Internet Applications, or RIAs, which bring a new world of real-time data and ease of use to the Web. These topics are far beyond the scope of motion tweens and animations. This chapter introduces you to the programming structure of ActionScript and explains how to start using code within your Flash movies.

 If you are new to scripting, we highly recommend that you review Part V, "Adding Basic Interactivity to Flash Movies," before you begin this chapter.

 For more information about ECMAScript 4, see the original proposal at www.mozilla.org/js/language/es4/.

Breaking Down the Interactive Process

Before you can become an ActionScript code warrior, realize that this isn't just a weekend activity—if you want to excel at Flash ActionScripting, you'll need to commit the time and energy necessary for the proper revelations to occur. It's not likely that you'll understand programming simply by reading this chapter (or the whole book). You need to create some trials for yourself, testing your textbook knowledge and allowing yourself to apply problem-solving techniques.

You might be thinking, "Oh no, you mean it's like geometry, where I'm given a problem, and I have to use theorems and postulates to create a proof?" Not exactly, but programming, like geometry, requires strong reasoning and justification skills. You need to be able to understand how values (for example, the height of a Movie Clip instance) are determined, what type of changes you can perform on those values, and how changes to one value might affect another value. Confused? Don't worry; we take this one step at a time.

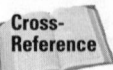

Cross-Reference   See Chapter 3, "Planning Flash Projects," for more detailed information regarding project planning and management.

Define your problems

Regardless of what interactive authoring tool you use (Macromedia Dreamweaver MX 2004, Macromedia Flash MX 2004, Macromedia Director MX, and so on), you can't begin any production work until you have a clear idea of the product. What is it that you are setting out to do? At this point in the process, you should use natural language to describe your problems; that is, define your objective (or problem) in a way that you understand it. For example, let's say that you want to make a quiz. You'll have to run through a list of goals for that interactive product:

✦ Is it a true/false test?

✦ Or will it be multiple choice?

✦ Or fill-in-the-blank?

✦ An essay test?

✦ How many questions will be in the quiz?

✦ Will there be a time limit for each question?

✦ Will you notify the person of wrong answers?

✦ How many chances does the person get to answer correctly?

Other questions, of course, could help define what your product will encompass. Don't try to start Flash production without setting some project parameters for yourself.

Clarify the solution

After you have defined the boundaries for the project, you can start to map the process with which your product will operate. This step involves the procedure of the experience (in other words, how the person will use the product you are creating). With our quiz example, you might clarify the solution as:

1. The user starts the movie and types his or her name.

2. After submitting the name, the user will be told that he or she has 10 minutes to complete a 25-question quiz that's a combination of true/false and multiple-choice questions.

3. Upon acknowledging the instructions (by pressing a key or clicking a button), the timer starts and the user is presented with the first question.

4. The timer is visible to the user.

5. The first question is a true/false question, and the correct answer is false.

6. If the user enters a true response, a red light graphic appears and the sound of a buzzer plays. The user is asked to continue with the next question.

7. If the user enters a false response, a green light graphic appears and the sound of applause plays. The user is asked to continue with the next question.

8. This process repeats until the last question is answered, at which point the score is tallied and presented to the user.

The preceding eight steps are similar to a process flowchart, as discussed in Chapter 3, "Planning Flash Projects." In real-life production, you would want to clarify Step 8 for each question in the same amount of detail as Steps 5 through 7 did. As you can see, once you start to map the interactive experience, you'll have a much better starting point for your scripting work. Notice that we're already using logic, with our `if` statements in Steps 6 and 7. We're also determining object properties such as `_visible` in Step 4. While we may not know all the ActionScript involved with starting a timer, we know that we have to learn how time can be measured in a Flash movie.

Note   We use the terms "scripting," "programming," and "coding" interchangeably through this chapter and other parts of the book.

Translate the solution into the interactive language

After you have created a process for the movie to follow, you can start to convert each step into a format that Flash can use. This step will consume much of your time as you look up concepts and keywords in this book, the *Flash MX 2004 ActionScript Bible* (Wiley, 2004), or Macromedia's new Help panel that ships with Flash MX 2004. It's likely that you won't be able to find a prebuilt Flash movie example to use as a guide, or if you do, that you'll need to customize it to suit the particular needs of your project. For our quiz example, we could start to translate the solution as:

1. Frame 1: Movie stops. User types name into a text field.

2. (a) Frame 1: User clicks a submit Button symbol instance to initiate the quiz. The instructions are located on frame 2. Therefore, the Button action uses a `gotoAndStop(2)` action to move the playhead to the next frame.

2. (b) Frame 2: Static text will be shown, indicating the guidelines for the quiz.

3. Frame 2: User clicks a start quiz Button symbol instance. An action on the Button instance starts a timer and moves the playhead to frame 3.

4. Frame 3: The current time of the timer is displayed in a text field, in the upper-right corner of the Stage.

5. Frame 3: The first question is presented in the center of the Stage. A button with the text True and a button with the text False are located just beneath the question. The correct answer for the question is hidden in a variable name/value. The variable's name is answer, and its value is false. This variable declaration appears as a frame action on frame 3. A variable, called score, will also be declared to keep track of the correct answer count. Its starting value will be 0.

6. (a) Frame 3: If the user clicks the True button, an if/else action checks whether answer's value is equal to true. If it is, an action sets the _visible of a green Light_mc Movie Clip instance to true, and initiates and plays a new Sound object for the applause.wav file in our Library. Also, the value of score increases by 1. If the value of answer is not true, then an action sets the _visible of a redLight_mc Movie Clip instance to true, and initiates and plays a new Sound object for the error.wav file in our Library. The value of score will be left as is.

6. (b) Frame 3: A Button instance appears, and when clicked, takes the user to frame 4.

7. (a) Frame 3: If the user clicks the False button, an if/else action checks whether answer's value is equal to true. If it is, an action sets the _visible of a green Light_mc Movie Clip instance to true, and initiates and plays a new Sound object for the applause.wav file in our Library. Also, the value of score is increased by 1. If the value of answer is not true, an action sets the _visible of a redLight_mc Movie Clip instance to true and initiates and plays a new Sound object for the error.wav file in our Library. The value of score is left as is.

7. (b) Frame 3: A Button instance appears, and when clicked, it takes the user to frame 4.

Although there is more than one way we could have translated this into ActionScript-like syntax, you'll notice that a few key concepts are presented in the translation: where events occur (frames or buttons), and what elements (for example, Button symbols or Movie Clip instances) are involved.

Most important, you'll notice that we used the same procedure for both the True and the False buttons. Even though we could hardwire the answer directly in the Button actions, we would have to change our Button actions for each question. By placing the same logic within each Button instance, we have only to change the value of the answer variable from frame to frame (or from question to question).

Granted, this example was already translated for you, and 90 percent of your scripting woes will be in the translation process — before you even have a testable Flash movie. You need to learn the basic terminology and syntax of the ActionScript language before you can start to write the scripting necessary for Steps 1 through 7. And that's exactly what the rest of this chapter (and the rest of Part VII of the book) will do.

Cross-Reference
Because the vocabulary of the ActionScript language has become so immense, Robert Reinhardt and Joey Lott have created a separate book, the *Flash MX 2004 ActionScript Bible*, to thoroughly address the syntax of ActionScript. If you are new to scripting and programming, we recommend that you start with our coverage of ActionScript here before reading the *Flash MX 2004 ActionScript Bible*.

The Basic Context for Programming in Flash

With the enhanced Actions panel (also known as the ActionScript editor) in Flash MX 2004, you can program interactivity by writing interactive commands directly into the Script pane of the Actions panel.

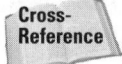

See our explanation of the Actions panel in Chapter 18, "Understanding Actions and Event Handlers."

Flash MX 2004 has replaced the Reference panel with a new Help panel that allows you to look up ActionScript terms, with definitions, usage, and code examples. We'll show you the Help panel later in this section.

In the Actions panel, you can type your code from scratch, as well as insert your code with the help of Action booklets. Syntactically, ActionScript looks and feels very much like JavaScript. Macromedia has gone to great lengths to make ActionScript compatible with ECMAScript 4 (the standard programming guidelines derived from JavaScript). And like other object-oriented languages, ActionScript is composed of many familiar building blocks: variables, operators, conditionals, loops, expressions, built-in properties, subroutines, and native functions.

The Actions panel no longer supports a Normal mode for ActionScript code creation.

Accessing ActionScript commands

All of the ActionScript commands are found in the Flash interface in the Action booklets or plus (+) button menu of the Actions panel. However, assembling actions with one another is not something Flash MX 2004 automatically performs. Although it is beyond the scope of this chapter to fully explain fundamental programming principles, we can give a sense of the whole of ActionScript by providing you with an organized reference to each of its parts.

Actions list organization in the Actions panel

In the Actions panel, you can cut, copy, and paste code within the Script pane from one area of your movie to another using Ctrl+X (⌘+X), Ctrl+C (⌘+C), and Ctrl+V (⌘+V), respectively. You are free to select partial or entire lines of code, and modify the code in any way you want. With Flash MX 2004, you can even edit your code in your preferred text editor! If you want to create your own programming macros in other programming applications, you can write your scripts outside of the Flash authoring environment and copy the final code into the Actions panel when you're done.

Using Esc Shortcut Keys for Actions

In Flash MX 2004, you can choose to show or hide shortcut keys in the Actions panel. In the options menu of the Actions panel, choose View Esc Shortcut Keys (if it's not already checked). Now, click the plus (+) menu of the Actions panel to access ActionScript commands. You'll notice that shortcut keys are defined after the name of the command. For example, loadMovie(), in the Global Functions ⇨ Browser/Network menu, has a keyboard shortcut of Esc+l+m. If you give the Actions panel focus and press the Esc key, then the l key, then the m key, the loadMovie action appears in the actions list of the Script pane, complete with placeholders for arguments. The shortcut will not work if you try to press the keys simultaneously—you must press the keys in sequence, as described in the previous example. Each key must be pressed and released before you type the following key(s) in the shortcut.

Tip

To make sure that you don't have any syntax errors after reorganizing code, click the Check Syntax button in the Actions panel toolbar. Flash alerts you if there are scripting errors by placing messages in the Output panel.

Also, use the new Script Navigator in the lower-left corner of the Actions panel to quickly switch back and forth between keyframe or object code. For example, you can choose one frame in the Script Navigator, copy its code, and then switch to another frame to paste the code.

The Help panel

Don't know what the methods of the Sound object are? Need to see if the getVersion() function will work in a Flash Player 4–compatible movie? Flash MX 2004 has revamped the help materials and conveniently nested everything in the Help panel. Among other items, the new Help panel contains all the syntax of the ActionScript language. You can access the Help panel in a few ways:

✦ Choose Help ➪ Help, or press F1.

✦ Click the Reference icon in the Actions panel.

✦ Right-click (or Control+click on Mac) an action in the left-hand Actions pane of the Actions panel and choose View Help in the contextual menu.

Let's quickly show you how to use the new Help panel in an actual Flash document:

1. Open a new document (File ➪ New).

2. Select frame 1 of Layer 1, and open the Actions panel by pressing F9.

3. Open the Global Functions booklet and click the Browser/Network booklet. Double-click the loadMovie action. The action will appear in the Script pane, as shown in Figure 24-1.

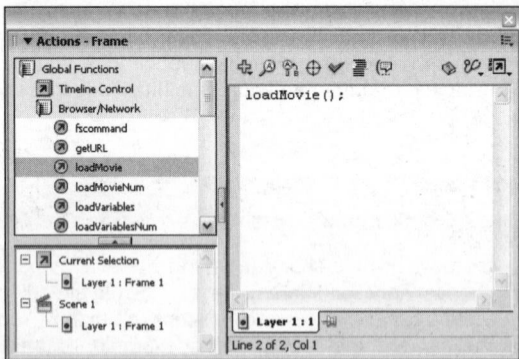

Figure 24-1: The Actions panel with a loadMovie() action in the Script pane

Using the #include Action

ActionScript has a processing directive hat enables you to insert external text files (with a .as file extension). You can write ActionScript in any text or script editor and save that text separately from the Flash document (.fla file). When you publish a Flash movie (.swf file) from the Flash document, Flash MX 2004 will retrieve the AS file and insert the actions to the action list where the #include action was issued. For example, the following code could be written in a contact.as file, which, as the name implies, contains a person's contact information for the Flash movie:

```
contactName = "Joseph Farnsworth";
contactStreet = "675 Locust Street";
contactCity = "Chicago";
contactState = "IL";
contactPhone = "312-555-1342";
contactEmail = "jfarnsworth@mycompany.com";
```

In a Flash document, you could insert this code into a keyframe of the Main Timeline (or a Movie Clip timeline) by using the #include action. You can use the #include action within any Flash event handler including keyframe, Button instance, onClipEvent, and so on:

```
#include "contact.as"
```

Make sure you do *not* insert a semicolon at the end of the #include line. Think of the #include action as a special tag for Flash MX 2004, letting it know that it should replace the #include line of code with all the code within the referred file. The following code will result in a "malformed" error in the Output window, upon testing or publishing the Flash document:

```
#include "contact.as";
```

Why is the #include action useful? For experienced programmers, the #include command allows freedom to write ActionScript in any text editor. You can define entire code libraries of custom functions. These .as libraries can then be reused from movie to movie. In ActionScript 2.0, custom classes *must* be defined in a separate AS file.

Note that the #include action is executed only upon publishing or testing the Flash movie. You cannot upload AS files to your Web server for "live" insertion of Flash ActionScript. Anytime you change the AS file, you will need to republish your Flash movie (.swf file).

You can find more information on the #include action in Chapter 34, "Managing and Troubleshooting Flash Movies." We use the #include action extensively in Chapter 32, "Creating a Portfolio Site in Flash." As we discuss in Chapter 3, "Planning Flash Projects", you can track all of the AS files in the new Project panel of Flash MX 2004 Professional as well.

4. Select the text loadMovie in the Script pane, making sure *not* to select the (); portion of the action. Click the Reference icon (that is, the blue book with the question mark) at the top right of the Actions panel. The Help panel will open, displaying the definition for the loadMovie() action, as shown in Figure 24-2.

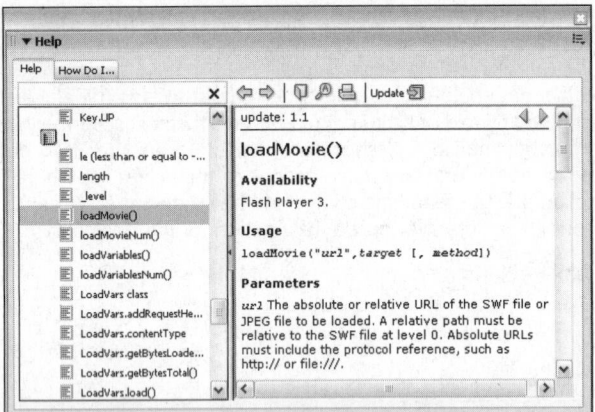

Figure 24-2: The Help panel with the definition for `loadMovie`

You can select other actions from the left pane of the Help panel and view their descriptions.

Tip   You can also print descriptions from the Help panel by choosing Print from the options menu at the top-right corner of the panel.

ActionScript 1.0 and 2.0

So what's all the fuss about ActionScript now? Let's make one thing clear right away: for most Flash designers and developers, or rather for most of the work you need to get done in Flash, the graduation of ActionScript 1.0 to 2.0 may mean next to nothing at all. This isn't to say that ActionScript 2.0 should be ignored or is not a monumental leap forward for Flash programming—we simply want to calm or allay any fears you might have after reading about Flash MX 2004's new features. If you've used ActionScript in Flash MX or Flash 5, then ActionScript 1.0 refers to the coding styles that those versions of the application used.

ActionScript 2.0 introduces a couple of major structural changes to the way in which you can code Flash ActionScript. To begin with, it uses strong data typing. You learn more about data typing in Chapter 26, "Using Functions and Arrays," but for now, know that ActionScript 2.0 imposes some rules on how you can assign values to variables, functions, and other constructors in your code. Unless you're creating code that uses custom classes and object-oriented programming concepts such as inheritance and prototypes, you won't really need to worry about whether your code will work as ActionScript 2.0 code. Another big change with ActionScript 2.0 is case-sensitivity. Prior to Flash MX 2004, most ActionScript terms were case-insensitive, meaning you could refer to object references or variables with varying cases, such as:

```
var firstName = "Robert";
var lastName = "Reinhardt";
var fullName = firstName + " " + lastName;
```

In ActionScript 1.0, you could have used the following code as the last line, without receiving an error:

```
var fullName = firstname + " " + lastname;
```

However, in ActionScript 2.0, that same line of code would be incorrect because `firstname` and `lastname` are not using the same case as the original variables.

Why should the distinction between ActionScript 1.0 and 2.0 even be an issue? For starters, when you publish a Flash movie for Flash Player 6 or 7, you need to decide how Flash MX 2004 will compile the ActionScript code in your document. In the Publish Settings dialog box, you can choose which ActionScript version to publish in the Flash tab. Unless directed otherwise, you'll publish most of the Flash movies for Part VII of this book as ActionScript 2.0, even though it pretty much looks and feels like ActionScript 1.0.

One Part of the Sum: ActionScript Variables

In any scripting or programming language, you will need some type of "memory" device — something that can remember the values and properties of objects or significant data. This type of memory device is referred to as a *variable*.

Variables are named storage places for changeable pieces of data (numbers and letters). One of the first obstacles for designers learning a scripting language is the concept that variable names in and of themselves have no meaning or value to the computer. Remember that the computer can't perform anything unless you tell it to. Even though any given scripting language has a certain set of built-in properties and functions, variables can simplify your scripting workload by creating shortcuts or aliases to other elements of the ActionScript language. One prime example of a "shortcut" variable is the pathname to a deeply nested Movie Clip instance, such as:

```
_root.birdAnim.birdHouse.birdNest.birdEgg
```

truncated to a variable named `pathToEgg` as:

```
var pathToEgg = _root.birdAnim.birdHouse.birdNest.birdEgg;
```

Once `pathToEgg` is declared and given a value, you can reuse it without referring to the lengthy path name, as in:

```
with(pathToEgg){
    gotoAndPlay("start");
}
```

The important concept here is that you could just as easily have given `pathToEgg` a different name, such as `myPath`, or `robPath`, or whatever word(s) you'd like to use. As long as the syntax and formatting of the expression is correct, you have nothing to worry about.

Another example of a variable that stores path information is the URL to a Web resource, such as a CGI script. Oftentimes, you may have different server URLs for testing and deployment. Instead of changing the URL in every action of the Flash document, you can use a variable name. That way, you only need to change your variable's value once. In the following sample code, a variable named `serverURL` is set to the actual URL you want to access. You then refer to that `serverURL` name in other actions, such as `getURL()`.

```
serverURL = "http://www.flashsupport.com/";
getURL(serverURL);
```

Note   Variables in ActionScript are "typed," meaning that their value is explicitly set to be either a string, number, Boolean, or object. When working with variables, you must therefore know what data type the value is. We discuss data typing in Chapter 26, "Using Functions and Arrays."

Variables in ActionScript are attached to the timeline of the movie or Movie Clip instance on which they are created. If you create a variable x on the Main Timeline, that variable is available for other scripting actions on that timeline. However, from other Movie Clip timelines, the variable is not directly accessible. To access the value of a variable on another timeline (such as a Movie Clip instance), enter the target path to the clip instance in which the variable resides, a dot (.); then enter the variable name. For instance, this statement sets the variable foo to be equal to the value of the variable bar in Movie Clip instance named ball:

```
var foo = _root.ball.bar;
```

This statement, on the other hand, sets the variable foo to be equal to the value of the variable bar on the Main Timeline:

```
var foo = _root.bar;
```

Tip   Variables in ActionScript 1.0 are not case-sensitive and cannot start with a number. Variables in ActionScript 2.0 are case-sensitive.

Flash Player 6 introduced a new location to store variables, independent of any timeline: _global. You can access global variables from any object or timeline in the Flash movie — hence the name global. You only need to specify the _global path to assign a value to the global variable. To read a global variable, you simply specify the name. For example, on frame 1 of the Main Timeline, you can specify the following ActionScript in the Actions panel:

```
_global.firstName = "George";
```

Then, if you wanted to use the firstName variable within a Movie Clip instance's timeline, you simply refer to the variable firstName. The following code will insert the firstName variable into a TextField object named user. This code would be placed inside of a Movie Clip symbol containing the TextField object:

```
user.text = firstName;
```

Even though the _global path is not specified, Flash Player 6 or 7 looks for a variable named firstName on the current timeline. If a variable by that name does not exist on the current timeline, Flash Player 6 looks in _global for the variable and returns any value for that variable.

Caution   You need to publish your Flash documents as Flash Player 6 or 7 movies to use the _global path. The global namespace can be used in ActionScript 1.0 or 2.0.

String literals

In programmer speak, a string is any combination of alphanumeric characters. By themselves, they have no meaning. It is up to you to assign something meaningful to them. For example, giving a variable the name firstName doesn't mean much. You need to assign a value to the variable firstName to make it meaningful, and you can do something with it. For example, if firstName = "Susan", you could make something specific to "Susan" happen.

You can also use much simpler name/value pairs, such as i = 0, to keep track of counts. If you want a specific Movie Clip animation to loop only three times, you can increment the value of i by 1 (for example, i = i + 1, i += 1, and i ++ all do the same thing) each time the animation loops back to the start. Then, you can stop the animation when it reaches the value of 3.

Expressions

Flash uses the term *expression* to refer to two separate kinds of code fragments in ActionScript. An expression is either a phrase of code used to compare values in a Conditional or a Loop (these are known as *conditional expressions*), or a snippet of code that is interpreted at runtime (these are known as *numeric expressions* and *string expressions*). We discuss conditional expressions later in this chapter.

Numeric and string expressions are essentially just segments of ActionScript code that are dynamically converted to their calculated values when a movie runs. For instance, suppose you have a variable, y, set to a value of 3. In the statement x = y + 1, the y + 1 on the right side of the equal sign is an expression. Hence, when the movie runs, the statement x = y + 1 actually becomes x = 4, because the value of y (which is 3) is retrieved (or "interpreted") and the calculation 3 + 1 is performed. Numeric and string expressions are an extremely potent part of ActionScript because they permit most of the parameters used in actions to be based on mathematical calculations and external variables rather than requiring fixed information. Consider these two examples:

✦ The parameter of a gotoAndPlay() action could be set as an expression that returns a random number in a certain range, sending the movie to a random frame:

```
this.gotoAndPlay(Math.random()*100);
```

✦ The URL option in a getURL() action could be made up of a variable that indicates a server name and a literal string, which is the file path:

```
var serverName = "http://localhost/";
var filePath = "resources/showRecent.cfm";
getURL(serverName + filePath);
```

As we mentioned in an earlier section, to change all the URLs in your movie from a staging server to a live server you'd just have to change the value of the server variable. So, to change the latter example's code for a live Web server, you'd simply change the serverName variable, as the following code demonstrates:

```
var serverName = "http://www.flashsupport.com/";
```

All of the other lines of code would stay the same, because you only needed to change the server location for the live Web site.

Anywhere that you see the word "expression" in any action options, you can use an interpreted ActionScript expression to specify the value of the option.

To use a string inside an expression, simply add quotation marks around it. Anything surrounded by quotation marks is taken as a literal string. For example, the conditional: if (status == ready) wrongly checks whether the value of the variable status is the same as the value of the nonexistent variable ready. The correct conditional would check whether the value of status is the same as the string "ready" by quoting it, as in: if (status == "ready").

You can even have expressions that indirectly refer to previously established variables. In ActionScript, you can use the dot syntax (and array access operators) to indirectly refer to variables, or you can use Flash 4's eval() function (to maintain backward compatibility).

We like to use the phrase "setting and getting" to help beginners understand how equations and expressions work in ActionScript code. An equation is any line of code that sets an object or variable to a new value. The order of syntax terms can be confusing to designers and developers new to code writing. Do you specify a value first? How do you know where to insert the equal sign (=)? If you remember the phrase "setting and getting," you'll know how to write basic equations. The variable you want to set (or assign a new value) is always on the left side of the equation, while the new value is always on the right:

```
what you want to set = the value you want to get
```

For example, if you wanted to set a variable named `currentTime` to the amount of time that has elapsed since the Flash movie started playing in the Flash Player, you would place `currentTime` on the left side of the equation and place the actual value of the time on the right side:

```
current time in the movie = the number of milliseconds that have elapsed
```

Translated into actual code, this would be:

```
var currentTime = getTimer();
```

Again, another important aspect of variables to remember is that the name of a variable is quite arbitrary. What we called `currentTime` could just as well be named `myTime`, `movieTime`, `elapsedTime`—or whatever you want to call it. As long as you consistently refer to your variable's name in subsequent ActionScript code, everything will work as expected.

Array access operators

If you have a variable called `name_1`, you can write the expression `_root["name_" + "1"]` to refer to the value of `name_1`. How is this useful? If you have more than one variable, but their prefixes are the same (for example, `name_1`, `name_2`, `name_3`, and so on), you can write an expression with two variables as a generic statement to refer to any one of the previously established variables: `_root["name" + i]`, where `i` can be any predefined number. This type of expression is most commonly found in a code loop; you learn more about loops later in this chapter.

eval() function and Flash 4's Set Variable

If you want to use old-fashioned ActionScript to indirectly refer to variable names and values, you have two ways to go about it:

✦ Use the `Set Variable` action, specifying the variable name as a Slash-notated expression:

```
set("/name_" add i, "Robert Reinhardt");
```

✦ Use the `eval()` function, specifying the variable as an expression:

```
eval("_root.name_" add i) = "Robert Reinhardt";
```

Note   This usage is specific to Flash Player 4 compatibility. Unless you are authoring movies to be compatible for this player, you should use the most current syntax.

Variables as declarations

In most scripting languages, you usually don't have to declare a variable without its value; that is, you don't need to say variable `firstName` and then address it again with a value. In Flash ActionScript, you don't need to pre-establish a variable in order to invoke it.

Note As you start to code more complex scripts in ActionScript 2.0, such as creating custom classes, you do need to pre-declare variable names. As you're starting out with more basic scripts, you do not need to be so thorough with your code.

If you want to create a variable on the fly from a Movie Clip to the Main Timeline, you can. Most variables that you use in Flash will be declared in a timeline's keyframes. Let's create a couple of simple variables in a Flash document:

1. Open a new Flash document (File ➪ New). In the New Document dialog box, choose Flash Document and click OK.

2. Rename Layer 1 to **actions**.

3. Select frame 1 of the actions layer in the Timeline window, and open the Actions panel by pressing the F9 key. Type the following action in the Script pane. (See Figure 24-3.)

```
var firstName = "Franklin";
```

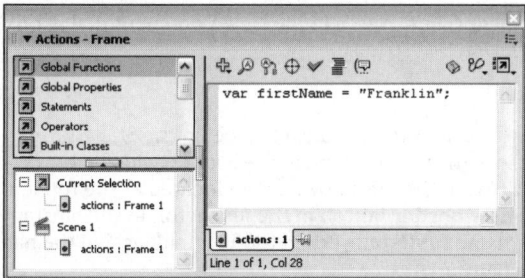

Figure 24-3: A variable declaration in the Actions panel

4. Save your Flash document as `variable_frame.fla`, and test it (Ctrl+Enter or ⌘+Enter). Choose Debug ➪ List Variables (Ctrl+Alt+V or Option+⌘+V). In the Output panel, you will see the following line of text:

```
Variable _level0.firstName = "Franklin"
```

As you can see in this example, the `firstName` variable is shown at `_level0`, which is the `_root` of the current Flash movie. All variables belong to a specific timeline or object.

On the CD-ROM You can find the sample file, `variable_frame.fla`, in the `ch24` folder of this book's CD-ROM.

Variables as text fields

Since Flash 4, text can be specified as *text fields*. A text field can be used as a dynamic text container whose content can be updated via ActionScript and/or the intervention of a server-side script (known in Flash MX 2004 as *Dynamic text*), or it can accept input from the user (known in Flash MX 2004 as *Input text*).

You can access a text field's properties by selecting the text field and opening the Property inspector. In the inspector, you can define the parameters of the text object, including its Var (for Variable) name and instance name.

Note Text fields in Flash MX 2004 are `TextField` objects. The instance name of a `TextField` object should be different from the Var name. In fact, we recommend that, as a general rule of thumb, you do not specify a Var name for text fields in Flash Player 6 or 7–compatible movies.

An Input text field is editable when the Flash movie is played in the Flash Player; the user can type text into the text field. This newly typed text becomes the value of the text field's Var name, or the `text` property of the text field. On a login screen, you can create an Input text field with an instance name `login_txt`, where the user enters his or her name, such as Joe. In ActionScript, this would be received as `login_txt.text = "Joe"`. Any text that you type into a text field during the authoring process will be that property's initial value.

To review this process of text fields and variable names, let's create a simple example:

1. Create a new Flash document (File ➪ New). In the New Document dialog box, choose Flash Document and click OK.

2. Rename Layer 1 to **textfield**.

3. In the Tools panel, choose the Text tool, and click once on the Stage. Extend the text field to accommodate at least five characters. In the Property inspector (Window ➪ Properties), choose **Input Text** in the drop-down menu located at the top-left corner of the inspector. Click the **Show border** button in the inspector. In the <Instance Name> field, assign the instance name **firstName_txt**. In the Var field, assign the name **firstName_var**. Refer to Figure 24-4.

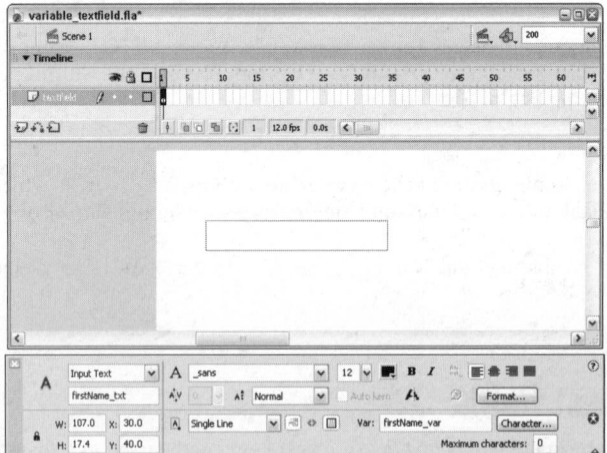

Figure 24-4: The Property inspector settings for the Input Text field

4. Save your Flash document as `variable_textfield.fla`, and test it (Ctrl+Enter or ⌘+Enter). In the Test Movie window, type your name into the `firstName_txt` text field. Then, choose Debug ➪ List Variables. Among other information, you will see the following lines of text:

```
Variable _level0.firstName_var = "Holly"
Edit Text: Target="_level0.firstName_txt"
    variable = "firstName_var",
    text = "Holly",
```

Note that this sample assumes that the name Holly was typed into the text field.

This simple exercise demonstrates how the Var assignment of a `TextField` object differs from the instance name assignment. The actual text displayed in the `TextField` object can be accessed in two ways: as a variable called `firstName_var`, or as a property of the `TextField` object, `firstName.text`. Dynamic text fields behave in the same manner as well.

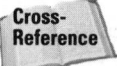

For an introduction to all of the different types of text fields, read Chapter 8, "Working with Text." We will explore more ActionScript-related aspects of text fields in Chapter 31, "Applying HTML and Text Field Formatting."

Declaring Variables in ActionScript

There are several ways to establish, or declare, variables in a Flash movie. You can create them directly with ActionScript (or with `TextField` objects, as shown in the last section), load them from a text file or server-side script, or include them in HTML tags.

Using actions to define variables

The most common way to create a variable is to type the variable's name and value in the Script pane of the Actions panel, on a specific timeline's keyframe. Most basic variables will have values that are string literals.

Note that the `var` syntax can be used for local variables that exist only for the duration of a function execution.

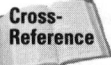

We discuss local variables in Chapter 26, "Using Functions and Arrays."

Loading variables from a predefined source

You can also establish variables by loading them from an external source, such as a text file located on your Web server or even through a database query or a server-side script. By using the `loadVariables()` action, you can load variables in this fashion. There are three primary parameters for the `loadVariables()` action: URL, target, and variables:

```
loadVariables(url, target, [,variables]);
```

The *variables* parameter is optional. In the Help panel pages in the ActionScript Dictionary, any parameters displayed with surrounding left and right brackets ([ ]) are optional.

Note There's more than one way to load data into Flash Player 6 and 7-compatible movies. See the cross-reference note at the end of this section.

URL specifies the source of the variables to be loaded. This can be a relative link to the variable source (you don't need to enter the full path of the resource). You can specify whether this URL value is a literal value (`"http://www.theMakers.com/cgi-bin/search.cfm"`) or an expression that uses a variable or a combination of variables (`serverURL + scriptPath + scriptApp`). If you want to point to a specific file, type its relative path and name here. If you want to access a database that returns dynamic data, insert the path to the script, such as `"http://www.domain.com/cgi-bin/search.pl"`.

The *target* parameter determines where the variables are to be loaded. You can send the name/value pairs to a level or a timeline target. If you want the variables to be available on the Main Timeline, use `_root` or `_level0`. You can also specify a Movie Clip target using a relative or absolute address. To load to the current Movie Clip (the one initiating the `loadVariables` action), use the target `this`.

The last option is *variables*, and this parameter specifies whether you are sending and loading (in other words, receiving) variables. If you want to load variables from a static source, such as a text file, you should omit this parameter. If you are sending a query to a database-driven engine, then you may need to specify either `"GET"` or `"POST"`. Note that the use of `loadVariables()` in the `GET` or `POST` method means that you are sending variables declared on the active timeline to the specified URL, which, in turn, will send name/value pairs back to the Flash movie.

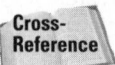

Cross-Reference In Chapter 30, "Sending Data In and Out of Flash," you learn how to send variables out of a Flash movie to a server-side script.

The formatting of name/value pairs is standard URL-encoded text. If you want to encode name/values in a text file (or a database), you need to use the following format:

```
variable=value&variable=value...
```

Basically, in URL-encoded text, name/value pairs are joined by an ampersand (&). To join multiple terms in a value, use the plus (+) symbol, as in:

```
name1=Joe+Smith&name2=Susan+Deboury
```

Cross-Reference There are several ways to load data into a Flash movie. Flash Player 6 introduced the `LoadVars` object, which gives you more control over dynamic data. The `LoadVars` object is discussed in Chapter 30, "Sending Data In and Out of Flash." You also learn more about URL-encoded text in that chapter.

Sending variables to URLs

You can also send variables to a URL by using the `getURL()` action. Any name/value pairs that are declared on the active timeline will be sent along with the `getURL()` action if a variable send method is defined (`GET` or `POST`). Note that `getURL()` is only used to send variables out of a Flash movie — it will not retrieve or load any subsequent name/value pairs. If you use a `getURL()` action on a Movie Clip timeline as follows:

```
var firstName = "Robert";
getURL("/cgi-bin/form.cgi", "_blank", "GET");
```

the Flash movie will send the following request to your server:

```
http://www.server.com/cgi-bin/form.cgi?firstName=Robert;
```

The output of the `form.cgi` script would be opened in a new browser window (`"_blank"`).

 **Note**   Any terms that follow a question mark (?) in a URL is called a *query string*. The name/value pairs in a query string are usually provided an input or filter to a server-side script.

Establishing variables with HTML

You can also send variables to Flash movies in the `<embed>` and `<object>` tags that call the Flash movie. In the SRC attribute of `<embed>` or the `param name="movie"` subtag of the `<object>` tag, attach the name/value pairs to the end of the Flash movie filename, separated by a question mark (?).

```
<object ... >
<param name="movie" value="flash.swf?name=Rob" />
<embed src="flash.swf?name=Rob" ... />
```

This method works with Flash Player 4 or later movies. However, Flash Player 6 and 7 can recognize a new HTML attribute, `flashvars`. Now, you can specify longer strings of name/value pairs that will be declared in the Flash movie as soon as it loads into the Flash Player. The previous method that we showed is limited to strings that are about 1,024 characters long (depending on the Web browser), which include the movie's full URL. With the newer `flashvars` attribute, you don't need to rely on the URL of the movie. Here's an example of declaring a few variables with the `flashvars` attribute:

```
<object ...>
<param name="movie" name="flash.swf" />
<param name="flashvars"
name="firstName=Gregory&lastName=Smith&address=1234+Hollywood+Way" />
<embed src="flash.swf"
flashvars="firstName=Greg&lastName=Smith&street=1234+Broadway" ... />
```

In practical use, you would not likely hard code the name/value pairs directly into the HTML document. You can use client-side JavaScript or server-side scripting (such as ASP.NET or ColdFusion) to dynamically "write" the name/value pairs into the HTML document before it is served to the user's Web browser.

Creating Expressions in ActionScript

You can write expressions either by manually typing in the primary option fields of ActionScript commands, or by dragging and dropping actions from action booklets in the Actions panel. There are no scripting wizards in Flash; Flash MX 2004 does not automatically script anything for you (not counting components, which already include many lines of code to perform specific tasks for you). However, Flash provides you with booklets of operators, objects, and functions available in the ActionScript language.

Operators

Operators perform combinations, mathematical equations, and value comparisons. See Table 24-1 for a list of common operators in the ActionScript language.

General and numeric operators

These operators are used for common mathematical operations of adding, subtracting, multiplying, and dividing. You can also use these operators to compare numeric values, such as > or <.

```
if (results > 1)
name = "Robert";
_root["name_" + i] = newName;
```

String operators

The Flash Player 4-specific operator add joins one value with another value or expression. If you want to concatenate two variables to create a new variable, use the add string operator. Again, this syntax should be used only for Flash Player 4 movies.

```
set ("fullName", firstName add " " add lastName);
```

Logical operators

These operators join several expressions to create conditions. We discuss these further in the "Checking conditions: If . . . Else actions" section of this chapter.

```
// Flash Player 5 and later syntax below

if (results > 1 && newResults < 10){
    // do something...
}

// Flash Player 4 syntax below

if (results > Number("1") and newResults < Number("10")){
    // do something...
}
```

Table 24-1 describes the ActionScript operators available in Flash 4 and higher syntax.

Table 24-1: ActionScript Operators

Flash 5+	Flash 4	Description
+	+	Adds number values (all player versions) and joins, or *concatenates*, strings in Flash Player 5 and later.
-	-	Subtracts number values.
*	*	Multiplies number values.
/	/	Divides number values.
=	=	Equals; used for assignment of variables, properties, methods, and so on in Flash Player 5 or later.
==	=	Numeric operator: Is equal to; used for comparison in if/else . . .else if conditions.
!=	<>	Numeric operator: Does not equal.
<	<	Less than.

Flash 5+	Flash 4	Description
>	>	Greater than.
<=	<=	Less than or equal to.
>=	>=	Greater than or equal to.
( )	( )	Groups operations together, as in $x = (x+y) * 3;$.
" "	" "	Indicates that the enclosed value should be interpreted as a string, not as an expression.
==	eq	String operator: Is equal to; for example, if (name == "derek") or if (name eq "derek").
=== (F6+)	N/A	Strict equality operator; both of the compared values must be the same data type and value. This operator is compatible only with Flash Player 6 or higher.
!=	ne	String operator: Is not equal to.
!== (F6+)	N/A	Strict inequality operator; both of the compared values must have different values and data types. This operator is compatible only with Flash Player 6 or higher.
<	lt	Alphabetically before; if the strings compared have multiple characters, the first character determines the alphabetical position.
>	gt	Alphabetically after.
<=	le	Alphabetically before or the same as.
>=	ge	Alphabetically after or the same as.
+	add	Joins two strings together or adds a string to a variable.
&&	and	Logical comparison; requires that two or more conditions be met in a single comparison.
||	or	Logical comparison; requires that one of two or more conditions be met in a single comparison.
!	not	Logical comparison; requires that the opposite of a condition to be met in a single comparison.

Checking conditions: if . . . else actions

Conditions lie at the heart of logic. To create an intelligent machine (or application), you need to create a testing mechanism. This mechanism (called a conditional) needs to operate on rather simple terms as well. Remember the true/false tests you took in grade school? if/else statements work on a similar principle: If the condition is true, execute a set of actions. If the condition is false, disregard the enclosed actions and continue to the next condition or action.

You can simply create isolated if statements that do not employ an else (or else if) statement. Solitary if statements are simply ignored if the condition is false. else statements are used as a default measure in case the tested condition proves false. else if statements continue to test conditions if the previous if (or else if) was false. Refer to following examples for more insight.

✦ **Basic** `if` **statement:** The code between the curly braces is ignored if the condition is false.

```
if (condition is true){
    then execute this code
}
```

✦ **Extended** `if...else if...else` **statement:** If the first condition is true, the code immediately after the first condition is executed and the remaining `else if` and `else` statements are disregarded. However, if the first condition is not true, the second condition is tested. If the second condition is true, its code executes and all other statements in the `if` group are ignored. If all conditions prove false, the code between the curly braces of the final `else` is executed:

```
if ( first condition is true){
    then execute this code
} else if (second condition is true){
    then execute this code
} else {
    otherwise, execute this code
}
```

In production, you could have an `if/else` structure that assigned the value of one variable based on the value of another, such as:

```
if (x == 1){
  name = "Margaret";
} else if (x == 2){
  name = "Michael";
} else {
  name = "none";
}
```

Caution   Do not use a single = sign in a condition, as this actually sets the variable's value. For example, if you wrote `if (x = 1){}`, ActionScript actually sets x = 1, and does not check whether x's value is equal to 1. Moreover, the condition always evaluates to `true`. In our experience, many beginners make this common mistake in their ActionScript code. We can't emphasize enough the importance of making sure you use an == operator in `if` and `else if` expressions for "is equal to" comparisons.

You can add an `if` statement in ActionScript by choosing the `if` action from the plus (+) button in the toolbar of the Actions panel, or by selecting it from the Statements ➪ Conditions/Loops booklet. Between the parentheses of the `if()` statement, shown as the term *condition* in the code hint, enter the expression that identifies what circumstance must exist for the actions in your conditional to be executed. Remember that, in your expression, literal strings must be quoted, and the == operator must be used for string or numeric comparisons. To add an `else` clause, position the text cursor after the closing curly brace (}) of the `if()` statement, and then double-click the `else` or `else if` action in the Statements ➪ Conditions/Loops booklet.

Note   There's nothing stopping you from just typing the actions directly in the Script pane as well. Use the booklets as a guide at first, to learn about the choices you have available.

You can join two conditions using logical compound operators such as and (&&), or (||), or not (!), as in:

```
if (results >1 && newResults < 10){
    gotoAndPlay ("end");
} else if (results > 1 ! newResults < 10) {
    gotoAndPlay ("try_again");
}
```

In this sample code, the first if statement has two expressions — both need to be true in order for the gotoAndPlay("end"); code to execute. If both are not true, the else if condition executes. If the first condition is true *and* the second condition is not true, the gotoAndPlay("try_again"); code executes. If neither the if nor the else if conditions are true, then no code is executed.

We'll take a look at a step-by-step example of if statements in the exercise at the end of this chapter.

Branching conditions with switch() and case

In ActionScript, you can also use switch() and case statements. switch() and case can replace extended if and else if actions. Instead of declaring a true/false expression (as with if statements), switch() uses an expression that can return any value — you are not limited to true and false conditions with switch(). In pseudo-code, a switch() code structure would look like this:

```
test a value
    if the value equals this expression
        then execute this code
    if the value equals this expression
        then execute this code
    if none of the expressions match the value
        then execute this code
end test
```

In the previous code example, one or more "if" statements (called case clauses) could execute. Meaning, the tested value could execute more than one segment of code nested within the clauses. You could translate the previous pseudo-code into the following ActionScript code:

```
var currentFrame = _root._currentframe;
switch(currentFrame){
    case 10:
        helpBox.gotoAndStop("products");
    case 20:
        helpBox.gotoAndStop("services");
    case 30:
        helpBox.gotoAndStop("contact");
    default:
        helpBox._x = _root._xmouse;
        helpBox._y = _root._ymouse;
}
```

In the previous code example, although it's only possible for `currentFrame` to equal one value, the `default` clause will also execute—regardless of the value of `currentFrame`. However, you may not want to execute the `default` clause (or multiple `case` clauses). In this situation, you need to use the `break` action to "escape" the `switch()` action. The `break` action prevents subsequent clauses from being evaluated.

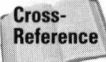

Cross-Reference   In the "Loops" section later in this chapter, the `break` action is discussed in more detail.

In the following code, only one clause can execute:

```
var currentFrame = _root._currentframe;
switch(currentFrame){
    case 10:
        helpBox.gotoAndStop("products");
        break;
    case 20:
        helpBox.gotoAndStop("services");
        break;
    case 30:
        helpBox.gotoAndStop("contact");
        break;
    default:
        helpBox._x = _root._xmouse;
        helpBox._y = _root._ymouse;
}
```

You can use `switch()` actions for many other situations. If you wanted to make a card game in Flash, you could use a `switch()` expression to pick a card suit based on a random number:

```
1.   var suitNum = Math.round(Math.random()*3);
2.   switch(suitNum){
3.       case 0:
4.           suit = "diamonds";
5.           break;
6.       case 1:
7.           suit = "spades";
8.           break;
9.       case 2:
10.          suit = "hearts";
11.          break;
12.      case 3:
13.          suit = "clubs";
14.          break;
15.  }
16.  cardFace.gotoAndStop(suit);
```

In this code, a random number is picked (line 1) and used as an expression in the `switch()` action (line 2). The random number (represented as a variable named `suitNum`) will then be matched to a `case` clause. The matching clause will set a variable named `suit` to equal a specific card suit and exit the `switch()` action (lines 3 through 15). A Movie Clip instance named `cardFace` will go to and stop on a frame named after one of the card suits (line 16).

Tip In a working example of a card game, the `switch()` code for the suit matching would occur within a function. We discuss functions in Chapter 26, "Using Functions and Arrays."

Note The `switch()`, `case`, and `default` actions can be used in Flash Player 4 or higher movies. Even though the `switch()` syntax was only introduced in Flash MX, the ActionScript will be compiled to be compatible with Flash Player 4 or 5 if you choose these versions in the Version menu of the Publish Settings' Flash tab.

Loops

A loop is a container for a statement or series of statements repeated as long as a specified condition is exists. A basic loop has three parts: the condition, the list of statements to be repeated, and a counter update. There are four types of loops in ActionScript:

✦ `while`

✦ `do . . . while`

✦ `for`

✦ `for . . . in`

Each of these loop types has a specific use. Depending on the repetitive actions you wish to loop, you need to decide how best to accommodate your code with loop actions.

Caution These types of code-based loops do not update the contents of the stage with each pass of a loop execution. If you want to automate changes over time on the stage through code, you'll need to use an `onEnterFrame()` event handler or a `setInterval()` function. You learn more about these types of actions in Chapter 25, "Controlling Movie Clips," and Chapter 33, "Creating a Game in Flash."

while (*condition*) { *actions* }

In this loop type, the condition of the loop is evaluated first, and, if it is true, the actions within the curly braces will be executed. The actions will loop indefinitely (causing a script error) unless there is a way out of the loop — a counter update. A counter update will increment (or decrement) the variable used in the `while` condition. Here you see a breakdown of a typical `while` loop. Note that a variable used in the condition is usually set just before the `while` action is executed.

```
count = 1;  // Initial variable
while (count <= 10){  // Condition
  _root["clip_" + count]._xscale = 100/count; // Statements to be repeated
  count = count + 1; // Counter update
}   // Termination of loop
```

In this example, a variable named `count` starts with a value of 1. The first time the `while` action executes, `count`'s value is less than (or equal to) 10. Therefore, the actions within the curly braces are executed. The first action in the loop uses the `count` value to form the name of a Movie Clip instance, `clip_1`, and alter its X Scale property by a value of 100/1 (which is equal to 100). Then the `count` variable is incremented by 1, giving it a new value of 2. The `while` condition is then re-evaluated.

The second time the `while` action is executed, `count`'s value, 2, is still less than (or equal to) 10. Therefore, the actions within the curly braces are executed again. This time, however, the first action in the loop will address the `clip_2` instance's X Scale property, and make that property's value 50 (100/2 = 50). Then, `count` will be incremented by 1, giving it a new value of 3. Again, the `while` condition is re-evaluated.

The `while` condition will continue to execute its nested actions until `count` exceeds a value of 10. Therefore, `clip_1` through `clip_10` will show a decrease in X Scale.

do { *actions* } while (*condition*);

This type of loop is very similar to the `while` loop discussed previously, with one important exception: The actions in the `do{}` nesting will always be executed at least once. In a `do . . . while` loop, the condition is evaluated after the actions in the loop are executed. If the `while` condition is `true`, the actions in the `do{}` nesting will be executed again. If the `while` condition is `false`, the loop will no longer execute.

```
count = 1;  // Initial variable
do{  // do loop
  _root["clip_" + count]._xscale = 100/count; // Statements to be repeated
  count = count + 1; // Counter update
} while (count <= 1); // Condition
```

In this example, the actions within the `do{}` nesting will execute automatically without checking any condition. Therefore, the X Scale of `clip_1` will be set to 100, and the `count` value will increase by 1, giving it a new value of 2. After the actions execute once, the condition is checked. Because the value of `count` is not less than (or equal to) 1, the loop does not continue to execute.

for (*initialize; condition; next*) { *actions* }

The `for` loop is a supercondensed `while` loop. Instead of assigning, checking, and reassigning a variable action in three different actions, a `for` loop enables you to define, check, and reassign the value of a counter variable.

```
for(i = 1; i <= 10; i++){ // Initial variable value, condition, and update
  _root["clip_" + i]._xscale = 100/i; // Statements to be repeated
}  // Termination of loop
```

This `for` loop does exactly the same as the `while` loop example we used earlier. When the loop is started, the variable `i` is given a starting value of 1. A condition for the loop is specified next, `i <= 10`. In this case, we want the loop to repeat the nested actions until the value of `i` exceeds 10. The third parameter of the `for` loop, `i++`, indicates that `i`'s value should be increased by 1 with each pass of the loop. Note that this parameter can use `++` (to increase by 1) or `--` (to decrease by 1) operators. You can also use expressions such as `i = i*2` for the update.

for (*variableIterant* in *object*) { *actions* }

The final type of loop, `for . . . in`, is the most complex looping mechanism. A `for . . . in` loop does not need a condition statement. Rather, this loop works with a find-and-replace keyword mechanism. Basically, a *variableIterant* is declared, which is simply a placeholder for a property or position index within an object or array, respectively. For every occurrence of the variableIterant, the actions within the for . . . in {} nesting will be executed. The for . . . in loop can only be used with objects and arrays, and even then, not all properties of this elements can be enumerated.

```
for(var name in _root){//Placeholder and object
  if(_root[name] instanceof MovieClip){ // Check the data type of the object
    _root[name]._xscale = 50; // Statements to be repeated
  } // end if statement
} // Termination of loop
```

In the preceding code example, the term name is used to designate a property of the _root timeline. In this case, we want to change all Movie Clip instances on the Main Timeline to a 50 percent X Scale value. We don't need to specify the actual target paths of each individual instance—the for . . . in loop will search for all instances on the Main Timeline, apply the change, and exit the loop.

Although this might look a bit confusing, it can be more helpful than you can imagine. Have you ever had a bunch of nested Movie Clip instances that all needed to play at the same time? In Flash 4, you would have had to use several tellTarget(){} actions, each one specifying the target path. You could use a while loop to shorten the lengthy code, but, even still, you would need to list the specific parts of the each Movie Clip path, as in:

```
count = 1;
while(count <= 10){
    path = eval("_root.clip_" + count);
    tellTarget(path){
        play();
    }
    count++;
}
```

In Flash 4, the preceding code block would tell clip_1 through clip_10 to start playing. But what if you didn't know (or care to remember) all the paths to several differently named Movie Clip instances? For example, if you had a Movie Clip instance named nestAnim with several nested Movie Clip instances with different names (for example, squareAnim, triangleAnim, and circleAnim), you would have to specifically name these instances as targets. In Flash 5 or MX, the for . . . in loop would let you control any and all nested Movie Clip instances simultaneously:

```
for(var name in nestAnim){
    nestAnim[name].play();
}
```

With just three lines of code, all Movie Clip instances in the nestAnim Movie Clip instance will start to play. How? Remember that the variableIterant name is simply a placeholder for a property of the nestAnim Movie Clip object. The for . . . in loop will find every occurrence of an instance inside of nestAnim. And the word name has no significance. We could use a variableIterant myName, and everything would still work fine. Think of the variableIterant as a wildcard in file searches or directory listings in MS-DOS or UNIX:

```
nestAnim[*].play();
```

Although this syntax won't work with ActionScript, it does illustrate the processing of a for . . . in loop. Everything and anything that is playable on the nestAnim timeline will play.

Check out the `mcPlay.fla` and `forInLoop.fla` files, located in the `ch24` folder of the CD-ROM that accompanies this book.

break

The `break` action is not a type of loop — it is an action that enables you to quickly exit a loop if a subordinate condition exists. Suppose you wanted to loop an action that hides, at most, `clip_1` through `clip_10` (out of a possible 20 Movie Clip instances), but you want to have a variable control the overall limit of the loop, as `upperLimit` does in the following code block. `upperLimit`'s value could change at different parts of the presentation, but at no point do we want to hide more than `clip_1` through `clip_10`. We could use a `break` action in a nested `if` action to catch this:

```
count = 1;
while(count <= upperLimit){
    if(count > 10){
        break;
    }
    _root["clip_" + count]._visible = false;
    count++;
}
```

Tip   You can use `break` statements to catch errors in your loops (such as during a debug process). However, you may want to check out Flash's breakpoint feature in the Actions and Debugger panels. For more information on this feature, read Chapter 34, "Managing and Troubleshooting Flash Movies."

continue

Like the `break` action, `continue` enables you to exit the execution of actions within a loop. However, a `continue` action won't exit the loop action. It simply restarts the loop (and continues evaluating the current condition). Usually, you will place a `continue` action with an `if` nest — otherwise, it will always interrupt the actions within the `loop` action. For example, if you wanted to omit a particular value from going through the `loop` actions, you could use the `continue` action to bypass that value. In the following code block, we hide `clip_1` through `clip_10`, except for `clip_5`:

```
count = 1;
while(count <= 10){
    if(count == 5){
        count++;
        continue;
    }
    _root["clip_" + count]._visible = false;
    count++;
}
```

Adding a loop to your actions list

To create a loop, add one of the loop-type actions in the Actions panel, using the plus (+) button in the toolbar of the panel (or selecting it from the Statements ⇨ Conditions/Loops booklet).

With code hints enabled, replace the *condition* code hint term with an expression that describes the conditions under which the loop should continue repeating. Before the end of the loop, be sure to update whatever the loop relies on in order to continue, usually a counter. If you forget to update a counter, you will be stuck forever in the loop, and Flash will imperiously stop the script from continuing.

Loops in ActionScript are not appropriate for running background processes that listen for conditions to become true elsewhere in the movie. While a loop is in progress, the screen is not updated and no mouse events are captured, so most Flash actions are effectively not executable from within a loop. Loop actions are best suited to abstract operations such as string handling (for example, to check each letter of a word to see whether it contains an @ symbol) and dynamic variable assignment.

Loops to execute repetitive actions over time, which affect tangible objects in the movie, should be created as repeating frames in Movie Clips. To create a permanently running process, make a Movie Clip with two keyframes. On the first frame, call the subroutine or add the statements that you want to execute; on the second frame use a gotoAndPlay(1); action to return to the first frame. Alternatively, you can use the onClipEvent(enterFrame), onEnterFrame() handler, or setInterval() function to execute repetitive actions.

The onClipEvent() and onEnterFrame() handlers are discussed in the next chapter, "Controlling Movie Clips."

Properties

Properties are characteristics (such as width and height) of movies and Movie Clips that can be retrieved and set. You can use variables to store the current value of a given property, such as:

```
var xPos = _root._xmouse;
```

which stores the current X position of the mouse pointer (relative to the Stage coordinates of the Main Timeline) in the variable xPos.

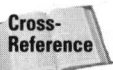

See Chapter 25, "Controlling Movie Clips," for more information on Movie Clip (and movie) properties.

Built-in functions

ActionScript contains a number of native programming commands known as *functions*. Among others, these functions include getTimer(), getVersion(), parseFloat(), parseInt(), escape(), and unescape(). It's beyond the scope of this chapter (and this book) to discuss the practical use of every new function and ActionScript element in Flash MX 2004. We do, however, discuss many built-in functions throughout this part of the *Macromedia Flash MX 2004 Bible*.

Because ActionScript has expanded so much over recent versions of the Flash authoring tool, Robert Reinhardt and Joey Lott created a companion book, the *Flash MX 2004 ActionScript Bible*, to specifically address all the terms of the ActionScript language.

Subroutines in Flash Player 4 Movies

To create a subroutine in Flash Player 4-compatible movies, first attach an action or series of actions to a keyframe. Next, give that keyframe a label. That's it, you have a subroutine. To call your subroutine from any other keyframe or button, simply add a `call()` action, and then enter the name of frame containing the subroutine as the parameter of the action. Use the following syntax: Start with the target path to the timeline on which the subroutine keyframe resides, enter a colon (`:`), and then enter the subroutine name (for example, `call ("/bouncingball:getRandom")`). When you call a subroutine, all the actions on the specified keyframe are executed. The subroutine must be present on the movie timeline (either as a keyframe or an embedded Movie Clip instance) for it to work.

Subroutines in Flash Player 4 movies do not accept passed parameters, nor do they return any values. To simulate passing and receiving variable values, set the necessary variable values in the action list that calls the subroutine before the frame is called, and then have the subroutine set other variables that can be retrieved afterward by any other actions.

Creating and calling subroutines

Whether they're called functions, subroutines, or methods, most programming languages provide a mechanism for programmers to create self-contained code modules that can be executed from anywhere in a program. ActionScript supports subroutines by using the ActionScript `function` constructor. You can create functions on any timeline, and, just like Movie Clip instances, functions have absolute or relative paths that must be used to invoke them. For example, if you have the following function on a Movie Clip named `functions_mc`, located on the Main Timeline:

```
function makeDuplicate(target, limit){
    for(var i=1; i<=limit; i++){
        _root[target].duplicateMovieClip(target + "_" + i, i);
    }
}
```

then to invoke it from another timeline, you would execute it as follows:

```
_root.functions_mc.makeDuplicate("clip",5);
```

Executing it creates five duplicates of the Movie Clip instance named `clip`, naming the duplicates `clip_1`, `clip_2`, `clip_3`, `clip_4`, and `clip_5`.

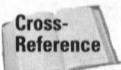
Cross-Reference   We discuss functions in greater detail in the Chapter 26, "Using Functions and Arrays."

Creating a Login Sequence with Variables

In this section, we show you how to use variables to create an interactive form in Flash that accepts or rejects user input. You will create two input text fields into which Web visitors will type a username and password. Using ActionScript, you will check the values of the entered data with predefined name/value pairs.

Caution
Do not use the following example for secure information over the Web. You could use a login sequence like this in a Flash adventure game, or modify it to work in a Flash quiz. The login information is not secure within the confines of a Flash movie (.swf file). This example is intended to demonstrate the procedure of using conditional statements in a Flash movie.

1. Open a new Flash document.

2. Create two text fields on one layer called **text fields**. Make each text field long enough to accommodate a single first name and/or password. For demonstration purposes, make the text in the text fields large—around 24 points. Make sure that you use a non-white fill color for the text.

3. Access the properties for each text field by selecting the text field (with the Selection tool) and opening the Property inspector, shown in Figure 24-5. In the Text Type drop-down menu, select the **Input Text** option for both fields. For the top text field, assign the instance name userEnter_txt. For the other text field, assign the instance name passwordEnter_txt, enable the Password option, and restrict the text length to 8 characters. Do *not* assign a Var name to either text field.

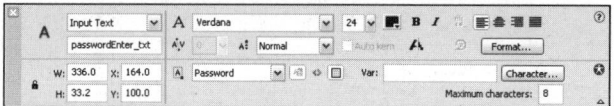

Figure 24-5: The passwordEnter_txt instance will be an input text field with the password option enabled and a restricted character length of 8 characters.

4. Create a new layer and name it **static text**. Create text blocks that describe the two text fields, as shown in Figure 24-6. For example, make a text block with the word **Login:** and another one with the word **Password:**. Align these text blocks to the left of the text fields. Note that these text blocks do not need the Input Text behavior; they should be **Static Text** blocks.

```
          Login:    [                    ]

     Password:    [                    ]
```

Figure 24-6: Here you have four text areas: two static text blocks on the left, and two input text fields on the right. The static text cannot be altered and/or "read" by ActionScript.

5. Create a new Movie Clip symbol (Ctrl+F8 or ⌘+F8), called **errorMessageClip**, that displays an error message, such as INVALID or LOGIN ERROR. Rename Layer 1 of its timeline to **actions**. On that layer, the first frame of the Movie Clip should be blank with a stop(); frame action.

6. Create another layer called **labels**. On frame 2 of this layer, make a keyframe and assign it the label **start** in the <Frame Label> field of the Property inspector.

7. Then, create a new layer called **anim** and move it underneath the actions layer. On this layer, create a tweening animation of your message fading in and out (or scaling up and down, and so on). Start the Motion tween on frame 2 of the anim layer, underneath the start label of the actions layer. You'll need to make the message a Graphic symbol of its own in order to tween the alpha state. Add enough frames and keyframes to cycle this message animation twice. The very last frame of the animation should have a frame action (on the actions layer) gotoAndStop(1);. When you are finished with this step, your Movie Clip timeline should resemble the one shown in Figure 24-7.

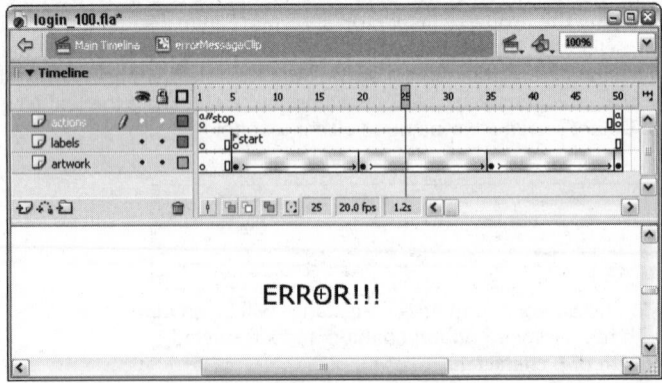

Figure 24-7: The errorMessageClip symbol contains an empty first frame and an animation that begins on the start label. This animation will play only if the user enters an incorrect login.

8. In the main movie timeline (Scene 1), create a new layer called **errorMessage_mc**. Drag the errorMessageClip symbol from the Library on to the Stage. Position it underneath the user and password text fields. Select the Movie Clip instance on the Stage and access its settings in the Property inspector. Assign the instance name of errorMessage_mc.

Tip   In the Property inspector, you can temporarily change the symbol type of the error Message_mc instance to a Graphic instance, and specify frame number 5 in the First field. This technique allows you to more accurately place a symbol that has an empty first frame. When you are finished positioning the instance, make sure you switch the instance behavior back to Movie Clip and rename the instance. Do not change the behavior of the symbol in the Library panel; this method only applies to the symbol behavior on an instance level.

9. Create another layer named **labels**. Assign a frame label of start to frame 1 of the labels layer. Add a keyframe to the frame 10 of the labels layer, and label it **success**. Make sure all other layers on frame 10 have empty keyframes.

10. Extend all the layers to frame 20 by selecting frame 20 across all of the layers and pressing F5.

11. Make a new layer called **success** and place a text block and/or other graphics suitable for a successful login entry. It should only appear on frame 10, so if necessary, move its initial keyframe to that frame. When you're finished with the step, your Stage and Main Timeline should resemble Figure 24-8.

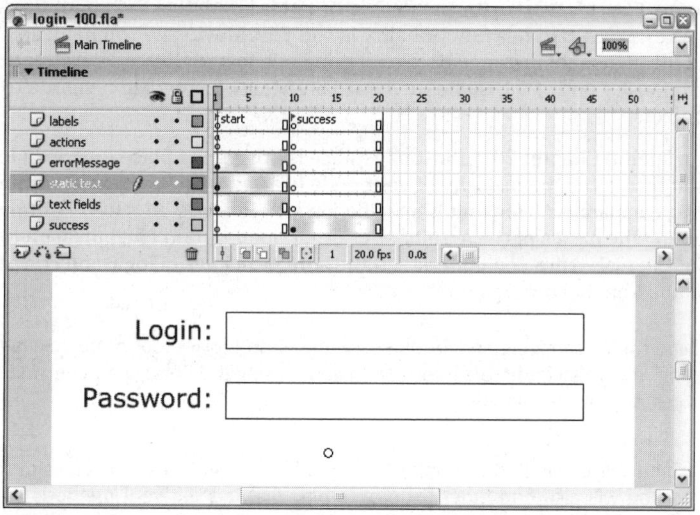

Figure 24-8: Your Main Timeline should have three key elements: a login frame, an error message Movie Clip, and a success frame.

12. Create a new layer on the Main Timeline called **button**, and make a Button symbol on it. You can make one of your own, or use one from Flash's Button library (Window ⇨ Other Panels ⇨ Common Libraries ⇨ Buttons). Place it to the right of or underneath the user and password fields. Select the Button symbol instance, and open the Actions panel. Add the following ActionScript code in the Script pane (note that the ⊃ character indicates a continuation of the same line of code; do not type or insert this character into your actual code):

```
on (release){
  if (userEnter_txt.text == "Sandra" && ⊃
    passwordEnter_txt.text == "zebra24"){
      this.gotoAndStop("success");
  } else {
      this.errorMessage_mc.gotoAndPlay("start");
  }
}
```

You can change the compared values for the `userEnter_txt.text` and `passwordEnter_txt.text` values to whatever string value you desire.

13. Add an empty keyframe (F7) on frame 10 of the button layer.

14. On the Main Timeline, create an **actions** layer, and place it at the top of the layer order. On the first frame, add a `stop();` frame action.

15. Save the Flash document as `login_100.fla`. Test the movie's functionality with the Test Movie command (Control ⇨ Test Movie).

Most login forms like this work with the Return or Enter key active to submit the information. However, this key press also has functionality in the Test Movie environment, so assign a key press to the Button symbol instance only *after* you have tested the initial ActionScript code. You can also choose Control ⇨ Disable Keyboard Shortcuts in Test Movie mode to avoid any key press conflicts.

As you'll learn later in Chapter 26, a Button instance is not a great place to store a lot of code — it's usually better to place the majority of your code in a keyframe, contained within a function, or better yet, in a separate AS file that is specified in an `#include` directive. For now, however, as you're learning the basics of the ActionScript programming, don't feel pressured to take on too much too fast; make sure you understand the core principles of logic and conditions before you move on to additional programming topics.

Cross-Reference See Chapter 34, "Managing and Troubleshooting Flash Movies" for more coverage of code debugging. You'll also find more information about using the Debugger panel and other useful features, such as breakpoints.

On the CD-ROM You can find the completed example, `login_100.fla`, in the `ch24` folder of this book's CD-ROM. You will also find other login examples that use different methods to make the user name and password comparisons.

Web Resource We'd like to know what you thought about this chapter. Visit `www.flashsupport.com/feedback` to fill out an online form with your comments.

Summary

✦ Before you begin to add complex interactivity to your Flash document, you need to break down the steps in the interactive process in a natural language that you can understand.

✦ After you know what you want your presentation to do, you can start to clarify the interactive steps and translate those steps into Flash-compatible actions.

✦ You can add ActionScript to your Flash document with the Actions panel. The Actions panel's Script pane is where you type or insert the actions that are invoked from elements in a Flash movie.

✦ Variables, a programming device, enable you to store property values, strings, paths, or expressions in order to reduce the redundancy of code and to simplify the process of computing information.

✦ Variables can be declared with actions, input, or dynamic text fields, or by loading them from an external data source, such as a server-side script, text document, or HTML-specified `flashvars` values.

✦ Expressions are equations that refer to a mathematical operation, a string concatenation, or an existing code object (another variable or object value).

✦ You can use `if...else if...else` actions to add intelligence to your interactive actions. These actions test a condition and execute a certain set of actions if the condition is true.

✦ Loop actions execute a given set of actions repeatedly until a loop condition is no longer true.

✦ ✦ ✦

Controlling Movie Clips

In This Chapter

Understanding the MovieClip object

Working with properties of the `MovieClip` object

Creating Mouse Drag behaviors

The MX event model explained

Making sliders that dynamically change properties

◆　　◆　　◆　　◆

In Chapter 19, "Building Timelines and Interactions," we established the key role that Movie Clips have within the Flash movie structure. By having a timeline that plays separately from other timelines, Movie Clips enable multiple events to occur — independently or as part of an interaction with other Movie Clips. This chapter explores how to manipulate Movie Clips beyond navigation actions such as `gotoAndPlay()` or `stop()`.

Movie Clips: The Object Overview

Since Flash 5, the implementation of ActionScript has resembled true object-oriented programming languages. Much like JavaScript, each element in a Flash movie has a data type. A data type is simply a category to which an element belongs. In the current version of ActionScript (including ActionScript 2.0), there are several data types available, among others `boolean`, `number`, `string`, `object`, `function`, and `movieclip`.

Tip　If you want to see a list of all data types in ActionScript, open the Actions panel (make sure code hints are turned on), and type `var a:`. After you type the colon (:), you'll see a list of supported data types.

For our purposes, a Movie Clip instance *is* an object, and we'll refer to it as such throughout Part VII of this book. An object is any element in Flash that has changeable and accessible characteristics *through ActionScript*. Objects can be user-defined (you create and name them) or predefined by the programming language. The `MovieClip` object is a predefined object, meaning that all of its characteristics are already described in the ActionScript language.

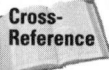

Cross-Reference　For a brief overview of object-oriented programming concepts, please review the "What Is Dot Syntax" sidebar located in Chapter 19, "Building Timelines and Interactions." For more information on basic data types, please see Chapter 26, "Using Functions and Arrays."

A MovieClip object is the same Movie Clip instance you've seen in previous chapters. Any instance of a Movie Clip is a unique object in ActionScript. However, you haven't treated it like an object in your scripting. Before we can proceed with a discussion of Movie Clips as Flash movie assets, you need to understand what predefined characteristics are available in the MovieClip object. See Figure 25-1 for more information.

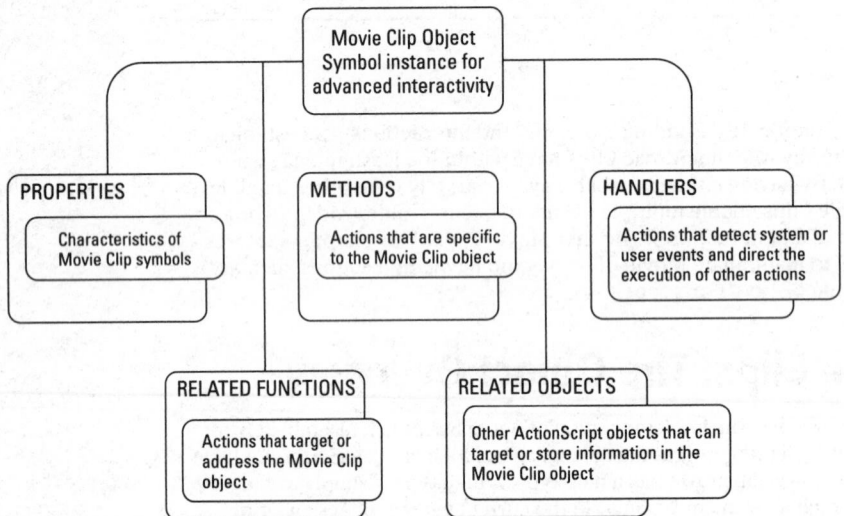

Figure 25-1: An overview of the MovieClip object

Movie Clip properties

Each Movie Clip instance has definable properties, or attributes, that control its appearance, size, and position. For example, you can move a Movie Clip instance to a new position on the stage by changing the value of its X or Y coordinate. This property in ActionScript is denoted as _x or _y, respectively. Some properties have read-only values, meaning these values can't be altered. One read-only property is _url, the value of which indicates the download location of the Movie Clip (or SWF file) such as http://www.yourserver.com/swf/background.swf. Figure 25-2 is a summary of the properties of the MovieClip object. For more information on each property, please refer to Table 25-1, " Flash Movie and Movie Clip Properties."

All properties are preceded by the underscore (_) character. In Table 25-1, each property has an "R" (as in "read") and/or "W" (as in "write") designation. All properties can be read, which means that you can retrieve that property's current value. The values of some properties can also be changed through ActionScript. The table represents these properties with the "W" designation.

Note In Flash Player 4 ActionScript, these properties were retrieved using the `getProperty()` action. Properties are altered using the `setProperty()` action. For Flash Player 5 or higher movies, you should avoid using these actions. Many free online Flash tutorials or samples at sites such as FlashKit.com will often be riddled with these deprecated actions.

Cross-Reference More advanced properties of the `MovieClip` object are not reviewed in this chapter. For the most comprehensive coverage, refer to the `MovieClip` object chapter of the *Flash MX 2004 ActionScript Bible* by Robert Reinhardt and Joey Lott (Wiley, 2004).

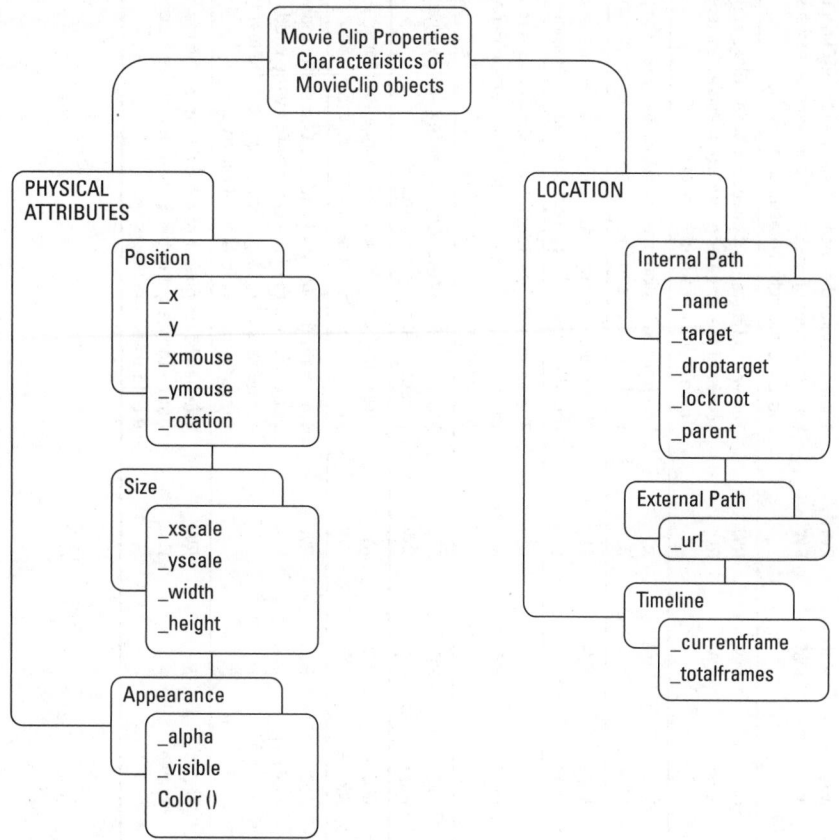

Figure 25-2: Properties of the MovieClip object

Table 25-1: Flash Movie and Movie Clip Properties

Category	Property	Timeline	Flash 4	Flash 5+	Definition
Position	_x	MC Movie	RW RW	RW RW	The horizontal distance between a Movie Clip's center point and the top-left corner of the stage upon which it resides. Increases as the clip moves to the right. Measured in pixels.
	_y	MC Movie	RW RW	RW RW	The vertical distance between a Movie Clip's center point and the top-left corner of the stage upon which it resides. Increases as the clip moves downward. Measured in pixels.
	_xmouse	MC Movie	N/A N/A	R R	The horizontal distance (in pixels) between the zero point of a Movie Clip (or the Movie) and the current position of the mouse pointer.
	_ymouse	MC Movie	N/A N/A	RW R	The vertical distance (in pixels) between the zero point of a Movie Clip (or the Movie) and the current position of the mouse pointer.
	_rotation	MC Movie	RW	RW RW	The amount (in degrees) that a Movie Clip is rotated off plumb. Returns values set both by the Transform panel (or Transform tool) and by ActionScript.
	_xscale	MC Movie	RW RW	RW RW	The width of a Movie Clip instance (or Movie) as a percentage of the parent symbol's actual size.
Size	_yscale	MC Movie	RW RW	RW RW	The height of a Movie Clip instance (or Movie) as a percentage of the parent symbol's actual size.
	_width	MC Movie	R R	RW R	The width (in pixels) of a Movie Clip or the main Movie Stage. Determined not by the width of the canvas but by the width of the space occupied by elements on the Stage (meaning it can be less than or greater than the canvas width set in Movie Properties).
	_height	MC Movie	R R	RW R	The height (in pixels) of a movie clip or the main movie Stage. Determined not by the height of the canvas but by the height of the space occupied by elements on the Stage.

Category	Property	Timeline	Flash 4	Flash 5+	Definition
Appearance	_alpha	MC Movie	RW RW	RW RW	The amount of transparency of a Movie Clip or Movie. Measured as a percentage: 100 percent is completely opaque; 0 percent is completely transparent.
	_visible	MC Movie	RW RW	RW RW	A Boolean value that indicates whether a Movie Clip instance is shown or hidden. Set to 1 (or true) to show; 0 (or false) to hide. Buttons in "hidden" movies are not active.
	Color()	MC Movie	N/A N/A	RW RW	Color() is an ActionScript object, not a property of the MovieClip object. Because Movie Clips can be specified as the target of the Color object, color values of a Movie Clip can be treated as a user-definable property. We discuss the Color object in Chapter 27
Internal Path	_name	MC Movie	RW R	RW R	Returns or reassigns the Movie Clip instance's name (as listed in the Property inspector).
	_target	MC Movie	R R	R R	Returns the exact string in Slash notation that you'd use to refer to the Movie Clip instance. To retrieve the dot syntax path, use eval(_target).
	_droptarget	MC Movie	R R	R R	Returns the name (in Slash notation) of the last Movie Clip upon which a draggable Movie Clip was dropped. To retrieve the dots syntax path, use eval(_droptarget). For usage, see "Creating Draggable Movie Clips" in this chapter.
	_lockroot	MC Movie	RW RW	RW RW	This new property, only available to Flash Player 7-compatible movies, allows you to control how a _root reference is interpreted. If the _lockroot property of a MovieClip object is set to true, then any child assets (nested MovieClip objects) will see the parent MovieClip object as _root. For example, if you load an SWF file into a MovieClip object (as you learn in Chapter 28), any _root target in the loaded SWF will point to the MovieClip object.
	_parent	MC Movie	N/A N/A	R R	Returns a reference to the parent timeline of the current MovieClip object. For example, if an instance named bird_1 exists within another instance named flock_mc, then bird_1._parent refers to the flock_mc instance. *._parent will return only a valid reference from the Main Timeline if the Flash movie is loaded into a MovieClip instance of another Flash movie.

Continued

Table 25-1 (continued)

Category	Property	Timeline	Flash 4	Flash 5+	Definition
External Path	_url	MC	R	R	Returns the complete path to the Flash movie (.swf file) in which the action is executed, including the name of the Flash movie (.swf file) itself. Could be used to prevent a movie from being viewed if not on a particular server.
		Movie	R	R	
Timeline	_currentframe	MC	R	R	Returns the number of the current frame (for example, the frame on which the Playhead currently resides) of the Movie or a Movie Clip instance.
		Movie	R	R	
	_totalframes	MC	R	R	Returns the number of total frames in a Movie or Movie Clip instance's timeline.
		Movie	R	R	
	_framesloaded	MC	R	R	Returns the number of frames that have downloaded over the network.
		Movie	R	R	
Global	_quality	Movie	N/A	RW	The visual quality of the Movie. The value is a string equal to: "LOW" (no anti-aliasing, no bitmap smoothing). "MEDIUM" (anti-aliasing on a 2 x 2 grid, no bitmap smoothing), "HIGH" (anti-aliasing on a 4 x 4 grid, bitmap smoothing on static frames), "BEST" (anti-aliasing on a 4 x 4 grid, bitmap smoothing on all frames).
	_focusrect	Movie	RW	RW	A Boolean value that indicates whether a yellow rectangle is shown around buttons when accessed via the Tab key. Default is to show. When set to 0, the Up state of the button is shown instead of the yellow rectangle.
	_soundbuftime	Movie	RW	RW	The number of seconds a sound should preload before it begins playing. Default is 5 seconds.

MC = Movie Clip; R = Read property (cannot be modified); W = Write property (can be modified)

On the CD-ROM

Use the propInspector Movie Clip in the Library of the property_inspector.fla file, located in the ch25 folder of the *Macromedia Flash MX 2004 Bible* CD-ROM to see the values of Movie Clip or Movie properties.

Movie Clip methods

Although the name might sound intimidating, don't be scared. Methods are simply actions that are attached to objects. As you now know, Movie Clips qualify as objects in ActionScript. A method looks like a regular action, except it doesn't (and in most cases, can't) operate without a dot syntax reference to a target or an object:

Action: `gotoAndPlay("start");`

becomes

Method: `myMovieClip.gotoAndPlay("start");`

As actions, interactive commands are executed from the timeline on which they are written. As methods, interactive commands are tied to specific (or dynamic) targets. Figure 25-3 lists many of the methods and Table 25-2 reviews them in more detail. Some methods can be used with Movie Clip instances and with the entire Flash movie (_root, _level0, and so on), while others can only be used with Movie Clip instances. The "Flash 4" column indicates if the method (when used as an action) is compatible in Flash Player 4. Some commands need to be written in dot syntax, as a method (designated as "M" in the table) of a timeline or `MovieClip` object. Other commands can be used as actions (designated as "A" in the table), meaning that the `MovieClip` object name need not precede the command.

Cross-Reference

Figure 25-3 and Table 25-2 do not contain all methods of the `MovieClip` object. For comprehensive description and usage of the methods, refer to the *Flash MX 2004 ActionScript Bible* by Robert Reinhardt and Joey Lott.

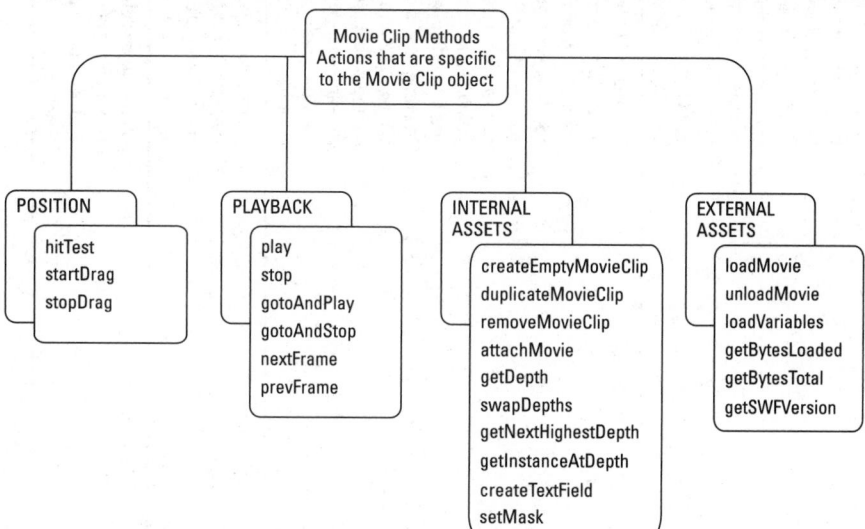

Figure 25-3: Common methods of the `MovieClip` object

Table 25-2: Common Movie and Movie Clip Methods

Category	Method	Flash 4	Definition	Usage

Position	hitTest
	M
		No	Determines if a MovieClip object overlaps with the boundaries of another MovieClip object, or if an X-Y coordinate intersects with a MovieClip instance. For more information on this method, see Chapter 27, "Interacting with Movie Clips."	*timeline.hitTest(MovieClip object);*
				OR
				timeline.hitTest(x coordinate, y coordinate, shapeFlag);
				`myMC.hitTest(myOther_mc);`
				`myMC.hitTest(_root._xmouse, _root._ymouse, true);`

	startDrag M, A	Yes	Enables the user to move a Movie Clip instance on the Stage. The Movie Clip moves (or drags) in tandem with the movements of the mouse. You can specify whether the mouse pointer locks to the center of the Movie Clip instance and if the drag area is constrained to a range of X and Y coordinates (in the parent symbol or timeline space). Constraining the drag area is useful for slider controls.	*timeline.startDrag(lock, min X, min Y, max X, max Y);* `myMC.startDrag(false, 200,0,200,200);`
	stopDrag M, A	Yes	Stops any startDrag action currently in progress. No target needs to be specified with this action.	*timeline.stopDrag();* `myMC.stopDrag();`

Playback	play
	M, A
		Yes	Starts playback from the current position of the Playhead on a specified timeline.	*timeline.play();*
				`_root.play(); // plays the Main Timeline`
				`_root.myMC.play(); // plays myMC`

Category	Method	Flash 4	Definition	Usage

	stop
	M, A
		Yes	Stops playback on a specified Timeline.	*timeline.stop();*
				`_root.stop(); // stops the Main Timeline`
				`_root.myMC.stop(); // stops myMC`

	gotoAndPlay
	M, A
		Yes	Jumps the Playhead of a specified timeline to a label, frame number, or expression, and starts playing from there.	*timeline.gotoAndPlay(position);*
				`_root.myMC.gotoAndPlay("start");`
				`// plays from the "start" label of the myMC timeline`

	gotoAndStop
	M, A
		Yes	Jumps the Playhead of a specified Timeline to a label, frame number, or expression, and stops playback.	*timeline.gotoAndStop(position);*
				`_root.myMC.gotoAndStop("mute");`
				`// stops playback on the "mute" label of myMC`

	nextFrame M, A	Yes	Moves the Playhead of the specified timeline to the next frame.	*timeline.nextFrame();* `_root.myMC.nextFrame();`
	prevFrame M, A	Yes	Moves the Playhead of the specified timeline to the previous frame.	*timeline.prevFrame();* `_root.myMC.prevFrame();`

Internal Assets	createEmptyMovieClip
	M
		No	Makes a blank (empty) Movie Clip instance on the Stage (or nested in another Movie Clip instance). The new instance is placed directly above the parent instance, at a specified depth. Higher depth numbers appear above lower depth numbers (for example, a Movie Clip at depth 2 is stacked above a Movie Clip at depth 1).
			
			This method works only in Flash 6 or higher movies played in Flash Player 6 or higher.
				timeline.createEmptyMovieClip(new name depth);*
				`_root.createEmptyMovieClip("myMC", 1);`
				`myMC._x = 50;`
				*You should not specify a new path for the copy. It will be located from the same root as the parent MC instance.

Continued

Table 25-2 (continued)

Category	Method	Flash 4	Definition	Usage
M, A	`duplicateMovieClip`	Yes	Makes a copy of an existing Movie Clip instance on the Stage (or nested in another Movie Clip). The new copy is placed directly above the parent instance, at a specified depth. Higher depth numbers appear above lower depth numbers (for example, a Movie Clip at depth 2 is stacked above a Movie Clip at depth 1).	*timeline.duplicateMovieClip(new name*, depth);* `myMC.duplicateMovieClip("myMC_2", 20);` `myMC_2._x = 200;` *You should not specify a new path for the copy. It will be located from the same root as the parent MC instance.
M, A	`removeMovieClip`	Yes	Deletes a previously duplicated Movie Clip instance. When used as a method, you do not need to specify a target. You cannot remove a Movie Clip instance that is manually inserted on any timeline frame from the Library.	*timeline.removeMovieClip();* `myMC_2.removeMovieClip();`
M	`attachMovie`	No	Places an instance of a Movie Clip symbol from the Library into the specified timeline. Each attached instance requires a unique name and depth. Attached Movie Clip instances can be deleted with `removeMovieClip`.	*timeline.attachMovie(ID*, new name, depth);* `_root.attachMovie("eye", "eye_1", 1);` *You need to specify a unique identifier to attached Movie Clip symbols in the Library, using the Linkage Properties.
M	`getDepth`	No	Returns the current depth of a duplicated (or attached) `MovieClip` object. This method only works in Flash 6 movies played in Flash Player 6.	*timeline.getDepth();* `_root.attachMovie("eye", "eye_1", 1);` `trace(eye_1.getDepth());` *If you attempt to retrieve the depth of a Movie Clip instance that you manually placed on the Stage, then ActionScript will return -16383 as the value of getDepth().

Category	Method	Flash 4	Definition	Usage
M	`swapDepths`	No	Switches the depth placement of two duplicated or attached Movie Clips. This method is useful for placing one Movie Clip instance in front of (or behind) another instance.	*timeline.swapDepths(depth);* *timeline.swapDepths(target);* `eye_1.swapDepths(10);` // depth `eye_1.swapDepths(eye_2);` // target
M	`getNextHighestDepth`	No	Determines if any objects currently exist within depth slots of the current `MovieClip` object, and returns a depth number one higher than an occupied slot. For example, if you duplicated a `MovieClip` object to a depth count of 2, this method would return 3. You can use this method in conjunction with any of the Movie Clip methods that require a depth parameter. This method works only when issued from a Flash Player 7-compatible movie.	*timeline.getNextHighestDepth();* `var nextSlot = myMC.getNextHighestDepth();`
M	`getInstanceAtDepth`	No	Returns the name of an object occupying the specified depth slot. If no object exists at the slot, `undefined` is returned. This method works only when issued from a Flash Player 7-compatible movie.	*timeline.getInstanceAtDepth(depthSlot);* `var isOccupied = myMC.getInstanceAtDepth(1);`
M	`createTextField`	No	Adds a new TextField object (that is, a dynamic or input text field) to the `MovieClip` object. This method allows you to add new text fields to your movie at runtime. This method is used extensively in Chapter 33, "Creating a Game in Flash."	*timeline.createTextField(name, depth, x position, y position, width, height);* `myMC.createTextField("display_txt", 1, 10, 10, 300, 50);`

Continued

Table 25-2 *(continued)*

Category	Method	Flash 4	Definition	Usage
			This method works only when issued from a Flash Player 6 or higher movie.	
	`setMask` M	No	Assigns a `MovieClip` object to be used as the mask for another `MovieClip` object. This method works only when issued from a Flash Player 6 or higher movie.	*timeline.setMask(instanceName);* `myMC.setMask(clip_mc);`

External Assets	`loadMovie`
	M, A
		Yes	Loads an external movie (.swf file) or JPEG file into the main movie. As one of the most powerful features of Flash, this method enables you to break up your Flash movie into several smaller components, and load them as needed. This method can load movies (.swf files) or JPEG images (.jpg files) into Movie Clip targets.
			
			Note: You can load only JPEG images with `loadMovie()` if you are publishing Flash 6 movies for use in Flash Player 6. We discuss the use of JPEG files with `loadMovie()` in Chapter 27.
				timeline.loadMovie(path, send variables*);
				`myMC.loadMovie("menu.swf");`
				OR
				
				`myMC.loadMovie("image.jpg");`
				*You can also send Flash variables to the newly loaded SWF file with an optional "GET" or "POST" parameter. This is discussed in Chapter 24.

	`unloadMovie` M, A	Yes	Removes an externally loaded movie (.swf file) from the main movie. This method enables you to dump movie assets when they are no longer needed. Use this method for assets loaded into Movie Clip targets.	*timeline.unloadMovie();* `myMC.unloadMovie();`

Category	Method	Flash 4	Definition	Usage
	loadVariables **M, A**	Yes	Loads external text-based data into the movie. This method enables you to access data (in the form of variable name/value pairs) from server-side scripts or text files, and place it in a Movie Clip target.	*timeline.loadVariables(path, send variables*);* myMC.loadVariables("info.txt"); *See note in loadMovie. We discuss loadVariables() and the new LoadVars object in Chapter 30.
	getBytesLoaded **M**	No	Returns the number of bytes that have streamed into the Flash Player for a specified Movie Clip (or movie).	*timeline.getBytesLoaded():* loadBytes = myMC.getBytesLoaded();

	getBytesTotal
	M
		No	Returns the total file size (in bytes) for a loading movie or Movie Clip. Combined with getBytesLoaded(), you can use this method to calculate the movie's loaded percentage.	*timeline.getBytesTotal():*
				totalBytes = myMC.getBytesTotal();
				loadBytes = myMC.getBytesLoaded();
				newPercent = (loadBytes/totalBytes)*100;

	getSWFVersion **M**	No	Returns the version of the Flash movie as a number. For example, if you create a Flash movie (.swf file) to be Flash Player 4-compatible, you can check the version number of that SWF from a Flash Player 7-compatible movie (SWF file). This method can only be invoked from Flash movies created for Flash Player 7 or higher.	*timeline.getSWFVersion():* myMC.getSWFVersion();

M = Method; A = Action

onClipEvent: The Original Movie Clip handler

In Flash 5, the onClipEvent handler was added to the ActionScript language. In Flash 4 or earlier, the only event handlers were keyframes and Button instances. In Flash 5 or higher movies, you can add actions to the wrapper of a Movie Clip instance — meaning that these actions are not added to keyframes on the Movie Clip's timeline. Nine events can be used with the onClipEvent handler. Refer to Table 25-3 for a summary of these events.

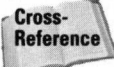

Cross-Reference

If you would like to read a review of events and event handlers, see Chapter 18, "Understanding Actions and Event Handlers."

Let's create a simple example of onClipEvent() in action:

1. Open a new Flash document (File ➪ New).

2. Draw any artwork you wish, and make the artwork a Movie Clip symbol.

3. Select the Movie Clip instance on the Stage. In the Property inspector, name the instance tracker_mc.

4. With the tracker_mc instance selected on the Stage, open the Actions panel (F9). Type the following code into the Script pane:

```
onClipEvent (mouseMove){
  this._x = _root._xmouse;
  this._y = _root._ymouse;
  updateAfterEvent();
}
```

This code uses onClipEvent() to track the position of the user's mouse, and apply that position to the MovieClip object — effectively moving the MovieClip object with the mouse pointer. The code is executed every time the user's mouse moves. The updateAfterEvent() action will tell the Flash Player to refresh the video display each time a mouse move is detected, resulting in a smoother movement of the object.

5. Save your Flash document as tracker_oce.fla, and test it (Ctrl+Enter or ⌘+Enter). As you move the mouse, the artwork will follow the mouse.

On the CD-ROM

You can find a completed version of the file tracker_oce.fla in the ch25 folder of the *Macromedia Flash MX 2004 Bible* CD-ROM.

Event methods: The MX Movie Clip handler

In Flash MX and MX 2004, event handlers for MovieClip objects can be written and executed from any other event handler. This means that you can code the same event handlers used for onClipEvent() in keyframe or Button instance actions. While this may not seem like a monumental leap forward, this new event model allows you to create event handlers that are not directly attached to physical instances of a Movie Clip on the Stage. For a summary of common event methods, see Table 25-3.

It is beyond the scope of this book to discuss all of the event methods available in ActionScript 1.0 and 2.0. Please refer to the *Flash MX 2004 ActionScript Bible* by Robert Reinhardt and Joey Lott for more information.

To get a better idea how this event model works, let's create a simple example:

1. Create a new Flash document.

2. Draw some artwork, and make it a Movie Clip symbol.

3. Select the new instance on the Stage. Name the instance `tracker_mc` in the Property inspector.

4. Create a new layer on the Main Timeline (that is, Scene 1). Name the layer **actions**.

5. Select frame 1 of the actions layer, and open the Actions panel (F9). Type the following code into the Script pane:

```
tracker_mc.onMouseMove = function (){
    this._x = _root._xmouse;
    this._y = _root._ymouse;
    updateAfterEvent();
};
```

This code adds an `onMouseMove()` method to the tracker instance. Each time the user's mouse moves, the function written for the method will execute. We discuss functions in the next chapter.

6. Save your Flash document as `tracker_eventmodel.fla`, and test it (Ctrl+Enter or ⌘+Enter). The artwork will follow your mouse pointer as you move it on the Stage.

You can find the completed document, `tracker_eventmodel.fla`, in the ch25 folder of the *Macromedia Flash MX 2004 Bible* CD-ROM. You will also find another document, `tracker_eventmodel_adv.fla`, which uses multiple event handlers.

You can continue to add more event methods to the tracker instance, in order for the instance to respond to mouse clicks, time elapsing, and so on.

The new event model for Flash movies only works in Flash Player 6 or higher. If you need to use events with Movie Clips that are compatible with Flash Player 5, then use `onClipEvent()` handlers.

Table 25-3: Common onClipEvent and MX Event Handlers

Category	onClipEvent	MX Event Handler	Definition	Usage

Playback	load	onLoad	This event is triggered when (a) a Movie Clip instance first appears on the Stage; (b) a new instance is added with attachMovie or duplicateMovieClip; or (c) an external Flash movie (.swf file) is loaded into a Movie Clip target.
			
			Note: The onLoad method does not function properly on individual instances. When a Flash movie (.swf file) loads into a level or a Movie Clip target, any existing methods will be overwritten, including onLoad. See the Usage example to see how onLoad can be used. The onLoad method, however, is useful for setting parameters for components that are added via ActionScript.
				```onClipEvent(load){```
				``` trace(_name + " has loaded.");```
				```}```
				OR
				```movieclip.prototype.onLoad = function(){```
				``` trace("A movie or Movie Clip has loaded.");```
				```};```
				For components:
				```var myButton = myclip_mc.attachMovie("Button", "cbtToggle", 1);```
				```myButton.onLoad = function(){```
				``` this.label = "Toggle Button";```
				```};```

Category	onClipEvent	MX Event Handler	Definition	Usage

unload	unload	onUnload	This event occurs when (a) a Movie Clip instance exits the Stage (just after the last frame has played on the Main Timeline), or (b) an external Flash movie (.swf file) is unloaded from a Movie Clip target. Actions within this handler type will be executed *before* any actions in the keyframe immediately after the Movie Clip's departure keyframe.	`onClipEvent(unload){`
				`    trace( _name + " has unloaded.");`
				`}`
				OR
				`holder_mc.onUnload = function(){`
				`    trace(this._name + " has unloaded.");`
				`};`

enterFrame	enterFrame	onEnterFrame	This event executes when each frame on a Movie Clip instance's timeline is played. The actions within this event handler will be processed *after* any actions that exist on the keyframes of the Movie Clip timeline. Note that enterFrame events will execute repeatedly (at the same rate as the movie's frame rate), regardless of whether any timelines within the movie are actually playing frames.	`onClipEvent(enterFrame){`
				`    trace( _name + " is playing.");`
				`}`
				OR
				`_root.holder.onEnterFrame = function(){`
				`    trace(_name + " is playing.");`
				`};`

Continued

Table 25-3 (continued)

Category	onClipEvent	MX Event Handler	Definition	Usage
User Input	mouseMove	onMouseMove	This event is triggered each time the mouse moves, anywhere on the Stage. All Movie Clip instances with this event handler defined receive this event. Combined with the hitTest() method, this event can be used to detect mouse movements over Movie Clip instances.	```onClipEvent(mouseMove){` ` var myX = _root._xmouse;` ` var myY = _root._ymouse;` ` if(this.hitTest(myX, myY, true) == true){` ` trace("Mouse move over MC.");` ` }` `}` `OR` `holder_mc.onMouseMove = function(){` ` var myX = _root._xmouse;` ` var myY = _root._ymouse;` ` if(this.hitTest(myX, myY, true)){` ` trace("Mouse move over " + this._name);` ` }` ` updateAfterEvent();` `};```
	mouseDown	onMouseDown	This event occurs each time the left mouse button is pressed (or down) anywhere on the Stage. All Movie Clip instances with this event handler receive this event.	```onClipEvent(mouseDown){` ` myX = _root._xmouse;` ` myY = _root._ymouse;` ` if(this.hitTest(myX, myY, true)){` ` trace("Mouse press on MC.");` ` }` `}` `OR` `holder_mc.onMouseDown = function(){` ` var myX = _root._xmouse;` ` var myY = _root._ymouse;` ` if(this.hitTest(myX, myY, true)){` ` trace("Mouse press on " + this._name);` ` }` `};```

Category	onClipEvent	MX Event Handler	Definition	Usage
mouseUp	mouseUp	onMouseUp	Each time the left mouse button is released (when the user lets up on the mouse button), this event is triggered. All Movie Clip instances with this handler receive this event.	```onClipEvent(mouseUp){` ` myX = _root._xmouse;` ` myY = _root._ymouse;` ` if(this.hitTest(myX, myY, true)){` ` trace("Mouse release on MC.");` ` }` `}``` OR ```holder_mc.onMouseUp = function(){` ` var myX = _root._xmouse;` ` var myY = _root._ymouse;` ` if(this.hitTest(myX, myY, true)){` ` trace("Mouse release on " + this._name);` ` }` `};```
keyDown	keyDown	onKeyDown	When the user presses a key, this event occurs. Combined with the Key.getCode method, you can use this event handler to detect unique key presses. **Note:** It's better to use Key.addListener() with a listener object to detect key down events. This advanced use of the Key object is discussed in the *Flash MX 2004 ActionScript Bible*.)	```onClipEvent(keyDown){` ` newKey = Key.getCode();` ` myKey = Key.UP;` ` if(newKey == myKey){` ` trace("UP arrow is pressed.");` ` }` `}```

Continued

Table 25-3 *(continued)*

Category	onClipEvent	MX Event Handler	Definition	Usage

	keyUp	onKeyUp	This event happens when the user releases a key (when the finger leaves the key). Same functionality as the keyDown event.
			
			Note: It's preferable to use Key.addListener() with a listener object to detect key down events. This advanced use of the Key object is discussed in the *Flash MX 2004 ActionScript Bible*.
				`onClipEvent(keyUp){`
				`  newKey = Key.getCode();`
				`  myKey = Key.LEFT;`
				`  if(newKey == myKey){`
				`    trace("LEFT arrow released.");`
				`  }`
				`}`

External Input	data	onData	This event is triggered when (a) the loadMovie action retrieves an external Flash movie (swf file) and puts it in a Movie Clip target, or (b) the data from a file or script with the loadVariables action (targeted at a Movie Clip instance) is finished loading.	`onClipEvent(data){`
				`  trace("New data received.");`
				`}`
				`OR`
				`holder_mc.onData = function(){`
				`  trace("New data received.");`
				`}`

Other objects and functions that use the MovieClip object

Movie Clips can be used with other ActionScript objects to control appearance and sounds, and to manipulate data.

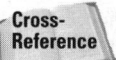

Cross-Reference: We will discuss the `Color`, `Sound`, and `Mouse` objects and the new `PrintJob` API in Chapter 27, "Interacting with Movie Clips."

Color object

This object requires a Movie Clip as a target. After a new object is created with the `Color()` constructor, you can control the color effects of the targeted Movie Clip.

Sound object

With this object, you can create virtual sound instances on a Movie Clip timeline and target them for later use.

Tip: If you are publishing Flash Player 6 or higher movies, you can load MP3 files directly into Sound objects. We'll discuss this feature in Chapter 28, "Sharing and Loading Assets."

Mouse object

This object controls the appearance of the mouse pointer within the Flash movie. After the `Mouse` object is hidden, you can attach a `MovieClip` object to the X and Y coordinates of the mouse pointer.

PrintJob API

Flash MX 2004 introduces a new ActionScript class, `PrintJob`. `PrintJob` objects allow you to dynamically create off-screen content that can be sent to a user's printer. The `PrintJob` class offers you more control over printing than previous versions of the Flash Player. You learn more about the `PrintJob` API in Chapter 27.

Note: You can still use the `print()` function for Flash Player 6 or earlier movies. This function prints a frame (or series of frames) in the targeted timeline. Each frame prints to one piece of paper. Use this function to print high-quality artwork. Note that alpha and color effects applied to `MovieClip` objects do not print reliably with this method — use the `printAsBitmap()` function instead.

with() action

This action enables you to avoid needless replication of object references and paths. By specifying a target for the `with()` action, you can omit the path from nested actions. We demonstrate the `with()` action in the next section.

tellTarget() action

This Flash Player 4-compatible action can direct actions to a specific Movie Clip timeline. To be compatible with Flash 4, you need to use Slash notation for the target path. We strongly discourage you from using `tellTarget()` actions if you are designing Flash Player 5 or higher movies.

Working with Movie Clip Properties

Now that you have a sense of what a Movie Clip can do (or be told to do), let's get some practical experience with the Movie Clip properties. This section shows you how to access Movie Clip appearance properties that control position, scale, and rotation.

Note   The following exercises use Button symbols from the prebuilt Common Libraries that ship with Flash MX 2004. To access buttons from the Common Libraries, use Window ⇨ Other Panels ⇨ Common Libraries ⇨ Buttons to open the Flash library file, and drag an instance of any button into your Flash document.

Positioning Movie Clips

You can change the location of Movie Clip instances on-the-fly with position properties such as _x and _y. How is this useful? If you want to create multiple Movie Clip instances that move randomly (or predictably) across the Stage, then you can save yourself the trouble of manually tweening them by writing a few lines of ActionScript code on the object instance:

1. Create a new Flash document (Ctrl+N or ⌘+N).

2. Rename Layer 1 to **circle_mc**.

3. On frame 1 of the circle_mc layer, draw a simple shape such as a circle. Select the shape and press F8 to convert it into a symbol. Choose the Movie Clip behavior in the Symbol Properties dialog box, and give the new Movie Clip symbol a unique name such as **circleClip**.

4. Select the instance on the stage of the Main Timeline, and in the Property inspector, name the instance circle_mc.

5. Create a new layer on the Main Timeline (that is, Scene 1), and name the layer **actions**.

6. Select frame 1 of the actions layer, and open the Actions panel (F9). Type the following code into the Script pane:

```
circle_mc.onEnterFrame = function(){
    this._x += 5;
};
```

7. Save your document as movieclip_x.fla, and test the movie (Ctrl+Enter or ⌘+Enter). The Movie Clip instance moves across the Stage.

On the CD-ROM   You can find the movieclip_x.fla in the ch25 folder of this book's CD-ROM.

How does this code work? In Step 4, you specified that the onEnterFrame() event method should be assigned to the Movie Clip instance circle_mc. Regardless of the number of frames on any playing Timeline, the enterFrame event is triggered continuously. Therefore, any actions nested within the handler will be executed repeatedly.

Our nest contains one action: `this._x += 5`. On the left side of the action, `this` refers to the object instance to which this handler and code has been applied. In our case, `this` refers to our `circle_mc` Movie Clip instance. Immediately after this is the property for X position, `_x`. By adding the property `_x` to the object `this`, Flash knows that we want to change the value of this property.

On the right side of the action are the operators `+=` and the value 5. By combining the + and = operators, you've created a shortcut to adding the value of 5 to the current X position of the `circle_mc` Movie Clip instance. Each time the `enterFrame` event occurs, the `circle_mc` object moves 5 pixels to the right.

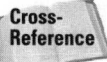

Cross-Reference   We dissect operators and expressions in Chapter 24, "Knowing the Nuts and Bolts of Code."

To show how quickly you can replicate this action on multiple Movie Clips, select the `circle_mc` instance on the Stage, and duplicate it (Ctrl+D or ⌘+D) as many times as you wish. Name each new instance with a different name in the Property inspector, such as `circle_2_mc`, `circle_3_mc`, and so on. For each instance you create, you can duplicate the code on frame 1, specifying the same actions. For example, for the two objects, `circle_2_mc` and `circle_3_mc`, you could write the following code on frame 1:

```
circle_2_mc.onEnterFrame = function(){
    this._x += 10;
}
circle_3_mc.onEnterFrame = circle_2_mc.onEnterFrame;
```

When you test your movie, each instance moves independently across the Stage. Notice that the `onEnterFrame()` handler for the `circle_3_mc` instance borrows the `onEnterFrame()` handler from `circle_2_mc`. Once a method has been defined for one object, you can reuse it with other objects' methods.

Tip   To move the instance diagonally across the Stage, add the action `this._y += 5` to the `onEnterFrame()` handler. This moves the instance down 5 pixels each time the handler is processed. Also, we'll show you how to consolidate duplicated actions in Chapter 26, "Using Functions and Arrays."

Scaling Movie Clips

In the last example, you learned how to access the `_x` and `_y` properties of the `MovieClip` object. The next example shows you how to use a Button symbol to enlarge or reduce the size of a Movie Clip on the Stage:

1. Create a new Flash document (Ctrl+N or ⌘+N).

2. Draw a shape (or multiple shapes), select the shape(s), and press F8 to convert the artwork into a symbol. Give the Movie Clip symbol a distinct name to identify it in the Library.

3. Select the instance of the Movie Clip on the Stage, and open the Property inspector. Give the Movie Clip a unique name. In this example, we've named the instance `circle_mc`.

4. From the Button library, drag an instance of a button onto the Stage.

5. Now create the ActionScript code that will enlarge the circle_mc Movie Clip instance. Select the Button instance on the Stage, and open the Actions panel. Type the following code into the Script pane:

```
on (release){
  with (circle_mc){
    _xscale += 10;
    _yscale += 10;
  }
}
```

This code uses the with() action to target the circle_mc instance with a nested group of actions. In this case, you've increased the values of the _xscale and _yscale properties by 10 percent. With each release event on the Button symbol instance, the scale properties of the circle_mc instance will be changed.

6. Save your document as movieclip_scale.fla, and test the movie (Ctrl+Enter or ⌘+Enter). Each time you click the Button instance, your circle_mc instance enlarges by 10 percent.

7. Duplicate the Button instance (Ctrl+D or ⌘+D). With the new copy of the Button instance selected, change the code in the Actions panel so that it reads:

```
on (release){
  with (circle_mc){
    _xscale -= 10;
    _yscale -= 10;
  }
}
```

By changing the += operator to -=, each click on this Button instance reduces (shrinks) the circle instance by 10 percent.

8. Resave your Flash file and test the movie again. Make sure that each Button instance behaves appropriately. If one doesn't work (or works in an unexpected manner), go back to the Flash document and check the code on both Button instances.

On the CD-ROM You can find the movieclip_scale.fla document in the ch25 folder of this book's CD-ROM.

Caution In this simple exercise, we haven't placed any limits on the how much the Movie Clip can be reduced or enlarged. If you click the reduce button enough times, the Movie Clip instance will actually start enlarging again. We look at creating conditions and logic for Movie Clips in Chapter 27, "Interacting with Movie Clips."

Rotating Movie Clips

Let's move along to the rotation property, _rotation, which is used to control the angle at which your Movie Clip is shown. In this sample, you'll use the same Flash document that you created in the previous section.

Note If you drew a perfect circle in past exercises for the `MovieClip` object, then you will want to edit your Movie Clip symbol to include some additional artwork that provides an indication of orientation and rotation. If you try to rotate a perfect circle, you won't see any visual difference on the Stage. Because the value of the rotation property is determined from the center point of the Movie Clip, you can also move the contents of the Movie Clip (in Edit mode) off-center to see updates in the `_rotation` value.

1. Select the Button instance you used to enlarge the `circle_mc` Movie Clip instance. Change the button's ActionScript in the Actions panel to:

```
on (release){
   circle_mc._rotation += 10;
}
```

2. Now, select the Button instance you used to shrink the `circle_mc` Movie Clip instance. Change the button's ActionScript in the Actions panel to:

```
on (release){
     circle_mc._rotation -= 10;
}
```

3. Save your document as `movieclip_rotation.fla`, and test the movie. Each button should rotate the `circle_mc` Movie Clip instance accordingly.

On the CD-ROM You can find the `movieclip_rotation.fla` document in the `ch25` folder of this book's CD-ROM.

At this point, you should have a general knowledge of how to access a Movie Clip's properties. Repeat these examples using other properties that can be modified, such as `_width` and `_height`. Try combining all the properties into one Button instance, or one event method or `onClipEvent()` handler.

Creating Draggable Movie Clips

Flash 4 introduced the drag and drop feature, which enables the user to pick up objects with the mouse pointer and move them around the movie Stage. Flash 5 added some other ways to use drag'n'drop with the `onClipEvent()` Movie Clip handler. As we briefly discussed, Flash MX and higher ActionScript can use a different event model for `MovieClip` objects. Drag'n'drop in Flash is based entirely on Movie Clips. The only objects that can be moved with the mouse are Movie Clip instances. So, if you want a drawing of a triangle to be moveable by the user, you have to first put that triangle into a Movie Clip, and then place a named instance of that clip onto the Stage. Flash's drag and drop support is fairly broad, but more-complex drag'n'drop behaviors require some ActionScript knowledge.

Drag-and-drop basics

In mouse-based computer interfaces, the most common form of drag and drop goes like this: A user points to an element with the mouse pointer, clicks the element to begin moving it, and then releases the mouse button to stop moving it. One method of adding drag and drop functionality is the use of a nested Button instance in a Movie Clip symbol. A `startDrag()` action is added to an `on()` handler for that Button instance. Let's try out this technique.

Note

This exercise can be used to make a Flash Player 5-compatible movie that contains a draggable object. In the "Making Alpha and Scale Sliders" section of this chapter, you learn how to use more cutting edge methods of creating draggable content.

1. Start a new Flash document.

2. Create a circle with the Oval tool. Select the artwork and press F8. In the Convert to Symbol dialog box, select the Button behavior. Name the symbol **dragButton**.

3. Now, you will nest the Button instance inside of a Movie Clip symbol. With the `dragButton` instance selected on the Stage, press F8 again. In this Convert to Symbol dialog box, select the Movie Clip behavior. Name the symbol **dragClip**.

4. With the new Movie Clip instance selected, open the Property inspector. Give the instance the name `drag_mc`.

5. Double-click the `drag_mc` instance to edit the symbol. With the nested Button instance selected on the Stage, open the Actions panel (F9). Type the following code into the Script pane:

```
on (press){
  this.startDrag();
}
```

Even though this `startDrag()` method will be applied to the same Movie Clip (`this`) that houses your button, a `startDrag()` method can target any Movie Clip from any button, or from any keyframe.

6. At this point, your button, when clicked, causes the `drag_mc` Movie Clip instance to start following the mouse pointer. Now you have to tell the Movie Clip to stop following the pointer when the mouse button is released. After the last curly brace (}) highlighted in the actions list of the Script pane, type the following code:

```
on (release, releaseOutside){
  this.stopDrag();
}
```

Caution

It is possible to use a button that is not contained in the draggable Movie Clip to stop the dragging action. If you use a button like that, remember that when your only event handler is `on (release)`, your action will not be executed if the mouse button is released when it is no longer over the button (which is likely to happen when the user is dragging things around). You should also add a `releaseOutside` event to capture all `release`-based events.

7. Save your Flash document as `movieclip_button_drag.fla`. Test your movie with Control ➪ Test Movie (Ctrl+Enter or ⌘+Enter). Click the circle and drag it around the Stage. To stop dragging, release the mouse button.

On the CD-ROM

You can find the `movieclip_button_drag.fla` document in the `ch25` folder of this book's CD-ROM.

Did it work? Great! Now we can tell you about the other basic settings for the `startDrag()` action. Next, you'll look at additional features of the `startDrag()` action. You may want to select an existing `startDrag()` action in the Script pane of the Actions panel and click the Reference icon in the panel's toolbar to more clearly see these options.

Lock mouse to center

This setting, which is the first option specified in the parentheses of the `startDrag()` method, controls how the Movie Clip instance will position itself relative to the position of the mouse pointer. There are two values for this option: `true` or `false`. When set to `true`, this option makes the dragged Movie Clip instance center itself under the mouse pointer for the duration of the drag movement. If the dragged Movie Clip instance is not already under the mouse pointer when the `startDrag()` action occurs, the instance will automatically be moved under the pointer, providing that the pointer is not outside the region defined by Constrain to Rectangle (discussed in the next section). The following code will "snap" the center of the Movie Clip instance `drag_mc` to the mouse pointer:

```
drag_mc.startDrag(true);
```

When this option is set to `false`, the Movie Clip instance moves with the mouse pointer from the point at which it was clicked. For example, if you click the draggable object on its left edge, then that's where the object will "snap" the mouse pointer:

```
drag_mc.startDrag(false);
```

Constrain to rectangle

In order to specify the limits of the rectangular region within which a draggable Movie Clip instance can be dragged, you can add parameters to the `startDrag()` method. First, determine the pixel locations of the four corners of the rectangle. The pixel coordinates are set relative to the top-left corner of the Stage upon which the draggable Movie Clip instance resides. For example, the following code would constrain the draggable Movie Clip instance named `drag_mc` to a 300-pixel square region in the top-left corner of the Main Timeline's Stage:

```
drag_mc.startDrag(false, 0, 0, 300, 300);
```

Note   If the draggable Movie Clip instance is located outside of the defined drag region when the `startDrag()` action occurs, the instance is automatically moved into the closest portion of the drag region.

Detecting the drop position: Using _droptarget

In "Drag and drop basics," we showed you how to make Movie Clip instances that the user can move around. But what if you want to force the user to move a Movie Clip object into a certain location before you let them drop it? For instance, consider a child's shape-matching game in which a small circle, square, and triangle should be dragged onto corresponding larger shapes. If the child drops the small circle onto the large square or large triangle, the circle returns to its original location. If, on the other hand, the child drops the small circle onto the large circle, the small circle should stay where it is dropped, and the child should receive a "Correct!" message. That kind of game is quite possible in Flash, but it requires some understanding of Movie Clip properties. Here's how it works — you'll use the circle as an example:

Note   In the following steps, we'll show you Flash Player 6 (and higher) methods of the `MovieClip` object that were introduced with Flash MX. These methods allow you to assign button behaviors to Movie Clip instances, without nesting a physical Button instance within the Movie Clip.

1. Open a new Flash document (File ➪ New).

2. Rename Layer 1 to **circle_mc**.

3. On frame 1 of the circle_mc layer, use the Oval tool to draw a circle that is 100 x 100 pixels. Convert the artwork to a Movie Clip symbol named **circleClip**, and name the instance `circle_mc`. Scale the artwork to 25 percent in the Transform panel. Position this instance along the bottom left of the Stage, as shown in Figure 25-4.

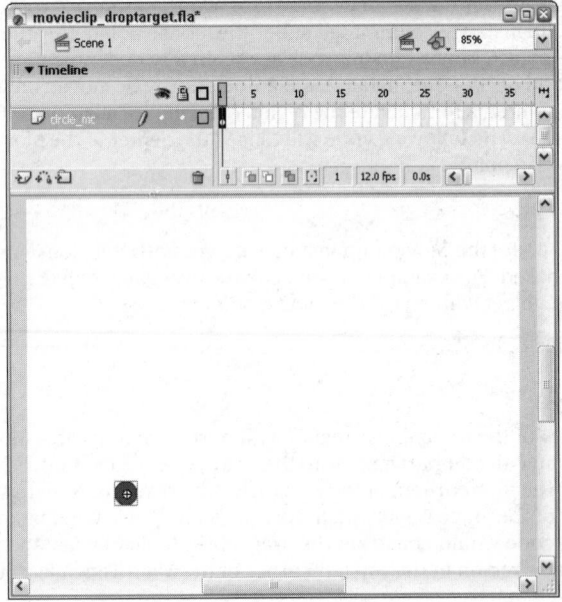

Figure 25-4: The `circle_mc` instance

4. Copy the `circle_mc` instance by selecting it on the Stage and choosing Edit ➪ Copy (Ctrl+C or ⌘+D).

5. Create a new layer, and name the layer **circleBig_mc**. Place the layer below the circle_mc layer.

6. On frame 1 of the circleBig_mc layer, choose Edit ➪ Paste (Ctrl+V or ⌘+V). Place the new copy above the original instance, as shown in Figure 25-5. Scale the artwork to 125 percent in the Transform panel, and name the instance `circleBig_mc` in the Property inspector.

7. Create a new Movie Clip symbol from scratch by choosing Insert ➪ New Symbol (Ctrl+F8 or ⌘+F8). Name the symbol **statusClip**. Inside of this symbol, create a short animation displaying the text "Correct!" Leave the first frame of the symbol empty, and create the text (and supporting tweens, if desired) on frame 2 and higher. Create a frame label named `correct` on frame 2 of a new layer named labels, as shown in Figure 25-6. Also, place a `stop();` action on frame 1 of an actions layer in the timeline.

8. Go back to the Main Timeline (that is, Scene 1), and place an instance of statusClip along the bottom of the Stage, centered. With the instance selected, open the Property inspector and name the instance `status_mc`.

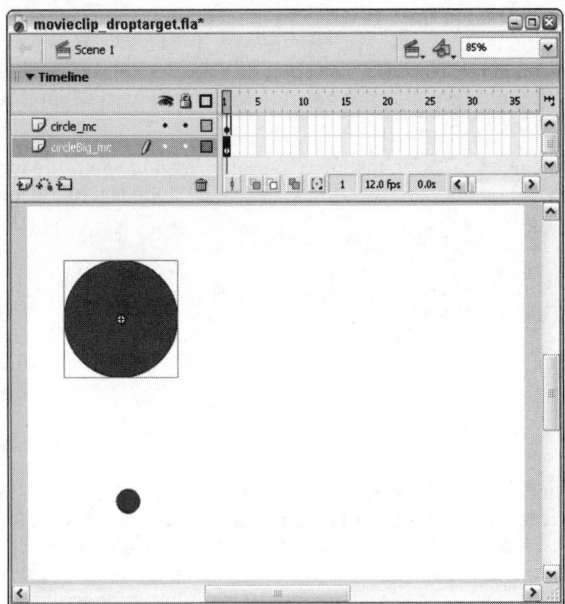

Figure 25-5: The `circleBig_mc` instance

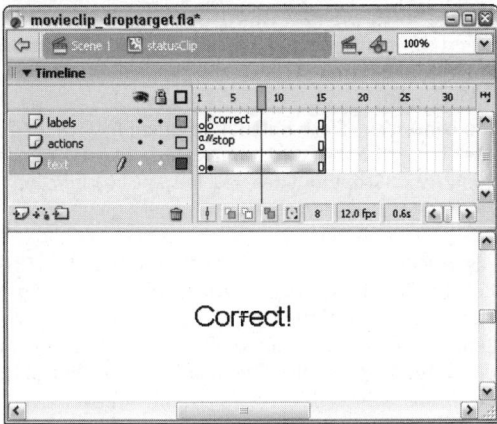

Figure 25-6: The statusClip symbol timeline

9. Now, you will make the `circle_mc` instance draggable by adding some frame actions — you won't use a Button instance as you did earlier in this chapter. On the Main Timeline, create a new layer named **actions** and place this layer above the other layers. Select frame 1 of the actions layer, and in the Actions panel type the following code into the Script pane:

```
circle_mc.onPress = function(){
  this.startDrag();
};
```

Here, the onPress() method of the MovieClip object is used to assign a button press behavior to the instance. In this code, you tell the circle_mc instance to start dragging when it is clicked on the Stage. Note that, as soon as a Movie Clip instance has a button event assigned to it, the mouse pointer will switch to a finger icon when it rolls over the area of the MovieClip object.

10. Next, you need to tell the circle_mc instance to stop dragging when the mouse button releases. Underneath the last line of the code from Step 4, type the following code:

```
circle_mc.onRelease = circle_mc.onReleaseOutside = function(){
  this.stopDrag();
  if ( eval(this._droptarget) == circleBig_mc ) {
    status_mc.gotoAndPlay ("correct");
  } else {
    this._x = 112;
    this._y = 316;
  }
};
```

This code uses the onRelease() method. The code for this method will be executed when the mouse button is released after a mouse click on the circle_mc instance. The instance is told to stop dragging, and then ActionScript evaluates if the current instance (this) is dropped on top of circleBig_mc. When the user drops any Movie Clip instance, the instance's _droptarget property is updated. The _droptarget property specifies the name of the Movie Clip instance upon which the dragged Movie Clip instance was last dropped. If no instance is underneath the dragged instance, _droptarget returns nothing (that is, an empty string). If the _droptarget is the large circle, then the dragged instance stays where it was dropped and the status_mc Movie Clip instance plays its "Correct!" animation. Otherwise, the dragged instance (circle_mc) returns to the X and Y coordinates of its starting point (112, 316).

Note The eval() function is used to convert the Slash notation returned by _droptarget into a "real" object reference. On its own, _droptarget returns Flash Player 4-compatible syntax. In order to use it with current ActionScript routines, use the eval() function to return a proper object reference.

11. Save your Flash document as movieclip_droptarget.fla, and test it (Ctrl+Enter or ⌘+Enter). Click and drag the circle_mc instance on top of the circleBig_mc instance. The dragged instance will stay put on top of the larger circle, and the "Correct!" message will animate. Click and drag the circle_mc instance off the circleBig_mc instance, and release the drag outside of the larger circle. The smaller circle will snap back to its original starting point.

You can continue this example with other shapes, using the same methodology. Create a separate onPress() and onRelease() method for each new drag interaction.

On the CD-ROM For further study, we've included this basic drag and drop game as a sample document called movieclip_droptarget.fla on the *Macromedia Flash MX 2004 Bible* CD-ROM in the ch25 folder.

Making alpha and scale sliders

A compelling use of a draggable Movie Clip is a slider that can alter the properties of another object. By checking the position of a Movie Clip, you can use the position's X or Y coordinate value to alter the value of another Movie Clip. In this section, we create two sliders (one for alpha and another for scale) that will dynamically change the transparency and size of a Movie Clip instance on the Stage. Many thanks to Sandro Corsaro (sandrocorsaro.com) for supplying the artwork of our dog Stella and the park sign.

On the CD-ROM

You need to copy the slider_basic_starter.fla file from the ch25 folder of the *Macromedia Flash MX 2004 Bible* CD-ROM. You'll use premade artwork to understand the functionality of startDrag, stopDrag, and duplicateMovieClip.

Assembling the parts

In this section, you set up the basic composition of the Stage, using elements from the slider_basic_starter.fla Library. You will add artwork of a dog and a park sign to the movie. The dog artwork will be duplicated using the duplicateMovieClip() method, and the duplicate instance will be manipulated by the sliders that you create in the next section. The park sign will be used to remove the duplicate instance using the _droptarget property and the removeMovieClip() method.

1. Open your copy of the slider_basic_starter.fla. Rename Layer 1 to **dog_1_mc**.

2. Access the document's Library by pressing Ctrl+L or ⌘+L. Open the dogElements folder, and drag the dogClip symbol onto the Stage. Place the instance in the upper-left corner of the Stage.

3. With the dogClip instance selected, open the Property inspector. In the <Instance Name> field, type dog_1_mc, as shown in Figure 25-7.

4. Using the Text tool, add the words **Original Dog** under the dog_1_mc instance. You don't need to make a new layer for this artwork.

5. Create a new layer and name it parkSign_mc. Move this layer below the dog_1_mc layer. Drag the parkSignClip symbol, located in the parkSignElements folder in the Library, to the lower-right corner of the Stage. In the Property inspector, assign the instance the name parkSign_mc. In the Transform panel, reduce the size of the parkSign_mc instance to **50%**, as shown in Figure 25-8.

6. Create a new layer called **actions**, and place it above all the other layers. Select the first keyframe of this layer. In the Actions panel, add the following actions:

```
dog_1_mc.duplicateMovieClip("dog_2_mc", 1, {_x: 350,_y:175});
```

This line of code duplicates the instance dog_1_mc, names the new instance dog_2_mc, and places it on the first depth layer of the current timeline (_root). However, Flash Player 6 (or higher) ActionScript allows us to do a little more with the duplicateMovieClip() method. You can assign an initObject parameter that is passed to the duplicated instance. In this example, you create an object with _x and _y properties that are passed to the dog_2_mc instance. This argument positions the dog_2_mc instance at the X coordinate of 350 (350 pixels from the left corner of the Main Timeline Stage) and the Y coordinate of 175 (175 pixels down from the left corner).

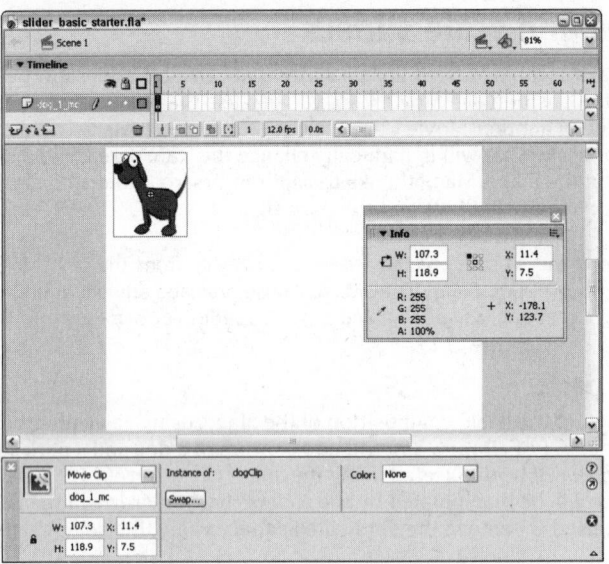

Figure 25-7: The dog_1_mc instance will be used as your reference MovieClip object. The scale and transparency of this dog instance will not be changed.

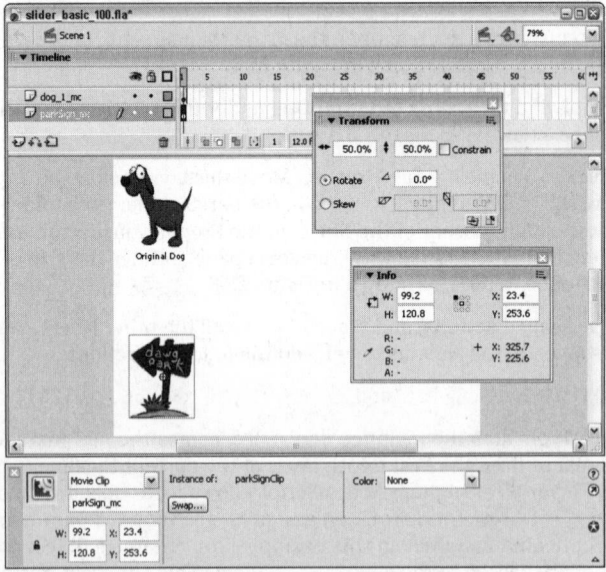

Figure 25-8: The parkSign_mc instance will be used to remove duplicates of the dog_1_mc Movie Clip instance.

7. Save your document as `slider_basic_100.fla`, and test the movie (Ctrl+Enter or ⌘+Enter). You should see a new instance of the `dog_1_mc` Movie Clip appear on the right side of the Stage (see Figure 25-9).

Figure 25-9: The `duplicateMovieClip()` method creates a new instance of a `MovieClip` object. Unless you alter the new instance's X and Y position, it will appear directly above the parent instance.

Now that you have some artwork on the Stage, you can manipulate the duplicated Movie Clip with a pair of dynamic sliders.

Building the sliders

In this section, you'll create two sliders: one for scale, and one for transparency. We'll need to make only one slider Movie Clip symbol and use a new instance for each slider. The basic "problems" of a dynamic slider are to (a) retrieve the position value of an object on the slider (we'll call this the **slider bar**), and (b) set the value of another object equal to (or some factor of) the position value of the slider bar. Finding the position of a slider bar is relatively straightforward. The difficulty lies in creating the value scale for the slider.

Because we have already determined the properties that will be altered (scale and transparency), you need to establish a range of values that each property can use. Luckily, both scale (as `_xscale` and `_yscale` in ActionScript) and transparency (as `_alpha`) use percentage units. However, scale can be any value that's greater than 0 percent and less than 3,200 percent. Alpha has a range of 0 to 100 percent. If you want to use the same parent slider for each property slider, you need to manipulate the position values of the slider bar differently for each property. Let's start with building the basic slider.

On the CD-ROM

Resume using the same file you finished in the previous section. Otherwise, you can open a copy of `slider_basic_100.fla`, located in the `ch25` folder of the *Macromedia Flash MX 2004 Bible* CD-ROM.

1. Create a new Movie Clip symbol (Ctrl+F8 or ⌘+F8) and name it **sliderClip**. In Edit mode, rename the first layer **sliderRule**. On this layer, drag an instance of the sliderRule Graphic symbol (located in the sliderElements folder of the Library) onto the Movie Clip Stage.

Note   The sliderRule artwork contains a line that is 200 pixels long, bound with a circle on each end. The length of this line determines the position range for the slider bar. Therefore, the absolute range is between 0 and 200.

2. With the sliderRule graphic selected, open the Info panel. On the right side of the Info panel (on the diagram of the square bounding box), make sure that the registration point is set to the top-left corner of the selection's bounding box. Then enter the values **–28.4** for the X coordinate and **–12.4** for the Y coordinate, as shown in Figure 25-10.

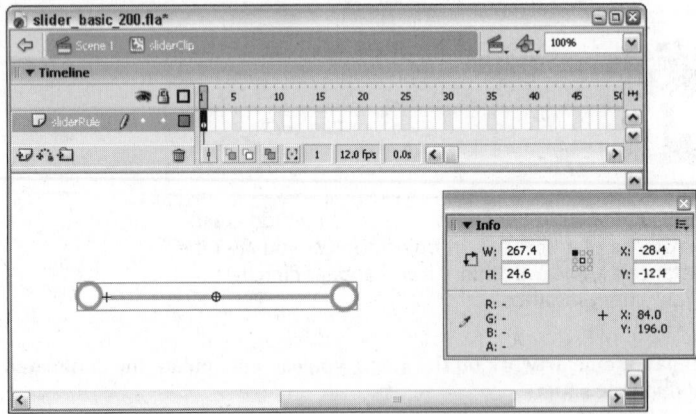

Figure 25-10: The sliderRule's starting point (just to the right of the first left-hand circle) needs to be at the slider Movie Clip's zero X coordinate.

3. Create another layer for the slider Movie Clip and name it **position_mc**. Drag an instance of the sliderBar Movie Clip (located in the sliderElements folder of the Library) to the sliderClip Movie Clip Stage.

4. With the sliderBar instance selected, open the Transform panel. Type **90** in the Rotate field, and press Enter. In the Info panel, click the center registration point in the bounding box diagram, and enter **100** for the X coordinate and **–0.3** for the Y coordinate.

5. To see the position of the sliderBar instance, you need to assign a unique instance name. Select the sliderBar instance and type position_mc in the <Instance Name> field of the Property inspector, as shown in Figure 25-11.

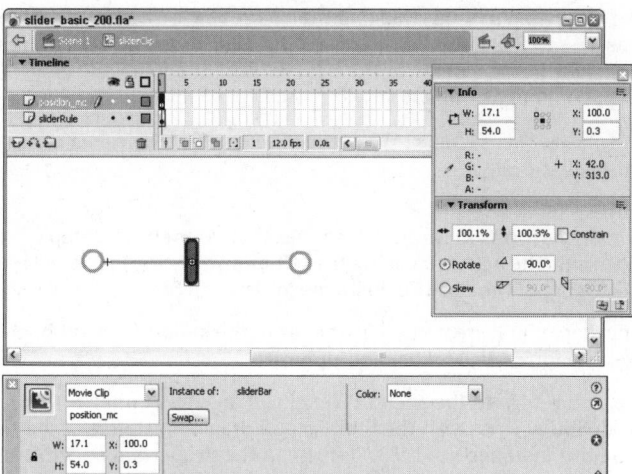

Figure 25-11: The starting X coordinate for the `position_mc` Movie Clip instance is set to 100. When the Flash movie starts, this value will be applied to the scale and alpha properties of the `dog_2_mc` instance on the Main Timeline.

6. Now you need to make the `position_mc` Movie Clip instance draggable. In this example, you're going to make a button-free draggable Movie Clip instance, using the newer `onPress()` and `onRelease()` methods for `MovieClip` objects — just as you did in the earlier exercise. Create a new layer in the slider symbol, name it **actions**, and move it above the position_mc layer. Open the Actions panel (F9). Type the following code in the Script pane:

```
position_mc.onPress = function(){
  this.startDrag(true, 10, 0, 200, 0);
};
```

To make the position instance draggable, you need to detect a mouse press event on the `position_mc` instance. When a mouse click occurs on the instance, the actions nested within the `onPress()` function are executed.

The second line of code enables the dragging behavior of the `position` instance by using the `startDrag()` method on `this`. Because it's used as a method and not as an action, you don't need to specify a target instance in the arguments. The arguments prescribed here lock the mouse to the center of the object and constrain the draggable region to a bounding box defined by 10, 0 and 200, 0. This effectively keeps the `position_mc` instance confined to the line of the sliderRule graphic.

Note We've limited the left end of the `startDrag()` to the X coordinate of 10. This keeps the scale properties from going below 10 percent. If you try to assign a value of 0 or less to the scale properties, Flash will start scaling the instance back up to positive values in an unpredictable manner.

7. Next, you need to be able to stop dragging the position_mc object when the mouse button is released. You'll use the onRelease() handler to define your actions. Open the Actions panel for frame 1 of the actions layer. Type the following code after the last curly brace of the onPress() function:

```
position_mc.onRelease = position_mc.onReleaseOutside = function() {
  this.stopDrag();
};
```

This block of code performs in the same manner that your code in Step 6 did. Once a mouse release event (the act of releasing the left mouse button) is detected (line 1), you stop the dragging of the position instance initiated in Step 6 (line 3).

In the following step, you'll create two instances of the sliderClip symbol on the Main Timeline Stage: one for scale, and one for alpha.

8. Exit Edit mode, and return to the Scene 1 Timeline (the Main Timeline). Create a new layer called **scaleSlider_mc**. Open the Library and drag an instance of the sliderClip to the Stage. Name this instance scaleSlider_mc in the Property inspector.

9. Move the scaleSlider_mc instance to the lower right of the Stage.

10. Create another layer called **alphaSlider_mc**. Drag another instance of the sliderClip symbol onto the Stage, and name the instance alphaSlider_mc. Rotate this instance **–90 degrees**. Place the instance near the right edge of the Stage, as shown in Figure 25-12.

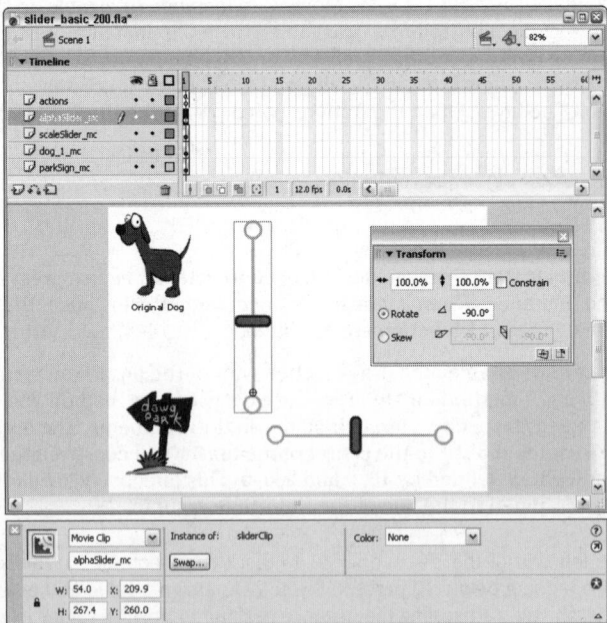

Figure 25-12: At this point, your Flash document's Stage should contain the dogClip and parkSignClip artwork, as well as two instances of the sliderClip symbol.

11. Save your Flash document as `slider_basic_200.fla`, and test it. You should be able to drag the position instances on both sliders.

Checking the positions of the sliders

Once you have a slider bar that is draggable, you need to access the new values of the `position_mc` instance and apply the values to the properties of the `dog_2_mc` instance. To do this, you need to have an event handler whose sole job is to check the X coordinate of the `position_mc` instance. In this section, you'll learn how to make an `onEnterFrame()` handler on the Main Timeline.

On the CD-ROM Resume using the Flash document that you created in the last section. If you didn't complete that section, make a copy of the `slider_basic_200.fla` file located in the `ch25` folder of the *Macromedia Flash MX 2004 Bible* CD-ROM.

1. Select frame 1 of the actions layer in the Main Timeline (that is, Scene 1). Open the Actions panel. In the Script pane, after the `duplicateMovieClip()` action, type the following code:

```
this.onEnterFrame = function(){
  var scalePos = scaleSlider_mc.position_mc;
  var alphaPos = alphaSlider_mc.position_mc;
  with(dog_2_mc){
    _xscale = scalePos._x;
    _yscale = scalePos._x;
    _alpha = alphaPos._x;
  }
};
```

Because the event method `onEnterFrame()` is specified for the Main Timeline (`this`), this block of code will execute continuously in your Flash movie. Why? Any timeline will continuously enter a frame for playback, even if a `stop()` action is applied to all timelines. The speed at which the `enterFrame` event occurs is determined by the frame rate of the Flash movie (as defined by the Modify ⇨ Document dialog box). The frame rate of 12 fps was already set in the sample file before you opened it. Therefore, this block will execute 12 times each second.

What happens on each execution of the `onEnterFrame()` handler? The second and third lines of code create variables that reference the `position_mc` instances with your two sliders. The fourth line of code uses the `with()` action to target the `dog_2_mc` object with the remaining nested actions. The fifth and sixth lines of code set the X and Y scale properties of the `dog_2_mc` instance to the value returned by the current X coordinate of the `position_mc` instance (relative to the coordinates within the sliderClip symbol) nested within the `scaleSlider_mc` instance. The seventh line sets the alpha property of the `dog_2_mc` instance equal to the X coordinate of the `position_mc` instance within the `alphaSlider_mc` instance.

2. Save your Flash document as `slider_basic_300.fla`, and test it. When you drag the bar on the bottom scale slider, notice how the *size* of the `dog_2_mc` instance increases as you drag it to the right. When you drag the bar down on the left alpha slider, you'll see that the *opacity* of the `dog_2_mc` instance decreases.

Note   You may be wondering why the X coordinate of the `position_mc` instance is used for the `alphaSlider_mc` instance, instead of the Y coordinate. Indeed, you do drag the bar on a vertical axis instead of a horizontal one. However, the `position_mc` instance exists within the space of the sliderClip symbol, which has a horizontal orientation in the Edit mode. The X coordinate is derived from the Stage of the Edit mode, regardless of the instance's orientation.

Okay, you have the sliders changing the size and opacity of the `dog_2_mc` instance. However, nothing happens as you drag the bar on the `alphaSlider` instance toward its upper limit. Because the X coordinate of the `position` instance starts at 100, you won't see any visual effect to the alpha property as it increases beyond 100 percent. The lower limit of the alpha slider is 10 percent — it's prevented from going below that value by the coordinate arguments of the `startDrag()` method. Therefore, it would be better to have the `alphaScale_mc` slider convert the X coordinate of the `position` instance to a true 0 to 100 range of values.

To do this, you need to develop an equation that will do the work of automatically remapping values to a 0–100 scale. We know that the lowest X coordinate of the `position_mc` instance is 10, and that the highest X coordinate is 200. If you want the highest position of the bar to provide 100 percent opacity, then you need to divide 200 by a number that will give you 100. Dividing 200 by 2 returns 100. How does that work for the low end? If the X coordinate returns the lowest value of 10, then your lowest opacity value will be 5.

3. With frame 1 of the actions layer of the Main Timeline selected, open the Actions panel (F9), and modify the seventh line of the `onEnterFrame()` handler function to read:

```
_alpha = alphaPos._x/2;
```

4. Save your Flash document and test it. Now, as you drag up with the bar for the `alphaSlider_mc` instance, the opacity increases. As you drag down, it decreases.

So far, so good. However, it would be useful if the `alphaSlider_mc`'s `position_mc` instance started with an X coordinate of 200. This would initialize the `dog_2_mc` instance with an opacity of 100 percent. You could physically move the `position_mc` instance within the sliderClip symbol to an X coordinate of 200, but that would increase the scale of the `dog_2_mc` instance to 200 percent at the start. To change only the `position_mc` instance of `alphaSlider_mc` at the start of the movie, you'll add another line of code to frame 1 of the actions layer on the Main Timeline.

5. Select frame 1 of the actions layer, and open the Actions panel. Add the following code to the Script pane, after all of the existing code:

```
alphaSlider_mc.position_mc._x = 200;
```

This block of code will execute once, when the `position_mc` instance (a Movie Clip object) first appears (or loads) on the Stage.

6. Save the Flash document and test it. This time, the `alphaSlider_mc`'s bar (its `position_mc` instance) will immediately start at the upper limit.

Removing Movie Clips

At this point in the chapter, you have two sliders that dynamically control the scale and alpha of the `dog_2_mc` Movie Clip instance on the Stage. What if you wanted to get rid the `dog_2_mc` instance? How would you delete it? The only way to remove a duplicated Movie Clip instance is to use the `removeMovieClip()` method or action. In this section, we show you how to use the `_droptarget` property and the `removeMovieClip()` method of the `MovieClip` object.

Resume using the same document, `slider_basic_300.fla`, that you created in the last section. Alternatively, you can open the `slider_basic_300.fla` file located in the `ch25` folder of the *Macromedia Flash MX 2004 Bible* CD-ROM.

1. Select frame 1 of the actions layer on the Main Timeline, and open the Actions panel. Type the following code after the last line of ActionScript currently in the Script pane:

```
dog_2_mc.onPress = function(){
  this.startDrag (true, 0, 0, 550, 400);
};
dog_2_mc.onRelease = dog_2_mc.onReleaseOutside = function(){
  this.stopDrag ();
  if(eval(this._droptarget) == parkSign_mc){
    this._parent.onEnterFrame = null;
    this.removeMovieClip();
  }
};
```

Most of this code is already familiar to you. Here we want to make only our duplicate dog instance (`dog_2_mc`) draggable.

When a mouse press event is detected on the `dog_2` instance, the function declared within the `onPress()` method for `dog_2_mc` will execute. The `startDrag()` method of the current dog instance (`this`) will be enabled and constrained to the dimensions of the Flash movie Stage.

When a mouse release event is detected over the `dog_2_mc` instance, then the `stopDrag()` method will be executed. The last `if` statement checks whether the `_droptarget` property of the current dog instance is equal to the target path of the `parkSign_mc` instance. If the `dog_2_mc` instance is over the `parkSign_mc` instance on the Stage when the dragging stops, then the current dog instance is removed.

Finally, if the `dog_2_mc` instance is removed, you must reset the `onEnterFrame()` method assigned to the Main Timeline, the parent of the `dog_2_mc` instance—otherwise, the `onEnterFrame()` method will generate errors in the Output window. By assigning a value of `null` to the Main Timeline's `onEnterFrame()` handler, the function established earlier will be deleted.

We use the `eval()` action on the `_droptarget` property because `_droptarget` returns the path of the target in Slash notation (for Flash 4 compatibility). If we use `eval()` on the `_droptarget` property, Flash returns the target path in dot syntax, as a true object reference.

2. Save your Flash document as `slider_basic_400.fla`, and test it. When you drag the `dog_2_mc` instance over the `parkSign_mc` instance, the `dog_2_mc` instance disappears.

You can find a completed version of `slider_basic_400.fla` in the `ch25` folder of the *Macromedia Flash MX 2004 Bible* CD-ROM. We've also included a more advanced version of the slider example, `slider_advanced_100.fla`, that assigns a callback handler to each slider instance and has a button handler to re-duplicate the `dog_2_mc` instance.

In the next chapter, you expand your knowledge of ActionScript code by using functions and arrays. These code devices enable you to organize code and data much more efficiently with ActionScript.

Web Resource We'd like to know what you thought about this chapter. Visit www.flashsupport.com/ feedback to fill out an online form with your comments.

Summary

✦ The MovieClip object has unique properties, methods, and handlers. Using dot syntax, you can access these characteristics of the MovieClip object.

✦ You can change a Movie Clip instance's position, scale, and rotation using ActionScript. Most physical attributes are accessed by specifying the Movie Clip's path followed by the property name, as in myMCinstance._rotation.

✦ You can create draggable Movie Clips in ActionScript without the use of any Button instances, by using the onPress() and onRelease() methods of the MovieClip object.

✦ The _droptarget property of Movie Clip instance (instance A) indicates the path of the Movie Clip instance (instance B) upon which a Movie Clip instance (instance A) is dropped.

✦ As the sliders example demonstrated, you can use the values of one Movie Clip instance's properties to change the property values of another Movie Clip instance.

✦   ✦   ✦

Using Functions and Arrays

Now that you've had some practice applying ActionScript to
MovieClip objects, you can start to explore the programming
concepts behind subroutines and arrays. This chapter introduces you
to data types, subroutines, arrays, and complex uses of functions.

In previous chapters, you may have found yourself repeating the
same actions (or type of actions) in several event handlers within a
movie. Functions allow you to group actions into code blocks,
referred to by custom names. Arrays are a different kind of grouping
mechanism—instead of grouping actions, an array is used to group
multiple items of data. Before we can discuss functions and arrays,
however, you need to understand the types of data that are available
in ActionScript.

What Are Data Types?

Simply put, ActionScript has several types of data that can be
declared (or loaded) into the Flash movie. So far, you have worked
primarily with three types of data in previous chapters: strings, numbers, and MovieClip objects. In this section, we define more data
types available in ActionScript.

 **Cross-
Reference**   With the release of Flash MX 2004, there are several data types not
discussed in this chapter. For the most comprehensive guide to
ActionScript, refer to the *Flash MX 2004 ActionScript Bible* (Wiley,
2004).

Understanding data types is rather straightforward. The most difficult aspect of working with data types is knowing which data types
work correctly with the operation you want to perform in ActionScript.
We will work with examples throughout this chapter to help you
understand how data types are used.

string

You've seen string data types throughout the *Macromedia Flash MX 2004 Bible* already. Anytime you have a value in quotes, it is typed as a string. If you have an expression that refers to string data types, then its data type will be a string as well. All of the following examples have a string data type:

```
var firstName = "Frank";
var lastName = "Houston";
var fullName = firstName + lastName;
var pathSuffix = "1";
```

Tip

All text contained with Input and Dynamic text fields have a data type of string. If you need to perform numeric operations with text field values, make sure you convert the string data to number data by using the Number() or parseInt() function. We discuss the number data type in the next heading.

Note

Feel free to try out the following code examples in new Flash document files. Create a new file, and rename layer 1 to actions. Using the Actions panel, add the code examples to frame 1 of the actions layer. After you type each code block, test the movie to see the output from the trace() actions appear in the Output panel.

If a variable has a string data type, then any of the String object methods can be used with that data. For example, if you want to convert the case of all characters in the value of firstName to uppercase (turn "Frank" into "FRANK"), you could do the following operation:

```
var firstName = "Frank";
var firstName = firstName.toUpperCase();
trace("firstName = " + firstName);
```

Here, the String object method toUpperCase() converts any lowercase characters in a string value to uppercase characters. Likewise, you can extract specific information from a string. For example, if you wanted to find where a space occurs within a string, and return the value of the string from the point in the value to the end of the value, you could use the following code:

```
var myVersion = "Netscape 4.72";
var startChar = myVersion.indexOf(" ") + 1;
myVersion = myVersion.substr(startChar);
trace("myVersion = " + myVersion);
```

In the preceding code, the indexOf() method searches for the first occurrence of a space (" ") within the string value for myVersion. indexOf(" ") for myVersion will return the position (as a number, counting from left to right) of the space character. For this example, indexOf(" ") will return a 9. Then, 1 is added to this value to determine the character position after the space. In this example, the tenth position of myVersion's value is a "4". Then, by using the slice() method, we can extract the rest of the string from the startChar value of 10. The –1 option tells Flash to continue all the way to the end of the string's value, from the starting point of startChar. Note that in this example, the final value of myVersion is a string value of "4.72".

Cross-Reference For more information on methods that can be performed upon `String` objects and string values, see the `String` object coverage in the *Flash MX 2004 ActionScript Bible*. You can also look up the `String` object in the Help panel.

number

A `number` data type is any value (or expression value) that refers to a discrete numeric value in ActionScript. A value must be typed as a number in order for it to work properly in mathematical operations.

```
var myAge = "27";
var futureYears = "5";
myAge = myAge + futureYears;
trace("I will be " + myAge + " years old in " + futureYears + " years.");
```

If this code was added to frame 1 of your Flash document and tested, the following `trace()` information would appear in the Output panel:

```
I will be 275 years old in 5 years.
```

Obviously, this isn't the answer we were looking for. Because `myAge` and `futureYears` were specified as string values (with quotes), ActionScript simply concatenated (joined) the two string values as `"27"` + `"5"`, which is `"275"`. To see these values as numbers, we need to change the code to the following:

```
var myAge = 27;
var futureYears = 5;
myAge = myAge + futureYears;
trace("I will be " + myAge + " years old in " + futureYears + " years.");
```

Now, the values of `myAge` and `futureYears` appear as real numbers to ActionScript, and the mathematical operation will add the values of `myAge` and `futureYears` correctly. The `trace()` output will now read:

```
I will be 32 years old in 5 years.
```

You can convert `string` data values to `number` data values by using the `Number()` function. In our string example from the last section, we could convert the `myVersion` string value to a number value by adding this line of code:

```
myVersion = Number(myVersion);
```

So, we can now perform mathematical operations on the `"4.72"` value of `myVersion`, which is now simply 4.72.

boolean

There will be times when you will designate a variable's value as either `true` or `false`. Variables that use `true` or `false` are said to have a Boolean value. Boolean values are useful for either/or situations, or when you need a toggle switch—just like a light switch, which is on or off. In the code that follows, a variable named `isLoading` is initialized with a `true` value, but later switched to a `false` value when loading is complete:

```
onClipEvent(load){
    var isLoading = true;
    trace("isLoading's type = " + typeof(isLoading));
}
onClipEvent(enterFrame){
    if(this._framesloaded >= this._totalframes){
        _isLoading = false;
    }
}
```

This code could be placed on a Movie Clip instance. When the Movie Clip instance appears on the Stage, the load event will occur, and the Output panel displays the following:

```
isLoading's type = boolean
```

You can check the data types of declared variables and objects with the typeof operator.

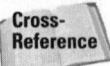

Cross-Reference You learn more about typeof operator in the "Checking data types with typeof" section later in this chapter.

movieclip

As the data type name implies, Movie Clip instances on the Stage have a data type of movieclip. ActionScript distinguishes MovieClip objects from other code-based objects so that you can more easily detect MovieClip objects in your code. The following variable value will be typed as movieclip:

```
var path = this.ballAnim;
```

As long as a Movie Clip instance named ballAnim exists on the current timeline (this), then path's data type will be movieclip. If ballAnim did not exist, then path's data type would be undefined. Because path is classified as a movieclip, methods of the MovieClip object can then be applied to it. In the following code, the gotoAndStop(1) method will be passed along to ballAnim:

```
path.gotoAndStop(1);
```

object

This data type refers to most code-based objects you create with ActionScript. For example, in the next chapter, you will use the Color and Sound objects to enhance interactive presentations. Each of the following variables would be typed as object:

```
var myColor = new Color(_root.ballAnim);
var mySound = new Sound();
var myList = new Array();
var myObject = new Object();
```

If you used this code in your Flash movie, you would see object types in the Output panel when Debug ⇨ List Variables is used in the Test Movie environment:

```
Variable _level0.myColor = [object #1, class 'Color'] {}
Variable _level0.mySound = [object #2, class 'Sound'] {}
Variable _level0.myList = [object #3, class 'Array'] []
Variable _level0.myObject = [object #4, class 'Object'] {}
```

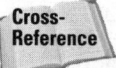

We discuss the new `instanceof` operator introduced with Flash MX later in this section. You can test the class of objects in ActionScript with this operator.

function

In ActionScript, you can define your own subroutines of ActionScript code. We discuss subroutines and constructor functions later in this chapter. The `function` data type will be assigned to any ActionScript code that begins with the `function` action, such as:

```
function myGoto(label){
gotoAndStop(label);
}
```

You can also use the following syntax:

```
var myGoto = function(label){
    gotoAndStop(label);
};
```

There is a difference between declaring a function with the first technique versus the second technique. If you declare a function with in the former method, then you can place the function anywhere within your code block, on any layer for a given frame — the function will be available to any other actions declared on that frame. If you use the latter method, the function will be available only to actions that occur below the function declaration and/or or layers beneath the layer on which it was declared.

undefined

If you check for the data type of a nonexistent code element, ActionScript will return a data type of `undefined`. For example, if you tried to create a variable that stored a reference to a `MovieClip` object that was not currently present on the Stage, a data type of `undefined` will be returned. Create a new Flash document with no elements on the Stage, in any frame. With the first frame of the document selected, type the following code into the Script pane of the Actions panel:

```
var myMovieClip = ballAnim_mc;
trace("the data type of myMovieClip is " + typeof(myMovieClip));
```

Test your Flash movie (Ctrl+Enter or ⌘+Enter). The Output panel will report:

```
the data type of myMovieClip is undefined
```

Checking data types with typeof

Now that you know the various data types in ActionScript, you'll want to know how to check the data type of a given piece of information. Using the `typeof` operator, you can determine the data type of an ActionScript element. The `typeof` operator accepts only one option: the name of the ActionScript element that you wish to test. For example, you can trace a variable (or object) type in the Output panel:

```
var firstName = "Robert";
trace("firstName has a data type of " + typeof(firstName));
```

Strict Typing in ActionScript 2.0

In ActionScript 2.0, introduced with Flash MX 2004, you can declare variables with a strict data type. The format for such declarations is:

```
var variableName:data type;
```

or

```
var variableName:data type = value;
```

For example, if you type the following code into the Actions panel, you will declare a strictly typed string variable:

```
var myName:String = "Robert";
```

In this example, the variable myName can only use values that have a data type of String. If a different data type is assigned to the variable, the ActionScript compiler will report an error when you publish or test your Flash movie. Try the following code in a new Flash document, on the first frame:

```
var myName:String;
myName = 4.72;
```

Once you have entered this code, choose Control ➪ Test Movie. The Output panel will report the following error:

```
**Error** Scene=Scene 1, layer=Layer 1, frame=1:Line 2: Type mismatch in
assignment statement: found Number where String is required.
    myName = 4.72;
```

Interesting, eh? That's a pretty specific error message, letting you know that you declared a number where a string value was expected. If you change the second line of code to:

```
myName = "Robert";
```

and retest the movie, you will no longer see the error message in the Output panel. So, why is strict typing important, after all is said and done? For the most part, strict typing forces you to carefully plan and map out the goals of your Flash movie, and discourages you from "free-form" coding, or coding haphazardly. By using strict typing with your ActionScript code, you can more easily debug problems in your Flash movies. In later chapters of Part VII, we'll put strict typing to use. For the most comprehensive coverage of ActionScript 2.0, refer to the *Flash MX 2004 ActionScript Bible*.

When this movie is tested, the Output panel will display:

```
firstName has a data type of string
```

You can use typeof in for . . . in loops, so that actions will be executed with specific data types. The following ActionScript code will take any string variables on the Main Timeline and move them to the _global namespace:

```
for(name in _root){
  if(typeof(_root[name])=="string" && _root[name] != _root["$version"]){
    _global[name] = _root[name];
```

```
    delete _root[name];
  }
}
```

The preceding code block will move all variables except the native `$version` variable to the new `_global` namespace.

On the CD-ROM   You can see the returned values of the `typeof` operator in the `typeof_simple_AS1.fla`, `typeof_simple_AS2.fla`, `typeof_advanced_AS1.fla`, `typeof_advanced_AS2.fla`, and `moveVariables.fla` files, located in the `ch26` folder of the *Macromedia Flash MX 2004 Bible* CD-ROM.

Checking class type with instanceof

Flash MX introduced a new operator to ActionScript: `instanceof`. With this operator, you can check the class type of a specific object in ActionScript. A class is similar to a data type, but a little more detailed. As you saw in the object data discussion, several different objects returned `object` as their data type. However, these objects belong to different classes. In fact, you probably noticed the class type showing up in the Output window when you chose Debug ⇨ List Variables.

Let's take a look at an example that compares `typeof` to `instanceof`. Create a new Flash document, and select frame 1 of the default layer. In the Actions panel, type the following code into the Script pane:

```
var currentDate = new Date();
trace("the data type of currentDate is " + typeof(currentDate));
```

After you've written this code, test the Flash movie (Ctrl+Enter or ⌘+Enter). The Output panel will display the following text:

```
the data type of currentDate is object
```

Now, let's use the `typeof` operator in an `if` statement. After the last line of code that you typed, enter the following code:

```
if(typeof(currentDate) == "object"){
  trace("currentDate has a data type of object");
}
```

When you save and test this movie, the last line of the Output panel will be:

```
currentDate has a data type of object
```

However, if you wanted to check what kind of object `currentDate` was, the `typeof` operator would not be able to help you out. Enter the `instanceof` operator. Add the following code to the actions list for frame 1:

```
if(currentDate instanceof Date){
  trace("currentDate is a Date object");
}
```

When you test the movie, you will see the following text display in the Output panel:

```
currentDate is a Date object
```

Now, let's try an `if`/`else` statement that compares `currentDate` to a different class, such as Sound. Add the following code into the Actions panel for frame 1:

```
if(currentDate instanceof Sound){
  trace("currentDate is a Sound object");
} else {
  trace("currentDate is not a Sound object");
}
```

When you test your movie, you will see the following text displayed in the Output panel:

```
currentDate is not a Sound object
```

While these are simple tests, you can start to see how `instanceof` allows you to check the class types of your data.

Note   When you use the `instanceof` operator, you do not wrap the compared value in quotes, as you do with `typeof`. For example, do not use `if(currentDate instanceof "Date")`. Simply refer to the class by name, without the quotes: `if(currentDate instanceof Date)`.

Overview of Functions as Procedures

A primary building block of any scripting or programming language is a procedure. A procedure is any set of code that you wish to reserve for a specific task. A procedure is useful for code that you wish to reuse in multiple event handlers (for example, Button instances and keyframes). In Flash ActionScript, procedures are called functions, and are created with the `function` action.

What functions do

A function (or procedure) sets aside a block of code that can be executed with just one line of code. Functions can execute several actions, and pass options (called *arguments* or *parameters*) to those actions. All functions must have a unique name, so that you know what to reference in later lines of code. In a way, functions are equivalent to your own custom additions to the Flash ActionScript language. In ActionScript, you can define a function on a specific timeline, and refer to its path and name to execute it.

Note   For Flash Player 4 compatible movies, use the `call()` action to execute code blocks located on other keyframes in the Flash movie.

When to create a function

For people new to scripting, perhaps the most confusing aspect of functions is knowing when to create them in a Flash movie. Use the following guidelines to help you determine when a function should be created:

✦ If you find yourself reusing the same lines of code on several Button instances, `MovieClip` objects, or keyframes, then you should consider moving the actions to a function. In general, you should not pile up ActionScript on any single Button or Movie Clip instance.

✦ If you need to perform the same operation throughout a Flash movie, such as hiding specific Movie Clip instances on the Stage, you should consider defining a function to take care of the work for you.

✦ When you need to perform operations to determine a value (such as determining the current day of the week or calculating values in a mathematical formula), you should move the operations to a function.

How to define a function

When you add a function to a keyframe on the Main Timeline or a Movie Clip timeline, you are defining the function. All functions have a target path, just like other objects in ActionScript. All functions need a name followed by opening and closing parentheses, but arguments (options to pass to the function) inside the parentheses are optional.

Tip Functions are usually defined at the very beginning of a Flash movie. We recommend only defining functions on timeline keyframes—you can, however, execute functions from any event handler in a Flash movie.

As a simple example, let's say you wanted to create a function that has one `gotoAndStop()` action. This function will have a shorter name than `gotoAndStop()`, and will be faster to type and use in our ActionScript code. Place this code on the first keyframe of the Main Timeline.

```
function gts(){
this.gotoAndStop("start");
}
```

This function, when evoked, will send the current timeline Playhead to the `start` label You could further expand the functionality of `gts()` by adding an argument, which we'll call `frameLabel`:

```
function gts(frameLabel){
    this.gotoAndStop(frameLabel);
}
```

In this version of the `gts()` function, instead of hard-coding a frame label such as `start` into the actual `gotoAndStop()` action, you specify an argument with the name `frameLabel`. Just like variable names, the names of your function and its arguments are entirely up to you— the name `frameLabel` has no significance. ActionScript simply knows that if you pass an argument to the `gts()` function, that it should place that argument where the `frameLabel` term occurs in your actions. An argument acts as a placeholder for information that will be supplied to the function on a per-use basis; that is, you can specify a different value for `frameLabel` each time you evoke the `gts()` function. You can also use as many (or as few) arguments as you need. Insert a comma between each argument in the function declaration:

```
function calculateRange (min, max){
   var diff = Math.abs(max - min);
   return diff;
}
```

Caution Beware of naming your functions (and arguments) after already existing ActionScript terms. If in doubt, you should probably choose a word that does not resemble any JavaScript syntax (with later upgrades to ActionScript in mind). You'll see many examples in tutorials or books in which programmers always prefix names with `my`, as in `myColor` or `myLabel`, to avoid any potential naming conflicts.

How to execute a function

After you have defined a function on a timeline's keyframe, you can create actions that refer to the function's actions. The standard method for executing a function is:

```
path to function.functionName(arguments);
```

At the end of the previous section, you defined a function named gts() on the Main Timeline. If you added a Button instance to our movie, you could then execute the function from the Button instance with the following code:

```
on(release){
this.gts("start");
}
```

When this Button instance is clicked, the function gts() on the current timeline (this) is executed, and passed the argument "start". In your function gts(), you defined frameLabel as an argument that occurs in the gotoAndStop() action. Therefore, the Main Timeline will go to and stop on the "start" frame label.

Later in this chapter, you use functions to create a dynamic reusable menu system in a Flash movie.

Caution   A function cannot be executed unless it was previously defined in the movie and recognized by the Flash Player. The keyframe containing the function declaration needs to be "played" before the function is available for use. For example, if you define a function on frame 10 of a Movie Clip instance that has stopped on frame 1 (and never played to frame 10), the Flash Player will not have registered the function in memory. For this reason, it's usually a good idea to place your functions on the first frame of the Flash movie.

Managing Related Data: The Array Class

Have you ever had a bunch of variables that have a lot in common? For example, do you have variables such as name_1, name_2, name_3, name_4, and so on? These variables look like lists of common information, such as:

```
var name_1 = "John";
var name_2 = "Vanessa";
var name_3 = "Jennifer";
var name_4 = "Frank";
```

In programming languages, an array is a list of values that can be addressed by their position in the list. An array is created by using the Array constructor:

```
var visitors = new Array();
```

The preceding code object simply creates the array container for data. You create an array with information already specified, such as:

```
var visitors = new Array("John","Vanessa","Jennifer","Frank");
```

or

```
var visitors = ["John", "Vanessa","Jennifer","Frank"];
```

Emulating Arrays in Flash Player 4 Movies

In Flash Player 4, you could only emulate arrays, using expressions for variable names. In the earlier array examples, you could create an array-like structure for a Flash 4 movie by using the following code:

```
var name_1 = "John";
var name_2 = "Vanessa";
var name_3 = "Jennifer";
var name_4 = "Frank";
```

Then you could use another variable, i, to refer indirectly to different name_ variables, as in:

```
var i = 2;
var currentName = eval("name_" add i);
message = "Hello " add currentName add ", and welcome!";
```

For Flash Player 4 compatibility, the add operator (instead of the + operator) and the eval() function are used to return the current value of the name_ variable we want to insert. If you traced the message variable, the Output window would display:

```
Hello Vanessa, and welcome!
```

We only mention array emulation in this section because many Flash developers may encounter clients who wish to have Flash movies (or sites) that will work with the Flash Player 4 plug-in, especially for Flash banner ads.

To access an item in visitors, you would use the array access operators with an array index number. To access the first position's data, you would use the following code:

```
var message = "Hello " + visitors[0] + ", and welcome.";
```

Here, visitors[0] will return the value "John". If you traced the message variable, it would read:

```
Hello John, and welcome.
```

In most programming languages, the first index value (the starting position) is 0, not 1. In the following table, you'll see how the index number increases with the sample visitors array.

Index Position	0	1	2	3
Index Value	John	Vanessa	Jennifer	Frank

You can set and get the values within an array using the array access operators. You can replace existing array values by setting the index position to a new value, and you can add values to the array by increasing the index number, as in:

```
var visitors = new Array("John","Vanessa","Jennifer","Frank");
visitors[3] = "Nicole";
visitors[4] = "Candice";
```

In the example, "Nicole" replaces "Frank", and "Candice" is added to the end of the array. You can also add elements to the array using the push() method of the Array class, as in:

```
visitors = new Array("John", "Vanessa","Jennifer","Frank");
var newLength = visitors.push("Nicole","Candice");
```

This code will add "Nicole" and "Candice" after "Frank", and set the variable newLength equal to the length of the visitors array. length is an Array property that returns the number of elements in the array. In the preceding example, newLength is equal to 6 because there are now six names in the array.

 **Cross-Reference** You can read more about methods of the Array class in the *Flash MX 2004 ActionScript Bible*.

You learn more about arrays in a function example later in this chapter.

Creating a Dynamic Reusable Flash Menu

In this section, you use arrays to create a dynamic code-built menu that you can adjust for any Flash movie. You create a Main Timeline with six sections for a mock photographer's site, and a menu that navigates to those four sections. While that sounds simple enough, you create the menu entirely from ActionScript code. Figure 26-1 displays the menu and its items, as it appears during runtime.

 **Note** Flash MX 2004 includes many components that enable you to create menu systems, but most of them require a more advanced understanding of ActionScript concepts such as listeners. You'll learn more about components in Chapter 29, "Using Components."

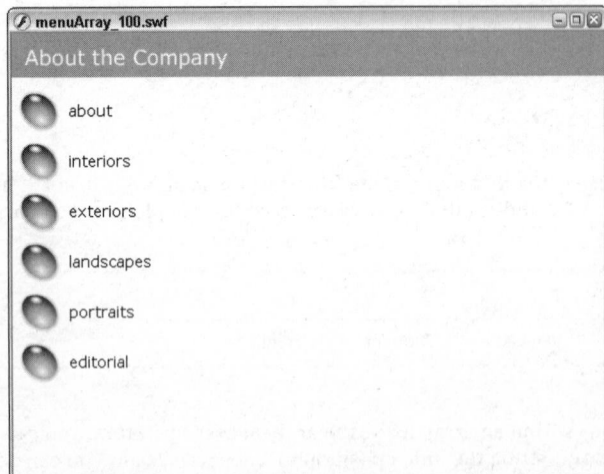

Figure 26-1: The completed Flash movie with the menu items

In the following steps, you build a Flash movie that uses this menu system.

1. Create a new Flash document (Ctrl+N or ⌘+N).

2. Rename Layer 1 **labels**. Create new keyframes (press the F6 key) on frames 2, 10, 20, 30, 40, and 50. Select frame 60 and press F5.

3. Starting on frame 2 of the labels layer, assign the following label names to the keyframes you created in Step 2: **about**, **interiors**, **exteriors**, **landscapes**, **portraits**, and **editorial**.

4. Add a new layer, and name it **actions**. Add a keyframe on frame 2 of the actions layer. With that keyframe selected, open the Actions panel and add a `stop();` action. In the Property inspector, type //**stop** in the <Frame Label> field. This creates a frame comment of stop. The `stop();` action on frame 2 prevents the Main Timeline from playing past the about section when the movie first loads.

5. Create another layer called **heading**. Add keyframes on this layer, matching the keyframes in the labels layer. Insert some graphics in each keyframe for each section. As a starting point, you can simply add text headings to each section (for example, About the Company, Interior Photography, and so on). You need this heading layer so that you have some indication that the Playhead on the Main Timeline actually moves when an item in the menu is clicked.

6. Create another layer called **background**. Place this layer at the bottom of the layer stack. Draw a filled rectangle that spans the top of the document, as shown in Figure 26-2.

7. Now you create an array that contains the names of each your frame labels. Add a new layer to the Main Timeline, and name it **menu actions**. Select the first keyframe on the menu actions layer. Open the Actions panel (F9), and add the following code (note that the ⤶ indicates a continuation of the same line of code; do not insert this character into your actual code):

```
var sectionNames = new Array("about", "interiors", ⤶
   "exteriors", "landscapes", "portraits", "editorial");
```

This line of ActionScript creates an `Array` object named `sectionNames`. You can now refer to each section of your timeline using array syntax, such as `sectionNames[0]`, `sectionNames[1]`, and so on. You use this array to build the actual button text in our menu.

8. In the same block of code, add the following line to the Script pane for frame 1 of the menu actions layer, after the existing code:

```
var sectionCount = sectionNames.length;
```

This code creates a new variable named `sectionCount`. The `length` property of an array will return the current number of elements inside of the array. Therefore, because you put six elements into the array (in Step 7), `sectionCount` will be equal to 6. You may be wondering why you just didn't manually insert the value 6 here. The reason for using an array is that you can change the elements of the array at any point, and the rest of your code will update automatically to reflect the changes. In this way, you are building a dynamic menu system.

9. Save your Flash document as `menuArray_100.fla`. At this point, your Flash document should resemble Figure 26-2.

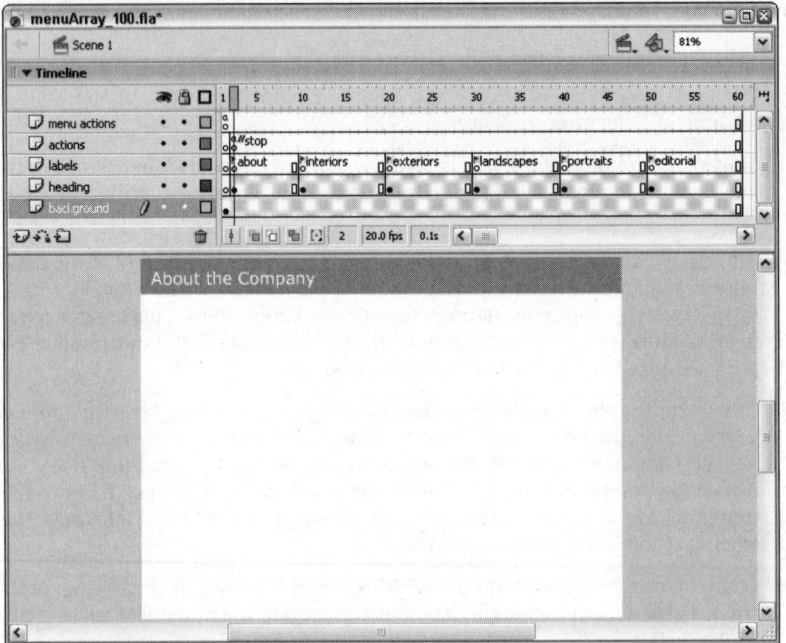

Figure 26-2: The Main Timeline has frame labels and artwork for each section of the presentation.

10. Now you need to create the menu element that you can use to build a dynamic menu from ActionScript. Create a new Movie Clip symbol by pressing Ctrl+F8 (⌘+F8). Name this symbol **itemClip**, and choose the Movie Clip behavior.

11. Within the timeline of the itemClip symbol, rename Layer 1 to **button**. On this layer, create or add a Button symbol. In our example, we used the Oval buttons — blue button from the Ovals folder of the Buttons library (Window ➪ Other Panels ➪ Common Libraries ➪ Buttons). This will be the actual button that appears in the menu. Center your Button instance on the Stage, using the Align panel.

12. Add a new layer to the itemClip symbol, and name it **textfield**. On this layer, create a Dynamic text field that can accommodate the longest name you specified in the sectionNames array. In the Property inspector, give this Dynamic text field the instance name label_txt. Use whatever font face you prefer. Place the text field to the right of the button, as shown in Figure 26-3.

13. Add another layer to the itemClip symbol, and rename it **actions**. Select frame 1 of this layer, and in the Actions panel add the following code:

```
label_txt.text = labelName;
stop();
```

This code will put the value of a variable named labelName into the label_txt text field. You will see how labelName is declared in the Step 18.

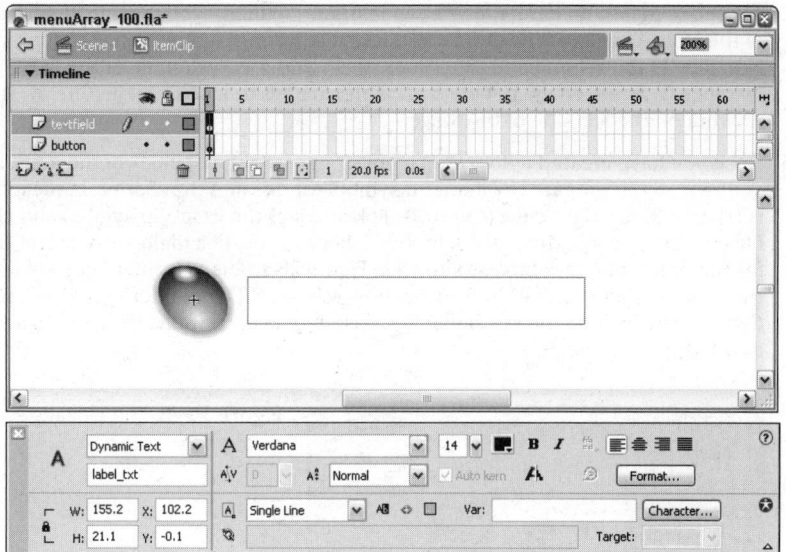

Figure 26-3: The itemClip symbol will be used to create each button in the dynamic menu. Using ActionScript, the label_txt field will be filled with the appropriate section name.

14. Select the Button instance that you added in Step 12. Open the Actions panel, and type the following code in the Script pane:

```
on(release){
    this.targetClip.gotoAndStop(labelName);
}
```

This code will use the value of a `labelName` variable as the frame label for the `gotoAndStop()` action. Notice that you will control the Playhead of a dynamically-assigned timeline, indicated by `this.targetClip`. This value will be assigned to each menu item with ActionScript in a later step.

You will use the itemClip symbol as a prototype for the real buttons in the menu. In the remaining steps of this exercise, you'll create a `MovieClip` object in ActionScript to hold several instances of the itemClip symbol.

15. Save your Flash document.

16. Go back to the Main Timeline (that is, Scene 1). Open the Actions panel for frame 1 of the menu actions layer. Add the following ActionScript to the Script pane, after the existing code:

```
var menu = this.createEmptyMovieClip("menu_mc", 1);
menu._x = 25;
menu._y = 70;
```

This code makes an empty MovieClip instance, named menu_mc, at the first depth slot of the Main Timeline (this). The variable menu returns a reference to the menu_mc instance. In the second and third lines, the X and Y coordinates of the menu_mc instance (referenced via the menu variable) are set to a position just below the heading artwork on the left side of the Stage.

17. Once you have created a MovieClip object to contain instances of the itemClip symbol, you're ready to prepare the itemClip symbol for use in ActionScript. In the Library panel (Ctrl+L or ⌘+L), right-click (Control+click on Mac) the itemClip symbol and choose Linkage in the contextual menu. In the Linkage Properties dialog box, select the Export for ActionScript check box, as shown in Figure 26-4. The Identifier field will auto-fill with the symbol's name, itemClip. You can now refer to this identifier in ActionScript, to dynamically include the symbol in the Flash movie at runtime. Click OK to accept the new linkage parameters.

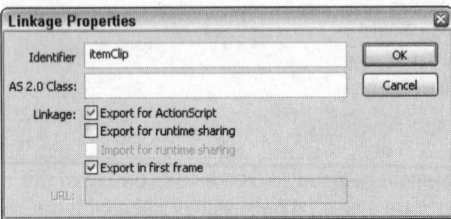

Figure 26-4: The Linkage Properties dialog box

18. Select frame 1 of the menu actions layer, and open the Actions panel. Now, you're ready to add the ActionScript code that will dynamically attach several instances of the itemClip symbol to the menu_mc instance created in Step 16. Note that the ⊃ indicates a continuation of the same line of code; do not insert this character into your actual code.

```
for(var i=0; i < sectionCount; i++){
  var depthCount = menu.getNextHighestDepth();
  var item = menu.attachMovie("itemClip", "item_" + i, ⊃
    depthCount);
  item.labelName = sectionNames[i];
  item.targetClip = this;
  item._y = i*45;
}
```

New Feature

This code uses the new MovieClip object method getNextHighestDepth(), which takes the guesswork out of determining which depth slots are unoccupied with existing elements.

This code inserts a for loop that will attach the itemClip symbol for each element in the sectionNames array. It will also set the value of labelName in each attached instance (item) to the name of the appropriate section name. Notice that you specify i for the index number of the sectionNames array because the position index of every array starts at 0 — your menu item numbering will also start at 0.

After an instance is attached for the section name, the targetClip variable (mentioned in Step 14) is set to the current timeline, this. All of your frame labels exist on the Main Timeline, where this code is being invoked.

You then position the item instance at multiples of 45. The first item is positioned at a Y coordinate of 0 (0 × 45 = 0), the second item is positioned at 45 (1 × 45 = 45), the third item is positioned at 90 (2 × 45 = 90), and so on.

Tip

Be sure to click the Check Syntax icon in the toolbar of the Actions panel, to make sure you didn't make a typo in the code. As an alternative, you can press Ctrl+T or ⌘+T while focus is in the Actions panel.

19. Save your Flash document again, and test it (Ctrl+Enter or ⌘+Enter). Unless you had a syntax error in your ActionScript, you will see a dynamic menu, built by ActionScript (as shown in Figure 26-1). Each menu item has a unique labelName value, which is used in the gotoAndStop() action by each Button instance.

You can enhance this dynamic menu by adding animation to the itemClip symbol timeline. You can also restructure the ActionScript to work with separate Movie Clips for each sectionName, instead of frame labels. If you use this properly, you may never need to script a menu again! Simply change the Button instance artwork and text styles for unique menu interfaces.

On the CD-ROM

You will find the completed menuArray_100.fla file in the ch26 folder of the *Macromedia Flash MX 2004 Bible* CD-ROM.

Functions as Methods of Objects

We've already discussed functions as procedure mechanisms in Flash movies. Functions can be used to define a set of actions that are later executed when the function is invoked. In ActionScript, you can also use functions as methods of other objects. Methods are actions mapped to other objects. Unlike properties and values, methods carry out a task with that object. In this section, we deconstruct a Flash document (.fla file) that uses a function to create a menu completely from ActionScript.

On the CD-ROM

Make a copy of the createMenu_100.fla file, located in the ch26 folder of the *Macromedia Flash MX 2004 Bible* CD-ROM.

Open a local copy of the createMenu_100.fla file in Flash MX 2004. You'll notice that the Main Timeline has a setup similar to the menuArray_100.fla file that was discussed in the last section. There are a series of labels, indicating sections of the Flash movie. Test this Flash movie, and you'll see a dynamic menu display. Clicking each button takes you to the corresponding section of the Flash movie.

Unlike our previous menuArray_100.fla example, however, notice that we have different text on the menu buttons than the text used in the frame labels. For example, the Our Products menu button takes you to the products label on the Main Timeline. For this Flash movie, a function with multiple arguments enables you to specify the text of the menu buttons separately from the targeted labels (and timelines).

Select the first frame of the functions layer. In the Actions panel, you'll see this function appear in the Script pane:

```
function createMenu(arrObj){
    var sectionCount = arrObj.length;
    for(var i=0; i < sectionCount; i++){
        var section = arrObj[i];
        var depthCount = this.getNextHighestDepth();
        var item = this.attachMovie("itemClip", "item_"+i, depthCount);
        item.label_txt.text = section.btext;
        item.targetClip = section.clip;
        item.labelName = section.flabel;
        item._y = i*45;
    }
}
```

The `createMenu()` function has one arguments: `arrObj`. The value of this argument will be supplied via a method of a Movie Clip instance when the function is executed. Similar to our previous `menuArray_100.fla` example, an array is used to store the values of frame labels, button text, and target clips. In this way, you can create ActionScript that correctly uses frame labels in other `goto` actions, without worrying about the text that is actually used as a button item.

Select frame 1 of the actions layer, and view the code in the Actions panel. Some of the same actions from the previous section's example are re-used here. An empty `MovieClip` object named menu_mc is created, positioned, and assigned the `createMenu()` function as a method, just as `duplicateMovieClip()` or `attachMovie()` is a method of the `MovieClip` object:

```
menu.createMenu = createMenu;
```

Note   We'll examine the revised `sectionNames` array in just a moment. For now, let's see how the `createMenu()` function is assigned to the menu_mc instance.

This line of code creates a new method called `createMenu`, specifically for the menu_mc instance (referenced via the menu variable) on the Stage. It also set this method to use the function `createMenu` as its value. Therefore, whenever you evoke the `createMenu` method of the menu object, the actions within the `createMenu` function will run.

Caution   The act of creating and assigning a method name for an object does not actually execute the method or the function. We're simply defining a method for the object, so that it can be evoked later. Do not use parentheses for method (and function) assignment—doing so will execute the function upon assignment.

Note that you can use any method name you prefer—it need not match the name of the function as our example does. So, you could write:

```
menu.customMenu = createMenu;
```

The function `createMenu` also uses the `this` syntax to make the function work in relation to the object that is executing it. `this` will correspond to menu_mc for the method assignment menu.createMenu = createMenu. However, if we had another menu instance, such as menu_2, that used the `createMenu` function as a method, `this` would refer to its path for its method.

Herein lies the power of a function as a method of an object — you can assign the same function (and arguments) to several unique objects (or Movie Clip instances) on the Stage.

To execute the method `createMenu` for the `menu` instance, specify the method and any arguments you will supply the method. In our example, the following line executes the `createMenu()` method for the `menu_mc` instance:

```
menu.createMenu(sectionNames);
```

In this line of code, the `sectionNames` variable is passed as the argument to the `createMenu` function. The `sectionNames` variable is an array of `Object` objects. Each object contains three properties:

✦ `flabel`: This property defines the frame label to be used in the menu item's `gotoAndStop()` action.

✦ `btext`: This property defines the text to appear to the right of the button.

✦ `clip`: This property declares which timeline should invoke the `gotoAndStop()` action.

In our example, three section objects are defined in the `sectionNames` array:

```
var sectionNames = [
                    {flabel: "main", btext: "Home", clip: this},
                    {flabel: "products", btext: "Our Products", clip: this},
                    {flabel: "services", btext: "Our Services", clip: this}
                    ];
```

When the `createMenu()` method is evoked, the `createMenu()` function parses the `sectionNames` array into the actions contained with the function. While you do not see the code structure of an array specified in the function, a local variable named `section` represents each object in the `sectionNames` array:

```
var section = arrObj[i];
```

where `arrObj`, as the argument of the `createMenu()` function, represents the passed value, `sectionNames`. In this more advanced usage of an array, each index of the array represents the section object with the three named properties. For example, when `arrObj[0]` is evaluated in the `for` loop, the following object is returned:

```
{flabel: "main", btext: "Home", clip: this}
```

The `section` variable is used to take each object and apply its properties to dynamically created instances of the itemClip symbol:

```
item.label_txt.text = section.btext;
item.targetClip = section.clip;
item.labelName = section.flabel;
```

The `section.clip` property is used to let each `item` instance know which timeline target it should address with its `gotoAndStop()` action (contained on the Button instance within the itemClip symbol in the Library). The `section.flabel` property assigns the proper frame label for the `gotoAndStop()` action for the Button instance, and the `section.btext` property assigns the text to the `label_txt` field within the `item` instance.

This movie also uses a `clearMenu()` function (and method) to delete the `item` instances.

Functions as Constructors for Objects

Functions can also be used with the new constructor to create objects with properties and methods assigned by the function. This means that you can use a function to create unique objects, based on parameters that you pass as arguments to the function upon invocation. In this section, we deconstruct another function example that creates an entire sound library with ActionScript, without using any Movie Clip instances.

On the CD-ROM Make a local copy of the soundObjects.fla file, located in the ch26 folder of the *Flash MX 2004 Bible* CD-ROM.

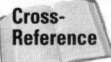

Cross-Reference You will learn about ActionScript for Sound objects in the next chapter.

Open your copy of the soundObjects.fla file in Flash MX 2004. You'll notice that there aren't any Movie Clips and/or physical elements on the Stage. Select the first (and only) frame on the actions layer. Open the Actions panel, and you'll see the following code:

```
function SoundLibrary(begin, end) {
  this.snd = new Array();
  for (var i = begin; i <= end; i++) {
    var depthCount = _root.getNextHighestDepth();
    var target = _root.createEmptyMovieClip("sndStorage_" + i, depthCount);
    this.snd[i] = new Sound(target);
    this.snd[i].attachSound("sound_" + i);
  }
}
soundLib = new SoundLibrary(1, 7);
soundLib.snd[1].start();
soundLib.snd[2].start();
```

There are three sections to this code: the function definition; the object creation and assignment; and the method execution of the Sound objects.

Function definition

The SoundLibrary() function has two arguments: begin and end. Again, these are user-defined function names and arguments. You could rename the function and arguments to your own preferred terms. The for loop in the SoundLibrary() function will create a snd array object within the calling object (this). This array will contain Sound objects that use the sound files in the Library. Note that each of the sounds in the Library have been set to export with the Flash SWF file, as defined by the Linkage Properties for each sound.

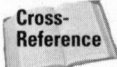

Cross-Reference See Chapters 28, "Sharing and Loading Assets," for more information on symbol linkage.

Object creation and assignment

After the SoundLibrary() function is defined, you can use it for new objects. In this example, a new object named soundLib is created after the function definition:

```
soundLib = new SoundLibrary(1,7);
```

First, the object is declared as being on the current timeline (this or _root). By not specifying _root directly, you can load this Flash movie into MovieClip objects in other Flash movies and retain proper targeting paths for the createLib() function. If you test this movie on its own, soundLib will be declared on _root or _level0. Using the new constructor, we create the snd array and Sound objects relative to the soundLib object. We are creating a unique object with specific properties and values. This enables you to make as many objects as you desire, all from one function:

```
soundLib_1 = new SoundLibrary(1,3);
soundLib_2 = new SoundLibrary(4,7);
```

These actions (not used in our example) would create two separate soundLib objects, each using a specific range of Sound objects that play linked sound files from the Library.

The numbers specified in the parentheses indicate the sounds to use from the Library. Remember that in our function SoundLibrary(), the begin and end arguments are used to form the linkage identifiers:

```
"sound_" + i
```

where i is defined by the begin argument, and incremented until the end argument value is reached.

Sound object method execution

Finally, after the Sound objects are created within the soundLib object, you can play the sounds with the built-in ActionScript start() method for Sound objects:

```
this.soundLib.snd[1].start();
this.soundLib.snd[2].start();
```

These lines of code tell the Sound objects located in the 1 and 2 index positions of the snd array (in this example, sound_1 and sound_2 from the Library) to play.

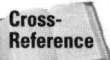
Cross-Reference Functions can also be used to return values to other variables in ActionScript. You learn how to use the return keyword in functions in Chapter 33, "Creating a Game in Flash."

This is just one way of using functions to create new objects. You can use functions to create other types of data-based objects for record storage and retrieval, as well as to create unique Color objects to reference with more than one Movie Clip target.

Caution During further testing, we discovered that the setVolume() method of the Sound Object controls all Sound objects linked to the same target timeline. This means that each Sound object must target a unique MovieClip object, in the new Sound() constructor. For example, if you wanted to separately control the volume of five individual sounds, make sure you use a different target MovieClip instance for each of those Sound objects. To safeguard for this condition, we used the `createEmptyMovieClip()` method in our example to allocate sound resources to a separate timeline, designated by the local variable `target` in the `SoundLibrary()` function.

We'd like to know what you think about this chapter. Visit `www.flashsupport.com/feedback` to fill out an online form with your comments.

Summary

✦ ActionScript has several data types, including `boolean`, `function`, `movieclip`, `number`, `object`, and `string`.

✦ The data type of an ActionScript element can be checked using the `typeof` operator.

✦ The most common use of a function is as a procedure, a set of actions that execute when the function's name is evoked.

✦ A procedure should be created when the same actions are repeated within a Flash movie, or when you want to avoid storing long action lists within Button instances.

✦ A function is defined with the `function` action, in the format `function name(arguments){actions}`.

✦ A function can be executed when the name of the function is evoked. The format of a function call is `targetPath.functionName(arguments);`, as in `createMenu(sectionNames)`.

✦ Arrays can manage related information, such as lists. An array is initiated with the `Array` constructor, as in `myArray = new Array();`.

✦ Array elements have an index number, indicating their position in the array. Array index numbers start with 0 and increment by 1 with each new element.

✦ Functions can be used as methods of ActionScript objects. A method is assigned by creating a unique method name after the object and setting the method's value equal to a function name (for example, `menu.createMenu = createMenu;`). Parentheses and arguments are omitted from the method assignment.

✦ Objects can be created with the function constructor. Functions intended for this use describe properties and methods for objects using the `this` target path. A new object is created by specifying an object name and setting its value equal to a new instance of the function name, as in `myObject = new SoundLibrary(1,7);`.

✦   ✦   ✦

Interacting with Movie Clips

✦ ✦ ✦ ✦

In This Chapter

Defining collisions

Using the hitTest()
method

Using the Color object

Accessing the Sound
object

Controlling the volume
and balance of a sound

Printing Flash content
with PrintJob

✦ ✦ ✦ ✦

This chapter continues your exploration of the `MovieClip` object in ActionScript. You explore the ins and outs of collision detection for `MovieClip` objects and learn how to control the visibility of the mouse pointer or to attach a custom cursor to the mouse pointer. You look at other ActionScript elements such as `Color` and `Sound` objects that work with `MovieClip` objects to create visual and audio effects, respectively.

 **New Feature** You will also learn how to print Flash content with the new `PrintJob` class, introduced with Flash MX 2004. The Flash Player creates high-quality output for hard copy artwork.

Movie Clip Collision Detection

Have you ever wanted to detect the intersection of two elements in a Flash movie? If two Movie Clip instances overlap on the Stage, how would you know? How would you tell ActionScript to look for an overlap? In ActionScript, there are two primary types of intersections (or collisions):

  ✦ **User-initiated collisions:** This type of intersection occurs when you click and drag an object (a `MovieClip` object) and overlap another `MovieClip` object as you drag or release. You can also consider the mouse pointer an "object" that can intersect with another object. For example, if you move the mouse pointer over a `MovieClip` object, you can detect when the mouse pointer enters the space of the `MovieClip` object.

  ✦ **Script- or time-based collisions:** This type of intersection between objects happens when randomly moving objects collide with one another, such as balls bouncing around the Stage, detecting the edges of the frame and responding to other boundaries or objects.

In this section, you look at examples in each of these categories. Let's begin with a quick review of the `_droptarget` property of the `MovieClip` object.

Using _droptarget

A collision between two MovieClip objects can occur if the user drags one Movie Clip instance to the location of another Movie Clip instance. We first examined the startDrag() action and method in Chapter 25, "Controlling Movie Clips." In the dog movie, you used the _droptarget property of a MovieClip object to detect whether the area of one MovieClip object occupied the area of another MovieClip object. To recap, you can test the intersection of two Movie Clips with the following code:

```
on(press){
 this.startDrag();
}

on(release,releaseOutside){
 trace(eval (this._droptarget));
 if(eval(this._droptarget) == level0.mcInstance1){
  trace("this MC instance overlaps mcInstance1");
 } else {
   trace("this MC instance OVERLAPS mcInstance1");
   trace("this MC instance OVERLAPS mcInstance1");
 }else{
   trace("this MC instance does NOT overlap mcInstance1"
 }
 topDrag ();
}
```

This code could occur on a Button instance within the first Movie Clip instance. When the user clicks the Button instance, the Movie Clip startDrag() method is invoked, and the user can drag the Movie Clip instance on the Stage. When the user releases the mouse, the _droptarget property (which returns target paths in Slash notation) is evaluated to convert the target path to dot syntax. If the _droptarget property returns the path to another instance, the if condition sees whether the path matches mcInstance2. If the paths match, the trace() action indicating an overlap is executed. Otherwise, a separate trace() action notifies us that the instance is not on top of mcInstance2.

Cross-Reference   To see a fully functional example of the _droptarget property in action, please review the section "Detecting the drop position: Using _droptarget" in Chapter 25, "Controlling Movie Clips."

Collision detection with hitTest()

You can also perform more advanced collision detection using the hitTest() method of the MovieClip object. hitTest() does exactly what it says — it tests to see whether a "hit" occurred between two elements. hitTest() has the following two formats:

```
mcInstance.hitTest(anotherInstance);
```

or

```
mcInstance.hitTest(x coordinate, y coordinate, shapeFlag);
```

With this method, you can determine whether the X and Y coordinates are within the space occupied by the Movie Clip instance. You can use `onClipEvents` such as `mouseMove` or newer event handlers such as `onMouseMove()` to check constantly for a hit occurrence:

```
onClipEvent(mouseMove){
  if(this.hitTest(_root._xmouse, _root._ymouse, true)){
   trace("A hit has occurred");
  }
}
```

or

```
myMC.onMouseMove = function(){
  if(this.hitTest(_root._xmouse, _root._ymouse, true)){
   trace("A hit has occurred");
  }
};
```

This code reports a `trace()` action anytime the mouse pointer is moved within the artwork of the Movie Clip instance to which the `onClipEvent` or `onMouseMove()` handler is attached. The shape flag attribute of `hitTest()` defines the actual test area for the hit. If the shape flag is set to `true`, a hit occurs only if the X and Y coordinates occur within the actual artwork of the Movie Clip instance. If the shape flag is set to `false`, a hit occurs whenever the X and Y coordinates occur within the bounding box of the Movie Clip instance. In Figure 27-1, if the left circle uses a shape flag of `true`, a hit is reported whenever the X and Y coordinates occur within the shape of the circle (not within the bounding box). If the right circle uses a shape of `false`, a hit is reported when the X and Y coordinates occur within the bounding box.

shape flag = true

shape flag = false

Figure 27-1: The shape flag determines the boundary of the Movie Clip instance for the hitTest() method.

On the CD-ROM

You can see a working example of shape flags and the `hitTest()` method in the `hitTest_xy.fla` file, located in the ch27 folder of the *Macromedia Flash MX 2004 Bible* CD-ROM. Open this Flash document, and test the movie. As you move your mouse within the space of each object, you will notice that the hit area is different for each object. You create your own Flash movie that uses `hitTest()` in our coverage of the `Mouse` object in this chapter.

The other format for the `hitTest()` method is to simply specify a target path to compare for a hit occurrence. With this syntax, you cannot use a shape flag option; if any area of the bounding box for a Movie Clip instance touches the bounding box of the tested instance, a hit occurs. For example, you can modify the ActionScript used earlier to indicate a hit between instances, instead of X and Y coordinates:

```
onClipEvent(mouseMove){
  if(this.hitTest(mcInstance2)){
   trace("A hit has occurred.");
```

```
      }
    }
```

or

```
  myMC.onMouseMove = function(){
   if(this.hitTest(mcInstance2)){
    trace("A hit has occurred.");
   }
  };
```

This code assumes that other actions are actually initiating a startDrag() action. Also, we have omitted the other half of the if condition in both this example and the previous example. If you omit a condition operator and test condition, ActionScript assumes that you are testing for a true result (as a Boolean value). The following if conditions are exactly the same:

```
  var myMouseClick = true;
  if(myMouseClick){
   trace("myMouseClick is true.");
  }
  if(myMouseClick == true){
   trace("myMouseClick is true.");
  }
```

Therefore, to test for a true value with any if statement, specify the variable (or method) that has a Boolean value. The hitTest() method yields either a true (a hit has occurred) or a false (no hit has occurred) result. Note that, with scripting languages, it is more common to use the former example for testing true conditions.

You can see a working example of targets and the hitTest() method in the hitTest_target.fla file, located in the ch27 folder of the *Macromedia Flash MX 2004 Bible* CD-ROM. You will create a Flash movie that uses this type of hitTest() method in our coverage of the Sound object later in this chapter.

Using the Mouse Object

With ActionScript, you can emulate custom mouse pointers (that is, the graphic shown for the mouse pointer) by using the startDrag() behavior (with lock to center true) on Movie Clips containing icon graphics. However, this technique does not hide the original mouse pointer — it appears directly above the dragged Movie Clip instance. ActionScript features a static Mouse object, which has the following two simple methods:

✦ show(): This method reveals the mouse pointer. By default, the mouse pointer appears at the start of a movie.

✦ hide(): This method turns off the mouse pointer's visibility. To reveal the mouse pointer again, execute the show() method.

Once the Mouse object (that is, the mouse pointer) is hidden, you can lock a MovieClip object containing a new icon graphic to the position of the mouse pointer. In this section, you create a Flash movie with a large circle `MovieClip` object. When the mouse pointer moves into the area of this object, you attach a smaller circle to the mouse pointer's position. The `hitTest()` method will be used to determine when the mouse pointer movies into the area of the large circle, and the `attachMovie()` method of the `MovieClip` object will affix the small circle to the mouse pointer's position.

1. Create a new Flash document (Ctrl+N or ⌘+N). Rename Layer 1 to **circle**.

2. Select the Oval tool, and draw a circle. In the Property inspector, set the circle's size to 25 x 25.

3. With the circle artwork selected, press the F8 key to convert the artwork into a Movie Clip symbol. Name the symbol **circleClip**.

4. Name the instance on the Stage **circleLarge_mc** in the <Instance Name> field of the Property inspector. Increase the size of this particular instance to 200 x 200, and apply a Tint effect to fill the instance with a different solid color. Center the instance on the Stage using the Align panel.

5. Now you have to link the circleClip symbol in the Library panel to the exported Flash movie (.swf file). Right-click (Control+click on the Mac) the circle symbol, and choose Linkage. Select the Export for ActionScript check box, and the Identifier field auto-fills with the text **circleClip**, as shown in Figure 27-2. Click OK to accept these settings.

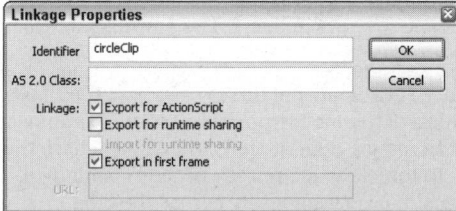

Figure 27-2: The circle symbol is now linked to the Flash movie.

Once the circle symbol is linked, you can dynamically insert the symbol into the Flash movie with ActionScript. Remember that you want to attach the circle to the mouse pointer when it enters the space of the `circleLarge_mc` instance.

6. On the Main Timeline (that is, Scene 1), create a new layer and name it **actions**. Select frame 1 of this layer, and open the Actions panel. Type the code shown in Listing 27-1 into the Script pane as follows:

Listing 27-1: The onMouseMove() Handler for the circleLarge_mc Instance

```
1. circleLarge_mc.onMouseMove = function() {
2.   if(this.hitTest(_root._xmouse,_root._ymouse, true)){
3.     if (!(circleSmall_mc instanceof MovieClip)) {
4.       _root.attachMovie("circleClip", "circleSmall_mc", 1);
5.     }
```

Continued

Listing 27-1 (continued)

```
6.    circleSmall_mc._x = _root._xmouse;
7.    circleSmall_mc._y = _root._ymouse;
8.    Mouse.hide();
9.    updateAfterEvent();
10.  } else {
11.    if(circleSmall_mc instanceof MovieClip){
12.       circleSmall_mc.removeMovieClip();
13.    }
14.    Mouse.show();
15.  }
16. };
```

Here, you use the event handler onMouseMove() for MovieClip objects. This handler is assigned to the circleLarge_mc in line 1. When the mouse moves in the Flash movie, the function(){} code executes.

If the X and Y position of the mouse pointer intersects with the circleLarge_mc instance, the if condition in line 2 executes. Line 3 checks to see if the new graphic (that is, the circleClip symbol in the Library) exists in the movie. If it doesn't, the symbol is attached to the Main Timeline (_root) in line 4. The new instance is named circleSmall_mc.

Lines 6 and 7 position the X and Y coordinates of the circleSmall_mc instance by referencing the current position of the mouse pointer (_root._xmouse and _root._ymouse). Line 8 hides the mouse pointer icon, while Line 9 uses the updateAfterEvent() function to force a video refresh of the Flash movie. This enables the circleSmall_mc to move very smoothly across the Stage.

Lines 10–15 execute if the mouse pointer is not within the space of the circleLarge_mc instance. Line 11 checks to see if circleSmall_mc exists in the movie — if it does, it is removed (line 12). The mouse pointer will also reappear when the mouse moves outside of the circleLarge_mc instance (line 14).

7. Save your Flash document as mouse_hitTest.fla, and test it (Ctrl+Enter or ⌘+Enter). In the Test Movie window, move the mouse pointer into the space of the large circle. When the mouse enters this area, the small circle from the Library attaches itself to the position of the mouse cursor and hides the original pointer. When you move the mouse out of the large circle, the small circle disappears and the original mouse pointer returns. See Figure 27-3 for these comparisons.

That might have seemed like a lot of work to hide a mouse pointer, but in the process, you learned how to attach your own icons to the mouse pointer. You can use this same methodology to add any custom graphic to the mouse pointer. Simply add a different linked symbol to the Library, and change the linkage ID in the attachMovie() method.

On the CD-ROM   You can find the completed example, mouse_hitTest.fla, in the ch27 folder of the *Macromedia Flash MX 2004 Bible* CD-ROM.

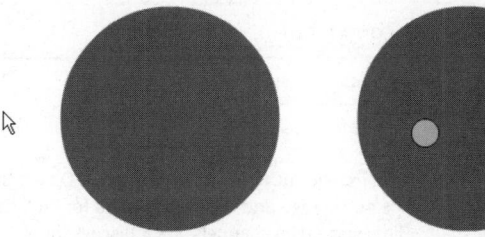

Figure 27-3: The left image shows the mouse outside the large circle, whereas the right image shows the mouse inside the large circle with the small circle attached.

Manipulating Color Attributes

The Color object in ActionScript gives you unprecedented control of the appearance of your MovieClip objects. By controlling the color (and transparency) of your artwork with ActionScript's Color object, you can:

✦ Create on-the-fly color schemes or "skins" for Flash interfaces.

✦ Enable users to select and view color preferences for showcased products on an e-commerce site.

✦ Instantly change the color attributes of a Flash design-in-progress for a client.

Because color is controlled through the Color object, we'll quickly review the unique methods available to this object. Refer to Table 27-1 for more information. Note that this table is organized by order of practical use.

Table 27-1: Methods for the Color Object

Method	Definition	Options
setRGB	Changes the RGB offset for the specified Color object (and targeted Movie Clip). This method changes all colors in the targeted instance to one solid RGB color.	*colorReference.setRGB(0xRRGGBB);* where: *colorReference* is the name of the Color object. We'll discuss the creation of Color objects in this section. *RR, GG,* and *BB* are the offset values (in hexadecimal) for the Red, Green, and Blue channels, respectively.
getRGB	Retrieves the values established with the last setRGB execution. If you want to reapply RGB offsets to a new Color object, use this method. You can also retrieve RGB numeric values of any Movie Clip instance on the Stage that has a Tint effect applied to it.	*colorReference.getRGB();* No options or arguments for this method.

Continued

Table 27-1 *(continued)*

Method	Definition	Options
setTransform	Changes the RGB offset and percentage values for the specified Color object (and targeted Movie Clip). This method produces visual results that resemble both left- and right-hand color controls in the Advanced Effect dialog box for the Advanced option in the Color menu of the Property inspector.	*colorReference.setTransform(colorTransformObject);* where: *colorTransformObject* is the name of a Object that has percentage and offset properties for Red, Green, Blue, and Alpha channels. We'll discuss the intricacies of these properties in the following sections.
getTransform	Retrieves the values established with the last setTransform execution. Use this method to reapply color transforms to new Color objects. You can also use this method to retrieve the color values of Movie Clip instances that have an Advanced Effect applied in the Property inspector.	*colorReference.getTransform();* No options or arguments for this method.

Creating a Color object

To manipulate the color attributes of a Movie Clip instance, you need to create a new Color object that references the Movie Clip instance. In the following steps, you learn to use the constructor for the Color object. Let's work out the steps required to take control of color properties.

On the CD-ROM   For the exercises with the Color object, make a copy of the dogColor_starter.fla document in the ch27 folder of the *Macromedia Flash MX 2004 Bible* CD-ROM. Thank you, Sandro Corsaro of www.sandrocorsaro.com, for supplying the dog artwork!

1. Select the instance of the dog graphic on the Stage. Open the Property inspector and name this Movie Clip instance dog_1_mc.

2. Create a new layer on the Main Timeline, and name the layer **buttons**.

3. Open the Components panel and drag an instance of the Button component onto the Stage. Place the instance near the left corner of the Stage. We discuss components in more detail in Chapter 29, "Using Components." For now, we'll guide you through the use of this component for the purposes of this exercise.

4. Select the `Button` component instance on the Stage, and open the Property inspector. Make sure the Parameters tab is selected in the inspector. Name this instance `cbtRed`. Type the text **Red** in the label field. Refer to the settings shown in Figure 27-4.

Note Flash MX 2004 components do not use a click or change handler in the same way that Flash MX components did. As you'll see shortly, there's a new event listener model for components.

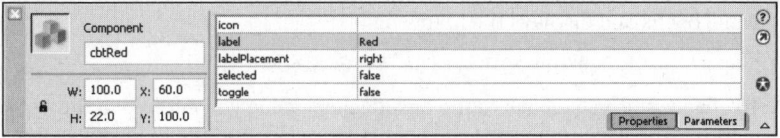

Figure 27-4: The parameters for this instance of the Button component

5. Now you need to create a `changeColor()` function in the movie. This function is executed by the `cbtRed` instance when it is clicked. Create a new layer on the Main Timeline and name it **actions**. Select frame 1 of the actions layer, and open the Actions panel (F9). In Expert mode, type the following code into the Script pane:

```
function changeColor(obj){
 var label = obj.target.label.toLowerCase();
 if(label == "red"){
  dogFill_1 = new Color(dog_1_mc);
  dogFill_1.setRGB(0xFF0000);
 }
}
cbtRed.addEventListener("click", this.changeColor);
```

In this function, the `obj` argument represents an event object that the `Button` instance passes to the function. When the `cbtRed` instance is clicked, `obj.target` will equal `cbtRed`. (You'll be adding another instance in short order.) Line 2 of this function establishes a variable named `label` that returns the label text inside of the `obj` instance and converts the label text to lowercase. If `label` equals "red" in line 3, lines 4 and 5 will execute. Line 4 creates a new `Color` object called `dogFill_1`, which refers to the `dog_1_mc` Movie Clip instance you made in Step 1. Once the `dogFill_1` object is initiated, you can access methods of the `Color` object, such as `setRGB()`. In line 5, you change the color of the Movie Clip instance to pure red, designated by `0xFF0000` in hexadecimal.

The last line of code, after the function declaration, tells the `cbtRed` instance to register the `changeColor()` function as a listener for click events. Whenever the `cbtRed` instance is clicked, the `changeColor()` function is invoked.

Tip Choose View Line Numbers in the options menu of the Actions panel to see line numbers next to your ActionScript code. The options menu is located at the top right corner of the panel.

6. Save the Flash document as `dogColor_100.fla`, and test the movie. Click the `cbtRed` instance on the Stage. The color of the `dog_1_mc` Movie Clip should change to bright red. Close the Flash movie, and return to the Flash MX 2004 authoring environment.

7. To see the getRGB() method in action, let's create some trace() messages for the Output panel. Go back to the changeColor() function on frame 1. Add the following line of code just before the closing curly brace (}) of the if() action. Type this as one line of code:

```
trace("dogFill_1's RGB numeric value = " + ↩
  dogFill_1.getRGB());
```

8. Save the document and test the movie. When you click the cbtRed instance, the Output panel opens and displays the following text:

```
dogFill_1's RGB numeric value = 16711680
```

9. To change this value back to the hexadecimal value you entered in the setRGB() method, you need to convert the value to base 16. Add the following action after the last trace() action from Step 6:

```
trace("dogFill_1's RGB hex value = " +
  dogFill_1.getRGB().toString(16));
```

10. Save the document and test the movie. When you click the cbtRed instance, the Output panel should open and display the new value:

```
dogFill_1's RGB numeric value = 16711680
dogFill_1's RGB hex value = ff0000
```

However, you won't need to convert getRGB()'s native return value to set another Color object equal to a previous setRGB() value. In the following steps, you will create another dog and Color object team.

11. Duplicate the dog_1_mc Movie Clip instance on the Stage (Edit ⇨ Duplicate), and name the new instance dog_2_mc in the Property inspector. Position the dog_2_mc instance to the right of dog_1_mc.

12. Duplicate the Button component instance on the Stage, and position the new instance below the original one. In the Property inspector, change its instance name to cbtPassRed. Change its label value to **Pass Red**.

13. Select frame 1 of the actions layer, and open the Actions panel. On the closing curly brace line of the existing if() code in the changeColor() function, add the code shown in bold in Listing 27-2.

Listing 27-2: **Checking for the Pass Red Label**

```
function changeColor(obj) {
  var label = obj.target.label.toLowerCase();
  if (label == "red") {
    dogFill_1 = new Color(dog_1_mc);
    dogFill_1.setRGB(0xFF0000);
    trace("dogFill_1's RGB numeric value = " + dogFill_1.getRGB());
    trace("dogFill_1's RGB hex value = " + dogFill_1.getRGB().toString(16));
  } else if (label == "pass red") {
    dogFill_2 = new Color(dog_2_mc);
```

```
    dogFill_2.setRGB(dogFill_1.getRGB());
  }
}
cbtRed.addEventListener("click", this.changeColor);
cbtPassRed.addEventListener("click", this.changeColor);
```

14. Save the Flash document and test the movie. When you click the `cbtRed` instance, the `dog_1_mc` Movie Clip instance turns red. When you click the `cbtPassRed` instance, the `dog_2_mc` Movie Clip instance turns red.

Note

If you click the second `Button` instance first, the `dog_2_mc` Movie Clip instance will turn black. Why? Because the first button's actions were not executed, and there was no previous `setRGB()` method execution for the `getRGB()` method to refer to. Moreover, there was no `dogFill_1` object either. Consequently, ActionScript returns a zero or null value for the `getRGB()` method. In hexadecimal color, zero is equivalent to black.

Now that you've had some experience with the `Color` object's `setRGB()` and `getRGB()` methods, let's move on to the more complex `colorTransformObject`. You'll use the Flash document from this exercise, so keep the dogs on the Stage!

On the CD-ROM

You can find the completed Flash document, `dogColor_100.fla`, in the ch27 folder of the *Macromedia Flash MX 2004 Bible* CD-ROM.

Creating a Transform Object

The two remaining methods of the `Color` object, `setTransform()` and `getTransform()`, require a more thorough understanding of RGB color space. Before the `setTransform()` method can be used with a `Color` object, you need to create a generic object using the object constructor. This generic object becomes a `colorTransformObject` once we have assigned color properties to the generic object.

The properties of the `colorTransformObject` are:

✦ `ra` — the Red channel percentage

✦ `rb` — the Red channel offset

✦ `ga` — the Green channel percentage

✦ `gb` — the Green channel offset

✦ `ba` — the Blue channel percentage

✦ `bb` — the Blue channel offset

✦ `aa` — the Alpha channel percentage

✦ `ab` — the Alpha channel offset

The *a* properties are percentage-based, ranging in value from –100 to 100. The *b* properties are offset-based, ranging from –255 to 255 (derived from 24-bit RGB color space, in which each 8-bit color channel can have a range of 256 values).

These properties and values may seem complex, so refer to the Advanced options of the Color menu for symbol instances in the Property inspector for guidance. With the Advanced option chosen in the Color menu, click the Settings button. In the Advanced Effect dialog box, the left-hand color controls are percentage-based, whereas the right-hand controls are offset-based. Admittedly, color is difficult to visualize from numbers. To accurately predict the color changes with setTransform(), we use the Advanced Effect dialog box to help us out.

On the CD-ROM Make a copy of the dogColor_100.fla if you didn't complete the previous section's exercise. This document is located in the ch27 folder of the *Macromedia Flash MX 2004 Bible* CD-ROM.

1. Using the same Flash document (.fla file) from the previous exercise, select the original dog_1_mc Movie Clip instance on the Stage. Open the Property inspector, and choose the Advanced option in the Color menu. Press the Settings button to the right of the menu. In the Advanced Effect dialog box, enter the following value on the left-hand side: **–100% Blue**. On the right-hand side, enter these values: **37 G** and **255 B**. Refer to Figure 27-5. Click OK to close the dialog box. With these values, the dog_1 instance should be a monochrome blue with yellow eyes. Normally, you would want to write these values down so that you had them to use later. Because you have them printed here in this book, erase them by choosing None from the Color menu in the Property inspector. The dog_1 instance should now appear in its original state.

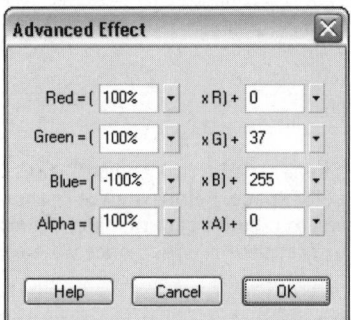

Figure 27-5: These settings will change the color of the dog_1 instance.

2. Duplicate one of the existing Button component instances on the Stage. Place the duplicated instance underneath the last Button component instance. Name the name instance cbtRabid. Change the label value to **Rabid**.

   With this new instance, you will create some code that will initiate a new Color object, and a new colorTransformObject. The colorTransformObject will be given properties that have the same values as those determined in Step 1. Then you'll execute the setTransform() method for the Color object, using the colorTransformObject's data for the color change.

3. Select frame 1 of the actions layer and open the Actions panel (F9). Starting on the line containing the last curly brace of the else if() action within the changeColor() function, add the bold code shown in Listing 27-3.

Listing 27-3: **Checking for the rabid Label**

```
function changeColor(obj) {
  var label = obj.target.label.toLowerCase();
  if (label == "red") {
    dogFill_1 = new Color(dog_1_mc);
    dogFill_1.setRGB(0xFF0000);
    trace("dogFill_1's RGB numeric value = "+dogFill_1.getRGB());
    trace("dogFill_1's RGB hex value = "+dogFill_1.getRGB().toString(16));
  } else if (label == "pass red") {
    dogFill_2 = new Color(dog_2_mc);
    dogFill_2.setRGB(dogFill_1.getRGB());
  } else if (label == "rabid") {
    dogColor = new Color(dog_1_mc);
    rabidLook = new Object();
    rabidLook.ba = -100;
    rabidLook.bb = 255;
    rabidLook.gb = 37;
    dogColor.setTransform(rabidLook);
  }
}
cbtRed.addEventListener("click", this.changeColor);
cbtPassRed.addEventListener("click", this.changeColor);
cbtRabid.addEventListener("click", this.changeColor);
```

In the preceding code, you created two objects: dogColor and rabidLook. rabidLook is assigned the ba, bb, and gb colorTransformObject properties. Each of these properties is given the values you determined in Step 1. Then you specified that the rabidLook object be used as the target for dogColor's setTransform() method.

4. Save the Flash document as dogColor_200.fla, and test the movie. Click the new Button instance that you added in Step 2. The colors of the dog_1_mc Movie Clip instance should change to match those you saw in Step 1. Close the Test Movie window, and return to the Flash MX 2004 authoring environment.

Now you will create a button that restores the original look of the dog_1_mc Movie Clip instance. The code structure resembles that of Step 3, but you use a different syntax to assign color properties to the colorTransformObject.

5. Duplicate one of the Button instances, and place the new instance underneath the last Button instance. In the Property inspector, name this component instance cbtRestore. Change the label value to **Restore**, and leave the Click Handler set to changeColor().

6. Select frame 1 of the actions layer, and open the Actions panel (F9). Add the bold code shown in Listing 27-4 to the Script pane.

Listing 27-4: **Checking for the Restore Label**

```
function changeColor(obj) {
  var label = obj.target.label.toLowerCase();
  if (label == "red") {
    dogFill_1 = new Color(dog_1_mc);
    dogFill_1.setRGB(0xFF0000);
    trace("dogFill_1's RGB numeric value = "+dogFill_1.getRGB());
    trace("dogFill_1's RGB hex value = "+dogFill_1.getRGB().toString(16));
  } else if (label == "pass red") {
    dogFill_2 = new Color(dog_2_mc);
    dogFill_2.setRGB(dogFill_1.getRGB());
  } else if (label == "rabid") {
    dogColor = new Color(dog_1_mc);
    rabidLook = new Object();
    rabidLook.ba = -100;
    rabidLook.bb = 255;
    rabidLook.gb = 37;
    dogColor.setTransform(rabidLook);
  } else if (label == "restore") {
    dogColor = new Color(dog_1_mc);
    restoreLook = {
      ra:'100',
      rb:'0',
      ga:'100',
      gb:'0',
      ba:'100',
      bb:'0',
      aa:'100',
      ab:'0'
    };
    dogColor.setTransform(restoreLook);
  }
}
cbtRed.addEventListener("click", this.changeColor);
cbtPassRed.addEventListener("click", this.changeColor);
cbtRabid.addEventListener("click", this.changeColor);
cbtRestore.addEventListener("click", this.changeColor);
```

In the restoreLook object, you define all the default properties using name/value pairs separated by the colon character (:). Notice that all the properties of the restoreLook object can be declared and given values within a { } nesting.

Caution   Do not insert a comma after the very last property assignment when you are using this syntax. Doing so will result in an ActionScript error.

7. Save the Flash document again, and test the movie. Click the cbtRabid instance you created in Step 2. After the dog_1_mc Movie Clip instance changes color, click the cbtRestore instance you created in Step 5. Voila! The dog_1_mc Movie Clip instance reverts to its original color. Click the cbtRed instance that you created in the previous section. This button (which uses the setRGB() method) changes the appearance of the dog_1_mc Movie Clip instance to a solid red color. Now click the cbtRestore instance—the dog_1_mc Movie Clip instance reverts to its original look!

You can find the completed document, dogColor_200.fla, in the ch27 folder of this book's CD-ROM.

While the setRGB() method can alter basic color properties of MovieClip objects, the setTransform() method is the color-control powerhouse. Any look that you can accomplish with the Advanced Effect dialog box, you can reproduce with the setTransform() method and the colorTransformObject.

Just as the getRGB() method can retrieve the values of a past setRGB() method, you can transfer past setTransform() values using the getTransform() method. You can also use getRGB() to retrieve manually set Tint values applied to Movie Clip instances and getTransform() to retrieve Advanced settings applied to Movie Clip instances with the Property inspector.

Enabling Sound with ActionScript

ActionScript offers many object types, and one of the most exciting objects to use is the Sound object. As with most objects, the Sound object has predefined methods that you can use to control each new Sound object. Table 27-2 provides an overview of the Sound object and its common methods.

Table 27-2: Common Methods for the Sound Object

Method	*Definition*	*Options*
attachSound	Creates a new instance of a sound file (AIF or WAV) available in the Library. The new instance becomes a part of the Sound object and can be targeted with Sound object methods. Unlike attached Movie Clips, attached sounds do not require a depth number.	*soundObject.attachSound(libraryID);* where: *soundObject* refers to the sound Object's name *libraryID* is the name of the sound in the Symbol Linkage properties (available in the Library)

Continued

Table 27-2 *(continued)*

Method	Definition	Options
loadSound	Loads a separate MP3 audio source (.mp3 file) into a Sound object. You can begin playback of the MP3 sound as soon as enough bytes have downloaded, or wait until the entire file has downloaded. We will show you how to use this new method in Chapter 28, "Sharing and Loading Assets."	*soundObject.loadSound(URL, isStreaming);* where: *URL* is the location of the MP3 file. This location can be a relative or absolute path. *isStreaming* determines if the loading sound will begin playback as soon as enough bytes have downloaded (true), or if the entire sound must download before playback can begin (false).
start	Plays the targeted Sound object. A sound must be attached to the Sound object before it can play.	*soundObject.start(inPoint, loopFactor);* where: *inPoint* is the time (in seconds) in the sound where playback should begin. *loopFactor* is the number of times the sound should be repeated. Both of these parameters are optional and can be omitted.
stop	Stops playback of the targeted Sound object. If no target is specified, all sounds are stopped. Note that this is not equivalent to pausing a sound. If a stopped sound is played later, it will start at the beginning (or at the *inPoint*).	*soundObject.stop(libraryID);* where: *libraryID* is the name of the sound in the Linkage properties (available in the Library)
setVolume	Changes the overall volume of the specified Sound object. This method accepts values between 0 and 100 (in percentage units). You can enter percentages greater than 100 percent to increase sound output beyond its original recording level, but you may notice digital distortion of the sound.	*soundObject.setVolume(volume);* where: *volume* is a number between 0 and 100

Method	Definition	Options
getVolume	Retrieves the current volume of the Sound object.	*soundObject.getVolume();*
		No options or arguments for this method.
setPan	Changes the offset of sound output from both the left and right channels.	*soundObject.setPan(panValue);*
		where:
		panValue is a value between –100 (full left-speaker output) and 100 (full right-speaker output). Use a value of 0 to balance sound output evenly.
getPan	Retrieves the values created with a previous setPan execution. Use this method to apply Pan settings consistently to multiple objects, or to store a Pan setting.	*soundObject.getPan();*
		No options or arguments for this method.
setTransform	Changes the volume for each channel of the specified Sound object. This method also enables you to play the right channel in the left channel and vice versa.	*soundObject.setTransform(soundTransformObject);*
		where:
		soundTransformObject is the name of an object that has percentage properties for left and right output for the left channel, and left and right output for the right channels.
getTransform	Retrieves the values established with the last setTransform execution. Use this method to reapply sound transforms to new Sounds objects, or to store setTransform values.	*soundObject.getTransform();*
		No options or arguments for this method.

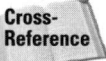

Cross-Reference

In Flash Player 6, ActionScript added two new properties, duration and position, and two methods, getBytesLoaded() and getBytesTotal(), for Sound objects. We will look at the new methods in Chapter 28, "Sharing and Loading Assets." For more detailed information on Sound objects, refer to the Sound object coverage in the *Macromedia Flash MX 2004 ActionScript Bible* (Wiley, 2004) by Robert Reinhardt and Joey Lott.

The following list of Sound object features offers reasons for using Sound objects over traditional sound Movie Clips or keyframe sounds:

✦ Dynamic event sounds that play in a random or user-defined order

✦ Precise control over volume and panning

✦ The ability to dump (or erase) a Sound object when the sound is no longer needed

Note All Sound objects are treated as Event sounds. You cannot use Sound objects to control the playback or frame rate like Stream sounds can. However, ActionScript does allow you to load MP3 files on the fly and "stream" their playback — these types of sounds, however, cannot control playback or frame-rate synchronization. For more information on Synch modes for sound, please refer to Chapter 15, "Adding Sound." (The usage of the term "stream" in this context does not imply real-time streaming, but rather a progressive download for the MP3 file.)

The Sound object uses sounds directly from the movie's library. You cannot use the Sound object to control sounds specified in the Property inspector for any given keyframes.

Tip You can, however, control Stream sounds attached to keyframes on a given timeline by controlling an empty Sound object. Any methods applied to the Sound object will be passed along to the Stream sound.

The next section shows you how to create Sound objects, using the object constructor with the attachSound() and start() methods.

Creating sound libraries with ActionScript

In the Chapter 19, "Building Timelines and Interactions," you learned how to use behaviors to identify and play sounds. From a conceptual point of view, manually creating each sound behavior enabled you to see and work with each sound "object" very easily. However, you can produce the sounds for a sound library much more quickly using your own ActionScript code.

On the CD-ROM In this section, you start with the linked sounds you created in Chapter 19. Make a copy of the pianoKeys_sounds.fla file from the ch19 folder of the *Macromedia Flash MX 2004 Bible* CD-ROM.

1. Using the Open External Library command in the File ⇨ Import menu, select your copy of the pianoKeys_sounds.fla file. Opening a Flash document as a Library enables you to access symbols and media in that file.

2. If you don't have a new untitled Flash document open, create a new Flash file (Ctrl+N or ⌘+N). Change the background color of the document to black in the Document Properties dialog box (Modify ⇨ Document).

3. Open the new document's Library panel (Ctrl+L or ⌘+L). Drag each of the key_ sounds from the pianoKeys_sound Library panel into the Library panel of your new document. When you are finished, you should see all seven sounds in your new document's Library panel, as shown in Figure 27-6.

4. Close the pianoKeys_sounds Library panel, and save your new Flash document as soundLib_ActionScript.fla.

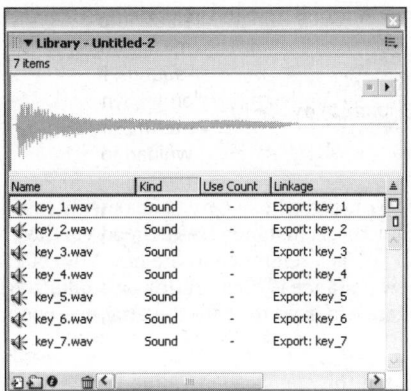

Figure 27-6: The imported sounds with their linkage identifiers displayed

5. Now, you need to add the ActionScript code that will create your Sound objects. You will construct a function that, when executed will form a list of sound instances. On the Main Timeline (that is, Scene 1), rename Layer 1 to **actions**. Alt+double-click (or Option+double-click on the Mac) frame 1 of this layer. This opens the Actions panel. Type the following code into the Script pane:

```
function createLib(num){
  var soundLib = this.createEmptyMovieClip("soundLib_mc", 1);
  this.sound_array = new Array();
  for(var i=1; i<=num; i++){
```

The first line establishes the name of your function, createLib(). You will want to dynamically change the number of sounds you create with this function. Therefore, we assign an optional parameter (called an argument) num that will be passed to the nested actions within the function.

The second line creates an empty MovieClip object, soundLib_mc. This instance will hold individual sound targets, which you create in the next step. The local variable soundLib creates a reference to the soundLib_mc instance within the createLib() function.

The third line creates a new Array object, sound_array. This array stores the Sound objects that createLib() function creates.

The fourth line starts a for loop that cycles its nested actions until the condition i<=num is no longer true. i starts (or initializes) with a value of 1, and the syntax i++ tells i to increase by 1 with each pass of the for loop.

In the next step, you want the for loop to create a new instance of the Sound object for each sound in the Library; and attach each sound in the Library to its new instance.

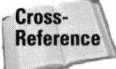
Cross-Reference

We do not discuss the overall structure and purpose of functions, arrays, and logic in this exercise. Refer to Chapter 26, "Using Functions and Arrays," for more information.

6. In the Actions panel, add the following ActionScript to the code from Step 5:

```
var target = soundLib.createEmptyMovieClip("sndStorage_"+i, i);
this.sound_array[i] = new Sound(target);
this.sound_array[i].attachSound("key_"+i);
 }
}
```

The first line creates a new MovieClip object, whose name starts with sndStorage_. This instance is stored with the soundLib_mc instance (referenced via the soundLib local variable). The local variable target is a reference to the new MovieClip object as well. With each pass of the loop, a new instance is created (for example, sndStorage_1, sndStorage_2, and so on). Each instance is used to store the attached sound later in the for loop.

The second line makes a new element in the sound_array object. The new element is a new Sound object that points to the timeline referenced by the target variable. Ultimately, your Sound objects will be tied to instances nested within the soundLib_mc Movie Clip instance, which you'll see later. Each element in an array has a number indicating its position in the array. Because the value of i increases with each pass of the for loop, each Sound object will have a unique position within the snd array.

The third line uses the attachSound() method to take a sound element in the Library and attach it to the Sound object in the sound_array object. The argument for the attachSound() method is specified as "key_" + i. On each pass of the for loop, this expression will return "key_1", "key_2", and so on until the limit prescribed by the num argument is reached.

The complete block of code on the first keyframe of the actions layer is shown in Listing 27-5.

Listing 27-5: The createLib() Function

```
function createLib(num) {
  var soundLib = this.createEmptyMovieClip("soundLib_mc", 1);
  this.sound_array = new Array();
  for (var i = 1; i<=num; i++) {
    var target = soundLib.createEmptyMovieClip("sndStorage_"+i, i);
    this.sound_array[i] = new Sound(target);
    this.sound_array[i].attachSound("key_"+i);
  }
}
```

7. Now that you have a function defined to create all the Sound objects, you need to invoke the function. With the code for frame 1 of the actions layer displayed in the Actions panel, type the following code after the createLib() function:

```
createLib(7);
```

This line of code invokes the createLib() functoin. In addition to executing the createLib() method, you're also sending the function the number 7 as the num argument. Therefore, seven Sound objects are created.

8. Save the Flash document and test it (Ctrl+Enter or ⌘+Enter). Although you won't hear or see anything special happen, choose Debug ⇨ List Variables in the Test Movie environment. The Output panel opens and displays the Sound objects, among other variables and objects:

```
Variable _level0.sound_array = [object #2, class 'Array'] [
    1:[object #3, class 'Sound'] {
      id3:[getter/setter] undefined,
      duration:[getter/setter] 1752,
      position:[getter/setter] 0
    },
    2:[object #4, class 'Sound'] {
      id3:[getter/setter] undefined,
      duration:[getter/setter] 1602,
      position:[getter/setter] 0
    },
    3:[object #5, class 'Sound'] {
      id3:[getter/setter] undefined,
      duration:[getter/setter] 1822,
      position:[getter/setter] 0
    },
    4:[object #6, class 'Sound'] {
      id3:[getter/setter] undefined,
      duration:[getter/setter] 1672,
      position:[getter/setter] 0
    },
    5:[object #7, class 'Sound'] {
      id3:[getter/setter] undefined,
      duration:[getter/setter] 1660,
      position:[getter/setter] 0
    },
    6:[object #8, class 'Sound'] {
      id3:[getter/setter] undefined,
      duration:[getter/setter] 1728,
      position:[getter/setter] 0
    },
    7:[object #9, class 'Sound'] {
      id3:[getter/setter] undefined,
      duration:[getter/setter] 1785,
      position:[getter/setter] 0
    }
  ]
]
```

9. Close the Test Movie window and return to the Flash MX 2004 authoring environment. Select frame 1 of the actions layer, and add this last bit of code to the Script pane:

```
sound_array[1].start();
```

The first line of code targets the first declared element, 1, of the sound_array object, and tells it to begin playback with the start() method of the Sound class. Remember that element 1 in the array is a Sound object, which references the key_1 ID in the Library.

The `for` loop in the `createLib()` function inserts the first `Sound` object at an index of 1, not 0. As we discussed in Chapter 25, usually the first element of an array is at the 0 index. With this function, though, the 0 index is skipped, in order to facilitate a one-to-one correlation with sound ID values in the library and the array index number.

10. Save the Flash document and test it. You will hear key_1 sound (`key_1.wav` or `key_1.aif`) play.

Now you should practice targeting these `Sound` objects from other event handlers such as buttons and more keyframes. To access a different sound, simply change the number in the array brackets. In the next chapter, you'll learn how to load a Flash movie (.swf file) into another Flash movie, as well as how to load MP3 files directly into the movie.

You can view the completed sound library movie, `soundLib_ActionScript.fla`, located in the ch27 folder of the *Macromedia Flash MX 2004 Bible* CD-ROM. We've also included a bonus file, `soundLib_onSoundComplete.fla`, that demonstrates the `onSoundComplete()` handler of the `Sound` class. This handler detects when a sound has finished playing. In the bonus example, each sound plays successively, from key_1 all the way through key_7.

During our testing of `Sound` object methods, we learned that you should attach only one sound per timeline (or Movie Clip instance). While you can create more than one `Sound` object instance on a timeline, you cannot use the `setVolume()` method of the `Sound` class to control each individual sound — the volume will be set for all `Sound` object instances on the targeted timeline.

Creating a soundTransformObject

Two other methods of the `Sound` class, `setTransform()` and `getTransform()`, work in the same manner as the transform methods of the `Color` class. You need to create a generic object using the object constructor before the `setTransform()` method can be used with a `Sound` object. This generic object will become a `soundTransformObject` once you have assigned sound channel properties to the generic object.

Luckily, the `soundTransformObject` doesn't have as many properties as the `colorTransformObject`, and they're much simpler to predict with trial-and-error testing. The properties of the `soundTransformObject` are:

✦ `ll` — the percentage of left channel output in the left speaker

✦ `lr` — the percentage of right channel output in the left speaker

✦ `rr` — the percentage of right channel output in the right speaker

✦ `rl` — the percentage of left channel output in the right speaker

The first letter of each property determines which physical speaker is being affected. The second letter determines which channel's output (or its volume) is played in that speaker. Each property can have a value between −100 and 100.

While -100 to 100 is the suggested range of values, you can use values well beyond this range. The Flash Player will do its best to amplify sounds that use values higher than 100. Be warned — you will likely notice severe digital distortion of the sound for extreme values.

The steps to produce and incorporate a `soundTransformObject` are nearly the same as the `colorTransformObject`. The only difference is that you specify paths to `Sound` objects rather than `MovieClip` objects for the `setTransform()` and `getTransform()` methods. Refer to the steps described earlier in this chapter for `colorTransform` objects.

Tip   Use the `soundTransformObject` to vary the output of the sounds in the soundLib example you created in this section. As with the `setTransform()` example for the `Color` object, create buttons that create and execute unique transform settings.

Creating volume and balance sliders for sounds

In this section, you learn how to control the volume and balance output from a `Sound` object using the slider mechanism from Chapter 25, "Controlling Movie Clips." The slider mechanism works by taking the X position value of the slider's bar and applying it a property of another object. In Chapter 25, you applied the position value of the bar to Movie Clip properties such as `_xscale`, `_yscale`, and `_alpha`. In this exercise, you apply the position values to the `setVolume()` and `setPan()` methods of the `Sound` object to control the volume and balance output, respectively.

On the CD-ROM   In this section, you need to use the `slider_basic_400.fla` file, located in the ch25 folder of the *Macromedia Flash MX 2004 Bible* CD-ROM. If you want to learn how this slider was built, read Chapter 25, "Controlling Movie Clips."

The first part of this exercise shows you how to add the slider to a new document, import a sound, and control the volume of the sound with the slider. In the last steps, you apply the same methodology to the balance slider.

1. Open your copy of the `slider_basic_400.fla` file via the File ➪ Import ➪ Open External Library command.

2. Create a new Flash document (File ➪ New). Rename Layer 1 to **volumeSlider_mc**.

3. Drag the sliderClip symbol from the `slider_basic_400.fla` Library panel to the new document's Stage. When you have finished, close the `slider_basic_400.fla` Library panel.

4. With the slider instance selected on the Stage, open the Property inspector. Name the instance `volumeSlider_mc`. In the Transform panel, rotate the instance –90 degrees. (You can also use the Free Transform tool to rotate the instance.)

5. Now you need to create a `Sound` object. Import a sound file into the Flash document. Use a sound file that is at least 20 seconds long. You can import the `atmospheres_1.wav` (or .aif) file located in ch15 folder of the *Macromedia Flash MX 2004 Bible* CD-ROM.

6. Once you have imported a sound file, select the sound in the Library panel. Right-click (Control+click on Mac) the sound file and choose Linkage in the contextual menu. In the Linkage Properties dialog box, select the Export for ActionScript check box and type `sound_1` in the Identifier field. Click OK to close the dialog box.

7. Create a new layer on the Main Timeline (that is, Scene 1), and name the layer **actions**.

8. Select frame 1 of the actions layer and open the Actions panel (F9). In the Script pane, type the following code:

```
var soundtrack:Sound = new Sound();
soundtrack.attachSound("sound_1");
soundtrack.start(0,999);
```

Note   This code uses ActionScript 2.0's strict typing feature to declare the soundtrack variable as a Sound data type. Notice that once you declare the data type of a variable, you'll see the code hints for the data type (in this case, the Sound class) appear after you type the variable's name, soundtrack.

This code creates the Sound object that the volumeSlider_mc instance controls. Line 1 uses the new Sound() constructor to establish a Sound object name soundtrack. Line 2 links the sound_1 asset (that is, the sound file in the Library) to the soundtrack object. Line 3 plays the sound, starting at the beginning of the sound (0), and looping it 999 times for indefinite playback.

9. Save your Flash document as soundSlider_100.fla. Test the movie (Ctrl+Enter or ⌘+Enter). You will hear the sound attached to the soundtrack object begin to play. However, if you click and drag the bar on the slider, you will not hear a volume change.

To change the volume of the soundtrack object, you need to take the position of the bar in the slider and apply its value to the setVolume() method of the Sound object. You'll use ActionScript's event handlers to accomplish this.

10. Select frame 1 of the actions layer on the Main Timeline. Open the Actions panel, and insert the following code after the last action in the Script pane:

```
volumeSlider_mc.onMouseMove = function():Void {
 var currentVolume:Number = this.position_mc._x/2;
  soundtrack.setVolume(currentVolume);
};
```

This code declares an onMouseMove() handler for the volumeSlider_mc instance. Each time a mouse move is detected, the function defined for this handler executes. The first line of the function retrieves the current _x value of the position_mc instance inside of volumeSlider_mc and divides it by 2. (See our coverage of the slider in Chapter 25 to learn more about this operation.) This value, declared as currentVolume, is then applied to the setVolume() method of the soundtrack object.

11. Save your Flash document again, and test it. Click and drag the bar on the slider. As you move it up, the sound increases in volume. As you move it down, the volume decreases.

Creating a slider that controls the balance output is almost identical to the process of creating the volumeSlider_mc. You will make another instance of the sliderClip symbol, and add a new onMouseMove() handler for the new instance.

12. Create a new layer on the Main Timeline, and name it **balanceSlider_mc**.

13. Drag an instance of the slider symbol from the Library to the Stage. Place the instance to the right of the volumeSlider_mc instance. In the Property inspector, name the instance balanceSlider_mc.

14. Select frame 1 of the actions layer, and open the Actions panel. After the last line of code in the Script pane, type the following code:

```
balanceSlider_mc.onMouseMove = function():Void {
 var currentPan:Number = this.position_mc._x - 100;
 soundtrack.setPan(currentPan);
};
```

This code declares an `onMouseMove()` handler for the `balanceSlider_mc` instance. When the mouse moves within the Flash movie, the function for the `onMouseMove()` handler executes. In this function, though, we need to translate the `_x` property of the `position_mc` instance differently. Because pan values are within a range of –100 to 100, we need to map the 0 to 200 range of the slider accordingly. In order for the lowest value (0) to equal –100 and the highest value (200) to equal 100, you simply subtract 100 from the current `_x` property value returned by the position instance. You then apply this value to the `setPan()` method of the `soundtrack` object.

15. Save your Flash document and test it. As you drag the bar on the `balanceSlider_mc` to the right, you should hear the sound play in the right speaker. As you drag the bar to the left, you should hear the sound play in the left speaker.

You may have noticed with both the `volumeSlider_mc` and `balanceSlider_mc` instances that the lowest value of `_x` for the `position_mc` instance is not 0 — it's 10. This low range restriction was added for the scale slider in Chapter 25. If you desire, you can modify the `startDrag()` method found on the Button instance inside of the `position_mc` instance to use 0 instead of 10 for the left drag limit value.

You can find the completed `soundSlider_100.fla` file in the `ch27` folder of the *Macromedia Flash MX 2004 Bible* CD-ROM.

Printing with ActionScript

Using the new PrintJob class introduced with Flash MX 2004 ActionScript, you can enable your Flash movies to output Flash artwork, text, and bitmaps. With these actions, you can do the following:

✦ **Create Flash ads that have printable specifications for e-commerce merchandise.** Imagine if the next car ad you saw on your favorite Web site automatically printed dealer locations and maps without having to go to the car manufacturer's Web site?

✦ **Make Flash coupons.** You could design printable coupons for e-tailers on the Web that can be printed and redeemed at their brick-and-mortar stores.

✦ **Automate dynamic Web-generated invoices and receipts at e-commerce sites.** With ActionScript, you can format ordered items and add dynamic data to printable sheets.

✦ **Print rich vector illustrations or photorealistic bitmaps from a Web site.** Design Flash portfolio sites that print samples of stock images, or create personalized vector artwork that can be print unique images for each visitor.

✦ **E-mail printable Flash artwork to clients.** The next time you have proof of concepts or finished artwork that needs final approval, you can e-mail your clients the Flash artwork in a standalone projector or SWF file.

✦ **Design custom contact information pages.** Are you sick of HTML tables that won't print your nice row-and-column–formatted pages of information consistently from browser to browser? Printable Flash frames print beautifully each time. You can even add a visitor's contact information to a dynamic database and print it.

Although we can't describe how to do all these tasks in the space of this chapter, we will show you how to get started with the last idea. The following exercise shows you how to use the new PrintJob class to build pages that can be sent to a user's printer. You'll also practice new ActionScript 2.0 coding conventions, using strict data types.

Note
Because Flash natively uses vector artwork, it translates best when output to a PostScript printer. Nevertheless, the Flash Player produces high-quality output to both PostScript and non-PostScript printers.

Caution
The PrintJob class is only available for use in Flash Player 7-compatible movies. If you need to generate printable output for Flash Player 5 or 6, use the older print() and printAsBitmap() functions, as discussed in the *Macromedia Flash 5 Bible* and the *Macromedia Flash MX 2004 Bible*.

1. Open the printjob_starter.fla in the ch27 folder of this book's CD-ROM. This document has sample artwork in the library that you can use to practice printing exercises.

2. Rename Layer 1 to **content_mc**.

3. Create a new Movie Clip symbol (Insert ➪ New Symbol) named **contentClip**. Inside of this symbol (in Edit mode), rename Layer 1 to **page border**.

4. Select frame 1 of the page border layer. Using the Rectangle tool, draw a non-filled rectangle with a black stroke. After you have drawn the rectangle, select the entire outline, and open the Property inspector. Choose a line style of Solid, at 1 px. In the width and height fields, enter values that are in the same aspect ratio as a 8.5" x 11" piece of paper. For example, as shown in Figure 27-7, the size 320 x 440 uses the same aspect ratio. Position the artwork's left corner at 0, 0.

5. Add another layer in the contentClip timeline, and rename this layer to **content**.

6. Open the Library panel (Ctrl+L or ⌘+L), and drag an instance of the siteLogo symbol to frame 1 of the content layer. Use the Free Transform tool to resize the artwork to fit within the frame artwork you created in Step 3. See Figure 27-8.

7. Save your Flash document as printjob_noscale.fla.

8. Go back to the Main Timeline (that is, Scene 1). On frame 1 of the content_mc layer, drag an instance of the contentClip symbol from the Library panel to the Stage. In the Property inspector, name this instance content_mc. Do not resize the instance. For now, just let the bottom edge of the instance run off stage.

9. On the Main Timeline, create another layer named **cbtPrint**. Place this layer above the content_mc layer. The cbtPrint layer will hold a Button component that the user can click to print the content_mc instance.

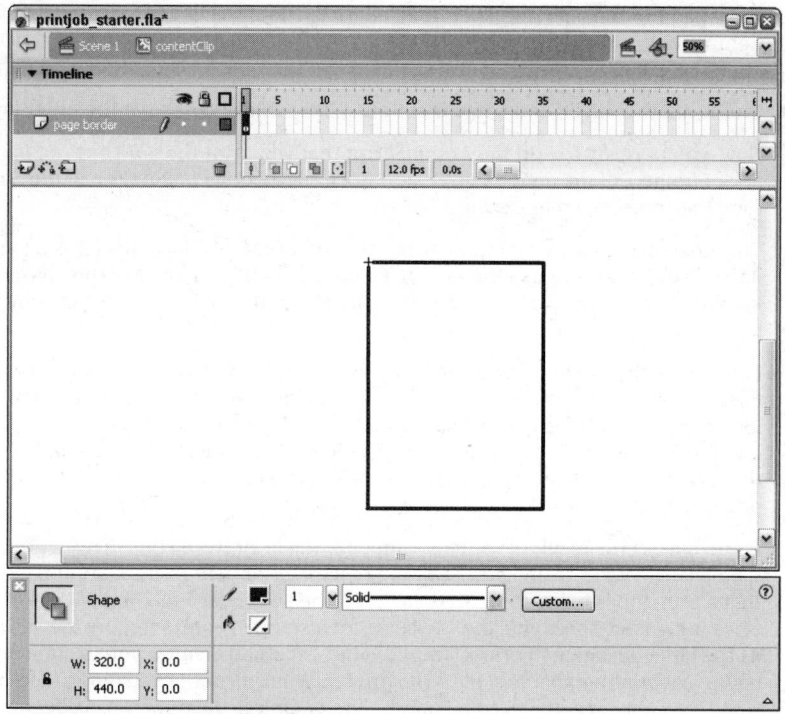

Figure 27-7: The frame artwork

Figure 27-8: The siteLogo artwork

10. On frame 1 of the cbtPrint layer, drag an instance of the Button component from the Components panel to the Stage. In the Property inspector, name this instance cbtPrint. In the Parameters tab of the inspector, type Print into the label field.

11. Create another layer, and name it **actions**. Place this layer above the other layers.

12. Now, you're ready to add the ActionScript that will print the content_mc instance. Select frame 1 of the actions layer, and open the Actions panel (F9). In the Script pane, type the code shown in Listing 27-6.

This code declares a printContent() function (line 1). Line 2 declares a local variable named output, set to use the PrintJob data type, which invokes the constructor for the PrintJob class. Line 3 creates a local variable named clip, pointing to the content_mc instance.

Line 4 uses the start() method of the PrintJob class to initiate a print session on the user's machine. When the start() method is invoked, the system's standard Print dialog box appears. If the user clicks OK in this dialog box, then lines 5 through 8 execute. If the user cancels the print request, lines 9 through 11 execute. If the user clicks OK, the local variable printInit is set to true. If the user cancels the dialog box, printInit is set to false.

Line 5 checks the result of the user's input in the Print dialog box. If printInit is true, then lines 6-8 execute. In line 6, a trace() message is sent to the Output panel, indicating that a print job is being submitted. In line 7, the addPage() method of the PrintJob class is invoked, specifying the content_mc instance, represented by the variable clip, as the target instance to print. The addPage() method enables you to submit individual pages in a print job that is sent to the printer. When all of the addPage() methods are finished, you must initiate a send() method to complete the print job, as demonstrated in line 8.

If the user cancels the Print dialog box, lines 9-11 execute. In line 10, a trace() message is sent to the Output panel, indicating that the print request was denied.

Finally, after the function is declared, the printContent() function is added as an event listener for the cbtPrint instance. Now, when the user clicks the Button component, the printContent() function will be invoked.

Listing 27-6: **The printContent() Function**

```
1.  function printContent(){
2.    var output:PrintJob = new PrintJob();
3.    var clip:MovieClip = content_mc;
4.    var printInit = output.start();
5.    if(printInit){
6.      trace("printing...");
7.      output.addPage(clip);
8.      output.send();
9.    } else {
10.     trace("print aborted by user");
11.   }
12. }
13. cbtPrint.addEventListener("click", this.printContent);
```

13. Save your Flash document, and test the movie. When you click the cbtPrint instance, you should see the Print dialog box. If you click OK, the Output panel displays the "printing..." message. The first frame of the content_mc instance will print at 100 percent on the outputted page. To accurately foretell what your printed dimensions will be in inches, divide the pixel width and height of your content clip by 72 — there are 72 pixels to an inch. So, 320 x 440 will print at a size of 4.4" x 6.1". You can, however, scale the content clip to be printed, so that it will fill the entire page. In the next step, you'll learn how to do just that.

14. Select frame 1 of the actions layer, and open the Actions panel. Add the bold code shown in Listing 27-7 to the printContent() function. Here, you use the pageWidth and pageHeight properties of the PrintJob object, output, to calculate a two variables, xScale and yScale. pageWidth and pageHeight return the size of the page output by the printer, in pixels. By dividing each value by the respective width and height of the content_mc instance (clip), you can determine how much you need to scale the content_mc instance to fill the entire page.

Listing 27-7: **Scaling Content in the printContent() Function**

```
function printContent(){
  var output:PrintJob = new PrintJob();
  var clip:MovieClip = content_mc;
  var printInit = output.start();
  if(printInit){
    trace("printing...");
    var pWidth:Number = output.pageWidth;
    var pHeight:Number = output.pageHeight;
    var xScale:Number = (pWidth/clip._width)*100;
    var yScale:Number = (pHeight/clip._height)*100;
    with(clip){
      _xscale = xScale;
      _yscale = yScale;
    }
    output.addPage(clip);
    output.send();
  } else {
    trace("print aborted by user");
  }
}
```

15. Save your Flash document as printjob_scale.fla, and test it. When you click the cbtPrint instance, the content_mc scales to a larger size. The printed output will fill the entire page with the content_mc instance's artwork.

16. The last step will be to scale the content_mc clip back to original size after the print output has been sent to the printer. Add the bold code shown in Listing 27-8 to the printContent() function.

Listing 27-8: Resetting the Scale of the clip Instance

```
function printContent(){
  var output:PrintJob = new PrintJob();
  var clip:MovieClip = content_mc;
  var printInit = output.start();
  if(printInit){
    trace("printing...");
    var pWidth:Number = output.pageWidth;
    var pHeight:Number = output.pageHeight;
    var origXscale:Number = clip._xscale;
    var origYscale:Number = clip._yscale;
    var xScale:Number = (pWidth/clip._width)*100;
    var yScale:Number = (pHeight/clip._height)*100;
    with(clip){
      _xscale = xScale;
      _yscale = yScale;
    }
    output.addPage(clip);
    output.send();
    with(clip){
      _xscale = origXscale;
      _yscale = origYscale;
    }
  } else {
    trace("print aborted by user");
  }
}
```

17. Save your Flash document, and test it. When you click the cbtPrint instance, the art-
    work no longer scales on the Stage, but the printed output will be scaled.

You can find the completed documents, printjob_noscale.fla and printjob_scale.
fla, in the ch27 folder of this book's CD-ROM.

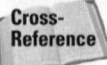

You can find complete coverage of all PrintJob properties and methods in the *Macromedia
Flash MX 2004 ActionScript Bible*.

We'd like to know what you thought about this chapter. Visit www.flashsupport.com/
feedback to fill out an online form with your comments.

Summary

✦ Collisions occur when two or more elements in a Flash movie touch each other. Whenever the space by one Movie Clip instance occupies the space of another, a collision, or "hit," has occurred.

✦ You can detect simple user-initiated collisions by using the startDrag() method and _droptarget property of the MovieClip object.

✦ Using the hitTest() method of the MovieClip object, you can detect the intersection of X and Y coordinates with a specified Movie Clip instance. You can also use hitTest in a similar fashion to _droptarget, where the overlap of two specific Movie Clip instances is detected.

✦ The Color object can store new color values and apply them to Movie Clip instances using the setRGB() and setTransform() methods.

✦ Sound libraries can be created in less time by using ActionScript and the Sound object. Sound objects are created by using Linkage identifiers for sound files in the movie's Library.

✦ ActionScript enables you to change the volume and pan values of any Sound object in your Flash movie.

✦ By using the new PrintJob class, you can output high-quality artwork to a PostScript or non-PostScript printer.

✦   ✦   ✦

Sharing and Loading Assets

Because most Flash movies are downloaded and viewed over the Web, ActionScript has a number of advanced actions that are dedicated solely to controlling the download and display of movies and Library assets. Actions that check the loaded bytes of a Flash movie (SWF file) or media file let developers prevent a movie from playing before a specified portion of it has finished loading. The `loadMovie()` and `unloadMovie()` actions enable movies to be broken into small pieces or assets downloaded only if required by user choice.

Tip   ActionScript allows you to load JPEG, MP3, and FLV files directly into Flash movies. These actions require the use of Flash Player 6 (or 7 for FLV files). We show you how to load these media files in this chapter.

Managing Smooth Movie Download and Display

When Flash movies are played back over the Internet, they *stream*, meaning that the Flash Player plug-in shows as much of the movie as it can during download, even if the whole file has not been transferred to the user's system or browser cache. The benefit of this feature is that users start seeing content without having to wait for the entire movie to finish downloading.

Note   Technically, a Flash movie file is not a streaming file format, but a progressive download file format, similar to an original Apple QuickTime 3 video movie. A *progressive download* can be viewed before the entire file has been received by the browser. Streaming file formats are never saved as actual files in the browser cache. You can't save a true streaming file, but you can typically save a shortcut or link to the file's location on the Web.

Nevertheless, streaming has potential drawbacks. First, during streamed playback, the movie may unexpectedly halt at arbitrary points on the timeline because a required portion of the movie has not yet downloaded. Second, ActionScript code is ignored when it refers to segments of the movie that have not downloaded. For example, if the movie invokes a `gotoAndPlay("main");` action, and the contents of the main frame have yet to download, the Flash Player ignores the action. These drawbacks can lead to unpredictable and often undesired playback results.

Thankfully, there's a solution. You can regulate the playback of the movie by using ActionScript code to prevent the movie from playing until a specified portion of it has downloaded. This technique is often referred to as *preloading*. A common preload sequence, or *preloader*, involves displaying only a short message, such as "Loading . . . Please Wait," while the movie loads. Once the appropriate amount of the movie has been retrieved, the movie is allowed to play. ActionScript provides basic and advanced methods of producing a preloader. This section of the chapter shows you how to use the following three different *internal* actions (or methods) to check the download status of a Flash movie:

✦ `ifFrameLoaded()`: This action has been around since Flash Player 3, and it enables you to check whether a specified frame label in the Flash movie has been downloaded by the plug-in. This is the simplest action to use to check a movie's download progress. If you are designing Flash Player 5 or later movies, this action is considered deprecated.

✦ `MovieClip._framesloaded` **and** `MovieClip._totalframes`: Introduced with Flash Player 4, these properties can be checked on a Movie Clip timeline or the Main Movie timeline (Scene 1, Scene 2, and so on). `_framesloaded` returns the current number of frames that have downloaded into the plug-in, whereas `_totalframes` returns the number of frames that exist on the specified target timeline.

✦ `getBytesLoaded()` **and** `getBytesTotal()`: These methods were introduced in Flash Player 5 ActionScript. The most accurate way to check the progress of a Flash movie download is to use these methods with other ActionScript code. You can use these methods for the following objects in ActionScript for Flash 6 movies: MovieClip (including loaded movies [SWF files] or JPEG images) and `Sound` objects that load MP3 files.

Note   Flash MX 2004 introduces a new method of monitoring the load progress: the `MovieClipLoader` class. The implementation of this class is used for external asset loading and is discussed later in this chapter.

In this edition of the book, we show you how to use the `getBytesLoaded()` and `getBytesTotal()` methods in ActionScript to check the download progress of movie assets.

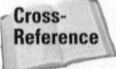

Cross-Reference   You can find our coverage of Flash 3 and 4 movie preloaders (as discussed in the *Flash 5 Bible*) on the book's Web site, `www.flashsupport.com/archive`.

Preloading a Flash Movie

In this section, you learn how to preload a Flash movie whose assets are all internal. You will construct a movie timeline containing a preload section. This section contains two consecutive frames that loop until the entire movie has loaded into the Flash Player. While the movie is loading, a loader graphic updates to display the progress of the download. In the following steps, you learn how to build such a preloader.

Note

The method described in this exercise is compatible with Flash Player 5 and higher. Later in this chapter, you learn how to adapt this method to a Flash Player 6 and higher routine.

On the CD-ROM

Make a copy of the `preloader_f5_starter.fla` file, located in the `ch28` folder of the *Flash MX 2004 Bible* CD-ROM.

1. With the starter file open in Flash MX 2004, resave the document as `preloader_f5_100.fla`.

2. Rename Layer 1 to **content**.

3. Create an empty keyframe (F7) on frame 10 of the content layer. Drag an instance of the pilonsImage Graphic symbol to the Stage on this keyframe. Center the instance on the Stage. Select frame 20 of the content layer and press the F5 key to extend the layer to this frame.

4. Create a new layer and rename it to **labels**. Place this layer at the top of the layer stack.

5. Add a keyframe on frame 2 of the labels layer. In the Property inspector, assign this frame a label of **preload**.

6. Add a keyframe on frame 10 of the labels layer and label this frame **main** in the Property inspector. Your document should now resemble Figure 28-1.

7. Create a new layer and name it **loader_mc**. Place this layer underneath the labels layer.

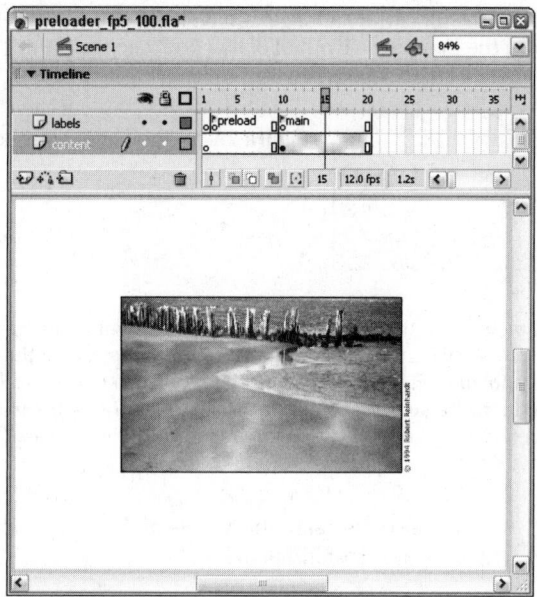

Figure 28-1: The content of this movie starts on the main label.

8. With frame 1 of the loader_mc layer highlighted, select the Rectangle tool. Make sure that you have a stroke and fill color specified in the Tools panel. Draw a rectangle on the Stage. In the Property inspector, size both the stroke and fill of the rectangle to 300 x 10. This rectangle is the progress bar that grows as the movie's bytes load into the Flash Player.

9. With the stroke and fill of the rectangle selected, press F8. In the Convert to Symbol dialog box, choose the **Movie clip** behavior. Name the symbol **loaderClip** and click the top left registration point, as shown in Figure 28-2. Click OK.

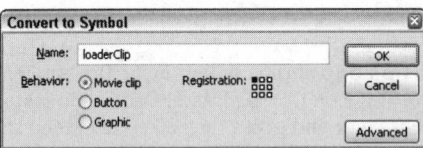

Figure 28-2: The rectangle artwork will be part of the loader symbol.

10. With the new instance selected on the Stage of the Main Timeline, name the instance loader_mc in the Property inspector.

11. Double-click the loader_mc instance on the Stage. In Edit mode, rename Layer 1 of the loader symbol to **bar_mc**. Create another layer and name it **frame**. Make sure the frame layer is above the bar_mc layer.

12. Select the stroke of the rectangle and cut it (Ctrl+X or ⌘+X). Select frame 1 of the frame layer and paste the stroke in place (Edit ⇨ Paste in Place, or Ctrl+Shift+V or ⌘+Shift+V).

13. On the bar_mc layer, select the fill of the rectangle. Convert this fill to a Movie Clip symbol named **barClip**. In the Convert to Symbol dialog box, choose the **middle left** registration point, as shown in Figure 28-3.

Figure 28-3: The barClip symbol settings

14. With the new instance selected on the Stage of the loaderClip symbol, name the instance bar_mc in the Property inspector. In the Transform panel, scale the width of the instance to 1.0%, as shown in Figure 28-4. When the movie first starts to load, you do not want the bar_mc instance scaled at full size (100%) — as the bytes of the movie load into the Flash Player, the _xscale of the bar_mc instance will increase. (You will insert the code to do this later.)

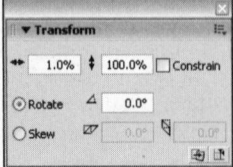

Figure 28-4: Decrease the X scale of the bar_mc instance to 1.0% in the Transform panel.

15. Create another layer and name it **text**. Place this layer at the bottom of the layer stack.

16. Select the Text tool and create a Dynamic Text field on frame 1 of the text layer. Place the text field underneath the `bar_mc` instance, as shown in Figure 28-5. In the <Instance Name> field of the Property inspector, assign a Var name of `percent`. You will use this text field to display the current percent loaded of the Flash movie. You do not need to enable the Show Border (or other options) for this text field.

Caution   Do not assign a `TextField` instance name to the field in the Property inspector. In order to make a Flash Player 5-compatible preloader, you can only control the contents of the field via the Var name.

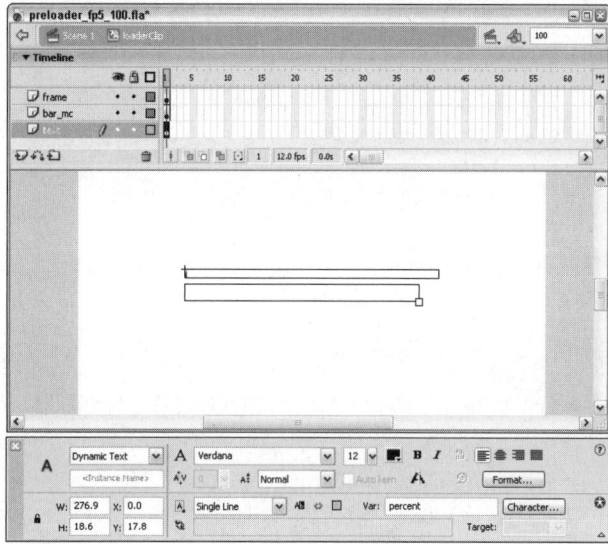

Figure 28-5: The `percent` field will display the current percent loaded of the movie.

17. Go back to the Main Timeline (that is, Scene 1). Select the `loader_mc` instance on the Stage and center it using the Align panel. Select frame 4 of the loader_mc layer and insert an empty keyframe (F7). You only need the loader instance to appear as the movie is preloading.

18. Create a new layer and name it **actions**. Place this layer underneath the labels layer.

19. Select frame 3 of the actions layer and insert an empty keyframe (F7). With this frame selected, open the Actions panel (F9). In the Script pane, type the code shown in Listing 28-1. Do not type the ⌐ character in your actual code. This symbol indicates a continuation of the same line of code. Each line of code is explained in comments within the code.

Note   In Listing 28-1, the variable named `count` is never declared with an initial value. As such, when the line `count++` is executed, the variable `count` is both initialized and incremented by 1. In ActionScript 2.0 syntax, you can't declare a variable and increment it at the same time.

Listing 28-1: **The Preloading Script Routine**

```
// lBytes stores the current bytes that have loaded

var lBytes = this.getBytesLoaded();

// tBytes stores the total bytes of the movie

var tBytes = this.getBytesTotal();

// percentLoaded calculates the percent of the movie that
// has loaded into the Flash Player.

var percentLoaded = Math.floor((lBytes/tBytes)*100);

// Apply the percentLoaded value to the X scale of the
// bar instance within the loader instance

loader_mc.bar_mc._xscale = percentLoaded;

// Fill the percent text field within the loader instance
// with the percentLoaded value followed by the text
// "% of " and the total kilobytes of the movie. For
// example, when half of a 64K movie has loaded, the text
// field will display "50% of 64K loaded."

loader_mc.percent = percentLoaded + "% of " + Math.floor(tBytes/1024) + ⤴
  "K loaded.";

// If the loaded bytes are greater than or equal to the
// total bytes of the movie and the total bytes are
// greater than 0

if (lBytes >= tBytes && tBytes > 0) {

  // Check to see if the count variable is greater than
  // or equal to 12. If it is, execute the nested code.
  // This if/else code pauses the movie once 100% of the
  // movie has loaded into the Flash Player.

  if (count>=12) {

    // exit the loading sequence

    gotoAndStop("main");

  // otherwise, if the movie has completely loaded and
  // count is less than 12.
```

```
  } else {

    // add 1 to the count variable
    count++;

    // continue to loop the loading sequence
    gotoAndPlay("preload");
  }

// if the movie hasn't finished loading into the Flash
// Player then execute this code

} else {

  // loop back to the "preload" frame label
  gotoAndPlay("preload");
}
```

20. Now make sure that the Flash movie (.swf file) is published as a Flash Player 5 compatible movie. Choose File ⇨ Publish Settings, and click the Flash tab. In the Version menu, choose **Flash Player 5**. Click OK to close the dialog box.

21. Save your Flash document and test it (Ctrl+Enter or ⌘+Return). When you enter Test Movie mode, choose View ⇨ Simulate Download or press Ctrl+Enter or ⌘+Return again. As shown in Figure 28-6, you will see the movie's download progress reflected in the _xscale property of the bar_mc instance as well as an updating percent value and total file size in the percent field. When the movie is fully loaded, the loader will pause for about a second and go to the main label.

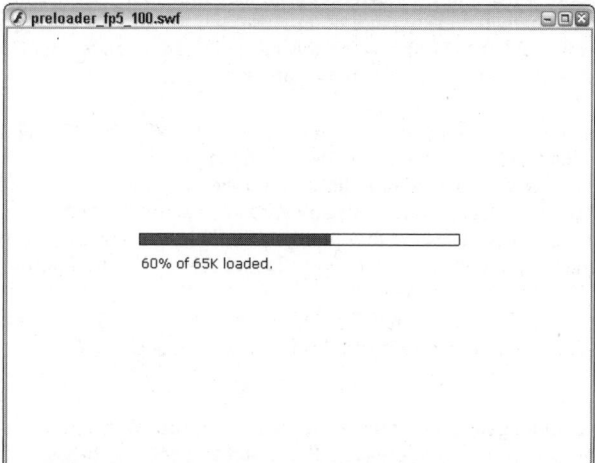

Figure 28-6: The progress bar grows as the movie loads into the Flash Player.

You can find the completed file, `preloader_f5_100.fla`, in the `ch28` folder of the *Flash MX 2004 Bible* CD-ROM. You can also find a Flash Player 6 or higher compatible version of this document, `preloader_f6_100.fla`, that uses a `setInterval()` routine. You learn more about this technique later in the chapter. And, while we recommed against using the ProgressBar component for internal preloading, we have supplied a sample file, `progressbar_fp6_100.fla`, on the CD-ROM. This new component is compatible with Flash Player 6 when the file is published with ActionScript 2.0 support. The reason we don't recommend using the `ProgressBar` component for internal loading is simply because the component itself is nearly 60 KB—the first frame of the movie will "pause" on an empty screen until the component has fully loaded. The `ProgressBar` component is designed to work more with external assets, as we discuss later in this chapter.

Loading Flash Movies

A long sequence of Flash animation or any Flash movie that contains many internal assets naturally requires the preloading described in the preceding section to guarantee smooth playback. But traditional information-based Web sites done in Flash require a different kind of download management. Suppose you're building a Web site with three sections: products, staff, and company history. Each section is roughly 100 KB in size. In a normal Flash movie, you'd place those sections in a sequential order on the Main Timeline or create a scene for each of them. The last section you place on the timeline would, of course, be the last section to download. Might sound fine so far, but here's the problem: What if the section that appears last on the timeline happens to be the first and only section the users want to see? They'd have to wait for the other two sections to download before they could view the one they want—but they don't even want to see the other two sections, so really they're waiting for nothing. The solution to this problem is the `loadMovie()` action.

Note

It's not just a matter of the user waiting for a Flash movie to load—it's also an issue of bandwidth. You can rack up unnecessary bandwidth usage fees with your Web hosting provider. You wouldn't want to download every page of an HTML site just to look at one page of it, and the same principle applies to Flash movies. Paying careful attention to your Flash movie architecture not only saves your users time, but it can save you real money.

`loadMovie()` provides a means of inserting one or more external SWF files into a Flash movie (whether that movie resides in a browser or on its own in the stand-alone player). `loadMovie()` can be used to replace the current movie with a different movie or to display multiple movies simultaneously. It can also be used, as in our company Web site example, to enable a parent movie to retrieve and display content kept in independent SWF files on a need-to-retrieve basis (similar to the way a frame in an HTML frameset can call external pages into different frames).

Tip

You can use the `loadMovie()` action to load JPEG images directly into your Flash Player 6 or higher movies. We show you how to load JPEG files later in this chapter.

Tip

If you are concerned about getting accurate usage statistics in your Web server's access logs, you will want to use `loadMovie()` to break up the content on your Flash-based site. If all of your content is stored in one Flash movie (.swf file), you will only see that the Web user has downloaded the site file—you have no idea which sections of the site the user has actually visited. By breaking up the Flash movie into several smaller files, your site's access logs will show which section SWF files were downloaded and viewed by the user.

Basic overview of Flash site architecture

You can produce and distribute straight Flash content on the Web in the following two primary ways:

✦ Create several small SWF files, with each one living within a standard HTML page on a Web site.

✦ Create one HTML page that hosts one main SWF file that loads additional content through the Flash Player plug-in.

Figure 28-7 illustrates these alternatives.

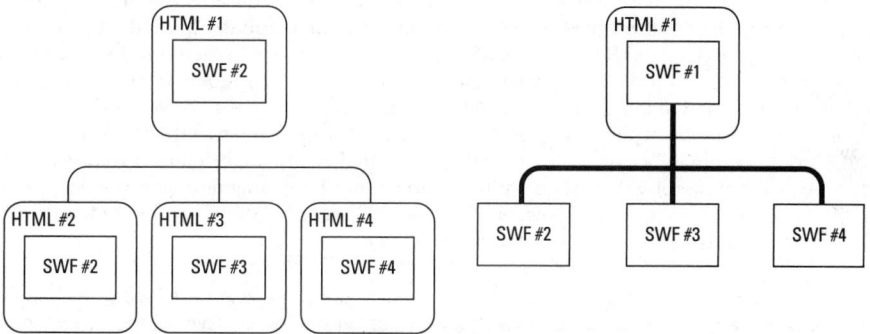

Figure 28-7: The diagram on the left illustrates a Web site that uses multiple HTML pages, each with an individual SWF file. The diagram on the right shows a Web site that uses one HTML page (or frameset) that has one primary SWF file, which loads other SWF files as needed.

If you decide to break up your Flash movies across several HTML pages, your Web visitors will experience the following:

✦ Short download times for each page

✦ Easier bookmarking of discrete sections of your Web site

✦ Abrupt transitions between each section of the Web site

However, if you use one primary Flash movie in one HTML page (or frameset), your visitors will benefit from:

✦ Short download times for each SWF file (Download times vary with file size)

✦ Seamless integration of new Flash content

✦ Controllable transitions between SWF asset changes

Which method should you use for your Flash projects? The answer depends on the specifics of each Web project. You may decide to use a combination of both methods, especially for larger sites that use several Web technologies (Apple QuickTime, Macromedia Flash and Shockwave, Real Systems RealOne, Microsoft Windows Media, and so on). In either scenario, you can use the loadMovie() action to manage Flash content more easily.

Tip   Because Flash Player 6 or higher allows you to download JPEG, MP3, and Flash movies with embedded video, you may not need to rely on other plug-in technologies for the Web sites you design and develop.

Storing multiple movies

You may already be wondering how these newly loaded movies are managed relative to the original movie. Macromedia Flash uses the metaphor of *levels* to describe where the movies are kept. Levels are something like drawers in a cabinet; they are stacked on top of each other and can contain things. You can place things in any drawer you like, but once a drawer is full, you have to take its contents out before you can put anything else in. Initially, the bottom level, referred to in ActionScript as _level0 ("Level 0"), contains the original movie, the first movie that loads into the Flash Player. All movies subsequently loaded into the Flash Player must be placed explicitly into a target level. If a movie is loaded into Level 1 or higher, it appears visually on top of the original movie in the Player. If a movie is loaded into Level 0, it replaces the original movie, removing all movies stored on levels above it in the process. When a loaded movie replaces the original movie, it does not change the frame rate, movie dimensions, or movie background color of the original Flash Stage. Those properties are permanently determined by the original movie and cannot be changed, unless you load a new HTML document into the Web browser. You can also use a getURL() action to load a new SWF file into the browser to "reset" the Flash Player.

Tip   You can effectively change the background color of the Stage when you load a new movie by creating a rectangle shape of your desired color on the lowest layer of the movie you are loading.

Loading an external SWF file into a movie

A new movie is imported into the Flash Player when a loadMovie() action is executed. In the following steps, you'll learn how to make a button click load an external movie named video_anchors.swf.

On the CD-ROM   Before you begin these steps, make a copy the video_anchors.swf file from the ch17/anchors folder of the *Macromedia Flash MX 2004 Bible* CD-ROM. Copy the file to the location on your hard drive where you will save the new Flash document in the forthcoming exercise.

1. Create a new Flash document (File ⇨ New). Save this document as loadMovie_100.fla in the same location as your copy of the video_anchors.swf file.

2. Rename Layer 1 to **loadButton**.

3. Drag an instance of the Button component from the Component panel to your document's Stage. Place the instance in the lower-left corner of the Stage. In the Property inspector, name the component loadButton. In the Parameters tab, select the label field and type Load Movie. Refer to Figure 28-8 to see these settings.

Cross-Reference   We discuss components more thoroughly in Chapter 29, "Using Components."

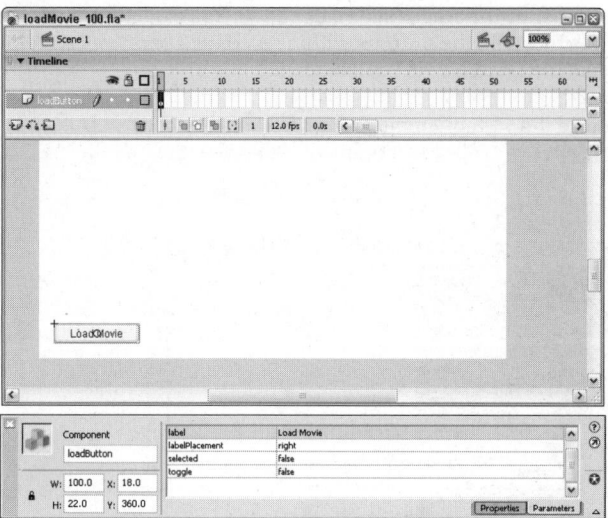

Figure 28-8: The loadButton instance

4. Create a new layer and rename it **actions**.

5. Select frame 1 of the actions layer and open the Actions panel (F9). In the Script pane, type the code shown in Listing 28-2. This code creates a listener for the loadButton instance. When the loadButton instance is clicked, the video_anchors.swf movie loads into Level 1.

Listing 28-2: **The Listener Code for the loadButton Instance**

```
var loader:Object = new Object();
loader.click = function(){
   loadMovieNum("video_anchors.swf", 1);
};
loadButton.addEventListener("click", loader);
```

Caution

The URL used in loadMovie() or loadMovieNum() actions contains the network path to the movie file that you want to load. That path must be specified relative to the location of the page that contains your main movie, not relative to the location of the movie itself. If you are designing a Web site for early browsers, pay attention to the URL path. Internet Explorer 4.5 (or earlier) for the Macintosh does not resolve paths correctly. For more information, please see Macromedia's tech note at:

www.macromedia.com/support/flash/ts/documents/mac_ie_issues.htm

6. Save your Flash document and test it by choosing Control ➪ Test Movie (Ctrl+Enter or ⌘+Return). When you click the loadButton instance, the video_anchors.swf will load

into the top-left corner of the Stage (see Figure 28-9). You can control the playback of the loaded SWF file by using the buttons within its control bar. You can reload the same SWF file by clicking the Load Movie button again.

Caution   Make sure you copied the `video_anchors.swf` file from the book's CD-ROM to the same location as the `loadMovie_100.fla` document. Otherwise, the `loadMovieNum()` action will fail.

Figure 28-9: The `video_anchors.swf` loads into the top-left corner of the Stage.

You can apply this technique to any SWF file that you wish to load into another Flash movie. You can make a series of buttons, each one loading a different SWF file. You can modify the `click()` method of the `loader` object to switch the URL of the loaded movie, depending on which button is pressed.

On the CD-ROM   You can find the completed example file, `loadMovie_100.fla`, in the ch28 folder of the *Flash MX 2004 Bible* CD-ROM. Note that you cannot run the `loadMovie_100.swf` file directly from the CD-ROM — to test this SWF file, you need to copy it and the `video_anchors.swf` file from the ch17/anchors folder to the same location on your hard drive.

When a movie is loaded above any other movie (including the main movie), the Buttons and Movie Clips in the movies on lower levels will continue to be active, even though they may not be visible. To prevent this undesired behavior, you need to send movies on lower levels to an idle or blank frame where no buttons are present. Do that by adding a `goto` action before your `loadMovie()` action that sends the current movie to the idle frame. This technique is known as "parking" the movie. If you have to park multiple movies, you'll need to know how to communicate between movies on different levels. This will be discussed shortly.

_level0 or _root: What's the Difference?

You may have seen the Main Timeline referred to as _root in ActionScript. If you don't employ Levels in a Flash movie, _root always refers to the Main Timeline of the Flash movie that is loaded into a browser. However, if you start to use levels to load external SWF files, _root will be relative to the level that's executing actions.

For example, if the main movie uses a _root reference in an action, such as:

```
_root.gotoAndStop(10);
```

the Main Timeline Playhead will go to frame 10 and stop.

If a loaded movie has the same action within its timeline, it will go to frame 10 on its timeline and stop.

While this works with movies that are loaded into level locations, it will not work with Movie Clip instance targets. As you'll see in the following sections, a movie loaded into a Movie Clip target becomes an instance located within the level that the Movie Clip target resides. Therefore, _root will still refer to a different timeline than that of the loaded SWF file.

Flash MX 2004 and Flash Player 7 has introduced a new property of MovieClip objects, _lockroot, that allows MovieClip objects to act as _root references to loaded movies. This property is discussed in Chapter 25, "Controlling Movie Clips."

How Flash handles loaded movies of differing dimensions

A movie loaded onto Level 1 or higher that is smaller in width and height than the Level 0 movie is positioned in the top-left corner of the Stage. We saw this occur with the example in the last section. In this situation, it is possible to have elements that are off-stage within the loaded SWF file. However, when you load a smaller SWF file Stage into a larger SWF file Stage, these off-stage elements are displayed on the Stage of the larger SWF file. To prevent objects from being displayed, you would have to create a curtain layer or a Mask layer above all the other layers in the Level 1 movie that covers up the *Work area* (the space outside the movie's Stage).

Movies loaded onto Level 0 that are smaller than the original Level 0 movie are automatically centered and scaled up to fit the size of the original movie. (The manner in which they are scaled depends on the Scale setting in the Publish settings.)

Movies loaded onto Level 0 that are larger than the original Level 0 movie are cropped at the right and bottom boundaries defined by the original movie dimensions.

Placing, scaling, and rotating externally loaded Flash movies

Especially when your movies have different width and height dimensions, it's not very convenient to have newly loaded movies dropped ingloriously in the top-left corner of the Stage. To give you more flexibility with the placement, rotation, and scale of your loaded movies, ActionScript provides the capability to load a Flash movie (.swf file) into a Movie Clip instance.

So far, this may not make a whole lot of sense. Loading a movie into a Movie Clip instance seems like a strange feature at first, until you find out what it can do—then it seems indispensable. The easiest way to understand what happens when you load a movie into a Movie Clip is to think of the loadMovie() action as a "Convert Loaded Movie to Movie Clip" action.

When a movie is loaded into a Movie Clip instance, many attributes of the original Movie Clip instance are applied to the newly loaded movie:

✦ The timeline of the loaded movie completely replaces the original instance's timeline. Nothing inside the original Movie Clip (including actions on keyframes) remains.

✦ The loaded movie assumes the following properties from the original Movie Clip instance:

- Instance name
- Scale percentage
- Color effects, including alpha
- Rotation degree
- Placement (X and Y position)
- Visibility (with respect to the _visible property)

✦ Any onClipEvent() handlers (and actions within them) that are written for the original Movie Clip instance will still be available (and executing) on the loaded movie.

✦ Any event handlers such as onMouseMove() or onEnterFrame() or variables assigned to the original Movie Clip instance will be erased once an external SWF file is loaded into the instance.

We like to refer to Movie Clips that are used to load other movies as Movie Clip holders. Usually, you load movies into empty Movie Clips that don't have any artwork or actions. However, because you may need a physical reference to the actual area your loaded movie will occupy on the Stage, it's useful to create temporary guides or artwork that indicates this area.

Tip

In Flash Player 6 or higher ActionScript, you can create empty MovieClip objects dynamically, using the createEmptyMovieClip() method. You can then load external SWF files into this empty MovieClip object using the loadMovie() method.

The following steps show you how to create a Movie Clip holder and how to load an external SWF file into it. We will use the same file you created in the previous section.

On the CD-ROM

If you didn't complete the example in the last section, make a copy of the loadMovie_100. fla file located in the ch28 folder of the *Flash MX 2004 Bible* CD-ROM. You will also need to copy the video_anchors.swf file from the ch17/anchors folder.

1. Open the loadMovie_100.fla document.

2. Create a new layer on the Main Timeline and rename the layer to **holder_mc**. Place this layer below the actions layer.

3. Select the Rectangle tool and draw a rectangle on frame 1 of the holder_mc layer. The shape should have the same dimensions as the external Flash movie's Stage, as defined in its Document Properties dialog box. For our example, size the rectangle to 320 x 240 using the Property inspector.

Note You do not need to include an outline (or stroke) with the rectangle artwork.

4. With the rectangle selected, choose Insert ➪ Convert to Symbol or press the F8 key to convert the artwork into a symbol. In the Convert to Symbol dialog box, name the symbol **holderClip** and choose the Movie Clip behavior. In the Registration grid, click the top-left corner point, as shown in Figure 28-10. Movies loaded into Movie Clip instances load from the top-left corner of the original target Movie Clip.

Figure 28-10: An instance of the holderClip symbol will hold the loaded SWF file.

5. With the new instance on the Stage selected, name the instance holder_mc in the <Instance Name> field of the Property inspector. Position the instance on the Stage, where you want the external SWF movie to appear. At this point, you can also tween, scale, or apply any color effect to the instance as well. For our example, apply a 50 percent alpha to the instance in the Property inspector.

Now, you need to modify the click() handler of the loader object called by the loadButton component instance (already on the document's Stage). This method needs to target the holder_mc instance.

6. Select frame 1 of the actions layer on the Main Timeline. Open the Actions panel (F9), and change the loadMovieNum() action to the following line shown in bold.

```
var loader:Object = new Object();
loader.click = function(){
    holder_mc.loadMovie("video_anchors.swf");
};
loadButton.addEventListener("click", loader);
```

Note The instance must be resident on Stage at the time the loadMovie() action occurs. Any instance can either be manually placed on the Timeline or created with ActionScript code, such as the duplicateMovieClip(), attachMovie(), and createEmptyMovieClip() methods. If any specification of the loadMovie() action is incorrect, then the movie will fail to load. The Flash Player will *not* start a request for an external SWF file if the Movie Clip instance target is invalid.

7. Save the Flash document as loadMovie_200.fla and test it (Ctrl+Enter or ⌘+Return). When you click the Load Movie button, the video_anchors.swf file will load into the top-left corner of the holder_mc instance. The 50 percent alpha applied to the holder_mc instance will also be applied to the loaded movie, as shown in Figure 28-11.

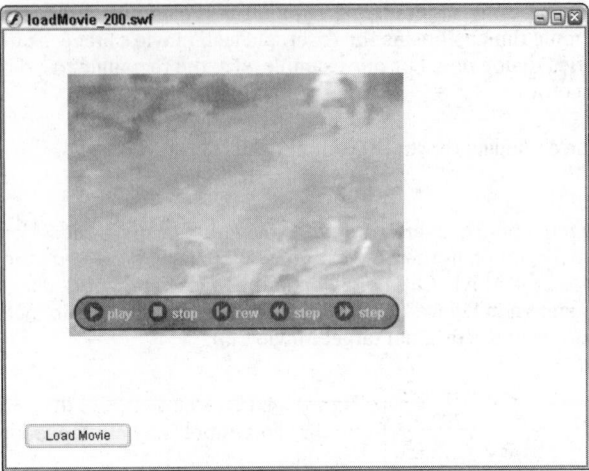

Figure 28-11: The SWF file loads into the holder instance when the component button is clicked.

To avoid seeing the rectangle artwork in your final Flash movie, go into the Movie Clip symbol for holderClip and turn the layer containing the rectangle artwork into a Guide layer. Guide layers will not export with the SWF file.

Caution   If you do not have any artwork in your target Movie Clip instance (or have converted the artwork to a Guide layer), you will not be able to scale the instance using the Transform tool or panel. You can, however, transform the instance before you remove the artwork (or convert it to a Guide layer) — the setting will "stick" even after you remove the artwork.

If you need to add functionality to the loaded movie, use ActionScript to control the new loaded movie instance. The next section shows you how to communicate with loaded movies.

On the CD-ROM   You can view the completed file, loadMovie_200.fla, in the ch28 folder of the *Flash MX 2004 Bible* CD-ROM.

loadMovie() versus loadMovieNum()

You may have noticed that a loadMovie() action is used with Movie Clip instances, whereas loadMovieNum() is used with a level location. Because you can specify variables (that point to dynamic targets) as a location value, ActionScript needs a way to distinguish a numeric level location from a Movie Clip instance.

Also, if you want a loadMovie() action to be compatible with Flash Player 4 (or earlier), you will need to specify the Movie Clip target name as a string (that is, enclosed in quotes).

Communicating between multiple movies on different levels

After a movie or two are loaded onto different levels, you may want each timeline to control the other, just as Movie Clips can control each other. To communicate between different levels, you simply need to address actions to the proper level. The method for addressing a level that controls a timeline on a different level is identical to the method for addressing a Movie Clip target that controls the timeline of another Movie Clip instance, except for one small change. You have to indicate the name of the level you want target rather than the name of the Movie Clip. Level names are constructed such as this: First, there's an underscore (_); then there's the word *level*; then there's the number of the level that you want your action to occur on.

This tells the movie loaded onto Level 1 to go to frame 50:

```
_level1.gotoAndStop(50);
```

This tells the Main Movie Timeline to go to frame 50:

```
_level0.gotoAndStop(50);
```

You can also target Movie Clips that reside on the timelines of movies on other levels. Here's an example:

```
_level3.products_mc.play();
```

This sends a play() action to the Movie Clip named products_mc on the timeline of the movie loaded onto Level 3.

Unloading movies

To lighten the memory required by your Flash movies in the Flash Player or to clear the loaded movie from the Stage, you can explicitly unload movies in any level or Movie Clip target by using the unloadMovie() action. The only option for unloadMovie() is the path to the desired location (for example, _level1, _root.instanceName).

You can see an example of an unloadMovie() action in the loadMovie_201.fla file located in the ch28 folder of the *Flash MX 2004 Bible* CD-ROM. Here, the loader object handles both the clicks from the loadButton and the unloadButton instances. The removeMovie() method of the loader object is assigned as a listener to the unloadButton instance, which clears the loaded movie.

If you want to replace an existing loaded movie with another external file, you do not need to unload the movie before loading the new one. A loadMovie() action implicitly unloads the existing content in the specified location. We have actually seen problems occur in Flash movies where unloadMovie() and loadMovie() actions are executed consecutively.

Loading External Files Through Proxy Servers

If you are creating Flash movies that will be loaded through proxy servers set up by large Internet service providers (ISPs) on the Internet, you may need to know how to trick them into loading "fresh" SWF files every time a user visits your site. What is a proxy server? With the growth of high-speed Internet connections, such as DSL and cable, many ISPs will process all outgoing HTTP requests through a go-between computer that caches previous requests to the same URL. Anytime you type a Web site URL into a browser, you're making an HTTP request. If that computer, called a *proxy server*, sees a request that was made previously (within a certain time frame), then it serves its cached content to the end user instead of downloading the actual content from the remote server.

Why do you need to be concerned about caching? If you or your client needs accurate usage statistics for a Web site, you will likely want to know which portions of the site your users are actively using (that is, downloading into their browsers). Your Web server will not log a request it never receives — if a proxy server delivers the content to the end user, you will not even know a user is looking at your content.

When a Flash movie makes an HTTP request with a `loadMovie()` action, a proxy server may serve the cached SWF file instead of the one that actually exists on your server. Why is this a problem? If you are updating that SWF file frequently or if you want precise Web usage statistics for your Flash movies and content, then you'll want users to download the actual SWF file on your server each time a request is made.

The question remains: How do you trick a proxy server into serving the real SWF file instead of its cached one? The proxy server knows what's in its cache by the URL for each cached item. So, if you change the name of the loaded Flash movie each time you make a request for it, the proxy server won't ever see an identical match with its cached content.

To change the name of a loaded Flash movie, simply add a random number to the end of the movie's name in the `loadMovie()` action. This random number won't actually be part of the movie's filename. Rather, it will appear as a query at the end of the filename. Place the following actions on the event handler that initiates a `loadMovie()` action:

```
var randomNum = Math.round(Math.random()*9999999999);
holder_mc.loadMovie("external_1.swf?" + randomNum);
```

In the preceding example, a variable called `randomNum` is established and given a random value, a number in the range of 0 to 9999999998. Each time the event handler calling these actions is executed, a different number is appended to the filename of the loaded movie. The proxy server thinks that each request is different and routes the request to your Web server.

Not only does this method prevent a proxy server from serving a cached Flash movie file; it prevents most browsers from caching the loaded movie in the user's local cache folder.

loadMovie() as a method for Movie Clip targets

Both `loadMovie()` and `unloadMovie()` can be used as either an ActionScript method or action for Movie Clip targets. What does this mean? You can apply some actions in ActionScript in two ways: as methods of a `MovieClip` object (or some other ActionScript object, as we have discussed in previous chapters) or as a stand-alone action.

As an action, loadMovie() and unloadMovie() start the ActionScript line of code. When you use actions in this manner, the target of the action is specified as an argument (option) within the action. In the following example, the file external_1.swf is loaded into the holder_mc instance:

```
loadMovie("external_1.swf", "holder_mc");
```

As a method, actions are written as an extension of the object using the action. Therefore, the target is already specified before the action is typed. The same example shown previously could be rewritten as a method of the holder_mc MovieClip object:

```
holder_mc.loadMovie("external_1.swf");
```

or

```
_root.holder_mc.loadMovie("external_1.swf");
```

Because we have specifically referenced the holder_mc instance as an object, the loadMovie() action (now a method) knows where to direct the loading of external_1.swf.

 When you use unloadMovie() as a method of the MovieClip object, you do not need to specify any arguments for the method. For example, holder.unloadMovie(); will unload any movie in the holder_mc instance.

Loading JPEG Images into Flash Movies

Flash Player 6-compatible ActionScript added the exciting capability to load JPEG images into Flash movies at runtime — while the movie plays in a Web browser! In previous versions of the Flash Player, all externally loaded content needed to be in the SWF format. However, starting with Flash Player 6, the doors have opened to download specific media formats directly into Flash movies.

 You cannot load JPEG images directly into Flash movies playing in Flash Player 5 or earlier. The user must have Flash Player 6 to use this feature.

Some basic rules for using JPEG images that are loaded into Flash movies are as follows:

✦ Use only standard JPEG files. You can not load progressive JPEG images into Flash movies playing in Flash Player 6.

✦ Watch the file size of JPEG files. Unless your JPEG files are extremely small and/or within a reasonable limit of your target audience's data rate, you will likely want to build a preloader for your JPEG files.

✦ All JPEG images that are loaded dynamically will be smoothed in Flash Player 6. Smoothed bitmaps may have an adverse effect on playback performance. You can control the global rendering of bitmaps and all artwork by using the _quality property of the MovieClip object. For example, _quality = "low"; turns off smoothing for all artwork. Use this property with care — most vector artwork and text looks unsightly with low-quality rendering.

✦ Control the physical characteristics of the JPEG image (X and Y coordinates, X and Y scale, rotation, and so on) by controlling those properties of the `MovieClip` object holding the image.

Caution

In practice, you should nest JPEG images within yet another instance in the holder instance. For a reason unbeknownst to us, when you load JPEG images into a `MovieClip` object, the holder instance stops behaving as a true `MovieClip` object. Some `MovieClip` methods will work with the holder, whereas others won't. To be safe, create another empty `MovieClip` object within the holder instance, and load the JPEG image into that "buffer" clip. If you need to make any changes to the `MovieClip` instance, control the outer holder instance.

✦ Check the user's version of the Flash Player with ActionScript or JavaScript. The user must have Flash Player 6 or higher installed to load JPEG images directly into Flash movies. We discuss Flash Player detection in Chapter 21, "Publishing Flash Movies," and Chapter 22, "Integrating Flash Content with Web Pages."

Cross-Reference

Keep in mind general issues for bitmap usage in Flash movies. Read our coverage of using bitmap images in Chapter 16, "Importing Artwork," and Chapter 35, "Working with Raster Graphics."

When in doubt, test the specific JPEG images with your Flash movies. If you encounter problems with loading the JPEG, check the following:

✦ **URL:** Make sure you have the correct path and filename specified in the `loadMovie()` action.

✦ **Target:** Does the target exist into which you want to load? Check the path to the level or `MovieClip` object that contains the image.

✦ **Format:** Is the JPEG image a standard format? Or does it use progressive encoding? Progressive JPEGs cannot be loaded into Flash Player 6 or 7.

Without further ado, let's create a Flash movie that dynamically loads a JPEG image. In this example, you will load a JPEG file located in the same directory as the Flash movie (.swf file). In ActionScript, the `loadMovie()` action is used to load JPEG images, using the following syntax:

```
instanceName.loadMovie(URL);
```

where *instanceName* is the `MovieClip` object that holds the JPEG image and *URL* is the relative or absolute path to the JPEG file. In the following code, a JPEG file named `cat.jpg` will be loaded into a `MovieClip` object named `holder_mc`:

```
holder_mc.loadMovie("cat.jpg");
```

or

```
holder_mc.loadMovie("http://mydomain.com/cat.jpg");
```

On the CD-ROM

For this exercise, you will use the `loadMovie_201.fla` document that was discussed earlier in this chapter. You can also make a copy of this completed file from the ch28 folder of the *Flash MX 2004 Bible* before you begin this exercise. You will need to copy the `beach.jpg` file in this location to your local folder as well.

In the following steps, you create a Flash movie that can load an external JPEG image:

1. Open a copy of the loadMovie_201.fla document. Create a new layer named **textfield**. Place the holder_mc layer at the bottom of the layer stack.

2. Save the Flash document as loadMovie_300.fla.

3. On frame 1 of the textfield layer, select the Text tool and create an Input text field underneath the holder_mc instance artwork. With the text field selected, open the Property inspector and type image_txt in the <Instance Name> field. Enable the Show Border option as well. When you are finished, your document's Stage should resemble Figure 28-12.

4. Select the loadButton instance on the Stage. In the Property inspector, change the label value to **Load JPEG**.

5. Select the unloadButton instance on the Stage. In the Property inspector, change the label value to **Unload JPEG**.

6. Select frame 1 of the actions layer and open the Actions panel. In the Script pane, edit the code to reflect the bold changes shown in Listing 28-3.

   Here, you retrieve the current text in the image_txt field and use it as the URL of the loadMovie() method of the holder_mc instance. When the loadButton component instance is clicked, the getMovie() method executes and loads the JPEG file specified in the image_txt field into the holder_mc instance. When the unloadButton instance is clicked, it does the same thing as it did before: it unloads the contents of the holder_mc instance.

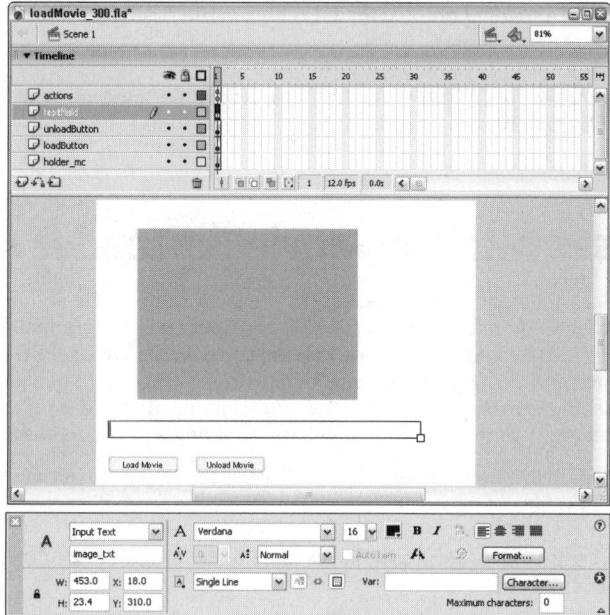

Figure 28-12: The image_txt field will specify the path to the JPEG image.

Listing 28-3: **Modifying the getMovie() Handler**

```
var loader:Object = new Object();
loader.getMovie = function(){
    holder_mc.loadMovie(image_txt.text);
};
loader.removeMovie = function(){
    holder_mc.unloadMovie();
};
loadButton.addEventListener("click", loader.getMovie);
unloadButton.addEventListener("click", loader.removeMovie);
```

7. Save your Flash document and test it (Ctrl+Enter or ⌘+Return). In the Test Movie window, type **beach.jpg** into the text field. When you click the Load JPEG button, the beach.jpg image will load into the holder_mc instance.

Try typing in other known image URL locations into the text field. For example, you can download the same image from the following location. Be sure to type the full URL, including the http:// protocol:

```
http://www.flashsupport.com/images/beach.jpg
```

You may want to go back to the Flash document and move the location of the holder_mc instance to better accommodate the size of the JPEG image you are loading. Remember, there is a 50 percent alpha effect applied to the holder_mc instance as well.

You will learn how to build a loading graphic for JPEG files in the "Using a Preloader for External Assets" section of this chapter.

You can find the completed file, loadMovie_300.fla, in the ch28 folder of the *Macromedia Flash MX 2004 Bible* CD-ROM.

Loading an Asset with the MovieClipLoader API

Flash MX 2004 ActionScript introduces a new class, MovieClipLoader. The actions associated with this class, collectively referred to as the API, or Application Programming Interface, allow you to more easily initiate and monitor the loading of external SWF or JPEG files into a Flash movie (.swf file) at runtime. One of the benefits of using the MovieClipLoader class is that you can handle loading errors within your code. For example, it would be good to know if a URL failed to load or if there were other difficulties with loading a particular asset.

In the following steps, you learn how to use a MovieClipLoader object to initiate the loading of an external SWF or JPEG file.

Use the loadMovie_300.fla document, in the ch28 folder of this book's CD-ROM, as a starting point for this exercise.

1. Open the `loadMovie_300.fla` document, and save it as `MovieClipLoader_100.fla`.

2. Select the `holder_mc` instance on the Stage. In the Property inspector, change the alpha of the instance to 100 percent.

3. Select frame 1 of the actions layer, and open the Actions panel (F9). Delete the existing code in the Script pane, and add the code shown in Listing 28-4.

In line 1, a `MovieClipLoader` object named `loader` is created, using the constructor function of the `MovieClipLoader` class.

In line 3, a listener object named `loadListener` is created. This object will receive events that are broadcasted from the `loader` object.

In lines 5 through 7, an `onLoadError()` handler is defined for the `loadListener` object. This handler is specific to `MovieClipLoader` listeners. If there is an error during the loading of an external asset via the `MovieClipLoader` object, `loader`, this handler will be invoked. The handler can accept two parameters, the `MovieClip` instance receiving the loaded asset (`targetClip`) and an error message indicating what went wrong with the loading (`errorCode`). In our example, on line 6, we simply throw the error message to the Output panel.

In line 8, the `loadListener` object is added as a bonafide listener of the `loader` object. Without this line of code, the `loader` object would not know to broadcast events to the `loadListener` object.

In lines 10 through 18, another listener is created, named `buttonListener`. (Note that this is effectively the same `loader` object we used in previous exercises of this chapter.) The `buttonListener` receives events from the `loadButton` and `unloadButton` instances (lines 20 and 21). When the `loadButton` instance is clicked, the `getMovie()` handler in lines 12 through 14 is invoked.

The difference from our previous exercises occurs primarily in line 13: instead of using the `loadMovie()` method, the `loadClip()` method of the `MovieClipLoader` class is used with the loader object. `loadClip()` takes two parameters: the URL of the SWF or JPEG asset to load, and the `MovieClip` object that will hold the asset.

In lines 16 through 18, the `removeMovie()` handler, invoked by a click from the `unloadButton` instance, uses the `unloadClip()` method of the `MovieClipLoader` class to unload the content from the `holder_mc` instance.

Listing 28-4: An Example of a MovieClipLoader Object at Work

```
1.  var loader:MovieClipLoader = new MovieClipLoader();
2.
3.  var loadListener:Object = new Object();
4.
5.  loadListener.onLoadError = function(targetClip, errorCode){
6.     trace("A loading error has occurred: " + errorCode);
7.  };
8.  loader.addListener(loadListener);
9.
```

Continued

Listing 28-4 *(continued)*

```
10. var buttonListener:Object = new Object;
11.
12. buttonListener.getMovie = function(){
13.    loader.loadClip(image_txt.text, holder_mc);
14. };
15.
16. buttonListener.removeMovie = function(){
17.    loader.unloadClip(holder_mc);
18. };
19.
20. loadButton.addEventListener("click", buttonListener.getMovie);
21. unloadButton.addEventListener("click", buttonListener.removeMovie);
```

4. Save your document, and test it (Ctrl+Enter or ⌘+Enter). Type a valid URL to an image or Flash movie asset, and click the Load JPEG button. The holder_mc instance will then display the image when it's finished loading. Click the Unload JPEG button, and type an *invalid* URL into the text field — just type any gibberish that comes to mind. Click the Load JPEG button, and the error message from the onLoadError() handler should display in the Output panel.

On the CD-ROM You can find the completed document, MovieClipLoader_100.fla, in the ch28 folder of this book's CD-ROM.

While this might not seem to be a revolutionary way to load an external JPEG or SWF file into a Flash movie, there are other reasons why MovieClipLoader objects are useful:

✦ You can queue several load targets. One instance of the MovieClipLoader class can be used to manage the loading of one or more external assets.

✦ You can integrate other components or code with additional methods of the MovieClipLoader class, not shown in this exercise. For example, you can tie a ProgressBar component to a MovieClipLoader object to monitor the downloading of an asset. You'll learn how to do this procedure later in the chapter.

✦ You can program fail-safes into your ActionScript code. In our simple example, we didn't do much with the onLoadError() handler. In your own work, though, you can use the onLoadError() handler to direct the user to alternate content or attempt to load the content from a backup server or to display an alert dialog box.

✦ You can invoke the onLoadComplete() and/or onLoadInit() handlers on a listener of a MovieClipLoader object to perform further operations with the loaded asset or the master Flash movie after loading has finished.

On the CD-ROM In the ch28 folder of this book's CD-ROM, you can find an example of an onLoadInit() handler that resizes JPEG images to fit the boundary of the holder_mc instance. This document is named MovieClipLoader_resize_100.fla.

Loading MP3 Audio into Flash Movies

If you thought JPEG image loading was exciting, wait to you see the support for MP3 audio loading into Flash Player 6 or higher movies. You can load MP3 files directly into Sound objects that you create with ActionScript.

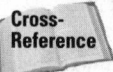

If you don't know how to use Sound objects, read our coverage of Sound objects in Chapter 27, "Interacting with Movie Clips." You may also want to read Chapter 15, "Adding Sound," if you are unfamiliar with general sound use in Flash movies. You can find expanded and more advanced coverage of Sound objects in the *Flash MX 2004 ActionScript Bible* (Wiley, 2004).

Here are a few tips for using MP3 files that will be loaded into Flash 6 movies:

✦ Watch file size. MP3 files, especially those of full-length songs, can be very large in file size, easily exceeding 3MB. Make sure your target audience can accommodate the file sizes you are loading.

✦ Test your specific MP3 encoding method(s) before you use the same encoding on several files that you intend to use with Flash Player 6 or higher movies. In our tests, we have not encountered problems with any MP3 files that we loaded into the Flash Player. However, there are several variations of CBR (Constant Bit Rate) and VBR (Variable Bit Rate) encoding methods available in several audio applications.

✦ Depending on the Flash Player release version, MP3 files may not cache on the user's hard drive. All MP3 files loaded through the Sound object in ActionScript are stored in the computer's virtual memory. Be careful with the number of MP3 files downloaded and stored in memory simultaneously.

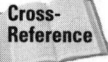

Review the troubleshooting tips we listed for loadMovie() and JPEG images in the last section. The same principles apply to MP3 files.

The core method to the Sound object that can access external MP3 files is the loadSound() method. With this method, you can specify a path to an MP3 file just like you did for JPEG images with the loadMovie() method. However, the loadSound() method has an additional argument, isStreaming. We'll discuss this in a moment. The syntax for using the loadSound() method is:

```
soundObject.loadSound(URL, isStreaming);
```

soundObject indicates the name of a Sound object created previously in ActionScript and *URL* is the relative or absolute path to the MP3 file. *isStreaming* is a Boolean value (true or false) that determines whether the MP3 file automatically begins playback as soon as enough bytes have loaded into Flash Player 6 (true) or whether the MP3 file must fully download before playback can begin (false).

Before you begin the following exercise, make a copy of the loadMovie_300.fla located in the ch28 folder of the *Macromedia Flash MX 2004 Bible* CD-ROM. You will modify the existing structure of the document that you built in earlier sections of this chapter. You will also need an MP3 file copied to the same location on your hard drive. You can use the atmospheres_1.mp3 file located in the ch28 folder as well.

In the following steps, you learn how to load an MP3 file into a Sound object.

1. Open the loadMovie_300.fla document. Resave this document as loadSound_100.fla.

2. Select the Load JPEG component instance on the Stage. In the Parameter tab of the Property inspector, change the label value to **Load MP3**.

3. Select the Unload JPEG component instance on the Stage. In the Property inspector, change the label value to **Unload MP3**.

4. Select the Input text field on the Stage and change the instance's name to sound_txt in the Property inspector.

5. Now you need to change the ActionScript in the document to use the Sound object and the loadSound() method. Select frame 1 of the actions layer and open the Actions panel (F9). Change the code in the Script pane to match the code shown in Listing 28-5.

In lines 2 through 5, the getSound() method of the loader listener (which is invoked by the Load MP3 component instance), a new Sound object named sound_1 is created (line 3). Then, in line 4, the loadSound() method of the object is then executed, using the URL specified in the sound_txt field. The isStreaming argument is set to true so that the MP3 automatically begins to play as soon as enough of the sound file has downloaded into the movie.

The removeSound() handler in lines 6 through 9 (which is executed by the Unload MP3 component instance) stops the sound playing in the sound_1 object and deletes the object from the movie.

Listing 28-5: **Using loadSound() for External MP3 Files**

```
1.  var loader:Object = new Object();
2.  loader.getSound = function(){
3.    sound_1 = new Sound();
4.    sound_1.loadSound(sound_txt.text, true);
5.  };
6.  loader.removeSound = function(){
7.    sound_1.stop();
8.    delete sound_1;
9.  };
10. loadButton.addEventListener("click", loader.getSound);
11. unloadButton.addEventListener("click", loader.removeSound);
```

6. Save your Flash document, and test it (Ctrl+Enter or ⌘+Return). In the Test Movie window, type **atmospheres_1.mp3** into the sound_txt field. Click the Load MP3 button, and the MP3 begins to play. When you click the Unload MP3 button, the sound stops playing.

Try using other URLs of MP3 files, either locally or remotely. You can specify the following URL to stream the same MP3 file from our Web server:

http://www.theMakers.com/sounds/atmospheres_1.mp3

Note It may take a few moments for remote sound files to load into Flash Player.

You can continue modifying the `Sound` object into which the MP3 file loads. For example, you can apply the same volume and balance output control from the examples in Chapter 27 to the `Sound` object in this Flash movie.

We will show you how to monitor the download progress of an MP3 file (and other external files) in the next section.

On the CD-ROM You can see the completed Flash document, `loadSound_100.fla`, in the `ch28` folder of the *Macromedia Flash MX 2004 Bible* CD-ROM.

Loading a Flash Video into a Flash Movie

Starting with Flash Player 7 and Flash MX 2004, you can now load Flash Video files (.flv files) directly into a Flash movie at runtime. In Flash Player 6 and Flash MX, such files needed to be embedded with a Flash movie (.swf file) and loaded with traditional `loadMovie()` actions.

Cross-Reference If you don't know what a Flash Video file (.flv file) is, see Chapter 17, "Embedding Video."

Tip You could — and still can — stream Flash Video files (.flv files) with the aid of Macromedia Flash Communication Server MX. In fact, to get the best performance out of FLV files, we still recommend that you consider Flash Communication Server as a solution for real-time audio/video streaming.

In this section, you learn how to progressively download an FLV file into a Flash movie at runtime.

On the CD-ROM You need to make a copy of the `loadMovie_300.fla` document used in earlier in this chapter, as well as the `sample_high_300k.flv` file found in the `ch17/squeeze` folder of this book's CD-ROM.

1. Open the `loadMovie_300.fla` document, and save it as `netstream_100.fla`.

2. Delete the `holder_mc` instance and layer in the document. Flash Video files are not loaded into `MovieClip` objects.

3. Select the `loadButton` instance on the Stage. In the Property inspector, change the label value to **Load FLV**.

4. Select the `unloadButton` instance on the Stage. In the Property inspector, change the label value to **Unload FLV**.

5. Select the `image_txt` instance, and in the Property inspector, change its instance name to `video_txt`.

6. Create a new layer, and rename it to **flv_video**. Place this layer at the bottom of the layer stack.

Note Delete the holder_mc layer, or turn that layer into a Guide layer. The holder_mc instance is no longer needed for this example.

7. Open the Library panel (Ctrl+L or ⌘+L). In the panel's options menu in the top right corner, choose **New Video**. A new empty Embedded Video object will appear in the Library panel.

8. With frame 1 of the flv_video layer selected, drag an instance of the Embedded Video symbol from the Library panel to the Stage. Position the instance in the same area that the holder_mc previously occupied. In the Property inspector, name this instance flv_video. Change the width to 320 pixels and the height to 240 pixels. See Figure 28-13.

9. Now, you're ready to add the ActionScript code necessary to load an external FLV file, and display it in the flv_video instance. Select frame 1 of the actions layer, and open the Actions panel (F9). Change the code to that shown in Listing 28-6.

Like previous examples, the behavior for each Button component is tied to respective methods of a listener object. In our example, the listener object is named loader. The getVideo() method of the loader instance, defined in lines 2 through 11, creates a NetConnection object named videoConn (line 3). The videoStream object in line 5 uses this connection. A NetStream instance is required to play an FLV file.

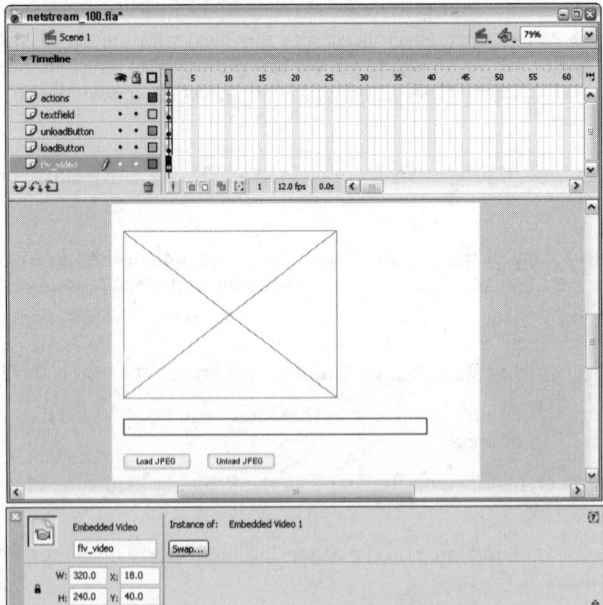

Figure 28-13: The flv_video instance will display the video from external FLV files.

In lines 6 through 10, an `onStatus()` handler is defined for the `videoStream` object. This handler is invoked whenever an event occurs on the stream. In this example, the handler simply outputs `trace()` messages to the Output panel, letting you know what's happening with the stream.

In line 11, the `attachVideo()` method of the Video class is invoked on the `flv_video` instance, the Embedded Video object you placed on the Stage in Step 8. The parameter for the `attachVideo()` method is the instance name of the `NetStream` object created in line 5.

In line 12, a buffer time is set for the stream. This value determines how many seconds of the stream must download before playback begins.

In line 13, the `play()` method of the `NetStream` class is invoked on the `videoStream` instance. For FLV files that are not accessed from a Flash Communication Server application, the parameter for the `play()` method is the http-based URL of the FLV file. You can use relative or absolute paths for this URL. In our example, you use the text from the `video_txt` field to determine the URL.

In lines 15 through 18, the `removeVideo()` method of the listener object is declared. This method is invoked when the `unloadButton` instance is clicked. In line 16, playback of the stream is stopped by invoking the `close()` method of the `videoStream` instance, and the image in the Embedded Video instance, `flv_video`, is blanked with the `clear()` method.

Listing 28-6: **Creating a NetStream Object to Access Flash Video Content**

```
1.  var loader:Object = new Object();
2.  loader.getVideo = function(){
3.    videoConn = new NetConnection();
4.    videoConn.connect(null);
5.    videoStream = new NetStream(videoConn);
6.    videoStream.onStatus = function(info){
7.      trace("videoStream.onStatus >");
8.      trace("   level: " + info.level);
9.      trace("    code: " + info.code);
10.   };
11.   flv_video.attachVideo(videoStream);
12.   videoStream.setBufferTime(5);
13.   videoStream.play(video_txt.text);
14. };
15. loader.removeVideo = function(){
16.   videoStream.close();
17.   flv_video.clear();
18. };
19. loadButton.addEventListener("click", loader.getVideo);
20. unloadButton.addEventListener("click", loader.removeVideo);
```

10. Save your Flash document. Make sure you have copied the `sample_high_300k.flv` file from the `ch17/squeeze` folder of this book's CD-ROM to the location where you saved the Flash document for this exercise. Test the movie (Ctrl+Enter or ⌘+Enter), and type the text `sample_high_300k.flv` into the `video_txt` field. Click the Load FLV button, and the video will play in the `flv_video` instance (see Figure 28-14). If you click the Unload FLV button, the playback stops and the image no longer appears in the `flv_video` instance.

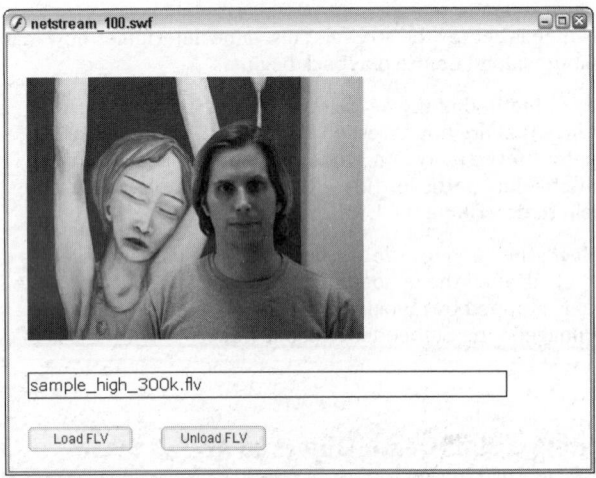

Figure 28-14: The video as it plays in the `flv_video` instance

You can find the completed file, `netstream_100.fla`, in the `ch28` folder of this book's CD-ROM.

Try creating some of your own Flash Video files and using them with this Flash movie. Remember to go back to Chapter 17, "Embedding Video," for more information on Flash Video encoding.

Using a Preloader for External Assets

In this section, you will learn how to add a preloader that monitors the download progress of any external asset, whether it is a SWF, JPEG, or MP3 file. This preloader combines the same methodology employed by the original `preloader_f5_100.fla` document you built earlier in this chapter. We've already taken the same loader Movie Clip symbol from that exercise and added ActionScript to its timeline. Let's take a quick look at what we've done.

Later in this chapter, you learn how to use the Preloader component in Flash MX 2004. In this section, you learn the fundamental building blocks of an asset preloader, from the ground up.

Open the `loader_100.fla` located in the `ch28` folder of the *Macromedia Flash MX 2004 Bible* CD-ROM. Open the Library panel and double-click the loaderClip symbol. Inside of this symbol, select frame 1 of the actions layer. Open the Actions panel, and you will see the following code in the Script pane. Note the ⤵ character indicates a continuation of the same line of code.

```
function checkLoad(obj) {
  var lBytes = target.getBytesLoaded();
  var tBytes = target.getBytesTotal();
  var percentLoaded = Math.floor((lBytes/tBytes)*100);
  bar_mc._xscale = percentLoaded;
  percent_txt.text = Math.floor(percentLoaded) + "% of " + ⤵
    Math.floor(tBytes/1024) + "KB loaded.";
  if (lBytes>=tBytes && tBytes>0) {
    if (count>=12) {
      clearInterval(checkProgress);
      _parent[loadExit]();
      obj.removeMovieClip();
    } else {
      count++;
    }
  }
  updateAfterEvent();
}
var count = 0;
var checkProgress = setInterval(checkLoad, 100, this);
stop();
```

While this may seem a bit overwhelming, it's nearly identical to the code you built on the Main Timeline of the `preloader_100.fla` document. The primary differences are as follows:

✦ The code is contained within a function named `checkLoad()`.

✦ Instead of a frame loop, the new `setInterval()` function is used to repeatedly execute the `checkLoad()` function. When the loading is finished, the `clearInterval()` function is called to stop the looping.

✦ The loader instance is dynamically placed in the movie to monitor the download progress of a specific asset — it does not monitor the load progress of the main movie SWF file.

> **Tip**
> The `setInterval()` and `clearInterval()` functions were introduced in Flash MX and Flash Player 6. These actions work only in Flash Player 6 or higher movies.

But that's not all of the code you'll need to get an asset preloader working. Even though there is code with a loaderClip symbol that continually checks the loading progress of an asset, you need some code that provides some input for the loaderClip symbol, such as what type of file is loading (SWF, JPEG, or MP3) and where the file is loading (a `MovieClip` object or a `Sound` object).

Let's take a look at one more chunk of code. Open the `loadfile.as` file located in the `ch28` folder of the *Macromedia Flash MX 2004 Bible* CD-ROM. You can use Macromedia

Dreamweaver MX 2004, Flash MX Pro 2004, or any other text editor to view the code. Here's what you'll see in the file:

```
function loadFile(){
    var fileExt = fileURL_txt.text.substr(-3);
    var loadObj = _root.createEmptyMovieClip("holder_mc",1);
    if(fileExt == "swf" || fileExt == "jpg"){
        loadObj.loadMovie(fileURL_txt.text);
    } else if(fileExt == "mp3"){
        sound_1 = new Sound(loadObj);
        sound_1.loadSound(fileURL_txt.text, true);
        loadObj = sound_1;
    }
    var initObject = {
        _x: fileURL._x,
        _y: fileURL._y - 40,
        target: loadObj,
        loadExit: null
    };
    _root.attachMovie("loaderClip", "loader_mc", 2, initObject);
}
function unloadFile(){
    if(typeof(holder_mc) != undefined){
        holder_mc.removeMovieClip();
    }
    if(typeof(sound_1) != undefined){
        sound_1.stop();
        delete sound_1;
    }
}
```

The `loadFile()` function takes a URL specified in a `fileURL_txt` text field (`fileURL_txt.text`) and loads it into a proper container. If the URL ends with "swf" or "jpg", the function will load the URL into a new Movie Clip instance named `holder_mc`. If the URL ends with "mp3", the function loads the URL into a new `Sound` object. The `initObject` contains the information that the loaderClip symbol needs to work. The X and Y position of the `loader_mc` instance is based on the position of the `fileURL_txt` text field. The `target` variable (which is specified in the `checkLoad()` function you saw earlier within the loader symbol) is set to either `holder` or `sound_1`, depending on what type of media file is being loaded. Finally, the `attachMovie()` method attaches the loaderClip symbol from the movie's library to the Main Timeline (`_root`), passing it the properties of the `initObject`.

Tip　The ability to pass an `initObject` to the `attachMovie()` method is a feature of Flash Player 6 and higher movies.

Note　For this example, the `loadExit` variable in the `checkLoad()` function is not used.

The unloadFile() function deletes the objects created by the loadFile() function. If either a holder_mc or sound_1 instance exists, it will be deleted or removed from the movie.

In the following steps, you combine the loaderClip symbol from the loader_100.fla with the loadfile.as file that you just examined. You integrate these elements into a new version of the loadSound_100.fla that you created in the previous section.

On the CD-ROM

Make a copy of the loader_100.fla, loadfile.as, and loadSound_100.fla files, located in the ch28 folder of the *Macromedia Flash MX 2004 Bible* CD-ROM.

1. Open the loadSound_100.fla document. Save this document as preloader_fp7_200.fla.

2. Choose File ⇨ Import ⇨ Open External Library, and choose the loader_100.fla document.

3. Drag the loaderClip symbol from the loader_100.fla Library panel to the Stage of the preloader_fp7_200.fla document. All of the symbols associated with the loaderClip symbol will be transferred to the preloader_fp7_200.fla document. Close the loader_100.fla Library panel.

4. Delete the instance of the loaderClip symbol from the Stage of the preloader_fp7_200.fla document. This symbol is linked in the Library of this document and will be attached to the movie's Stage via ActionScript.

5. Delete the holder layer in the Main Timeline. You will not need a physical Movie Clip instance on the Stage in which to load assets. The code within the loadFile() function creates a holder_mc instance on the fly.

6. Select the Load MP3 component instance on the Stage. In the Property inspector, change the label value to **Load File**.

7. Select the Unload MP3 component instance on the Stage. In the Property inspector, change the Label value to **Unload File**.

8. Select the Input text field on the Stage and open the Property inspector. Change the instance name of the field to fileURL_txt. At runtime, the text that is typed into this field will be used by the loadFile() function, which will be executed by the listener of the loadButton instance when the button is clicked.

9. Select frame 1 of the actions layer. Open the Actions panel (F9), and replace the existing code in the Script pane with the following code:

```
#include "loadfile.as"

loadButton.addEventListener("click", this.loadFile);
unloadButton.addEventListener("click", this.unloadFile);
```

The #include directive fetches the contents of the loadfile.as file when you publish or test the movie (at compile time) and insert the code into the Flash movie on this keyframe. The original listener object, loader, was removed because the loadFile() function (this.loadFile) was directly inserted as the callback listener handler for the loadButton instance, just as the unloadFile() function (this.unloadFile) was added as a listener for the unloadButton instance.

10. Save the Flash document, and test it (Ctrl+Enter or ⌘+Return). Type a URL into the Input text field. You can use the following test URL:

```
http://www.flashsupport.com/images/beach.jpg
```

Alternatively, you can type the name of a file in the same location as the tested movie on your hard drive. Click the Load File button, and the loader instance will appear above the Input Text field, indicating the progress of the file's download. See Figure 28-15. When you click the Unload File button, the media will unload from the Flash movie.

Figure 28-15: The `loader_mc` instance appears when you click the Load File button.

Try a URL for each of the media formats that Flash Player 6 can load dynamically. If a file fails to load, check the same URL in a Web browser.

On the CD-ROM   You can find the completed document, `preloader_fp7_200.fla`, in the `ch28` folder of the *Macromedia Flash MX 2004 Bible* CD-ROM.

Using the Loader and ProgressBar Components

If you're thinking it takes too much effort to create your own ActionScript code for preloaders in ActionScript, you may be in luck. Flash MX 2004 includes two new components, `Loader` and `ProgressBar`, which make the task of loading external files into Flash movies at runtime very simple.

You might be wondering why we even bothered to have you get your hands dirty, per se, with our earlier coverage. It's extremely important for you to be able to build your own functionality into your projects. Chances are, you'll come across situations where components won't do exactly what you need them to. As such, you'll need to know how to build interactivity into your movie on your own. Now that you have a solid understanding of how to load external files into a Flash movie, you can greater appreciate the features we're about to demonstrate.

Adding a Loader component to your Flash movie

The Loader component can automatically load an external JPEG or SWF file into your Flash movie, and it's incredibly simple to use. One of the nice features of the Loader component is that it can scale the image to fit within the boundaries of the component.

1. Create a new Flash document, and save it as fmx2004_loader_100.fla.

2. Rename Layer 1 to **loader_mc**.

3. Open the Components panel, and open the UI Components grouping. Drag the Loader component to the Stage. Place the instance near the top left corner of the Stage.

4. Select the new instance, and name it loader_mc in the Property inspector. Select the Parameters tab in the Property inspector. Leave the autoload setting at its default value (true). In the contentPath field, type **http://www.flashsupport.com/images/beach.jpg**. Make sure the scaleContent setting is **true**. See Figure 28-16.

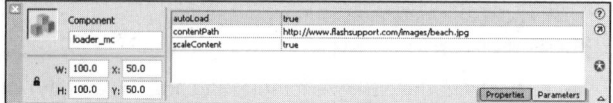

Figure 28-16: The parameters of the Loader component

5. The Loader component, when used in this fashion, gives you a live preview of the loaded asset. Deselect the instance on the Stage, and reselect it. Doing so should force the instance to update, displaying the image within the area of the loader_mc instance. You can resize the loader_mc instance to change the size of the loaded image.

6. Save the document, and test it. You can watch the asset load into the Flash movie.

On the CD-ROM

The fmx2004_loader_100.fla document can be found in the ch28 folder of this book's CD-ROM. z

You can use this procedure to load "fixed" content into your Flash movie. Meaning, if you don't need to change the URL of the loaded asset for a given presentation, using the component with hard-coded values in the Property inspector can take care of your needs. However, if you want to be able to change or display several images in the same instance over the course of your presentation, you'll need to know how to change the parameters of the Loader component instance in ActionScript. In the next section, you learn how to do just that.

Dynamically changing the source of a Loader component

You can also set the URL to the content of a Loader component instance using ActionScript. In the following steps, you learn how to integrate the Loader component with one of the earlier examples you created in this chapter.

On the CD-ROM Make a copy of the `preloader_fp7_200.fla` and `loadfile.as` documents from the `ch28` folder of this book's CD-ROM. Alternatively, you can use your own version of these documents if you built it in the earlier exercise of this chapter.

1. In Flash MX 2004, open the `preloader_fp7_200.fla` document. Resave the document as `preloader_fp7_comps_200.fla`.

2. Create a new layer, and rename it **loader_mc**. On frame 1 of this layer, add a Loader component instance, as outlined in Step 3 in the previous section.

3. In the Property inspector, name the new instance `loader_mc`. Do not specify any additional parameters for the component. You can resize the component instance so that it fills up more of the Stage.

4. Select frame 1 of the actions layer, and open the Actions panel (F9). Change the first line of the script to the following bold code. Here, you change the reference to the included .as file to `loadfile_component.as`. In the next step, you see how the code in the new .as file is altered.

```
#include "loadfile_component.as"

loadButton.addEventListener("click", this.loadFile);
unloadButton.addEventListener("click", this.unloadFile);
```

5. Open the `loadfile.as` file from the earlier example, and add (or modify) the code to the bold code shown in Listing 28-7.

Here, instead of creating an empty MovieClip object to store the loaded SWF or JPEG asset, lines 4 and 5 tell the `loader_mc` instance to load the asset specified by the URL entered into the `fileURL_txt` field. The `load()` method of the Loader component essentially acts as the `loadMovie()` method, bringing the external asset into the movie.

Line 7 creates an empty MovieClip object for `Sound` objects, because the Loader component is designed for visual assets such as JPEG and SWF files.

Line 18 changes the name of the attached clip to `progress_mc`. In previous examples, we used `loader_mc` as the name, but this name is already in use by the Loader component instance.

Lines 28-30 modify the `unloadFile()` method to remove the asset, which can be referenced via the `content` property of the Loader component.

Listing 28-7: The Modified loadfile_component.as Script

```
1.   function loadFile(){
2.       var fileExt = fileURL_txt.text.substr(-3);
3.       if(fileExt == "swf" || fileExt == "jpg"){
4.           var loadObj = loader_mc;
5.           loadObj.load(fileURL_txt.text);
6.       } else if(fileExt == "mp3"){
7.           var loadObj = _root.createEmptyMovieClip("holder_mc",1);
```

```
8.          sound_1 = new Sound(loadObj);
9.          sound_1.loadSound(fileURL_txt.text, true);
10.         loadObj = sound_1;
11.     }
12.     var initObject = {
13.         _x: fileURL_txt._x,
14.         _y: fileURL_txt._y - 40,
15.         target: loadObj,
16.         loadExit: null
17.     };
18.     _root.attachMovie("loaderClip", "progress_mc", 2, initObject);
19. }
20. function unloadFile(){
21.     if(typeof(holder_mc) != undefined){
22.         holder_mc.removeMovieClip();
23.     }
24.     if(typeof(sound_1) != undefined){
25.         sound_1.stop();
26.         delete sound_1;
27.     }
28.     if(loader_mc.content != undefined){
29.         loader_mc.content.removeMovieClip();
30.     }
31. }
```

6. Save the `loadfile.as` file as `loadfile_component.as`.

7. Save the Flash document, and test the movie. Type a URL into the `fileURL_txt` field, such as:

   `http://www.flashsupport.com/images/beach.jpg`

   Click the Load File button, and the asset should load into the `Loader` component. Notice that the custom preloader still works with the Loader component as well.

On the CD-ROM You can find the `preloader_fp7_comps_200.fla` and `loadfile_component.as` file in the `ch28` folder of this book's CD-ROM.

Applying the ProgressBar component

Now you learn how to use the `ProgressBar` component with the example you created in the previous section. The `ProgressBar` component displays the download progress of a loading asset, and can be used with the `Loader` component or your own custom loader Movie Clips.

1. Open the `preloader_fp7_comps_200.fla` and `loadfile_component.as` files from the last section. Save these as `preloader_fp7_comps_201.fla` and `loadfile_progressbar.as`, respectively.

2. With the `preloader_fp7_comps_201.fla` document active, open the Components panel and drag an instance of the `ProgressBar` component to the Stage.

3. Delete the new instance of the `ProgressBar` component from the Stage. You need to have only the `ProgressBar` component in the Library panel for use in this exercise.

> **Note**   You can open the Library panel to see the `ProgressBar` component and its linkage identifier.

4. Select frame 1 of the actions layer, and open the Actions panel. Change the .as file referenced in line 1 to the following code, shown in bold.

```
#include "loadfile_component.as"

loadButton.addEventListener("click", this.loadFile);
unloadButton.addEventListener("click", this.unloadFile);
```

5. Switch over to the `loadfile_progressbar.as` file, and add or modify the code shown in Listing 28-8 (lines 17-22).

In line 17, an instance of the `ProgressBar` component is added from the Library. The instance is named `progress_mc`.

In line 18, a new listener object named `progListener` is created. This listener needs a method that can be invoked by the `Loader` component when the asset has finished loading. This method, named `complete()`, is defined in lines 18-21. The purpose of this listener is to remove the `progress_mc` instance 1 second after the loading of the asset has finished. Line 20 uses the `setInterval()` function to invoke an anonymous function which does just that.

In line 22, the listener object is added to the `Loader` component instance, referenced with the `loadObj` variable created in line 4.

Listing 28-8: **Modifying the Code for the ProgressBar Component**

```
1.   function loadFile(){
2.     var fileExt = fileURL_txt.text.substr(-3);
3.     if(fileExt == "swf" || fileExt == "jpg"){
4.       var loadObj = loader_mc;
5.       loadObj.load(fileURL_txt.text);
6.     } else if(fileExt == "mp3"){
7.       var loadObj = _root.createEmptyMovieClip("holder_mc",1);
8.       sound_1 = new Sound(loadObj);
9.       sound_1.loadSound(fileURL_txt.text, true);
10.       loadObj = sound_1;
11.     }
12.     var initObject = {
13.       _x: fileURL_txt._x,
14.       _y: fileURL_txt._y - 40,
15.       source: loadObj
16.     };
17.     var progClip = _root.attachMovie("ProgressBar", "progress_mc", 2, ⤵
         initObject);
18.     progListener = new Object();
```

```
19.     progListener.complete = function(eventObj){
20.        progID = setInterval(function(obj){obj.removeMovieClip(); ↪
             clearInterval(progID);}, 1000, progress_mc);
21.     };
22.     loadObj.addEventListener("complete", progListener.complete);
23. }
24. function unloadFile(){
25.    if(typeof(holder_mc) != undefined){
26.       holder_mc.removeMovieClip();
27.    }
28.    if(typeof(sound_1) != undefined){
29.       sound_1.stop();
30.       delete sound_1;
31.    }
32.    if(loader_mc.content != undefined){
33.       loader_mc.content.removeMovieClip();
34.    }
35. }
```

6. Save both documents, and test the `preloader_fp7_comps_201.fla` document. When you type a URL into the `fileURL_txt` field and click the Load File button, the `ProgressBar` component instance displays on the Stage, as shown in Figure 28-17. When the loading has finished, the `ProgressBar` component is removed from the movie.

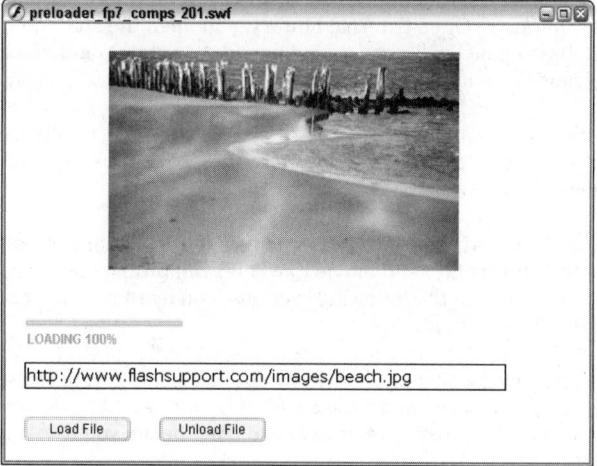

Figure 28-17: The `ProgressBar` component in action

You can find the completed documents, `preloader_fp7_comps_201.fla` and `loadfile_progressbar.as`, in the `ch28` folder of this book's CD-ROM.

Accessing Items in Shared Libraries

Since Flash 5, Web designers and developers have had the fortune of using an exciting feature to manage assets in Flash movies: the capability to link the symbols, sounds, bitmaps, and font symbols within external SWF files to other Flash movies that you use on your Web site. These external SWF files, called *shared libraries,* are different than loaded SWF files. Flash MX 2004 continues to expand the potential of shared libraries and has improved the interface and dialog boxes used to create shared items.

Tip   Flash MX 2004 allows you to easily update shared assets in the Flash documents (.fla files) that use them. Flash MX 2004 refers to shared assets as *runtime sharing*. We'll take a look at this feature in just a moment.

The primary benefit of using a shared library SWF file is that it needs to be downloaded only once, even though several other Flash movies may need to access the same element. For example, if you want to use Blur Medium as an embedded font in several Flash movies (.swf files), you would need to embed the font into each movie. A font can easily consume over 30 KB in each movie. Multiply that by 10 or 20 files in your Web site that use the font, and you may be eating up a lot of bytes just for the font usage. Instead, if you added a Font symbol to one Shared library SWF file and used that shared asset in all of the Flash movies, you would need to download the font only once, even though it's used by several movies.

A shared library SWF file doesn't load into a level or a Movie Clip instance location. Instead, you set up the Library of a Flash document (.fla file) with assets that you want to use in other Flash movies. This document is the basis of the shared library SWF file. After you assign an identifier to each asset in the Library, you save the Flash document, publish a Flash movie (.swf file) from it, and close the Flash document. Then, you open another Flash document (.fla file) and, using File ⇨ Import ⇨ Open External Library, you open the shared library Flash document (.fla file). Its Library panel will open (in a dimmed gray state), and you can drag and drop assets to your new Flash movie file.

Note   Even though the assets are linked to the external Shared library SWF file, the Flash document (.fla file) actually stores copies of the assets. However, they will not be exported with the published Flash movie.

After you have established a shared library file, any changes to the actual contents of the Shared library Flash document (.fla file) and movie (.swf file) will propagate to any Flash movie that uses the shared assets. In the following sections, you learn how to create a shared library file and use it with other Flash movies.

Caution   It is recommended that you use only small (low byte size) elements in your shared libraries to ensure that they are downloaded and available for Flash movies that use them. As with any Web production, make sure that you test early and often before you develop an entire project.

Setting up a shared library file

To share assets among several Flash movies, you need to establish a shared library file (or files) available to other Flash movie files. To create a shared library file, follow these steps:

1. Create a new Flash document (Ctrl+N or ⌘+N).

2. To place Flash artwork into the Library, draw the shapes and other elements (text, lines, gradients, and so on). Select the artwork and choose Insert ⇨ Convert to Symbol (F8). In the Convert to Symbol dialog box, choose a symbol type (for example, Graphic, Button, or Movie Clip) that best suits the nature of your artwork.

   Flash MX 2004 also allows you to define export parameters directly in this dialog box. Click the Advanced button; and in the extended options, check the Export for runtime sharing. Specify a linkage identifier name, and type the relative or absolute URL for the shared SWF file in the URL field. This URL should simply be the path to this Flash movie on the Web server, such as `http://mydomain.com/files/sharedLib.swf`. Alternatively, if you know all of your Flash movies will be stored in the same directory on the Web server, you can simply type the name of the SWF file, as shown in Figure 28-18.

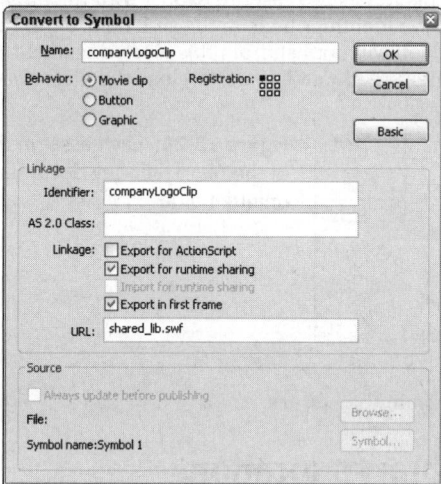

Figure 28-18: Flash MX 2004 allows you to add runtime-sharing information directly in the Convert to Symbol dialog box.

3. To place bitmaps and sounds into the Library, import the source files as you normally would, using File ⇨ Import ⇨ Import to Library.

4. Delete all artwork that you have placed on the Stage. Every asset that you want to share should be in the Library panel.

5. To place an entire font (or typeface) into the Library, open the Library panel and choose New Font from the options menu located at the top-right corner of the Library panel. In the Font Symbol Properties dialog box, type a reference name for the font, choose the font face from the Font menu, and select a faux font style (Bold or Italic) to be applied (optional). See Figure 28-19.

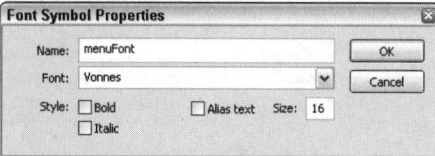

Figure 28-19: Give each embedded font face a descriptive name that indicates its functionality within the Flash movie.

Note   In Flash MX 2004, you can now specify alias text and size settings in the Font Symbol Properties dialog box. However, in our tests, we could not see any visible difference in the way in which a shared font (or any Font symbol) was rendered.

Assigning names to assets

After you have placed each asset into the Library of your starter Flash document (.fla file), you'll need to assign a unique identifier to each asset.

1. Select the symbol, bitmap, sound, and font in the Library. Right-click (or Control+click on Mac) the selected asset and choose Linkage. Alternatively, you can select the item and choose Linkage from the Library panel's options menu.

2. In the Linkage Properties dialog box, shown in Figure 28-20, choose Export for runtime sharing for the Linkage option. This forces the asset to export with the published SWF file. Then, type a unique name in the Identifier field. In the URL field, enter the intended final location of the SWF file that you will publish from this Flash document. We discuss this option in more detail in the next section. Click OK to close the dialog box.

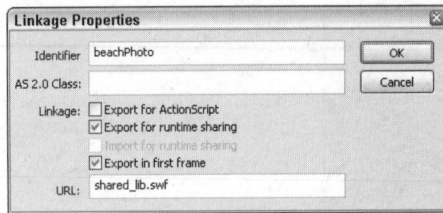

Figure 28-20: Each asset in the Library of the Shared library document needs a unique name.

3. Repeat Steps 1 and 2 for each asset in the Library.

Specifying the shared library's location

A required setting for each asset of the Shared library document is the relative or absolute path (as a URL) to the shared library SWF on your Web server. To change the URL for all of the assets with the current Shared library document, follow these steps:

1. In the options menu in the Library panel, choose Shared Library Properties.

2. In the URL field, type the location of the shared library SWF file (or where you intend to publish it on the Web). This location will be appended to each shared asset's identifier in the movies that use the assets.

Caution   Make sure that you specify this URL before you start using the shared library document (.fla file) with other Flash documents (.fla files). The URL location is stored within each document that uses the shared library SWF file, and it will not update if you decide to change the URL later in the Shared library FLA file.

Publishing the shared library movie file

After the assets of the Flash document have been assigned identifiers and the URL of the shared library has been set, you need to publish a SWF file of the Flash document.

1. Save the Flash document (.fla file). Use a descriptive name that notifies other members of your Web production team that this is a shared library file, such as shared_lib.fla.

2. Publish the Flash movie as a SWF file. No other publish formats are necessary. In the Publish Settings (File ⇨ Publish Settings), select only the Flash format in the Format tab. Click OK. Choose File ⇨ Publish to create a SWF file from your document.

3. Close the Flash document.

Linking to assets from other movies

After the shared library SWF file is published, you can use the shared assets in other Flash movies.

1. Create a new Flash document or open an existing one.

2. Using the File ⇨ Import ⇨ Open External Library command, browse to the folder where your shared library Flash document (.fla file) was saved. For testing purposes, you should keep this document in the same folder as the other Flash documents that share it. Select the shared library FLA file and click Open. A separate grayed-out Library panel for the shared library FLA file will open in the Flash MX 2004 authoring environment.

3. Drag the asset(s) that you wish to use into the new Flash document's Library or onto its Stage. Even though Flash MX 2004 will copy the contents of each shared asset, the asset will load from the separate shared library SWF file at runtime.

4. To see whether an asset is native to the Flash movie or from a shared library SWF file, right-click (or Control+click on Mac) the symbol or asset in the Library. Select Linkage from the contextual menu. The Linkage Properties dialog box, shown in Figure 28-21, will indicate whether the symbol (or asset) will be imported from an external shared library SWF file.

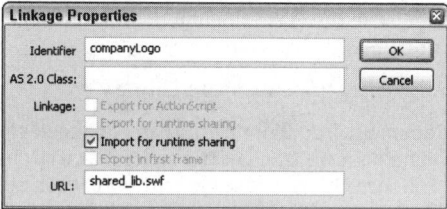

Figure 28-21: If a Shared library asset is used in another movie, the Linkage Properties indicate the name (and path) of the shared library SWF file.

When you are done dragging the assets from the shared library file, close its Library panel. When you publish the new Flash movie(s) that use the shared library SWF file, make sure you put all of the files on your Web server for live testing. If you used relative URL locations for the shared library SWF file(s), make sure the files are stored in the proper directories on your Web server.

You can find a shared library document and Flash document that uses the shared assets in the `ch28/sharedLib` folder of the *Macromedia Flash MX 2004 Bible* CD-ROM.

Updating shared assets

Flash MX 2004 has an update feature to assets that have been imported from a shared library document. To see which assets in your current document are imported, expand the width of the Library panel to view the Linkage column, as shown in Figure 28-22.

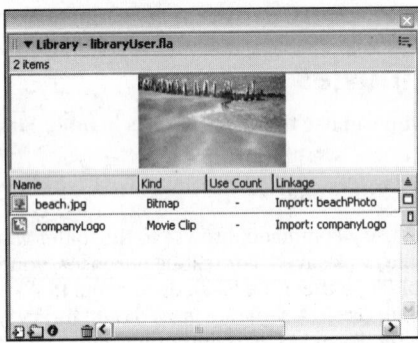

Figure 28-22: The Library panel allows you to quickly view the Linkage settings for each item.

If you have changed the contents of an asset in a shared library document (.fla file) and published the new Flash movie (.swf file), you can choose to update the reference assets in other Flash documents that use the shared assets. Let's walk through the complete process of updating a shared library asset.

1. Open the shared library document (.fla file).

2. Open the Library panel and edit the shared asset you wish to update. For example, if you need to change the artwork with a Movie Clip symbol, double-click the symbol and edit the symbol's content.

3. When you're done editing the asset, save the Flash document and publish a Flash movie. Close the Shared library document.

4. Open a Flash document that uses an asset from the shared library.

5. Open the Library panel for the document. You'll notice that any changed elements still appear as they did before the update occurred. Select the asset that was changed in the shared library document and choose Update from the Library panel's options menu. Or right-click (Control+click on Mac) the asset and choose Update from the contextual menu. The Update Library Items dialog box appears, as shown in Figure 28-23. Select the check box next to the asset's name you wish to update and then click the Update button.

You can also select multiple items in the Library panel and chose Update in the Options menu to update several items at once.

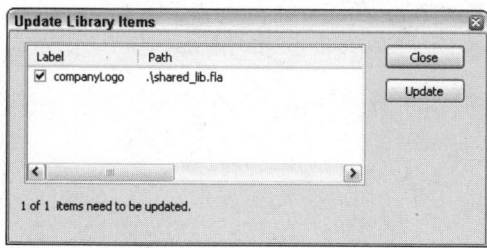

Figure 28-23: You can update shared assets in other Flash documents that use them.

We'd like to know what you think about this chapter. Visit www.flashsupport.com/feedback to fill out an online form with your comments.

Summary

✦ If you want to make sure that your larger Flash movies don't pause during playback over the Web, you may want to make a preloader for each Flash movie you make.

✦ Preloaders can use three different ways to test the download progress of the Flash movie SWF file: ifFrameLoaded(), _framesloaded/_totalframes, and getBytesLoaded()/getBytesTotal(). The most accurate mechanism uses the getBytesLoaded()/getBytesTotal() methods.

✦ You can break up large Flash projects into several smaller Flash movie components that are loaded into a primary Flash movie when they're needed.

✦ The loadMovie() action enables you to download SWF files into level or Movie Clip instance locations.

✦ You can load JPEG images with the loadMovie() action in Flash Player 6 or higher movies.

✦ MP3 files can be downloaded directly into Flash Player 6 or higher movies using the loadSound() method of the Sound object.

✦ The new MovieClipLoader class can make the job of loading and monitoring asset loading much easier.

✦ The new Loader and ProgressBar components can quickly add external asset loading features to your Flash movies.

✦ You can share Flash assets with the shared library feature. Assets are stored in one or more shared library SWF files and referenced by other Flash movies.

✦   ✦   ✦

Using Components

A major change in Flash MX 2004 is the addition of a whole new set of components, known as V2 components, and the architecture that they use. Components offer an easy way to reuse complicated elements within your movie without having to build them on your own. Flash MX 2004 continues to develop upon the same components introduced in Flash MX — you probably have already noticed a panel including several built-in components. Although it's beyond the scope of this book, you can also build your own custom components. In this chapter, we take a look at what components are, their parameters, and how to work with the many of the components included with Flash MX 2004.

New Feature Flash MX 2004 ships with 13 components, whereas Flash MX Professional 2004 has 30 components. Many of the Pro version's components are derived from previous Macromedia Developer Resource Kits (DRKs).

 **Cross-Reference** The *Macromedia Flash MX 2004 Bible* focuses on the UI components that are found in both versions of Flash MX 2004. Many more components are discussed in the *Macromedia Flash MX 2004 ActionScript Bible* (Wiley, 2004).

What Are Components?

Components are complex Movie Clips with parameters that you define during the authoring process. They are essentially a container, holding many assets, which work together to add enhanced interactivity, productivity, or effects to your movies. Components can be used to control your movie, such as moving from one frame to another, or to perform more complex tasks, such as sending data to and from a server.

Additional components can be downloaded from Macromedia and third-party developers, to add to those already bundled with Flash MX 2004 and Flash MX Professional 2004. Many of the most useful and regularly used elements are already included with the program, such as buttons, combo boxes, and lists. We look at many of the components found in the UI Components set in this chapter.

Different from Flash MX Components

You may already be familiar with the use of Flash MX's components. The original components are now referred to as V1 components. V1 components use a different event model than the new V2 components that ship with Flash MX 2004 and Flash MX Professional 2004.

If you had a large investment in V1 components, you can continue using them in Flash MX 2004 documents, but you will be restricted to publishing ActionScript 1.0 movies. You may also find that you need to publish your movies for Flash Player 6 as well. To reuse your V1 components from Flash MX in Flash MX 2004, do the following:

1. Copy the Flash document (.fla file) for the component set (for example, the Communication Components.fla for the Flash Communication Server MX 1.5 components) from the Flash MX `First Run\Components` directory to your Flash MX 2004 First Run\Components folder.

2. Restart Flash MX 2004. The older components should appear in the Components panel.

Why Use Components?

Components make it easy for you to share your work with other Flash developers who work in your production team, or to share your innovations with other developers in the Flash community.

While this chapter focuses on the components bundled with the release of Flash MX 2004, the way in which these components are used will also help you understand how other components work—from Macromedia or a third-party. Components you download sometimes come in *sets*, which may include many similar small applications. A current example of this is a component set made by Macromedia comprised of several graphing utilities, which you could use in conjunction with XML to dynamically set values and have them displayed in a graph at runtime. These sets are essentially a Flash document (.fla file) stored on your computer. You may need the Macromedia Extension Manager to install them into Flash MX 2004.

Cross-Reference   For more information on exchanging and downloading components, please see the section "Exchanging and acquiring components" at the end of this chapter.

One of the arguments against using components is the file size they add to your productions. Even though this may be the case, there are several reasons to use components apart from the ease of dragging them to your Stage and modifying the parameters.

Caution   Many of the V2 components in Flash MX 2004 are substantially large in file size. Go to `www.flashsupport.com/mx2004/component_comparison/` for a comparison of Flash MX and Flash MX 2004 component sizes.

First of all, usability is an integral part of effective interface design. Components are an extremely effective way of ensuring that your end user understands how to use certain elements of your Flash movie. A predictable interface does not have to be boring or cliché. Furthermore, because components can be skinned, they can have a unique look from one site to the next. The components shipped with Flash MX 2004, for the most part, are also reliable, given they were built, developed, and tested by professionals. This is not to say that the same level of construction cannot be achieved by thousands of others, but the time and effort spent in complicated coding and testing has already been done for you. And because components are a quick solution to common interface requirements, you will have more time to spend on more complicated and interesting creative tasks instead of repetitive authoring.

Caution   Exercise care with third-party components — even those that you can download from the Macromedia Exchange. Not all components have been thoroughly tested, and some are specifically developed for one particular use in mind. Be sure to test your implementation of a component throughout the development process.

A new symbol type for components

A component is made up of one or more internal assets. One of the changes in Flash MX 2004's component architecture, though, is that components are now compiled. This means that when you add a component to the Flash document and open your Library panel, you'll only see one symbol for the component (see Figure 29-1). In Flash MX, the same component may have added many folders and symbols that are used by the component (see Figure 29-2).

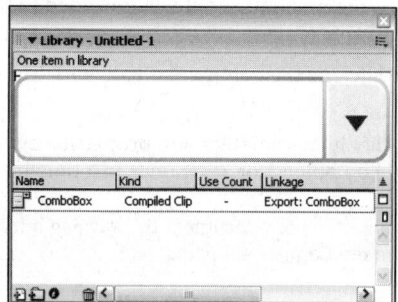

Figure 29-1: The ComboBox component in Flash MX 2004

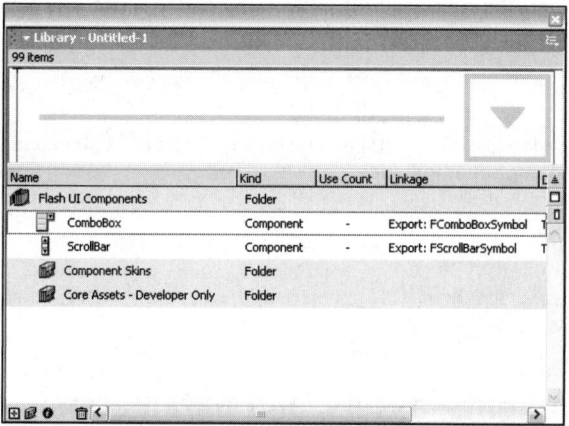

Figure 29-2: The ComboBox component in Flash MX

The new symbol type for components in Flash MX 2004 is a called Compiled Clip. There are a couple of major differences with this new component architecture:

✦ You can no longer edit the symbols of a component that has been compiled. As such, you need to use ActionScript code to change the appearance of a component.

✦ Developers can now create and distribute components without the user being able to see the code used to create the component. This is a big "win" for developers who used Flash MX and were concerned about their intellectual property rights.

If you were familiar with components in Flash MX 2004, other differences between V1 and V2 components are highlighted throughout this chapter.

How to add a component

You can add a component to your Stage in the following ways:

1. Open the Components panel by going to Window ⇨ Development Panels ⇨ Components or by pressing Ctrl+F7 or ⌘+F7.

2. Add a component to the Stage by:

   • **Double-clicking:** You can double-click a component, and it will be added to the center of your Document window's workspace.

   • **Dragging:** You can add an instance by clicking the component icon and dragging it onto the Stage.

After your component is on the Stage, you can modify its parameters and properties manually in various panels or by using ActionScript code on objects or keyframes in a timeline.

Note   You can add additional instances of your component to your document by dragging it from your Library panel onto the Stage instead of from the Component panel.

You can also add a component to your movie by using the `MovieClip.attachMovie()` method in ActionScript after the instance is added to your library. An example of adding a `Button` component to the Stage and setting a few properties using ActionScript is as follows: (This code uses standard ActionScript 1.0 syntax.)

```
var myButton = _root.attachMovie("Button", "myButton ", 1);
myButton.label = "Music";
```

This creates an instance of a push button on the stage, labeled with "Music." You can also use ActionScript 2.0 to create a new component instance:

```
import mx.controls.Button;
this.createClassObject(Button, "myButton", 1, {label: "Test Button"});
```

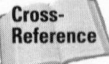

Cross-Reference   For more information on using the `MovieClip` object and `attachMovie()`, refer to Chapter 25, "Controlling Movie Clips."

Where to find components, assets, and parameters

You can find, control, and edit your components in many areas of the Flash interface. Understanding each of these areas will help you add custom features to your Flash movies that use components.

Components panel

You can find this panel, shown in Figure 29-3, by going to Window ⇨ Development Panels ⇨ Components or by using the Ctrl+F7 or ⌘+F7 shortcut. This panel includes all of the components that ship with Flash MX 2004 or Flash MX Professional 2004.

Note   As mentioned earlier in this chapter, the Professional version of Flash MX 2004 has many more components than the standard version.

If you add components that you have downloaded from other Web sites, such as the Macromedia Exchange, you will be able to access the sets from this panel as well. Each set appears as a new nesting.

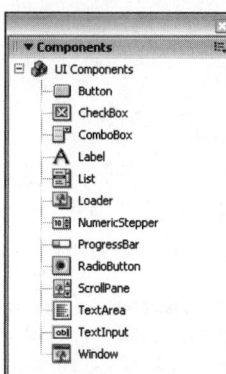

Figure 29-3: The Components panel, featuring a new look in Flash MX 2004

New Feature   In the previous release of Flash MX, you would change component sets in a drop-down menu at the top of the panel. Now, the Components panel uses a tree structure, in which every set is shown in the panel. The components of each set are nested with each node.

Property inspector

The Property inspector includes two tabs when you have a component selected. The Parameters tab includes an area similar to the Component Inspector panel (discussed next), where you can change the values of each parameter depending on how you need to use the component. Figure 29-4 shows the parameters of a ComboBox component.

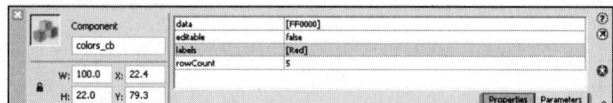

Figure 29-4: The Property inspector enables you to quickly configure a component.

The Properties tab enables you to add color effects, such as Brightness, Tint, Alpha, or a combination of these attributes — just as you can with any other symbol in Flash. You can also swap the instance with another symbol from this tab.

Component Inspector panel

The Component Inspector panel is a new addition to the Flash authoring environment. It combines the Component Parameters panel of Flash MX with extended options in Flash MX Professional 2004. You can find this panel by choosing Window ⇨ Development Panels ⇨ Component Inspector or by using the Alt+F7 or Option+F7 shortcut. In the standard edition of Flash MX 2004, this panel has only one tab named Parameters (see Figure 29-5). In this tab, you can set values for each parameter of a component instance, just as you can with the Property inspector. This tab can also be used to display custom user interface movies (SWF files) for components.

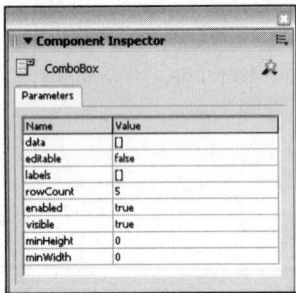

Figure 29-5: The Component Inspector as seen in the standard edition of Flash MX 2004

Tip   The Component Inspector panel also features a new Component Wizard icon. If a component was built to employ a wizard, clicking this button will initiate the wizard.

If you are using Flash MX Professional 2004, the Component Inspector features two additional tabs: Bindings and Schema (see Figure 29-6). These tabs are used for more advanced data features of many extra components that ship with Flash MX Professional 2004.

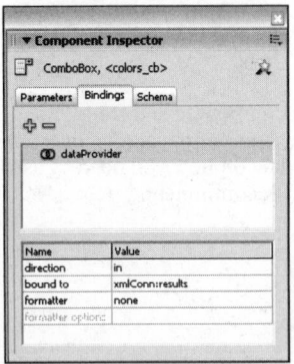

Figure 29-6: The Component Inspector panel as seen in Flash MX Professional 2004

Note   The Bindings and Schema tabs can also be used with UI Components, but you can only see these tabs if you are using Flash MX Professional 2004. If you had used the Firefly components that were available for Flash MX, you'll be familiar with the use of these tabs as well.

For more information on binding data to components via the Bindings and Schema tabs, refer to the *Macromedia Flash MX 2004 ActionScript Bible*. You can also find examples of their usage in the Help panel by searching with the phrase "data binding."

Library panel

After dragging a UI component to the Stage, you will notice a new Compiled Clip symbol for the component added to your Library. If you want to remove a component from your Flash document, be sure to delete it from the Library as well as from the Stage.

A V1 component, or any component designed to work with the original release of Flash MX, usually adds several folders and the assets associated with their construction to the Library panel.

Actions panel and ActionScript

Not only is there ActionScript hidden within the compiled components that ship with Flash MX 2004, but you can also write ActionScript to control components or modify their appearance. The built-in components that ship with Flash MX 2004 have several methods and properties that you can use to customize their functionality. Later in this chapter, you learn how to tap some of these scripted resources.

You can also use behaviors, found in the Behaviors panel, with several of the components.

Modifying component color properties and parameters

There are several ways you can easily modify the appearance and functionality of your components. In the UI components of Flash MX 2004, you can customize the face color of each instance with little effort. Let's look at how this is accomplished.

First of all, open the Property inspector. As you have already seen, the Parameters and Properties tabs contain information on the attributes of your component. This is possibly the easiest and quickest way to change the appearance of your component. Simply by selecting the Properties tab and then the Color menu, you can alter the Brightness, Tint, Alpha, or a combination of these elements by choosing Advanced. You can see the changes made to the face of your component after publishing or previewing your movie.

The Parameters tab enables you to change the built-in component parameters to ones better matching your site or the usage of your component. For example, on a ScrollPane instance, you can change the horizontal and vertical scroll attributes (visibility) in this area by clicking the value area and selecting an option from the list. The Component Inspector panel (and the Component Definition dialog box, if applicable) is another area that enables you to modify or customize the functionality of your components.

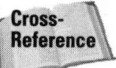

For more information on changing the look of components please refer to the section later in this chapter called "Modifying Components."

For Uncompiled Components Only: Component Definition Dialog Box

If you use V1 components or if you create your own custom components in Flash MX 2004, you can access the definitions used by a component by right-clicking (or Control+clicking on Mac) the component in the Library (or using the Library's options menu) and choosing Component Definition. This dialog box enables you to add or remove parameters from pre-built or custom components. You are also able to customize or alter the functionality of the component. Other options in this dialog box include setting the ActionScript 2.0 class name, Custom UI, Live Preview, and Description. This dialog box is generally intended for advanced component users or authors.

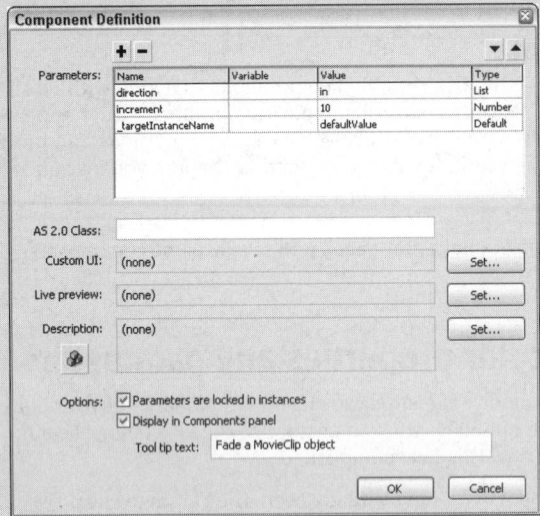

The Component Definition dialog box enables you to add and remove parameters and functions of uncompiled components.

Once a component is compiled, the user of the component no longer has access to the Component Definition settings.

Removing components from your movie

It is important to understand how to properly remove components from your movie. Removing V2 components is usually very straightforward: Select the compiled clip in the Library panel, and delete it.

V1 components, on the other hand, can often be linked to many other assets spread across several folders in the Library panel. Some V1 components share assets, such as the V1 Scrollbar component. Therefore, care must be taken when removing assets from the Library.

You should have a solid understanding of component structure and asset usage if you attempt to manually remove items from the Flash UI Component folder in the Library.

Components in Flash MX 2004

Flash MX 2004 includes several UI components, which provide *user interface* elements and functionality frequently used by developers. You should be able to find a use for some or all of these components at one time or another. Let's take a look at what each of the core UI components does and how to use them in your movies. After dragging any component instance to your Stage, open up the Property inspector and select the Parameters tab to view the parameters discussed in this section.

New Feature Most of the V2 components feature a new Halo skin, with colors and effects that resemble modern day operating systems' interfaces.

Tip Most UI components in Flash MX 2004 will function properly in Flash Player 6 movies. If you're in doubt, simply publish or test your Flash movie as a Flash Player 6 movie and see if the component works as expected. Make sure you set the ActionScript version to ActionScript 2.0 in the Publish Settings as well.

Note The new V2 component framework does not use click or change handlers in the same way that V1 components from Flash MX did. Refer to the section titled "Understanding the Listener Event Model for V2 Components" later in this chapter for more information.

The parameters for each component discussed in the following sections are also the respective names of each component's properties. Note that not all of a component's properties may be exposed in the Property inspector.

Button component

This component is essentially a standard button with built-in up, over, and down states. The button is designed to resemble an HTML form button (such as a submit button), but with the new Halo theme for V2 components. The Button component, shown in Figure 29-7, is very easy to use and can aid in quick development of mockups or modified to suit more aesthetically inclined productions.

Figure 29-7: The Button component as it appears in a Flash movie at runtime

Caution Do not confuse a Button component with a Button symbol. The Button component replaces the V1 PushButton component from Flash MX. In this chapter, any reference to Button instance implies a Button component, not a Button symbol.

Parameters

The Button parameters are perhaps some of the easiest to manage. As with other components, you can enter text for the button's label and set a function to execute when the button is pressed.

✦ `icon`: This optional parameter specifies the linkage ID of a symbol in the Library that will appear next to the label text of the button. The placement of the label in relation to the icon symbol is determined by the `labelPlacement` parameter (discussed later in this list).

✦ `label`: This is the text appearing on the button face. The default text is simply "Button."

✦ `labelPlacement`: This optional parameter is a menu with left, right, top, or bottom options. This setting determines how the label text is aligned to the button's icon symbol. The default value is right. If you do not use an icon symbol for the instance, this setting has no effect.

✦ `selected` **and** `toggle`: These two parameters work together to enable a Button component instance to act as an on/off button. As a toggle button, the rim of the instance displays an "on" color (green is the default Halo theme) if `selected` is set to `true`. The `selected` property has no effect if `toggle` is not set to `true`. The default value for both `selected` and `toggle` parameters is `false`.

Caution   If you use the Property inspector to set the `selected` parameter to `true`, the `Button` instance (unfortunately) will not appear with a selected state when you publish or test the movie. The selected property must be set in ActionScript to work properly.

How it works

An instance of a `Button` component can have regular, disabled, or active states, which can be customized graphically. It is a very quick way to add interactivity to your movie. For additional functionality of the button, you will need to write ActionScript using the `Button` methods.

Tip   The `click` event is sent to any listeners when a `Button` component instance is clicked. You can use an `on(click)` event handler directly on a `Button` component instance to initiate further actions when the instance is clicked.

Cross-Reference   You can find several examples of the `Button` component throughout many chapters of this book. You can also search for "button component" in the Help panel to find more information on the Button component. If you search for "button component class," you'll find the primary page describing the methods and properties of the Button component.

CheckBox component

The `CheckBox` component, as the name implies, is a user interface element that has a selection box next to text. As with HTML form check boxes, the `CheckBox` component enables you to easily add form options to a Flash movie. The `CheckBox` component returns a `true` or `false` value. If the box is checked, it returns a `true` value; if not, it returns a `false`. These states are shown in Figure 29-8.

☑ Subscribe to news   ☐ Subscribe to events

Figure 29-8: A selected (true) check box, left, and a cleared (false) check box, right

Parameters

CheckBox parameters can be changed to customize the default label text and its placement in relation to the check box graphic. You can also set the initial state and have the option of setting a function, executing as soon as the button state changes.

✦ `label`: This is the name appearing next to the check box. The default value is set to "CheckBox."

✦ `labelPlacement`: This parameter sets the label to the left, right (default), top, or bottom of the check box.

Tip Make sure to set the height of the instance appropriately to accommodate top and bottom alignment.

✦ `selected`: Assigning a `true` value checks the box initially, although the default value for this is set to `false` (unchecked).

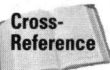

Cross-Reference Refer to the exercise, later in this chapter, called "Using components in your movie," for an example of how to use a listener with a `ComboBox` instance.

How it works

The `CheckBox` component has a hit area that encompasses the check box itself, as well as the label next to it. The width of a `CheckBox` instance can be transformed to accommodate more text. Added functionality using ActionScript is possible by using the methods, events, and properties of the `CheckBox` class.

ComboBox component

The `ComboBox` component is similar to any standard HTML drop-down list. When you click the component instance, a list of options appears below the default value in the list. You can also navigate the list using the up-arrow, down-arrow, Page Up, Page Down, Home, and End keys. This component is very useful and essentially has the following two different functionalities:

✦ As a regular combo box, the component can display a list of choices from which the user can select an option. If the combo box has focus, the user can type a letter to jump to a label starting with the same letter. See Figure 29-9.

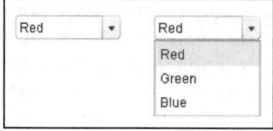

Figure 29-9: A standard ComboBox instance, shown closed (left) and open (right)

✦ An editable combo box, a user can enter text into the top field to specify a value that is not displayed in the list. The typed value is the active value for the `ComboBox` instance. Figure 29-10 shows a value being entered into the `ComboBox` instance at runtime.

Figure 29-10: An editable ComboBox instance, shown with default display (left) and entered text (right)

Parameters

ComboBox parameters can be changed to set labels and data for each item in the drop-down box, set the top of the pull-down to be a text input box (an editable combo box), and customize how many items are viewable when the arrow is selected.

✦ data: This array is composed of values that correspond to each label value entered in the array for the labels parameter. For example, if you had a label value of "Red," you may want a data value of "FF0000." Similarly, if you have catalog of items, the product's name may be the label value and its catalog number is the data value. The user does not see the data value(s).

> **Note** When you set values for the data or labels array in the Property inspector, the values will be typed as strings. You need to set the data values in ActionScript if you want to type the values differently.

✦ editable: This parameter is set to define whether the ComboBox instance can have text entered into the top of the list to specify a value not listed in the menu. This typed value can be passed as data to the movie using the value property of the ComboBox class.

✦ labels: This array of values determines the list of text entries that the user sees when viewing the drop-down box.

✦ rowCount: The number entered here represents how many labels are seen on the drop-down before a scrollbar appears. The default value is set to 5.

How it works

When you click the data or labels field in the Property inspector, you will notice a magnifying glass icon next to the drop-down area. This button, when clicked, opens a Values panel where you can enter the array of values using the + or - buttons.

> **Tip** The values for these parameters use a zero-based index, which means the first item in your array is listed as [0].

Functionality can be added using ActionScript, and the ComboBox class's methods, properties, and event handlers can be used with each instance of this component.

List component

The List component also allows you to create lists just as the ComboBox does, but the list menu is always visible (see Figure 29-11). If there are more items than the height of the instance allows, a scroll bar is automatically added to the list. This component allows selection of one of more items. As with the ComboBox component, keyboard navigation is allowed, and a zero-based index system is used for the arrays populating the label and data parameters.

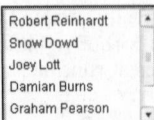

Figure 29-11: The List component at runtime

Parameters

The List component parameters include an additional option to select multiple values. Other settings in this tab are similar in function to components mentioned earlier.

✦ **data:** This parameter is an array of values associated with the values set in the labels parameter.

✦ **labels:** Values entered into this area will be the labels on each list item.

✦ **multipleSelection:** Set to either true or false. A true value allows end users to select multiple values at once when holding down the Ctrl or ⌘ key. The default value of false allows only one selection to be active at any time.

✦ **rowHeight:** This parameter control the pixel height of each item in the list. This value does not control the size of the text used for each item. Rather, it indicates the active "hit" area of the item. If you specify a value that's smaller than the pixel height of the text, cropping of the item's label is the result. The default value is 20 pixels.

How it works

This component's functionality is very similar to that of the ComboBox component. The main difference in a List component is the visibility of the labels and the ability to select multiple values. If you wish to add functionality using ActionScript, the methods, property, and events of the List class are used.

RadioButton component

The RadioButton component looks and feels similar to those found in HTML forms. Based on the design of radio button functionality, only one radio button can be selected within a group of buttons. Figure 29-12 shows a group of RadioButton instances in a Flash movie.

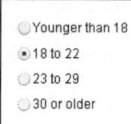

Figure 29-12: A group of RadioButton instances

Parameters

The RadioButton component has the unique attribute for setting a Group name, which will associate the instance with others on the Stage. Other parameters resemble those of components discussed earlier.

✦ **data:** The value entered here is associated with the label value of the RadioButton instance.

✦ **groupName:** The value of this parameter specifies which group of RadioButton instances on the Stage the particular instance is associated with. Therefore, only one radio dot appears in this group at one time. You can have several groups, each with its own set of associated RadioButton instances. The default value is radioGroup.

✦ **label:** This is the text you see alongside the RadioButton instance.

✦ labelPlacement: By default, the label placement is set to the right of the radio button. The acceptable options include left, right, top, and bottom.

✦ selected: This parameter sets the initial state of the button to be true or false (default). A false selection is clear. All buttons having the same group name will allow only one radio button to be selected at one time. If you set more than one RadioButton instance in the same group to initially have a true value, the last instance will be selected when you publish your movie.

How it works

The groupName parameter is important to understand. Groups of buttons can be added to your document, and in each group, only one button can be selected at one time. The width and height of an instance can be resized with the Free Transform tool, the Property inspector, or the Transform panel to accommodate your label alignment parameter. The hit area of the RadioButton instance surrounds both the button and the label area. Added functionality can be controlled using the RadioButton class's methods, properties, and events in ActionScript.

Note   It is important to consider the interactive design of your movie when you add radio buttons or check boxes to your movies. Your decision should not be based on the "look" of a radio button versus a check box. Radio buttons should only be used when you need *one* selection to be made from several choices, and a radio button should never exist outside of a group (that is, you shouldn't have a single radio button appearing on its own). Check boxes should be used when you need to allow *one or more* selections to be made from several choices. You can also use a check box for a single option (for example, a form may have a check box asking if you want to receive promotional e-mails for a product). We recommend that you carefully consider how these elements are designed for use in applications, because this enhances the usability of your production.

ScrollPane component

The ScrollPane component is potentially a very powerful and diverse tool. It adds a window with vertical and horizontal scrollbars on either side and is used to display linked Movie Clip symbols from the Library on to the Stage. Because the component features scroll bars, you are able to accommodate more content within a smaller footprint on the Stage. Figure 29-13 shows a ScrollPane instance displaying a linked Movie Clip symbol.

Figure 29-13: The ScrollPane component at runtime

Parameters

Parameters for the ScrollPane component will link it to a Movie Clip symbol and also control how your end user will be able to manipulate the ScrollPane content. You can also control scroll bar positioning and visibility with these parameters.

✦ contentPath: Enter a text string to set to the Linkage ID of the Movie Clip you want to appear in the ScrollPane instance.

Caution

The ScrollPane component can also use external paths (or URLs) for displayed content, but in our tests at the time of this writing, the content displayed horribly. External JPEG or SWF files were not masked properly. Check Macromedia's Web site for updates to the V2 components for potential fixes to this problem.

✦ hLineScrollSize: This value determines how much the content in the ScrollPane instance will move when the left or right arrows along the horizontal scroll bar are pressed. The default value is 5 pixels.

✦ hPageScrollSize: This parameter specifies how much the content moves when the user clicks the scroll track on either side of the horizontal scroll bar's middle scroller. The default value is 20 pixels.

✦ hScrollPolicy: This parameters controls how the horizontal scroll bar for the window is displayed. The default setting of auto means a horizontal scroll bar only appears if necessary. A value of true ensures it is always visible, and a false value turns it off.

✦ scrollDrag: Setting this parameter to true enables your users to drag the area within the instance window in order to view the content. A setting of false (default) requires scroll bars to be used instead.

✦ vLineScrollSize: This parameter functions the same way as the hLineScrollSize parameter, but for the vertical scroll bar of the window.

✦ vPageScrollSize: This parameter behaves in the same way as the hPageScrollSize parameter, but for the vertical scroll bar of the window.

✦ vScrollPolicy: This parameter controls if the vertical scroll bar is visible. See the description for the hScrollPolicy for more details.

How it works

The ScrollPane component only displays Movie Clips with linkage IDs, so you will need to convert any other symbol types or bitmap images to Movie Clips for the images to display. Linkage IDs must be set between the Movie Clip and the scroll content parameter. The Movie Clip simply has to be in the Library and have the Export for ActionScript setting checked in the Linkage Properties dialog box.

TextArea component

The TextArea component, shown in Figure 29-14, can be thought of as a ScrollPane component for text. The purpose of the TextArea component is to display text or HTML formatted text within a display window, complete with vertical and/or horizontal scroll bars. The TextArea component is meant as a replacement for the V1 ScrollBar component and text fields in the original release of Flash MX.

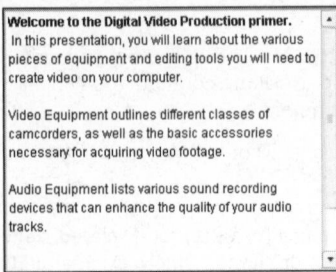

Welcome to the Digital Video Production primer.
In this presentation, you will learn about the various pieces of equipment and editing tools you will need to create video on your computer.

Video Equipment outlines different classes of camcorders, as well as the basic accessories necessary for acquiring video footage.

Audio Equipment lists various sound recording devices that can enhance the quality of your audio tracks.

Figure 29-14: The TextArea component displaying HTML-formatted text

Parameters

The settings for the TextArea component in the Property inspector control the text that is displayed in the instance.

✦ editable: This parameter controls whether or not the user can change the text in the instance at runtime. The default value is true. If set to false, the user cannot change the text.

Caution   We strongly recommend that you get in the habit of setting the editable parameter to false. You usually won't want users to change the contents of your TextArea component.

✦ html: This parameter determines how the value for the text parameter is interpreted. If html is set to true, any HTML tags format the text accordingly. If html is set to false, the text parameter displays "as is." The default value is false.

✦ text: The value of this parameter is the actual text displayed in the instance's text field.

Tip   For larger blocks of text, draft the text in a separate text editor and copy and paste the text into the text parameter field of the Property inspector.

✦ wordWrap: This parameter controls how the text wraps in the instance. If set to true (default), the text wraps at the visible horizontal boundary of the display area. If the parameter is set to false, the text wraps only when a carriage return or line break is specifically embedded in the text value, with a <br/> or <p> tag in HTML formatted text.

Note   Horizontal scrollbars will be added only to TextArea instances if wordWrap is set to false and the text width for a line extends beyond the visible display area.

How it works

The TextArea component takes the text parameter value and displays it within the visible area of the instance. The TextArea component can be further enhanced or controlled with ActionScript, by utilizing the methods, properties, and event handlers of the TextArea class.

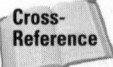

Cross-Reference   You can see the TextArea component in Chapter 20, "Making Your First Flash MX 2004 Project."

Understanding the Listener Event Model for V2 Components

While it's rather simple to drag and drop components on to the Stage of your Flash document and use the Property inspector to set up initial values for them, the result of any component behavior needs to be described *by you*, in your own ActionScript code. When the user interacts with a component, a specific event — tailored for the component — is sent out to the Flash movie. Just as you can yell alone in an empty forest, these broadcasted events will just be ignored by the Flash movie unless you create something to listen to the events. Such objects are called listeners because their sole purpose is to intercept broadcasted messages from other objects that generate events — such as components.

What a typical listener looks like

Just about any object in a Flash movie can be a listener. You can add custom methods to `MovieClip` objects, for example, or you can create an instance of the `Object` class that exists only in ActionScript. To create a generic object, use the following syntax:

In ActionScript 1.0:

```
var myListener = new Object();
```

or

```
var myListener = {};
```

In ActionScript 2.0:

```
var myListener:Object = new Object();
```

or

```
var myListener:Object = {};
```

Once you have created an object that behaves as a listener, you can create methods for the listener geared toward the behavior of the component it observes. For example, if you wanted to do something when a `Button` component instance is clicked, you can add a `click()` method (or handler) to the listener object.

```
myListener.click = function(){
    trace("---listener received an event broadcast");
};
```

In this simple example, a `trace()` message is sent to the Output panel. You could add further actions to the `click()` method, performing more tasks necessary for your Flash movie.

Letting the component know who its listeners are

Once a listener has a method to invoke, you need to assign the listener object (or its method) to the component that will be broadcasting events. For our previous example, you could assign the listener to a `Button` component instance named `myButton` by using the following code:

```
myButton.addEventListener("click", myListener);
```

or

```
myButton.addEventListener("click", myListener.click);
```

The addEventListener() method takes two parameters: the event being broadcast and the listener object (or method). Each component has its unique event names. The Button component, used in this example, has a click event, which is broadcast to all listeners when the user clicks the Button component instance.

Most components also broadcast additional information to the listeners, passed as parameters to the listener's method. All of the UI components pass an event information object to their listeners. The exact properties of this object vary from one component to the next, but some are consistent. In the following listener method, the eventInfo parameter from the Button instance contains several properties, including eventInfo.target, which is a reference to the Button instance.

```
myListener.click = function(eventInfo){
    trace(eventInfo.target + " was clicked.");
    trace("The broadcasted event was " + eventInfo.type );
};
```

Note   You can change the parameter name to any term you wish. In our example, the parameter is referred to as eventInfo, but you can use a term such as eventObj. Just be sure to use the term consistently throughout your listener's method.

The type property, as you can see in the example code, can tell the listener what type of event was broadcast to it. In this way, you can create one method for a listener and have it handle different event types with specific code.

On the CD-ROM   You can find a sample click listener for the Button component in the button_listener. fla found in the ch29 folder of this book's CD-ROM.

Using Components in Your Movie

In the following exercise, you use various components in a movie to activate and deactivate a series of elements. It provides an example of how you may use components in your movie to create interactivity.

On the CD-ROM   The source file for this exercise called components_starter.fla is located in the ch29 folder on the *Macromedia Flash MX 2004 Bible* CD-ROM. You will notice several components have been added to the Stage and have been given instance names. You'll also need to copy the component.txt file from this folder as well.

1. Open the components_starter.fla and locate the TextArea instance on the first frame. This instance is already named ctaInfo. You will write the ActionScript code to dynamically load a text file named component.txt into the movie at runtime. If you open component.txt in a text editor, you'll see that this file declares a variable named strIntro, whose value will be used by the TextArea component. Add the code shown in Listing 29-1 to frame 1 of the actions layer, before the existing actions.

Here, a LoadVars object named text_data loads the component.txt file, and sets the text property of the ctaInfo component instance to the strIntro variable declared in the component.txt file.

Listing 29-1: The text_data **object**

```
var text_data:LoadVars = new LoadVars();
text_data.onLoad = function(success) {
   if(success){
      trace("---text file loaded successfully");
      ctaInfo.text = this.strIntro;
   } else {
      trace("---text file did not load.");
   }
};
text_data.load("component.txt");
```

Cross-Reference

For more information on the LoadVars object, refer to Chapter 30, "Sending Data In and Out of Flash."

Tip

Throughout this chapter, you'll see that component instances have a specific name convention. All component instance names start with the letter "c," for component, which is then followed by a two-letter abbreviation of the component's name. For example, a prefix of cta denotes a TextArea component. This is our own naming convention; feel free to make one of your own.

2. Save the Flash document as components_100.fla, and test it (Ctrl+Enter or ⌘+Enter). When the movie loads, you should see a trace() message appear in the Output panel indicating whether or not the text file loaded successfully. If it did load, the TextArea component should have filled with the text described in the component.txt file.

3. Now that text is loading into the TextArea component, you will group the two RadioButton instances on the Stage so that they cannot be selected at the same time. On frame 1 of the Main Timeline, select each instance of the RadioButton components. In the Property inspector, enter the same text string into the groupName parameter for each instance. Let's give the radio buttons a group name of newsletter, which best describes their purpose in the movie. This identifier places both buttons in the same group.

4. Give each instance a different value in the data field in the Property inspector's Parameters tab. This data is what is returned to the movie indicating the selection. Give the first RadioButton instance, crbDigest, a value of digest. For the crbNormal instance, assign a data value of normal.

5. It is also a good practice to have one radio button already selected by default. In the Parameters tab for the crbDigest instance, set the selected value to true.

Note The live preview of the `RadioButton` component does not update the Stage to show the radio button as selected. You need to test your movie to see the selection occur.

6. Now you are ready to have the "sign me up" button (the `cbtSignup` instance) send the movie to the right location, based upon which `RadioButton` instance is selected. Add the code shown in Listing 29-2 after the code you inserted in Step 1.

In the `signupListener` object, the current value of the `newsletter` group is assigned to a local variable named `radioData`. Notice that the way in which you can retrieve the value of a radio buttons' group is through the `selection.data` property. If `radioData` is equal to `"digest"` (the `data` value for the `crbDigest` instance), the movie goes to the `digest` frame label. If `radioData` is equal to `"normal"` (the `data` value for the `crbNormal` instance) the movie goes to the `normal` frame label.

Listing 29-2: The click listener for the `Button` **component**

```
var signupListener:Object = new Object();
signupListener.click = function(eventInfo){
    trace(eventInfo.target + " clicked");
    var radioData:String = newsletter.selection.data;
    if (radioData == "digest") {
        eventInfo.target._parent.gotoAndStop("digest");
    } else if (radioData == "normal") {
        eventInfo.target._parent.gotoAndStop("normal");
    }
};
cbtSignup.addEventListener("click", signupListener.click);
```

---

7. Save your Flash document, and test it (Ctrl+Enter or ⌘+Enter). When you click the "sign me up" button, the movie should jump to the `digest` frame label. Click the Home button to go back to the first frame of the movie. Now, choose the Normal radio button, and click the "sign me up" button. The movie will jump to the `normal` frame label.

8. Let's activate the `ComboBox` instance, `ccbSections`, so users who select an item from the menu are automatically taken to a certain area of your movie. This is very similar to what you have accomplished with the `RadioButton` instances, although you will use a different method this time. The instance name of the ComboBox has already been set to `ccbSections`. The values for the combo box's labels and data have also already been entered for you into the `label` and `data` fields, respectively. You can activate the instance of the `ComboBox` in two different ways. Because the data and labels are the same names, you could simply create a `Button` component instance and enter the following code onto the button:

```
on (click) {
    this._parent.gotoAndStop(this._parent.ccbSections.value);
}
```

However, if you are not using the same data and frame label names, you need to do something a bit more complex, which can easily be applied to many different components. To avoid putting a lot of code on a button, and to make your drop-down box automatically take your user to a different area of the movie, you create a listener object for the ccbSections instance. Add the code shown in Listing 29-3 after the code you inserted into frame 1 from Step 6.

Here, a listener named comboListener is created. Its dropdown() method retrieves the current selected value from the ccbSections instance (eventInfo.target.value) and sets that as the value of a local variable named comboValue.

The switch() action is much like using if . . . else but much cleaner. Notice that each data value of the ccbSections instance is defined in a case statement. Each case contains a gotoAndStop() action from the appropriate frame in the Flash movie.

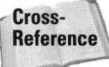

Cross-Reference

For more information on the switch() action, read Chapter 24, "Knowing the Nuts and Bolts of Code."

Listing 29-3: The listener object for the ComboBox **component**

```
var comboListener:Object = new Object();
comboListener.dropdown = function(eventInfo){
    var comboValue:String = eventInfo.target.value;
    switch (comboValue) {
        case "new" :
            _root.gotoAndStop("new");
            break;
        case "free" :
            _root.gotoAndStop("free");
            break;
        case "trade" :
            _root.gotoAndStop("trade");
            break;
        case "buy" :
            _root.gotoAndStop("buy");
            break;
        case "links" :
            _root.gotoAndStop("links");
            break;
        default :
            trace("no action matched");
    }
};
ccbSections.addEventListener("close", comboListener.dropdown);
```

---

9. Save your Flash document, and test it. Click the ComboBox instance, and choose a section name. When you make a choice, the movie goes to the appropriate frame of the Flash movie.

10. Now add a ScrollPane instance to the movie. The ScrollPane component enables you to add a Movie Clip symbol to a scrollable window. On frame 15 of the pages layer, drag an instance of the ScrollPane component onto the Stage from the Components panel.

11. Open the Library panel. Select the file named `headedit1.png`, and drag it to the Stage. Convert it to a Movie Clip symbol by pressing the F8 key. In the Convert to Symbol dialog box, name the symbol **pictureClip**. Assign a registration point in the top-left corner. Click the Advanced button in the dialog box. Select the Export for ActionScript check box (which also selects the Export in first frame check box). The linkage identifier should also automatically be set to `pictureClip`. Refer to Figure 29-15 for these details.

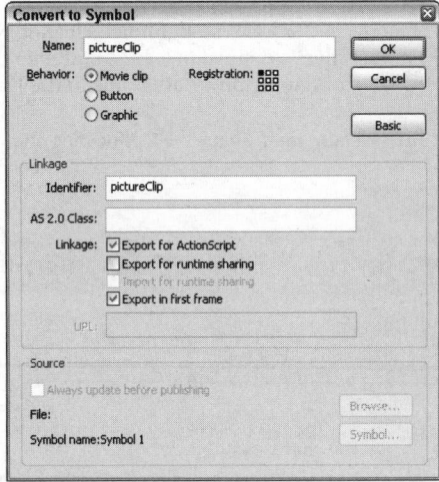

Figure 29-15: The settings for the pictureClip symbol

12. Select the instance of the `ScrollPane` component on your Stage. Open the Property inspector, and name the instance `cspPicture`. Select the Parameters tab. For the `contentPath` parameter, enter the string `pictureClip` that you set as your symbol's linkage ID.

13. Save your Flash document, and test the movie. Choose `new` from the `ComboBox` instance, and, on the new frame, you will see the image within the `ScrollPane` window. If you want to be able to drag the picture with the mouse, go back to the Parameters tab in the Property inspector and change `scrollDrag` to **true**.

On the CD-ROM You can find the finished file, `components_100.fla`, in the `ch29` folder of this book's CD-ROM.

Modifying Components

We have already discussed how to alter the color, alpha, or brightness of your component, allowing you to match it to the content on your production. It is a bit more complicated, but not difficult, to change more than just the symbol's effects in the Property inspector. There are three ways in which you can change the look-and-feel of Flash MX 2004 components:

✦ Use the Styles API

✦ Apply a theme

✦ Modify or replace a component's skins

For the purposes of this introduction to components, you'll learn how to change the look of components using styles.

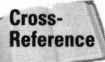

Cross-Reference For more information on themes and changing component's skins, search the Help panel with the terms "customizing components overview."

Global style formats

You can use ActionScript to change the look of your components. Using ActionScript to change properties is often much easier than doing so manually or making your own graphics. Luckily, you can change attributes of components on an instance or global level—with the help of ActionScript. Most of these changes will be limited to colors, alignment, and text.

In Flash MX 2004, you can control the look-and-feel of all components in your Flash movie by using the new _global.style object.

On the CD-ROM Open the components_100.fla document from the ch29 folder of this book's CD-ROM to test this new feature.

1. Create a new layer, and rename it to global styles. Place this layer at the top of the layer stack.

2. On frame 1 of the global styles layer, open the Actions panel (F9), and add the code shown in Listing 29-4.

   Here, the setStyle() method is used to apply various style changes, from color to font face.

Listing 29-4: An example of using the _global.style **object**

```
_global.style.setStyle("color", 0x336699);
_global.style.setStyle("themeColor", "haloBlue")
_global.style.setStyle("fontSize", 10);
_global.style.setStyle("fontFamily", "Verdana");
_global.style.setStyle("backgroundColor", 0xE2C7C7);
```

---

3. Save the Flash document as components_101.fla, and test it. All of the components will change to the new style settings.

On the CD-ROM You can find the components_101.fla document in the ch29 folder of this book's CD-ROM.

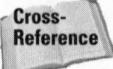

Cross-Reference

Search the Help panel for "supported styles" to see the various style properties that can be set and changed with ActionScript.

Changing styles for individual instances

It is relatively easy to change the font color and face on individual component instances now that you understand style formats. You can accomplish this task by using single lines of ActionScript. Because this code uses fonts in the system, it is important to remember that a default system font will be displayed if your end user does not have the particular font installed on his or her system.

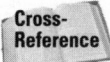

Cross-Reference

Using custom font faces and embedded fonts with buttons is covered in the section, "Using Embedded Fonts with Components."

1. Create a new Flash document, and save it as component_style.fla.

2. Rename Layer 1 to **myButton**. On frame 1 of this layer, add an instance of the Button component from the Components panel. In the Property inspector, name this instance myButton.

3. Make a new layer, and name it **actions**. On frame 1 of this layer, add the following lines of code in the Actions panel.

```
myButton.setStyle("fontFamily", "Arial");
myButton.setStyle("themeColor", "haloOrange");
myButton.setStyle("fontWeight", "bold");
myButton.setStyle("color", 0x333333);
```

This will set your button font face as Arial, and the second line of ActionScript tells it to use the orange Halo theme. Line 3 sets the font style to bold for the label text, and line 4 sets the color of label text to dark gray.

Tip

There are three built-in halo themes: haloGreen, haloBlue, and haloOrange. The themes, by and large, control the outline color used by components.

4. Save the Flash document, and test it. The Button component instance should now have a different appearance.

On the CD-ROM

In the ch29 folder of the *Macromedia Flash MX 2004 Bible* CD-ROM, you can find the completed file, component_style.fla.

Using embedded fonts with components

In this section, you will explore how to use a custom font for a Button component. There are two ways to accomplish this: use a dummy text field that embeds the font you want to use in the component, or add a Font symbol set to export from the Library panel. Both involve some ActionScript. First of all, let's look at the easier of the two methods.

1. Open the component_style.fla document from the last section, and resave the document as component_embedded_font.fla.

2. Select frame 1 of the actions layer, and change the existing code to the following code:

```
myButton.setStyle("fontFamily", "Charcoal");
myButton.setStyle("embedFonts", true);
```

This code sets the font face of the Button component to Charcoal. The second line tells the component that it should only display embedded fonts. If you tested your movie at this point, the label text for the component would be empty because the Charcoal font is not embedded in the movie.

3. Create a new layer and name it **dummy_txt**. On frame 1 of this layer, select the Text tool and make a Dynamic text field off-stage. Give the field an instance name of dummy_txt in the Property inspector. In the font menu of the Property inspector, choose Charcoal. (If you don't have Charcoal, pick a different font name, and be sure to change the name in the code of Step 2.) Next, click the Character button in the Property inspector. In the Character Options dialog box (shown in Figure 29-16), click the **Specify Ranges** radio button. Ctrl+click (or ⌘+click on the Mac) the **Uppercase**, **Lowercase**, and **Numerals** options. Click OK to accept these settings. You have now embedded the Charcoal font in the Flash movie.

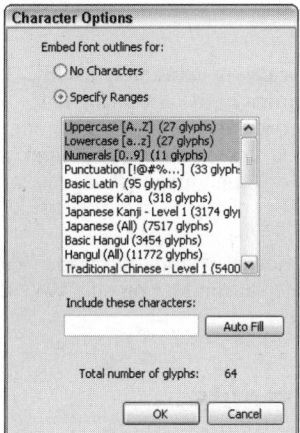

Figure 29-16: The Character Options dialog box

4. Save your Flash document, and test it. The Charcoal font (or your substituted font, if applicable) is the font used by the myButton instance.

On the CD-ROM You can find the completed document, component_embedded_font.fla, in the ch29 folder of this book's CD-ROM.

If you don't want to use a dummy text field as this example illustrated, there is another way you can use an embedded font with a component. You can add a Font symbol to the Library panel, and set the font to export with the Flash movie. This method, however, will significantly add more weight (in bytes) to the movie's file size because all characters in the font are exported with the movie. We highly recommend you use an empty TextField instance with specific character ranges to minimize the size of your Flash movies.

Custom Components

One of the most exciting aspects of components in Flash MX 2004 is being able to make your own creations for distribution or reuse. Custom components usually require a significant amount of ActionScript or at least a solid understanding of the language in order to modify an established component. If you learn how to make your own components to suit common requirements, you will inevitably save a lot of valuable development time. Components were created to be easily reused among projects, and they also allow simple modifications without having to alter the ActionScript code in the component. Given the robust nature of components, you should be able to develop complex applications, detailed right down to custom icons for the library. While we will not go into detail on how to create custom components in this chapter due to their complexity, many resources are available to you for learning more about this subject, including the *Macromedia Flash MX 2004 ActionScript Bible*.

New Feature

As you learned earlier in this chapter, components can now be compiled clips. Flash MX 2004 allows you to compile your own custom components so that you can distribute the components without giving away your source code.

Live Preview

If you are creating custom components, a Live Preview can be extremely useful. This feature enables you to create an updated view of your component in the authoring environment, so you do not have to publish your movie to view the current state of your component. Creating a Live Preview requires a number of steps to set up your movie structure properly and also ActionScript to activate. It is definitely worth it if you are spending a lot of time creating your own components.

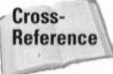

Cross-Reference

This feature is beyond the scope of this chapter. However, more information on creating a Live Preview can be found in the Support center at the Macromedia Web site, www. macromedia.com/support/flash/.

Exchanging and acquiring components

After you have made your own components, you may be interested in distributing them. Or you may also be looking for a place to find new pre-built elements for your Web site. Luckily, there are many extensive resources online where you can find components for download or for submission. A good place to start searching is at Macromedia:

    www.macromedia.com/exchange/flash

To install components, you need to download the free Extension Manager 1.6 (or higher), which is the first version to be compatible with Flash MX 2004. There is also a specific method for making your components ready for exchange. You need to package it into an MXI file, which this Manager can read. The file tells the Manager information regarding the file and the creator. Information about making your components ready for the Extension Manager is available from the same section of the Web site, which includes help and FAQ links.

Web Resource

We'd like to know what you thought about this chapter. Visit www.flashsupport.com/ feedback to fill out an online form with your comments.

Summary

✦ Components are a fast and easy way to add interactivity to a movie. They save time and increase usability through consistency, intuitiveness, and solid ActionScript.

✦ Flash MX 2004 components are called V2 components, whereas Flash MX components are now called V1 components.

✦ The UI components that ship with Flash MX 2004 are a new symbol type, compiled clips. All of the component's assets and code are condensed into a single symbol. You cannot edit a component's assets in its compiled version.

✦ Some of the most useful UI elements are already built into Flash MX 2004, including radio buttons, click buttons, combo boxes, lists, and scrolling panes. Using these facilitates user friendliness with your Flash projects because they emulate the user interface elements commonly used across the Internet and on many desktop applications.

✦ You can change the look and feel of your components by using the setStyle() method of the individual component or of the _global.style object.

✦ If you are changing the fonts on your components, you probably want to embed them to avoid problems if your end user does not have the font you are calling for.

✦ Advanced users of Flash may want to create their own custom components. Custom components can be reused from movie to movie, exchanged, or sold on the Internet. You can download additional components to add to your own movie from online resources, such as the Macromedia Exchange.

✦   ✦   ✦

Sending Data In and Out of Flash

A powerful feature of ActionScript is the extraordinary control of data acquisition and management it provides within a Flash movie. You can load external text data into Flash movies, making it possible to include fresh dynamic content every time a Flash movie is viewed over the Web. In this chapter, you will learn how to access text data stored in a variety of formats that are separate from the actual Flash movie.

Using Text Fields to Store and Display Data

Before we can discuss sending and receiving data with Flash movies, you need to know the basic mechanisms of input and output. Most of the time, your data in Flash will be text-based, which means that you will gather information from the user and display new and updated information with text. In ActionScript, Input text fields gather data from the user, while Dynamic text fields can be used to display live and updated text to the user.

Input text fields

Input text fields can be created with the Text tool. In the Property inspector, the top-left drop-down menu must be set to Input text for the selected text field. In Flash MX 2004, a text field can be an actual object with an instance name. However, an Input text field has a variable name (designated by Var in the Property inspector) to remain backward-compatible with Flash Player 5 or 4 movies. The text typed inside of an Input text field is the value of that variable (specified by the Var name), and it is the value of the `text` property of the text field's instance name. For example, if you create an Input text field and assign it the Var name `visitorInput`, anything that is typed into that text field during runtime will become the value of `visitorInput`. If you assigned an instance name of `visitor_txt` to the text field, you would access the contents of the text field with the `text` property. To test this, let's create a simple Input text field.

Caution If you are developing Flash Player 6 or higher movies (that is, Flash Player 6 or 7 is the version listed in the Flash tab of the Publish Settings dialog box), we strongly recommend that you use the instance name of the text field to access the contents of the field.

1. Using the Text tool, create a text field on the Main Timeline of a Flash document. Make the box long enough to hold 20 characters. You can type a temporary word or phrase into the text field, but delete these characters before proceeding to the next step.

2. In the Property inspector, select Input Text in the top-left menu. In the <Instance Name> field, type **visitor_txt**. In the Var field, enter the text **visitorInput**. Click the Show Border option as well. Refer to Figure 30-1 for these settings.

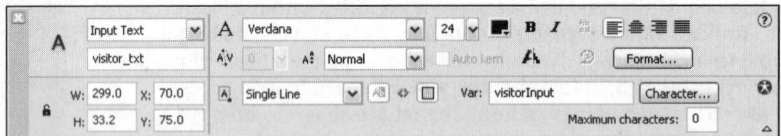

Figure 30-1: The Property inspector controls the settings for text fields.

3. Save your Flash document as `inputText.fla` and test the movie (Ctrl+Enter or ⌘+Return). In the Test Movie window, click the text field and type your first name into the field.

4. Choose Debug ➪ List Variables, and the `visitorInput` variable will display the value you typed in Step 3. In addition, you will see the `visitor_txt` text field object display along with several properties of the `TextField` object. In our example, we entered the name **Charlie**. Therefore, the Output panel displays (among other text):

```
Variable _level0.visitorInput = "Charlie"
Edit Text: Target="_level0.visitor_txt"
    variable = "visitorInput",
    text = "Charlie",
```

Note The List Variables command always shows the `$version` variable and value, indicating the Flash Player version currently playing the movie.

5. If you change the text in the `visitor_txt` text field, the value will automatically update for the `visitor_txt.text` value or the `visitorInput` variable. You need to choose List Variables from the Debug menu to see the updated value.

Input text fields not only accept input from the user, but they can also be set to an initial value or updated with a new value with ActionScript code. You can test this with the preceding Flash movie example.

6. If you are viewing the `inputText.swf` file from Step 5, close the Test Movie window to return to the Flash MX 2004 authoring environment. Create a new layer, and rename it **actions**. Select the first frame of the actions layer and press F9 to open the Actions panel. Add the following code to the Script pane:

```
visitor_txt.text = "enter your name here";
```

7. Save your Flash document and test it. You should see the text "enter your name here" in the `visitor_txt` text field.

You can find the `inputText.fla` document in the `ch30` folder of this book's CD-ROM.

As you can see, Input text fields can accept text input from the user, just like an HTML form. Later in this chapter, you use Input text fields to create a fully functional Flash form that can send and receive information with a server-side script.

While you should use the Var name attribute of text fields for Flash movies that require compatibility with Flash Player 5 or 4, we strongly recommend that you leave the Var name blank in the Property inspector for any Flash Player 6 or higher movies.

Dynamic text fields

If you want to display text information to people viewing Flash movies, you have two options: (a) create Static text blocks whose contents cannot be updated with ActionScript or (b) create Dynamic text fields that can be filled with internal Flash data or external text data.

Do not use Input or Dynamic text fields unless you need to accept or display live data to the user. Static text is perfectly fine for text used for graphical purposes, where the text does not need to be changed during the presentation.

Dynamic text fields are also objects with instance names, just as Input text fields. The only difference between Input and Dynamic text fields is that you can type into Input text fields. Dynamic text fields are most useful for display of text information that will be changed by the movie (via ActionScript), rather than the user. Using Dynamic text fields, you can display news articles that change on a daily (or hourly) basis, a player's score during a Flash game, and the system time and date, just to name a few.

Both Input and Dynamic text fields can use HTML text formatting tags to change the display of text. We discuss HTML use within text fields in Chapter 31, "Applying HTML and Text Field Formatting."

In the following steps, you create a Dynamic text field updated with an ActionScript variable action. You can also load external variables for use in Dynamic text fields, which we discuss in the next section. To insert text into a Dynamic text field:

1. Create a new Flash document (File ➪ New), and rename Layer 1 to **textfield**.

2. Using the Text tool, create a text field on the Main Timeline of a Flash document. Make a field large enough to accommodate multiple lines of text, as shown in Figure 30-2. Choose a normal font size, such as 12.

3. In the Property inspector, select Dynamic Text in the top-left menu. Select Multiline from the Line type menu. In the <Instance Name> field, enter the text `output_txt`. Click the Selectable and Show Border options. Refer to Figure 30-2 for these settings.

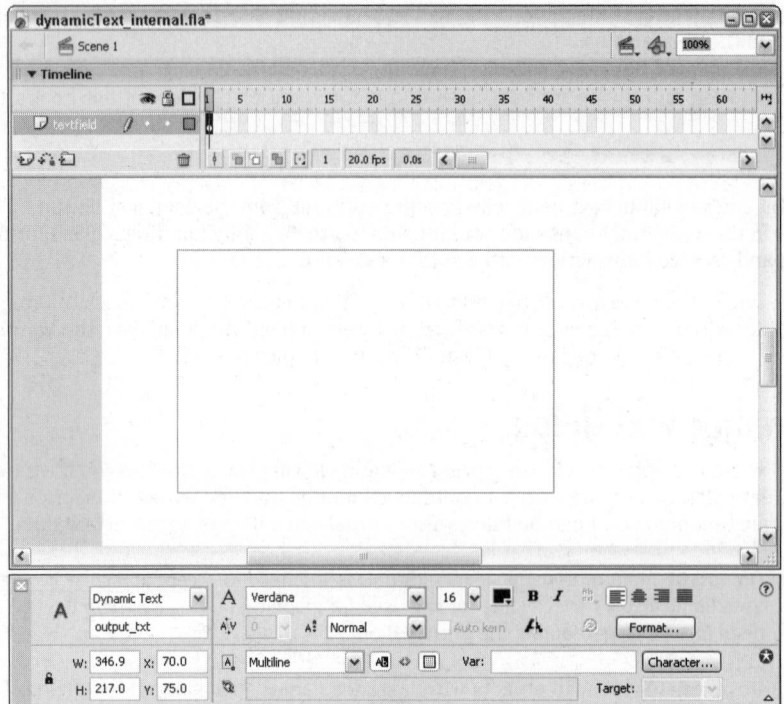

Figure 30-2: The Dynamic text field settings in the Property inspector

4. Add a new layer and name it **actions**. Select the first keyframe of the actions layer and press F9 to open the Actions panel. Enter the following code on one single line in the Script pane. (You can enable word wrapping in the options menu if you wish.)

```
output_txt.text = "WANTED: Flash Input & Output\r\rA start-up
  dotcom company is looking for a qualified Web
  technology that will present text input and output to
  Web visitors in a more compelling animated and visually
  stunning environment than that possible with HTML.
  Please call:\r\r1-800-555-CODE";
```

In this code, you specify string values (denoted with quotes) for the actual text you want to insert into the output_txt Dynamic text field instance. To insert a carriage return in the text, the \r character entity is inserted between string values.

5. Save the Flash document as dynamicText_internal.fla.

6. Test the movie (Ctrl+Enter or ⌘+Enter). The output_txt Dynamic text field updates with the value assigned to the text property of the output_txt instance in ActionScript.

On the CD-ROM

You can find the dynamicText_internal.fla document in the ch30 folder of this book's CD-ROM.

You can also load text data into Input and Dynamic text fields. This data can be returned from a simple text file (TXT file) or from an application that resides on your Web server. In the next section, you learn how to send and receive text from a Flash movie.

Defining a Data Process with States

When you manipulate text fields with internal ActionScript properties of the `TextField` object, the data for the text fields is available for use immediately. Meaning, if you declare a variable and a value for that variable, any text field can be given that value as well. When you want to load external data into a Flash movie, you need to create the appropriate steps, or *states,* in your movie to make sure that the data is available for use in the Flash movie. For example, suppose you want to retrieve a news article from a Web server, and the text for that article is contained within a variable named `article_1`. You can't use or assign the value of `article_1` to any other Flash element *unless* the article has fully downloaded to the Flash movie.

So, how do you know when data is available in a Flash movie? Any Flash movie that relies on data exchange between the Flash movie and the Web server should contain four separate states:

✦ An *input* state to gather the information from the user or the movie

✦ A *send* state in which a Flash action sends the data out of the movie

✦ A *wait* state during which the data downloads to the movie

✦ The *output* state in which the data can be used by the Flash movie in text fields and other ActionScript code

Input state

The first step for data exchange requires that you have something to send out of the Flash movie. The input can be a Flash form into which a user types text. The data could be environment variables, such as the time of the day, or the Flash Player version. There could be various substeps in the input state, such as multiple forms or the completion of a quiz to calculate a test score that will be sent to the Web server.

Note   Not all data transactions require input. For example, if you need to retrieve the latest stock quotes or news article from a Web server application, you may simply need to send a request for that data without providing any additional information to the Web server application.

Send state

After the input data has been set or retrieved in the Flash movie, you're ready to send the data to another host, such as an application or script on your Web server. The following actions or object methods can be used to send data out of the Flash movie:

✦ `getURL()`

✦ `loadVariables()` or `MovieClip.loadVariables()`

✦ `loadMovie()` or `MovieClip.loadMovie()`

✦ `LoadVars.load()`

✦ LoadVars.send() or LoadVars.sendAndLoad()

✦ XML.load()

✦ XML.send() or XML.sendAndLoad()

✦ XMLSocket.send()

✦ Flash Remoting or Flash Communication Server calls

Of these actions, getURL(), LoadVars.send(), and XML.send() are restricted to a one-way data path; that is, you can only send data out with these actions — you cannot receive external data with them. getURL() must target the sought URL to the current browser (or frame) or a new browser window. In many situations, you may only need to send data out of the Flash movie without needing to receive any further data. To send information with the user's e-mail client, you can use a simple mailto: URL in a getURL() action on a Button instance. Note that the ⊃ character indicates a continuation of the same line of code:

```
on(release){
  var email = "admin@server.com";
  var subject = escape("Visitor Feedback");
  var body = escape("Please let us know how you feel.");
  getURL("mailto:" + email + "?subject=" + subject + ⊃
    "&body=" + body);
}
```

In the preceding code block, the variables email, subject, and body are inserted into the getURL() action. Note that you can automatically set subject and body text for the e-mail message as well. To add specific variables to a URL string, you should use the escape() function in ActionScript, which converts illegal URL characters such as spaces and ? into URL form-encoded text (for example, a space is converted into %20).

Wait state

If you are sending data from the Flash movie with loadVariables(), loadMovie(), or any of the object load() or sendAndLoad() methods, you need to know when the requested data is received by the script or application running on your Web server. One way to detect the download state of data into the Flash movie is to use a terminal tag — a name/value pair in the downloaded data that indicates the end of the data string. For example, if the value of the text property for the output_txt instance that you used in the last section was converted to a name/value pair in a TXT file (as URL form-encoded text), the value would appear as the following (URL-converted characters are shown in bold, and the terminal tag is underlined):

```
article=WANTED%3A%20Flash%20Input%26%20Output%0AA%20start%2Dup%20
Dot%20com%20company%20is%20looking%20for%20a%20qualified%20web%20
technology%20that%20will%20present%20text%20input%20and%20output%20to
%20web%20visitors%20in%20a%20more%20compelling%20animated%20and%20
visually%20stunning%20environment%20than%20that%20possible%20with%20
HTML%2E%20Please%20call%3A%0A%0A1%2D800%2D555%2DCODE&success=1
```

At the end of this line of text (or at the very end of a long line of variables), we have inserted a terminal tag success=1. With this variable in place, you can set up a frame loop within a Flash movie to detect the existence (loading) of the terminal tag variable. After the terminal tag is loaded, the Flash movie will be directed to the appropriate output state.

Note You can use GET or POST to send Flash variables to a URL from the SWF file.

All wait states should have a timeout condition: If the data fails to load within a certain time frame, you will assume the Web server (or script) is not functioning correctly. If the timeout condition proves true, the Flash movie will go to the appropriate output state. You create a wait state for our Flash form in the next section.

Tip You can avoid the use of terminal tags with the LoadVars object in ActionScript. You can also use the Movie Clip data event, which is specified with the onClipEvent() action. We present the LoadVars object in the "Creating a Flash Form" section, later in this chapter.

Output state

The final step in a data exchange is the actual display of any received data in the Flash movie. However, as indicated in the last state, there are two separate output states: a success display or an error display. If the data was properly received during the wait state, the Flash movie will display the success output state. If the server failed to return any data to the Flash movie, the movie will display an error output state, indicating that there was a problem with the server.

Creating a Flash Form

In this section, you create a Flash form that submits user-entered information to a server-side ColdFusion script that e-mails the data to an e-mail address that you specify in the script. By accessing a remote ColdFusion script, you make a Flash movie with five data exchange states: input, send, wait, output, and error. You learn how to submit name/value pairs from Flash to remote URLs and learn how to check the receipt of variables from the ColdFusion script using the LoadVars object. The LoadVars object can detect the loading of the external variable data.

On the CD-ROM You can find the ColdFusion script (sendmail.cfm) and supporting Flash documents for this section in the ch30 folder of this book's CD-ROM. Note that you need a ColdFusion MX 6.1-enabled Web server to configure and use the sendmail.cfm script. We have also included the sendmail.asp script (Microsoft ASP version) and the sendmail.pl script (Perl 5) that were included with previous editions of the *Flash Bible*. The ASP script requires the installation of the free w3 JMail Personal ASP component available at:

http://tech.dimac.net/websites/dimac/website/products/w3JMail

Web Resource You can download a trial version of ColdFusion MX 6.1 at:

www.macromedia.com/software/coldfusion

You can also find installation instructions on the Web site.

Flash forms are user data entry forms (just like HTML forms) created in Flash MX 2004 using Input text fields. When a user types information in these text fields, the information is stored as a property of the text field instance (text). The values of these properties are assigned to variable names and are then sent to a specified Web server using standard GET or POST communication. These variables are available to the Web server and can be processed there by a server-side program or script. Server-side programs can be written to e-mail this information, manipulate it, store it in a database, or perform many other applications. The same server-side script can also return values to the Flash movie — these can then be displayed or used by the originating Flash movie.

In this exercise, the Flash form solicits feedback from visitors, giving them an opportunity to submit comments, report bugs, or make suggestions for improvement. As each form is submitted, it's e-mailed directly to the e-mail address that you specify in the ColdFusion script.

1. Open a new Flash document (Ctrl+N or ⌘+N).

2. Rename Layer 1 to **labels**. Create keyframes (F6) on frames 5, 15, 25, and 35. Give these keyframes the labels **input**, **wait**, **output**, and **error**, respectively. (Do not give frame 1 a label.) Select frame 45 and press F5 to insert more empty frames at the end of the layer.

3. Create a new layer and name it **actions**. On frame 5 of the actions layer, insert a keyframe (F6) and select it. Open the Actions panel and add a `stop();` action. In the Property inspector, add a comment of `//stop` in the <Frame Label> field.

4. Create a new layer, and name it **text fields**. Insert keyframes on frames 5, 15, 25, and 35.

5. On frame 5 of the text fields layer, insert three separate Input text fields. From top to bottom, assign the following instance names to the Input text fields (in the Property inspector): `fromName_txt`, `fromEmail_txt`, and `comments_txt`. The `fromName_txt` and `fromEmail_txt` text fields should accommodate one line of text, while the `comment_txt` field should be set to Multiline in order to hold multiple lines of text. All of the Input text fields should have the Show Border option selected, unless you plan to create your own background graphics. Make each text field long enough to accommodate about 45 characters of text. The comments field should be able to show between five and ten lines of text. (See Figure 30-3.)

6. Create a new layer, and name it **static text**. Insert keyframes on frames 5, 15, 25, and 35. On frame 5, add Static text blocks to the left of the text fields, indicating the purpose of each field, as shown in Figure 30-3.

7. On frame 15 of the static text layer (underneath the `wait` label), insert a Static text block indicating that the information is being sent to the server and that the movie is waiting for confirmation. In our example, we used the text "Checking the server. . . ."

8. On frame 25 of the static text layer (underneath the `output` label), insert a Static text block containing a successful receipt of the visitor's information. In our example, we used the text "Thank you. Your feedback was received at:".

9. You can see that you are setting up the output state to display the time that the server received the data (Figure 30-4). The ColdFusion script returns the time and date of the receipt to the Flash movie. On frame 25 of the text fields layer, create a Dynamic text field with an instance name of `receipt_txt` and place it underneath the Static text you just made.

10. On frame 35 of the static text layer (underneath the `error` label), insert Static text that indicates the data was not successfully received. In our example, we used the text "Sorry, the server is down."

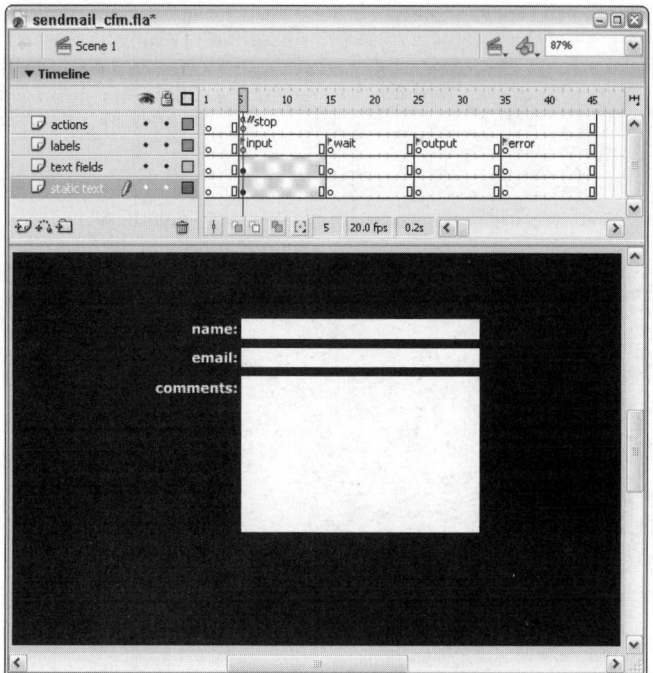

Figure 30-3: These text fields accept input from your site visitors.

11. Save your Flash document as sendMail_cfm.fla.

Now you have all your states defined with placeholder artwork. You can go back later and refine the text and graphics to suit your particular needs. Next, you need to add a function to transfer the data from the text fields to a LoadVars object and send the data to the Web server.

These actions need to put on the appropriate Flash event handlers. Start by defining a function named sendComments() that creates two LoadVars objects: one to send the data and another to receive the data. The data from the Input text fields is then copied to variables within the sending LoadVars object. The data is then sent to the ColdFusion script using the sendAndLoad() method of the LoadVars object. When the data is received by the ColdFusion script, the Web server will return some confirmation data to the Flash movie, including the time and date the user's comments were received. When this data loads completely into the Flash movie, the movie will then go to and stop on the output frame label.

Before you define these functions, however, let's add a Button component to the Stage. This component button will initiate the sendComments() function.

12. Create a new layer and name it **button**. Insert keyframes on frames 5 and 15 of this layer.

13. On frame 5 of the button layer, drag an instance of the Button component from the Components panel to the document's Stage.

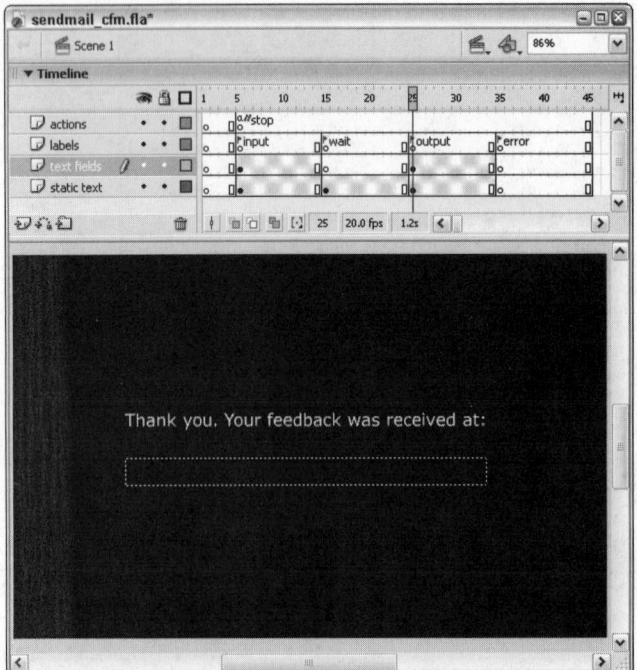

Figure 30-4: The receipt_txt field will display the time that the server received the Flash form data.

14. With the component selected, open the Property inspector. Name the instance `cbtSend`. In the label field, type `Send Comments`. You may need to stretch the width of the `Button` instance to accommodate the label text.

15. When this component button is clicked in the Flash movie, the `sendComments()` function will need to be executed. As such, you'll need to add a listener to the `cbtSend` instance. Select frame 5 of the actions layer, and type the following code before the existing `stop()` action. You'll define the `sendComments()` function in later steps.

```
cbtSend.addEventListener("click", this.sendComments);
```

16. Create a new layer on the Main Timeline, and rename it **functions**. Place this layer at the top of the layer stack. Select frame 1 of this layer, and open the Actions panel (F9). In the Script pane, add the code shown in Listing 30-1. This code defines the `sendComments()` function used by the `cbtSend` instance.

This function establishes all of the data that the `sendmail.cfm` requires for successful operation. Line 1 declares the function and its name, `sendComments`. The function starts by creating two `LoadVars` objects, named `sender` (line 2) and `responder` (line 3). The `sender` object will send the data from the Flash movie, while the `responder` object will handle the data received from the server.

Line 4 declares a local variable named `scriptURL` that stores the path to the ColdFusion script. If you have installed the ColdFusion script on your local machine or Web server, change the path of this variable to reflect the new location.

Lines 5–12 define an onLoad() handler for the responder object. Here, an anonymous function will be executed when the responder object receives any external data from the Web server script. In this example, if the data was successfully received (line 6), a global variable named serverTime is set to the variable named timeDate received by the responder object (line 7). On line 8, the Main Timeline (_root) will go to and stop on the output frame label. If the data was not received or there was an error in sending the data (line 9), the Main Timeline will go to and stop on the error frame label (line 10).

Lines 13–15 establish the variables that the ColdFusion script expects to see in the data transmission: fromEmail, fromName, and body. These variables retrieve their values from the appropriate TextField objects in the Flash movie.

Note   You can change the values of the Form.toEmail and Form.subject variables in the sendmail.cfm script to change where the server sends the data from the Flash movie. If you use the live script located on the www.flashsupport.com site, Mr. Reinhardt will receive all of your test e-mails, so please be careful.

Line 16 executes the sendAndLoad() method of the sender object that sends the fromEmail, fromName, and body variables to the sendmail.cfm script on our Web server. The responder reference indicates that any output from the sendmail.cfm script should be directed to the responder.onLoad() method.

After the sendAndLoad() method is executed, the Main Timeline will jump to the wait frame label (line 17).

In line 19, after the function ends, the _lockroot property of the Main Timeline (this) is set to true. This feature, introduced in Flash MX 2004 and supported by Flash Player 7, makes sure that all of the _root references will work if the Flash movie is loaded into another Flash movie.

Listing 30-1: **The** sendComments() **function**

```
1.  function sendComments() {
2.     var sender:LoadVars = new LoadVars();
3.     var responder:LoadVars = new LoadVars();
4.     var scriptURL:String = "http://www.flashsupport.com/sendmail.cfm";
5.     responder.onLoad = function(success){
6.        if (success) {
7.           _global.serverTime = this.timeDate;
8.           _root.gotoAndStop("output");
9.        } else {
10.          _root.gotoAndStop("error");
11.       }
12.    };
13.    sender.fromEmail = fromEmail_txt.text;
14.    sender.fromName = fromName_txt.text;
15.    sender.body = comments_txt.text;
16.    sender.sendAndLoad(scriptURL, responder, "POST");
17.    _root.gotoAndStop("wait");
18. }
19. this._lockroot = true;
```

17. Finally, add a keyframe to frame 25 of the actions layer. With this keyframe selected, open the Actions panel and add the following action:

```
receipt_txt.text = _global.serverTime;
```

This action takes the time and date returned by the server (in line 7 of Listing 30-1), and uses its value for the `text` property of the `receipt_txt` instance.

18. Save your Flash document again and test it (Ctrl+Enter or ⌘+Return). Type some information into the text fields and click the Send Comments button. If the server script is available, you should see the output state display the time/date receipt from the server.

The server script supports either GET or POST methods. Remember, every data exchange with a Flash movie should use input, wait, output, and error states.

On the CD-ROM   Use the `sendmail.cfm` script on `www.flashsupport.com` only for development and/or testing purposes. Do not try to use the script for demanding, high-volume Web sites. Remember that live Flash movies on a Web server can only access server-side scripts on the same server. While you can use the `sendmail.cfm` script on `www.flashsupport.com` for local testing in the Flash MX 2004 authoring environment, it will not work once you upload your Flash movie to your own Web server—you'll have to install the `sendmail.cfm` script (or equivalent) on your own Web server. The same ColdFusion script is available on the *Macromedia Flash MX 2004 Bible* CD-ROM, in the `ch30` folder. You can find the completed version of the Flash document, `sendmail_cfm.fla`, in the `ch30` folder. We have modified another version of this file, `sendmail_asp.fla`, to work with the `sendmail.asp` script from the *Flash MX Bible*. There's also a Perl script from the *Flash 5 Bible* as well, `sendmail.pl`— the Flash document for that script is named `sendmail_perl.fla`.

Using XML Data in Flash Movies

Flash Player 5 or higher movies can load (and send) external XML data. This is a very powerful feature, as XML has quickly become a standard data structure for e-commerce purposes and for news services, as well as for easier control over HTML formatting (and style sheets) in the Web browser. You can organize external data with simple XML formatting and use the XML data for text fields and ActionScript code in your Flash movies.

Note   It is beyond the scope of this book to give a thorough explanation of XML. We examine the basic structure of XML and show you how to use XML data in a Flash movie. We recommend that you read the *XML Bible* by Elliotte Rusty Harold for more information on XML. You can also find more detailed ActionScript coverage of XML objects in the *Macromedia Flash MX 2004 ActionScript Bible* by Robert Reinhardt and Joey Lott (Wiley, 2004).

Understanding XML

XML is an acronym for e*X*tensible *M*arkup *L*anguage. *Extensible*, in this case, means that you can create your own markup tag names and attributes. While there are a few additional rules with XML, its structure very much resembles traditional HTML:

```
<tag name opener>Information here</tag name closer>
```

For basic XML-Flash usage, your XML document needs one "container" tag in which all other subordinate tags will be nested. Each opener and closer tag set is called a node. In the following XML example, the `<section>` tag is the primary container tag, and the `<article>` tags are nodes of the `<section>` tag:

```
<section>
     <article>First article node</article>
     <article>Second article node</article>
</section>
```

You can create as many *child* nodes as you need. In the preceding example, the `<section>` tag has two child nodes: the first occurrence of `<article>` . . . `</article>` and the second occurrence of `<article>` . . . `</article>`. In the following example, the first `<article>` node has two child nodes:

```
<section>
     <article>
        <title>WANTED: New Computer</title>
        <description>Insert description here
        </description>
     </article>
     <article>Second article node</article>
</section>
```

`<title>...</title>` is the first child node of the first `<article>...</article>` node. The value of `<title>` is also considered a child of `<title>`. In the previous example, "WANTED: New Computer" is the child of `<title>`.

Caution   Early releases of Flash Player 5 do not ignore white space in XML documents. For this reason, you may not want to format your XML documents with indented tags or carriage returns between tags. Otherwise, you will need to create an ActionScript routine that removes the white space. Flash Player 6 and 7 support the `ignoreWhite` property of the `XML` object, which can tell ActionScript to ignore any white space within the XML document.

Loading an XML document into a Flash movie

Once you have an XML document structured to use in a Flash movie, you can use the XML document tree in the Flash movie. When an XML document is loaded into a Flash movie, the structure and relationship of all nodes are retained within the Flash Player.

The XML object

Before you can load an XML document into Flash, you need to make an object that will hold the XML data. To do this, use the `XML` constructor function, as in:

```
var myXML = new XML();  // ActionScript 1.0
```

or

```
var myXML:XML = new XML();  // ActionScript 2.0
```

Just as you created new objects for the `Color` and `Sound` objects in ActionScript, you can create as many new instances of the `XML` object as you need for your movie. You can also use an `XML` object to store Flash-created XML structures and send them to a server for further processing.

The load method of the XML object

After you have established an object, like the `myXML` variable in the previous heading, you can invoke built-in methods of the `XML` object. The `load()` method enables you to specify an external source (such as a URL or filename) that holds the XML data. If you had an XML document called `articles.xml` in the same directory as your SWF file, you could load it by writing the following code:

```
var myXML:XML = new XML("articles.xml");
```

or

```
var myXML:XML = new XML();
myXML.load("articles.xml");
```

The onLoad() method of the XML object

After the document is loaded into the Flash movie, you can specify another function (or action) to occur, using the `onLoad()` method of the `XML` object. The `onLoad()` method simply defines a function to be executed when the XML document is finished loading—it does not actually execute the function (or actions) when the `onLoad()` is first processed. In the following example, the `onLoad()` handler is executed when the XML document, articles.xml, is finished loading:

```
var myXML:XML = new XML();
myXML.onLoad = function(success){
    if(success){
        //perform more XML methods upon the XML data
    } else {
        // indicate that the XML document (or data)
        // did not load.
    }
};
myXML.load("articles.xml");
```

In the preceding code example, the `onLoad()` handler has one argument, `success`. The `onLoad()` method is passed a Boolean value of `true` or `false`. If the `load()` method successfully loaded the `articles.xml` document, the `onLoad()` method will be executed and passed a `true` value for the `success` argument. This `true` value is inserted into the `if` condition. If `success` is equal to `true`, the nested `if` actions will be executed. Otherwise, the `else` actions will be executed.

On the CD-ROM   Check out the XML document load examples on this book's CD-ROM in the `ch30/xml` folder. These examples demonstrate how XML node values can be manipulated with Flash arrays. You may want to review Chapter 26's coverage of the `Array` object before looking at these examples.

Using XMLSockets with a Flash Movie, *by Shane Elliott*

In this tutorial, you learn to employ the XMLSocket class in a Flash movie. You will find all of the associated files on the *Macromedia Flash MX 2004 Bible* CD-ROM. Be aware that this example utilizes a Java server, which requires the Java SDK in order to run and work with the Flash movie interactions.

On the CD-ROM You can find Shane's files in the ch30/S_Elliott folder of this book's CD-ROM.

ActionScript in Flash 5 introduced the capabilities of opening a socket that connects to a back-end database or server and keeping an open line of communication between the Flash movie and the server. Previously, if you wanted to send data back and forth between a server and Flash, you would use the loadVariables() action and connect to a back-end program, such as a Perl script, Java servlet, or some other middleware solution. With this older system, name/value pairs would be sent to and from the Flash movies to get a dynamic data flow, allowing data to be served on the fly. Feedback could be initiated by the user or by some system event (such as a timer or upon completion of a set of tasks). With XMLSockets in ActionScript, not only can you open a direct flow of data between your movie and the server, but you can receive the data as nicely formatted XML. This information structure is easier to handle and much more organized. Even though they're called XMLSockets in Flash, they don't require you to send your data as XML to the server, nor do you have to receive it as such. And although the XMLSocket object and methods are set up to handle XML elements, you have the option of sending String data as well, providing greater flexibility for database connectivity.

You might ask, "When do I need to use these sockets, and, more important, how do I use them?" Even though you can still use loadVariables() in ActionScript, you must make a request from within the Flash movie to be able to receive data from the server. With XMLSockets, you have a constant open connection. You can tell Flash to do a certain set of actions any time it detects data across this open socket. It's very useful for low-latency client-server applications, such as a chat room, where you want your messages to be sent immediately, or, in the case I describe next, for a Flash login movie. Now, instead of requiring a user to log in to my site or online resource using a standard form and CGI script, I can give the user a much better looking, and possibly more consistent, uninterrupted experience by allowing login through my Flash movie.

Before starting, you need certain graphic elements to be present on your Stage. I created a very simple login page that is focused completely on functionality—an aesthetically pleasing interface would follow this example in a real-world production environment. You need two Input text fields: one for the username and one for the password. Name these input fields **userid** and **password** in the <Instance Name> field of the Property inspector. Include some Static text to label these fields for the user. You also need a Dynamic text field instance named **fromServer** to display the server response. Again, add some Static text to identify the Dynamic text field on the Stage. Last, but not least, you need a login button. I just grabbed one out of the Common Libraries (Window ➪ Common Libraries ➪ Buttons), but you can create one of your own if you prefer. You can put all of these graphic elements on one layer, or separate the graphics across multiple layers. When you're finished adding the graphic elements to the Stage, create a new layer for your actions. In our example, the actions layer is named **action script**.

At this point, there should be only one frame in the Main Timeline (for example, Scene 1). Now, go to the first frame of your actions layer, select that frame, and open the Actions panel (Window ➪ Actions). On this frame, we define our socket and tell Flash how to handle the events regarding it.

The following code goes in the Actions panel:

```
function myOnConnect(success) {
  if (success)
    fromServer.text += newline + "Connected...";
  else
    fromServer.text += newline + "Unable to Connect...";
}
function myOnXML(doc) {
  var e = doc.firstChild;
  if(e!=null && e.nodeName == "MESSAGE") {
    fromServer += newline + e.attributes.response;
    // Code here to take you into the protected area
  }
  else {
    fromServer += newline + e.attributes.response;
    // Code here to take you to an exit screen etc...
  }
}

myXML = new XML();
loginTag = myXML.createElement("login");
loginSocket = new XMLSocket();
loginSocket.onConnect = myOnConnect;
loginSocket.onXML = myOnXML;
loginSocket.connect("localhost",8080);
```

Now let's take a look at each line and go over what it's doing. Skip the function definitions for now and jump down to the following lines:

```
myXML = new XML();
loginTag = myXML.createElement("login");
```

The first line in the preceding code creates a new XML element on the Main Timeline. We will be sending the login information (username and password) in XML format to the Java server. The second line creates a new XML element named login, which is the equivalent to XML that looks like the following:

```
<login />
```

Now we need to create a socket for communication with the server. That's where the following line of code comes in:

```
loginSocket = new XMLSocket();
```

When you create a new XMLSocket object, the constructor doesn't accept arguments. They're not needed at this point anyway. We don't define any of its options until we actually connect to the server. At this point, we have our XMLSocket object created, and we're ready to move on to the next step. We need to define some of the callback functions that are built into the Flash ActionScript language.

Flash ActionScript recognizes three event-handler methods for the XMLSocket object. The Flash movie calls these functions at an internally known time or after a certain event whether you define them or not, but without indicating the event occurrence to you. If we don't define a set of actions to occur for these events, these functions don't do anything in our Flash movie. They're simply there so that you can define (and, in a sense, override) them. Table 30-1 describes the three methods.

Table 30-1: Common Methods of the XMLSocket Object

Method	Description
onConnect(*success*)	Executed when a connection request initiated through the XMLSocket.connect method either succeeds or fails. (The success variable indicates true or false to tell you whether the connection was a success or not.)
onXML(*object*)	Called when the specified XML object containing an XML document arrives over your XMLSocket connection. The *object* is an instance of the XML object containing the XML document received from the server.
onClose()	Initiated when an open connection is closed by the server.

Note   Just as we use on(release) as an event handler for mouse events on Button instances, other objects have predefined event handlers and events. With data objects and methods, these events tend to occur when data is sent or received by the Flash movie.

The only two methods we use in this example are onConnect and onXML. Although Flash knows when to call these methods, there's nothing innately performed by them. Therefore, we must define our own methods to give them customized functionality.

```
loginSocket.onConnect = myOnConnect;
loginSocket.onXML = myOnXML;
```

These two lines simply assign these event handler methods to our customized versions of these methods. The myOnConnect and myOnXML functions tell our movie exactly what to do when a connection either succeeds or fails (onConnect), and what to do when data is received from the server through our socket (onXML), respectively.

Now let's go back to the two function definitions in the Flash movie. In frame 1 of the Main Timeline, we defined `myOnConnect` to execute some commands based on the status of the attempted connection. Flash sends the `myOnConnect` function a `success` argument, as a Boolean value (`true` or `false`), so that it knows whether a connection has been established. Then we add an `if . . . else` statement to handle either case. The function sends a notification to the user by setting the `fromServer` variable (which we defined at the beginning of the movie) to give the user updates on the status of his/her login. You could add more lines of code here if you wanted to jump to another Movie Clip or perform some other action specifically designed for your application.

The `myOnXML` function is a bit more complex. This function is basically looking for data from the server in XML format, and when it detects that data (which has been sent to the Flash socket), it assigns it to `doc` or whatever argument you put into your custom version of `onXML`. In this example, I used `doc` for document. Whatever you choose, just know that it will be used as an `XML` object that's received from the server. Therefore, it must be treated as one throughout your function. You can convert it to a `String` object or parse it like I did in the `myOnXML` function. Once `e` is set to be the `doc.firstChild`, I can access that node's elements and name, as you learned when using `XML` objects earlier in this chapter.

It's important at this stage of your development that you know the formatting of the XML data the server application will be sending you. If you're not writing the server application yourself, make sure you stay in close contact with the XML developer.

The reason I know to look for the `nodeName` of `MESSAGE` is that I wrote my own Java server application to interact with my Flash movie. Again, I have an `if` statement that performs actions based on the server response. You could add more here as well.

Now, let's look at the last line of code, which is the most important line so far because it actually attempts to make the connection (open the socket) between our Flash movie and our server.

```
loginSocket.connect("localhost",8080);
```

To do that, I use the `connect(host, port)` method. The `connect` method takes two arguments: `host` and `port`. The `host` argument refers to one of the following:

* A fully qualified DNS name, such as `http://www.timberfish.com`

* An IP address, such as 205.94.288.213

* A computer's name on a LAN, such as Zeus or Atlas

* `null`, which means to connect to the host server on which the movie resides

I use `localhost` for the host argument because that (like `null`) also refers to the machine that my Flash movie is running on, which happens to also be where my Java server is residing. Whatever you choose here, just remember the `host` must be the location of the server with which you'll be communicating.

The next argument is the `port`, which refers to the TCP port number on the host used to establish the connection. For security reasons, this number cannot be below 1024. I chose 8080 because I know my computer isn't using that port for anything significant. Some examples of commonly used ports for TCP connections are:

FTP Transfers = 21

HTTP = 80

Telnet = 23

POP3 = 110

Whatever you choose, remember the previous rules and try to make sure nothing else on your computer is using that port number. Now, that last line of code automatically connects the Flash movie to my server when playback begins. Now that we have everything set up graphically and our code is ready to react to our socket events, we need to give some functionality to the login button so that our users can log in to the server. That code looks like this:

```
on (release, keyPress "<Enter>") {
  loginTag.attributes.username = userid.text;
  loginTag.attributes.password = password.text;
  myXML.appendChild(loginTag);
  loginSocket.send(myXML);
}
```

With the preceding code, we are detecting when the user clicks the button or presses the Enter key on the keyboard. When either event is detected, the username and password are sent to the server for verification. With those events detected, let's look at the nested code in the on handler.

Remember the loginTag XML element we made earlier? Here, we are giving that node some attributes and assigning those attributes to be the userid and password that the user has entered into our Input text fields. Then, loginTag is appended as a child to the myXML object. The entire XML object is sent through the XMLSocket object named loginSocket.

When we use the send method, we don't necessarily have to have an XML object as its argument. In this case, we do (myXML), but we could just as easily put a string value in its place. As long as the server knows what to expect, we can use any data type or structure. If it's looking for an XML-formatted string and we send it something similar to "hello", the server might become confused. Either way, the send method is taking whatever it has as its argument, converting it to a string, and then sending it. So, suppose I, as a user, enter shane as my username and flash as my password and submit that information as my login. My server receives the following string value from the Flash movie:

```
<login password="flash" username="shane" />
```

I can choose to parse that string and compare the values in my server code, but now that it has left Flash, I'm no longer responsible for what happens to it until the server sends back a response. When the server does send back a response, we have our myOnXML function set up to handle it and tell our user whether he/she got in or not.

You can see the final FLA file of my Flash work on the *Macromedia Flash MX 2004 Bible* CD-ROM, in a file called XML_SignIn.fla, located in the ch30/S_Elliott folder. To try the login example, you need to run the Java program name flashlogin.jar and then run the Flash movie that you created. There is also a text file named data.txt on the CD-ROM that contains the usernames and passwords that the server recognizes as valid. If you'd like to modify this file so that you can try your own login info, feel free to do so. Just remember to put a semicolon at the end of every name/value pair.

Caution   When the XML send() method is used, it sends a u\0000 termination character at the end of its string value to let you know when the data is completely sent. You must send this character back to Flash to get the onXML() function to recognize that it has received data. Without this termination character, you'll find yourself facing a few problems!

Unifying the Web, by Colin Moock

In Flash 5, Macromedia added the XMLSocket class, which can be used to create multi-player applications, such as games, chat, and shared whiteboards. Applications based on XMLSocket require the use of a server-side application, often called a "socket server" (much like e-mail requires a mail server and Web sites require a Web server). A socket server receives connections from the Flash Player and manages communication between connected users (a.k.a. "clients").

The canonical example of a multiuser application is a chat room, where two or more users type text that is sent to each other. To create a chat room in Flash, you need some client-side code that creates the connection and sends and receives text. You also need a socket server that receives and sends messages between the connected Flash clients.

At the skeletal level, the code for a Flash chat client looks something like this:

```
// Create the socket object.
mySocket = new XMLSocket();
// Assign callbacks to respond to connection events and incoming XML.
mySocket.onConnect = handleConnect;
mySocket.onClose = handleClose;
mySocket.onXML = handleIncoming;
// Connect to the socket server.
mySocket.connect("www.someserver.org", 2001);

// *** Event handler to respond to the completion of a connection attempt.
function handleConnect (succeeded) {
  // If handleConnect's succeeded argument is true,
  // the connection has been established.
  if (succeeded) {
    incoming += "Connection established.\n";
  } else {
    incoming += "Connection failed.\n";
  }
}

// *** Event handler called when server kills the connection.
```

```
function handleClose () {
  // Tell the user that the connection was lost.
  incoming += ("The server has terminated the connection.\n");
}

// *** Event handler to receive and display incoming messages.
function handleIncoming (messageObj) {
    // Add the message to the chat window
    incoming += ("New message: " + messageObj.toString + "\n");
}

// *** Sends a new XML object to the server
function sendMessage() {
  // Create the message to send as an XML source fragment.
  var message = '<MESSAGE><USER> ' + userID + '</USER>'
                      + '<TEXT>' + outgoing + '</TEXT>'
                      + ' </MESSAGE>';
  mySocket.send(message);
}
```

Of course, as the chat room becomes more complex, the code expands. The most challenging aspect of developing a multiuser application is formulating the logic that controls how users interact over the network. For example, even in a simple tic-tac-toe game, messages must be created to manage player moves, to tell each user when the game has started and ended, and to allow users to start and exit games. On both the server side and the Flash client, logic must be created to respond to these messages.

For the past three years, I've worked closely with Derek Clayton to develop a framework that generalizes the logic that governs multiuser interaction. The framework is called *Unity*. Now in its second major version, Unity's goal is to provide Java and Flash developers with a complete toolkit for developing multiuser applications. It also lets Flash-only developers create multiuser applications without the need for server-side code.

The theory of Unity 2 is surprisingly simple: all multiuser applications include groups of connected users that communicate by sharing data and invoking methods on each other. Correspondingly, Unity's core concepts include:

   clients (users connected to the server)

   rooms (groups of clients)

   namespaces (groups of rooms)

   room attributes (shareable and storable data pertaining to rooms)

   client attributes (shaerable and storable data pertaining to clients)

   remote method invocation (invoke methods on any user, or on the server)

If you are considering developing a multiuser application, I invite you to visit www.moock. org/unity/.

If you're new to multiuser application development, Unity 2's architecture will give you the guidance you need to create your application. If you're experienced at multiuser application development, you'll save valuable time using Unity 2 (because you won't waste it creating fundamental multiuser services).

The Unity site also includes a great deal of instructive material and sample code that is free for use even without the purchase of a server. In particular, see the Unity 2 uSimpleChat Tutorial for a four-part walkthrough of the multiuser application development process: `www.moock.org/unity/docs/client/simplechat/`. Note also that Unity is free for academic and artistic use.

For further reading on multiuser application development in Flash, see Jon Williams' article, "The Tao of Pong," at:

```
hotwired.lycos.com/webmonkey/multimedia/shockwave_flash/
tutorials/tutorial9.html.
```

Other commercial and noncommercial socket servers are available at the following sites:

Branden Hall's AquaServer, www.figleaf.com/development/flash5/aquaserver.zip

Jon Williams's MultiServer, www.shovemedia.com/multiserver/

Xadra's Fortress, www.xadra.com/products/main.html

NowMedia's FlashNow, www.nowcentral.com/

You can do incredibly powerful data exchanges with Macromedia Flash Remoting MX, a gateway server that interfaces with popular application servers such as Macromedia ColdFusion MX 6.1, Microsoft .NET, and J2EE. To learn more about Flash Remoting and the AMF format, refer to Joey Lott's *Complete Flash Remoting MX* (Wiley, 2003).

You can also perform real-time data synchronization with Macromedia Flash Communication Server MX 1.5, including live audio/video streaming. For more resources on Flash Communication Server and Rich Internet Applications, visit the book's Web site, `www.flashsupport.com`.

We'd like to know what you thought about this chapter. Visit `www.flashsupport.com/feedback` to fill out an online form with your comments.

Summary

✦ Input text fields can accept text data from anyone viewing the Flash movie (SWF file) with Flash Player 4 or higher. Input text fields are treated as ActionScript variables if you access them via their Var name. If you use instance names with text fields, the Flash movie will work only in Flash Player 6 or higher.

✦ Dynamic text fields can display any string values retrieved with ActionScript in the Flash movie.

✦ Any data exchange between Flash and a remote application or server-side script should use four steps, or states: input, send, wait, and output.

✦ A Flash form can be used to gather feedback from your site's visitors. The form's data can be sent to a properly configured server-side script for further data processing, such as sending the data in an e-mail to the site administrator.

✦ The LoadVars object can send and load text data to a Web server script or application.

✦ XML data structures are quickly becoming an interbusiness standard for data exchange over the Web. Flash can use XML data structures to send and receive data from your Web server.

✦   ✦   ✦

Applying HTML and Text Field Formatting

This chapter shows you how to control text-field formatting and focus using internal HTML tags and ActionScript. Flash gives you an incredible amount of control over text field formatting by using the `TextFormat` object with `TextField` objects (that is, Input and Dynamic text fields). You also learn how to highlight text within text fields by using the `Selection` object.

New Feature As you learn in this chapter, Flash MX 2004 has added style sheet support to `TextField` and `TextFormat` objects. You can also dynamically insert images, linked symbols, or SWF files into `TextField` objects!

Exploring HTML Usage in Text Fields

As you have been using Flash MX 2004, you may have noticed the HTML button in the Property inspector for text fields. Even though one of the primary advantages of using Flash movies is that you can avoid the fuss of HTML page layout, you can use HTML formatting tags within Input and Dynamic text fields. You can use `<font>` tags to specify multiple typefaces, colors, styles, and sizes within one text field. You can also use `<a href>` tags to link to internal ActionScript functions or external URLs!

Caution In Flash Player 4 movies, you cannot specify more than one set of formatting specifications for any text field. For example, if you create a text field that used black Verdana text at 18 points in faux bold, you can't insert any other typeface, color, or size in that text field.

Supported HTML tags

You can use the following HTML tags to format your Flash text fields. You can insert these tags into ActionScript variable values, or you can apply them (without knowing or writing the syntax) using the Property inspector. As you already know, text fields in ActionScript are real objects with instance names. As such, you need to address specific properties of the `TextField` object to insert HTML text. In previous chapters, you've used the following syntax to assign text to a text field instance:

```
instanceName.text = "Enter your last name here";
```

You cannot assign HTML tags in the `text` property of a `TextField` object. You must use the `htmlText` property to assign HTML formatted text, such as:

```
instanceName.htmlText = "Enter your <b>last</b> name here.";
```

Here, the `<b>` tag is used to bold the text "last" in the text field instance. In a moment, you will create your own examples that use the `htmlText` property. Let's review the HTML tags that are available to use in ActionScript:

Font and paragraph styles

The basic `<font>` and physical "faux" styles for text (bold, italic, and underline) can be applied to Flash text.

✦ **<b>:** Placing `<b></b>` tags around Flash text in string values for text field variables applies **bold** formatting to the enclosed text.

✦ **<i>:** Placing `<i></i>` tags around Flash string values *italicizes* the enclosed text.

✦ **<u>:** The `<u></u>` tags <u>underline</u> the enclosed text.

✦ **<p>:** The `<p>` tag inserts a paragraph break between lines of text. You can use the `align` attribute to specify `left`, `right`, `center`, or `justify`, to apply the respective justifications to the Flash text.

✦ **
:** The `<br/>` tag inserts a carriage return at the point of insertion. This is equivalent to the `newline` operator in ActionScript.

✦ **<font color='#hex code'>:** The `<font>` tag with the `color` attribute can change the color of your Flash text. This color is specified in hexadecimal values, just as with regular HTML. For example, `"<font color='#FF0000>This is red text.</font>"` uses full red for the text color.

✦ **<font face>:** The `<font>` tag with the `face` attribute enables you to specify a specific typeface to the enclosed text. You can specify Flash device fonts for the `face` value, such as `<font face='_sans'>` to use the Sans Serif device font.

✦ **<font size>:** The `size` attribute of the `<font>` tag enables you to specify the point size of Flash text. You can use absolute values (in pt sizes), such as `<font size='18'>`, or relative values, such as `<font size='+1'>`, to change the size of text.

✦ **<textformat>:** This tag is a Flash-specific formatting tag that you won't find in traditional HTML. `<textformat>` has four attributes: `indent`, `leading`, `leftmargin`, and `rightmargin`, that control the margin and line spacing of text within the text field. Each of these attributes uses pixels as the unit of measurement. To get a feel for how these attributes work, create a Static text with a paragraph of text, click the Format button in the Property inspector for the selected text field, and change the settings in the Format Options dialog box.

Tip   The `<textformat>` tag was introduced in Flash MX. You can only use this HTML tag within text fields for Flash Player 6 or higher movies. Make sure the Version menu in the Flash tab of the Publish Settings (File ➪ Publish Settings) is set to Flash Player 6 or Flash Player 7.

✦ `<span>`: As with its real HTML counterpart, `<span>` enables you to apply a style from a style sheet to the encompassed range of text. This tag has only one supported attribute, `class`. This attribute can be set to the name of the style class declared in the style sheet. For example, `<span class="heading">` applies the style named `heading` to the enclosed text.

✦ `<img>`: A potentially exciting tag now supported in Flash HTML is the `<img>` tag, short for image. As you may have guessed, this tag enables you to insert images inline with other text in a text field. This tag supports the following attributes: `src`, `id`, `width`, `height`, `align`, `hspace`, and `vspace`. The `src` attribute can be set to one of the following: the linkage identifier of a symbol in the library, the external URL to a SWF file, or the external URL to a standard JPEG image (progressive JPEGs are not supported).

New Feature   The `<img>` and `<span>` tags have been introduced with Flash MX 2004. As such, you must publish your Flash movie for Flash Player 7 in order for these tags to function. You learn how to use these new tags later in this chapter.

URL and ActionScript Linking

You can use the anchor, or `<a>`, tag with the `href` attribute to apply URL links within Flash text fields. For example, you can insert the following HTML into a string value for the `htmlText` property of a text field instance, to link the text [*the*MAKERS] Web site to the appropriate URL:

```
<a href='http://www.theMakers.com'>the Makers Web site</a>
```

You can also specify a `target` attribute for the `<a>` tag. The `target` attribute determines which browser window or frame displays the URL link in the `href` attribute. As with regular HTML, you can use the default `_top`, `_parent`, `_self`, or `_blank` values, as described for the `getURL()` action. Later in this section, you also learn how to execute internal ActionScript functions from `<a href>` tags.

Caution   You cannot type HTML tags directly into any text block or field — the actual tags show up in the text field as the Flash movie runs in the Flash Player. The formatting tags are specified in ActionScript code or are "hidden" in Static text. (The Property inspector applies the formatting.)

Formatting text with the Property inspector

You don't necessarily need to write out HTML tags to apply them to your Flash text. You can use the Property inspector to assign HTML formatting to all Text types (that is, Static, Input, and Dynamic). For Input and Dynamic text fields, you need to enable HTML formatting by pressing the Render text as HTML button in the Property inspector. In this section, we demonstrate the use of HTML formatting within Static and Dynamic text fields.

1. Open a new Flash document (Ctrl+N or ⌘+N). If the background color of your document is a nonwhite color, then set the background color to white in the Document Properties dialog box (Ctrl+J or ⌘+J). Save your Flash document as `htmlText_static.fla`.

2. Select the Text tool and open the Property inspector. Make sure the Text type menu (in the top-left corner of the inspector) is set to Static Text. Click once on the Stage and type the following text (with carriage returns) in the text block, using Verdana at 18 points:

   ```
   Flash MX 2004 Bible
   by Robert Reinhardt & Snow Dowd
   ```

3. With the text block still active, select the Flash MX 2004 Bible text and, in the Property inspector, change the point size to **24** and click the **B** (for bold) option, as shown in Figure 31-1. Enter the following URL in the URL field of the Property inspector and choose **_blank** in the Target menu.

   ```
   www.amazon.com/exec/obidos/ASIN/0764543032
   ```

   Tip   The Property inspector allows you to assign a target window for URL-linked text.

Figure 31-1: You can selectively change text within one text block or field.

4. With the text block still active, select the Robert Reinhardt text, and, in the Property inspector, enter the following text for the URL field:

   ```
   mailto:robert@theMakers.com
   ```

5. Now, select the Snow Dowd text and enter the following text in the URL field of the Property inspector:

   ```
   mailto:snow@theMakers.com
   ```

   See Figure 31-2 for an example of how the URL-linked text will appear.

Figure 31-2: URL-linked text appears with dashed underlines. You will not see this dashed underline in the actual Flash movie (SWF file).

6. Save the Flash document, and test the Flash movie (SWF file) in your Web browser by choosing File ⇨ Publish Preview ⇨ HTML. When you click the Flash MX 2004 Bible text, the browser loads the Amazon.com page for the *Macromedia Flash MX 2004 Bible* in a new window. When you click either author's name, your e-mail client opens a new message window.

On the CD-ROM

You will find the completed `htmlText_static.fla` document in the `ch31` folder of the *Macromedia Flash MX 2004 Bible* CD-ROM.

Try making another example with your own text and URL links. You can even add `javascript:` commands to URL links.

Cross-Reference

If you want to learn how to send an e-mail message from a Flash movie without relying on an e-mail client and the `mailto:` method, read Chapter 30, "Sending Data In and Out of Flash."

Inserting HTML tags into text fields with ActionScript

In this section, we continue with the previous example that you created in the last section. You convert the Static text block into a Dynamic text field and manipulate the formatting with ActionScript.

1. Resave your Flash document from the last section as `htmlText_dynamic.fla`. You will convert this Static text into a Dynamic text field, so you'll want to keep your original Static text example for future reference.

2. Select the text block and open the Property inspector. Change the text type to Dynamic Text and make sure the HTML option is enabled. In the `<Instance Name>` field, type the name `book_txt`. Now, this text field can be updated with ActionScript directed at the `book_txt` instance. You can also disable the Show Border option if you don't want to see a bounding box around your text.

3. Save the Flash document and test it (Ctrl+Enter or ⌘+Return). While the Flash movie is playing in the Test Movie window, choose Debug ⇨ List Variables. You should see the HTML formatting tags displayed in the Output window. The `book_txt` object has several properties and values. The `htmlText` property reads as one continuous line displaying the following markup:

```
htmlText = "<TEXTFORMAT LEADING=\"2\"><P ALIGN=\"LEFT\"><FONT FACE=
\"verdana\" SIZE=\"24\" COLOR=\"#000000\"><A HREF=\"http://www.amazon.
com/exec/obidos/ASIN/0764543032\" TARGET=\"\"><B>Flash MX 2004
Bible</B></A></FONT></P></TEXTFORMAT><TEXTFORMAT LEADING=\"2\">
<P ALIGN=\"LEFT\"><FONT FACE=\"verdana\" SIZE=\"18\" COLOR=\"#000000\">
by <A HREF=\"mailto:robert@theMakers.com\" TARGET=\"\">Robert Reinhardt
</A> &amp; <A HREF=\"mailto:snow@theMakers.com\" TARGET=\"\">Snow Dowd
</A></FONT></P></TEXTFORMAT>",
```

You can observe the proper ActionScript syntax for HTML formatting in the Output panel. Note that any quotes around values of tag attributes are preceded by a backslash, as in `<font face=\"verdana\">`. Because the value of `htmlText` is already a string data type surrounded by quotes, any internal quotes need to be declared with a backslash character.

Note HTML tag names are not case-sensitive in Flash. We prefer to use XHTML compliant code; as such, you'll see our examples use all lowercase characters in HTML tag and attribute names. The values of attributes, such as file URLs in `href` or `src`, require attention to case-sensitivity.

4. Close the Test Movie window and go back to the Main Timeline of your Flash document. Create a new Dynamic text field, and in the Property inspector, enable the HTML option. Make sure the text field is set to Multiline. In the `<Instance Name>` field, type the name `book_2_txt`. The text field should be somewhat wider than the previous text field.

5. Add a new layer, and name it **actions**. Select the first frame of the actions layer and open the Actions panel (F9). In the Script pane, specify an HTML-formatted string value for the `htmlText` property of the `book_2_txt` instance, such as the following code:

```
book_2_txt.htmlText = "<font face=\"Verdana\" size=\"24\" color=
\"#0000FF\"><b><a href=\"http://www.amazon.com/exec/obidos/ASIN/
0764543547\">Flash MX 2004 ActionScript Bible</a></b></font><br/>
<font size=\"18\" color=\"#000000\">by <a href=\"mailto:robert@
theMakers.com\">Robert Reinhardt</a> & <a href=\"mailto:joey@
person13.com\">Joey Lott</a>";
```

Note This code should appear as one line number in the Script pane of the Actions panel.

6. Save the Flash document and test it. The `book_2_txt` text field displays the HTML-formatted value that you specified in the actions layer.

You can also use variables in expressions for HTML-formatted text fields, such as the following (note that the `bookURL` variable and value should appear on one line of code):

```
var bookURL:String = "http://www.amazon.com/exec/obidos/ASIN/0764543547";
var bookName:String = "Flash MX 2004 ActionScript Bible";
book_2_txt.htmlText = "<a href=\"" + bookURL + "\">" + bookName + "</a>";
```

By using other ActionScript variables and methods, you can apply specific text formatting to external data sources that have been loaded into the Flash movie, such as database records or lists. In the next section, you learn how to format text within text fields using the new `TextFormat` object in ActionScript.

On the CD-ROM   You can find the completed `htmlText_dynamic.fla` document in the `ch31` folder of the *Macromedia Flash MX 2004 Bible* CD-ROM.

Formatting fields with the TextFormat object

ActionScript offers a wide range of options for the `TextField` object. Many properties of the `MovieClip` object, such as `_x` and `_y`, can be controlled with `TextField` objects, too. One interesting method of the `TextField` object is the `setTextFormat()` method. This method allows you to control the formatting of text within a `TextField` object without relying on HTML tags. The `setTextFormat()` method works much like the `setTransform()` methods of the `Color` and `Sound` objects that we cover in Chapter 27, "Interacting with Movie Clips." Like `setTransform()`, `setTextFormat()` requires another object — a `TextFormat` object — that contains individual properties and values in order to adjust the targeted instance's text contents.

Tip   ActionScript in Flash Player 6 and 7 compatible movies can also create text fields on the fly using the `createTextField()` method of the `MovieClip` object.

In this section, you create a Flash movie that makes a dynamic text field on the fly and applies formatting to the field with the `TextFormat` object. You also use the `TextFormat` object to determine the dimensions of the `TextField` instance.

1. Create a new Flash document (Ctrl+N or ⌘+N).

2. Rename Layer 1 to **actions**. ActionScript creates the entire contents of this movie. You will not use any tools from the Tools panel to create the text.

3. Select frame 1 of the actions layer and open the Actions panel. In Expert mode, type the following code into the Script pane:

```
var titleStyle:TextFormat = new TextFormat();
titleStyle.font = "Verdana";
titleStyle.bold = true;
titleStyle.color = 0x0000FF;
titleStyle.url = "http://www.flashsupport.com/";
titleStyle.target = "_blank";
```

This code creates a new `TextFormat` object named `titleStyle` (line 1). This formatting is used for site links displayed in the Flash movie. Within this object, properties of the site link text are specified. Lines 2 through 6 assign the `font`, `bold`, `color`, `url`, and `target` properties of the style. In later steps, you apply this style to a `TextField` instance.

4. Within the same actions list shown in Step 3, add the following code:

```
var site_1:String = "FlashSupport.com";
var fieldSize:Object = titleStyle.getTextExtent(site_1);
```

This code declares a `site_1` variable, which contains the text of the first site link the movie displays. `fieldSize` is an object created by the `getTextExtent()` method of the `TextFormat` object. This method allows you to determine the pixel dimensions of text with formatting applied to it before you actually create the `TextField` object displaying the text. `fieldSize` contains two properties (among others): `textFieldWidth` and `textFieldHeight`. You access these properties in the next step.

New Feature

The `TextFormat.getTextExtent()` method has been greatly improved for Flash Player 7. The following properties are now returned by the method: `descent`, `ascent`, `textFieldHeight`, `textFieldWidth`, `height`, and `width`. Refer to the Help panel for more information on these properties or read the coverage in the *Flash MX 2004 ActionScript Bible* (Wiley, 2004).

5. After the last line of code listed in Step 4, add the following code. Note that the ⊃ character indicates a continuation of the same line of code:

```
this.createTextField("siteList_txt", 1, 10, 10, ⊃
   fieldSize.textFieldWidth, fieldSize.textFieldHeight);
siteList_txt.html = true;
siteList_txt.text = site_1;
siteList_txt.setTextFormat(titleStyle);
```

The first line of code uses the `createTextField()` method of the `MovieClip` object to make a new Dynamic text field named `siteList_txt` at a depth 1 on the current timeline (`this`). The field is positioned at the X and Y coordinates of 10, 10, with a width and height specified by the `fieldSize` object created earlier.

The second line of code enables the `siteList_txt` field to use HTML text.

The third line fills the text field with the value of the `site_1` variable, "Flash Support."

The fourth line applies the `titleStyle` TextFormat object to the entire contents of the `siteList` field.

6. Save the Flash document as `textFormat_100.fla` and test it (Ctrl+Enter or ⌘+Return). The `siteList_txt` text field appears in the top-left corner of the Stage. When you click the text, the default Web browser opens, displaying the URL for `flashsupport.com`.

On the CD-ROM

You can find the completed `textFormat_100.fla` file in the ch31 folder of the *Macromedia Flash MX 2004 Bible* CD-ROM.

You can continue to develop this Flash document, adding more sites to the `siteList_txt` text field. You don't necessarily need to make more text fields — create more `site_` variables and add their expressions together as the contents of the `siteList_txt` instance.

Cross-Reference

It is beyond the scope of this chapter to discuss all of the methods, properties, and event handlers for `TextField` and `TextFormat` objects. For more detailed information, read the *Flash MX 2004 ActionScript Bible*.

Applying style sheets to text fields

In this section, you learn how to load an external style sheet, as a CSS file, and apply its styles to text in a Flash movie. This capability is new to Flash Player 7 and Flash MX 2004 ActionScript.

Making the style sheet

Before you can apply an external style sheet to Flash text, you need to create the CSS file describing the styles. In the following steps, use any text editor such as Notepad or TextEdit.

1. Create a new text document.

2. Define two custom styles, h1 and h2. These styles should use bold 14 and 12 px type, respectively. The font face should be Verdana for both. Refer to Listing 31-1.

3. Now, define a body style. This style will be used for regular text in paragraphs. This style will use Arial at 10 px. The color of this text will be dark gray, using the hexadecimal value #666666. Refer to Listing 31-1.

4. Save your text file as styles.css.

Listing 31-1: **The h1, h2, and body styles**

```
.h1 {
    font-family: Verdana;
    font-weight: bold;
    font-size: 14px;
}

.h2 {
    font-family: Verdana;
    font-weight: bold;
    font-size: 12px;
}
.body {
    font-family: Arial;
    font-size: 10px;
    color: #666666;
}
```

Loading the style sheet into a Flash movie

Once you have a CSS file ready, you can create the ActionScript required to load the style sheet into a Flash movie. In the following steps, you'll do just that.

1. Create a new Flash document (File ➪ New).

2. Rename Layer 1 to **actions**.

3. Select frame 1 of the actions layer, and open the Actions panel (F9). Type the code shown in Listing 31-2 into the Script pane.

In line 1 of this code, you create a new `StyleSheet` object, which is actually a subclass of the `TextField` class. The `StyleSheet` object is named `movieStyle`.

In line 2, you define the `onLoad()` method of this object. The `onLoad()` handler is invoked when the external CSS file has finished loading into the movie. If the loading was successful, lines 3 through 5 are invoked, sending a `trace()` message to the Output panel and invoking another function named `showText()`. You define the `showText()` function in the next section.

If the CSS style could not be loaded (that is, if the URL or filename was incorrect, or if the style sheet could not be parsed by the Flash Player), lines 6 through 8 are invoked in the `onLoad()` handler. Line 7 sends a message indicating the result to the Output panel.

Line 10 invokes the `load()` method of the `movieStyle` object. This line of code tells the Flash Player to get the `styles.css` file and attempt to load it.

Tip   It's always a good idea to define the `onLoad()` handler of an object before you initiate the `load()` method. There's a slight chance that the `onLoad()` handler won't be invoked if you declare it after the `load()` method.

Listing 31-2: The `movieStyle` **object**

```
1.  var movieStyle:TextField.StyleSheet = new TextField.StyleSheet();
2.  movieStyle.onLoad = function(success){
3.     if(success){
4.        trace("loaded external CSS file");
5.        showText(this);
6.     } else {
7.        trace("CSS file did not load.");
8.     }
9.  };
10. movieStyle.load("styles.css");
```

4. Save your Flash document as `css_styles_100.fla`, in the same location where you saved your `styles.css` file from the previous section. Test the movie (Ctrl+Enter or ⌘+Enter). You should see the following text appear in the Output panel:

```
loaded external CSS file
```

Applying the styles to Flash text

Once you have the external style sheet loaded into a Flash movie, you're ready to apply the defined styles to text used in dynamic or input text fields. In the remaining steps, you learn how to apply each of the styles to text displayed in a dynamic text field.

1. In the Flash document that you created in the previous section, go back to frame 1 of the actions layer. Open the Actions panel (F9), and add the code shown in Listing 31-3 *before* the existing code. Note that the ⊋ character indicates a continuation of the same line of code. Do not type this character into your actual code.

Line 1 declares the function's name, showText, and defines one argument, named style. Remember that in Listing 31-2, when the showText() function is invoked in the onLoad() handler, a reference to the movieStyle object (this) was passed to this function.

Line 2 creates a text field named display_txt. Line 3 sets the styleSheet property of the display_txt instance to that of the style argument (in this case, movieStyle). Lines 4 through 6 setup basic properties of the display_txt instance, allowing it to display HTML text (line 4), and display wrapping text over multiple lines (lines 5 and 6).

Lines 7 through 10 create a long string of text that will be inserted into the display_txt field. Here, you can see that each of the styles is used, defined in the class attributes of various <span> and <p> tags. Finally, in line 11, the htmlText property of the display_txt instance is set to the value of the bodyText variable.

Listing 31-3: **The** showText() **function**

```
1.   function showText(style){
2.      this.createTextField("display_txt", 1, 10, 10, 400, 400);
3.      display_txt.styleSheet = style;
4.      display_txt.html = true;
5.      display_txt.multiline = true;
6.      display_txt.wordWrap = true;
7.      var bodyText:String = "<span class='h1'>Flash MX 2004 Style ⤸
           Support</span><br/>";
8.      bodyText += "<p class='body'>You can now use style sheets in your ⤸
           Flash movies with Flash Player 7.</p><br/>";
9.      bodyText += "<span class='h2'>Supported styles</span><br/>";
10.     bodyText += "<p class='body'>More text here...</p>";
11.     display_txt.htmlText = bodyText;
12. }
```

2. Save your Flash document, and test it. You should see nicely formatted text, specified by the details of the style sheet, as shown in Figure 31-3.

Figure 31-3: The formatted text

You can find the completed files, styles.css and css_styles_100.fla, in the ch31 folder of this book's CD-ROM.

You can also use other nonsystem fonts in style sheets, but you'll need to make sure that you have created linked Font symbols in your movie's library or that you have created empty text fields that include the embedded fonts.

Cross-Reference   To learn more about Font symbols, see Chapter 28, "Sharing and Loading Assets." You can also find more expanded coverage of style sheet usage in the Help panel of Flash MX 2004 (use the search term, "styles") and in the *Flash MX 2004 ActionScript Bible*.

Inserting images into text fields

In this section, you learn how to load a JPEG image into a TextField object. Continue using the same Flash document you created in the last section.

On the CD-ROM   Open the css_styles_100.fla document from the ch31 folder of this book's CD-ROM if you didn't complete the previous section.

1. In the css_styles_100.fla document, select frame 1 of the actions layer, and open the Actions panel (F9). Change the showText() function to the code shown in Listing 31-4. Remember that you shouldn't include the ⏎ character in your actual code. This character denotes a continuation of the same line of code.

   This code uses the same structure of the showText() function from the last section. However, in line 1, you include the bio.as file, which you can find in the ch31 folder of this book's CD-ROM. A copy of this file should exist in the same location as your FLA file. The bio.as file declares a string variable named bioText, containing a sample biography.

Tip   For a final production version of this Flash movie, you may want to load the data stored in the bio.as into the Flash movie at runtime. For example, the biography text could be stored in an XML document and loaded with an XML object, or it could be loaded from a server-side script. For more information on data loading, read Chapter 30, "Sending Data in and Out of Flash."

   In line 9, you use the new <img> tag to include a JPEG image, portrait.jpg, in the display_txt field. You can find this JPEG file in the ch31 folder of this book's CD-ROM, and it's also located at the URL shown in line 9. Lines 10 and 11 add the text for the biography, and line 12 sets the htmlText property of display_txt to all of the HTML created in lines 8 through 11.

Listing 31-4: **The modified** showText() **function**

```
1.   #include "bio.as"
2.   function showText(style){
3.      this.createTextField("display_txt", 1, 10, 10, 415, 350);
4.      display_txt.styleSheet = style;
5.      display_txt.html = true;
6.      display_txt.multiline = true;
7.      display_txt.wordWrap = true;
8.      var bodyText:String;
```

```
9.       bodyText = "<img src='http://www.flashsupport.com/bio/portrait.jpg' ⊃
         id='portrait_mc' width='200' height='200' vspace='4' hspace='8' ⊃
         align='left'>";
10.      bodyText += "<span class='h1'>Robert Reinhardt</span><br/>";
11.      bodyText += bioText;
12.      display_txt.htmlText = bodyText;
13. }
```

2. Save your Flash document as `img_insert_100.fla`, and test it. When the movie loads, you should see the header and biography text wrap around the JPEG image, as shown in Figure 31-4.

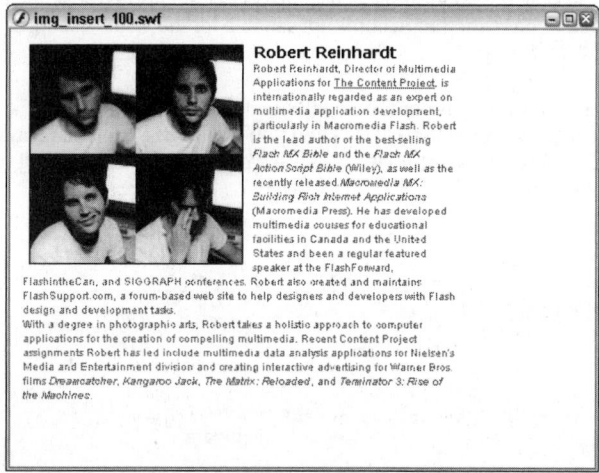

Figure 31-4: The JPEG image with wrapping text

On the CD-ROM

You can find the completed document, `img_insert_100.fla`, in the ch31 folder of this book's CD-ROM. This document also features a `drawBorder()` function, which dynamically draws a border around the JPEG image.

You can also use symbol linkage identifier names as the value of the `src` attribute of the `<img>` tag. However, you may find that if you use several `<img>` tags in a text field, not all of the images load and/or display. In some of our experiments, we noticed that text realigned itself when text with URLs was rolled over. Be sure to test your Flash movies with the latest Flash Player 7 revisions, as Macromedia releases them.

Using asfunction in anchor tags

Not only can you use HTML formatting in Flash text; you can execute Flash actions from your text fields using the `<a>` tag and a `href` attribute value of `asfunction:function,argument`. For example, if you wanted to link text to a function that loads a new Flash movie (SWF file) into a Movie Clip target, you can create a custom function that uses the `loadMovie()` action and reference that action from your `<a href>` tag for a text field. See the following code (note that the ⊃ indicates a continuation of the same line of code; do not insert this character into your actual code):

```
function getSWF(name){
  holder_mc.loadMovie(name);
}
myField.htmlText = "<a href=\"asfunction:getSWF,movie.swf\">Click to load ⊃
  movie</a>";
```

In this code example, the text within the `<a></a>` tags executes the `getSWF()` function, passing the string `movie.swf` as the `name` argument.

Tip

The `asfunction` can only pass one string value. You do not need to enclose the argument in quotes. If you need to pass another ActionScript variable for the value, use the `+` operator to add it to the HTML text string.

If you need to pass more than one argument, you will need to send all the values as one string separated by a comma (or preferred character). Then you would use the `split` method as follows (note that the ⊃ indicates a continuation of the same line of code; do not insert this character into your actual code):

```
function getSWF(name){
    var tempArgs:Array = name.split(",");
    var mcTarget:MovieClip = eval(tempArgs[0]);
    var swfUrl:String = tempArgs[1];
    mcTarget.loadMovie(swfUrl);
}
var myArgs = "holder_mc,movie.swf";
myField.htmlText = "<a href=\"asfunction:getSWF," + myArgs + "\"> ⊃
  Click to load movie</a>";
```

In this example, the `getSWF()` function takes the `name` argument and creates an array with the `split` method. This array's name is `tempArgs`. The elements of the `tempArgs` array are the two string values separated by a comma in the `myArgs` variable.

On the CD-ROM

You can see examples of HTML-formatted Flash text and the `asfunction` in the `ch31/asfunction` folder of the *Macromedia Flash MX 2004 Bible* CD-ROM.

Controlling Text Field Properties

Input and Dynamic text fields have several properties that are accessible with ActionScript. Two of these, `scroll` and `maxscroll`, control the viewable area of a text field that has more lines of text than the text field can show.

  ✦ `scroll`: This property can retrieve the current line number (from the top of the field), and it can also move to a new line number in a text field.

  ✦ `maxscroll`: This property returns the maximum value of the scroll property for a given text field. You can only retrieve this value — you cannot set it.

To understand how these properties work, you need to see how lines are enumerated in a text field. Suppose you had ten lines of text as a string value for a variable called `myText`. If you want to use this text in a Dynamic text field named `article_txt`, which only has a viewable area of five lines, then the remaining five lines of the `myText` variable will not be seen in the text field. To make the text field "scroll" to the next line of text by showing lines 2 to 6 (instead of lines 1 to 5), you can create a Button instance, such as a down-arrow button, with ActionScript to advance the lines:

```
on(release){
   article_txt.scroll = article.scroll + 1;
}
```

or

```
on(release){
   article_txt.scroll += 1;
}
```

The `maxscroll` property returns the maximum value for the top line number in a text field. In our previous ten-line text value example, the `maxscroll` property would equal 6. If you had 20 lines of text in the `article` text field, then the `.maxscroll` property would return a value of 16.

New Feature

Flash MX 2004 has a `TextArea` component that automatically creates a text field and scrollbar. You can find more information on components in Chapter 29, "Using Components." Also, the `ScrollBar` component from Flash MX is no longer available as a stand-alone component in Flash MX 2004. It's highly likely that Macromedia will release updates to the components, so if you're looking for it, check the Macromedia Exchange at `www.macromedia.com/exchange`.

On the CD-ROM

In the `ch31/scroll` folder of the *Macromedia Flash MX 2004 Bible* CD-ROM, you will find a Flash document named `scrollProp_simple.fla`. This movie demonstrates the use of the `scroll` property to view the entire Gettysburg Address within a text field. A more advanced scrolling mechanism can be found in the `scrollProp_advanced.fla`, which features a draggable scroll bar.

Manipulating Text with the Selection Object

The last text feature that we discuss in this chapter is the `Selection` object. The `Selection` object is similar to the `Mouse` object — you don't create instances of the `Selection` object as there can only be one active highlighted item at any given time.

Several object classes can use the `Selection` object, including `TextField` objects. The `Selection` object can uses a string reference to the text field's variable (Var) name or its instance name to perform its methods. We discuss the methods of the `Selection` object in the following sections.

Note

In Flash 4 movies, there is no way of checking which text field was active. You could turn off a focus rectangle for Flash 4 text fields and Button instances, but you can't control tab order or automatically set a text field to active.

getBeginIndex()

This method detects and returns the starting position of a highlighted selection in a text field. The method returns –1 if there is no active text field and/or there is no selection inside the text field. As with the Array object, selection indexes start position values at 0. You do not need to specify a target path for this method — only one text field can have a selection at any given point. Therefore, as a variable startIndex, the getBeginIndex() method would look like:

```
this.onMouseMove = function(){
var startIndex = Selection.getBeginIndex();
trace("startIndex = " + startIndex);
};
```

In the Output panel, the trace() action would reveal startIndex = -1 until you made a selection within a text field in the movie, as shown in Figure 31-5.

On the CD-ROM

In the ch31/selection folder of the *Macromedia Flash MX 2004 Bible* CD-ROM, review the getBeginIndex_trace.fla to see how the getBeginIndex() method returns values for a text field. Each of the following sections also has a Flash document to demonstrate its respective method.

| test this text field with a selection |

Figure 31-5: A text field with a starting selection index of 3

getEndIndex()

Similar to the getBeginIndex() method, this method returns a number indicating the index position at the end of a highlighted selection in a text field, as shown in Figure 31-6. If there is no active selection, then a value of –1 is returned.

| test this text field with a selection |

Figure 31-6: A text field with a starting selection index of 5 and an ending index of 9

getCaretIndex()

This method of the Selection object returns the current cursor position (as an index value) within an active text field, as shown in Figure 31-7. As with the two previous methods, if you use the getCaretIndex() method when there is no active cursor in a text field, it returns a –1.

| test this text field with a selection |

Figure 31-7: A text field with a caret index of 5

getFocus()

This method returns the current active text field's Var or instance name as an absolute path; that is, if you have selected or inserted the cursor position inside a text field instance named myOutput_txt on the Main Timeline, then Selection.getFocus() returns _level0.myOutput_txt. If there is no active text field, then this method returns null.

Note   If a text field does not have an instance name but does have a Var name, the Var name and path will be returned. A text field's instance name, when available, will be returned by this method.

setFocus()

Perhaps the best enhancement to controlled text field activity is the setFocus() method. This method enables you to make a text field active automatically—the user doesn't need to click the mouse cursor inside the text field to start typing. To use this method, simply indicate the setFocus() method of the Selection object and the path to the text field as its argument:

```
Selection.setFocus(testInput_txt);
```

This code sets the current focus to the testInput_txt text field. If any text exists in the text field, it will be highlighted as a selection. You can only use string data types as the setFocus() argument for Flash Player 5 compatability, but you can use instance names for Flash Player 6 or higher.

setSelection()

Another method available for the Selection object is setSelection(). This method enables you to make a specific selection within an active text field. The method takes two arguments: a start index and an end index. Using the same index numbering as getBeginIndex() and getEndIndex(). Note that this method will not work unless a text field is already active. The following code creates a selection span from index 5 to 9 of the testInput_txt text field:

```
Selection.setFocus(testInput_txt);
Selection.setSelection(5,9);
```

Caution   You may find that the setSelection() method does not show any results in the Test Movie environment. Always test your Flash movies in a Web browser or the stand-alone player to analyze your results.

Cross-Reference   Our coverage of the Selection object will get you on your way to selection and highlight control within your Flash movies. It is beyond the scope of this book to provide further explanations of Selection object methods and handlers. You can continue to read more about the Selection object in the *Flash MX 2004 ActionScript Bible*. There, you will also find detailed information about the new addListener() and removeListener() methods of several ActionScript classes, including the Selection object.

Web Resource   We'd like to know what you think about this chapter. Visit www.flashsupport.com/feedback to fill out an online form with your comments.

Summary

✦ You can use HTML text formatting within Flash text fields. Only basic HTML text formatting is allowed.

✦ You can insert HTML tags into the values of ActionScript variables that refer to Input or Dynamic text fields. Any quotes used with HTML attributes should be preceded by a backward slash, \.

✦ The `TextFormat` object enables you to create object-based styles that can be applied to text within `TextField` objects.

✦ You can now apply style sheets to text within Flash movies that are compatible with Flash Player 7. The TextField object can also display inline artwork with the HTML `<img>` tag.

✦ The `asfunction` parameter for the `HREF` attribute of the `<A>` tag enables you to execute ActionScript functions from text fields. You can pass one argument to the specified function.

✦ The `scroll` property of Input and Dynamic text fields enables you to control the portion of a text field value that is displayed within the text field. `maxscroll` returns the highest top line number for a given set of text in a text field.

✦ The `Selection` object in ActionScript enables you to control the focus and highlighted selection spans of text fields in a Flash movie.

✦   ✦   ✦

Creating a Portfolio Site in Flash

There are probably as many different approaches to building a Flash project as there are designers, but getting insight into how other designers choose to work can help you build your own best process. Whether you work independently or as part of a team, the fundamental pieces of a project that have to be put together are similar.

This chapter walks you through the production workflow that the authors used for building a sample portfolio site for artist/designer Daisy Reinhardt. The organizational principles and the basic structure of this project can be adapted to suit a variety of content. As a two-person core team with one more design-oriented partner and one more code-oriented partner [the MAKERS] has addressed many of the issues that come up in any collaborative effort. Centralizing assets and approaching the site structure as a modular assembly of various individual files help to make the best use of both partners' skills while minimizing redundant effort.

The project development process described in this chapter will help you review and apply the Flash production techniques covered in earlier chapters of the book. The workflow progresses from the basic strategy of design to adding the ActionScript needed to load assets and control dynamic color and scale effects.

Each phase of the project includes a step-by-step workflow outline, but you should refer to the relevant chapters if you need a more detailed reminder of how to complete specific tasks.

Creating an Extensible Site Structure

Depending on the project, you may begin your planning by designing a structure and then sorting content to fit that structure; or more likely, you will first evaluate the content and then design a structure to accommodate it. For this portfolio project, we began with the basic premise of having a main page and some individual sections that would highlight different kinds of design work. Although the limited number of images that we are starting with could easily be accommodated in one page with an interface for navigating through the various items, we have decided to build a site that can accommodate more content in the future. As with most projects, it is helpful to look ahead and consider how new portfolio content will be integrated with the original site structure.

The goal is to create a site that grows painlessly, without major overhaul of the navigation system or other core features. No matter what the content of your project might be, the features you should consider when designing an *extensible* site structure are similar:

✦ **Asset organization:** Create logical categories for content, even if you currently have only a limited number of assets.

✦ **Titles and graphic text:** Make site section titles and navigation text or icons descriptive, but keep them generic enough that they will not have to be changed as the site content is updated. For example, it would be better to have a site section titled "Company News" than to have a section titled "April Newsletter." In the portfolio site we are designing, we have titled a section simply "Costumes," rather than "Mermaid Costumes," because this allows the designer to add other costumes in the future without having to modify the site structure.

✦ **Navigation:** Consider how your navigation interface accommodates added content. It may be better to number assets and to create a generic Movie Clip that can load preview icons than to manually name assets and create thumbnails that will have to be modified whenever the content is updated. If you plan carefully, your interface will work equally well with 10 items or 100 items.

✦ **Consistency:** Although the site structure and layout should suit the content, it will make your life difficult if each asset has to be placed and aligned manually. Wherever possible, define a consistent area of the site for loaded assets and format the content to fit the site instead of changing the site to fit the content. Think of your site design as architecture rather than as window dressing. If you do your research and create a site that is appropriate for the content, you shouldn't have to modify the site to accommodate additions or changes (at least on a regular basis). If you're planning an extensible site, create a layout and choose colors and fonts that support a range of content rather than making a design that only "goes with" a very specific asset.

On the CD-ROM

The files referred to in this chapter are in the `ch32` folder of the *Macromedia Flash MX 2004 Bible* CD-ROM. You will find the Flash MX 2004 project files as well as the various planning documents included for your reference.

Planning the basic site structure

It's not really surprising how many developers can't be bothered to make a formal plan before jumping in and putting valuable time into working out the visual aspects of a design—after all, that's the fun part, right? Unfortunately, this can easily put you in a situation where you waste initial enthusiasm, not to mention production time, working without perspective on how the whole project will come together. Doing a bit of groundwork before you start designing empowers you to focus your production efforts and enables you to avoid the dreaded pitfalls of plan-as-you-go production: The animation you just spent three hours on doesn't fit into the site anywhere. The detailed menu graphics that you designed all have to be redone because it turns out the navigation has to be oriented vertically instead of horizontally, and the whole site has to be finished by Monday and you're missing 15 photos and three product descriptions. Isn't this fun?

The two simple tools you can use to help you avoid haphazard and painful production scenarios are site flowcharts and the technical specification documents. You have probably seen examples of these at some point, but you may not have paid much attention or considered making them for yourself. Even if you aren't the most enthusiastic paper-pusher, you can probably find a way to make these tools work for you in some shape or form.

There are many options for authoring your planning documents. You can make flowcharts and tables for technical specification documents in most basic text-editing programs or in your preferred graphics program (such as Illustrator or Fireworks). Some terrific specialized programs make the task of creating charts and tables much easier. More detailed descriptions of these various document types are discussed in Chapter 3, "Planning Flash Projects."

Before getting too carried away with rough page layouts, it is helpful to establish the site "skeleton" or a flowchart of how the content will be organized. Flowcharts can range in complexity from thumbnail sketches on coffee-stained napkins to highly detailed and beautifully rendered presentation boards. Unless you're trying to sell a client on your designs, the beauty of your charts isn't as important as the basic logic that they represent.

The important thing to establish with a flowchart is how visitors will move through the content. Spending the time now to work out the hierarchy and navigation paths of the site will save a lot of confusion and potentially wasted effort down the road. This step is also important because it may be the first time that you can start to really see how the content can be broken down into balanced categories. If all goes well, you will also be able to identify missing elements or weaknesses in the plan early enough to make improvements without disrupting work that you've already completed.

Daisy's portfolio site did not require a lot of text or sound assets. If you will be handling a lot of text and/or sound files in a project, you may want to create a script of these assets that can be used as a reference for recording sound or finalizing text. In the same way that images are numbered for Daisy's site, sounds or text docs can be numbered to indicate how they match up with different scenes or pages in your site design.

The flowchart should, at the very least, identify basic site sections and navigation paths, but it can also be developed to a level of detail that describes all the individual elements on every page of the site. As shown in Figure 32-1, the flowchart we created for the portfolio site is a very simple "tree" that shows the navigation paths, the main category names, the background colors, and the numbering scheme for loaded images (SWF and JPEG files).

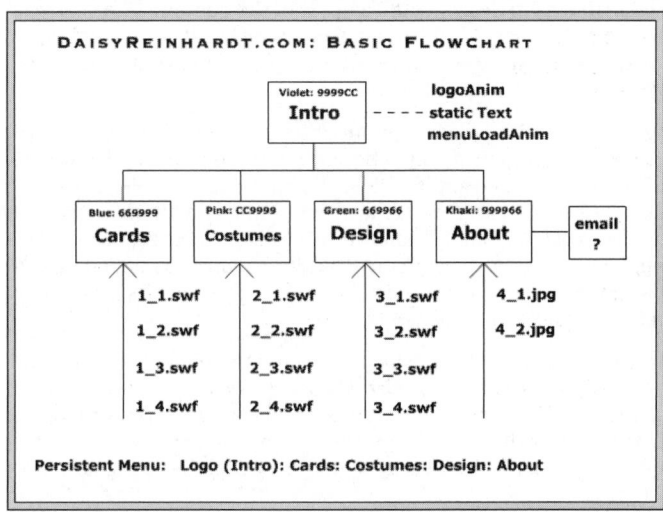

Figure 32-1: A basic flowchart helps when planning even small projects.

The next step in detailing the logic and structure of your site design is to begin compiling *functional specifications*. As with flowcharts, functional specs can be simple or highly detailed, but the main purpose is to itemize all the elements that will be put together to make your final site. The document should include the following information, regardless of how it is organized:

✦ A naming convention for assets and interface elements.

✦ A description of any special technique or content required to complete each element.

✦ An explanation of the purpose that each element serves in the site. (If you can't come up with a brief and compelling reason for including a particular element, you may want to consider removing it from your design plan.)

If the term *functional specification* is too off-putting, you can think of this document in terms of a film script — name all the characters (who are they and why are they included?), explain the plot (what happens and in what order?), and list any special effects, locations, or props needed to complete the story (what skills and assets will be needed?).

On the CD-ROM   The functional specification document for the portfolio site described in this chapter is included in the ch32 folder of the *Macromedia Flash MX 2004 Bible* CD-ROM in both Word and PDF documents.

As work progresses on a project, both the flowchart and the functional specs will most likely need to be updated to reflect small changes or additions. These documents are only as useful as you make them; if they are simply done as a convention and not tailored to your specific needs or kept up to date, chances are that these documents will simply get lost in the shuffle. If you make an ongoing effort to make these documents actually work for you and others on your team, it will make your production go more smoothly in almost every way. Honest!

Establishing key elements

To establish a visual site layout for artist and designer Daisy Reinhardt, we experimented with different designs and tested each design with samples of the content. The goal was to find a consistent layout scheme that would "fit" a range of content. Aside from bitmaps of her designs, Daisy had a logo that was placed as a key element in the site layout. Figure 32-2 shows a rough layout of the main elements of the site.

If we were going to design this site with no consideration for extensibility, we would probably design each page of the site as a separate layout — perhaps even adding modifications to the layout to accommodate individual loaded assets. However, our goal with this project is to create a framework that allows the loaded assets to change without having to modify any key elements. The first step toward establishing a framework is to convert the information we have gained from the rough layouts (shown in Figure 32-2) into a more simplified sketch that maps out the space in our page design. As shown in Figure 32-3, this "map" should indicate the approximate size and placement of key elements.

The most important thing to establish is the maximum size and the boundaries for loaded content — the layout should work visually when loaded assets of various sizes are aligned consistently. In our map, the loaded images will be aligned with ActionScript within the border of the image area, as they are loaded. This keeps the layout balanced while accommodating smaller square images of cards and larger vertical images of costume designs.

Figure 32-2: By roughly placing key elements and samples of the artwork, we can begin to establish a site layout.

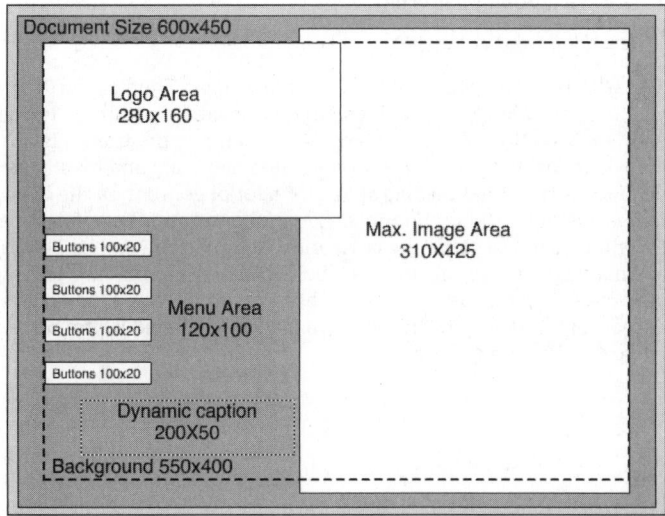

Figure 32-3: To create an extensible structure that accommodates various loaded assets, it is important to define a consistent image area and to position navigation elements.

To make it easy to update the content of the site without having to reauthor the main Flash document, we're going to use loaded text for the image captions.

On the CD-ROM The custom *description* component that Robert created to facilitate loading the caption text (`description.fla`) is included in the `ch32/site` folder on the CD-ROM. You can reuse this component for any site structure that requires loaded text to be associated with specific assets.

Organizing the document

When you have a general map of the content and the layout, you can begin to organize and label your main Flash document. For this portfolio site, we have decided to use a document size of 600 x 450 pixels, with a medium-gray background color.

With all Flash projects, we always start with a basic layer structure that makes it easy to identify and edit content in the future. The layers in the document for the portfolio site are as follows:

- ✦ Layer 1: actions
- ✦ Layer 2: labels
- ✦ Layer 3: logo
- ✦ Layer 4: mainMenu
- ✦ Layer 5: secondMenu (forward and back arrows)
- ✦ Layer 6: caption (for loaded and static text)
- ✦ Layer 7: imageMC (for loaded images)
- ✦ Layer 8: bgTexture (for background patterns)
- ✦ Layer 9: bgColor (for background color tile)

Now that you have a layer structure, the next step is to start building a Timeline structure. In the *labels* layer, insert evenly spaced keyframes and use the frame label field in the Property inspector to add names for each section of your project. The spacing of the frames is not critical at this point, because we are using Movie Clips for animated elements and loading images dynamically. We don't need to worry about making space for a lot of content on the Main Timeline (just be sure to leave enough frames after each keyframe to keep the label names visible). The frame labels will be used to guide the navigation ActionScript, so it is best to use consistent and logical naming conventions for the labels. Otherwise, you have to keep reminding yourself of what crazy label names you used while you are creating the scripts for various parts of your navigation interface. For this site, we made six labeled keyframe sections, about ten frames apart, on the Main Timeline:

- ✦ Label 1: preload
- ✦ Label 2: intro
- ✦ Label 3: cards
- ✦ Label 4: costumes
- ✦ Label 5: design
- ✦ Label 6: about

The last four sections are obvious, but the first two sections merit some explanation. (They are described in detail later in this chapter.) The *preload* keyframe is used to hold a looping animation that plays while the interface loads. And what about *intro?* Don't we want to skip intro as a general rule? Although we don't condone forcing users to watch long animated sequences before they can make any other choices, they do have to start from somewhere; and obviously if they are dumped straight into one of the specific categories, it may be confusing. The intro section could also be considered the Home page or the Welcome page as it introduces visitors to the site and lets them decide what section they want to look at first. You will notice in our flowchart of the site that the mainMenu is persistent — visitors can move among sections without having to return to the intro page. In fact, we have "hidden" the link back to the intro page in the logo graphic because visitors are not likely to need to get back to the intro. The link just gives the logo a secondary purpose and rewards the user for exploring.

Preparing Graphics

We have now established the placement and approximate size of core elements, and we can move on to adding visual flair. The same principles of consistency and modular production should be kept in mind when creating visual elements. Wherever possible, we've reused symbols and kept the scale, color, and style of the graphics consistent from section to section.

For this project, we had multiple sources for the graphics, and the challenge was to try to unify the look of the images and then to optimize everything for use in Flash.

Acquiring original portfolio images

Daisy had high-quality photographs of some of her designs, but only snapshots or laser-printed *copies* of snapshots for others. She also sent us actual samples of her card designs to include on the site. The challenge was to find the best way of getting all the images edited so that they would be as clean and consistent as possible.

Capturing images

The first step was to get all the assets digitized and saved as high-resolution source files. We used the following different methods for the various image sources:

✦ **High-quality photo prints:** 4-x-6-inch images scanned at actual size, millions of colors, and 100 dpi resolution. The scanned images were brought into Photoshop for cropping and saved in TIFF format with descriptive names.

Note

Because the photo prints were already larger than we needed the final images to be — and for this project, we wanted to keep our resources streamlined for Web use only — we chose to scan at 100 dpi. If you are working with smaller originals or you plan to use details of the final images, than it is important to scan at a higher resolution setting. The final image scaled to the largest size you need it should be no less than 100 dpi resolution. If there is some chance that you will be using the images in printed graphics, then it is also important to have high-resolution source files (minimum 300 dpi at final size).

✦ **Rough copies of photos:** Some of the images were provided as low-resolution ink-jet prints. Instead of trying to smooth the pixel pattern that would have been exaggerated by scanning these images, we decided to "copy" them by shooting a digital still of the printed pages. The result was a digital image that had a less noticeable ink pattern and enough resolution for retouching and scaling to the final size.

✦ **Physical card samples:** We considered scanning the cards but decided that they would have more depth if we photographed them instead. We used a white background and even lighting to get consistent color. It was also important to get good separation between the colorful cards and the clean, monochrome background to make it easier to make clipping paths later on. To keep the size and framing of each shot consistent, we used a "locked" tripod setup for the digital camera and were as precise as possible with positioning the cards in the same place for each shot. The captured images were saved on a Sony memory stick, so we were able to upload them directly to our server. These images were also brought into Photoshop for cropping and down-sampled from the original capture resolution to about 500 x 500 pixels.

Retouching images

In an ideal production environment, all the images for a given project would be delivered on Photo CD from the same source, with consistent lighting, resolution, and formatting. In reality, we're usually dealing with a motley collection of images gathered from various sources. The trick, especially when handling images that may not be as high quality as you would like, is to find a way of editing the images so that they're more consistent. If you're lucky, you'll be able to take a little bit of artistic license with the images to create whatever hybrid photo illustration looks best.

The card photos that we created in a controlled studio environment didn't require a lot of work to get them Web-ready. We used Photoshop to clean up the images, size them, and add an alpha channel. Using the fixed-ratio option for the Photoshop Cropping tool made it easy to crop the images consistently to the same size and position within the frame (see Figure 32-4).

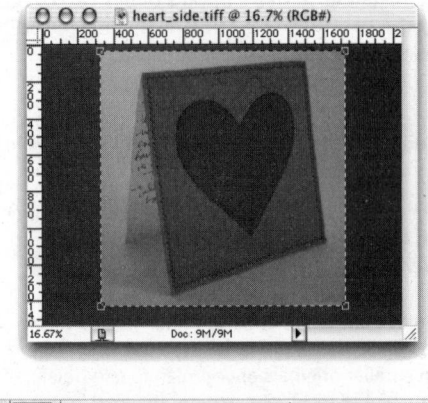

Figure 32-4: The constrained cropping feature in Photoshop ensures that the framing and resolution for each image in the series will be consistent.

The next step was to add a Levels layer to improve the contrast of the image, which was a little too dark originally. Finally, the Magnetic Lasso tool made it quick to create an accurate selection around the edges of the card. This selection was used to define a Mask for the card image, eliminating the background cleanly (see Figure 32-5).

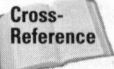

Cross-Reference A step-by-step explanation of the process for creating mask layers in Adobe Photoshop is included in Chapter 35, "Working with Raster Graphics."

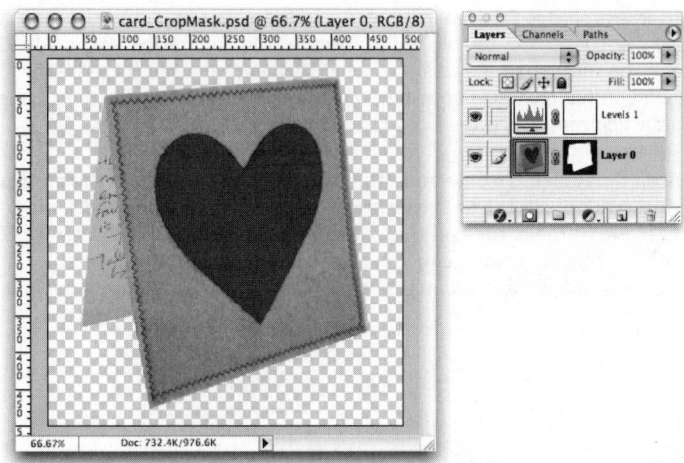

Figure 32-5: Using layers for levels adjustment and a mask to crop out the background allows *nondestructive* edits. (The original image is kept intact in its own layer.)

After saving the layered Photoshop file in PSD format (in case we need to make any changes later), the final step was to use the Save for Web command to choose the format and size of our final image (see Figure 32-6). We saved the images in PNG-24 format to preserve the alpha channel so that the mask we added would transport to Flash.

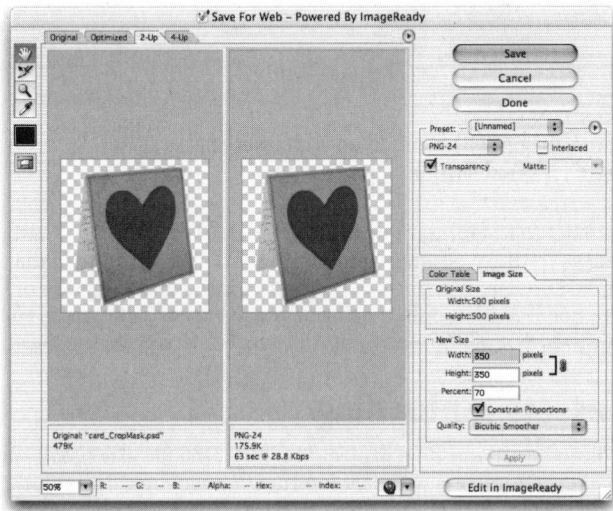

Figure 32-6: The Save for Web window in Adobe Photoshop provides a preview of the final image with the selected export settings.

Tip
Although you can always change the filenames later, it will save time and potential confusion if you use the naming convention established in the site planning for the Web-ready PNG files. It is helpful if you include an indication of what section of the site these files will be used for and a number that relates to how they will be organized on the site (for example, you might name the first card image `1_1_card.png`).

For the design photos on Daisy's site, we decided that the focus should be on the clothes, not on the backgrounds or the people in the images. Using Photoshop, we made the same basic adjustments that were made to the cards and then did some additional work to stylize the images. After some cloning, filled masking, and selective application of the Watercolor art filter, the final image has the funky illustrated quality that suits the style of Daisy's designs (see Figure 32-7).

Figure 32-7: The rough original image (left) is modified with layered effects in Photoshop for a more polished illustrated look (right).

These images were also saved in PNG-24 format to preserve the masking. The same retouching was applied to all the images for the costumes and design sections of the site to make them look as consistent as possible. The two portraits of Daisy for the about section of the site only required levels adjustment and cropping. Because these images didn't need to have any transparency, they were saved out of Photoshop in JPEG format to reduce the file sizes.

Preparing image assets for loading

If we place all the PNG files directly into our final project file (FLA), the file size bloats, making it a long and painful download even for users with fast Internet connections. The solution to this aspect of developing image-heavy sites is to structure the site so that images load individually when the visitor wants to view them. This way, the download doesn't have to happen all at once, and the user won't be forced to wait for images they may not even look at.

Flash supports dynamic loading of JPEG images. This is a terrific option for sites that have large numbers of images or images that need to change often. The only restriction is that the JPEG format doesn't support transparency, so the image backgrounds can't be masked out. For the photos in the about section that are loaded into a graphic "frame," we can use loaded JPEGs; but the other portfolio images need to be loaded with masking intact. The best way to accomplish this is to use loaded SWF files. By placing the original PNG files into individual SWFs, we can load the images dynamically with masking preserved. The other advantage of creating SWF files for each image is that we can add any other graphic details or text that may go with the individual photos. This keeps our main project file uncluttered and makes it easy to modify the image files independently for updates or changes.

The process for creating the individual SWF files is straightforward. The only thing to keep in mind is that the SWFs should all have a consistent size, and the alignment and scale of the imported photos on the Stage should also be kept as consistent as possible from one image to the next. The process we used to generate a series of SWF files is as follows:

1. To export a Flash movie (SWF file), we obviously need to make a Flash document (FLA file) first. For the card images, we created a document sized to 310 x 300 pixels. The **image** layer holds the placed bitmap image and the dashed line detail that frames the image (see Figure 32-8).

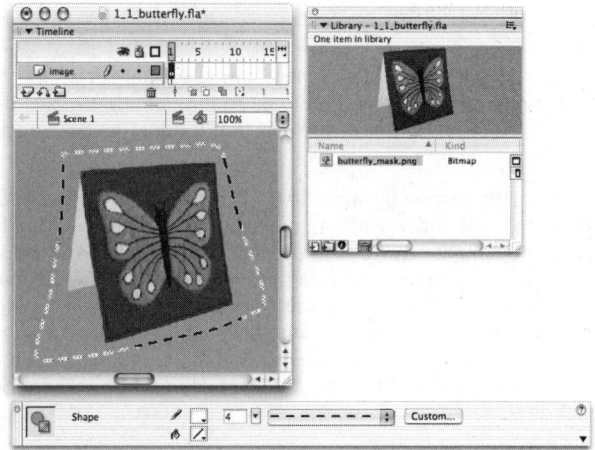

Figure 32-8: The first PNG image imported with a vector line added to frame it

2. The **caption** layer holds an instance of a custom component that will be used to enter variable text descriptions for each image. When the component is selected on the Stage, the Property inspector shows a Description field where the image caption can be entered (see Figure 32-9). The text won't be visible in the exported SWF file, but it will be attached information so that it can be loaded into our main project file (as described later in this chapter).

Figure 32-9: The description component allows a caption to be entered and stored with each image SWF file.

3. Save the Flash document (FLA) with a descriptive name, so that revisions can be made later if needed. We used the name **1_1_butterfly.fla** to indicate that this is the first image in the first portfolio category of the site and that it contains the butterfly card image.

4. To simplify the ActionScript needed for loading the images, we want to publish Flash movies (SWF files) that are identified with only the numbers that describe the section and sequence that they belong in. By default, the Flash movie will have the same name as the document (as noted in Step 3). The Flash movie can always be renamed manually after it has been published, but there is another way that you can control naming of exported files from Flash. In the Publish Settings dialog box (shown in Figure 32-10), you can modify the default name shown in the Flash (SWF) field. Now when you publish your file, the Flash movie will have the name you've specified rather than the same name as the original document.

New Feature

A very useful addition to the Publish Settings dialog box is the option to specify different locations for published files. This makes it much easier to organize files without having to manually move them into different folders after they are published. To send SWF files to a different folder than your saved FLA files, simply click the folder icon to the right of the **File** text field and browse to the folder where you want to store the published SWF files. As you can see from the files on the CD-ROM, in our portfolio site, the SWFs are saved in the top-level `cards` folder, whereas the FLA files are saved in a subfolder named `flaFiles`.

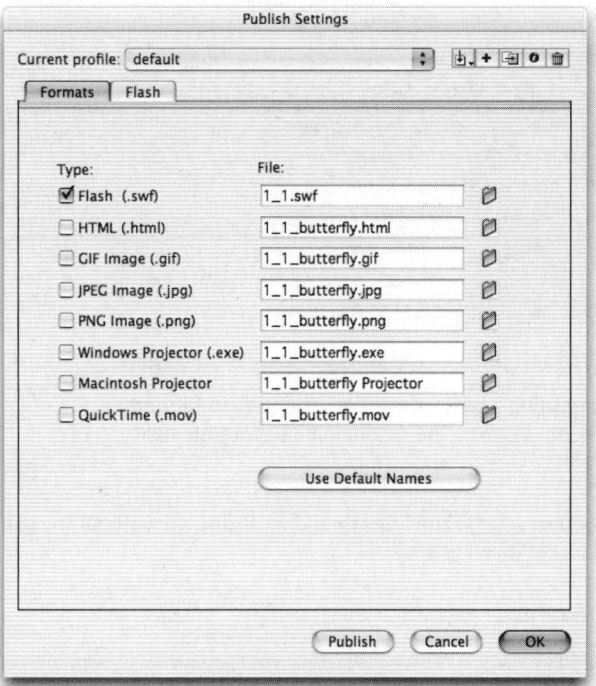

Figure 32-10: Use the Publish Settings dialog box to modify the name specified for the final Flash movie (SWF).

5. Instead of creating a new Flash document (FLA) from scratch for each image, it is much faster to work from one document with the correct size and layer structure to support any other text or graphic elements related to the images. To prepare the next image in our card series, keep the current document open and proceed to Step 6.

6. Use the Bitmap Properties dialog box to import the next image — "replacing" the first PNG with the second PNG in our series of card images. The benefit to using this method is that you will be certain that the import settings are consistent and that any sizing or alignment adjustments made with the first image will be applied to each new image. As shown in Figure 32-11, the new image that you select for import displays in the preview window of the Bitmap Properties dialog box, but the filename field still shows the name of the original PNG. To make it less confusing when you come back to the files later on, change the name of the bitmap in the text field before clicking **OK** to import the image to your Flash file.

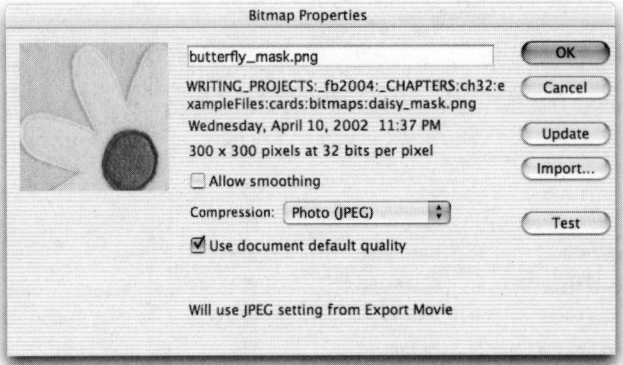

Figure 32-11: Importing a new image from the Bitmap Properties dialog box allows you to swap the original image with the next image in the series.

7. The new image will now be in the Library and on the Stage, with all the same attributes as the first card image (see Figure 32-12).

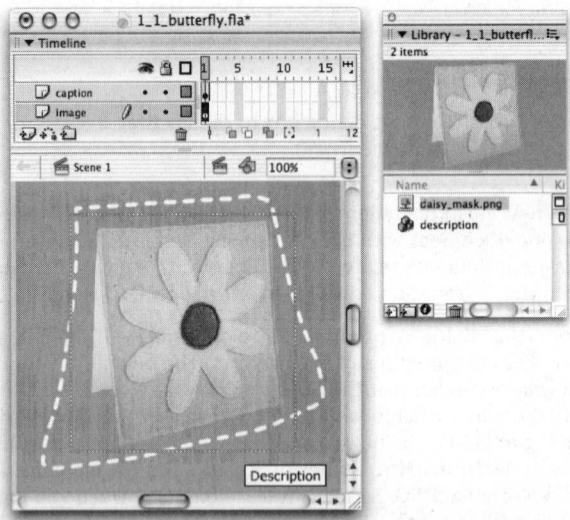

Figure 32-12: The new image replaces the original bitmap in the Library and appears in your layout at the same scale and position as the original image.

8. Select the description component instance on the **caption** layer and modify the caption text to fit the new image.

9. Be cautious when saving the FLA file. If you accidentally use a direct save, the file you saved with the first image will be overwritten. Use **Save As** and assign a new name to the file that indicates its place in the sequence (**1_2_daisy.fla**).

10. Before publishing the Flash movie (SWF), be sure to change the name specified in the **Flash** tab of the Publish Settings dialog box.

And that's it! Repeat Steps 6 through 10 for each of the images in the card sequence. If all of your image assets have the same aspect ratio, you can continue to use the same document size. In this portfolio, the design and costume images are much taller than the card images, so we changed the document size to 310x425 before starting to import the PNG images for those sections. You'll also notice that the dashed line was consistent on each card image, but for the designs and costumes, we added a unique outline to fit each image. To ensure that the URLs used to locate the images for loading into the main project file will be logical, the final SWF files are placed in named category folders inside the main site folder. The FLA files should be archived in case you need to make changes in the future, but you don't need them in the main site folder.

Formatting logo graphics and other vector art

If you're creating all your artwork directly in Flash, then you don't need to worry about file compatibility and color consistency. However, it's common to receive graphic art created in other applications, and the best method for translating these files to Flash depends on the original format and the content of the file.

 **Cross-Reference** Some of the most common workflows for integrating vector artwork in other formats with Flash projects are described in Chapter 36, "Working with Vector Graphics."

Using logo art created in Illustrator

For this project, the logo was originally designed as vector artwork in Adobe Illustrator (see Figure 32-13).

Figure 32-13: The original logo in Adobe Illustrator with paths describing the outlined shapes on layers

The easiest way to get the vector artwork into Flash with all the color and outlines intact is to use the new direct import feature of Flash MX 2004. When the AI file is imported to the Flash authoring environment, it appears as a group of various vector shapes with the original Illustrator layers preserved (see Figure 32-14).

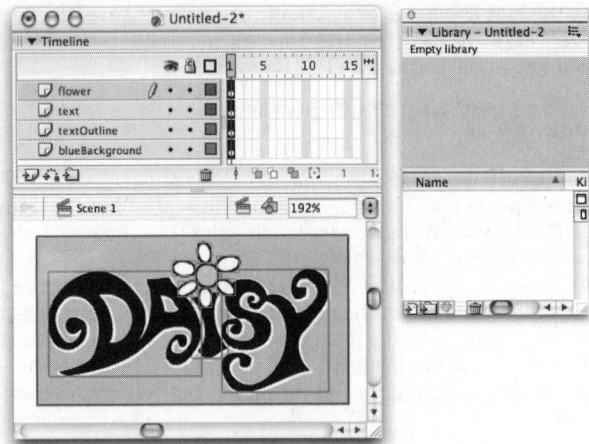

Figure 32-14: The imported AI file comes into Flash as grouped shapes with the original layer structure preserved.

To optimize the file for use in our project, the groups are reorganized and converted into logical graphic symbols that can be nested inside animated Movie Clips and Button symbols (see Figure 32-15).

Figure 32-15: The basic shapes are converted into graphic symbols used to build other animated elements.

Giving these symbols descriptive names and sorting them into a single labeled folder in the Library makes it easy to transfer them into other project files when they're needed. Note that all the animation is contained on symbol timelines rather than on the Main Timeline. Also, if you open the **Logo_final.fla** (in the ch32/sourceImageSamples/logo folder on the CD-ROM,) you can see that the animated symbols in the Library are all created by nesting and reusing other symbols wherever possible.

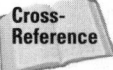

Cross-Reference For a review of how to convert primitive shapes into symbols for optimized Flash files, refer to Chapter 6, "Symbols, Instances, and the Library."

Creating backgrounds

To make the site lively and fun, we decided to give each section of the site a unique background color. The colors for the backgrounds were chosen to complement colors that Daisy uses in her designs. However, in order to make them work with different artwork and to keep them from overpowering the loaded images, we used slightly muted tones.

To create a custom palette, you can use the Eyedropper tool to sample colors from images and then use the Color Mixer panel to modify the colors as needed. To change the background color in different sections of our site, we made a white filled rectangle sized to match our document (600 x 450 pixels) and saved it as a graphic symbol. Instances of this graphic symbol can then be reused and tinted using the Color Effects settings available in the Property inspector to change the "background" color for different sections of the site.

Note As described later in this chapter, our final solution uses ActionScript to control a single background "tile" so that color transitions can be animated between different site sections dynamically.

Because we also wanted to add some texture to the backgrounds and to make the designs as flexible and easy-to-update as possible, we created separate graphic symbols and drew patterns in white. This allowed us to apply the textures as alpha overlays on any background color and to scale them as needed. Figure 32-16 shows one of the individual texture patterns and an instance of the Graphic symbol placed onto the background color with alpha and scaling applied.

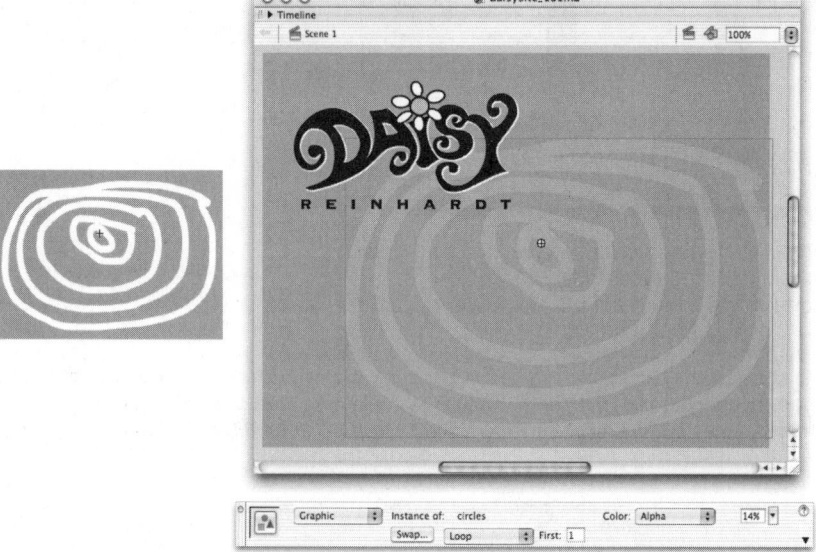

Figure 32-16: Graphic symbols in a neutral color (left) can be layered over different background colors and modified with Color Effects and scaling to suit the layout (right).

Cross-Reference For a review of working with the color tools and panels, refer to Chapter 7, "Applying Color." For a review of using Color Effects on symbol instances, refer to Chapter 9, "Modifying Graphics."

Using symbols to organize graphic elements

The remaining vector artwork, for interface elements and decorative graphics are created with the Flash drawing tools and organized in symbol timelines. Even simple elements, such as the "photo frame" used in the *about* section of the Web site to frame loaded JPEG images, are built in layers to keep all the graphics as easy to modify as possible (see Figure 32-17). To keep the file structure manageable, elements that work together should also be nested inside symbols rather than stacked or grouped on the Main Timeline in the master project file. For example, the *JpegFrame* Graphic symbol has the *JpegHolder* Movie Clip used as the target for loaded JPEGs nested under the frame art and above the white mat art.

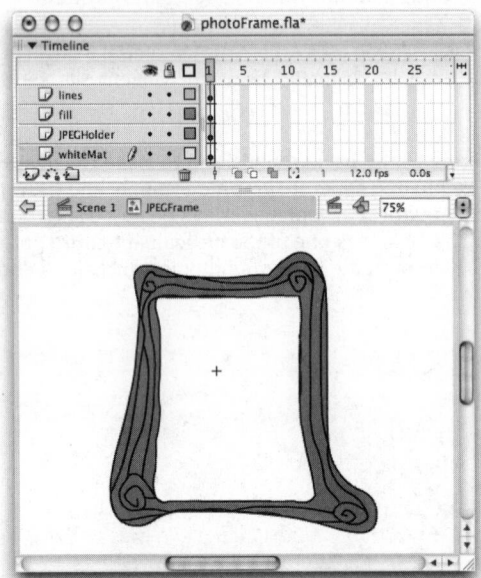

Figure 32-17: Nesting artwork and related elements on symbol timelines in individual FLA files keeps files modular and manageable.

On the CD-ROM To see how the elements described in this section are structured, you can look at the Flash documents (FLA files) for the individual examples found in the `ch32/site/prototype` folder in the `ch32` folder of the *Macromedia Flash MX 2004 Bible* CD-ROM.

Putting It All Together

While one designer is working on preparing the graphic elements, the coder on your team can be developing scripts for animation or other features of the site that will be controlled with ActionScript. As long as you're both working from the same plan, you should be able to make progress independently until it's time to start putting everything together. The first step toward assembling your project is usually to drop in any static graphic elements or persistent navigation elements that do not require scripting. The next step is to add the simple scripting needed to control the Main Timeline. When these elements are in place, start putting in placeholders for the dynamic content. This should be a fairly quick and painless process if you've managed to stick to your original "map" of the various elements.

To see the various stages of the site as it is put together, refer to the incrementally numbered Flash documents in the **site** folder in the ch32 folder of the *Macromedia Flash MX Bible* CD-ROM. Starting with daisySite_100.fla and finishing with daisySite_107.fla, you can scrub through the timelines and check out the symbols stored in the Library for each document to see what elements are added as we work toward the finished site.

In our example files, text on menu or logo elements has been broken apart to avoid layout problems that might be caused by font substitution. In production files, you should leave text editable in most cases until the very final stage of design, unless you are concerned about font issues that might be caused by opening FLA files on different workstations. Ideally, team production environments should include a centralized font source, such as a project fonts folder on a server that everyone can access. Extensis Suitcase Server is a good option for centralized font management, even in a cross-platform environment.

Placing static elements and text

We start assembling the site by opening up daisySite_100.fla (the file described earlier that has the basic folder and Timeline labels in place). The first elements that we add to the project file are as follows:

✦ **Logo:** The first element to add is the animated symbol of the logo (logoAnimMC). As you can see in Logo_final.fla, the Timeline of the animated symbol is set up with the final sized static logo on frame 1 before the logo animation starts on frame 2. This allows us to use the same symbol instance in all the site sections (instead of using one animated symbol for the intro and another static symbol for the other sections of the site). There are two ways that you can move the logo from the source file (Logo_final.fla) to the project file (daisySite_100.fla):

  • Open both files and copy and paste the symbol instance of logoAnimMC onto the Stage in the **intro** keyframe of the **logo** layer of daisySite_100.fla.

  • Open daisySite_100.fla and use the File ➪ Import ➪ Open External Library command to open only the Library of Logo_final.fla. Drag the folder of logo symbols from the source library into the project library (daisySite_100.fla) before placing logoAnimMC onto the Stage in the **intro** keyframe of the **logo** layer.

✦ **Background Textures:** The Graphic symbols for the various background patterns are placed into their respective **category keyframes** on the **bgTextures** layer. The Graphic symbol instances are each assigned an **alpha** value of **15** in the Property inspector so that they blend better with the background.

Tip

We could have used an alpha fill to create the original background patterns, but using a solid fill and then using Color Effect to change the alpha value of the symbol instances gives us more options. It is easier to preview how different alpha values look on the Stage and to quickly make adjustments in the Property inspector than to go back inside each symbol and modify the alpha value of the original fill color.

✦ **Static Text:** The text for the **intro** and the **about** sections of the site is entered in static text fields. To keep track of these elements, we converted them to Graphic symbols. (Now they're stored in the Library.) An instance of the relevant text symbol is placed on the **caption** layer of the **intro** keyframe and the **about** keyframe, respectively. The intro text is actually placed on a new keyframe that is a few frames ahead of the keyframe that marks the start of the intro section. This gives the logo animation time to start before the intro text pops up on screen.

The intro text symbol includes the decorative vector elements that dress up that text. Again, the goal is to make the project file easy to navigate and edit without having to dig through the items on the Stage in each area of the Timeline.

Note

Because Robert prefers to work in Windows XP for coding and Snow prefers to work in Mac OS X for design, the font display is sometimes inconsistent when Rob opens the files. However, Rob doesn't have to worry about editing the layout, so he just views the file with a default substitute font while adding code. The final files are saved and published from the OS X machine.

✦ **JPEG Frame:** As discussed earlier, we will not be using the same SWF image-loading convention for the photos in the **about** section of the site. For this section, we will be loading JPEG files directly into an empty Movie Clip. To add a bit of polish to the JPEGs (that will load with a flat white border,) the empty Movie Clip is nested inside a Movie Clip that contains vector artwork of a photo frame. This element was created and saved in a separate FLA file (photoFrame.fla). An instance of the final **JpegFrame** Movie Clip is placed on the **imageMC** layer of the **about** keyframe. To fit the layout, the instance is scaled down to 50 percent of the original symbol size. Option+drag (Alt+drag) the instance to create a second frame with the same scaling and position it in the layout.

To see the project file after these items are added, open **daisySite_101.fla** from the site folder on the CD-ROM. (Figure 32-18 shows a sample frame from the site at this stage.)

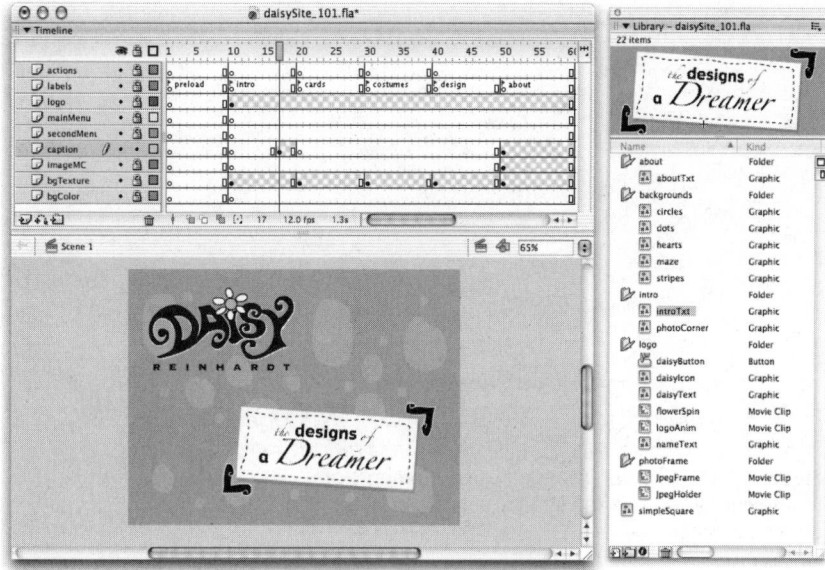

Figure 32-18: The project file, with the first graphic elements added

Basic Timeline navigation

Although some of the navigation needs to be finalized after the placeholders for dynamic content have been added, we can start building the navigation that allows visitors to view each category that we have labeled on the Main Timeline.

✦ **mainMenuMC:** The text menu that is persistent throughout the site can be prebuilt in a separate Flash document. (See **mainMenu.fla** in the ch32/site/prototype folder on the CD-ROM.) The individual Button symbol instances are contained in a Movie Clip symbol and the actual text that appears in the button is converted into Graphic symbols so that any changes to the text style will propagate to each frame of the Button symbol Timeline automatically. The nested file structure makes it easy to move or scale the menu as a single element while still allowing quick edits to the contents of each button at any time. (The hierarchy of menu elements is visible in the location label of the Document window shown in Figure 32-19.)

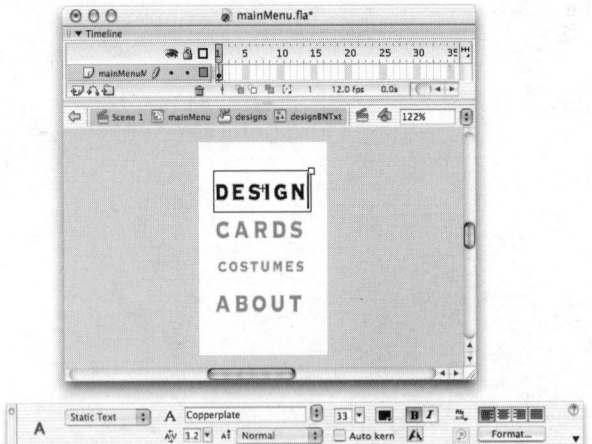

Figure 32-19: Clicking into the nested elements of
mainMenuMC reveals the structure in the location label
above the Stage.

Tip

Because we're using text as the only visible content of our buttons, it is important to remember to set the Hit state of the button as a solid filled rectangle, rather than using the Graphic symbol of the text box. Often times we need a basic filled rectangle to define elements of the site, such as invisible buttons, hit states, or masks. Instead of making a new shape each time you need a rectangle, it's better to create a single Graphic symbol of a rectangle that can be reused wherever it's needed. In this project, a black filled rectangle is stored in the Library as a Graphic symbol named "basicSquare."

To set up the buttons for navigating to the different site sections, make sure to include the following steps:

1. Place an instance of the mainMenuMC Movie Clip onto the **intro** keyframe of the **mainMenu** layer of the project file. Because the menu is consistent for all sections of the site, you don't need to make keyframes anywhere after the intro keyframe on the mainMenu layer.

2. Modify the ActionScript for each Button instance in the menu to correctly target the corresponding category frame label with a goto action, composed as follows:

```
on (release){
  _root.gotoAndStop("cards");
}
```

✦ **secondMenu:** At this stage of the project, we also added the Button instances of **arrowBN** and aligned them in the layout on the keyframes for each image category in the **menuSecond** layer. The rollOver and Down animation for the button is working now, but the ActionScript needed to control the loaded images will be added later.

✦ **Contact button:** A simple text button (**contactBN**) is added to the **about** keyframe on the **menuSecond** layer. The scripting needed to make this button launch an email window will be added later.

To see the project file after these navigation elements are added, open `daisySite_102.fla` on the CD-ROM. (Figure 32-20 shows a sample frame from the site at this stage.)

Figure 32-20: The project file, with the navigation elements added

Load functions and intro animation

Although there aren't any images in the Main Timeline (that is, Scene 1) of our project, the graphic interface may still take a bit of time to load on a slow connection, so we have left room at the beginning of the Timeline for a preloader (after the interface is loaded, the preloader will not appear again if the visitor returns to the intro section of the site). This same preloader is reused throughout the site, whenever a new asset is loaded into an empty Movie Clip.

Cross-Reference For a review of building and using preloaders, refer to Chapter 28, "Sharing and Loading Assets."

The animation for the preloader (shown in Figure 32-21) was organized in a separate document (`loader_101.fla`). The only thing unique about the preloader used in this example is that the percent loaded is equated with a frame on the animation Timeline, rather than being equated with an increase in the X scale of a standard loader bar. The daisy graphic has ten petals and each petal represents 10 percent of the total site size. As the site loads, the petals are added until, at 100 percent, all ten are in place.

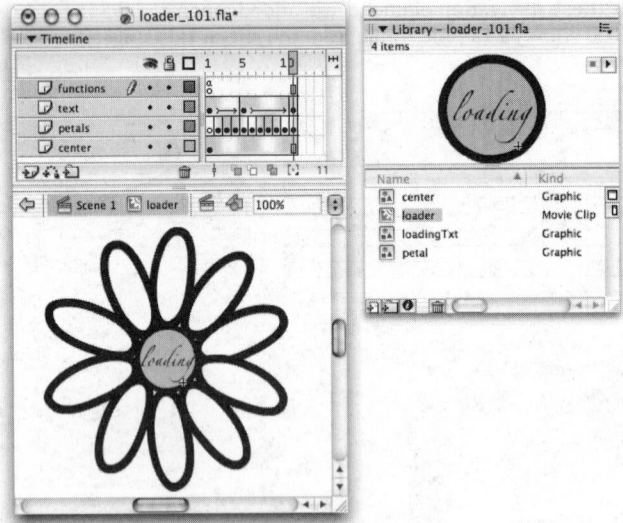

Figure 32-21: The Movie Clip Timeline for the loader animation

On the CD-ROM

We don't include the ActionScript as part of our discussion in this section. However, if you want to see the Timeline structure and code used for the loader, open `loader_101.fla` from the `ch32/site/prototype` folder and look at the ActionScript on the first frame of the Main Timeline and also on the first frame of the loader Movie Clip Timeline.

The steps taken to integrate the loader with our main project file are as follows:

1. Create a new layer titled **functions** at the top of the layer stack (above the **actions** layer,) on the Main Timeline of `daisySite_102.fla`.

2. Add the ActionScript on the first keyframe of the **functions** layer that will monitor loading and control the loader animation. Because we aren't describing in detail how the code is structured in this example, you can autoload the preauthored ActionScript by adding just one line of code to the keyframe:

```
#include "scripts/addLoader.as"
```

Inside of this script file is an ActionScript function named `addLoader()`. When this function is executed, the code creates a Movie Clip named `holder` to hold the loaded Flash movies. The function also grabs a Movie Clip symbol named `loader` from the Library and places it on the movie's Stage — as the movie runs in the Flash Player. The `addLoader()` function tells the new `loader` instance which asset download it is monitoring. For this section, it will monitor the progress of the Main Timeline (`_root`), in the master movie (SWF file).

On the CD-ROM

The ActionScript is not printed here, but it is included on the CD-ROM for you to review or reuse. You will find the code in the **scripts** folder.

3. Now you can add the actual loader Movie Clip. Use the File ⇨ Import ⇨ Open External Library command (Shift+Ctrl+O or Shift+⌘+O) to open the Library for loader_101.fla and drag the **loader** Movie Clip into the main Library. You will notice that the Graphic symbols used in the Movie Clip will be transferred also. To keep the Library organized, we create a new folder named **preloader** and store all the loader assets together.

4. Add the following actions on the first keyframe of the **actions** layer:

```
addLoader("main", _root, {x: 300, y: 225});
stop();
```

The next step is to add the ActionScript that will start the logo animation when the intro loads. Remember that we currently have a stop action on the first frame of the logoAnim Movie Clip, so the logo works as a static graphic throughout the site.

1. Select the instance of **logoAnim** on the first keyframe of the **logo** layer and give it an instance name of logoAnim in the Property inspector.

2. Double-click the symbol instance to access the Movie Clip Timeline and remove the stop(); action from the first keyframe of the actions layer.

3. Go back to the Main Timeline (that is, Scene 1). On frame **10** of the **actions** layer (above the first keyframe for **intro**), add the following ActionScript to trigger the logoAnim Movie Clip to play.

```
logoAnim.gotoAndPlay(2);
stop();
```

To see the project file after these navigation elements are added, open daisySite_103.fla on the CD-ROM. Because the changes we've made are not visible on the Stage unless the file is viewed in the Test Movie environment, Figure 32-22 shows the changes visible in the Timeline window and in the Library.

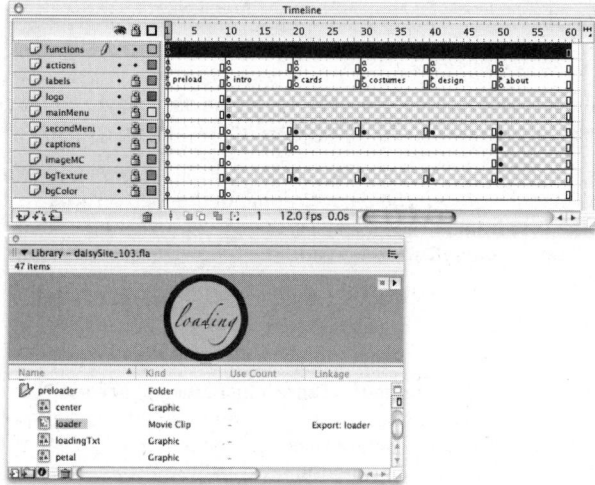

Figure 32-22: The modified Main Timeline and new assets added to the Library in daisySite_103.fla

Navigation for loaded assets

The next step is to add the Dynamic text field to hold the image captions attached to the loaded SWF images. A function is called that will enable switching of loaded images. Next, actions on the secondMenu buttons and the actions layer of the Main Timeline are edited to control navigation of the image sequences. We also set up a function to clear the Stage so that images don't accidentally overlap when the visitor moves from section to section. We will walk through the steps for the first portfolio section on the Main Timeline, marked by the keyframe label "cards."

Note You may have noticed earlier that the order of the category keyframe labels doesn't match the order of the categories in the main menu list — design is the last portfolio keyframe label, but it's the first menu item — but we didn't! Aside from proving that even when you're really trying to be organized, little things can still go wrong, this anomaly illustrates clearly that the exact order of sections on the Main Timeline doesn't control how visitors will actually navigate through the site. Because the playback of the Main Timeline is completely subordinate to the actions on our buttons, the viewer will never know how the Timeline is really organized. As long as all the ActionScript correctly references keyframe labels and Movie Clip instance names, the movie should function smoothly. The main reason to try and match up the order of the Timeline with the navigation menu is to make it easier to find our way around while editing the project file (FLA).

Once you've followed these steps, you can repeat the same edits on the other two portfolio sections ("costumes" and "design").

1. **Create a caption field:** Add a Dynamic text field on the first keyframe of the **cards** section (frame 20) on the **caption** layer and give it an instance name of `caption` in the Property inspector (see Figure 32-23).

2. **Bring in ActionScript for loading images:** In the first keyframe of the **functions** layer, add the following code to autoload the preauthored ActionScript (provided in the scripts folder on the CD-ROM):

```
#include "scripts/switchImage.as"
```

This `#include` directive loads and "stores" the code in the functions layer so that it can be called by the navigation elements when they need to load an image SWF.

3. **Note:** An update was also made to the ActionScript on the button nested inside the **logoAnim** Movie Clip, so that clicking on the daisy graphic of the logo returns visitors to the intro section. On the first frame of the **daisy** layer on the Movie Clip Timeline of **logoAnim**, select the instance of **daisyButton** and add the following ActionScript:

```
on (release) {
  _root.gotoAndStop("intro")
}
```

4. **Edit secondMenu:** In the cards section, name the Button instances of **arrowBN** on the **secondMenu** layer as `nextButton` (right-pointing arrow) and `prevButton` (left-pointing arrow), respectively. Next, add actions to each of these Button instances to call the relevant image load functions (imported to the function layer in Step 2).

On the `prevButton` instance add:

```
on(release){
  prevImage();
}
```

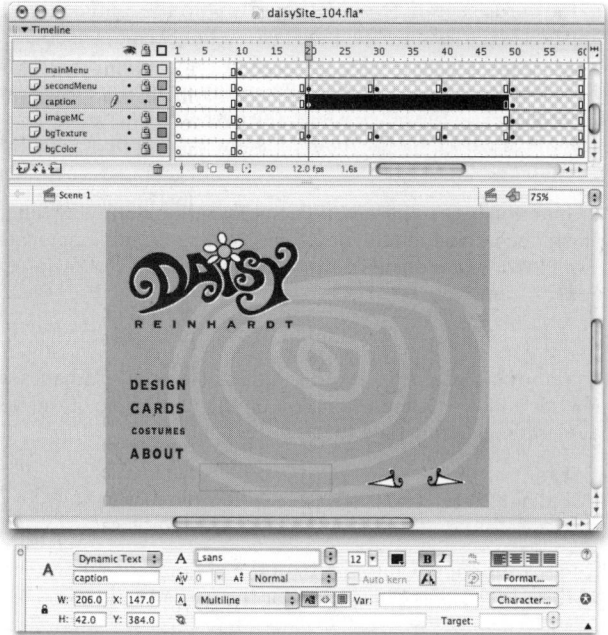

Figure 32-23: The settings in the Property inspector for the caption text field that will display the text variables attached to the loaded image SWFs

On the `nextButton` instance add:

```
on(release){
  nextImage();
}
```

5. **Define the cards section with code:** Add the following Actions to frame **20** of the **actions** layer to configure the cards section of the site. Note that the ⟲ should not appear in your actual code—it indicates a continuation of the same line of code:

```
_global.sectionName = "cards";
_global.sectionNum = 1;
_global.currentImage = 1;
_global.imageLimit = 4;
_global.holderPos = {x: 260, y: 75};
_global.loaderPos = {x: 445, y: 215};
addLoader(sectionName, currentImage, ⟲
  {x: loaderPos.x, y: loaderPos.y});
checkButtons();
stop();
```

This code sets up the cards section to work properly with the addLoader() function you added previously. The _global object in Flash ActionScript is used to store the current section's configuration, specifying its number (sectionNum), the starting image in the SWF sequence (currentImage), how many images are in the sequence (imageLimit), the position on the Stage where the SWF files will load (holderPos), and the position on the Stage where the loader instance will appear (loaderPos) while the SWF files are loading.

The addLoader() function is then passed this configuration data. The function creates a holder instance into which the first SWF file for this section, located in cards/1_1.swf, will load. The filename path is formed with the following expression inside the addLoader() function:

```
var file = section+"/"+sectionNum+"_"+currentImage+".swf";
```

6. **Add a function to remove content:** To avoid accidental overlap of images when a visitor moves to a new section, we define a function on the first frame of the **functions** layer that can be referenced at any time to clear the Stage:

```
function clearStage(){
  masterHolder.holder.removeMovieClip();
}
```

7. **Execute** clearStage() **function:** On frame 10 of the **actions** layer, add the following code to "activate" the clearStage() function for the cards section:

```
clearStage();
```

The project file with these changes is saved as daisySite_104.fla, and it is included on the CD-ROM for you to review.

Duplicating the functionality

Now that you have followed the step-by-step changes that were needed to develop the cards section of the site, you can use **daisySite_105.fla** (on the CD-ROM) as a guide to help you duplicate the same functionality on the other two portfolio sections of the site as follows:

1. Name the arrowBN instances (prevButton and nextButton) in the **secondMenu** layer for the **costumes** and **design** sections of the site.

We included a gap of four empty frames between each section's buttons to make sure that instances would be "refreshed" when the Timeline jumps to the new frame. In our tests, we found that Button instances from previous sections show up in new sections, overwriting the position of the placed instances there. By inserting empty keyframes between the instances, each section "clears" the old instances before the new ones load.

2. Add actions to all the buttons in the **secondMenu** layer for each section. Copy and paste the actions from the buttons in the **cards** section to make the work go faster and to reduce the margin of error (typing can be dangerous, especially when you get tired!).

3. Add actions to the **actions** layer for each section. Copy and paste the code used for cards, but customize the code where needed to fit each section (section names, section numbers, and so on).

And that completes the steps needed to create a functional navigation system for the portfolio images. Figure 32-24 shows a frame of the Flash movie as it should appear in the Test Movie environment with the loaded images.

Figure 32-24: Dynamically loaded portfolio images will be visible only in the published SWF of the main project movie (or in the Test Movie environment).

Setting up placeholders for loaded JPEGs

Remember those photo frames that we placed in the about section of the site? It's finally time to get them ready to load the JPEG images dynamically.

1. Name the instances of the JpegFrame symbol on the **imageMC** layer in the **about** section to image_1 (top) and image_2 (bottom,) respectively, in the Property inspector.

2. In the first keyframe of the **actions** layer for the **about** section (frame 50), add the ActionScript to load the JPEG images:

```
image_1.holder.loadMovie("about/4_1.jpg");
image_2.holder.loadMovie("about/4_2.jpg");
clearStage();
```

Note The clearStage() action is only necessary for the **intro** and **about** sections because the holder instance is automatically replaced with new content in the other sections.

While we're working on the about section, we also add a getURL action to the **contact** Button symbol instance on the **menuSecond** layer:

```
on(release){
   getURL("mailto:daisy@daisyReinhardt.com");
}
```

After these changes are made, the project file is saved as **daisySite_105.fla**. Figure 32-25 shows how the about section of the published SWF will appear with the dynamically loaded JPEG images.

Figure 32-25: JPEG images loaded into the frames on the about section of the main movie (SWF)

ActionScript for final functionality

Now that the basic asset loading is in place, we can move on to doing something about that dull gray background. Rather than placing static filled rectangles in each section (which would change abruptly), we're going to use ActionScript to control the color of a background color tile. Using the Color object in ActionScript, we can change the color of a dynamically added rectangle graphic, and gradually fade the color using the _alpha property of the Movie Clip object.

On the CD-ROM

To see how this effect works on the site, you can look at the Flash movie for the final project file (daisySite_107.swf), saved in the site folder of the ch32 folder on the CD-ROM.

Adding actions to change the background color

To give you a "shortcut" for developing the more complex features of this project, we have included some custom components that you can reuse in other projects too. The first component controls the color changes and is saved in a document titled bgFader_100.fla (in the prototypes folder). This fade component is nested inside of another symbol named bgTile.

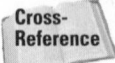

Cross-Reference

The fade component is described in more detail in Chapter 20, "Making Your First Flash MX 2004 Project."

To integrate the component with our current project, follow these steps:

1. With daisySite_105.fla active, open bgFader_100.fla as a Library and drag a copy of the **bgTile** Movie Clip symbol into the main document Library. When all the new assets are transferred, move them into the **background** folder in the main Library.

2. Rename the **bgColor** layer to **bgFader**.

3. Create an empty Movie Clip by choosing Insert ⇨ New Symbol. In the Create New Symbol dialog box, name the symbol **emptyMC**, choose the Movie Clip behavior, and click **OK**.

4. Return to the Main Timeline. In frame **10** of the **bgFader** layer, place an instance of the emptyMC symbol in the top-left corner of the Stage (0,0). (You may need to unlock the layer.) Name the placed instance `bgFader` in the Property inspector.

5. To bring in the function that will change the color of the background tile, add the following code to the first keyframe of the **functions** layer:

```
#include "scripts/changeColor.as"
```

6. In the **actions** layer, add the following code to each category section to define the colors:

For intro:

```
changeColor("purple",0x9999CC);
```

For cards:

```
changeColor("blue",0x669999);
```

For costumes:

```
changeColor("pink",0xCC9999);
```

For design:

```
changeColor("green",0x669966);
```

For about:

```
changeColor("khaki",0x999966);
```

Adding a scale effect to loaded images

Now that the background colors are changing more subtly, we need to make the transition from one loaded image to another a bit more polished. A `setScale.as` script is included in the scripts folder if you want to deconstruct how it was coded. Otherwise, just enjoy using the script wherever you want something to scale dynamically. To integrate the preauthored script with our current project file, follow the same steps used to call functions in previous steps:

1. On the first keyframe of the **functions** layer add the following code:

```
#include "scripts/setScale.as"
```

The `setScale()` function described in this .as file is already incorporated into the functions defined in the `switchImage.as` script file. You can cross-reference the functions in the script files to see how the loaded Flash movie is dynamically scaled.

2. Save the Flash document, and test it (Ctrl+Enter or ⌘+Return). Go into any section that loads external Flash movies (such as **cards**). When you click the **next** button, the current image will scale down and the next image will scale up.

Fixing details for final Flash movie

There are a few last-minute things that need to be taken care of before the Flash movie (SWF file) is published for the final project.

✦ Adjust the position of the `holder` instance for each section in the main document. The holder instance is targeted by the `addLoader()` function to display the loaded SWF files. You can adjust the position of the `holder` instance in the following line of code, found in each section's keyframe on the **actions** layer:

```
_global.holderPos = {x: 260, y: 13};
```

Simply change the X and Y numeric values to indicate the position of the top-left corner of the loaded assets for each section. With this method, it is possible to change the position for the assets for each section — but not for the individual images in a series. If any of the images in a series require unique adjustment, you must open the Flash document that contains the imported PNG file and change the alignment or size of the bitmap on the Stage before republishing a new movie (SWF) to load into the Empty Movie Clip in the main project file (FLA). This can be a slightly tedious process of trial and error as you try to get the images exactly right — you will have to keep publishing SWF files to test how the images align in the project layout.

✦ Adjust the position of the `loader` instance for each section in the main document. The same notes apply from the previous point. To change the position of the loader instance in each section, adjust the following line of code found in each section's keyframe on the **actions** layer:

```
_global.loaderPos = {x: 445, y: 215};
```

✦ Make any last-minute changes to the graphics or effects used in the movie. For example, we decided that we wanted the introTxt graphic in the intro section to only display after the `logoAnim` instance was finished playing. So, we selected the introTxt graphic on the Stage, switched the instance's behavior to a Movie Clip, and named it `introTxt` in the Property inspector. We then added the following code to the actions layer keyframe for the intro section:

```
introTxt._visible = false;
```

This code turns off the visibility of the `introTxt` instance. Then we went inside of the logoAnim symbol and inserted this action on its last keyframe:

```
_root.introTxt._visible = true;
```

This code shows the `introTxt` instance when the animation finishes.

✦ The other changes you will notice in our final version of the site layout are in the **about** section. We decided to make one of the photo frames (and the loaded JPEG) larger and we added an instance of the **arrow** Graphic symbol to point out the **contact** button text.

To modify the size of the photo frame Movie Clip, select the `image_1` instance of JpegFrame and change the scale in the Transform panel from 50 percent to 60 percent size. In the **about** keyframe of the **actions** layer, you will see the code added to modify the alignment and scale of the loaded JPEG image so that it will align correctly with the new larger frame.

✦ Publish an index.html file for your main Flash document. Use the Publish Settings to specify the name of the .html file, and use the HTML tab to adjust the parameters for the `<EMBED>` and `<OBJECT>` tags that will be included in the published .html file.

Tip

You may need to publish a different filename for the main HTML document for your particular Web server. For example, Microsoft IIS servers commonly use default.htm as the primary document in a Web server directory.

✦ Publish a final Flash movie for the main document. We usually use a generic name such as `main.swf` for the final "master" movie. Again, use the Publish Settings to specify this name.

Note

In the final Flash document (`daisySite_final.fla`) available on the CD-ROM, we converted any graphic text to outlines by using the Break apart command. In this way, you can see the typeface we're using for the document. However, you should not break apart the text in your own Flash documents. Presumably, you'll always have access to the fonts you're using throughout the project.

Other than sorting out the files you will need to upload to the server, you should be home free. We hope that you're happy with your project and feel confident that you can reuse some of what you've learned on the next project you decide to tackle.

On the CD-ROM

As we've mentioned throughout this chapter, all the files you will need in order to deconstruct the project and reuse the ActionScript or the components are included in the `ch32` folder on the CD-ROM. Although the logo graphic and some of the source portfolio images are also included, we ask that you please respect the copyright on those elements of the project.

Uploading the final files to the Web server

After you've made any last-minute changes to the final document, you're ready to transfer the files to your site's Web server. Using Macromedia Dreamweaver MX 2004 or your preferred FTP client, upload the following files to the Web server:

✦ index.html (or equivalent)

✦ main.swf (the master movie file)

✦ A subfolder named **about**, containing all of the numbered JPEG images

✦ A subfolder named **cards**, containing all the numbered SWF files

✦ A subfolder named **costumes**, containing all the numbered SWF files

✦ A subfolder named **design**, containing all the numbered SWF files

Note

You do not need to upload the .as script files because they're automatically included with the main movie (SWF file) when you publish it.

When you're finished uploading the files, test the site in a Web browser. Make sure the files load properly. ***Remember:*** UNIX servers are case-sensitive with filenames, so be certain to specify the same case in your folder and filenames that you used in your ActionScript code.

 You can also decide to add further functionality to the site by adding a Flash Player detection mechanism to the first HTML document that loads for your site. You can learn more about detection in Chapter 22, "Integrating Flash Content with Web pages."

 We'd like to know what you think about this chapter. Visit `www.flashsupport.com/feedback` to fill out an online form with your comments.

Summary

✦ The principles of extensible design can be applied to any project to reduce redundant production work as the content grows or changes.

✦ Site maps, technical specification sheets, and other design planning documents are useful tools for guiding development on projects of all sizes.

✦ Building a site from a series of smaller pieces that are brought together with ActionScript facilitates collaboration.

✦ Leveraging the strongest skill sets of different members of a production team and reducing redundant effort will enhance the work and make it faster to create.

✦ Centralizing assets for dynamic loading and decentralizing the structure of your site by breaking it down into smaller Flash documents (FLA files) makes it easier to delegate production tasks while maintaining design consistency.

✦ Custom components are a great way for developers to strategically "deploy" ActionScript in a format that will be manageable for less code-fluent designers (or clients who may want to take on more control of their own sites).

✦ Components are also a flexible way for coders to repurpose custom ActionScript behaviors. Components are portable and easy to reuse, minimizing the need to rearchitect solutions that may be useful in more than one project.

✦   ✦   ✦

Creating a Game in Flash

Creating a game requires much more than programming. It is a combination of many skills — game design, interaction design, visual and sound design, and scripting — that brings it all together. These skills also represent the different phases of game design and are covered in this chapter. You must devote attention to all these aspects of design to produce a successful game.

To illustrate the different aspects of game design, we deconstruct a simple game, the universally known Hangman.

On the CD-ROM

Before reading through this chapter, copy the `hangman.fla` and the `hangman.swf` files from the `ch33` folder of the CD-ROM onto your hard drive. Double-click the SWF file to play the game and become acquainted with our project. Now, open the `hangman.fla` file and look at the two sections (or frame labels) on the Main Timeline. The second frame label, game, creates the game itself and is addressed first. The first label, `init`, collects and displays the user's personal information and is covered last.

The Game Plan: Four Phases of Game Design

Game development includes the four phases introduced earlier. The following sections discuss those phases in detail.

Note

Many thanks to Jonathan Brzyski for contributing his illustrations to the Flash movie used in this chapter. You can learn more about Jonathan at `www.humanface.com/brzyski`. This edition of the Macromedia Flash MX 2004 Bible uses a modified version of the original `hangman.fla` file created by Veronique Brossier, as discussed in the Macromedia Flash MX Bible (Wiley, 2002).

Game design

Designing a game is creating a fantasy world, a story and characters with defined roles and goals. It establishes a structure with a clearly defined set of rules and a scoring system. In a single-player computer game, such as the one we created for this chapter, the computer acts both as the opponent and the referee.

This traditional Hangman game presents the user with a number of empty slots corresponding to the letters of a word. The player must guess the word, entering one letter at a time. When a player guesses correctly, the letter appears in the appropriate slot. A wrong guess, and the hangman is revealed, one body part at a time. It is clearly understood that the hangman is a representation of the state of the user in the game. Being hanged represents defeat, but no harm is done. If the user guesses the word before the body is complete, he or she wins the round; otherwise, the man is hanged, and the round is lost.

Interaction design

Interaction design is creating the visual representation of the mechanisms of a game: It determines how to play the game and communicates the rules to the user.

The interaction of our game is very simple, and our design should be just as simple. To keep the interface to a minimum, the alphabet is used both to represent the choices and to display the user's selection. The character's physical state is a character representation of the user as well as an indication of the score within one round.

For the Hangman interface, we need the following:

✦ Text fields to display the empty slots for the letters of the word to guess.

✦ A listing of the alphabet that indicates letters already selected as well as ones that remain. This listing is also the device by which the user can select a letter.

✦ A field for feedback from the computer referee.

✦ An area to display the score.

✦ The hangman character.

Visual and sound design

The visual design is essential because it is the first and longest-lasting impression. It communicates the mood of the game. Ours is fun, colorful, and somewhat humorous.

This particular game is fairly limited, with not much of a narrative. Nonetheless, the character drawing and animation should keep the user entertained: The hangman is now an alien character going back to the mother ship. Each round was designed with a different set of colors to give some visual diversity. The alien choice is meant to be humorous, both as a homage to the old computer games that used such characters and as a spoof of the multitude of computer demonstrations and illustrations using aliens.

The alien character and the background, including the selection of color schemes, were created by Jonathan Brzyski, a talented artist with a sense of humor (see Figure 33-1).

Of course, good sound effects are an important complement to the visual. They translate a mood and are helpful to indicate a win or a loss. They also are crucial in supporting and reinforcing animation.

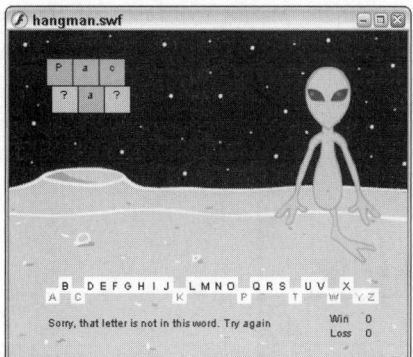

Figure 33-1: Our version of the hangman is a tribute to aliens and old computer games.

Programming

Programming a game is the task of asking a series of questions and making decisions, including asking new questions based on the answers, in a language and syntax that the computer can understand. Writing short and task-specific functions is helpful to break down the logic of the game into discrete elements.

The programmer must deconstruct the game in terms of a dialogue between the computer and the player. It must address every detail, no matter how obvious it seems. By thinking of the flow of events ahead of time, you will be able to write code that can handle several aspects of a problem at different times of your game cycle.

Finally, with every new update, Flash provides new functions to simplify our scripting task. Becoming acquainted with them streamlines this process and makes your code easier to write and more elegant.

Building the Project

This section discusses the creation of the art and assets for the interface and then talks about assembling the game's mechanics.

In the tradition of character animation, the alien puppet is constructed of independent Movie Clips for each body part for maximum flexibility. (Figure 33-2 shows the timeline of the headClip symbol in the hangMan ⇨ hangMan elements folder of the document's Library panel.) Each Movie Clip in the hangMan elements folder is made of nine frames used for the nine rounds of the game. Each frame displays the same Movie Clip symbol with different advanced color effects. You can view the color settings by selecting the Movie Clip symbol, opening the Property inspector, and clicking the Settings button to the right of the Color menu. Note that by using the color effects, we can use the same symbols over and over, keep our file small, and still develop a very large visual vocabulary.

When the game is a loss and the alien is complete, an animation is triggered. This animation uses the beamClip symbol and the fade component. Both of these symbols are attached dynamically in ActionScript, which you'll see later in this chapter.

We discuss the custom Fade component in Chapter 20, "Making Your First Flash MX 2004 Project."

Cross-
Reference

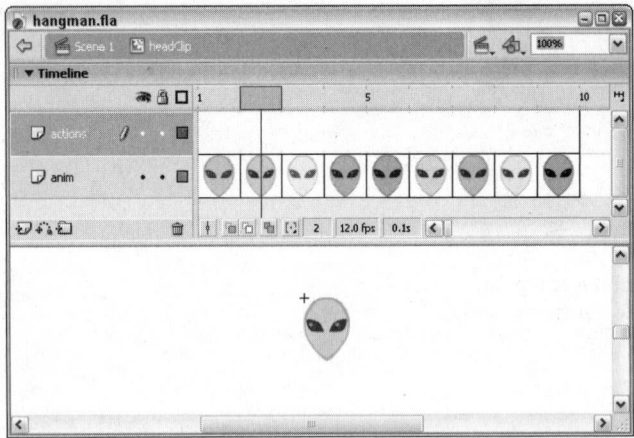

Figure 33-2: The headClip symbol uses the head symbol and displays it with different color schemes. This timeline is shown with the Preview in Context option enabled in the Timeline window.

Scripting the Game

The Hangman game consists of a series of rounds, corresponding to the number of available words to guess. In each round, the computer randomly chooses a word and generates slots as placeholders for the letters. The user attempts to guess the word one letter at a time. For each right guess, the letter appears. For each wrong guess, a piece of a character appears. After six wrong guesses, the alien character is completed, does a little animation for us, and the round is over. The score for each round appears on the screen.

The three steps to the game are the setup, user input, and interpretation of the user input. Most of the code for this aspect of the game is located in the AS files located in the ch31 folder of this book's CD-ROM.

The game has an additional feature: The user name and his or her score are saved on the local machine, and the data is available the next time the user plays the game. Most of the code for this feature is located on frame 1 of the actions layer. This feature, however, is covered last.

Tip   The SharedObject class, introduced in Flash MX, allows you to save data locally, similarly to the way a cookie saves data in a Web browser. This feature is only available for Flash Player 6 and higher movies.

Initializing Variables and Creating Sound Objects

Before examining the functions used by the game, you learn about a few of the variables that are vital to structure of the game.

The `wordSelection` array is an array containing the words to guess. You can find the code for this array on frame 5 of the actions layer. For our game, the user must guess the names of old computer games. Note that some of the words contain a space, which represent a carriage return and is used as an indicator to place words on multiple lines. This additional feature is to make the word easier to guess as well as create a more attractive layout.

```
var wordSelection:Array = ["Asteroids", "Defender", "Donkey Kong", ⊃
    "Pac Man", "Paddle", "Pong", "QBert", "Space Invaders", "Tetris"];
```

 Note   As mentioned in Chapter 26, "Using Functions and Arrays," you can implicitly create an `Array` object by using the array access operators, [ ]. This "shortcut" is equivalent to writing `var wordSelection:Array = new Array();` and then adding the elements to the array.

Two `Sound` objects, `soundWin` and `soundLoss`, are created for this project, and a sound is attached to each of them. These sounds provide audio feedback for the score.

```
var soundWin:Sound = new Sound(this);
var soundLoss:Sound = new Sound(this);
soundWin.attachSound("applause");
soundLoss.attachSound("error");
```

The `roundNumber` variable keeps track of the round to inform the user at the beginning of every round. It is assigned a value of 0.

The `editedWord` variable stores the number of letters in a word (minus any spaces) and determines when a word is complete.

The `delayCounter` variable gives a time delay between rounds in association with the `setInterval()` method. `setInterval()`, introduced in the last version of Flash, is used to call a function at a specific time interval.

The `win` and `loss` variables increment as the score changes. The `saveWinScore()` and `saveLossScore()` functions are created in the `save.as` document. However, they will be discussed last in the "Added Feature: Storing User and Game Information" section of this chapter. For now, note that they are passed the value of `win` and `loss`.

```
var win:Number = 0;
var loss:Number = 0

saveWinScore(0);
saveLossScore(0);
```

Building the Interface

ActionScript can create primitives and text fields in Flash Player 6 or higher movies. We will take advantage of this feature to create the rest of our assets.

Creating text fields

The createTextField() method creates a new empty text field as a child of a MovieClip object. Note that the createTextField() takes several parameters: the instance name, the depth, x position, y position, width, and height.

One of the core functions of the game is the buildInterface() function, found in the ui_controls.as file. This function controls much of the layout for each state of the game. When a game starts (with an activeState argument of "startgame" in the buildInterface() function), several text fields are created. A TextFormat object also can be created and applied to each of these text fields. In the createStyles() function, found in lines 3–22 of the ui_controls.as file, you'll see several TextFormat objects created, including one named fieldStyle defined in lines 10–15:

```
fieldStyle = new TextFormat();
with (fieldStyle) {
  font = "Arial";
  size = 10;
  align = "left";
}
```

> **Note**
>
> We don't use the var keyword here because we want the style variables to be scoped to the Main Timeline of the movie. In this way, we can access the styles from various functions throughout the game.

The createStyles() function is invoked in line 5 of frame 1 of the actions layer, as soon as the movie starts. Several score text fields are created, as well as the feedback text field in the buildInterface() function, lines 55–65. We then invoke the setNewTextFormat() method with the instance name of the TextFormat object to apply its settings (line 62). To target all the field dynamic text fields, we use the for . . . in action and search all instance for all TextField instances (line 59). We also use the getNextHighestDepth() method of the MovieClip object, new in Flash Player 7, to make sure each text field is created at a unique depth.

```
this.createTextField("fieldWon_txt", this.getNextHighestDepth(), 300, 255, ⮐
  50, 15);
this.createTextField("fieldLost_txt", this.getNextHighestDepth(), 300, 268, ⮐
  50, 15);
this.createTextField("fieldFeedback_txt", this.getNextHighestDepth(), 35, ⮐
  259, 260, 20);
for (var name in this) {
  if (this[name] instanceof TextField) {
    with (this[name]) {
      selectable = false;
      setNewTextFormat(fieldStyle);
    }
  }
}
```

To create the content of the score text fields, we concatenate, respectively, the string `"Win"`, the variable `win`, the string `"Loss"`, and the variable `loss`:

```
fieldWon_txt.text = "Win\t" + win;
fieldLost_txt.text = "Loss\t" + loss;
```

Tip   You can use the `\t` backslash pair to insert a tab between characters in a text field.

Figure 33-3 calls out the text fields created in these lines of code.

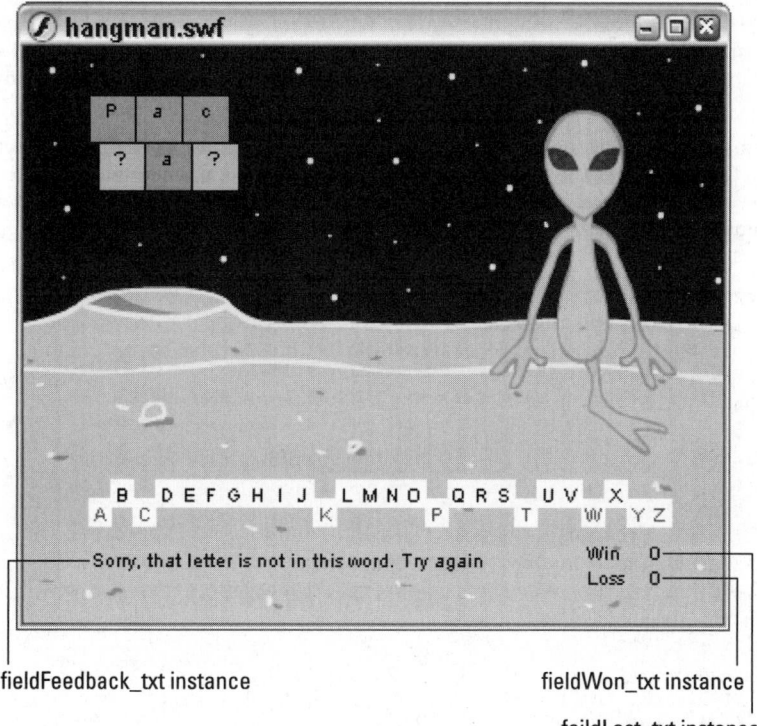

fieldFeedback_txt instance   fieldWon_txt instance

                                              feildLost_txt instance

Figure 33-3: The fieldFeedback_txt field displays comments throughout the game. The fieldLost_txt and the fieldWin_txt instances display the score.

Creating the alphabet

Movie Clips can be created dynamically using the `createEmptyMovieClip()` method. This method takes two parameters: an instance name and a depth. Furthermore, with ActionScript's event model, Movie Clips can be used as buttons as you learned in earlier chapters.

We use the alphabet as both visual feedback of the user selection and input device for the user to make a selection. To take care of both aspects, we are going to create dynamic Movie Clips and then create text fields as their children.

The `createStyles()` function also made the following style:

```
centeredStyle = new TextFormat();
with (centeredStyle) {
  font = "Arial";
  size = 10;
  align = "center";
}
```

ASCII characters can be created using the `String.fromCharCode()` method, which uses the number corresponding to a letter and returns its corresponding string (A=65, B=66, and so forth). Each letter of the alphabet is displayed in a dynamically created text field, as shown in Figure 33-4.

Note that we are also defining an `onRelease()` handler for each letter Movie Clip that will be invoked when the user clicks the letter. When the mouse is released, the letter is checked for a match. The `readyToPlay` variable prevents the call to the function from being executed between rounds and at the end of the game. The following function, `createAlphabet()`, is defined in lines 4–31 of the `letter.as` file:

```
function createAlphabet() {
   trace("createAlphabet() invoked");
   var alphabet:MovieClip = this.createEmptyMovieClip("alphabet_mc", ⟳
     this.getNextHighestDepth());
   with(alphabet){
     _x = 35;
     _y = 225;
   }
   var objX:Number = 0;
   for (var i = 65; i <= 90; i++) {
     var letter:String = String.fromCharCode(i);
     var field:MovieClip = alphabet.createEmptyMovieClip(letter + "_mc", ⟳
       alphabet.getNextHighestDepth());
     field.id = letter;
     field._x =  objX;
     field.createTextField("character_txt", 1, 0, 0, 13, 15);
     with (field.character_txt) {
        selectable = false;
        setNewTextFormat(centeredStyle);
        background = true;
        text = letter;
     }
     field.onRelease = function() {
        if (readyToPlay) {
           checkInput(this.id);
        }
     };
     objX += 12;
   }
}
```

The createAlphabet() function is invoked from the buildInterface() function, on line 68, after the text fields are created.

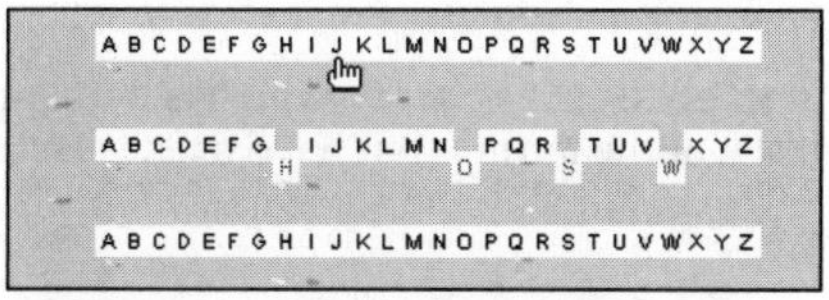

Figure 33-4: Our alphabet Movie Clips work as both text fields and buttons.

Starting the Game

The functions that we cover next are built with the framework of the game in a circular fashion: All the functions are used within one game cycle and again within the next game cycle. This kind of flow is specific to games and must be kept in mind when writing code. In particular, variables need to be reset properly at the beginning of a new cycle.

At the beginning of each round, some of our assets need to be edited and some variables initialized. The newRound() function, defined in lines 93–105 of the ui_control.as file, takes care of it by incrementing the variable roundNumber, setting the value of variable editedWord to 0 and setting readyToPlay to true.

```
roundNumber++;
editedWord = 0;
readyToPlay = true;
```

newRound() also prepares the alien character: The hangManState array is created to store the instance names of the body parts. A for loop hides these Movie Clips. These Movie Clips go to the frame number corresponding to the roundNumber to display a new color scheme.

```
_global.hangManState = new Array(hangMan_mc.head_mc, hangMan_mc.body_mc, ⊃
  hangMan_mc.leftArm_mc, hangMan_mc.rightArm_mc, hangMan_mc.leftLeg_mc, ⊃
  hangMan_mc.rightLeg_mc);
for (var i = 0; i < _global.hangManState.length; i++) {
  var item:MovieClip = _global.hangManState[i];
  item._visible = false;
  item.gotoAndStop(roundNumber);
}
```

Note   We use the _global name space here just to make sure we can easily access the array from any location in the Flash movie. It could have just as easily been declared as an object on the Main Timeline for the purposes of this game.

Putting the Movie Clips' instance names in an array comes in handy during the game when we want to reveal the hangman's elements, one at a time. We also use the hangManState array to check the status of the game.

Display the letters of the alphabet

The newRound() function also invokes the positionAlphabet() function, which is declared in lines 34–44 of the letters.as document.

This function stores each letter of the alphabet in a lettersLeft array, which is populated by the letters of the alphabet. It is used to keep track of the letters that have been selected by the user. It also moves the vertical position of the Movie Clips by the same name. This is used in the circular fashion mentioned earlier.

```
function positionAlphabet() {
    trace("positionAlphabet() invoked");
    lettersLeft = new Array();
    for (var i = 65; i <= 90; i++) {
        var letter:String = String.fromCharCode(i);
        lettersLeft[lettersLeft.length] = letter;
        var item = this.alphabet_mc[letter + "_mc"];
        item._y = 0;
        item.character_txt.textColor = 0x000000;
    }
}
```

Choose a random word

The selection of words is stored in an array called wordSelection, which is defined at the beginning of the game, on frame 5 of the actions layer. A random number, generated using the Math.random() function, defines the index in the array and stores its element in the variable randomWord. Lastly, the selected word is removed from the array using the splice() method so that it doesn't get chosen again. You can find this functionality in the startGame() function, declared in lines 84–91 of the ui_controls.as file:

```
function startGame() {
    newRound();
    fieldFeedback_txt.text = "Round " + roundNumber;
    randomNumber = Math.floor(Math.random() * wordSelection.length);
    randomWord = wordSelection[randomNumber];
    wordSelection.splice(randomNumber, 1);
    createWord(randomWord);
}
```

Note   In this version of the game, a word is randomly selected from a pool for each round. As such, the difficulty of each word (number of characters, number of words, and so on) is not ranked. You can modify the game to create a series of word arrays, each one varying in level of difficulty. As the player progresses to the next round, a word from another array can be chosen.

Create the slots for the letters of the word

The createWord() function, invoked from the startGame() function mentioned in the previous section, sets the number of slots corresponding to the letters. You can find the createWord() function in lines 46–77 of the letters.as file.

At the beginning of the `createWord()` function, we create a `MovieClip` object named `word_mc`, to hold the individual letters of the chosen word. Again, because we are working in a cycle between rounds, this would remove the letter text fields created in a previous round before creating new ones.

```
if(this.word_mc != null){
   this.word_mc.removeMovieClip();
}

var challengeWord:MovieClip = this.createEmptyMovieClip("word_mc", ⊃
   this.getNextHighestDepth());
with(challengeWord){
   _x = 35;
   _y = 25;
}
```

Looking back at the `wordSelection` array, you will notice that some of the elements have a space character in the string (such as "Donkey Kong"). We use code that detects entries with multiple words and place each word on its own line. When the system sees a space, the `for` loop ignores the rest of the statement block and goes back to the top of the loop using the `continue` action.

In all other cases, a text field is created, using the `objX` and `objY` variables as coordinates. Flash assigns the text field a text format, and its text becomes a question mark as a cue to the user.

The variable `editedWord` is incremented. This variable keeps track of the number of letters in the word and is used to check when the word is complete. Figure 33-5 shows a game in play with some letters already guessed.

```
var objX:Number = 0;
var objY:Number = 0;
for (var i = 0; i < word.length; i++) {
   if (word.substr(i, 1) == " ") {
      objX = 5;
      objY = 25;
      continue;
   }
   challengeWord.createTextField("letter_" + i, ⊃
      challengeWord.getNextHighestDepth(), objX, objY, 25, 25);
   with (challengeWord["letter_" + i]) {
      border = true;
      background = true;
      backgroundColor = 0x99CCFF;
      setNewTextFormat(centeredStyle);
      text = "?";
   }
   editedWord++;
   objX += 25;
}
```

Figure 33-5: The slots correspond to the number of characters in the word to guess. At the beginning of a round, all slots display a question mark. When a selection is correct, the ? character is replaced by the letter.

The User Input

The user enters his or her selection by clicking one of the Movie Clip letters (remember how the Movie Clips now function as buttons).

On release, the checkInput() function is called, and the Movie Clip instance name is passed. Its instance name corresponds to the letter of the alphabet it represents.

Interpreting the User Input

This is the bigger part of our project. A series of questions are asked, and their answers determine the next step in the process. You can find the checkInput() function on lines 80–87 of the letters.as file:

```
function checkInput (guess) {
  trace("checkInput("+guess+") invoked");
  if(isLeft(guess)){
    lookForMatch(guess);
  } else {
    fieldFeedback_txt.text = "Sorry, you already tried that letter";
  }
}
```

The isLeft() function looks to see if the selected letter was already chosen, and the lookForMatch() function checks the letter against the word to guess.

Was the letter selected before?

Using a for loop, the isLeft() function compares the lettersLeft array to the chosen letter, one element at a time. If the letter is contained in the array, the vertical position of its corresponding Movie Clip is offset by 10 pixels, and the color of its text field is modified. The letter is deleted from the array, and the function returns true.

```
function isLeft(char):Boolean {
    trace("isLeft("+char+") invoked");
    for (var i = 0; i < lettersLeft.length; i++) {
        if (lettersLeft[i].toLowerCase() == char.toLowerCase()) {
            var letterObj:MovieClip = this.alphabet_mc[char + "_mc"];
            trace("letterObj = " + letterObj);
            letterObj._y = 10;
            letterObj.character_txt.textColor = 0x666666;
            lettersLeft.splice(i, 1);
            return true;
        }
    }
    return false;
}
```

Note   In ActionScript 2.0 code, you can specify the data type of the returned value from the function. The data type is declared after the parentheses of the arguments, separated by a colon (:) character. In the isLeft() function, the data type of the return value is Boolean.

Is the letter part of the word?

The lookForMatch() function, found in lines 104–126 of the letters.as file, compares the selected letter to the variable randomWord, one character at a time. The toLowerCase() method converts the character to lowercase so that the two compared elements would match if they are the same letter, regardless of their case.

If the letter is found in the randomWord variable, the corresponding letter text field gets assigned a new background color, and its text is changed to reveal the letter. Also, the variable match is assigned the value of true.

```
for (var i = 0; i < randomWord.length; i++) {
    if (randomWord.substr(i, 1).toLowerCase() == char.toLowerCase()) {
        this.word_mc["letter_" + i].text = randomWord.substr(i, 1);
        this.word_mc["letter_" + i].backgroundColor = 0x9999FF;
        var match = true;
    }
}
```

For a match, we also want to start a sound and display a feedback message; but because we want to execute it only once, it is placed outside the repeat loop. The variable match keeps track of a match.

```
if (match) {
    trace("found match");
    soundWin.start();
    fieldFeedback_txt.text = "Correct! " + fieldGuess.text + " is in the word";
}
```

The letter is not part of the word

If the character is not contained in the array, the `shift()` method deletes the first element in the `hangMan` array and makes the corresponding Movie Clip visible to reveal a piece of the alien. It also displays a text message and starts the sound effect that corresponds to a wrong choice.

```
} else {
    trace("didn't find match...");
    var hangPiece:MovieClip = _global.hangManState.shift();
    trace("hangPiece = " + hangPiece);
    hangPiece._visible = true;
    fieldFeedback_txt.text = "Sorry, that letter is not in this word. Try again";
    soundLoss.start();
}
```

Tip　You could also construct a hangman Movie Clip symbol that uses several keyframes to animate the progression of the hangman. Instead of using an array, the Movie Clip instance could be told to advance one frame further with `nextFrame()` to proceed to the next stage of the hangman.

Checking the Status of the Game

The last step in our process is to check the status of the game. More specifically, is the word complete, is the character complete, and/or is the game complete? The function `gameStatus()`, defined in lines 107–139 of the `ui_control.as` file, asks all these questions. The following sections discuss questions and conditions that exist in the game and the programming logic behind their answers and actions.

Is the word complete?

To check whether the word is complete, we check for any remaining ? characters in the letter text fields. We use a `for` loop (with the value of the `editedWord` variable as the condition to exit the loop). Note how the Boolean variable `allMatch` is assigned the value of `true` if the word is complete and of `false` if the word is not complete.

```
for (var i = 0; i <= editedWord; i++) {
    if (this.word_mc["letter_" + i].text == "?") {
        allMatch = false;
        break;
    } else {
        allMatch = true;
    }
}
```

The word is complete

If the word is complete (and `allMatch` has a value of `true`), the `fieldFeedback_txt` instance displays the corresponding message. The variable `win` is incremented, and the new score displays on the screen.

```
if (allMatch) {
  fieldFeedback_txt.text = "You won this round!";
  win++;
  fieldWon_txt.text = "Win    " + win;
  saveWinScore(win)
  reset = true;
```

Is the alien complete?

If the word is not complete (and allMatch has a value of false), we need to check that the status of the alien: If it has all its parts, the round is lost. The fieldFeedback_txt instance displays the corresponding message. The variable loss is incremented, and the new score displays on the screen. The movie moves forward on the Timeline to play the losing animation.

```
} else if (_global.hangManState.length <= 0) {
  fieldFeedback_txt.text = "You lost this round";
  loss++;
  fieldLost_txt.text = "Loss    " + loss;
  saveLossScore(loss);
  reset = true;
  removeHangMan();
}
```

In both cases, the reset variable is set to true. This is a flag to indicate that this round is over and to proceed to the next step. Only if reset is true, the process continues. Otherwise, it is complete, and the game is ready for the next user input.

Removing the hangman

The removeHangMan() function, invoked in the code mentioned in the last section, is defined in lines 147 through 150 of the ui_control.as file.

```
function removeHangMan(){
  var beam:MovieClip = this.attachMovie("beamClip", "beam_mc", ⤵
    this.getNextHighestDepth(), {_x: 242, _y: 0});
  beam.targetClip = "hangMan_mc";
}
```

This function attaches the beamClip symbol from the library to the Stage, as an instance name beam_mc, above the alien hangman instance (hangMan_mc). A variable on the beam_mc instance (referenced via the beam local variable) named targetClip is set equal to the instance name, as a string, of the hangMan_mc instance. This variable is used by yet another attachMovie() method, found inside of the beamClip symbol.

In the Library panel, open the beamClip symbol. On frame 7 of the actions layer on this symbol's timeline, you'll find the following code:

```
var fader:MovieClip = this._parent.attachMovie("fadeBehavior", "fader_mc", ⤵
  this._parent.getNextHighestDepth(), {direction: "out", increment: 10, ⤵
  _targetInstanceName: this.targetClip});
```

Here, the fade symbol, linked as fadeBehavior in the Library panel, is dynamically attached to the Main Timeline (which is the parent timeline of the beam_mc instance added earlier). The fade component, which we used in Chapter 20, "Making Your First Flash MX 2004 Project," uses three parameters: direction, increment, and _targetInstanceName. In this `attachMovie()` method, we pass these parameters and their values in the `initObj` argument. The `fader_mc` instance is then set up to make the alien hangman (`hangMan_mc`, as set by the `this.targetClip` parameter) fade from the stage.

Is the word selection empty?

If the `wordSelection` array is empty, it is the end of the game, and the `fieldFeedback_txt` instance displays a "thank you" message.

```
if(wordSelection.length == 0){
readyToPlay = false;
  fieldFeedback_txt.text = "Thanks for playing!";
```

There are more words to guess

If it is the end of a round but not the end of the game, a delay is created before calling the next game.

```
else if (reset){
readyToPlay = false;
  delayNextRound = setInterval(createDelay, 2000);
}
```

The `readyToPlay` variable prevents interactivity on the letters Movie Clips when it is set to `false`. This is to prevent the user from making selections between rounds or at the end of the game.

Adding a delay before the next round

Let's add a delay so the user has the time to view the result before moving on to the next round. ActionScript provides a way to add a timer without having a script going between two frames or on an `enterFrame` event. The `setInterval()` method calls a function at the time increment you choose. It keeps running until you call the `clearInterval()` method, at which point the `startGame()` function is invoked again. Because we used a time interval of 2000 milliseconds in the `gameStatus()` function, this function invokes 2 seconds after the `setInterval()` function is called.

```
function createDelay() {
    clearInterval(delayNextRound);
    delete delayNextRound;
    startGame();
}
```

Added Feature: Storing User and Game Information

Being able to save information opens new dimensions to game development. For example, users particularly enjoy playing a multilevel game if they know the next time they visit the site, they can pick up where they left off because the computer remembers which level they last completed and their current score.

For our Hangman game, the following section demonstrates a very simple application of saving data onto the user's local hard drive and recalling it when the player returns to the game at a later time.

Flash Player 6 introduced a new feature, the SharedObject class, which allows you to save data locally, similar to a Web browser cookie. The next time the user runs the game, it displays the saved information. The information can be saved in two ways: when the movie ends or as soon as the information is entered. For our game, the information is saved right away, in frame 1 of the actions layer. The SharedObject.getLocal() method creates a new object called localInfo.

```
var localInfo:SharedObject = SharedObject.getLocal("hangMan");
```

To store data in a SharedObject instance, you access the data property of the instance, followed by a variable name. For example, to store a variable named firstName in a SharedObject instance named localInfo, you could use the following code:

```
var localInfo.data.firstName = "Damian";
```

For the purposes of this game, we check that the data was saved for the user name and the win and loss scores. If any of this information is missing, the movie stops at frame 1

```
if (localInfo.data.winScore == undefined || localInfo.data.lossScore == ⏎
  undefined || localInfo.data.user == undefined) {
    buildInterface("init");
```

and two text fields are created dynamically, as shown in Figure 33-6. One is an input form for the user to enter his/her name, and the second is an instruction of what to do. Lines 28–45 of the buildInterface() function, in ui_control.as, does just that:

```
this.createTextField("nameLabel_txt", this.getNextHighestDepth(), 50, 232, ⏎
  200, 20);
_global.activeElements.push(nameLabel_txt);
with (nameLabel_txt) {
   selectable = false;
   setNewTextFormat(openingStyle);
   text = "Please Enter Your Name";
}
this.createTextField("nameEntry_txt", this.getNextHighestDepth(), 50, 250, ⏎
  150, 18);
_global.activeElements.push(nameEntry_txt);
with (nameEntry_txt) {
   setNewTextFormat(openingStyle);
   background = true;
   type = "input";
}
submit_btn.onRelease = function() {
   saveName(nameEntry_txt.text);
   gotoAndStop("game");
};
```

Figure 33-6: The input form

Figure 33-6 shows the first frame you see when you first come to the game. Not unlike a registration form, you enter your name. Every time after that, your name and score are remembered and displayed.

After the user enters his/her name and clicks the orange button (submit_btn) on the screen, the data is saved by calling the saveName() function, found in the save.as file:

```
function saveName(name) {
   localInfo.data.user = name;
   localInfo.flush();
}
```

Note   The flush() method of the SharedObject class forces the data to be written to the local data file.

In the first frame of the movie, if the user has already played the game, the buildInterface() function is passed the "showstats" argument, invoking lines the function showUserInfo() is also declared but is only used on the second frame:

```
this.createTextField("displayData_txt", this.getNextHighestDepth(), 50, ⤵
   220, 150, 100);
displayData_txt.setNewTextFormat(openingStyle);
displayData_txt.text = localInfo.data.user + "," + newline + "This is ⤵
   your last score:" + newline + "you won " + localInfo.data.winScore + ⤵
   " rounds and lost " + localInfo.data.lossScore + "." + newline + ⤵
   "Good luck on your new game!";
_global.activeElements.push(displayData_txt);
submit_btn.onRelease = function() {
   gotoAndStop("game");
};
```

If the data is stored on the local drive, the movie displays the information by calling these lines in the function. This function populates a text field, which is created dynamically. The field displays a message, including the user's name and score, as shown in Figure 33-7.

The saveWinScore() function and the saveLossScore() function are called from within the game at the end of each round and store the win and loss scores.

```
function saveWinScore(win) {
  localInfo.data.winScore = win;
  localInfo.flush ();
}
function saveLossScore(loss) {
  localInfo.data.lossScore = loss;
  localInfo.flush();
}
```

Figure 33-7: The second time you play the game and every time after that, your name and previous score are displayed.

We'd like to know what you think about this chapter. Visit www.flashsupport.com/feedback to fill out an online form with your comments.

Summary

✦ Creating a game is much more than programming. It involves other talents, such as game design, interaction design, and visual and sound design.

✦ Before writing code, it is helpful to deconstruct the game into small detailed steps.

✦ Scripting a game is asking a series of questions and responding to them appropriately, depending on the user input.

✦ Arrays are helpful to store, retrieve, and manipulate information. In our game, we use them for the selection of words to guess as well as for the alien character's body parts.

✦ Functions are essential to intelligent programming. Writing small, task-focused functions allows for greater flexibility, particularly for complex games.

✦ With the event model of ActionScript, functions can be defined for objects and executed when events, such as a mouse event, are triggered. We are using this new model to create functions for the alphabet Movie Clips. Instead of writing the code on each Movie Clip, the functions are created within a repeat loop only once on a frame script. The code no longer needs to be on the object itself.

✦ Movie Clips and text fields can be created dynamically. Additionally, text fields' properties can be manipulated via ActionScript. In addition to adding flexibility, it reduces the weight of your movie.

✦ The new setInterval() action can be used as a timer to call a function over time without having the playhead move between frames. Here, we are using it to create a delay between rounds.

✦ Using the SharedObject class is a great way to save data on the local drive. We are using it to store the user's name as well as the game's score.

✦   ✦   ✦

Managing and Troubleshooting Flash Movies

◆ ◆ ◆ ◆

In This Chapter

Controlling code hints and syntax coloring

Organizing and editing code

Using the Output panel

Knowing the Flash Debugger panel

Assigning breakpoints

Debugging a Flash movie remotely

External code files

Troubleshooting guidelines

Community help

◆ ◆ ◆ ◆

Is there anything worse than sitting at your computer, scratching your head utterly frustrated because something won't work as planned? Chances are it is something really minor. This chapter focuses on tools, methods, and techniques you can use to fix these sorts of problems.

Many problems can occur while creating your movie. ActionScript errors, movie structure and design, external technologies, such as XML and server-side processes may cause problems. Debugging your Flash document can seem like an overwhelming task but in this chapter, we'll review a few tools to help you. At the end of the chapter you will find a Good Practices list, troubleshooting guidelines and testing matrices, which can be used to sort out common issues and problems that often occur when developing with Flash.

Customizing the Actions Panel

The Actions panel in Flash MX 2004 (and the Script editor in Flash MX Professional 2004) is the primary place for adding interactivity to your movies, by writing your own ActionScript code.

Note   Even though the Actions panel no longer includes a Normal mode, it does offer some excellent features that can make it easier to author and edit your code.

Code hints

If you have code hints enabled when you are typing ActionScript, a pop-up window appears containing relevant syntax, method, and event completion tips. This very useful tool helps when you are writing ActionScript because it reveals the suggested syntax of the function or method. Flash MX 2004's code hints, however, work best when it knows what class of object you are addressing. For example, if you name your Movie Clip instance with a _mc suffix, the Actions panel knows that the object is a MovieClip object. When writing code, the most relevant action out of several suggestions is highlighted in the code hints pop-up menu, as shown in Figure 34-1.

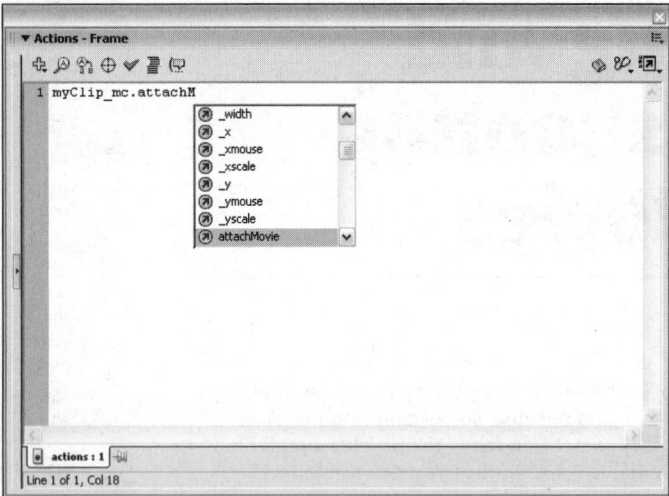

Figure 34-1: The Code Hints menu

If you press the Enter key at this time, the method or function is completed for you. The cursor is then positioned at the end of the line and a tooltip pops up, providing necessary parameters for the function or method you are typing. As you type your code, the tooltip makes the parameter you are writing bold. Refer to Figure 34-2 for an example of the Code Hints tooltip.

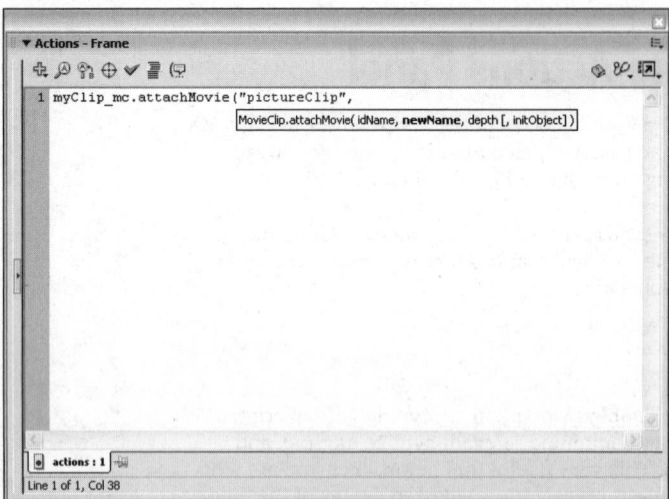

Figure 34-2: The Code Hints tooltip indicates the correct parameters for the attachMovie() method.

If you use ActionScript 2.0's strict typing for variable declarations, you can forego the use of suffixes for your instance names. Flash MX 2004 can automatically show you the code hints for a class of objects if you declare the object's type. For example, if you type the following code into the Actions panel, Flash MX 2004 knows that `myClip` is a `MovieClip` object.

```
var myClip:MovieClip = this.createEmptyMovieClip("holder_mc", 1);
```

 Tip

If you're following along and typing this code into the Actions panel, notice that the Code Hints menu appears after you type the colon (:) following the `myClip` term. This hint menu displays most of the class names available in ActionScript.

Then, if you refer to `myClip` later in your code (as shown in Figure 34-3), the code hints for the `MovieClip` class appear.

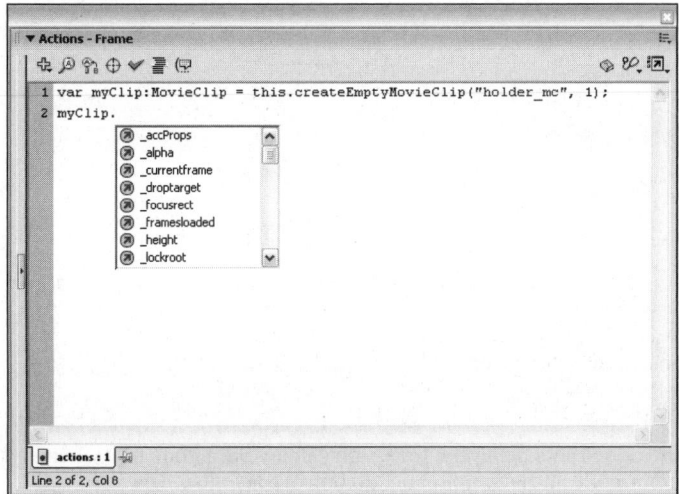

Figure 34-3: Code hints work for ActionScript 2.0 declared objects as well.

Code hints remove a lot of the guesswork from writing ActionScript. Using this feature is often faster than traversing the massive list of nodes in the Actions toolbox. There are a few settings you can modify to customize the way code hints work and act.

Let's walk through the options to customize code hints:

1. Select Edit ➪ Preferences (Windows) or Flash ➪ Preferences (Mac OS X).

2. Select the **ActionScript** tab. We will focus on the **Editing options** section.

 Tip

You can also access this tab in the Preferences dialog box by selecting **Preferences** from the Actions panel options menu.

3. The **Automatic indentation** check box should already be selected. When you type code into the Script pane, this option controls how your code indents. Adjust the **Tab size** value to increase or decrease the spacing of the indentation.

4. Make sure the **Code hints** check box is selected in order to enable them. We recommend keeping the **Delay** slider at a value of **0 seconds**, which makes the code hints appear automatically as you type. Refer to Figure 34-4 to see how the ActionScript Editor tab should appear.

Figure 34-4: The default settings for the Actions panel

If you prefer not to have Code Hints on all the time, you can invoke a code hint whenever needed. While typing your code in the Script pane, do one of the following:

✦ Click the Show Code Hint button in the Action panel's toolbar.

✦ Select Show Code Hint from the Actions panel options menu.

✦ Press Ctrl+Spacebar (Windows) or Control+Spacebar (Mac).

Syntax coloring

A feature that was added in the original release of Flash MX was the ability to choose how your ActionScript is colored. Flash MX 2004 has this feature as well. This is known as "syntax coloring," and it helps to visually "divide" your ActionScript. There are many elements to ActionScript such as variables, functions, constants, and statements. Using syntax coloring makes it much easier to read ActionScript. Set up your Syntax color settings so that they are easy to read, but also follow common "standards" in syntax highlighting.

1. Create a new Flash document by selecting File ➪ New.

2. Select the first frame of Layer 1 and open the Actions panel by selecting Window ➪ Development Panels ➪ Actions (F9).

3. Enter the code shown in Listing 34-1 into the Actions panel. This code can be used for testing and modifying syntax coloring because it uses most of the different elements of ActionScript.

Listing 34-1: **Sample code to aid syntax color settings**

```
#include "externalActions.as"

// This is a one line comment.

/*
This is a multiple line comment.
*/

var number:Number = 30;
var text:String = "string";

if (number != 4) {
    var soundObj:Sound = new Sound(this.targetMC);
    soundObj.loadSound("soundFile.mp3");
} else {
    _root.fakeMC._alpha = this.targetMC._alpha;
}
```

4. Open the Preferences dialog box (to the ActionScript tab) by selecting **Preferences** from the Actions panel options menu. See Figure 34-5.

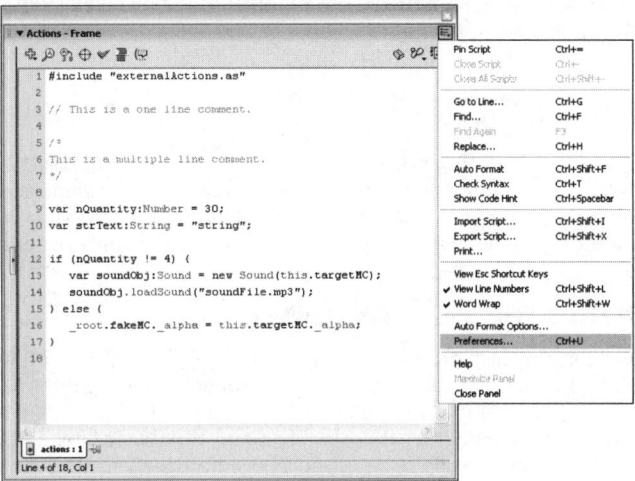

Figure 34-5: Accessing the Preferences from the Actions panel

5. Refer to the **Syntax coloring** section in the ActionScript tab. You can turn syntax coloring on or off by selecting or clearing the check box next to Syntax coloring, respectively.

6. Select the **Foreground** color chip and choose black (#000000) from the pop-up swatch menu. The Foreground option sets the default color of the text in the Actions panel. (Unless you changed this setting earlier, the default value should already be black.)

7. Select the **Keywords** color chip and choose blue (#0000FF) from the pop-up swatch menu. This blue color highlights all keywords such as var, if, and else.

8. Select the **Identifiers** color chip and choose a medium green (#009900). This color is used to highlight terms that are methods and properties of classes, as well as class names themselves.

9. Set the **Background** color chip to white (#FFFFFF). White should be used because it is likely you will spend hours at a time typing ActionScript and black text on a white background has high contrast and is more forgiving on your eyes than a colored background might be. (Unless you changed this setting earlier, the default value should already be white.)

10. Set the **Comments** color chip to a bright orange (#FF9900). Most programming applications use a gray for the comment color. We have chosen an orange as we believe that commenting code is a very important (and often neglected) part of authoring (and learning) code. Using a more visible color helps comments stand out more easily from the rest of the code.

11. Finally, select red (#FF0000) in the **Strings** color chip. Red is a common color for strings in many programming packages that have syntax coloring.

12. Click **OK** to close the Preferences dialog box. Make sure you have the Actions panel open and frame 1 of Layer 1 selected so that you can see the colors in use.

You can modify these colors if you prefer something different — the point of these steps is to illustrate where you can change the colors of your ActionScript code and visibly see those changes on the test code we provided.

Managing Your Code

In this section, we'll discuss methods and options for storing, writing and positioning your code. In Flash MX 2004, there is often more than one way to perform the same action — if you don't thoroughly think about why and where to place your code, you can run into trouble quickly. Using the following methods and suggestions will help you avoid common mistakes.

Using Replace in the Actions panel

Writing online applications in Flash often requires you to write a lot of code. While writing code, it is easy to name an object or variable without thoroughly thinking it through. Naming your objects and variables descriptively is a good idea. If you don't, you will find it hard to come back to your files and remember what each object and variable is intended for. Using Search and Replace allows you to easily rename poorly or improperly named variables or objects. It allows you to identify and change the incorrect string in one step, leaving Flash to replace all occurrences of the string.

However, there are traps when doing this. The following list contains points to remember:

✦ If you change the name of a variable, you must also change each reference to the variable across all timelines.

✦ Search and Replace replaces strings even if they make up a larger part of a code string. For example the following line: `sou = new Sound();` will be modified to this line: `sit = new Sitnd();` when you replace `ou` with `it`. So, if you use this feature, be mindful of the implications of searching for strings existing within other strings. A good method of avoiding this problem is to use a space whenever possible, remembering to replace the initial space with another in the replacement string. This step is necessary so your code formatting isn't modified.

Step through the following example to learn how to use Search and Replace to modify a block of code:

On the CD-ROM
You will find `component_definition.fla` in the `ch34` folder on the *Macromedia Flash MX 2004 Bible* CD-ROM. Copy this file to a location on your hard drive. We use this example code in a Search and Replace function.

1. Select File ➪ Open and browse to the folder on your hard drive where you saved component_definition.fla. Highlight it and click OK.

2. Select frame 1 in the actions layer.

3. Open the Actions panel (F9).

4. Open the Replace dialog box by doing one of the following:

   • Choose **Replace** from the options menu of the Actions panel or

   • Press Ctrl+H (Windows) or Shift+⌘+H (Macintosh).

5. Type "[Author name]" (without the quotes) into the **Find what** field.

6. Type your name (for example, "John Smith") in the **Replace with** field. You will be replacing "[Author name]" with your name.

7. From here you can search for each instance of the string before choosing to replace it. To do this, click **Find Next**. However, if you want to simply replace all instances of "[Author name]" choose **Replace All**. For this example, choose Replace All.

Choosing Find Next is a good method for overcoming the problem when a string is found within a larger string. You can choose Find Next; when it finds the string on its own, you can replace it by choosing Replace. If it finds the search string within a larger string, simply choose Find Next to move forward.

New Feature
You can also use the new global Find and Replace feature in Flash MX 2004 to search your entire document for specific ActionScript terms. Choose Edit ➪ Find and Replace, and make sure the ActionScript check box is selected. Clicking one of the found results takes you directly to the script where the term was found.

How and where to place your code

There are several ways to position your code effectively, but first there are two considerations to make. On one hand, your code needs to be effective and work well; it must be positioned properly in order for the application to work successfully. On the other hand, you need to make the application easy to build and edit. It needs to be quick and simple in order to modify sections without being laborious and taking up valuable time better spent coding.

The project requirements also dictate how you place your code. We use the scenario that follows to explain some good coding concepts and how and where to place your code.

You are creating a coloring book aimed toward children. The requirements state the application must have a paintbrush tool with different brush styles and sizes, a line tool with different widths available and a stamp tool used to place user-defined images on the drawing canvas. Each of the tools has a corresponding button and a range of options used to modify the properties of the tool. The user clicks on the canvas to start drawing or stamping. Building this application would require a combination of different functions. Functions can be grouped into the following two main categories:

✦ **Multipurpose functions:** A multipurpose function can be used many times and by more than one source. A multipurpose function should be written in the most generic way possible, but still meet its criteria. The coloring book application would benefit from a multipurpose function used to modify the cursor. For example, when the user clicks the line tool, the function changeDrawingTool() might be called with the string "line" parsed as the parameter. This function would then call changeCursor() to handle the cursor being changed and modifyOptions() to modify the options panel, which would reflect the current tool being used.

✦ **Chain functions:** The most effective functions are self-contained, perform one specific task, and can be used by many sources. However, there is an exception to the rule: chain functions. Chain functions group many other functions to perform several actions at once. Using chain functions allow you to write neater code and make it easier to understand.

An example of a chain function for the coloring book application would be startDrawing(). This might call the following functions: getColor(), would get the current color ready to draw; followMouse(), is used to trace the path of the mouse, and draw() which would actually draw the path to the canvas using values from followMouse().

A major benefit of using chain functions is you split up code into smaller chunks, which can then be easily accessed by other methods. For example, the startDrawing() function could have all of the code from the getColor(), followMouse(), and draw() functions within it. However, it would make the getColor() function inaccessible. This function could be used for more than one purpose. For example, if you parsed red, green, and blue values to the function, it could *set* the color for the user, rather than just *retrieving* the value the user has set.

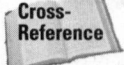

Cross-Reference

The Hangman game discussed in Chapter 33, "Creating a Game in Flash," uses many functions chained together.

Note After you start to write more sophisticated code such as chain functions, you may want to explore the concepts of true object-oriented programming in ActionScript. Refer to the *Flash MX 2004 ActionScript Bible* (Wiley, 2004) for examples that use OOP structures.

Centralized code

There are many places you can write code in Flash; in a frame, in and on Movie Clips, and on buttons. Your code can interact with any other object within the current movie structure including all levels and nested objects. This makes ActionScript an easy language to use for referencing and modifying objects from anywhere within a movie structure. It also allows poor coding placement, however. It is very important to take note of where you place your code. "Spaghetti code" is a common term to describe poorly placed code residing on multiple timelines and interlinked in an unclear way. It is quite easy to run into the trap of creating such code.

Centralized code is the key to making an application easy to use and edit. Centralized code does not necessarily mean all of your code should be written on frame 1 of the Main Timeline. Creating centralized code means making observations about what the code is being used for, where it applies, how often it will be used and how many objects will use the code.

Creating centralized code is different for each project. Here is a list of key concepts to follow when centralizing your code:

✦ **Reusable code:** Determine if a certain block of code is going to be reused by more than one object. If so, it is suitable for turning it into a function or a method, or possibly even a listener for objects that broadcast events.

✦ **Same code, multiple objects:** If a block of code is going to be used across a range of objects, such as buttons, you should place the code in a function and execute it from each button.

✦ **Function parameters:** Use functions to your advantage. If you have a block of code repeated across a number of objects referring to the objects' properties, you can centralize the code and make it much more manageable. Create a function in a central location and set up parameters to parse needed information about each object to the function. When you want to modify the block of code, you only need do it once instead of on every object.

Naming conventions

A naming convention is a method and style used to name objects, variables, frames, symbol instances, and many other aspects of Flash development. You can have different naming conventions for each area, such as frames and variables. However, this practice should be kept to a minimum and used only if necessary. There are common naming conventions used by most ActionScript and JavaScript code writers. Here is a list of rules that you may use to help you to create a naming convention:

✦ **Alternate Capitalization:** The first word is entirely lowercase, all subsequent words start with a capital letter, and all spaces are removed. This method is also known as InterCaps or "camel hump" and is used by many programming languages. ActionScript's predefined functions also follow this rule. A good example of this is the method name `createEmptyMovieClip()` of the `MovieClip` object — notice that the e, m, and c of this keyword are capitalized. This rule can be applied to objects, variables, frame names, and symbol instance names.

Caution   Now that Flash Player 7 forces case-sensitivity in ActionScript code, regardless of whether it's ActionScript 1.0 or 2.0, be extremely diligent about adhering to your own naming conventions in code.

✦ **Descriptive:** Creating successful names for your ActionScript elements is a careful process. The most effective names are descriptive, making them easy to read in context and easy to understand the next time you read the code. Try to shorten names as much as possible while keeping them descriptive. For example, a function used to get the current local time could be named `getLocalTime` because it is descriptive and short.

✦ **Object/Class Capitalization:** Many coders don't use this rule, but it does help when creating large applications with dozens of variables, functions, and objects. You can capitalize every word of your object names rather than every subsequent word after the first. This makes it easy when coding to distinguish between variables and functions, or objects.

✦ **Acronyms:** Using an acronym when creating global variables, functions, or objects is a great idea. This ensures when you mix your ActionScript with someone else's you won't have conflicting names. Your acronym should be short and have something to do with the project you are creating. For example, if you are creating an online e-mail reading/sending/writing program named FlashMail, you might want to add FM to all variable names, functions, and objects, such as `FMComposeNewMessage`.

Commenting

A particular problem with writing ActionScript is returning to your code to modify it at a later date — most of us don't have computer-like memories. Commenting your ActionScript while writing it is an excellent idea that overcomes this problem by helping you remember how the code is constructed and/or works. It may take slightly longer to write your code with commenting, but it is worth the trouble. Follow these rules to effectively comment your code:

✦ **Blocks of code:** You don't need to comment every line in your code. Rather than doing this, comment each block or the different sections of your code. If the ActionScript is obvious, such as setting a `MovieClip` object's X position to 10, you wouldn't write `// Set the movie clip's position to 10`. A more effective comment would be `// Align the movie clip with other objects`.

✦ **Natural language and punctuation:** Your comments should contain all punctuation and grammar, as if you are writing a formal letter. It is quite easy to write something that makes sense to you but not to others, but using punctuation ensures that your comments are easy to understand to everyone who reads them.

✦ **Be descriptive:** It is important to be as descriptive as possible. This also helps you remember what your code is doing when you come back to it.

✦ **Multi-line or single-line comments:** There are two methods to comment in ActionScript. You can use `/* comment in here */` or `// comment here`. The first method is used to create multi-line comments; you can enter down to a new line and what you type will still be commented. The second method is used for single line comments. A good practice is to reserve multi-line style commenting for more important comments or if you want to catch the readers attention.

Strong (or strict) typing

As you have seen earlier in this chapter and other chapters in the book, Flash MX 2004's ActionScript 2.0 language can use strong data type declarations. If you are starting a project from scratch in Flash MX 2004 for Flash Player 6 or 7, we strongly recommend that you try to use ActionScript 2.0 and strong typing. This simply means that you declare variables with data types. If you try to perform an illegal operation with a specific data typed-variable or object, Flash MX 2004 will inform you in the Output panel — this is definite bonus for developers during the debugging process.

Add the code shown in Listing 34-2 to frame 1 of an otherwise empty Flash document. If you click the Check Syntax button in the toolbar of the Actions panel, you'll see the following error in the Output panel:

```
**Error** Scene=Scene 1, layer=Layer 1, frame=1:Line 3: Type mismatch in
assignment statement: found Number where String is required.
```

Listing 34-2: **A sample script using strong data typing**

```
var nPercent:String = (nLoaded/nTotal)*100;
var nLoaded:Number = this.getBytesLoaded();
var nTotal:Number = this.getBytesTotal();
var nPercent:String = (nLoaded/nTotal)*100;
```

The error message tells you that the expression used to set the value of nPercent returns a Number data type, not a String. If you change the data type of nPercent to a Number, then the code will not return an error:

```
var nPercent:Number = (nLoaded/nTotal)*100;
```

Declaring data types with your variable declarations forces you to think clearly about how your code will be used.

Using the Output Panel

The Output panel is used to send messages and notifications while troubleshooting your movies. When you test a Flash movie (SWF file), Flash MX 2004 checks your ActionScript for syntax errors and sends any error messages to the Output panel.

Note   Many author applications such as Macromedia Director won't let you leave the script window until the syntax is correct. With Flash, it's entirely possible to write incorrect syntax within a block of code and close the Actions panel with the error intact. Flash notifies you, though, when you publish or test the movie if it finds an error.

The Output panel itself is packed with functionality allowing you to do the following:

✦ Print the contents of the panel.

✦ Copy the contents of the panel to the clipboard.

✦ Save the contents of the panel to a text file.

✦ Search for a specific string within the contents of the panel.

✦ Clear the current contents of the panel.

These commands can be accessed via the options menu in the upper-right corner of the Output panel.

trace() action

The Output panel is not only used by Flash MX 2004 to send syntax error messages to you, but you can also use it to view any data while testing a movie.

Using the trace() action can be a valuable tool when you debug your code. It is very simple to use and is sometimes better used than the Debugger panel, which we discuss later in this chapter. Each time you call the trace() action a new line is created and nothing is replaced. This makes it a great asset when debugging code such as for loops. All data sent to the Output panel can also be saved to a text file and later reviewed. A debugging session with the Debugger panel can't be saved.

Note   You can use the Output panel and the Debugger panel together to more effectively analyze every aspect of your Flash movie during testing.

In this exercise, you create a simple frame loop and repeatedly send some information to the output window.

1. Open Flash MX 2004 and create a new file by selecting File ➪ New.

2. Rename Layer 1 to **actions**.

3. Select the first frame of the actions layer and open the Actions panel (F9). Add the following code to the Script pane:

```
var count:Number = 0;
```

This code declares a variable named count, with a Number data type. Its value is set to 0.

4. Select frame 2 of the actions layer and press the F7 key to insert an empty keyframe. Select frame 2, and open the Actions panel. Insert the following code:

```
trace(count++);
```

This code will send the value of count to the Output panel and then increment the value of count by one.

5. Select frame 3 of actions layer and insert an empty keyframe (F7). With frame 3 selected, open the Actions panel (F9). Add the following code:

```
this.gotoAndPlay(2);
```

This action tells the Flash movie to constantly loop the second frame. As such, the trace() action repeatedly sends messages to the Output panel.

6. Test the movie to see the result of using the trace() action by choosing Control ➪ Test Movie (Ctrl+Enter or ⌘+Enter). You should see the value of count repeatedly sent to the Output panel, as shown in Figure 34-6. You can close both the Test Movie and Output windows.

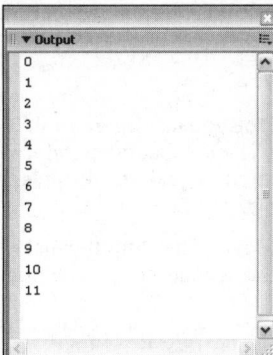

Figure 34-6: Your Output panel should look similar to this figure once you have completed Step 6.

Caution If you close the Output panel before closing the Test Movie window it will continue to re-open because the `trace()` action will be executed the next time frame 2 is played.

Tip You can slow down the rate of `trace()` messages for this example by changing the movie's frame rate in the Modify ➪ Document dialog box to a lower value such as 1 fps.

On the CD-ROM You can find this example, `trace_loop.fla`, in the `ch34` folder of this book's CD-ROM.

The `trace()` action can also send expressions to the Output panel. In this example, you write an expression inside the `trace()` action and the result is sent to the Output panel.

1. Create a new file by selecting File ➪ New.

2. Rename Layer 1 to **actions**, and select the first frame. Open the Actions panel ➪ (F9). Type the following code into the Script pane of the Actions panel:

```
var foo:Number = 5;
var bar:Number = foo;

trace(bar == foo);
```

The first line of this code declares a variable `foo`, which is equal to 5. The second line declares a variable named `bar`, which is equal to `foo`. The expression inside the `trace()` action uses the equality operator to evaluate if `bar` is equal to `foo` and sends the result to the Output panel. The equality operator is used to compare two expressions. If the two expressions are equal, the result is `true`. If they aren't equal, the result is `false`.

3. Test the movie by selecting Control ➪ Test Movie. When you test the movie the Output panel should open and display the Boolean value `true`. This is because the value of `bar` is equal to the value of `foo`.

4. Close the Test Movie window and the Output panel and add the following line of code to the end of the actions list:

```
trace(bar != foo);
```

This code uses the inequality operator instead of the equality operator in the expression. Again, the result is sent to the Output panel. The inequality operator is used to compare two expressions. If the two expressions aren't equal, the result is true. If the two expressions are equal, the result is false.

5. Test the movie again by selecting Control ➪ Test Movie. The Output panel will display true for the first trace() action, and false for the second trace() action.

On the CD-ROM You can find the completed file, trace_expression.fla, in the ch34 folder of this book's CD-ROM.

Although these are simple examples, the trace() action can be used to send the result of almost any equation that can be written on one line to the Output panel, assuming all variables referenced in the expression have been predefined.

Simulating the trace() Action Online

The trace() action can only be used in Test Mode within Flash MX 2004, or when you use the Debugger panel with a remote Flash movie. You might like to use something similar to the trace() action when testing in a browser. Follow these steps to make a Flash/JavaScript version of the trace() action using a JavaScript alert dialog box:

1. Open Flash MX 2004 and create a new file by selecting File ➪ New.

2. Select the first frame of Layer 1 and enter the following code using the Actions panel. This code simulates a trace() action. It uses a JavaScript alert dialog to display any information you send to the alert function. When testing this in Flash MX, a browser window is opened to display messages.

```
function alert (alertString) {

    getURL("javascript:alert('" + alertString + "');");

}

alert("this is a test");
```

3. Anytime you want to send an alert to the browser, use alert("any text or expression in here").

List Objects & List Variables

The Output panel is used for troubleshooting, displaying syntax errors and viewing trace action values. It can also be used to view all objects or variables currently in your movie.

The List Object and List Variables commands, available in the Debug menu of the Test Movie environment, are very useful when debugging large applications in Flash MX 2004.

✦ **List Variables:** This command sends all properties of any ActionScript objects, variables, and any XML data currently in your Flash movie to the Output window. Functions are also listed when this command is executed.

✦ **List Objects:** This command sends the current level, frame number, symbol names, Button, Movie Clip, or text field instance names, target paths, text blocks, and vector shapes to the Output window. The List Objects command displays the information in a hierarchal format. If you have five objects within a Movie Clip instance named `foo`, each of these objects will be indented beneath the `foo` declaration.

List Objects is frame dependent. If frame 1 of a movie has different objects to frame 5, executing List Objects on each of those frames sends different results to the Output panel.

The data sent to the Output panel from the List Objects command is a little confusing. It reports a vector graphic as being a "shape:" However, a Graphic symbol is also reported as being "shape:" Hence, there is no way to distinguish whether it is a vector shape or a graphic. Similarly, both dynamic text fields and input text fields are reported as "Edit Text:" and a text block (static text) is reported as "Text:"

Follow these steps to test the List Objects and List Variables commands.

1. Open Flash MX 2004 and create a new file by selecting File ➪ New.

2. Populate frame 1 with multiple objects, inserting a Movie Clip instance, a text field, a Button instance, a block of text (Static text), and a simple vector shape. You might try nesting some objects three or four Movie Clips deep to see the hierarchy of information within the Output window.

3. Test your movie by selecting Control ➪ Test Movie.

4. Select Debug ➪ List Objects. The Output panel will appear, containing the list of all objects on the current frame. Take a look to see how it reports the objects.

Knowing the Flash Debugger Panel

ActionScript has evolved as a language with each release of Macromedia Flash. Indeed, if you're only starting to use Flash and ActionScript, it can seem quite overwhelming. Because there's so much you do with ActionScript, Macromedia has included a Debugger panel (see Figure 34-7), which has been available since the release of Flash 5.

The Debugger panel allows you to find errors in your code while your movie is playing in the Flash Player. As well as debugging local movies in Test Mode, you can also debug remote Flash movies that reside on a server. The Debugger panel can be a valuable tool when testing your movie and solving problems.

To Activate the Debugger and test your movie select Control ➪ Debug Movie. You must push the Play button in the Debugger panel before your movie will start playing.

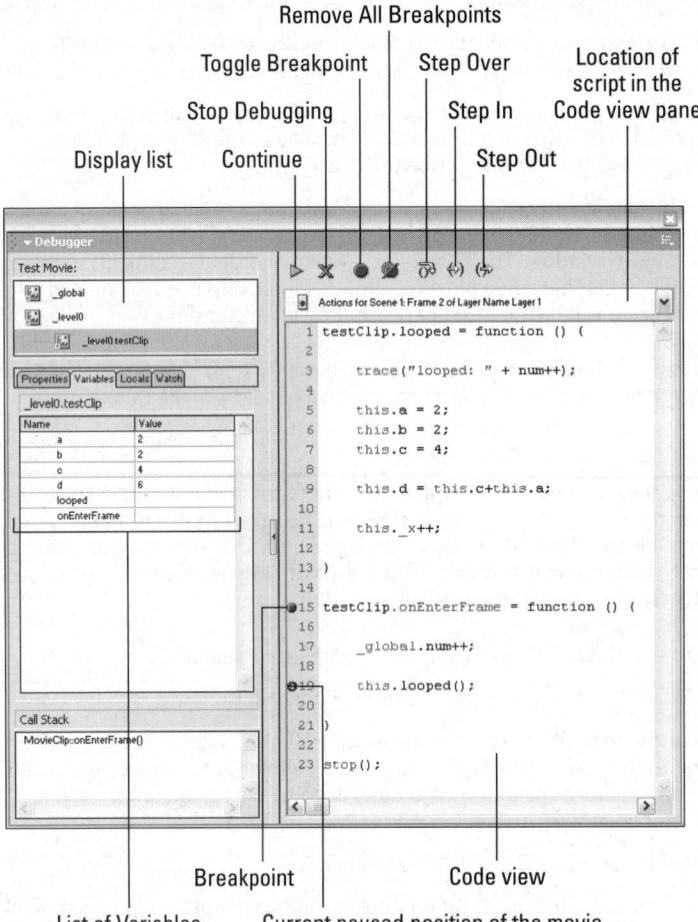

Figure 34-7: The Debugger panel, showing all buttons and element names

Displaying and modifying variables

While you are testing, you can use the Debugger panel to view or modify all variables in your movie. This is very useful because you will see the results of any change in a variable's value straight away as your movie is running.

Displaying a variable

These simple steps should be followed to view variables in the Debugger that exists in your movie.

You can find `debugging_code.fla` in the `ch34` folder on the *Macromedia Flash MX 2004 Bible* CD-ROM. Copy this file to a location on your hard drive. We will use it in the next few examples.

1. Select File ➪ Open and browse to the folder on your hard drive where you have saved `debugging_code.fla`. Highlight it and select OK.

2. Enter Debug mode by selecting Control ➪ Debug Movie.

3. Select Continue (that is, the play button in the toolbar of the panel) to start the movie playing.

4. Select the Variables tab. This is where all of the variables are displayed.

5. Select the `_level0.testClip` Movie Clip from the Display list to see the variables that exist in that Timeline.

6. Select the `_level0` target to see the variables change in the Variables tab. See Figure 34-8 for an example of `_level0`, displaying the `$version` variable.

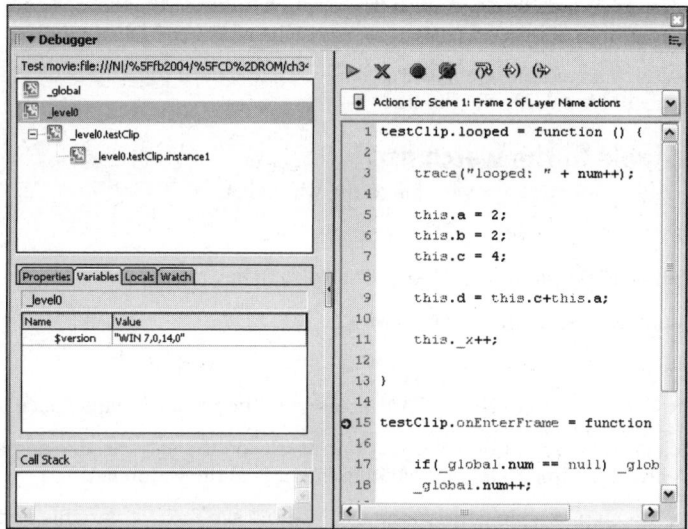

Figure 34-8: The Variables tab showing the `$version` variable from `_level0`. This variable refers to the version of the Flash Player you are using to debug your movie.

Modifying a variable

These simple steps should be followed to modify variables in the Debugger panel that exist in your movie.

1. Open the debugging_code.fla document.

2. Enter Debug mode by selecting Control ➪ Debug Movie.

3. Select Continue to start the movie playing.

4. Select the _global target from the Display list.

5. Select the Variables tab.

6. Double-click on the Value field for the num variable and enter 70 as its new value. When you click the Continue button, you will see how the value of the num variable increases to 70 and increments from there.

Tip   All objects, either user defined or predefined ActionScript objects will appear in the variable list. However, you can only change the values of some properties and variables.

The Watch list

Using the Debugger panel to monitor the value of multiple variables can get quite confusing, especially if you need to compare variables that exist on different timelines. The Watch list is an easy way to monitor the value of certain variables in a manageable way.

Once you have added a variable to the watch list, you can view it regardless of which Movie Clip you have selected in the Movie Clip list.

Adding a variable to the watch list

There are two options for adding a variable to the Watch list.

1. Open the debugging_code.fla document.

2. Start a debugging session by selecting Control ➪ Debug Movie.

3. Select Continue to start the movie playing.

4. Select the _global target from the Display list.

5. Select the Variables tab to show all variables from the _global namespace.

6. Right-click (Windows) or Control-click (Macintosh) on the num variable and select **Watch**. A little blue dot appears indicating that it is in the watch list.

7. Select the Watch tab to view the Watch list. You will see the num variable and its value you change as you progress through the debugging session.

Alternatively, you can perform the following steps to add a watch to the Flash movie.

1. Repeat Steps 1 and 2 from the previous method.

2. Select the Watch tab.

3. From the Debugger panel's options menu, choose Add Watch. Alternatively, you can right-click (Windows) or Control+click (Mac) the empty area of the Watch tab and choose Add.

4. Double-click the new entry (`<undefined>`) in the Named column and type in the correct path and name of the variable you want to watch.

Caution If you type in an incorrect path or variable name, the variable value will be undefined in the Watch list.

Removing a variable from the watch list

There are three methods to remove a variable from the watch list. The first method involves the following steps:

1. Navigate to the variable using the Display list and the Variables tab.

2. Right-click (Windows) or Control+click (Mac) the variable you wish to remove and deselect the Watch command. The little blue dot will be removed.

The second method involves these steps:

1. Select the Watch tab.

2. In the Watch list, right-click (Windows) or Control+click (Mac) on the desired variable and select Remove.

Alternatively, the third method involves these steps:

1. Select the Watch tab.

2. Highlight the variable you no longer need and select Remove Watch from the Debugger options menu.

Editing and displaying movie properties

The Properties tab of the Debugger panel displays the properties of all the Movie Clip instances, including the Main Timeline (`_root`, displayed as `_level0`) in your movie. Follow these steps to view and edit movie properties while debugging.

Follow these steps to view the properties of any Movie Clip timeline in the movie:

1. Open a file that you want to debug.

2. Enter Debug Mode by selecting Control ⇨ Debug Movie. In the Debugger panel, click Continue.

3. Select a Movie Clip instance from the Display list. Choose something other than `_global`.

4. Select the Properties tab to view the properties of the selected Movie Clip instance. The properties that appear in a different color from the majority of the properties are read-only and cannot be changed.

Tip For processor intensive applications in Flash MX 2004 that use the drawing API, try changing the `_quality` property of the `_level0` timeline to "LOW" to see increased performance.

Perform these steps to edit a specific property of a timeline or object in the Debugger panel:

1. Follow Steps 1 through 3 of the previous exercise.

2. Double-click the Value field of the property you wish to alter and enter the new value.

Note If you enter an incorrect value, such as a string when a number is required, the Debugger panel ignores the change, reversing the value to its last valid state the next time you reselect that Movie Clip instance.

Assigning Breakpoints

Perhaps one of the most useful features of the Debugger panel is the option to set and use breakpoints. A breakpoint is a position in your ActionScript code that halts playback of a movie while you are in Debug mode.

Using breakpoints, the Debugger panel allows you to step through a block of ActionScript line by line. You can define when the Flash movie will halt and when it will proceed. You can choose to execute a function or to step through the function. Choosing to step through a function will halt your movie on every line of the function waiting for your action. This is very valuable and makes it easier to find (often simple) problems in your ActionScript.

On the CD-ROM You can find the `debugging_code.fla` file in the `ch34` folder of the *Macromedia Flash MX 2004 Bible* CD-ROM. Make a copy of this file to a location on your hard drive. This file is used in the next few sections.

Adding or removing breakpoints in the Actions panel

You can set, delete, or remove all breakpoints in the Actions panel while authoring a Flash document.

Follow these steps to apply a breakpoint to specific line of ActionScript code:

1. Open the `debugging_code.fla` document.

2. Select frame 2 of the actions layer, and open the Actions panel (F9).

3. Place the cursor on line 15. The Debugger stops the movie at a line where a breakpoint exists, only executing the code before the breakpoint. Breakpoints should be positioned on lines where you think an error exists or just before the point where you think an error is occurring.

4. Do one of the following:

   • Click the Debug Options button in the toolbar of the Actions panel (look for the stethoscope icon) and from its menu choose Set Breakpoint.

   • Right-click (Windows) or Control+click (Mac) the line of code and select Set Breakpoint. A red dot in the gutter indicates lines that have breakpoints, as shown in Figure 34-9.

Breakpoint

Gutter   Script pane   Debug Options

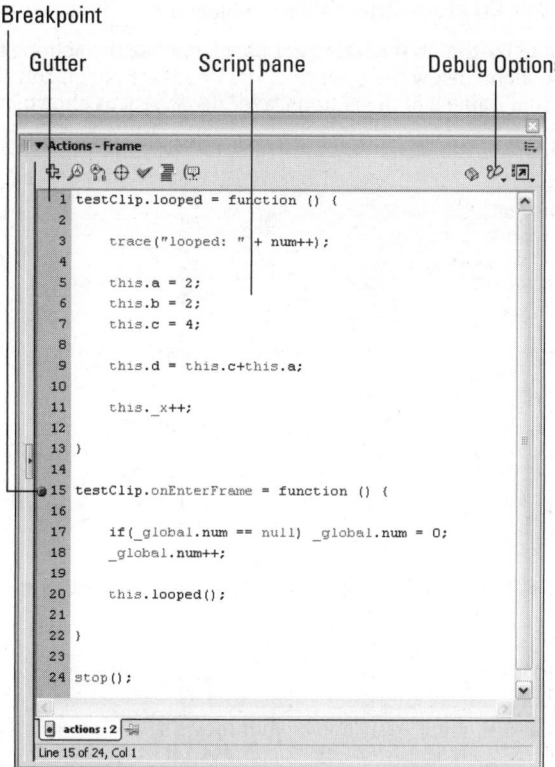

Figure 34-9: You can see the breakpoint icon residing in the gutter of the Actions panel.

Perform the following steps to delete a breakpoint from a line of code in the Actions panel:

1. Place the cursor on the line where a breakpoint exists.

2. Do one of the following: Click the Debug Options button and choose Remove Breakpoint, or right-click (Windows), or Control+click (Mac) and select Remove Breakpoint. The red dot will be removed.

Tip   To remove all breakpoints from the code, follow steps 1 – 2 and select Remove All Breakpoints instead of Remove Breakpoint.

Adding and removing breakpoints in the Debugger panel

Once you have started debugging your movie you can add and remove breakpoints. You can remove a single breakpoint or remove all breakpoints.

Follow these steps to add a breakpoint in the Debugger panel:

1. Open a fresh copy of the `debugging_code.fla` document from this book's CD-ROM.

2. Select frame 2 of the actions layer.

3. Enter Debug mode by selecting Control ➪ Debug Movie.

4. *Before* you press the Continue button on the Debugger panel, choose the actions for frame 2 from the drop-down menu below the toolbar of the Debugger panel. You should see the ActionScript code from frame 2 of the actions layer displayed, as shown in Figure 34-10.

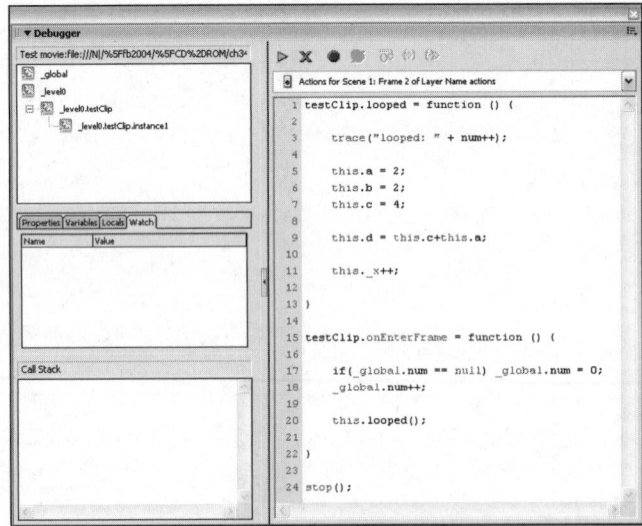

Figure 34-10: You can look at just about every line of your movie's code in the Debugger panel.

5. Place a cursor on the line 11.

6. Do one of the following: Click the Toggle Breakpoint button in the toolbar of the Debugger, which will add a breakpoint if none exists on that line. (It will remove a previously defined breakpoint if one exists.) Alternatively, right-click (Windows) or Control-click (Mac) and select Set Breakpoint.

   When the debugger reaches the line where you placed the breakpoint, it halts playback of the movie, waiting for your response.

7. Once the breakpoint is set, click the Continue button. The debugger pauses the movie when the code execution reaches your breakpoint. When the breakpoint is reached, you can analyze various aspects of the movie in the Variables, Properties, and Watch tabs of the Debugger panel. You need to click the Continue button to resume playback of the movie.

To remove a breakpoint in the Debugger panel, follow these steps. This example continues from above. You should use the same file, so make sure you are still in Debug Movie mode.

1. Place the cursor on line 11.

2. Do one of the following: (a) Click the Toggle Breakpoint button, which removes the breakpoint. If you push it a second time, the breakpoint will be re-set. (b) Right-click (Windows) or Control+click (Mac) and select Remove Breakpoint.

Caution Changes you apply to breakpoints while using the Debugger panel in Debug Movie mode only exist for that debugging session. When you return to authoring mode, the breakpoints added (or removed) during the debugging session will not be saved.

Stepping through your code

Using breakpoints and the Debugger panel, you can step through lines of your code while the movie is playing. This is a very powerful feature, enabling you to pin-point the exact position of a problem in your code.

When you start a debugging session by selecting Control ➪ Debug Movie, the movie is paused in the Flash Player so you can modify and set new breakpoints before you start the debugging session. You need to push the Continue button to allow your movie to play.

On the CD-ROM Make a copy of the `debugging_breakpoints.fla` document from the `ch34` folder of this book's CD-ROM.

1. Open the `debugging_breakpoints.fla` document. The ActionScript in this movie was built to demonstrate the process of stepping through lines of code.

2. Debug the movie by selecting Control ➪ Debug Movie.

3. As the movie is initially paused, click the Continue button to start debugging. Refer to Figure 34-11 to easily locate the Continue button.

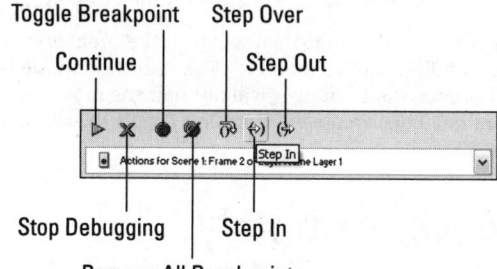

Figure 34-11: Using a breakpoint on a line in which a function is being called is very useful. From there you can Step In, Step Over, or Step Out of the function.

4. When the Debugger panel reaches the first breakpoint at the line `testClip.onEnterFrame = function ()`, it will stop and wait for you to choose action. The little yellow arrow in the gutter indicates the current position of the movie.

You can choose one of the following actions:

- **Step Out:** If you are debugging inside a user-defined function, Step Out will cause the debugger to execute everything within the function and continue playing, until it reaches the next breakpoint outside of the function. However, if there is a breakpoint below the line where you have selected Step Out within the function, the debugger will halt the movie and wait for your action.

Note If you click Step Out on a line that is not inside a function it performs the same actions as if you had clicked Continue.

- **Step In:** If you position a breakpoint on a line where a function is called, such as line 15 in frame 2 on the actions layer of `debugging_code.fla`, the debugger will move to line 3; the first line within the function you "stepped into." Click Step In to proceed to the next line in the function. Pressing Step In within a function will proceed and pause the movie to the next line, regardless if it has a breakpoint. Click Continue to move through the lines until another breakpoint is reached, skipping lines without one.

Note If you click Step In on a line that is outside of a function, it performs the same action as if you had clicked Continue.

- **Step Over:** Clicking Step Over on a breakpoint tells the Debugger to ignore the line of code where the breakpoint occurs and moves the player to the next line of your code. If you choose "Step Over" on a line where a function is called, it moves to the next line and calls the function in the process.

Note If you click Step Over on a line where a function is called and the function has a breakpoint inside of it, the Debugger will halt the movie at the breakpoint line.

- **Continue:** Choosing Continue will start the movie playing until the next breakpoint is reached.

- **Stop Debugging:** Selecting this option will stop the Debugger from processing the actions any further. However, your movie will still continue to play.

- **Toggle Breakpoint:** If you click this button, it will turn the breakpoint off because one already exists on that line. You will need to click either Continue or Step In to advance the movie. However, the Debugger will not halt the movie at this line again as the breakpoint has been removed. Pressing Toggle Breakpoint a second time will set a breakpoint.

Debugging a Flash Movie Remotely

You can debug a Flash movie (.swf file) using the stand-alone, ActiveX, or plug-in versions of Flash Debug Player 7. Debugging your file remotely is very useful if you have a Flash movie that references server-side scripts on your production server.

On the CD-ROM You can find the `debugging_code.fla` file in the `ch34` folder of the *Macromedia Flash MX 2004 Bible* CD-ROM. Make a copy of this file on a location on your hard drive.

Note You need a Web server to use this feature of the Debugger panel. If you have a Web server on your local machine, you can test your files there. Otherwise, you need to upload your files to a remote Web server.

Follow these steps to enable remote debugging and debug the example Flash movie (.swf file):

1. Open Flash MX 2004 and open the `debugging_code.fla` document.

2. Open the Publish Settings by selecting File ⇨ Publish Settings.

3. Clear the HTML check box. You can test by directly referencing the Flash movie (.swf file) on your server — you don't necessarily need the HTML document to debug the movie.

4. Select the Flash tab of Publish Settings and select the Debugging Permitted check box. If you want your Flash movie to be protected from prying eyes, you should enter a password into the Password field. The password will not be hidden in the authoring document. Anyone who has access to the Flash document (FLA file) will be able to view the password.

5. Press the Publish button in the Publish Settings dialog box. This creates a Flash movie (.swf file) with debugging enabled. Flash MX 2004 also generates a Flash debug file (.swd file). Flash Debug Player uses this file when remotely debugging a movie. Both of these files should be uploaded to the same directory of your Web server.

Note   If you do not upload the SWD file you can still debug remotely. However, you will not be able to step through the code, because breakpoints will be ignored.

6. Press OK to close the Publish Settings.

7. Open the Debugger panel by selecting Window ⇨ Development Panels ⇨ Debugger.

8. Enable Remote Debugging in Flash MX 2004 by selecting Enable Remote Debugging from the Debugger panel's options menu. You have now finished all the steps needed to remotely debug the Flash movie.

9. Upload the Flash movie (.swf file) and debug file (.swd file) to your Web server.

10. Make sure Flash MX 2004 is open. Without Flash MX open, you will not be able to debug the movie.

11. In your preferred Web browser, open the remote Flash movie (.swf file). You must make sure Flash Debug Player 7 is installed in the browser you choose. See the "Installing the Flash Debug Player 7" sidebar later in this chapter.

12. The Remote Debug dialog box will open as soon as the Flash movie loads into the browser (refer to Figure 34-12).

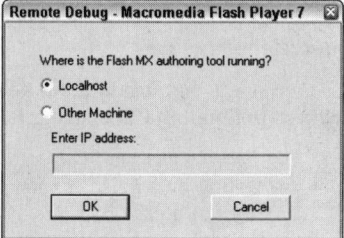

Figure 34-12: The Remote Debug dialog box as it appears from the browser running the debugged Flash movie

Caution If the Remote Debug dialog box didn't open, it means that the Flash Debug Player 7 couldn't find the SWD file. You can still remotely debug your movie, but any breakpoints will be ignored. Right-click (Windows) or Control-click (Macintosh) any area of the Flash movie's stage and select Debugger from the player's contextual menu.

13. From the Remote Debug dialog box, select either of the following options:

- **Localhost:** Select this option if the Flash MX 2004 authoring application is on the same machine that's running the remote Flash movie in the browser.

- **Other Machine:** Select this option if the Flash movie (.swf file) you are debugging and the Flash MX 2004 application aren't on the same machine. In this case, you need to enter the IP address of the machine with the Flash MX 2004 application.

Tip Don't lose sight of how powerful the "Other Machine" option is during debugging. If a movie is working correctly on your computer but not on an associate's machine, you can have your associate download and install the debug player. When your associate goes to the remote Flash movie in his/her browser, supply the tester with your machine's public IP address in the Other Machine field of the Remote Debug dialog box. Your machine must have Flash MX 2004 running, and your machine must not be behind a firewall in order for the debugging session to work properly. Note that the tester does not need to have Flash MX 2004.

14. Once the Flash movie (.swf file) and the Debugger have successfully connected, a password prompt will appear. Enter the password and select OK.

Note If you didn't enter a password when you published your Flash movie, leave the password field blank and click OK.

15. You will be automatically taken into Flash MX 2004. You can start debugging just as if the movie was running in Debug Movie mode on your computer. The only difference is that you will need to switch back and forth between the Web browser and Flash MX 2004 to see any visual changes in the Flash movie.

Using Flash Debug Player 7

Two versions of Flash Player 7 ship with Flash MX 2004: the Debug version and the release version. When you enter the Debug Mode of Flash MX 2004 by selecting Control ⇨ Debug Movie, the debugging features of the Flash Player 7 are used.

In order to debug a remote SWF file you need to use the debug version of Flash Player for your browser. You will find it in the following directory: `<Flash MX 2004 program directory>\Players\Debug`. Run the appropriate installer for your preferred browser.

In `<Flash MX 2004 program directory>\Players\Release` you will find the Release version of Flash Player 7. You can reinstall the original plug-in (without the debugging features) at any time.

Periodically, Macromedia may release updates to both the Debug and Release versions of the Flash Player. Check `www.macromedia.com/support/flash` for updates.

Testing across mediums

Macromedia has successfully deployed Flash Player technology over the years. You can now find the Flash Player on many platforms including Windows, Macintosh Linux, but it also exists on devices such as the Pocket PC (PDA handhelds), mobile phones, and the Sony PlayStation.

With the availability of the Flash Player on many platforms and devices, it is very important that you test your Flash movies across all possible mediums. Thorough testing your movie on multiple player versions is a very important step in planning a successful application built with Flash MX 2004. Doing this can save you much trouble further down the road if your application is more successful than you initially planned.

Testing Matrix

Figure 34-13 and Figure 34-14 are examples of testing matrices. These should be used before a launch of any commercial application. Testing across all of these different configurations can be a little time consuming but ensure maximum compatibility of your application. There is little point to releasing a product that doesn't correctly work for your target audiences.

Regular testing of your product, both at the end of the development and especially during the development cycle will ensure an easier transition from development to release.

	Win 95	Win 98	Win 2000	Win NT	Win ME	Win XP	Mac OS 9	Mac OS X
IE 6.0								
IE 5.5								
IE 5.0								
IE 4.0								
NS 6.0								
NS 4.7								
NS 4.5								
NS 4.0								
AOL 5								
AOL 4								

Figure 34-13: Test Matrix 1 should be used for Flash movies that will be viewed and used within a browser. It covers a wide range of available and commercially used browsers.

	Pocket PC 2002	Cell Phone
Casio Cassiopeia		
Compaq iPaq		
Hewlett Packard Jornada		

Figure 34-14: Test Matrix 2 should be used for Flash movies that will be used on a mobile device. This includes PDAs and handhelds.

Storing Code in External Files

Flash MX 2004 is easily extensible, as there are various areas in which you can place code. This can be the cause of major problems — because there are many available options, you need to make sure the code is correctly placed so your movie is manageable and easy to use. In Flash MX 2004, you have the option to store your code in an external .as file.

The #include command

Once you have an .as file to use in a project, it is easy to make the ActionScript within the file available to your movie. The #include command is used to load any code from an external file and put it in the Flash movie (.swf file) published or tested by Flash MX 2004. If you edit the .as file included in your movie, the changes will not automatically become part of an already-published Flash movie (.swf file). The #include command is only executed at the time you publish or test the SWF file.

This simple example shows you how to include an external ActionScript file in a movie.

On the CD-ROM

You can find externalActions.as in the ch34 folder on the *Macromedia Flash MX 2004 Bible* CD-ROM. Make a copy of this file to a folder on your hard drive. external Actions.as contains a trace() action which will appear in the Output panel once you have entered Test Mode.

1. Create a new Flash document by selecting File ➪ New.

2. Save the Flash document to the same location on your hard drive where you copied the externalActions.as file.

3. Select the first frame of Layer 1 and open the Actions panel (F9). In the Script pane, type the following code:

```
#include "externalActions.as"
```

4. Test the movie by selecting Control ➪ Test Movie. In the Output panel, the words "Traced from externalActions.as" should appear. This is the result of the trace() action in the externalActions.as file.

Now that you know how to use the #include directive, you can start to store larger amounts of code within .as files. One of the primary benefits of using .as files is that you can easily share the same ActionScript code from one Flash document to another.

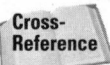
Cross-Reference

Read Chapter 32, "Creating a Portfolio Site in Flash," and Chapter 33, "Creating a Game in Flash," to see more Flash documents that use the #include directive.

Import Script command

If you prefer not to use the #include command to incorporate the code in your Flash movie (.swf file) at runtime, you can simply import the file directly into Flash MX 2004 using the Actions panel.

On the CD-ROM

Continue to use the externalActions.as file for this exercise.

1. Open Flash MX 2004 and create a new Flash document.

2. Save this file to the same location as the externalActions.as file.

3. Select the first frame of Layer 1 and open the Actions panel (F9).

4. Select **Import Script** from the options menu of the Actions panel.

5. Browse to the folder where you saved `externalActions.as`, highlight it, and select OK. Flash MX 2004 will import the file and put it in your movie.

Caution When you import ActionScript from a file using this method, the content of the Script pane will be overwritten and replaced with the contents from the ActionScript file.

Tip Flash MX 2004 does not parse the file and check for incorrect syntax when importing. You should check the syntax of the code once it has imported to make sure it is correct. To do this, choose Check Syntax from the options menu of the Actions panel.

Export Script command

Just as you can import the contents of an external file, you can export the contents of the Script pane to an .as file. This will enable you to take advantage of the editing capabilities in the Actions panel while still leveraging the usefulness of external ActionScript files.

1. Open a Flash document that contains some ActionScript code. You can use the `debugging_code.fla` document from the exercise earlier in this chapter.

2. Select a frame containing ActionScript code, and open the Actions panel.

3. Select **Export Script** from the options menu of the Actions panel.

4. Save the new .as file to a preferred location on your system.

Team environments

When working with a team of developers on the one project, it can get quite difficult to manage the development of an application. Many "newbie" applications are built within one FLA file, which poses a problem because only one person can work on the file at any given time. It can become very confusing and file versioning errors may occur.

A great way to reduce dependency on other team members is to break the FLA file up as much as possible. This may include breaking a project into several Flash documents (.fla files), which are then combined using the `loadMovie()` method command at runtime. Another effective method is to use external code files for storing data. For each block of code performing a separate task, or each custom object you are using in your application, you can store the ActionScript in an external file. This makes it easy for many people to work simultaneously on one application.

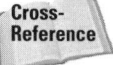

Cross-Reference For more information on Flash project management, see Chapter 3, "Planning Flash Projects." This chapter discusses the new Project panel featured in Flash MX Professional 2004.

ActionScript libraries and classes

With Flash MX 2004, you can build ActionScript routines (and even your own custom classes) suitable for re-use across a variety of situations. For instance, you may have a block of code that you use to initiate a connection to a server-side script, or a Flash Communication Server application. Storing such code in external code files is an easy way to include them in your next project without much effort.

An ActionScript library is a set of code used for a specific purpose. It can be any block of ActionScript, from simple variable declarations to more advanced ActionScript objects. This sort of code is well suited for being stored in an external text file, and easily included in many projects.

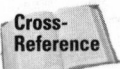

Cross-Reference

It's beyond the scope of this book to discuss the use of custom class files in Flash MX 2004. Refer to the *Flash MX 2004 ActionScript Bible* for more details.

Troubleshooting Guidelines

Troubleshooting problems with a Flash movie can be quite difficult. Depending on the complexity of your movie(s) it can be quite involved. The two main areas where you can experience problems with your movie are as follows: the structure and design of your movie, or your ActionScript code. However, this can be extended to other technologies your movie may use. For example if you use a Web server that relays XML data back and forth, the problem could lie in the connection and processing of data and may have nothing to do with the Flash movie. Similar issues can exist if you're using Flash Remoting or Flash Communication Server applications. We have compiled these troubleshooting checklists to help you solve some problems that may occur during your Flash development.

Good practices

The following list will help you alleviate the need for troubleshooting your movie and prevent many problems from occurring.

✦ **Planning:** Planning can be a tedious task. However, it can also be the start to a very successful project. If you plan your project from start to finish, you can pinpoint potential problem areas before you have even begun.

Note

We are not referring to a time schedule, but the processes and methods you use to satisfy the requirements of a project.

✦ **Incremental File Saving:** A major problem may arise in your movie that can slow production. It may be easier to revert to the last saved version in your movie. This can be an easy task by incrementally saving a new copy of your movie at each milestone.

Note

We suggest using the following naming convention file name_version number as a useful naming structure. Some examples of this convention are `movie_01.fla`, `movie_02.fla` and so on.

A *milestone* should be considered a significant point in your project; a step closer to completion of your project.

✦ **Regular testing:** While you create your movie, you should start testing early in the development process. Regular and thorough testing can help to point out problems that may occur down the track.

Not only should you test regularly but you should also test in the target environment (you can use the testing matrices discussed earlier in this chapter).

✦ **Comments:** When you write ActionScript code, you should comment each function or block of code. Many problems can arise as a result of simply not remembering what each function or block of code does. Without comments, you could accidentally skim over the exact trouble location because you can't remember what the function does or how it works. Comments should be short and concise going into detail if necessary.

Not only should you comment your ActionScript, but you should also comment your frames. Have a layer named "comments" in your movie. On any given keyframe of this layer place a comment in the Frame Label field of the Property inspector to remind yourself what a particular frame does or is used for.

✦ **Naming Conventions:** Make sure all aspects of your movie are named properly, including ActionScript. Make sure you've given each function a descriptive name. This should also be applied to variables and objects. Your naming conventions should extend beyond ActionScript; you should name each layer, scene, and symbol descriptively.

✦ **Rest:** If you find a lot of simple problems occurring, chances are you are just tired and overworked. A lot of problems arise when you are mentally exhausted. Often the best thing to do is get some sleep and come back refreshed. Typos are a common problem when you get tired. Take regular breaks also — they really do help.

General troubleshooting checklist

The following is a list of guidelines, which you should follow when you are not too sure where your movie is faulting. Both developers and designers should read these general guidelines; often, simple mistakes cause problems in your structure and ActionScript.

✦ **Locked, hidden, or Guide layers:** A common problem occurs when you accidentally lock or hide a layer. It is easy to overlook ActionScript that resides on an object that you can't see, due to the layer being locked or hidden. Also, any object residing in a Guide layer will not be included in the generated SWF file.

Caution

ActionScript code on a Guide layer will be exported with your Flash movie. If you're intentionally using a Guide layer to prevent elements on that layer from being exported, make sure you don't have any conflicting ActionScript on any keyframes of the Guide layer.

✦ **Naming conflicts:** It is quite easy to give multiple objects the same name. This can occur in ActionScript or in naming frames and objects. A good practice is to make sure that each variable, function, object, and property has a unique name.

✦ **swLiveConnect:** When working with Flash movies in combination with JavaScript and `fscommand()` action, the `swLiveConnect` attribute of the `<embed>` tag in HMTL has to be set to true. Without it, Flash movies cannot communicate with JavaScript in Mozilla or Netscape browser — nor can you use the `fscommand()` in your code. You can learn more about this type of interactivity in Chapter 22, "Integrating Flash Content with Web Pages."

Designer troubleshooting checklist

This checklist is a simple guide to problems that are focused on the structure and layout of your movies.

✦ **Graphics or Movie Clips:** Problems occur when you think an object is a Movie Clip when it is really a Graphic symbol. You can't name a Graphic symbol or reference it in ActionScript code. This will cause problems if you're under the presumption that a Graphic symbol is actually a Movie Clip.

✦ **Edit mode:** It is quite easy to become confused as to which Timeline or editing mode you are in. You may think you are editing on the Main Timeline, when in fact you are two timelines deep. Look at Figure 34-15 for an indication of where to look to find out which Timeline you are currently on.

Back button

Nested Movie Clip

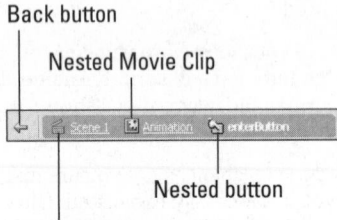

Nested button

Scene 1 (Main Timeline)

Figure 34-15: Refer to this portion of the Document window to view which Timeline or object you are currently editing.

✦ **Action placement:** Be sure you haven't confused the type of action you are using on a particular object. There are three types of action modes in Flash MX 2004: Frame, Movie Clip, and Button actions. Often, these are confused and become a problem. For example, you may accidentally add actions to a keyframe when you meant to add them to a Movie Clip instance.

Web Resource While not related to ActionScript or coding, a common bitmap problem that designers encounter is bitmap shift. See the following tech note at Macromedia's site:

www.macromedia.com/support/flash/ts/documents/bitmaps_shift.htm

Developer troubleshooting guidelines

This is a list of common problems that may occur when writing ActionScript. Problems in your project can spread wide and far; these might be caused by one or more trouble areas covered in either of the general, designer, or developer guidelines. It would be advantageous to read all areas to maximize the chance of solving problems.

✦ **Object and Frame Label Names:** Make sure you have correctly named your objects and frame labels using the Property inspector. This can alleviate many problems, which may be caused by a result of a poor naming structure. Names are case sensitive in Flash Player 7! As such, make sure you have the name correct, both on the frame or object and in your ActionScript code where you are referencing the frame or object.

✦ **Paths:** When referencing objects, frames, or variables, make sure you have the path correct. It can get quite confusing using relative paths such as `this` and `_parent` which can often be the source of major problems.

Tip　You can use the Insert Target Path button in the Actions panel to help target nested Movie Clip instances. See Chapter 19, "Building Timelines and Interactions," for more details.

✦ **Conflicting namespace:** When creating an object or declaring a variable make sure it isn't the same as a predefined object or variable name in ActionScript. Likewise, make sure you have unique objects and variable names.

✦ **Conflicting frame actions:** Many simple problems are caused by conflicting frame actions. You may have a `stop()`; action on Layer 1 at frame 20 and a `play()`; action on Layer 2 at frame 20 which would stop your movie from stopping. For more information on this topic, see the sidebar "Layer Order and Execution Order" in this chapter.

✦ **Confining the problem:** Make sure the problem exists with the Flash movie. When you work with server-side elements, the problem could be on the server. You may have a problem with the connection or with database information being passed back and forth. Make sure you test your server-side scripts for errors also. Oftentimes, developers will create non-Flash interfaces in HTML to test the functionality of server-side elements to isolate any problems before integrating the same data with a Flash movie.

✦ **Strings or Expressions:** A common problem is using a string when an expression should be used and an expression where a string should be used. When you are writing code in the Actions panel, make sure you have quotes when you are writing a string and no quotes when you are referring to an object, function, or variable. For example, this code `trace(test)`; will try to send the value of test to the Output panel, rather then sending the string "test" to the Output panel.

Layer Order and Execution Order

The order of your layers determines the order in which your ActionScript is executed. This can cause problems in your ActionScript code. Follow these steps to set up an example to illustrate this problem:

1. Open Flash MX 2004 and select File ➪ New to create a new file.

2. Select Insert ➪ Layer three times so you have a total of 3 layers in the movie.

3. Open the Actions panel by selecting Window ➪ Actions.

4. Select frame 1 of the top layer and enter this code: `var i = 20;`

5. Select frame 1 of the middle layer and enter this code: `var i = 30;`

6. Select the frame 1 of the bottom layer and enter this code: `trace(i);`

7. Test the movie by selecting Control ➪ Test Movie. The value of `i` will be sent to the Output panel and it should be 30.

Continued

Continued

8. Drag the top most layer beneath the second layer, so you have reversed the i declaration order.

9. Test the movie by selecting Control ➪ Test Movie. The value of i will be sent to the Output panel and it should now say 20. As you can see, the last declaration of i sticks and the first one is over written. This can affect any type of ActionScript object: variables, functions, or objects.

The layer order specified on the Flash tab of the Publish Settings dialog box also controls the order in which Flash draws the layers over a slow network or modem connection.

Community Help

There are many Web sites out there built solely for the Flash community. You should leverage from the huge knowledge base available at these Web sites. Post your messages in forums and mailing lists; more often than not, others have come across the same problems. Most of these sites also have a huge resource of downloadable open source code, which you can peruse to work out how certain tasks are performed.

These resources are invaluable and an excellent way to learn more about Flash. However, you should download the examples and figure out how they work. If you simply download them and use them you won't learn anything. Working through all of the code is an excellent method for learning Flash.

The following list of excellent Web sites is devoted to the Flash community:

✦ **FlashSupport:** www.flashsupport.com

✦ **Ultrashock:** www.ultrashock.com

✦ **Moock.org:** www.moock.org

✦ **Person13.com:** www.person13.com

✦ **FlashKit:** www.flashkit.com

✦ **FlashPlanet:** www.flashplanet.com

✦ **ShockFusion:** www.shockfusion.com

✦ **Were-Here.com:** www.were-here.com

✦ **ActionScript.com:** www.actionscript.com

 Web Resource   We'd like to know what you think about this chapter. Visit www.flashsupport.com/feedback to fill out an online form with your comments.

Summary

✦ Use code hints in the Actions panel to help you determine the correct syntax for your ActionScript code.

✦ While you develop an application, testing regularly — including testing on target mediums — can make the difference between a good application and an excellent application. You should get in the habit of testing the Test Matrices to ensure that your product will perform on most commercially available and accepted programs and platforms.

✦ You can often remove the need for troubleshooting through regular testing. However, if you think a problem lies within your ActionScript, use the Debugger in combination with the Troubleshooting guidelines to find and fix the problem.

✦ When you create code-intensive projects, use the Debugger regularly; you can use Breakpoints effectively and to your advantage. Using Breakpoints regularly to debug your code is often the most effective method because of its flexibility and ease of use.

✦ You can design and use your own Testing Matrices if the ones that are provided in this chapter aren't conclusive enough for your platform. You may need to update the Testing Matrices over time as the Flash player becomes available on more platforms.

✦　　✦　　✦

Expanding Flash

If you've done nearly everything you can do in Flash and you're wondering what else is possible - this is the section that will give you an introduction to the best applications and workflows for expanding your projects beyond pure Flash. We could have called this section the "Working With" section because all of the chapters included here cover applications that work with Flash and the techniques you can use to work with these programs to enhance your multimedia project development.

In Parts 1 through VII, you learned that Flash can tackle some of the most complex graphic, animation, sound, and interactive projects. But, as we all know, no one program can do it all (or do it all *best*). For optimum efficiency and creative options, most of us work with a toolbox of multiple programs that fit together in various ways. In an effort to help you find the best place for Flash amongst the other key applications that you might be using, we have included this section on "Expanding Flash."

We have compiled coverage of the most relevant applications that you can leverage for specialized tasks and use to discover new creative possibilities. If Macromedia FreeHand, Fireworks, Dreamweaver, or Director are part of your toolbox, this section will provide guidance on how to make the most of these programs in your Flash workflow. We also include coverage of the latest versions of Adobe's most popular programs, Illustrator and Photoshop.

Working with Raster Graphics

Although Flash can generally hold its own for vector art creation, you need another application to acquire, finesse, and export bitmap images for use in your Flash projects. Flash MX 2004 is an amazingly versatile application that can import and export just about any raster (a.k.a. *bitmap*) image format. This chapter shows you how to create bitmaps for Flash in image-editing applications such as Macromedia Fireworks and Adobe Photoshop.

Preparing Bitmaps for Use in Flash MX 2004

Regardless of the specific effects that you apply to your images in other programs, the key features to consider when preparing bitmaps for use in Flash are size, compression, and transparency.

✦ **Size:** It is important to know what the maximum image size will be in your final Flash layout. You may choose to size your bitmaps slightly larger than the final size to accommodate browser scaling. Although you can scale multiple instances of the same image to different sizes in Flash, if you intend to use many smaller thumbnails and only a single instance of the image at a larger size, it will be worthwhile to make a smaller copy of your image to import into Flash in addition to the original, larger image.

✦ **Compression:** Different compression schemes will work better on some images than on others. With experience, you will learn to select the most appropriate compression to maximize the quality of your images, while minimizing file size. For example, if you are working with a black and white photo that has high contrast or a bitmap image of a line-art illustration, you might find that GIF compression is actually more effective than JPEG compression.

Some images need to be very high-resolution to maintain details, while other images (such as abstract background images) can be down-sampled significantly, while still serving their purpose in your design. Although you can always add additional compression to your images in Flash with the native JPEG options, it is helpful to decide on a baseline for an image and reduce it to the highest quality that you will actually need in your final presentation. If you choose to add JPEG compression to your images *before* importing them to Flash, make sure to select the **Use Imported JPEG data** check box when you import the files to Flash. The Launch and Edit functionality of Fireworks ensures that you will always have the option of making changes to your source image, even if you use a flattened JPEG version of the image for authoring in Flash.

✦ **Transparency:** There are many different ways of adding transparency (or *Alpha*) to an image; you might need a very subtle fade of one image over another, or you might simply need to eliminate the white space around a central image. Deciding on the final effect that you need and then finding the best way to achieve this while keeping your file size small is the challenge. Bitmap file formats that support true transparency in Flash include PNG, PICT (Mac), BMP (Win), and TIFF. These file formats all have *lossless* native compression schemes, making them ideal for high-quality images. However, these benefits come with a high price in terms of file size. If you can achieve the effect that you need by applying a vector mask in Flash, or by cropping the original image, it is much better to take that approach.

Enhancing Web Production with Fireworks

Macromedia Fireworks has upped the ante on what you can expect from a Web-imaging application. The many features of Fireworks MX 2004 enable you to do more of your Web-image production from start to finish without ever going to another application.

With Fireworks, designers have the freedom to import work that they have created in Photoshop, Illustrator, FreeHand, Flash, Poser, After Effects, LiveMotion, or even 3D Studio Max — while maintaining the option to edit the files. Unlike most other Web design programs, Fireworks combines the ease of vector-based editing with the tools required for advanced bitmap editing.

Along with its advanced, yet familiar, tools Fireworks also sports a superior optimization engine for exporting files, and for the automation of custom command batch processing. It includes the indispensable option to implement a Find and Replace for elements within a graphic project. For designers working on Flash projects that require integration of numerous source images, one of Fireworks' most powerful features is its capability to prepare (and optimally compress) huge quantities of bitmap files for import.

Perhaps the most important feature of Fireworks is that the native PNG formatted files can be imported directly to Flash without any other file export or format conversion required. All vectors, bitmaps, animations, and even multi-state button graphics will be preserved in the Flash authoring environment. This workflow finally breaks down the barrier between raster files and vector art or text, enabling you to take advantage of the best features of these different formats without having to switch modes or break your artwork up into multiple files. Going the other way, Fireworks is equally capable of receiving files from Flash and optimizing them for inclusion on HTML sites.

Here's a quick overview of some of the core features of Fireworks, which make it a preferred partner for Flash:

✦ **Macromedia common user interface (UI):** Just like Flash MX 2004, Fireworks MX 2004 has a streamlined interface (shown in Figure 35-1). All the tools and options are laid out in dockable panels that are distinguished by unique icons and names. Also, the **Property inspector** provides intuitive, centralized information and controls relevant to the active tool or element.

Figure 35-1: The sleek interface for Fireworks MX 2004 is consistent with the UI you'll see in other Macromedia MX 2004 Studio programs.

✦ **Create and edit text directly:** In Fireworks you can create and edit text directly on the canvas without having to use a separate text editor. You can modify text settings at any time directly in the Property inspector.

✦ **Bitmap tools:** Fireworks flaunts a set of bitmap-editing tools that will make designers requiring detailed image editing options very happy. These include Blur, Sharpen, Dodge, Burn, and Smudge.

✦ **Gradient tool:** Fireworks also has a user-friendly Gradient tool that can be used to fill pixel selections, vector objects, and text.

✦ **Batch Processing:** The user interface for Batch Processing makes it easy to optimize large quantities of images. You can also run scripts during a batch process.

✦ **Quick Export button:** Fireworks gives developers a shortcut to their other Macromedia MX Studio programs. As shown in Figure 35-2, this icon at the top of the Document window provides a drop-down menu of various options for file export or transfer to other core development programs.

✦ **Extend Fireworks with custom commands made in Flash:** Fireworks MX (and MX 2004) allows you to enhance the Fireworks JavaScript Extensibility API by combining prebuilt or custom commands with interfaces created in Flash using ActionScript and components. Visit the Macromedia Exchange to download user-built commands.

✦ **Selective JPEG compression:** Fireworks enables you to add a JPEG Mask to an area of your image. This mask can have a different JPEG compression setting than the rest of the image.

Figure 35-2: The Fireworks Quick Export button provides a shortcut to other core programs and common file options.

✦ **Launch and Edit:** You can easily edit PNG image files while authoring documents in Flash or in Dreamweaver by using the **Edit With** option, as shown in Figure 35-3. When a PNG image is opened in Fireworks from another application, Fireworks will let you know that you're in "Launch and Edit" mode. The changes made in Fireworks will automatically be applied to the image in your document and can also be saved to update the original source PNG file.

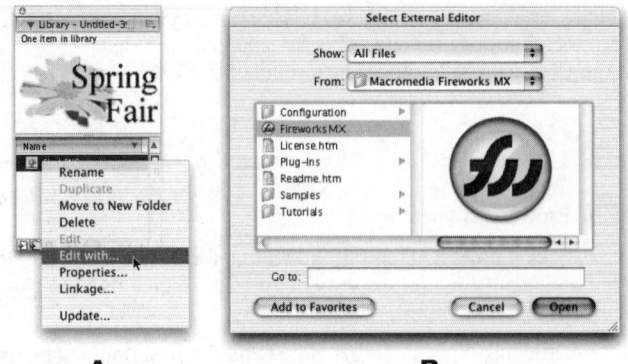

Figure 35-3: The Flash Edit With option allows you to choose an image-editing application to modify raster images that you've placed in Flash.

✦ **Reconstitute image tables:** Fireworks MX will rebuild an editable source PNG file from an image table in an HTML file. Fireworks will import the slices with Web behaviors, such as rollovers or pop-ups, still attached. The graphic can be edited in Fireworks and then exported with all of the behaviors intact.

✦ **Streamline Web production tasks in Fireworks:** The Fireworks Data-driven Graphics Wizard takes automated production a step further by supporting variable-assignment for graphic elements and Web objects in a Fireworks template document. This reduces repetitive production time for designers authoring multiple copies of the same elements. Also, Fireworks offers instance-level button properties, making it easier than ever to make multi-button navigation bars or pop-up menus by assigning unique text and URLs in the Property inspector.

✦ **Director export:** Fireworks can export files in a format suitable for Director use. This export requires an additional plug-in for Director.

✦ **FreeHand reader:** You can import or copy and paste FreeHand files from versions 7 and higher into Fireworks.

Note Although Fireworks supports the direct import of FreeHand files, if you plan to move vector artwork *from* Fireworks *to* FreeHand (or any vector graphics program other than Flash), you will need to export your files from Fireworks in Illustrator 7.0 format.

There's plenty more to Fireworks, and we get you on your way by introducing some solutions for Fireworks and Flash integration. Fireworks is an incredibly robust program that offers many features for Web production that go beyond the scope of this book.

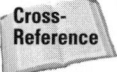

Cross-Reference For more detailed information on working with Fireworks MX 2004 (a core product in the Macromedia MX 2004 Studio), refer to the online help that is offered by Macromedia or the *Macromedia Studio MX Bible* (Wiley, 2004).

Transferring Fireworks images with transparency to the Flash authoring environment

The Fireworks tools and options will be familiar to anyone who has some experience with photo-editing — we will have to leave you to explore all the possible effects on your own. To introduce you to the various export options available in Fireworks for images with bitmap or vector masking, we will walk through the steps for moving a logo with bitmap and vector elements into Flash from Fireworks.

On the CD-ROM You can find the files used for this example in the FireworksMask folder in the `ch35` folder on the CD-ROM.

1. You can add mask layers to your bitmap file in Fireworks to isolate the areas of the bitmap image that you want visible in the final image. As shown in Figure 35-4, text created in Fireworks is automatically "masked"; it will float on any background color without additional clipping paths or masking.

Figure 35-4: In Fireworks you can easily add complex masks and editable text to your bitmap images.

2. By saving the file in Fireworks' native PNG file format, you will preserve all masking, bitmap images, and editable text.

3. Open Flash and create a new document (or open an existing FLA file that you want to add a new element to).

4. Select the Timeline and the frame that you want to import the artwork to. You may choose to create a new symbol before importing the artwork, or you can import directly to the Main Timeline and convert the graphic into a symbol later on.

5. Select File ➪ Import ➪ Import to Stage from the main application menu and find the Fireworks PNG file you saved in Step 2. When you select Open, the Fireworks PNG Import Settings dialog box appears. To import our static graphic with masking, while preserving editable text, select the options as shown in Figure 35-5.

Figure 35-5: Import Settings for translating Fireworks PNG files to the Flash authoring environment

The various options will interpret the PNG file as follows:

- **File Structure:** The first option (**Import as movie clip and retain layers**) automatically inserts the content of the Fireworks PNG file into a Movie Clip symbol in Flash. All the layers from the original Fireworks file will be preserved as individual Flash layers. The second option (**Import into new layer in current scene**), imports all of the content of the Fireworks PNG file into a single new layer on the current Flash Timeline — you can manually convert individual elements into symbols after the file has been imported.

- **Objects:** These options determine how Fireworks vector artwork is interpreted when imported to Flash. The first option (**Rasterize if necessary to maintain appearance**) converts any special vector effects or fills that are not supported by Flash into raster images to preserve the visual look of the artwork, but you will no longer be able to modify the original vector elements in Flash. The second option (**Keep all paths editable**) preserves vector artwork as editable elements, but any special effects or fills that are not supported by Flash are lost when the file is imported.

- **Text:** If you are working with text that has special formatting that may not be supported by Flash, this is an important option to select. If the text will not require further editing in Flash — such as an illustrative text element or logo — the first option (**Rasterize if necessary to maintain appearance**) ensures that any special formatting is preserved, but the text may appear in Flash as a bitmap element and the resulting file size may be larger. If the priority is to maintain editable text, it is best to select the second option (**Keep all text editable**), even if special formatting that is not supported by Flash may be lost.

- **Flatten:** The final option listed at the bottom of the Import Settings dialog box (**Import as a single flattened bitmap**) cancels all of the other options and simply flattens and rasterizes all of the elements in the Flash PNG file. This option is useful if you want to simplify a complex graphic that you know will not require further editing. It makes the graphic easy to place and may produce a smaller final file size.

6. After choosing the settings that are appropriate for the content of your Fireworks file, select **OK** to import the graphics to your Flash document as specified. Presto! As shown in Figure 35-6, the example Fireworks file has been placed on a single layer on the Main Timeline in Flash. The editable text box is preserved and the bitmap (with masking applied) is automatically placed in the Library.

Figure 35-6: The masked bitmap and editable text block from the Fireworks PNG file are preserved in the Flash authoring environment.

It is also possible to copy and paste content from Fireworks to Flash with the following cautions:

- ✦ Standard copy (Ctrl+C or ⌘+C) and paste of content from a Fireworks file to a Flash document renders all of the copied graphics as a single flattened bitmap image in Flash. The visual appearance of the graphics is maintained, but the image will not have any transparency.

- ✦ The **Copy as Vectors** allows you to preserve editable Fireworks text and vector artwork when it is pasted into Flash, but bitmap images may not be transferred correctly with this method.

Preparing other bitmap formats in Fireworks

Flash accommodates most common raster formats without any difficulty. The process for optimizing files with the various compression settings available in Fireworks is straightforward. The various View tabs in the Document window allow you to compare different image formats and compression settings that can be chosen in the Optimize panel (see Figure 35-7).

Figure 35-7: Preview tabs in the Fireworks Document window and the Optimize panel for choosing file formats and compression settings

The other option that can help you to preview the effect of different optimization settings is the Export Preview window, which is invoked by selecting File ➪ Export Preview (Ctrl+Shift+X or ⌘+Shift+X.) As shown in Figure 35-8, this window also includes all the familiar settings that affect how your final file displays when imported to other applications.

Figure 35-8: The Fireworks Export Preview window provides all the options you need to decide on the settings to use for the final exported image.

Note the color swatches available from the Matte drop-down menu; these let you define the background color to match when complex clipping paths are exported.

One other consideration when saving JPEG files for use in Flash MX 2004 is that you can now use imported JPEG data on images that have been exported from Fireworks with the Progressive check box selected. In Flash MX, images saved for progressive download were *not* recognized as optimized files and the option to Use imported JPEG data was not available in the Bitmap Properties dialog box.

Batch processing bitmap sequences with Fireworks

Consider a Flash project — a catalog or a portfolio, for example — that requires many bitmaps and bitmap animations. How do you get all those nicely rendered images into Flash? Suppose you have an animation created in a bitmap program such as Adobe After Effects, 3D StudioMax, QuickTime Pro, or Poser; all of these programs have an option to export the animation as a sequence of files, usually as a sequence of PICT, PNG, or BMP images. Often, this will be a sequence of **filename_01**, **filename_02**, **filename_03**, and so on. The obvious challenge of working with such file sequences is that they have the potential to add up to hundreds of individual files, all needing to be prepared and optimized for Flash import. Often, in dealing with such a sequence, the files are the wrong dimension, or need to have other changes made. Batch processing in Fireworks, and the capability to run custom commands during a batch process, easily saves the day (and your wrists).

On the CD-ROM You'll find all of the required assets for this project in the `ch35` folder of the CD-ROM. To work through this example, copy the exported PCT sequence to a separate folder on your hard drive.

Setting up Fireworks to batch process

To batch process efficiently, you first need to consider the several changes that might be required to prep the file sequence for Flash:

1. All of the files are the wrong dimensions. For the images to fit nicely into our Flash project, we need to change the dimensions from 320 x 240 to 200 x 150.

2. We also want to change the hue and saturation of the files to match the color scheme of the Flash project.

3. The art director decided to shake things up; he actually wants you to flip the sequence horizontally.

4. Finally, we need to convert all the files from the PCT format to JPEG format so that they will perform efficiently in Flash.

Let's get started. Open the first file of the sequence (`ch35/sequence/videoStills/ sleepyStella 01.pct`) and make a copy. Then, working on just this one file, make all of the changes that need to be done, per your list (as explained previously). This will be your test file.

Tip A similar workflow can be accomplished using custom Actions in Photoshop. Although we will not cover the step-by-step process in both programs, if you are familiar with Photoshop you should be able to adapt the Fireworks process to an equivalent process in Photoshop.

Creating a Fireworks command

Let's assume that you found the perfect settings and are completely pleased with the results on your test file. If not, undo and repeat the process until it comes out just right. Then, the next step is to use the History panel to create a Fireworks command. To make this custom command, we need to make the necessary changes to the sample file to get our desired final result:

1. Resize the image to 200 pixels wide (Modify ⇨ Canvas ⇨ Image Size).

2. Change the hue/saturation to a warm color (PI ⇨ Effects ⇨ Adjust Color ⇨ Hue/Saturation).

3. Flip the image horizontally (Modify ⇨ Transform ⇨ Flip Horizontal)

Open the History panel, to see every action or event that's been done to the file listed as steps (as shown in Figure 35-9).

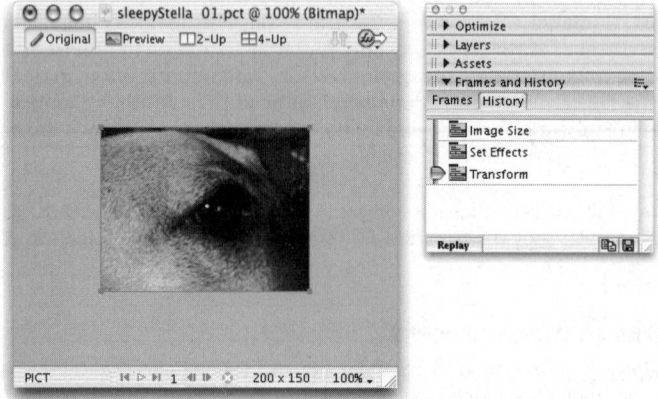

Figure 35-9: The History panel records your editing steps in sequential order.

This is how Fireworks commands are created. However, here's a word of caution about the History panel: Not every step in Fireworks can be used in a command. When you select steps that cannot be translated into a command, Fireworks will notifies you with a dialog box. Fireworks also gives you two visual clues for steps that cannot be applied as sequential commands: One is the step icon with a red X over it, and the other is not so obvious — it's a horizontal line break between steps. However, there are workarounds. To get around these continuity glitches, we'll just make two commands for the batch process.

To create the first command:

1. In the History panel, select the first step.

2. Click the **Save** icon at the bottom of the History panel.

3. Save the new command as **Resize**, and click **OK.**

You've just made a custom command in Fireworks. The custom command can then be accessed in the Command menu for future use.

For the second command, while still in the History panel, select the last two actions applied to the image (color effect and flip horizontal), and save this command as **Colorize & Flip.**

With these two custom commands saved, the next step is to customize the compression settings for the PNG sequence.

Creating custom export settings

Fireworks ships with two default preset quality options for exporting JPEGs: **better quality** (80 percent), and **smaller file** (60 percent). However, we need more compression than 60 percent. So, we simply create our own custom export setting:

1. Open the Export Preview dialog box (Shift+Ctrl+X or Shift+⌘+X).

2. Select the Options tab at the top of the Export Preview window and experiment with the JPEG compression settings in the **Quality** field, until you finally conclude that 50 percent is ideal for this project.

3. Set the JPEG quality to **50** percent.

4. Click the small plus icon (+) in the top-right corner of the Export Preview window to add your custom setting to the available export options.

5. Save this new custom setting as **JPEG 50**.

6. Click **OK** to close the Export Preview dialog box.

Launching the batch process

Now that we have two custom commands and a custom compression setting, we're ready to initiate the Fireworks batch process. Here's how:

1. Go to File ➪ Batch process and navigate to the folder that contains the (original) files to be processed.

2. Select the files to batch by opening the folder where all the images reside, clicking **Add All**, and then clicking **Next**.

3. This invokes the Batch Options dialog box. Here, you can choose what commands to apply to the selected files. A word of caution, however: To get the desired effect, the commands need to be arranged in a specific order. The order of the commands should be **Colorize & Flip**, **Resize**, and then **Export**. Select each command in sequence and click the **Add** button. (Refer to Figure 35-10.)

Figure 35-10: Custom commands added in sequential order for a batch process

Note Although the two custom commands don't have any extra options, the **Export** command does. With the Export command selected, click the drop-down menu for Export Settings, and then select the **JPEG 50** setting that we created earlier. Click **Next**.

4. This last step of the batch process asks where to place the new files and what to do with the originals. It is always a good idea to create a new folder for the modified images, rather than overwriting your source files. After you specify a folder, click the **Batch** button. While batch processing, Fireworks opens a feedback window indicating how many files are completed and how many files have yet to be processed. With a long sequence the process can take several minutes.

Tip Note the **Save Script** option in the Batch Options dialog box; this is used to save the current batch process settings as a reusable JavaScript command. This is useful if there's even a remote possibility that there may be more than one set of files to batch with the same edits.

After you have sized, flipped, and optimized all the files, you'll be ready to import them into Flash. The JPEG files will be imported and placed into sequential keyframes on the Timeline, as shown in Figure 35-11.

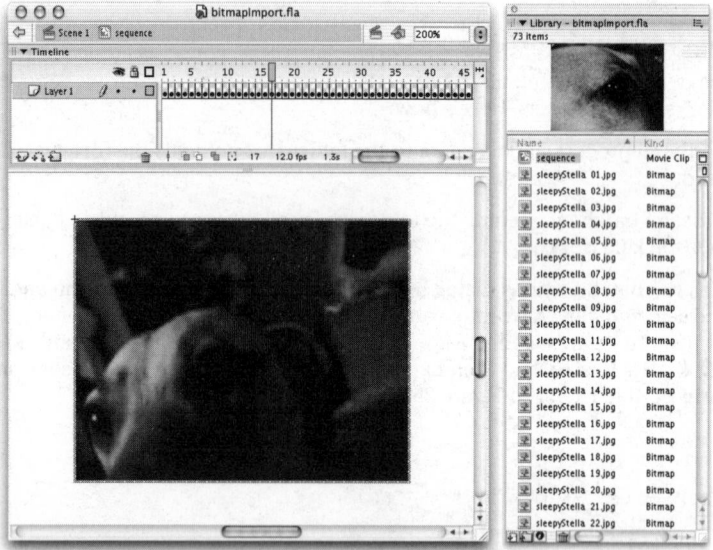

Figure 35-11: Import the JPEG sequence to a Movie Clip Timeline as a series to automatically place each image on a new keyframe.

Tip It is usually best to import the image files to a Movie Clip symbol Timeline so that they are easier to modify or move within your Flash project. Flash will auto-detect a numbered sequence and give you the option of importing all of the images in the sequence to individual frames on the current Flash timeline.

Creating Flash/GIF ad banners in Fireworks

Not only does Fireworks excel at preparing file sequences for Flash, but it's equally suited for *importing* Flash animations. It really is a two-way street with these programs. So, if you're already comfortable creating animations in Flash, why waste time learning how to animate in any other program? Fireworks can import anything you've done in Flash!

Flash banner ads continue to gain in popularity; however, many clients still require animated GIF banners. Someday, we can hope to work in a world of pure Flash advertising and rich-media banners. Meanwhile, we'll be in a transitional period where we still need to turn Flash ad banners into animated GIFs.

Tip   The templates that come pre-built with Flash go a long way toward encouraging consistent standards for rich-media banners. To start your design with any of these templates as a guideline simply open Flash MX 2004 and choose File ⇨ New; then select the **Templates** tab to choose a template available in the **Advertising** category.

Before we make a cool animated banner with Flash, we need to know the basic restrictions on banners. Here are some basic guidelines for animated banners: Target file size ranges from 12 KB on the high end, to an acceptable 5 KB, and on down to the ideal of a mere 3 KB. Typical dimensions are 468 x 60, 392 x 72, and 125 x 125.

Now we need to create an exciting animated banner ad that will work on all browsers. (That means it has to be an animated GIF.) The dimensions of the movie are 468 x 60 and the file size limitation is that it can be no more than 12 KB.

With these limitations in mind, we can begin designing our banner in Flash:

1. In the Document Properties dialog box (which is accessed from the Property inspector or from the application menu under Modify ⇨ Document), set the movie size to the specified dimensions.

2. Also in the Document Properties dialog box, set the frame rate to no more than 10 fps. That's because we know we have to make this animation into an animated GIF and, to stay within our file size limit, the lower the frame rate, the better our chances.

3. While creating the animation, watch out for file size. Try to design a simple animation with few colors and few frames. Fewer colors with fewer frames make it more likely to land within our target file size.

Tip   Color gradients are one of the most gratuitous file bloaters around. If you get a design comp for a banner ad that includes a color gradient and you need to reduce the file size, find a way to replace the gradient with solid colors.

Which format is best for export?

Once the animation works to your liking, the next step is to decide how to export it. If the animation has a lot of colors or images, then the best option is usually to export the animation as a PNG sequence with File ⇨ Export Movie. But if the animation has very few colors and only vector graphics, it's often best to export it as an animated GIF, either from the Publish Settings dialog box or with Export Movie.

Colorful animation export

Because the hypothetical animation is very colorful, we choose to export a PNG sequence. PNG is ideal for this, due to the amount of information that the format can hold, which is 24-bit color plus an alpha channel.

1. Still in Flash, choose File ➪ Export Movie.

2. In the Export Movie dialog box, choose **PNG Sequence** from the Format drop-down menu. Then, name the animation, choose a location for the exported file sequence, and click **Save**.

3. Now, open Fireworks and create a document that matches your Flash banner size. To import the PNG sequence as one file, choose File ➪ Open, and then navigate to the folder containing the PNG sequence. The next step is important.

4. If, at this point, we were to Shift+click all the files that we want to open and then open them, Fireworks would open each file individually, which would make it more difficult to create our animated GIF. So, we need to make sure to check the **Open as Animation** option, *before* we click Open. With this option, Fireworks places each selected file in its own frame within a single Fireworks file, in numerical order. Now click **Open**.

5. This new Fireworks file should have the file sequence set for export as an **Animated GIF**. But we're not done yet. To reduce the file size, we still have to go to work with the color palette.

6. Select the **Preview** tab to see how our animation will look when exported. In preview mode, Fireworks indicates the file size that will result with the current compression settings. Now it's necessary to focus on the **Optimize panel**, which is where the file type is chosen.

7. Select **Animated GIF** in the Optimize panel. Once a file type is selected, various optimization options appear. For an animated GIF, begin by editing the number of colors, either (a) choosing from a range of default color settings, with 256, 128, 64, 32, 16, 8, 4, or 2 colors in the color palette, or (b) entering a specific number of colors. Note that with every change to the color range or adjustment to the Optimize panel, the preview window updates with the file size. To ease comparison, Fireworks gives the option to view compression schemes with the 2-up and 4-up preview modes, viewing either two or four settings side by side.

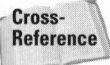
Cross-Reference   To see an illustration of how the various GIF color settings will affect color range in an image, refer to the samples printed in the color insert pages.

The trick to compression is finding a balance between appearance and file size. Too much compression, and the graphic looks like dirt, although the file size is ideal; too little compression and, while the graphic looks beautiful, the file size threatens to choke the fastest connections. So what can you do after trying to find that balance between image quality and file size, without success? What can you do when the image quality can't go any lower, but the file size is still way too large? As mentioned earlier, there is a second factor to the file size of animated GIFs: the number of frames. When image optimization fails, change your focus from the Optimize panel to the **Frames panel**.

The Fireworks Frames panel is used to control several animation playback settings. These are:

✦ The number of frames in the animation.

✦ The frame delay for each frame — should this frame hold for a second or two or just breeze right through as quickly as possible?

✦ The loop settings for the animation. Will the animation loop ten times, five times, never, or forever?

To further reduce the file size of an animated GIF, remove some frames. To remove a frame, simply select the frame in the Fireworks Frames panel, and then click the trashcan icon at the bottom of the panel.

Keep deleting frames, judiciously, and continuously preview the animation until you've brought the animation down to the required file size. Throughout this process, the preview mode will update its display of the file size every time a change is made. Unfortunately, you will find that as you delete frames from the animation, the animation will not play back as smoothly as originally designed and intended. But that's just a limitation of animated GIFs and a compelling reason to start creating pure Flash banner ads!

When the file's been brought down to an acceptable size, the next step is to edit the timing of each frame. Each frame in the Frames panel has a name on the left and a number on the right. The number signifies the delay length for each frame, measured in one-hundredths of a second. The default setting is 20 — or $^{20}/_{100}$ of a second. So, to pause a frame for 3 seconds, set the frame delay to 300.

The last adjustment to set is the looping of the animation. At the bottom left of the Frames panel is a loop icon. Select it and choose a loop setting. Finally, it's time to export this file as an animated GIF and send it off to the Web. Use File ➪ Export Preview. In the Export Preview window, select **Animated GIF** from the format pull-down menu. Now press the **Export** button to name the file and place it within the desired location. Click **Save** and you are ready to go.

Alternative workflow

If an animation is created in Flash with few colors, there's no need to export it as a PNG sequence. Instead, export the animation directly from Flash as an animated GIF. Use the application menu to select File ➪ Export Movie, and then choose **Animated GIF** from the Format drop-down menu; or use the Publish Settings dialog box, and first select the **GIF** check box, and then from the GIF tab, choose **Animated**. In either case, use the largest possible color palette in order to defer color crunching to Fireworks, where the controls over the color palette are generally more accurate and effective.

The exported animated GIF is easily imported into Fireworks by choosing File ➪ Open, and then selecting the single animated GIF file. Fireworks imports each frame with the frame delay settings intact. From here, the animation may be optimized per the previous instructions, proceeding from the color palette, to the number of frames and loop settings.

Preparing Images for Flash with Photoshop CS

Adobe Photoshop CS is an exciting upgrade to this premiere image-editing program. When you're preparing bitmaps for use in Flash, Photoshop adds some extremely useful and powerful Web features that make saving high-quality JPEGs and PNGs a snap. The PNG-24 format is a great format to use with Flash, because this file format has lossless compression and can support an alpha channel (a.k.a. *transparency mask*). In this section, we show you how to export a Photoshop image (PSD file) as a PNG-24 image to use in Flash.

New Feature   Flash MX 2004 now supports import of alpha channels in PSD format files. The workflow described in the following section is still valid, but you now have the choice of saving your final file in PNG-24 or PSD format. We have included files in both formats on the CD-ROM so you can try importing either file and the alpha channel will be preserved.

Photoshop has excellent selection and masking tools for the most complex images. Although some third-party plug-ins can make the task a littler simpler, some basic know-how with Photoshop tools can also go a long way toward completing your task with ease. In the following tutorial, we take an image of some houses along the beach and mask the background sky. This lesson assumes that you have a working knowledge of Photoshop layers and layer masks.

On the CD-ROM   Use the sample image `beachhouses.psd` in the `ch35/PhotoshopAlpha` folder of the CD-ROM that accompanies this book. The completed PSD and PNG versions of the masked image titled `beachhouses_masked.psd` and `beachhouses_masked.png` are also on the CD-ROM in the same folder.

1. Open the `beachhouses.psd` file from the CD-ROM. If you receive a message about a color profile mismatch, choose **Don't Convert**. For more information about color profiles and Flash, see the "Color Management in Photoshop" sidebar in this section.

2. To more easily separate the color tones of the sky from the foreground, add a separate Levels adjustment layer for the image on Layer 0. Do *not* use the regular Levels command, which permanently applies its effect to the image. We need only a temporary Levels adjustment layer to increase the contrast (see Figure 35-12).

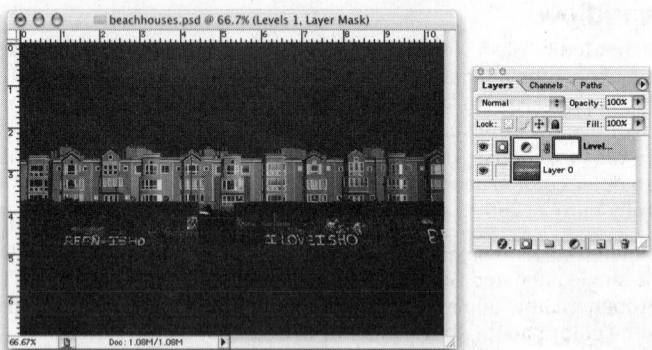

Figure 35-12: The image with a Levels adjustment layer

On the CD-ROM   You can achieve the correct level values in the Levels layer by loading the `separation.alv` file into the Levels dialog box, using the Load button when you first create the new Levels layer. This file is in the `ch35` folder of the CD-ROM that accompanies this book.

3. Select the Magic Wand tool in the Photoshop Tools palette. In the Magic Wand settings of the Option bar, enter **15** in the Tolerance field, and make sure **Anti-Aliased** and **Contiguous** are checked. Click the uppermost area of the now-darkened sky to select it. Shift+click additional areas with the Magic Wand tool until the entire sky is selected. If you grab anything in the foreground, either undo or start over (Select ⇨ None). See Figure 35-13.

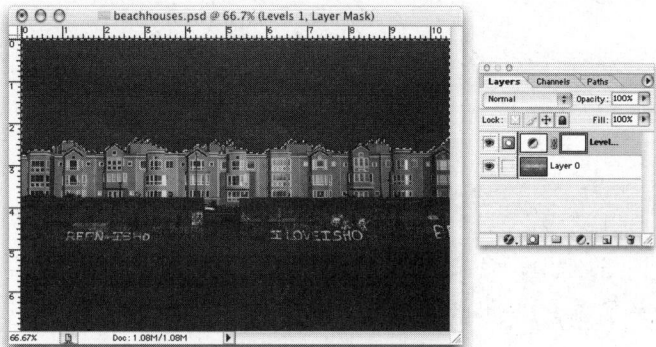

Figure 35-13: When you're creating your selection, pay particular attention to the edges of the rooftops.

4. With Layer 0 highlighted in the Layers window, Alt+click (Windows) or Option+click (Mac) the Add a mask icon at the bottom of the Layers window. This applies the current selection of the sky as a mask (see Figure 35-14). If the Add a mask icon was clicked without holding Alt or Option, the foreground elements would have been masked instead.

Figure 35-14: Alt+clicking (Windows) or Option+clicking (Mac) the Add a mask icon uses the active selection as the black area of a layer mask.

5. Now that we have masked out the sky, we don't need the Levels effect anymore. Turn off the Levels adjustment layer, or delete it.

Caution   Make sure you double-check the layer mask by viewing it separately in the Channels window. If any faint gray lines appear along the top edges of the mask, paint over them with a black brush. If any gray appears in the black area of the mask, it shows up in the Flash movie as hints of the original image.

6. Before we save this image as a PSD or PNG-24 file, we should crop all unnecessary information from the image. In this example, the masked sky should be nearly eliminated. See Figure 35-15.

Figure 35-15: It's always a good idea to crop unnecessary information (especially if it's hidden by a mask) from the image before importing it into Flash.

7. In Chapter 16, "Importing Artwork," we discussed the effects of larger-than-necessary bitmaps. Because the image width is currently larger than the default Flash movie width, we use the Image ⇨ Image Size command to change the width from 755 pixels to 550 pixels. Be careful when using the Image Size command. For this example, the **Constrain Proportions** and **Resample Image: Bicubic** options should be checked.

8. We're ready to save the image as a PSD or PNG-24 file. To save in Photoshop format (PSD) simply use the Save command (Ctrl+S or ⌘+S).

Note   If you *don't* want to overwrite the original unmasked image, use the **Save As** command (Shift+Ctrl+S or Shift+⌘+S) and give the file a new name.

9. To choose settings for saving the file in PNG-24 format, use the **Save for Web** command located in the File menu (Ctrl+Shift+Alt+S or Option+Shift+⌘+S). After you've chosen this command, the image appears in Live Preview mode within the Save for Web dialog box (see Figure 35-16). Click the **2-Up** tab to view the original image with the optimized version.

In the Settings section, choose the PNG-24 preset. Make sure the **Transparency** option is checked—this exports the layer mask as an alpha channel in the PNG file. Do not use the Interlaced or Matte options for Flash import. Click **OK**; Photoshop will ask you to specify a location and filename for the PNG-24 image. **Images Only** should be chosen from the Format drop-down menu. You can leave the Settings option as **Default** and the Slices option as **All Slices**.

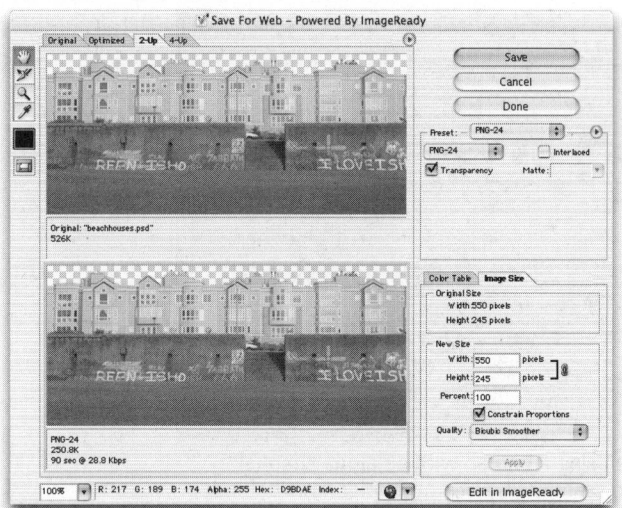

Figure 35-16: The Save for Web command enables fast Web image previews in Photoshop. You may need to resize this dialog box in order to display horizontal images on top of each other, as shown in this figure.

Tip
The Save for Web dialog box has many other cool features. While the 4-Up preview is not necessary for PNG-24 files (there are no compression options to worry about), you can preview your original with three different JPEG or GIF versions, each at a different compression setting. You can use the Preview Menu to see the effect of 8-bit browser dither (by checking the Browser Dither option), and you can use color profiles using Photoshop Compensation or Uncompensated Color. For PNG-24 files, always use the Uncompensated Color preview because it is the most accurate for Flash use. See the sidebar "Color Management in Photoshop" for more information on color compensation.

Note
You can also resize the optimized image in the Image Size tab, instead of performing this action as we did in Step 7.

10. We're ready to import the PSD or PNG file into Flash, which recognizes the alpha channel saved with our image. Open a document in Flash (or create a new one), and choose File ➪ Import ➪ Import to Stage (Ctrl+R or ⌘+R). Set the Show criteria to **All Files** in the Import dialog box. Select the PSD or PNG image and Flash places the image on the current frame of the active layer. Remember that all bitmaps are stored in the Flash Library. If you delete the instance of the bitmap on the Stage, you can always replace it with the bitmap in the Library. That's it! You've successfully imported an image with an alpha channel into Flash (see Figure 35-17).

Figure 35-17: Using a bitmap with an alpha channel enables you to seamlessly place other elements behind the bitmap in a Flash movie.

Check out the finished sample Flash document, `alphaBitmap.fla`, in the `ch35/PhotoshopAlpha` folder of the CD-ROM that accompanies this book.

The various options for controlling Flash JPEG compression of imported bitmaps are discussed in Chapter 16, "Importing Artwork," and in Chapter 21, "Publishing Flash Movies."

Color Management in Photoshop

Many strategies exist for color calibration on desktop computer systems. Macintosh computers have had a leg up in this area of graphics creation and output ever since the development of ColorSync. Apple's ColorSync software provides one of the most complete system-level color management solutions for desktop publishing. Unfortunately, while Windows systems do include ICC profile support, it's not as comprehensive as Apple's ColorSync system. Since the release of Photoshop 5.0, it has been possible to specify and attach ICC color profiles to most image file formats. In a nutshell, ICC profiles describe the color capabilities of a given input or output device, such as a computer monitor, printer, or scanner. When an ICC profile is attached to an image the profile tells the application that is using the image how the colors in the image should be interpreted. If every program in your workflow supports ICC profiles, then, theoretically, this provides a consistent display and output of all graphics.

Adobe has made an effort to address the complex subject of color management by including a direct link to information and tutorials on color management in the new Welcome screen in Photoshop CS — taking the time to review this information will give you a good start on understanding how color profiles are set up and managed.

However, while Photoshop and most page-layout programs recognize ICC profiles, the majority of Web development applications do not. Some Web browsers do not support embedded image profiles, although Apple has proposed many ICC tags to make color management a reality for the Web (visit `www.apple.com/colorsync/benefits`). More importantly, Flash MX 2004 does not support ICC profiles. Neither does the current implementation of the PNG-24 format. The JPEG file format is the only current Web image format that supports embedded profiles. Moreover, ICC profiles typically add about 500 to 800 bytes to an image's file size.

This is why the Save for Web feature (introduced with Photoshop 6.0) and its Preview Menu are so invaluable. They enable you to see how the JPEG, GIF, or PNG looks without Photoshop Compensation.

If you work primarily with Web or screen graphics, then you should use Photoshop's new Color Settings presets (Photoshop 6 or higher only) to quickly switch color spaces. For Web work, always use Web Graphics Default. For ColorSync management on the Mac, choose ColorSync Workflow. On the PC, choose a setting that best matches your printing needs (ColorSync is an Apple-only management system).

In Photoshop 5.5, change your RGB working space to sRGB, or turn off Display Using Monitor Compensation if you continue to use other RGB spaces. Either method enables you to work with your images so that the Photoshop Compensation and Uncompensated Color settings render the image exactly the same within the Save for Web preview panes. Also, disable ICC profile embedding in the Profile Setup preferences (File ⇨ Color Settings ⇨ Profile Setup) by deselecting all the boxes under the Embed Profiles heading.

Exporting Raster Images from Flash

If you've been wondering how to use your artwork in Flash with other raster-based applications, then this section is for you. Many people prefer to use Flash as their primary drawing and illustration tool, thanks to Flash's uniquely intuitive set of vector drawing tools. Combined with a pressure-sensitive graphics tablet, Flash can indeed be a powerful illustration program.

Why would you want to export raster-based images from a vector-based application? The answer is quite simple: Some applications work better with raster (or bitmap) images than they do with vector images. Video-editing applications and other motion graphics programs intended for producing broadcast content usually prefer to work with bitmaps instead of vectors. If the application in which you want to use Flash artwork *does* support vector file formats such as EPS or AI, then it's generally better to use those instead of bitmap-based formats such as BMP or PCT.

Cross-Reference

We discuss using external vector applications in Chapter 36, "Working with Vector Graphics." If you want the best-quality vector artwork exported from Flash, jump to that chapter.

If you are unsure of the format to use in your graphics program, refer to Table 35-1. Afterward, we show you how to export a frame's artwork as a static raster image.

Table 35-1: Raster Image Formats for Flash Export

Flash Export Format	File Extension	Comments
BMP (Win only), Windows Bitmap	.bmp	Can be used with all Windows and some Mac applications. Variable bit depths and compression settings with support of alpha channels. Supports lossless compression. Ideal for high-quality graphics work.
GIF Image, Graphics Interchange File	.gif	Limited to a 256-color (or less) palette. Not recommended as a high-quality Flash export format, even for Web use.
JPEG, Joint Photographic Experts Group	.jpg	Supports 24-bit RGB color. No alpha channel support. Recommended for most high-quality graphics work that will not need to be re-edited. Note that this format throws out color information due to its lossy compression method.
PICT , Picture	.pct	Can be used with many Windows and all Mac applications. Variable bit depths and compression settings with support of alpha channels. Supports lossless compression. Can contain vector and raster graphics. Ideal for high-quality graphics work.
PNG, Portable Network Graphic	.png	Supports variable bit depth (PNG-8 and PNG-24) and compression settings with alpha channels. Lossless compression schemes make it an ideal candidate for any high-quality graphics work.

To export a raster image format from Flash MX 2004:

1. Move the Playhead in the Flash Timeline to the frame that contains the artwork that you wish to export.

2. Choose File ⇨ Export ⇨ Export Image.

3. Select a destination folder and enter a filename. Select your preferred raster image format in the Format drop-down menu.

4. Depending on the file format you selected, you are presented with an export dialog box with options specific to that file format. We look at the general options and at some file-specific settings next.

General export options in raster formats

Every raster image format in Flash's Export Image dialog box has the same basic options. All of these pertain to the image size, resolution, and bit depth (or number of colors) for the exported image. You can also trim any unused Stage area from the final exported image. As you will see in the next section, for each specific raster format there are other unique settings in addition to the main options described here:

✦ **Dimensions:** The Width and Height options control the image's width and height, respectively, in pixels. Note that the aspect ratio of these values is always locked. You cannot control the Width value independently of the Height value.

✦ **Resolution:** Measured in dpi (dots per inch), this setting controls the quality of the image in terms of how much information is present in the image. By default, this setting is 72 dpi. If you want to use Flash artwork in print or high-resolution graphics work, enter a higher value, such as 300 or 600. If you change this setting accidentally, pressing the Match Screen button reverts the value to 72 dpi, the resolution of most computer monitors. Note that changing the value for this setting also changes the Width and Height values in the Dimensions setting.

✦ **Include:** This drop-down menu determines what Flash content is included in the exported image.

- **Minimum Image Area:** When this option is selected, the image size (a.k.a. *dimensions*) is reduced to the boundary of Flash artwork currently on the Stage. This means that if you have only a circle in the middle of the Stage, the dimensions of the exported image match those of the circle — the rest of the Flash Stage or background won't be included.

- **Full Document Size:** When this option is selected, the exported image looks exactly like the Flash Stage. The entire frame dimensions and contents are exported.

✦ **Color Depth (or Colors):** This drop-down setting controls the color range of the raster image. The higher the bit depth, the wider the color range. Depending on the file format, not all options are identical. We define the most frequently occurring options here. This option is not available for JPEG images, as that format must always be 24-bit. The options include the following:

- **8-bit grayscale:** This option limits the image to 256 levels, or values, of gray. It is equivalent to a typical scan of a black –and white photograph.

- **8-bit color:** This option reduces the image to 256 colors. You may notice unsightly dithering in the image as a result. See Chapter 21, "Publishing Flash Movies," for more information regarding dither.

- **24-bit color:** This option allows the image to include any of the 16.7 million colors available in true RGB color space. Use this option for the best color quality.

- **32-bit color w/ alpha:** This option enables the same range of colors as 24-bit color, but also adds an alpha channel using the Flash movie's background color as a matte. If your raster image program can read alpha channels, then the Flash background color is transparent.

Other raster file format options

Each specific file format Export dialog box will also have some additional export options. In this section, we look at the additional options available for BMP (Windows only), PCT or PICT, and GIF.

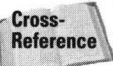

The JPEG, GIF, and PNG format options are discussed in Chapter 21, "Publishing Flash Movies." Because a problem exists with publishing adaptive GIFs in the Macintosh version of Flash, however, we explore the GIF export options here.

Export BMP (Windows only) options

The Windows Bitmap (.bmp) file format has numerous options. In addition to the general export settings (described previously), the BMP Export dialog box has an options setting containing a check box for **Smooth**. When this option is selected, Flash anti-aliases all Flash artwork, making the edges nice and smooth. If this option is unchecked, Flash artwork is rendered in an aliased fashion, in which edges may appear jagged and rough.

Caution   In most external graphics applications, the **32 bit w/ alpha** option in the Colors drop-down menu is not supported. You should use the 24-bit option if you experience difficulties using 32-bit BMP files. If you need to export an image with alpha channel support, use the PNG format in the Windows version of Flash.

Export PICT options

The PICT (short for Picture) format is a standard Macintosh graphic file format. Any Mac OS application that uses graphics can use it, and, with QuickTime, you can also use PICT (or PCT) files on Windows computers. PICT files can contain both vector and raster (bitmap) information. Usually, only raster-based PICT files are truly cross-platform (see Figure 35-18).

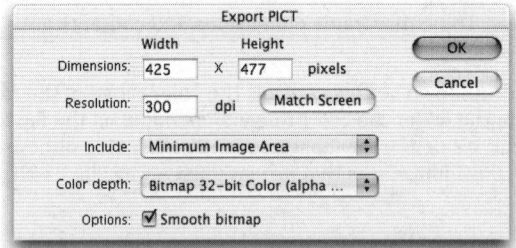

Figure 35-18: The PICT format has a unique Objects option (in the Color Depth drop-down menu) in addition to traditional raster-based options.

The following options can be used to control how your Flash artwork is converted to PICT format:

✦ **Color Depth:** This drop-down menu is the same as the Colors setting for other raster-image file formats. (It has a few peculiarities that are defined in the next section.) There are six different color depth options, as follows:

• **Objects:** Because PICT files will support vector or raster information, you can specify Objects to export Flash artwork as vector-based images.

Caution   Selecting the **Object** color option enables you to select **Use PostScript** in the Options setting. Use PICT output that contains PostScript with caution, as it can produce undesirable results. If you need PostScript with your output, it is better to use Illustrator or EPS as the export format.

• **Bitmap 1-bit B/W:** This option converts all colors to either black or white, with no intermediate values of gray. It is equivalent to the Bitmap image mode in Photoshop, and gives a fax document look to your Flash artwork.

- **Bitmap 8-bit Gray:** This option converts your Flash artwork colors to 256 values of gray.

- **Bitmap 8-bit Color:** This option creates an adaptive palette of 256 colors for the exported image.

- **Bitmap 24-bit Color:** This option produces the highest-quality raster-based PICT files, enabling any color in the RGB color space to be represented. This is usually the preferred color setting for images that will be used for graphics work in other applications.

- **Bitmap 32-bit Color (alpha channel):** This option has the same color depth as 24-bit color, with the addition of an alpha channel (or transparent mask). Any unoccupied areas of the Flash Stage are used to determine the transparent areas of the alpha channel.

✦ **Options:** The PICT Export dialog box displays only one other option. The options that are displayed vary depending on the Color Depth setting.

- **Smooth bitmap:** If you choose any of the Bitmap color options in Color Depth, then you have the option of anti-aliasing (or smoothing) Flash artwork. Smoothing produces cleaner edges on Flash vector-based artwork.

- **Include PostScript:** If you choose Objects from the Color Depth menu, you can enable the Include PostScript option. This option optimizes the file's settings for output to a PostScript-compatible printer.

Export GIF options

The check box options in the Colors section of the GIF Export dialog box (see Figure 35-19) are discussed in the "Using the GIF settings" section in Chapter 21, "Publishing Flash Movies." The Colors drop-down menu is slightly different, however. Also, as mentioned in a previous note, the Publish settings in the Macintosh version of Flash do not create adaptive GIF images (even if you have selected the option to do so).

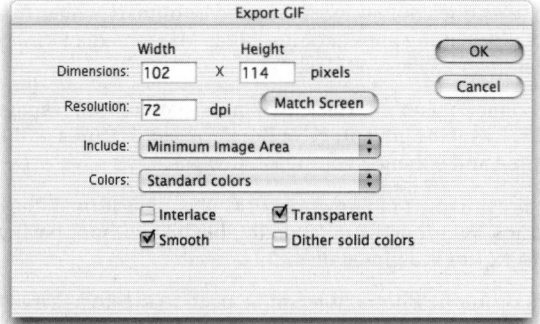

Figure 35-19: Export Options that are specific to the GIF format

On the CD-ROM

You can see the effect of each of these color options by looking at a series of GIF images created from a test Flash movie, `gifcolors.fla`, located in the `ch35/GIFexport` folder of the CD-ROM that accompanies this book. Each GIF color depth setting was applied to this movie and saved as a separate GIF image. These images are also printed for your reference in the color insert pages of the book.

✦ **Colors:** As stated in the discussion regarding general options, this setting controls the range of colors contained in the exported image. GIF images can use a variety of bit depths with the overall 8-bit color depth setting. The fewer the colors, the smaller the resulting GIF file. The three different approaches to color conversion are as follows:

- **Black & White:** This option is equivalent to a 2-bit color depth, and converts all Flash colors to one of three colors (Web hex in parentheses): black (#000000), middle gray (#808080), or white (#FFFFFF).

- **4, 8, 16, 32, 64, 128, or 256 colors:** These options create the respective color ranges within the GIF format. Flash determines which colors are used for each setting, similar to the adaptive palette type in Photoshop.

- **Standard Colors:** This option creates GIF images that use the 216 Web-Safe Palette.

Using Raster Animation Tools

Although the main appeal of Flash is the sleekness of vector-based animation, there are occasions when you might want to try something a little different. Whether you choose to start your animation in a raster program because you are more comfortable in the authoring environment or because you simply like the look of the artwork, you can easily integrate your raster artwork with Flash projects. An increasing number of programs natively support export to the SWF format. However, the workflow described earlier in this chapter for optimizing a bitmap sequence for Flash can be used to integrate raster image sequences from any program that may not support direct export to the SWF format.

Web Resource We'd like to know what you think about this chapter. Visit www.flashsupport.com/feedback to fill out an online form with your comments.

Summary

✦ Flash is a vector artwork tool that does not support creation of bitmap images from scratch. You need to use an image-editing application such as Macromedia Fireworks to create, modify, and optimize bitmap images for Flash.

✦ Fireworks and Flash share a common user interface, making it simpler for Flash users to learn the tools in Fireworks. By taking advantage of the strongest features of different programs, you can save time and enhance your Flash designs.

✦ Flash MX 2004 supports the direct import of Fireworks PNG files. This format allows you to preserve bitmap graphics, vector artwork, and editable text without having to change authoring modes or to export individual files.

✦ Either Macromedia Fireworks or Adobe Photoshop can be used to create a PNG-24 image with an alpha channel. Flash MX 2004 also supports import of PSD files with alpha channels. Flash renders the black area of an alpha channel transparent (or semi-transparent) on the Flash Stage, which allows other elements in a Flash movie to show through the foreground bitmap.

✦ Flash can export a variety of raster image file formats, which enables you to transfer your Flash artwork to other graphics programs. You can specify the exported image's quality and size in the Export Image dialog box.

✦ ✦ ✦

Working with Vector Graphics

As the Flash authoring environment has matured, more designers have realized that much (if not all) of their design and artwork for Web projects can easily be created directly in Flash. Designers have also begun to integrate Flash as part of a streamlined production process to deliver consistent design to clients who have a presence in print and broadcast as well as on the Web.

Even if your designs are intended only for the Web, adding a few other programs to your toolkit enables you to take advantage of specialized features that can enhance your Flash projects and save production time. Custom brush styles, creative text controls, and libraries of reusable Graphic symbols are just a few of the "extras" that come with most professional vector design programs.

Flash MX 2004 offers more options than ever for integrating artwork created in other authoring programs. With a few simple steps, the process of importing or exporting vector artwork between Flash and most professional graphics programs can be seamless. This chapter discusses some of the most common workflow options and gives you the background you need to keep artwork and page layouts consistent when moving from one program to another.

Optimizing Vector Graphics for Use in Flash

Macromedia FreeHand and Adobe Illustrator are two of the most commonly used vector programs, and there are many other programs that also offer tools or techniques that can add a special touch to your Flash designs. The best effects are often complex, and a detailed description of specific techniques in other programs is beyond the scope of this book. However, with an understanding of how Flash interprets imported vector files, you will be able to apply the information in this chapter to optimize your workflow, regardless of what specific programs you choose to work with.

Cross-Reference
For coverage of how imported vector files can be modified in the Flash authoring environment, refer to Chapter 16, "Importing Artwork." If you are looking for more detailed information on production techniques in Macromedia programs beyond Flash, a good place to start is the *Macromedia Studio MX 2004 Bible* (Wiley, 2004).

Maintaining color consistency

Flash can only use an RGB color space, meaning that it renders colors in an additive fashion — full red, green, and blue light added together produce white light. Whenever possible, you should use RGB color pickers in your preferred drawing application. If you're using FreeHand or Illustrator, specifying colors with the RGB color picker ensures that both copied-and-pasted objects and exported files will appear as you see them in the original workspace. If you use CMYK, then you will notice color shifts when the artwork is imported into Flash.

Caution   Some vector file formats cannot save artwork color values in RGB space. If you're using Adobe Illustrator and you choose to save to Illustrator 6 or lower format, RGB values will not be saved, and color shifts will result.

Macromedia FreeHand (version 9 and higher) includes Clipboard options that can be customized. These settings are accessible from the main application menu via File ➪ Preferences (FreeHand MX ➪ Preferences on Mac). In the Windows version of FreeHand, click the Export tab of the Preferences dialog box. In the Mac version of FreeHand, click the Export Category of the Preferences dialog box. There, you find a Convert Colors To drop-down menu. If you're using a mix of CMYK and RGB color in a FreeHand document, choose CMYK and RGB. However, this may still render CMYK artwork differently when imported to Flash. To have WYSIWYG (What You See Is What You Get) color between FreeHand and Flash, opt to use the solitary RGB option (as shown in Figure 36-1). This option converts all artwork to RGB color space, regardless of the original color picker used to fill the object(s).

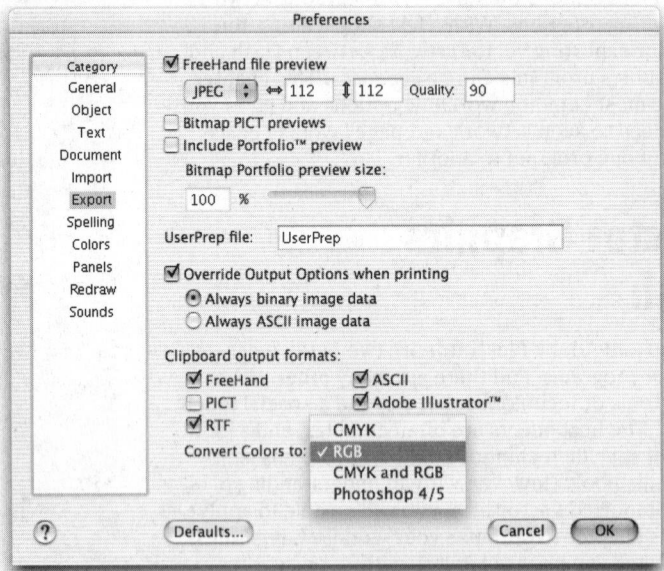

Figure 36-1: Setting the Convert Colors preference in FreeHand to RGB ensures color consistency when creating artwork for use in Flash.

Tip

If you're exporting EPS files from FreeHand 8, use the **Setup** (Windows) or **Options** (Mac) button in the Export Document dialog box to access the same color options available in the FreeHand Preferences for more recent versions of FreeHand.

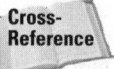

Cross-Reference

For more coverage of color issues related to Flash production, please refer to Chapter 7, "Applying Color."

Saving in the proper file format

As long as you save your file to the correct format and version, Flash MX 2004 can import most common vector formats, with a few limitations on support for editable text and layers. Both Macromedia FreeHand (version 9.0 or higher) and Adobe Illustrator (version 9.0 or higher) support export to the SWF format — this is one of the most consistently compatible vector formats for importing graphics to Flash.

Note

If you are working with Adobe Illustrator 11, use the File ➪ Export command to save your file in a format that will import to Flash reliably. The most compatible formats include Illustrator Legacy (.ai), Illustrator Legacy EPS (.eps), or Macromedia Flash (.swf). AI and EPS files saved directly (with the Save or Save As command) from Illustrator 11 do not always import correctly to Flash. Officially, Flash MX 2004 only supports AI files version 10 or lower, PDF files version 1.4, and EPS files 3.0 and earlier.

Native FreeHand files (.fh), PDF, and AI files can be imported to Flash with layers and symbols preserved, but EPS files will be flattened into a single layer. The various methods for importing files into Flash from FreeHand and Illustrator are further discussed later in this chapter.

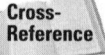

Cross-Reference

For detailed discussion of some of the issues related to rendering imported artwork in Flash, refer to Chapter 16, "Importing Artwork."

Converting text to outlines

Many of the designs you import from other programs may consist only of vector shapes, but there are times when you also need to handle text. An important aspect of vector graphics that comes up especially when working with other designers is font linking and embedding. With most vector file formats, such as Illustrator, FreeHand, or EPS, you can link to fonts that are located on your system. However, if you give those files to someone else who doesn't have the same fonts installed, he or she won't be able to work with or view your file as it was originally designed. Some formats (such as PDF) enable you to embed fonts into the document file, which circumvents this problem. However, whether the fonts are linked or embedded, you may be unnecessarily bloating the size of the graphic file by including all of the font information when you need to render only a few letters in a logo.

You can convert any text into outlines (a.k.a. *paths*) in most drawing or illustration programs. In FreeHand, select the text as a text block (with the Selection tool, not the Text tool) and choose Text ➪ Convert to Paths. In Illustrator, select the text as an object and choose Type ➪ Create Outlines.

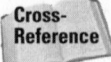

Converting text to outlines is discussed in more detail in Chapter 16, "Importing Artwork."

When importing files from FreeHand to Flash directly (in .fh format), any text with special effects is automatically converted to outlines. Text with special formatting, such as tabs or centered alignment, will be preserved as editable text; however, it will be broken into a series of smaller text blocks to maintain the layout. For more detail on converting artwork from FreeHand to Flash, refer to "Enhancing Flash Production with Macromedia FreeHand" later in this chapter.

If you have a lot of body text in the file, you may want to copy the text directly into a Flash text box and use a _sans, _serif, or _typewriter device font. These fonts do not require any additional file information (unlike embedded fonts) when used in a Flash movie and will result in smaller SWF files than if you included outlines of all the text.

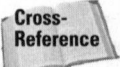

For more detailed information on optimizing and managing fonts in Flash projects, refer to Chapter 8, "Working with Text."

Tracing to convert rasters to vectors

A handful of applications, including Flash, let you trace raster artwork to create a vector "drawing." In the section "Enhancing Flash Production with Macromedia FreeHand," later in this chapter we cover the workflow for tracing images in FreeHand. Although you can trace images in Adobe Illustrator, Adobe has a better stand-alone product that is specifically designed for tracing raster artwork—Streamline 4.0.

Although Streamline has not been updated since version 4.0 and will only run on OS X in Classic mode, it does offer extensive conversion options and optimization commands. If tracing bitmaps will be an important step in your workflow, it is worth looking into this tool. Get more info and find demo downloads on Adobe's Web site at www.adobe.com:80/products/streamline/main.html.

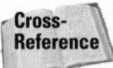

For coverage of Flash's native **Trace Bitmap** command, refer to Chapter 16, "Importing Artwork."

With any tracing application, keep these points in mind:

✦ Higher resolution images always yield better "traced" vector artwork. With more pixels to define edges, the application can better detect shapes.

✦ Sharper images (such as clearly focused images) and higher contrast images produce better traced artwork. Applying Photoshop art filters to reduce the complexity of a photographic image can make it easier to trace.

✦ One-color images or scans, like those of hand-drawn sketches with pencil or ink, produce the best traced results.

With all of the software and tool options available, it can be difficult to keep track of all the variables. The most important thing to decide is how you want your final artwork to look. For example, if you want a minimal silhouetted vector look, then it may actually be better to create a clipping path from the bitmap and fill it with solid color manually than to use an auto-trace tool. On the other hand, if you are trying to maintain detail in an image and your goal is simply to reduce your file size, it may be best to import an optimized bitmap directly into Flash (where you can then apply the Break apart command and erase any unnecessary parts of the image).

The two traps that you want to avoid in production are bloated file sizes and needless quality loss. There are certainly times when you will have to compromise on image size or resolution in order to keep your Flash movies streamlined, but don't make the mistake of assuming that the worse the image looks, the smaller your file will be—this is not always the case.

Caution

Surprisingly, the results of some traced raster images can produce even larger vector images. Remember that vectors were designed for solid colors, limited blends, lines, and points. Every file format has its purpose, and sometimes raster images are smaller than their traced counterparts. With a little practice, you'll be able to judge what kind of images will produce effective traced versions.

Figure 36-2 compares the same bitmap image in a series of different workflow options. As you can quickly see, the differences in file size do not always have the same relationship to image quality as you might expect.

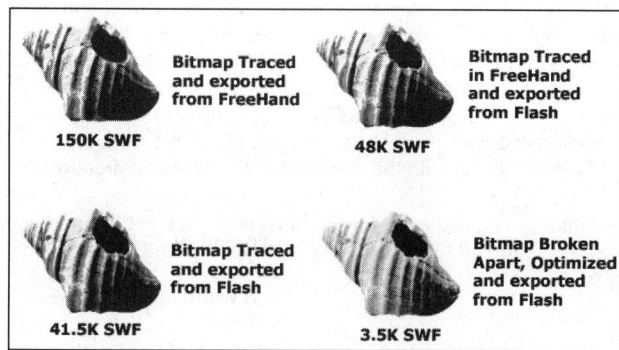

Figure 36-2: Even when the final image quality is similar, the file sizes that are achieved with different workflow options can vary widely.

In our production testing overall, Flash MX 2004 proves to be the first choice for achieving high image quality and small file sizes with traced or optimized bitmaps. The lesson we've learned is that unless we need a special effect that can't be created directly in Flash, it's best to import high-quality images (scaled appropriately for the movie size) directly to Flash and use the native Flash authoring tools to modify the image if needed.

Reducing vector complexity

Although Flash MX 2004 provides robust tools for modifying the complexity of vector artwork, if you're creating artwork in other applications, you have some options for streamlining the artwork before bringing it into your Flash project.

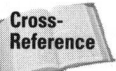

Cross-Reference

For coverage of the Flash MX 2004 native tools for modifying artwork, refer to Chapter 9, "Modifying Graphics," and Chapter 16, "Importing Artwork."

Combining paths

You can use the Pathfinder panel (View ➪ Pathfinder) in Illustrator or the Modify ➪ Combine menu in FreeHand to control how overlapping paths are combined. Not only does this reduce the complexity of the path, but it also makes the graphic easier to edit or move. Both programs offer several different options for combining overlapping paths, including merging or cropping specific sections to create custom shapes.

Note   The default behavior of ungrouped shapes in the Flash authoring environment achieves a kind of "automatic" optimization by combining or merging overlapping shapes on the same layer. This takes a little getting used to, but it eliminates the need to spend time analyzing and combining separate paths to optimize your graphics.

To apply a command for combining separate paths, select the overlapping paths by Shift+clicking each object (or by dragging a selection box around all of the elements you want to modify). In the Illustrator Pathfinder panel, or in the FreeHand Modify ➪ Combine menu, select an option to combine the overlapping elements and create a unified path shape.

Note   The stacking order of overlapping shapes may affect how paths are combined—if your first try doesn't work, analyze the shapes you are trying to combine and make sure that you have them in the right order for the combine commands to work. For example, if you want to modify a shape by "trimming" it with some other shapes in Adobe Illustrator or in Macromedia FreeHand, you need exactly opposite stack orders to create the same effect. In Illustrator, you must make certain that the shapes you want to use as "trimmers" are behind the main shape in the stack before using the Minus Back command. To achieve the same effect in FreeHand, you must move your main shape to the back of the stack and use the Punch command to trim the main shape with the shapes that are stacked in front of it.

Figure 36-3, shows three individual oval outlines in Adobe Illustrator (left) combined using the Merge option (center), and the Minus Back option (right) to create unified paths that describe different simplified polygons.

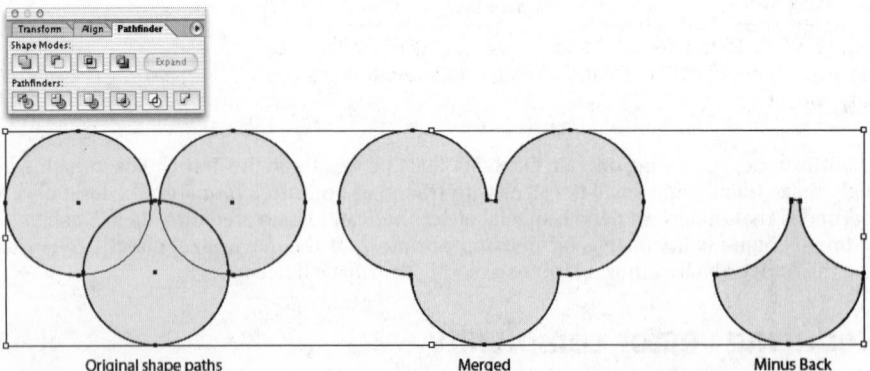

Original shape paths   Merged   Minus Back

Figure 36-3: The Pathfinder panel in Illustrator offers a variety of options for combining overlapping paths.

Simplifying paths

In addition to combining paths, complex artwork can be simplified by reducing the number of points used to describe the path (or a set of paths). The controls available for simplifying paths in Adobe Illustrator are slightly more sophisticated than the controls in Macromedia FreeHand (as shown in Figure 36-4), but the final result in either program is similar to Smoothing or Straightening in Flash. Simplifying reduces the number of the points that define the lines and curves of a vector graphic to make the file smaller and easier to edit. The goal is to remove as many extraneous points along individual paths as you can without distorting the final shape too much.

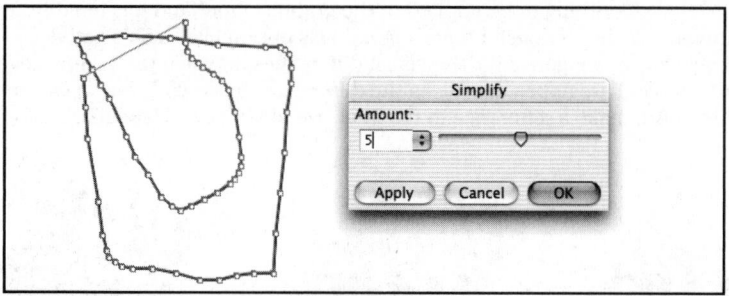

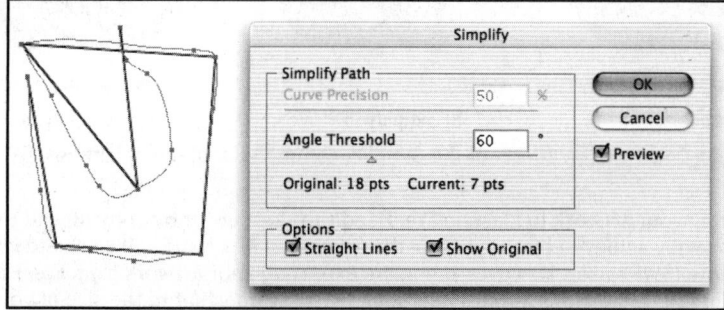

Figure 36-4: The Simplify dialog box in Macromedia FreeHand (top) and in Adobe Illustrator (bottom) for modifying the points in the paths that describe a vector shape

To simplify vector artwork, select the paths that describe the object and choose the Simplify command and settings available in your program of choice. The commands and settings for Illustrator and for FreeHand are as follows:

✦ In Illustrator, select Object ⇨ Alter Path ⇨ Simplify. Along with controls for **Curve Precision** (lower values result in more simplified shapes, higher values can actually *add* points to your shapes) and **Angle Threshold,** the Illustrator Simplify dialog includes three handy options:

  • **Preview:** Select this check box to see a live preview of your settings. When you make changes, the preview may not always update until you deselect and reselect the Preview check box.

  • **Straight Lines:** Select this check box to favor straight lines over curves — similar to the Straighten modifier in Flash. Use this option in concert with the Angle Threshold control to define the allowable range of angles in the graphic. An Angle Threshold of 0 degrees will allow any angle in the selected shape, a setting of 90 degrees will convert all angles to right angles, and the highest setting of 180 degrees will reduce the shape to a single line defined by two points (with a relationship of 180 degrees).

- **Show Original:** Select this check box to keep an outline view of your original shape for comparison as you preview various simplify settings.

✦ In FreeHand, select Modify ⇨ Alter Path (or Xtras ⇨ Cleanup). The Simplify option in either menu invokes the Simplify dialog box (shown in Figure 36-2), where you can choose a level of smoothing to be applied to the graphic. FreeHand has ten different simplification levels, but it doesn't have a multi-pass option like Flash's native Optimize command. As shown in Figure 36-5, the visual differences between the various levels of Simplify in FreeHand are not as drastic as the differences between levels of Optimize in Flash, but they can make a difference in the final size of your FreeHand file.

a) Original artwork   b) Simplify "5"   c) Simplify "8"

Figure 36-5: Compare the effects of the Simplify command at different settings.

If you are importing your artwork to Flash in FreeHand (.fh) format (or by copying and pasting), the file size saving achieved by simplifying the artwork in FreeHand will translate into smaller Flash movie (SWF) sizes. However, if you are exporting your artwork from FreeHand directly to SWF format, the various **Simplify** settings are less important to the size of your SWF files than the **Path Compression** settings chosen in the Export process. This setting controls the file size of artwork exported in SWF format from FreeHand and is found in the Movie Settings dialog box (accessed from the Setup button in the Export dialog box.) The process for exporting SWF files directly from FreeHand is described later in this chapter, along with the SWF export options available from Illustrator.

Creative Type Layouts

The text-handling features of Flash have improved with every version, but there are still some layouts that are much easier to accomplish using a program such as Macromedia FreeHand or Adobe Illustrator. Aside from precise settings for kerning and line spacing, these programs include controls that make it easy to create custom text block shapes, curved type, runarounds, and multicolumn spreads.

Curved paths

If you've ever spent time manually placing individual text characters along a curved guide in Flash, you will appreciate how painless custom type paths can be with the right tools. Figure 36-6 shows type aligned on shaped paths and the various controls for creating and modifying type in FreeHand (top) and in Illustrator (bottom).

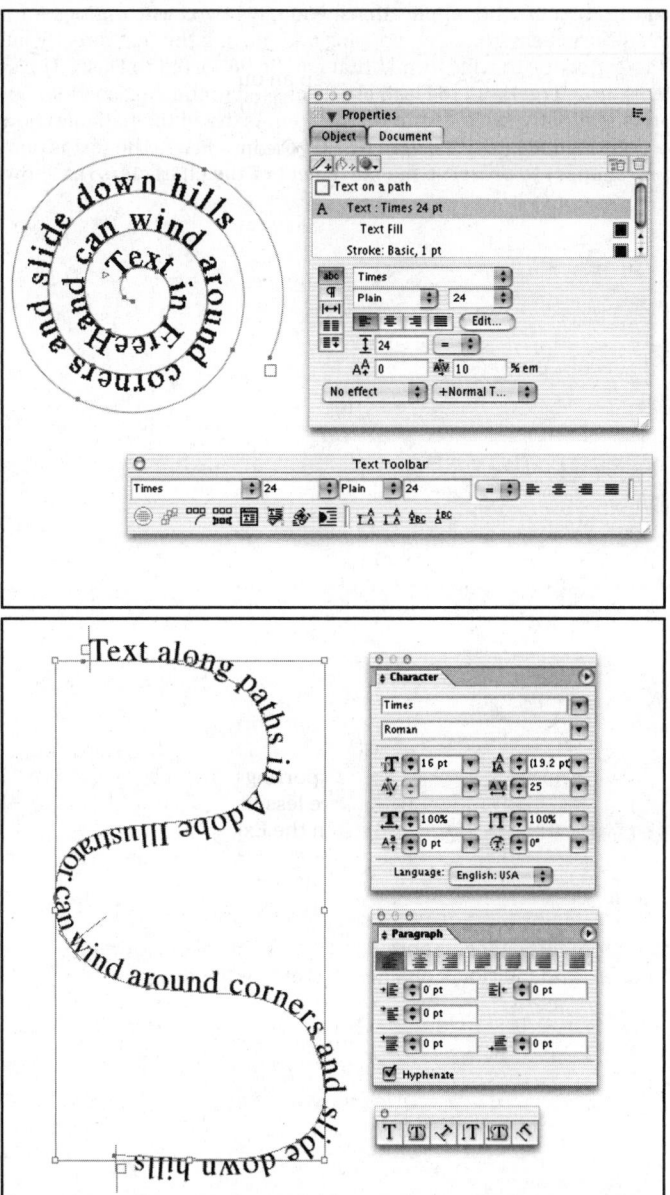

Figure 36-6: Curved text paths are quick to create with the right tools and are almost infinitely variable. (Macromedia FreeHand, top. Adobe Illustrator, bottom.)

When you are working with text in other applications, you have two basic options for moving the text into the Flash authoring environment: copying and pasting the text directly into a Flash text box or saving/exporting to a file format that can be imported to Flash. The specific steps for moving artwork from FreeHand to Flash are discussed in the next section, but the way that Flash interprets text paths will depend on the complexity of the path and how it is saved. If you import a FreeHand file (.fh10) with a text layout into Flash, the text is converted into individual outlines (shapes) to preserve the placement of the characters (as shown in Figure 36-7.)

Figure 36-7: Text with custom formatting imported to Flash in FreeHand format (.fh) is converted automatically to individual outlines to preserve the design.

If you export a SWF file from FreeHand, the text will be converted to outlines, but the character shapes will be translated into Graphic symbols so that your file is optimized. When you import the SWF into the Flash authoring environment (FLA), the symbols are loaded into the Library, and the type layout is preserved on the Stage (see Figure 36-8).

If you are working in FreeHand and you prefer not to have text reduced to shapes when it is imported to Flash, save your files in *Editable EPS* format using the **Save As** command, or to *Generic EPS* format using the **Export** command. Either of these formats will preserve editable text, although the text will be broken into smaller text blocks to preserve special formatting (see Figure 36-9).

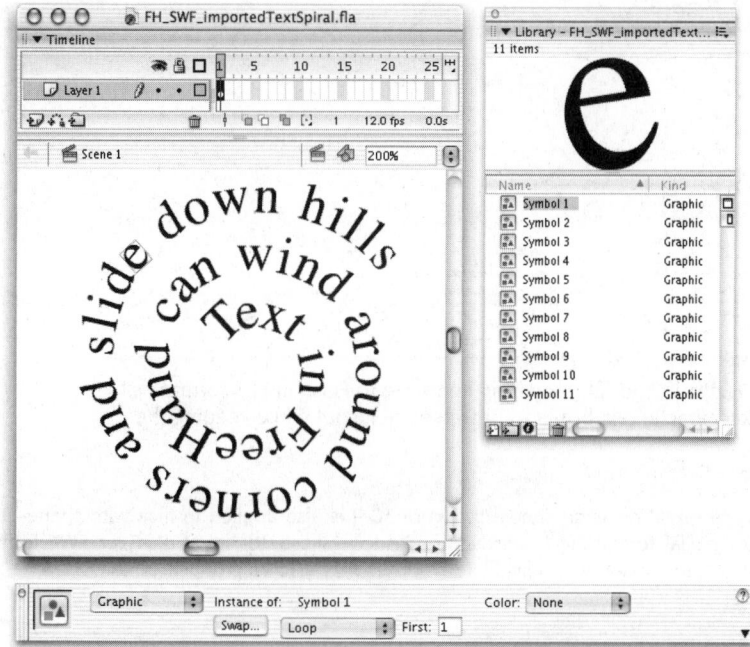

Figure 36-8: SWF files exported from FreeHand will optimize custom text as Graphic symbols that are preserved when imported to the Flash authoring environment (FLA).

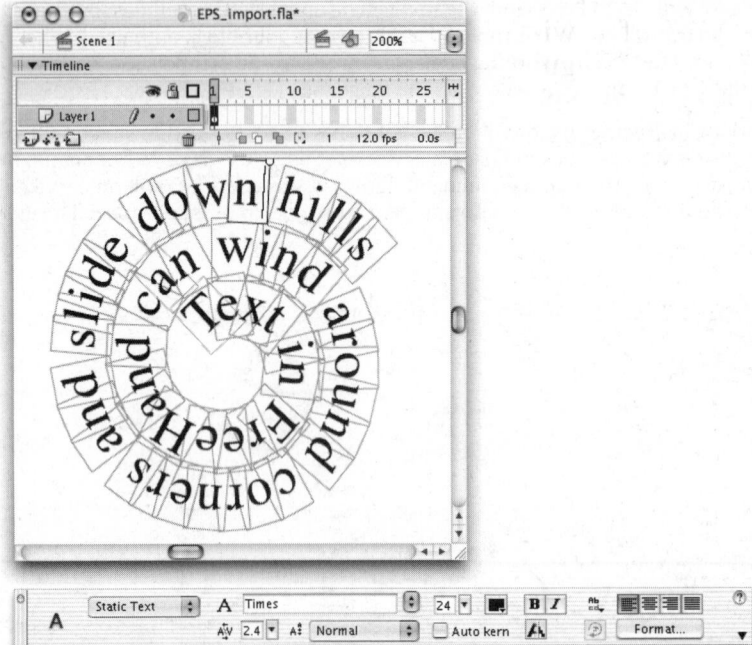

Figure 36-9: Text with special formatting imported to Flash in EPS format will be broken into character text boxes to preserve the layout while keeping the text editable.

Note   The style of text conversion shown in Figure 36-9 is also applied to files with shaped text paths or special formatting imported from Adobe Illustrator in AI, PDF, or SWF format, although in some cases, the individual text boxes may also be grouped on the Stage.

Columns and runarounds

Two standard text effects that are difficult to create manually in Flash are multicolumn layouts and runarounds (or custom text wrapping). Both FreeHand and Illustrator provide text-editing options that make it easy to create and modify text blocks with multiple columns and custom runarounds. After you design your layout in FreeHand or Illustrator, you have many choices for file formats that the file can be saved to, but these all result in one of two basic results for how the file is converted on import to Flash. Figure 36-10 illustrates the same multicolumn layout converted to outlines (top), and converted into multiple editable text boxes (bottom) on import to the Flash Stage.

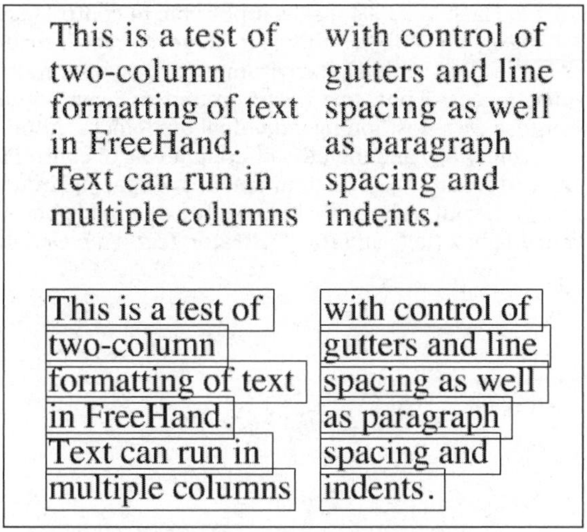

> This is a test of two-column formatting of text in FreeHand. Text can run in multiple columns with control of gutters and line spacing as well as paragraph spacing and indents.

> This is a test of two-column formatting of text in FreeHand. Text can run in multiple columns with control of gutters and line spacing as well as paragraph spacing and indents.

Figure 36-10: Multicolumn text imported to Flash will be interpreted as outlines (top) or as multiple editable text fields (bottom).

The following workflows result in conversion of text with special formatting to outlines:

✦ Direct import of a FreeHand file (.fh) to the Flash Stage

✦ Copying and pasting a text block as an object from Illustrator or FreeHand to the Flash Stage

✦ Exporting a file with special text formatting to SWF format from FreeHand before importing the SWF file to the Flash Stage

✦ Converting text to outlines in FreeHand or Illustrator before saving the file and importing it to Flash in any compatible format

The following workflows result in conversion of text with special formatting to editable text boxes:

✦ Saving (or exporting) a file from FreeHand or Illustrator to EPS or PDF format before importing to the Flash Stage

✦ Exporting a file with special text formatting to SWF format from Illustrator before importing the SWF to the Flash Stage

✦ Saving (or exporting) an Illustrator file in AI format for version 10 or lower before importing the file to the Flash Stage

Note
If editable text is your main objective and you are not concerned about preserving the layout created in FreeHand or Illustrator, you may choose to copy and past text from a text field in either of these programs into a Flash text field. The difference between this workflow and copying and pasting the text block as an *object* is that you use the text selection tool to copy the text to the Clipboard and then select an existing text box in Flash before pasting the text to the Flash Stage.

Although the expanded HTML support in Flash MX 2004 makes it possible to control text flow around images in a layout with HTML tags, it can still be tedious to achieve precise spacing between images and text characters in the Flash authoring environment. In layout programs such as Illustrator and FreeHand, you can control how text wraps around an image without having to manually space your text or fuss with positioning individual text blocks. Although different programs may use different terminology and include different levels of control for modifying text flow or runaround, the end result is a consistent amount of spacing around items placed near text characters in your layout. Figure 36-11 shows the difference between the FreeHand *Flow Around Selection* dialog box (left) and the Illustrator *Text Wrap Options* dialog box (right).

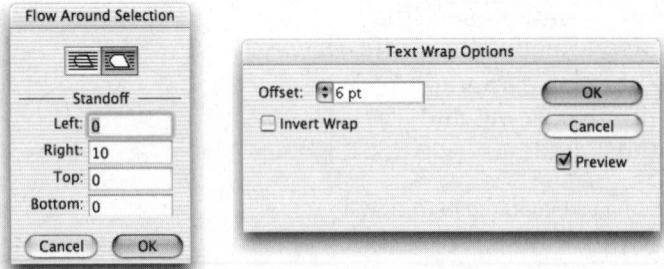

Figure 36-11: Terms and controls for creating spacing between text and other items in a layout will differ in various programs: this space is referred to as *Standoff* in Macromedia FreeHand (left) and *Offset* in Adobe Illustrator (right).

To invoke the FreeHand dialog box for controlling text runaround (shown in Figure 36-11), select the item that you want to flow the text around and choose Text ⇨ Flow Around Selection from the application menu or click the Flow icon in the Text toolbar. To invoke the Illustrator dialog box for controlling text wrap (also shown in Figure 36-11), select the item that you want to flow text around and choose Object ⇨ Text Wrap ⇨ Make Text Wrap from the application menu. After you choose the amount of standoff or offset that you want to maintain between the selected item and the closest text characters, the text should flow around the placed image or other item. A simple example of runaround (or text flow) is shown in Figure 36-12.

Text editing tools in layout programs such as FreeHand and Illustrator make it much easier  to control text flow around images. You can modify the margin between placed images and text without any manual adjustment.

Figure 36-12: When you apply text flow or runaround to an item, the amount of space you specify is placed between the item and the closest text characters.

The options described earlier in this section for preserving multicolumn layouts for import to Flash can also be applied to preserve a layout with placed graphics and defined text flow.

Enhancing Flash Production with Macromedia FreeHand

Macromedia's robust print and design application, FreeHand, includes many features that can support Flash production—and the tight integration of these two programs makes transfer of assets intuitive and hassle-free. If you're not familiar with FreeHand, take a look at the features that it offers:

✦ Transferable symbols and actions for simple navigation that translate to Flash

✦ Powerful text tools for creating custom layouts—including curved paths, runarounds, and columns

✦ Live raster and vector effects that can be added to an item without altering the original

✦ An Extrude tool that can be used to render 3D effects with lighting and surface options

✦ A Perspective Grid that believably distorts the scale of artwork

✦ Fill options for creating complex gradients in different styles

✦ Blending effects that automatically produce intermediate steps between two pieces of artwork

✦ Trace tool and Cleanup tools for optimizing vector artwork

✦ Support for SWF export *and* SWF import

✦ Release to Layers feature that exports drawings to Flash as animated frames

Creating complex gradients in FreeHand

It is possible to create more complex gradients and blends in FreeHand than in Flash, but when these elements are imported to Flash, they will be interpreted as Graphic symbols with masks and clipping paths (see Figure 36-13). Although the visual translation of your custom gradient is fairly seamless, the graphic elements are difficult to edit after they have been converted to Flash, and you should be mindful of the effect they can have on your final SWF size. A raster version of the same gradient may produce smoother blends and smaller file sizes.

Caution

A bug with FreeHand MX causes a whole series of extra symbols to be added to the Flash Library when you import shapes and gradients from FreeHand. These symbols are nested in folders inside the FreeHand Objects folder. If you did not use any custom brush tips in your FreeHand artwork, it is generally safe to delete the entire Brush Tips folder without damaging the graphic that you have imported. Another way to sort out symbols that should be saved from symbols that can be deleted is to refer to the Use Count listed in the Library panel. To make sure that counts are current, choose **Update Use Counts Now** from the Library options menu—symbols that show a count of 0 are not relevant to the graphic that you imported to the Flash Stage and can be deleted.

Figure 36-14 shows how the Flash Library looked after a contour gradient was imported from FreeHand and before the file was cleaned up for the screen shot shown in Figure 36-13. Unused symbols are not exported with your published Flash SWF, so final file size is not a concern, but your working file size and the organization of your Library will benefit from deleting unused symbols.

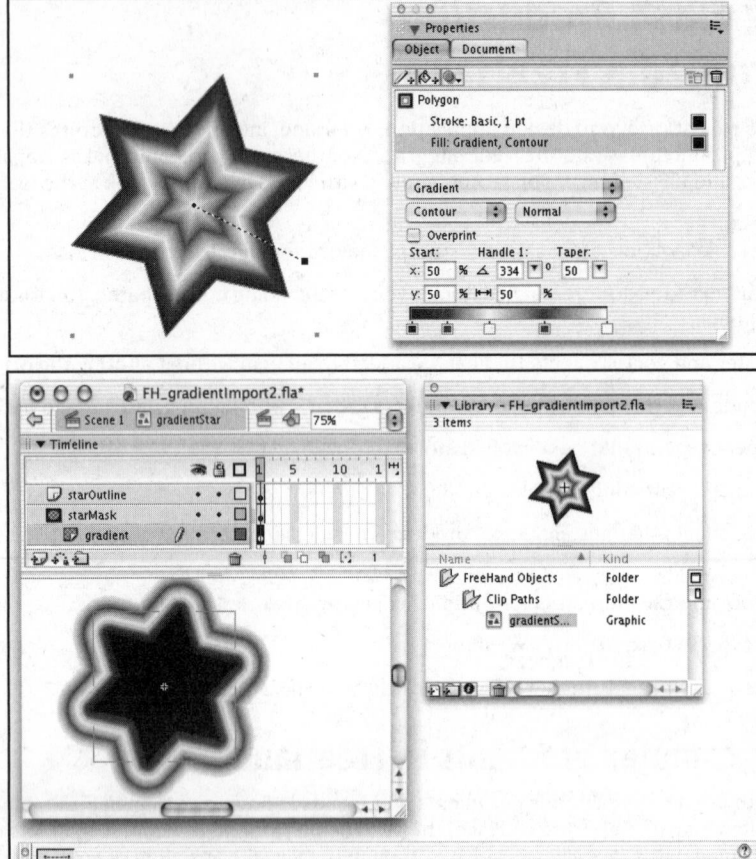

Figure 36-13: A contour gradient created in FreeHand (top) is interpreted by Flash as a series of grouped shapes nested in a Graphic symbol with masking to reproduce the FreeHand clipping paths (bottom).

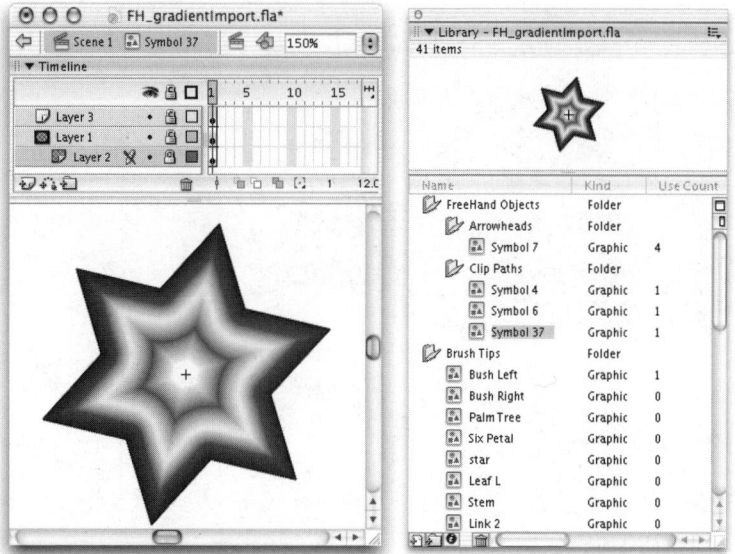

Figure 36-14: Files imported from FreeHand may add a series of symbols to the Flash Library that are not really needed to render the graphic on the Stage. To optimize your FLA file, check Use Count numbers in the Library list and delete unused symbols in the FreeHand Objects folder.

Creating 3D graphics with the Extrude tool

There is a range of programs that have been developed to assist designers in creating 3D artwork for use in Flash, but humble FreeHand actually offers a powerful and user-friendly tool to add depth and render lighting effects for Flash-compatible artwork. The Help files that ship with FreeHand offer handy tutorials on how to use the Extrude tool, so we will not go into depth on how to use this tool here. But to give you an idea of what is possible, we will illustrate a basic example of how extruded artwork can be brought into Flash to create a faux 3D animation. Figure 36-15 shows a series of star shapes that have been extruded (with the Extrude tool selected in the Tools panel) and then rotated incrementally using the y-axis Rotation control under the Object tab of the Properties panel.

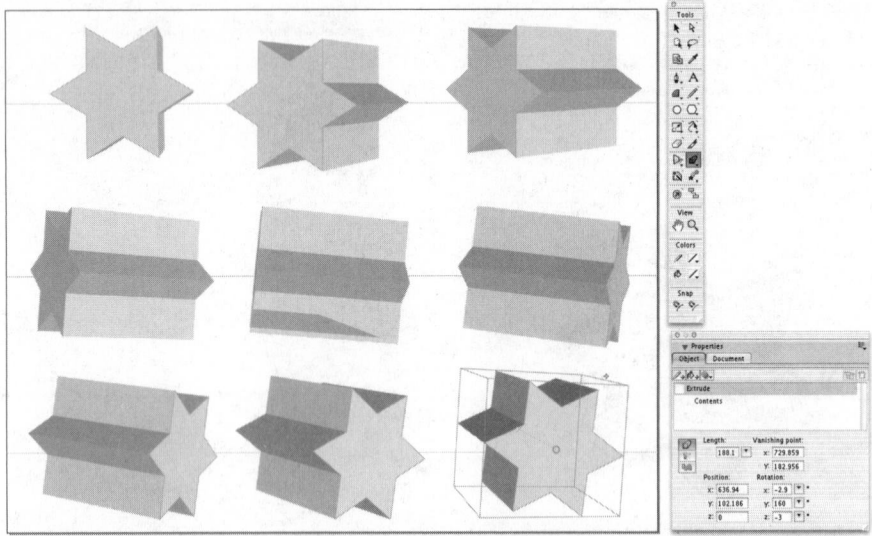

Figure 36-15: A FreeHand star shape can be extruded and then copied and rotated incrementally to create a series of shapes ready for import to Flash.

Cross-Reference   For an explanation of the various options available for moving FreeHand artwork into Flash and some tips that will help smooth your workflow, refer to the section later in this chapter on "Moving artwork from FreeHand to Flash."

To import a faux 3D sequence from FreeHand, follow these steps:

1. After you have created a series of shapes in FreeHand that you think will work as frames in an animated sequence, save the file in FreeHand (.fh) format or export it as a Flash movie (.swf).

Tip   Ideally, you will place each shape that you want to use in an animated Flash sequence on a unique layer in FreeHand, stacked in the order that you want the images to appear when converted to Flash frames. This will look cluttered in the FreeHand file, but it makes it easy to align the elements and when you import the file to Flash or export it from FreeHand to SWF format, you have the option of converting the layers directly to Flash frames.

2. Create a new Flash file with dimensions that will accommodate the item that you intend to animate from the FreeHand sequence. There are some tricks to setting up a FreeHand file so that it will align correctly to your Flash Stage; these tricks are described in the section later in this chapter "Moving artwork from FreeHand to Flash."

3. Select a frame on the Timeline (you may wish to create a Movie Clip symbol to nest your FreeHand sequence as a contained animated element).

4. Select File ➪ Import to Stage from the application menu (Ctrl+R or ⌘+R), browse to the SWF or FH file that contains your extruded artwork, and click **Import**.

5. If you have organized your sequence on FreeHand layers, opt to convert these layers into Flash frames in the FreeHand Import dialog box (shown in Figure 36-16), as a quick shortcut to eliminate the work of manually aligning and moving the graphics onto sequential Flash frames. Click **OK**.

Figure 36-16: The Flash FreeHand Import dialog box includes options for converting FreeHand layers to Flash frames.

6. Depending on the workflow that you've chosen, the extruded artwork will appear in Flash in one of three ways:

   • If you organized your artwork on FreeHand layers and converted the layers to Flash frames with the FreeHand Import dialog box, you should have a ready-made animated sequence after the artwork is imported to the Flash Timeline. However, you may wish to ungroup some of the shapes to modify them or you may want to optimize the file by converting some of the shapes into symbols.

   • If you left all your artwork on a single layer in FreeHand, it will be dumped onto a single frame in the Flash Timeline so you will have to manually move each graphic in the sequence onto a unique keyframe to create an animation. If you export the FreeHand file to SWF format before importing the file to Flash, you can at least optimize the graphics by converting them to symbols that will be stored in the Flash Library, as shown in Figure 36-17.

   • If you exported your *layered* FreeHand file to SWF format and chose **Animate** for Layers in the Movie Settings dialog box, you will not only get optimized artwork stored in the Library as symbols, but you will also end up with a ready-made Timeline animation when you import the SWF to your Flash Stage. This is the most efficient workflow for converting a series of FreeHand images into a Flash animation sequence.

Shaded extruded shapes consist of numerous individual pieces that can really add to your file size. If you export the FreeHand file to SWF format, the file is analyzed and the individual pieces that appear more than once will automatically be converted to symbols that are reused. You can see just how much the file is optimized by reading the **Use Count** listed for each symbol in the Library after the file is imported to Flash. (See Figure 36-17.) If you had imported the same series of graphics in raw FreeHand format, each piece would have been added to the file as a unique shape and the file size would have been bloated.

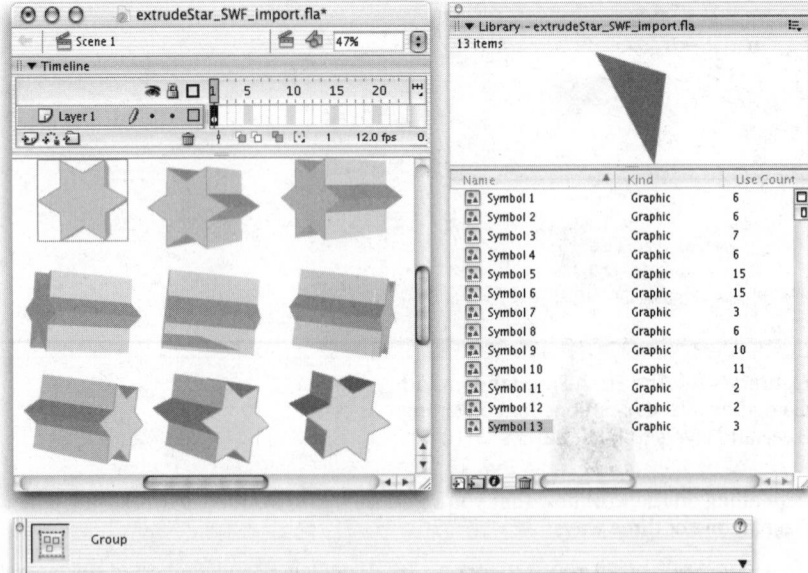

Figure 36-17: FreeHand files exported in SWF format for import to Flash will result in optimized files by converting raw graphics into symbols that are reused, as shown by the Use Counts in the Flash Library.

After the graphics are imported to the Flash Stage (either in one frame or to a series of frames), you can ungroup them and use any of the drawing or layout tools in Flash to modify the shapes. You can reorder the sequence by moving keyframes to new locations in the Timeline and you can adjust the pace of the sequence by adding or dropping frames between each keyframe. If you're lucky (and you've taken advantage of the layer features in FreeHand and the SWF conversion workflow), your animation will be ready to go as-is and you can enjoy the fruits of your labor by scrubbing the Timeline or using the Test movie command (Ctrl+Enter or ⌘+Return) to preview your final faux 3D animation.

On the CD-ROM

We have included a Flash file with the animated extruded star sequence for you to review. To play the faux 3D animation, open extrudeStar_optimize.swf from the ch36 folder on the CD-ROM. To see how the shapes have been converted into Flash symbols, open extrudeStar_optimize.fla from the CD-ROM, also in the ch36 folder.

FreeHand's Trace tool

The Trace tool in Macromedia FreeHand works like a magic wand, allowing you to selectively trace areas of a bitmap based on color. You can access the Trace tool in the FreeHand Tools panel; double-clicking the icon invokes the Trace tool settings dialog box (shown in Figure 36-18). The FreeHand Trace tool offers numerous settings that control how bitmap artwork will be converted to vectors.

Figure 36-18: The FreeHand Trace tool offers an array of options for precise tracing.

When you're ready to trace the bitmap, there are two ways to choose an area to trace. To trace the entire image within a selected area, simply click-drag a marquee selection with the Trace tool active, and FreeHand traces everything within the selected area. To select specific color regions, click areas of the image with the Trace tool wand. (Shift+click to add areas to your selection.) After you have selected the area that you want to trace, double-click inside the selection to invoke the Wand options dialog box (shown in Figure 36-19). The Wand options dialog box makes it possible to choose whether you want to trace everything inside the current selection (**Trace Selection**) or just the edge of the selection (**Convert Selection Edge**). Click **OK** after you have chosen an option, and FreeHand traces the specified area.

Figure 36-19: When you have selected an area with the Trace tool wand, the Wand Options dialog box lets you choose how the selection will be traced.

Tip   Use the magic wand method if you want to extract a traced image from a bitmap that contains multiple elements or an irregular shape. For example, if you have a picture of many people and you want to trace just one of them, the magic wand can help you isolate that one person. If you want to trace all the people as well as the background, trace the entire image by dragging a selection box around the whole picture.

Because the nature of bitmapped artwork varies by subject matter, finding the optimal settings for the FreeHand Trace tool may require a bit of trial and error. If the results are not satisfactory, simply undo the trace and try a different setting.

FreeHand retains the original bitmapped artwork behind the traced vector artwork; to see the traced image, select it and move it to a new position on the page (as shown in Figure 36-20.) If you no longer need the bitmapped version, delete the bitmap image after you have moved the traced objects to a new location. Group the traced objects for greater ease in moving them.

Figure 36-20: FreeHand preserves the original bitmap (left) beneath the traced graphic (right).

When you import a traced vector image into Flash directly from FreeHand, the file is brought in as multiple grouped shapes. To make it easier to modify the graphic as a single element, ungroup the imported items until you are able to select the graphic as a unified shape (see Figure 36-21.)

Moving artwork from FreeHand to Flash

Macromedia has invested a lot of development time in its quest to create a seamless workflow between FreeHand and Flash — and it shows! The result is that it's much easier and more efficient to use these applications together. Many of the options for importing graphics to Flash from FreeHand have been mentioned in this chapter already; in this section we will clearly explain the steps for moving artwork from one program to another and the options available with different workflows.

You have at least six ways to get your vector artwork from FreeHand to Flash MX 2004: the SWF export feature from FreeHand, the EPS export feature from FreeHand, the PDF export feature from FreeHand, copy and paste, drag and drop, or opening the FreeHand files directly in Flash.

Figure 36-21: Traced vector graphics imported from FreeHand should be ungrouped in Flash, so that they can be edited as a unified shape.

Opening FreeHand files directly into Flash

With the continuity between FreeHand and Flash available in the recent versions, Flash development and concept design started in FreeHand is even more easily integrated with your final project. FreeHand 9 introduced symbols that function much like Graphic symbols in Flash. Consequently, symbols that are created in FreeHand 9 or higher will be maintained — along with layers and guides — when the FreeHand file is opened in Flash. Let's take a look at the basic steps for importing a FreeHand file into Flash.

1. Open a new Flash file and set the movie size to match the page size of the FreeHand file that you will be importing.

2. Use File ⇨ Import to select your FreeHand file.

3. A dialog box appears with a number of options specific to FreeHand import (see Figure 36-16) that control how you want your file translated. Select the desired options and click **OK**.

4. Layers should be preserved if you have chosen that option and any symbols created in FreeHand will be stored in the Flash Library. Some text or vector artwork may be translated from FreeHand to Flash as grouped elements. To edit individual shapes or text characters, simply ungroup the items in Flash until they can be isolated.

5. Now that you have your FreeHand artwork in Flash (intact and organized just as it was in FreeHand), you are ready to develop your Flash project.

Caution   If you plan to open your FreeHand files directly in Flash, be aware of the following issues while working in FreeHand: Use symbols in FreeHand to start the optimization process. Only use Type 1 PostScript fonts. You may have problems with TrueType Fonts. Only use image formats supported by Flash — JPG, PICT, BMP, and PNG.

Using FreeHand SWF export for layouts

Opening FreeHand files directly into Flash is very convenient because it retains a good deal of structure, including layers and guides. However, the FreeHand SWF Export feature is also an excellent method for translating FreeHand files into Flash movies because it not only creates the most optimized result, it also does much of the tedious work for you. For example, exporting a SWF from FreeHand can automatically convert any custom text into smaller text blocks or outlines and will convert shapes into Graphic symbols to preserve the layout while optimizing the file and keeping editable text intact wherever possible.

Tip   If you prefer to manually select the typography elements in your FreeHand layout and convert them to paths, simply select the text blocks that you want to change and apply the Text ⇨ Convert to Paths command.

Before you export a FreeHand document as a Flash file, you need to prepare the FreeHand artwork for optimal export. In the FreeHand file, select all the objects on a page that you want to export and *align the upper left-hand extents of objects with the upper left-hand extents of the page*. If you only need to export a few elements from a detailed FreeHand layout, it is best to select and copy those elements and paste them into a new FreeHand page before exporting.

Caution   When you export a SWF, the file will be sized to center the artwork in the middle of the movie. If you've been working on a vertical page layout in FreeHand with a lot of empty space above and below your artwork, the SWF will contain a lot of blank space, too. If you align your artwork in the top-left corner of the FreeHand page, then the exported SWF will not have extra empty space. Alignment is an issue that will also affect your artwork when importing FreeHand files into the Flash authoring environment. Although the empty white space of the FreeHand page will not be visible when you import your artwork to Flash, you may find your artwork placed far below the Stage area because Flash "reads" and includes the space that was above the artwork in the original FreeHand layout.

New Feature   The Movie Settings dialog box available from FreeHand MX includes a small but powerful new option for eliminating any unwanted empty space in your layout that can bloat your files and throw off the alignment of artwork when it is imported to the Flash Stage. To ensure that the exported SWF is only as big as you need it to be and that your artwork is centered in the movie, simply select **Size to match contents** in the Movie Properties section of the Movie Settings dialog box.

You can access the FreeHand SWF Export feature by choosing File ⇨ Export (Ctrl+Shift+R or ⌘+Shift+R) and selecting **Flash SWF** (Windows) or **Macromedia Flash SWF** (Mac) in the Save as Type (Windows) or Format (Mac) drop-down menu. Click the **Setup** button to access the Movie Settings used to convert the FreeHand file into a Flash SWF, as shown in Figure 36-22.

The first section of the new Movie Settings dialog box makes it simpler to choose Export Options for converting your FreeHand file to SWF format. With the **Movie** radio buttons, you can choose to export a **Single** SWF or **Multiple** SWFs, depending on the content of your FreeHand file. With the **Layers** radio buttons, you can opt to **Animate** the content in your FreeHand layers by exporting them into sequential Flash keyframes, or you can simply **Flatten** the layers into a single keyframe.

The **Page Range** options enable you to specify which pages of your FreeHand file you want to include in the exported SWF file. If you are working with a single page file, the default setting of **All** will work fine.

The settings in the Movie Properties section of the Movie Settings dialog box can be left at their default settings unless you plan to use the exported SWF as-is without importing it to Flash for further editing. If you plan to use the SWF as a finished presentation, you can choose a frame rate, as well as settings to control whether the content of the SWF file can be printed from a Web browser or imported to the Flash authoring environment. FreeHand includes the option to select a background color for the SWF file, which is handy if you plan to use the SWF in an HTML file or if you want to match it with another existing Flash layout. For artwork that will be imported to the Flash authoring environment for further modification, the background color option can be left at its default setting which is **None** (or no color).

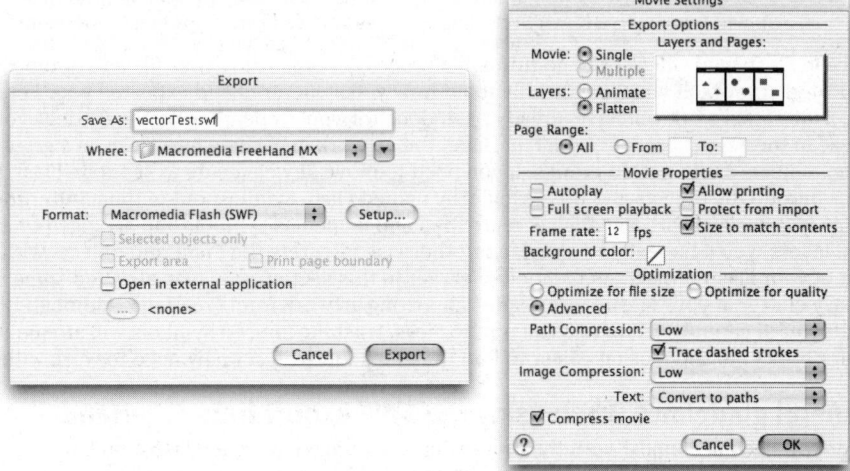

Figure 36-22: The Export dialog box (left) allows you to access the Movie Settings (right) with the Setup button.

The Optimization section of the Movie Settings dialog box includes another MX improvement: rather than making individual selections for each of the Optimization settings, you can simply choose between radio buttons to **Optimize for file size** or to **Optimize for quality**. These buttons automatically set the other options for you to convert your FreeHand file to a Flash SWF with priority given either to creating a streamlined file or to creating a high fidelity file that will most closely match the original layout, respectively. If you prefer to set each option manually, select the **Advanced** radio button to access the menus for **Path Compression**, **Image Compression**, and **Text**, and the check box for **Trace dashed strokes**.

In FreeHand 10, you could choose Flash 2, 3, 4, or 5 as the SWF version format, any of which is perfectly fine for Flash MX artwork. Because the Flash MX SWF format has not changed any artwork specifications that were used in earlier versions, this option was removed from FreeHand MX.

If this export is a transition from FreeHand to Flash and *not* a final file, you can eliminate any file degradation by setting the Path Compression and Image Compression drop-down menus to **None**.

To preserve editable text wherever possible, select the **Maintain blocks** option from the Text drop-down menu in the Settings dialog box. Text with custom FreeHand effects (such as columns, runarounds, or paths) will automatically be converted to smaller text blocks, individual characters, or letter-shape symbols as needed to preserve the layout in Flash. If you do *not* need to edit your text in Flash, choose **Convert to paths** from the Text drop-down menu. This converts all the text to paths and creates symbols of each character in the process.

FreeHand automates editable text conversion when you export to the SWF format with the **Maintain blocks** option selected. If you import files with special text formatting directly to Flash in FreeHand format (.fh), Flash converts the text to outlines to preserve the layout.

Click **OK** to close the Movie Settings dialog box and then choose **Export** from the Export dialog box. You will now have a Flash SWF that can be imported into your Flash document (FLA.)

Once in Flash, you will want to go through a process of organizing your file and optimizing the imported artwork. If you were careful about how you structured and exported your FreeHand file, a lot of this work will have already been done for you. Depending on the settings you chose in the export process from FreeHand, the artwork may come into Flash as a group — often, objects are in nested groups. If you need to move key elements to separate Flash layers, ungroup the objects and create logically named Flash symbols out of them. After the scene is organized with the objects regrouped and named as symbols and arranged on their own layers, you'll be ready to animate or otherwise integrate the FreeHand objects with the rest of your Flash project. As mentioned earlier in this section, you may also find some unnecessary clutter in your Flash Library after importing artwork from FreeHand. Although it takes a little bit of careful sorting to clean up the mess, trashing unused symbols will streamline your project file and make it easier to find the items that you actually need to work with.

General guidelines when using the SWF export from FreeHand

After you become familiar with the process of exporting artwork to Flash, you'll discover that it's relatively simple. However, it's helpful to keep some guidelines in mind:

✦ When exporting SWF files from FreeHand, do not include large amounts of body text with custom formatting. Recreate the body text (for example, copy and paste the text into a text box) in Flash.

✦ Remember that elements from FreeHand will be put into groups, often stacked or nested within other groups. If you can't edit an element, ungroup it or break it apart.

✦ Symbols automatically created by FreeHand when you export a SWF should be renamed in your Flash Library after you import the file, or at the very least stored in a folder with a meaningful name, such as "extruded Star shapes."

✦ Organize your FreeHand artwork into logical Flash layers. Nest Timeline animation in Movie Clip symbols. Develop a consistent system that you and others on your team can recognize and implement.

✦ You must be using FreeHand 8.01 or greater to export Flash SWF files.

Streamlined Workflow: FreeHand and Flash, by Todd Purgason

Author's Note: Todd originally developed this tutorial for the Flash 5 Bible, but the Juxt workflow translates seamlessly to the current version of Flash; and his insight on optimizing Web and print production is invaluable, so we have included it in this edition.

Flash is a powerful tool for developing intelligent, sophisticated Web sites and interactive environments. But as most of us in the digital design arena know, no single tool does it all. We've all mastered many applications that enable us to design and produce the images and interfaces that are imagined in our mind's eye. The old cliché about "the right tool for the job" holds just as true in the digital arena as it does in your grandpappy's garage. By adding FreeHand to your Flash Tools panel, you go from having four drawers of specialized tools to having eight drawers of specialized tools. FreeHand is a proven illustration and typography tool that brings more than ten years of research, design, and refinement to all your Flash projects. By tapping the strengths of FreeHand, your Flash applications can be that much more effective.

What advantages can FreeHand give to Flash projects?

For starters, familiarity: For some designers, Flash is a new tool with a new paradigm for creating vector-graphic artwork. Many of us have become quite proficient with programs, such as FreeHand and Illustrator, and setting these skills aside would be a terrible waste. But FreeHand brings much more than familiarity to the table. It has very powerful tools for illustration and — my personal favorite — typography.

A huge benefit of using FreeHand in the Flash design process is conceptualizing a design. By using the FreeHand multipage format, you can lay out moments in time or keyframes to visualize and study the interface and motion graphics that you will be executing in Flash. This is a big advantage of using FreeHand instead of Illustrator for your conceptualizing needs: Illustrator is limited to one-page documents. In addition, Macromedia has spent a great deal of time and effort on features, such as the Release to Layers command and SWF export in FreeHand, which enable FreeHand to live symbiotically in the same design space as Flash. Flash MX brought this synthesis to completion by allowing direct import of FreeHand files to Flash and import of Flash SWF files to FreeHand. You can preserve layers, guides, text, and even symbols that you have created in FreeHand when you import directly to Flash.

I think that the greatest asset that FreeHand brings to the Flash table is *print*. Ooooo . . . that nasty word: the old medium of print. Don't we live in the paperless society yet? Not quite. While developing your design in FreeHand, you're actually doing production and composition at the same time. After you have visualized an animation over several pages in FreeHand, it's a very simple task to bring those pages together onto a large format presentation board that you can output to a printer. These presentations blow the clients away! After you get approval, it's on to Flash, where you breathe life into the design that you've been carefully planning in FreeHand. If your clients are like mine, they'll come back and want you to do print promotions, ads, and even identity materials based on the Web site. You already have all the print assets developed in your page compositions. What a bonus! I just hate getting more billable work, don't you?

Developing a process model

Because the complexity of this process would require several chapters, I walk you through the key steps, using visuals from one of my recent projects, an in-house marketing project titled "The Process." It's a reflection of our creative philosophy at Juxt Interactive. Visit this project at `www.juxinteractive.com/theprocess`.

Design planning

Many Flash projects are orchestrated over one or more layouts that are called *scenes*. The term *scene is* appropriate because, oftentimes, they are just that — scenes in a Flash movie. After I've developed a concept in my head and scribbled sketches on paper, I go to FreeHand and start sketching out scenes. Figure 36-23 is an example of a scene.

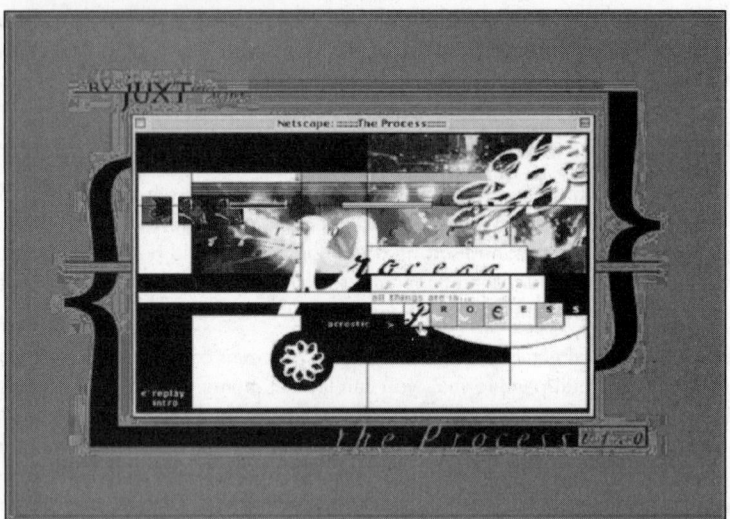

Figure 36-23: The *Process* scene from the JUXT site, as seen in a Web browser by using the Flash Player plug-in

Next, I start building moments in time — or keyframes — which bring elements (characters) into the scene to be laid out and experimented with. I typically start by developing a moment in time that is very heavy visually — often the end of the first major scene. Once I am happy with the scene and the way the elements or characters are working together, I duplicate the page in FreeHand. Then, working with the duplicated page(s), I experiment with the relationships of all the characters. During this step, I'm mindful of the motions that will get me to and from each moment in time. I continue to develop a number of keyframes that form the framework of what I intend to do. The renowned film title designer Kyle Cooper, of Imaginary Forces, has been a great inspiration to me. He once said, "I think that, in the end, I should be able to pull any frame out of my title sequences, and it should be able to stand on its own as an effective illustration." By studying my design as snapshots in time in FreeHand, I hope to ensure that the motion won't destroy the concept but instead enhance its effectiveness.

Impact of presentation

Now, I have many pages that help me to understand just how to pull this project off. I take those keyframe pages and lay them out onto a large format sheet that will be printed on our large format HP Design Jet at roughly 30" x 40". Many people ask me why I continue to print in this day and age. I will tell you why: communication. Half of the job of design is selling the design you create, especially if you are asking the client to take risks pushing the envelope that they are accustomed to. A digital presentation has many advantages, but so does a good old tangible printed piece.

We have developed a presentation process at Juxt that I affectionately call the two-by-four approach. It is based on the old aphorism, "How do you get the attention of a donkey?

Hit him over the head with a two-by-four." Don't get me wrong — I'm not insulting any clients, but the point is to make an impact. When we go into a presentation, we intend to exceed the client's expectations. With a presentation board (such as the one shown in Figure 36-24), I can show many keyframes or screens simultaneously as I walk the client through the animation, explaining the process of the motion or the interaction of the interface without, at this early stage, committing the resources to create an actual working prototype.

However, as a communication tool, the advantages are far greater than saving time. Here's why: The digital medium is abstract, whereas print is tangible and real. With a presentation board, the clients can absorb the design when it is all laid out for them. They can see how their brand is working across the piece. Because the print piece is so very tangible, they can grasp the wholeness of it — which means that they can take ownership of it emotionally. But most important, it communicates to the client that you are good at what you do. Consequently, they'll have more faith in the decisions that you'll make for them during the process of creating the project.

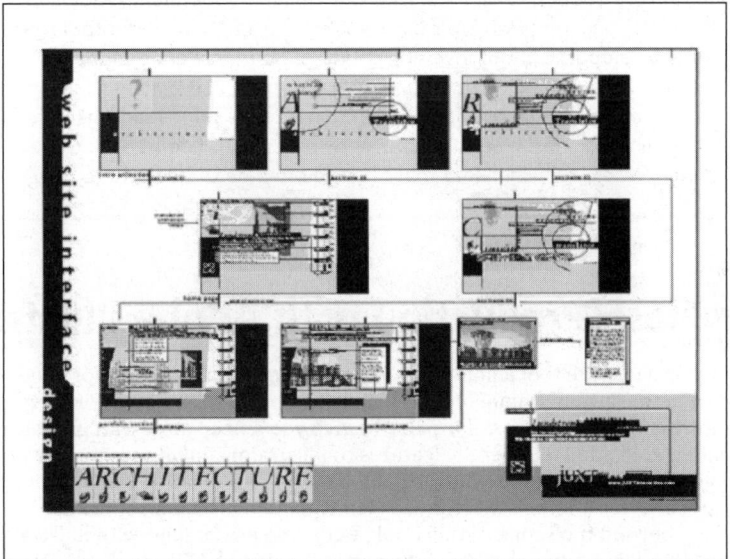

Figure 36-24: Here's an example of the presentation board, which is used as a printed presentation for clients.

Instant changeability

Like Flash MX 2004, FreeHand also has the capability to globally replace colors and fonts. So you've finished presenting the project, your client is sold on your design, but then his partner walks in and says, "Eww . . . I just hate that green." You try to explain its purpose and the importance of that color to the design, but he won't budge. Fortunately, you can change that green to tan across the entire piece — in about five seconds. You simply select the new tan color in the FreeHand Web-Safe Color Palette, drag and drop it on top of the banished green in the color list, and — *voilà* — every instance of the green is now tan. Anywhere there were green lines, files, patterns, text, or colored bitmaps, all are now tan.

Before you have time to gloat, the client's graphics guru tells you that you were given the old corporate design standards manual. Instead of Franklin Gothic (the font you used on 75 percent of the typography), you are supposed to be using Meta Plus. Well, you can simply use the graphic search-and-replace feature to instantly change every bit of Franklin Gothic to Meta Plus. After a few minutes of double-checking kerning effects, you are back to where you started. The files are ready to go to press or to be imported to Flash. Now go ahead and feel proud of yourself. Your client will love that these changes won't cost the company a dime.

Conclusion

Starting your Flash project by using FreeHand gives you huge advantages that won't detract from Flash as a tool. Instead, FreeHand can enhance your understanding of animation and interactive concepts. With FreeHand, you'll have a fast, powerful tool to study your design and develop it, without investing countless hours in work that may or may not make the final cut. Furthermore, you will have fantastic print deliverables to sell your design approach. For me, this is the icing on the cake — I have print-ready materials if the client needs anything from the FreeHand concepts. That means I don't have to create my artwork or designs twice — which means that I have more time to dedicate to design.

Enhancing Flash Production with Adobe Illustrator

Adobe Illustrator is a favorite tool among logo designers and graphic artists for good reason — it offers a robust authoring environment with lots of "extras." The various brush styles, graphic libraries, and even prebuilt color palettes give you a head start with graphic content. Adobe has continued to add Web-friendly features to Illustrator, and in version 9 or higher you will even find graphics for multi-state buttons and a system for creating symbols and adding JavaScript to graphics for interactive interface elements. The full scope of features available in Illustrator 11 is beyond the scope of this book, but if you are familiar with Illustrator, you will be pleased to find that your workflow between Illustrator and Flash can be seamless. To ensure color consistency, always set your Illustrator document color mode to RGB before creating artwork for use in Flash (File ⇨ Document Color Mode).

Note   Most vector artwork created in Illustrator (including special brush styles and most graphic symbols) will import or copy and paste into Flash without becoming rasterized. The important exception to this rule is for artwork that includes gradients. Copied and pasted Illustrator gradients are converted into a series of masked filled shapes or into a bitmap that will more or less preserve the appearance of the gradient but not the option to modify it in the Color Mixer panel. The most reliable way to preserve editable gradients in most Illustrator graphics is to use the Export to SWF option and then import the SWF into your Flash project file.

Another advantage of using Illustrator is that you have plenty of export options that make Illustrator a good choice for authoring content that can be used in a variety of contexts. If you use Adobe Illustrator 9 or higher, you can export your artwork for Flash as:

✦ Encapsulated PostScript format (.eps file extension)

✦ Adobe Illustrator format (.ai file extension)

✦ Portable Document format (.pdf file extension)

✦ Flash movie format (.swf file extension)

Depending on the nature of your artwork, you may choose to use any of these file formats for import to Flash. The native Illustrator format and PDF format provide the most options for importing content to Flash — making it possible to preserve layers, editable text, simple gradients, and placed bitmaps.

As mentioned earlier in this chapter, Flash MX 2004 does not officially support import of Illustrator files saved directly from version 11. In our testing, we found that basic layouts often import without any problem, but files with special text formatting or complex gradients can be corrupted or have unexpected import results unless they are saved as version 10 or earlier. Version 8 still seems to be the most consistently compatible with Flash. To save files to earlier versions from Illustrator 11, use the File ➪ Export command (rather than Save As) and select **Illustrator Legacy** (.ai) or **Illustrator Legacy EPS** (.eps) from the Format drop-down menu. After you make a format selection and click **Export**, the Legacy Options dialog box opens (shown in Figure 36-25), where you can choose Version 10, 9, 8, or 3, before you click **OK** to complete the export process.

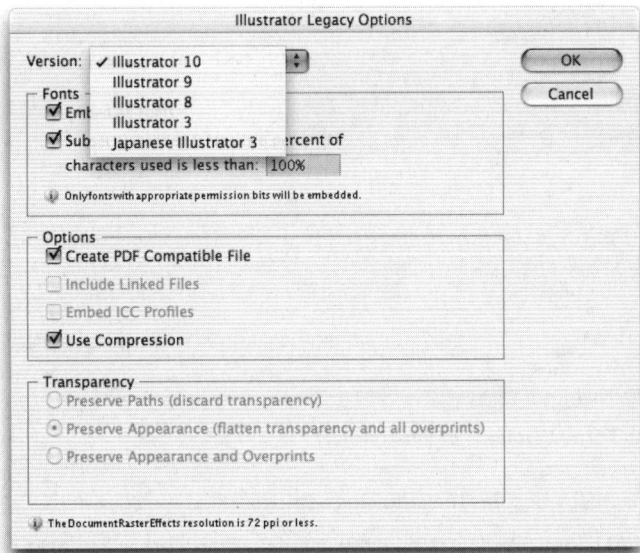

Figure 36-25: The Legacy Options dialog box available from Adobe Illustrator 11 makes it possible to save your file to an earlier version format to ensure consistent import to Flash.

> **Tip** If you use Illustrator 8, you can still export artwork as SWF files if you download and install Macromedia's free Flash Writer plug-in, which is available at www.macromedia.com/support/flash/download.

Using SWF Export from Illustrator 9 or higher

A feature that was introduced with Adobe Illustrator 9 is the capability to export SWF files without the use of an additional plug-in. To export a SWF file directly from Illustrator 9 or higher, follow these steps:

1. Open your Illustrator (AI or EPS) file.

2. Select **Export** from the File menu and choose **Flash (SWF)** from the Format drop-down menu. Type a name for your new SWF file and choose a folder to store the file; then click **Export** to open the Flash Format Options dialog box.

3. In the Flash (SWF) Format Options dialog box (shown in Figure 36-26), you can choose how you want your Illustrator artwork to translate to the SWF format.

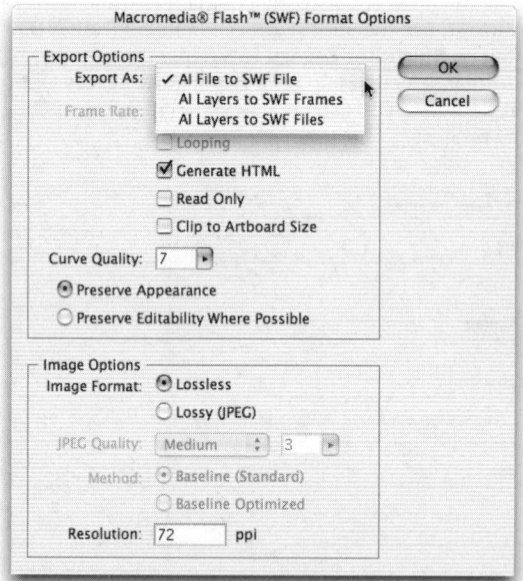

Figure 36-26: Flash Format Options in Illustrator 11

The Export Options dialog box has the following settings:

- **Export As:** If AI File to SWF File is selected, all of your artwork will appear on one keyframe and in one layer in the Flash movie. AI Layers to SWF Frames will export each layer as separate sequential keyframes on the Flash movie Timeline. If this option is selected, then you can enter a Frame Rate as well. AI Layers to SWF Files exports a separate SWF file for each Illustrator layer.

- **Frame Rate:** As mentioned in the Export As description, you can specify a frame rate for your SWF animation if you chose the AI Layers to SWF Frames option. By default, this option is 12 fps. For faster animations, enter a higher frame rate.

- **Looping (AI 10 or higher only):** If you are intending to place your SWF directly on the Web without any further editing in Flash, this option will control playback of the frames in the SWF file generated by Illustrator. If you want a multiframe sequence to repeat after it has finished playing through the first time, choose AI Layers to SWF Frames from the Export As drop-down menu and select the Looping check box before you export the file.

- **Generate HTML (AI 10 or higher only):** Like the looping option, this option was added to the SWF Format Options for files that you intend to use on the Web without any further editing in Flash. This will create an HTML file that you can load into a browser to preview your SWF file.

- **Read Only:** To prevent your SWF file from being imported into the Flash authoring environment, select this check box.

- **Clip to Artboard Size:** This option forces the SWF's movie dimensions to match the page size of your Illustrator document, even if your artwork doesn't occupy the whole page.

- **Curve Quality:** This setting enables you to specify the accuracy of paths exported from Illustrator. Higher settings (up to 10) result in better accuracy but larger file sizes. Lower settings produce smaller file sizes, at the expense of line quality. We recommend that you use the default setting of 7.

- **Image Options:** These standard settings control how any placed bitmap images will be compressed when the SWF is exported from Illustrator.

- Radio buttons were added to Illustrator 11 that allow you to choose either **Preserve Appearance** or **Preserve Editability Where Possible**. I'm not certain that "editability" is a word, but I do know that these options make it possible to influence the conversion process from Illustrator to Flash. Select the first option to favor image fidelity—converting text to outlines or rasterizing artwork where necessary. Or select the second option to favor editable content—preserving text blocks and converting artwork to shapes in Flash, with masks to emulate clipping paths if needed.

4. Click **OK**, and Illustrator exports a new SWF file. You can import the new file into another Flash document (FLA) or use it directly in Web presentations.

Note

In addition to most of the options described for more recent versions of Illustrator, Illustrator 9 includes an option to **Auto-create Symbols**. This setting converts each piece (or group) of Illustrator artwork into a Flash symbol that can be accessed from the Flash Library. Use this setting if you want to import the SWF file into Flash for further editing and for reuse in other Flash movies. This feature adds a duplicate keyframe for each symbol when imported into Flash. As odd as this may seem, it's necessary for Flash to recognize the symbols on import. Make sure that you remove the second keyframe before you publish your final SWF from Flash.

Using the Save for Web command to preview export settings

Illustrator 10 or 11 offers the handy option of using the File ➪ Save for Web command to invoke the Save for Web window (as shown in Figure 36-27). This allows you to preview how your file will appear with different export settings. Although the settings are not as extensive as those in the Export Options dialog box (described previously), the Save for Web dialog box does allow you to alter the file's dimensions and to see a preview of how the file size is affected by the different Curve Quality settings.

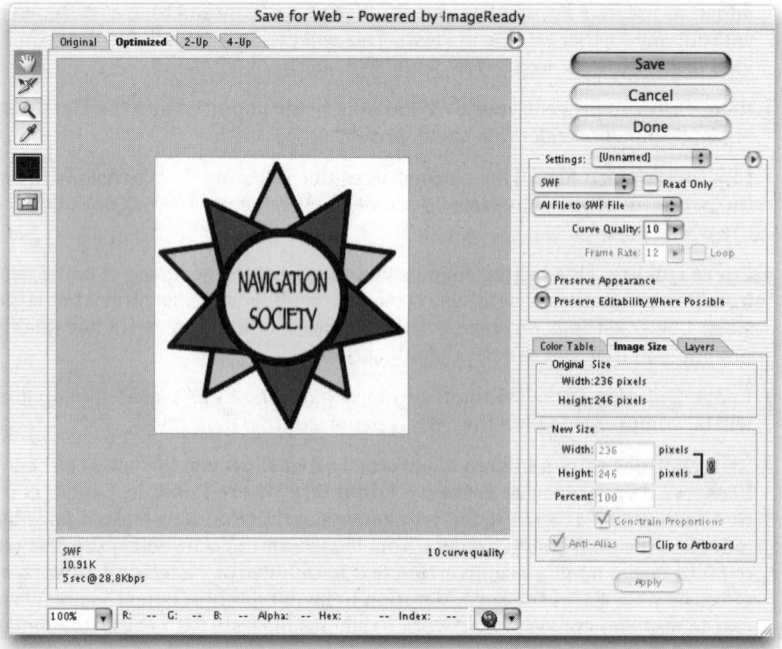

Figure 36-27: The Illustrator Save for Web window allows you to see a preview of the file size and quality as you choose settings for the exported SWF.

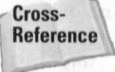

Cross-Reference   For more information on importing and editing vector artwork from other applications in Flash, refer to Chapter 16, "Importing Artwork."

Exporting Vector Graphics from Flash

In the previous chapter, you learned to export raster image formats from Flash. If you've created artwork in Flash that you want to share with other drawing applications, then you can export any frame (or series of frames) from Flash — in any of the popular vector file formats.

Why would you want to export vector-based images from Flash? If you're a design or graphics professional, then you probably need to reuse your artwork in a number of different media for print, multimedia, or broadcast delivery. As such, you don't like wasting valuable time recreating the same artwork. Most Flash artwork exports flawlessly to the file formats listed in Table 36-1.

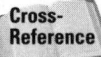

Cross-Reference If you want to export a series of vector images from a Flash movie to use with video or other multiframe applications, check out Chapter 14, "Exporting Animation."

If you are unsure of the format to use in your graphics program, refer to Table 36-1. Afterward, we show you the steps for exporting artwork in a Flash frame as a static vector image.

Table 36-1: Vector Image Formats for Flash Export

Flash Export Format	File Extension	Comments
EPS 3.0 (Encapsulated PostScript)	.eps	Universal vector format recognized by most applications. Note: Gradients created in Flash will not export well with this format.
Adobe Illustrator	.ai	Proprietary file format mainly used by Adobe applications. Note: Gradients created in Flash will not export well with this format.
AutoCAdDXF (Drawing eXchange Format)	.dxf	AutoCAD 2D/3D file format used for high-end rendering of blueprints, models, and other detailed or technical vector drawings.
PICT — Mac only (Picture)	.pct	The Macintosh PICT format can contain both vector and raster information.
WMF/EMF — PC only (Windows Meta File/ Extended Meta File)	.wmf, .emf	Only some Windows applications support these formats. These files are not used often on either Mac or PC systems.

To export artwork as a vector file format from Flash MX 2004, follow these steps:

1. Move the Playhead in the Flash Timeline to the frame that contains the artwork you wish to export.

2. Choose the File ➪ Export Image command from the application menu.

3. Enter a filename and select your preferred vector image format in the Save as Type (or Format) drop-down menu. Select a destination folder for the saved file.

4. Click **Save** and you now have a file that you can use in your drawing or illustration program, either by opening the file directly or by importing or placing it in an existing file.

Note Unlike exported raster image formats from Flash, the exported vector file formats do not have any additional settings for image quality, contents, or size because these settings are not necessary for vector file formats. By their nature, vector graphics can be scaled at any size.

A word of caution: Using vector formats from Flash

Generally, the quality of exported vector files from Flash is less than desirable. Although it would seem that Flash's vector exports would be better than its raster exports, this simply isn't the case. Because RGB color space (as the end product) is relatively new to the world of print-based production, most vector file formats need to encode color information as CMYK. This presents a couple of problems, as you'll see in the following sections.

Color consistency

Flash works within an RGB color model, which means that all color is defined by three numbers, one assigned to each color channel of the image (for example, red, green, and blue). Most standard vector file formats do not encode the color information in this manner. Rather, they use CMYK (cyan, magenta, yellow, and black) colors that have a much more restricted color *gamut* (range) than RGB.

As such, most, if not all, of your Flash artwork will display quite differently when exported as a vector file format, such as EPS or AI. Is this yet another reason to start projects intended for multiple media formats in Macromedia FreeHand? Yes and no. While starting projects in FreeHand lends itself to greater flexibility for the reuse or repurposing of artwork, you do have another alternative to exporting vector files from Flash: good old copy and paste. If you select Flash artwork, choose Edit ➪ Copy, switch to your illustration program, and choose Edit ➪ Paste; the newly pasted artwork should match your original Flash artwork.

Why is this so? Most likely it is because the Flash vector export file formats (or the versions of these formats) default to CMYK colors. However, the Clipboard can support a multitude of data types, and Adobe Illustrator and FreeHand can recognize RGB colors. Therefore, the copied-and-pasted colors show up as RGB colors in these programs — as long as the document you are pasting into is set to RGB color space (or mode) *before* you paste artwork from Flash.

Note Interestingly, if you choose Adobe Illustrator (AI) as the export file format from Flash, you can only choose up to and including Illustrator 6 formats. RGB color support was first introduced to Adobe Illustrator in version 7.

Flash gradients

Another troublesome spot for exported vector files from Flash is the re-rendering of Flash gradients as CMYK *blends*. Depending on the vibrancy of the original gradient in Flash, the exported vector equivalents might end up very muddy or brownish — especially in the middle range of the gradient. Again, you can avoid this color shifting by copying and pasting the Flash gradients directly between applications. Note that this still converts Flash gradients to blends, but it will retain the RGB color values of the original Flash gradient.

Tip If you need perfect exported material from Flash, you might consider exporting high-resolution bitmap (a.k.a. *raster*) files instead. For coverage of bitmap export from Flash, refer to Chapter 35, "Working with Raster Graphics."

 **Web Resource** We'd like to know what you think about this chapter. Visit www.flashsupport.com/feedback to fill out an online form with your comments.

Summary

✦ You can use Flash to import and export many vector formats to support designs for print, broadcast, or other media.

✦ To maintain color consistency when you're creating artwork in other programs, it is important to work in RGB color whenever possible. This will avoid unexpected color shifts in the artwork when you import it to Flash.

✦ FreeHand offers specialized tools for handling text and complex vector artwork, which can greatly enhance your Flash designs.

✦ FreeHand is used by top designers, such as Todd Purgason, to plan and print high-impact presentations that help sell clients on Flash project proposals before production begins in the Flash authoring environment.

✦ Many vector programs offer tools for converting raster images into vector images, but the final artwork can result in larger file sizes than the original bitmaps imported directly to Flash.

✦ Finding the best workflow requires a balance between the visual effect and the final file size constraints. It's important to decide first what look you are trying to achieve with your graphics. The next step is testing different format and compression options to find the best way of keeping the image quality high and the file size streamlined.

✦ ✦ ✦

Working with Dreamweaver MX 2004

Macromedia Dreamweaver is the most popular HTML authoring tool for professional Web developers. Dreamweaver MX 2004, as its name suggests, is designed to integrate with the other programs in the Macromedia MX 2004 Studio suite. While there are many other site management and HTML authoring tools available, when it comes to integrating Flash with your Web site, there's no other tool that compares to the capabilities of Dreamweaver.

The latest version builds on the award-winning foundations of Dreamweaver MX. Tools for visual designers and application developers have been expanded and enhanced, the interface has been updated and there is tighter integration with Flash and Fireworks to make production easier and faster.

 **On the CD-ROM**   A demo version of Dreamweaver MX 2004 is available in the software folder of the *Macromedia Flash MX 2004 Bible* CD-ROM.

Why Use Dreamweaver with Flash?

Dreamweaver is much more than an HTML authoring tool. It provides many options for site management; not only is it a great tool for HTML pages, but it's also excellent for keeping track of site assets such as images, source files, and Flash movies.

Flash movies are rarely viewed as standalone objects. People point their browsers to HTML pages that contain SWF files; they don't usually load a standalone Flash movie if they are browsing the Web. Although Flash can generate basic HTML pages using the Publish feature, Macromedia Dreamweaver enables you to gain more control over the visual placement of your Flash movie, to customize plug-in settings and to manage your Web site more effectively.

Dreamweaver MX 2004 includes many excellent page layout templates and examples. These include image placeholders and sample text for a range of common pages — from text layouts to registration forms to shopping carts — these files give you a jump-start on building various HTML frameworks that Flash can be added to.

Building sites with Dreamweaver can vary in complexity. Developing data-driven sites or rich Internet applications always involves several other necessary components — a Web server and a database, to name but two. In this chapter we're going to explore the simpler option of adding Flash to basic sites with Dreamweaver.

Additional information and examples of dynamic Web applications can be found at www.macromedia.com/devnet/mx/dreamweaver.

Of course, of all the features in Dreamweaver, we are particularly interested in those features that make our lives easier as Flash developers. These include the following:

✦ **Flash elements:** Dreamweaver MX 2004 takes Flash integration to a new level by allowing developers to convert Flash movies into Dreamweaver components that can be distributed and customized in the Dreamweaver authoring environment using settings and properties in the Tag inspector.

The two Flash objects that ship with Dreamweaver MX 2004 — Flash Button and **Flash Text** — have been available since Dreamweaver 4. So what's different about the new Flash elements in Dreamweaver MX 2004? Flash elements can be authored by other Flash developers and *added* to the Flash elements category of the Insert bar, so you are no longer limited to using the original Flash objects that ship with the program. Although only one Flash element ships with Dreamweaver MX 2004, this new architecture supports the potential for developers to easily create and share (or sell) Flash elements for Dreamweaver and opens new possibilities for expanding your toolkit.

✦ **Launch and edit Flash from within Dreamweaver:** If you have used this feature with any of the other Studio programs, you'll realize how helpful this can be. It's very easy to change a SWF file from a Dreamweaver page. By just clicking one button, Dreamweaver opens Flash with the correct FLA and enables you to make your changes. When you finish editing, one more click automatically exports the SWF, saves the FLA, and takes you back to the updated page in Dreamweaver.

✦ **ActionScript editing:** The Dreamweaver coding environment supports code hinting and color coding for ActionScript and the *ActionScript Reference Guide* is built-in. Because Dreamweaver also supports several key scripting languages, some developers prefer to use Dreamweaver for authoring and editing all code files on complex projects. Code files can be saved in a variety of formats from Dreamweaver, including XML, JavaScript, ColdFusion and ActionScript (.as format), which can be imported to Flash for integration or modification.

Dreamweaver's capability to transfer code back and forth between applications, keeping your preferred formatting intact, is referred to as "roundtrip" editing — Dreamweaver will not overwrite or reformat your own code as many other HTML authoring tools are known to do.

✦ **Link updates:** From within Dreamweaver, you can change URL links within Flash movies and have the change propagate to both the Flash movie (SWF) and to the Flash document (FLA).

What's New in Dreamweaver MX 2004?

You may like to create your pages visually or prefer to get your hands dirty with the behind-the-scenes coding. Either way, Dreamweaver is a robust and powerful and flexible authoring tool. New features in Dreamweaver MX 2004 include the following:

✦ **MX 2004 interface update:** The Dreamweaver interface has been modified to make it more space-efficient and intuitive. New features are consistent with other MX 2004 Studio programs, including the new Start page that makes it possible to access recent files as well as templates, tutorials, and Help content.

✦ **Enhanced performance:** As with Flash MX 2004, Dreamweaver MX 2004 has been re-architected and optimized to improve performance for key tasks such as opening and saving files, switching context or jumping in and out of the program.

✦ **MX elements for HTML and for Flash:** Prebuilt components for interactive UI elements make it easier to build animated interfaces. Support for editable Flash elements opens new possibilities for publishing hybrid Flash/HTML content from Dreamweaver.

✦ **More editing options:** Edit images with built-in Fireworks technology. Copy and paste from Microsoft Word or Excel directly into Flash while preserving fonts, colors, and CSS styles.

✦ **Improved CSS support:** An integrated Tag inspector with CSS rules and behaviors, a CSS-based Text Property inspector, CSS Rule inspector, CSS-based Page Properties panel, CSS code hints, and an improved Design view all make it easier to author and render complex CSS-based layouts.

✦ **Full Unicode support:** You can now use, render, and save any font and encoding supported by your operating system, including double-byte character sets.

✦ **Secure FTP:** Fully encrypt all file transfers to prevent unauthorized access to your data, files, usernames, and passwords.

✦ **Automatic cross-browser validation:** Specify which browsers to target and Dreamweaver checks your documents for cross-browser compatibility issues when saving.

✦ **Improved coding environment:** Timesaving features include more robust Find and Replace options, a selection inspector for comprehensive property editing and new context menus for quick access to table editing and code formatting or conversion options.

Cross-Reference

We have highlighted only the new features most relevant to general Web authoring in Dreamweaver. For a more complete list of new features and tips on server-side topics, refer to: www.macromedia.com/devnet/mx/dreamweaver.

Importing Flash into Dreamweaver

Although the Flash Publish feature takes a lot of the guesswork out of placing Flash movies into HTML pages, you might want to add HTML graphics and text to the page, too.

In this section, we look at the fundamentals of using Flash movies with Dreamweaver and HTML.

Cross-Reference To follow the steps in this section, you need to have a SWF file published from Flash. For more information on using the Flash Publish Settings to export files from Flash, refer to Chapter 21, "Publishing Flash Movies." You may also find it helpful to review Chapter 22, "Integrating Flash Content with Web Pages," before proceeding with this chapter.

Inserting your Flash movie

After you've created an animation or some interactive content in Flash and have exported the file into the SWF format, you're ready to put the file into your HTML document.

Let's get started. First, create a new document in Dreamweaver — you have the following two options:

✦ Select HTML from the Create New list in the Start page.

✦ Select File ⇨ New (Ctrl+N or ⌘+N) to invoke the New Document dialog box and choose HTML from the Basic page category.

Next, insert the Flash file by selecting Insert ⇨ Media ⇨ Flash from the application menu, or by clicking the Flash icon in the Media submenu on the Insert bar (when the Common category is loaded) as shown in Figure 37-1.

New Feature The tabbed insert menu structure from Dreamweaver MX has been replaced with a nested menu structure that reduces clutter in the interface. The same options that were available in the tab-style insert menu are still available; you simply have to select the relevant main category from the drop-down menu on the left side of the Insert bar to see the icons that lead to submenus for specific insert types.

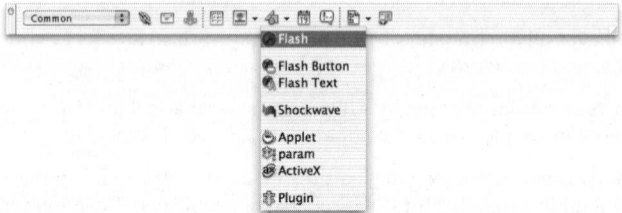

Figure 37-1: Click the Flash icon in the Media submenu on the Insert bar to import a Flash SWF to your Dreamweaver page.

After you select a file type from the insert menu, the Select File dialog box appears — this enables you to browse folders until you find the Flash movie (SWF) that you want to insert. Choose a Flash movie (SWF) and click Select.

Tip If you prefer to use keyboard shortcuts, use Ctrl+Alt+F or Option+⌘+F to invoke the Select File dialog box directly.

If the file you choose to import is not located in the same folder (directory) as your current Dreamweaver file, you will be given the option to copy the SWF to the active site folder. This is optional, but if you do keep related project files together in the same location on your system, it makes the file linking less complex.

Cross-Reference Publish profiles in Flash MX 2004 include options for controlling where SWF files are placed when you publish them from an FLA. This feature really promotes good organization of your various project files. For more information about managing Flash files and using Publish profiles, refer to Chapter 3, "Planning Flash Projects."

After the SWF is imported and inserted on your HTML document, you should see a gray preview rectangle with a small Flash symbol in the Design view of the Dreamweaver Document window. You should also notice that when the SWF (icon) is selected, the Property inspector displays the most commonly used settings and info related to your Flash item, as shown in Figure 37-2. (Refer to Table 37-1 for a description of these properties.) The animated Flash graphics are only visible if you press the Play button on the Property inspector. If the Property inspector is not visible, access it with Window ➪ Properties (Ctrl+F3 or ⌘+F3). If all of the properties are not displayed, click the expand arrow in the lower-right corner or double-click the inactive areas of the inspector.

Note The new Class menu visible in the Property inspector is used for defining CSS styles and does not apply to Flash items.

Some of the controls visible in the Property inspector are similar to those you've seen in the Property inspector in Flash, but others are specific to the Dreamweaver authoring environment.

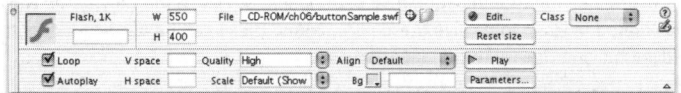

Figure 37-2: The Property inspector in Dreamweaver MX 2004 (on Mac)

Table 37-1: **Flash Properties in the Property Inspector**

Property	Description
Name	Identifies the movie for scripting purposes. It is always a good habit to name all your elements in Dreamweaver.
W and H	Represents the size of the SWF in default pixels. The dimensions can also be set to pc (picas), pt (points), in (inches), mm (millimeters), cm (centimeters), or % (percent). By default, this information is automatically set to the SWF's original dimensions.
File	The SWF file's path/location. The information for your current file should automatically appear in this field. Click the folder icon to the right of the text field to invoke the Select File dialog box if you want to re-link or replace the file.
Src	Holds the source file (FLA) for the Flash movie, enabling the launch and edit feature to function from within Dreamweaver.
Align	Determines how the movie is aligned on the page (left, middle, right). The default is align left.

Continued

Table 37-1 *(continued)*

Property	Description
Bg	Specifies a background color for the movie area. This color also appears while the movie is not playing (while loading and after playing). This setting can also be selected within Flash in the Property inspector or in the Document Properties dialog box (Modify ⇨ Document or shortcut keys Ctrl+J or ⌘+J).
V Space and H Space	Specifies the number of pixels for white space around the movie. V Space pertains to the white space above, and below, while H space defines the space on the left and right sides of the movie.
Quality	Sets the quality parameter for the object and embed tags that run the movie. The settings to choose from are Low, Auto Low, Auto High, and High.
Scale	Sets the scale parameter for the OBJECT and EMBED tags that place the movie. Scale defines how the movie is placed within the browser window when the width and height values are percentages.
Loop	Makes the Flash movie automatically loop if no stop actions occur on the main Timeline.
Autoplay	Plays the movie's main Timeline automatically when the page loads.
Parameters	Opens a dialog box for entering additional parameters to pass to the movie. The movie must be created in Flash to receive these parameters. These can be hard-coded, or they can be dynamic and drawn from a database.
Reset Size	Examines the SWF file and resets it to the original size it was created within Flash.

Positioning your movie

The best way to center your Flash movie within the browser window is to surround the `<EMBED>` and/or `<OBJECT>` tags with the `<CENTER></CENTER>` tags. Unlike scale options, this method preserves the original aspect ratio of your Flash movie and will not stretch or expand the size. This also ensures that items outside the Stage area of the Flash movie will not be visible.

Tip   The easiest way to add this code is to type it into the Code view window directly, if you use the Split view, you will be able to see how adding the `<CENTER>` tags in the Code view adjusts the position of the SWF preview in your Design view.

Another way to center the Flash movie in the browser is to set the width and height dimensions to 100 percent in the Dreamweaver Property inspector. However, this method might cause some unwanted effects by altering how your movie is framed in the browser window. For example, if you had items in the Flash-authoring environment that bled off the Stage area and into the Work area, items off Stage are normally "cropped" by the dimensions of the movie. When the Flash movie is imported to Dreamweaver, Dreamweaver adheres to the original dimensions, giving you the cropping and the clean edge that you expect. However, when the width and height are set to 100 percent in Dreamweaver, items in the Flash work area that were meant to be cropped may be visible, creating a "sloppy" edge on the movie. Although most Web sites are viewed in full-screen capacity, some users scale their browser to their own desired size, which may adversely impact the aspect ratio (the height and width ratio) of your movie. The scale options in the Dreamweaver Property inspector enable you to select from three display settings to control how the SWF appears in browser windows. These options are as follows:

✦ **Default (Show all):** Makes the entire movie visible in the specified area. The aspect ratio of the SWF is maintained, and no distortion occurs. Borders may appear on two sides of the movie.

✦ **No Border:** Forces the movie to scale to fit the browser window. The aspect ratio of the movie is maintained, and no distortion occurs — but portions of the movie may be cropped if the browser window does not match the aspect ratio of the SWF.

✦ **Exact Fit:** Forces the movie to stretch or squash to fill the entire visible area of the browser window, even if the aspect ratio does not match the original SWF. This option is rarely used because the aspect ratio of the movie is not maintained, and distortion may occur.

Specifying Window Mode

Chapter 21, "Publishing Flash Movies," describes how the Publish Settings dialog box within Flash has a Window Mode setting used to make Flash movies transparent and show DHTML content that would otherwise be hidden behind them. The window mode parameter, WMODE, enables the background of a Flash movie to drop out, so that HTML or DHTML content can appear in place of the Flash movie background. You have probably seen Flash ads that use this feature so that they can "float" on top of other content in your browser window.

Note Since the mid-release of the Flash Player 6.0, this feature is supported by Mozilla-compatible browsers, such as Netscape and Apple Safari in addition to Internet Explorer 4.0 or higher for Windows (95/98/ME/NT/2000/XP).

Tip If you are using browser detection on your Web pages, you can divert visitors using these browsers to specialized Flash and DHTML Web pages, while routing visitors with older systems to standard pages that don't use Window Mode. For more information on using browser detection, refer to Chapter 22, "Integrating Flash Content with Web Pages."

You may have noticed that there is no equivalent of the Window Mode option in the Dreamweaver Property inspector. If you want that option in Dreamweaver, you have to specify it a little more directly. If you want to try it out, it's pretty simple.

The three options for Window Mode are as follows:

✦ **Window:** This is the "standard" player interface, in which the Flash movie plays as it would normally, in its own rectangular window on a Web page.

✦ **Opaque:** Use this option if you want the Flash movie to have an opaque background and have DHTML or HTML elements behind the Flash movie.

✦ **Transparent:** This option "knocks out" the Flash background color so that other HTML elements can show through. Note that the Flash movie's frame rate and performance may suffer on slower machines when this mode is used because the Flash movie needs to composite itself over other non-Flash material.

If you want to animate other material behind or in front of the Flash movie, make sure that your Flash movie is on its own DHTML layer.

1. In your Dreamweaver page, select the Flash movie (SWF).

2. Click the Parameters button in the Property inspector.

3. The Parameters dialog box appears. Enter WMODE for the Parameter and TRANSPARENT, OPAQUE, or WINDOW for the value, as shown in Figure 37-3.

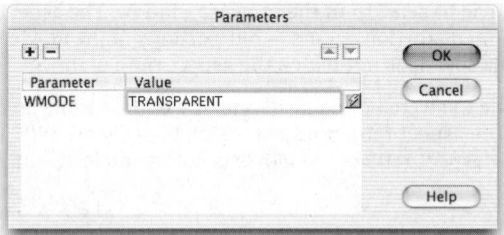

Figure 37-3: Specifying Window Mode in Dreamweaver

4. Click OK. Preview your page by pressing F12 or by choosing File ⇨ Preview In Browser.

Launch and Edit Flash from Dreamweaver

You can't edit your imported Flash movies (SWFs) directly in the Dreamweaver authoring environment, so you must go to the Flash document (FLA) to make any significant changes to the Flash content. Before Dreamweaver MX, this entailed opening up Flash and navigating through your files to find the source Flash document, which might even be in a different location than the Flash movie placed in Dreamweaver, with no inherent mechanism for tying the two together. You'd edit in Flash, export the SWF and finally go back to Dreamweaver, hoping that you'd exported to the correct location. This could be a surprisingly time-consuming task on a large site and even on simpler sites could certainly interfere with workflow and add unnecessary steps to what should be an easy routine. Fortunately, since Dreamweaver MX was introduced we have a simpler method.

After you specify a site for your files to be associated with, Dreamweaver can store basic information about an inserted Flash SWF: most important, its associated FLA file. This can be viewed in the Src element of the Property inspector. The first time you decide to change a SWF file from within Dreamweaver, you will be prompted to specify the location of the original FLA file, but once you enter this information, it will be stored in the Dreamweaver file. To launch Flash from Dreamweaver follow these steps:

In your Dreamweaver page, select the SWF you want to edit. Do one of the following:

✦ Click the Edit button in the Property inspector.

✦ Right-click (Control-click) the Flash movie placeholder and choose Edit with Flash from the contextual menu.

✦ Hold down the Ctrl (Windows) or ⌘ (Mac) key and double-click the placeholder movie.

If Dreamweaver does not know the location of the FLA file, you will be prompted to supply it. Flash then opens the FLA and you can edit it in Flash as you normally would. The only indication that you are working on a file linked to a file placed in Dreamweaver are the icons at the top of the Document window and the text that says "Editing From Dreamweaver," as shown in Figure 37-4.

Figure 37-4: Editing a Flash file from Dreamweaver

When you are finished editing the Flash movie, click the Done button. Flash exports the Flash movie (SWF), saves the Flash document (FLA), and returns you to the Dreamweaver authoring environment where the modified SWF will be visible in your HTML page.

Note   Dreamweaver MX 2004 uses Design Notes to track any changes made to Flash objects or other media objects originating from Dreamweaver.

Using Built-in Flash Objects

Dreamweaver includes some simple but useful options for adding Flash content without having to use the Flash authoring tool. These options can be found in the Media submenu of the Insert panel. (Refer to Figure 37-1.)

New Feature   A whole new category has been added to the Insert bar to accommodate customizable Flash elements. Flash elements are an exciting new area of development, but the basic Flash objects that ship with Dreamweaver are still a great option for adding interactive buttons or text — the most commonly needed interface items.

Adding a Flash Button object

Since version 4.0, Dreamweaver has had the capability to create Flash Button objects based on predetermined button styles. The styles available in Dreamweaver MX 2004 look much like the Button Library that ships with Flash MX 2004. In addition to choosing from a wide variety of styles for these buttons you can easily edit the text labels and links in Dreamweaver. Dreamweaver creates a Flash movie (SWF file) based on your selections and stores it in the same directory as the current HTML document.

Note   You must save your document before inserting a Flash Button or Text object. If you have not saved your document, Dreamweaver prompts you to do so. Dreamweaver needs to know where the HTML file resides before it can create the Flash movie (SWF file).

To create a Flash Button object in Dreamweaver follow these steps:

1. Select the Flash Button icon from the Media submenu of the Insert Panel, or select Insert ➪ Media ➪ Flash Button from the application menu. Using either of these methods enables you to access the Insert Flash Button dialog box, shown in Figure 37-5.

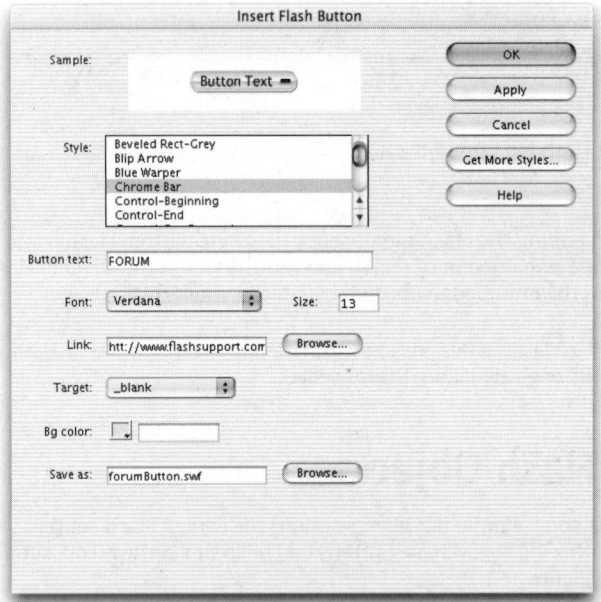

Figure 37-5: The Insert Flash Button dialog box

2. Now select a button from the **Style** list provided. Dreamweaver displays a live preview of the currently selected button style in the **Sample** window and you can click and roll over the preview button to see how it behaves. However, you will not be able to preview any changes to the text or Bg color in this window.

3. Next, in the **Button text** field, type the text that you would like to add. This field doesn't work for every button style, as VCR-style Play and Stop buttons don't have text. If the button preview has the words Button Text on the button, then you will be able to type in your own text. Also, the amount of text is limited to the width of the button.

4. From the **Font** menu (optional), select a font for the text. Enter a font size in the **Size** text field or leave it at the default value—make sure this is not too small to be legible or too big to fit your button text.

5. For the **Link** field (optional), type a filename (or URL) or click the Browse button to locate the file to link to. The link can be either a document-relative or absolute link for the button.

6. The **Target** field (optional) enables you to choose a target frame or target window from the drop-down menu.

7. The **Bg color** chip and text field (optional) enable you to choose a background color to fill in the rectangular space around your Flash button. You can either type in a hexadecimal color value (for example, #0066FF) or use the pop-up color swatches to select a background color. Generally, the button Bg color should match the background color of the HTML page that the button appears in.

8. For the **Save as** field, enter a name for the new Flash movie (SWF file) that will be saved to store your button, or accept the default button name. You could also specify a different location for the Flash movie to be saved in by clicking the Browse button and locating or creating a new folder on your system.

9. If you can't find a button style that suits you, click the Get More Styles button to connect to the Macromedia Exchange site to download even more button styles.

10. Finally, click either Apply to see the button with the current settings displayed in the Design view of your Dreamweaver document or OK to insert the Flash button and close the Insert Flash Button dialog box.

Editing a Flash button

As shown in Figure 37-6, some editing options are available directly in the Property inspector when the button is selected.

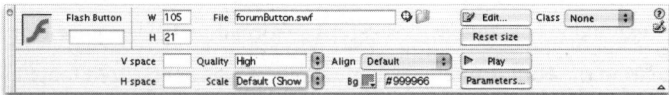

Figure 37-6: These editing options become available in the Property inspector when a Flash button is selected.

If you need to access more editing options there are two ways to reopen the Insert Flash Button dialog box so you can modify any of the original settings:

✦ Double-click the Flash button in the Design view of the document window.

✦ Select the Flash button in the Design view and click the Edit button in the Property inspector.

Inserting a Flash Text object

The Flash Text object enables you to insert a body of Flash text with a simple rollover effect. The text renders correctly in the browser even if the font you specify is not available on a viewer's machine. Inserting the Flash Text object is very similar to inserting the Flash Button object. Simply select the Flash Text icon from the Media submenu of the Insert Panel, or select Insert ➪ Media ➪ Flash Text from the application menu. Using either of these methods enables you to access the Insert Flash Text dialog box, shown in Figure 37-7.

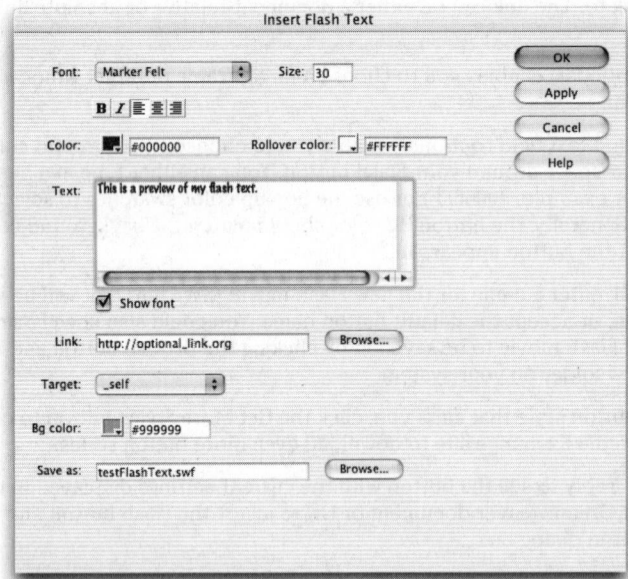

Figure 37-7: The Insert Flash Text dialog box. Dreamweaver MX enables you to place anti-aliased Flash Text within an HTML document. Dreamweaver creates the necessary SWF file and saves it with your HTML document.

Using the Insert Flash Text dialog box, follow these steps to format and insert your text:

1. Select a font face from the **Font** drop-down menu. You can use specialized fonts in the Flash text object and not have to worry about how it displays. The font information is embedded in the SWF, so the text always appears as you designed it.

2. Enter a font size (in points) in the **Size** field.

3. Select style attributes by clicking the Bold, Italic, and Text Alignment buttons.

4. Choose a text **Color** by entering a hexadecimal color (for example, #0066FF) or by choosing a specific color from the color pop-up menu. You can also choose a separate rollover color for your text.

5. Type in your desired text in the **Text** field. The text is not constrained to the preview window size and it does not auto-wrap, so it continues on one long line unless you manually enter breaks with the Return (or Enter) key.

6. Add a document-relative or absolute HTML **Link** (optional).

7. Choose an HTML **Target** window or target frame (optional).

8. Choose a background color (optional) from the **Bg color** swatches. The background color for Flash Text objects fills in the rectangular text box around your type. Leave this setting at Default if you want it to match the background of your current HTML document.

9. Type in a file name for the **Save as** field or accept the default name (for example, text1.swf).

10. To preview all of your settings, click Apply to insert the Flash Text without leaving the dialog box.

11. To insert the Flash Text and exit the dialog box, click OK.

The static text is visible in the Design view window, but to see any animated rollover effects, you need to preview the document in a browser window (F12) or select the Flash Text and click the Play button in the Property inspector.

Editing a Flash Text object

To modify the inserted Flash Text, use the settings in the Property inspector or reopen the Insert Flash Text dialog box in one of two ways:

✦ Double-click the Flash Text object in the Design view window.

✦ Select the Flash Text object click the Edit button in the Property inspector.

Using Flash Elements

Dreamweaver MX 2004 ships with only one example of a Flash element, but it is an exciting preview of what is to come for designers building hybrid Flash-HTML applications. In this section we go through the steps for using the Image Viewer Flash element that ships with Dreamweaver MX 2004.

Note   The topic of authoring custom Flash elements (also called *components* or *objects*) is beyond the scope of this chapter, but the API Reference in the Dreamweaver Help Center is a good place to start (Help ➪ Extending Dreamweaver ➪ API Reference). Look under Utility APIs ➪ Flash Integration.

Web Resource   Visit the Macromedia Developer Center to find articles and tutorials on Flash integration, as well as many others related to expanding Dreamweaver and Flash: www.macromedia.com/devnet.

Inserting the Picture Viewer Flash element

Inserting a Flash element is just as easy as inserting one of the Flash objects described in the previous section; however, there is a separate category for elements in the Insert bar. Choose **Flash Elements** from the Category menu and you will see one lonely icon for the Picture Viewer, as shown in Figure 37-8. The good news is that Picture Viewer is a fun, functional example and there is plenty of room for you to add more Flash elements as they become available.

Figure 37-8: Picture Viewer is the first Flash element available
in Dreamweaver MX 2004.

Note   At the time of this writing, not many new Flash elements for Dreamweaver MX 2004 were
yet available, but keep an eye on the Dreamweaver Exchange. Hopefully, we can look forward to a whole range of new Flash elements from developers taking advantage of the
tighter integration between Flash MX 2004 and Dreamweaver MX 2004.

When using a Flash element that interacts with multiple files (such as the bitmaps that we are
going to load into the Picture Viewer), the organization of your files becomes very important.
To begin the example for this section, I actually defined a new site called PictureViewer so
that I could specify the location for the HTML files, Flash file, and source image files. The
HTML file and the SWF file generated by Dreamweaver can both be stored in my main directory and the JPEGs are all stored in a subfolder called "images." This is a simplified structure
and a real-world project might include many more files, but this is a good start for a logical
system.

**On the
CD-ROM**   You can find all of the files for the Picture Viewer example described in this section in the
"FlashElement" folder in the `ch37` folder on the CD-ROM. To view the final result, open
`flowerViewer.htm` in a browser window.

After you define a site (or specify a location for saving your various files), create a new HTML
document as described for the Flash object examples earlier in this chapter. To insert the
Picture Viewer Flash element, follow these steps:

1. Load the Flash Elements Category in the Insert bar and click the Picture Viewer icon, or
   choose Insert ➪ Media ➪ Image Viewer from the application menu.

2. A Save Flash Element dialog box appears that enables you to specify a location and to
   enter a name for the SWF file that will be generated from the Picture Viewer Flash element in Dreamweaver. We used the name **flowerGallery** for our example file. Click Save
   to insert the Flash Viewer element into your HTML page and close the dialog box.

3. A gray preview with a Flash element icon should appear in the Design view of your
   Dreamweaver document and if you look at Code view, you will notice that a chunk of
   HTML has been added to the file to define the various parameters of the Flash element.

Using the Tag inspector to define Flash element parameters

Although you can edit or modify the parameters for a Flash element manually in the Code
window it is much easier to use the new integrated Tag inspector that has been added to
Dreamweaver MX 2004:

1. Open the Tag inspector from the application menu (Window ⇨ Tag Inspector) or press the F9 shortcut key.

2. Select a placed Flash element in the Design view of your Document window to load the relevant editable parameters into the Tag inspector — the Flash element tab also becomes visible, replacing the various tabs related to HTML or CSS elements. When the Picture Viewer element is selected, the list of parameters in the Tag inspector can be set or modified, as shown in Figure 37-9.

Figure 37-9: The Tag inspector provides a quick interface for modifying the parameters of the Picture Viewer Flash element.

The settings for the Picture Viewer enable you to create an interactive slide presentation from a series of images and to choose a range of options for controlling the playback of the file and the animated transitions. These settings save an enormous amount of time and the end result is a clean, professional-looking slide presentation with cool transitions and a functioning UI. Aside from the standard Dreamweaver settings for fonts, colors, border elements and links, there are pace, style, and playback options for the Flash SWF presentation generated by the Picture Viewer Flash element. Although you can make choices for these settings before you load in a series of images, it makes sense to choose your images first so that you have something to look at when you test the file.

Working with image arrays

If you are a code-oriented designer (or a design-savvy coder) the title of this section will not sound intimidating, but if you are the type of person who usually runs from anything that sounds like "programming," don't give up yet. The real beauty of the simple interface-based architecture of Flash elements is that it makes it very easy for almost anyone to edit little pieces of the code used to generate an interactive Flash movie without having to get overwhelmed by a lot of syntax or a complicated menu system. All you need to know is that the imageURL line in the Tag inspector controls what images load in the Picture Viewer and the order in which they appear.

1. To specify the images that will be displayed in your Picture Viewer presentation, click once in the text area to the right of the `imageURLs` parameter listing. This makes the text field active so that you can manually edit the array, but it also makes a very small icon visible at the far right of the text of the Tag inspector. This button invokes the Edit Array dialog box, as shown in Figure 37-10.

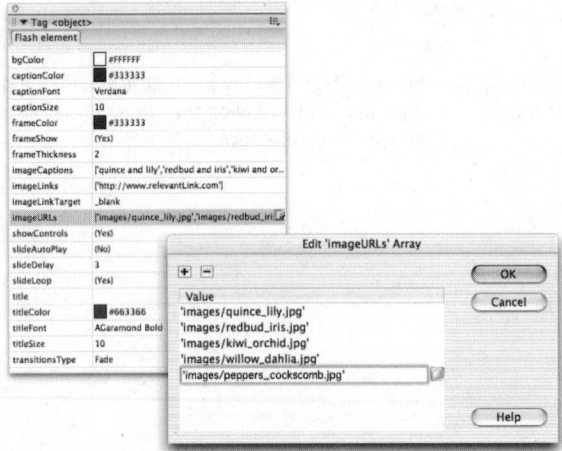

Figure 37-10: The Edit Array dialog box makes it possible to specify the images you want to load in the presentation by typing the path to each image or by browsing to select them one-by-one from your file list.

2. As each line of text in the dialog box is selected, a folder appears to the right that can be clicked to browse to a specific image that you want to load into the Picture Viewer presentation.

3. By default, three items are listed in the array, to add or remove image URLs, simply click the small plus (+) or minus (–) buttons at the top of the dialog box.

4. After you have specified a list of images to load into your presentation, click OK to close the dialog box.

The other two (optional) arrays that relate to the images you have added to the presentation are:

✦ **imageCaptions:** Click in this parameter line to activate the text field. You can type in any name that you want for each of the images, but pay careful attention to the syntax of the array if you are typing directly in the Tag inspector. If you prefer to add captions in the Edit Array dialog box, click the small icon that appears to the right when the imageCaptions parameter line is active. Captions can be entered without array syntax and Dreamweaver will automatically add the syntax after you click OK to load the caption text into the `imageCaptions` array. The captions must be in the same order as the image names appear in the `imageURLs` array so that the correct text appears with each image.

✦ **imageLinks:** The `imageLinks` array is used to add links to the images in your presentation. URLs and Links serve different purposes in these image arrays. Whereas `imageURLs` are used to specify the path to the image that is visible in the Image Viewer, `imageLinks` are used to specify a link to another HTML page or Web address that can be triggered by clicking one of the images. The `imageLinks` array can be edited in the same way as the `imageURLs` array and the link addresses should also appear in the same order as the image names so that they are linked correctly.

Previewing animated Flash elements

After you have added some images — and perhaps some captions and links — to load into the Picture Viewer, you can preview the animated presentation in the following two ways:

✦ Get a live preview in the Dreamweaver authoring environment by selecting the preview in the Design Code and then clicking the Play button in the Property inspector. The Play button is actually a toggle that can be used to play and stop the preview.

✦ Load the presentation into a browser window by choosing an available browser from the File ➪ Preview in Browser menu or use the F12 shortcut key to load the presentation into the current primary browser (defined in Dreamweaver Preferences).

Figure 37-11 shows what the published Picture Viewer looks like in a browser window with the images and captions we have added.

Figure 37-11: The finished FlowerViewer.html file with the Picture Viewer Flash element file (FlowerGallery.swf) visible in a browser window

Editing Flash element parameters

If you are not yet impressed by the functionality of the Picture Viewer Flash element, you can adjust the transition animations or to the other graphic elements in the presentation by changing settings in the Property inspector or by opening the Tag inspector to edit parameters until you are satisfied with the final result. Click the text line of any parameter in the Tag inspector to access available menu options or to edit the text directly. Some of the parameters are simple on/off toggles, but the `transitionsType` parameter can be set with a range of options available from a drop-down menu, as shown in Figure 37-12.

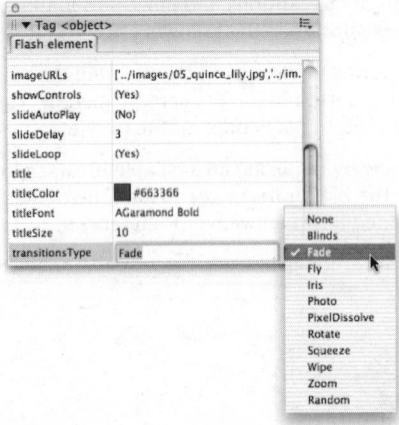

Figure 37-12: The various transition styles available from the transitionType drop-down menu in the Tag inspector can be used to change the Flash animation in your Picture Viewer presentation without ever touching a keyframe in Flash or typing a single line of code.

Try out a few of these transition styles and think for a moment about how long it might have taken to author the Flash animation manually. Then think about how much fun you will have with a whole library of Flash elements — smiling yet?

Adding Dreamweaver Behaviors

Dreamweaver MX 2004 includes several prewritten JavaScript behaviors to supply a variety of different client-side interactions. These include routines to perform image rollovers and DHTML functions. There are two routines that are of particular interest to Flash developers: the Check Plugin behavior and the Control Shockwave or Flash behavior.

Check Plugin behavior

While this is not the most foolproof way of detecting Flash, it's quick and easy to use.

1. Create a new Dreamweaver document or open an existing one.

2. Select an element on the page such as an image or a link. If you want to apply the behavior to the entire page, click the <body> tag in the tag selector at the bottom left of the Document window.

3. In the Behaviors panel (Window ⇨ Behaviors or Shift+F3) click the Add (+) button and select the Check Plugin behavior.

4. The Check Plugin dialog box opens, as shown in Figure 37-13. Select Flash from the Plugin drop-down menu.

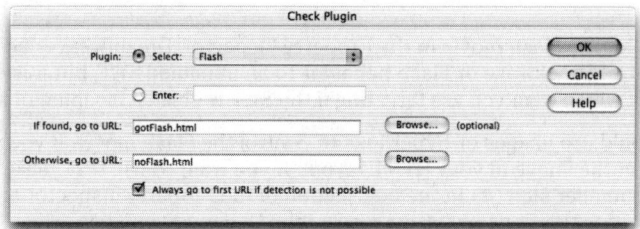

Figure 37-13: The Check Plugin behavior enables you to apply simple Flash detection easily.

5. In the **If found, Go to URL** field; enter the path to the page that you want to load if the visitor has the Flash Player. This can be a relative or absolute address.

6. In the **Otherwise, go to URL** field; specify an alternative page to go to if the visitor does not have the Flash Player. This can be a relative or absolute address.

7. Click **OK**. The Behaviors panel should show the Check Plugin behavior and the event on which it happens, typically the onLoad event, shown in Figure 37-14.

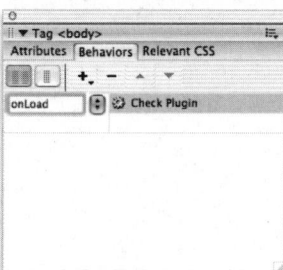

Figure 37-14: The event associated with the behavior can be changed, but onLoad is generally used for the Check Plugin behavior.

Should you need to modify the behavior settings, double-click the behavior text in the Tag inspector to reopen the Check Plugin dialog box. You can also click once in the event text area of the Tag inspector to activate the drop-down menu used to select a different trigger event for the behavior.

Control Shockwave or Flash behavior

This enables simple JavaScript control of a Flash movie, telling the movie to Play, Stop, Rewind, or Go To a certain frame. You can apply these behaviors to regular HTML images or hyperlinks and use them to control the timeline of your Flash movie.

1. Add a Flash movie (SWF) to your Dreamweaver page.

Note This behavior is dimmed in the Behaviors panel if there is no Shockwave or Flash content in the current HTML document.

2. Add a name for the Flash movie in the Property inspector. Dreamweaver enables you to add the Control Shockwave or Flash behavior to an unnamed SWF, but it is easier to keep track of which item you are targeting if the SWF is given a meaningful name.

3. Typically, you'd use images or hyperlinks to control the Flash movie. If you want to use images, select the image in your HTML layout. If you want to use text, make sure you at least have a number sign (#) in the link section of the Property inspector and that the text is selected in the Code or Design view of the Document window.

Note Behaviors cannot be added to plain text, but you can add a behavior to a link. The best way to attach a behavior to text is to add a null link (or a link that won't take the user to another document). Entering a number sign (#) in the Link field of the Property inspector will work to convert the text into a null link, but it is preferable to enter javascript:; (include the colon and the semicolon) because using a number sign will cause some browsers to jump to the top of the document when the user clicks the null link.

4. In the Behaviors tab of the Tag inspector panel (Window ➪ Behaviors), Click the Add (+) button and choose **Control Shockwave or Flash**. The Control Shockwave or Flash dialog box appears, shown in Figure 37-15.

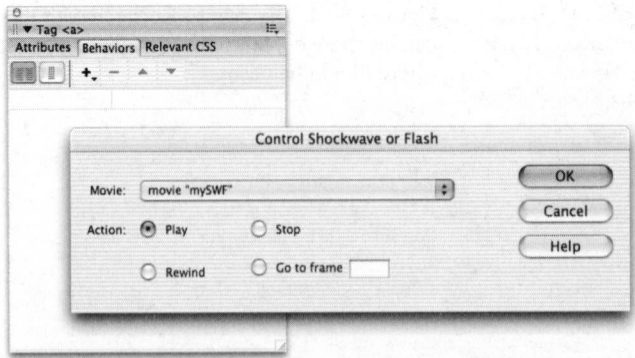

Figure 37-15: The Control Shockwave or Flash dialog box

5. If you have more than one movie on your page, choose the correct one from the drop-down list. Choose whether you want to Play, Stop, Rewind, or Go To a frame. When choosing Go To Frame, enter the frame number.

6. Click OK. Check that the event (onMouseOver, onMouseDown) is correct.

Note   For more about JavaScript behaviors and events in Dreamweaver, check the Help documentation and Macromedia's Dreamweaver support area at www.macromedia.com. Other behaviors are also available for download at the Macromedia Exchange.

Site Map & Link Checker

One of the most common—and often most tedious—tasks in site management is keeping links updated and changing out-of-date URLs. Dreamweaver has long supplied many Find/Replace options for searching entire sites of HTML pages and changing one link to become a different link, but when your site consists of both Flash and HTML content, it was always a manual process to change all the links within the Flash movies.

Since Dreamweaver MX, this is no longer a limitation. You can change links even in Flash movies (SWF files). The Files panel (Window ⇨ Files, or F8) includes drop-down menus for choosing a site that you want to view and for setting a view style. The view shown in Figure 37-16 is set by choosing **Map and Files** from the Site Map drop-down menu (available from the site map icon at the top of the Files panel).

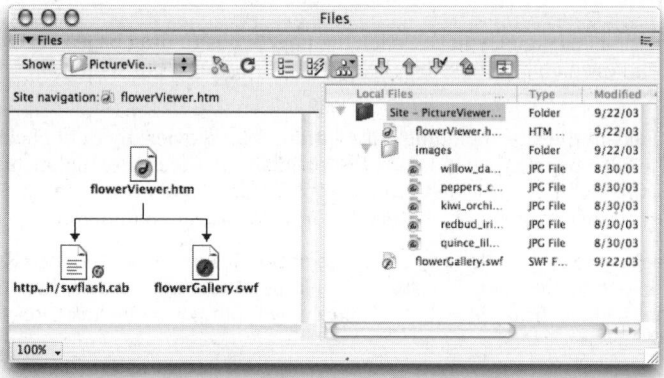

Figure 37-16: The Files panel Map and Files view enables you to see a hierarchical view of the pages and links in your site, including links from Flash movies.

To be able to see this level of detail in the Site Map, you must have a page defined as your Home page in your site definition and also be able to view any dependent files. You can specify this in the Site Map Layout section of the Site Definition dialog box as shown in Figure 37-17. To load the Site Definition dialog box, select Site ⇨ Manage Sites from the application menu (or from the Files panel options menu), and then click the Edit button in the Edit sites dialog box.

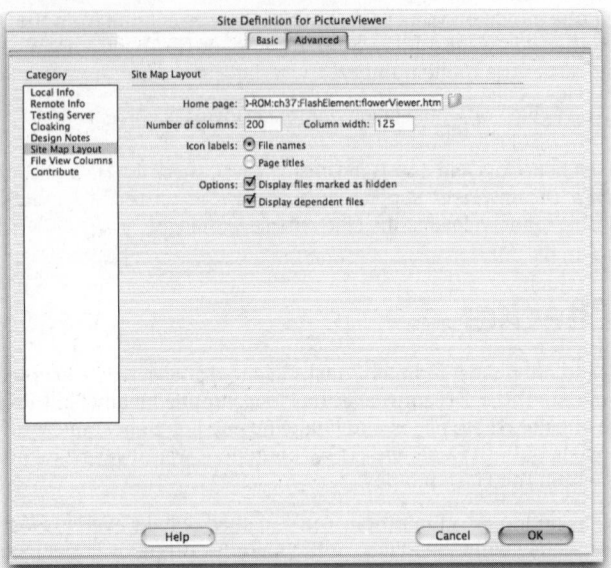

Figure 37-17: You can select a Home page and choose to
Show Dependent Files in the Site Map Layout section of the
Site Definition dialog box.

In the Site Map view of the Files panel, you can click the page icons to drag pages into different relative positions and even change links by clicking and dragging a link icon from one
page to another page.

You can check all the links in the site, including links within Flash movies, by right-clicking in
the Site Map area of the Files panel and choosing Check Links from the contextual menu. You
can also choose Site ➪ Check Links Sitewide from the application menu, or use the Alt+F8 or
Option+F8 shortcut keys. You can check the entire site or just a subset of folders.

The results of this check appear in the Link Checker tab of the Results panel (refer to Figure
37-18). You can then view them by category—broken links, external links and orphaned
files—and also change the links from this window simply by typing over the link URLs.

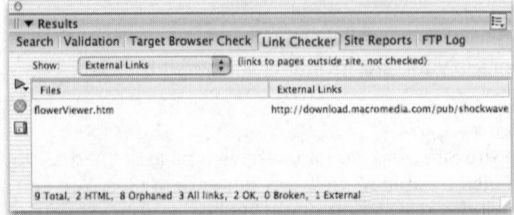

Figure 37-18: The Link Checker tab in the Results
panel enables you to view and change the links within
your site, even within Flash movies (SWF files).

Writing ActionScript with Dreamweaver

When creating large Flash movies, many programmers choose to keep their ActionScript in external text files — typically saved with the .as file extension. There are many benefits to this method.

✦ You can start building libraries of code external to your FLA files, making it easier to reuse code in Flash movies that share common routines.

✦ You don't have to work in the ActionScript window in Flash, which some coders find cramped and difficult to navigate, especially when writing large amounts of code.

✦ You can modularize your code files, allowing different developers to work on different parts of the same Flash movie simultaneously.

✦ When code files are stored externally, you can use a version control system to track changes.

Since Dreamweaver MX, the Dreamweaver coding environment has supported external ActionScript files with full syntax coloring and code hinting features. This makes the process of creating code files much less error-prone than it was in early versions of Dreamweaver, where most methods of editing external ActionScript didn't offer any means of syntax checking.

Code hinting in Dreamweaver creates pop-up menus that automatically appear when typing the name of an object, as in the ActionScript panel in Flash. For example, if your object name ends in _mc, the code hint menu will show the methods and properties for a `movieClip` object. If your object name ends in xmlsocket, you see the methods and properties for an `XMLSocket` object. If you aren't using the suggested suffixes and want to force code hints to appear, press Ctrl+Spacebar (⌘+Spacebar).

To create an ActionScript .as file in Dreamweaver MX 2004, follow these steps:

1. In Dreamweaver, click More in the Create New column of the Start page (or if you are already in the authoring environment choose File ⇨ New from the application menu). Select ActionScript from the Basic page Category in the New Document dialog box and click the Create button.

2. A new page opens in Code view with a comment at the start to indicate an ActionScript document file. You can begin writing ActionScript by typing directly in the code window.

3. When you save the file it is automatically given the .as extension, this is the format that will be recognized by Flash.

Some ActionScript is well-suited to being written in external files — long routines, groups of functions, and object definitions, for example. Though it may seem counter-intuitive, it's practical to have more — rather than fewer — external files when writing code. A common method is to use a separate .as file for each object definition within your Flash project.

In the Flash authoring environment, use the `#include` command in your Flash movie to load the code from an external file. External ActionScript is only included in the Flash movie when the SWF is published, so it will not be added to your FLA file. If you change any code in the external file, you'll need to publish the SWF again to include the changed ActionScript.

 For more information about using the #include directive to load external ActionScript from .as files into Flash movies (SWFs), refer to Chapter 32, "Creating a Portfolio Site in Flash."

Dreamweaver also has support for creating a wide range of other code format files, including ActionScript Communication documents (.asc files) and ActionScript Remote documents (.asr files). These are used with advanced ActionScripting features.

 For more details on ActionScript remoting and communications, refer to the *Flash MX 2004 ActionScript Bible* (Wiley, 2004) by Robert Reinhardt and Joey Lott.

Summary

✦ Dreamweaver is a robust and powerful tool for HTML authoring and site management and allows more sophisticated control over the placement of Flash objects within an HTML framework than is possible in the Flash authoring environment.

✦ You can easily add Flash buttons and Flash text objects from within Dreamweaver without ever opening Flash.

✦ Flash elements are an amazing resource for designers creating hybrid Flash/HTML projects. Leveraging the new SWC format makes it possible for developers to build sophisticated source files in Flash that can then be loaded into Dreamweaver and modified with predefined parameters accessed through a simple interface. The finished, Web-ready SWF file is generated from Dreamweaver.

✦ Dreamweaver comes with many built-in JavaScript behaviors that are easy to apply, including methods for detecting plug-ins and simple control of Flash movies.

✦ Dreamweaver includes full ActionScript code editing abilities, including code hinting and syntax coloring.

✦ URL links in Flash movies can be checked and edited within the Dreamweaver environment without opening Flash.

✦ You can launch Flash and edit Flash movies from within Dreamweaver, making the process of updating Flash files inserted in an HTML site environment much faster.

✦   ✦   ✦

Working with Director MX

Macromedia Director has been the industry-standard, multi-media authoring application for DVD-ROMs, CD-ROMs, kiosk presentations, and Shockwave game development on the Web. Since version 6.5 of Director, you could import Flash movies (.swf files) via the Flash Asset Xtra. With Director MX, you can take even more control of your Flash movies in Director. Moreover, the latest versions of the Shockwave plug-in automatically install the Flash Asset Xtra on Web browsers. This means that you can count on Shockwave-enabled visitors being able to view your Flash-Director Shockwave content.

New Feature   With the use of Lingo, Director's scripting language, you can now create Flash objects dynamically without importing Flash movies (.swf files) into a Director cast.

Why would you want to use Director in combination with Flash? With any multimedia project, you should use the technology that enables you to accomplish your goals. Flash Player 7 has once again expanded the capabilities of Flash movies, but the player does have a few limitations. Macromedia Director can augment the toolset of Flash MX 2004, and enable you to take your multimedia projects to a higher plane of interactive experiences.

Caution   As of this writing, Macromedia Director MX could import only Flash 6 or earlier movies (.swf files). If you want to use Flash MX 2004 to create Flash movies for Director movies, make sure you publish Flash 6 movies. Director 7.02 and 8.0 can use Flash 4 or earlier movies, and Director 8.5 can import Flash 5 or earlier movies. You can set the version of the Flash movie in the Version menu of the Publish Settings Flash tab (File ➪ Publish Settings). Check www.macromedia.com/software/director for the latest Flash Asset Xtra updates.

Advantages of Director over Flash

Flash MX 2004 has added many improvements upon its predecessor, Flash MX. With the continuing growth and maturity of the ActionScript language and the support for embedded and real-time streaming video, it may seem that a tool such as Director is no longer necessary. The following reviews some of the current benefits of Director movies and its authoring environment:

✦ **The Xtra architecture:** The functionality of Director can be expanded with the use of Xtras, which are similar to Flash components in the sense that both enable you to expand the capabilities of your movies. However, Xtras are much more integrated with the actual playback engine of Director movies. Many of Director's standard features, such as importing Flash movies (.swf files), are controlled by Xtras. Third-party Xtras can add additional runtime file support to your Director movies (such as MIDI and PDF files) or enable custom data types or server connections to be employed by your Director movies. You can find more information on Xtras at `www.macromedia.com/ software/xtras/director/`.

✦ **A faster playback engine:** The Shockwave Player plug-in and Director projector executable, while only available on Windows and Macintosh platforms, outperform the playback speed of the Flash Player. Director movies usually have faster screen redraws and process data much more quickly than Flash movies in Flash Player 7.

✦ **An extended drawing API:** In Director 8, a new `image` object was introduced to Lingo, the scripting language used within the Director authoring environment. The `image` object enables you to control, at a pixel level, lines and fills on the Director stage. Flash ActionScript also enables you to create artwork with code, but Lingo's implementation of the `image` object enables you to create visual effects not easily achieved (or possible) with ActionScript.

✦ **A built-in 3D engine:** Director 8.5 introduced the ability to use high-impact, textured, 3D graphics and models. Flash movies can not import true 3D models — you can only simulate 3D effects with Flash artwork and animation. Using Lingo, you can manipulate 3D models and apply lighting effects. Check out Flash pioneer Yugo Nakamura's site `www.yugop.com` for an extensive collection of inspiring Shockwave 3D movies.

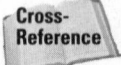

Cross-Reference To learn more about the new drawing features of Flash ActionScript, read the *Flash MX 2004 ActionScript Bible* by Robert Reinhardt and Joey Lott (Wiley, 2004).

Advantages of Flash over Director

Of course, you're reading the *Macromedia Flash MX 2004 Bible* instead of the *Director Bible* — clearly, something's drawn you to Flash MX 2004. Flash is slowly taking on more features that used to be strictly Director's domain. Let's take a quick look at the benefits of Flash MX 2004 development:

✦ **Flash Player penetration:** Simply put, the Flash Player dominates the Web. While the Flash Player is available for several operating systems and mobile devices, Director movies can only be viewed on Windows and Macintosh desktop computers. The Flash Player is also a much smaller download than the Shockwave Player — even with its new video capabilities, Flash Player 7 is still under 1MB! You can develop Flash movies that deliver high-quality content over the Internet to a wide audience.

Note While the ActiveX Control for Flash Player 7 is still under 1MB, the file size for other versions of the plug-in installer is slightly over 1MB.

✦ **Superior drawing and animation tools:** Flash started as a vector-based animation tool. Everyone from traditional animators to interactive designers can easily learn how to use the drawing toolset in Flash MX 2004 to create animated content.

✦ **Leaner file sizes:** While you can create small Director movies (.dcr files) for distribution on the Web, Flash movies by and large tend to be much smaller for equivalent use of graphics and interactive elements. Because most artwork in Flash movies is vector-based, file sizes remain quite small.

Note Just as a SWF file is the document type used by the Flash Player, a DCR file is the file type used by the Shockwave Player. A DIR file, the authoring document for Director movies, is the equivalent of the FLA file for a Flash movie.

✦ **Easier access to new server-side technologies:** When Director MX was introduced, Macromedia discontinued development of the Shockwave Multi-User Server (MUS). In its place, Macromedia has encouraged developers to use Flash Communication Server to provide real-time connectivity between multiple clients on the Internet. Flash Remoting MX was also introduced in 2002 to provide efficient and fast delivery of dynamic data. Both of these server technologies are Flash-based, and while Director supports these technologies, it's often easier to do everything in Flash ActionScript instead of Director Lingo.

✦ **A broad range of support options:** Many Flash developers are surprised at the lack of Director resources on the Web. You won't find equivalents to ultrashock.com, Flash Kit (`http://flashkit.com`), and We're Here (`http://were-here.com`) for Director developers. These sites offer hundreds (if not thousands!) of Flash tutorials and example files. While there is a Director community on the Web, the number of Flash developers sharing information with one another far exceeds the number of Director developers doing so.

Benefits of Flash Assets in Director

Flash MX 2004 has been another monumental leap forward for Flash interactivity, especially for the development of Rich Internet Applications (RIAs). With the ever-growing scope of the ActionScript language and the improved media handling capabilities that Flash movies employ, many of the previous Flash-Director scenarios or workarounds are no longer needed. However, if you're already familiar with Director and Lingo (Director's scripting language), you may find integrating Flash movies into Director projects easier than learning advanced scripting with ActionScript in Flash MX 2004. The following describes some of the benefits of using Flash movies in Director projects:

✦ **Vector control:** Even though Director has vector shape-drawing tools, it doesn't use the same intuitive drawing mechanism that Flash does. Use Flash for any complex vector drawing and animation, and then bring it into your Director project.

✦ **The ability to implement existing projects:** With the ability to use Flash movies in Director, you need not duplicate efforts if material already exists in one format or the other. Therefore, if you've already developed some cool animations in Flash for your company's Web site, you can reuse the same Flash .swf files in your Director projects.

✦ **Similar scripting environments:** Both Flash and Director use a form of dot syntax for their scripting languages. Flash ActionScript resembles JavaScript much more closely than Director Lingo does. Director Lingo uses a different model of command and event control than Flash does. Also, now that ActionScript 2 adheres more closely to ECMA3 and ECMA4 specifications, seasoned programmers who use other languages can more easily develop Flash movies in Flash MX 2004, publish a Flash movie, and import it into a Director movie.

Flash and Director both have means to communicate with each other. Data can be sent from Flash to Director, or Director to Flash, via Lingo. Just as Flash Movie Clips can be self-contained interactive modules within one overall Flash movie (.swf file), Flash movies can be elements of a much larger and media-rich Director movie. To get you started with Director-Flash interactivity, the next section shows you how to send events from Flash movies to Director movies.

The following sections are intended for readers who already know the basics of Director movie production. If you need more information on the Director authoring environment, refer to the *Director 8 Bible*. You can also find more advanced Flash-Director integration coverage in the *Flash MX 2004 ActionScript Bible*.

Creating Director-Specific Actions in Flash

You can use Flash movies (.swf files) in any number of ways with Director. If you just want to use a Flash animation for graphic content within a Director presentation, you can simply use the same Flash movie (.swf file) you generated for the Web. Use the Flash Asset Xtra import box (see the more in-depth discussion later in this section) to set the parameters of playback without needing any Lingo. However, if you want Flash actions in frames or on buttons to do something in your Director movies, then you need to know how to get Lingo's attention. The drawback to this type of "dual" interactivity is that you need to plan ahead with both your Flash and Director movies. As with any project, you should outline a storyboard before embarking on a task such as this.

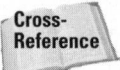

Use a project planner such as Microsoft Visio to plan an interactive project. By creating interactive hierarchies and flowcharts (for example, determining which scenes will link to other scenes), you can manage projects with greater ease. The importance of interactive project planning is discussed in Chapter 3, "Planning Flash Projects."

You can use three methods within a Flash movie to communicate with Director Lingo, all involving the getURL() action. You can assign any of these methods the same way you would with any other Flash interactivity — attach these actions to buttons, frames, or ActionScript conditions.

The standard getURL command

On a Flash button or frame, open the Actions panel and assign a getURL() action. This is the preferred method of sending information to Director movies because you can deal with the result of the action in Director — you do not need to specify what Director does with the string from the Flash movie. In the getURL() action, create a string to be passed to an event handler in Lingo. In Figure 38-1, a getURL() action is assigned to a frame in Flash. The string ProjectOne is entered as the parameter of the action. This string, in turn, is received by Lingo.

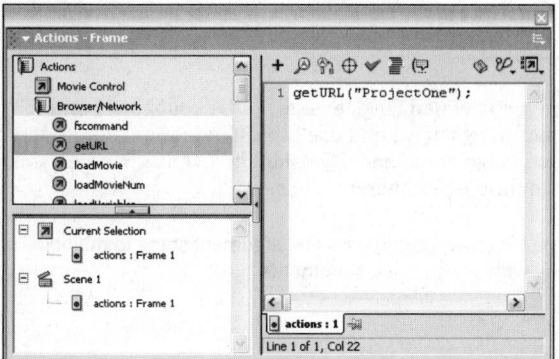

Figure 38-1: You can enter any word or series of characters (that is, a string) as the parameter of the getURL() action. This string is then passed to Lingo.

In Director, you need to attach a behavior script to the Flash sprite so that the getURL() action and string can be received by Lingo. We discuss the actual implementation of this example later in this chapter in the "Controlling Flash Movies in Director" section. In Figure 38-1, the string ProjectOne was assigned to getURL(). In Director, you could tell Lingo to go to the frame marker called ProjectOne:

```
on getURL me, FlashString
   go to frame FlashString
end
```

When the Flash sprite plays in Director and the getURL() action is executed, the ProjectOne value of getURL() is passed as the FlashString argument of the Lingo event handler, on getURL. Lingo directs the playback of the Director movie to the frame marker ProjectOne.

The event: command

You can also specify an event: handler as the parameter of the getURL() action. This method is useful if you would like to describe an event that is repeatedly used in Flash, but needs customized settings with each use. For example, if you want to add a mouse click to go to a different Director frame depending on which button was clicked, you could use the following string in the getURL() action:

```
event: FClick 'ProjectOne'
```

In Director, you then write a behavior that would receive the FClick event:

```
on FClick me FlashString
   go to frame FlashString
end
```

How is this different from the last example? If you want to have several events in one script that perform different Lingo commands, you need to label each one with a separate event, such as:

```
on FClickButton01 me FlashString
   go to frame FlashString
end
```

```
on FClickButton02 me FlashString
  quit
end
```

In the preceding example, there are two defined Flash events, FClickButton01 and FClickButton02, which do different things. If we had used the standard getURL() action, we could only pass the string to one Lingo command. By using the event: handler, you can create one handler that processes multiple parameter values.

Tip   With a bit more programming in Lingo, you could pass one argument string to multiple Lingo commands by testing the string with if...else statements.

The lingo: command

The last getURL() method of sending events to Lingo is the most direct method of communicating with Director movies. In the URL field, a lingo: handler is used to specify a Lingo statement. This is the most inflexible method of sending events to Director—insofar as you cannot do anything in Director to modify or direct the event. For example, if you add the following code to a Button instance in Flash:

```
on (release){
    getURL("lingo: quit");
}
```

the Director movie quits (or the Director projector closes) when that button is clicked.

With lingo: statements in getURL() actions, you do not need to specify any further Lingo in the Director movie, unless you are setting the value of a prescripted variable or executing an event described in the Director movie script.

Controlling Flash Movies in Director

You can import and use Flash movies (.swf files) in Director just as you would any other cast member. Director controls Flash movies with the Flash Asset Xtra. This section shows you how to import Flash movies and use them in the Director Score window. You should already be familiar with the Director authoring environment and basic behavior use.

The Flash Asset Xtra: Importing Flash movies

Since Director 6.5, the Flash Asset Xtra has enabled Flash movies to play within Director movies. Again, make sure you have Director MX in order to use Flash 6 movies. If you have Director 8.5 or 8.0, you'll need to export your Flash 5 or 4 movies, respectively, from Flash MX 2004.

Note   As mentioned earlier in this chapter, you can not currently use Flash 7 movies in Director MX. You must publish your Flash documents as Flash 6 or earlier movies for use in Director. By the time this book is published, it's highly likely that a new Flash Asset Xtra will be available for Flash 7 movies.

On the CD-ROM This file was published to be compatible with Flash Player 5 and higher. For this section, we use the `makers_rotate.swf` file, which is located in the `ch38` folder on the CD-ROM.

To import a Flash movie (.swf file), perform the following steps:

1. Start a new Director movie (.dir file) or open an existing movie.

2. Use the File ➪ Import command (Ctrl+R or ⌘+R) to select a Flash movie (.swf file). Double-click the filename in the upper portion of the Import dialog box (see Figure 38-2), or select the filename and choose Add. You can select several files of different types and import them all at once. When you are done adding files, click Import to bring the Flash movie(s) into the internal cast.

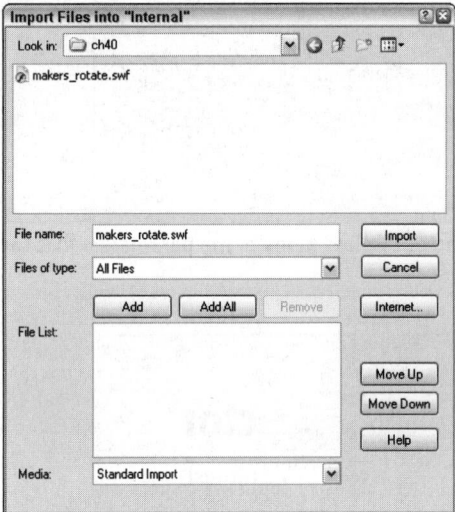

Figure 38-2: You can import several files at once with the Import command. (The Windows version is shown here.)

3. Open the Cast window (Ctrl+3 or ⌘ +3). Select the Flash movie that was imported, and open the Property inspector (Window ➪ Property Inspector). An overview of the Flash cast member properties are displayed (see Figure 38-3). If you click the Options button in the inspector, you can access all of the Flash movie properties in the Flash Asset Properties dialog box (see Figure 38-4). The top section of the dialog box is used to link to external or remote Flash movies (see the following tip and the sidebar "Using Lingo to Preload Flash Movies"), whereas the lower section sets the playback attributes:

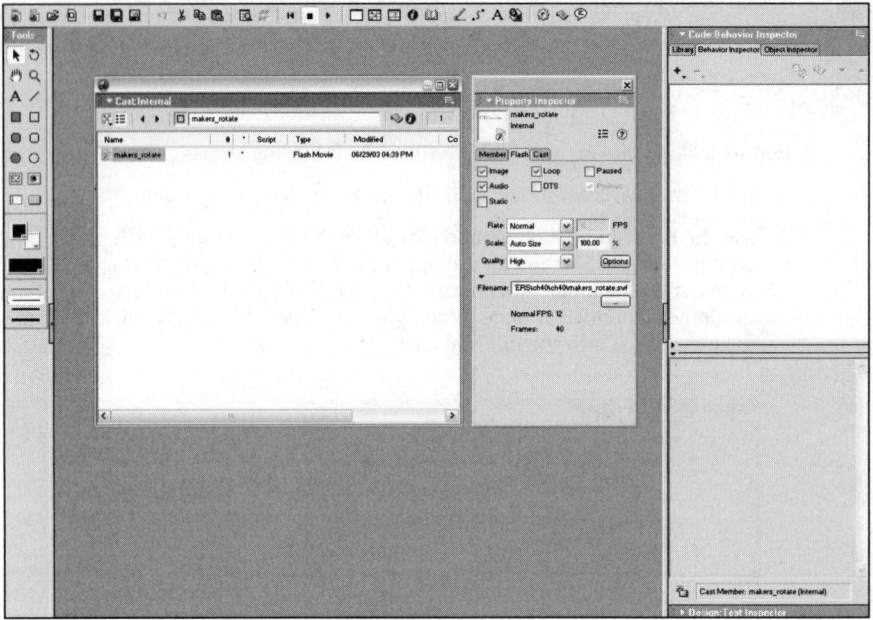

Figure 38-3: The Property inspector displays many of the parameters that can be set for cast members.

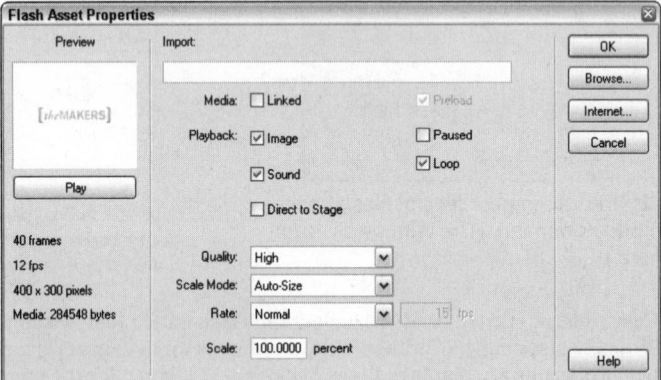

Figure 38-4: The Flash Asset Properties dialog box enables you to specify how the Flash movie functions in the Director movie.

• **Media:** This setting has two options, Linked and Preload. If you don't want to store a Flash movie within the Director movie, check Link and specify the path to the Flash movie. Unless you want to link to a Flash movie on the Internet, you should store the Flash movie in the Director movie—Flash movies are usually very small due to their vector structure. If Link is checked, then you can also enable Preload. Preloading will force Director to load (or download) the entire .swf file before it starts playing the Flash movie. Otherwise, Director starts playing the Flash movie as soon as it starts to stream the Flash cast member. See the sidebar "Using Lingo to Preload Flash Movies" for more information on linked Internet files.

* **Playback:** This setting has five options that control how Director displays the Flash movie:

The Image option, checked by default, determines whether Director shows the graphic content of a Flash movie.

The Sound option determines whether Director plays the audio content of a Flash movie.

The Direct to Stage option tells Director to give priority to the Flash movie sprite over all other sprites currently on the stage. Although this option may enable Flash movies to play back more smoothly, Director ignores any ink effects applied to the sprite (see the "Flash movies as sprites" subsection for more information on ink effects), and the Flash movie always displays on top of other sprites.

The Paused option is akin to adding a `stop()` Flash action to the first frame of the Flash movie — you can force Director to display the movie in a paused state.

The Loop option enables continuous playback of the Flash movie. If this option is checked, the Flash movie repeats as soon as it reaches the last frame unless the last frame has a `stop()` Flash action. It continues to repeat while the Flash sprite is present in the Director Score, or until it is paused by a Lingo command.

* **Quality:** This setting has a drop-down menu with the some of the same Quality settings found in the Flash environment's Publish Settings. By default, this setting is High. For more information on the Quality property of a Flash movie, see Chapter 21, "Publishing Flash Movies."

* **Scale Mode:** By default, this setting uses Auto-Size, which enables Director to automatically resize the Flash movie's width and height according to the sprite's bounding box on the Director stage. This means that, if you resize the sprite, the Flash movie should fit the size of the sprite box. Auto-Size automatically sets the Scale setting to 100 percent. Conversely, No Scale keeps the Flash movie at the size specified by the Scale setting (covered in a moment) and any subsequent resizing of the sprite bounding box may crop the Flash movie. The remaining options, Show All, No Border, and Exact Fit operate the same as the Publish Settings options in Flash MX 2004 (see Chapter 21, "Publishing Flash Movies").

* **Rate:** Perhaps one of the most powerful settings in the Flash Asset Properties dialog box, Rate controls how fast or slowly the Flash movie plays in a Director Score — irrespective of the Tempo setting used in the Score. The Flash Asset Properties' Rate setting has two options: a drop-down menu and an fps text field. If Normal or Lock-Step is selected, then the fps text field is disabled. Normal plays the Flash movie at its native frame rate, as set in the Flash application via the Modify ⇨ Document dialog box.

Lock-Step plays one Flash movie frame for every Director frame that its sprite occupies (for example, if the Flash movie occupies four frames of the Director score, then only the first four frames of the animation plays back in Director).

Therefore, Lock-Step inherits the frame rate of the Director movie as established in the Tempo setting in the Score.

Fixed Rate enables you to specify a new frame rate for the Flash movie, independent of the original frame rate specified in Flash (via Modify ➪ Document) or the Director Tempo setting in the Score.

Caution   If your Director movie uses a frame rate (or tempo) slower than the Flash movie, you will not be able to force the Flash movie to refresh its display faster (that is, use a faster frame rate) unless the Director to Stage option is enabled for the Flash sprite.

- **Scale:** This setting works hand-in-hand with the Scale Mode setting. If anything other than Auto-Size is selected in Scale Mode, you can specify the percentage of the original Flash movie used for the Flash sprite. If 50 percent is used for the Scale of a 550 x 400 Flash movie and Exact Fit is chosen in Scale Mode, the movie displays at 225 x 200 in the original placed Flash sprite on the Stage. If you resize the sprite box, it continues to maintain a 50 percent portion of the sprite box area.

Tip   You can also use the Insert ➪ Media Element ➪ Flash Movie command to import Flash movies via the Flash Asset Properties dialog box. Simply click the Browse button and select a Flash movie (.swf file). Both the File ➪ Import and Flash Asset Property dialog boxes enable you to enter Internet URLs for the filename path.

4. After specifying the settings you wish to use for your Flash movie, you can then place the Flash cast member as a sprite on to the Director Stage. Open the Score window (Window ➪ Score) and drag the `makers_rotate` cast member from the Cast window to frame 1 of sprite channel number 1 in the Score window. Your Flash sprite will automatically occupy 28 frames in this channel.

5. Save your Director movie as `makers_rotate.dir`. You'll come back to this movie later in the chapter.

On the CD-ROM   You can find the `makers_rotate_starter.dir` file in the `ch38` folder of the book's CD-ROM.

Using Lingo to Preload Flash Movies

As with other Director cast members, you can control how a Flash movie cast member is loaded into a Shockwave movie or standalone Director projector. While you author a Director movie with a Flash movie cast member, it's useful to have a linked .swf file included in the internal cast. However, when you launch a Shockwave movie on the Web, you may want to make changes to the .swf file only and leave the Director .dcr file unchanged. Moreover, the path of a locally linked file is different from a file linked remotely over the Internet. This problem is easy to fix with a little Director Lingo.

For any Director movie that uses .swf files that you intend to update on a regular basis, you should dynamically set the filename property of the Flash cast member with Lingo. The following steps show you how to detect where the Director movie is being played (for example, from a standalone projector or from the Shockwave Player), and how to change the source of a linked Flash cast member.

1. Create or add the following Lingo to the movie script for your Director movie (note that the ↺ indicates a continuation of the same line of code):

```
on prepareMovie
    global URLRootPath
    global shockPlayer
    if (the runMode contains "Projector") OR (the ↺
    runMode contains "Author") then
        shockPlayer = false
    else
        shockPlayer = true
        URLRootPath = "http://www.theMakers.com/swf/"
    end if
end prepareMovie

on initLoad me
    global URLRootPath
    global myNetID
    global flashPath
    flashPath = URLRootPath & "sliders.swf"
    set myNetID = preloadNetThing(flashPath)
end initLoad
```

For the variable `URLRootPath`, change the value of the path to your Flash files on your Web server. Don't forget the ending forward slash character, as a filename is appended to this path in the `initLoad` handler. In the `initLoad` handler, change the `flashPath` variable to specify the filename of the Flash movie (.swf file) that you want to load into the Director movie.

2. In the Director Score window, reserve a section of ten frames at the very beginning of the Score. Create a frame marker named `initPreload` on frame 1, and on frame 5, create a marker named `loadLoop`. Also, make sure that you have a marker on the frame where your Director movie's first interactivity takes place (for example, wherever the movie starts beyond these first ten frames for the preload sequence). In this example, we use the name `intro`.

3. On frame 1, add the following frame script:

```
on enterFrame
    global shockPlayer
    if shockPlayer = true then
        initLoad
    else
        go to "intro"
    end if
end
```

Continued

Continued

Here, we check whether the `prepareMovie` handler returned a `true` or `false` value for the `shockPlayer` variable. If the movie is being played in a Web browser, then `shockPlayer` will equal `true`. If that's the case, then execute the `initLoad` handler (in the movie script). Incidentally, handlers in Lingo work much like functions in ActionScript and JavaScript.

If the movie is being played in the authoring environment or a projector, then `shockPlayer` will equal `false`. Therefore, the `else` condition will execute, moving the Director playhead to the `intro` marker.

4. On frame 10, add the following frame script:

```
on exitFrame
    global myNetID, flashPath
    if netDone(myNetID) = true then
        member("sliders").fileName = flashPath
        go to "intro"
    else
        go to "loadLoop"
    end if
end
```

Here, we check whether the `preloadNetThing` command that was executed in the `initLoad` handler has finished loading the Flash movie (.swf file). If it has, then the path of the linked (or stored) cast member sliders is changed to the Internet path described in `flashPath`. Then, the Director playhead moves to the `intro` frame marker to start the movie. If the Flash movie file isn't finished loading, then the Director playhead moves back to the `loadLoop` frame marker. The playhead will continue looping the frames between `loadLoop` and frame 10 until the Flash movie loads.

You will want to change the name of the cast member sliders to the name of the Flash movie cast number that was used in your Director movie.

These are the basic steps to preloading and changing the source file for Flash cast members. We didn't include error handling in the frame 10 script. As you may well know, Web servers can crash, Internet connections may falter, or a file may have been deleted or moved to another location. Refer to the Lingo Dictionary included with Director MX to see the various `netDone` and `netError` return values.

Using Director's Property inspector

Director 8 introduced a new look and feel to the authoring environment. In addition to a resizable Stage window, you can change the Cast window to view by list or thumbnail, and you can quickly modify sprite, cast member, and movie attributes (among others) with the Property inspector.

The Property inspector (shown earlier in Figure 38-3) enables you to quickly change most of the Flash Asset properties for any Flash cast member. You can click the Options button on the Property inspector to access the traditional Flash Asset Properties dialog box, which enables you to change Import (the path to remotely or locally linked Flash movies) and Media (Linked and Preload) properties. You cannot preview Flash movies in the Property inspector.

Tip You may have noticed that the Flash Asset Properties dialog box takes a few seconds to load, as it requires the entire Flash Asset Options Xtra to load into memory. Why? In order to use the Play button in the Flash Asset Properties dialog box, the Flash Player contained within the Flash Asset Options Xtra must be loaded. Because the Property inspector doesn't include a preview/play option, you can change Flash movie settings much more quickly in the inspector.

Flash movies as sprites

In Director, any item that is used in a movie becomes part of a cast, and is referred to as a *cast member*. When a cast member is placed on the stage, it becomes a sprite. A sprite is an instance of the cast member used in the Score. The relationship between a Flash symbol and a symbol instance is similar to the relationship between a Director cast member and its sprite(s).

To place a Flash cast member on the Director stage, simply click and drag its cast member icon (or thumbnail) from the Internal Cast window to the stage or the score. If you drag a cast member to the stage, it automatically becomes a sprite on the first sprite channel (see Figure 38-5). If you drag a sprite to the score, it is automatically centered on the stage.

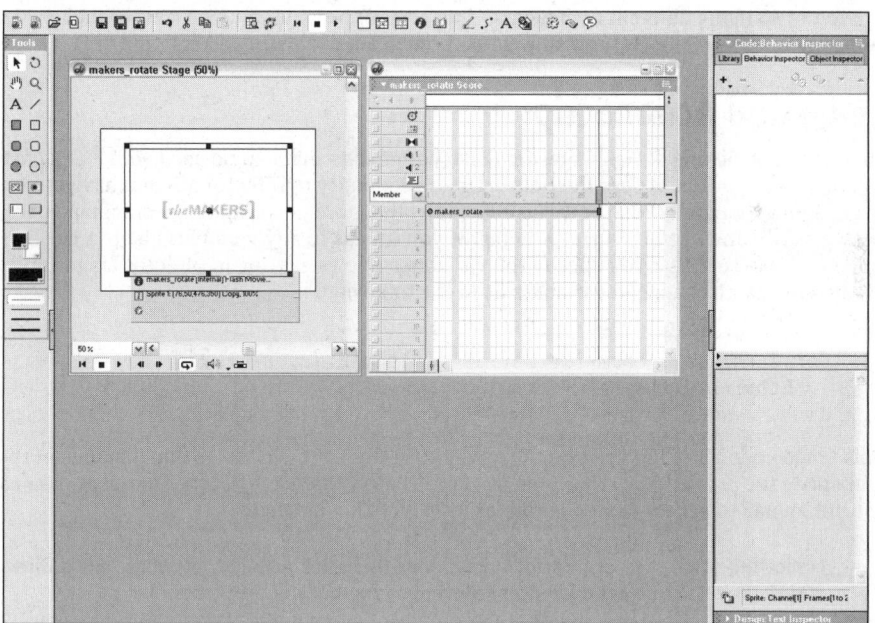

Figure 38-5: A Flash sprite on Director's stage (on the left), and a Flash sprite in Director's Score window (on the right)

Although Flash sprites perform almost the same as other Director sprites, you should be aware of certain sprite properties before proceeding with Lingo behaviors and Flash sprites.

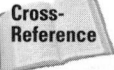

Cross-Reference For more information on basic animation features of Director, consult the *Macromedia Using Director MX Shockwave Studio* manual that comes with the Director software.

✦ **Sprite duration:** The duration of a sprite appears in the score. By default, the duration of every sprite that is dragged to the score or stage is 28 frames. As with digital video and sound sprites, Flash sprites play only as long as their frame duration enables them. For example, if a Flash movie that is 30 Flash frames long (and has a Lock-Step rate) is inserted as a 15-frame Flash sprite in Director, Director shows only the first half of the Flash movie.

✦ **Sprite inks:** Inks are akin to the color/alpha effects you can apply to Flash instances. In Director, the ink setting controls how the background area of a sprite appears. Of all the inks available to sprites, only Copy, Transparent, and Background Transparent have any noticeable effect on Flash sprites. Copy makes the Flash movie background opaque, in the same color that you specified in the Flash authoring environment. Transparent and Background Transparent hide the background of a Flash movie, so that the Director movie background (and other Director sprites) shows through.

Controlling Flash Movies with Lingo

Not only can you send events from Flash movies to Director movies, but you can also control Flash movies from Director with Lingo. More than 80 Lingo commands exist that are specific for Flash movie assets in a Director movie. Unfortunately, it is beyond the scope of this book to explore so many different commands. This section provides an overview of the new Lingo commands for Flash movie, and shows you how to alter the size and rotation of Flash sprites.

Lingo and ActionScript

For a complete listing of Flash-specific Lingo commands that can be used with Flash cast members and sprites, access the Help ➪ Lingo Dictionary in Director MX and navigate to Using Lingo ➪ Lingo by Feature ➪ Flash. Some of the more powerful Lingo commands are `getVariable` and `setVariable`, which give you access to any variables inside a Flash 4, 5 or 6 movie. Make sure that you specify the variable name as a string in Director Lingo (unless it's also the name of a Lingo variable), as in the following:

```
on beginSprite me
   sprite(me.spriteNum).setVariable("init_mc.currentURL", ⤶
     "http://www.theMakers.com")
end
```

This Lingo code gives the variable `currentURL` in the `init_mc` Movie Clip instance of the current sprite (`me.spriteNum`) the value of `http://www.theMakers.com`. Therefore, you can use dot syntax to access nested variables in Movie Clip instances.

Note   Notice the similarities of Director's dot syntax to Flash's ActionScript syntax. Both Director and Flash can use object references followed by methods or properties.

New Feature   With Director MX Lingo, you can use Dots notation to specify target paths. In previous versions of Director, you needed to use the older Slashes notation to access Flash Movie Clip paths.

Similarly, the `getFlashProperty` and `setFlashProperty` Lingo commands can access Movie Clip or Main Timeline properties:

```
on enterFrame me
  global dog_ScaleX
  dog_ScaleX = sprite(me.spriteNum).getFlashProperty("_root.dog_mc", ⏎
    #scaleX)
end
```

This Lingo code retrieves the current X scale of the _root.dog_mc Movie Clip instance and makes it the value of a global Director variable named dog_ScaleX. As you'll see next, though, you can harness the power of ActionScript features more directly with Director MX Lingo.

> **Note** In Director 8.5, Macromedia expanded the Lingo hitTest method (which can be used to detect whether an arbitrary point in the Flash movie is the transparent background area, a normal "fill" area, or a Flash button) to include an #editText return value to detect Flash 4, 5, or 6 editable text fields. The Lingo hitTest method works much like the hitTest() ActionScript method. For more information on Director's hitTest method, refer to the Help ⇨ Lingo Dictionary. Refer to Chapter 27, "Interacting with Movie Clips," for more information on Flash's hitTest() method.

With Director MX Lingo, you can now tap the methods, functions, and properties of native objects within the Flash sprite directly, without using older Lingo expressions. Using a new parameter with the Lingo getVariable method of Flash sprites, you can return a reference to any object within the Flash sprite, from Movie Clips to basic data objects constructed from classes such as Array, Object, and Date (just to name a few). In the following example, Lingo targets a Flash Movie Clip instance named anim_mc and tells it to play:

```
on mouseUp me
  global flashMC
  flashMC = sprite(me.spriteNum).getVariable("anim_mc", false)
  flashMC.play()
end
```

With this new syntax, you can access any of the methods and properties of MovieClip objects directly, without using a setVariable or tellTarget reference in Lingo — as you would have needed to do in Director 8.5 or earlier. The false parameter in the getVariable method tells Lingo to return a reference to the object, not the object's actual value.

More importantly, you can even construct and manipulate new ActionScript-based objects in Lingo, and pass them back to a Flash sprite. In the following example, a Lingo reference is made to the Main Timeline (_level0) of the Flash sprite, and a new instance of the Object class is created and named tempObj, using the newObject Lingo method. Properties of this object are created and set with new values. Then, the object is passed to a function named initMe() on the Main Timeline of the Flash sprite.

```
on mouseUp me
  flashRoot = sprite(me.spriteNum).getVariable("_level0", false)
  tempObj = sprite(me.spriteNum).newObject("Object")
  tempObj.name = "Roger"
  tempObj.age = 27
  tempObj.hair = "brown"
  flashRoot.initMe(tempObj)
end
```

> **Note** You can specify one of several class names as the parameter of the newObject Lingo method.

Changing the rotation of Flash sprites

As mentioned earlier in this chapter, you can control the properties of a Flash sprite with Lingo, giving you complete control of the entire Flash movie. With the `makers_rotate.swf` example used earlier, we can rotate the Flash movie in Director. For this exercise, you won't access any objects that exist within the Flash sprite. You'll simply control the entire sprite within the Director movie.

1. Open the same Director movie you created earlier in this chapter, `makers_rotate.dir`. Double-click frame 1 in the Behavior channel of the Score window. In the Script window, add the following code:

```
on exitFrame me
    go the frame
end
```

This Lingo code tells the Director movie to loop on frame 1. After you have entered this code, close the Script window.

2. Select the Flash sprite on the stage. Right-click (or Control-click on the Mac) the sprite, and choose Script. In the Script window, remove the `on mouseUp` code, and add the following code to the Flash sprite:

```
on mouseEnter me
    repeat while sprite(me.spriteNum).rotation < 720
        sprite(me.spriteNum).rotation = ⤶
            sprite(me.spriteNum).rotation + 10
        updateStage
    end repeat
end

on mouseLeave me
    sprite(me.spriteNum).rotation = 0
end
```

This script tells the Flash sprite to rotate a full 720 degrees — two revolutions — when the mouse enters the Flash sprite. Here, the `rotation` property is manipulated. Notice that when the mouse leaves the sprite, the rotation is reset to 0.

Note You may be surprised by the smoothness of the rotation animation. Director's playback engine is still far superior to that of the Flash Player, especially with intensive graphics and high frame rates.

3. To view the current Flash sprite properties in Director's Message window, you can add the following lines of code to the sprite's script:

```
on mouseUp me
    sprite(me.spriteNum).showProps()
end
```

When the Flash sprite is clicked, the `showProps` command displays the current properties of the Flash sprite and cast member (see Figure 38-6).

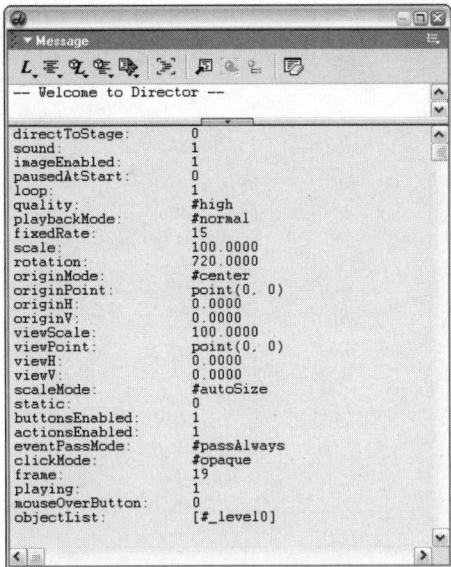

Figure 38-6: Director's Message window, displaying the current Flash sprite properties

4. Save your Director movie.

On the CD-ROM

Open the `makers_rotate.dir` file in the `ch38` folder of this book's CD-ROM to see the completed movie.

Summary

✦ Macromedia Director has traditionally been used for more advanced multimedia projects for CD-ROMs, DVD-ROMS, and presentations that don't require network connections.

✦ Director MX can integrate most multimedia file formats and play them within a Shockwave movie over the Web.

✦ Carefully weigh the goals of a multimedia project to determine which technology (or combination of technologies) will most effectively fulfill the requirements. While Flash MX 2004 can create rich media presentations, you may need the extended functionality of Director for more advanced projects.

✦ Flash and Director movies can communicate with one another via Lingo (Director's scripting language) or ActionScript (Flash's scripting language). You can control Flash movie playback from Director movies, or send commands from Flash movies to control the interactivity of a Director movie.

✦ ✦ ✦

Appendixes

◆ ◆ ◆ ◆

In This Part

Appendix A
Keyboard Shortcuts

Appendix B
Digital Audio Basics

Appendix C
Digital Video Basics

Appendix D
Using the CD-ROM

Appendix E
Guest Experts
Information

◆ ◆ ◆ ◆

Keyboard Shortcuts

It is surprising how long some developers will go before learning shortcut keys, but after you begin to make them a part of your workflow, you will realize how much time you can save. Not only will your Flash production be more efficient, but you may just save yourself the pain of *carpal tunnel syndrome* — a chronic condition that can result from overusing your "mouse arm."

In order to make Flash shortcut keys more consistent with other Macromedia programs and to fix some conflicts that were caused by Flash MX keyboard shortcuts, there have been some shortcut changes in Flash MX 2004. Tables A-1 through A-5 are intended to serve as a quick reference for the shortcut keys used for common tasks.

There are many other shortcut key combos, and you always have the option of adding or modifying these shortcuts to suit your own workflow. To review or change existing keyboard shortcuts, select File ⇨ Keyboard Shortcuts (Windows) or Flash ⇨ Keyboard Shortcuts (Mac).

Table A-1: Tool Shortcut Keys

Tool	Shortcut	Tool	Shortcut
Selection tool	V	Subselection tool	A
Line tool	N	Lasso tool	L
Pen tool	P	Text tool	T
Oval tool	O	Rectangle tool	R
Pencil tool	Y	Brush tool	B
Free Transform tool	Q	Fill Transform tool	F
Ink Bottle tool	S	Paint Bucket tool	K
Eyedropper tool	I	Eraser tool	E
Hand tool	H (Spacebar)	Zoom tool (magnifier)	Z (M)

Table A-2: View Shortcut Keys

Menu Item	Windows Shortcut	Macintosh Shortcut
100 percent View scale	Ctrl+1	⌘+1
Show Frame	Ctrl+2	⌘+2
Show All	Ctrl+3	⌘+3
Zoom In	Ctrl+= (equal)	⌘+= (equal)
Zoom Out	Ctrl+- (minus)	⌘+- (minus)
Hide Edges (Mesh)	Ctrl+Shift+E	⌘+Shift+E
Grid (Show/Hide)	Ctrl+' (apostrophe)	⌘+' (apostrophe)
Guides (Show/Hide)	Ctrl+; (semicolon)	⌘+; (semicolon)
Rulers (Show/Hide)	Ctrl+Shift+Alt+R	⌘+Shift+Option+R
Outlines	Ctrl+Shift+Alt+O	⌘+Shift+Option+O
Work Area (On/Off)	Ctrl+Shift+W	⌘+Shift+W

Table A-3: Panel & Window Shortcut Keys

Menu Item	Windows Shortcut	Macintosh Shortcut
Actions panel	F9	F9
Accessibility panel	Alt+F2	Option+F2
Align panel	Ctrl+K	⌘+K
Color Mixer panel	Shift+F9	Shift+F9
Color Swatches panel	Ctrl+F9	⌘+F9
Components panel	Ctrl+F7	⌘+F7
Component inspector	Alt+F7	Option+F7
Debugger window	Shift+F4	Shift+F4
Document properties	Ctrl+J	⌘+J
Find & Replace	Ctrl+F	⌘+F
Help panel	F1	F1
Hide/Show (all) panels	F4	F4
History panel	Ctrl+F10	⌘+F10
Info panel	Ctrl+Alt+I	⌘+Option+I
Library panel	F11 (or Ctrl+L)	F11 (or ⌘+L)

Menu Item	Windows Shortcut	Macintosh Shortcut
Movie Explorer panel	Alt+F3	Option+F3
New Document window	Ctrl+N	⌘+N
New Flash document	Ctrl+Alt+N	⌘+Option+N
Output window	F2	F2
Preferences	Ctrl+U	⌘+U
Preview in browser	F12	F12
Project panel (Pro only)	Shift+F8	Shift+F8
Property inspector	Ctrl+F3	⌘+F3
Publish Flash Movie	Shift+F12	Shift+F12
Publish Settings	Ctrl+Shift+F12	Shift+Option+F12
Scene panel	Shift+F2	Shift+F2
Strings panel	Ctrl+F11	⌘+F11
Test Movie	Ctrl+Enter	⌘+Return
Timeline window	Ctrl+Alt+T	⌘+Option+T
Tools panel	Ctrl+F2	⌘+F2
Transform panel	Ctrl+T	⌘+T

Table A-4: Edit & Modify Shortcut Keys

Menu Item	Windows Shortcut	Macintosh Shortcut
Break Apart	Ctrl+B	⌘+B
Copy	Ctrl+C	⌘+C
Copy Frames	Ctrl+Alt+C	⌘+Option+C
Cut	Ctrl+X	⌘+X
Cut Frames	Ctrl+Alt+X	⌘+Option+X
Clear Frames	Alt+Enter	Option+Delete
Distribute to Layers	Ctrl+Shift+D	⌘+Shift+D
Duplicate	Ctrl+D	⌘+D
Edit Symbols (in Edit mode)	Ctrl+E	⌘+E
Group	Ctrl+G	⌘+G
Ungroup	Ctrl+Shift+G	⌘+Shift+G

Continued

Table A-4 *(continued)*

Menu Item	Windows Shortcut	Macintosh Shortcut
Import to Stage	Ctrl+R	⌘+R
Open	Ctrl+O	⌘+O
Optimize (shape)	Ctrl+Shift+Alt+C	⌘+Shift+Option+C
Paste in Center	Ctrl+V	⌘+V
Paste Frames	Ctrl+Alt+V	⌘+Option+V
Paste in Place	Ctrl+Shift+V	⌘+Shift+V
Save	Ctrl+S	⌘+S
Save As	Ctrl+Shift+S	⌘+Shift+S
Select All	Ctrl+A	⌘+A
Deselect All	Ctrl+Shift+A	⌘+Shift+A
Insert Frame	F5	F5
Remove Frame	Shift+F5	Shift+F5
Convert to Keyframe	F6	F6
Clear Keyframe	Shift+F6	Shift+F6
Convert to Blank Keyframe	Shift+F7	Shift+F7
Convert to Symbol	F8	F8
Create New Symbol	Ctrl+F8	⌘+F8
Remove Transform	Ctrl+Shift+Z	⌘+Shift+Z
Undo	Ctrl+Z	⌘+Z
Redo	Ctrl+Y	⌘+Y

Table A-5: Align & Arrange Shortcut Keys

Menu Item	Windows Shortcut	Macintosh Shortcut
Rotate 90 degrees CW	Ctrl+9	⌘+9
Rotate 90 degrees CCW	Ctrl+7	⌘+7
Align Left	Ctrl+Alt+1	⌘+Option+1
Align Center Vertical	Ctrl+Alt+2	⌘+Option+2
Align Right	Ctrl+Alt+3	⌘+Option+3
Align Top	Ctrl+Alt+4	⌘+Option+4
Align Center Horizontal	Ctrl+Alt+5	⌘+Option+5
Align Bottom	Ctrl+Alt+6	⌘+Option+6
Align Distribute Widths	Ctrl+Alt+7	⌘+Option+7
Align Make Same Width	Ctrl+Shift+Alt+7	⌘+Shift+Option+7
Align to Stage	Ctrl+Alt+8	⌘+Option+8
Align Distribute Heights	Ctrl+Alt+9	⌘+Option+9
Align Make Same Height	Ctrl+Shift+Alt+9	⌘+Shift+Option+9
Send to Back	Shift+Alt+↓	Shift+Option+↓
Bring to Front	Shift+Alt+↑	Shift+Option+↑
Send Backward	Ctrl+↓	⌘+↓
Bring Forward	Ctrl+↑	⌘+↑

✦   ✦   ✦

Digital Audio Basics

If you plan carefully and pay attention to technical detail, sound can add dimension to your Flash projects. That's because sound introduces another mode of sensory perception. Coordinated with visual form and motion, sound deepens the impact and can even enhance the ease of use of your Flash creation.

Cross-Reference For detailed information on adding sound to your Flash productions, refer to Chapter 15, "Adding Sound." Chapter 15 fully explains how to work with imported sound in Flash MX 2004, covering topics from codecs and compression to syncing to behaviors.

Understanding the Basics of Sampling and Quality

Before you begin integrating sound with your Flash project, it's important to understand the basics of digital audio. To help you with this, this appendix is dedicated to sampling, bit resolution, and file size.

What is sound?

Sound, or hearing, is one of our five senses; it's the sense that's produced when vibrations in the air strike the aural receptors located within your ears. When you hear a sound, the volume of the sound is determined by the intensity of the vibrations, or sound waves.

The *pitch* that you hear — meaning how high (treble) or low (bass) — is determined by the frequency of those vibrations (waves). The frequency of sound is measured in hertz (abbreviated as Hz). Theoretically, most humans have the ability to hear frequencies that range from 20 to 20,000 Hz. The frequency of the sound is a measure of the range of the sound — from the highest high to the lowest low. It's important to note here that, when starting to work with sound, the most common error is confusing the frequency of the sound with the recording sample.

What affects the quality and size of sound files?

When you add sound to a Flash movie, a number of factors affect the final quality of the sound and the size of the sound file. The quality of the sound is important because it determines the aesthetic experience of the sound. The file size is important because it determines how quickly (or slowly) the sound arrives at the end user's computer. The primary factors that determine the quality and size of a sound file are sample rate and bit resolution.

Sample rate

The sample rate, measured in hertz (Hz), describes the number of times an audio signal is sampled when it is recorded digitally. In the late 1940s, Harry Nyquist and Claude Shannon developed a theorem, which said that, for optimal sound quality, a sampling rate must be twice the value of the highest frequency of a signal. Thus, the higher the sample rate, the better the audio range. Generally, higher sample rates result in a richer, more complete sound. According to Nyquist and Shannon, in order for the audible range of 20 to 20,000 Hz to be sampled correctly, the audio source needs to be sampled at a frequency no lower than 40,000 Hz, or 40 kHz. This explains why CD audio, which closely resembles the source sound, is sampled at 44.1 kHz.

Note   A sound *sample* refers to one "analysis" of a recorded sound, whereas a sound *file* refers to the entire collection of samples recorded, which compose a digital recording.

The less a sound is sampled, the further the recording will deviate from the original sound. However, this tendency toward loss of the original quality of the sound yields one advantage: When the sample rate of a sound file is decreased, the file size drops proportionately. For example, a 300 KB, 44.1 kHz sound file would be 150 KB when saved as a 22.05 kHz file. See Table B-1 for more details on how sample rate affects quality.

Table B-1: Audio Sample Rates and Quality

Sample Rate	Quality Level	Possible Uses
48 kHz	Studio quality	Sound or music recorded to digital medium such as miniDV, DAT, DVCam, and so on
44.1 kHz	CD quality	High-fidelity sound and music
32 kHz	Near-CD quality	Professional/consumer digital camcorders
22.050 kHz	FM radio quality	Short, high-quality music clips
11.025 kHz	Acceptable for music	Longer music clips; high-quality voice; sound effects
5 kHz	Acceptable for speech	"Flat" speech; simple button sounds

Because the native playback rate of most common audio cards is 44.1 kHz, sound that is destined for playback on any computer should be a multiple of 44.1. Thus, we recommend sample rates of 44.1 kHz, 22.05 kHz, and 11.025 kHz for *any* use on computers. (Although sample rates that deviate from the rule of 44.1 may sound fine on your development platform, and may sound fine on many other computers, some may have problems. This simple rule will go a long way toward reducing complaints of popping and distorted sound.) This becomes more important with Flash. When Flash imports sounds that are not multiples of 11.025, the sound file is resampled, which causes the sound to play at a lower or higher pitch than the original recording. This same logic applies to sound export, which is discussed in Chapter 15. Finally, although Flash menus list sample rates as 11, 22, and 44, these are abbreviations for the truly precise sample rates of 11.025, 22.05, and 44.1 kHz.

Bit resolution

The second key factor that influences audio quality is bit resolution (or bit depth). Bit resolution describes the number of bits used to record each audio sample. Bit resolution is increased exponentially, meaning that an 8-bit sound sample has a range of 2^8, or 256, levels, whereas a 16-bit sound sample has a range of 2^{16}, or 65,536, levels. Thus, a 16-bit sound is recorded with far more information than an 8-bit sound of equal length. The result of this additional information in a 16-bit sound is that background hiss is minimized, while the sound itself is clearer. The same sound recorded at 8 bits will be noisy and washed out.

A 16-bit sound file is twice the size of the same file saved at 8-bit quality. This is due to the increase in the amount of information taken to record the higher quality file. So, if your sound is too big, what can you do? Well, a sound that's been recorded at a higher bit resolution can be converted to a lower bit resolution, and a sound with a high sample rate can be converted to a lower sample rate. Although a professional studio might perform such conversions with hardware, either of these conversions can also be done with software.

For more information on down sampling and conversion, refer to the archived chapter, "Working with Audio Applications," from the last edition of the *Flash Bible* at www.flash-support.com/archive.

If you're having difficulty understanding the significance of bit depths yet are familiar with the intricacies of scanning photographic images, consider the difference between an 8-bit grayscale image and a 24-bit color image of equivalent dimensions. The file size for the 8-bit grayscale image (such as a black-and-white photograph) is much smaller than the 24-bit color image (such as a color photograph). The grayscale image doesn't have as much tonal information — only 256 levels of gray — yet the 24-bit color image records a range of 16.7 million colors. Unlike photographs, sound samples don't require anything close to a range of 16.7 million values. 16-bit sound samples deliver a dynamic range of over 64,000 values, which is more than the human ear can detect.

Table B-2 lists the various bit depths of sound along with their quality level and possible uses.

Table B-2: Audio Bit Resolution and Quality

Bit Depth	Quality Level	Possible Uses
16-bit	CD quality	High-fidelity sound and music
12-bit	Near-CD quality	Professional/consumer digital camcorder audio
8-bit	FM radio quality	Short, high-quality music clips
4-bit	Acceptable for music	Longer music clips; high-quality voice; sound effects

Note   As hardware technology improves, we're seeing even better audio bit resolution beyond the 16-bit and 44 kHz range. The new DVD-Audio format, for example, offers audio bit resolutions of 16, 20, or 24, and sampling rates of 48, 96, or 192 kHz. Obviously, these extraordinarily high-fidelity recordings are appreciated by extreme audiophiles who have superior playback devices and speakers. Don't worry if your multimedia presentations don't utilize such extremes—trust me when I say that 16-bit 44 kHz audio will be more than enough quality for average computer-audio devices and speakers.

Refer to Figures B-1 and B-2 for a comparison of the differences between sounds at different sample rates and bit depths. Both figures show a wave form derived from the same original sound file, differing only in their sample rates and bit depths. The waveform of the 16-bit 44.1 kHz sound has twice as many "points"—or samples of information—as the 8-bit 11.025 kHz sound. Because the 16-bit 44.1 kHz sound has more samples, the gap between each sample isn't as large as the gaps of the 8-bit 11.025 kHz sound. More samples result in a much smoother, cleaner sound.

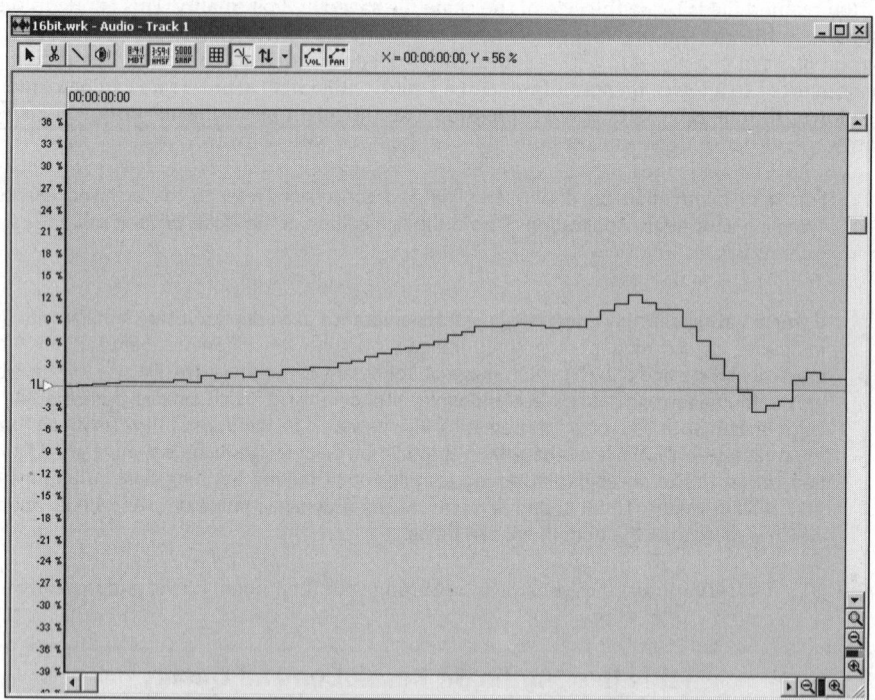

Figure B-1: A waveform of a sound sampled at 44.100 kHz with a 16-bit resolution, as displayed in a high-end sound application

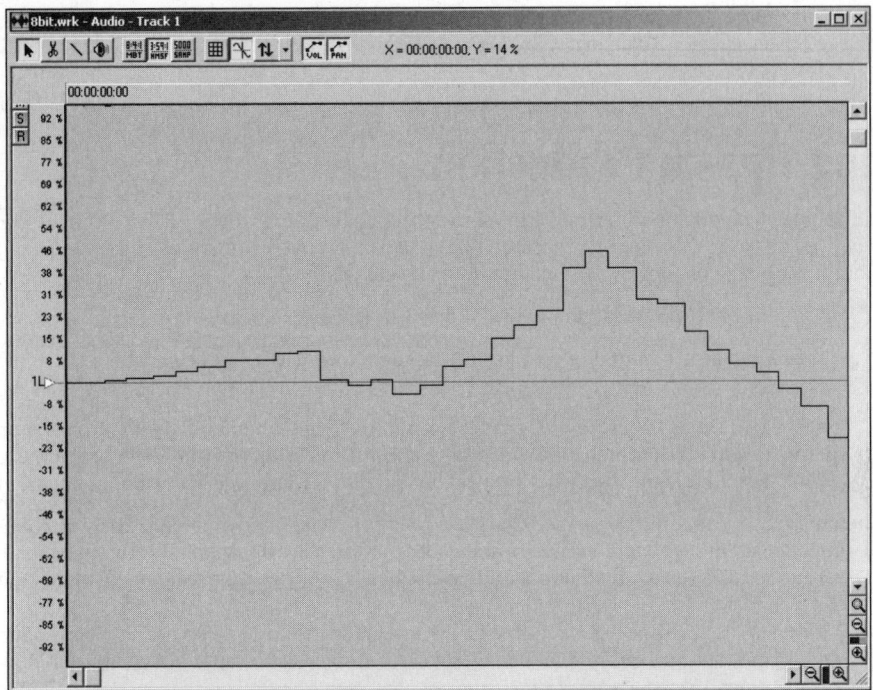

Figure B-2: The same sound as shown in Figure B-1, but down-sampled to 11.025 kHz with an 8-bit resolution

Tip
A common mistake novices make with sound is the assumption that 8-bit audio is acceptable, especially because it ought to result in a much smaller files than 16-bit sound. This is wrong for at least two reasons. First, 8-bit is unacceptable because it sounds far worse than 16-bit sound. Second, the horrible sound will not pay for itself in diminished file size because most compression codecs (especially those used by Flash) won't work with 8-bit sound.

Channels

Audio files are either mono (single channel) or stereo (dual channel: left and right). Stereo files are twice the size of mono files because they have twice the information. Most audio-editing applications offer the option to mix the two stereo channels together and either save or export a stereo sound to a one-channel mono sound. Most audio applications also have the ability to save the right or left channel of a stereo sound separately as a WAV or AIF file.

With the more robust, multitrack-editing applications, such as Deck 3.5, ProTools, Sound Forge, or Cool Edit, it's not unusual to work with eight or more audio tracks — limited only by your system configuration. As you may imagine, these applications give the sound artist greater control over the final sound mix. For use in Flash, these multitrack audio project files need to be "bounced" or mixed down to a stereo or mono file in order to be saved as WAV or AIF files.

Web Resource   For a more detailed description of this process, refer to the *Macromedia Flash MX Bible's* archived chapter, "Working with Audio Applications," available at www.flashsupport. com/archive.

Getting Tips on Production

The primary goal of sound optimization for limited delivery networks (such as the Internet) is to deliver an acceptable quality without a large file-size "cost." You should be concerned about the file size of your audio clips for several reasons.

✦ Sound files require a large amount of drive space.

✦ Managing large sound files and importing them into Flash can be cumbersome and slow.

✦ Download times for large, elaborate sound clips (even when heavily compressed upon export from Flash) can be detrimental to the appreciation of your Flash project, even if your target audience has what may be considered a high-speed Internet connection.

When working with audio clips, it's important to create the shortest audio clips possible. That means trimming off any excess sound that you don't need, especially any blank lead-in or lead-out *handles* (also called in and out points) at either the beginning or the end of a clip.

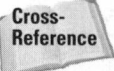

Cross-Reference   Trimming excess sound is discussed briefly in Chapter 15, with reference to Flash's sound tools. The topic is explained in greater detail in the archived chapter, "Working with Audio Applications," found at www.flashsupport.com/archive.

If you plan to have a background music track in your Flash project, it's a good idea to use a small audio clip that can be looped.

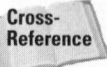

Cross-Reference   Looping audio clips are described in Chapter 15.

Here is a simple formula to determine the file size, in bytes of a given audio clip:

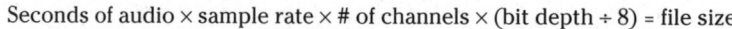

Seconds of audio × sample rate × # of channels × (bit depth ÷ 8) = file size

Note   In the preceding formula, the sample rate is expressed in hertz, not kilohertz. The bit depth is divided by 8 because there are 8 bits per byte.

Thus, a 20-second stereo audio loop at 8 bits, 11 kHz would be calculated like this:

20 sec × 11,025 Hz × 2 channels × (8 bits ÷ 8 bits/byte) = 441,000 bytes = 430KB

There are two schools of thought regarding the ideal quality of sound files for import into Flash. These schools are pretty much divided into those who have high-end sound-editing tools and those who don't. In an effort to delineate the best path for each group, we've noted the following:

✦ If you don't have high-end sound tools available, you may be among those who always prefer to start with audio source files of the highest possible quality (16-bit, 44.1 kHz is ideal), and then use the Flash sound settings to obtain optimal compression upon export.

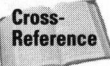

Cross-Reference See Chapter 15 for detailed information on the sound export settings for Flash movies.

✦ If you do have high-end sound tools available, you may prefer to compose most of your clients' music from scratch and that you very rarely work with the MP3 format before importing into Flash. You may also disagree with those who advise that one should bring their sound into Flash at the highest quality before optimizing. This workflow difference may be attributable to the plethora of options that are available to those with high-end sound tools. We know of one sound engineer who converts all of his audio to 16-bit 22.1 kHz mono files, "with major bass reduction," before importing into Flash.

Web Resource For more information on high-end sound tools, refer to the archived *Macromedia Flash MX Bible* chapter, "Working with Audio Applications," at www.flashsupport.com/archive. As with so many things, individual mileage may vary.

You should always keep in mind that Flash can retain imported MP3 compression settings only with those MP3 files that will be used for non-Stream sync options. Anytime you set a sound to use Stream sync on a timeline, Flash needs to recompress the file with the Stream export settings found in the Publish Settings dialog box.

Finally, all linked sounds, or those set to export from the Library and played back via ActionScript, are treated as non-Stream sounds. If you use linked sounds, you may find it useful to import precompressed MP3 files at your preferred bit rate. Flash will not recompress the MP3 file upon export to a SWF file.

✦   ✦   ✦

Digital Video Basics

As you begin to create more complex Flash presentations that include digital video, you need to know how to achieve the highest quality image and playback. In this appendix, you learn how to prepare a digital video file for use in a Flash MX 2004 document.

Cross-Reference After you have successfully created a digital video file, you can learn how to import and use digital video files within a Flash MX 2004 document by reading Chapter 17, "Embedding Video."

Before you consider importing digital video footage into Flash MX 2004 or exporting your video with the Flash Video Exporter tool, you need to plan how the video will be used within the Flash movie (or Web site). Will you be using several video clips for product demonstrations, interviews, or prerecorded events? Will you be using video for special effects such as a time-lapse effect of moving clouds or the sun setting? The more footage you plan to use, the more important it is to make sure you're acquiring the footage properly—you wouldn't want to redo all your footage after you've seen the results in the Flash movie! In this appendix, tips are provided for making sure you have the best possible video quality for your Flash presentations.

Garbage In, Garbage Out: Knowing What Affects a Video's Quality

You may have heard this phrase before, which means that you can't get something from nothing. Ever tried making a soup with bad ingredients and thought it would still taste good? The same principle holds true for video production. Four primary factors influence the quality of your video footage: source format, image quality, sound quality, and subject matter.

Source format

The source format is the container in which the video is stored, whether it's a digital recording encoded on miniDV or DVCAM tape, an analog recording on VHS or Hi8 tape, or a direct MPEG file recorded on your digital camera. Each recording medium has inherent resolution limitations—some formats can store more information than others. The more information the medium stores, the higher the quality of the recording.

The following list outlines the resolution capacities of common recording mediums. For the purposes of our discussion, this list is restricted to video formats and excludes film formats, such as 35mm or 16mm motion picture film. The video formats are compared by *line resolution,* which is the number of horizontal scan lines the format can capture. Line resolution is not the definitive attribute for video quality, but it does measure the capacity of potential visual information captured by the camera or recording device. The most important factor to remember when comparing line resolutions is that video is primarily targeted at television screens that, in North America, display 525 lines of resolution.

Note
Practically speaking, television sets display a maximum of 483 lines of visible resolution – the remaining lines convey other information such as the sync pulse. Although HDTV (High Definition TV) is capable of displaying 1,080 lines of resolution, most multimedia producers will not be using HD cameras to record video.

✦ **VHS, VHS-C or 8mm videotape:** These tape formats, especially VHS, are the most common video formats in use by consumers today. The average household VCR records video in VHS format. These tape formats can record about 240 lines of resolution. This resolution is less than half of the potential scan lines that can be shown on a TV screen, which is why the VHS recordings of your favorite TV shows don't exactly match the live broadcasts. These tape formats are analog in nature – the signal they record is not digital and can deteriorate from copy to copy. To translate this tape format into digital video for use in a multimedia production, you need to capture the footage with an analog video capture card.

✦ **S-VHS or Hi8 videotape:** S-VHS and Hi8 video use the same tape sizes as their VHS and 8mm equivalents, but they capture up to 400 lines of resolution. This resolution capacity comes very close to the 525 lines of resolution that a television can display. You probably won't encounter many S-VHS camcorders anymore, but Hi8 video camcorders are still very popular and in wide use today. While the video quality is a noticeable improvement, the video signal is still analog, so as with VHS, you must capture it with an analog video capture card.

✦ **miniDV, Digital8, or DVCAM tape:** The new breed of video recording devices for consumer, prosumer, and professional use is the DV (Digital Video) format. DV formats use the DV codec to digitally record video, while storing audio at near-CD or CD-quality sampling rates. The native resolution for the DV format is 525 lines, but the actual resolution a DV camcorder will record varies from model to model. Most high-end DV camcorders are considered broadcast quality, meaning the video image is good enough to use on a television show such as the evening news. Many computer systems today ship with an IEEE 1394 (also known as FireWire or iLink) port to capture digital video from DV recording devices. When video is transferred digitally from a camera to a computer over an IEEE 1394 connection, there is no loss of quality.

✦ **Betacam SP, Digital Betacam:** These tape formats are for serious video professionals who work in the television industry. Betacam SP has been the industry standard for network television for over 30 years. While Betacam SP is an analog format, Digital Betacam (also known as DigiBeta) records video with a proprietary Sony codec. Both formats capture 550 or more lines of resolution.

✦ **MPEG file recording:** Many digital cameras can also record MPEG video at various sizes and resolutions. Most digital cameras use the MPEG-1 codec, which was used in the original Video CD (or VCD) format. Sony recently introduced a new Micro MV format, which records video in the MPEG-2 format used by DVD Video discs, at similar line resolutions to DVD Video (525 lines). Most MPEG recording devices capture at line resolutions equal to or less than VHS quality.

As a general guideline, we recommend using a miniDV camcorder to record video that you intend to use for multimedia presentations within a Flash movie. Several factors beyond the recording format affect the quality of any recording. In the next two sections, we discuss variables that influence the visual and audio portions of a recording.

Web Resource If you're a beginner videographer and want to know more about video resolution, check out the following links:

> www.bealecorner.com/trv900/respat/
> hometown.aol.com/ajaynejr/vidres.htm
> www.elitevideo.com

Image quality

Regardless of the source format that you use for your video recording, the recording device may have other limitations. The recorded resolution of your camera may be significantly lower than the upper limit of your recording format's line resolution. For example, the DV format is capable of storing 525 lines of resolution. However, your specific DV camcorder may have an effective resolution of 490 lines. The following variables can affect the quality of the picture recorded by the camera. Note that this list is by no means exhaustive for the professional videographer—we chose these topics as a general summary to guide you in your video production.

✦ **Optics:** The characteristics of the lens (or lens system) that your camera uses are known as the optics. The optical quality of video camcorders varies wildly. Many camcorders boast Carl Zeiss lenses, which are known for their precision and accuracy. Some lenses are constructed of plastic, whereas others are glass. Neither lens type is necessarily better than the other, but the only way to accurately judge the optical system of your camera is to conduct extensive testing with a resolution target.

✦ **CCD:** The CCD, or charged-coupled device, is the electronic plate that captures the image being rendered by the camera's lens. You can think of the CCD as the digital film that's being exposed to the light coming through the lens. CCDs come in a variety of sizes, ranging from ¼ inch to 1 inch. Although these sizes may sound incredibly small, even ¼ inch CCDs can capture amazing detail. The larger a CCD is, however, the more information it can capture. Most cameras only have one CCD, but some cameras have three CCDs—one for each color of the RGB (red, green, and blue) spectrum. These are known as 3-chip or 3-CCD cameras, and they have better color fidelity than single-chip CCD cameras. Color fidelity, simply put, is the measure of how closely the recorded color of an image matches the original colors of the subject.

✦ **Tape quality:** The quality of the tape on which you record the video can also affect the quality of the overall image. Each tape brand has unique characteristics, such as the type of metal particles that are magnetized onto the tape. Some brands (or stocks) are more durable and can withstand the rigors of repeated recordings. In general, you should always record on a fresh tape—and preferably one listed as premium or high quality.

Tip Make sure you use the same brand and model of tape consistently throughout a given shoot. There are slight color variations and differences in quality in each brand and tape type. Preferably, all of the tapes used for a given shoot should be manufactured from the same batch, and as such, you should buy bulk boxes of your preferred tape brands and formats.

✦ **Shutter mechanism:** The shutter mechanism is the device that controls how quickly the CCD samples the image rendered by the lens. Most camcorders have shutters that record interlaced video, which records two interwoven fields (or separate halves of a picture) to create one frame of video. Have you ever noticed how the image on your TV flickers when you pause a VHS recording? You're seeing the two fields of the frame alternating. Computer monitors do not display interlaced video. Rather, they use progressive scanning, to minimize a flicker effect. Some higher-end camcorders have progressive scan shutters that record the image with higher apparent resolution. De-interlacing video is discussed later in this appendix.

✦ **Exposure:** You should make every effort to properly shoot your video footage with the correct exposure. Exposure refers to the amount of light captured by the CCD and the shutter mechanism. Some camcorders do not allow you to control the exposure — it's all automatic. The biggest pitfall for most videographers is underexposing your video footage or shooting in low light. When you try to record a poorly lit subject, you tend to see noise in the darkest areas of the image. Video noise is a random pattern of dots that show up on the image. Finally, make every effort to properly white balance your shot — some camcorders enable you to control the color temperature. You'll notice the effects of color temperature in the video samples on the CD-ROM. You learn more about white balance later in this appendix.

So what do all these variables boil down to? In a nutshell, we recommend that whenever possible, you should shoot video with a camcorder that has a superior optical system with three CCDs, using high-quality tapes and properly controlling your exposure. Avoid shooting in low light, unless you are shooting with a particular effect in mind, such as infrared lighting.

Sound quality

Every videographer should consider how audio is recorded during production. Most video camcorders have a decent built-in stereo microphone, but professional videographers equip themselves with accessories beyond those that ship with the camera. Review the following guidelines for capturing sound with your video recording:

✦ **External microphones:** To achieve the best audio recording, put an external microphone as close as possible to the source of the sound. If you want to record a person talking, an external microphone, such as a wireless lavaliere mic that's pinned to the person's shirt, collar, or tie, will produce a much cleaner recording than the microphone on the camera.

✦ **Balanced vs. unbalanced audio:** Most microphones you will find at electronics stores use a stereo or mono 3.5mm mini-adapter that plugs into the microphone jack on your camcorder. These microphones are considered "unbalanced" audio sources, due to the nature of their internal wiring. For many video shoots this may not pose a problem. However, professional audio engineers use balanced audio for all sound sources. The cabling for balanced audio tends to be a heavier gauge than that of the consumer variety. Many balanced microphones have a 3-pin XLR connector, and most camcorders require an XLR adapter to connect these sources to the mini microphone jack. Many professional video cameras have built-in XLR jacks.

✦ **Sampling rate and bit-depth:** Unless you're using a DV format camcorder, it's likely that you will have little or no control over the specific sampling rate and bit-depth used to record audio on the camera. DV camcorders enable you to record with either 32 kHz or 48 kHz. 32 kHz audio is recorded at 12-bit, which is suitable for recording dialog and live action. 48 kHz is recorded at 16-bit, which is suitable for recording live musical performances or any other scene requiring high fidelity.

✦ **Audio levels:** One of the most overlooked aspects of video production is monitoring the audio levels of your source while recording. Most camcorders only record audio with AGC, or Automatic Gain Control. This "feature" allows the camcorder to determine how much an audio signal should be boosted or minimized during recording. Professional audio engineers prefer to manually monitor and adjust sound levels while the recording is taking place. Undesirable side effects of using AGC include amplified background noise during silent periods, audio distortion, and sudden jumps or drops in audio levels. Whenever possible, listen to your audio source through headphones connected to the camera.

✦ **Unwanted noise:** Do your best to minimize any background noise when you are recording. The microphone(s) connected to your camera will pick up more noise than you may realize. Each microphone has a different "pick-up" pattern, determining the range and direction of sound that it will receive.

In summary, you should record audio as close as possible to the source, using balanced microphones and monitoring the audio feed with headphones connected to the camera. For most video recording, either the 32 kHz or 48 kHz sampling rates will yield superior audio reproduction.

Subject matter

Last, but by no means least, the type of subject matter you are shooting can influence the results of video compression in Flash MX 2004. When it comes to video compression, the most important factor to remember is variability from frame to frame. Simply put, how much and how often does your subject matter change? Are you recording the Indy 500, panning fast racecars accelerating at incredibly fast speeds? Or, are you recording a time lapse of a flower blooming? In general, you will achieve the best results with video compression if the subject matter does not move randomly and wildly.

Here are some general guidelines when choosing and shooting your subject matter:

✦ **Use a tripod:** One of the most common mistakes amateur videographers make is to handhold the video camcorder. Unless you need to freely move with your camera or intentionally want to introduce shakiness to your video image, always mount your camera on a tripod.

✦ **Avoid quick and jerky movements:** If you need to follow your subject matter by panning the head on the tripod, practice the movement a few times before recording. Try to be as slow and fluid as possible. The quicker you pan a video camera while recording, the more likely you'll see compression artifacts show up in your final video in the Flash movie.

✦ **Avoid zooming:** While it may be tempting, do not zoom the lens while recording your subject matter. It's better to use the zoom to frame the shot before you record. Of course, you may intentionally want to using wild zooming effects to recreate the next "Blair Witch" mockumentary, but be aware that any rapid movement from zooming the lens will likely compress very poorly in the Flash movie.

✦ **Lock focus:** All camcorders can auto-focus the lens. If you plan to record a stationary object, you may want to switch to manual focus. If your subject matter moves away from the focus "spot" used by the camera, it may refocus on areas behind the subject matter. This type of focus drifting may yield very unpleasant compression artifacts in the Flash video.

✦ **Watch white balance:** White balance refers to how the camera interprets color. You might notice that your skin looks much less appealing under fluorescent light than it does under an incandescent or soft white indoor light bulb. The human eye can "correct" the perception of a light source's color (or color temperature) with greater ease than an automatic setting on your camera. Be sure to match the white balance setting on your camcorder to the predominant light source in your video composition. Most cameras have at least two white balance settings: indoor and outdoor. Some cameras enable you to perform a custom white balance. To set a custom white balance, focus the entire viewing area on a solid field of white and engage the white balance lock on your camera.

Another factor to consider is the area of the video composition that changes from frame to frame. In a previous example, I mentioned panning a racecar. In that example, the entire picture changes in every frame. Compression works best on video footage with the least amount of movement per pixel in the frame. For example, if you mount your camera on a tripod and keep the camera motionless, you can record the motion of a single subject, such as the flight of a bee between flowers. In such an example, the video compression with the Sorenson Spark codec is much more effective than it would be in the example of the racecar.

Tip　While we mention these general rules for better looking video shoots, it is more important is to develop a look and feel for whatever you are shooting. Establish a set of rules that apply to everything in the shoot. For example, perhaps you *want* to shoot everything handheld, rack the focus regularly, underexpose the image slightly, dutch the angle on all wide shots, and so on. With today's cutting-edge video and film effects, it is more important to develop a style and operate under a consistent look than to worry excessively over conventional do's and don'ts.

Comparing Video Sources

On the *Macromedia Flash MX 2004 Bible* CD-ROM, you will find three video samples in the `appC` folder. You can use these examples to test compression settings in Flash MX 2004, the Flash Video Exporter tool, or a third-party utility such as Sorenson Squeeze or Wildform Flix. Each sample was recorded with a different camera.

✦ **sample_low.mpg:** This video file was recorded with a Sony DSC-S70 Cybershot camera. While this camera is designed to shoot stills, it can also record MPEG-1 video files. This file was recorded in high quality mode at 320 x 240, 15 frames per second. The microphone on this camera is mono (single-channel).

✦ **sample_med.avi:** This video file was recorded with a Sony DCR-PC100 miniDV camcorder. This camcorder has a stereo built-in microphone and a single CCD. The quality captured by this camera is average for most DV camcorders. Compare the color temperature of this recording to that of `sample_higher.avi` and `sample_highest.avi`.

✦ **sample_high.avi:** This video file was recorded with a Sony DSR-PD150 mini-DVCAM camcorder. This professional camera has superior exposure and color temperature control. Among other differences with the previous samples, the audio was recorded with a wireless Shure microphone and an UP4 receiver, which uses a 3-pin XLR output. The PD150 can accept this XLR output.

When you open these files in a video viewer such as Windows Media Player or Apple QuickTime Player, notice that the files recorded by the DV camcorders appear stretched horizontally. The DV format uses non-square pixels, whereas most display devices such as computer monitors use square pixels. Unless the video viewer compensates for non-square pixels, the video image will appear stretched. Flash MX 2004 will not compensate for non-square pixel footage, so you should either convert the footage to square pixels in a video application such as Apple Final Cut Pro, Adobe Premiere, or QuickTime Player Pro edition. The FLV Exporter tool, Sorenson Squeeze, and Wildform Flix can automatically compensate their output for square pixels. Alternatively, you can import the footage "as is" into Flash MX 2004 and transform the width to correctly render the picture. This latter method, however, will still import the extra pixels used in the nonsquare footage, making your Flash movie's file size (as a .swf file) larger than necessary.

I offer you these samples so that you may experiment with them in Flash MX 2004. You will find that cleaner video (such as that shot with the high-end video camcorder) will exhibit less video noise in the Spark-compressed version within the Flash MX 2004 document.

Editing Footage

After you have recorded the video with your camcorder, it's time to start editing the footage in a digital video editor such as Adobe Premiere or Apple Final Cut Pro.

New Feature Flash MX 2004's Video Import Wizard enables you to edit and sequence cuts within your source video file before it is imported into the Flash document. See Chapter 17 for more information.

It's beyond the scope of this book to fully explain the process of editing video footage, but I offer the following pointers to maximize the compression benefits of the Spark codec that the Flash Player uses for video:

✦ **Watch transitions and filter effects:** Keep the general rule in mind that we mentioned previously — refrain from global changes to the entire frame. Some effects and transitions, such as cross-fades and slow dissolves, introduce rapid changes to successive frames of video. These changes require more keyframes to retain quality, and these keyframes add significant weight to the file size of the compressed video in the Flash document. Otherwise, if you don't want the extra weight, you'll have to accept less quality in the overall image.

✦ **Minimize duration:** The shorter you make your finished video clip, the smaller the file size of your Flash movie (.swf file). While you can stream video content just like any Flash content, you should keep in mind the data rate of your target audience.

✦ **Enable necessary tracks:** Use video and audio tracks only if you need both in your final Flash movie. While you can disable the audio in the Flash document's Publish Settings, you can prevent major headaches by importing only the essential material you require.

When you finish editing your video, make a master version that can serve for other purposes beyond your Flash movie presentation. You may even want to output a final version of the edited footage to DV tape. In the next section, we discuss what output format to use for your edited footage. Later, this output format will be compressed and embedded in the Flash document.

Choosing an Import Format

After you complete the editing phase for your video footage, you're ready to output a final version of your video project that you can import into a Flash document. The following checklist should help you determine how to get the most effective use out of the Flash Player's video codec, Sorenson Spark. Just as you don't want to re-JPEG a JPEG (that is, save a JPEG file again with more JPEG compression), you will find that it's best to retain as much original quality from the video as possible before you bring it into Flash MX 2004.

✦ **Frame size:** Most video sources are captured and edited at full frame NTSC sizes, such as 640 x 480 and 720 x 480. It's unlikely that you'll want to expend the bandwidth required to display this full frame size. A starting frame size should be 320 x 240; work your way down from there. If you are targeting Web users with dial-up connection speeds such as 28.8 or 56 Kbps, you may want to consider a frame size of 160 x 120. Remember, when you scale down a bitmap-based element in the Flash authoring environment, you don't actually throw away any pixels — the full size of the graphic is retained in the final Flash movie (.swf file).

✦ **Frame rate:** When you capture video from your camcorder to your desktop video editing application, the video has a frame rate of 29.97 fps (NTSC) or 25 fps (PAL). This frame rate, as with regular video frame sizes, will consume massive amounts of bandwidth in a Flash movie. As a general rule, keep your video frame rate as close as possible (or lower than) the frame rate of your Flash movie, as defined in the Document Properties dialog box (Modify ➪ Document). Most video on the Internet has a frame rate of 12 or 15 fps.

✦ **Video Compression:** Keep your final video file in the codec in which it was originally captured. For example, if you captured and edited the video with the DV codec, use the DV codec for the video file you create to import into Flash MX 2004. You can also use the Uncompressed option when you save your final video file, available in Apple QuickTime Player Pro or any video editing application such as Adobe Premiere or Apple Final Cut Pro.

✦ **Audio Compression:** Follow the same guidelines for video compression. DV-formatted video stores audio uncompressed. Flash MX 2004 will recompress audio in a video file that has been imported. As such, it's not ideal to apply any compression to the audio track before you bring it into Flash MX 2004.

✦ **De-interlacing:** We mentioned earlier in this chapter that video recorded by camcorders is interlaced. However, computer monitors (and the graphics displayed on them) are progressively scanned and do not require interlacing. (You may notice how "soft" your DV footage appears in most desktop video editing applications; this is due to the even and odd "interlaces" being multiplied to accommodate the progressive scanning of computer video.) The general rule of thumb is to use a de-interlace filter (or export option) on any video footage that you intend to use for computer playback. However, if you resize your video to 320 x 240 or smaller and decrease the frame rate from its original rate, you effectively de-interlace the video footage. Usually, you will not see any difference enabling a de-interlace filter on top of these reductions.

After you have gone through this checklist for your video footage, export a final video file that you can import into Flash 2004. Most video applications (including Apple QuickTime Player Pro) can re-save a finished video file with a new frame size, frame rate, video and audio compressions, and other options such as de-interlacing. Flash MX 2004 can import a variety of video file formats, listed in Table C-1.

Table C-1: Video Import Formats for Flash MX 2004

Format	Platform	Required drivers	Description
AVI (.avi) Audio Video Interleaved Macintosh	Windows	DirectX 7 or higher, or QuickTime 4 or higher	Standard Windows video format; usually the format in which video is captured on Windows; can use any combination of video and audio codecs.
DV (.dv) Digital Video stream	Windows Macintosh	QuickTime 4 or higher	Format saved from applications such as Adobe Premiere or Apple QuickTime Player Pro; uses the DV codec for video and uncompressed audio.
MPEG (.mpg, .mpeg) Motion Picture Experts Group	Windows Macintosh	DirectX 7 or higher, or QuickTime 4 or higher	Precompressed video in the MPEG-1 or MPEG-2 codec; a format used by many digital cameras that save to media format such as Compact Flash (CF) and Memory Stick.
QT (.mov) Apple QuickTime	Windows Macintosh	QuickTime 4 or higher	Standard video format on the Mac; usually the format in which video is captured on the Mac; can use any combination of video and audio codecs.
WMV (.wmv, .asf) Windows Media files	Windows	DirectX 7 or higher	Precompressed video in a modified MPEG-4 codec developed by Microsoft to use with the Windows Media Player.

Of the formats listed in Table C-1, I recommend that you import formats that don't apply any recompression to the original source format of your video. If you can avoid using compressed video such as Windows Media and MPEG files, you can prevent further artifacts from being introduced into the video by Flash's video compressor. Compression artifacts are areas in the video frame where detail is lost. The process of compressing a file already using compression is known as recompression.

Caution If you try to import MPEG files into the Macintosh version of Flash MX 2004, you will not be able to use the audio track in the Flash document (or Flash movie). Only Windows' DirectX driver will successfully convert both the video and audio tracks in a MPEG file to a format usable in the Flash MX 2004 document. To import a MPEG via QuickTime on the Mac, you will need to use an application such as Discreet Cleaner 5.1 (or higher) to convert the MPEG to a QuickTime movie that uses another codec.

✦   ✦   ✦

Using the CD-ROM

T his appendix provides you with information on the contents of
the CD-ROM that accompanies this book.

Note
For the latest version of this appendix, including any late-breaking
updates, please refer to the ReadMe file located in the root directory of the CD-ROM.

Here is what you will find on the CD-ROM:

+ System requirements

+ Example SWF and FLA files

+ Reusable ActionScript

+ Tips for installing and using plug-ins and applications

+ Listing of relevant applications and software trials

Before loading up the CD-ROM, make sure that your computer meets
the minimum system requirements listed in this section. If your computer doesn't match up to most of these requirements, you may have
a problem using the contents of the CD-ROM.

**For Windows 9*x*, Windows 2000, Windows NT4 (with SP 4 or later),
Windows Me, or Windows XP:**

+ PC with a Pentium II processor running at 300 MHz or faster

+ At least 96MB of total RAM installed on your computer; for best
performance, we recommend at least 128MB. Note that additional RAM is needed to open other programs with Flash.

+ 16-bit color monitor capable of 1,024 x 768 (millions of colors)
or better

+ 510MB of available hard-disk space to install applications

+ A CD-ROM drive

For Macintosh:

+ Power Mac G3 running OS X 10.1 and higher

+ At least 96MB of total RAM installed on your computer; for best
performance, we recommend at least 128MB

+ 16-bit color monitor capable of 1,024 x 768 (millions of colors)
or better

+ 510MB of available hard-disk space to install applications

+ A CD-ROM drive

Reviewing Example SWF and FLA Files

Many of the examples discussed in the text and in step-by-step tutorials are included in the relevant chapter folder on the CD-ROM. Opening the Flash movie (SWF) is the quickest way to see how the finished example is supposed to look. The fonts should display correctly, and as long as you haven't moved the file to a new location, any loaded assets should also work.

When you open a Flash document (FLA), you may get a warning about missing fonts. This warning simply means that you do not have the same fonts installed on your machine as the original author of the file. Select a default font and you will be able to review and edit the Flash document on your machine. However, without the proper fonts installed, the layout may not appear as it was originally designed.

Note The only font files included on the CD-ROM are Craig Kroeger's vector-based Miniml fonts, described in Chapter 8. Other fonts are copyrighted material, and, as such, cannot be distributed on this CD-ROM.

Installing and Using Plug-Ins and Applications

In the software folder of the CD-ROM, you'll find the trial versions of both versions of Flash MX 2004. Additional plug-ins and trial versions of applications discussed in Part VIII of this book can be found online. The `links.html file` included on the CD-ROM is a good reference for finding these Web resources.

On a Macintosh, go to the specific application's folder and double-click the installation file. Then follow the installer's instructions to proceed.

On a PC, go to the specific application's folder, and either unzip the installation ZIP file or double-click the installation EXE file.

Installing and Using the sendmail Scripts

Chapter 30, "Sending Data In and Out of Flash," introduces the concept of creating Flash forms that interact with server-side scripts. These scripts need to be installed on a live Web server in order to work properly with the Flash movies created in the lesson. You may need the assistance of your Web-server administrator to get the appropriate script working correctly.

sendmail.cfm

This ColdFusion script can be installed on a ColdFusion MX (or higher) server. On line 10 of this script, the `<cfmail>` tag assumes that your SMTP server is located on the same server, using an IP address of 127.0.0.1 on port 25. You will need to edit the `server` (and `port`, if applicable) attributes of the `<cfmail>` tag if your SMTP server is located on another machine.

More importantly, be sure to edit line 3 of the script:

```
<cfparam name="Form.toEmail" type="string" default="robert@theMakers.com" />
```

Change the `default` attribute to specify your e-mail address (or the e-mail address to which you want the comment form values sent).

You can download a trial version of ColdFusion MX 6.1 at Macromedia's site at:

    www.macromedia.com/downloads/

ColdFusion MX 6.1 can be easily integrated with Microsoft IIS (Internet Information Service), which is part of Microsoft Windows 2000 Pro or Microsoft Windows XP Pro.

sendmail.asp

This script is written in ASP (Active Server Page) for use on a Microsoft IIS Web server (or equivalent). This script works in conjunction with a free version of the w3 JMail server component. While the sendmail.asp script file is in the ch30 folder of the CD-ROM, you will need to download the latest version of the w3 JMail component at:

    http://tech.dimac.net/

Download the free personal edition of this software if you are using this example for educational or personal use. Follow the standard installation steps for the JMail component, and place the sendmail.asp script in a directory on the IIS server where ASP scripts have permission to run and execute.

In a text editor such as Notepad, BBEdit, or Macromedia Dreamweaver, you will need to change the location of the SMTP server information in the sendmail.asp script. In lines 3 and 4 of the sendmail.asp file, you will see:

    smtpServer = "127.0.0.1"
    smtpPort = 25

Change the value of smtpServer to the SMTP server for *your* Web hosting provider or ISP (Internet Service Provider). Most SMTP servers use port 25 — if your SMTP server requires a different port number, specify it for the smtpPort value.

Once the script and the component are installed on your IIS server, you will be able to create your own custom Flash form as described in Chapter 30.

sendmail.pl

To use Joey Lott's sendmail.pl Perl script, you need to have Perl 5 or higher installed on your Web server. You may need the assistance and permission of the system administrator of your Internet service provider (ISP) or Internet presence provider (IPP) to install (or use) Perl 5. After it is installed, upload the script file sendmail.pl to a directory or folder that is accessible by Perl. This folder may need to have proper permissions in order for Web users to execute the script file.

In a text editor such as Notepad, BBEdit, or Macromedia Dreamweaver, you may need to edit the first line of the script to indicate the path to the Perl files on your server. On line 19, you can remove the comment code (#) and specify a default e-mail to which output from the script will be sent. Meaning, if you wish to omit a variable in the Flash movie ActionScript, you can specify an e-mail address on line 19. If you are receiving errors from the script during trials, you may need to adjust the location parameter of the Web server's sendmail program (*not* the script file, but the actual program the server uses to send e-mail), specified in line 24.

After you have the script installed, follow the section "Creating a Flash Form" in Chapter 30 to create a fully functional form in your Flash movies.

Note You need to modify the LoadVars object actions to refer to your script's URL instead of the flashmxbible.com script URL.

Applications

The CD-ROM included with this book aids you with many examples and tutorials by providing relevant files and software trials, including the following:

✦ Trial versions (Macintosh and Windows) of Macromedia Flash MX 2004 and Flash MX Professional 2004.

✦ Limited edition versions of Craig Kroeger's vector-based fonts from miniml.com, as described in Chapter 8.

✦ Limited-edition version of the new sendmail.cfm and sendmail.asp script used for the Flash form lesson in Chapter 30. This ASP script requires Microsoft IIS (Internet Information Server) or equivalent. You can also find the original sendmail.pl script (written in Perl) that Joey Lott created for the *Flash 5 Bible*. Please refer to the explanation of how to use these scripts, included in the previous section of this appendix.

✦ Prebuilt components for alpha effects and text loading, scripted by Robert Reinhardt and integrated with project examples in Chapters 20 and 32.

✦ Just about every FLA and SWF file that is discussed in the book, including those shown in examples from guest experts.

Web Resource Other applications or utilities discussed in the book can be found online. For a list of relevant Web links, refer to the links.html document included in the main directory of the CD-ROM.

Shareware programs are fully functional, trial versions of copyrighted programs. If you like particular programs, register with their authors for a nominal fee and receive licenses, enhanced versions, and technical support. *Freeware programs* are copyrighted games, applications, and utilities that are free for personal use. Unlike shareware, these programs do not require a fee or provide technical support. *GNU software* is governed by its own license, which is included inside the folder of the GNU product. See the GNU license for more details.

Trial, demo, or evaluation versions are usually limited either by time or functionality (such as being unable to save projects). Some trial versions are very sensitive to system date changes. If you alter your computer's date, the programs will "time out" and will no longer be functional.

Troubleshooting

If you have difficulty installing or using any of the materials on the companion CD-ROM, try the following:

✦ **Turn off any anti-virus software that you may have running.** Installers sometimes mimic virus activity and can make your computer incorrectly believe that it is being infected by a virus. (Be sure to turn the anti-virus software back on later.)

✦ **Close all running programs.** The more programs you're running, the less memory is available to other programs. Installers also typically update files and programs; if you keep other programs running, installation may not work properly.

✦ **Reference the ReadMe:** Please refer to the ReadMe file located at the root of the CD-ROM for the latest product information at the time of publication.

If you still have trouble with the CD-ROM, please call the Wiley Customer Care phone number: (800) 762-2974. Outside the United States, call 1 (317) 572-3994. You can also contact Wiley Customer Service by e-mail at techsupdum@wiley.com. Wiley Publishing, Inc. will provide technical support only for installation and other general-quality control items; for technical support on the applications themselves, consult the program's vendor or author.

✦　✦　✦

Guest Experts Information

Bazley, Richard
Bazley Films
Corsham, England, UK
richard@bazleyfilms.com
www.bazleyfilms.com
* Animation examples from The Journal of Edwin Carp in Part III.

⇨ Was a Lead Animator on such films as Disney's *Hercules* and Warner Bros.' *The Iron Giant* ⇨ Now heads a studio that can deliver top notch animation in 2D or 3D for film and broadcast ⇨ Clients include the BBC, Channel 5, High Eagle Ent., Telemagination, 4:2:2, Grove International, Mousepower Productions, The ALKEMI Group, Future Publishing, Varga, Hahn Film, Bermuda Shorts and Hart TV ⇨ Richard was one of the first to use Flash for a theatrically released animated short, *The Journal of Edwin Carp* sponsored by Macromedia and Wacom and featuring the voice of Hugh Laurie (*Stuart Little, 101 Dalmatians*).

Brown, Scott
Los Angeles, California, USA
sbrown@artcenter.edu
www.spicybrown.com
* Tutorial: "Designing for Usability," in Chapter 3

⇨ Graduated from Art Center College of Design with a degree in product design ⇨ Has worked in new media development for guess.com and did interface design for rampt.com ⇨ Teaches Flash classes for Art Center College of Design ⇨ Scott currently does Web development for tekniondna.com, an office furniture design company in Pasadena.

Corsaro, Sandro
sandro corsaro animation
Hermosa Beach, California, USA
info@sandrocorsaro.com
www.sandrocorsaro.com
* Tutorial: "Flash Character Design Strategies," in Chapter 13

⇨ A pure Flash animation specialist trained in traditional animation ⇨ Has created projects for Intel, McDonalds, MCA Records, Nestle, and E Music ⇨ Author of *The Flash Animator* (New Riders Publishing, 2002) ⇨ A featured speaker at leading conferences including SIGGRAPH,

FlashKit, and FlashForward ➪ Sandro has taught Flash animation seminars for Art Center of Pasadena and for `lynda.com`'s Ojai Digital Art Center ➪ Currently working with Warner Bros. studios on animation projects for broadcast and theatrical release.

Elliott, Shane
Timberfish
Studio City, California, USA
`shane@timberfish.com`
`www.timberfish.com`
* Tutorial: "Using XML Sockets with a Flash Movie," in Chapter 30

➪ A designer, programmer, teacher, and writer with nine years of online design and Web experience ➪ Has worked with top advertising agencies Saatchi & Saatchi and TBWA\Chiat\Day as well as many large institutions such as Siebel, Energizer, Toyota and Infiniti to create compelling client-driven Flash designs and applications ➪ Recently developed a university-level Flash course with `education2Go.com` ➪ Shane now focuses on his creative endeavors at `www.timberfish.com` and continues to expand his writing and design portfolio.

Kroeger, Craig
Miniml
Milwaukee, WI, USA
`craig@miniml.com`
`www.miniml.com`
* Sidebar: "Using Miniml Fonts in Flash," in Chapter 8

➪ Creates Flash-friendly, vector-based pixel fonts perfect for large or small screen applications; available at `www.miniml.com` ➪ The purpose behind miniml is to encourage functional and beautiful design by providing inspiration and resources ➪ Craig's miniml fonts are also featured in *Flash Enabled* (New Riders Publishing, 2002) ➪ Miniml.com was nominated for typography in the Flash Film Festival at FlashFoward NYC, 2003.

Lott, Joey
Valley Village, California, USA
`joey@person13.com`
`www.person13.com`
* Tutorial: "Adding New Tools to Flash MX 2004," Chapter 4 and sendmail.pl script on the CD-ROM: Cross-Reference in ch30

➪ Coauthor of the *ActionScript Bible* (Wiley Publishing, 2002) ➪ Author of *Complete Flash Remoting MX* (Wiley Publishing, 2003) and the *ActionScript Cookbook* (O'Reilly & Associates, 2003) ➪ Note from the authors: Joey is too busy writing books to write a long bio, but he is a friendly guy so e-mail him if you really want to know more!

Moock, Colin
Toronto, Ontario, Canada
`colin@moock.org`
`www.moock.org`
`www.moock.org/unity`
* Tutorial: "Unifying the Web" in Chapter 30

➪ An independent Web guru with a passion for networked creativity and expression ➪ Author of the world-renowned guide to Flash programming, *ActionScript: The Definitive Guide* (O'Reilly & Associates, 2001) ➪ Runs one of the Web's most venerable Flash developer sites ➪ Colin's latest project is Unity, a Flash socket server for multiuser content.

Perry, Bill
Pocket PC Flash
Santa Monica, California, USA
bill@pocketpcflash.net
www.pocketpcflash.net
* Tutorial: "Adding Custom Templates for Devices," in Chapter 4

⇨ A freelance developer who focuses on application development for smart devices, including Pocket PCs ⇨ Maintains www.pocketpcflash.net, a Macromedia Flash development resource for Pocket PCs ⇨ A member of Team Macromedia, he has spoken at leading Flash conferences ⇨ Contributing author to the book, *Flash Enabled* (New Riders Publishing, 2002) ⇨ Currently, Bill is exploring alternative uses of Macromedia Flash applications with smart devices in wireless environments.

Purgason, Todd
JUXT Interactive
Newport Beach, CA, USA
toddhead@juxtinteractive.com
www.juxtinteractive.com
www.juxtinteractive.com/deconstruction
www.juxtinteractive.com/toddhead
* Tutorial: "Streamlined Workflow: FreeHand and Flash," in Chapter 36

⇨ Creative Director for JUXT Interactive ⇨ Cited as one of today's top ten Web designers in the world by *Create Online* magazine and the Internet Professional Publishers Association (IPPA) ⇨ An author and international speaker on the subject of interactive Web design ⇨ Completed a book titled, *Flash deCONSTRUCTION* (New Riders, 2001) ⇨ Todd has led Juxt in creating innovative work for clients such as Sketchers, Billabong, Macromedia, Kawasaki, Reef, Red Bull, OmniSky, Nortel, Toshiba, Fujitsu, J.F.Shea Companies, TBWA\Chiat\Day, FCB, and many others.

Spiridellis, Gregg & Evan
JibJab Media, Inc.
Raleigh Studios
Manhattan Beach, CA, USA
getinfo@jibjab.com
www.JibJab.com
* Tutorial: "Filter Effects for Classic Broadcast Animation," in Chapter 13

⇨ JibJab Media creates and produces original Internet and broadcast animation ⇨ Gregg and Evan Spiridellis founded JibJab in November 1999, seizing the opportunity to broadcast their creative productions directly to a worldwide audience ⇨ Since then, millions of people have visited JibJab.com ⇨ JibJab's productions have been broadcast on FOX, ABC, CNN, WB, Noggin and Nickelodeon.

Turner, Bill
Turnertoons Productions, Inc.
Melbourne, Florida, USA
bill@turnertoons.com
www.turnertoons.com
* Animation examples and Tutorial: "Lip-Syncing Cartoons," in Chapter 13

⇨ Author of the book *Flash 5 Cartoons and Games FX/Design* (Coriolis, 2001) ⇨ Coauthor of *Flash the Future* (No Starch Press, 2002), a book on the subject of graphics and games specific to Pocket PCs ⇨ Bill created one of the first interactive animated cartoon sites, "Dubes," in early 1996.

Wan, Samuel
samuel@samuelwan.com
www.samuelwan.com/information
www.samuelwan.com/expressionbyproxy
* Tutorial: "Using Custom Timeline Effects," in Chapter 11

⇨ Coauthor of *Object-Oriented Programming with ActionScript* (New Riders Publishing, 2002) ⇨ Contributed to several other books, including *New Masters of Flash (Friends of Ed, 2001)*, and *Flash 5 Magic* (New Riders, 2001) ⇨ A featured speaker at leading Flash conferences ⇨ Nominated in the Best Storytelling category for the Flash Film Festival at FlashForward, London 2002 and a collaborator on the winning entry for Best Application at FlashForward, NYC 2003 ⇨ Sam is a generous and inspirational member of the Flash elite — those developers who lead the way and share knowledge as they continue to innovate.

Winkler, Tom
doodie.com
Hollywood, California, USA
tomwink@earthlink.net
www.doodie.com
* Animation examples in Chapter 10

⇨ A former *Simpsons* animator, Winkler has directed, animated, and cartooned in Hollywood for ten years ⇨ His whimsical style can be seen daily on doodie.com — the ultimate site for potty humor animation ⇨ Winkler continues to push forward with his superhero *doodieman* and is available as director for hire and for freelance Web or broadcast animation ⇨ Credits include ABC, Warner Bros., Discovery Channel, adamsandler.com, MCA, spamarrest.com, and blink182 ⇨ Winkler says; "I was happy to contribute . . . Giving back to the animation community is something I felt was my duty."

✦   ✦   ✦

Index

Continued

Continued

Continued

Continued

Wiley Publishing, Inc.
End-User License Agreement